Handbook of
the Sociology
of Mental Health

Handbooks of Sociology and Social Research

Series Editor:
Howard B. Kaplan, *Texas A&M University, College Station, Texas*

HANDBOOK OF THE SOCIOLOGY OF EDUCATION
Edited by Maureen T. Hallinan

HANDBOOK OF THE SOCIOLOGY OF GENDER
Edited by Janet Saltzman Chafetz

HANDBOOK OF THE SOCIOLOGY OF MENTAL HEALTH
Edited by Carol S. Aneshensel and Jo C. Phelan

A Continuation Order Plan is available for this series. A continuation order will bring delivery of each new volume immediately upon publication. Volumes are billed only upon actual shipment. For further information please contact the publisher.

Handbook of
the Sociology
of Mental Health

Edited by

Carol S. Aneshensel

University of California, Los Angeles
Los Angeles, California

and

Jo C. Phelan

Columbia University
New York, New York

Kluwer Academic/Plenum Publishers
New York   Boston   Dordrecht   London   Moscow

ISBN: 0-306-46069-6

© 1999 Kluwer Academic / Plenum Publishers
233 Spring Street, New York, N.Y. 10013

10 9 8 7 6 5 4 3 2 1

A C.I.P. record for this book is available from the Library of Congress

Though this be madness, yet there is method in't.
WILLIAM SHAKESPEARE, *Hamlet*, II, 2:211

Contributors

Pauline Agbayani-Siewert, Department of Social Welfare, School of Public Policy and Social Research, University of California, Los Angeles, Los Angeles, California 90095-1656

Carol S. Aneshensel, Department of Community Health Sciences, School of Public Health, University of California, Los Angeles, Los Angeles, California 90095-1772

William R. Avison, Centre for Health and Well-Being, The University of Western Ontario, London, Ontario, Canada N6A 5C2

Carol A. Boyer, Institute for Health, Health Care Policy, and Aging Research, Rutgers University, New Brunswick, New Jersey 08903-5070

Evelyn J. Bromet, Department of Psychiatry and Behavioral Sciences, State University of New York at Stony Brook, Stony Brook, New York 11794-8790

Kendrick T. Brown, Department of Psychology, Macalester College, St. Paul, Minnesota 55105

Tony N. Brown, 5006 Institute for Social Research, University of Michigan, Ann Arbor, Michigan 48106-1248

Martha Livingston Bruce, Department of Psychiatry, Weill Medical College of Cornell University, White Plains, New York 10605

Mary Amanda Dew, Departments of Psychiatry, Psychology, and Epidemiology, University of Pittsburgh School of Medicine and Medical Center, Pittsburgh, Pennsylvania 15213

George W. Dowdall, Department of Sociology, St. Joseph's University, Philadelphia, Pennsylvania 19131

William W. Eaton, Department of Mental Hygiene, School of Public Health, The Johns Hopkins University, Baltimore, Maryland 21205

Linda K. George, Department of Sociology and Center for the Study of Aging and Human Development, Durham, North Carolina 27710

Allan V. Horwitz, Institute for Health, Health Care Policy, and Aging Research, Rutgers University, New Brunswick, New Jersey 08903-5070

James S. Jackson, 5006 Institute for Social Research, University of Michigan, Ann Arbor, Michigan 48106-1248

Ronald C. Kessler, Department of Health Care Policy, Harvard Medical School, Boston, Massachusetts 02115

Stuart A. Kirk, Department of Social Welfare, School of Public Policy and Social Research, University of California, Los Angeles, Los Angeles, California 90095-1656

Neal Krause, Department of Health Behavior and Health Education, School of Public Health, University of Michigan, Ann Arbor, Michigan 48109-2029

Bruce G. Link, Division of Epidemiology, School of Public Health, Columbia University, New York, New York 10032

Keri M. Lubell, Department of Sociology, Indiana University, Bloomington, Indiana 47405

Jane D. McLeod, Department of Sociology, Indiana University, Bloomington, Indiana 47405

John Mirowsky, Department of Sociology, The Ohio State University, Columbus, Ohio 43210-1353

Joseph P. Morrissey, Sheps Center for Health Services Research, Chapel Hill, North Carolina 27599-7590

James M. Nonnemaker, Department of Sociology, University of Minnesota, Minneapolis, Minnesota 55455

Rosavinia W. Pangan, Department of Community Health Sciences, School of Public Health, University of California, Los Angeles, Los Angeles, California 90095-1772

Leonard I. Pearlin, Department of Sociology, University of Maryland at College Park, College Park, Maryland 20742-1315

Bernice A. Pescosolido, Department of Sociology, Indiana University, Bloomington, Indiana 47405

Jo C. Phelan, Division of Sociomedical Sciences, School of Public Health, Columbia University, New York, New York 10032

Michael F. Polgar, Center for Mental Health Services Research, Washington University, St. Louis, Missouri 63105-2198

Sarah Rosenfield, Institute for Health, Health Care Policy, and Aging Research, Rutgers University, New Brunswick, New Jersey 08903-5070

Catherine E. Ross, Department of Sociology, The Ohio State University, Columbus, Ohio 43210-1353

Jaya Sastry, Late of the Department of Sociology, Duke University, Durham, North Carolina, 27710

Sherril L. Sellers, 5006 Institute for Social Research, University of Michigan, Ann Arbor, Michigan 48210-1353

Galen E. Switzer, Departments of Medicine and Psychiatry, University of Pittsburgh School of Medicine and Medical Center, Pittsburgh, Pennsylvania 15213

David T. Takeuchi, Department of Sociology, Indiana University, Bloomington, Indiana 47405

Mark Tausig, Department of Sociology, University of Akron, Akron, Ohio 44325-1905

Peggy A. Thoits, Department of Sociology, Vanderbilt University, Nashville, Tennessee 37235

J. Blake Turner, Division of Sociomedical Sciences, School of Public Health, Columbia University, New York, New York 10032

R. Jay Turner, Department of Sociology, University of Miami, Coral Gables, Florida 33146

Debra Umberson, Department of Sociology and Population Research Center, University of Texas, Austin, Texas 78712-1088

Blair Wheaton, Department of Sociology, University of Toronto, Toronto, Ontario, Canada M5T 98 ZZ245

David R. Williams, Institute for Social Research, University of Michigan, Ann Arbor, Michigan 48106-1248

Kristi Williams, Department of Sociology and Population Research Center, University of Texas, Austin, Texas 78712-1088

Yan Yu, Department of Sociology, University of Maryland, College Park, Maryland 20742

Shanyang Zhao, Department of Health Care Policy, Harvard Medical School, Boston, Massachusetts 02115

Preface

Within American society, mental disorder is commonly understood as an attribute of the individual. This intuitive understanding reflects the experiential reality that it is individuals who are beset by feelings of fear and despair, confused by intrusive or jumbled thoughts, addicted to drugs, and so forth. In this regard, everyday thinking is consistent with contemporary psychiatry, which also individualizes pathology, increasingly in biological terms.

The contributors to this handbook collectively articulate an alternative vision, one in which the individual experience of psychopathology is inextricably embedded within its social context. This theme—the interface between society and the inward experience of its constituents—is developed here in a more encompassing manner than has been previously undertaken. Although this perspective may seem self-evident, especially in a handbook on the sociology of mental health, the widespread adoption of a medical model of aberrant states, especially by sociologists, has, we submit, obscured the relevance of social organization and processes.

This problem is tackled at its most fundamental level by several authors who question our basic understanding of mental illness as illness. One aspect of this critique points to the historical and cultural specificity of the medical model, thereby calling attention to its socially constructed nature. Some question the often tacit assumption that mental disorders exist as objective states that can legitimately be assessed with universal and standardized criteria, especially with regard to comparisons among culturally disparate groups. Several authors also call attention to the impact of social, economic, cultural, and political forces on our science, including the methods we use, how we interpret data, and the conclusions we draw about the mental health impact of these very same forces. Throughout this volume, then, the authors confront the dilemma that even the manner in which we think about mental disorder is shaped by the nature of the society in which we live and conduct our research.

Most of this handbook is devoted to the explanation of one elementary observation: Disorder is not uniformly distributed throughout society, but occurs more densely within some social strata than others. The explanation of social variation in risk has engaged the attention of sociologists since the earliest community-based surveys revealed an inverse association with socioeconomic status. It continues to do so.

The most influential idea running through this body of work—the idea that connects work on gender, socioeconomic status, race, ethnicity, age, and poverty—is that social group differences in disorder are somehow linked to corresponding differences in exposure to the social conditions that cause disorder. This idea does not dispute the etiological significance of biological factors but sets these influences to the side, held in reserve to account for individual (as distinct from group) differences. The explanation of group differences in disorder necessarily entails casual agents whose own occurrence also depends (at least in part) on group membership. Social factors best fit this criterion.

This one idea is key to understanding the distinctive vision that sociologists bring to the study of mental health. From a clinical perspective, disorder is abnormal and its origins lie in anomalous experiences or attributes (an admittedly overly simplistic account). For the sociologist, the occurrence of abnormality is a normal by-product of the routine functioning of society. In other words, the social arrangements and processes that serve the interests of some segments of society inevitably harm others. The sources of systematic differences in disorder, then, lie not in the bizarre or happenstance, but in the repetition and reproduction of the commonplace. Thus, it is not surprising that social stratification and inequality are prominent themes in this handbook.

The influence of social forces, however, is perhaps most evident in the aftermath of the onset of mental, emotional, or behavioral problems. Here, we see that individuals with essentially the same disorder often follow divergent sequences of societal response, which determine (at least in part) the course of the disorder—its duration, the likelihood of recovery, and the chances of relapse or recurrence. One dimension of the societal response is the definition of the problem in medical terms and associated processes of help seeking and treatment, as well as the institutional contexts within which these processes unfold. Stigma constitutes a second dimension of societal response, sometimes counterbalancing the potentially restorative effects of treatment. And perhaps the most social aspect of mental illness concerns its impact on others, especially the family.

The course of a particular disorder over time displays considerable variation at the individual level. Response to treatment, including reactions to powerful pharmaceutical agents, is often defined in biological or intrapsychic terms. However, there are pronounced group differences in the course and consequences of mental illness as well, differences that once again point to the equally powerful influence of the social factors that differentiate one group from another. The impact of gender, race, age, and socioeconomic status are apparent at virtually every juncture, pointing once again to the significance of systems of stratification and inequality.

These perspectives have characterized the sociological study of mental illness for nearly a half-century. In this sense, this handbook can be viewed as a historical record of the emergence of the field and its current state, a description of a work-in-progress. It presents the state of the art in theory, method, research, and interpretation. Its authors, however, have gone one step further, offering their vision of what lies on the horizon or just beyond it, presenting a sociological agenda for the future. This agenda, we submit, is the reintegration of individual psychopathology into society.

It is our immodest hope, too, that this handbook will foster a reintegration of the sociological study of mental health. Just as the discipline has become increasingly specialized, so too has the subdiscipline. As Toffler (1984) notes, one of the most highly developed skills in contemporary Western civilization is dissection—the splitting up of problems into their smallest possible components—a skill perhaps most finely honed in science. Yet in editing this handbook, we have seen the same themes emerge repeatedly in somewhat different guises. Our initial pleasure at what seemed like a fortuitous outcome has given way to the realization that this outcome was inevitable because its authors have all been describing one and the same thing: the social experience of mental illness. The many stages and transitions of this process have generated areas of specialization that have obscured continuities across time and place. We as a field should assume responsibility for tending these commonalities with the same commitment we have brought to each unique manifestation.

Finally, in undertaking this handbook, we began with what we knew best and branched out to create what we thought of as an encyclopedic perspective. Having reached the end of this task, we see now all too clearly other topics that rightfully have a place in the table of contents. Thus, we expect that the next handbook on this topic will differ from the present one—as indeed it should.

CAROL S. ANESHENSEL
JO C. PHELAN

REFERENCE

Toffler, A. (1984). Science and change: Foreword. In I. Prigogine & I. Stengers (Eds.), *Order out of chaos: Man's new dialogue with nature* (pp. xi–xxvi). New York: Bantam Books.

Acknowledgments

This book is about people who suffer, and it is fitting to recognize and appreciate their pain. Thus, we acknowledge the many people whose lives have been affected by mental illness and whose life experiences are reflected at least partially in the content of this book. We are especially indebted to the persons who participated in the various research projects recounted here. These individuals have generously taken the time to tell us their stories, answer our questions, and fill out our forms, even though these activities were at times painful or at the very least tedious. Our debt to these persons is enormous, far greater than we can acknowledge here.

Similarly, we would like to take this opportunity to thank those who conducted the original scholarly work that informs this handbook. Some of these individuals are to be found among the authors of this volume. Most appear only in the text and references, however, insofar as their work constitutes the body of knowledge that we refer to as the sociology of mental health.

We would also like to thank the many colleagues and friends who contributed chapters to this handbook. We sought out the leading experts in the field, and so the fact that each chapter offers an authoritative summary and critique of its respective subject comes as no surprise. However, these authors also took on the difficult task of extending this knowledge base beyond its past accomplishments. Their creativity, critical thinking, and occasional outrageousness have gratified and delighted us. The success of this volume is due to their enthusiastic commitment to the project, the goodwill with which they responded to our suggestions for revisions, and their acquiescence to demanding deadlines. To these outstanding authors, we express our special appreciation.

The work presented in this volume is the result of the collective efforts of a large number of people working in several institutions, most of which are acknowledged by individual authors, but several have played a more fundamental role in facilitating this project. In particular, our gratitude goes to the Mental Health Section of the American Sociological Association for its support and sponsorship of this book. This official backing no doubt lent credence to the undertaking and helped gain the participation of the respected scholars whose work is collected here.

Dr. Aneshensel also wishes to thank the University of California, Los Angeles, for a three-month hiatus from her teaching responsibilities, which enabled this project to get off the ground. I am especially grateful to Carmi Schooler, Director of the Socio-Environmental Studies Laboratory at the National Institute of Mental Health (NIMH), and Leonard I. Pearlin, research professor in the Sociology Department, University of Maryland, College Park. During my leave, both provided a rich intellectual atmosphere, congenial companionship, supportive resources, and, perhaps most important, space. Both Len and Carmi also shared with me their firsthand recollections of the emergence of the sociological study of mental health, which gave me a greater appreciation of the critical role played by a small group of social scientists working within the Socio-Environmental Studies Laboratory at NIMH.

Dr. Phelan also wishes to thank Bruce Link, Sharon Schwartz, and the Psychiatric Epidemiology Training Program at Columbia University for their ongoing intellectual inspiration and nurturance and for the excellent schooling they provide in issues relating to the social sources, meanings, and consequences of mental illness.

We also wish to thank Howard Kaplan for developing and editing the larger series of which this handbook is a part and for offering us the opportunity to edit this particular volume. We are especially pleased to have had the privilege of crafting its theme and the good fortune to work with its distinguished authors. We are also grateful to our editor, Eliot Werner, who has shepherded this project to its completion.

Finally, there is you, the reader of this volume. We thank you in advance for your critical attention to this material, with the hope that it contributes to your own work.

Contents

PART I

Introduction

Alternative Understandings of Mental Health

CHAPTER 1

The Sociology of Mental Health

Surveying the Field

CAROL S. ANESHENSEL
JO E. PHELAN

This handbook describes the ways in which society shapes the mental health of its members and further shapes the lives of those who have been identified as mentally ill. The terms *mental health* and *mental illness* encompass a broad collection of cognitive, emotional, and behavioral phenomena. Mental illness includes, for example, the experiences of a person who speaks to a companion whom no one else can see; someone who sits silently in her room, alone, eating little and sleeping less, contemplating death; a person suddenly overwhelmed with intense anxiety for no apparent reason; an individual whose consumption of alcohol makes it difficult for him to hold a job or maintain friendships; the person who is frequently sick with no identifiable physiological disease; and, someone who lies even when the truth would be personally advantageous and feels no remorse when others are injured by his actions. Although the classification of these states as "illness" has been questioned, the very use of the term *mental health* in the title of this handbook and in the designation of the sponsoring section of the American Sociological Association reflects widespread acceptance of this perspective among sociologists.[1]

Mental illness is a multifaceted concept whose understanding requires the insights of

---

[1] The terms *mental health* and *mental illness* are often used as antonyms, although the concept of health usually includes dimensions of well-being that go beyond the mere absence of illness.

CAROL S. ANESHENSEL • Department of Community Health Sciences, School of Public Health, University of California, Los Angeles, California 90095-1772.   JO C. PHELAN • School of Public Health, Columbia University, New York, New York 10032.

Handbook of the Sociology of Mental Health, edited by Carol S. Aneshensel and Jo C. Phelan. Kluwer Academic/ Plenum Publishers, New York, 1999.

several disciplines, each contributing a distinctive viewpoint. Psychiatry brings intraindividual considerations to the forefront, for example, whereas cross-cultural variations occupy this position in anthropology. This volume seeks to articulate a distinctively sociological orientation. This is a fool's errand insofar as there is not one but several sociological perspectives, each sharing features with those of other disciplines. Moreover, it is intellectually more fashionable to call for multidisciplinary perspectives. Nevertheless, we have undertaken this task out of a conviction that social arrangements and processes are fundamental to understanding the causes of mental illness and its consequences.

This assertion rests first and foremost on a foundation of empirical research demonstrating repeatedly and convincingly that mental disorders are not randomly distributed throughout society, but tend to cluster more densely within some social strata than others. Much of this volume is dedicated to describing and explaining these distributions. Here it suffices to note that a person's chance of developing and maintaining a healthy mental state throughout the life course is influenced by his or her social status, for example, by gender, race or ethnicity, and socioeconomic status (SES). These characteristics also influence the ways in which disorder is likely to be experienced and expressed, for example, as depression versus alcoholism. Although some of the covariation between social status and mental health may reflect social selection processes, especially for severe and persistent disorder, the weight of the empirical evidence favors a social causation interpretation (Aneshensel, 1992; Link & Phelan, 1995). Thus, social variation in the prevalence of disorder demonstrates incontrovertibly that some aspects of mental illness are social in origin.

The evidence concerning social consequences is equally compelling. Being identified as mentally ill is itself a social transformation. One's identity is altered, often irrevocably, to include what is generally regarded as a socially undesirable and stigmatizing attribute. This transformation has profound repercussions for one's subsequent social relationships. For example, after people recover from depression, their husbands and wives often remain apprehensive about the future and fear relapse, foreboding that may become self-fulfilling prophecy (Coyne et al., 1987).

However, most people who are beset by signs and symptoms of mental illness do not see themselves as being mentally ill, nor are they identified in this way by others—by friends, family, employers, physicians, or mental health professionals. Few seek treatment; involuntary commitment is even less common. Each of these outcomes is influenced by the person's social characteristics. For example, irrespective of the intensity of symptoms, women are more likely than men to recognize emotional problems, to identify these problems as depression, to seek help, and to obtain treatment (Yokopenic, Clark, & Aneshensel, 1983). Social characteristics also shape interactions with the professions and institutions that treat those who are mentally ill. For example, the likelihood that a diagnosis will be assigned to a given set of symptoms depends upon seemingly irrelevant characteristics such as race and gender (Loring & Powell, 1988; Rosenfield, 1982). In addition, sociocultural factors shape ideas about how disorder can be ameliorated and the means to achieve this end, for example, through psychotherapeutic or psychopharmaceutical treatment.

Mental illness is a fertile field for sociological inquiry, then, because social characteristics and processes are implicated in both the etiology of disorder and in its consequences. The characteristics that have been most important to sociological inquiry have been those that signify status within stratified social systems, including SES, gender, age, and race or ethnicity. Also attracting considerable sociological attention are characteristics that reflect the occupancy of major social roles, especially marriage, parenting, and employment. Role-related research has also examined the mental health impact of entrances into and exits from social roles, as well as the quality of experience within roles, especially their capacity to generate stress or provide support.

The remainder of this chapter introduces three substantive areas that are of particular interest to the sociology of mental health. The first concerns the socially constructed nature of mental illness. The second and third areas deal, respectively, with the social antecedents and consequences of mental health. We then conclude the chapter with an overview of the remainder of the text.

MENTAL ILLNESS OR SOCIAL CONSTRUCTION?

The very concept of mental illness is of profound sociological interest, because there is considerable sociocultural variation in how mental illness is manifest and understood, both across societies and within the various strata comprising a given society. In the extreme, sociologists disagree over whether mental illness exists as anything other than a social construction manufactured primarily by the institution of psychiatry (Scheff, 1966). As observed by Eaton (1986), the controversy is not over the occurrence of bizarre behaviors—by which he means human activities that are rare, culturally deviant, and inexplicable—which seem to occur in all cultures and historical periods; rather, the issue is the contrary ways of comprehending these behaviors.

The importance of relativity, subjectivity, and frame of reference can be seen in Davidson and Layder's (1994, pp. 26–27) description of the proverbial Martian who visits Earth seeking to conduct research on madness:

> What absolute, external criteria could it use to define madness? Unhappiness? Then all those who have recently been bereaved or suffered some other tragedy would be classified insane, along with countless others who live lives of quiet despair brought about by poverty, injustice, racism, war, famine and disease. Cruelty and brutality are not the exclusive property of mad people, but are regularly practiced in many of our most cherished institutions; auditory and visual hallucinations are not considered untoward in the feverish, the religious fanatic, the psychic or the drug user; no therapeutic intervention has been designed to "cure" the grandiose self-importance of statesmen, prelates, and pop stars, and our political leaders' mendacity and ability to simultaneously maintain wholly inconsistent and contradictory positions is not taken as an indication that they are deranged.

This passage introduces several themes that resound throughout this volume.

First, madness appears in many guises: disturbances of feeling—unrelenting sorrow, sudden euphoria, paralyzing anxiety, reckless abandon; breakdowns in thinking—irrational, intrusive, jumbled ideas, hallucinations, delusions; and bizarre behavior—purposeless acts, unintelligible talk, rigid immobility. These states, which collectively comprise the category of human experience labeled mental illness, have little in common with one another—schizophrenia, for example, bears virtually no resemblance to major depression—except in being extreme, troublesome, and socially inappropriate. This hodgepodge quality means that the concept of mental illness is often too amorphous to be useful except as a way of speaking about the conglomerate subject matter of psychiatry.

Second, the attribution of madness to aberrant thoughts, feelings, or behaviors is not inherent to the state, but rather contingent upon the context within which these states occur. As the previously quoted passage makes clear, this attribution is not made when there are other reasonable explanations for these states. Thus, extreme emotions are not seen as indicators of mental illness when the affect is appropriate to the situation (Thoits, 1985), such as, for example, a parent's grief over the death of a child. The identification of a state as aberrant, then, is not absolute, but relative to circumstances.

Third, whether the attribution of madness is made depends not only on the setting, but also on the person's characteristics. There is greater tolerance of deviance among rock stars, for example, than among office workers. The characteristics of the observer matter as well. For example, families often tolerate extremely peculiar behavior, behavior that would certainly prompt a mental health professional to apply a diagnostic label, because people are reluctant to apply the label of mental illness to a loved one and fear the consequences of doing so. The line between eccentricity and insanity, therefore, is not fixed, but moves according to extrapsychic criteria.

These considerations point to the socially constructed nature of mental illness. It does not exist in a material way, but only as an abstraction inferred on the basis of subjective and sometimes arbitrary standards. These standards, in turn, can be found only in societies with worldviews that include the concept of mental illness. Here, we speak not only of clinical definitions of mental illness as found in the diagnostic labels used by psychiatry, but also of lay understandings such as being "crazy" or "insane," "having a nervous breakdown," or going "berserk," or "postal." The existence of these ways of categorizing human experience is a necessary precondition for classifying any particular person as being in this condition. Recognition that mental illness is a social fabrication superimposed on some states and persons has led some social critics to claim that mental illness is a "myth" (Szasz, 1974).

Nevertheless, the kinds of thoughts, emotions, and actions commonly referred to as "mental illness" are experienced across diverse cultures, social structures, physical environments, and historical epochs. The pervasive presence of these troublesome states suggests that the social construction of mental illness is connected to an objective reality (albeit not in a one-to-one correspondence). The interpretation of this reality, however, has varied widely across place and time. The historical development of the social constructions culminating in current concepts of mental illness has been described in detail elsewhere (Eaton, 1986; Foucault, 1965; Szaz, 1974; see also Chapters 3 and 4). Here, we merely highlight two traditions that are especially consequential for sociology.

The first is a religious or moral interpretation that views aberrant states as resulting from possession by evil spirits, demonology, witchcraft, or sinfulness. Indeed, it was the close analogy between religion and witchcraft on the one hand, and psychiatry and mental illness on the other, that led Szasz (1970) to his heretical declaration that mental illness was a fraud perpetrated on helpless victims by institutional psychiatry. As we shall see, this tradition is important for sociology because it links mental illness to the study of social deviance and the associated processes of labeling and stigmatization (see below and Chapter 23 in this volume).

The second tradition emphasizes natural or physical causes, such as Hippocrates's contention that both mental and physical diseases are attributable to imbalances of the four bodily humors (blood, phlegm, black bile, and yellow bile). The modern version of this tradition understands mental illness as a disease, placing madness squarely within the province of medicine. Although a variety of understandings of aberrant states have some currency in the modern Western World, the medical model dominates.

The Medical Model

The defining characteristic of the medical model is the assumption that mental disorder is a disease or a disease-like entity with a physiological, genetic, or chemical base that can be treated through medical means (Cockerham, 1996; Kirk & Kutchins, 1992).[2] Terms such as *disease* and *illness* are used literally to connote identical meanings as in the physical realm, not as metaphors that simply call attention to certain similarities between mental and physical dysfunction. Troublesome thoughts, feelings, and actions are seen as signs and symptoms of underlying pathology. The designation of these states as "signs and symptoms" is the quintessence of the medical model and, as we shall see, the basis for its critique. From this perspective, the appropriate means of treatment are medical interventions, principally psychopharmacology.

This orientation has gained considerable scientific and lay acceptance in recent years, partly due to the effectiveness of various psychotropic medications, and partly due to actions taken by psychiatry to formalize diagnostic criteria to enhance its scientific base within the field of medicine (Chapter 26). The medical model has one seemingly fatal shortcoming, however: No demonstrable organic pathology has been established for most disorders. There are exceptions to this generalization, such as Alzheimer's disease, in which the accumulation of beta amyloid causes plaques in the brain that result in dementia, although even in this case, the cause of these accumulations is uncertain. Most mental, emotional, and behavioral disorders, however, lack identifiable brain abnormalities in anatomical structure or in chemical composition or functioning (Klerman, 1989). The absence of identified physiological causes has led some critics of the medical model to question whether these conditions can properly be thought of as diseases.

Biopsychiatry has countered with the claim that the medical model is validated when symptoms subside following the administration of substances that alter the brain's chemistry, even in the absence of information about what caused the symptoms in the first place. In other words, the remedy authenticates the disease, or so the argument goes. The successes of the psychopharmacological approach have indeed been impressive (side effects notwithstanding), especially for some severely disabling conditions such as schizophrenia, bipolar disorder, and major depression.

However, physiological correlates do not demonstrate that the origin of the condition itself is physiological (Cockerham, 1996). Furthermore, critics point out that drug treatments provide temporary symptom control but do not cure the putative disease that causes the symptoms. This palliative effect is no small feat, enabling many to function within society who would otherwise be beyond even rudimentary participation in basic social life. Nevertheless, the claim that symptom alleviation is evidence of an underlying disease is compromised by the absence of curative effects.

The Medicalization of Deviance

The medical model of mental illness is a problem for sociology. True, some sociological research enthusiastically embraces this model, in particular epidemiological research concerned with discrete diagnostic entities (as defined by the American Psychiatric Association [APA] and the National Institute of Mental Health [NIMH]; see, for example Chapters 3 and 7). However, other sociologists reject the model's most fundamental premise that what is wrong can legitimately be considered a disease or an illness, or, indeed, that any-

---

[2] Sociologists usually distinguish between the concept of disease as a pathological condition and illness as the subjective awareness of being unwell. This distinction is less commonly used in the mental health area because of the controversy over whether these states can legitimately be considered diseases.

thing is wrong. Still other sociologists study disorders or symptoms but are ill at ease with some of the assumptions of the medical model or its implications. This ambivalence is evident throughout this volume as authors struggle with definitions and search for a vocabulary that does not rely on the nomenclature of psychiatry.

The primary sociological alternative to the medical model was articulated in the sixties and seventies as part of the antipsychiatry critique, which portrays mental illness as socially unacceptable behavior that is successfully labeled by others as being deviant. Key proponents of this position include Szasz (1970, 1974), who contends that mental disorders are "myths," labels used to control socially devalued behavior; Scheff (1966), who argues that the mental illness label is disproportionately applied to socially devalued persons; and Laing (1967), who asserts that these are sane responses to an insane world, responses that serve to dissociate the individual from intolerable circumstances. These views share the idea that there is nothing inherently bad about the behaviors conventionally defined as mental illness. From this perspective, the fact that these definitions are used is more informative about the society doing the labeling than about the persons or behaviors being labeled. The causes of such "mental illness," therefore, are social, political, and economic, not medical.

Critics of labeling theory, however, conclude that the empirical evidence contradicts some of its most crucial tenets and puzzle over its continuing influence within sociology (e.g., Gove, 1982). Most problematic is the notion that mental illness exists *only* in the eye of the beholder (Szasz, 1974). The most damaging evidence against this proposition is the presence of similar "symptom" profiles across disparate cultures and social systems—clusters of emotions, cognitions, and actions that tend to occur together, to be subjectively distressing, and to create impairment. That specific clusters of "symptoms," such as those defining depression and schizophrenia, arise in heterogeneous settings among diverse peoples demonstrates that these phenomena have an objective reality apart from their subjective interpretation (Eaton, 1986). The sameness of these clinical profiles has been proffered as evidence that these individuals are all suffering from the same thing, and, furthermore, that this "same thing" is mental illness.

The presence of similar states in dissimilar settings discredits the idea that mental illness is defined solely by the observer, without any basis in the behavior of the labeled individual. It does not, however, demonstrate that these ubiquitous phenomena are illnesses. Indeed, in many settings, the states we refer to as mental illness are defined in decidedly different terms, as evidence, for example, of soul loss (see Chapter 2). Across different settings, the states being described resemble one another, but the names applied to these profiles differ. Although the phenomena themselves exist, universally treating these phenomena as "symptoms" of a disease may be problematic. In other words, abnormal behavior, incoherent thoughts, and painful emotions are ubiquitous phenomena, but the understanding of these conditions as disease is culture-specific.

In accordance with the foregoing arguments, subsequent critiques of the psychiatric perspective have taken as given the deviant status of the behaviors identified as mental illness but question the construction of these deviant behaviors in medical terms. These critiques note the lack of empirical evidence supporting a medical interpretation for many of these conditions, as discussed earlier. Of equal importance, they emphasize several negative social, personal, and scientific consequences of adopting a medical model.

Conrad and Schneider (1980), for example, describe a historical shift toward the "medicalization" of deviance. Among the consequences they cite is a lessening of individual responsibility for one's behavior, insofar as the deviating individual is considered "sick," not "bad." Moreover, the medical model diverts attention away from the social sources of deviance because it focuses on processes internal to the individual. An additional problem is the illusory moral neutrality of medicine, which obfuscates its social control function, a function that is more visible when exercised by the state or church. Furthermore, they argue that medicalization removes deviance from the realm of public discussion, because only medical experts are considered qualified to have opinions about illness.

The Debate over Diagnosis

In recent years, the debate over the nature of the phenomena being investigated has taken place in a methodological forum: Should mental health be measured as discrete diagnostic-type entities or as continuous attributes? This debate was ignited by the development and widespread use of the Diagnostic Interview Schedule (DIS; Robins, Helzer, Croughan, & Ratcliff, 1981), an instrument that yields diagnostic-type assessments based on information obtained by lay interviewers in community-based surveys. The DIS rapidly ascended to the status of instrument-of-choice via its sponsorship by NIMH, its large scale application in the Epidemiologic Catchment Area (ECA) study (Regier et al., 1985), and events occurring within the American Psychiatric Association (APA), specifically the development of the *Diagnostic and Statistical Manual of Mental Disorders* (DSM; American Psychiatric Association, 1987; Kirk & Kutchins, 1992; see Chapter 26).

The DIS displaced the symptom checklist, which had been the principal tool used by sociologists studying mental health. Large-scale community-based research, the bread and butter of sociological research into mental health, thus came increasingly under the conceptual control of those whose job it is to make diagnoses, that is, psychiatrists. However, sociologists retained their expertise in the methods of survey research and the analysis of the data it generates. As a result, sociologists have been among the lead researchers in all of the major epidemiological research conducted within this diagnostic protocol, including the ECA project and the National Comorbidity Study (Kessler et al., 1994; see Chapter 7).

The diagnostic approach, however, has come under heavy fire from sociologists. In particular, Mirowsky and Ross (1989a,b) have articulated the limitations of this approach, focusing on the ways in which it impedes scientific understanding of the phenomena under study. Specifically, they criticize the practice of "reifying diagnostic categories": describing observable attributes (such as hallucinations and flattened affect) in terms of hypothetical underlying entities (such as schizophrenia). They contend that reification diverts attention away from the causes of the real attributes and toward the hidden and possibly nonexistent biological causes of socially constructed psychiatric entities. They also call attention to the methodological weaknesses inherent in artificially reducing continuous phenomena into dichotomous categories, such as the presence or absence of a diagnosable disorder. In addition, the specific diagnostic categories of DSM have been criticized because the system is atheoretical and, consequently, impedes scientific research progress (Carson, 1996; Follette, 1996; Follette & Houts, 1996).

These views remain controversial. Those advocating diagnostic-type assessments argue that disorder is indeed a discrete entity, qualitatively distinct from seemingly similar normal states, and that symptom checklists measure ephemeral distress of limited clinical importance, "problems in living" (Klerman, 1989; Swartz, Carroll, & Blazer, 1989; Tweed & George, 1989). Critics of diagnostic-type measures contend that these instruments reify mental illness and trivialize the distress that is most common and consequential in the general population (Mirowsky & Ross, 1989a,b; Pearlin, 1989). Note, however, that neither side asserts that the phenomena do not exist, or are not abnormal. Instead, the issue is whether these phenomena are extreme forms of normal states or qualitatively distinct from normality. To some extent, this debate reflects tension between the borders of sociology and psychiatry over what constitutes worthwhile areas of inquiry. It also embodies, we submit, sociology's continuing discomfort with the idea that mental illness is an illness.

Dis-ease over Disease

The unresolved nature of this debate is evident in the content of this handbook. Some authors use one perspective or the other, diagnosis or distress, whereas other authors shift back and forth, including both alternatives. This heterogeneity reflects ambivalence within sociology about the phenomena under investigation. It reflects as well concerns about legitimization in a field dominated by another discipline (psychiatry).

This tension reflects two distinct traditions within the sociology of mental health: the social etiology of mental illness and the social construction of mental illness. The etiological approach implicitly assumes that psychic distress can meaningfully be understood as mental illness and sets as its prime task the identification of the social factors that are likely to cause it. In contrast, the constructionist approach takes as problematic the translation of aberrant states into an illness metaphor. This orientation illuminates the subjective and relative nature of mental illness but does not account for the original emergence of states that come to be construed as illnesses. Conversely, the etiological orientation addresses the latter issue, but does so by setting to the side issues concerning whether these states are legitimately treated as illnesses. Thus, each perspective takes as given that which is problematic in the other perspective. As a result, these two orientations have developed along largely independent lines (see Chapter 4).

For a variety of sociopolitical reasons, including, importantly, the policies of NIMH, the primary source of funding for mental health research, the issues raised by the antipsychiatry critique have become bracketed off to the side of mainstream sociological research, which typically adopts, at least implicitly, a medical model of mental illness. This practice does not mean that these issues have been laid to rest, but rather that the debate about the nature of the phenomenon being investigated has been conducted at the periphery of substantive sociological research rather than at its core.

For example, there are marked gender differences in the prevalence of specific disorders, with depression and anxiety being more common among women than men, and substance abuse and personality disorders being more common among men than women. One of many interpretations of these countervailing gender differences is that men and women are socialized into gender-appropriate modes of expressing distress, specifically that socialization practices inhibit emotional expression among men and discourage aggression among women (see Chapter 11). The idea that social learning shapes the types of disorder that people are likely to develop, and the manner in which disorder is displayed, is wholly inconsistent with the idea that these are signs and symptoms of an underlying disease (Kirk & Kutchins, 1992). Yet the question of whether alcoholism is the functional equivalent of depression typically does not take up the more fundamental issue of whether alcoholism and depression are diseases.

The majority of sociologists working in this specialty area begin with the recognition that the phenomena that form the subject matter of this book are extremely consequential for individuals and societies, and concern themselves with uncovering the social origins and consequences of these phenomena. Some sociologists working on such problems accept the illness model, whereas others remain agnostic as to the nature and meaning of these phenomena. What is common across these orientations is the acknowledgment that some persons suffer from bizarre thoughts, painful emotions, and problematic behaviors; that these states are more common among some subgroups of the population than others; and that these states have social antecedents as well as social consequences.

SOCIAL ANTECEDENTS OF MENTAL ILLNESS

Although the origins of sociological interest in mental health can be traced to Durkheim's (1951/1897) *Suicide*, contemporary research has been influenced most directly by early community surveys of mental health conducted in the decades following World War II (e.g., Gurin, Veroff, & Feld, 1960; Hollingshead & Redlich, 1958; Srole, Langner, Opler, & Rennie, 1960). These studies demonstrated certain key regularities in the distribution of disorder, especially its inverse association with SES. These patterns remain evident in more recent epidemiological research (Kessler et al., 1994; Mirowsky & Ross, 1989c; Robins et al., 1984) including the work reported in this volume (see Chapter 7). Virtually all of this descriptive epidemiology has been conducted by sociologists or with their substantial collaboration.

In addition to identifying social strata at especially high risk of mental disorder, sociologists have also sought to explain why these differentials exist. Although many disciplines are engaged in the task of uncovering the causes of mental illness, a key aspect of sociological research concerns the connection between these causes and one's location within society (Aneshensel, 1992; Pearlin, 1989; Link & Phelan, 1995). True, some etiological factors tend to occur randomly. For example, virtually everyone is at risk of exposure to unforeseen natural disasters, exposure that may induce posttraumatic stress disorder (PTSD). Randomly distributed etiological factors, however, are of limited value in explaining why some social groups have higher rates of disorder than others. At the risk of belaboring the obvious, the unequal distribution of disorder across social strata cannot be accounted for by etiological factors that are uniformly distributed throughout society.[3]

Sociological explanations for the occurrence of mental disorder, therefore, tend to emphasize causal factors that are consequences of one's social standing. Much of this explanatory work utilizes the stress process model, especially as it has been elaborated for stress mediators, including prominently social and personal resources, such as social support and mastery (Pearlin, 1989; Pearlin, Lieberman, Menaghan, & Mullan, 1981). A key feature of this research is an emphasis on socioeconomic disadvantage and the unequal distribution of material and psychosocial resources that might otherwise ameliorate the harmful impact of exposure to social stressors (Aneshensel, 1992; Pearlin, 1989). Still other work emphasizes sociocultural influences, such as the impact of minority-group status and inequality on mental health.

The sociological approach is also distinctive in its emphasis on ordinary aspects of

---

[3] Etiological factors may exert stronger effects among some groups than others, however, thereby generating group differences in disorder even when the groups have similar exposures. However, this apparent effect modification, sometimes referred to as differential vulnerability, is in actuality a proxy for the differential distribution of the resources that exert this modifying effect (Aneshensel, 1992).

social life. Many clinical theories of psychopathology, in contrast, link abnormal emotions, thoughts, and behaviors to anomalous social circumstances—to traumatic childhood experiences, deviant family dynamics, chaotic environments, and so forth. From this perspective, mental illness is an aberration whose origins lie in deviations from normal experience. The sociological orientation views abnormality in individuals as a by-product of the routine functioning of society. From this perspective, pathology is not evidence of some breakdown in the social system, but rather the unfortunate yet inevitable outcome of society functioning as usual (Aneshensel, 1992). The arrangements that are functional for society as a whole are seen as creating conditions that are dysfunctional for some persons.

For example, involuntary unemployment is a potent source of emotional distress. Although losing one's job is not an ordinary or routine experience for most individuals, the occurrence of job loss is a commonplace feature of most contemporary economies. Thus, some individuals will inevitably experience the mental health consequences of unemployment. The question is not whether there will be unemployment-related disorder, but rather who is at greatest risk for unemployment and, hence, disorder.

The sociological approach articulated in this volume, therefore, seeks the origins of psychopathology in ordinary aspects of social organization and routine social processes. For example, one productive line of research emphasizes connections between social roles and mental health, probing not only the occupancy of various roles and role constellations, but also the quality of experience within these roles (see Chapters 12 and 13). An important application of this perspective has been the explanation of gender differences in mental health (see Chapter 11). Although being married and being employed are each associated with better mental health, the impact of these roles depends at least in part on gender. Variation within roles also is influenced by gender, with men and women encountering somewhat different sets of stressors on the job and in the home. Thus, the ways in which society is organized around family and work are consequential to the mental health of men and women.

In summary, sociological research into the social antecedents of mental illness tends to adopt a structural approach: The sources of disorder are sought in the basic social arrangements that constitute society. Within this framework, a major goal is to explain why disorder is more common among some segments of society than others. The emphasis is on etiological factors that are consequences of one's location within society, that is, risk that derives from systems of social stratification and inequality. This approach often utilizes the stress process as the connection between structure and mental health outcome: High levels of disorder among certain groups can be attributed to their extreme exposure to social stressors or limited access to ameliorative psychosocial resources.

SOCIAL CONSEQUENCES OF MENTAL ILLNESS

The occurrence of mental illness sets in motion a variety of social processes with important consequences for the person with the disorder, for his or her family, and for society in general. From this vantage point, questions concerning the nature of mental illness and its antecedents give way to questions concerning its consequences. The occurrence of something identifiable as mental illness is taken as given, and the focus of inquiry shifts to accounting for its social repercussions. Although research into the social antecedents of mental illness tends to use a structural approach, research into its consequences more often uses a symbolic interactionist framework.

This approach predominates in research concerned with one of the most consequential issues, the labeling of persons as mentally ill, especially the adverse impact of stigma for psychiatric patients (see Chapter 23). One aspect of this work concerns the ways in which people come to see themselves as being "troubled." For example, Karp (1996) observes that depressed people initially attribute their emotional distress to external situations, and convert to an internal attribution that "Something is seriously the matter with me" when the situation changes but the distress continues. Thoits (1985) suggests that such self-attributions are likely to arise when the person becomes aware that his or her emotional reactions are inappropriate to the situation, a discrepancy that is also likely to lead others to view the person as emotionally disturbed.

In this framework, the individual comes to adopt as his or her own the real or imagined responses of others, that is, to view the self as others do, as mentally ill. Not all distressed persons, however, come to see themselves as being troubled or in need of help. In this situation, the person's self-perception may be seriously at odds with the perceptions of others, including importantly family members, agents of social control such as the police, or mental health professionals. These conflicting perspectives may lead to the imposition of an official label as mentally ill, a label the person may strenuously resist.

Work conducted within this tradition usually sets to the side questions concerning the origins of the primary deviance (i.e., the signs and symptoms of mental illness) that prompts the application of the label "mentally ill." Rather, it deals with the secondary deviance and other consequences that result from having had this label applied to oneself. The work of Scheff (1966) was especially influential in the development of this perspective, particularly his assertion that labeling is the single most important cause of a career of mental illness. From this perspective, a stable pattern of secondary deviance emerges because persons who are labeled mentally ill are treated in ways that tend to reinforce social stereotypes of the mentally ill; in particular, they may be punished when they attempt to return to their customary roles and rewarded for conforming to the role of mental patient. Social attributes are important not because they contribute to acts of primary deviance, but because they shape whether these acts are construed by others as mental illness.

Critics of labeling theory argue that stigmatization of mental illness is relatively rare and inconsequential, and, therefore, not capable of generating the adverse outcomes observed among mental patients (Gove, 1982). Instead, these outcomes are a result of the deviant behavior itself. Proponents of the modified labeling theory, however, dispute the idea that stigmatization is negligible. At issue is whether labeling effects offset any benefits of psychiatric treatment, which entails not only therapy but also labeling in the form of diagnosis (Link, Struening, Rahav, Phelan, & Nuttbrock, 1997; Rosenfield, 1997; see Chapter 23).

Within this context, the issue of self-attribution of mental illness is crucial because it differentiates coerced help seeking and involuntary commitment from help seeking by choice and elective treatment. Classic sociological work, such as Goffman's (1961) analysis of asylums as total institutions, necessarily emphasized processes within mental hospitals, because this was the site of most treatment, at least for serious and persistent mental illness (Chapter 25). Following deinstitutionalization, treatment research has emphasized pathways to treatment among the general population.

A key sociological issue with regard to treatment is the identification of the social determinants of help-seeking behavior, especially the tendency of distressed persons to not seek help. The types of formal health services used also have garnered substantial attention, particularly the preferential use of general medical care rather than specialty sources of psychiatric treatment. Research into the use of health services necessarily entails examination of the formal institutions that interface with mentally ill people. Important issues here include socially patterned differences in access to health care; reluctance to use mental health services; availability of appropriate and affordable services; managed care; involuntary commitment; social stigma; and other consequences of having been treated as a mental patient, especially within the confines of a psychiatric ward or a mental hospital.

Finally, the social consequences of mental illness necessarily include its impact on the family. One strand of inquiry addresses the role of the family in accounting for variation in the course of disorder, including its duration and chronicity, most notably with regard to the relapse of former psychiatric patients. Other work examines the impact of patients upon the health and well-being of family members. In this instance, mental illness is treated as a cause of stress and emotional distress for others (see Chapter 24).

OVERVIEW OF THE HANDBOOK

In summary, mental illness is of interest to sociologists because social arrangements and processes define the very construct of mental illness, shape its occurrence, and channel its consequences. These three themes form the framework around which this handbook is organized. Specifically, the chapters that follow examine mental illness as a social product, analyze its social etiology, and explore its social impact.

The handbook starts with a consideration of how social processes shape understandings of mental health, including the ways in which we as social scientists go about studying its occurrence and consequences. Part I deals with issues of definition and social construction. Two perspectives are discussed in detail: cultural variations in the conceptualization of mental illness (Chapter 2), and the medical model that predominates in contemporary Western psychiatry and is implicit in much of the mental health research conducted by sociologists (Chapter 3). The concluding chapter in this section seeks to illuminate the contributions made by alternative approaches to defining mental health (Chapter 4). Part II continues with issues of definition and conceptualization, but in a more concrete fashion, dealing with alternative measurement and analytic strategies (Chapters 5 and 6). It also sets the stage for the substantive sections that follow by introducing key methodological issues that cut across specific content areas.

The second theme addressed in this handbook concerns the social origins of mental illness. Part III begins with a general description of how mental illness is distributed throughout society (Chapter 7), followed by discussions of specific indicators of social stratification, including social class; race, ethnicity, and culture; age; and gender (Chapters 8–11). It also considers two major life domains especially relevant to mental health: the family (Chapter 12) and work (Chapter 13). The chapters in this section describe how mental illness varies according to one's social characteristics and the social roles one fills. Each chapter goes beyond description, however, and seeks to further our understanding of how these social patterns are created. Part IV continues this focus on social causation, examining the stress process as a crucial link between social stratification and mental health (Chapters 14, 16, and 19). This section emphasizes psychosocial mediators of the stress process, including social integration and support (Chapter 15), self-concept and identity (Chapter 17), and personal control (Chapter 18). It additionally emphasizes the social contexts of the stress process, including, importantly, social stratification and inequality (Chapters 16 and 19). Also included in this section is a conceptual examination of the process of social contagion as it related to mental health (Chapter 20).

The third theme represents a substantial shift in emphasis from the social antecedents of mental illness to its consequences. Part V begins with an analysis of treatment for mental illness, focusing on both the individual's help-seeking behavior (Chapter 21) and the system of mental health services (Chapter 22). The chapters on treatment are followed by two chapters that consider possible consequences of mental illness and treatment. One focuses on stigma and its impact relative to any benefits of treatment (Chapter 23). The second deals with the impact of mental illness on the family (Chapter 24). Part VI examines two institutional contexts for the processes surrounding treatment and its impact. One is the mental hospital, whose changing role over time has resulted in the deinstitutionalization of many persons with severe mental illness who now live in the community without being part of it (Chapter 25). The other is the NIMH, whose institutional life coincides with the emergence of the sociology of mental health, and whose programs, policies, and funding priorities have shaped the current state of the discipline (Chapter 26).

This handbook concludes with two chapters that present frameworks for integrating its diverse topics. The penultimate chapter takes a life-course perspective, examining how mental health problems ebb and flow over time, emphasizing the connections between mental health and the other trajectories of a person's life, such as work and family (Chapter 27). The final chapter examines the internal organization of a career of mental illness as it evolves over time (Chapter 28). Both of these chapters consider not only the onset of disorder but also its course over time, including issues of chronicity and recurrence, and its impact on the totality of the individual's life.

The sociological approach articulated in this volume emphasizes communalities in experience among people having similar social characteristics as distinct from the personal experience of any single person. In some important respects, each instance of mental illness is distinctly different from all others. The trajectories of one's personal history that converge and combine in the experience of confused thinking, strange behavior, or emotional distress are unique, as are the interpersonal actions and reactions that shape the course of disorder and its aftermath. Nevertheless, social regularities in the occurrence and consequences of disorder are not produced by idiosyncratic experience. This volume is dedicated to identifying and explaining these social patterns.

ACKNOWLEDGMENTS: We wish to thank Leonard I. Pearlin for his constructive critique of an early version of this chapter. Preparation of this chapter was supported in part by a grant from the National Institute of Mental Health (2 RO1 MH40831).

REFERENCES

American Psychiatric Association. (1987). *Diagnostic and statistical manual of mental disorders* (3rd ed., rev.). Washington, DC: Author.

Aneshensel, C. S. (1992). Social stress: Theory and research. In J. Blake (Ed.), *Annual review of sociology* (Vol. 18, pp. 18–38). Palo Alto, CA: Annual Reviews.

Carson, R. C. (1996). Aristotle, Galileo, and the DSM taxonomy: The case of schizophrenia. *Journal of Consulting and Clinical Psychology, 64*, 1133–1139.

Cockerham, W. C. (1996). *Sociology of mental disorder.* (4th ed.). Upper Saddle River, NJ: Prentice Hall.

Conrad, P., & Schneider, J. W. (1980). *Deviance and medicalization: From badness to sickness.* St. Louis, MO: Mosby.

Coyne, J. C., Kessler, R. C., Tal, M., Turnbull, J., Wortman, C. B., & Greden, J. F. (1987). Living with a depressed person. *Journal of Consulting and Clinical Psychology, 55,* 347–352.

Davidson, J. O., & Layder, D. (1994). *Methods, sex and madness*. London: Routledge.

Durkheim, E. (1987). *Suicide: A study in sociology*. New York: Free Press. (Original published 1951)

Eaton, W. W. (1986). *The sociology of mental disorders*. (2nd ed.). New York: Praeger.

Follette, W. C. (1996). Introduction to the special section on the development of theoretically coherent alternatives to the DSM system. *Journal of Consulting and Clinical Psychology, 64*, 1117–1119.

Follette, W. C., & Houts, A. C. (1996). Models of scientific progress and the role to theory in taxonomy development: A case study of the DSM. *Journal of Consulting and Clinical Psychology, 64*, 1120–1132.

Foucault, M. (1965). *Madness and civilization: A history of insanity in the age of reason*. New York: Vintage Books.

Goffman, E. (1961). *Asylums*. Garden City, NY: Doubleday, Anchor Books.

Gove, W. R. (1982). The current status of the labelling theory of mental illness. In W. R. Gove. (Ed.), *Deviance and mental illness* (pp. 273–300). Beverly Hills, CA: Sage Publications.

Gurin, G., Veroff, J., & Feld, S. (1960). *Americans view their mental health*. New York: Basic Books.

Hollingshead, A. B., & Redlich, F. C. (1958). *Social class and mental illness: A community study*. New York: Wiley.

Karp, D. A. (1996). *Speaking of sadness: Depression, disconnection, and the meanings of illness*. Oxford, UK: Oxford University Press.

Kessler, R. C., McGonagle, K., Zhao, S., Nelson, C., Hughes, M. Eshleman, S. Wittchen, H., & Kendler, K. (1994). Lifetime and 12-month prevalence of DSM-III-R psychiatric disorders in the United States: Results from the National Comorbidity Survey. *Archives of General Psychiatry, 51*, 8–19.

Kirk, S. A., & Kutchins, H. (1992). *The selling of DSM: The rhetoric of science in psychiatry*. New York: Aldine de Gruyter.

Klerman, G. L. (1989). Psychiatric diagnostic categories: Issues of validity and measurement. *Journal of Health and Social Behavior, 30*, 26–32.

Laing, R. D. (1967). *The politics of experience*. New York: Ballantine.

Link, B., & Phelan, J. (1995). Social conditions as fundamental causes of disease. *Journal of Health and Social Behavior, Extra Issue*, 80–94.

Link, B. G., Struening, E., Rahav, M., Phelan, J. C. & Nuttbrock, L. (1997). On stigma and its consequences: Evidence from a longitudinal study of men with dual diagnoses of mental illness and substance abuse. *Journal of Health and Social Behavior, 38*, 177–190.

Loring, M., & Powell, B. (1988). Gender, race, and DSM-III: A study of the objectivity of psychiatric diagnostic behavior. *Journal of Health and Social Behavior, 29*, 1–22.

Mirowsky, J., & Ross, C. E. (1989a). Psychiatric diagnosis as reified measurement. *Journal of Health and Social Behavior, 30*, 11–25.

Mirowsky, J., & Ross, C. E. (1989b). Rejoinder—Assessing the type and severity of psychological problems: An alternative to diagnosis. *Journal of Health and Social Behavior, 30*, 38–40.

Mirowsky, J., & Ross, C. E. (1989c). *The social causes of psychological distress*. New York: Aldine de Gruyter.

Pearlin, L. I. (1989). The sociological study of stress. *Journal of Health and Social Behavior, 30*, 241–256.

Pearlin, L. I., Lieberman, M. A., Menaghan, E., & Mullan, J. (1981). The stress process. *Journal of Health and Social Behavior, 22*, 337–356.

Regier, D. A., Myers, J. K., Kramer, M., Robins, L. N., Blazer, D. G., Hough, R. L., Eaton, W. W., & Locke, B. Z. (1985). Historical context, major objectives, and study design. In W. W. Eaton & L. G. Kessler (Eds.), *Epidemiologic field methods in psychiatry: The NIMH Epidemiologic Catchment Area Program* (pp. 3–19). New York: Academic Press.

Robins, L. N., Helzer, J. E., Croughan, J. L., & Ratcliff, K. S. (1981). The NIMH Diagnostic Interview Schedule: Its history, characteristics, and validity. *Archives of General Psychiatry, 38*, 381–389.

Robins, L. N., Helzer, J. E., Weissman, M. M., Orvaschel, H., Gruenberg, E., Burke, J. D., & Regier, D. A. (1984). Lifetime prevalence of specific psychiatric disorders in three sites. *Archives of General Psychiatry, 41*, 949–958.

Rosenfield, S. (1982). Sex roles and reactions to primary deviance of mental patients. *Journal of Health and Social Behavior, 23*, 18–24.

Rosenfield, S. (1997). Labeling mental illness: The effects of received services and perceived stigma on life satisfaction. *American Sociological Review, 62*, 660–672.

Scheff, T. J. (1966). *Being mentally ill: A sociological theory*. Chicago: Aldine.

Srole, L., Langner, T. S., Opler, M. K., & Rennie, T. A. C. (1960). *Mental health in the metropolis: The midtown study*. New York: McGraw-Hill.

Swartz, M., Carroll, B., & Blazer, D. (1989). In response to "Psychiatric Diagnosis as Reified Measurement." *Journal of Health and Social Behavior, 30*, 23–34.

Szasz, T. (1970). *The manufacture of madness: A comparative study of the inquisition and the mental health movement.* New York: Dell.

Szasz, T. (1974). *The myth of mental illness* (rev. ed.). New York: Harper & Row.

Thoits, P. (1985). Self-labeling processes in mental illness: The role of emotional deviance. *American Journal of Sociology, 91*, 221–249.

Tweed, D., & George, L. K. (1989). A more balanced perspective on "Psychiatric Diagnosis as Reified Measurement." *Journal of Health and Social Behavior, 30*, 35–37.

Yokopenic, P. A., Clark, V. A., & Aneshensel, C. S. 1983. Depression, problem recognition, and professional consultation. *Journal of Nervous and Mental Disease, 171*, 15–23.

CHAPTER 2

Mental Illness in a Multicultural Context

PAULINE AGBAYANI-SIEWERT

DAVID T. TAKEUCHI

ROSAVINIA W. PANGAN

How does culture affect the expression and prevalence of mental illness? This question reflects a critical tension in scientific investigations of mental health and illness that is revealed in the history of the development of the *Diagnostic and Statistical Manual of Mental Disorders* (DSM). The DSM provides a description of different "accepted" mental disorders and the clinical criteria for assessing each. Since the American Psychiatric Association (APA) first published the DSM in 1952, it has become widely used by clinicians, psychiatric researchers, and social scientists for different purposes. As a foundation, DSM assumes that mental disorders are discrete biomedical entities that are explained by biomedical processes. It is often implicitly assumed that psychiatric symptoms or syndromes are universally distributed and uniformly manifested. This assumption is unwarranted, because groups vary in how they define such constructs as "distress," "normality," and "abnormality." These variations affect definitions of mental health and mental illness, expressions of psychopathology, and coping mechanisms (White & Marsella, 1982).

The changes from DSM-I to the latest version, DSM-IV, mirror some of the social and institutional changes that have taken place in the United States over this 45 year period

PAULINE AGBAYANI-SIEWERT • Department of Social Welfare, School of Public Policy and Social Research, University of California, Los Angeles, Los Angeles, California 90095.   DAVID T. TAKEUCHI • Department of Sociology, Indiana University, Bloomington, Indiana 47405.   ROSAVINIA W. PANGAN • Department of Community Health Sciences, University of California, Los Angeles, Los Angeles, California 90095.

Handbook of the Sociology of Mental Health, edited by Carol S. Aneshensel and Jo C. Phelan. Kluwer Academic/ Plenum Publishers, New York, 1999.

(Rogler, 1997; see Chapter 26). As DSM-IV was being developed, social scientists and policy makers pressured the manual developers to consider cultural factors in the assessment of mental disorders. As a result, DSM-IV includes an appendix of culture-bound syndromes and statements about "specific cultural features" within each disorder section. Although the concession to include cultural factors in DSM was seen by some as a marked improvement, it did leave the DSM with a somewhat shaky foundation. Social and cultural explanations may not be consistent with the psychiatric tendency to focus on standardized discrete classifications of mental disorders (Aneshensel,1992; Kleinman, 1988).

The debate about the role and significance of culture and mental illness is not new, nor is it recent. This chapter begins with a review of the historical basis for the debate, examines the sources for the current interest in these issues, and provides a summary of the theoretical perspectives that guide empirical research on the role that culture plays in expressing, reporting, and responding to mental illness. The chapter concludes by advocating the integration of structural and cultural perspectives with conventional methodologies when investigating psychological distress and more serious forms of mental illness in ethnic minority communities.

HISTORICAL CONTEXT

Cultural relativists contend that explanations of mental illness cannot be separated from the individual's social and cultural context. In contrast, the universalists argue that a biological similarity and unity among people supersedes culture. Both perspectives agree that culture plays a role in the perception of mental illness. However, conceptual and theoretical disagreements continue unresolved regarding the impact of culture on the etiology, experience, expression, responses, and outcome of mental illness.

Each perspective comes with a voluminous body of theoretical and empirical research that supports its respective explanation of mental illness. Inherent in each explanation is a set of beliefs that frames research questions and methodology, guides diagnosis, and implies prevention and treatment techniques and strategies. Changing definitions and explanations of mental illness provide evidence for a cultural and social constructionist perspective. At the same time, a biomedical perspective maintains that historical evidence supports the argument that mental illness is a universal phenomenon that has consistently occurred throughout history and continues to afflict humankind. From this perspective, changing definitions and explanations are viewed merely as differences in interpretation based on available knowledge for any given period in time (see Chapter 4).

The Cultural Perspective

Cultural theories have disputed psychiatry's biological reductionism (Fabrega, 1995). During the 1950's, social construction theorists questioned the validity of a medical model and argued that mental illness was socially and politically constructed (Szasz, 1960). Biomedical explanations of mental illness as a disease similar to physical diseases were contested (Foucault, 1957). Although anatomical and physiological links were made for physical diseases, none could be made for the majority of identified mental disorders. Cultural theorists argued that our perceptions and responses to mental illness are shaped through social interactions, which are themselves formed by the cultural and sociopolitical context of society. Concepts of mental illness are not fixed, but are specific to a culture at a given time in its history (Foucault, 1965; Szasz, 1961).

A Euro-Mediterranean orientation of madness was dominant from the Medieval to Renaissance periods. Individuals who manifested patterns of symptoms outside the normal boundaries of behavior were labeled as mad. Dominant religious beliefs and symbols were reflected in definitions and explanations of madness, which was perceived as a conflict between the external supernatural forces of good and evil. Intervention was generally apathetic, and the afflicted were ostracized, left to wander, or were imprisoned. The perception and response to mentally ill persons began to change parallel to a restructuring of the economic system from a peasant economy to a capitalist one. Perceptions of the mad as victims of supernatural conflicts shifted to one of individual moral corruption and sinfulness. By the sixteenth century, persons believed to be mentally ill were institutionalized in hospitals originally established for lepers. These institutions played an important socioeconomic function of protecting the status quo by ensuring that a cheap source of labor was readily available and by tempering uprisings by the unemployed and homeless (Foucault, 1965).

Perceptions of mental illness during the American Colonial period also incorporated religious ideology (Manning & Zucker, 1976). The concept of mental illness did not exist prior to the nineteenth century, and affected individuals were referred to as "distracted." Emotional distress was expressed through religious idioms that reflected the dominant religious ideology and generally consisted of a blending of medical and religious treatment. As the United States began a transition from an agricultural to an industrial economy, the perceptions of mental illness caused by supernatural forces shifted to individual moral blame. Overindulgence, idleness, and masturbation were the prominent explanations given for behavior patterns perceived as insane. A biological basis for insanity also emerged during this historical period. The chronically afflicted were thought to have had an incurable hereditary disposition to insanity. Thus, two perceptions of mental illness existed: Individuals either caused their own insanity or inherited a predisposition for developing it. Asylums established to treat the chronically insane were largely occupied by the poor and homeless, who rarely were discharged. The affluent were treated in private sanitariums and had a more successful treatment outcome than those placed in asylums. Differences in social class influenced perceptions of insanity, its course, treatment, and outcome (Manning & Zucker, 1976).

With a predominant orientation that mental illness was a myth and nonexistent, early social constructionist theories were viewed as "antipsychiatry" and were ineffective in redirecting psychiatry's momentum toward a biological explanation of mental illness (Fabrega, 1995). With their roots in social construction, sociological theories such as social labeling and symbolic interaction also fell from prominence as primary explanations of mental illness. Although these theories did not dispute a biomedical explanation of mental illness, they redirected the focus of attention from the individual to society by conceptualizing mental illness as a product of societal response (see Chapter 4). Anthropological research made significant contributions toward a cultural understanding of mental illness and was a prominent leader in the cultural relativity movement beginning in the midtwentieth century. Anthropology has generally tended to focus and rely on cross cultural studies of mental disorders with populations in preindustrial, non-western, "exotic" cultures. Although this research significantly contributed to the clarification and development of concepts and theory in cross-cultural research on mental illness, it was seldom applied or tested in the same manner with racial and ethnic minorities who were considered culturally different in modern, mainstream Western societies such as the United States.

The Biomedical Perspective

The historical evolution of psychiatry's perception of mental illness as a universal phenomena began during the early twentieth century as it moved toward a scientific medical model of mental illness (Jimenez, 1988). The twentieth century ushered in the concept of psychiatry as an official branch of the medical sciences. Although moral and ethical issues were still believed to be related to the causes of mental illness, psychiatry, wanting to share in the medical knowledge and developments of the twentieth century, began to move purposely toward "scientific" explanations of mental illness (Pilgrim & Rogers, 1993). It was also assumed that an alignment with the medical sciences would bring recognized legitimization to a somewhat nebulous profession. Thus, psychiatrists began to use scientific idioms such as diagnosis, treatment, and outcome to categorize mental illness according to a medical model. The focus shifted, then, from the individual to a disease. The discovery of encephalitis, epilepsy, and paresis with its origin in syphilitic infection provided convincing evidence that mental and physical disorders were linked (Grob, 1983). Eventually, biological explanations of mental illness have found acceptance in the general public's attitudes and beliefs through popular media and literature, along with the popularized use of some medications (e.g., Prozac) that have become common household words.

Although social science research continues to advance a greater understanding of the cultural and social origins of distress, psychiatric research continues to strengthen its biomedical perspective of mental illness. Hereditary predisposition is the current theme that dominates perceptions and treatment interventions of mental illness (Fabrega, 1987; Kleinman, 1988). As psychiatry becomes more entrenched in medical explanations and as the biological orientation of mental illness is strengthened, the role of structural and cultural factors becomes increasingly minimized.

ETHNIC AND RACIAL MINORITIES IN THE UNITED STATES

The United States is becoming increasingly diverse as we move into the twenty-first century. Currently, ethnic and racial minority groups comprise 31% of children and 23% of the entire population (Hollman, 1993). By the year 2025, nearly one-third of all adults and one-half of all children will be from ethnic minorities (Lewit & Baker, 1994). In the past decade alone, the majority of people in some major urban cities, such as Los Angeles and New York, are from ethnic minority groups. Thus, the racial makeup of the United States. is changing dramatically, while our understanding of ethnic minority mental health and illness has not significantly increased since the 1980s. A critical component of these changes is attributed to immigration from non-European geographical areas such as Mexico, Asia, Cuba, and Haiti. The rate of immigration parallels that at the turn of the century, when large numbers of Europeans entered the United States. Although still the largest of the racial and ethnic minority groups in the United States., African Americans are projected to be the second largest group next to Latinos by the year 2025 (Lewit & Baker, 1994). Immigrants from other countries will increasing alter the composition of ethnic and racial minority groups in the United States.

As the United States undergoes continued demographic changes, there is renewed interest in studying cultural factors in the distribution of mental illness within ethnic minority communities. When examining prevalence rates of specific disorders, we find great variation in both cross-national studies and among ethnic groups in the United States. For example, a wide range has been observed in lifetime prevalence rates for major depression across different countries: Taiwan; 1.5%, Edmonton, Canada, 9.6%; Savigny, France, 16.4%; United States, 17.1%; Christchurch, New Zealand, 11.6%; Korea, 2.9% (Weissman et al., 1996; Kessler et al., 1994).

Rates of Minority Mental Illness

In attempting to understand the impact of cultural factors on mental illness, a common research strategy has been to describe the distribution of mental illness across different racial and ethnic categories. In the early part of this century, data based on hospital and clinic admissions and treatment were used to draw conclusions about the prevalence and type of mental disorders found in ethnic and racial minority communities. Using a treated-case-method approach, late nineteenth- and early twentieth-century research consistently reported a high prevalence rate of schizophrenia among African Americans (Bell & Mehta, 1980). Reportedly low rates of depression were explained as African Americans lacking the psychic makeup to experience sadness and depression (Bevis, 1921). Conversely, other research suggests that repeated misdiagnosis of African Americans led to higher rates of schizophrenia and lower rates of affective disorders (Bell & Mehta, 1980; Jones & Gray, 1986; Simon, 1973; Spitzer, Endicott, & Robins, 1978).

Although African Americans were reported to have high rates of mental illness, Asian Americans were described as a relatively problem-free population (Kimmich, 1960; Kitano 1962; Sue & McKinney, 1975; Yamamoto, James, & Palley, 1968). Findings from these studies supported a belief that Asian Americans had lower rates of mental disorders than most other groups in the United States, including Euro-Americans.

The rates of mental illness for nonwhite Hispanic groups vary widely, and it is often unclear if these rates of mental illness are similar to or different from other groups (Martinez, 1993). Data are mixed and sometimes contradictory on nonwhite Hispanic rates of mental illness (Vega & Miranda, 1985). Research has indicated lower, similar, and higher rates of overall and specific disorders (Jaco, 1960; Malzberg & Lee, 1956; Vega & Miranda, 1985).

Treatment data, however, have been criticized for not adequately reporting true prevalence rates. For example, researchers have repeatedly demonstrated the underutilization of mental health services by some ethnic minority group members, whereas others have questioned the validity of clinical diagnosis (Jones & Gray, 1986, Rogler, Malgady, & Rodriquez, 1989; Sue & Morishima, 1982).

AFRICAN AMERICANS.   By the middle of the twentieth century, survey research became a more prominent means of documenting the level of treated and untreated cases of mental illness in communities. A shift from treated populations to community surveys brought with it contradictions of earlier assumptions and understanding of ethnic and racial minorities. For example, unlike the wide discrepancies found in treatment data between African Americans and whites, community surveys demonstrate only modest or no differences in diagnostic disorders (Adebimpe, 1994).

Unlike rates under treatment data, Epidemiologic Catchment Area study (ECA) data showed no differences in the rates of schizophrenia between whites and African Americans after controlling for age, sex, socioeconomic status, and marital status (Adebimpe 1994). Adebimpe suggests that the disparity in findings found between community and treated samples can be attributed to an interaction between racism, sociodemographic, and experiential differences between whites and African Americans that necessarily affect treatment. For example, racial stereotypes and assumptions about African Americans have resulted in this history of receiving more severe diagnoses misdiagnosis, and differential treatment than whites (Adebimpe, 1994). The ECA study also found that African Americans had higher 6-month prevalence rates of cognitive impairment, drug abuse, panic attacks, and phobia (Griffith and Baker, 1993, p.152). Griffith and Baker caution that significantly higher cognitive impairment may be related to substance abuse, anxiety disorders, panic attacks, and other medical problems. Although the ECA offers new information about the prevalence and types of mental disorders experienced by African Americans, Williams (1986) warns that the ECA sampling methodology significantly undersampled middle- and upper-income African Americans, seriously limiting the extent to which the study's findings can be generalized.

Within-group variability has been generally neglected in epidemiological research with African Americans. Although stereotypes have led to an assumption that the majority of African Americans are poor and disadvantaged, about 10% are found in the upper classes and approximately 40% are middle class (Sue & Sue, 1990). Differences between Euro-American and African American rates of psychiatric illness are typically attributed to race. In a review of community surveys on African American mental disorders, Williams (1986) concluded that most findings of racial differences can be accounted for by socioeconomic variables. However, the fact remains that African Americans are overrepresented in lower socioeconomic levels, and, as such, may be more vulnerable to stressors linked to psychological distress. In an analysis of 21 cross-national studies, including the United States, Dohrenwend et al. (1980) concluded that the severest psychopathology is twice as common in lower socioeconomic classes.

ASIAN AMERICANS.   Asian Americans were not specifically recruited for inclusion in the ECA study. However, the notion that Asian Americans are generally well adjusted and problem free has been challenged by other research (Sue & Sue, 1974). Low utilization rates are not necessarily indicative of low prevalence rates, but may be a reflection of cultural factors, such as a stigma associated with perceptions of mental illness, the presence of family support, cultural incompatibility of Western forms of treatment, and differential meanings associated with mental illness. Uba (1994) conducted an extensive review of the research literature on Asian American emotional distress and concluded that Asian Americans have a rate of mental illness higher or equal to Euro-American rates. In addition, variations in rates and types of mental disorders vary across the numerous subgroups that comprise the Asian American category. For example, Southeast Asians have higher rates of posttraumatic stress syndromes than other Asian American groups, whereas Filipino Americans reportedly have higher rates of depression than most other Asian groups (Kuo, 1984) and the general population (Tompar-Tiu & Sustento-Seneriches, 1994).

NATIONAL COMORBIDITY STUDY AND ETHNIC AND RACIAL MINORITIES

A decade after the ECA study, the National Comorbidity Survey (NCS), another large-scale psychiatric epidemiological survey was launched (see Chapter 7). It was the first time that a structured interview schedule, the Composite International Diagnostic Interview (CIDI; World Health Organization 1990) was used on noninstitutionalized random sample of the national population. The CIDI is based on DSM-III-R nosology because revisions to what would become DSM-IV were still in progress at the time. Spanning 17 months of lay interviews across the 48 contiguous states, the NCS looked at the comorbidity of substance disorders and nonsubstance psychiatric disorders (Kessler et al., 1994).

Kessler et al. (1994) reported a 48% lifetime prevalence of one or more psychiatric disorders (i.e., affective, anxiety, substance use, and other disorders) (see Chapter 7). Meanwhile, nearly 30% had at least one disorder within the past 12 months. Major depressive episode (17.1%), alcohol dependence (14.1%), social phobia (13.3%), and simple phobia (11.3%) had the highest lifetime prevalence rates. Of those with a history of mental disorder (48%), more than half (56%) had two or more DSM-III-R disorders. Overall, NCS findings were similar to those reported from the ECA study, although the NCS rates are generally higher in the absolute.

However, notable differences emerged between the two studies in relation to race. Controlling for age, income, and education, Kessler divided race into four categories—"white," "black," "Hispanic" and "other"—and found that blacks were 50% less likely than whites to have had any kind of disorder within their lifetime or within the past year. Hispanics, on the other hand, showed no significant differences in lifetime or 12-month prevalence of any disorder compared to non-Hispanic whites. Neither the ECA nor NCS studies actively focused on Asian Americans.

Mexican Americans

Until recently, the ECA project was considered one of the most sophisticated and comprehensive in epidemiological research on Mexican American mental illness. Findings showed that Mexican Americans and non-Hispanic whites in Los Angeles were very similar across selected mental disorders, whereas whites had higher rates of drug abuse/dependency (Karno et al., 1987). Research has been mixed about the role of immigrant status on psychological distress and mental illness. Some studies have reported a greater vulnerability toward mental distress by immigrants than nonimmigrants, whereas others have concluded the opposite (Burnam, Hough, Karno, Escobar, & Telles, 1987; Rogler, Cortes, & Malgady 1991; Warhiet, Vega, Auth, & Meinhardt, 1985).

The ECA data suggest that structural and cultural factors play a powerful role in shaping rates of mental illness. Burnam et al. (1987) examined the relationship of acculturation, mental disorder, and immigrant status. Mexican Americans who were native born and highly acculturated had the highest lifetime prevalence rates across five disorders: major depression, dysthymia, phobia and alcohol and drug abuse/dependence. Immigrant Mexican Americans had lower prevalence of major depression and drug abuse/dependency than nonwhite Hispanics, whereas native Mexican Americans had higher prevalence than non-Hispanic whites of dysthymia, phobia, and alcohol abuse/dependency. The differential rate of mental distress between native born and immigrant groups has been attributed to structural and cultural factors, including an association between acculturation and a sense of status deprivation; selective immigration, with the disproportionate immigration of the most healthy individuals (Burnam et al., 1987); and, traditional cultural factors, such as strong family cohesiveness and support, and perceptions of mental illness (Shuval, 1982). Although these explanations point out important differences among Mexican Americans related to acculturation, they do little to advance an understanding of the cultural sources for these differences. In research with ethnic minorities, acculturation has been used to measured either the extent to which one has learned a new culture or the psychological changes experienced by the individual as a result of being in contact with other cultures and participating in the process of acculturation. Thus, the operationalization of acculturation as a social learning or psychological construct does not directly measure culturally related factors.

Explanations of Group Differences

Generally, there appear to be both similarities and differences across racial and ethnic categories. Differential rates between groups and within groups indicate a need to examine cultural and structural factors. When group differences are found, cultural explanations are often neglected in favor of explanations based on ethnic or racial differences, or factors related to cultural conflict. For example, differences in levels of acculturation have been used to explain greater immigrant vulnerability to psychological distress such as depression (Vega, Warheit, Auth, & Meinhardt, 1984), adjustment problems (Abe & Zane, 1990), and unhappiness (Padilla, Alvarez, & Lindholm, 1986). Conversely, recent data have indicated that immigrants have less psychological distress and mental disorders than their native-born cohorts. However, little is known about how the acculturation process creates psychological distress, nor is it clear whether acculturation protects individuals or makes them more vulnerable to mental disorders. Generally, level of acculturation does not communicate much information except to point out that people come from different cultures and describe the extent to which they hold on to traditional ways. Minimal information is revealed on the sources of cultural differences and how cultural content affects the etiology, expression, and treatment of mental disorders. Research on ethnic and racial minorities has tended to superimpose empirically untested cultural descriptions of a group onto findings in an attempt to understand and explain observed ethnic and racial differences in rates of mental disorders. For the most part, cultural factors are not directly examined but are inferred. Thus, we are left to speculate about the role of culture in mental disorders and how culture affects rates of mental illness for ethnic and racial minorities.

Figure 2.1 illustrates the two models of mental health research with ethnic and racial minorities discussed earlier. The conventional model examines how social factors directly affect mental health outcomes, unless the elaborated model allows for the integration of social, structural, and cultural factors. The conventional model is based on an assumption that one's place in society, such as membership in ethnic minority group, or as immigrant, is analogous with cultural factors such as beliefs, attitudes, and values, and as such can predict the expression, response, and prevalence of psychological distress and psychopathology. An empirical examination of the direct effect of cultural variables on mental health outcomes is oftentimes circumvented and replaced with conceptual descriptions of a group's culture. One problem with this approach is that we lose sight of the fact that cultural factors are only inferred and are not empirically based. The conventional model also assumes that all individuals within a particular category are similar based on their shared membership. For example, research has tended to focus on four general ethnic minority categories. However, each category is comprised of within group differences that may conceal more than they inform (Takeuchi, Uehara, & Maramba, 1997). The category Asian American encompasses numerous subgroups with distinct cultural, educational, historical, and socioeconomic differences. The elaborated model proposes to directly examine cultural factors and their impact on mental health outcome, while continuing to include social factors.

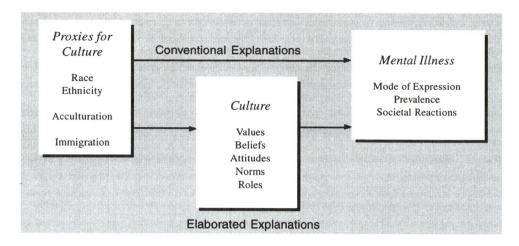

FIGURE 2.1. Conventional and Elaborated Explanations of Culture and Mental Illness

CULTURAL THEMES

Two major themes emerge from the literature examining ethnic and racial group differences in psychopathology: structural factors and cultural factors. Social structural factors can enhance or constrain the manner in which cultures express distress (Linsky, Bachman, & Straus 1995). Although a number of channels of expression for psychiatric distress may exist universally, whether a society is individualistic or collectivistic, for example, could pave specific pathways and affect the manifestation of symptoms. A study of the Hutterites in North America illustrates how structural factors influence the expression of mental illness. Alternately, cultural factors may also influence modes of expressing mental illness such that these modes are more acceptable in some groups than others. The preference of the Chinese for a clinical diagnosis of "neurasthenia" as opposed to depression, for example, illustrates how culture affects the manner in which individuals present psychological distress. The next two sections will briefly discuss the Hutterite and Chinese cultures to illustrate these two themes.

The Hutterites

The Hutterites are members of the Anabaptist sect that originated in Central Europe during the sixteenth century. Severe religious persecution in 1565 drove them out from Moravia (a geographic region in the former Czechoslovakia) and into other countries, including the Ukraine. A large number of Hutterites eventually migrated to the United States beginning in 1874, and in 1918 to Canada, where they have remained in religious communes. As a socially (and genetically) homogeneous group, the Hutterites provide an interesting insight into the effects of sociostructural factors on mental health.

An NIMH-funded study on the Hutterites conducted in the early 1950s by sociologist Joseph Eaton, in collaboration with psychiatrist Robert Weil, showed high rates of psychoses (Eaton & Weil, 1955). This finding was unexpected. After a thorough investigation, Eaton claimed that "the Hutterite way of life, despite the good mental health reputation of its members, provides no immunity from severe psychiatric disorders" (p. 53). The sect ranked third among nine other groups (e.g., an urban district in Baltimore, an arctic village in Norway, Williamson County in Tennessee). But rather than interpret the results as indicative of the Hutterites' proneness to psychotic illness, Eaton was more inclined to propose that the high expectancy ratio was "a function of the thoroughness of the survey methods" (p. 76). Since methodology has often been a source of disagreement among researchers, it is indeed relevant to meaningful comparisons of diverse groups. However, the various rates presented by Eaton in his analyses, and results of more recent cross-national studies, highlight a more striking observation: Culture has a profound impact on the expression and interpretation of psychological distress, which manifests in the different rates that have been reported in the psychiatric epidemiological literature.

Eaton and Weil (1955) found a lifetime morbidity of 199 in a population of 8,542, or one case per 43 Hutterites. A breakdown of the diagnostic categories revealed that 74% of psychotic cases (n = 53), were of the manic-depressive kind. These 39 Hutterites showed psychotic symptomatology characterized by a depressed mood with "mental and motor retardation, perplexity, or agitation" (p. 100). Meanwhile, other categories were discovered to be much less prevalent than manic-depressive reaction. A recent reanalysis of Eaton's data by Torrey (1995) using DSM-III-R criteria showed strikingly low rates of schizophrenia (0.9 per 1,000) and bipolar disorder (0.6 per 1,000). Thirty-two (3.7 per 1,000) were rediagnosed with major depression.[1]

That depression among Hutterites is four times more prevalent than schizophrenia and six times more common than bipolar disorder brings some intriguing questions to the fore: What is it in the Hutterite way of life that contributes in the expression of psychological distress, specifically depression? How does a Hutterite view her or his depressive condition?

Hutterites reside in agricultural colonies called *Bruderhöfe*, and practice a highly conservative, Christian way of life. They are isolated from more modern communities surrounding their enclaves, decline involvement in political issues, and are strict pacifists. Crime is almost unheard of and transgressions against one another are highly discouraged. The collectivistic orientation of this society requires every individual, child or adult, to give up selfish motives for the good of the group. Thus, a theocratic system coupled with a heavy emphasis on collectivistic values work hand in hand in the formation of a Hutterite culture.

The Hutterites' religious orthodoxy influences this group's depressive symptomatology. Eaton and Weil (1955) observed that "the content of the delusions and the verbal production [seemed] to be greatly colored by their notion that their disorder [was] a spiritual or religious trial by God" (p. 101). The Hutterites referred to depression as *Anfechtung*, meaning "temptation by the devil" (p. 101). It was believed that *Anfechtung* befalls "good people" (p.102); hence, its victims did not need to feel stigmatized for having the disease. Despite the supportive atmosphere in the colonies, the depressives nevertheless experienced a loss of self-esteem and felt sinful. Eaton claimed that "the culture of a Hutterite village [was] conducive to the development of such sentiments" (pp. 105–106).

Psychoanalytical theories and research on anger and its relationship to mental health

---

[1] At the time of Eaton's study, individuals who have had an episode of depression of any state (mild, acute, or depressive stupor), may be diagnosed with manic-depressive psychosis without having a prior history of manic attacks. Conversely, it could also be used on individuals who have had manic attacks only. Torrey's (1995) reanalysis using DSM-III-R criteria reflects the breakdown of Eaton's single category into three separate diagnoses—schizophrenia, bipolar disorder, and major depression.

may provide some insight into the high prevalence of depression among the Hutterites. Abraham (1927) attributed depression to repressed violence, and Freud (1993) conceptualized it as anger turned inward. Modern theories of depression suggest a similar causal link (White, 1977). A number of empirical studies have indeed found a positive correlation between suppressed anger and depression (Biaggio & Godwin 1987; Moore & Paolillo 1984; Riley, Treiber, & Woods 1989; Clay, Anderson, & Dixon 1993).

Laden with guilt for experiencing a socially unacceptable emotion such as anger, a Hutterite who has been conditioned to control overt display of a basic human emotion has little choice but to internalize her or his aggression. In addition, Hutterites are socialized at an early age to find guilt within themselves instead of their brethren (Eaton & Weil, 1955, p. 86). Not surprisingly, Eaton found that among the manic-depressives in the sect, only a few expressed verbal threats, and there were no incidents involving physical injury. Thus, the Hutterites' constant suppression of aggressive impulses to maintain group harmony may have drastic repercussions on their mental health.

That depression was found to be a common reaction to the Hutterite way of life is a classic example of culture's profound influence on the ways individuals respond to their environment. Thus, the context in which mental disorders appear should be treated with equal gravity as their prevalence. This concept has been clearly elucidated by Bales (1946) in his attempt to identify the social structural factors that influence rates of alcoholism within society. He suggested that (1) levels of stress or "inner tensions"; (2) societal attitudes toward drinking (abstinence, ritualistic, "social drinking," utilitarian); and (3) the availability of means other than drinking to relieve stress work simultaneously and may have differential effects in any particular culture. In a recent study testing Bales's theory, Linsky et al. (1995) found that levels of societal stress and degree of permissiveness toward drinking were correlated with indicators of alcohol problems (death rate from cirrhosis and average consumption of alcohol) at the state level of analysis. These results support Bales's theory and further emphasize the importance of cultures and social structures in the expression of mental disorders.

The Chinese

Neurasthenia. Numerous studies on depression among the Chinese have verified the prominence of somatic complaints presented by depressive individuals (Cheung, Bernard, & Waldmann, 1981; Kleinman, 1977, 1980, 1982; Marsella, Kinzie, & Gordon, 1973; Tseng, 1975). Chinese depressive symptomatology is markedly different from the affective and dysphoric manifestations of the disorder that are more common in the West. Lin (1982) remarks that "one may even wonder if one is not looking at a distinctly different illness" (p. 240). Additionally, results of these studies reveal significantly lower prevalence rates of depression among the Chinese compared with Western populations. However, some researchers ascribe these findings to culturally biased diagnostic criteria being used inappropriately in these epidemiological studies (Kleinman, 1977; Lin, 1982; Zhang, 1995). Thus, Chinese depressives whose primary symptoms are somatic are systematically being undercounted as a result of using culturally irrelevant instruments. Kleinman (1977) refers to this error as "category fallacy," a major source of error in the interpretation of cross-cultural epidemiological studies.

Although major depressive disorder has been found to have low prevalence among the Chinese, researchers have reported high rates of "neurasthenia." Furthermore, the disorder also appears to be the most common clinical diagnosis in this population (Cheung, 1989; Ming-Yuan, 1989). A term introduced by American neurologist George Beard in 1869, neurasthenia's symptoms include physical and mental fatigue, memory loss, insomnia, palpitations, dizziness, hypochondriasis, depressed mood, phobias, and headache—to name but a few of the 70 some symptoms described by Beard (1880). From the late 1800s until the mid-1900s, neurasthenia became a popular diagnosis worldwide. It gradually lost its foothold in the psychiatric community when biological etiologies failed to explain the constellation of neurasthenic manifestations and its symptoms overlapped with newly developed categories (e.g., depressive, anxiety, and somatoform disorders). Despite the APA's decision to exclude neurasthenia in DSM-III (and in subsequent editions), it has remained an indispensable category in the Chinese psychiatric nosology. Instead of concurring with Kleinman's (1986) conclusion that neurasthenia is but "a culturally salient form of chronic somatization that acts as a final common pathway for several distinctive types of pathology, of which major depressive disorder is the principal disease" (p.165), some researchers maintain that neurasthenia should be kept a separate construct, not a subtype of depression (Ming-Yuan, 1989; Yan, 1989; Young, 1989). Young (1989) asserts that "the elimination of the category only indicates change of diagnostic concept without definite direction" (p. 138).

In addition to the narrowly defined depressive criteria that are built into research instruments, unique aspects of the Chinese culture may mask depression altogether, thereby favoring the diagnosis of neurasthenia. Language, absence of body–mind dualism, shame and loss of face, family privacy issues, and a somatopsychic orientation of traditional Chinese medicine are factors that have been repeatedly cited in the literature (Draguns, 1996; Lin, 1985). As a "nosological dilemma," Rin and Huang (1989) have found that the diagnosis of neurasthenia is preferred by patients because it does not carry the stigma that is often associated with mental disorders. Consequently, clinicians favor using neurasthenia to establish rapport with their clients and their family.

Neurasthenia is a culturally sanctioned disease category among the Chinese. Moreover, its status as a "heterogeneous disease" (Yan, 1989) clearly warrants further investigation. Thus, it may be premature to jettison this disorder given the repercussions it may have on future cross-cultural comparisons.

CONCLUSIONS

The effect of culture on the expression and prevalence of mental illness has been relatively ignored in epidemiological research. As discussed earlier, culture is typically addressed only indirectly with the proxies of ethnic and racial categories, immigration, and acculturation. This approach precludes a direct examination of cultural and structural explanations. Using ethnic and racial categories to imply cultural explanations tells us little about how culture shapes the perceptions, expression, and responses to mental illness. In the future, studies must begin to develop and include measures that function to directly assess the multiple facets of culture.

Figure 2.2 depicts a working illustration of the elaborated model that integrates social factors and directly examines the effect of cultural variables on mental health outcome.

For example, using the construct of individualism–collectivism, Triandis (1993) proposed that mental health and psychological well-being are associated with an individual's set of cultural values and beliefs. The construct of individualism–collectivism is defined as

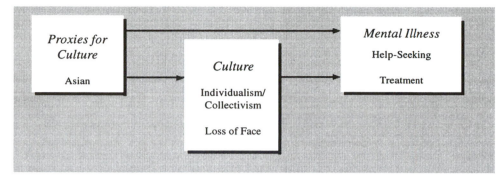

FIGURE 2.2. Cultural Explanation of Responses to Mental Illness among Asians

a cultural syndrome such as shared beliefs, attitudes, norms, roles, and values organized around a theme that is manifested in individual and group behavior. Individualism emphasizes autonomy, with personal goals taking precedence over group goals. Collectivism, in contrast, makes minimal distinction between personal and group goals. Collectivists will not generally perceive individual personal problems as sufficiently important reasons to seek professional help (Tracey, Leong, & Glidden, 1986). They tend to rely on collective forms of coping that make facing life's challenges more manageable (Kashima & Triandis, 1986). Collective coping may help to explain why some ethnic groups seemingly underutilize mental health services and instead, rely on family members to care for mentally ill relatives. The measure of individualism–collectivism goes beyond ethnic and racial categories to an in-depth examination of underlying cultural structures that affect perceptions, expression, and response to mental disorders.

Another example of a culturally specific construct is "loss of face." Defined within the context of an individual's strong identification with a specific collective, "loss of face" pertains to "a threat [to] or loss of one's social integrity" (Zane, 1993, p. 1). Extant literature on Asian culture has consistently alluded to or directly identified loss of face as an important construct in social dynamics. In examining various putative factors that prevent Asian Americans from seeking treatment for substance abuse, loss of face to the family and the ethnic community has been recognized as a significant cultural component (Ja & Aoki, 1993). As illustrated in Figure 2.2, cultural constructs should serve a key function when probing for unique explanations and causations in mental health research in areas such as modes of expression, social reactions, help-seeking behaviors, and the utilization of services.

In addition to a direct examination of the structural and cultural variables discussed earlier, the predictive ability of an elaborated model requires that outcome measures be culturally appropriate and relevant. Epidemiological research has tended to examine Western conceptualizations of mental disorders. Social and cultural explanations of mental disorders may not be consistent with the psychiatric tendency to focus on standardized, discrete classifications of mental disorders. Examining symptoms or clusters of symptoms based on Western conceptualizations of mental disorders or psychological distress may not be valid for use with ethnic and racial minorities (Rogler et al., 1989). The symptoms chosen as indicators of the various mental disorders may not represent the experiences of some groups. For example, exposure to stress can affect groups in different ways. Recent immigrants may respond to distress in ways that are similar to those found in their country of origin. Statistical equivalence-of-scale measures between groups do not necessarily translate into conceptual equivalence (Vernon & Roberts, 1982). Measurement error may occur, because the symptoms that comprise diagnostic categories may be interpreted differently across different groups. It may prove useful to consider constructs that are common in other cultures (e.g., *susto* for Mexicans and neurasthenia for the Chinese), because variations in rates of mental illness may reflect differences in how an immigrant group perceives, experiences, and expresses psychological distress.

Rates of mental disorders may be affected by the types and number of outcomes used in epidemiological research. By expanding the spectrum of outcomes measured, we could gain a better understanding of the cultural and structural factors that account for variation in rates of mental illness. The recent ECA study left out the majority of DSM-III diagnostic categories, leaving us to speculate on possible alternative expressions of psychological distress. The inclusion of multiple outcomes may avoid biased over- or underreporting of mental disorders. Fabrega, Rubel, and Wallace (1967) reported Mexican American gender differences in the expression of internalized distress. Women tended to express their distress as depression and anxiety, whereas men used alcohol and aggressive behavior. Examining recent ECA data, Aneshensel, Rutter, and Lachenbruch (1991) demonstrated that gender differences in the expression of stress are disorder-specific and that there is no difference between men and women's vulnerability to stress. Stress exposure was related to depression for women and to substance use for men. If only depression had been measured, the findings would have led to an incorrect conclusion that women were more vulnerable to stress than men. The extension of this issue to race, ethnicity, and cultural groups is self-evident.

Rates of mental disorders may also be affected by a group's cultural perceptions, attitudes, and beliefs regarding mental illness through the methods of data collection. For example, loss of face may result in a response bias to Western concepts of psychological distress, resulting in the underreporting of mental disorders. Similarly, overreporting results biases findings when excessively compliant respondents answer questions regarding their mental health status (Rogler et al.,1989).

Since each group constitutes a unique set of social and cultural structures and beliefs, mental illness will be processed differently with concomitant variances in rates of psychopathology, treatments, and outcomes. Ethnocentric cultural assumptions about abnormal behavior and symptoms make it difficult to accurately assess true differences in mental disorders across groups or culturally influenced expressions of psychological distress (Good & Good, 1986). It may be more helpful to examine the level of functioning, such as daily routines that are related to definitions of normal and abnormal behavior, within a particular culture, along with assessing the individual's ability to fulfill culturally specific psychological, social and occupational role expectations (see Waxler 1974). Without fully rejecting a biological basis of mental illness, evaluating the individual's level of functioning incorporates the structural and cultural context of mental illness (Lemert 1951). It also redirects the focus of attention from the individual to society by viewing mental illness as the product of a process of societal interaction and reaction. This perspective represents a person-in-environment model that integrates biomedical, sociostructural, and cultural factors.

Epidemiological studies are especially vulnerable to problems of instrument validity and cultural biases in the reporting and understanding of mental illness among ethnic and racial minority groups. Current epidemiological studies, with a reliance on traditional methodologies, will do little to unravel the sources of variations in rates of mental disorders.

Until these issues are addressed, it is not clear if findings represent a biased or valid report of psychological distress and mental illness. Extant literature strongly suggests the prominent role of culture in the perception, experience, response, treatment, and outcome of mental illness. Along with a biomedical perspective, epidemiological research on mental disorders needs to include a person-in-environment perspective that more accurately represents the reality of ethnic and racial minorities. Because of the nature of their methods, researchers using large-scale epidemiological studies will have difficulties in fully understanding the cultural factors that help to explain the distribution of mental illness. If the intent is to understand reasons for ethnic differences in rates of mental illness or more systematically understand cultural factors, it may be prudent in the future to supplement large scale community surveys with more ethnographic investigations and/or in-depth interviews. By incorporating and integrating different approaches to the study of culture, we will have a more complete grasp of the cultural contexts that so profoundly shape and affect people's lives.

ACKNOWLEDGMENTS: Support for this chapter was provided by National Institute of Alcohol Abuse and Alcoholism Grant No. AA09633 and National Institute of Mental Health Grant No. MH44331.

REFERENCES

Abe, J. S. & Zane, N. (1990). Psychological maladjustment among Asian and White American college students: Controlled for confounds. *Journal of Counseling Psychology, 37,* 437–444.

Abraham, K. (1927). *Selected papers of Karl Abraham.* London: Hogarth Press.

Adebimpe, V. R. (1994). Race, racism, and epidemiological surveys. *Hospital and Community Psychiatry, 45,* 27–31.

Aneshensel, C., Rutter, C. & Lachenbruch, P. (1991). Social structure, stress and mental health: Competing conceptual and analytic models. *American Sociological Review, 56,*166–78.

Aneshensel, C. (1992). Social stress: Theory and research. *Annual Review of Sociology, 18,* 15–38.

Bales, R. F. (1946). Cultural differences in rates of alcoholism. *Quarterly Journal of Studies on Alcohol, 6,* 480–499.

Beard, G. M. (1880). *A practical treatise on nervous exhaustion (neurasthenia).* New York: W. Wood & Co.

Bell, C. C. & Mehta, H. (1980). The misdiagnosis of Black patients with manic depressive illness. *Journal of the National Medical Association, 72,* 141–145.

Bevis, W. (1921). Psychological traits of the southern Negro with observations as to some of his psychosis. *The American Journal of Psychiatry, 78,* 69–78.

Biaggio, M. K. & Godwin, W. H. 1987. Relation of depression to anger and hostility constructs. *Psychological Reports, 61,* 87–90.

Burnam, M. A., Hough, R., Karno, M., Escobar, J., & Telles, C. (1987). Acculturation and lifetime prevalence of psychiatric disorders among Mexican Americans in Los Angeles. *Journal of Health and Social Behavior 28,* 89–102.

Cheung, F. M. (1989). The indigenization of neurasthenia in Hong Kong. *Culture, Medicine and Psychiatry, 13,* 227–241.

Cheung, F. M., Lau, B. W. K. & Edith Waldmann. 1980-1981. Somatization among Chinese depressives in general practice. *International Journal of Psychiatry in Medicine, 10,* 361–374.

Clay, D. L., Anderson, W. P. & Dixon, W. W. (1993). Relationship between anger expression and stress in predicting depression. *Journal of Counseling and Development, 72,* 91–94.

Dohrenwend, B. P., Dohrenwend, B. S., Gould, M. S., Link, B., Neugebauer, R., & Wunsch-Hitzig, R. (1980). *Mental illness in the United States: Epidemiological estimates.* New York: Praeger Publishers.

Draguns, J. G. (1996). Abnormal behaviour in Chinese societies: Clinical, epidemiological, and comparative studies. In M. H. Bond (Ed.), *The handbook of Chinese psychology,* (pp. 412–428). Hong Kong: Oxford University Press.

Eaton, J. W., & Weil, R. J. (1955). *Culture and mental disorders: A comparative study of the Hutterites and other populations.* Glencoe, IL: Free Press.

Fabrega, H. (1995). Cultural challenges to the psychiatric enterprise. *Comprehensive Psychiatry, 36,* 377–383.

Fabrega, H. (1992). The role of culture in a theory of psychiatric Illness. *Social Science Medicine, 35,* 91–103.

Fabrega, H. (1987). Psychiatric diagnosis: A cultural perspective. *Journal of Nervous and Mental Disease, 175,* 383–394.

Fabrega, H., Rubel, A. J., & Wallace, C. A. (1967). Working class Mexican psychiatric outpatients. *Archives of General Psychiatry, 16,* 704–712.

Foucault, M. (1957). *Mental illness and psychology.* Berkeley, CA: University of California Press.

Foucault, M. (1965). Madness and civilization; a history of insanity in the age of reason. New York: Pantheon Books.

Freud, S. (1993). *Mourning and melancholia.* Madison, CT: International Universities Press.

Griffith, E. & Baker, F. M. (1993). Psychiatric care of African Americans. In A. C. Gaw (Ed.), *Culture, ethnicity, and mental illness,* (pp. 147–174). Washington, DC: American Psychiatric Association.

Grob, G. (1983). *Mental illness and American society, 1875–1940.* Princeton, NJ: Princeton University Press.

Hollman, F. W. (1993). *U.S. population estimates by age, sex, race, and Hispanic Origin: 1980–1990.* Current Population report, Series P-25, No. 1095, Washington DC: U.S. Printing Office.

Ja, D. Y., & Aoki, B. (1993). Substance abuse barriers in the Asian-American community. *Journal of Psychoactive Drugs, 25,* 61–71.

Jaco, E. G. (1960). *The social epidemiology of mental disorders: A psychiatric survey of Texas.* New York: Russell Sage Foundation.

Jimenez, M. A. (1988). Chronicity in mental disorders: Evolution of a concept. *Journal of Contemporary Social Work. 69,* 627–633.

Jones, B. E., & Gray, B. A. (1986). Problems in diagnosing schizophrenia and affective disorders among blacks. *Hospital and Community Psychiatry, 37,* 61–65.

Karno, M., Hough, R., Burnam, A., Escobar, J., Timbers, D., Santana, F., & Boyd, J. (1987). Lifetime prevalence of specific psychiatric disorders among Mexican Americans and non-Hispanic whites in Los Angeles. *Archives of General Psychiatry, 44,* 695–701.

Kashima, Y., & Triandis, H. (1986). The self-serving bias in attributions as a coping strategy: A cross-cultural study. *Journal of Cross-Cultural Psychology, 17,* 83–98.

Kessler, R. C., McGonagle, K. A., Zhao, K. A., Nelson, C. B., Hughes, M., Eshleman, S., Wittchen, H. U., & Kendler, K. S. (1994). Lifetime and 12-month prevalence of DSM-III-R psychiatric disorders in the United States: Results from the National Comorbidity Study. *Archive of General Psychiatry, 51,* 8–19.

Kimmich, R. A. (1960). Ethnic aspects of schizophrenia in Hawaii. *Psychiatry, 23,* 97–102.

Kitano, H. H. L. (1962). Changing achievement patterns of the Japanese in the United States. *Journal of Social Psychology, 58,* 257–264.

Kitano, H. H. L. (1962). Japanese American mental illness. In S. C. Plog & R. B. Edgerton (Eds.), *Changing perspectives in mental illness* (pp. 256–284). New York: Holt, Rinehart & Wilson.

Kleinman, A. (1988). *Rethinking Psychiatry: From cultural category to personal experience.* New York: Free Press.

Kleinman, A. 1986. *Social Origins of Distress and Disease.* New Haven, CT: Yale University Press.

Kleinman, A. (1982). Neurasthenia and depression: A study of somatization and culture in China. *Culture, Medicine and Psychiatry, 6,* 117–190.

Kleinman, A. (1977). Depression, somatization and the "new cross-cultural Psychiatry". *Social Science and Medicine, 11,* 3–10.

Kuo, W. (1984). Prevalence of depression among Asian-Americans. *Journal of Nervous and Mental Disease, 172,* 449–457.

Lemert, E. M. (1951). *Social pathology: A systematic approach to the theory of sociopathic behavior.* New York: McGraw-Hill.

Lewit, E. M., & Baker, L. (1994). Race and ethnicity: Changes for Children. *The Future of Children, 4,* 134–144.

Lin, T-Y. (1985). Mental disorders and psychiatry in chinese culture: characteristic features and major issues. In W. S. Tseng and D. Y. H. Wu (Eds.), *Chinese mental health,* (pp. 369–93). New York: Academic Press, Inc.

Lin, T-Y. (1982). Culture and psychiatry: A Chinese perspective. *Australian and New Zealand Journal of Psychiatry, 16,* 235–245.

Linsky, A. S., Bachman, R., & Strauss, M. S. (1995). *Stress, culture, and aggression.* New Haven: Yale University Press.

Malzberg, B. & Lee, E. S. (1956). *Migration and mental disease: a study of first admissions to hospitals for mental diseases*. New York: Social Science Research Council.

Manning, P. K. & Zucker, M. (1976). *The sociology of mental health and illness*. Indianapolis, IN: Bobbs-Merrill.

Marsella, A. J., Kinzie, D. & Gordon, P. (1973). Ethnic variations in the expression of depression. *Journal of Cross-Cultural Psychology, 4*, 435–458.

Martinez, Jr., C. (1993). Psychiatric care of Mexican Americans. In A.C. Gaw (Ed.), *Culture, Ethnicity and Mental Illness*, (pp. 431–466). Washington, D.C.: American Psychiatric Press, Inc.

Ming-Yuan, Z. (1989). The diagnosis and phenomenology of neurasthenia: A Shanghai study. *Culture, Medicine and Psychiatry, 13*, 147–161.

Mirowsky, J. & Ross, C. (1989). *Social causes of psychological distress*. New York: de Gruyter.

Moore, T. W., & Paolillo, J. G. (1984). Depression: Influence of hopelessness, locus of control, hostility, and length of treatment. *Psychological Reports, 54*, 875–881.

Padilla, A. M., Alvarez, M., & Lindholm, K. J. (1986). Generational status and personality factors as predictors of stress in students. *Hispanic Journal of Behavioral Sciences, 8*, 275–288.

Pilgrim, D., & Rogers, A. (1993). *A sociology of mental health and illness*. Bristol, PA: Open University Press.

Riley, W. T., Treiber, F. A., & Woods, G. (1989). Anger and hostility in depression. *Journal of Nervous and Mental Disease, 177*, 668–674.

Rin, H., & Huang, M. G. (1989). Neurasthenia as a nosological dilemma. *Culture, Medicine and Psychiatry, 13*, 215–226.

Rogler, L. (1997). Making sense of historical changes in the *Diagnostic and Statistical Manual of Mental Disorders*: Five propositions. *Journal of Health and Social Behavior, 38*, 9–20.

Rogler, L. H., Malgady, R. G., & Rodriguez, O. (1989). *Hispanics and mental health: A framework in research*. FL: Robert E. Krieger.

Rogler, L. H., Cortes, D., & Malgady, R. (1991). Acculturation and mental health status among Hispanics. *American Psychologist, 6*, 585–597.

Spitzer, R., Endicott, J., & Robins, E. (1978). Research diagnostic criteria: rationale and reliability. *Archives of General Psychiatry, 35*, 773–782.

Shuval, J. T. (1982). Migration and stress. In L. Goldberger & S. Breznitz (Eds.), *Handbook of stress: Theoretical and clinical aspects* (pp. 677–691). New York, NY: Free Press.

Sue, D. W., & Sue, D. (1990). *Counseling the culturally different: Theory and practice* (2nd ed.). New York: John Wiley.

Sue, S. & McKinney, H. (1975). Asian Americans in the community mental health care system. *American Journal of Orthopsychiatry, 45*, 111–118.

Sue, S. & Morishima, J. K. (1982). *The mental health of Asian Americans*. San Francisco, CA: Jossey-Bass.

Sue, S. & Sue, D. (1974). MMPI comparisons between Asian-American and non-Asian students utilizing a student health psychiatric clinic. *Journal of Counseling Psychology, 21*, 423–427.

Szasz, T. (1960). The myth of mental illness. *American Psychologist, 15*, 113–118.

Szasz, T. (1961). The uses of naming and the origin of the myth of mental illness. *American Psychologist, 16*, 59–65.

Takeuchi, D. T., Uehara, E. S., & Maramba, G. G. (In Press). Cultural diversity and mental health treatment. In A. Horwitz & T. Scheid (Eds.), *Sociology of mental health and illness*. Cambridge, MA: Cambridge Press.

Tompar-Tiu, A., & Sustento-Seneriches, J. (1994). *Depression and other mental health issues: the Filipino American experience*. San Francisco: Jossey-Bass.

Torrey, E. F. (1995). Prevalence of psychosis among the Hutterites: A reanalysis of the 1950–53 study. *Schizophrenia Research, 16*, 167–170.

Tracey, T., Leong, F., & Glidden, C. (1986). Help-seeking and problem perception among Asian Americans. *Journal of Counseling Psychology, 33*, 331–336.

Triandis, H. (1993). Collectivism and individualism as cultural syndromes. *Cross-Cultural Research, 27*, 155–180.

Tseng, W. (1975). The nature of somatic complaints among psychiatric patients: The Chinese case. *Comprehensive Psychiatry, 16*, 237–245.

Uba, L. (1994). *Asian Americans: Personality patterns, identity, and mental health*. New York: Guilford.

Vega, W., & Manuel M. (1985). *Stress and Hispanic mental health: Relating research to service delivery*. Rockville, MD: U.S. Department of Health and Human Services, Alcohol, Drug Abuse, and Mental Health Administration.

Vega, W., Warheit, G., & Meinhardt, K. (1985). Mental health issues in the Hispanic community: The prevalence of psychological distress. In W. Vega & M. Miranda (Eds.), *Stress and Hispanic mental health: Relating research to service delivery* (pp. 30–47). Rockville, MD: National Institute of Mental Health.

Vega, W., Warheit, G., Auth, J. B., & Meinhardt, K. (1984). The prevalence of depressive symptoms among Mexican Americans and Anglos. *American Journal of Epidemiology, 120,* 592–607.

Vernon, S., & Roberts, R. (1982). Prevalence of treated and untreated psychiatric disorders in three ethnic groups. *Social Science and Medicine, 16,* 1575–1582.

Warheit, G., Vega, W., Auth, J. B., & Meinhardt, K. (1985). Psychiatric symptoms an dysfunctions among Anglos and Mexican Americans: An epidemiological study. *Research in Community Mental Health, 5,* 3–32.

Waxler, N. E. (1974). Culture and mental illness: A social labeling perspective. *Journal of Nervous and Mental Disease, 159,* 379–395.

Weissman, M. M., Bland, R. C., Canino, G. J., Faravelli, C., Greenwald, S., Hwu, H.-G., Joyce, P. R., Karam, E, G., Lee, C.-K. Lelouch, J., Lepine, J.-P., Newman, S. C., Rubio-Stipec, M., Wells,, J. E., Wickramaratne, P. J., Wittchen, H.-U., & Yeh, E.-K. 1996. Cross-national epidemiology of major depression and bipolar disorders." *Journal of the American Medical Association, 276,* 293–299.

White, R. B. (1977). Current psychoanalytic concepts of depression." Pp. 127–141 In *Phenomenology and Treatment of Depression*, W. E. Fann, I. Karacan, A. D. Pokorny, & R. L. Williams (Eds.), (pp. 127–141). New York: Spectrum.

White, G. M., & Marsella, A. J. (1982). Introduction: Cultural conceptions in mental health research and practice. In A. J. Marsella & G. M. White (Eds.), *Cultural conceptions of mental health and therapy* (pp. 1–38). Boston, MA: D. Reidel Publishing Company.

Williams, D. H. (1986). The epidemiology of mental illness in Afro-Americans. *Hospital and Community Psychiatry, 37,* 42–49.

World Health Organization. (1990). *Composite International Diagnostic Interview (CIDI)*, Version 1.0. Geneva, Switzerland.

Yamamoto J., James, Q. C., & Palley, N. (1968). Cultural problems in psychiatric therapy. *Archives of General Psychiatry, 19,* 45–49.

Yan, H.-Q. (1989). The necessity of retaining the diagnostic concept of neurasthenia. *Culture, Medicine and Psychiatry, 13,*139–45.

Young, D. (1989). Neurasthenia and related problems" *Culture, Medicine and Psychiatry, 13,*131–138.

Zane, N. (1993). An empirical examination of loss of face among Asian Americans. Los Angeles: University of California, Los Angeles, National Research Center on Asian American Mental Health.

Zhang, D. (1995). Depression and culture—A Chinese perspective. Canadian *Journal of Counselling, 29*(3), 227-233.

CHAPTER 3

Mental Illness as Psychiatric Disorder

MARTHA LIVINGSTON BRUCE

INTRODUCTION

To the sociologist, perhaps the single most important characteristic of the psychiatric perspective is that psychiatry views mental illness as a real illness, as distinct from being a socially constructed myth. Whereas some social perspectives might argue that "mental illness" is a label applied by society or social groups to subsets of unusual, unappealing, or disruptive behaviors and feelings, the psychiatric perspective would argue that these behaviors and feelings are themselves the signs and symptoms of true underlying disease or disorder states. Psychiatry uses the term *mental illness* for a spectrum of syndromes that are classified by clusters of symptoms and behaviors considered clinically meaningful in terms of course, outcome, and response to treatment. The purpose of this chapter is to describe how psychiatry defines and organizes these syndromes and to identify the kinds of clinical features associated with the syndromes most relevant to sociological inquiry. The overall goal is to show how the psychiatric perspective of mental illness encompasses more than a single dichotomous category—indeed, even more than a series of dichotomous diagnoses—for use as outcome variables. Rather, psychiatric notions of heterogeneity along a number of clinical axes within and among psychiatric disorders offer considerable richness to a sociological understanding of the risks and outcomes of mental illness.

MARTHA LIVINGSTON BRUCE • Department of Psychiatry, Weill Medical College of Cornell University, White Plains, New York 10605.

Handbook of the Sociology of Mental Health, edited by Carol S. Aneshensel and Jo C. Phelan. Kluwer Academic/ Plenum Publishers, New York, 1999.

Modern psychiatry's conceptualization of mental illness as disease or disorder has found increasing support in recent years because of evidence of genetic or biological risk factors and of physiological mechanisms (as indicated by brain scans, blood levels, and response to pharmacotherapy). The medical model of mental illness has ramifications for how individuals with psychiatric disorder are viewed by others. By suffering a disease or disorder, persons with mental illness become eligible for what sociologists call the "sick role." In the sick role, individuals are not considered personally responsible for their condition. The sick role contrasts with other models of mental illness in which individuals can elicit such pejorative labels as "bad," "weak," or "immoral" (Mechanic, 1978, 1995). The power of a medical label for the public persona of mental illness is well understood by advocacy groups, such as the National Alliance for the Mentally Ill, which prefers the even more medically oriented term, *brain disorder* for psychiatric problems. At the same time, evidence of the contribution of personal behavior (e.g., smoking, exercise, sexual practice, and diet) in the risk of cancer, hypertension, AIDS, and numerous other diseases diffuses boundaries between personal responsibility and disease risk even within the medical model. From that perspective, labeling behaviorally linked conditions such as alcohol dependence or drug abuse as psychiatric disorders becomes somewhat more consistent with the current medical model of disease than sometimes argued (see below).

Psychiatry's medical model of disease by no means negates the role of social factors in the study of mental illness. First, the sociologist's task of determining how and to what extent social factors contribute to, modify, or mediate the risk, course, and outcomes of psychiatric disorders is arguably easier when biological factors are better defined and measured. Second, the medical model's classification of persons with mental illness as having a disease or disorder places an obligation on society to care for those persons, and an obligation on persons with the illness to accept the privileges and constraints of such care. Sociologists continue to investigate the extent to which the willingness and ability of social groups to provide affordable and accessible care for persons with mental illness varies by a range of social factors, including the characteristics of the group, the characteristics of the individuals with the disorder, the kinds of treatment available, and the characteristics of the disorder itself. For example, public acceptance of medication therapy for major depression has increased rapidly in the past decade with the introduction of a class of antidepressants that are easier to use and have fewer side effects. Yet, as noted later, younger adults with major depression are more likely to be treated than older adults with major depression, in part because of the public perception that depression is an expected and therefore normal consequence of aging. Finally, the extent to which a person with a history of mental illness can function in society is an inherently sociological question, as any society can choose or not choose to structure itself in such a way as to facilitate housing, jobs, and companionship for persons with a wide range of capacities and needs. For example, various social and medical trends, including the advent of more efficacious antipsychotic medications in the 1950s, the community mental health movement in the 1960s, and the rise in managed care in the 1990s, have resulted in dramatically shortened hospital stays for persons with even severe mental illness. These changes, however, have not necessarily been mirrored by the development of sufficient treatment and support services for these individuals to maintain viable and productive lives in the community (Greenley, 1990).

The remainder of this chapter describes the psychiatric perspective of mental illness in greater detail in order that this information can enrich sociological research on these and other questions about mental illness. The chapter is organized into three major parts. The first two parts describe how psychiatry classifies mental illness. The first part examines issues concerning the processes of classification and diagnosis that are particularly relevant to sociology. The second part is a catalogue of major psychiatric diagnoses and their criteria. This section may be particularly useful to readers unfamiliar with the fourth edition of the *Diagnostic and Statistical Manual of Mental Disorders* (DSM-IV; American Psychiatric Association, 1994). Other readers may want to skip ahead to the final section, a discussion of several other dimensions (labeled "clinical features") of mental illness, as viewed from the psychiatric perspective, that are not often incorporated into sociological studies of mental illness but have particular relevance to sociology.

PSYCHIATRY'S APPROACH TO CLASSIFYING MENTAL ILLNESS

Modern psychiatry justifies its conceptualization of mental illness as a disorder or disease in great part by the extent to which reliable diagnoses are both possible and related to a specific course, etiology, and response to treatment (Mechanic, 1978; Klerman, 1989). The two major diagnostic systems are those of the American Psychiatric Association and the World Health Organization as described in the DSM-IV, and the International Classification of Disease (ICD-10; World Health Organization, 1990), respectively. These systems are purposefully similar. For the most part, these systems of modern psychiatry use phenomenonology as their fundamental classification tool. Diagnoses form the major types of category and are defined, in large part, by clusters of signs and symptoms that are clinically meaningful in terms of personal distress, associated loss of functioning, or risk of negative outcomes such as death, disability, or loss of independence. This section considers some general caveats about this approach before reviewing the most sociologically relevant diagnoses covered in DSM-IV.

This emphasis on phenomenology, as distinct from theories of etiology or other organizing principals, represents a change in modern psychiatry, codified in 1980 by DSM-III (American Psychiatric Association, 1980; Rogler, 1997). The development of DSM-III reflected efforts of the research community to standardize diagnostic criteria. DSM-III drew on, for example, the Research Diagnostic Criteria (RDC; Spitzer & Endicott, 1978) and Feighner Criteria (Feighner et al., 1972) and corresponding research instruments. A goal of DSM-III and its successors has been to encourage reliability in making psychiatric diagnoses by providing operationalized criteria for both clinicians and researchers. The strength of this approach is in offering a mechanism to increase the consistency with which diagnoses are made across individual clients, clinicians, institutions, and geographic regions. Reliability does not, of course, confer validity, and the emphasis on reliability has left DSM-III and successors vulnerable to considerable criticism from a wide range of theoretical perspectives (see Millon, 1983; Rogler, 1997). (See Chapter 5 for a discussion of the interplay between reliability and validity in the assessment of mental health.)

To the sociologist, the potential pitfalls in relying on phenomenology to make psychiatric diagnoses are quite obvious. Even if we accept the psychiatric assumption that the disorders are "real," we also know that how individuals perceive, experience, and cope with disease is based in large part on cultural explanations of sickness and expectation about illness behavior (Kleinman, Eisenberg, & Good, 1978). As culture is highly influential in shaping the subjective experience of disease, objective indicators of disease are only imperfectly related to the reported subjective experience of the illness (Angel & Thoits, 1987). The lack of objective indicators has large implications for clinical and population-based mental health research because assessment necessarily relies upon the individual's self-reported appraisal of his or her own symptoms. These self-appraisals contribute directly or indirectly to virtually all mental health measures used in studies of the risk, help-seeking behavior, treatment, and outcomes of health conditions.

The lack of correspondence between objective and subjective measures also has implications for the accuracy of diagnoses made in clinical practice. For example, group differences in the language used to express and give meaning to symptoms affect the diagnostic process. Additional, perhaps more subtle, potential sources of bias are expectations of providers based on irrelevant characteristics of the patient, such as race and ethnicity, socioeconomic status, age, or some combination of those characteristics. In the case of depression, for example, providers often believe that depressive symptoms are normal reactions to the stresses and losses associated with aging and low socioeconomic statuses. The elderly and the poor, therefore, may be underdiagnosed (and underserved) because their symptomatology is not seen as problematic. The problem arises in finding the right line between "over medicalizing" what might be a normal reaction to these events and conditions versus ignoring a debilitating yet treatable disease (NIH Consensus Development Panel, 1992).

A second potential problem in the DSM's phenomenological approach is the distinction between "mental" and "physical" conditions. In introducing its classification schema, the authors of the DSM-IV acknowledge the problem in using the term *mental disorder* with the implication of a distinction from physical disorders:

> a compelling literature documents that there is much "physical" in "mental" disorders and much "mental" in "physical" disorders. The problem raised by the term "mental" disorders has been much clearer than its solution, and, unfortunately, the term persists in the title of DSM-IV because we have not found an appropriate substitute, (American Psychiatric Association, 1994, p. xxi).

Although DSM-IV relies heavily on phenomenology, differentiating "mental" from "physical" introduces decisions based on etiology. DSM-IV warns not to include symptoms that are clearly due to a general medical condition, but does not explain how to accomplish this task. This problem is especially difficult for disorders such as depression with high levels of medical comorbidity and for the study of psychiatric disorders among the medically ill (Katz, 1996). There is no gold standard, laboratory test, or methodology generally accepted by the field for distinguishing symptoms of depression from those associated with medical illness. Cohen-Cole and Stoudemire (1987) differentiate four common approaches to this problem: (1) *Inclusive*, when symptoms of depression are counted whether or not they might be attributable to a primary physical problem, which increases sensitivity at the expense of specificity; (2) *Etiologic*, when symptoms count toward the diagnosis of depression only if they are not "caused" by physical illness, which is the approach stipulated by DSM-IV and the decision rule for the assessment tools such as the Structured Clinical Interview for Axis I DSM-IV Disorders (SCID; Spitzer, Gibbon, & Williams, 1995), although neither explains how to accomplish this task; (3) *Substitutive*, when additional psychological, affective, or cognitive symptoms are substituted for somatic symptoms in making the diagnosis (e.g., Clark, Cavanaugh, & Gibbons, 1983); and (4) *Exclusive,* when somatic items are eliminated from the existing criteria and the diagnosis is made on the basis of nonsomatic symptoms. The strategy chosen has profound implications for the estimated rates of disorder, especially in medically ill populations. For example, in a sample of elderly medical inpatients, Koenig, George, Peterson, and Pieper (1997) report a twofold difference (from 10.4% to 20.7%) in the prevalence rate of major depression depending upon which of these strategies is used. Other potential sources of variation are the instrument used for making the diagnostic assessment and who determines the attribution of symptoms to medical or mental etiology. In highly structured interviews, such as the Diagnostic Interview Schedule (DIS; Robins, Helzer, Ratcliff, & Seyfried, 1982), the interviewee makes this decision, whereas in structured clinical interviews, such as the SCID (Spitzer et al., 1995), the interviewer makes a clinical judgment.

Rates of medical illness are disproportionately high in older relative to younger adults, making the likelihood that psychiatric symptoms will be misattributed to medical illness highest in the elderly (Small, 1991). This problem is exacerbated by cohort differences in the amount of stigma associated with mental health problems and psychiatry (Leaf, Bruce, Tischler, & Holzer, 1987). Consequently, older individuals are more likely to interpret symptoms of depression or anxiety as indicative of medical morbidity (Hasin & Link, 1988) and to seek care from medical rather than mental health clinicians in response to these symptoms (Leaf et al., 1988). These factors most likely contribute to the relatively low correspondence between scoring high on a symptom assessment of depression or anxiety and meeting diagnostic criteria for these disorders in older age groups compared to younger age groups.

Although differences in classification criteria do not change the phenomena, or their underlying condition per se, the label attached to these signs and symptoms has far reaching implications. From the individuals' perspective, the type of diagnosis given will affect the type and range of formal medical or psychosocial treatment offered to them and the expectations placed on them for physical, emotional, and functional recovery by clinicians, family, friends, and employers. From society's perspective, the type of diagnosis assigned will affect findings generated from research on the risk, outcomes, and potential treatment of these phenomena. These points concern not just the diagnostic decisions made in more complex situations, such as medically ill patients, but for all psychiatric diagnoses. For these reasons an understanding of the criteria currently used by psychiatry to diagnose specific types of mental illness is an essential tool for any sociological investigation of mental illness.

TYPES OF PSYCHIATRIC ILLNESS

This section briefly introduces the characteristics of the major psychiatric disorders comprised by DSM-IV. DSM-IV attempts to describe the full range of psychiatric conditions, referred to as diagnoses and their subtypes, using a system of mutually exclusive and jointly exhaustive categories. DSM-IV's categorical orientation and focus on diagnostic dichotomous boundaries have drawn thoughtful criticism (Mirowsky & Ross, 1989; Rogler, 1997). A major concern is the notion that a person either has or does not have a symptom, or that a person either has or does not have a diagnosis. Critics argue that symptoms and conditions rest on a continuum, with individuals potentially having different degrees of symptomatology. Dichotomizing psychiatric states loses information about the degree of symptomatology in both groups. Although acknowledging this criticism and admitting to the impreciseness of classificatory boundaries, the authors of DSM-IV also argue that the categorical approach—that is, defining diagnostic cases—is "thus far" still more pragmatic in clinical settings and useful in stimulating research (American Psychiatric Association, p. xxii). The classification system is reinforced by financial reimbursement strategies, which usually determine payment based on whether or not a patient meets diagnostic criteria for a specific disorder.

For each DSM-IV diagnosis, the criteria are defined first by the presence of a specified cluster of signs and symptoms, usually occurring together and for a minimum duration of time. Second, these signs and symptoms—individually or in combination—must reach a minimum threshold of severity, usually indicated by functional impairment or level of distress. Third, exclusion criteria are applied, so that a symptom does not count toward a diagnosis if the symptom, for example, is due to a medical illness, medication use, or substance use. Although, in a small number of cases, DSM-IV does not permit certain diagnosis to exist in the context of another diagnoses (e.g., major depression is not possible if a person has a bipolar disorder), psychiatric comorbidity (i.e., a person meeting criteria for more than one DSM-IV diagnosis) is not only possible but fairly common (Kessler et al., 1994).

The subset of DSM-IV disorders covered in this chapter was chosen for several reasons. The first group, schizophrenia and other psychotic disorders, was included because it represents the majority of conditions labeled "serious mental illness." These conditions have been a primary concern of sociology since Faris and Dunham introduced the debate over social causation versus social selection when they identified socioeconomic patterns in the housing location of patients discharged from mental hospitals in the 1930s. The second two disorder groups, depression and anxiety, became more focal to sociological research with the advent of community-based surveys because the self-report questionnaires used in these studies were heavily laden with symptoms indicative of these two disorders. Depression and anxiety are the most prevalent disorders in adult women. Substance-related disorders are included both because they are also very prevalent, especially in men, and because of their inherent interest to the sociologist. Unlike psychotic, depressive, and anxiety disorders, a substance-related diagnosis such as alcohol dependence is based more on a voluntary behavior (e.g., drinking) than on an internal feeling state. Together, these first four sets of disorders comprise the great majority of psychiatric disorders observed in community populations (Kessler et al., 1994). The two final sets of disorders discussed in this chapter were chosen for their relevance to children and elderly adults, two groups that have relatively less power and fewer resources compared to working-age adults. Additionally, because children are usually, and elderly often, dependent on other people for care and guidance, mental illness in these two groups often has an especially large impact on family and friends.

Schizophrenia and Other Psychotic Disorders

Psychotic disorders, including schizophrenia, have particular relevance to sociology because they comprise a large proportion of the conditions labeled as "severe mental illness." Schizophrenia is usually described as a rare disorder affecting approximately 1% of the population over the lifetime, yet this 1% represents as many as 4 million people in the United States today (Keith, Regier, & Rae, 1991). Schizophrenia is severe because it not only brings considerable personal suffering but also because people with schizophrenia very often are unable to complete their education, maintain a job, and otherwise function as normally expected in our society. One reason schizophrenia and related disorders are interesting to sociologists, then, is that these conditions serve as a kind of mirror for the capacities needed to live successfully in our society. In addition, the kinds of lives lived by people with schizophrenia speak to the level of intolerance in our society of people who do not have those capacities.

Historically, the term *psychotic* has been defined in a variety of ways, none with universal acceptance. Compared to earlier versions, DSM-IV uses a relatively narrow definition, with psychosis referring to delusions, prominent hallucinations (usually without insight, that is, recognition by the individual as being an hallucination), disorganized speech (an indicator of disorganized thinking), or disorganized or catatonic behavior. Delusions are erroneous beliefs that usually involve a misinterpretation of perceptions or experiences. The bizarreness, that is, implausibility, of delusions can be difficult to judge, especially across cultures (Rogler, 1996). Hallucinations are distortions or exaggerations of sensory perception, most often hearing things no one else hears, but also seeing, smelling, tasting or feeling things that are not present. Hallucinatory experiences are a normal part of religious experience in some cultures, making the judgment of bizarreness or abnormality particularly difficult.

Among the major DSM-IV diagnoses characterized by psychosis are schizophrenia, schizo–affective disorder, and schizophreniform disorder. *Schizophrenia* is defined as a disturbance lasting at least 6 months and, in its active phase, including two or more of the five symptom groups: (1) delusions; (2) hallucinations; (3) severely disorganized speech; (4) grossly disorganized or catatonic behavior, or (5) negative symptoms (e.g., affective flattening, alogia/poverty of speech, and avolition/inability to initiate and persist in goal-directed activities). These negative symptoms reportedly account for much of the morbidity associated with schizophrenia because they generally interfere with social and occupational functioning. *Schizophreniform* disorder is similar to schizophrenia but with shorter duration and the possibility of less functional decline. *Schizo–affective disorder* is a disturbance in which a mood episode (i.e., depression or mania) and the active phase symptoms of schizophrenia occur together and are preceded or followed by at least 2 weeks of delusions and/or hallucinations without mood symptoms.

Depression and Other Affective Disorders

Although the early community-based studies of mental illness, most notably the Midtown Manhattan Study and Stirling County Study, aimed to assess all forms of mental illness, much of what they measured was depression and anxiety. This result occurred because the questionnaires largely tapped into these conditions, and because both conditions are highly prevalent. In more recent decades, investigations into depression have formed the backbone of social stress research. Depression is an appealing topic for study because its high prevalence (as much as 17% over the lifetime; Kessler et al., 1994) makes it relatively easy to study in population samples and also makes the findings from such a study relevant to a large population. The relative commonness of depression, however, also makes it difficult to study because the very term *depression* is used both casually and with a wide range of meanings that may or may not be linked upon the same continuum. For this reason, knowledge of the diagnostic criteria is useful for precision and clarity.

The predominate feature of depression and other kinds of affective disorders is mood. The major types of disturbances, usually experienced as episodes, are characterized by either mania or depression. These episodes form the major components of the affective diagnoses, with bipolar disorder defined by episodes of mania often interspersed with episodes of depression, and major depressive disorder defined by episodes of depression without a history of mania.

DEPRESSION.   The essential feature of a major depressive episode, as defined by DSM-IV, is a period of at least 2 weeks during which there is depressed mood or the loss of interest or pleasure in nearly all activities. In children, the mood may be more irritability than sadness. To meet full criteria for an episode of major depression, individuals must also concurrently experience symptoms, also lasting 2 weeks or more, from at least four out of a list of seven groups: (1) changes in weight or appetite; (2) changes in sleep; (3) changes in psychomotor activity; (4) decreased energy; (5) feelings of worthlessness or guilt; (6) difficulty thinking, concentrating, or making decisions; and (7) recurrent thoughts of death or suicidal ideation, plans, or attempts. Symptoms must be entirely new or significantly worse than normal. Symptoms also must be severe, which means they are associated with clinically significant distress and/or impairment in social, occupational or other types of functioning.

Major depression is diagnosed when an individual experiences one or more major depressive episodes without history of mania (defined below). In contrast to the episodic nature of major depression, dysthymia is defined by chronically depressed mood that occurs for most of the day, more days than not, for at least 2 years, with at least two additional depressive symptoms and no history of mania. An individual can be chronically dysthymic and experience periodic episodes of major depression. Recent studies also suggest that acute but relatively mild episodes of depressive symptoms (i.e., minor, subsyndromal, subthreshold depression) may also have clinical relevance and impact on outcomes such as functional status and institutionalization (Judd, Rapaport, Paulus, & Brown, 1994; Meyers, 1994; Sherbourne et al., 1994). Although not formally recognized by DSM-IV, minor depression has been included in the section labeled "needing more study." The research criteria proposed by DSM-IV for minor depression are similar to major depression but with fewer symptoms (two vs. five).

MANIA.   A manic episode is defined by a distinct period (1 week or more) during which there is abnormally and persistently elevated, expansive, or irritable mood. Concurrently, an individual must experience at least three additional symptoms from a list of seven symptom groups: (1) inflated self-esteem or grandiosity; (2) decreased need for sleep; (3) increased talkativeness; (4) racing thoughts; (5) distractibility; (6) increased goal-directed activity or psychomotor agitation; and (7) excessive involvement in pleasurable activities that have a high potential for painful consequences (e.g., buying sprees, sexual indiscretions, or foolish business investments). These symptoms must be severe enough to cause marked impairment in functioning. Variations on the manic episode include *mixed* episodes (e.g., symptoms of both depression and mania for at least 1 week) and milder *hypomanic* episodes.

Most sociological studies that assess depression using symptom scales do not differentiate between respondents with and without a history of mania. Using DSM-IV criteria, however, a history of mania changes the type of diagnosis given to a person who is currently depressed. *Bipolar I* disorder is defined by a history of manic or mixed episodes, with or without a history of major depressive episodes. *Bipolar II* disorder is characterized by a history of major depressive episodes, as well as episodes of hypomania. *Cyclothymic* disorder is also defined by hypomania episode but with interspersed subsyndromal depressive symptoms.

Anxiety Disorders

Although the most highly prevalent set of psychiatric disorders, the anxiety disorders have not received the same level of research attention from sociologists as have depression and schizophrenia. As noted earlier, however, many of the self-report measures of overall mental illness used in early sociological studies—indeed, even those currently used to assess depression—actually contain symptom indicators of anxiety. Perhaps not surprisingly, then, sociological research has begun to document the strong influence of society on the risk and outcomes of anxiety disorders as has been observed for other mental disorders.

Anxiety disorders encompass a range of diagnoses characterized by excessive worry, fear, or avoidance behavior. The major forms of DSM-IV anxiety disorders include: (1) panic disorder without agoraphobia; (2) panic disorder with agoraphobia; (3) agoraphobia without history of panic; (4) specific phobia; (5) social phobia; (6) obsessive–compulsive disorder; (7) posttraumatic stress disorder; (8) acute stress disorder, and (9) generalized anxiety disorder.

Panic disorder, which can occur with or without comorbid agoraphobia, is diagnosed by a history of two or more panic attacks. These attacks are discrete periods characterized by sudden onset of intense apprehension, fearfulness, or terror, often associated with feelings of impending doom in situations in which most people would not feel afraid. The criteria for a panic attack demand at least four out of 13 additional somatic or cognitive symptoms, for example, shortness of breath, palpitation, chest pain or discomfort, choking or smothering sensations, and fear of "going crazy" or losing control. Attacks have a sudden onset and short duration (i.e., 10 minutes or less). Panic attacks are often experienced as a heart attack or similar physical condition, resulting in exacerbated worry by the sufferer and family, as well as substantial use of medical resources (Eaton, Dryman, & Weissman, 1991).

Phobia, or fear, is the basis of several of the anxiety disorders. Important to the diagnosis of phobias is the difference between manageable fear, which many of us have to specific stimuli, versus fear that is both excessive and leads to clinically significant impairment. *Agoraphobia* is anxiety about (or avoidance of) places or situations from which escape might be difficult, or in which help might not be available if needed. Individuals with agoraphobia often stay inside their homes most of the time. Agoraphobia often coexists with panic disorder. *Specific phobias* (previously called simple phobias in DSM-III) refer to clinically significant anxiety provoked by exposure to a specific feared object or situation (e.g., snakes, bridges), often leading to avoidance behavior. *Social phobia* is also characterized by clinically significant anxiety, in this case, provoked by exposure to certain types of social or performance situations, often leading to avoidance behavior.

Obsessive–compulsive disorder is characterized by obsessions, which cause marked anxiety or distress, and/or compulsions, which serve to neutralize anxiety. These obsessions or compulsions must be severe enough to be time consuming (i.e., lasting at least 1 hour per day), or to cause marked impairment/distress. As defined by DSM-IV, obsessions are persistent ideas, thoughts, impulses, or images that are experienced as intrusive and inappropriate (i.e., outside the individual's control), cause marked anxiety or distress, and are not simply excessive concerns about real-life problems. Examples include thoughts about contamination (e.g., from shaking hands), doubts (e.g., Did I leave the iron on?), need for things to be in a particular order (e.g., symmetrical), and sexual imagery. Compulsions are repetitive behaviors (e.g., washing hands, returning home to check the iron) or mental acts (e.g., praying, counting). The goal of these compulsions is to prevent or reduce anxiety or distress as opposed to providing pleasure or gratification. Generally, compulsions are attempts to reduce anxiety about an obsession, so that, for example, excessive worry about germ contamination from shaking hands is linked to excessive hand washing, and excessive doubts about the iron burning down the house are linked to countless trips home to ensure that the iron has been turned off. For the diagnosis of obsessive–compulsive disorder, compulsions or obsessions must cause marked distress, be time consuming, or significantly interfere with normal functioning.

Posttraumatic stress disorder (PTSD) is characterized by the reexperiencing of an extremely traumatic event (e.g., war, rape, assault) accompanied by symptoms of increased arousal, and by avoidance of stimuli associated with the trauma. In contrast to other diagnoses, PTSD is explicitly defined in reference to an etiological agent. The symptoms of *acute stress disorder* are similar to those of PTSD but occur in the immediate aftermath of an extremely traumatic event.

Generalized anxiety disorder (GAD) is arguably the most common and least severe of all the anxiety disorders, if not of all DSM-IV diagnoses (Blazer, Hughes, George, Schwartz, & Boyer, 1991). GAD is defined by 6 months of persistent and excessive anxiety and worry about events or activities. The individual experiencing GAD finds it hard to control the worry, which is accompanied by three or more symptoms including: (1) restlessness; (2) fatigue; (3) difficulty concentrating; (4) irritability; (5) muscle tension; and (6) sleep disturbance. To satisfy GAD diagnostic criteria, excessive anxiety must cause distress and/or interfere with accomplishing normal tasks.

Substance-Related Disorders

The interplay among personal behavior, societal expectations, and biology is especially obvious in the class of conditions labeled substance-related disorders in DSM-IV. In DSM-IV, "substance" refers in large part to a "drug of abuse" obtained either legally (e.g., alcohol, caffeine, nicotine) or illegally (e.g., PCP, opioids). "Substance" also refers to medications and toxins. Substance-related disorders are problematic conditions related to consuming these substances. Perhaps more than many of the diagnoses included in DSM-IV, the sociologist may question the reasons for including substance-related conditions as psychiatric disorders because the causes of these "problematic conditions" (i.e., drinking alcohol or using drugs) are self-induced and often (especially in the case of alcohol) socially sanctioned behaviors. The logic for their inclusion, however, is consistent with DSM-IV's reliance on phenomenology rather than etiology or cause. DSM-IV's criteria focus on the signs and symptoms (e.g., craving, physiological withdrawal) rather the drinking per se. Society's ambivalence regarding the classification of substance-related conditions is reflected in the separation of alcohol, drugs, and mental health into three separate institutes of the National Institute of Health and in the ways in which many states organize and finance their services in terms of these three categories.

The essential feature of *substance dependence* is a cluster of cognitive, behavioral, and physiological symptoms indicating that the individual continues to use the substance despite significant problems related to its use. A pattern of repeated self-administration usually results in tolerance (i.e., need for markedly increased amounts to achieve a desired effect or markedly diminished effect for a given amount), withdrawal, and compulsive drug-taking behavior. *Substance abuse* is less severe than substance dependence and is characterized by a maladaptive pattern of substance use, manifested by recurrent and significant adverse consequences (e.g., repeated failure to fulfill role obligations, use when physically hazardous, or multiple legal, social, and/or interpersonal problems). Compared to substance dependence, the symptoms of substance abuse tend to be defined by social rather than biological or psychological problems.

Disorders in Childhood

Although children suffer from a number of psychiatric disorders that are also common among adults (e.g., depression and anxiety), an additional set of disorders is defined by onset during childhood. Among these are mental retardation, learning disorders, pervasive developmental disorders, and attention-deficit/hyperactivity disorder (ADHD).

Of these, *ADHD* is both relatively common (prevalence of approximately 3–5%) and very disruptive to the life of the affected child and family. In DSM-IV, ADHD is characterized by persistent inattention and/or hyperactivity in more than one setting (e.g., home and school) at a level greater than normally observed in children at a similar developmental stage. To meet diagnostic criteria, at least some ADHD symptoms must appear before age 7. In addition, a child needs to demonstrate 6 or more maladaptive symptoms lasting six months or more related either to *inattention* (e.g., careless mistakes at school, difficulty sustaining attention in tasks, not listening, not following through on instructions, difficulty organizing tasks, avoiding tasks that require sustained effort, losing tools needed for a task, being easily distracted or forgetful) or *hyperactivity/impulsivity* (e.g., fidgeting, leaving one's seat inappropriately, leaving the room inappropriately, difficulty playing quietly, being always on the go, talking excessively, blurting out answers prematurely, having difficulty waiting one's turn, interrupting others). In ADHD, these symptoms result in considerable impairment in family, school, and social groups, and children with ADHD are often disruptive to these settings. Because many of these symptoms mirror the normal behaviors of very young children, these symptoms cannot be easily evaluated or identified until at least age 4, an age at which children are developmentally ready to pay sustained attention to tasks and more able to control their own behavior.

Childhood behavioral disorders are of particular interest to sociologists because it is even more evident than usual that the line between normal and abnormal behavior is drawn by cultural or even subgroup norms rather than by some absolute criterion. Indeed, ADHD usually does not get diagnosed until a child enters school and is confronted with more constraints on his or her behavior than in the home. On the other hand, a hallmark of ADHD is the inability to constrain one's behavior to social expectations as opposed to a lack of willingness. From this perspective, ADHD brings huge and unwanted problems to a child. As with most psychiatric illnesses, ADHD also greatly burdens and is a source of stress for the family, which puts family members at risk for other negative outcomes.

Dementia and Delirium

Dementia and delirium are predominately problems of aging adults. The risk of dementing disorders is frightening to many older people not only because of the loss in cognitive capacity per se but also because dementia generally results in the loss of physical independence. Families assume much of the responsibilities for the older person with dementia, providing either direct care or coordinating care from formal providers or institutions. As noted for children with mental disorders, the perceived emotional and financial burden of caring for a family member with dementia is often stressful and increases the risk for depression and other health problems.

The predominant disturbance of dementia and delirium is a clinically significant deficit in cognition or memory. In both conditions, the cognitive and memory deficits represent a significant change from previous functioning, differentiating them from mental retardation. Also unlike mental retardation, dementia and delirium are disorders associated with aging and old age.

DSM-IV *dementia* criteria include evidence of memory impairment as well as disturbance of one or more of the following functions: (1) language (aphasia); (2) motor activity (apraxia); (3) recognition (agnosia); and (4) planning, organizing, and abstracting (executive function). To meet diagnostic criteria, the level of disturbance must result in significant functional impairment. Subtypes of dementia are differentiated by their etiology with major types, including: (1) *Alzheimer's type dementia*; (2) *vascular dementia*; and (3) less common dementias resulting from other medical conditions (e.g., HIV, head trauma), substance use (e.g., alcohol), or indeterminate etiology. Alzheimer's dementia and vascular dementia differ by their patterns of onset and course. The onset of Alzheimer's disease is gradual, and decline continues gradually, often for many years, resulting in great disability and functional dependence. Only very recently have drugs become available that effectively help slow the course of Alzheimer's dementia. Vascular dementia is associated with cerebrovascular disease. In contrast to Alzheimer's dementia, the onset of vascular dementia is often, although not always, very rapid and in direct response to a recognized cerebrovascular event (e.g., a stroke). In vascular dementia, recovery of memory and cognitive functioning is possible. The term *pseudodementia* has been used to describe dementia-like symptoms in depressed elderly patients. In many of these patients, the true diagnosis is confirmed only when the dementia-like symptoms resolve with antidepressant treatment. Recent evidence suggests, however, that this set of depressed patients is at disproportionately high risk for subsequent onset of confirmed dementia (Alexopoulos, Young, & Meyers, 1993).

Delirium is characterized by disturbance of consciousness and change in cognition over a short period of time that are not accounted for by preexisting dementia. Delirium is particularly prevalent in older, hospitalized medical patients, often in response to the medical condition itself or to the medication and/or other treatment factors used for the medical condition.

CLINICAL FEATURES OF PSYCHIATRIC DISORDERS

In describing the diagnostic criteria of the major psychiatric diagnoses contained in DSM-IV, the previous section focused on the differences in the signs and symptoms among these disorders. From the psychiatric perspective, the process of using these signs and symptoms to make a judgment (i.e., to diagnose) about the kind of problem a patient may have (i.e., a diagnosis) is a critical step is recommending appropriate treatment and care (Klerman, 1989). As noted previously, diagnostic classification has been criticized by sociologists for losing information about what are often continuous phenomena. Yet diagnostic classification is usually only one (often the first) step. Most clinically oriented researchers and clinicians also assess patients along a number of other dimensions. These other dimensions are not often incorporated into sociological mental health research yet have great potential for enriching our understanding of the contribution of social factors to the etiology and course of psychiatric disorders and of the ways in which psychiatric problems affect an individual's social functioning, social status, and social environment. Although these different dimensions have overlapping qualities, they are organized below for convenience sake into three sets: (1) severity, (2) episode duration, and (3) onset and illness course

Severity

Severity is a measure of the magnitude or intensity of an illness. For sociologists oriented toward continuous measures, measures of severity are intuitively appealing, as they move beyond a dichotomous indicator of "sick/not sick" to a degree of illness. The notion of severity of illness is embedded, implicitly or explicitly, in many sociological theories about the etiology, care, and outcomes of mental illness, with hypotheses such as the greater the stress, the greater the severity of the resulting illness, or that the effect of predisposing factors on seeking help will be weaker in the context of more severe mental illness than in the context of less severe illness.

Severity, measured in terms of number of symptoms, is perhaps the most familiar clinical feature to sociologists given that it lies at the heart of most symptom scales, including those designed for use in epidemiological samples, such as the Centers for Epidemiologic Study–Depression Scale (CES-D; Radloff, 1977), and those designed for use with diagnosed patients, such as the Hamilton Depression Scale (Hamilton, 1960). Although symptom scales differ in the time period assessed (e.g., current state vs. past month) and the detail provided by possible responses (e.g., yes/no vs. some of the time/much of the time/all of the time), most scales produce a continuous outcome measure ranging from little or no symptomatology to considerable symptomatology (see Chapter 5, this volume). Well-designed symptom scales generally correlate highly with diagnostic criteria, so that respondents who score high on symptom scales (e.g., depressive symptoms) are most likely to also meet criteria for the corresponding disorder (e.g., major depression), but this correspondence is far from perfect. Symptom scales are also used to designate individuals with subsyndromal or subthreshold conditions.

Symptom scales do not perfectly correlate with diagnoses, in part because they do not incorporate the inclusion and exclusion criteria used in making psychiatric diagnoses. In particular, symptom scales assess the presence or duration of symptoms but not whether this constellation of symptoms meets severity criteria in terms of associated distress or functional impairment. An individual may experience a great number of psychiatric symptoms, but these symptoms may be mild enought to allow an individual to continue to function well in home and work roles. In contrast, a different individual may report only the minimum symptoms necessary to meet diagnostic criteria (or only subthreshold criteria), yet the depression may be severely debilitating or lead to negative outcomes such as job loss or disability (e.g., Blazer, Hughes, George, 1987; Broadhead, Blazer, George, & Tse, 1990; Bruce, Seeman, Merrill, & Blazer, 1994).

Arguably, less methodological progress has been made in knowing how to assess syndrome severity than in developing strategies for assessing the presence of symptoms and operationalizing whether or not these symptoms fit the structure of a given psychiatric diagnosis. Assessing severity is complicated, in part, because social factors may well have an even greater influence on the assessment of both distress and functional impairment than on the assessment of symptom presence. Gender differences in the willingness of men and women to acknowledge symptoms of depression, for example, suggest similar differences in the willingness of men and women (or across other sociocultural groups) to acknowledge that a behavioral symptom (e.g., weight gain, distractibility, shortness of breath) is upsetting to the individual (Newmann, 1986). Similar subgroup variation might be expected in the willingness to report that symptoms interfere with normal functioning or lead to help-seeking behavior.

Syndrome severity is also affected by variation in the number and kinds of roles typically filled by an individual. An example comes from Boyd, Weissman, Thompson, and Myers (1982, p. 1198) who compared depression assessed using the CES-D (Radloff, 1977) and Schedule for Affective Disorders and Schizophrenia (SADS/RDC; Spitzer & Endicott, 1978) in 482 community-dwelling adults. The authors describe an 85-year-old woman who scored very high on the CES-D but did not meet criteria for major depression using the SADS. The woman lived alone, had almost no social contact, and was homebound due to fear of both crime and medical morbidity. She, in essence, had no family, work or other social roles. Although the woman affirmed almost all the SADS depression items, the items could not be scored positive because she had not sought help and, having no role to impair, reported no role impairment. Although this example sounds extreme, the very factors that reduced this woman's functional scope—social isolation, homebound status, and medical morbidity—are disproportionately prevalent in older adults and have been implicated as major risk factors for first-onset major depression (Bruce & Hoff, 1994). More generally, individuals' normal role structures can influence both the likelihood of meeting diagnostic criteria and our ability to assess severity among those who have been diagnosed with a mental disorder.

Misconceptions about severity also have an impact on beliefs about treatment. One example stems in part from the sociological literature linking depression to life events. This literature is concordant with much of popular culture, where there seems to be general acceptance that symptoms of depression are common, if not normative, after bad things happen. This cultural acceptance of the depressive reactions to negative events has several sequelae. First, although DSM-IV generally excludes etiology from its diagnostic criteria, an exception is made for depressive episodes that follow bereavement. In DSM-IV, bereavement serves as an exclusion criterion for major depressive episodes, although similar exclusions are not made for other negative life events (e.g., job loss, injury, divorce). The cultural acceptance of depressive symptoms as normal reactions to events also contributes to the notion that such symptoms are normal and should not be medicalized by treatment. This attitude is particularly pervasive with regard to elderly adults, many of whom experience numerous losses in terms of their physical function, loved ones and friends, and residential independence. For example, an influential article in the popular press severely criticized geriatric psychiatry for making a disorder out of the normal reactions to the difficulties of aging (Jacobson, 1995). What is lost in this kind of argument is the notion of severity in terms of the pervasiveness of symptoms, the duration of symptoms, and the impact these symptoms have on distress and functioning (Katz, 1996). Ironically, perhaps the most sociologically interesting observation is that attitudes about whether a person deserves treatment can reflect knowledge and assumptions about the etiology of a condition (e.g., virus vs. events) rather than the efficacy of treatment in relieving distress and improving functioning.

Episode Duration

Time provides an additional dimension by which to describe mental disorders, both in terms of characterizing a specific episode and the long-term course of the illness (next section). Criteria for most DSM-IV disorders require that symptoms be present for at least some minimal amount of time. For example, symptoms of depression must be present most of the day on most days for at least a 2-week period. Accordingly, some episodes of depression can last as little as 2 weeks, whereas others can persist for months or years. Some disorders, such as schizophrenia, are predominately *chronic,* with at least some symptoms usually persisting over much of the individual's lifetime after initial onset. Other disorders are more episodic in nature. Major depression, for example, is usually characterized by periodic episodes, often lasting at least 6 months. A small proportion of depressive episodes last 2 years or more; these are labeled as chronic.

An important question, then, for characterizing a disorder is when the current episode began. Whether a "psychiatric case" is identified by random selection from the community or from a persons seeking treatment from a mental health facility, researchers rarely interview their subjects at the very beginning of a psychiatric episode. Most survey research, then, produces samples with considerable heterogeneity in the duration of these conditions. Research evidence suggests that for many disorders, the duration of the episode is associated with the risk of various clinical and social outcomes (Callahan, Hui, Nienaber, Musick, & Tierney, 1994; Katon et al., 1994; Sargeant, Bruce, Florio, & Weissman, 1990). Other evidence suggests that episode duration differentiates potential risk factors (Alexopoulos et al., 1996; Sirey, Myers, & Bruce, in press). This evidence argues for the inclusion of duration indicators in sociological analyses of risk factors and outcomes. For example, a considerable body of recent research has documented high rates of major depression in various medical care populations or in populations experiencing losses or other life events. These studies tend to assess the patients either at one period of time or only with a long-term follow-up, so that little is known about the extent to which these depressions are transient, self-limiting reactions to the experiences associated with needing care versus persistent, high-risk conditions that would potentially benefit from intervention.

Onset and Illness Course

Whether a given episode is a first or a recurrent episode is an important source of heterogeneity within a diagnostic category. For most psychiatric disorders, the strongest risk factor for the onset of an episode is whether or not the individual has a history of previous episodes (American Psyciatric Association, 1994; see also Kessler & Magee, 1994). Some evidence suggests that other risk factors also differ depending upon past psychiatric history. For example, Post (1992) argues that life events have a greater impact on the risk of a first episode of depression than on the risk of a recurrent episode. The rationale is that life events provide some of the kindling needed to ignite the initial depressive episode. Once started, the history of depression fuels subsequent episodes, regardless of life events. Similarly, the prognosis of any given episode tends to be worse if the individual has a history of previous episodes.

The terms used to describe the course of mental illness have traditionally been ill-defined and inconsistently used. To understand the kinds of phases characterizing an episodic course, the conceptualization developed by Frank and colleagues (1991) for major depression is illustrative. As the operationalizations of these definitions are purposefully vague and depend upon the diagnostic schema and the assessment instruments used, they are presented both to suggest the ways in which the elements of course can be incorporated into sociological inquiry and to provide a common language for this kind of analysis.

In this schema, an *episode* is the period during which an individual meets full symptomatic criteria for the disorder. In DSM-IV depression, for example, symptoms must last at least 2 weeks. *Remission* from the episode is defined as the interim period (e.g., 2 weeks to 6 months) during which the individual's symptoms have decreased sufficiently that he or she has only minimal symptoms and no longer meets full diagnostic criteria. *Partial remission* is a period of decline from the episode to full remission. *Response* (i.e., to treatment) is the point at which partial remission begins. *Recovery* from the episode (but not necessarily from the illness per se) occurs when an individual remains minimally symptomatic beyond the defined period of remission (e.g., more than 6 months*). Relapse* occurs when symptoms meeting full diagnostic criteria reappear during the period of remission (but before recovery). *Recurrence* occurs with the reappearance of a new episode once recovered.

Heterogeneity with respect to past history has important implications for survey research on psychiatric illness. A random community sample will generally yield a disproportionately large number of recurrent or chronic cases compared to first-onset cases so that analyses of both risk factors and outcomes will need to control for, or stratify by, past history. In many samples, the number of first-onset cases will be too small for rigorous analysis. Other complicating factors are the tendency for respondents to forget or otherwise misreport previous psychiatric episodes and the need to control for previous subclinical conditions in respondents without a history of diagnoses (Bruce & Hoff, 1994).

Additionally, history of previous psychiatric episodes calls into question the independence of potential risk factors from the illness itself. The goal of teasing apart the impact of sociological variables in the course of the illness from the impact of the illness on the social environment is particularly challenging with retrospective data but is also difficult in longitudinal studies. What may be most important—or at least, most attainable—is that the interplay among social and psychological factors through the course of time is incorporated into the conceptual framework of the data analyses and their interpretation (Link, Mesagno, Lubner, & Dohrenwend, 1990; Miller et al., 1986).

Although identifying age of onset is essential for determining past psychiatric history, age of onset has also been implicated as a source of heterogeneity in psychiatric illness. In depression research, for example, patients whose first episode of depression occurs later in life (e.g., after age 60) tend to experience a different constellation of symptoms during their initial episode and have a different course and outcome than do comparably aged patients whose first onset was when they were younger (Alexopoulos et al., 1993). In the case of late-life depression, patients with late onset tend to have a greater prevalence of vascular risk factors as well as more comorbid cognitive impairment, suggesting a different etiologic path (Alexopoulos et al., 1997). Age of onset in this context represents a proxy indicator for some underlying source of heterogeneity among individuals meeting the same diagnostic criteria.

CLOSING THOUGHTS

The past 40 years of sociological research on the risk for and outcomes of mental illness can be characterized by increasing concern with heterogeneity in psychiatric conditions. Assessment of overall mental illness was replaced with assessment of specific types of psychiatric problems. This chapter has focused on sources of heterogeneity within specific psychiatric disorders, specifically, dimensions such as severity, duration, onset, and course. One of the interesting questions in the face of increased differentiation in the psychiatric variable—whether as the dependent variable or as the risk factor for other outcomes—is whether the links to social phenomena will be equally specific. Evidence points to both specificity and generalization. For example, in a prospective analysis of women who developed breast cancer, those with a history of major depression were significantly more likely than controls to be diagnosed with late-stage breast cancer (predicting poorer chances of recovery), whereas women with anxiety disorders were significantly more likely than controls to be diagnosed with early-stage breast cancer (Desai, Bruce, & Kasl, in press). These findings underscore the differences between anxiety and depression, in this case, in terms of women's help-seeking behavior and/or the clinical interaction between patient and provider. In contrast, other studies report shared social risk factors across different disorders. For example, poverty is associated with an increased risk of depression, alcohol abuse, and phobia (Bruce, Takenchi, & Leaf, 1991). Evidence of potential "fundamental causes" of psychiatric outcomes (Link & Phelan, 1995) pose equally important questions about the ways in which biological, social, and/or cultural factors link general risk factors to specific psychiatric phenomena.

Finally, whether mental health is assessed using continuous measures or diagnostic indicators, investigations into the relationships between mental health and social factors can be strengthened by incorporating additional psychiatric dimensions into these analyses. In particular, we need to incorporate more carefully the notion of time into our analyses and examine how social factors interact with the risk, expression, course, and outcomes of mental illness, taking into account the longer term context, at least in terms of age of onset, duration of the episode, history of past episodes, time to recovery, and so forth. Equally important is the assessment of severity. As noted earlier, current approaches to assessing severity, especially in terms of role functioning, are methodologically weak and could benefit greatly from sociological contributions. Well-measured indicators of severity offer great potential for specifying the ways in which social and psychiatric factors interact over time.

REFERENCES

Alexopoulos, G. S., Meyers, B. S., Young, R. C., Kakuma, T., Feder, M., Einhorn, A., & Rosendahl, E. (1996). Recovery in geriatric depression. *Archives of General Psychiatry, 53,* 305–312.

Alexopoulos, G. S., Meyers, B. S., Young, R. C., Kakuma, T., Silbersweig, D., & Charlson, M. (1997). Clinically defined vascular depression. *American Journal of Psychiatry, 154,* 562–565.

Alexopoulos, G. S., Young, R. C., & Meyers, B. S. (1993). Geriatric depression: Age of onset and dementia. *Biological Psychiatry, 34,* 141–145.

American Psychiatric Association. (1980*). Diagnostic and Statistical Manual of Mental Disorders* (3rd ed.). Washington, DC: Author.

American Psychiatric Association. (1994). *Diagnostic and statistical manual of mental disorders* (4th ed.). Washington, DC: Author.

Angel, R., & Thoits, P. (1987). The impact of culture on the cognitive structure of illness. *Culture, Medicine, and Psychiatry, 11,* 465–494

Blazer, D. G., Hughes, D. C., & George, L. K. (1987). The epidemiology of depression in an elderly community population. *Gerontologist, 27,* 281–287.

Blazer, D. G., Hughes, D., George, L. K., Swartz, M., & Boyer, R. (1991). Generalized anxiety disorder. In L. N. Robins & D. A. Regier (Eds.), *Psychiatric disorders in America: The epidemiologic catchment area study* (pp. 180–203). New York: The Free Press.

Boyd, J. H., Weissman, M. M., Thompson, W. D., & Myers, J. K. (1982). Screening for depression in a community sample. *Archives of General Psychiatry, 39,* 1195–1200.

Broadhead, W. E., Blazer, D. G., George, L. K., & Tse, C. K. (1990) Depression, disability days, and days lost from work in a prospective epidemiologic sample. *JAMA, 264,* 2524–2528.

Bruce, M. L., & Hoff, R. A. (1994). Social and physical health risk factors for first onset major depressive disorder in a community sample. *Social Psychiatry and Psychiatric Epidemiology, 29,* 165–171.

Bruce, M. L., Seeman, T. E., Merrill, S. S., & Blazer, D. G. (1994). The impact of depressive symptomatology on physical disability: MacArthur Studies of Successful Aging. *American Journal of Public Health, 84,* 1796–1799.

Bruce, M. L., Takeuchi, D. T., & Leaf, P. J. (1991). Poverty and psychiatric status: Longitudinal evidence from the New Haven Epidemiologic Catchment Area Study. *Archives of General Psychiatry, 48,* 470–474.

Callahan, C. M., Hui, S. L., Nienaber, N. A., Musick, B. S., & Tierney, W. M. (1994). Longitudinal study of depression and health services use among elderly primary care patients. *Journal of the American Geriatrics Society, 42,* 833–838.

Clark, D. C., Cavanaugh, S., & Gibbons, R. D. (1983). The core symptoms of depression in medical and psychiatric patients. *Journal of Nervous and Mental Disease, 171,* 705–713.

Cohen-Cole, S. A., & Stoudemire, A. (1987). Major depression and physical illness: Special considerations in diagnosis and biological treatment. *Psychiatric Clinics of North America, 10,* 1–17.

Desai, M., Bruce, M. L., & Kasl, S. (in press). Psychiatric status and stage of breast cancer diagnosis in a community sample of women. *International Journal of Psychiatry in Medicine.*

Eaton, W. W., Dryman, A., & Weissman, M. M. (1991). Panic and phobia. In L. N. Robins & D. A. Regier (Eds), *Psychiatric disorders in America: The epidemiologic catchment area study* (pp. 155–179). New York: The Free Press.

Feighner, J. P., Robins, E., Guze, S. B., Woodruff, R. A., Winokur, G., & Munoz, R. (1972). Diagnostic criteria for use in psychiatric research. *Archives of General Psychiatry, 26,* 57–63.

Frank, E., Prien, R. F., Jarrett, R. B., Keller, M. B., Kupfer, D. J., Lavori, P. W., Rush, A. J., & Weissman, M. M. (1991). Conceptualization and rationale for consensus definitions of terms in major depressive disorder: Remission, recovery, relapse, and recurrence. *Archives of General Psychiatry, 48,* 851–855.

Greenley, J. R. (1990). Mental illness as a social problem. In J. R. Greenly (Ed), *Research in community and mental health,* (Vol. 6, pp.7–40). New York: Plenum Press.

Hamilton, M. (1960). A rating scale for depression. *Journal of Neurology, Neurosurgery, and Psychiatry, 23,* 56–62.

Hasin, D., & Link, B. (1998). Age and recognition of depression: Implications for a cohort effect in depression. *Psychological Medicine, 18,* 683–688.

Jacobson, S. (1995, April). Overselling depression to the old folks. *Atlantic Monthly,* pp. 46–51.

Judd, L. L., Rapaport, M. H., Paulus, M. P., & Brown, J. L. (1994). Subsyndromal symptomatic depression: A new disorder? *Journal of Clinical Psychiatry,* 55, 18–28.

Katon, W., Lin, E., von Korff, M., Bush, T., Walker, E., Simon, G., & Robinson, P. (1994). The predicator of persistence of depression in primary care. *Journal of Affective Disorders, 31,* 81–90.

Katz, I. R. (1996). On the inseparability of mental and physical health in aged persons. *American Journal of Geriatric Psychiatry, 4,* 1–16.

Keith, S. J., Regier, D. A., & Rae, D. . (1991). Schizophrenic disorders. In L. N. Robins & D. A. Regier (Eds), *Psychiatric disorders in America,* (pp. 33–52). New York: The Free Press.

Kessler, R. C., & Magee, W. J. (1994). The disaggregation of vulnerability to depression as a function of the determinants of onset and recurrence. In W. R. Avison & I. H. Gotlib (Eds.), *Stress and mental health: Contemporary issues and prospects for the future* (pp. 239–258). New York: Plenum Press.

Kessler, R. C., McGonagle, K. A., Zhao, S., Nelson, C. B., Hughes, M., Eshleman, S., Wittchen, H. U., & Kendler, K. S. (1994). Lifetime and 12-month prevalence of DSM-III-R psychiatric disorders in the United States: Results from the National Comorbidity Survey. *Archives of General Psychiatry, 51,* 8–19.

Kleinman, A., Eisenberg, L., & Good, B. (1978). Culture, illness, and care. *Annals of Internal Medicine, 88,* 251–258.

Link, B. G., & Phelan, J. C. (1996). Understanding sociodemographic differences in health—the role of fundamental social causes. *American Journal of Public Health, 86,* 571–572.

Klerman, G. L. (1989). Comment to Mirowsky and Ross. *Journal of Health and Social Behavior, 30,* 26–32.

Koenig, H. G., George, L. K., Peterson, B. L., & Pieper, C. F. (1997). Depression in medically ill hospitalized older adults: Prevalence, characteristics, and course of symptoms according to six diagnostic schemes. *American Journal of Psychiatry, 154,* 1376–1383.

Leaf, P. J., Bruce, M. L., Tischler, G. L., Freeman, D. H., Weissman, M. M., & Myers, J. K. (1988). Factors affecting the utilization of specialty and general medical mental health services. *Medical Care, 26*(1), 9–26.

Leaf, P. J., Bruce, M. L., Tischler, G. L., & Holzer, C. E. (1987). The relationship between demographic factors and attitudes toward mental health services, *Journal of Community Psychology, 15,* 275–284.

Link, B. G., Mesagno, F. P., Lubner, M. E., & Dohrenwend, B. P. (1990). Problems in measuring role strains and social functioning in relation to psychological symptoms. *Journal of Health and Social Behavior, 31,* 354–369.

Mechanic, D. (1978) *Medical sociology* (2nd ed.). New York: The Free Press.

Mechanic D. (1995) Sociological dimensions of illness behavior. *Social Science and Medicine, 41*, 1207–1216.

Miller, P. M., Dean, C., Inghan, J. G., Kreitman, N. B., Sashidharan, S. P., & Surtees, P. G. (1986). The epidemiology of life events and long-term difficulties, with some reflections on the concept of independence. *British Journal of Psychiatry, 148*, 686–696.

Millon, T. (1983). The DSM-III: An insiders' perspective. *American Psychologist, 38*, 804–814.

Meyers, B. S. (1994). Epidemiology and clinical meaning of "significant" depressive symptoms in later life: The question of subsyndromal depression. *American Journal of Geriatric Psychiatry, 2*, 188–192.

Mirowsky, J., & Ross, C.E. (1989). Psychiatric diagnosis as reified measurement. *Journal of Health and Social Behavior, 30*, 11–25.

Newmann, J. P. (1986). Gender, life strains, and depression. *Journal of Health and Social Behavior, 196*(27), 161–178.

NIH Consensus Development Panel on Depression in Late Life. (1992). Diagnosis and treatment of depression in late life. *Journal of the American Medical Association, 192*(268), 1018–1024.

Parker G. (1987). Are the lifetime prevalence estimates in the ECA study accurate? *Psychological Medicine, 17*, 275–282.

Post, R. M. (1992). Transduction of psychosocial stress into the neurobiology of recurrent affective disorder. *American Journal of Psychiatry, 149*, 999–1010.

Radloff, L. S. (1977).The CES-D scale: A self-report depression scale for research in the general population. *Applied Psychological Measurement, 1*, 385–401.

Robins, L. N., Helzer, J. E., Ratcliff, K. S., & Seyfried, W. (1982). Validity of the diagnostic interview schedule, version II: DSM-III diagnoses. *Psychological Medicine, 12*, 855–870.

Rogler, L. H. (1996). Framing research on culture in psychiatric diagnosis: The case of the DSM-IV. *Psychiatry, 59*, 145–155.

Rogler, L. H. (1997). Making sense of historical changes in the *Diagnostic and Statistical Manual of Mental Disorders*: Five propositions. *Journal of Health and Social Behavior, 38*, 9–20.

Rogler, L. H., & Cortes, H. E. (1993). Help-seeking pathways: A unifying concept in mental health care. *American Journal of Psychiatry, 150*, 554–561.

Sargeant, J. K., Bruce, M. L., Florio, D. P., & Weissman, M. M. (1990). Factors associated with 1-year outcome of major depression in the community. *Archives of General Psychiatry, 47*, 519–526.

Sherbourne, C. D., Wells, K. B., Hays, R. D., Rogers, W., Burnam, A., & Judd, L. L. (1994). Subthreshold depression and depressive disorder: Clinical characteristics of general medical and mental health specialty outpatients. *American Journal of Psychiatry, 151*, 1777–1784.

Small, G. W. (1991). Recognition and treatment of depression in the elderly. *Journal of Clinical Psychiatry, 52*(Suppl. 6), 11–22.

Spitzer, R. L., & Endicott, J. (1978). *Schedule for Affective Disorders and Schizophrenia*. New York: Biometrics Research Division, New York State Psychiatric Institute.

Spitzer, R. L., Gibbon, M, & Williams, J. B. (1995). *Structured Clinical Interview for Axis I DSM-IV Disorders (SCID)*. Washington, DC: American Psychiatric Association Press.

Williams, B. W., Gibbon, M., First, M. B., Spitzer, R. L., Davies, M., Borus, J., Howes, M. J., Kane, J., Pope, Jr. H. G., Rounsaville, B., & Wittchen, H. U. (1992). The Structured Clinical Interview for DSM-III-R (SCID): II. Multisite test–retest reliability. *Archives of General Psychiatry, 49*, 630–636.

World Health Organization. (1990). *International classification of diseases and related health Problems* (10th ed.). Geneva: Author.

CHAPTER 4

The Sociological Study of Mental Illness

A Critique and Synthesis of Four Perspectives

ALLAN V. HORWITZ

INTRODUCTION

For both laypeople and mental health professionals, the nature, causes, and cures of mental illness are found in the symptoms of specific disordered individuals. Mental illness, as a cultural category, is rooted in the personality or, more recently, in the brain. These individualistic conceptions of mental illness are entrenched in both common sense and in the large and powerful mental health professions—psychiatry, psychology, social work, and nursing—that define, study, and treat mental illness. Sociologists who study mental disorders must confront deeply rooted asociological models that have a high degree of social legitimation.

In this chapter, I outline four sociological styles of thinking about mental disorder. Each reacts in a distinct way to the dominant individualistic model of mental illness. The most common style accepts the prevalent definition of mental illness and searches for the social causes of mental disturbances in individuals. A second style, more common in anthropological and historical than in sociological studies, examines how symptoms that emerge in individuals are cultural products of particular sociohistorical contexts. Both address the social causes of symptoms but make different assumptions about whether psychiatric symptoms emerge independently of cultural contexts or are cultural products.

ALLAN V. HORWITZ • Department of Sociology and Institute for Health, Health Care Policy, and Aging Research, Rutgers University, New Brunswick, New Jersey 08903.

Handbook of the Sociology of Mental Health, edited by Carol S. Aneshensel and Jo C. Phelan. Kluwer Academic/Plenum Publishers, New York, 1999.

Two other sociological orientations do not address how symptoms arise in individuals, but focus instead on how social and cultural factors affect responses to mental disorder. One style uses traditional measures of mental illness as a base and studies the variation in the reaction to these symptoms. The other imputes no significance to mental disorders apart from the cultural constructions of reactors; in this view, mental disorders are social definitions.

Figure 4.1 presents a highly oversimplified classification of these sociological explanations of mental disorder. Two dimensions form this table. The first is whether studies seek to explain, on the one hand, how symptoms emerge in individuals or, on the other hand, the social response to symptomatic persons. Both (I) etiological and (II) sociological psychology dimension study how particular individuals develop mental disorders. In contrast, the (III) social response and (IV) social constructionist schools explain the ways in which social groups define and respond to individuals displaying mental symptoms. The second basis of classification is whether the basic aspects of mental symptoms are viewed as cultural products; In this regard, (I) etiological and (III) social response studies either see symptoms as emerging independently of culture or take the nature of symptoms for granted. In contrast, the major goal of both (II) sociological psychology and (IV) social constructionist explanations is to understand how categorizations of symptoms themselves are culturally produced.

The remainder of this chapter discusses the strengths and weaknesses of these four styles of sociological explanation of mental disorder and the extent to which each style is compatible with or divergent from the others. Although these styles encompass the dominant sociological approaches to mental disorder, neither this classification nor the discussion that follows captures the great heterogeneity within each style. In addition, any classification of this sort necessarily reifies the fuzzy boundaries between the styles. My goal is to illuminate the most general assumptions of each style as well as to indicate: when these assumptions are complementary, contradictory, or mutually exclusive. In my view, there is no single distinctively sociological style of explaining mental illness but a variety of explanations that can illuminate a phenomenon that is not generally considered to be within the social domain at all.

ETIOLOGICAL STUDIES

The dominant tradition in the sociological study of mental illness examines how social factors influence variation in rates of mental illness (see e.g. Dohrenwend & Dohrenwend, 1969; Pearlin, 1989). The outcome this style attempts to explain is the same as that used by investigators from mental health disciplines—symptomatology in individuals. Diagnoses or scales that can be applied across many different cultural contexts measure mental symptoms. In this sense, the etiological study of mental illness is comparable to the study of physical illnesses. Both mental and physical illnesses are clusters of symptoms whose nature is independent of the cultural context in which they arise. This assumption is implicit, rather than explicit; indeed, many, or most, investigators in this tradition would probably even reject it. Nevertheless, their research uses measures that do not vary across cultural contexts and do not take into account the possible historical and culture aspects of symptoms.

The distinctly sociological aspect of this approach is not the conception of mental disorder, but rather how mental symptoms arise from individuals' positions in the social structure (Mirowsky & Ross, 1989a; Pearlin, 1989). In contrast to other mental health

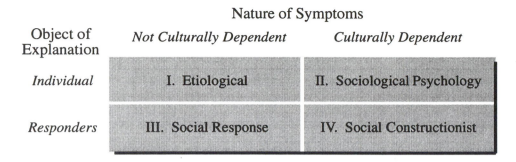

FIGURE 4.1. Sociological explanations of mental disorder.

disciplines, sociological research explores how the properties of social systems are related to the development of mental disorder. This orientation emphasizes the etiological role of chronic strains such as poverty or single parenthood; acute life events such as unemployment or marital dissolution; aspects of social roles such as role conflict, role overload, or role strain; and the degree of social support people can rely on when they deal with stressors (e.g., Aneshensel, 1992; Kessler, Price, & Wortman, 1985; Turner, Wheaten, & Lloyd, 1995). The explanatory variables are aspects of the social environment that are external to the personalities or brains of individuals, although these aspects of individuals may mediate the impact of social factors. Sociological studies also are concerned with differing rates of mental disorder across different social locations (nations, cities, regions, etc.) or groups (social class, gender, age, etc.), rather than with why particular individuals develop symptoms of mental illnesses (e.g., Barrett & Rose, 1986; Schwab & Schwab, 1978). Finally, sociologists study samples of community members, most of whom have not been professionally treated for mental illness, not just clinical samples of treated individuals (Weissman, Myers, & Ross, 1986).

Because etiological studies do not search for the reasons particular individuals develop illnesses, hut for differences in rates of mental illness across social locations, groups, and positions, these studies must adopt certain conceptualizations of mental illness. The only way to establish comparability across settings is to use standard and reliable measures that vary minimally from application to application (Hahn, 1995). Only standardized and comparable scales can measure symptoms across settings. Idiosyncratic aspects of personal experience or social context are, in theory, if not always in practice, controlled for and, ideally, eliminated.

There have been two major strands in the etiological study of mental disorder (see Part III of this volume). One focuses on the social causes of particular mental disorders. Durkheim's *Suicide* (1897/1951), which studied social variation in suicide rates among different groups, is the first systematic study of this sort. The initial American study of this type is Faris and Dunham's (1939) research on variation across Chicago neighborhoods in treated rates of schizophrenia and manic-depression. This explanatory style dominates contemporary studies of psychiatric epidemiology, which explore sex, age, ethnic, and social class variations in the incidence and prevalence of particular diagnostic categories such as major depression, anxiety disorders, substance abuse/dependence, and antisocial personality disorder in community populations (Kessler et al., 1994; Robins et al., 1984).

A second strand of etiological research uses global symptoms of distress rather than particular psychiatric disorders as the object of explanation. This research tradition, which began in sociology with the Midtown Manhattan Studies of the 1950s (Srole, Langner, Michael, Opler, & Rennie, 1962), is grounded in the psychodynamic assumption that mental disorders are not distinctive symptom clusters but are continuous with normal behavior (Grob, 1991; Hale, 1995). The boundary between mental health and mental illness is fluid rather than rigid. Nor is psychological distress sharply separated from physical distress, because both represent nonspecific, generalized responses to the same stressors (Cassel, 1974; Selye, 1956). Measures of this concept do not use symptoms of particular disorders but, rather, continuous scales of depression, anxiety, and psychosomatic symptoms that indicate generalized distress (e.g., Langner. 1962; Radloff, 1977). Although these scales do not provide diagnoses, they indicate the global mental health consequences of different social arrangements and examine variation in well-being across groups—social class, age, sex, ethnic, and so on (Aneshensel, Rutter, & Lachenbruch, 1991).

Some of the most heated contemporary controversies in the sociology of mental disorder arise between advocates of continuous and diagnostic measurements of disorder (see especially Klerman, 1989; Mirowsky & Ross, 1989b). Proponents of continuous models believe they more accurately represent the underlying realities of psychiatric symptoms; upholders of diagnostic models think they more suitably classify, explain, and treat mental disorders. Nevertheless, from a broader perspective, both styles embody the same explanatory mode. Both use standardized measures of mental illness abstracted from any particular context to explain social variation in the occurrence of disorder. The diagnostic model is best suited to understand the social correlates of particular disorders, and the continuous model best measures the stressful consequences of different social arrangements (Aneshensel et al., 1991). As general styles of explanation, however, their similarities outweigh their differences.

The diagnostic and continuous etiological models have made major contributions to the study of mental disorder. One is to indicate how mental disorders can result from the external environment, including long-term structural strains such as impoverishment, environments that induce hopelessness for the future, or single parenthood, as well as more discrete stressful life events such as marital dissolution, unemployment, or natural disasters (Avison & Turner, 1988; Holmes & Rahe, 1967; Turner et al., 1995; Wheaten, 1990). Another contribution is to show the wide variation across groups in both the type and amount of mental disorder (Dohrenwend et al., 1980). For example, younger people report more: disorder than older people, and rates of disorder among the young may have grown in recent decades (Klerman, 1988); men report far more substance abuse disorders than women, while women consistently display more disorders marked by depression and anxiety (Horwitz, White, & Howell-White, 1996); disorders are more prevalent in lower than in higher socioeconomic groups (Kessler & Cleary, 1980) although blacks paradoxically do not report more disorder than whites (Kessler et al., 1994; Robins et al., 1984). The distinctively sociological contribution of these studies is to show how social factors external to the brains and personalities of individuals produce mental disorders.

Social variation in rates of disorder also call into question the adequacy of clinical samples that are used to establish the presumably biological and psychological origins of disorder. A contribution of etiological research has been to show that clinical samples are not representative of the kinds of individuals who suffer from various disorders. For example, rates of disorder among people who are ethnic minorities, poorly educated, older, and male far exceed their presence in psychiatric treatment (Horwitz, 1987; Olfson & Pincus 1994a). Psychiatric epidemiology now routinely assumes that only community samples provide accurate estimates of disorder in general populations.

A final strength of etiological studies is their usefulness for cross-cultural research. Because these studies assume that the characteristics of mental disorders (whether continuous or diagnostic) arise independently of social contexts, symptoms can be isolated from the cultural settings in which they emerge and then compared across cultures. For example, the major cross-cultural study of mental disorders—the World Health Organization's study of schizophrenia—uses diagnostic schedules applied in nine widely varying settings (Wittchen et al., 1991). The findings indicate both a high degree of comparability across countries in rates of core symptoms of schizophrenia and widely varying rates of symptoms beyond the core (Sartorius et al., 1986). The use of symptoms that are extracted from particular settings allows for the comparative study of disorders across different settings.

Several weaknesses are also apparent in etiological models. One is the failure to establish valid standards of mental illness. Continuous measures of generalized distress are so vague and global that what they measure: is not clear. They are analogous to measures of body temperature in which elevations indicate that something is wrong, but not what is wrong (Dohrenwend & Dohrenwend, 1982). The problem of validity is equally serious for diagnostic studies, which lack criteria for the inclusion of any particular diagnosis in the general category of mental illness (Wakefield, 1992a). *The Diagnostic and Statistical Manual of Mental Disorders* (4th ed.) (DSM-IV) (American Psychiatric Association, 1994, pp. xxi-xxii) defines mental disorders (in theory, although not in practice) as patterns of thought and behavior associated with distress and functional impairment resulting from dysfunction in the individual and not from expectable responses to events or from deviant behavior. Yet etiological studies make no attempt to separate mental disorders that are individual dysfunctions from disorders that emerge as reactions to stressors. Nor do they justify why some diagnoses such as alcohol and drug abuse or antisocial personality disorders indicate individual dysfunctions rather than patterns of deviant behavior (Wakefield, 1992b). Etiological studies show social variation in particular symptoms but not why these symptoms are indicators of mental illness.

A related problem of etiological studies is the tendency to overestimate rates of mental disorder in community populations (Wakefield, 1997). Depending on the context, virtually all of the particular symptoms that comprise continuous or diagnostic measures can indicate either normal or abnormal responses to stressors. The lack of valid criteria of mental illness may account for findings that one-fourth of the population have a mental illness over the course of a year and more than 50% over their lifetimes (e.g., Kessler et al., 1994). In contrast to clinical studies, which deal with people who can be presumed to have problematic conditions because they have sought professional help, studies or untreated populations cannot assume that symptoms represent mental illness rather than understandable, ordinary, and transitory reactions to life experiences. Because they do not separate symptoms that are individual dysfunctions from those that are expectable responses to stressors or deviant behaviors, etiological studies are prone to an abundance of Type II errors in which nondisordered people are counted as having disorders (Wakefield, 1997). Until etiological studies develop and use a valid concept of mental disorder, they likely will continue to provide inflated estimates of disorder.

Etiological studies also face the problem of whether the same symptom reports reflect the same underlying disorder in different types of people. If members of different groups manifest disorders in unlike ways, comparing rates of the same standardized symptoms will not provide good estimates of group differences. For example, etiological studies consistently show that women report far more depression and generalized distress more than men. Yet if men respond to stressors through different expressions, such as problematic use of alcohol, gender comparisons of depression only or alcohol problems only will inaccurately represent gender differences in reactions to stressors (Horwitz et al., 1996). Likewise, if people of higher social-class status are prone to commit suicide in the same circumstances that make lower class people prone to homicide, social-class comparisons of rates of suicide alone or of homicide alone would be misleading (Henry & Short, 1954). Different rates of the same disorder among groups could represent many things, including differential exposure to stress, various coping strategies, or different styles of expressing distress. This problem again points to the need for development of valid measures of mental illness that are sensitive to possible variations in the way diverse groups develop and express disorders.

Etiological studies have made many contributions to explain social variation in the emergence of mental disorders. Directly confronting some fundamental conceptual issues that are currently ignored would maximize their ability to illuminate important aspects of the sociology of mental disorder.

SOCIOLOGICAL PSYCHOLOGY STUDIES

The etiological model has dominated mainstream studies in the sociology of mental disorder. As a result, mental illness has been viewed, at least implicitly, as consisting of culture-free symptoms measurable through standardized scales. In etiological approaches, social and cultural factors affect rates of psychiatric disorders, but not the basic nature of these disorders themselves. The model of sociological psychology makes fundamentally different assumptions about the nature of mental illness. Although rarely used in recent sociological studies, this model has flourished in anthropological and historical studies of psychiatric disorder. Its basic principle Is that cultural contexts fundamentally shape the types of mental disorder that individuals experience and display. Psychiatric symptoms develop from culturally specific patterns of socialization, norms of appropriate emotional display, and general cultural schemas, rather than from culture-free disease processes.

In sociological psychology models, mental disorders do not develop independently of their cultural context but are products of particular times and places. Major aspects of the central psychiatric illnesses found in contemporary U.S. society—such as depression, anxiety disorder, substance abuse, or personality disorder—could not arise in different socio-historical eras (e.g., Nuckolls, 1992). Conversely, the types of disorders that develop in fundamentally different cultural contexts could not emerge here. The goal of research is to show how aspects of the broader social, cultural, and historical context shape the types of mental disorders that individuals develop. Thus, etiological and sociological psychology models differ not only in their basic assumptions about the nature of mental illness, hut also in their fundamental goals: The first model explains social variation in universal symptoms of mental disorder; the second explains the social and cultural origins of the kinds of mental disorders that emerge in particular contexts.

There are several predecessors of current studies of sociological psychology. One is the neo-Freudian movement led by Erich Fromm (1941), Karen Horney (1937), and Henry Stack Sullivan (1953). Despite differences among prominent neo-Freudians, all criticized traditional psychiatric thought, psychoanalysis in particular, for ignoring the social shaping of psychiatric symptoms and character disorders. For neo-Freudians, individual psychology was social psychology: Social and Cultural institutions determine character structures, symptoms, and neuroses. Fromm (1941, p. 231) captures this aspect of neo-Freudian thought:

"The essential nucleus of the character structure of most members of a group . . . has developed as the result of the basic experiences and mode of life common to that group." For example, the oedipal complex stems from the types of family relationships found in patriarchal societies, or the anal character structure emerges from the values of rationality, retention, and order that capitalist societies emphasize. Likewise, the contradictions of capitalist society may be responsible for many of the typical neurotic conflicts of contemporary women, such as masochistic character traits (Horney. 1937). As social structures and cultural values change, modal personalities and psychopathological styles that typify an era will also change. To the extent that models grounded in sociological psychology are correct, the symptom scales used in seemingly objective measures reflect culture-bound manifestations of pathology rather than context-free signs of illness.

Another precursor of sociological psychology is the culture and personality school in anthropology, which emerged concurrently with the neo-Freudian movement (Harris, 1968, Chapter 15, 16). This anthropological tradition also developed as a reaction against the presumed universality of mental disorders and character structures in psychoanalytic theory. Instead, anthropologists emphasized the cultural shaping of personality. Customs and social organization, rather than universal psychic dimensions and mechanisms, shaped abnormal, as well as normal, thoughts and feelings in group members (Dubreuil & Wittkower, 1976). Anthropologists viewed Freudian and other Western psychiatric theories as culturebound manifestations of Western thought that were not inherently superior to ethnopsychiatries established in other cultures. The nature and symptoms of personality problems in non-Western societies were unlike those emphasized by Western psychiatry (Kardiner, 1939). A considerable amount of cross-cultural research in this vein associated culturally specific institutions of child rearing with the development of particular personality types (Whiting & Child, 1953). This research crossed over to sociology in such major works of the 1950s as Reisman, Glazer, and Denney's *The Lonely Crowd* (1951) and Whyte's *The Organization Man* (1956), which located major forms of character structure in dominant forms of social organization. Although it is now unfashionable, the culture and personality school is an intellectual precursor of an active "new" anthropology of mental illness.

Contemporary anthropological studies are not likely to trace types of mental illness to styles of childhood socialization. Instead, they argue that culture shapes mental illnesses through providing the symbolic expressions of meaning that organize all thought and action (Geertz, 1973; Sewall, 1992; Swidler, 1986). The "new" cross-cultural psychiatry emphasizes how the most fundamental aspects of selves, personal experiences, and symptoms of disorder are culturally produced and determined, not as childhood products of socialization, but as ongoing accomplishments of everyday experiences. Cultural forces shape not only relatively superficial aspects of psychiatric symptoms, such as the content of delusions, but also define essential aspects of mental illnesses (Littlewood, 1990). The taken-for-granted notion in Western psychiatry that experience is rooted in separate, individual selves does not hold in cultures that experience and interpret symptoms as physiological or as disturbances in interpersonal relationships (Hopper, 1992; Kleinman, 1988).

For example, the Chinese may use physiological expressions to display the same distressing symptoms that Westerners manifest through psychogenic idioms (Kleinman, 1986). It might be technically possible to translate diagnostic categories and symptom scales of depression into other languages but the data obtained from such cross-cultural comparisons of Western psychiatric entities may be no more valid than epidemiological surveys of "soul loss" among middle-class North Americans (Hopper, 1992). The same diagnosis of "depression" cannot capture the radical difference between symptoms experienced as guilt-ridden despair and those processed as lower back pain (Kleinman, 1987). Cultural differences in the experience and manifestation of symptoms are so profoundly that the two forms of expression cannot be encompassed within the same diagnostic category. From this perspective, a valid understanding of how individuals experience psychiatric symptoms can arise only within the framework of the relevant cultural context (e.g. Guarnaccia, 1993).

The study of the cultural production of mental disorders has flourished among historians as well as anthropologists. Writing with the advantage of hindsight, historians can document how disorders that seemed natural and universal to observers during a prior era retrospectively become anachronistic and culture-bound entities.

Edward Shorter (1992, 1994) has developed a general model of psychiatric disorder in historical context. He assumes that universal biological and psychological factors present in all cultures produce very general predispositions to express psychosomatic, depressive, and anxious symptoms. But the mind must interpret the distressing sensations that emerge from the brain, so that people can answer questions about the nature, causes, and course of symptoms. Culturally appropriate styles of symptom formation and the dominant fashions of the medicopsychiatric profession mold vague and incoherent feelings of suffering into specific symptom patterns. Individuals do not make these interpretations idiosyncratically, but through culturally learned and rewarded patterns that provide recognizable interpretations of experience. Without these interpretations, it would be impossible for people to make sense of their disturbing perceptions. The result is that very general predispositions to distress become culturally recognizable patterns of hysteria, neurasthenia, chronic fatigue syndrome, anorexia, multiple personality disorder, and so forth. Although diffuse biological or psychological vulnerabilities might provide underlying predispositions, the actual, manifest disorders reflect the symptom pool available in the particular cultural context.

A good illustration of this theory is hysteria—once; the paradigmatic psychiatric disorder. A plethora of studies demonstrate how the symptoms of hysteria manifest the particular cultural, professional, and scientific assumptions of the time (see especially Goldstein, 1987; Micale, 1995). Some of these assumptions stemmed from the repressive sexual practices in late nineteenth century Western societies, some from the diagnostic practices used in psychiatry in this period, others from the culturally produced and rewarded models of appropriate symptom formation, and still others from the presence of a charismatic medical leader, John-Martin Charcot. When the social factors that gave rise to the particular symptom display found in hysteria changed, the characteristics of this disorder disappeared and mutated into other disorders such as neurasthenia, chronic fatigue syndrome, and other psychosomatic disorders (Shorter, 1992). A corollary of the historical approach is that disorders that seem natural and universal at the present time will prospectively be viewed as culture-bound products of a particular time and place. For example, anorexia might represent a comparable culture-bound syndrome that develops where food supplies are abundant, thinness is a valued cultural norm, and outward appearance takes precedence over inner character (Brumberg, 1989).

The emphasis of current anthropological and historical studies on how social, cultural, and professional factors shape the kinds of symptoms that individuals experience would seemingly be very congenial to sociological styles of explaining mental disorders. Yet studies of how expressions of personal distress might be cultural products are virtually absent from the sociological literature. Instead, sociologists who reject standardized measures of mental disorder found in etiological models have ignored the study of personal experience and focused instead on the ways in which professionals create and apply psychiatric diagnoses. The unfortunate result is that sociologists have ceded to anthropologists, historians, psychologists, philosophers, and literary critics the study of the cultural shaping and internalization of such contemporary psychiatric experiences as anorexia and bulimia (Brumberg, 1989), chronic fatigue syndrome (Shorter 1994), multiple personality disorder (Hacking. 1995), alien abduction (Showalter, 1997), and repressed memory of sexual abuse (Ofshe & Watters, 1994).

The strength of sociological psychology studies is their focus on how social factors influence not only variability of rates of mental disorder but also the nature of psychiatric symptoms themselves. Unless sociologists believe that mental symptoms do reflect culture-free disease processes, there is no reason why the social shaping of the form of psychiatric outcomes should be any less powerful than the social shading of rates of disorders. The most common psychiatric symptoms of distress—anxiety, depression, and the like— are very amorphous and amenable to channeling into a variety of particular manifestations. Showing how particular cultural and social factors shape incoherent predispositions to distress into definitive psychiatric syndromes ought to be, but has not been, a high priority of sociological research.

Another strength of sociological psychology studies is their potential to show how different symptoms might reflect the same underlying disorder: for example, women who now display multiple personality disorders could possibly have developed hysteria in the late nineteenth century. Conversely, behaviors with surface similarity might reflect very different types of phenomena: Starvation behavior of fourteenth-century Italian nuns, for example, may reflect a religious mentality far removed from the self-starvation of modern adolescent girls (cf. Bell, 1985; Brumberg, 1989). Studies of how underlying cultural and social dynamics shape particular symptom formations can lead to more valid comparative studies of psychiatric disorders.

Sociological psychology models also have the potential to understand how "appropriate" symptom pools develop and are used in particular sociohistorical contexts (Shorter, 1992). Both general cultural currents and professional fashions shape the manifestations of symptoms. Sufferers actively, albeit unknowingly, select culturally appropriate ways of expressing distress: They are not passive recipients of professional labels. How the experience of sufferers interacts with popular symptom interpretations among mental health professionals will be a fruitful topic of study.

Studies of the cultural grounding of psychiatric disorders also face difficult problems. One problem is the need to develop standards to compare symptoms across cultures. Claims that the Chinese are likely to manifest depression physiologically, whereas Westerners display depression psychologically (Kleinman, 1986), or that anorexia at the end of the twentieth century is analogous to hysteria at the end of the nineteenth century (Shorter, 1994), are impossible to verify in the absence of standards that are themselves not culturally specific but underlie different manifestations of psychiatric disorders (Leff, 1990). The absence of culture-free grounds for comparison across cultures renders all disorders idiosyncratic, which precludes the development of a more general theory of how cultures produce styles of disorder.

To this point, sociological psychology studies have not established how particular aspects of social and cultural arrangements and professional ideologies lead to various styles of pathology. No general theory explains how particular factors, including family structures, cultural goals, identity categories, and changing professional models of illness, lead styles of psychiatric disorder to emerge, flourish, and disappear. For example, it is not clear whether culture primarily shapes expressions of mental disorder through socialization styles that create enduring personality predispositions or through contemporaneous currents of thought and action that provide "appropriate" symptom styles that channel distress. The best sociological explanations will not just assert that culture in general shapes the nature of psychiatric symptoms, but will explain how certain styles of psychiatric expression emerge from particular social and cultural contexts.

SOCIAL RESPONSE STUDIES

Both of the models discussed thus far, etiological and sociological psychology models, examine psychopathology in individuals. Etiological models explain why some types of people, but not others, develop symptoms of mental illness; sociological psychology models explain how people express their distress in culturally patterned ways. In contrast, social response models do not study the emergence of psychiatric symptoms but, instead study the responses that people make to these symptoms. This orientation addresses different kinds of questions than the first two models, such as "When do responders label behavior as 'mental illness' rather than another type of behavior?"; "How are social characteristics of labelers and labelees related to variation in the labeling of the mentally ill?"; or, "How do social factors affect the treatment of people after they have been labeled mentally ill?" The kinds of questions asked by social response models shift the object of explanation from the people who develop symptoms to those who respond to symptoms (Horwitz, 1982).

No grand theoretical tradition encompasses social response theories. Instead, this style of research emerged from empirical studies in the 1950s and 1960s that examined how factors such as family structures (Clausen & Yarrow, 1955; Freeman & Simmons, 1963; Myers & Roberts, 1959; Sampson, Messinger, & Towne, 1964), social class (Hollingshead & Redlich, 1958), or culture (Kadushin, 1969) influence responses to mental symptoms. Mechanic's (1968) concept of "illness behavior" provides the first general distinction between these studies and traditional studies of the causes of mental illness. "Illness behavior" encompasses the responses of disordered persons themselves, other lay reactors, and professionals. These responses include the definitions of what sort of condition people have, decisions regarding what to do about the condition, and the consequences of these decisions for the course of the illness. Studies of illness behavior do not explain how symptoms of illness develop in the first place but how, given the presence of symptoms, sufferers themselves and others around them define, classify, and respond to their experiences of illness (Mechanic, 1962).

Studies in the social response tradition find many social variations in the response to mental symptoms (Kessler, Brown, & Broman, 1981; Leaf et al., 1985; Veroff, Kulka, & Douvan, 1981). For example, people with greater educational attainment are more likely than poorly educated people to attribute personal difficulties to mental symptoms and to seek help from mental health professionals (Olfson & Pincus, 1994a). Likewise, women are more likely than men to make psychological attributions for problems and view mental health professionals as appropriate remedial agents (Horwitz, 1987). Or elderly people are far more likely than middle-aged or younger people to make physical interpretations of problems and approach general medical, rather than mental health, professionals for help (Leaf et al., 1985). Cultural factors also influence how families respond to their mentally ill members. Ethnic minorities, for example, often undertake more informal caretaking, suffer less burden from providing care, and rely less on professionals than white families (Jenkins, 1988; Horwitz & Reinhard, 1995; Lefley, 1987). All these findings address different issues than the question of why psychological symptoms emerge, so they art: compatible with any explanation for the development of symptoms.

Some recent social response studies investigate variation in reactions to disorders identified in etiological studies of community populations (Narrow, 1993; Regier et al., 1993). This research-compares who, among people that community surveys define as mentally ill, either seek no professional treatment, help from nonpsychiatric professionals, or help from mental health professionals. These studies indicate that most people who are identified as mentally ill through symptom scales either seek no formal treatment or seek help from nonpsychiatric professionals, or from alternative healing sources (Regier et al., 1993). Social and cultural factors systematically influence these responses: Those entering mental health treatment are more likely to be women, middle-aged, highly educated, and white (Olfson & Pincus, 1994b). "Unmet need" for psychiatric services—defined as identified psychiatric conditions where people with diagnoses have not sought professional help-is presumed to be especially acute among ethnic minorities, people with little education, and the elderly (Narrow, Regier, Rae, Manderscheid, & Locke, 1993).

This research gives less prominence to the corresponding finding that nearly half of people who do enter psychiatric treatment have no Psychiatric disorder, even as defined by the generous standards of contemporary psychiatric epidemiology (Regier et al., 1993). Those who enter and, especially, those who remain in mental health treatment, are highly educated, upper income, middle-aged females who have the lowest rates of psychiatric disorder (Olfson & Pincus, 1994b). Epidemiological studies of help seeking thus point not only to underuse by people who may benefit from mental health services, but also to possible overuse by those with little apparent need of these services.

The social response model has also generated some strong comparative research. The World Health Organization (WHO) studies of schizophrenia, noted earlier, show not only similarities in rates and types of certain symptoms of schizophrenia across cultures but also divergences across cultures in the course of these symptoms over time (Sartorius et al., 1976). In particular, outcomes of schizophrenia are better in the less developed countries than in the more developed countries, where schizophrenia has a more chronic course. The varying responses to people with schizophrenic symptoms in different cultures seem responsible for the prognosis of the disorder. Compared to more economically developed societies, less developed societies have lower expectations for performance and place less stigma on the mentally disordered (Hopper, 1992; Waxler, 1974).

One strength of social response studies is to show how the nature of psychiatric symptoms only partly determines how people react to psychiatric disorder. A variety of factors-including the relationship to the person who is ill, ethnicity, social class, age, gender, social networks, and culture—affect the definition, classification, and reaction to symptoms (Horwitz, 1982). In addition, studies of social response can make important contributions to understanding the sociological factors that can either impede or enhance the optimal provision of mental health services (Mechanic, 1987). Response studies can indicate the social variations in response to the kinds of untreated, as well as treated, disorders uncovered in epidemiological research. Because this orientation complements, rather than challenges, the prevailing psychiatric paradigm of mental disorder held by clinical researchers, these studies are often conducted in interdisciplinary teams of sociologists and other mental health researchers.

Despite their useful empirical and policy contributions to the study of mental illness, no major theory has emerged concerning the social and cultural conditions leading to varying responses to mental illness (see, however, Freidson, 1970; Horwitz, 1982; Pescosolido, 1992). The lack of a general theory that links particular aspects of societies to certain kinds of responses to mental disorder limits the contribution of this style of research.

Another problem of response studies lies in their often unquestioning assumption that professional mental health treatment is beneficial. The presence of symptoms in the absence of treatment is assumed to indicate "unmet need" for services instead of, for example, successful lay response to disorder. Better questions for sociological research would be to ask about the *costs* as well as benefits of professional treatment and the *benefits* as well as the costs of lay treatment. How definitions and responses of community members keep people out of, as well as propel them into, professional treatment is virtually unstudied, as are the consequences of both types of response on the future course of symptoms (Rogler & Cones, 1993). Response studies should also pay more attention to how macro-level determinants at the group, neighborhood, and societal levels, as well as social characteristics of individuals, affect responses to mental disorder (e.g., Catalano, Dooley, & Jackson, 1981).

SOCIAL CONSTRUCTIONIST STUDIES

A fourth and final style of sociological explanation asserts that abnormality and normality are not aspects of individual behavior at all but are cultural definitions applied to certain types of behavior. Unlike the first two sociological styles of explanation, the object of study is not disordered individuals, but how cultural categories of mental illness arise, are applied, and change. Yet unlike social response studies that either bracket the issue of the nature of mental illness or use notions of "real" mental illness as abase to explain variations in social reaction, social constructionist studies directly challenge the view that psychiatric symptoms are properties of individuals. Hence, they are not compatible with traditional views but are radically different and mutually exclusive ways of looking at mental disorder.

The central assumption of constructionist explanations of psychiatric disorder is that the essence of mental disorders resides in cultural rules that define what is normal and abnormal(e.g., Coulter, 1973; Gaines, 1992; Szasz, 1961). The problems addressed in this orientation are how these rules arise and change from one era to another and who has the power to enforce definitions of normality and abnormality. The symptoms of individuals that evoke social judgments are viewed as unimportant apart from the rules that define these symptoms as abnormal or normal. The objects of explanation are cultural definitions and rules, not the individuals who manifest the behaviors to which the rules are applied.

The historical origins of the social constructionist view of mental illness are found in Durkheim's *The Rules of Sociological Method* (1895/1966). In this work (unlike in *Suicide*), Durkheim views all sorts of deviant behavior as violations of social rules. Crime (and by implication, mental illness) has no reality apart from the cultural rules that define its existence. What is defined as criminal is not dependent on individual behavior, but on the value systems of collectivities that define and apply rules of appropriate and inappropriate behaviors. The "same" behavior manifested in different conditions can be defined in multiple ways depending on the system of classification applied by the particular group. Durkheim's contribution was to move the object of analysis in studies of deviance from the behavior of individuals to the cultural definitions that define deviance.

The first application of Durkheim's approach in the study of mental illness was Ruth

Benedict's (1934) "Anthropology and the Abnormal." Benedict questioned the validity of Western definitions of normal and abnormal behavior. She asserted that the sorts of behavior that Western psychiatry defines as abnormal—such as paranoia, seizures, trances, and the like—are often considered normal in other cultures. Among the Shasta Indians in California or the native people of Siberia, for example, seizures are not viewed as dreaded illnesses but as signs of special connections to a supernatural power that singles out people for authority and leadership. In ancient Greece, homosexuality was presented as a major means to a good life rather than as abnormality. Among the Dobuans of Melanesia, a constant fear of poisoning that runs through life is seen as normal rather than paranoiac behavior. Conversely, behaviors that are normalized and even rewarded in our culture, such as megalomania, would be considered abnormal in other cultures. The Dobuans, for example, would regard a cheerful, helpful product of the Dale Carnegie school as crazy. Normality resides in culturally approved conventions, not in universal psychological standards of appropriate functioning. For Benedict and the anthropologists who followed her, "all our local conventions of moral behavior and of immoral are without absolute validity" (p. 79).

The hugely popular writing of the French philosopher Michel Foucault (e.g., 1965, 1973) extend the Durkheimian vision into the history of mental illness in Western civilization. Like Benedict, Foucault viewed madness as a property of cultural categories rather than as the symptoms of individuals. What makes the mentally ill mad is not anything they do but how their cultures categorize their behaviors. These categories are not constant but change according to the dominant modes of thinking in each time period. For Foucault (1965), mental illness did not exist until the seventeenth century, when the madman replaced the leper as the signifier of threat and disorder in Europe. He asserted that before then, madness was linked with wisdom and insight and since then, with alien forces that must be controlled by reason or by chains.

Thomas Scheff (1966) brought the social constructionist viewpoint on mental illness into American sociology in his study, *Being Mentally Ill*. Scheff (1996, p. 32), following Becker (1963, p. 9), defines deviance as "not a quality of the act the person commits, but rather a consequence of the application by others of rules and sanctions to an offender'." Thus, psychiatric symptoms are "considered to be labeled violations of social norms" rather than intrapsychic disturbances of the individual (Scheff, 1966, p. 25). Scheff renamed psychiatric symptoms as "residual rule-breaking," which refers to norm-violating behavior that lacks an explicit cultural label. "Residual rules" do not refer to how disordered individuals behave, but to how *observers* categorize certain kinds of rule-violating behaviors. "Mental illness" is a category observers use to explain rule-violating behavior when they are unable to explain it through other culturally recognizable categories.

Scheff's concept of "residual rule-breaking" refers to a different object of explanation than the concept of psychiatric disorder used by etiological or culture and personality studies. It does not explain symptoms that develop in individuals but, rather, the responses made to these symptoms. Yet, it is also different from the concept of "illness behavior" used by social response studies. For Scheff, psychiatric symptoms are violations of residual rules; it is only possible to recognize symptoms through the cultural categories that classify what sort of phenomenon they are. Unlike the social response concept of mental illness, responses cannot vary around a given base of mental symptoms, because these symptoms cannot be defined except through the definitions used to classify them as symptoms. Scheff's view does not complement but, instead, challenges traditional studies of mental illness.

Scheff's actual use of the notion of residual-rule breaking does not follow from and is, in fact, inconsistent with his concept of this phenomenon (see Horwitz, 1979). One would expect this concept to be used in studies of how observers interpret and classify rule-breaking behavior and the conditions under which they apply labels of mental illness, or other labels, to behaviors. In practice, however, residual rule breaking comes to be synonymous with the traditional concept of mental illness. Scheff, and those who followed him (e.g., Haney & Michielutte, 1968; Rosenhan, 1973; Scheff, 1974; Wenger & Fletcher, 1969), studied whether labels of mental illness were correctly or incorrectly applied to individuals, a question that presupposes the validity of a traditional psychiatric notion of mental illness that provides a standard for when labels have been correctly applied.

The most influential strand of subsequent labeling studies ignores the notion of residual rule breaking entirely and uses labels of mental illness as a factor in the environment that may exacerbate or alleviate mental symptoms (Link, Cullen, Frank, & Wozniak, 1987; Link, Cullen, Struening, Shrout, & Dohrenwend, 1989). This work uses social concepts of mental disorder as one important factor contributing to why some mentally ill people function better or worse than others. Labeling becomes an aspect of the social environment that explains the course of mental illness, an endeavor similar to response studies that explain the course of mental symptoms after their initial development, but one far removed from constructionist concerns with the nature of the rules that define what mental illness is. One reason for the poverty of constructionist studies of mental illness following *Being Mentally Ill* may be the fundamental conceptual confusion that lies at the heart of this work.

Research embodying social constructionist styles of explaining mental illness has not developed far beyond Scheff's initial statement. The best empirical studies examine how particular categories of disorder such as homosexuality (Bayer, 1987), premenstrual syndrome (Figert, 1996), or posttraumatic stress disorder (Scott, 1990) either succeed or fail to gain recognition from professionals as "official" categories of mental illness. Other good studies in this vein indicate how mental health professionals legitimize their authority to define and manage mental illness (Kirk & Kutchins, 1992; Scull, MacKenzie, & Hervey, 1996). Recent constructionist studies, however, do not connect professional constructions of mental illness with lay processes of self-labeling (see, however, Thoits, 1985; Weinberg, 1997). The creation of a distinctly sociological explanation of how systems of interpretation and classification of mental illness arise and change as a result of social and cultural forces remains unrealized.

The greatest strength of social constructionist views of mental illness is their sociological conceptualization of the nature of mental symptoms, a conceptualization that does not rely on psychology or biology. Social constructionist studies demonstrate that taken-for-granted categorizations do not simply reproduce symptoms, but are socially contingent systems that develop and change with social Circumstances (Berger & Luckmann. 1966). Biological psychiatry, for example, which defines mental illness as a disease of the brain, legitimizes a particular construction of social reality that has great credence in contemporary Western societies and is an orientation that may reduce the stigma placed on mental illness through its emphasis on disease processes. The legitimacy provided symptoms viewed as products of brain disorders results not from the actual locus of symptoms in the brain, but from the credence that a particular culture gives to disorders thought to result from brain malfunctions. Attributing symptoms to elevated levels of serotonin has no more inherent validity as a cultural explanation than attributing them to unconscious forces or to demonic possession. The explanation and functioning of social systems of classification are questions independent of the explanation of the types of symptoms individuals develop.

The constructionist perspective also entails a number of weaknesses. One is its inability to deal with any inherent constraints that biology creates in the manifestations of mental illness (Leff, 1990). Not everything about mental illness is socially constructed, because some aspects of psychiatric disorders would create problems, regardless of how they are defined (Murphy, 1976). Especially when symptoms emanate from disturbances of brain functioning, there may be limited variation in the societal reaction to them. Constructionist studies have yet to develop a language to deal with the impact of, say, massive alcohol consumption, psychotropic drugs, elevated levels of serotonin, or schizophrenia, apart from their social definitions.

Another problem of constructionist models stems from their view that mental disorder is whatever is considered as such in a particular cultural context. Despite this assumption, constructionists typically present their work as a critique of traditional psychiatric views rather than as a different way of examining mental symptoms. Yet their concept of mental disorder provides no logical or scientific grounds for claiming that any view of mental illness is better, or worse, than any other view. A constructionist has no criteria to critique, for example, the labeling practices of nineteenth century English psychiatrists, who claimed that women who had orgasms during sexual intercourse were mentally disordered, or their American counterpart, who diagnosed runaway slaves as suffering from the disorder of mania (Wakefield, 1994). A pure constructionist perspective has no extracultural criteria for why labels are right or wrong and, therefore, cannot judge the adequacy of any classification of mental symptoms (Hahn, 1995).

Another problem constructionists face is the possibility of conducting comparative work in the absence of grounds to compare mental disorders across different contexts. Benedict, and those who followed her, asserted that universal standards of mental illness do not exist, because all definitions of mental illness are culturally specific. If so, how is it possible to compare the phenomena that indicate the "same" behavior in two different contexts? If, for example, the Dobuans see paranoia as normal and altruism as disordered, what criteria can distinguish "paranoid" or "altruistic" behaviors from the cultural definitions of these phenomena? The constructionist is unable, without self-contradiction, to separate the unclassified behavior (e.g., suspicion of others people's motives) from the social definitions of the behaviors to compare unclassified symptoms across contexts. Whenever the rules used to classify mental disorder are considered to be purely products of the particular setting, comparisons across settings become a conceptual impossibility. Yet the constructionist view lacks criteria at a more generalized level than the particular culture: under study that could provide standards for comparing concepts of mental disorder across different cultures. Only a generalized concept of mental disorder as a certain type of violation of cultural rules in any setting (e.g., "incomprehensibility" or "harmful dysfunction") will allow the comparison of labels of mental illness beyond particular settings (Horwitz, 1982; Wakefield, 1994).

Constructionist studies also suffer from the almost purely coercive model of psychiatry that they embrace (Micale, 1995). Psychiatric practice tends to be equaled with exploitative social control without therapeutic aspects. Similarly, constructionist views have tended to see patients as passive victims of coercive psychiatric practices. Yet patients are generally active participants and shapers of their treatment, both because they initiate the vast majority of psychiatric help seeking, and because mental health professionals rely on patient descriptions of their symptoms. Indeed, very often, patients desire more treatment than professionals are willing to give them. Borges and Waitzkin (1995), for example, find that female help seekers are commonly disappointed by the failure of physicians to prescribe desired psychotropic drugs.

A final weakness of constructionist studies is that the view of mental illness as a cultural label ignores the genuine suffering of people with psychiatric disorders. In the constructionist literature, it appears as if the problems of labeled individuals would disappear if only they were not labeled as mentally ill. This ignores the deep pain that inheres in unlabeled, as well as labeled, symptoms. The political extension of the constructionist view that labeling is responsible for symptoms can also extend to political advocacy that attacks governmental support for the mentally ill (e.g., Breggin, 1991; Szasz, 1961).

The social constructionist view can lead to multiple insights about the nature of mental illness. When constructionists engage in a different sort of enterprise, which is posed at a different level of analysis, than other styles of explanation they can illuminate the: cultural aspects of mental illness (Holstein, 1993). Like Durkheim, their insights speak to the operation of society and culture, not to the functioning of individual personalities or brains.

A SYNTHESIS OF PERSPECTIVES

There is no single style of sociological explanation of mental illness. Neither do styles easily split into "objectivist" versus "subjectivist" or "medical" versus "labeling" models. Even the four general styles presented here represent a great simplification of how sociologists study mental disorder. A central issue is whether these varying styles of explanation are distinct ways of studying mental illness, or whether they can be synthesized.

The possible integration of styles depends on the nature of the questions that each seeks to answer. Whenever two different styles address the same question, it makes sense to ask whether the basic assumptions that underlie each can be reconciled. However, when styles address different questions, they may in some cases be complementary but in other cases irreconcilable, so attempts to integrate them are bound to fail.

Traditional etiological research must be grounded in standardized measures that can be applied across various groups. Although it requires the use of comparable measures, it can benefit from culturally sensitive research that might reveal how "the same" can actually mean different things in different settings. Adding a cultural dimension to etiological research would enhance its ability to ensure that standardized measures in fact measure the same thing for different people, and in different settings. Likewise, greater sensitivity to the fact that members of different groups might manifest distress in different ways could indicate that symptoms of presumably different disorders may actually measure the same underlying psychiatric disturbance. Attention to issues of cultural specificity can help etiological research attain its central goal of comparing rates of mental disorder across different groups.

Conversely, research in sociological psychology can benefit from understanding which aspects of mental disorder are comparable, as well as which are different, across settings. Indeed, cross-cultural comparisons of different types of psychiatric symptoms are impossible in the absence of some criteria that identify how different styles of symptom presentation are variants of the same general concept of mental disorder. A central question for sociological psychology studies should be the cultural variation in the presentation of universal types of human distress. The cultural basis of particular types of psychiatric disorders does not preclude the development of standardized measures of disorder that can also be applied in other settings. Indeed, if research shows that different symptoms represent the same underlying syndrome in different groups, the sociological psychology model would make a basic contribution to traditional etiological work.

Social response models are highly compatible with both etiological and sociological psychology studies. The study of illness behavior begins with the question of how people interpret, define, and respond to symptoms. The study of how people respond to symptoms is compatible and complementary with any sort of explanation of how these symptoms arise in the first place. Studies that begin with the presence of psychiatric disorders identified in etiological studies that examine the social variation in the response to these disorders are stronger than studies of social response alone, because they provide a point of comparison—the presence of psychiatric disorder—that would otherwise be absent. Whether disorders are manifestations of universal or culturally specific mental illnesses is irrelevant: Social response studies are compatible with either the etiological or sociological psychology styles of explanation.

In contrast to the ease of integrating social response styles with studies of the causes of disorder is the difficulty of synthesizing constructionist with most other styles of explanations. For the constructionist, mental symptoms *are* cultural categories with no reality outside of the cultural definitions that form their essential properties. Their epistemology is so distinct from traditional studies of mental disorder that there is no consistent way to combine the two types of study. Scheff's *Being Mentally Ill* provides a good case study of the dangers of using constructivist assumptions about the nature of mental illness to answer conventional etiological questions: A conceptual apparatus in which mental symptoms are viewed as properties of cultural systems is irreconcilable with explaining why some individuals, but not others, develop mental symptoms.

Constructivist and etiological explanations do not explain the same phenomena; therefore, although each can and should attend to the findings of the other, these orientations cannot fruitfully be synthesized. For example, suppose that schizophrenia is shown to stem from faulty biochemistry in the brain. This would not invalidate a constructionist conception, because the resulting changes, if any, in social conceptions of schizophrenia become pan of the cultural understanding of the disorder. Schizophrenia as a brain disorder that is invariant across societies is a distinct entity from the cultural conception of schizophrenia as a brain disorder, which can only arise and have consequences in particular cultures. The debates between proponents of the etiological and constructionist styles of explanation can never be resolved fruitfully unless both sides agree that they are engaged in different types of research enterprises. Similarly, although response and constructionist explanations do not conflict with each other, each has a different goal: Constructionists critique what social response studies take for granted—the definition of mental disorder; conversely, response studies coexist with definitions of mental disorder that constructionists reject. The two types of studies do not compete, but they have different research ends.

Constructivist explanations are more readily integrated with sociological psychology studies. Indeed, one of the central flaws of constructivist research—ignoring the experiential aspect of mental disorder—can be overcome by viewing disorders as culturally specific but experientially real. In addition, the synthesis of these two perspectives introduces needed lay perspectives into a constructionist model that has been too exclusively focused on the behavior of mental health professionals. A synthesis of these orientations could show that many people considered mentally ill are not passive victims of professional labelers but actively use culturally constructed conceptions of psychiatric disorder to attain valued personal and social goals. Likewise, sociological psychology studies can benefit from attention to the constructionist emphasis on how various types of cultural labels arise, as well as how individuals come to internalize them.

CONCLUSION

Sociologists have made, and will continue to make, major contributions to the study of mental disorder. Some of these contributions will complement the findings of biological and psychological research, others will contradict these findings, and still others afford a distinctively sociological perspective on mental illness. None of the styles of explanation considered here is inherently superior to the others, and, if used well, all provide distinctive insights about the nature of mental illness. Optimal sociological insight will come, however, when users of any style do not accept the commonsense view of the nonsociological nature of mental disorders, but critically analyze the nature of the phenomenon they seek to understand. Not only the causes but also the nature of psychiatric symptoms have social and cultural aspects that biologists and psychologists are trained to ignore. Some fundamental aspects of psychological disorders may turn out not to be psychological at all.

REFERENCES

American Psychiatric Association. (1994). *Diagnostic and statistical manual of mental disorders* (4th ed.). Washington, DC: Author.

Aneshensel, C. S. (1992). Social stress: Theory and research. *Annual Review of Sociology, 18*, 15–38.

Aneshensel, C. S., Rutter. C. M.. & Lachenbruch. P. A. (1991). Social structure, stress, and mental illness. *American Sociological Review 56*, 166–178.

Avison, W. R., & Turner, R. J. (1988). Stressful life events and depressive symptoms: Disaggregating the effects of acute stressors and chronic strains, *Journal of Health and Social Behavior, 29*, 253–264.

Barren, J., & Rose R. (1986). Mental disorders in the community: *Findings from psychiatric epidemiology*. New York: Guilford.

Bayer, R. (1987). *Homosexuality and American Psychiatry: The politics of diagnosis*. Princeton, NJ: Princeton University Press.

Becker, H. S. (1963). *Outsiders*. New York: Free Press.

Bell, R. M. (1985). *Holy anorexia*. Chicago: University of Chicago Press.

Benedict, R. (1934). Anthropology and the Abnormal. *Journal of General Psychology, 10*, 59–80.

Berger. P. L., & Luckmann, T. (1966). *The social construction of reality*. Garden City. NY: Doubleday.

Borges, S., & Waitzkin. H. (1995). Women's narratives in primary care medical encounters. *Women and Health, 23*, 29–42.

Breggin, P R. (1991). *Toxic Psychiatry*. New York: St. Martin's Press.

Brumberg, J. 1. (1989). *Fasting girls: The history of anorexia nervosa*. New York: Plume.

Cassel, J. (1974). Psychosocial processes and stress: Theoretical formulation. *International Journal of Health Services, 4*, 471–482.

Catalano, R., Dooley. D.. & Jackson. R. (1981). Economic predictors of admission to mental health facilities in a nonmetropolitan community. *Journal of Health and Social Behavior 22*, 284–297.

Clausen. J. A.. & Yarrow M. R. (Eds.). (1955). The impact of mental illness on the family. *Journal of Social Issues, II*, entire issue.

Coulter, J. (1973). *Approaches to insanity: A philosophical and sociological study*. New York: Wiley.

Dohrenwend. B. P., & Dohrenwend. B. S. (1969). *Social status and psychological disorder*. New York: John Wiley.

Dohrenwend, B. P, & Dohrenwend, B. S. (1982). Perspectives on the past and future of psychiatric epidemiology. *American Journal of Public Health, 72*, 1271–1279.

Dohrenwend. B. P. Dohrenwend. B. S., Gould, M. S., Link, B., Neugebauer, R., & Wunsch-Hitzig, R. (1980). *Mental illness in the United States: epidemiological estimates*. New York: Praeger.

Dubreuil, G., & Wittkower. E. D. (1976). Psychiatric epidemiology: A historical perspective. Psychiatry, 39, 130–141.

Durkheim, E. (1966). *The rules of sociological method*. New York: Free Press. (Original published 1895)

Durkheim, E. (1951). *Suicide: A study in sociology*. New York: Free Press. (Original published 1897).

Faris, R. E. L.. & Dunham. H. W. (1939). *Mental disorders in urban areas*. New York: Hafner.

Figett, A. E. (1996). *Women and the ownership of PMS: The structuring of a psychiatric disorder*. New York: Aldine de Gruyter.

Foucault, M. (1965). *Madness and civilization: A history of insanity in the age of reason*. New York: Pantheon.

Foucault, M. (1973). *The birth of the clinic*. New York: Random House. Freeman, H. E., & Simmons, O. G. (1963). *The mental patient comes home*. New York: Wiley.

Freidson, E. (1970). *Profession of medicine*. New York: Dodd, Mead.

Fromm, E. (1941). *Escape from freedom*. New York: Rinehart.

Gaines, A. (1992). From DSM-I to III-R; voices of self, mastery, and the other: A cultural constructivist reading of U.S. psychiatric classification. *Social Science and Medicine, 35*, 3–24.

Geertz, C. (1973). *The interpretation of cultures*. New York: Basic Books.

Goldstein, J. (1987). *Console and classify: The French psychiatric profession in the nineteenth century*. New York: Cambridge University Press.

Grob, G. (1991). *From asylum to community*. Princeton, NJ: Princeton University Press.

Guanaccia, P (1993). Ataques De Nervios in Puerto Rico: Culture-bound syndrome or popular illness? *Medical Anthropology, 15*, 157–170.

Hacking, I. (1995). *Rewriting the soul: Multiple personality and the sciences of memory*. Princeton, NJ: Princeton University Press.

Hahn, R. A. (1995). *Sickness and healing: An anthropological perspective*. New Haven, CT: Yale University Press.

Hale, N. G. (1995). *The rise and crisis of psychoanalysis in the United States: Freud and the Americans, 1917–1985*. New York: Oxford University Press.

Haney, C. A., & Michielutte, R. (1968). Selective factors operating in the adjudication of incompetency. *Journal of Health and Social Behavior. 9*, 233–242.

Harris, M. (1968). *The rise of anthropological theory: A history of theories of culture*. New York: Thomas Y. Crowell.

Henry, A. F., & Short, J., Jr. (1954). *Suicide and homicide*. New York: Free Press.

Hollingshead, A. B., & Redlich, F. C. (1958). *Social class and mental illness*. New York: Wiley.

Holmes, T. H., & Rahe, R. H. (1967). The Social Readjustment Rating Scale. *Journal of Psychosomatic Research, 11*, 213–218.

Holstein, J. A. (1993). *Court-ordered insanity: Interpretive practice and involuntary commitment*. New York: Aldine de Gruyter.

Hopper, K. (1992). Some old questions for the new cross-cultural psychiatry. *Medical Anthropology Quarterly, 7*, 299–330.

Homey, K. (1937). *The neurotic: personality of our time*. New York: W. W. Norton.

Horwitz, A. V. (1979). Models, muddles, and mental illness labeling. *Journal of Health and Social Behavior, 20*, 296–300.

Horwitz, A. V. (1982). *The social control of mental illness*. New York: Academic Press.

Horwitz, A. V. (1987). Help-seeking processes and mental health services. In D. Mechanic (Ed.), Improving mental health services: What the social sciences can tell us (pp. 33–45). San Francisco: Jossey-Bass.

Horwitz. A. V. & Reinhard, S. C. (1995). Ethnic differences in caregiving duties and burdens among parents and siblings of persons with severe mental illnesses. *Journal of Health and Social Behavior, 36*, 138–150.

Horwitz, A. V., White, H. R., & Howell-White, S. (1996). The use of multiple outcomes in stress research: A case study of gender differences in marital dissolution. *Journal of Health and Social Behavior 37*, 278–291.

Jenkins, J. H. (1988). Conceptions of schizophrenia as a problem of nerves: A cross-cultural comparison of Mexican-Americans and Anglo-Americans. *Social Science and Medicine, 12*, 1233–1243.

Kadushin, C. (1969). *Why people go to psychiatrists*. New York: Athenon.

Kardiner, A. (Ed.). (1939). *The individual and his society*. New York: Columbia University Press.

Kessler, R. C., Brown, R. L., & Broman, C. L. (1981). Sex differences in psychiatric help-seeking: Evidence from four large-scale surveys. *Journal of Health and Social Behavior 22*, 49–64.

Kessler, R. C., & Cleary, P D. (1980). Social class and psychological distress. *American Sociological Review, 45*, 463–478.

Kessler, R. C., McGonagle, K. A., Zhao. S., Nelson. C. B., Hughes. M., Eshleman, S., Wittchen. H.-U., & Kendler, K. S. (1994). Lifetime: and 12-month prevalence of DSM-III-K psychiatric disorders in the United States. *Archives of General Psychiatry, 51*, 8–19.

Kessler, R. C., Price. K. H., & Wortman, C. B. (1985). Social factors in psychopathology: Stress, social support, and coping processes. Annual *Review of Psychology, 36*, 531–572.

Kirk, S. A. & Kutchins, H. (1992). *The selling of DSM: The rhetoric of* science *in psychiatry*. New York: Aldine de Gruyter.

Kleinman, A. (1986). *Social origins of distress and disease: Depression, neurasthenia and pain in modern China*. New Haven, CT: Yale University Press.

Kleinman, A. (1987). Anthropology and psychiatry: The role of culture in cross-cultural research on illness. *British Journal of Psychiatry, 152*, 447–454.

Kleinman, A. (1988). *Rethinking psychiatry: From cultural category to personal experience*. New York: Free Press.

Klerman, G. L. (1988). The current age of youthful melancholia: Evidence for increases in depression among adolescents and young adults. *British Journal of Psychiatry, 152*, 4–14.

Klerman, G. L. (1989). Psychiatric diagnostic categories: Issues of validity and measurement. *Journal of Health and Social Behavior, 30*, 26–32.

Langner, T. S. (1962). A twenty-two item screening score of psychiatric symptoms indicating impairment. *Journal of Health and Social Behavior 3*, 269–276.

Leaf, P. J., Livingston, M. M., Tischler, G. L., Weissman, M. M., Holzer, C. E., & Myers, J. K. (1985). Contact with health professionals for the treatment of psychiatric and emotional problems. *Medical Care, 23*, 1322–1337.

Leff, J. (1990). The new cross-cultural psychiatry: A case of the baby and the bathwater. *British Journal of Psychiatry, 156*, 305–307.

Lefley, H. P. (1987). Culture and mental illness: The family role. In A. Hatfield & H. Lefley (Eds.). *Families of the mentally ill: Coping and adaptation* (pp. 30–59). New York: Guilford Press.

Link, B. G., Cullen, F. T, Frank, J., & Wozniak. J. F. (1987). The social rejection of former mental patients: Understanding why labels matter. *American Journal of Sociology, 92*, 1461–1500.

Link, B. G., Cullen, F. T., Struening, E., Shrout, P, & Dohrenwend, B. P (1989). A modified labeling theory approach to mental disorders: An empirical assessment. *American Sociological Review, 54*, 400–423.

Littlewood, R. (1990). From categories to context: A decade of the "new cross-cultural psychiatry." *British Journal of Psychiatry, 156*, 308–327.

Littlewood, R., & Lipsedge, M. (1987). The butterfly and the serpent: Culture, psychopathology and biomedicine. *Culture, Medicine, and* Psychiatry, *11*, 289–335.

Mechanic, D. (1962). Some factors in identifying and defining mental illness. *Mental Hygiene, 46*, 66–74.

Mechanic, D. (1968). *Medical sociology: A comprehensive rut*. New York: Free Press.

Mechanic, D. (Ed.). (1987). *Improving mental health services: What the social sciences can tell us*. San Francisco: Jossey-Bass.

Mechanic, D., & Volkart, E. H. (1960). Illness behavior and medical diagnosis. *Journal of Health and Human Behavior, 1*, 86–921.

Micale, M. A. (1995). Approaching hysteria: Disease and its interpretations. Princeton, NJ: Princeton University Press.

Mirowsky, J., & Ross, C. E. (1989a). *Social causes of psychological distress*. New York: Aldine de Gruyter.

Mirowsky, J., & Ross, C. E. (1989b). Psychiatric diagnosis as reified measurement. *Journal of Health and Social Behavior, 30*, 11–25.

Murphy, J. M. (1976). Psychiatric labeling in cross-cultural perspectives. *Science, 191*, 1019–1028.

Myers, J. K., & Roberts, B. H. (1959). *Family and class dynamics in mental illness*. New York: Wiley.

Narrow, W. E., Regier, D. A., Rae, D. S., Manderscheid, R. W., & Locke, B. Z. (1993). Use of services by persons with mental and addictive disorders. *Archives of General Psychiatry, 50*, 95–107.

Nuckolls, C. W. (1992). Toward a cultural history of the personality disorders. *Social Science and Medicine, 35*, 37–47.

Ofshe, R., & Watters, E. (1994). *Making monsters: False memories*, psychotherapy, and sexual hysteria. New York: Scribner's.

Olfson, M., & Pincus, H. A. (1994a). Outpatient psychotherapy in the United States I: Volume, costs, and user characteristics. *American Journal of Psychiatry, 151*, 1281–1288.

Olfson, M., & Pincus, H. A. (194b). Outpatient psychotherapy in the United States II: Patterns of utilization. *American Journal of Psychiatry, 151*, 1289–1294.

Pearlin, I. (1989). The sociological study of stress. *Journal of Health & Social Behavior, 30*, 241–56.

Pescosolido, B. A. (1992). Beyond rational choice: The social dynamics of how people seek help. *American Journal of Sociology, 97*, 1096–1038.

Radloff, L. S. (1977). The CES-D Scale: A self-report depression scale for research in the general population. *Applied psychological Measurement, 3*, 249–265.

Regier, D. A., Narrow, W. E., Rae, D. S., Manderscheid, R. W., Locke, B. Z., & Goodwin, F. K. (1993). The de facto US mental and addictive disorders service system. *Archives of General Psychiatry 50*, 85–94.

Reisman, D., Glazer, N., & Denney, R. (1951). *The lonely crowd*. New Haven, CT: Yale University Press.

Robins, L. N., Helzer, J. E., Weissman, M. M., Orvaschel, H., Gruenberg, E., Burke, J. D., Jr.. & Regier, D. A. (1984). Lifetime prevalence of specific psychiatric disorders in three sites. *Archives of General Psychiatry, 41*, 949–956.

Rogler, L. H., & Cortes, D. E. (1993). Help-seeking pathways: A unifying concept in mental health care. *American Journal of Psychiatry, 150*, 554–561.

Rosenhan, D. L. (1973). On being sane in insane places. Science, 179, 250–258.

Sampson, H., Messinger, S., & Towne, R . (1964). *Schizophrenic women: Studies in marital crisis*. New York: Atherton.

Sartorius, N., Jablensky, A., Korten, A., Ernberg, G., Anker, M.. Cooper, J. E., & Day, R. (1976). Early manifestations and first-contact incidence of schizophrenia in different cultures. *Psychological Medicine, 16*, 909–928.

Scheff, T. J. (1966). *Being mentally ill: A sociological theory*. Chicago: Aldine.

Scheff, T. J. (1974). The labeling theory of mental illness. *American* Sociologica*l Review, 39,* 444–452.

Schwab, J. J., & Schwab, M. E. (1978). *Sociocultural roots of mental illness: An epidemiological survey*. New York: Plenum Press.

Scott, W. (1990). PTSD in DSM-III. A case of the politics of diagnosis and disease. Social Problems, 37, 294–310.

Scull, A., MacKenzie, C., & Hervey, N. (1996). *Masters of bedlam: The transformation of the mad-doctoring trade*. Princeton, NJ: Princeton University Press.

Selye, H. (1956). *The stress of life*. New York: McGraw-Hill.

Sewall, W. H., Jr. (1992). A theory of structures: Duality, agency, and transformation. *American Journal of Sociology, 98*, 1–29.

Shorter, E. (1992). *From paralysis to fatigue: A history of psychosomatic illness in the modern era*. New York: Free Press.

Shelter, E. (1994). *From the mind into the body: The cultural origins of psychosomatic symptoms*. New York: Free Press.

Showalter, E. (1997). *Hystories: Hysterical epidemics and modern media*. New York: Columbia University Press.

Srole, L., Langner, T. S., Michael, S. T., Opler, M. K., & Rennie, T.A.C. (1962). *Mental health in the metropolis: The midtown Manhattan study*. New York: McGraw-Hill.

Sullivan, H. S. (1953). *The interpersonal theory of psychiatry*. New York: W.W. Norton.

Swidler, A. (1986), Culture inaction: Symbols and strategies. *American Sociological Review 1*, 273–286.

Szasz, T. S. (1961). *The myth of mental illness*. New York: Harper.

Thoits, P. A. (1985). Self-labeling processes in mental illness: The role of emotional deviance. *American Journal of Sociology, 91*, 221–149.

Turner, R. J., Wheaten, B. & Lloyd, D. A. (1995). The epidemiology of social stress. *American Sociological Review, 60*, 104–125.

Veroff, I., Kulka, R. A., & Douvan, E. (1981). *Mental health in America: Patterns of help-seeking from 1957 to 1976*. New York: Basic Books.

Wakefield, J. C. (1992a). The concept of mental disorder: On the boundary between biological facts and social values. *American Psychologist, 47*, 373–388.

Wakefield, J. C. (1992b). Disorder as harmful dysfunction: A conceptual critique of DSM-III-R's definitions of mental disorder. Psychological Review, *99,* 232–247.

Wakefield, J. C. (1994). Is the concept of mental disorder culturally relative? In S. Kirk & S. Einbinder (Eds.), *Controversial issues in mental health* (pp. 111–117). Boston: Allyn & Bacon.

Wakefield, J. C. (1997). But are they psychiatric disorders? Conceptual validity of DIS diagnostic criteria and ECA prevalence estimates. Rutgers University. New Brunswick, NJ. unpublished manuscript.

Waxler, N. E. (1974). Culture and mental illness: A social labeling perspective. *Journal of Nervous and Mental Disease, 159*, 379–395.

Weinberg, D. (1997). The social construction of non-human agency: The case of mental disorder. *Social Problems, 44*, 217–234.

Weissman, M. M., Myers, J. K., & Koss, C. E. (Eds.). (1986). Community surveys of psychiatric disorders. New Brunswick, NJ: Rutgers University Press.

Wenger. D., & Fletcher. C. R. (1969). The effect of legal counsel on admissions to a state mental hospital: A confrontation of professions. *Journal of Health and Social Behavior, 10*, 66–72.

Wheaton, B. (1990). Life transitions, role histories, and mental health. *American Sociological Review, 55*, 209–223.

Whiting, J., & Child, I. (1953). Child training and personality: A cross-cultural study. New Haven, CT: Yale University Press.

Whyte, W. H., Jr. (1956). *The organization man.* New York: Simon & Shuster.

Winchen, H.-U., Robins, L. N., Cottler, L. B., Sartorius, N., et al. (1991). Cross-cultural feasibility, reliability and sources of variance: in the composite international diagnostic interview (CIDI). *British Journal of Psychiatry, 159*, 645–653.

PART II

Observing Mental Health
in the Community

CHAPTER 5

Issues in Mental Health Assessment

Galen E. Switzer
Mary Amanda Dew
Evelyn J. Bromet

Biosocial and sociocultural factors leave imprints on mental health which are discernible when viewed from the panoramic perspectives provided by a large population.

SROLE (1962)

Deviations from "normal" emotional functioning have been recognized and documented for as long as written accounts of history have existed. Parables concerning mental disorder appear in the written works of all major religions, and statutes concerning the mentally ill were a part of early Roman law (Eaton, 1980). Depending on the particular historical period in which they lived, those whose behavior did not conform to accepted norms were labeled variously as possessed, holy, mad, or insane. In the late nineteenth and early twentieth centuries, as mental disorders increasingly came under the purview of medical science, the previous broad categories of mental disorder (e.g., raving, melancholic, lunatic, idiot; Jarvis, 1971) began to be subdivided into more specific "diagnostic" categories. This categorization process, or nosology, has continued to the present day and is currently embodied in its most specific form as the American Psychiatric Association's *Diagnostic and*

GALEN E. SWITZER • Departments of Medicine and Psychiatry, University of Pittsburgh School of Medicine and Medical Center, Pittsburgh, Pennsylvania 15213.   MARY AMANDA DEW • Departments of Psychiatry, Psychology, and Epidemiology, University of Pittsburgh School of Medicine and Medical Center, Pittsburgh, Pennslavania 15213.   EVELYN J. BROMET • Department of Psychiatry and Behavioral Sciences, State University of New York at Stony Brook, Stony Brook, New York 11794.

Handbook of the Sociology of Mental Health, edited by Carol S. Aneshensel and Jo C. Phelan. Kluwer Academic/ Plenum Publishers, New York, 1999.

Statistical Manual of Mental Disorders (DSM-IV; American Psychiatric Association, 1994), and the *International Classification of Diseases* (ICD-10; World Health Organization, 1992), which describe the symptoms and diagnostic criteria of more than 250 psychiatric disorders. In this chapter, we briefly describe the historical roots, current practical issues, and future directions of the assessment of mental health in community-based populations. Our focus on macro, community-level assessment stems, in part, from the fact that sociologists have generated much of the literature and instrument development for group mental health assessment. In general, we focus on instruments designed for, and studies conducted with, adults.

Although in modern times, the process of evaluating and diagnosing mental disorders in clinical/treatment settings has been primarily the work of psychiatrists, cross-fertilization has led to increased interest in mental health and disorder in several other disciplines. Figure 5.1 depicts four major parent disciplines concerned with mental health issues in terms of the domains on which they draw in conceptualizing the study of mental health and disorder.

In general, psychiatry and psychology have traditionally focused relatively more heavily on internal states, whereas epidemiology and sociology have focused on characteristics external to the individual in examining mental health issues. In terms of examining internal states, psychiatry, especially, tends to emphasize physical, organic factors in the etiology of and solutions to mental disorders. In contrast, psychology places relatively more emphasis on cognitive and affective processes. Sociology and epidemiology both focus to a greater degree on external factors, although sociology tends to give greater weight to societal-level structures and processes, whereas epidemiology, more than any of the other disciplines, emphasizes physical environmental factors in mental disorder. Each discipline contributes

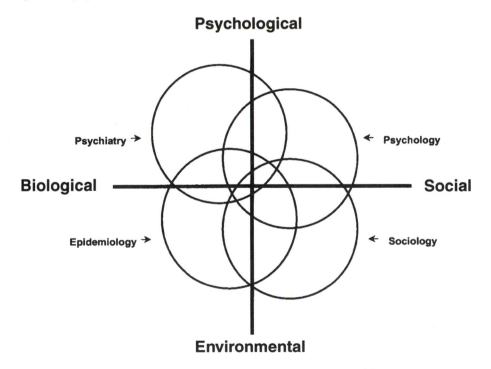

FIGURE 5.1. Major disciplines concerned with mental health issues.

a unique perspective and emphasizes slightly different, but overlapping, sets of variables as predictors and outcomes of mental disorders.

Where a discipline theoretically locates the "causes" of mental disorders is a critical determinant of how mental health will be assessed. Thus, psychiatrists and psychologists typically assess mental health individually with clinical interviews, neurological exams, and behavioral observation, whereas epidemiologists and sociologists are more likely to conduct population-based studies using community surveys, interviews, and secondary data sources. Nevertheless, across the disciplines, there is some consensus that mental health and disorder involve the interaction of unique personal characteristics with societal and environmental factors. This multifactorial perspective has produced several hybrid areas of study, including psychiatric sociology, social psychiatry, and psychiatric epidemiology. Each of these hybrids has focused on applying and evaluating the assumptions and theories of its parent discipline (e.g., sociology, epidemiology) to mental health issues. Among these hybrids, the psychiatric subdisciplines of sociology and epidemiology stand out as fields that seek to combine elements from all four domains (see Figure 5.1). Consequently, the history of these areas will be adopted as the organizing perspective from which to view the development of community mental health assessment research in the past 150 years.

Brief History of Community Mental Health Assessment

Although this chapter focus primarily on relatively recent developments in assessment instruments and techniques, a brief discussion of the evolution of community mental health evaluation seems warranted. Dohrenwend and Dohrenwend (1982) identified several distinct periods or eras of instrumentation and methodological developments that have culminated in what they refer to as "third generation" studies. Each of the three generations of studies and instrument types has distinctive characteristics, which are summarized in Table 5.1.

Conducted prior to World War II, the first set of community mental health studies attempted to assess broad patterns of mental disorder in the community by gathering information from informants, medical records, and, occasionally, from direct interviews (e.g., Jarvis, 1971). One of the first systematic efforts to assess treated prevalence of mental disorder in the community was conducted by Faris and Dunham (1939). These sociologists reviewed all medical records of Illinois state mental hospitals from 1922 through 1931 and drew inferences about the rates of diagnosed general mental disorder, and of schizophrenia

TABLE 5.1. **Characteristics of Three Generations of Epidemiological Research**

	Timespan	Method	Assessor	Primary goal	Limitations
First generation	1850–1950	Key informant Agency records Direct interview	Clinician	General disorder type	Validity Reliability
Second generation	1950–1980	Direct interview	Clinician or lay interviewer	Impairment	Validity
Third generation	1980–present	Direct interview Self-report survey Computer assisted	Clinician, lay interviewer, or self	Diagnosis or impairment	Validity

Source. Based on Dohrenwend & Dohrenwend (1982).

specifically, in the adult population living in and around Chicago. Their expectation was supported that a variety of sociological factors would result in higher rates of general disorder and schizophrenia in more densely populated, less affluent, inner-city areas. This application of sociological and epidemiological methodology to the assessment of mental disorder in the community was a significant departure from the traditional individualized methods used in clinic settings. The clinical setting tends to emphasize the unique aspects of each individual's personal history as distinct from the commonalities that exist across groups of similar persons, or among those exposed to similar environmental conditions.

The primary limitation of such first-generation community mental health studies was the fact that prevalence estimates were based on treated (rather than general population) samples; rates of individuals seeking mental health treatement were used directly to estimate rates of disorder in the population. It is now well established that only a fraction of those with mental disorders ever seek treatment, meaning that these initial community studies almost certainly underestimated "true" prevalence rates (Dohrenwend & Dohrenwend, 1982). In addition, the lack of standardized guidelines for diagnosing disorders at that time led to problems with comparability among these studies (Faris & Dunham, 1939).

The involvement of the United States in World War II ushered in the second generation of assessment studies. In the 1940s, the Neuropsychiatric Screen Adjunct (NSA) was developed by the U.S. Army to eliminate from the armed forces those individuals who could not serve effectively as soldiers (Star, 1950; Stouffer et al., 1950). The NSA, designed to assess general psychiatric status, found much higher prevalence rates of psychiatric impairment than expected based on pre–World War II studies. The necessity of evaluating large numbers of individuals for military service, coupled with the strikingly high observed rates of impairment, provided the impetus for the further development and refinement of instruments for use in community settings in the postwar period.

Two classic studies from this second generation—the Midtown Manhattan study in New York (Srole et al., 1962), and the Stirling County study in Nova Scotia (Leighton, Harding, Macklin, Macmillan, & Leighton, 1963)—were designed and conducted by sociologist Leo Srole and psychiatrist Alexander Leighton, respectively. Both studies drew on, and expanded, the Selective Service NSA items as a basis for rating individuals along 5- or 6-point continuums of psychiatric impairment ranging from completely well to completely or severely impaired. Both studies used relatively sophisticated techniques—including solicitation of a diverse set of expert opinions, pilot testing items, and assessment agreement between interview items and psychiatric ratings—to improve their instruments. In addition, these studies used state-of-the-art probabilistic sampling methods to select several hundred respondents who were representative of their respective communities. Advantages of these second-generation studies over previous efforts to assess population-based mental health included the use of community samples and direct interviewing, methods that had not previously been feasible. These new methods were made possible by the fact that these new instruments could be administered by nonclinician lay interviewers rather than psychiatrists, making them substantially less costly. Finally, there was growing evidence that instruments developed during this second phase of epidemiological investigation were considerably more reliable than their predecessors (Dohrenwend, 1995).

However, second-generation efforts did evoke some of the same validity concerns as first-generation studies. First, instruments used in these studies did not adequately assess the full range of clinical diagnostic categories, including impairment resulting from behavioral disorders or substance abuse. Second, and perhaps more important, there was ample evidence that psychiatric impairment, as defined by instruments used in the community, was not comparable to disorder as defined by psychiatrist clinicians; impairment was measured on a continuous scale quite different from discrete diagnostic categories (Srole et al., 1962; Leighton et al., 1963). Given that diagnosis of disorder was not the central purpose, however, it is important to acknowledge that many of these instruments did provide relatively stable dimensional assessments of areas such as general distress and depression (Link & Dohrenwend, 1980). Finally, additional validity concerns arose during this period as researchers and psychiatrists noticed large differences in the rates of psychiatric disorders between countries. The most striking example involved reported rates of manic–depressive psychosis in Britain that were 20 times those found in the United States (Kramer, 1961), which led to a large multisite study in the two nations (Cooper et al., 1972). This collaborative study—in which the Present State Examination (PSE) was chosen as the standard instrument—revealed that the cross-national differences had been produced by disparities in instrumentation and methods of diagnosis, findings that led to further refinement and standardization of community diagnostic instruments.

In a reflexive process, the demand for reliable instruments for epidemiological and clinical-based research spurred the psychiatric community to undertake several major revisions in its core diagnostic manual. Increasing detail and specificity of the DSM, in turn, led to the development of a third generation of instruments based on the more specific diagnostic categories found in the DSM. In response to the high cost of having clinicians administer these instruments in the community, the National Institute of Mental Health (NIMH) developed a fully structured interview that could be administered by lay interviewers. The Diagnostic Interview Schedule (DIS; Robins et al., 1988), based on the DSM-III, was designed for use in the Epidemiologic Catchment Area (ECA) studies conducted at five sites in major U.S. cities and has now been translated into several other languages (Regier & Robins, 1991; see Chapter 26 of this volume). In the past two decades, the number and variety of psychiatric assessment instruments designed specifically for use in the community has proliferated. Currently, a variety of fully structured and semistructured diagnostic instruments are available for community-based research.

REVIEW AND SUMMARY OF MAJOR ASSESSMENT TECHNIQUES

In general, mental health measures used in community settings currently fall into two categories, referred to here as dimensional and diagnostic. Dimensional instruments—also called screening instruments or symptom inventories (depending on how they are used and the type of data they gather) and designed for use by lay interviewers in research contexts—were designed to provide information about an individual's relative symptom level rather than a discrete diagnosis. These instruments can be fully structured (no deviations in how questions are asked) for lay interviews, semistructured (with probes as needed to gather maximum information) for clinician interviews, or self-administered questionnaires.

In contrast, diagnostic instruments—also called schedules or examinations—are based very closely on the specific symptoms described by the DSM-IV, or, more recently, the ICD-10, used to make diagnostic judgments in the clinic. One of the central goals in the development of diagnostic instruments was to allow nonclinicians to conduct fully or semistructured interviews that provide the equivalent of psychiatric *diagnoses*. Although there are many differences between diagnostic and dimensional instruments, perhaps the central distinction is that diagnostic instruments categorize individuals into dichotomous outcomes (e.g., meets criteria for major depression or not), whereas dimensional instruments place individuals along a continuum of symptom severity (e.g., more or less depressed).

The debate over the relative advantages and disadvantages of diagnostic versus dimensional approaches continues both at academic and policy levels. Proponents of the diagnostic approach argue that discrete categorization of mental illness is necessary from the practical standpoint of determining who is eligible for insurance and/or social service assistance. In addition, they assert that diagnostic typology, founded on consistent decision rules, will produce more precise assessment of mental status than will dimensional systems (Regier et al., 1984; Weissman, 1987). Moreover, they argue that mental illness is more than a matter of degree of severity along a continuous dimension; conditions such as schizophrenia and major depression are qualitatively distinct from normal human functioning. In contrast, proponents of a dimensional approach suggest that diagnostic approaches rely too heavily on microbiological models that view individuals as either diseased or not diseased. Mirowsky and Ross (1989a) argue that the discipline of psychiatry is inherently motivated to adhere to this medical model in order to retain its traditional preeminence over other disciplines concerned with mental health issues. They contend that discrete measurement of nondiscrete psychological phenomena (1) disregards useful information about the degree and characteristics of psychological distress; (2) confounds information on symptoms, causes, and consequences of distress; and (3) provides assessments that are relatively insensitive to changes in mental status (see Mirowsky & Ross, 1989a, 1989b). Clearly, the controversy over techniques for community mental health assessment will continue, and we suggest that prior to selecting an instrument, researchers become familiar with the major arguments on both sides of the issue.

Tables 5.2 and 5.3 list psychiatric assessment instruments that have been widely used in community studies. Instruments are divided into two tables corresponding to whether they provide a diagnostic (dichotomous; Table 5.2) or dimensional (continuous; Table 5.3) assessment of mental disorder.

Diagnostic Instruments

As noted earlier, proponents of categorical instruments argue that each mental disorder is qualitatively distinct from other disorders and from normality (Clementz & Iacono, 1993). All the diagnostic or categorical instruments listed in Table 5.2 are based on the DSM or ICD and assess lifetime and/or current psychiatric status for a broad set of disorders. Most were developed originally for use in clinical research as opposed to epidemiological field studies (Ustun & Tien, 1995; with a few exceptions, most notably the DIS and the Composite International Diagnostic Interview [CIDI]), because they were generated for use in a clinical setting, where the ultimate goal was to treat psychiatric disorders. These instruments generally assign only one primary diagnosis using a hierarchical system. One of the drawbacks of using these instruments (e.g., Structured Clinical Interview for DSM-IV [SCID] and PSE) in a hierarchical format is that, although assigning a single primary diagnosis may be useful for guiding treatment decisions in clinic settings, the high degree of comorbidity in psychiatric disorders may make it less desirable for assessing prevalence of psychiatric disorders in the population.[1] Additionally, diagnostic instruments can be fairly lengthy, because they cover a broad range of areas and may lead to respondent fatigue.

---

[1] These instruments, however, may be used in an alternate format that includes administration of the entire item set, which allows the investigator to evaluate comorbidity.

TABLE 5.2. Frequently Used Diagnostic Schedules

Diagnostic schedule	Source	Format: fully vs. semi-structured interview vs. self-administered questionnaire	Domains assessed	Administration format
CIDI Composite International Diagnostic Interview	Robins et al., 1988	Full	Axis I[a]	Lay interview
DIGS Diagnostic Interview for Genetic Studies	Nurnberger et al., 1994	Full	Axis I	Clinician interview
DIS (III, IIIA, IIIR, IV) Diagnostic Interview Schedule	Robins et al., 1981	Full	Axis I	Lay interview
DIPD-R Diagnostic Interview for Personality Disorders	Zanarini et al., 1987	Full	Axis II	Lay interview
PAF Personality Assessment Form	Shea et al., 1987	Semi and rating scale	Axis II	Clinician or lay interview
PDE/IPDE Personality Disorder Examination	Loranger, 1988 WHO, 1992a	Full	Axis II	Lay interview
PDQ/PDQ-R/PDQ-4 Personality Diagnostic Questionnaire, 4th ed.	Hyler et al., 1994	Self-report	Axis II	Questionnaire
PRIME-D	Spitzer et al., 1995	Self-report	Depression	Questionnaire
PSE Present State Examination	Wing et al., 1961 Wing et al., 1974	Full	Axis I	Lay interview
SADS/SADS-L Schedule for Affective Disorders and Schizophrenia	Endicott & Spitzer, 1978	Semi	Axis I	Clinician
SCAN Structured Clinical Assessment for Neuropsychiatric Disorders	Wing et al., 1990	Semi	Axis I	Clinician or lay interview
SCID/SCID-II Structured Clinical Interview for DSM-IV	Spitzer et al., 1992	Semi	Axis I Axis II	Clinician interview
SIDP/SIDP-R Structured Interview for DSM-IV Personality Disorders	Pfohl et al., 1982 Pfohl et al., 1989	Semi	Axis II	Lay interview

[a]Axis 1 includes the following clinical disorders: dementia-related, organic, substance-related, schizophrenia, mood, anxiety, somatoform, factitious, dissociative, sexual/gender, eating, sleep, impulse-control, and adjustment. Axis 2 includes the following personality disorders: paranoid, schizoid, schizotypal, antisocial, borderline, histrionic, narcissistic, avoidant, dependent, obsessive-compulsive, and mental retardation.

TABLE 5.3. **Frequently Used Dimensional Scales**

Dimensional scales	Source	Format[a]
Anxiety		
BAI Beck Anxiety Inventory	Beck & Steer, 1990	Self-administered
STAI State-Trait Anxiety Index	Spielberger, 1984	Self-administered
Depression		
BDI Beck Depression Inventory	Beck et al., 1961	Self-administered
CES-D Center for Epidemiologic Studies Depression Scale	Radloff, 1977	Self-administered
HDRS/HDI Hamilton Depression Rating Scale/Inventory	Hamilton, 1960 Reynolds & Koback, 1995	Self-administered
ZUNG Zung Depression Scale	Zung, 1963	Self-administered
Personality		
MCMI-III Millon Clinical Multiaxial Inventory	Millon, 1987	Self-administered
MMPI Minnesota Multiphasic Personality Inventory	Dahlstrom et al., 1972	Self-administered
MPI Maudsley Personality Inventory	Eysenk, 1947	Self-administered
MPQ Multidimensional Personality Questionnaire	Tellegen, 1993	Self-administered
NEO NEO-Personality Inventory	Costa & McCrae, 1985	Self-administered
Social Adjustment		
SAS Social Adjustment Scale	Weissman & Bothwell, 1976	Self-administered
K-SAS Katz Social Adjustment Scale	Katz & Lyerly, 1963	Self-administered
Multiple Domains		
GHQ General Health Questionnaire	Goldberg, 1972	Self-administered
HSCL/SCL-90/BSI Hopkins Symptom Checklist Symptom Checklist Brief Symptom Inventory	Parloff et al., 1954 Derogatis et al., 1974 Derogatis & Cleary, 1977	Self-administered
PERI Psychiatric Epidemiology Research Instrument	Dohrenwend et al., 1986	Semistructured Self-administered
POMS Profile of Mood States	McNair, Lorr, & Droppleman, 1992	Self-administered

[a]Most measures listed as self-adminstered can also be administered in a fully structured interview format.

Traditionally, diagnostic instruments used in the community have demonstrated only moderate reliability and relatively low validity (Ustun & Tien, 1995). For example, researchers using a variety of diagnostic instruments, including the DIS (Robins, Helzer, Ratcliff, & Seyfried, 1982), the SCID (Williams, 1992), and the Schedule for Affective Disorders and Schizophrenia (SADS; Bromet, Dunn, Connell, Dew, & Schulberg, 1986) have typically found fewer reported symptoms when the instrument is administered a second time to the same individuals (Robins, 1985). One of the difficulties in establishing reliability for diagnostic instruments is that the criteria for verifying reliability are relatively strict. To be deemed reliable, a diagnostic instrument must identify the same individuals as cases and as noncases in a second administration of the schedule as in the initial administration (Robins, 1985; Dohrenwend, 1989). This dichotomous, or "hard," approach to reliability is generally more stringent than the correlation coefficient used to establish reliability of a dimensional scale.

Validity concerns about diagnostic instruments are currently even more pressing than reliability concerns. Although category definitions have become much more specific and well defined—improving the face validity of included items—diagnostic instruments may still lack criterion validity. For example, DIS diagnoses obtained during the ECA studies (Anthony et al., 1985; Helzer et al., 1985) differed significantly from the number and type of diagnoses assigned to the same samples through clinical interviews (Anthony et al., 1985; Shrout, 1994). As Murphy (1995) notes, however, there is some controversy over whether clinical interviews should serve as the gold standard by which to assess the validity of community-based instruments. In the ECA studies, prevalence rates assigned by psychiatrists, as well as those assigned by the DIS, varied significantly across the metropolitan administration sites (Robins, 1985), suggesting that neither assessment technique provides completely reliable and valid estimates of prevalence.

Similarly, concerns have been raised about the construct validity of diagnostic instruments. The primary technique for validating diagnostic measures has been to assess the degree of correspondence of diagnoses obtained in the community with psychiatrists', clinical psychologists', or psychiatric social workers' diagnoses of the same individuals through clinical interviews. Thus, experienced clinicians' diagnoses—rather than a latent condition particular to the individual—become the construct represented in diagnostic instruments (Mirowsky & Ross, 1989a). Given the considerable variance in clinician-assigned diagnoses for individuals exhibiting similar symptoms and mental health histories, it has been argued that validating instruments against such diagnoses is tenuous at best (Mirowsky & Ross, 1989a).

Dimensional Instruments

Although dimensional instruments have been developed to assess a wide variety of impairment types, we focus here on five categories of impairment that are most frequently assessed: anxiety, depression, personality, social adjustment, and multiple distress domains. Anxiety, depression, and social adjustment (the ability to function effectively in social contexts) are generally considered to be state-like, or episodic in nature. Anxiety and depression are embodied in several of the primary Axis I disorders recognized by the DSM-IV and also are the most frequently assessed subcomponents on multiple distress instruments. In contrast, personality is typically regarded as an enduring trait, and is the central component of DSM-IV Axis II disorders. Measures in these five domains typically contain a series of items asking respondents to rate the presence–absence, frequency, and/or intensity of psychiatric symptoms during a timeframe of the past 1–2 weeks. Dimensional instruments, such as those listed in Table 5.3, differ from diagnostic instruments in several important ways. First, many of these instruments assess only one or two areas of symptomatology rather than a broad range of disorders, as found in most diagnostic instruments. Second, rather than defining caseness as a dichotomy, these instruments provide an overall score for the area of distress, based on a sum or average of the individual items in the instrument. Subscale scores for particular types of symptoms may also be computed. Symptoms are presumed to reflect quantitative departures from normal functioning (Clementz & Iacono, 1993). Most published dimensional instruments do, however, provide cutpoints or threshold levels that differentiate between "cases" and "noncases," where caseness is typically defined as a high, clinically significant level of symptomatology, or as showing a high likelihood of meeting psychiatric diagnostic criteria in a formal clinical assessment. These cutpoints may, however, have very low convergence with diagnoses based on clinical interviews and ratings (Dohrenwend, 1995). Finally, most dimensional instruments measure only current distress—as opposed to past episodes or lifetime rates—limiting the amount and type of information they provide.

Like diagnostic instruments, dimensional instruments have suffered from criticisms concerning reliability and validity. Although the internal consistency of established scales is relatively high—in the range of .80 to .85—test–retest reliability has been less consistent (Murphy, 1985). Variability in test–retest reliability may in part reflect the fact that some instruments (e.g., General Health Questionnaire [GHQ]) conceptualize and assess symptomatology or distress as acute (atypical, time-discrete symptoms), whereas others (e.g., Hopkins Symptom Checklist [HSCL]) focus on more chronic aspects of the symptomatology (may be typical and enduring symptoms). As might be expected, instruments assessing chronic symptomatology tend to have higher test–retest coefficients than those assessing episodic or acute symptoms (Murphy, 1995) in part because the phenomenon being assessed is inherently more stable over time.

Link and Dohrenwend (1980) found that early versions of dimensional instruments demonstrated very low correspondence with diagnosable disorder, thus raising serious questions about the validity of such instruments as measures of psychiatric disorders. Even more recently developed instruments (e.g., Center for Epidemologic Studies—Depression Scale [CES-D]) may exhibit this weakness (Breslau, 1985). However, positive evidence concerning validity has been found for some dimensional scales (e.g., Hopkins Symptom Check List [HSCL], Symptom Check List [SCL-90]), which have relatively stable underlying factor structures that seem to correspond to specific clinical syndromes (Derogatis & Cleary, 1977). However, as noted by Dohrenwend and Dohrenwend (1965, 1982), the high correlations among virtually all dimensional instruments (even when they were designed to assess different domains of psychiatric impairment) raise serious questions about the legitimacy of interpreting the measures as assessing different constructs. Instead, these instruments all may be measuring a more general factor such as nonspecific distress or demoralization (Dohrenwend & Dohrenwend, 1965, 1982).

In general, although diagnostic and dimensional instruments were developed with divergent goals, their application in community assessment studies may be quite similar. Dimensional instruments assess symptomatology on a continuous scale but are frequently published with a threshold or cutpoint above which individuals are defined as "cases," or as experiencing "significant distress." Conversely, in addition to reporting caseness, studies using diagnostic instruments often report continuous variables such as the number of symptoms endorsed or average level of symptom severity. This merging of diagnosis and dimensionality and intensity may be the ultimate future of community mental health assessment.

PRACTICAL ISSUES IN ASSESSMENT

We have grouped several practical assessment issues into three broad categories—sampling, instrument selection, and instrument administration—that we discuss here in detail.

Sampling Considerations

Because several excellent chapters and texts have been written on sampling considerations in community-based research (e.g., Fowler, 1984), only the most critical issues are mentioned here. The ultimate usefulness of a study assessing prevalence or incidence of mental disorder in the community is contingent on the generalizability of the findings. It is therefore critical to assemble a representative study sample. In sociological and epidemiological studies of mental disorder, samples are typically drawn from the community at large. However, in some circumstances, they may be drawn from new admissions or existing patients at hospitals and clinics (Bromet et al., 1992). Three major sources of potential bias in these samples include selection effects, nonresponse, and attrition (Dillman, 1978; Fowler, 1984; Goldstein & Simpson, 1995; Zahner, Chung-Cheng, & Fleming, 1995).

For community samples, selection effects are most likely to occur when a probability sample (one in which every person has an equal or known probability of being selected) is not obtained. Certain characteristics of individuals with psychiatric disorders may make them under- or overrepresented on lists from which community samples are often selected. For example, those with moderate to severe impairment may be less likely to be living independently, have established credit, have their own telephone, have a record of military service, or be registered voters. Conversely, they may be more likely to have had contact with the social service and criminal justice systems, and to have required medical assistance. Techniques for minimizing sampling bias in community samples include establishing (1) well-delineated sampling frames, (2) clear definitions of inclusion–exclusion criteria, and (3) explicit procedures for selection (Fowler, 1984).

Among patients admitted to hospitals or clinics, important selection effects have already occurred prior to the researcher's attempts to draw a sample. First, the level of symptom severity in a treated population is likely to be higher than that in the community. This is true despite the fact that many people with diagnosable disorders never seek treatment (Burke & Regier, 1994; Regier, Goldberg, & Taube, 1978). In addition to differences in symptom severity, comorbidity of mental and somatic disorders may further increase the probability that "cases" will be admitted to a hospital setting, known as Berkson's Bias (Berkson, 1946). Finally, important patient demographic characteristics (ethnicity, income, education) are known to be associated with access to health care—African Americans, for example, are less likely to receive services for most types of mental disorder than are European Americans (Cheung, 1990; Horwath, Johnson, & Hornig, 1993; Padgett, 1994; Sue, Fujino, Hu, & Takeuchi, 1991). These same demographic and social characteristics are also associated with type of treatment setting; those with higher socioeconomic status (SES) are more likely to be treated in private as opposed to public facilities. All these factors underscore the importance of basing prevalence rates on general, rather than treated, populations.

A second potential threat to obtaining a representative sample comes from differential rates of survey/interview completion—also called nonresponse bias (Dillman, 1978). In community samples, for example, individuals with some forms of mental disorder may be more likely to refuse to participate in interviews. Furthermore, severe symptom levels may prevent individuals with disorders from responding reliably in interviews or completing self-administered instruments. Efforts to minimize this form of bias should include special efforts to (1) secure participation from individuals who may be at most risk of having disorders, (2) ensure that study instruments can be completed even by individuals with low functioning levels, and (3) gather "objective" information from secondary sources (e.g., interviews with informants, collection of data from billing records, insurance files, and/or medical records) in order to examine and control for differences between responders and nonresponders. Additionally, sophisticated statistical techniques that take into account, and adjust for, characteristics of nonresponders have been used successfully in large epidemiological studies such as the National Comorbidity Survey (Kessler et al., 1994).

A similar type of potential bias exists for longitudinal studies in the form of study attrition due to morbidity or mortality. The debilitating effects of mental disorders may make individuals with such disorders—both in community and institutional settings—more likely to drop out of a study due to increased mortality or psychiatric morbidity. Although few proactive options are available for completely eliminating attrition-related bias, it is important to gather and utilize baseline and secondary source information about those individuals lost to attrition to assess and statistically account for demographic, psychosocial, and psychiatric differences.

Instrument Selection

There are several important issues to consider in selecting an instrument for research. Of key importance is whether the instrument provides reliable and valid assessments of the particular construct(s) of interest. Although the initial identification of possible instruments to assess depression, for example, may be relatively simple, determining whether the instruments have been proven reliable and valid may be more difficult, especially given the profusion of choices currently available. The Health and Psychosocial Instrumentation database (HaPI-CD; Behavioral Measurement Database Services, 1997) is an excellent resource for identifying and obtaining psychometric information on currently available instruments.

Most basic sociology, psychology, and epidemiology texts describe methods for evaluating the psychometric properties of instruments, including the critical factors for determining whether the instrument is reliable and valid, so only a brief overview is presented here. In establishing reliability, it is important to evaluate (1) whether the items that comprise the measure are internally consistent (i.e., measure a single underlying construct), and (2) whether an instrument provides similar symptom estimates or diagnoses for a person across reasonably short timespans and in different formats (e.g., clinician interview, lay interview, self-report). The most commonly used method of establishing the internal consistency of a measure is Cronbach's alpha (Cronbach, 1951), which provides a score ranging from 0.00 to 1.00, indicating the degree of "interrelatedness" among items included in the analysis; higher scores indicate better internal consistency. The test–retest method—in which the same instrument is administered to the same individuals on separate occasions—is often used to determine whether impairment or diagnosis is consistently assessed across time (Burke & Regier, 1994; Shrout, 1995).

Although there are several types of validity that can be evaluated, perhaps the two most relevant types are criterion and construct validity (Goldstein & Simpson, 1995). Evidence of criterion validity can be established by assessing the degree of correspondence between scores obtained with the instrument (e.g., a diagnosis of major depression) and some observable phenomenon (e.g., eating and sleeping disturbances), or between scores on two or more instruments intended to measure the same condition (e.g., Beck Depression Inventory and Zung Depression Scale). Construct validity can be established by showing that hypothesized relationships between scores on the measure and specific predictors or outcomes are empirically supported and/or that the measure does not correlate as highly with variables hypothesized to represent different constructs (Carmines & Zeller, 1979; Nunnally, 1978). Construct validity can therefore be established only in the context of a model or a set of well-defined theoretical relationships among variables. For example, a researcher assessing dysthymia using a newly created measure could generate a set of hypotheses about psychosocial factors that should be associated with dysthymia. If these predicted relationships are empirically established, the researcher has evidence that the underlying construct of dysthymia is indeed being assessed.

A second important issue is to determine whether a diagnostic instrument, dimensional instrument, or some combination of the two techniques should be used. A primary consideration should be the overall goal of the project in terms of how the data will be used. For example, if the goal is to describe differences between cases and noncases, or to isolate risk factors for a particular disorder, a diagnostic instrument would be appropriate. If the goal is to assess the general degree of impairment, or to describe the comorbidity and intensity of psychiatric dysfunction, a dimensional instrument would be more suitable. Characteristics of the population under examination should also be considered. The prevalence and incidence of many psychiatric disorders in the general population are low (Robins & Regier, 1991). Thus, studies using strict diagnostic criteria to define cases of a disorder may have difficulty generating enough cases to examine in relation to other variables. In addition, it has been suggested that a combined, or multimethod, approach might draw on the relative strengths of diagnostic and dimensional instruments and maximize the quality of information gathered (Dohrenwend, 1995; Duncan-Jones & Henderson, 1978; Ustun & Tien, 1995). One multimethod approach utilizes both types of instruments in a sequential process first to screen and then diagnose individuals who meet initial criteria (for examples of this technique, see Dohrenwend & Dohrenwend, 1981; Dohrenwend, Levar, & Shrout, 1986, Duncan-Jones & Henderson, 1978).

A third issue to consider is the appropriateness of the instrument for the study population. Most psychiatric instruments are based on middle-class, Western European/North American assumptions about mental health and illness. For example, many of the classic symptoms of schizophrenia (delusions, hallucinations, disorganized speech) are part of the religious ceremonies or daily spiritual experiences of many cultural groups (Eaton, 1980).[2] Conversely, it appears that some mental disorders—for example, *ataques de nervios* among Puerto Ricans—are recognized only among non-European cultures (Guarnaccia, Good, & Kleinman, 1990). Culture-bound assumptions pervade both the DSM and epidemiological

---

[2] There is evidence, however, that distinct subsets of what Western culture defines as symptoms of schizophrenia appear in and are defined as mental disorder by most other cultures (Eaton, 1980; Murphy, 1976).

instruments based on DSM categories. Consequently, it is important to determine whether the instrument has been used successfully with the particular cultural/ethnic groups included in the sample. Other demographic, medical status, and psychosocial characteristics (e.g., age, education, language skills, motivation for participating in the study) of the population are also important to consider in this regard. For example, there is concern that some instruments (e.g., the Beck Depression Inventory [BDI]) may not be appropriate for less educated populations due to the relatively complex response options. Other instruments—for example, those that include a relatively high proportion of somatic symptom items—may be inappropriate for physically ill groups in whom such symptoms may reflect medical status rather than emotional distress (Dew, 1998).

Instrument Administration

Depending on the study instrument, researchers may have several choices about how to gather information from respondents. An initial consideration should be the feasibility of using a particular instrument with the population of interest. Feasibility issues include the burden to potential respondents and the financial cost per subject of gathering the information. Community respondents may be reluctant to complete a lengthy interview or survey, because of both the time involved and perceptions that they will be asked to give confidential or sensitive information. Treated populations may have had more experience with the types of questions asked in mental health instruments, but, depending on the nature or severity of their illnesses, may also have more difficulty in completing certain types of assessments such as self-administered questionnaires. Some reluctance to participate may be addressed with careful explanation of the study procedures and how the data will be used, assurances of anonymity, and with monetary or other types of incentives offered to participants. Incentives will not only increase participation rates but will also substantially increase the cost per participant of gathering data (Dew, 1993; Dillman, 1978).

Another important cost consideration in determining feasibility is the cost of the assessment modality, and of the services of the person who will administer the assessment. Clinician interviewers are most costly, followed by trained lay interviewers (training periods for lay interviewers may range from a few days to a few weeks), research-assistant-administered questionnaires/interviews, and self-administered questionnaires. If it is necessary to use interviewers with some clinical experience to gather the data, it may be most feasible to employ individuals with master's level psychology, social work, or other social/behavioral science backgrounds.

In terms of the format of data gathering, in-person interviews are generally the most costly mode of assessment, followed by telephone interviews and self-administered questionnaires. Although self-report forms have been developed for most of the dimensional instruments (e.g., BDI, GHQ, Psychiatric Epidemiological Research Instrument [PERI]), this administration method is limited by the respondent's ability to read and understand questions, and is also less amenable to moving respondents through complicated question sequences. Telephone interviews may provide a middle ground in terms of cost and quality of information gathered. They also have been shown to yield highly reliable mental health data if the interviewers are carefully trained and supervised (Aneshensel et al., 1982a, 1982b; Aneshensel & Yokopenic, 1985; Fenig, Levar, & Yelin, 1993; Paulsen, Crowe, Noyes, & Pfohl, 1988; Wells, Burnam, Leake, & Robins, 1988). The use of computers to aid in recording responses to both interviews and self-administered questionniares has also become more prevalent. Self-administered computerized versions of several instruments (e.g., DIS, PSE, BDI, Clinical Interview Schedule [CIS], Health Assessment Questionnaire [HAQ]) have been developed and evaluated, and seem to provide a reliable, valid, and highly efficient means of assessing disorder/impairment (Brugha, Kaul, Dignan, Teather, & Wills, 1996; Dignon, 1996; Erdman et al., 1992; Kobak, Reynolds, & Greist, 1993; Lewis, 1994; Steer, Rissmiller, Ranier, & Beck, 1994; Thornicroft, 1992; for a review, see Kobak, Greist, Jefferson, & Katzelnick, 1996).

Each method of administration—clinical interview, interview, self-administered questionnaire—has its own sources of bias. A potential source of bias common to all forms of assessment is the motivation of the respondent for participating in the assessment. Individuals whose psychiatric status is linked to social and monetary benefits (e.g., social services, housing, public assistance) may be motivated to overreport symptomatology to ensure that these benefits are not withdrawn. Conversely, individuals who believe they might be stigmatized by family, friends, and work or educational colleagues may be motivated to underreport symptoms.

Even when they are motivated to report symptoms accurately, respondents may have difficulty recalling and accurately reporting information. Recall bias may especially threaten the validity of instruments assessing lifetime prevalence of psychiatric disorders; respondents may simply not remember the range of symptoms or duration of episodes occurring many years in the past. If this bias is assumed to be distributed randomly across population groups, it will contribute to overall measurement error and decrease the statistical power to detect differences among groups. If the bias is systematic (e.g., treated groups may be more attuned to current and past symptoms than nontreated groups), then artifical associations may be produced with risk factors or with outcomes. For example, recent studies have indicated that poor recall of earlier psychiatric episodes among the elderly may cause older cohorts to underreport psychiatric episodes relative to younger cohorts (Giuffra & Risch, 1994; Weissman et al., 1984). This tendency may have led researchers falsely to conclude that rates of mental disorder are rising in more recent cohorts. Because of the serious threat that this form of bias poses to the validity of instruments attempting to document psychiatric history, several techniques, such as the Life Chart Interview, which was pilot-tested at the Baltimore site of the ECA study, are being developed to improve the accuracy of autobiographical recall (Lyketsos, Nestadt, Cwi, Heithoff, & Eaton, 1994).

Another source of bias may be the order or format in which questions are asked. For example, an instrument that places general questions about daily functioning after a specific set of symptom-related questions may produce artificially low functioning estimates because the impairment has been made salient by the symptom questions. Additionally, extensive research on survey and interview techniques indicates that item wording, structure, and response categories all affect how participants respond to particular items (Schwarz, Hippler, Deutsch, & Strack, 1985; Tanur, 1992). When instruments are administered in an interview rather than a self-report format, there is the additional potential for interviewer bias (Dew, 1993; Dillman, 1978). Interviewer effects are most dangerous when interviewers are not blinded to the study hypotheses but can also occur anytime interviewers selectively probe for additional information on particular items or with particular participants, or give nonverbal expressions of approval or disapproval toward participants.

Finally, even if all these sources of potential bias are eliminated, there is still the possibility that the measure itself will provide biased estimates of disorder or symptom severity scores because of misclassification or measurement error. As with other forms of error, random misclassification reduces statistical power. If misclassification is systematic, however, examination of group differences may produce misleading conclusions. For example, if, despite experiencing similar symptomatology, Group A finds it easier to endorse (or acquiesce to) certain symptoms than Group B, the instrument will have produced artificial group differences.

There are several strategies to address threats to validity present in the instrument administration context. To counteract the potential that participants will be unmotivated or unable to provide accurate information, it is critical to establish interpersonal rapport with participants and to assure participants that their responses will be confidential. The researcher's interest in the topic should be clearly explained, and the researcher's links to other community or educational organizations that might be respected or valued by the participant should be noted. Several techniques can be used to assist the participant in recalling past events such as (1) working backward chronologically from present to past (Loftus, Smith, Klinger, & Fielder, 1991), (2) providing autobiographical landmarks—linking recall to important events in the participants' lives (Friedman, 1993), and (3) conducting a "life chart interview," which combines these techniques and provides a visual interactive memory aid for interviewees (Lyketsos et al., 1994).

To avoid biases that might occur as a result of item wording and format, as well as biases introduced by the interviewer, it is critical to pilot-test instruments for readability and flow, and to observe and evaluate interviewers. In conjunction with pilot testing and administration of the measure for "real" data collection purposes, it is important to establish and update question-by-question instructions for interviewers, to conduct ongoing interviewer training and/or refreshers, and periodically to have interviewers observe and critique each other.

Although several steps can be taken to reduce biases that come from the interviewer or respondent, it is more difficult to address biases inherent in the instrument itself. Simply identifying misclassification bias may not be possible in the context of a single research project unless several measures of the same disorder are included and compared. Psychometric analysis including item and factor analysis within sample subgroups, and group comparisons using multiple measures of the same construct, or multiple sources of data (Fenig et al., 1994), may be the primary means of combating misclassification.

CONTROVERSIES IN MENTAL HEALTH ASSESSMENT: RELIABILITY AND VALIDITY ISSUES

As opposed to the very practical issues covered in the previous section, this section deals with the more philosophical issues in mental health assessment. The first issue concerns the tension between reliability and validity, and the second section extends the discussion of validity to include the context within which mental health issues are studied.

Maximizing Reliability at the Expense of Validity?

Most individuals interested in research understand that a measure's ability to perform consistently (reliability), and to measure the targeted underlying construct (validity), are both highly desirable and necessary elements of the assessment process. The relationship between reliability and validity concerns is sometimes less explicitly stated. First, reliability is a necessary but not sufficient condition for establishing validity (i.e., an unreliable measure can never be valid). Second, validity is neither a necessary nor a sufficient condition for establishing reliability (i.e., a measure's reliability is independent of its validity). Finally, because it is a precondition for, and generally much easier to achieve than validity, reliability tends to be the focus of psychometric analysis of instrumentation.

The history of the DSM, and of community-based instruments founded on DSM definitions (e.g., CIDI and DIS), is one of increasing specificity in nomenclature, in diagnostic criteria, and in the number of different disorders identified. The increasing specificity and detail of these measures and continued refinement of items and assessment techniques has led to great improvements in the reliability of clinical research and community mental health assessment. However, this improvement should not be interpreted as an indication that the measures are simultaneously becoming increasingly valid (see Kirk & Kutchins, 1992). Although it is true that community assessment techniques must produce consistent results if they are to be claimed as valid, it is also true that a measure may be 100% reliable and 0% valid. Thus, while community-based measures have become increasingly reliable, there are enduring questions about their validity (Dohrenwend, 1995; Murphy, 1995). These questions stem in part from the lack of correspondence between diagnoses assigned to patients by community assessments and those assigned by expert clinicians; the severity of this problem varies according to the type of disorder being diagnosed. Although it is not clear if either assessment technique should be used as the "gold standard," the lack of agreement between the two assessment modalities raises serious validity concerns. Because the DSM, and community-based diagnostic instruments based on it, rely on conservative criteria for diagnosis—typically, observable behavioral criteria—community-based measures may tend to underestimate the prevalence of some disorders.

Assessment Context

We close the body of this chapter by coming full circle to the issue of the broader context within which beliefs about, descriptions of, and attempts to assess mental health and disorder take place. Although such issues are addressed from other perspectives elsewhere in this volume, our discussion of assessment issues would not be complete without a caution about the limitations of measurement techniques. Assessment techniques are tools created in a particular social context to gather information about the empirical world. As such, these instruments are not "objective" and can be no better or worse than the assumptions on which they are founded. A society's beliefs about the causes of mental disorders and their likely solutions will ultimately be reflected in the instruments used to assess mental health by that society. More broadly, the particular social arrangements—including the distributions of power, status, and resources—will all influence the creation, selection, and administration of instruments.

Numerous examples of the influence of social and political context on the definition and assessment of mental disorders can be found simply by charting the flow of diagnostic categories into and out of the DSM. The recent creation and addition of posttraumatic stress disorder (PTSD) to the DSM was a direct result of concerted post-Vietnam War lobbying efforts by American military veterans. The elimination of homosexuality as a diagnostic category was a result of lobbying by gay and lesbian organizations, changes in prevailing societal attitudes, and the greater willingness on the part of the medical community to acknowledge the lack of empirical evidence that homosexuality reflects psychopathology. The fact that posttraumatic symptoms and homosexuality have been a consistent part of human experience while their status as mental disorders has changed dramatically in the last 15 years is evidence of the subjective and transmutable nature of psychiatric categorization. These same societal forces have, at various times, defined broad population groups (e.g., women, ethnic minorities) as being "by nature" more vulnerable to psychiatric disorders. The emphasis on genetic or organic factors as a source of mental disorders has demonstrated the power of such explanations for some disorders (e.g., Alzheimer's disease), and their failure for others (e.g., major depression). The increased specificity of organic and genetic explanations—by helping to define both what biology can and cannot explain—has actually fostered the growth of sociological and epidemiological explanations for and investigations of mental health issues. The disciplines of mental health currently find themselves in a social context that encourages interdisciplinary efforts to assess and weigh the importance of physical, psychological, social, and environmental factors as precursors of mental disorder.

FUTURE DIRECTIONS

Finally, there are at least three growing movements in mental health assessment that are worth noting: interdisciplinary collaboration, multimethods approaches, and psychometric advances. First, as mentioned earlier, this is a time of increasing interdisciplinary collaboration that has the potential to produce more complex and multivariate examinations of the predictors and outcomes of psychiatric disorders. Sociologists have already contributed valuable insights to the study of mental health issues. Sociology offers a unique and valuable perspective to this process, including its focus on macrolevel historical, political, and economic forces on the definition and assessment of mental disorder that might otherwise be absent. Sociological models of mental health should continue to expand to incorporate biological variables in order to achieve a fully integrated perspective of the interactions between personal characteristics and broader societal forces.

Second, as is noted by several authors (e.g., Dohrenwend, 1995; Usten & Tien, 1995; Fenig et al., 1994), there is increasing application of, and great future potential for, multimethods and/or multisource approaches to the assessment of community mental health and disorder. As we noted earlier, there are enduring concerns about the reliability and validity even of state-of-the-art mental health assessment techniques. Dohrenwend (1995) suggests that the strengths of dimensional and diagnostic instruments can be used symbiotically to overcome the weaknesses of each. For example, individuals could be screened using a relatively inexpensive dimensional self-report instrument (e.g., the PERI), and then subsamples with severe symptomology could be further evaluated using a diagnostic instrument (e.g., the SADS). In this manner, the ability of dimensional instruments to provide reliable estimates of general disorder in the population could be combined with the ability of diagnostic instruments to provide finer-grained estimations of disorder near the diagnostic cutpoint. In addition to the use of more than one type of instrument, the use of multiple sources of data (e.g., medical records or informants) should significantly improve the ability to ascertain symptoms of mental disorder (Fenig et al., 1994).

Finally, recent advances in the psychometric evaluation of instruments may dramatically alter the structure and administration of psychiatric assessments. Perhaps the most notable is the increasing application of item response analysis to the process of evaluating instruments (Hambleton & Jones, 1993; McKinley, 1989; Steinberg & Thissen, 1996; Thissen & Steinberg, 1988). Although the statistical techniques underlying item response analysis were developed about 40 years ago, the lack of powerful computer systems to conduct these analyses efficiently prevented the ideas from being widely applied. The basic tenets of the theory are that (1) an individual's responses to an item reflects his or her position on a single, continuous, latent variable, and (2) the probability that the individual will give a certain response (e.g., one that indicates that he or she is depressed) can be determined based on the individual's position on the latent variable.

Although a detailed description of the technique is beyond the scope of this chapter, potential applications to psychiatric assessments include identifying the fewest number of items that need to be asked of a given respondent in order to adequately assess the construct (e.g., depression), altering the wording or "difficulty" of each item so that it provides unique and nonoverlapping information about an individual, and designing assessments to be most powerful at certain levels of the latent construct (e.g., to distinguish among fine gradations of minor depression). These evaluative techniques can also be applied to information gathered using well-standardized instruments. Ultimately, developments in item analysis may lead to the use of computer adaptive testing (CAT) in diagnostic evaluation. In this method—already used in education and achievement testing (McKinley, 1989)—a computer presents an individual with a series of items specifically tailored on the basis of his or her previous responses. For example, if an individual's initial responses indicated moderate levels of depression, the computer would select only items that would help to specify exactly where in the moderate range the person was located (i.e., no indicators of very high or very low levels of depression would be presented). Thus, rather than being presented with many items that do not provide additional information, an individual is presented with the fewest items that can accurately assess his or her position in the latent construct. This is a promising technique that may increase the efficiency and accuracy of psychiatric evaluation and substantially decrease the burden for interviewers and for study participants.

In summary, there has been dramatic progress in our ability to assess community mental health and disorder during past 150 years. Technical advances, such as the development of improved sampling methods, more reliable instruments, and more powerful analytical tools have been accompanied by the emergence of an increasingly complex interdisciplinary paradigm to explain mental disorder. Sociologists and epidemiologists, as relative newcomers to the field of mental health assessment, have provided valuable insights not only about how to conduct broad-based community studies but also about the critical effects of environmental and social forces on mental health. The future seems to hold continued interdisciplinary collaboration, further development of instruments combining the strengths of diagnostic and dimensional instruments and/or use of multimethod techniques, and increasing application of computer technology to mental health assessment.

REFERENCES

American Psychiatric Association. (1994). *Diagnostic and statistical manual of mental disorders* (4th ed, rev.). Washington, DC: Author.

Aneshensel, C. S., Frerichs, R. R., Clark, V. A., & Yokopenic, P.A. (1982a). Measuring depression in the community. *Public Opinion Quarterly, 46,* 110–121.

Aneshensel, C. S., Frerichs, R. R., Clark, V. A., & Yokopenic, P.A. (1982b). Telephone versus in-person surveys of community health status. *American Journal of Public Health, 72*(9), 1017–1021.

Aneshensel, C. S., & Yokopenic, P. A. (1985). Tests for the comparability of a causal model of depression under two condition of interviewing. *Journal of Personality and Social Psychology, 49*(5), 1337–1348.

Anthony, J. C., Folstein, M., Romanoski, A. J., Von Korff, M. R., Nestadt, G. R., Chahal, R., Merchant, A., Hendricks Brown, C., Shapiro, S., Kramer, M., & Gruenberg, E. (1985). Comparison of the lay diagnostic interview schedule and a standardized psychiatric diagnosis: Experience in Eastern Baltimore. *Archives of General Psychiatry, 42,* 667–675.

Beck, A. T., & Steer, R. A. (1990). *Manual, Beck Anxiety Inventory.* San Antonio, TX: Psychological Corporation, Harcourt Brace Jovanovich.

Beck, A. T., Ward, C. H., Mendelsohn, M., Mock, J., & Erbaugh, J. (1961). An inventory for measuring depression. *Archives of General Psychiatry, 4,* 561–571.

Behavioral Measurement Database Services. (1997). *HaPI-Health and Psychosocial Instruments.* Pittsburgh, PA: Author.

Berkson, J. (1946). Limitation of the application of fourfold table analysis to hospital data. *Biomedical Bulletin, 2,* 47–53.

Breslau, N. (1985). Depressive symptoms, major depression and generalized anxiety: A comparison of self-reports on CES-D and results from diagnostic interviews. *Psychiatry Research, 15,* 219–229.

Bromet, E. J., Dunn, L. O., Connell, M. M., Dew, M. A., & Schulberg, H. C. (1986). Long-term reliability of diagnosing lifetime major depression in a community sample. *Archives of General Psychiatry, 43,* 435.

Bromet, E., Schwartz, J. E., Fennig, S., Geller, L., Jandorf, L., Kovasznay, B., Lavelle, J., Miller, A., Pato, C., Ram, R., & Rich, C. (1992). The epidemiology of psychosis: The Suffolk County Mental Health Project. *Schizophrenia Bulletin, 18,* 243–255.

Brugha, T. S., Kaul, A., Dignon, A., Teather, D., & Wills, K. M. (1996). Present state examination by microcomputer: Objectives and experience of preliminary steps. *International Journal of Methods in Psychiatric Research, 6*(3), 143–151.

Burke, J. D., Jr., & Regier, D. A. (1994). Epidemiology of mental disorders. In R. E. Hales, S. C. Yudofsky, & J. A. Talbott (Eds.), *The American Psychiatric Press textbook of psychiatry* (2nd ed., pp. 81–104). Washington, DC: American Psychiatric Association Press.

Carmines, E. G., & Zeller, R. A. (1979). *Reliability and validity assessment. Quantitative applications in the social sciences* series (J. L. Sullivan, series ed.). Beverly Hills, CA: Sage.

Cheung, F. K. (1990). Community mental health and ethnic minority populations. *Community Mental Health Journal, 26*(3), 277–291.

Clementz, B. A., & Iacono, W. G. (1993). Nosology and diagnosis. In A. S. Bellack & M. Hersen (Eds.), *Psychopathology in adulthood* (pp. 3–20. Needham Heights, MA: Allyn & Bacon.

Cooper, J. E., Kendell, R. E., Gurland, B. J., Sharpe, L., Copeland, J. R. M., & Simon, R. (1972). *Psychiatric diagnosis in New York and London.* London: Oxford University Press.

Costa, P. T., & McCrae, R. R. (1985). *The NEO Personality Inventory.* Odessa, FL: Psychological Assessment Resources, Inc.

Cronbach, L. J. (1951). Coefficient alpha and the internal structure of tests. *Psychometrika, 16,* 297–334.

Dahlstrom, W. G., Welsh, G. S., & Dahlstrom, L. E. (1972). *An MMPI handbook: Vol. I. Clinical interpretation.* Minneapolis: University of Minnesota Press.

Derogatis, L. R., & Cleary, P. A. (1977). Confirmation of the dimensional structure of the SCL-90: A study in construct validation. *Journal of Clinical Psychology, 33,* 981–989.

Derogatis, L. R., Lipman, R. S., Rickels, K., Uhlenhuth, E. H., & Covi, L. (1974). The Hopkins Symptom Checklist (HSCL): A self-report symptom inventory. *Behavioral Science, 19,* 1–15.

Dew, M. A. (1993). Assessment and prevention of expectancy effects in community mental health studies. In P. D. Blanck (Ed.), *Interpersonal expectations: Theory, research and application* (pp. 437–453). New York: Cambridge University Press.

Dew, M. A. (1998). Psychiatric disorder in the context of physical illness. In B. P. Dohrenwend (Ed.), *Adversity, stress and psychopathology* (pp. 177–218). New York: Oxford University Press.

Dew, M. A., & Bromet, E. J. (1993). Epidemiology. In A. S. Bellack & M. Hersen (Eds.), *Psychopathology in adulthood* (pp. 21–40). Needham Heights, MA: Allyn & Bacon.

Dignon, A. M. (1996). Acceptability of a computer administered psychiatric interview. *Computers in Human Behavior, 12*(2), 177–191.

Dillman, D. A. (1978). *Mail and telephone surveys: The total design method.* New York: Wiley.

Dohrenwend, B. P. (1995). The problem of validity in field studies of psychological disorders. In M. T. Tsuang, M. Tohen, & G. E. P. Zahner (Eds.), *Textbook in psychiatric epidemiology* (pp. 3–20). New York: Wiley.

Dohrenwend, B. P. (1989). The problem of validity in field studies of psychological disorders revisited. *Psychological Medicine, 20,* 195–208.

Dohrenwend, B. P., & Dohrenwend, B. S. (1982). Perspectives on the past and future of psychiatric epidemiology. *American Journal of Public Health, 72,* 1271–1279.

Dohrenwend, B. P., & Dohrenwend, B. S. (1981). Socioenvironmental factors, stress, and psychopathology—Part 1. Quasi-experimental evidence on the social causation–social selection issue posed by class differences. *American Journal of Community Psychology, 9,* 146–159.

Dohrenwend, B. P., & Dohrenwend, B. S. (1965). The problem of validity in field studies of psychological disorder. *Journal of Abnormal Psychology, 70,* 52–69.

Dohrenwend, B. P., Levav, I., & Shrout, P. E. (1986). Screening scales from the Psychiatric Epidemiology Research Interview (PERI). In M. M. Weissman, J. K. Myers, & C. E. Ross (Eds.), *Community surveys of psychiatric disorders* (pp. 349–375). New Brunswick, NJ: Rutgers University Press.

Duncan-Jones, P., & Henderson, S. (1978). The use of a two-phase design in a prevalence survey. *Social Psychiatry, 13,* 231–237.

Eaton, W. W. (1980). *The sociology of mental disorders.* New York: Praeger Publishers.

Endicott, J., & Spitzer, R. L. (1978). A diagnostic interview: The Schedule for Affective Disorders and Schizophrenia. *Archives of General Psychiatry, 35,* 837–844.

Erdman, H. P., Klein, M. H., Greist, J. H., Skare, S. S., Husted, J. J., Robins, L. N., Helzer, J. E., Goldring, E., Hambruger, M., & Miller, J. P. (1992). A comparison of two computer-administered versions of the NIMH Diagnostic Interview Schedule. *Journal of Psychiatric Research, 26*(1), 85–95.

Eysenk, H. J. (1947). *Dimensions of personality.* London: Routledge & Kegan Paul.

Faris, R. L., & Dunham, H. W. (1939). *Mental disorders in urban areas.* Chicago: University of Chicago Press.

Fenig, S., Bromet, E. J., Jandorf, L., Schwartz, J. E., Lavelle, J., & Ram, R. (1994). Eliciting psychotic symptoms using a semistructured diagnostic interview: The importance of collateral sources of information in a first admission sample. *Journal of Nervous and Mental Disease, 182*(1), 20–26.

Fenig, S., Levav, I., Kohn, R., & Yelin, N. (1993). Telephone vs. face-to-face interviewing in a community psychiatric survey. *American Journal of Public Health, 83*(6), 896–898.

Fowler, F. J. (1984). *Survey research methods.* Beverly Hills, CA: Sage.

Friedman, W. J. (1993). Memory for the time of past events. *Psychological Bulletin, 113,* 44–66.

Giuffra, L. A., & Risch, N. (1994). Diminished recall and the cohort effect of major depression: A simulation study. *Psychological Medicine, 24*(2), 375–383.

Goldberg, D. P. (1972). *The detection of psychiatric illness by questionnaire: A technique for the identification and assessment of non-psychotic psychiatric illness.* London: Oxford University Press.

Goldstein, J. M., & Simpson, J. C. (1995). Validity, defintions and applications to psychiatric research. In M. T. Tsuang, M. Tohen, & G. E. P. Zahner (Eds.), *Textbook in psychiatric epidemiology* (pp. 229–242). New York: Wiley.

Guarnaccia, P. J., Good, B. J., & Kleinman, A. (1990). A critical review of epidemiological studies of Puerto Rican mental health. *American Journal of Psychiatry, 147*(11), 1449–1456.

Hambleton, R. K., & Jones, R. W. (1993). Comparison of classical test theory and item response theory and their applications to test development. *Educational Measuremen: Issues and Practice, 12*(3), 38–47.

Hamilton, M. (1960). A rating scale for depression. *Journal of Neurology, Neurosurgery, and Psychiatry, 23,* 57–62.

Hamilton, M. (1967). Development of a rating scale for primary depression illness. *British Journal of Social and Clinical Psychology, 6,* 278–296.

Helzer, J. E., Robins, L. N., McEnvoy, L. T., Spitznagel, E. L., Stoltzman, R. K., Farmer, A., & Brockington, I. F. (1985). A comparison of clinical and diagnostic interview schedule diagnoses: Physician reexamination of lay-interviewed cases in the general population. *Archives of General Psychiatry, 42,* 657–666.

Horwath, E., Johnson, J., & Hornig, C. D. (1993). Epidemiology of panic disorder in African-Americans. *American Journal of Psychiatry, 150*(3), 465–469.

Hyler, S. E. (1987). *The Personality Diagnostic Questionnaire* (4th ed.). *(PDQ-4).* New York: New York State Psychiatric Institute, Biometrics Research.

Jarvis, E. (1971). *Insanity and idiocy in Massachusetts.* Cambridge, MA: Harvard University Press.

Karoly, P. (1985). The logic and character of assessment in health psychology: perspectives and possibilities. In P. Karoly (Ed.), *Measurement strategies in health psychology* (pp. 3–45). New York: Wiley.

Katz, M. M., & Lyerly, S. B. (1963). Methods for measuring adjustment and social behavior in the community: I. Rationale, description, descriminative validity, and scale development. *Psychological Reports Monograph, 13,* 503–535.

Kessler, R. C., McGonagle, K. A., Zhao, S., Nelson, C. B., Hughes, M., Eshleman, S., Wittchen, H-U., & Kendler, K. S. (1994). Lifetime and 12-month prevalence of DSM-III-R psychiatric disorders among persons aged 15–54 in the United States: Results from the National Comorbidity Survey. *Archives of General Psychiatry, 51,* 8–19.

Kirk, S. A., & Kutchins, H. (1992). *The selling of DSM: The rhetoric of science in psychiatry.* New York: Aldine de Gruyter.

Kobak, K. A., Greist, J. H., Jefferson, J. W., & Katzelnick, D. J. (1996). Computer administered clinical rating scales: A review. *Psychopharmacology, 127*(4), 291–301.

Kobak, K. A., Reynolds, W. M., & Greist, J. H. (1993). Development and validation of a computer-administered version of the Hamilton Rating Scale. *Psychological Assessment, 5*(4), 487–492.

Kramer, M. (1961). Some problems for international research suggested by observations on differences in first admission rates to the mental hospitals of England and Wales of the United States. *Proceedings of the Third World Congress of Psychiatry, 3,* 153–160.

Langner, T. S. (1962) A twenty-two item screening score of psychiatric symptoms indicating impairment. *Journal of Health and Human Behavior, 3,* 269–276.

Lavrakas, P. A. (1987). *Telephone survey methods: Sampling, selection, and supervision.* Newbury Park, CA: Sage.

Leighton, D. C., Harding, J. S., Macklin, D. B., Macmillan, A. M., & Leighton, A. H. (1963). *The character of danger.* New York: Basic Books.

Lewis, G. (1994). Assessing psychiatric disorder with a human interviewer or a computer. *Journal of Epidemiology and Community Health, 48*(2), 207–210.

Link, B., & Dohrenwend, B. P. (1980). Formulation of hypotheses about the true prevalence of demoralization in the United States. In B. P. Dohrenwend, B. S. Dohrenwend, M. S. Gould, B. Link, R. Neugebauer, & R. Wunsch-Hitzig (Eds.), *Mental illness in the United States: Epidemiological estimates* (pp. 114–132). New York: Praeger.

Loftus, E. F., Smith, K. D., Klinger, M. R., & Fielder, J. (1991). Memory and mismemory for health events. In J. M. Tanur (Ed.), *Questions about questions* (pp. 102–137). New York: Sage.

Loranger, A. W. (1988). *Personality Disorders Examination (PDE).* Yonkers, NY: DV Communications.

Lyketsos, C. G., Nestadt, G., Cwi, J., Heithoff, K., & Eaton, W. W. (1994). The life chart interview: A standardized method to describe the course of psychopathology. *International Journal of Methods in Psychiatric Research, 4,* 143–155.

Macmillan, A. M. (1957) The health opinion survey: Technique for estimating prevalence of psychoneurotic and related types of disorder in communities. *Psychological Report, 3,* 325–329.

McKinley, R. L. (1989). Methods, plainly speaking: An introduction to item response theory. *Measurement and Evaluation in Counseling and Development, 22,* 37–57.

McNair, D. M., Lorr, M., & Droppelman, L. F. (1992). *Edits manual for the Profile of Mood States.* San Diego: Educational Testing Service.

Millon, T. (1983). *Millon Clinical Multiaxial Inventory* (3rd ed.). Minneapolis, MN: National Computer Systems.

Mirowsky, J., & Ross, C. E. (1989a). *Social causes of psychological distress.* New York: Aldine de Gruyter.

Mirowsky, J., & Ross, C. E. (1989b). Psychiatric diagnosis as reified measurement. *Journal of Health and Social Behavior, 30,* 114–125.

Murphy, J. M. (1976). Psychiatric labeling in cross-cultural perspective. *Science, 191,* 1019–1028.

Murphy, J. M. (1995). Diagnostic schedules and rating scales in adult psychiatry. In M. T. Tsuang, M. Tohen, & G. E. P. Zahner (Eds.), *Textbook in Psychiatric Epidemiology* (pp. 253–271). New York: Wiley.

Murphy, J. M., Neff, R. K., Sobol, A. M., Rice, J. X., & Olivier, D. C. (1985). Computer diagnosis of depression and anxiety: The Stirling County Study. *Psychological Medicine, 15,* 99–112.

Nunnally, J. C. (Ed.). (1978). *Psychometric theory* (2nd ed.). New York: McGraw-Hill.

Nurnberger, J. L., Blehar, M. C., Kaufmann, C. A., York-Cooler, C., Simpson, S. G., Haskary-Fieldman, J., Se???, J. B., Malaspira, D., & Reich, T. (1994). Diagnostic interview for genetic studies: Rationale, unique features, and training. *Archives of General Psychiatry, 51*(11), 849–859.

Padgett, D. K. (1994). Ethnicity and the use of outpatient mental health services in a national insured population. *American Journal of Public Health, 84*(2), 222–226.

Parloff, M. B., Kelman, H. C., & Frank, J. D. (1954). Comfort, effectiveness, and self-awareness as criteria of improvement in psychotherapy. *American Journal of Psychiatry, 111,* 343–351.

Paulsen, A. S., Crowe, R. R., Noyes, R., & Pfohl, B. (1988). Reliability of the telephone interview in diagnosing anxiety disorders. *Archives of General Psychiatry, 45*(1), 62–63.

Pfohl, B., Blum, N., Zimmerman, M., & Stangl, D. (1989). *Structured Interview for the DSM-III Personality Disorder (SIDP-R).* Iowa City: University of Iowa Press.

Pfohl, B., Stangle, D., & Zimmerman, M. (1982) *Structured Interview for the DSM-III Personality Disorder (SIDP).* Iowa City: University of Iowa, Department of Psychiatry.

Radloff, L. S. (1977). The CES-D Scale: A self-report depression scale for research in the general population. *Applied Psychological Measurement, 1,* 385–401.

Regier, D. A., Goldberg, I. D., & Taube, C. A. (1978). The de facto U.S. mental health services system. *Archives of General Psychiatry, 35*(6), 685–693.

Regier, D. A., Myers, J. E., Kramer, M., Robins, L. N., Blazer, D. G., Hough, R. L., Eaton, W. W., & Lock, B. Z. (1984). The NIMH Epidemiologic Catchment Area program: Historical context, major objectives, and study population characteristics. *Archives of General Psychiatry, 41,* 934–941.

Regier D. A., & Robins, L. N. (1991). Introduction. In L. N. Robins & D. A. Regier (Eds.), *Psychiatric disorders in America* (pp. 1–10). New York: Free Press.

Reynolds, W. M., & Kobak, K. A. (1995). Reliability and validity of the Hamilton Depression Inventory: A paper and pencil version of the Hamilton Depression Rating Scale clinical interview. *Psychological Assessment, 7*(4), 472–483.

Robins, L. N. (1977). Estimating addiction rates and locating target populations: How decomposition into stages helps. In J. D. Rittenhouse (Ed.), *The epidemiology of heroin and other narcotics* (pp. 25–39). Washington, DC: U.S. Government Printing Office.

Robins, L. N. (1985). Epidemiology: Reflections on testing the validity of psychiatric interviews. *Archives of General Psychiatry, 42,* 918–924.

Robins, L. N., Helzer, J., Croughan, J., & Ratcliff, K. S. (1981). The NIMH Diagnostic Interview Schedule: Its history, characteristics and validity. *Archives of General Psychiatry, 45,* 1069–1077.

Robins, L. N., Helzer, J., Ratcliff, K. S., & Seyfried, W. (1982). Validity of the Diagnostic Interview Schedule, Version II: DSM-III diagnoses. *Psychological Medicine, 12,* 855–870.

Robins, L. N., & Regier, D. A. (Eds.). (1991). *Psychiatric disorders in America: The epidemiologic catchment area study.* New York: Free Press.

Robins, L. N., Wing, J. K., Wittchen, H. U., Helzer, J. E., Babor, T. F., Burke, J., Farmer, A., Jablenski, A., Pickens, R., Regier, D. A., Sartorius, N., & Towle, L. H. (1988). The Composite International Diagnostic Interview: An epidemiologic instrument suitable for use in conjunction with different diagnostic systmes and in different cultures. *Archives of General Psychiatry, 45,* 1069–1077.

Schwarz, N., Hippler, H. J. Deutsch, B., & Strack, F. (1985). Response scales: Effects of category range on reported behavior and comparative judgments. *Public Opinion Quarterly, 49*(3), 388–395.

Shea, M. T., Glass, D. R., Pilkonis, P. A., Watkins, J., & Docherty, J. P. (1987). Frequency and implications of PD's in a sample of depressed outpatients. *Journal of Personality Disorders, 1,* 27–42.

Shrout, P. (1995). Reliability. In M. T. Tsuang, M. Tohen, & G. E. P. Zahner (Eds.), *Textbook in psychiatric epidemiology* (pp. 213–227). New York: Wiley.

Shrout, P. (1994). The NIMH Epidemiologic Catchment Area program: broken promises and dashed hopes? *International Journal of Methods and Psychiatric Research, 4,* 113–122.

Spielberger, C. D. (1984). *State-Trait Anxiety Inventory: A comprehensive bibliography.* Palo Alto, CA: Consulting Psychologists Press.

Spitzer, R. L., Kroenke, K., Linzer, M., Hahn, S. R., Williams, J. B., DeGruy, F. V., III, Brody, D., & Davies, M. (1995). Health-related quality of life in primary care patients with mental disorders: Results from the PRIME-D 1000 Study. *Journal of the American Medical Association, 274,* 1511–1517.

Spitzer, R. L., William, J. B., Gibbon, M., & First, M. B. (1992). The Structured Clinical Interview for DSM-III-R (SCID): I. History, rationale, and description. *Archives of General Psychiatry, 49,* 624–629.

Srole, L., Langner, T. S., Michael, S. T., Opler, M. K., & Rennie, T. A. C. (1962). *Mental health in the metropolis.* New York: McGraw-Hill.

Star, S. A. (1950). The screening of psychoneurotics in the army: Technical developments of tests. In S. A. Stouffer, L. Guttman, E. A. Suchman, P. F. Lazarsfeld, S. A. Star, & J. A. Clausen (Eds.), *Measurement and prediction* (pp. 486–547). Princeton, NJ: Princeton University Press.

Steinberg, L., & Thissen, D. (1996). Use of item response theory and the testlet concept in the measurement of psychopathology. *Psychological Methods, 1*(1), 81–97.

Steer, R. A., Rissmiller, D. J., Ranieri, W. F., & Beck, A. T. (1994). Use of the computer administered Beck Depression Inventory and Hopelessness Scale with psychiatric inpatients. *Computers in Human Behavior, 10*(2), 223–229.

Stouffer, S. A., Guttman, L., Suchman, E. A., Lazarsfeld, P. F., Star, S.,A., & Clausen, J. A. (1950). *The American soldier: Measurement and prediction* (Vol. IV). Princeton, NJ: Princeton University Press.

Sue, S., Fujino, D. K., Hu, L., & Takeuchi, D. T. (1991) Community and mental health services for ethnic minority groups: A test of the cultural responsiveness hypothesis. *Journal of Consulting and Clinical Psychology, 59*(4), 533–540.

Tanur, J. M. (1992). *Questions about questions: Inquiries into the cognitive bases of surveys.* New York: Russell Sage Foundation.

Tellegen, A., & Waller, N. G. (1982). Exploring personality through test construction: Development of the Multidimensional Personality Questionnaire. In S. R. Briggs & J. M. Cheek (Eds.), *Personality measures: Development and evaluation* (Vol. 1). Greenwich, CT: JAI Press.

Thissen, D., & Steinberg, L. (1988). Data analysis using item response theory. *Psychological Bulletin, 104*(3), 385–395.

Thornicroft, G. (1992). Computerised mental health assessments. In G. Thornicroft, C. R. Brewin, & J. Wing (Eds.), *Measuring mental needs* (pp. 258–272). London: Gaskell/Royal College of Psychiatrists.

Ustun, T. B., & Tien, A. Y. (1995). Recent developments for diagnostic measures in psychiatry. *Epidemiologic Reviews, 17*(1), 210–220.

Weissman, M. M. (1987). Advances in psychiatric epidemiology: Rates and risks for major depression. *American Journal of Public Health, 77,* 445–451.

Weissman, M. M., Klerman, G. L., Paykel, E. S., Prusoff, B., & Hanson, B. (1974). Treatment effects on the social adjustment of depressed patients. *Archives of General Psychiatry, 30,* 771–778.

Weissman, M. M., & Bothwell, S. (1976). Assessment of social adjustment by patient self-report. *Archives of General Psychiatry, 33,* 1111–1115.

Wells, K. B., Burnam, M. A., Leake, B., & Robins, L. N. (1988). Agreement between face-to-face and telephone-administered versions of the depression section of the NIMH Diagnostic Interview Schedule. *Journal of Psychiatric Research, 22*(3), 207–220.

World Health Organization. (1992). *International Personality Disorder Examination.* Geneva: Author.

Williams, J. B. W. (1992). The structured clinical interview for DSM-III-R (SCID): II. Multisite test–retest reliability. *Archives of General Psychiatry, 49,* 630–636.

Wing, J. K. (1961). A simple and reliable subclassification of chronic schizophrenia. *Journal of Mental Sciences, 107,* 862–875.

Wing, J. K., Babar, T., Brugha, T., Burke, J., Cooper, J. E, Giel, R., Jablenski, A., Regier, D., & Sartorius, N. (1990). SCAN: Schedule for clinical assessment in neuropsychiatry. *Archives of General Psychiatry, 47,* 589–593.

Wing, J. K., Cooper, J. E., & Sartorius, N. (1974). *Measure and classification of psychiatric symptoms: An instructional Manual for the PSE and CATEGO Programs.* Cambridge, UK: Cambridge University Press.

Wittchen, H. U. (1994). Reliability and validity study of the WHO–Composite International Diagnostic Interview (CIDI): A critical review. *Journal of Psychiatric Research, 28,* 57–84.

World Health Organization. (1992a). International Personality Disorder Examination. Geneva: Author.

World Health Organization. (1992). *International statistical classification of diseases and related health problems: ICD-10* (Vol I, 10th ed. rev.). Geneva: Author.

Zahner, G. E. P., Chung-Cheng, H., & Fleming, J. (1995). Introduction to epidemiologic research methods. In M. T. Tsuang, M. Tohen, & G. E. P. Zahner (Eds.), *Textbook in psychiatric epidemiology* (pp. 23–53). New York: Wiley.

Zanarini, M., Frankenberg, F., Chauncey, D., & Gunderson, J. G. (1987). The diagnostic interview for personality disorders: Inter-rater and test–retest reliability. *Comprehensive Psychiatry, 28,* 467–480.

Zung, W. W. K. (1963). A self-rating depression scale. *Archives of General Psychiatry, 12,* 63–70.

CHAPTER 6

Analyzing Associations between Mental Health and Social Circumstances

John Mirowsky

STATISTICAL EXPLANATION AND VANISHING ASSOCIATION

Comparison serves as the fundamental procedure of sociological research. Graduate training emphasizes the core sociological question, Compared to whom? If sociologists hear someone say, Workers are anxious, they immediately begin to wonder, Compared to whom? The unemployed? Housewives? Retirees? Which workers are we talking about? Under what circumstances? Are we comparing workers to others in general? To others from similar backgrounds? To others like themselves? In what ways?

Sociological research begins by demonstrating the existence of an association or correlation in a defined population. That association takes the form of a distinct difference between groups in the amount of a measured attribute. The researcher may begin by showing, for example, that adults who as children experienced parental divorce feel depressed more often than those whose parents stayed together, or that young adults feel anxious and angry more often than middle-aged or older adults, or that the frequency of malaise drops more rapidly in early adulthood for men than for women. The researcher first demonstrates that an association really exists and is not a ghost of random juxtaposition or a mirage of biased measurement. Convinced of that, the researcher then tries to explain why the association exists.

Explaining an association means demonstrating the conditions under which it no longer

John Mirowsky • Department of Sociology, The Ohio State University, Columbus, Ohio 43210.

Handbook of the Sociology of Mental Health, edited by Carol S. Aneshensel and Jo C. Phelan. Kluwer Academic/ Plenum Publishers, New York, 1999.

exists. If an association vanishes under specific conditions, then it is the presence (or absence) of those conditions that accounts for the association. The sociologist's game, then, has two goals: show an association exists, then find the conditions under which it vanishes (Cole, 1972; Davis, 1985; Susser, 1973). This chapter describes strategies for achieving the second goal—strategies for explaining the association of mental or emotional well-being with aspects of circumstance, identity, belief, or personal history.

Data analysts have two basic methods for demonstrating the conditions under which an association vanishes (Wheaton, 1985): progressive adjustment and interaction modeling. Progressive adjustment looks for mediators of the association. A mediator is something that results from one of the associated variables and causes the other, forming a bridge between them. For example, young adults are less secure economically than older adults. If being young increases the likelihood of economic insecurity, which in turn increases the level of anxiety, then economic insecurity mediates some of the relationship between age and anxiety. Interaction modeling looks for moderators of the association. A moderator regulates the size and direction of the association between two variables. For example, young children in the home might increase depression among women when the father avoids child care and child support, but otherwise not increase women's depression. If so, then the father's child care and child support moderate the association among women between having young children and feeling depressed. Moderators can be external or internal. External moderators apply to everyone, whereas internal moderators only apply to people in a specific situation. For example, the effect of marriage on depression may depend on a person's level of education and on the quality of the marriage. If so, then education acts as an external moderator, because everyone has some level of education whether married or not. The quality of the marriage acts as an internal moderator, because the quality of the relationship applies only to those who are married.

The rest of this chapter describes and illustrates progressive adjustment, to find the mediators of an association, and interaction modeling, to find the external and internal moderators of an association. It also discusses a methodological problem that often arises in studies of psychopathology. Skewness in the dependent variable reduces the precision of results. Logarithmic transformations solve the problem, providing the extra precision needed for assessing interactions.

PROGRESSIVE ADJUSTMENT

Progressive adjustment constitutes the single most valuable procedure for explaining associations. The technique is to sociological research what anatomical dissection is to biological research. Progressive adjustment peels away the layered components of an association. Contemporary researchers use sophisticated statistical regression programs for progressive adjustment. However, the procedure predates modern statistical techniques (Cole, 1972; Susser, 1973). The idea behind it is simple: Show that an association exists, propose a hypothetical mediator of the association, and show that holding the mediator constant reduces or eliminates the association.

Step 1: Specifying the Association, Explanation, and Model

Progressive adjustment begins by stating a theoretical explanation for an observed or hypothesized association. Suppose, for example, a researcher has demonstrated that U.S. adults whose parents separated or divorced in their childhood feel depressed more fre-

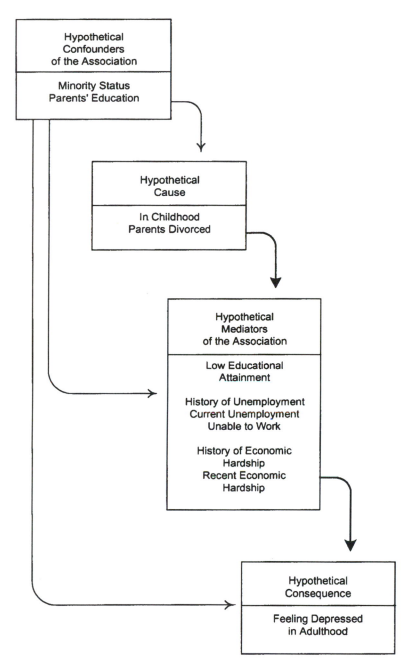

FIGURE 6.1. Hypothetical model explaining the correlation between the divorce of one's parents in childhood and feeling depressed in adulthood.

quently than others. What explains the association? The analysis begins by stating a theoretical explanation that describes a sequence of events or circumstances that might link the hypothetical cause to its hypothetical consequence. What effect of that parental breakup years ago may have had lasting and depressing consequences? Low educational attainment seems to be a possibility. We know that the frequency of depression increases in segments of the population with progressively lower levels of education. Many of education's consequences protect and reward the spirit: employment, prestige, prosperity, security, refinement, proficiency. We know that a parental breakup reduces the average educational attainment of the children. Emotional turmoil disrupts studies. Economic abandonment, in whole or in part, depletes the household's educational resources. Perhaps lower educational attainment and its consequences explain the higher frequency of depression among persons exposed to a childhood parental divorce.

After stating a theoretical explanation, the analyst looks for measurable variables that will allow a corresponding statistical explanation. Figure 6.1 illustrates a hypothetical model corresponding to the argument that low educational attainment and its consequences for employment and economic well-being explain why depression is greater among adults who experienced childhood parental divorce. The measures include the person's total years of education, a history of being unemployed and looking for work for 6 months or more at least once, current unemployment, current inability to work, a history of not having the money to pay bills or buy household necessities some time in the past, and recent trouble paying bills or buying necessities. These measures represent the ideas expressed in the theoretical explanation.

After stating a theoretical explanation and finding corresponding measures, the analyst proceeds to the statistical explanation. The idea behind statistical explanation is simple. If a mediator explains an association, then holding that mediator constant reduces or eliminates the association. In the example, if education alone mediates the whole association between adulthood depression and childhood parental divorce, then holding education constant will eliminate the association. The statistical analysis compares persons who attained the same level of education but had different childhood experiences. If there is no difference in their frequency of depression, then lower education explains the greater depression of adults whose parents divorced in childhood.

The variants of matched comparison go by several names. Researchers speak of the association "adjusting for education," "holding education constant," or "net of education." Contemporary researchers rarely would actually match sets of individuals with the same education but different childhood experiences. Today, most sociologists use some form of multiple regression to achieve the statistical equivalent of matching. Multiple regression gives the researcher far more flexibility in testing a variety of possible explanations efficiently. Imagine having to match each person from a divorced childhood home to someone else of the same age, education, sex, race, income, and employment status from an intact childhood home. The practical difficulties of matching grow geometrically with the number of variables considered. Multiple regression uses the variation and covariation within a sample to achieve the same end. The analytic goal remains the same: Measure the association and then adjust for variables representing hypothetical explanations until the association vanishes.

Social scientists typically need to consider many possibilities at once when trying to explain an association. The critical link might lie hidden in a long sequence of consequences that generate subsequent conditions with their own consequences. More commonly, the initial event might have several consequences, each generating trains of consequences. The explanation of the original association may lie in these knitted events and circumstances considered as a whole. To explain an association, the analyst progressively adjusts for variables that represent the steps in a hypothetical sequence linking exposure to outcome (Cole, 1972; Davis, 1985; Susser, 1973).

Step 2: Measuring the Total Association

After the conceptual model has been specified, the second step of the progressive adjustment technique is to measure the total association. Table 6.1 shows a progressive adjustment of the association between adult depression and parental divorce in one's childhood using a multiple linear regression. Depression is measured by asking questions such as "How many days in the past week have you felt sad? How many days did you feel unable to get going?" The interview asks about seven common symptoms of depression. The depression index takes the arithmetic mean of the seven responses. Thus, it measures the average number of days per symptom (during the past week).

Model 1.1 in Table 6.1 shows the total association. The variable labeled "Parents divorced" takes a score of 1 for persons who say that in their childhood their parents sepa-

Table 6.1. Progressive Adjustment: Regressions Showing Differences in Depression[a] between Persons Who Experience Parental Divorce or Separation in Childhood and Others, Adjusting Progressively for Socioeconomic Origins and Consequences of the Breakup[b]

Row	Regressor	Predicted Mean Frequency of Symptoms				
		Model 1.1	Model 1.2	Model 1.3	Model 1.4	Model 1.5
1	Parents divorced	.236*** (3.398)	.244*** (3.496)	.170* (2.455)	.149* (2.274)	.066 (1.039)
2	Minority		.156* (2.262)	.157* (2.318)	.050 (.774)	-.025 (-.405)
3	Mother's education—12 [c]		-.012 (-1.152)	.003 (.277)	.007 (.661)	.003 (.297)
4	Father's education—12 [c]		-.021* (-2.278)	-.008 (-.832)	-.007 (-.811)	-.009 (-1.036)
5	Person's education—12 [c]			-.090*** (-8.768)	-.069*** (-7.055)	-.047*** (-4.871)
6	Unable to work				1.921*** (13.907)	1.657*** (12.283)
7	History of long [d] unemployment				.557*** (8.202)	.374*** (5.570)
8	Current unemployment				.569*** (3.802)	.392** (2.702)
10	Economic hardship ever [e]					.105* (12.017)
11	Recent economic hardship [e]					.470*** (12.017)
12	Intercept	.889***	.837***	.995***	.827***	.611***

$p < .050$, ** $p < .010$, *** $p < .001$, one-tailed t test
[a] Depression is measured with an index of seven symptoms. Numbers represent the weekly number of days per symptom.
[b] Unstandardized coefficients with t values in parentheses below.
[c] Education is measured as the difference between the person's actual years of formal education and 12 years.
[d] Long unemployment is any period of 6 months or more during adulthood when the person was looking for a job or wanted a job but could not find one.
[e] Economic hardship ever contrasts people who say they have had at least one period in their adult lives of difficulty paying bills or buying food, clothing, medicine, or other needs with people who say they have not. Recent economic hardship is measured on a scale with zero indicating no difficulties in the past 12 months, 1 indicating some difficulties but not very often, 2 indicating difficulties fairly often, and 3 indicating difficulties very often.
Note. The regressions in this table use data from a 1995 U.S. survey of 2,539 adults ages 18 through 95, contacted by random-digit-dialing and interviewed over the telephone. The survey was funded by a grant from the National Institute on Aging (NIA 1R01-AG12393; John Mirowsky P.I., Catherine E. Ross Co-P.I.).

separated or divorced. It takes a score of zero for others. The intercept (row 12) represents the average level of depression for persons with scores of zero on all the independent variables. In Model 1.1, the intercept indicates an average weekly frequency of .889 days per symptom among adults who did not experience a breakup (because $.889 + .236(0) = .889$). The regression coefficient for parental divorce (row 1) indicates that adults who had that experience report an average of .236 more days per symptom than the reference group, for a total of 1.125 (because $.889 + .236(1) = 1.125$). The statistical significance test indicates less than 1 chance in 1,000 that a sample would show a difference this large if it were drawn from a population with no difference in depression between the two groups.

Some arithmetic suggests that the difference may be substantively significant as well. The adults who say their parents divorced report about 26.5% greater frequency of the symptoms than others (because $100(.236/.889) = 26.5$). Put another way, they would have the symptoms of depression 21.0% less often if they had them at the same frequency as others (because $100(.236/1.125) = 21.0$).

Step 3: Adjusting for Precursors

The third step of progressive adjustment controls for precursors of the observed association, which may act as confounders producing spurious association. A precursor is a trait or condition that existed before the hypothetical cause came to be. A precursor may have produced both the hypothetical cause and its hypothetical consequence, creating a spurious association between them. Suppose that parental divorce years ago and elevated depression today both result from a common cause. Perhaps that antecedent of the divorce, and not the divorce itself, causes subsequent depression. Something might have strained the parents' relationship or weakened its resistance to other social stresses. For example, parents with low or disadvantaged social status may divorce more often than other parents, and also may give their children few of the advantages needed to find success, security, and happiness later in life. If so, then the parents' low or disadvantaged status might produce both their divorce and their child's later adult depression, accounting for the correlation between these two variables.

Model 1.2 of Table 6.1 adjusts the association between parental breakup and adult depression for three measures of childhood family status. The variable labeled "Minority" takes a score of 1 for persons who say they are black, Hispanic, Native American, or Asian, and a value of zero for others. The variables labeled "Mother's education—12" and "Father's education—12" represent each parent's total years of formal education completed. They are centered on 12, meaning that they measure the number of years short of or beyond a 12th-grade education (Aiken & West, 1991). Thus, the intercept represents the average level of depression predicted for nonminority persons whose parents both had 12 years of education and remained together when the person was a child. As expected, the results indicate that members of minority groups feel depressed more often than others and that persons whose parents had higher levels of education feel depressed less often. (Readers should not make too much of the fact that the father's education appears more important than the mother's. The mother's education correlates highly with the father's education. In some samples, the mother's education appears more important.)

The association between parental breakup and depression does not vanish with adjustment for the three measures of childhood family status. In fact, the adjustment produces no appreciable change in the measured association. The coefficient for parental divorce (row 1) remains essentially unchanged. (The tiny increase from .236 to .244 lies well within the range of random noise in the estimate, as indicated by its standard error. The difference is .244 - .236 = .008, which is much smaller than the standard error of .244/3.496 = .070.) The two regressions (Model 1.1 and Model 1.2) show no support for the hypothesis that the association is spurious due to childhood family status. These two regressions imply that if we matched on minority status and parental education, the difference in depression associated with parental divorce would remain unchanged.

Step 4: Adjusting for Mediators

The fourth step of progressive adjustment controls for hypothetical mediators of the association. A mediator joins the cause to its consequence: It represents a link in the causal chain. Multiple regression as a statistical procedure does not distinguish mediators from confounders, but the interpretation of results must distinguish between them. Analysts sometimes fail to make the distinction, leading to serious misinterpretation. When held constant by adjustment, both confounders and mediators reduce the association between a hypothetical cause and its apparent consequence. The distinction between confounders and mediators follows from their relationships to the hypothetical cause, as illustrated in Figure 6.1. A confounder precedes both the hypothetical cause and the apparent consequence. When an association vanishes with adjustment for a precursor, the association is spurious: The consequence does not result from the hypothetical cause. In contrast, a mediator results from the hypothetical cause but precedes the apparent consequence. When an association vanishes with adjustment for a mediator, the mechanism of the effect is revealed: the consequence results from the cause through the mediator.

Typically the adjustment for hypothetical mediators proceeds in stages. Each step adds adjustment for a block of variables. Sometimes the blocks represent alternative hypothetical mechanisms, and sometimes they represent sequential developmental steps. Analyses can blend these approaches, as in the model represented in Figure 6.1 and estimated in Table 6.1. The model hypothesizes that the association between childhood parental divorce and adulthood depression is mediated by disrupted schooling, periods of unemployment, and periods of difficulty meeting household needs. The blocks of hypothetical mediators might act as alternative mechanisms, with each creating a separate part of the association. Alternatively, the blocks might act as a single causal chain, with parental divorce lowering educational attainment, which increases the frequency of unemployment, which creates economic hardship, which makes adults feel depressed.

The progressive adjustment in Table 6.1 tests the argument that divorce of parents in one's childhood increases depression in adulthood by disrupting education, thereby undermining employment and creating economic hardship, which makes people feel depressed. The results seem partly consistent with the account. Adding adjustment for the person's own educational attainment (Model 1.3) reduces the association by 30.3% (100 × [.244 - .170] / .244 = 30.3). In other words, if those whose parents divorced achieved the same level of education as others, the difference in depression between these two groups would be about 30.3% smaller than the observed difference (net of background status). That reduction seems sizable, but most of the association (69.7%) remains unexplained.

Model 1.4 adds adjustment for being unable to work because of a disability, having been unemployed for 6 months or more during adulthood, and being currently unemployed. Adjustment for these variables further reduces the association, making it about 38.9% smaller than in Model 1.2. (Interestingly, this adjustment essentially eliminates the association between minority status and depression.) Model 1.5 adds adjustment for past or recent difficulties paying bills or buying food, clothing, medicine, or other necessities. The adjustment further reduces the association, making it 73.0% smaller than in Model 1.2. The remaining difference of .066 days per symptom per week is only about 7.4% of the base rate among persons raised in intact families. The t test for statistical significance indicates a probability of .294 that a sample drawn from a population with no difference would show a .066 difference purely by chance. Disrupted education and a history of unemployment and economic hardship appear to explain the association between divorce of parents in one's childhood and depression in adulthood.

Step 5: Revising the Explanation and Model

The final step in a progressive adjustment revises the theoretical explanation so that it conforms to the statistical results and states alternative or supplemental explanations for future analysis. As in the example, a single mediator rarely explains all of the association between the hypothetical cause and consequence. Adjusting for differences in education explains some of parental divorce's apparent effect on depression, but not most of it. The progressive adjustment in Table 6.1 tested the viability of an account focused on education and its consequences for employment and economic well-being. Disrupted education does seem to play a part, but the results suggest some other connection too. The results in Table 6.1 imply that the parental divorce leads to unemployment and economic hardship, and thus to depression, for additional reasons. What might those be?

An alternative explanation might focus on interpersonal consequences. The parental divorce might leave some children fearful about relationships with other people and unable to form supportive ones as adults. Indeed, an analysis not shown here (Mirowsky & Ross, 1999) finds that adults whose parents separated or divorced have had more marriages, are less happy with their present marriages, think of divorce more often, and feel more suspicious of others in general than persons from intact families. Adjusting for those variables also eliminates most of the association between the parental breakup and depression. Perhaps the childhood parental divorce has two major effects, with interweaving consequences raising the frequency of adulthood symptoms. It may be that interpersonal doubts increase the risk of depressing adulthood unemployment and economic hardship.

The analyst also may want to revise the explanation by making it more specific. For example, the analyst might ask which aspect of separation and divorce produces the apparent consequences. Is it the simple fact that one parent left the household? The conflict leading up to that event? The disruption of daily life before and after? The hostility shown by each parent to the other? The sense of personal loss? The sense of abandonment? The decline in household economic well-being?

Each progressive adjustment ends with a reconsideration and revision of the theoretical explanation. The revisions begin a new cycle of analysis.

INTERACTION MODELING

Interaction models specify the moderators that regulate the size of an association. By definition, a moderator enlarges, diminishes, or reverses the association between two other variables (Wheaton, 1985). The search for moderators constitutes a second form of statistical explanation that is distinct from the search for mediators. In the sense that a moderator determines the size and direction (positive or negative) of an association between two variables, the state of the moderator explains their association.

The distinction between mediators (discussed in the previous section) and moderators (discussed in this section) can seem elusive at first. Analysts need to make the distinction because mediators and moderators embody different types of theoretical explanation with different statistical representation. On the theoretical level, a mediator results from the hypothetical cause and produces its consequence, thus forming the link between them. In contrast, a moderator changes the relationship between the hypothetical cause and consequence. A moderator could be completely uncorrelated with the hypothetical cause, yet determine the extent or direction of its effect on the hypothetical consequence. Some moderators are necessary for an effect to occur, as when a precipitating stress is necessary to turn a predisposition into a disorder. Some moderators buffer potentially damaging shocks, as when a supportive marriage lessens or absorbs the shock of a stressful event such as the death of a parent. Some moderators aggravate stresses, irritations, or threats, as when children in the household magnify the distress associated with unemployment. By definition, a moderator regulates the direction or strength of the relationship between two other variables.

Moderators can be external or internal. External moderators are attributes that describe everyone in all categories of exposure, whereas internal moderators only describe the members of one category. The distinction can be difficult to grasp when stated in abstract terms, but a concrete example makes it clear. The effect on depression of being married rather than unmarried may depend on a person's number of previous marriages and on the quality of the current marriage. Whether married or not, everyone has some number of previous marriages. The number may be zero or one, or two, or three or more. The important thing is that everyone, whether currently married or not, has some number of previous marriages. If the number of previous marriages alters the effect of current marital status on depression, then the number of previous marriages acts as an external moderator of that association. In contrast, only married people can be unhappy with the marriage and thinking of divorce. Unmarried people can not be described and compared in these terms. If unhappiness with the marriage and thoughts of divorce cancel the beneficial effect of marriage on depression, then these variables act as internal moderators of that association.

Most discussions of interaction modeling focus on external moderators, but modeling the internal moderators can be useful too. Both types of interactions describe the conditions that strengthen, weaken, eliminate, or invert an association. The rest of this section illustrates the models that describe external and internal moderators.

External Moderators

The key to understanding interaction models lies in thinking of regression coefficients as variables. In the absence of significant interaction, the same regression slope applies to everyone. In the presence of significant interaction, the slope depends on the moderator. Most data analysts learn to think of regression coefficients as constants, but these coefficients actually portray associations that may change depending on circumstances. The product-term interaction model represents the most prevalent model from a family that includes latent growth curves, hierarchical linear models, and nonlinear regressions. Product-term interaction models provide the simplest way to describe regression slopes that vary across segments of the population (Aiken & West, 1991).

BIVARIATE, MULTIPLE, AND CONDITIONAL REGRESSION.   To understand product-term interaction models, one needs to distinguish conditional regression equations from bivariate and multiple regression equations. Consider, for example, the effect of marriage on depression, which might depend on the number of previous marriages. In the equations below, D represents the frequency of feeling depressed, M represents the state of being married (scored 1) or not (scored zero), and P represents the number of previous marriages.

A *bivariate regression* describes the total association between two variables. Equation 1 represents the bivariate regression. In it b_1 describes the average difference in depression between married people and others, and b_0 represents the average frequency of depression among unmarried people.

$$\hat{D} = b_0 + b_1 M \qquad\qquad (1)$$

Model 2.1 in Table 6.2 shows the bivariate regression estimates. The intercept indicates a mean of 1.179 days per symptom among persons who are not currently married $(1.179 - .432(0) = 1.179)$. The coefficient for being currently married (row 1) indicates that married persons average .432 fewer days per symptom than the unmarried, or .747 days per symptom (because $1.179 - .432(1) = -.747$).

A *multiple regression* describes the association holding constant one or more other variables. Equation 2 represents the multiple regression controlling for the number of previous marriages. In this equation, b_1 describes the average difference in depression between married people and others who have the same number of previous marriages, and $b_0 + b_2 P$ represents the average frequency of depression among unmarried people with P previous marriages.

$$\hat{D} = b_0 + b_1 M + b_2 P \qquad\qquad (2)$$

Table 6.2.   Modeling External Interactions: Regressions Showing Differences in Depression[a] between Adults Who Currently Are Married and Those Who Are Not, Depending on the Number of Previous Marriages[b]

Row	b_i	Regressor	Predicted Mean Frequency of Symptoms		
			Model 2.1	Model 2.2	Model 2.3
1	b_1	Married currently	-.432*** (-8.401)	-.361*** (-6.634)	-.430*** (-6.505)
2	b_2	Previous marriages		.142*** (3.955)	.083* (1.751)
3	b_3	Married × previous marriages			.133* (1.843)
4	b_0	Intercept	1.179***	1.064***	1.111***

$p < .050$, ** $p < .010$, *** $p < .001$, one-tailed t test
[a] Depression is measured with an index of seven symptoms. Numbers represent the weekly number of days per symptom.
[b] Unstandardized coefficients with t values in parentheses below. See Note, Table 6.1.

Model 2.2 shows the multiple regression estimates. Unmarried people with no previous marriages average about 1.064 days per symptom. Each previous marriage adds an average of about .142 days per week to an unmarried person's frequency of each symptom. By comparison, married people average about .361 fewer days per symptom than unmarried people with the same number of previous marriages. The multiple regression's b_1 of -.361 is smaller than the bivariate regression's b_1 of -.432, because part of the association is spurious. Previous marriages increase depression and some of the lower depression among married people reflects the fact that they have had fewer previous marriages.

A *conditional regression* describes how the association depends on the value of a moderator. Equation 3 represents the conditional regression of depression on marriage, showing how it depends on the number of previous marriages. In the equation, $b_1 + b_3P$ describes the average difference in depression between married people and others with P previous marriages, and $b_0 + b_2P$ represents the average frequency of depression among unmarried people with P previous marriages. In Equation 3, the slope, as well as the intercept, depends on the number of previous marriages.

$$\hat{D} = (b_0 + b_2P) + (b_1 + b_3P)M \tag{3}$$

Notice that we can rewrite Equation 3 as follows, where $a_0 = b_0 + b_2P$ and $a_1 = b_1 + b_3P$.

$$\hat{D} = a_0 + a_1M \tag{4}$$

Equations 3 and 4 are called the conditional or simple (Aiken & West, 1991) regression equations. Each distinct value of P implies a different value of the slope and intercept that describe the relationship between depression and marriage. Model 2.3 of Table 6.2 shows the conditional regression estimates for our running example. Unmarried people average about $1.111 + .083P$ days per symptom. Married people differ from them by an average of $-.430 + .133P$ days per symptom. Each previous marriage adds an average of about .083 days a week to an unmarried person's frequency of each symptom, and adds an average of .133 days to a married person's frequency. Table 6.3 shows the conditional or simple regression coefficients for zero through five previous marriages. According to Model 2.3, each additional previous marriage increases the average frequency of depression among married people more than among unmarried people. Thus, the apparent benefits of marriage decline with the number of previous marriages and disappear once that number reaches about three.

When significant interaction exists, a multiple regression coefficient such as b_1 in Model 2.2 equals the mean value of the conditional regression coefficient a_1. In the example, the mean number of previous marriages is .512. That makes the mean value of the conditional regression coefficient a_1 equal $-.430 + .133 \times .512 = -.363$. This value is within rounding error of the -.361 estimated as the value of b_1 in Model 2.2. If the effect of marriage depends on P, its multiple regression coefficient adjusting for P represents its average effect. That beneficial average effect might get smaller in the future if the average number of previous marriages increases.

EXTERNAL PRODUCT TERMS.   The conditional regression model has one drawback. Standard regression programs cannot directly estimate coefficients such as a_1 that depend on other variables. Product terms provide the easiest and most common way to model interac-

Table 6.3. Conditional or Simple Regressions: Regressions Showing Differences in Depression^a between Adults Who Currently Are Married and Those Who Are Not, Depending on the Number of Previous Marriages $(P)^b$

P	Predicted Mean Frequency of Symptoms				Percent of sample
	$b_0 + b_2 P$	$b_1 + b_3 P$	a_0	a_1	
0	$1.111 + .083 \times 0$	$-.430 + .133 \times 0$	1.111	-.430	60.9
1	$1.111 + .083 \times 1$	$-.430 + .133 \times 1$	1.194	-.297	29.5
2	$1.111 + .083 \times 2$	$-.430 + .133 \times 2$	1.277	-.164	7.4
3	$1.111 + .083 \times 3$	$-.430 + .133 \times 3$	1.360	-.031	1.6
4	$1.111 + .083 \times 4$	$-.430 + .133 \times 4$	1.443	.102	0.4
5	$1.111 + .083 \times 5$	$-.430 + .133 \times 5$	1.526	.235	0.1

^{a} Depression is measured with an index of seven symptoms. Numbers represent the weekly number of days per symptom.
^{b} Unstandardized coefficients with t values in parentheses below. See Note, Table 6.1.
Note. See Equations 3 and 4 for notation.

tions. A product term is a new variable created by multiplying together two other variables. Multiplying through Equation 3 and collecting terms produces Equation 5, which shows how product terms solve the estimation problem. The researcher computes a new variable that equals the product of two others (such as $P \times M$), and enters all three (P, M, and $P \times M$) as independent variables in a regression. Product terms allow the data analyst to estimate and test interaction models using standard regression programs.

$$\hat{D} = b_0 + b_1 M + b_2 P + b_3 (P \times M) \tag{5}$$

The product term's coefficient b_3 represents the effect of the moderator (P) on the association between the other two variables (D and M). The t test for the product term's coefficient b_3 tests the null hypothesis that there is no interaction. The results in Table 6.2 show a t value of 1.843 for this coefficient. For a one-tailed test, the t value indicates that there is less than a 5% chance that a random sample of 2,539 persons would yield the observed coefficient of .133 by chance if there were no real interaction in the population from which the sample is drawn. Thus, it seems reasonable to reject the null hypothesis of no interaction. If b_3 were not significant, then we could remove the product term from the model and proceed on the assumption that marriage has the same effect regardless of the number of previous marriages. Because b_3 is significant, we must proceed on the assumption that the effect of marriage depends on the number of previous marriages.

Adding a product term to a regression model changes the meaning of the coefficients associated with the component variables. In the multiple regression of Model 2.2, the coefficient b_1 represents the effect of marriage holding previous marriages constant, or the effect given the mean number of previous marriages. In contrast, the coefficient b_1 in Model 2.3 represents the effect of marriage on depression *among people with no previous marriages* $(P = 0)$. The t test for b_1 in Model 2.3 tests the null hypothesis that there is no significant difference in depression between married and unmarried people with no previous marriages $(P = 0)$. Likewise the t test for b_2 in Model 2.3 tests the null hypothesis that there is no significant effect of previous marriage among persons who are currently unmarried $(M = 0)$. Data analysts must remember that adding the product term changes the meaning of the "lower order" coefficients. The coefficient of a lower order term represents the effect of that factor when the other term in the product term equals zero.

EXTERNAL CRITICAL POINTS.   When an interaction exists, the association may vanish when the moderator takes a particular value. Data analysts call that value the critical point. It divides the conditions under which the association is negative from the ones under which it is positive. In the example, the emotional benefits of marriage get smaller as the number of previous marriages increases. At some point, the benefits of marriage may vanish altogether. The data analysts can use the results from the product-term model to find such critical points, such as the critical number of previous marriages P_c. Setting the conditional regression coefficient a_1 to zero and solving for P_c tells us the number of previous marriages at which the emotional benefits of marriage disappear.

$$a_1 = b_1 + b_3 P_c = 0 \tag{6}$$

$$P_c = -b_1/b_3 \tag{7}$$

According to the results for Model 2.3, the dividing line is at $.430/.133 = 3.233$. Thus, the model implies that people with one or two previous marriages are less depressed if currently married. People with more than three previous marriages are more depressed if currently married.

CAUTIONS ABOUT EXTERNAL INTERACTIONS AND CRITICAL POINTS.   Reading the model by working out its implications provides insight. However, the analyst must remember several things. First, an estimated critical point such as P_c may lie in a region where data are sparse. In the data used for the regressions of Table 6.2, only 12 people have had more than three previous marriages, half of 1% of the sample. Only 42 people, or 1.6%, have had three previous marriage. Indeed 60.9% have had no previous marriages, and 29.5% have had only one, for a total of 90.4%.

Second, some aspects of the model represent untested assumptions. The product-term model implies that the association may switch from negative to positive at some point. An alternative form of model might imply that the association approaches zero but never switches. Such an alternative might fit the data as well as the product-term model, or better.

Finally, the regression coefficients used in the calculations are estimates with some degree of inaccuracy. The t value of 1.843 indicates that the standard error of the product term's coefficient is more than half the value of the coefficient $(1/1.843 = .543)$. If a crossover point really exists, its true value might be considerably higher or lower than the estimate because of imprecision. A later section describes how to sharpen the accuracy of the regression coefficients used to estimate critical points.

Internal Moderators

Sometimes the qualities of a situation determine the effect of being in it (Ross & Mirowsky, 1992). Internal moderators represent differences applicable only to the individuals in a particular situation that affects outcomes. We often wish to compare these internal variations to the effect of being outside the situation. For example, the effect of employment on emotional well-being might depend on the job's pay, level of authority, prestige, and the like, making some jobs more distressing than not working. In the case of marriage, its association with depression might depend on the quality of the marriage. Individuals who are unhappy with their marriages and think often of divorce may be as depressed or even more depressed, on average, than persons who are not married.

Historically most investigations of moderators have concentrated on testing external ones. However, some theories describe internal moderators. In the example, common sense tells us that the emotional benefits of a marriage may depend on qualities of the marriage itself. How can researchers measure the effects of those qualities on the emotional benefits of marriage? Many investigators study internal mediators by limiting the sample. In the example, that would mean looking only at married people and studying the effect of unhappy marriages and thoughts of divorce on depression. The trouble with limiting the sample is that it loses the comparison to unmarried people. That comparison might be important.. For example, people might get divorced when their marriages are so depressing that unmarried people are less depressed. Or they might seek help.

INTERNAL MODERATOR MODELS. Analysts usually find it useful to score moderators so that zero represents the mean, median, mode, or some other typical value used as the point of reference (Aiken & West, 1991). This especially applies to internal moderators. Equation 8 shows an internal moderator model, where U is unhappiness with the current marriage and T is thoughts of divorce (Cohen, 1968). As before, P is the number of previous marriages, D is the average weekly frequency of seven symptoms of depression, and M equals 1 for married persons and zero for others. Most married persons report being very happy with their marriages and never thinking about divorce. They are assigned scores of zero on U and T. Thus b_1 represents the effect of marriage on depression for persons with no previous marriages ($P = 0$) who say they are very happy with their marriages ($U = 0$) and never think of divorce ($T = 0$). Individuals who say they are very unhappy with their marriages are assigned a score of 1 on U. Thus, b_4 represents the difference in the effect of marriage for people in very unhappy marriages compared to those in very happy marriages. Similarly, individuals who say they think of divorce very often are assigned a score of 1 on T. Thus, b_5 represents the difference in the effect of marriage for them compared to the effect for persons who never think of divorce. Intermediate responses on U and T have scores of .333 and .667.

$$\hat{D} = (b_0 + b_2 P) + (b_1 + b_3P + b_4 U + b_5T) M \tag{8}$$

Equation 8 describes a conditional regression in which a_0 equals $b_0 + b_2P$ and a_1 equals $b_1 + b_3P + b_4U + b_5T$. Table 6.4 shows the estimated regression coefficients. According to Model 4.1 the difference in depression associated with being married rather than unmarried equals $-.459 + .095P + .948U + .525T$. The model implies that people in their first marriages who are very happy with their marriages and never think of divorce are less frequently depressed than unmarried people with no previous marriages ($-.459 + .095 \times 0 + .948 \times 0 + .525 \times 0 = -.459$). In contrast, people in their first marriages who are very unhappy with their marriages and often think of divorce are much more frequently depressed than unmarried people with no previous marriages ($-.459 + .095 \times 0 + .948 \times 1 + .525 \times 1 = 1.014$).

INTERNAL PRODUCT TERMS. Multiplying through Equation 8 and collecting terms show the variables needed to estimate the model (Cohen, 1968). In Equation 9, all of the product terms equal zero for unmarried persons. Thus, the product term $U \times M$ equals zero for unmarried persons and U for married persons. Likewise, the product term $T \times M$ equals zero for unmarried persons and T for married persons. This does not mean that the model equates being unmarried (scored zero on both products) with being very happily married

Table 6.4. Modeling Internal Interactions: Regressions Showing Differences in Depression[a]
Between Adults[b] **Who Currently are Married and Those Who Are Not, Depending**
on the Number of Previous Marriages and, If Married, the Degree of Unhappiness
with the Marriage and the Frequency of Thoughts about Divorce[c,d]

Row	b_i	Regressor	Frequency Model 4.1	Logged Frequency[e] Model 4.2
1	b_1	Married currently	-.459***	-.689***
			(-7.062)	(-9.905)
2	b_2	Previous marriages	.094*	-.026
			(1.999)	(-.525)
3	b_3	Married × previous marriages	.095	.238***
			(1.334)	(3.125)
4	b_4	Married × unhappy with marriage	.948***	1.016***
			(4.821)	(4.833)
5	b_5	Married × think about divorce	.525***	.651***
			(4.821)	(5.151)
6	b_0	Intercept	1.002***	-.730***
7	F	Goodness of fit	33.667***	47.965***

$p < .050$, ** $p < .010$, *** $p < .001$, one-tailed t test
[a] Depression is measured with an index of seven symptoms. Numbers represent the weekly number of days per symptom.
[b] Very happy with the marriage is coded 0, somewhat happy is coded .333, somewhat unhappy is coded .667, and very unhappy is coded 1.
[c] Never thinking of leaving the relationship is coded 0, rarely thinking of it is coded .333, sometimes thinking of it is coded .667, and often thinking of it is coded 1.
[d] Unstandardized coefficients with t values in parentheses below.
[e] Individuals who reported having none of the seven symptoms in the previous week were assigned a score of .5/7 before taking the natural log.
See Note Table 6-1.

and never thinking about divorce (also scored zero on both products). The model distinguishes between those states by including M.

$$\hat{D} = b_0 + b_1 M + b_2 P + b_3 (P \times M) + b_4 (U \times M) + b_5 (T \times M) \tag{9}$$

INTERNAL CRITICAL POINTS. Each internal moderator potentially may change the expectation for persons in a situation until it matches the expectation for persons not in it. In the example, unhappiness with the marriage and thoughts of divorce may eliminate the expected difference in depression between married persons and others. Combined with the number of previous marriages, the internal moderators determine the coefficient representing marriage's effect. Setting that effect to zero and solving for a moderator yields its critical value.

$$a_1 = b_1 + b_3 P + b_4 U + b_5 T = 0 \tag{10}$$
$$P_c = (-b_1/b_3) + (-b_4/b_3)U + (-b_5/b_3)T \tag{11}$$
$$U_c = (-b_1/b_4) + (-b_3/b_4)P + (-b_5/b_4)T \tag{12}$$
$$T_c = (-b_1/b_5) + (-b_3/b_5)P + (-b_4/b_5)U \tag{13}$$

The critical value of each moderator depends on the states of the other moderators. For example, the critical level of unhappiness with the marriage at which its salutary effect vanishes is $U_c = (.459/.948) + (-.095/.948)P + (-.525/.948)T = .484 - .100P - .554T$. If someone has no previous marriages and never thinks of divorce, then .484 is the critical level of unhappiness with the marriage. That score corresponds to being somewhat unhappy with the marriage. However, if the person has one previous marriage ($P = 1$) and sometimes thinks about divorce ($T = .333$), then the critical level of unhappiness with the marriage is much less: $.484 - (.100 \times 1) - (.554 \times .333) = .200$. That score corresponds to being somewhat happy with the marriage. The internal and external moderators operate collectively. Each one defines the critical values of the others.

INDEXES OF PATHOLOGY AND THE EFFICIENCY OF REGRESSION ESTIMATES

Random errors in regression estimates pose a special problem for interaction analysis. By their nature, interaction models test the effects of combinations of traits. The important combinations might be uncommon. When testing interactions, researchers need to take special care to maximize the efficiency of the regression estimates. An efficient estimate varies little across samples from the true population value. Greater efficiency increases the power of significance tests, thus increasing the probability of detecting the effect of an uncommon combination of traits. Greater efficiency also increases the accuracy of critical-point estimates, which use two or more regression coefficients.

Indexes of pathology often have one feature that reduces the efficiency of regression estimates: highly skewed distributions. Most people most often have no symptoms or only a few. Indexes that count symptoms typically produce scores that cluster near the minimum value of zero. The more skewed the dependent variable, the less efficient the regression estimates. Inefficient estimates have high standard errors, which means that two samples taken from the same population often produce very different results. Skewed dependent variables decrease efficiency because they create a correlation between the predicted value and the variance of the prediction error, called heteroscedasticity. Transformations that reduce the skewness of the distribution reduce the correlation between the error variance and the prediction and thus improve efficiency (Hamilton, 1992).

Texts on interaction modeling typically recommend one method for improving efficiency: centering variables before calculating product terms (e.g., Aiken & West, 1991). Centering is scoring a variable so that zero represents a typical value such as the mean, median, or mode. Centering makes it easier to read the regression results, but it also has a purely statistical effect. Centering the interacting variables reduces the correlation of the product term (e.g., $M \times P$) with its lower order factors (M and P). That greatly increases the efficiency of the coefficients associated with the lower order terms. Unfortunately, it has no effect on the efficiency of the coefficient associated with the product term (Aiken & West, 1991, p. 35). In contrast, transformations that reduce skewness in the distribution of the dependent variable can increase the efficiency of the product term's coefficient. As a consequence, a transformation that reduces the skewness of the dependent variable can improve the power to detect effects of uncommon combinations and improve the precision of estimated critical points.

Transformation to Reduce Skew

Several transformations can reduce the positive skew in symptom counts (Hamilton, 1992). The two most common transformations take the square root or the log. Taking the log produces a model that is easier to interpret than one taking the square root. However, the log of zero is undefined. (Punch zero into your scientific calculator and hit the "ln" key. It will say you have made an error.) Often, many cases report no symptoms. In the data for the examples, 777 persons reported no symptoms of depression. Before taking the log, it is necessary to assign a nonzero value to persons who reported having no symptoms. The lowest observed nonzero score comes from having one of the seven symptoms in the index on one day of the week, for a score of $1/7 = .143$. Half that frequency, or one symptom one day every other week, would be a score of $.5/7 = .071$. Assigning that value to cases that reported no symptoms in the past week makes it possible to take the log without losing cases due to undefined values.

The natural-log transformation of the depression scale reduces the skewness of its distribution from 2.111 to .171 (where zero is ideal). Table 6.4 shows the gain in efficiency. The F ratio measures the overall goodness of fit. It increases from 33.667 in the Model 4.1 to 47.965 in Model 4.2. The t values associated with the product terms all increase compared to their corresponding values in the unlogged Model 4.1. The t value of the coefficient b_3, representing the interaction between current and previous marriage, increases markedly from 1.334 in Model 4.1 to 3.125 in Model 4.2. That means the standard error of the estimate drops from 75.0% of the coefficient's value ($1/1.334 = .750$) to 32.0% ($1/3.125 = .320$). The standard error of b_1 (in row 1) also drops, from 14.2% of the coefficient to 10.1%.

Together, the more accurate coefficients locate the critical points more precisely. For example, Model 4.1 implies that the critical number of previous marriages P_c equals $4.832 - 9.974U - 5.526T$, whereas Model 4.2 implies that P_c equals $2.895 - 4.269U - 2.735T$. Thus, the unlogged model implied that it would take five previous marriages for the emotional benefits of a happy marriage with no thoughts of divorce to vanish. The logged model implies that it would take only three previous marriages.

Only one coefficient (b_2) appears more significant in the unlogged Model 4.1 than in the logged Model 4.2. Among unmarried persons, previous marriages significantly increase the predicted frequency of symptoms, but not the predicted log frequency. Given the lower overall efficiency of Model 4.1, the apparent statistical significance of b_2 is probably a false positive. If the true value of a parameter is zero, greater efficiency puts sample estimates closer to that true value.

Mean Logs and Geometric Means

Transformation of the dependent variable changes more than just the efficiency of estimates. It changes the form of the model and the central tendency that it predicts. By design, a regression model describes the mean value of the dependent variable expected for given specific values of the predictors. A predicted symptom count carries intuitive meaning. In Model 4.1, people who are not married and never have been average 1.002 days per symptom. Everyone knows the meaning of a day. In Model 4.2, people who are not married and never have been married average -.730 logged days per week (base e). What does that mean? Logged days carry little intuitive meaning. To grasp the magnitude the prediction must be translated back into days. The function $e^{Y^{\wedge}}$, or $EXP(Y^{\wedge})$, changes the predicted log of days into predicted days. Thus $EXP(-.730) = .482$ days per symptom.

The exponentiated mean of a logged variable is called its geometric mean. Exponentiating the predicted log yields the predicted geometric mean. Notice that the predicted arithmetic mean of 1.002 days per symptom is much larger than the predicted geometric mean of .482 days per symptom. The geometric mean is like a median. In fact, the closer the logged distribution is to normal, the closer the geometric mean is to the median. Thus, the logged model implies that approximately half of the people who are not married and never have been married report fewer than .482 days per symptom and half report more.

To calculate a predicted geometric mean, calculate the predicted log and then exponentiate. The geometric mean predicted for happily married persons who never think of divorce and were never married before is EXP([-.730 - .026 × 0] + [-.689 + .238 × 0 + 1.016 × 0 + .651 × 0] × 1) = EXP(-1.419) = .242, which is 50.2% of the geometric mean predicted for unmarried persons (.242/.482 = .502). A happy first marriage appears to cut the median frequency of depressive symptoms in half.

Multiplicative Coefficients

The log transformation of the dependent variable changes the interpretation of the regression coefficients as well as the interpretation of the predicted values. Exponentiating the predicted log produces a fully multiplicative model, as illustrated in Equations 14 and 15.

$$\ln \hat{D} = a_0 + a_1 M \tag{14}$$

$$\hat{D} = e^{\ln \hat{D}} = e^{a_0 + a_1 M} = e^{a_0} e^{a_1 M} = m_0 m_1^{M} \tag{15}$$

Exponentiating a regression coefficient from Model 4.2 yields a multiplier. Each multiplier describes the geometric mean predicted for persons with a score of one on the variable as a fraction of the geometric mean predicted for persons with a score of zero, other things being equal. For example, the coefficient b_1 in Model 4.2 equals -.689. Raising e to that power yields a value of .502. Thus, the geometric mean predicted for happily married persons who never think of divorce and were never married previously is about 50.2% of the geometric mean predicted for never married persons. Notice that this is the same value calculated in the preceding paragraph by computing the prediction for each group and taking the ratio.

CONCLUSION

Searching for mediators and moderators constitutes two main strategies of sociological research on mental health. Although distinct, the two approaches share a tactical goal: the specification of circumstances under which an association vanishes.

The examples in this chapter address two of many questions about emotional well-being that interest sociologists. The literature on the two topics provides additional examples of the methods that readers may want to review. McLeod (1991) and Aseltine (1996) used progressive adjustment to find mediators between depression and childhood parental divorce. McLeod studied the effect of the divorce on adulthood depression. She found that the childhood parental divorce reduced educational attainment and adulthood income, reduced the age at first marriage, increased the number of marriages, and decreased the quality of current marriages. She found that the reduced quality of current marriages accounted for most of the association between adult depression and childhood parental divorce.

Aseltine studied the effects of parental divorce on adolescent depression. He found that economic hardship associated with being in one-parent households accounted for most of the lasting effects of parental divorce on adolescent depression.

Wheaton (1990) and Jekielek (1998) used interaction modeling to study conditions that might reduce the distress associated with divorce. Wheaton found that divorce generally increased an adult's distress over the short run (about 2 years), but eventually decreased distress compared to predivorce levels for persons whose marriages had lacked affection, companionship, and sharing. Jekielek found that children from high-conflict families were psychologically better after a parental divorce than before, and better than children who remained in high-conflict families.

Once sociologists know that an association exists, they want to know why. Why are women more depressed than men? Why are men more destructive than women? Why are young adults more anxious than old adults? The chapters that follow summarize the results of many studies that used progressive adjustment and interaction modeling to answer such questions. Through the dissection of statistical correlation, sociologists find insights, answers, and new questions.

ACKNOWLEDGMENTS: The analyses reported here were supported by a grant from the National Institute on Aging (AG12393).

REFERENCES

Aseltine, R. H. (1996). Pathways linking parental divorce with adolescent depression. *Journal of Health and Social Behavior, 37*, 133–148.

Aiken, L. S., & West, S. G. (1991). *Multiple regression: Testing and interpreting interactions* Newbury Park, CA: Sage.

Davis, J. A. (1985). *The logic of causal order.* Beverly Hills, CA: Sage

Cohen, J. (1968). Multiple regression as a general data-analytic system. *Psychological Bulletin, 70*, 426–443.

Cole, S. (1972). *The sociological method.* Chicago: Markham.

Hamilton, L. C. (1992). *Regression with graphics: A second course in applied statistics.* Pacific Grove, CA: Brooks/Cole.

Jekielek, S. (1998). Parental conflict, marital disruption and children's emotional well-being. *Social Forces, 76,* 905–935.

McLeod, J. D. (1991). Childhood parental loss and adult depression. *Journal of Health and Social Behavior, 32,* 205–220.

Mirowsky, J., & Ross, C. E. (1999). Well-being across the life course. In A. V. Horowitz & T. L. Scheid (Eds.), *The sociology of mental health and illness* (pp. xxx–xxx). New York: Cambridge University Press.

Ross, C. E., & Mirowsky, J. (1992). Households, employment, and the sense of control. *Social Psychology Quarterly, 55*, 217–235.

Susser, M. (1973). *Causal thinking in the health sciences: Concepts and strategies of epidemiology.* New York: Oxford University Press.

Wheaton, B. (1985). Models for the stress-buffering functions of coping resources. *Journal of Health and Social Behavior, 26*, 352–364.

Wheaton, B. (1990). Life transitions, role histories, and mental health. *American Sociological Review, 55*, 209–223.

PART III

The Social Distribution
of Mental Illness

CHAPTER 7

Overview of Descriptive Epidemiology of Mental Disorders

RONALD C. KESSLER

SHANYANG ZHAO

INTRODUCTION

Epidemiology is the study of the distribution and correlates of illness in the population. The three stages of epidemiological investigation are descriptive, analytic, and experimental. Descriptive epidemiology is concerned with the distribution of illness onset and course, whereas analytic epidemiology is concerned with the use of nonexperimental data to elucidate causal processes involved in illness onset and course, and experimental epidemiology is concerned with the development and evaluation of interventions aimed at modifying risk factors to prevent illness onset or to modify illness course. Most epidemiological studies of psychiatric disorders are either descriptive or analytic. Historically, much of the important work in these areas has been done by sociologists. Experimental psychiatric epidemiology is more rare. A challenge for sociologists working in psychiatric epidemiology is to refine their analytic models sufficiently to establish the basis for structural interventions. See Rothman (1986) for an introduction to epidemiology overall and Tsaung, Tohen, and Zahner (1995) for an introduction to psychiatric epidemiology.

The chapters in this section of the handbook review recent work in descriptive psychiatric epidemiology. The focus is on areas that the sociology of mental illness has traditionally focused on most intently: class and race, age and gender, marriage and work. Intrigu-

---

RONALD C. KESSLER AND SHANYANG ZHAO • Department of Health Care Policy, Harvard Medical School, Boston, Massachusetts 02115.

Handbook of the Sociology of Mental Health, edited by Carol S. Aneshensel and Jo C. Phelan. Kluwer Academic/ Plenum Publishers, New York, 1999.

ing patterns have been found and continue to be explored in all these areas. These patterns provide hints as to the ways in which social structure influences the distribution, manifestation, recognition, labeling, and societal responses to mental illness. These hints are the raw materials used by sociologists to develop, refine, and empirically test theories about the social antecedents and consequences of mental illness. The present chapter sets the stage for those later in the section by providing an overview of current knowledge about descriptive psychiatric epidemiology. We begin with a historical overview and then present recent statistics on the prevalence and sociodemographic correlates of mental illness.

HISTORICAL OVERVIEW

Although descriptive studies comparing admission to and discharge rates from asylums were carried out as early as the seventeenth century, it was not until the early nineteenth century that studies began to appear that linked social structure to individual illness outcomes (Hunter & Macalpine, 1963). The latter consistently documented associations that were interpreted as showing that environmental stresses, especially those associated with poverty, can lead to psychiatric disorders. For example, in one of the best known of these early studies, Burrows (1820) documented a time series association between admission rates to British mental asylums and crop failures, and argued that this association showed financial adversity to be a cause of insanity. Later in the century, in the most famous psychiatric epidemiological study carried out in nineteenth-century America, Jarvis (1855) documented a relationship between poverty and insanity in the 1850 Massachusetts Census and interpreted this association as being due to the stresses of poverty.

Research using archival statistics continued to be the mainstay of descriptive psychiatric epidemiology up to the middle of the twentieth century. Important sociological studies in this tradition included Durkheim's (1951) famous study of suicide, the work of Faris and Dunham (1939) on the social ecology of schizophrenia, and the Hollingshead and Redlich (1958) study of social class and mental illness. These classic studies set the agenda for much of the current work reviewed in this section of the handbook.

Most of these early studies were hampered by the fact that they focused on archival data, which confounded information about help seeking and labeling with information about illness prevalence. In the few cases where population data were used rather than treatment statistics, such as the Jarvis study, there existed concerns about the accuracy of case assessment. Indeed, the initial data collected by the Massachusetts census takers for Jarvis's study were so clearly biased by underreporting that Jarvis had to carry out a second census of over 1,700 physicians, clergy, and other key informants to identify the insane people in their communities. This key-informant method continued to be the main approach to studying the population prevalence of psychiatric disorders until the end of World War II. Although this method was useful in avoiding the help-seeking biases associated with treatment studies and the concealment biases associated with self-report studies, key informants tended to miss people whose disorders were characterized more by private distress than public acting out. This approach led to an underestimation of disorder overall as well as a distorted picture of disorders being much more prevalent among men than women.

The end of World War II brought with it a growing appreciation of these methodological problems as well as a growing concern about the prevalence of mental illness. This concern was heightened by the fact that many Selective Service recruits for World War II were found to suffer from emotional disorders and to return from the war with what is now known as posttraumatic stress disorder. One response was the initiation of a number of local and national surveys of psychiatric disorders based on direct interviews with representative community samples.

The earliest of these postwar surveys were either carried out by clinicians or used lay interview data in combination with record data as input used in clinician evaluations of caseness (e.g., Leighton, 1959; Srole, Langer, Michael, Opler, & Rennie, 1962). In later studies, clinician judgment was abandoned in favor of less expensive self-report symptom rating scales that assigned each respondent a score on a continuous dimension of nonspecific psychological distress (e.g., Gurin, Veroff, & Feld, 1960). Controversy surrounded the use of these rating scales from the start, focusing on such things as item bias, insensitivity, and restriction of symptom coverage (e.g., Dohrenwend & Dohrenwend, 1965; Seiler, 1973). Nonetheless, these measures continued to be the mainstay of community psychiatric epidemiology through the 1970s.

There were three factors that accounted for the attraction of symptom rating scales in these studies. First, these scales were much less expensive to administer than clinician-based interviews. Second, as compared to dichotomous clinician caseness judgments, continuous measures of distress dealt directly with the actual constellations of signs and symptoms that existed in the population, as distinct from the classification schemes imposed on these constellations by the psychiatrists who created the official diagnoses of the *Diagnostic and Statistical Manual of Mental Disorders* (DSM) of the American Psychiatric Association (APA). Third, the clinician-based diagnostic interviews available during this period of time did not have good psychometric properties when administered in community samples (Dohrenwend, Yager, Egri, & Mendelsohn, 1978).

However, there were also disadvantages of working with rating scales. Perhaps the most important of these was that there was nothing in these measures themselves that allowed researchers to discriminate between people who did and did not have clinically significant psychiatric problems. This differentiation was less important to social scientists, whose main concern was characterizing the range of distress associated with structural variations, than to clinicians and social policy analysts who wanted to make decisions regarding such things as the number of people in need of mental health services. A division consequently arose within the field of psychiatric epidemiology that lingers to this day, with sociologists focusing much of their research on studies of dimensional distress, and psychiatric epidemiologists focusing their research on studies of dichotomous caseness designations.

A middle ground between these two positions was sought by some researchers who developed rules for classifying people with scores above a certain threshold of distress scales as psychiatric "cases" (e.g., Radloff, 1977) and studied both continuous and dichotomous outcomes. The precise cutpoints used in this research were usually based on statistical analyses that attempted to discriminate optimally between the scores of patients in psychiatric treatment and those of people in a community sample. However, as noted earlier, considerable controversy surrounded the decision of exactly where to specify cutpoints. Dichotomous diagnostic measures allowed this sort of discrimination to be made directly, based on an evaluation of diagnostic criteria, but these interviews were not precise due to lack of agreement on appropriate research diagnostic criteria and absence of valid instruments for carrying out research diagnostic interviews.

It was not until the late 1970s that the field was able to move beyond this limitation with the establishment of clear research diagnostic criteria (Feighner, Robins, & Guze, 1972) and the development of systematic research diagnostic interviews aimed at operationalizing these criteria (Endicott & Spitzer, 1978). The early interviews of this type required administration by clinicians, which yielded rich data but limited their use in epidemiological surveys because of the high costs associated with large-scale use of clinicians as interviewers. The majority of interviewers in these studies were clinical social workers. In light of the high costs and logistical complications of mounting a large field operation using professionals of this sort as interviewers, it is unsurprising that only a handful of such studies were carried out and that these studies were either quite small (e.g., Weissman & Myers, 1978), based on samples that were not representative of the general population (e.g., Kendler, Neale, Kessler, Heath, & Eaves, 1992), or were carried on outside the United States in countries where the cost of clinician interviewing was much lower (e.g., Dohrenwend, Levav, Shrout, & Schwartz, 1992).

Two responses to this situation occurred in the late 1970s. The first was the refinement of two-stage screening methods in which an inexpensive first-stage screening scale could be administered by a lay interviewer to a large community sample and followed with more expensive second-stage, clinician-administered interviews for the subsample of initial respondents who screened positive, plus a small subsample of those who screened negative (Newman, Shrout, & Bland, 1990). The hope was that two-stage screening would substantially reduce the costs of conducting clinician-administered community epidemiological surveys. However, problems associated with reduced response rates due to the requirement that respondents participate in two interviews and the increased administrative costs associated with logistical complications in this design prevented it from being used widely in community surveys, although it was, and continues to be, used in surveys of captive populations, such as schoolchildren in classrooms.

The second response was the development of research diagnostic interviews that could be administered by lay interviewers. The first instrument of this type was the Diagnostic Interview Schedule (DIS; Robins, Helzer, Croughan, & Ratliff, 1981), which was developed with support from the National Institute of Mental Health (NIMH) for use in the Epidemiologic Catchment Area (ECA) study (Robins & Regier, 1991). Several other interviews, most of them based on the DIS, have subsequently been developed. The most widely used of these is the World Health Organization's Composite International Diagnostic Interview (CIDI; WHO, 1990).

The remainder of this chapter provides a selective overview of the results regarding the descriptive epidemiology of psychiatric disorders in the United States, based on recent surveys that have used the DIS or CIDI. The focus is on the prevalence of dichotomously defined disorders as set forth in the DSM of the APA. Although a number of versions of the DSM classification scheme exist, most of the results reported here are based on the revised third edition (DSM-III-R: American Psychiatric Association, 1987), because this is the system that has been the basis for most recent general population research on the prevalence of psychiatric disorders.

It is important to recognize that there is an inherent ambiguity in making the dichotomous decision that is required in the DSM to define some people as "cases" and others as "noncases." This ambiguity is recognized by the clinicians who are involved in work to establish diagnostic criteria (Frances, Widiger, & Fyer, 1990). In some ways, this ambiguity is not terribly different from the situation in areas of physical medicine where yes–no treatment decisions have to be made based on continuous data, such as the decision of where to draw the line in blood pressure readings to define hypertension. Decisions of this sort are usually made on the basis of actuarial evidence regarding subsequent risk of some fairly well-defined outcome (e.g., stroke) associated with the continuous measure, but there is certainly no expectation that all of the people on one side of the line will experience the outcome or that none on the other side of the line will do so. However, the situation is more difficult in the area of psychiatric assessment because there are no relatively unequivocal dichotomous outcomes equivalent to having a heart attack or stroke that can be used as a gold standard. Nonetheless, despite this ambiguity, it is necessary for social policy purposes to make dichotomous diagnostic distinctions of this sort. That is why we do so here.

Data Sources

The need for general population data on the prevalence of mental illness was recognized two decades ago in the report of President Carter's Commission on Mental Health and Illness (President's Commission on Mental Health and Illness, 1978). It was impossible to undertake such a survey at that time due to the absence of a structured research diagnostic interview capable of generating reliable psychiatric diagnoses in general population samples. As noted earlier, the NIMH, recognizing this need, funded the development of the DIS, a research diagnostic interview that could be administered by trained interviewers who are not clinicians. The DIS was first used in the ECA study, a landmark effort in which over 20,000 respondents were interviewed in a series of five community epidemiological surveys (Robins & Regier, 1991; see Chapter 26 this volume). The ECA has been the main source of data in the United States on the prevalence of psychiatric disorders and utilization of services for these disorders for the past decade (Bourdon, Rae, Locke, Narrow, & Regier, 1992; Regier, Narrow, Rae, Manderscheid, Lock, & Goodwin, 1993; Robins, Locke, & Regier, 1991) and is a major source of data for the review presented in this chapter.

General population reliability and validity studies of the DIS (Anthony et al., 1985; Helzer et al., 1985) showed generally low agreement between DIS classifications and the classifications independently made by clinical reinterviews. However, these validity problems were found to be concentrated mong respondents who either fell just short of meeting criteria or barely met criteria, with the errors due to false positives and false negatives tending to balance out to produce fairly consistent total population prevalence estimates (Robins, 1985). Although this observation provides no assurance that the different errors are counterbalanced in all important segments of the population (Dohrenwend, 1995), the documentation that this is true in the population as a whole suggests that the ECA results yield useful overall prevalence data.

The ECA Study was carried out in five metropolitan areas in the United States. The results consequently tell us nothing about the 20% of the United States population that live in rural areas. This problem was subsequently addressed when the NIMH funded the National Comorbidity Survey (NCS; Kessler, McGonagle, Zhao, et al., 1994), a household survey of over 8,000 respondents, ranging in age from 15–54 that was carried out in a widely dispersed (174 counties in 34 states) sample designed to be representative of the entire United States. The NCS interview used a modified version of the DIS known as the CIDI (Robins et al., 1988). The CIDI expanded the DIS to include diagnoses based on DSM-III-R criteria. WHO field trials of the CIDI have documented adequate reliability and validity for all diagnoses (for a review, see Wittchen, 1994). However, it is important to recognize that most of the WHO field trials were carried out in clinical samples. Previous research has shown that the estimated accuracy of diagnostic interviews is greater in clinical samples than in general population samples (Dohrenwend et al., 1978). Therefore, the same caution regarding diagnostic accuracy, as noted earlier in the discussion of the ECA, is needed in interpreting the results of the NCS.

A final point regarding data sources that needs to be mentioned here concerns diagnostic coverage. Almost all of the diagnoses are Axis I disorders in the DSM-III and DSM-III-R diagnostic systems. Not all Axis I disorders are covered in these surveys. However, the most commonly assessed Axis I disorders are Mood Disorders (Major Depression, Dysthymia, Mania), Anxiety Disorders (Generalized Anxiety Disorder, Panic Disorder, Phobia, Obsessive–Compulsive Disorder, Posttraumatic Stress Disorder), Addictive Disorders (Alcohol Abuse and Dependence, Drug Abuse and Dependence), and Nonaffective Psychoses (Schizophrenia, Schizophreniform Disorder, Schizoaffective Disorder, Delusional Disorder, Brief Psychotic Reaction).

Axis II disorders, which include personality disorders and mental retardation, are generally not covered, although Antisocial Personality Disorder (ASPD) and some measures of cognitive impairment are often assessed. The absence of information on personality disorders other than ASPD is a major omission but was necessitated by the fact that valid structured diagnostic interview methods to assess personality disorders did not exist at the time these surveys were carried out.

This situation is changing rapidly, however, as several groups are working to develop measures of personality disorders that are appropriate for use in general population surveys (e.g., Lenzenweger, Loranger, Korfine, & Neff, 1997; Pilkonis et al., 1995) and we can anticipate, based on this work, that future large-scale epidemiological surveys will include comprehensive evaluations of personality disorders. For now, though, our review of evidence regarding the prevalence of personality disorders other than ASPD has to rely on the results of a small number of surveys from around the world that have been carried out using one of the recently developed assessment methods.

LIFETIME AND RECENT PREVALENCES OF AXIS I DSM-III-R DISORDERS

We focus on results from the NCS because this is the only nationally representative survey in the United States to have assessed the prevalences of a broad range of DSM-III-R disorders. The results in Table 7.1 show prevalence estimates for the 15 lifetime and 12-month disorders assessed in the core NCS interview. Lifetime prevalence is the proportion of the sample that ever experienced an episode of the disorder, whereas 12-month prevalence is the proportion reporting an episode of the disorder in the 12 months prior to the interview.

As shown in Table 7.1, the most common psychiatric disorder assessed in the NCS is major depression. However, in terms of broad classes of disorder, addictive disorders and anxiety disorders are somewhat more prevalent than mood disorders. Approximately one in every four respondents reported a lifetime history of at least one addictive disorder, and a similar number reported a lifetime history of at least one anxiety disorder. Approximately one in every five respondents reported a lifetime history of at least one mood disorder. Anxiety disorders, as a group, were considerably more likely to occur in the 12 months prior to interview than either addictive disorders or mood disorders, suggesting that anxiety disorders are more chronic than either addictive disorders or mood disorders. The prevalence of other NCS disorders is much lower. As shown in the last row of Table 7.1, almost half of the sample reported a lifetime history of at least one disorder and one in three had at least one disorder in the preceeding year.

Although there is no meaningful sex difference in the overall prevalence, there are sex differences for specific disorders. Consistent with previous research (Bourdon et al., 1992; Robins et al., 1981, 1991), men are much more likely to have addictive disorders and

Table 7.1. Lifetime and 12-Month Prevalences of Psychiatric Disorders, NCS[a]

	Total				Male				Female			
	Lifetime		12-month		Lifetime		12-month		Lifetime		12-month	
	%	(se)	%	(se)	%	(se)[b]	%	(se)	%	(se)	%	(se)
I. Mood disorders												
Major depression	17.1	(0.7)	10.3	(0.6)	12.7	(0.9)	7.7	(0.8)	21.3	(0.9)	12.9	(0.8)
Dysthymia	6.4	(0.4)	2.5	(0.2)	4.8	(0.4)	2.1	(0.3)	8.0	(0.6)	3.0	(0.4)
Mania	1.6	(0.3)	1.3	(0.2)	1.6	(0.3)	1.4	(0.3)	1.7	(0.3)	1.3	(0.3)
Any mood disorder	*19.3*	*(0.7)*	*11.3*	*(0.7)*	*14.7*	*(0.8)*	*8.5*	*(0.8)*	*23.9*	*(0.9)*	*14.0*	*(0.9)*
II. Anxiety disorders												
Generalized anxiety disorder	5.1	(0.3)	3.1	(0.3)	3.6	(0.5)	2.0	(0.3)	6.6	(0.5)	4.3	(0.4)
Panic disorder	3.5	(0.3)	2.3	(0.3)	2.0	(0.3)	1.3	(0.3)	5.0	(1.4)	3.2	(0.4)
Social phobia	9.1	(0.7)	7.9	(0.4)	11.1	(0.8)	6.6	(0.4)	15.5	(1.0)	9.1	(0.7)
Simple phobia	13.2	(0.6)	8.8	(0.5)	6.7	(0.5)	4.4	(0.5)	15.7	(1.1)	13.2	(0.9)
Agoraphobia	3.8	(0.4)	2.8	(0.3)	3.5	(0.4)	1.7	(0.3)	7.0	(0.6)	3.8	(0.4)
Posttraumatic stress disorder	5.4	(0.5)	3.9	(0.4)	4.8	(0.6)	2.3	(0.3)	10.1	(0.8)	5.4	(0.7)
Any anxiety disorder	*24.7*	*(0.9)*	*19.3*	*(0.8)*	*22.6*	*(1.2)*	*13.0*	*(0.7)*	*34.3*	*(1.8)*	*25.0*	*(1.5)*
III. Addictive disorders												
Alcohol abuse	9.4	(0.5)	2.5	(0.2)	12.5	(0.8)	3.4	(0.4)	6.4	(0.6)	1.6	(0.2)
Alcohol dependence	14.1	(0.7)	7.2	(0.5)	20.1	(1.0)	10.7	(0.9)	8.2	(0.7)	3.7	(0.4)
Illicit drug abuse	4.4	(0.3)	0.8	(0.1)	5.4	(0.5)	1.3	(0.2)	3.5	(0.4)	0.3	(0.1)
Illicit drug dependence	7.5	(0.4)	2.8	(0.3)	9.2	(0.7)	3.8	(0.4)	5.9	(0.5)	1.9	(0.3)
Any addictive disorder	*26.6*	*(1.0)*	*11.3*	*(0.5)*	*35.4*	*(1.2)*	*16.1*	*(0.7)*	*17.9*	*(1.1)*	*6.6*	*(0.4)*
IV. Other disorders												
Antisocialp Personality	2.8	(0.2)	—	—	4.8	(0.5)	—	—	1.0	(0.2)	—	—
Nonaffective psychosis[c]	0.5	(0.1)	0.3	(0.1)	0.3	(0.1)	0.2	(0.1)	0.7	(0.2)	0.4	(0.1)
V. Any NCS disorder	*49.7*	*(1.2)*	*30.9*	*(1.0)*	*51.2*	*(1.6)*	*29.4*	*(1.0)*	*48.5*	*(2.0)*	*32.0*	*(1.6)*

[a]The prevalence estimates are presented without exclusions for DSM-III-R hierarchy rules.
[b]se = standard error
[c]Nonaffective psychosis (NAP) = schizophrenia, schizophreniform disorder, schizoaffective disorder, delusional disorder, and atypical psychosis. It is important to note that the diagnosis of NAP was based on clinical reinterviews using the SCID rather than on the lay CIDI interviews.
Sources: Modified from Kessler, McGonagle, Zhao, et al. (1994) and Kessler, Abelson, & Zhao (1998). Copyright 1994, 1998 by Cambridge University Press. All disorders are operationalized using DSM-III-R criteria ignoring diagnostic hierarchy rules. Mania has been redefined based on methodological refinements described by Kessler, Rubinow, Holmes, Abelson and Zhao (1997). Agoraphobia is defined here without panic; it was defined with or without panic in Kessler, McGonagle, Zhao, et al. (1994a). They did not report on posttraumatic stress disorder because it was assessed only in the Part II NCS sample. Nonaffective psychosis is redefined based on methodological refinements described by Kendler et al. (1996). As documented elsewhere (Kendler, Gallagher, Abelson, & Kessler, 1996), the prevalence estimate for NAP based on the CIDI was considerably higher but was found to have low validity when judged in comparison to the clinical reappraisals.

ASPD than women, whereas women are much more likely than men to have mood disorders (with the exception of mania, for which there is no sex difference) and anxiety disorders. The data also show, consistent with a trend found in the ECA (Keith, Regier, & Rae, 1991), that women in the general population are more likely to have nonaffective psychoses than men.

It is instructive to compare these NCS results with the results of the earlier ECA study.

As noted earlier, the ECA was carried out in five communities around the country, and the results were subsequently combined and weighted to the population distribution of the United States on the cross-classification of age, sex, and race in an effort to make national estimates (Regier et al., 1993). To the extent that this poststratification succeeded in adjusting for the lack of representativeness of the local samples, it should be possible to make valid comparisons between the ECA and NCS results. A limitation is that the ECA was based on an unrestricted age range of adults, whereas the NCS included only persons 15–54 years of age. Another limitation is that the ECA diagnoses were based on DSM-III criteria (American Psychiatric Association, 1980), but the NCS diagnoses were based on DSM-III-R criteria (American Psychiatric Association, 1987). These two diagnostic systems differ substantially in a number of respects. Furthermore, the NCS, but not the ECA, used special motivation and memory probes to enhance recall and reporting of lifetime disorder. In order to reconcile these differences, collaborative ECA–NCS comparative analyses have been carried out in which subsamples in the 18–54 age range in both samples were compared using common measures that operationalized DSM-III criteria (which can be reconstructed from the NCS data, although DSM-III-R criteria cannot be reconstructed from the ECA data) and the combined two waves of ECA data to approximate the effects of the NCS memory probes. Although some discrepancies were found, especially in higher rates of depression and social phobia in the NCS than ECA, the overall pattern was one of considerable consistency between the two surveys, both in the prevalence of individual disorders and in overall prevalence of having any disorder (Regier et al., 1998).

SERIOUS MENTAL ILLNESS

Mental illnesses, like physical illnesses, vary in their severity. Several classification schemes have been developed to make distinctions among mental disorders based on seriousness. For example, the NIMH's National Advisory Mental Health Council (1993) defined "severe and persistent mental illness" (SPMI) as including manic–depressive disorder, nonaffective psychosis, autism, and severe forms of major depression, panic disorder, and obsessive–compulsive disorder. A broader definition of "serious mental illness" (SMI) was proposed in Public Law 102-321 to include mental illnesses that "substantially interfere" with "one or more major life activities." Addictive disorders are not included in either of these definitions.

The 12-month prevalences of SPMI and SMI were estimated in a combined analysis of the ECA and NCS data projected to the total US population using DSM-III-R criteria (Kessler, Berglund, et al., 1996). Results are reported in Figure 7.1. The prevalences of SPMI and SMI are estimated at 2.6% and 5.4%, respectively, compared to a prevalence of 23.9% for any DSM-III-R mental disorder. Although a substantial proportion of the population has experienced a mental disorder, the major burden of mental illness is concentrated in a fairly small part of the population.

PERSONALITY DISORDERS

Although the concept of personality disorder can be traced back to the beginnings of nineteenth-century psychiatry (for a review, see Tyrer, Casey & Ferguson, 1991), it has only recently become the subject of epidemiological research, because standardized diagnostic

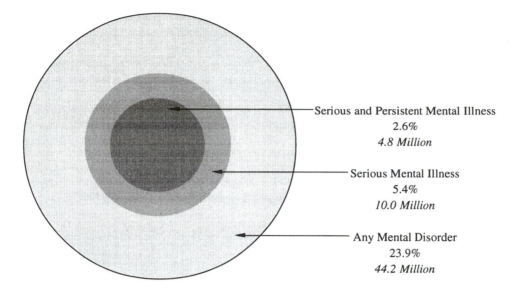

Serious and Persistent Mental Illness
2.6%
4.8 Million

Serious Mental Illness
5.4%
10.0 Million

Any Mental Disorder
23.9%
44.2 Million

FIGURE 7.1. One-year prevalence of mental illness and affected population. Adults, aged 18–54 DSM-III-R criteria. Pooled Baltimore ECA and NCS Data. Excludes homeless people and residents of institutions such as nursing homes, prisons, and long-term-care facilities; an additional estimated 2.2 million persons with SMI, for 12.2 million in total population. *Source:* Adapted from Kessler & Zhao (in press). Copyright 1999 by Cambridge University Press. Reprinted with permission of Cambridge University Press.

criteria only became available for the first time in the WHO's International Classifications of Diseases (ICD; WHO, 1990) and DSM-III (American Psychiatric Association, 1980). Unfortunately, it has proven to be difficult to develop reliable and valid measures of personality disorders (Perry, 1992; Zimmerman, 1994). Furthermore, there are a number of differences between the ICD and DSM systems (Blashfield, 1991), as well as substantial changes within each of these systems in recent revisions (Morey, 1988) that add to the complexity of synthesizing the available epidemiological evidence. Both the ICD and DSM classification schemes recognize three broad clusters of personality disorder, each defined by a series of traits that must be manifest habitually in a number of life domains to qualify as a disorder. These three are the odd (e.g., paranoid or schizoid personality disorders), dramatic (e.g., histrionic or borderline personality disorders), and anxious (e.g., avoidant or dependent personality disorders) clusters.

A recent comprehensive international review found only four fairly small community studies that assessed personality disorders in all three of these clusters using valid assessment methods (de Girolamo & Reich, 1993). These four studies yielded very consistent lifetime prevalence estimates for overall personality disorders ranging from 10.3% to 13.5%. Caution is needed in interpreting these results, however, because prevalence estimates vary substantially depending on whether full diagnostic criteria for personality disorders are required, as in these surveys, or whether respondents are counted if they manifest some traits of personality disorders on dimensional scales (Kass, 1985).

There have also been a number of community surveys that included assessments of one or more specific personality disorders without attempting to assess the full range of personality disturbances. The most commonly studied by far has been ASPD, a disorder characterized by persistent evidence of "irresponsible and antisocial behavior beginning in childhood or early adolescence and continuing into adulthood" (American Psychiatric Association, 1987). Irritability, aggressiveness, persistent reckless behavior, promiscuity, and the absence of remorse about the effects of behavior on others are cardinal features of ASPD. A number of epidemiological surveys, including both the ECA and NCS, have found lifetime prevalences of ASPD averaging about 1% among women and 4–5% among men (De Girolamo & Reich, 1993; Merikangas, 1989). Much less is known about the prevalences of other individual personality disorders, although the available evidence suggests that none of them alone has a prevalence greater than about 2% in the general population (De Girolamo & Reich, 1993; Merikangas, 1989; Weissman, 1993).

COMORBIDITY

An important aspect of the results in Table 7.1 is that the sum of the individual prevalence estimates across the disorders in each column consistently exceeds the prevalence of having any disorder in the last row. This pattern means that there is a good deal of comorbidity among these disorders. This comorbidity is quite important for understanding the distribution of psychiatric disorders in the United States. Although it is beyond the scope of this chapter to delve into the many different types of comorbidity that exist in the population (see Kessler, 1995), it is important to review some aggregate results.

The results in Table 7.2 (Kessler, McGonagle, Zhao, 1994), document the fact that comorbidity is very important in understanding the distribution of psychiatric disorders in the United States. The four rows represent the number of lifetime disorders reported by respondents. The set of disorders considered here is somewhat smaller than in Table 7.1, which accounts for the fact that 52% of respondents are estimated as never having had any NCS/DSM-III-R disorder, (or 48% as having one or more such disorders which is slightly less than the 50% in Table 7.1). Only 21% of all the lifetime disorders occurred to respondents with a lifetime history of just one disorder, which means that the vast majority of lifetime disorders (79%) are comorbid disorders. Furthermore, an even greater proportion of 12-month disorders occurred in respondents with a lifetime history of comorbidity. Close to six out of every ten (58.9%) disorders in the past year, and nearly nine out of ten (89.5%) severe disorders during this time, occurred to the 14% of the sample having a lifetime

Table 7.2. Lifetime and 12-Month Psychiatric Disorders among Persons with Lifetime Comorbidity, NCS

Number of lifetime disorders	Proportion of sample %	(se)[b]	Proportion of lifetime disorders %	(se)	Proportion of 12-month disorders %	(se)	Proportion of respondents with severe 12-month disorders[a] %	(se)
0	52.0	(1.1)	—	—	—	—	—	—
1	21.0	(0.6)	20.6	(0.6)	17.4	(0.8)	2.6	(1.7)
2	13.0	(0.5)	25.5	(1.0)	23.1	(1.0)	7.9	(2.1)
3 or more	14.0	(0.7)	53.9	(2.7)	58.9	(1.8)	89.5	(2.8)

[a]Severe 12-month disorders = active mania, NAP, or active disorders of other types that either required hospitalization or created severe role impairment.
[b]se = standard error
Sources. Modified from Kessler, McGonagle, Zhao, et al. (1994); Kessler, Abelson, & Zhao (1998). Copyright 1994, 1998 by Cambridge University Press. Reprinted with permission of Cambridge University Press.

history of three or more disorders. These results show that although a history of some psychiatric disorder is quite common among the adult population of the United States, the major burden of psychiatric disorder is concentrated in a group of highly comorbid people who constitute about one-sixth of the population.

Given this evidence, it is of some interest to learn more about detailed patterns of comorbidity. The ECA investigators were the first to examine this in a community sample, documenting the fact that over 54% of ECA respondents with a lifetime history of at least one disorder had a second disorder as well (Robins et al., 1991). Compared to respondents with no mental disorder, those with a lifetime history of at least one mental disorder had relative-odds of 2.3 of having a lifetime history of alcohol abuse or dependence and a relative-odds of 4.5 of some other drug use disorder (Regier et al., 1990). Similar results were found in the NCS. The results in Table 7.3 show the proportion of people with specific lifetime disorders who reported at least one other lifetime disorder. As shown, lifetime comorbidity is the norm, with percentages ranging from a low of 62.1% for alcohol abuse to a high of 99.4% for mania. The average proportion of comorbidity among disorders is 86.6%. This does not mean that 86.6% of people with one or more lifetime disorders are comorbid, though, because those with comorbidity are counted multiple times in the table. Instead, 59.8% of the people who ever had one of the disorders considered in the NCS also had one or more other disorders.

Table 7.3. Distribution of Lifetime Psychiatric Comorbidity by Disorder, NCS

	Proportion with lifetime comorbidity among those having the disorder	
	%	(se)
I. Mood disorders		
Major depression	83.1	(2.2)
Dysthymia	91.3	(1.8)
Mania	99.4	(0.6)
Any mood disorder	82.2	(2.1)
II. Anxiety Disorders		
Generalized anxiety disorder	91.3	(1.5)
Panic disorder	92.2	(1.9)
Social phobia	81.0	(1.5)
Simple phobia	83.4	(1.5)
Agoraphobia	87.3	(2.9)
Posttraumatic stress disorder	81.0	(3.3)
Any anxiety disorder	74.1	(1.5)
III. Addictive disorders		
Alcohol abuse	62.1	(2.6)
Alcohol dependence	80.6	(2.4)
Illicit drug abuse	89.0	(2.6)
Illicit drug dependence	95.7	(2.0)
Any addictive disorder	73.3	(1.3)
IV. Other disorders		
Antisocial personality	96.2	(1.0)
Nonaffective psychosis	93.0	(4.4)
V. Any NCS disorder	59.8	(1.2)

Source. Modified from Kessler, McGonagle, Zhao, et al. (1994); Kessler, Abelson, & Zhao (1998). Copyright 1994, 1998 by Cambridge University Press. Reprinted with the permission of Cambridge University Press.

AGE OF ONSET

The ECA and NCS studies both collected retrospective data on the age of first onset of each lifetime disorder. These studies were consistent in showing that simple and social phobia have a much earlier age of onset than the other disorders considered here (Burke, Burke, Rae, & Regier, 1991; Magee, Eaton, Wittchen, McGonagle, & Kessler, 1996), with simple phobia often beginning during middle or late childhood and social phobia during late childhood or early adolescence. Substance abuse was found to have a typical age of onset during the late teens or early 20s. A substantial proportion of people with lifetime major depression and dysthymia reported that their first episode occurred prior to the age of 20. Some other disorders, such as generalized anxiety disorder and mania, had a later age of onset, but the most striking overall impression from the data as a whole is that most psychiatric disorders have first onsets quite early in people's lives.

SOCIODEMOGRAPHIC CORRELATES

Bivariate, cross-sectional sociodemographic associations are reported for groupings of disorders in Table 7.4 (lifetime) and Table 7.5 (12-month). We also include three or more disorders as an outcome variable in Tables 7.4 and 7.5, because the majority of disorders, and the vast majority of severe disorders, occur to people with a history of three or more disorders. Associations are shown in the form of odds ratios (ORs) with 95% confidence intervals. The focus is on the same set of sociodemographic factors that are considered in subsequent chapters in this section of the handbook: class, race, age, gender, marriage, and work. We also look at urban–rural differences.

Social Class

Although many previous studies have documented inverse relationships between socio-economic status (SES) and mental illness (e.g., Bruce, Takeuchi, & Leaf, 1991; Canino et al., 1987; Holzer et al, 1986; Myers, 1984; Robins et al., 1991; Stansfeld & Marmot, 1992), few studies have studied class in the Marxian sense of the term. NCS analyses show no strong associations between social class, as indexed by ownership of the means of production, and any of the psychiatric outcomes considered here, after controlling for income and education. However, as shown in Tables 7.4 and 7.5, we do find strong associations with SES, with the rates of almost all disorders declining monotonically with income and with education. The ORs for education are somewhat more variable than those for income, but the general pattern is still one of decline from the lowest to highest education groups. One noteworthy exception is that lifetime substance use disorder is significantly higher in the *middle* education group than among those with either the least or most education. The significant ORs for income and education are consistently larger for 12-month than lifetime prevalence, which implies that SES is associated not only with onset but also with course of disorder. Finally, there is a consistent tendency for SES to be more power-fully related to anxiety disorders than mood disorders, suggesting indirectly that the resources associated with SES are more protective against worries and fears than sadness. We are unaware of any previous research on this issue, although this consistent pattern in our data suggests that this might be a fruitful area for future investigation.

Table 7.4. Demographic Correlates of Lifetime Psychiatric Disorders, NCS

	Any affective		Any anxiety		Any substance		Any disorder		Three or more disorders	
	OR	(95% CI)	OR	(95% CI)	OR	(95% CI)	OR	(95% CI)	OR	(95% CI)
Income										
0–19,000	1.6	(1.2, 2.0)	2.0	(1.7, 2.4)	1.3	(1.1, 1.5)	1.5	(1.3, 1.8)	2.5	(1.9, 3.2)
20–34,000	1.2	(0.9, 1.6)	1.5	(1.2, 1.9)	1.1	(0.8, 1.4)	1.2	(1.0, 1.5)	1.7	(1.2, 2.4)
35–69,000	1.2	(0.9, 1.5)	1.5	(1.2, 1.9)	1.1	(0.8, 1.4)	1.2	(1.0, 1.5)	1.6	(1.1, 2.2)
> = 70,000	1.0	—	1.0	—	1.0	—	1.0	—	1.0	—
Education										
0–11	1.0	(0.8, 1.2)	1.9	(1.5, 2.3)	1.0	(0.8, 1.3)	1.2	(1.0, 1.4)	2.2	(1.6, 2.9)
12	1.0	(0.8, 1.2)	1.8	(1.4, 2.2)	1.3	(1.1, 1.5)	1.3	(1.1, 1.5)	2.1	(1.5, 2.9)
13–15	1.1	(0.9, 1.3)	1.4	(1.2, 1.8)	1.2	(1.0, 1.4)	1.2	(1.0, 1.4)	1.7	(1.3, 2.4)
> = 16	1.0	—	1.0	—	1.0	—	1.0	—	1.0	—
Race										
White	1.0	—	1.0	—	1.0	—	1.0	—	1.0	—
Black	0.6	(0.5, 0.9)	0.8	(0.6, 1.0)	0.4	(0.3, 0.5)	0.5	(0.4, 0.6)	0.7	(0.5, 1.0)
Hispanic	1.0	(0.7, 1.3)	0.9	(0.7, 1.2)	0.8	(0.6, 1.0)	0.9	(0.7, 1.1)	1.0	(0.7, 1.4)
Age										
15–24	0.9	(0.7, 1.1)	1.1	(0.9, 1.4)	1.4	(1.0, 1.8)	1.2	(0.9, 1.4)	1.2	(0.9, 1.6)
25–34	1.0	(0.8, 1.2)	1.1	(0.9, 1.4)	2.0	(1.5, 2.6)	1.4	(1.1, 1.7)	1.5	(1.1, 2.0)
35–44	1.1	(0.8, 1.4)	1.1	(0.8, 1.3)	1.6	(1.3, 2.0)	1.2	(1.0, 1.5)	1.2	(0.9, 1.6)
45–54	1.0	—	1.0	—	1.0	—	1.0	—	1.0	—
Gender										
Male	1.0	—	1.0	—	1.0	—	1.0	—	1.0	—
Female	1.8	(1.6, 2.1)	1.9	(1.6, 2.2)	0.4	(0.3, 0.5)	1.0	(0.8, 1.1)	1.2	(1.0, 1.5)
Marital status										
Never married	1.0	(0.8, 1.2)	0.9	(0.8, 1.0)	0.9	(0.7, 1.0)	0.9	(0.8, 1.1)	1.0	(0.8, 1.1)
Previously married	2.0	(1.7, 2.5)	1.4	(1.2, 1.8)	1.0	(0.8, 1.3)	1.4	(1.0, 1.9)	1.4	(1.1, 1.8)
Currently married	1.0	—	1.0	—	1.0	—	1.0	—	1.0	—
Employment										
Working	1.0	—	1.0	—	1.0	—	1.0	—	1.0	—
Homemaker	2.0	(1.6, 2.6)	3.2	(2.5, 4.1)	0.9	(0.7, 1.2)	2.2	(1.7, 2.9)	1.8	(1.3, 2.3)
Student	1.0	(0.8, 1.3)	1.2	(1.0, 1.5)	0.7	(0.6, 0.9)	1.1	(0.9, 1.3)	0.9	(0.8, 1.2)
Other	2.2	(1.6, 2.9)	2.1	(1.6, 2.8)	2.0	(1.5, 2.7)	2.5	(1.8, 3.5)	2.9	(2.2, 3.8)
Urbanicity										
Metro	1.3	(0.9, 1.8)	1.0	(0.7, 1.3)	1.1	(0.8, 1.5)	1.1	(0.8, 1.5)	1.2	(0.9, 1.7)
Urban	1.2	(0.9, 1.7)	1.0	(0.7, 1.4)	1.1	(0.8, 1.5)	1.1	(0.8, 1.5)	1.2	(0.8, 1.7)
Rural	1.0	—	1.0	—	1.0	—	1.0	—	1.0	—

Note. Results concerning ASPD exclude respondents ages 15–17 because the diagnosis requires that the respondent be at least 18 years of age.
Source. Modified from Kessler, McGonagle, Zhao, et al. (1994). Copyright 1994 by Cambridge University Press. Reprinted with the permission of Cambridge University Press.

Table 7.5. Demographic Correlates of 12-Month Psychiatric Disorders, NCS

	Any affective		Any anxiety		Any substance		Any disorder		3 or more disorders	
	OR	(95% CI)	OR	(95% CI)	OR	(95% CI)	OR	(95% CI)	OR	(95% CI)
Income										
0–19,000	1.7	(1.3, 2.3)	2.1	(1.6, 2.8)	1.9	(1.4, 2.7)	1.9	(1.5, 2.4)	3.4	(2.0, 5.8)
20–34,000	1.1	(0.8, 1.6)	1.6	(1.2, 2.1)	1.1	(0.8, 1.6)	1.2	(1.0, 1.6)	2.1	(1.2, 3.8)
35–69,000	1.0	(0.8, 1.4)	1.5	(1.2, 2.0)	1.1	(0.8, 1.6)	1.2	(0.9, 1.6)	1.7	(1.0, 2.7)
> = 70,000	1.0	—	1.0	—	1.0	—	1.0	—	1.0	—
Education										
0–11	1.8	(1.3, 2.4)	2.8	(2.3, 3.5)	2.1	(1.56, 2.8)	2.3	(1.9, 2.8)	3.8	(2.5, 5.8)
12	1.4	(1.0, 1.9)	2.1	(1.7, 2.7)	1.8	(1.4, 2.3)	1.8	(1.5, 2.2)	2.5	(1.7, 3.8)
13–15	1.4	(1.0, 1.8)	1.6	(1.2, 2.2)	1.7	(1.2, 2.4)	1.6	(1.3, 2.0)	2.1	(1.2, 3.6)
> = 16	1.0	—	1.0	—	1.0	—	1.0	—	1.0	—
Race										
White	1.0	—	1.0	—	1.0	—	1.0	—	1.0	—
Black	0.8	(0.5, 1.1)	0.9	(0.7, 1.3)	0.5	(0.4, 0.6)	0.7	(0.6, 0.9)	1.0	(0.5, 2.1)
Hispanic	1.4	(1.0, 1.9)	1.2	(0.9, 1.5)	1.0	(0.7, 1.5)	1.1	(0.9, 1.4)	1.9	(1.2, 2.8)
Age										
15–24	1.7	(1.1, 2.4)	1.4	(1.1, 1.8)	3.6	(2.3, 5.8)	2.1	(1.7, 2.6)	2.1	(1.2, 3.7)
25–34	1.3	(0.9, 2.0)	1.1	(0.9, 1.5)	2.6	(1.7, 4.1)	1.5	(1.2, 1.9)	1.7	(0.9, 3.2)
35–44	1.4	(0.9, 2.0)	1.0	(0.8, 1.3)	2.0	(1.3, 3.1)	1.2	(0.9, 1.6)	1.4	(0.8, 2.5)
45–54	1.0	—	1.0	—	1.0	—	1.0	—	1.0	—
Gender										
Male	1.0	—	1.0	—	1.0	—	1.0	—	1.0	—
Female	1.8	(1.4, 2.2)	2.2	(1.9, 2.6)	0.4	(0.3, 0.4)	1.2	(1.1, 1.3)	1.6	(1.2, 2.1)
Marital Status										
Never married	1.5	(1.3, 2.0)	1.1	(0.9, 1.3)	1.8	(1.5, 2.2)	1.5	(1.3, 1.6)	1.3	(1.0, 1.6)
Previously married	2.3	(1.7, 3.1)	1.4	(1.1, 1.8)	1.3	(1.0, 1.7)	1.5	(1.2, 1.8)	2.1	(1.5, 2.9)
Currently married	1.0	—	1.0	—	1.0	—	1.0	—	1.0	—
Employment										
Working	1.0	—	1.0	—	1.0	—	1.0	—	1.0	—
Homemaker	2.4	(1.8, 3.1)	3.2	(2.4, 4.2)	0.7	(0.5, 1.1)	2.4	(1.8, 3.1)	2.9	(1.9, 4.4)
Student	1.6	(1.2, 2.1)	1.6	(1.3, 2.1)	1.4	(1.0, 1.9)	1.7	(1.4, 2.0)	1.4	(1.0, 2.0)
Other	3.2	(2.3, 4.5)	2.4	(1.8, 3.2)	3.0	(2.4, 3.8)	3.3	(2.5, 4.4)	3.5	(2.5, 4.8)
Urbanicity										
Major metro	1.2	(0.8, 1.9)	1.0	(0.8, 1.4)	1.1	(0.8, 1.5)	1.1	(0.8, 1.5)	1.4	(1.0, 2.1)
Other urban	1.1	(0.7, 1.8)	1.2	(0.9, 1.6)	1.1	(0.8, 1.6)	1.1	(0.8, 1.6)	1.4	(1.0, 2.0)
Rural	1.0	—	1.0	—	1.0	—	1.0	—	1.0	—

Source. Modified from Kessler, McGonagle, Zhao, et al. (1994). Copyright 1994 by Cambridge University Press. Reprinted with the permission of Cambridge University Press.

Race

Blacks in the NCS have significantly lower prevalences of mood disorders, substance use disorders, and lifetime comorbidity than whites. There are no disorders for which either lifetime or 12-month prevalence is significantly higher among blacks than whites. More detailed analyses (not reported here) show that these effects cannot be explained by controlling for income and education. The lower prevalence of mood disorders is consistent with, but more pronounced than, the ECA finding of a slightly lower rate in the 30–64 year age range among blacks than whites (Weissman, Bruce, Leaf, Florio, & Holzer, 1991). The lower prevalence of substance use disorders among blacks is consistent with the ECA finding of higher prevalence of drug and alcohol abuse and dependence among young whites compared to young blacks (Anthony & Helzer, 1991; Helzer, Burnam & McEvoy, 1991). Our failure to find black–white differences in anxiety disorders (or, in more detailed analyses not reported here, in either panic disorder, simple phobia, or agoraphobia) is consistent with the ECA finding that blacks and whites have similar prevalences of panic disorder (Horwath, Johnson, & Hornig, 1993), but inconsistent with the ECA finding that blacks have nearly twice the lifetime prevalence of simple phobia and agoraphobia (Eaton, Dryman, & Weissman, 1991).

Hispanics in the NCS have significantly higher prevalences of mood disorders and active comorbidity than non-Hispanic whites. There are no disorders in which either lifetime or active prevalence is significantly lower among Hispanics than among non-Hispanic whites. The higher rate of mood disorders is inconsistent with the ECA, which found higher lifetime rates among whites and no difference in active prevalence (Helzer et al., 1991). The failure to find a white versus Hispanic difference in anxiety disorders is inconsistent with the ECA finding that Hispanics have significantly lower lifetime rates of panic disorder (Bruce et al., 1991). Furthermore, the NCS does not replicate the ECA finding that Hispanics have elevated rates of alcohol use disorders compared to whites (Anthony & Helzer, 1991).

Age

In the absence of extremely young age of onset, cohort effects, differential mortality, selection bias associated with age, and age-related differences in willingness to report symptoms, one would expect to find increasing lifetime prevalence of all disorders with age. However, the results in Table 7.4 show quite a different pattern, with the highest prevalences generally in the 25–34 year age group and declining prevalences at later ages. This pattern is broadly consistent with the results of other recent epidemiological surveys (Cross-National Collaborative Group, 1992; Robins & Regier, 1991) in documenting increasing psychopathology in more recent cohorts. The pattern is even more pronounced in Table 7.5, with 12-month disorders consistently most prevalent in the youngest cohort (ages 15–24) and generally declining monotonically with age.

There are a number of ways to interpret these results, but the most plausible *substantive* interpretation is that the prevalence of psychiatric disorders has increased in recent cohorts. A graphic representation of this cohort effect using retrospective age of onset reports is shown in Figure 7.2 in the form of cohort-specific Kaplan–Meier (1958) cumulative probability of onset curves for any NCS/DSM-III-R disorder. The curves show that the proportion of respondents who reported having at least one of these disorders by a particular

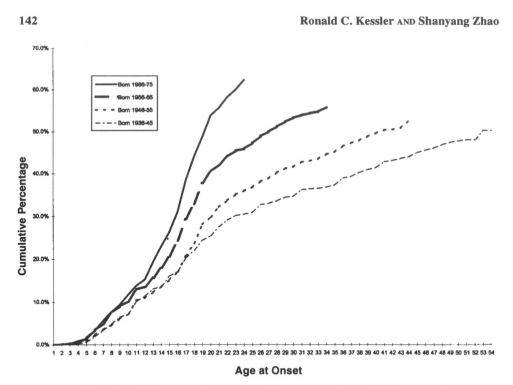

FIGURE 7.2. Cohort differences in the cumulative lifetime onset of any NCS/DSM-III-R disorder.

age is largest in the youngest NCS cohort and successively smaller in older cohorts. Disaggregated analyses show that these cohort effects are significant for most individual disorders (Blazer, Kessler, McGonagle, & Swartz, 1994; Magee et al., 1996; Warner, Kessler, Hughes, Anthony, & Nelson, 1995).

Caution is needed in interpreting these results to indicate a genuine increase in the prevalences of these disorders. *Methodological* interpretations are equally plausible, such as selective recall bias or differential attrition mortality associated with age. If the results are genuine, though, they are important for at least two reasons. First, they document that psychiatric disorders are a rapidly increasing public health problem. The dramatic increase in the prevalences of these disorders over the past few decades, coupled with the fact that many psychiatric disorders have an early age of onset, a chronic course, and serious role impairment, have led the World Health Organization to estimate that the societal costs of psychiatric disorders are among the highest of any illness category in the world (Murray & Lopez, 1996).

Second, these results are important because they indirectly speak to a hotly contested question of whether genetic or environmental factors are more important in accounting for the prevalence and distribution of psychiatric disorders. Twin studies have estimated that genetic factors explain a substantial part of the variance in liability to most commonly occurring psychiatric disorders (Kendler et al., 1995). Yet critics have argued that the assumptions used in these twin studies to estimate the contribution of genetic factors are implausible (Brown, 1997). The evidence of substantial cohort effects documented here argue against the genetic argument, because the genetic makeup of the population does not change so rapidly that it could explain increases in prevalence as dramatic as those shown in Figure 7.2. If these cohort effects are real, then changing environmental factors must be responsible.

Gender

As noted in the discussion of Table 7.2, the NCS data are consistent with previous epidemiological studies in finding that women have higher prevalences of mood disorders than men (with the exception of mania, for which there is no sex difference), anxiety disorders, and nonaffective psychoses (NAP), and that men have higher rates than women of substance use disorders and ASPD. Furthermore, we find that women have higher prevalences than men of both lifetime and 12-month comorbidity of three or more disorders. More detailed analyses reported elsewhere have also found that the gender differences in most disorders have decreased in recent cohorts. Men are beginning to catch up to women in rates of anxiety and depression (Kessler, McGonagle, Nelson, et al., 1994; Magee et al., 1996), while women are beginning to catch up to men in rates of addiction and ASPD (Warner et al., 1995). These changes strongly indicate that environmental factors are involved in these gender differences and that biological differences between men and women are not dominant influences.

Marital Status

Consistent with previous research (Kessler & Essex, 1982; Robins & Regier, 1991), the results in Tables 7.4 and 7.5 show that previously married people (separated, divorced, or widowed) have higher rates of most disorders than married people. This observation is especially true for depression. Never-married people, in comparison, do not have higher rates of lifetime disorder than married people, but they do have higher rates of past-year disorders, especially addictive disorders. An interesting distinction not shown in Table 7.5 is that these differences vary by gender and marital quality. There is a strong relationship between self-reported marital quality and the disorders considered. This relationship is significantly stronger among women, however, consistent with other evidence that marital quality is more important to the well-being of wives than husbands (Conger et al., 1993; McGonagle & Kessler, 1990). So important is marital quality for women, in fact, that the current mental health of married women in bad marriages is worse than that of divorced women. The opposite is true of men, though, in whom mental health is better among those in bad marriages than among the divorced.

Employment Status

The results in Table 7.4 show that workers and students have better lifetime mental health than homemakers and respondents in other occupational statuses (including the disabled, the unemployed, and the retired). The results in Table 7.5, in comparison, show that workers have better past-year mental health than people in all other occupational statuses. Homemakers have especially high rates of lifetime and recent anxiety disorder, whereas the unemployed, the disabled, and the retired as a group have especially high rates of recent mood and addictive disorder. More detailed results not reported in these tables show that employment is much more strongly related to the mental health of men than women, a result that is consistent with a great deal of previous sociological research on gender differences (Gove, 1978; Ross, Mirowsky, & Huber, 1983).

Urbanicity

Urbanicity is examined here at the county level by distinguishing major metropolitan counties, urbanized counties that are not in major metropolitan areas, and rural counties. The effects of urbanicity at the county level are generally not significant. The single exception is that residents of major metropolitan counties are more likely than residents of rural counties to have comorbidity in the 12 months prior to the interview (OR = 1.44). The coefficient comparing residents of other urbanized counties to residents of rural counties on the same outcome is very similar in magnitude (OR = 1.41) and significant at the .06 level, which means that it is the low rate of comorbidity in rural America rather than a high rate in major metropolitan counties that underlies this pattern. This one significant coefficient could have occurred by chance (given that 22 different comparisons were made, two urbanicity coefficients for each of 11 outcomes), although there is a general trend in the data for rural residents to have the lowest levels of disorder (in 10 of the 11 outcomes in Tables 7.4 and 7.5). It is noteworthy that other NCS analyses have shown that rates of treatment are considerably lower in rural than in urban areas (Kessler, Zhao, et al., 1999) despite the fact that disorder prevalences are not lower. The extent to which this pattern is due to lower access to services or to other objective or subjective barriers is not clear, but it is clear that the problem of unmet need for treatment appears greater in rural America than elsewhere in the country.

SOCIAL CONSEQUENCES

It is important to recognize that the previous associations documented between acquired social statuses (SES, marital status, and employment status) and psychiatric disorders could be due either to causal influences of the statuses (or their correlates) on the disorders, causal influences of the disorders (or their correlates) on the statuses, or some combination. As reviewed in chapters later in this section, most sociological research on psychiatric disorders has emphasized the importance of social factors as causes of mental illness. We know, for example, that job loss (Kessler, House, & Turner, 1987) and marital disruption (Aseltine & Kessler, 1993) can both provoke anxiety and depression. However, it is important to appreciate that psychiatric disorders can also have adverse effects on acquired social statuses.

A number of recent studies of this issue have documented that psychiatric disorders have substantial personal costs for individuals who experience them as well as for their families and communities in terms of both finances (Kessler, Foster, Saunders, & Stang, 1995) and role functioning (Rhode, Lewinsohn, & Seeley, 1990; Wells et al., 1989; Wohlfarth, van den Brink, Ormel, Koeter, & Oldehinkel, 1993). NCS analyses show that early-onset psychiatric disorders are strongly related to subsequent teen childbearing, school dropout, marital instability, and long-term financial adversity (Kessler, Berglund, et al., 1997; Kessler, & Forthofer, 1999; Kessler et al., 1995). These results document hidden societal costs of psychiatric disorders not only in the indirect sense of threats to our ability to maintain an educated and well-functioning citizenry and workforce, but also in the direct sense that the outcomes documented here are associated with increased use of entitlement programs, such as unemployment and welfare, that are paid for by all taxpayers. These costs need to be taken into consideration in policy evaluations of the societal cost–benefit ratio of providing mental health treatment irrespective of ability to pay compared to the costs of failing to do so. And these costs need to be taken into consideration before inter-preting significant associations between social statuses and psychiatric disorders as neces-sarily documenting a causal impact of the statuses on the disorders.

Another type of social cost involves workplace productivity. There is increasing aware-ness that people with psychiatric disorders have considerably more work loss days than others (Broadhead, Blazer, George, & Kit, 1990; Johnson, Weissman, & Klerman, 1992). Concerns have been raised that psychiatric disorders might also be related to workplace accidents and voluntary job leaving, both of which are very costly for employers. These considerations have led some commentators to argue that employer-sponsored health in-surance that offers generous provisions for mental health coverage should be seen as an investment opportunity rather than a cost of doing business (Kessler & Frank, 1997). Some sense of the magnitude of the lost productivity due to psychiatric disorders can be seen in the NCS analyses of average numbers of monthly work loss days and work cutback days reported by all respondents associated with pure and comorbid psychiatric disorders (Kessler & Frank, 1997). On a base of approximately 140 million people in the age range of the NCS in the United States, the significantly elevated averages among people with psychiat-ric disorders compared to those free of these disorders translated into annual estimates of over 50 million work-loss days and over 300 million work cutback days.

CONCLUSION

The results reviewed here show that psychiatric disorders are highly prevalent in the gen-eral population. Although no truly comprehensive assessment of all Axis I and Axis II disorders has ever been carried out in a general population sample, it is almost certainly the case that such a study would find that a majority of the population meet criteria for at least one of these disorders at some time in their life. Such a result might initially seem remark-able, but it is actually quite easy to understand. The DSM classification system is very broad. It includes a number of disorders that are usually self-limiting and not severely impairing. It should be no more surprising to find that half the population has met criteria for one or more of these disorders in their life than to find that the vast majority of the population have had the flu or measles, or some other common physical malady at some time in their lives.

The more surprising result is that although many people have been touched by mental illness at some time in their life, the major burden of psychiatric disorder in the population is concentrated in the relatively small subset of people who are highly comorbid. A pile-up of multiple disorders emerges as the most important defining characteristic of serious mental illness. This result points to the previously underappreciated importance of research on the primary prevention of secondary disorders (Kessler & Price, 1993). It also means that epidemiological information about the prevalence of individual disorders is much less important than information on the prevalence of functional impairment, comorbidity, and chronicity. These are topics that have not traditionally been the focus of psychiatric epide-miology, but they are likely to become so in the years ahead.

ACKNOWLEDGMENTS: Preparation of this chapter was supported by National Institute of Mental Health Grant Nos. R01-MH46376, R01-MH49098, RO1 MH52861 and K05-MH00507. Some of the figures and tables and portions of the text previously appeared elsewhere: Kessler and Zhao (in press); Kessler, Abelson, and Zhao (1998); Kessler, McGonagle,

Zhao, et al. (1994); Kessler, Nelson, et al. (1996); Kessler, Berglund, et al. (1996); Kessler et al. (1997); Kessler and Frank (1997). More detailed results of the National Comorbidity Survey can be obtained from the NCS Home Page: http://www.umich.edu/~ncsum/.

REFERENCES

American Psychiatric Association. (1980). *Diagnostic and statistical manual of mental disorders* (3rd ed.). Washington, DC: Author.

American Psychiatric Association. (1987). *Diagnostic and statistical manual of mental disorders* (rev. 3rd ed.). Washington, DC: Author.

Anthony, J. C., Folstein, M., Romanoski, A. J., VonKorff, M. R., Nestadt, G. R., Chahal, R., Merchant, A., Brown, C. H., Shapiro, S., Kramer, M., & Gruenberg, E. M. (1985). Comparison of the lay Diagnostic Interview Schedule and a standardized psychiatric diagnosis: Experience in eastern Baltimore. *Archives of General Psychiatry, 42*, 667–675.

Anthony, J. C., & Helzer, J. E. (1991). Syndromes of drug abuse and dependence. In L. N. Robins & D. A. Regier (Eds.), *Psychiatric disorders in America: The epidemiologic catchment area study* (pp. 116–154). New York: Free Press.

Aseltine, R. H., Jr., & Kessler, R. C. (1993). Marital disruption and depression a community sample. *Journal of Health and Social Behavior, 34*, 237–251.

Blashfield, R. K. (1991). An American view of the ICD-10 personality disorders. *Acta Psychiatrica Scandinavica, 82*, 250–256.

Blazer, D. G., Kessler, R. C., McGonagle, K. A., & Swartz, M. S. (1994). The prevalence and distribution of major depression in a national community sample: The National Comorbidity Survey. *American Journal of Psychiatry, 151*, 979–986.

Bourdon, K. H., Rae, D. A., Locke, B. Z., Narrow, W. E., & Regier, D. A. (1992). Estimating the prevalence of mental disorders in U.S. adults from the Epidemiologic Catchment Area Study. *Public Health Report, 107*, 663–668.

Broadhead, W. E., Blazer, D. G., George, L. K., and Kit, T. C. (1990). Depression, disability days, and days lost from work in a prospective epidemiologic survey. *Journal of the American Medical Association, 264*, 2524–2528.

Brown, G. W. (1997). Genetics of depression: A social science perspective. *International Review of Psychiatry, 8*, 387–401.

Bruce, M. L., Takeuchi, D. T., & Leaf, P.J. (1991). Poverty and psychiatric status: Longitudinal evidence from the New Haven Epidemiologic Catchment Area Study. *Archives of General Psychiatry, 48*, 470–474.

Burke, K. C., Burke, J. D., Rae, D. S., & Regier, D. A. (1991). Comparing age of onset of major depression and other psychiatric disorders by birth cohorts in five US community populations. *Archives of General Psychiatry, 48*, 789–795.

Burrows, G. M. (1820). *An inquiry into certain errors relative to insanity; and their consequences; physical, moral, and civil.* London: Thomas and George Underwood.

Canino, G. J., Bird, H. R., Shrout, P.E., Rubio-Stipec, M. B., Bravo, M., Martinez, R., Sesman, M., & Guevara, L. M. (1987). The prevalence of specific psychiatric disorders in Puerto Rico. *Archives of General Psychiatry, 44*, 727–735.

Conger, R. D., Lorenz, F. O., Elder, G. H., Simons, R. L., & Ge, X. (1993). Husband and wife differences in response to undesirable life events. *Journal of Health and Social Behavior, 34*, 71–88.

Cross-National Collaborative Group. (1992). The changing rate of major depression. *Journal of the American Medical Association, 268*, 3098–3105.

De Girolamo, G., & Reich, J. H. (1993). *Epidemiology of Mental Disorders and Psychosocial Problems: Personality Disorders.* Geneva: World Health Organization.

Dohrenwend, B. P. (1995). The problem of validity in field studies of psychological disorders—revisited. In M. T. Tsuang, M. Tohen, & G. E. P. Zahner (eds.), *Textbook in psychiatric epidemiology* (pp. 3–22). New York: Wiley.

Dohrenwend, B. P., & Dohrenwend, B. S. (1965). The problem of validity in field studies of psychological disorder. *Journal of Abnormal Psychology, 70*, 52–69.

Dohrenwend, B. P., Levav, I., Shrout, P. E., & Schwartz, S. (1992). Socioeconomic status and psychiatric disorders: The causation selection issue. *Science, 255*, 946–952.

Dohrenwend, B. P., Yager, T. J., Egri, G., & Mendelsohn, F. S. (1978). The psychiatric status schedule (PSS) as a measure of dimensions of psychopathology in the general population. *Archives of General Psychiatry, 35*, 731–739.

Durkheim, E. (1951). *Suicide*. Glencoe, IL: Free Press.

Eaton, W. W., Dryman, A., & Weissman, M. M. (1991). Panic and phobia. In L. N. Robins & D. A. Regier (Eds.), *Psychiatric disorders in America: The epidemiologic catchment area study* (pp. 116–154). New York: Free Press.

Efron, B. (1988). Logistic regression, survival analysis, and the Kaplan–Meier Curve. *Journal of the American Sociological Association, 83*, 414–425.

Endicott, J., & Spitzer, R. (1978). A diagnostic interview: The Schedule for Affective Disorders and Schizophrenia. *Archives of General Psychiatry, 137*, 837–844.

Faris, R. E. L., & Dunham, H. W. (1939). *Mental disorders in urban areas*. Chicago: University of Chicago Press.

Feighner, J. P., Robins, E., & Guze, S. B. (1972). Diagnostic criteria for use in psychiatric research. *Archives of General Psychiatry, 26*, 57–63.

Frances, A., Widiger, T. & Fyer, M. R. (1990). The influence of classification methods on comorbidity. In J. D. Maser & C. R. Cloninger (Eds.), *Comorbidity of mood and anxiety disorders* (pp. 41–59). Washington, DC: American Psychiatric Association.

Gove, W. R. (1978). Sex differences in mental illness among adult men and women: An evaluation of four questions raised regarding the evidence on the higher rates of women. *Social Science and Medicine, 12B*, 187–198.

Gurin, G., Verogg, J., & Feld, S. (1960). *Americans view their mental health*. New York: Basic Books.

Helzer, J. E., Burnam, A., McEvoy, L. T. (1991). Alcohol abuse and dependence. In L. N. Robins & D. A. Regier (Eds.), *Psychiatric disorders in America: The epidemiologic catchment area study* (pp. 81–115). New York: Free Press.

Helzer, J. E., Stoltzman, R. K., Farmer, A., Brockington, I. F., Plesons, D., Singerman, B., & Works, J. (1985). Comparing the DIS with a DIS/DSM-III-based physician reevaluation. In W. W. Eaton & L. G. Kessler (Eds.), *Epidemiologic field methods in psychiatry* (pp. 285–308). Orlando, FL: Academic Press.

Hollingshead, A. B., & Redlich, F. C. (1958). *Social class and mental illness: A community study*. New York: Wiley (Science Editions).

Holzer, C. E., Shea, B., Swanson, J. W., Leaf, P. J., Myers, J. K., George, L., Weissman, M. M., & Bednarski, P. (1986). The increased risk for specific psychiatric disorders among persons of low socioeconomic status. *American Journal of Psychiatry, 6*, 259–271.

Horwath, E., Johnson, J., & Hornig, C. D. (1993). Epidemiology of panic disorder in African-Americans. *American Journal of Psychiatry, 150*, 465–469.

Hunter, R., & Macalpine, I. (Eds.). (1963). *Three hundred years of psychiatry*. Oxford: Oxford University Press.

Jarvis, E. (1855). *Report on insanity and idiocy in Massachusetts by the Commission on Lunacy under resolve of the legislature of 1854*. Boston: William White Printer to the State.

Johnson, J., Weissman, M. M., & Klerman, G. L. (1992). Service utilizationand social morbidity associated with depressive symptoms in the community. *Journal of the American Medical Association, 267*, 1478–1483.

Kaplan, E. L., & Meier, P. (1958). Nonparametric estimation from incomplete observations. *Journal of the American Statistical Association, 53*, 281–284.

Kass, F. (1985). Scaled ratings of DSM-III personality disorders. *American Journal of Psychiatry, 142*, 627–630.

Keith, S. J., Regier, D. A., & Rae, D. S. (1991). Schizophrenic disorders. In L. N. Robins & D. A. Regier (Eds), *Psychiatric disorders in America: The epidemiologic catchment area study* (pp. 33–52). New York: Free Press.

Kendler, K. S., Gallagher, T. J., Abelson, J. M., & Kessler, R. C. (1996). Lifetime prevalence, demographic risk factors and diagnostic validity of nonaffective psychosis as assessed in a U.S. community sample: The National Comorbidity Survey. *Archives of General Psychiatry, 53*, 1022–1031.

Kendler, K. S., Neale, M. C., Kessler, R. C., Heath, A. C., & Eaves, L. J. (1992). A population based twin study of major depression in women: The impact of varying definitions of illness. *Archives of General Psychiatry, 49*, 257–266.

Kendler, K. S., Walters, E. E., Neale, M. C., Kessler, R. C., Heath, A. C., & Eaves, L. J. (1995). The structure of the genetic and environmental risk factors for six major psychiatric disorders in women. *Archives of General Psychiatry, 52*, 374–383.

Kessler, R. C. (1995). Epidemiology of psychiatric comorbidity. In M. T. Tsuang, M. Tohan, & G. E. P. Zahner (Eds.), *Textbook in psychiatric epidemiology* (pp. 356–365). Baltimore: Williams & Wilkins.

Kessler, R. C., Abelson, J. M. & Zhao., S. (1998). *The epidemiology of mental disorders*. In J. B. W. Williams & K. Ell (Eds.), *Advanced in mental health research: Implications for practice* (pp. 3–24). Washington, DC: National Association of Social Workers Press.

Kessler, R. C., Berglund, P. A., Foster, C. L., Saunders, W. B., Stang, P. E., & Walters, E. E. (1997). The social consequences of psychiatric disorders: II: Teenage parenthood. *American Journal of Psychiatry, 154,* 1405–1411.

Kessler, R. C., Berglund, P. A., Zhao, S., Leaf, P., Kouzis, A. C., Bruce, M. L., Friedman, R. M., Grosser, R. C., Kennedy, C., Kuehnel, T. G., Laska, E. M., Manderscheid, R. W., Narrow, B., Rosenheck, R. A., Santoni, T. W., & Schneier, M. (1996). The 12-month prevalence and correlates of serious mental illness (SMI). In R. W. Manderscheid & M. A. Sonnenschein (Eds.), *Mental health, United States, 1996* (pp. 5–70). Washington, DC: U.S. Government Printing Office.

Kessler, R. C., Crum, R. M., Warner, L. A., Nelson, C. B., Schulenberg, J., & Anthony, J. C. (1997). The lifetime co-occurence of DSM-III-R alcohol abuse and dependence with other psychiatric disorders in the National Comorbidity Survey. *Archives of General Psychiatry, 54,* 313–321.

Kessler, R. C., & Essex, M. (1982). Marital status and depression: The importance of coping resources. *Social Forces, 61,* 484–507.

Kessler, R. C., & Forthofer, M. S., (1999). The effects of psychiatric disorders on family formation and stability. In J. Brooks-Gunn & M. Cox (Eds.), *Family risk and resilience: The roles of conflict and cohesion* (pp. 301–320). New York: Cambridge University Press.

Kessler, R. C., Foster, C. L., Saunders, W. B., & Stang, P. E. (1995). Social consequences of psychiatric disorders, I: Educational attainment. *American Journal of Psychiatry, 152,* 1026–1032.

Kessler, R. C., & Frank, R. G. (1997). The impact of psychiatric disorders on work loss days. *Psychological Medicine, 27,* 861–873.

Kessler, R. C., House, J. S., & Turner, J. B. (1987). Unemployment and health in a community sample. *Journal of Health and Social Behavior, 28,* 51–59.

Kessler, R. C., McGonagle, K. A., Nelson, C. B., Hughes, M., Swartz, M. & Blazer, D. G. (1994). Sex and depression in the National Comorbidity Survey. II: Cohort effects. *Journal of Affective Disorders, 30,* 15–26.

Kessler, R. C., McGonagle, K. A., Zhao, S., Nelson, C. B., Hughes, M., Eshleman, S., Wittchen, H.-U., & Kendler, K. S. (1994). Lifetime and 12-month prevalence of DSM-III-R psychiatric disorders in the United States: Results from the National Comorbidity Survey. *Archives of General Psychiatry, 51,* 8–19.

Kessler, R. C., Nelson, C. B., McGonagle, K. A., Edlund, M. J., Frank, R. G., & Leaf, P. J. (1996). The epidemiology of co-occurring addictive and mental disorders: Implications for prevention and service utilization. *American Journal of Orthopsychiatry, 66,* 17–31.

Kessler, R. C., & Price, R. H. (1993). Primary prevention of secondary disorders: A proposal and agenda. *American Journal of Community Psychology, 21,* 607–634.

Kessler, R. C., Rubinow, D. R., Holmes, C., Abelson, J. M., & Zhao, S. (1997). The epidemiology of DSM-III-R bipolar I disorder in a general population survey. *Psychological Medicine, 27,* 1079–1089.

Kessler, R. C., & Zhao, S. (In press). The prevalence of mental illness. In A. V. Horwitz & T. L. Scheid (Eds.), *Sociology of mental health and illness*. New York: Cambridge University Press.

Kessler, R. C., Zhao, S., Katz, S. J., Kouzis, A. C., Frank, R. G., Edlund, M., & Leaf, P. (1999). Past year use of outpatient services for psychiatric problems in the National Comorbidity Survey. *American Journal of Psychiatry, 156,* 115–123.

Leighton, A. H. (1959). *My name is legion: Vol. I of the Stirling County Study*. New York: Basic Books.

Lenzenweger, M. F., Loranger, A. W., Korfine, L,. & Neff, C. (1997). Detecting personality disorders in a non-clinical population: Application of a 2-stage procedure for case identification. *Archives of General Psychiatry, 54,* 345–351.

Magee, W. J., Eaton, W. W., Wittchen, H. U., McGonagle, K. A., & Kessler, R. C. (1996). Agoraphobia, simple phobia, and social phobia in the National Comorbidity Survey. *Archives of General Psychiatry, 53,* 159–168.

McGonagle, K. A., & Kessler, R. C. (1990). Chronic stress, acute stress, and depressive symptoms. *American Journal of Community Psychology, 18,* 681–706.

Merikangas, K. R. (1989). Epidemiology of DSM-III personality disorders. In R. Michels & J. O. Cavenar, Jr. (Eds.), *Psychiatry* (Vol. 3, pp. 1–16). Philadelphia: Lippincott.

Morey, L. C. (1988). Personality disorders in DSM-III and DSM-III-R: Convergence, coverage and internal consistency. *American Journal of Psychiatry, 145,* 573–577.

Murray, C. J., & Lopez, A. D. (1996) *The global burden of disease.* Boston: Harvard University Press.

Myers, J. K. (1984). Social factors related to psychiatric disorders. *Social Psychiatry, 19,* 53–61.

National Advisory Mental Health Council. (1993). Health care reform for Americans with severe mental illness. *American Journal of Psychiatry, 150,* 1447–1465.

Newman, S. C., Shrout, P. E., & Bland, R. C. (1990). The efficiency of two-phase designs in prevalence surveys of mental disorders. *Psychological Medicine, 20,* 183–193.

Perry, J. S. (1992). Problems and considerations in the valid assessment of personality disorders. *American Journal of Psychiatry, 149,* 1645–1653.

Pilkonis, P. A., Heape, C. L., Proirette, J. M., Clark, S. W., McDavid, J. D., & Pitts, T. E. (1995). The reliability and validity of two structured diagnostic interviews for personality disorders. *Archives of General Psychiatry, 52,* 1025–1033.

President's Commission on Mental Health and Illness. (1978). *Report to the President from the President's Commission on Mental Health, Volume 1* (Stock No. 040-000-00390-8). Washington, DC: U.S. Government Printing Office.

Radloff, L. S. (1977). The CES-D Scale: A self-report depression scale for research in the general population. *Applied Psychology Measurement, 1,* 385–401.

Regier, D. A., Farmer, M. E., Rae, D. A., Locke, B. Z., Keith, B. J., Judd, L. L., & Goodwin, F. K. (1990). Comorbidity of mental health disorders with alcohol and other drug abuse. *Journal of the American Medical Association, 264,* 2511–2518.

Regier, D. A., Kaelber, C. T., Rae, D. S., Farmer, M. E., Knauper, B., Kessler, R. C., & Norquist, G. S. (1998). Limitations of diagnostic criteria and assessment instruments for mental disorders: Implications for research and policy. *Archives of General Psychiatry, 55,* 109–115.

Regier, D. A., Narrow, W. E., Rae, D. S., Manderscheid, R. W., Locke, B. Z., & Goodwin, F. K. (1993). The de Facto U.S. Mental and Addictive Disorders Service System: Epidemiologic Catchment Area prospective 1-year prevalence rates of disorders and services. *Archives of General Psychiatry, 50,* 85–94.

Rhode, P., Lewinsohn, P., & Seeley, J. (1990). Are people changed by the experience of having an episode of depression? A further test of the scar hypothesis. *Journal of Abnormal Psychology, 99,* 264–271.

Robins, L. N. (1985). Epidemiology: Reflections on testing the validity of psychiatric interview. *Archives of General Psychiatry, 42,* 918–924.

Robins, L. N., Helzer, J. E., Croughan, J. L., & Ratcliff, K. S. (1981). National Institute of Mental Health Diagnostic Interview Schedule: Its history, characteristics and validity. *Archives of General Psychiatry, 38,* 381–389.

Robins, L. N., Locke, B. Z., & Regier, D. A. (1991). An overview of psychiatric disorders in America. In L. N. Robins & D. A. Regier (Eds.), *Psychiatric disorders in America: The Epidemiologic Catchment Study* (pp. 328–366). New York: Free Press.

Robins, L. N., & Regier, D. A. (1991). *Psychiatric disorders in America: The Epidemiologic Catchment Area Study.* New York: Free Press.

Robins, L. N., Wing, J., Wittchen, H., Helzer, J. E., Babor, T. F., Burke, J. D., Farmer, A., Jablenski, A., Pickens, R., Regier, D. A., Sartorius, N., & Towle, L. H. (1988). The Composite International Diagnostic Interview: An epidemiologic instrument suitable for use in conjunction with different diagnostic systems and in different cultures. *Archives of General Psychiatry, 45,* 1069–1077.

Ross, C. E., Mirowsky, J., & Huber, J. (1983). Dividing work, sharing work, and in-between: Marriage patterns and depression. *American Sociological Review. 48,* 809–823.

Rothman, K. J. (1986). *Modern epidemiology.* Boston: Little, Brown.

Seiler, L. H. (1973). The 22-item scale used in field studies of mental illness: A question of method, a question of substance, and a question of theory. *Journal of Health and Social Behavior, 14,* 252–264.

Srole, L., Langer, T. S., Michael, S. T., Opler, M. K., & Rennie, T. A. C. (1962). *Mental health in the metropolis. The midtown manhattan study.* In Thomas A. C. Rennie Series in Social Psychiatry, Vol. I. New York: McGraw-Hill.

Stansfeld, S. A., & Marmot, M. G. (1992). Social class and minor psychiatric disorder in British Civil Servants: A validated screening survey using the General Health Questionnaire. *Psychological Medicine, 22,* 739–749.

Tsuang, M. T., Tohen, M., & Zahner, G. E. P. (1995). *Textbook of psychiatric epidemiology.* New York: Random House.

Tyrer, P., Casey, P., & Ferguson, B. (1991). Personality disorder in perspective. *British Journal of Psychiatry, 159,* 463–471.

Warner, L. A., Kessler, R. C., Hughes, M., Anthony, J. C., & Nelson, C. B. (1995). Prevalence and correlates of drug use and dependence in the United States: Results from the National Comorbidity Survey. *Archives of General Psychiatry, 52*, 219–229.

Weissman, M. M. (1993). The epidemiology of personality disorders: A 1990 update. *Journal of Personality Disorders, 7*, 44–62.

Weissman, M. M., Bruce, M. L., Leaf, P. J., Florio, L. P., & Holzer, C., III. (1991). Affective disorders. In L.N. Robins & D. A. Regier (Eds.), *Psychiatric disorders in America. The epidemiologic catchment area study* (pp. 53–80). New York: Free Press.

Weissman, M. M., & Myers, J. K. (1978). Affective disorders in a U.S. urban community. *Archives of General Psychiatry, 35*, 1304–1311.

Wells, K., Stewart, A., Hays, R., Burnam, M., Rogers, W., Daniels, M., Berry, S., Greenfield, S., & Ware, J. (1989). The functioning and well-being of depressed patients: Results from the Medical Outcomes Study. *Journal of the American Medical Association, 262*, 914–919.

Wittchen, H. U. (1994). Reliability and validity studies of the WHO–Composite International Diagnostic Interview (CIDI): A critical review. *Journal of Psychiatric Research, 28*, 57–84.

Wohlfarth, T. D., van den Brink, W., Ormel, J., Koeter, M. W., & Oldehinkel, A. J. (1993). The relationship between social dysfunctioning and psychopathology among primary care attenders. *British Journal of Psychiatry, 163*, 37–44.

World Health Organization. (1990). *International classification of diseases—10 classification of mental and behavioral disorders: Diagnostic criteria for research*. Geneva: Author.

World Health Organization. (1990). *Composite International Diagnostic Interview (CIDI, Version 1.0)*. Geneva: Author.

Zimmerman, M. (1994). Diagnosing personality disorders: A review of issues and research methods. *Archives of General Psychiatry, 51*, 225–245.

CHAPTER 8

Socioeconomic Status and Mental Health

Yan Yu
David R. Williams

In 1912, the British luxury liner, the *Titanic*, struck an iceberg off the coast of Newfoundland on its maiden voyage from Southampton, England, to New York City. This accident was one of the worst marine disasters ever, with two-thirds of the more than 2,200 persons aboard losing their lives. As the *Titanic* sank, women and children had preferential access to the lifeboats. However, the death rates for women on the *Titanic* were not random but strikingly linked to their social status. Among women passengers aboard the *Titanic*, only 3% of first-class passengers lost their lives, compared to 16% of second-class passengers, and 45% of those in third class (Carroll & Smith, 1997); that is, the quality and cost of accommodation, a marker of social ranking, clearly predicted the probability of survival. The relationship between social location and survival is not unique to the *Titanic*. A positive association between socioeconomic status (SES) and health has been found for most indicators of health status in virtually every society where it has been examined (Adler, Boyce, Chesney, Folkman, & Syme, 1993; Antonovsky 1967; Bunker, Gomby, & Kehrer, 1989; Krieger et al., 1993; Marmot, Kogevinas, & Elston, 1987; Williams, 1990; Williams & Collins, 1995). Mental health status is no exception to this pattern. Sociologists have long noted that one of the most firmly established patterns in the social distribution of psychiatric morbidity is an inverse association between SES and mental illness (Dohrenwend & Dohrenwend, 1969).

Almost a decade ago, Dohrenwend (1990) indicated that research interest in the asso-

Yan Yu • Department of Sociology, University of Maryland, College Park, Maryland 20742.   David R. Williams • Institute for Social Research, University of Michigan, Ann Arbor, Michigan 48106.

Handbook of the Sociology of Mental Health, edited by Carol S. Aneshensel and Jo C. Phelan. Kluwer Academic/ Plenum Publishers, New York, 1999.

ciation between SES and mental illness was waning. However, in recent years, there has been a dramatic increase in research focusing on the health consequences of SES, with a heavy emphasis on physical health outcomes (Kaplan & Lynch, 1997). This growth in research attention to the SES–health linkage is driven in part by the growing awareness, across a range of scientific disciplines, of the ubiquity and robustness of the association between SES and health and by the increasing recognition that SES differences in health in both the United States and Europe appear to be widening as economic inequalities in society widen (Krieger, Williams & Moss, 1997; Williams & Collins, 1995). This chapter provides a brief overview of early studies that assess the association between SES and mental illness. It then considers in more detail recent findings on the association between socioeconomic position and psychiatric disorders from two large, population-based studies in the United States. Finally, we consider some of the major unresolved issues in research on SES and mental illness.

EARLY STUDIES

Some of the early evidence of this association in the United States comes from studies that examine the relationship between measures of socioeconomic position and treatment for psychiatric illness. Faris and Dunham (1939), for example, studied the association between the social and economic characteristics of Chicago residential areas and the rates of first admission into mental hospitals for schizophrenia, manic–depressive disorder, drug addiction, alcohol psychosis, and old-age psychosis. They found that these mental disorders were all concentrated in and around the relatively undesirable and "socially disorganized" residential areas of the central business district. In another classic early study, Hollingshead and Redlich (1958) identified all residents of New Haven, Connecticut, who were receiving psychiatric treatment by contacting private psychiatrists and all public and private institutions in Connecticut. They found an inverse relationship between mental illness and social class.

These early studies also shed light on some of the processes by which social position affects the context of treatment. For example, the New Haven data demonstrated that high SES persons with schizophrenia entered treatment earlier than their lower SES peers. In addition, schizophrenic persons from the higher SES groups were typically referred to treatment through medical channels, whereas those from lower SES groups were referred through legal ones. The type of treatment also varied by social status. High SES persons with schizophrenia were more likely to receive psychotherapy, while their low SES peers received organic treatment or, in some cases, did not receive any treatment. High SES patients were also more likely than their low SES counterparts to be discharged to their families and communities.

These findings highlight a major problem with the early studies that used treated prevalence to study the association between SES and mental illness. These rates do not include the psychiatric problems of persons who have not entered treatment and are thus importantly affected by health care access and financing options, distance to treatment, available transportation, the client's economic status, and other structural and/or cultural barriers that affect the likelihood of seeking and receiving medical care, as well as being appropriately diagnosed. For example, recent national data of population-based rates of treated and untreated cases of mental illness indicate that only 40% of persons who have met the criteria for psychiatric illness have ever received treatment (Kessler et al., 1994). At the same time, almost half of all persons in treatment do not have a current psychiatric illness. Data from treatment samples, therefore, provide biased estimates of the occurrence of mental illness in the general population.

In the post–World War II era, community surveys were increasingly used to study the social distribution of mental health problems. These surveys avoided selection biases associated with treatment samples by using probability methods to select persons representative of the total community. However, psychiatry lacked consensus on the criteria for the formal diagnosis of discrete psychiatric disorders, as well as the technology to obtain standardized information based on structured or semistructured interviews. Accordingly, instead of assessing the occurrence of specific types of psychiatric disorders, these studies use scales of psychological distress. These scales captured nonspecific emotional symptoms and served as useful indicators of overall levels of impairment. They were not time-consuming, were easy to administer, and provided information on the distribution of mental health status on a continuum. Typically, these measures assessed depressed mood, anxiety, psychological distress, and somatic symptoms. These studies provided further evidence for an inverse association between psychological distress and SES (Kessler, 1979, 1983; Ilfeld, 1978).

Historically, mental disorder and normal functioning have been viewed by some as polar ends of a scale, with self-reported symptoms of psychological distress or depression being on a continuum with defined psychiatric disorders. Thus, some researchers viewed scales of psychological distress as substitutes for measures of psychiatric illness. There is growing recognition that scales of psychological distress capture qualitatively different phenomena than measures of psychiatric disorder (see Chapter 5, this volume). For example, research has shown that although most clinically depressed persons have scores in the depressed range on self-report questionnaires, relatively few persons from community samples who have high scores on self-report scales of depression meet diagnostic criteria for clinical depression (Downey & Coyne, 1991). In addition, the social correlates of self-reported symptoms differ from those of interview-generated diagnoses of clinical depression. Some have suggested that psychological distress scales capture not clinical diagnosis, but aspects of demoralization that are especially likely to be common at the low end of SES (Link & Dohrenwend, 1980). Some have suggested that even when assessing only symptoms associated with one specific disorder, symptom counts are better at measuring mild than severe forms of psychiatric impairment (Robins et al., 1984; Weissman, Myers, & Ross, 1986).

Several issues around the measurement of mental health status have been raised. Mirowsky and Ross (1989) have argued that scales that assess mental health status on a continuum, such as scales of psychological distress, do a better job of describing the psychiatric status of community populations than diagnostic instruments that provide dichotomous distinction between cases and noncases. Accordingly, they claim that symptom scales are more appropriate for studying the association between social status and mental health (see Chapter 6, this volume). Nevertheless, the emphasis in recent epidemiological research has been on diagnostic-type assessment.

RECENT POPULATION-BASED STUDIES

The Epidemiologic Catchment Area Study (ECA) is the largest community mental health survey ever conducted in the United States (Robins & Regier, 1991). Between 1980 and

1983, the ECA interviewed almost 20,000 adults in five communities, and estimated the prevalence and incidence of specific psychiatric disorders in samples of institutionalized and noninstitutionalized persons. An important methodological advance in the 1970s was the development of nosological systems for defining psychiatric illness by a standardized set of signs and symptoms (see Chapter 5, this volume). This innovation allowed for the development of structured interviews to obtain standardized information about symptoms. These data could then be used to create computer-generated diagnoses of specific psychiatric illnesses. The ECA utilized the Diagnostic Interview Schedule (DIS), a fully structured, lay administered interview that follows an algorithm to operationalize psychiatric diagnoses based on the presence, severity, and duration of symptoms (Robins, Lee, Helzer, Croughan, & Ratcliff, 1981). Its structured nature allows for the assessment of psychiatric illness without clinical judgment, which facilitates its use in community-based studies but raises questions about the meaning of caseness in the community context.

Table 8.1 presents the distribution of recent psychiatric disorders by SES in the ECA. The analyses in this table used a composite SES measure that combines rank orderings based on formal education, occupation, and household income. The any disorder category is a summary measure of any of the DIS disorders assessed in the ECA surveys, excluding phobias and cognitive impairment. This composite includes the following major mental disorders: alcohol abuse and dependence, drug abuse and dependence, anorexia, antisocial personality, bipolar disorder, major depression, dysthymia, obsessive–compulsive disorder, panic disorder, somatization, and schizophrenia/schizophreniform. Findings are also presented in Table 8.1 for select diagnoses: major depression, alcohol abuse and dependence, and schizophrenia. The table presents the odds ratios from logistic regression models, adjusted for age and gender, for the lowest, second, and third SES quartiles, compared to the highest quartile. A value of 1.00 in the last column of Table 8.1 indicates that the highest SES quartile serves as the reference category. An odds ratio greater than 1.0 indicates a higher prevalence of that disorder for those in the specified category relative to those in the reference category.

The table reveals that there is a consistent inverse relationship between socioeconomic position and psychiatric disorders, although the strength of the association between SES and psychiatric illness varies by the type of disorder under consideration. The rate for the composite DIS disorder category in the ECA was almost three times higher at the lowest SES quartile, compared to the highest. The rate in the second was twice as great, and even the adjacent third quartile is about one and a half times greater than the highest SES group. Although a significant association between SES and depression is not always found

Table 8.1. Odds Ratios[a] for Psychiatric Disorders (in the Last 6 Months) by Socioeconomic Status, Epidemiologic Catchment Area Study ($N = 18,572$)

| Disorder | Socioeconomic status quartiles | | | |
	Lowest	Second	Third	Highest[b]
Any disorder[c]	2.86	2.04	1.55	1.00
Major depression	1.79	1.92	1.51	1.00
Alcohol abuse/dependence	3.59	2.19	1.59	1.00
Schizophrenia	7.85	3.84	2.72	1.00

[a]Adjusted for age and sex.
[b]Reference category.
[c]Any of the DIS disorders excluding phobias and cognitive impairment.
Source. Adapted from Holzer et al. (1986).

(Dohrenwend, 1990), persons in the two lowest SES quartiles are almost twice as likely to meet criteria for major depression as those in the highest SES quartile. For alcohol abuse and dependence, the association is even stronger, with the lowest SES group having a rate of alcohol abuse and dependence that is almost four times greater than the highest SES group. Consistent with other research, there is a marked relationship between SES and the diagnosis of schizophrenia. Schizophrenia occurs almost eight times more frequently among persons in the lowest SES quartiles, compared to adults in the highest SES quartile. Thus, in the ECA, the association between SES and psychiatric disorder is strongest for schizophrenia. It is least pronounced for major depression, although even for this disorder, the risk almost doubles across the spectrum of SES.

The National Comorbidity Study (NCS) is another recent large study of psychiatric disorder in the United States (Kessler et al., 1994; see Chapter 7, this volume). The NCS interviewed over 8,000 persons aged 15–54 and is the first study to use a national probability sample to estimate psychiatric disorders. The psychiatric disorders assessed in the NCS include major depression, mania, dysthymia, panic disorder, agoraphobia, social phobia, simple phobia, generalized anxiety disorder, alcohol abuse, alcohol dependence, drug abuse, drug dependence, antisocial personality disorder and nonaffective psychosis. Table 8.2 presents odds ratios for the levels of broad categories of psychiatric disorders by years of education and categories of income in the NCS. Unlike the odds ratios in Table 8.1 which were adjusted for age and sex, these are bivariate associations. Although there is some variation across type of disorder, similar to that observed in the ECA data, there is a strong graded relationship between both indicators of SES and the occurrence of psychiatric illness, with the lowest rates at the highest level of SES and a general monotonic decline across categories of income and education.

Persons who have not completed high school are 1.8 times more likely to be diagnosed with a major affective disorder than those who have a college education or more. Similarly, those in the lowest income category are 1.7 times more likely to meet criteria for a depressive disorder than those in the highest income category. This inverse association is on the same order of magnitude evident in the ECA for major depression for the composite index of SES (see Table 8.1). Instructively, Hollingshead and Redlich (1958) had found a positive association between depression and social class that has been replicated in several subsequent studies, although some studies have found no relationship between SES and major depression (Ortega & Corzine, 1990). It is not clear if the differences in findings for SES and major depression reflect temporal changes in the true association, differences in

Table 8.2. Odds Ratios for Psychiatric Disorders (in the Last 12-Months) by Years of Education and Annual Income, National Comorbidity Study (*N* = 8,098)

Disorder	Years of education				Income (K = thousands of dollars)			
	0–11	12	13–15	16+[a]	0–19K	20K–34K	35K–69K	70K+[a]
Any disorder	2.33	1.79	1.58	1.00	1.92	1.24	1.20	1.00
Any affective disorder	1.79	1.38	1.37	1.00	1.73	1.13	1.01	1.00
Any anxiety disorder	2.82	2.10	1.60	1.00	2.12	1.56	1.50	1.00
Any substance abuse/ dependence disorder	2.10	1.80	1.70	1.00	1.92	1.12	1.11	1.00
Three or more disorders[b]	3.76	2.54	2.06	1.00	3.36	2.10	1.66	1.00

[a]Reference category.
[b]Three or more of the specific psychiatric disorders assessed in the NCS.
Source. Adapted from Kessler et al. (1994).

the assessment of depressive disorder over time, or are artifacts of treatment samples. It is also noteworthy that for both indicators of SES in Table 8.2, the association between SES and disorder is somewhat larger for the anxiety disorders than for the affective disorders. Kessler et al. (1994) suggest that the resources associated with SES may be more effective in buffering the individual from worries and fears than from sadness.

Low income persons are 1.9 times more likely to have a substance abuse disorder than persons in the highest income group, whereas persons who have not graduated from high school are 2.1 times more likely to have a substance abuse disorder than college graduates. However, the pattern for the intermediate SES categories varies by the indicator of SES utilized. In the case of education, there is a linear graded relationship, while in the case of income, the contrast is between the two extreme categories.

The NCS data also document that comorbidity among psychiatric disorders is relatively common in the general population. In both the NCS and the ECA, about 60% of respondents with a history of at least one disorder had two or more disorders (Kessler et al. 1994). Instructively, the strongest pattern of association for both income and education in the NCS is among persons who have three or more disorders. Among the lowest income category, the prevalence of three or more disorders is triple the rate among the highest income category. Similarly, for education, this differential is almost four times for the extremes of less than high school versus college graduates.

For both income and education, the odds ratios are consistently larger for 12-month prevalence rates of psychiatric disorder than lifetime prevalence (not shown) in the NCS (Kessler et al., 1994). A similar pattern (not shown) was evident in the ECA data (Williams, Takeuchi, & Adair, 1992). This pattern suggests that SES is associated not only with the onset, but also with the course of disorder. At the same time, findings for lifetime measures of SES must be interpreted with caution (Williams et al., 1992). On the one hand, lifetime rates of disorder avoid confounding the occurrence of disorder with its duration, as is the case for current rates of disorder. At the same time, there are many problems with lifetime measures, including impaired recall (Robins et al., 1984). Respondents probably have considerable difficulty in accurately recalling and dating psychiatric episodes that occurred over their lifetime (Rogler, Lloyd, Malgady, & Tyron, 1992). Years of formal education and level of language proficiency are probably associated with the accuracy of recall. Thus, lifetime psychiatric disorder may be underestimated, especially among low SES persons.

RACE, ETHNICITY, AND SOCIOECONOMIC STATUS

In the United States, race is strongly associated with SES, with Native Americans, Hispanics, blacks, and some subgroups of the Asian and Pacific Islander population having lower levels of education, income, and employment than the white population (Williams, 1996b). In some early health studies, racial status was used as a proxy for SES. The general trend of an inverse association between social class and mental illness is generally consistent across racial and ethnic groups, although distinctive patterns of variation by ethnicity are sometimes evident. For example, Williams et al. (1992) analyzed the relationship between education, income, occupation, and a composite SES measure and psychiatric illness separately for the black and white subsamples of the ECA study. They found that the patterns were generally consistent across racial groups, but some distinctive patterns were also evident. For example, the current rate of depression was unrelated to SES among African

Americans but inversely related for whites. Also, income was unrelated to either current or lifetime rates of psychiatric disorders for black males.

There is growing awareness that the association between race, SES, and mental health status is neither simple nor straightforward. Kessler and Neighbors (1986) reanalyzed data from eight epidemiological surveys and found an interaction between race and SES; that is, at the lower levels of SES, African Americans had higher rates of psychological distress than similarly situated whites. This racial difference diminished as SES increased. A similar pattern was found by Ulbrich, Warheit, and Zimmerman (1989); however, Cockerham (1990) found no racial differences in psychological distress at low levels of SES, but higher income blacks had lower levels of distress than higher income whites. Williams et al. (1992) tested for interactions between race and SES in the ECA data. They found that the interaction between race and SES varied by gender. Low SES black women had higher rates of alcohol and drug abuse disorders than their white counterparts. At the same time, low SES white males had *higher* rates of psychiatric disorder than their low SES black counterparts.

There are several possibilities that might account for this unexpected pattern for males. First, low social status for a white male in a white-dominated culture may be so dissonant from societal expectations that it can produce serious psychological consequences. Alternatively, this finding may reflect biased estimates of the distribution of disease among African American males due to the selective coverage of this population in community-based epidemiological studies. In addition to high rates of nonresponse in community samples, black males are disproportionately represented in institutional (e.g., prison) and marginal (e.g., homeless) populations, where the rates of mental illness are likely to be high, settings usually not included in community-based samples. Finally, these differences could reflect the differential access of low SES groups by race to psychosocial resources that might shield them from the negative effects of exposure to low SES conditions. Some research suggests that a number of adverse risk factors, to which blacks are more exposed, have larger negative impacts on the health of whites than of blacks (Williams & Collins, 1995). Kessler (1979) also documented that comparable stressful events more adversely affect the mental health of whites and higher SES persons, than of blacks and low SES persons, respectively. It is possible that African Americans have greater access than whites to some coping resources, such as religious involvement, that may reduce some of the negative effects of some types of stress on their mental health (Williams, 1996a; Williams, Yu, Jackson, & Anderson, 1997).

Many researchers have viewed race as a proxy for SES or regarded SES as a confounder of the relationship between race and health. Others argue that SES is part of the causal pathway by which race affects health (Cooper & David, 1986; Krieger et al., 1993; Williams, 1997); that is, race is an antecedent and determinant of SES, and SES differences between racial groups in the United States reflect, in part, the impact of economic discrimination as produced by large-scale societal structures and processes. Understanding the role of race in mental health will require more explicit attention to the macrosocial forces that produced this social category in the first place, and to the race-related conditions of life that can enhance or impair mental health functioning.

Researchers have also given increased attention to the nonequivalence of SES indicators across racial and ethnic groups (Williams & Collins, 1995; Krieger et al., 1993). It has been argued, for example, that racial differences in income understate racial/ethnic differences in economic status, because racial/ethnic differences in wealth are considerably larger than those for income, with white households having a net worth that is about ten times that of black and Hispanic households. These racial differences in wealth exist at all levels of income but are largest at the lowest levels of income (Eller, 1994). For example, for persons in the lowest quintile of income in the United States, the median net worth of whites is $10,257, compared to $1 for African Americans and $645 for Hispanics. Recent studies have found that measures of assets, such as home or car ownership, are predictive of health, independent of traditional indicators of SES (Krieger et al., 1997). Income returns for a given level of education also vary by race/ethnicity, with blacks and Hispanics receiving considerably lower levels of income for a given level of education than whites. College-educated blacks are almost four times more likely than their white peers to experience unemployment (Wilhelm, 1987), and employed blacks are considerably more likely than their white peers to be exposed to hazards and carcinogens in workplace settings, even after controlling for job experience and formal education (Robinson, 1984). The purchasing power of a given level of income also varies by race, with blacks facing higher prices than whites for a broad range of goods and services in society, including food and housing.

The complex interactions between race and SES suggest that analyses that utilize a single measure of SES may fail to capture the complex ways in which social stratification shapes racial/ethnic differences in health (Krieger et al., 1997). For example, it is unclear if it is possible fully to control for SES in racial contrasts. Sampson and Wilson (1995) indicate that the residential ecological context of blacks and whites differs so dramatically that it is not possible to compare blacks and whites who truly reside in comparable socioeconomic contexts. They argue that high rates of female-headed households, male joblessness, and concentrated poverty create distinct ecological contexts. They found that in *none* of the 171 largest cities in the United States was the proportion of blacks living in poverty equal to or less than that of whites, nor was the proportion of black families with children headed by a single parent equal to or less than that of white families. Accordingly, the worst urban context in which whites reside are considerably better than the average context of black communities (Sampson & Wilson, 1995, p. 41). Mental health researchers need to demonstrate greater sensitivity to the imprecision of the currently used SES measures and to the complex interactions between race and SES in the collection, analysis, and interpretation of data on racial differences.

SOCIAL CAUSATION VERSUS SOCIAL SELECTION

There are two major explanations for the striking pattern of association between SES and mental illness. Selection, or "drift," hypotheses argue that the association between SES and mental illness is a function of health-related downward mobility. According to this view, the presence of psychiatric illness keeps individuals from obtaining or keeping jobs that would maintain their SES position or enhance social mobility. Thus, mental illness causes individuals to drift into lower SES groups or to fail to climb out of low SES positions at rates comparable to that of healthy adults. In contrast, the social causation hypothesis views the higher rates of mental illness in lower SES groups as due to the socioeconomic adversities linked to low SES position. Low SES environments are viewed as having high levels of pathogenic conditions and fewer resources for dealing with them than higher SES environments.

Much of the research seeking to address the direction of the causal dynamics between SES and mental health has used cross-sectional data. However, several strategies have been employed to assess the extent to which cross-sectional analyses can provide clues to the nature of the underlying causal processes. Some studies have attempted to monitor changes in social status over time by comparing adult SES attainment with parental SES (Fox 1990). Other studies have compared patterns of illness among various ethnic and social class groups (Dohrenwend et al., 1992). Still other studies attempt to establish a temporal ordering of mental illness and occupation by gathering information to date the age of onset for psychiatric illness compared to the age of job entry (Link, Bruce, Dohrenwend, & Skodol, 1986). Recent analyses of the NCS's data indicate that about 14% of high school and 4% of college dropouts are due to mental illness (Kessler, House, Anspach, & Williams, 1995). This suggests that early onset of disorder does hinder educational attainment and job training.

It also appears that social selection and social causation may be differentially involved for specific psychiatric disorders (Dohrenwend et al., 1992; Ortega & Corzine 1990). In general, the selection and "drift" hypotheses are more consistent with genetic explanations for variation in the risk of illness, whereas the social causation hypothesis is consistent with explanations that give primacy to exposure to environmental risks. The social causation explanation is heavily focused on the stressful characteristics of lower SES environments, as well as on the differential distribution by SES of effective resources and coping styles to deal with the adversities of lower SES life.

The available longitudinal data from community samples suggest that processes of social selection and social causation may be operating simultaneously. In a 16-year follow-up study of Sterling County residents, Murphy and colleagues (1991) documented that lower SES respondents were at increased risk of developing first episodes of both depression and anxiety over the follow-up period. At the same time, the overall pattern of the association was not very strong and was more pronounced for depression than for anxiety. However, they also found empirical support for the drift hypothesis. Respondents who were diagnosed as depressed or anxious at baseline tended to be more downwardly mobile over the follow-up period, although this pattern was not significant. Using short-term follow-up data from the New Haven site of the ECA, Bruce, Kim, Leaf, and Jacobs (1990) found that persons who were poor were twice as likely as the nonpoor to develop major depression, phobia, and alcohol abuse/dependence within a 6-month follow-up period. In contrast, Broadhead, Blazer, George, and Tse (1990), using data from the Durham site of the ECA, found that baseline depression increased the risk of subsequently developing work-related disability. These studies suggest that the causal dynamic may operate in both directions.

Power and Manor (1992) used data from the 1958 British Birth Cohort Study to examine the relationship between occupational class and mental health among 23-year-olds. They found the expected association between social class and mental health, with members of lower SES groups having higher scores on a malaise inventory and being more likely to have sought help for psychological problems between the ages of 16 and 23. They examined the relative contribution of social class at birth, housing tenure, behavioral problems, school absences due to ill health, health behaviors, unemployment, and educational attainment. They found that each of these factors made a contribution to the SES differences in mental health status. Moreover, once accounting for these earlier circumstances, SES differences were no longer significant. These data suggest that there may be complex underlying processes by which SES affects mental health.

On balance, it appears that processes of social causation and social selection are both operative. What is needed at this time are theoretically informed analyses from prospective studies that identify how a range of social, psychological, and biological factors relate to each other and combine to affect mental health and adaptive functioning. This will require

more careful delineation and specification of the specific causal processes by which biological vulnerabilities combine with social adversities and individual and social resources to
affect the risk of mental illness. In general, processes of social drift and selection may be
more important in the origins of severe mental illness, while social causation may play a
more central role in the development of less severe disorders (Dohrenwend et al., 1992;
Ortega & Corzine 1990). More specifically, it is suggested that social causation plays a
larger role in depression, while processes of social selection and drift may be more important in schizophrenia.

CHALLENGES FOR FUTURE RESEARCH

Measuring Socioeconomic Position

One of the problems in the literature on SES and health is inattention to the appropriate
conceptualization and measurement of the SES variable (Krieger et al., 1997). One of the
important needs in future research is appropriately to conceptualize socioeconomic position in its multiple dimensions and to use the measure of social status that is most relevant
to the causal hypothesis being tested.

Researchers need more clearly to distinguish measures of SES from those of social
class. The term *social class* is used very loosely in the literature to refer to any indicator of
social stratification. Social class is conceptually and analytically meaningful only within
the context of a specific theory of class, whereas SES is a broader term that can characterize various aspects of social stratification. A greater emphasis on the construct of social
class could inform our research questions and enhance our understanding of the environmental forces responsible for producing inequalities in mental health. Social classes are
hierarchically arranged, socially interdependent groups that reflect the inequities in economic and political power and resources in society. Social class membership determines
the nature and quality of daily life experiences and the available resources to manage demands and uncertainties.

Income, education, and occupational status are the most widely used indicators of
SES. There is growing recognition that each of these terms can capture distinctive aspects
of social stratification and are not necessarily interchangeable. Each SES indicator has its
own set of advantages and disadvantages (Krieger et al., 1997; Liberatos, Link, & Kelsey,
1988; Williams & Collins, 1995). For example, education is fairly stable beyond early
adulthood, but it fails to capture the volatility in economic status that is experienced by a
surprisingly large proportion of U.S. households (Duncan, 1988). Several longitudinal studies
indicate that measures of long-term income that capture the dynamic nature of SES are
more strongly linked to child and adult health outcomes than are single-year indicators of
economic status (Duncan, Brooks-Gunn, & Klebanor, 1994; McDonough, Duncan, Williams, & House, 1997; Miller & Korenman, 1994; Takeuchi, Williams, & Adair, 1991).
Thus, among adults, income and occupation are more relevant than educational status in
evaluating the potential role of the "drift hypothesis" (how changes in health status affects
SES and vice versa).

There is also increased recognition that SES operates at multiple levels. It can be
measured at the level of the individual, the household, and the community. These three
levels are complementary, but each reflects exposure to distinctive risk factors and resources (Krieger et al., 1997). Recent studies suggest that neighborhood-level indicators of

economic deprivation are associated with physical health status, independent of the association with individual SES (Krieger et al., 1997). In addition, a major problem in the literature is a heavy emphasis on the assessment of current SES. An individual's health is importantly affected by exposures to risk factors and resources over the entire life course. SES can be meaningfully assessed at critical points of the life span, including infancy, childhood, adolescence, and adulthood. The relevant time periods for measurement should be based on the hypothesized exposures and causal pathways. Research that gives more explicit attention to the assessment of the SES variable can enhance our understanding of the underlying dynamics by which location in social structure affects health and well-being.

A major debate in the literature has been whether the association between SES and mental illness reflects the effects of absolute deprivation or of relative inequality (Marmot, 1989). The deprivation argument suggests that there is some minimal threshold of social and economic resources that is necessary to facilitate good mental health. The deprivation hypothesis would predict that the SES–mental health relationship would be driven by elevated levels of illness at the lowest level of SES compared to all other SES groups. In contrast, the relative deprivation hypothesis suggests that the health status advantage of low SES groups is not driven by an absolute standard of well-being. Instead, the risk of mental illness is linked to one's relative social standing with each higher level of SES associated with better health status. The results in Table 8.1 and 8.2 suggest that the influence of SES appears to be largest at the lowest SES level, and that the pattern with income for some disorders is consistent with a threshold effect. At the same time, there is also ample evidence of stepwise progression of risk in the association between some indicators of SES and some measures of disorder. Future research must seek to identify the conditions under which particular measures of socioeconomic position have linear or nonlinear associations with the incidence, prevalence, duration, severity, recovery, and co-occurrence of specific psychiatric disorders and other indicators of mental health status. We need to identify the thresholds after which weaker effects of SES are observed and the social, psychological, and material resources and risks that are present at each level of SES.

Measuring Mental Health Status

Another emerging issue in the measurement of psychopathology is the extent to which the standardized diagnostic instruments measure the same things for persons belonging to different SES groups. It is not uncommon in survey research studies for respondents to respond to questions that they do not fully understand or to attribute to a question meaning that is different from that intended by the investigator. In-depth cognitive interviewing is a strategy increasingly being used in the health field to identify subgroup differences in the understanding and interpretation of questions. The literature has focused on potential differences between racial and cultural subgroups, but the issues are equally applicable to potential educational status differences between groups. Cognitive interviewing techniques are designed to identify the extent of variation in comprehension and other cognitive processes, such as the response editing of sensitive questions, that survey respondents use in answering standardized questions (Forsyth & Lessler, 1991). If major gaps exist between different SES groups in the meaning of questions, then significant response errors can be introduced.

Integration of data on physical health status may also shed light on the SES–mental health association. As noted earlier, physical impairment, morbidity, and mortality are also strongly patterned by SES. Physical health status is a risk factor for the onset of psychiatric illness (Kennedy, Kelman, & Thomas, 1991; Oxman, Berman, Kasl, Freeman, & Barrett, 1992;) and psychiatric disorders increase the risk of mortality (Broadhead et al., 1990; Bruce & Leaf, 1989). Thus, physical health status may play an important intervening role in processes of social drift and social causation.

Stress and Socioeconomic Status

The stress literature indicates that acute life events and chronic stress or deprivation due to lack of income or chronic problems in work, marriage, parenting, and other social roles are associated with an increased risk of physical and mental illness, although these associations have been typically modest in size (Cohen, Kessler, & Underwood, 1995). Recent developments in the measurement of stress indicate that comprehensive measures of stress account for substantially more variability in mental health status than previous studies of stress have suggested (Turner, Wheaton, & Lloyd, 1995; Wheaton, 1994). All models of the stress process also recognize that there is a range of social and psychological resources that can affect the impact of stress on mental health. Psychosocial variables that have emerged as major risk factors for health status or as buffers or moderators of the impact of stressful experiences on health include social relationships, self-esteem, perceptions of mastery or control, anger or hostility, feelings of helplessness or hopelessness, and the repression or denial of emotions (Kessler et al., 1995). Neither stress nor the resources to cope with it are randomly distributed in society. The social conditions in which SES groups are embedded are important determinants of exposure to stress and resources to confront and deal with stressful experiences (Mirowsky & Ross, 1989; Pearlin, 1989; Williams & House, 1991). Prior studies have not simultaneously characterized the full range of stressors and psychosocial resources for various SES groups and the contribution that these factors, singly and in combination, make to SES differences in mental health.

An adequate understanding of the role of stress in SES variations in mental health will require not only the comprehensive assessment of stress, but also unifying or integrative models of life stress and mental health that incorporate the role of psychological and biological factors in the stress process (Cohen et al., 1995). For example, although, the neuroendocrine system has long been thought to play a critical role in the causal pathway that links stress to adverse changes in health status (Selye, 1974), few epidemiological studies with broad-based populations have examined the relationship between the social environment and stress hormones. A recent study from the anthropology literature, which examined the association between salivary cortisol and behavioral observations in 247 children over an 8-year period in a small Caribbean village, documented a strong relationship between salivary cortisol and psychosocial stress (Flinn & England, 1997). This study found that traumatic family events, such as severe punishment of the child, family fights, residence change, family alcohol abuse, and the child being shamed, were all associated with changes in cortisol levels. Hard physical work, competitive play, physical fights, and quarrels with peers also influenced salivary cortisol levels. The study also found that the current family environment and developmental traumas were related to cortisol levels. Children with severe caretaking problems in infancy (neglect, parental alcoholism, or maternal absence) exhibited either unusually low basal cortisol with occasional high spikes or chronically high levels of cortisol. The first profile was more common in males and associated with antisocial behavior, while the second profile was more common in girls and associated with anxiety and withdrawal behavior. These data provide impressive evidence of how the social context can influence cortisol levels.

There is a need for integrative models that seek to understand how environmental demands, appraisal processes, emotional states, and behavioral and physiological responses relate to each other and combine with inherited susceptibilities to increase the risk for psychiatric illness. At the present time, we know little about the relationship among various risk factors and resources or how they combine additively or interactively to affect physical and mental health. A more comprehensive, multidisciplinary, and integrated approach could contribute to a better understanding of the mechanisms and processes through which personal and social resources operate to affect mental health and SES inequities in health.

CONCLUSION

The association between SES and mental health has been observed for a long time. However, our understanding of the mechanisms and processes by which these relationships occur is still limited from both a scientific and policy perspective. There is clearly a need for more research to identify the underlying causal dynamics. Research of this kind must distinguish the basic or fundamental causes of inequalities in health from surface causes (House et al., 1990; Link & Phelan, 1995; Williams, 1990); that is, researchers must give greater attention to the ways in which risk factors measured at the individual level are clustered and rooted in a common set of upstream causal forces (Kaplan, 1995). Importantly, such an approach recognizes that effective societal interventions are possible even if all of the intervening biological and psychological mechanisms are not well understood.

Larger societal trends suggest that a large and potentially increasing segment of the population may be especially vulnerable to mental health problems. There is growing inequality in income and wealth and an absolute decline in the economic status of at least some racial minority populations compared to whites in the United States (Williams & Collins, 1995). Continued corporate downsizing, restructuring, and retrenchment ensures that the experience of downward social mobility and its attendant psychological sequelae may be increasingly commonplace (Newman, 1989). Research has long demonstrated that there is a strong positive relationship at the societal level between adverse changes in the economy and increases in suicide, first admissions and readmissions to mental hospitals, and alcohol abuse (Brenner, 1995). Thus, there is a need for a renewed commitment to reduce the inequalities in societal institutions that appear to be the basic causes of social inequalities in health (Williams & Collins, 1995).

ACKNOWLEDGMENTS: Preparation of this chapter was supported by a grant from NIMH on Psychosocial Factors in Mental Health and Illness (5 T32 MH16806) and a grant from NIMH on Race, Stress and Mental Health (1 R01 MH57425-01) and by the MacArthur Network on Socioeconomic Status and Health.

REFERENCES

Adler, N. E., Boyce, T., Chesney, M. A., Folkman, S., & Syme, S. L. (1993). Socioeconomic inequalities in health: No easy solution. *Journal of the American Medical Association, 269,* 3140–3145.

Antonovsky, A. (1967). Social class, life expectancy and overall mortality. *Milbank Memorial Fund Quarterly, 45,* 31–73.

Brenner, M. H. (1995). Political economy and health. In B. C. Amick, III, S. Levine, A. R. Tarlov, & D. C. Walsh (Eds.), *Society and Health,* (pp. 211–246). New York: Oxford University Press.

Broadhead, W. E., Blazer, D. G., George, L. K., & Tse, C. K. (1990). Depression, disability days, and days lost from work in a prospective epidemiologic survey. *Journal of the American Medical Association, 264,* 2524–2528.

Bruce, M. L., Kim, K., Leaf, P. J., & Jacobs, S. (1990). Depressive episodes and dysphoria resulting from conjugal bereavement in a prospective community sample. *American Journal of Psychiatry, 147,* 608–611.

Bruce, M. L., & Leaf, P. J. (1989). Psychiatric disorders and 15-month mortality in a community sample of older adults. *American Journal of Public Health, 70,* 727–730.

Bunker, J. P., Gomby, D. S., & Kehrer, B. H. (Eds.). (1989). *Pathways to health: The role of social factors.* Menlo Park, CA: Henry J. Kaiser Family Foundation.

Carroll, D., & Smith, G. D. (1997). Health and socioeconomic position: A commentary. *Journal of Health Psychology, 2,* 275–282.

Cockerham, W. C. (1990). A test of the relationship between race, socioeconomic status and psychological distress. *Social Science Medicine, 31,* 1321–1326.

Cohen, S., Kessler, R. C., & Underwood, L. G. (1995). *Measuring stress.* New York: Oxford University Press.

Cooper, R. S., & David, R. (1986). The biological concept of race and its application to public health and epidemiology. *Journal of Health and Politics, Policy and Law, 11,* 97–116.

Dohrenwend, B. P. (1990). Socioeconomic status (SES) and psychiatric disorders. *Psychiatry and Psychiatric Epidemiology, 25,* 41–47.

Dohrenwend, B. P., & Dohrenwend, B. (1969). *Social status and psychological disorder: A casual inquiry.* New York: Wiley.

Dohrenwend, B. P., Levav, I., Shrout, P. E., Schwartz, S., Naveh, G., Link, B. G., Skodol, A. E., & Stueve, A. (1992). Socioeconomic status and psychiatric disorders: The causation-selection issue. *Science, 255,* 946–952.

Downey, C., & Coyne, J. (1991). Social factors and psychopathology: Stress, social support and coping processes. *Annual Review of Psychology, 42,* 401–425.

Duncan, G. J. (1988). The volatility of family income over the life course. In P. Bates, D. Featherman, & R. Lerner (Eds.), *Life span development and behavior.* Hillsdale, NJ: Erlbaum.

Duncan, G. J., Brooks-Gunn, J., & Klebanov, P. K. (1994). Economic deprivation and early childhood development. *Child Development, 65,* 296–319.

Eller, T. J. (1994). *Household wealth and asset ownership: 1991.* U.S. Bureau of the Census, Current Population Reports, P70-34. Washington, DC: U.S. Government Printing Office.

Faris, R. E. L., & Dunham, H. W. (1939). *Mental disorders in urban areas: An ecological study of schizophrenia and other psychoses.* Chicago: University of Chicago Press.

Flinn, M. V., & England, B. (1997). Social economics of childhood glucocorticoid stress response and health. *American Journal of Physical Anthropology, 102,* 33–53.

Forsyth, B. H., & Lessler, J. T. (1991). Cognitive laboratory methods: A taxonomy. In P. P. Biemer, R. M. Groves, L. E. Lyberg, N. A. Mathiowetz, & S. Sudman (Eds.), *Measurement Errors in Surveys* (pp. 393–418). New York: Wiley.

Fox, J. W. (1990). Social class, mental illness, and social mobility: The social selection-drift hypothesis for serious mental illness. *Journal of Health and Social Behavior, 31,* 344–353.

Hollingshead, A. B., & Redlich, F. C. (1958). *Social class and mental illness: A community study.* New York: Wiley.

Holzer, C., Shea, B., Swanson, J., Leaf, P., Myers, J., George, L., Weissman, M., & Bednarski, P. (1986). The increased risk for specific psychiatric disorders among persons of low socioeconomic status. *American Journal of Social Psychiatry, 6,* 259–271.

House, J. S., Kessler, R. C., Herzog, A. R., Mero, R., Kinney, A., & Breslow, M. (1990). Age, socioeconomic status, and health. *Milbank Memorial Fund Quarterly, 68,* 383–411.

Ilfeld, F. (1978). Psychological status of community residents along major demographic dimensions. *Archives of General Psychiatry, 35,* 716–724.

Kaplan, G. A. (1995). Where do shared pathways lead? Some reflections on a research agenda. *Psychosomatic Medicine, 57,* 208–212.

Kaplan, G. A., & Lynch, J. W. (1997). Editorial: Whither studies on the socioeconomic foundations of population health? *American Journal of Public Health, 87,* 1409–1411.

Kennedy, G. J., Kelman, H. R., & Thomas, C. (1991). Persistence and remission of depressive symptoms in late life. *American Journal of Psychiatry, 148,* 174–178.

Kessler, R. C. (1979). Stress, social status, and psychological distress. *Journal of Health and Social Behavior, 20,* 259–273.

Kessler, R. C. (1983). Methodological issues in the study of psychosocial stress. In H. B. Kaplan (Ed.), *Psychosocial stress: Trends in theory and research* (pp. 267–341). New York: Academic Press.

Kessler, R. C., House, J. S., Anspach, R., & Williams, D. R. (1995). Social Psychology and Health. In K. S. Cook, G. A. Fine, & J. S. House (Eds.), *Sociological Perspectives on Social Psychology* (pp. 548–570). Boston: Allyn & Bacon.

Kessler, R. C., McGonagle, K. A., Zhao, S., Nelson, C. B., Hughes, M., Eshleman, S., Wittchen, H.-U., & Kendler, K. S. (1994). Lifetime and 12-month prevalence of DSM-III-R psychiatric disorders in the United States. *Archives of General Psychiatry, 51,* 8–19.

Kessler, R. C., & Neighbors, H. W. (1986). A new perspective on the relationships among race, social class, and psychological distress. *Journal of Health and Social Behavior, 27,* 107–115.

Krieger, N., Rowley, D. L., Herman, A. A., Avery, B., & Phillips, M. T. (1993). Racism, sexism, and social class: Implications for studies of health, disease, and well-being. *American Journal of Preventive Medicine, 9*(Suppl. 6), 82–122.

Krieger, N., Williams, D. R., & Moss, N. (1997). Measuring social class in U.S. public health research: Concepts, methodologies, and guidelines. *Annual Review of Public Health, 18,* 341–378.

Liberatos, P., Link, B., & Kelsey, J. (1988). The measurement of social class in epidemiology. *Epidemiologic Reviews, 10,* 87–121.

Link, B., & Dohrenwend, B. P. (1980). Formulation of hypotheses about the true prevalence of demoralization. In B. P. Dohrenwend (Ed.), *Mental Illness in the United States: Epidemiological estimates* (pp. 114–132). New York: Praeger.

Link, B., Dohrenwend, B. P., & Skodol, A. E. (1986). Socio-economic status and schizophrenia: Noisome occupational characteristics as a risk factor. *American Sociological Review, 51,* 242–258.

Link, B., & Phelan, J. (1995). Social conditions as fundamental causes of disease. *Journal of Health and Social Behavior*, extra issue, 80–94.

Marmot, M. (1989). Responses to four background papers. In J. P. Bunker, D. S. Gomby, & B. H. Kehrer (Eds.), *Pathways to health: The role of social factors* (pp. 97–126). Menlo Park, CA: Henry J. Kaiser Family Foundation.

Marmot, M. G., Kogevinas, M., & Elston, M. A. (1987). Social/economic status and disease. *Annual Review of Public Health, 8,* 111–135.

McDonough, P., Duncan, G. .J., Williams, D. R., & House, J. (1997). Income dynamics and adult mortality in the U.S., 1972–1989. *American Journal of Public Health, 87,* 1476–1483.

Miller, J. E., &. Korenman, S. (1994). Poverty and children's nutritional status in the United States. *American Journal of Epidemiology, 140,* 233–243.

Mirowsky, J., & Ross, C. R. (1989). *Social causes of psychological distress.* New York: Aldine de Gruyter.

Murphy, J. M., Olivier, D. C., Monson, R. R., Sobol, A. M., Federman, E. B., & Leighton, A. H. (1991). Depression and anxiety in relation to social status. *Archives of General Psychiatry, 48,* 223–229.

Newman, K. S. (1989). *Falling from grace: The experience of downward mobility in the American middle class.* New York: Vintage Books.

Ortega, S. T., & Corzine, J. (1990). Socioeconomic status and mental disorder. *Research in Community and Mental Health, 6,* 149–182.

Oxman, T. E., Berman, L. F., Kasl, S. V., Freeman, D. H., & Barrett, J. (1992). Social support and depressive symptoms in the elderly. *American Journal of Epidemiology, 135,* 356–368.

Pearlin, L. (1989). The sociological study of stress. *Journal of Health and Social Behavior, 30,* 241–256.

Power, C., & Manor, O. (1992). Explaining social class differences in psychological health among young adults: A longitudinal perspective. *Social Psychiatry and Psychiatric Epidemiology, 27*(6), 284–291.

Robins, L. N., Helzer, J. E., Croughan, J., & Ratcliff, K. S. (1981). The NIMH Diagnostic Interview Schedule: Its history, characteristics and validity. *Archives of General Psychiatry, 28,* 381–389.

Robins, L. N., Helzer, J. E., Weissman, M. M., Orvaschel, H., Gruenberg, E., Burke, J. D., Jr., & Regier, D. A. (1984). Lifetime prevalence of specific psychiatric disorders in three sites. *Archives of General Psychiatry, 41,* 949–958.

Robins, L. N., & Regier, D. A. (1991). *Psychiatric disorders in America: The Epidemiologic Catchment Area Study.* New York: Free Press.

Robinson, J. (1984). Racial inequality and the probability of occupation-related injury or illness. *Milbank Memorial Fund Quarterly, 62,* 567–590.

Rogler, L. H., Malgady, R., & Tyron, W. W. (1992). Evaluation of mental health: Issues of memory in the Diagnostic Interview Schedule. *Journal of Nervous and Mental Disease, 180,* 215–222.

Sampson, R. J., & Wilson, W. J. (1995). Toward a theory of race, crime, and urban inequality. In J. Hagan & R. D. Peterson (Eds.), *Crime and inequality* (pp. 37–54). Stanford, CA: Stanford University Press.

Sezler, H. (1974). *Stress without distress.* Philadelphia: Lippincott.

Takeuchi, D., Williams, D. R., & Adair, R. K. (1991). Economic stress in the family and children's emotional and behavioral problems. *Journal of Marriage and the Family, 52,* 1031–1041.

Turner, R. J., Wheaton, B., & Lloyd, D. A. (1995). The epidemiology of social stress. *American Sociological Review, 60,* 104–125.

Ulbrich, P., Warheit, G., & Zimmerman, R. S. (1989). Race, socioeconomic status, and psychological distress: an examination of differential vulnerability. *Journal of Health and Social Behavior, 30,* 131–146.

Weissman, M. M., Myers, J. K., & Ross, C. E. (1986). *Community surveys of mental disorders.* Series in Psychosocial Epidemiology. New Brunswick, NJ: Rutgers University Press.

Wheaton, B. (1990). Life transitions, role histories, and mental health. *American Sociological Review, 55,* 209–223.

Wheaton, B. (1994). Samplilng the stress universe. In W. R. Arison & J. A.. Gotlib (Eds.), *Stress and mental health: Contemporary issues and prospects for the future* (pp. 77–114). New York: Plenum Press.

Wilhelm, S. M. (1987). Economic demise of blacks in America: a prelude to genocide? *Journal of Black Studies, 17,* 201–254.

Williams, D. R. (1996a). The health of the African American population. In S. Pedraza & R. Rumbaut (Eds.), *Origins and Destinies: Immigration, Race, and Ethnicity in America* (pp. 406–416). Belmont, CA: Wadsworth.

Williams, D. R. (1996b). Race/ethnicity and socioeconomic status: Measurement and methodological issues. *International Journal or Health Services, 26,* 483–505.

Williams, D. R. (1997). Race and health: Basic questions, emerging directions. *Annals of Epidemiology, 7,* 322–333.

Williams, D. R. (1990). Socioeconomic differentials in health: A review and redirection. *Social Psychology Quarterly, 53,* 81–99.

Williams, D. R., & Collins, C. (1995). U.S. socioeconomic and racial differences in health. *Annual Review of Sociology, 21,* 349–386.

Williams, D. R., & House, J. S. (1991). Stress, social support, control and coping: A social epidemiologic view. In B. Badura & I. Kickbusch, (Eds.), *Health promotion research: Towards a new social epidemiology* (pp. 147–172). Copenhagen: World Health Organization.

Williams, D. R., Takeuchi, D., & Adair, R. (1992). Socioeconomic status and psychiatric disorder among blacks and whites. *Social Forces, 71,* 179–194.

Williams, D, R., Yu, Y., Jackson, J. S., & Anderson, N. B. (1997). Racial differences in physical and mental health: Socioeconomic status, stress and discrimination. *Journal of Health Psychology, 2,* 335–351.

CHAPTER 9

Race, Ethnicity, and Culture in the Sociology of Mental Health

TONY N. BROWN
SHERRILL L. SELLERS
KENDRICK T. BROWN
JAMES S. JACKSON

INTRODUCTION

The growing racial and ethnic heterogeneity of the U.S. population will require mental health researchers to think more seriously about sociocultural variation. To date, researchers have not given sufficient attention to how race, ethnicity, and culture are linked to one another and to mental health. For instance, race can be an important factor in predicting exposure and vulnerability to stress, coping strategies, social support, and, in turn, mental health status. Race, however, grossly aggregates people and often hides subtle, and not so subtle, variations in mental health status and functioning. This aggregation masks and perhaps distorts ethnic differences and cultural influences within racial groups. It is neither scientifically nor clinically valid to categorize, sample or theorize about racial groups—such as Whites, Asians, Hispanics, or Blacks—without recognizing the ethnic variation and cultural influences within these populations.

Despite this heterogeneity, many social scientists are content to "control" for race or

TONY N. BROWN, SHERRILL L. SELLERS, AND JAMES S. JACKSON • Institute for Social Research, University of Michigan, Ann Arbor, Michigan 48106.   KENDRICK T. BROWN • Department of Psychology, Macalaster College, St. Paul, Minnesota 55105.

Handbook of the Sociology of Mental Health, edited by Carol S. Aneshensel and Jo C. Phelan. Kluwer Academic/Plenum Publishers, New York, 1999.

ethnicity (i.e., to include race as a background factor in statistical models) without fully considering the sociological meaning of these constructs. They are content to make disclaimers about the difficulties in sampling and studying discrete ethnic groups, or the difficulties in accounting for the complexities of cultural influences. For these reasons, we have an incomplete understanding of how race, ethnicity, and culture individually, and in interaction, influence mental health.

This chapter briefly highlights the complexity of studying race, ethnicity, and cultural influences, specifically as these three constructs relate to the sociology of mental health. We argue that race, ethnicity, and culture influence mental health status in three important ways. First, the reliable and valid *assessment* of mental health is hindered by an inadequate sampling of racial and ethnic groups. Second, race and ethnicity are *social statuses* that can be associated with stressful experiences among subordinate groups. For example, conflicting cultural influences, experiences of discrimination, and immigration are often associated with, and directly related to, adverse mental health outcomes. Third, and finally, *predictors* of mental health outcomes can vary in important ways depending upon race, ethnicity, and cultural influences.

These three issues provide the organizing framework for this chapter. Though broad in scope, our discussion is not meant to be exhaustive; rather, we aim to illustrate the implications of these issues for the study of mental health within a sociological framework and thus to provide a directive for researchers in the mental health field. To adequately explore these issues, we first define the concepts of race, ethnicity, culture, and cultural influences. We then briefly review what is currently known about the distribution of mental health outcomes across several racial and ethnic populations. We conclude this chapter by suggesting a research plan for the next millennium, a period that will see phenomenal changes in racial, ethnic, and cultural diversity in the United States.

UNCONFOUNDING RACE, ETHNICITY, AND CULTURE: A MURKY MESS OF MISCONCEPTIONS

In secular and academic circles, the concepts "race," "ethnicity," and "culture" are frequently used but rarely defined (Adebimpe, 1994; Wilkinson & King, 1987; Williams, Lavisso-Mourey, & Warren, 1994). In some cases, these terms are used interchangeably. For example, published articles in the sociological literature describe "Hispanics" or "American Indians" as racial groups (Williams, 1997). Such classifications fail to distinguish between race and ethnicity. In addition, culture, and "cultural influences," are not well understood. In particular, sociologists often fail to consider the impact of cultural influences on individuals and racial groups. This oversight often leads to the discussion of cultural influences as "residual effects." The confounding of these terms complicates the study and understanding of mental health status and functioning in the United States. The following sections define the constructs of race, ethnicity, and cultural influences in a theoretically meaningful way. These definitions establish a common language that will allow us to discuss the mental health implications of these constructs in a clear way.

Defining Race

Race is undoubtedly one of the least understood sociological terms in use today (Wilkinson & King, 1987; Williams, 1997). Some scholars believe that race is a biological category that is fairly immutable. It is hypothesized to be a category that distinguishes among groups of individuals on the basis of a select number of shared genetic characteristics and the distribution of a constellation of genes. The evidence for the biological basis of racial categorization is fairly weak and often conflicting (Cooper, 1984; Williams, 1997). Racial classifications based upon biology, although often thought of as valid and scientific, tend to vary arbitrarily depending upon the social, political, or economic climate, and on the biases of the individuals responsible for creating the racial taxonomy.

Other researchers are reluctant to adopt such a strictly biological definition of race. Instead, they choose to conceptualize race as a socially constructed category that is based on observed phenotypic manifestations of presumed, underlying genetic differences (Cooper, 1984; Schaefer, 1990). This definition suggests that race is viable as a biological concept only in that there are ascriptive markers (e.g., skin color) that have important social consequences. We agree with those scholars who adhere to the position that race is essentially a socially constructed category. Racial classifications usually identified in the United States are White, Black, Asian, Hispanic, and American Indian (Williams, 1997).

Defining Ethnicity

The conceptual difficulty associated with operationalizing ethnicity in the United States is evidenced in standard measures of race. In commonly used measures of race, the "ethnic" categories of Hispanic and American Indian are often included as racial categories. It is also evidenced in the scarcity of standardized measures of ethnicity. Generally, *ethnicity* is a term that refers to a grouping of persons according to a shared geographic, national, or cultural heritage (Berreman, 1991). Ethnicity taps into a "putative" connectedness grounded in geographic proximity and in shared norms and values passed on from generation to generation. We use the word *putative* because, in many contexts, mixtures of various ethnic groups can become almost completely racialized (e.g., Whites in the United States are comprised of various ethnic groups). Race and ethnicity tend to be confounded because of racism and racialization in this country (Adebimpe, 1994; Williams & Fenton, 1994). Nonetheless, members of a particular race can be further classified and described according to their ethnicity.

Most scholars would agree that humans are not born with an ethnicity. It is a learned characteristic. The content of socialization to ethnicity (i. e., culture) can include things such as language, styles, prejudices, daily activities, values, and so on. (Berreman, 1991). Ethnicity and culture are inextricably bound together, and each binds groups of individuals together. Examples of ethnic groups in the United States include Haitians, Hopi Indians, Cubans, Mexicans, Europeans, and Filipinos. These examples include a number of groups that range broadly in terms of factors such as size, phenotypic distinctiveness, and salience of ethnic identity. Each individual group shares some common geographic origin, and shares some collective norms and values. Some of these groups are themselves comprised of multiple ethnic groups. For example, the umbrella category of Hispanic comprises Puerto Ricans, Mexicans, Dominicans, Cubans, and many other Spanish-speaking ethnic groups.

Defining Culture and Cultural Influences

Culture is the general canvas on which the ethnic and racial mosaic of the United States is painted (e.g., American culture; Western culture). Culture is also a phenomenon associated with a specific group (e.g., Vietnamese). Thus culture has multiple-level, bidirectional influences on both aggregate groups and individuals. For instance, whereas American culture has an impact on Asians, the presence of Asians in the United States affects American culture. Culture can be conceived of as a factor that transcends supposedly rigid categorical memberships (e.g., race or ethnicity). It is "unbounded" (Kroeber & Kluckhorn, 1952; Swindler, 1986). Unboundedness refers to the fact that individuals, regardless of their racial or ethnic status, can be exposed to and affected by multiple cultural influences. Culture, therefore, can have both general and specific influences on any given person. An individual living in the United States, for example, may be exposed to the general American culture, while simultaneously nurturing the specific culture associated with his or her ethnic heritage (e.g., German).

Culture should be conceptualized as a dynamic paradigm that shapes how one sees oneself in relation to the social environment, and how one functions as a way of life (Geertz, 1973, Kroeber & Kluckhorn, 1952). Swindler (1986) defines culture as a symbolic vehicle of meaning, including beliefs and rituals as well as informal practices such as language and activities of daily life. Consistent with Swindler, we believe that cultural influences transmit dynamic and action-oriented ways of living devised by people to meet biological and psychosocial needs. These ways of living are passed on from generation to generation but may change over time and across regions in response to larger sociological forces.

Figure 9.1 illustrates the relationships between race, ethnicity, and culture. This figure can be used to understand a person's link to a racial and ethnic group while accounting for multiple cultural influences. The shape of each construct is different, illustrating that each construct has a unique meaning. At the same time, however, the shapes overlap somewhat to illustrate their interconnectedness and are posted on the background of a general culture. For example, within the White racial group, there are many ethnic groups (e.g., Poles, Germans, Italians). Although each ethnic group has a distinct culture, they may all share a general culture (e.g., American). The same is true of racial groups that share a general culture (e.g., some African Americans share a Southern culture in the United States). Strictly speaking, racial groups (e.g., Hispanics, Blacks) do not have cultures, but ethnic groups within racialized groups can have a specific culture (e.g., Cuban culture; African American culture).

A systematic approach to conceptualizing race, ethnicity, and cultural influences is necessary if we are adequately to comprehend their joint impact on mental health outcomes. We must develop measures that account for the racialization of groups and yet consider the viability of ethnicity and culture influences. Such measures must become standard to any and all data collection instruments in which social scientists desire to gather reliable and valid data. Figure 9.2 illustrates an example of a series of questions that may permit the comprehensive disaggregation of data into categories that aim specifically to untangle race, ethnicity, and culture. The first question asks about racial group membership. The second question asks about ethnic group membership. The final question asks potential respondents about culture and cultural influences. With the information collected from this set of questions, mental health researchers and other social scientists would be in a position to address many assumptions about race, ethnicity, and culture. For example, with access to data yielded from a series of questions such as those in Figure 9.2, mental health researchers who study acculturation and immigration would be able to explore previously unexamined nuances. Researchers could compare those respondents who self-identify as Asian, claiming a Chinese ethnicity, and Chinese and American cultural influences, to

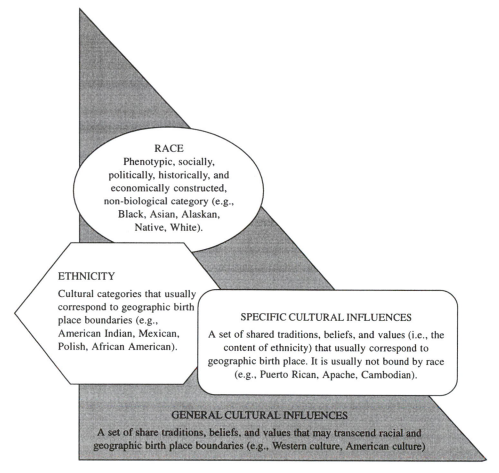

FIGURE 9.1. The conceptual distinction between race, ethnicity, and cultural influences.

those who self-identify as Asian and claim a Chinese ethnicity but indicate only Chinese cultural influences.

THE IMPORTANCE OF RACE, ETHNICITY, AND CULTURE IN THE STUDY OF MENTAL HEALTH

The fundamental issue that we address in this chapter is how race, ethnicity, and culture influence mental health. We propose that race, ethnicity, and culture influence mental health through at least three interrelated ways: (1) through *assessment* of mental health in terms of definition, measurement, sampling, and diagnosis; (2) by association with *social statuses* that embody stressful experiences; and (3) by altering relationships with *predictors* of mental health. The following section addresses these issues.

Which category best describes you?

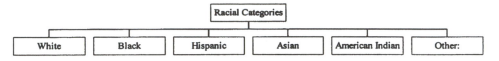

What category best describes you? (Check all that apply)

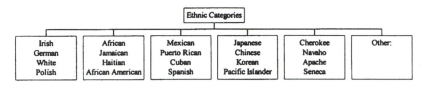

Which culture(s) is most important to you? (Check all that apply)

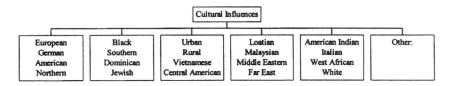

FIGURE 9.2.   Measuring race, ethnicity, and culture in the United States.

Assessment

We argue that race, ethnicity, and culture can directly influence the assessment of mental health. This influence can occur in the estimation of psychiatric disorders in treatment settings and in epidemiological community surveys. Assessment is also influenced by such things as clinical misdiagnosis (Adebimpe, 1981; Neighbors, Jackson, Campbell, & Williams, 1989; Rogler, 1996a,b), differential item interpretation by race or ethnicity (Gallo, Cooper-Patrick, & Hochman, forthcoming; Lawson, 1986), and clinical misinterpretation and misclassification of symptoms (Rogler, 1996a,b; Wade, 1993). Culture-bound syndromes (Alarcon, 1995; Levine & Caw, 1995) also present an assessment issue, because the appropriate measurement of particular disorders is partly determined by cultural influences. We further note the difficulty in attaining a representative sample of racial and ethnic groups in community epidemiological surveys (e.g., American Indians and Alaskan Natives) (Meketon, 1983; Norton & Manson, 1996). Many factors, such as residential racial segregation, geographic isolation, geographic clustering, systematic census undercounting (Williams & Harris-Reid, forthcoming), and the small size of some ethnic groups (Sue, Sue, Sue, & Takeuchi, 1995) all affect sample quality. The problem of appropriate and representative sampling is fundamentally related to our understanding of race, ethnicity, and cultural influences. We advocate, as do others (Sue et al., 1995; Williams & Harris-Reid, forthcoming), that truly representative, large samples of one or two racial and ethnic groups within a culturally sensitive framework will advance our overall knowledge of mental health issues more than small samples multiple groups.

The prevalence and incidence of psychiatric disorder and symptomatology can be estimated in community epidemiological surveys due to recent advances in survey diagnostic tools assessing mental health (Kessler et al., 1994; Robins, Helzer, Croughan, & Ratcliff, 1981; Robins & Regier, 1991). The development of the structured diagnostic interview allows lay interviewers to collect data that can be used to measure the incidence and prevalence of psychiatric disorders. Unfortunately, many psychiatric epidemiological studies do not collect data on sufficient numbers of individuals representing various racial or ethnic groups to make reliable comparisons. This is particularly true for early studies that had small samples of non-White ethnic and racial groups, at times as low as 1%. Despite large epidemiological studies such as the National Comorbidity Study (NCS; Kessler et al., 1994) and the Epidemiologic Catchment Study (ECA) (Robins et al., 1981; Robins & Regier, 1991), coverage problems remain. For instance, low response rates among certain segments of ethnic groups (e.g., African American men) continue to bias findings for many studies. Because of undercounting, even weighting to make the sample comparable to U.S. census estimates does not overcome the nonresponse problem (Williams & Harris-Reid, forthcoming). Moreover, the interracial, interethnic, and intercultural applicability of structured diagnostic interview schedules has not been sufficiently tested (Hendricks, 1983; Rogler, 1993b). Thus, general conclusions about the mental health status of various racial and ethnic groups are often offered without considering the representativeness of the sample, the adequacy of the measures, or unmeasured heterogeneity within and between particular groups.

Heterogeneity within and between racial and ethnic groups, including multiple cultural influences, affects researchers' ability to make comparisons and generalizations, and to frame theoretical and policy implications. For example, research indicates that some racial and ethnic minority groups are more likely to engage in the somatization of psychological problems (Kuo, 1984); that is, these individuals manifest psychological problems as physical symptoms. Yet a number of the symptom checklists used to determine disorders are designed to rule out physical health problems. This can result in underreporting of mental health problems among minority groups (Vega & Rumbaut, 1991).

Misdiagnosis of particular psychiatric disorders is also an issue for members of racial and ethnic groups (Adebimpe, 1994; Neighbors et al., 1989). Even though we focus on Blacks, other racialized and ethnic groups face the same issues. Many studies show that among comparable patient samples, Whites are more likely to be diagnosed with a mood disorder, whereas Blacks are more likely to be given a diagnosis of schizophrenia (see Neighbors, 1997, for a review). Psychiatrists tend to give correct diagnoses for a clear schizophrenic case description or personality disorder case description when no identifying racial information on the patients is given. When race is specified, however, regardless of psychiatrists' race, Black patients with identical symptoms are more likely than White patients to be given more severe diagnoses (Loring & Powell, 1988). Black inpatients and outpatients compromise double or more of the cases of diagnosed schizophrenia compared to White patients in the entire mental health system (Lawson, Hepler, Holladay, & Cuffel, 1994). Even when instructed to use DSM-III-R criteria in reviewing the charts of Black patients, clinicians still are significantly more likely to diagnose Black patients as schizo-phrenic (Strakowski, Shelton, & Kolbrener, 1993) than White patients with comparable symptom profiles. Raskin, Crook, and Herman (1975), in a study of diagnostic bias, found that Blacks are more likely to be diagnosed with some form of schizophrenia, whereas white patients with comparable symptoms are diagnosed as depressed (Adebimpe, 1981). This trend in clinical misdiagnosis is evidence that race, ethnicity, and cultural influences can alter the assessment of mental health and adversely influence the interaction between researcher/clinician and respondent/client.

Social Statuses

Race and ethnicity are stratifying social statuses that place some groups higher on the socioeconomic ladder (e.g., status, education, income, employment) than other groups be-cause of barriers, for example, conflict in cultural influences, racism, nativity and immigra-tion status (Adebimpe, 1994; Burke, 1984; Carter, 1993; Gary, 1991; Kaplan & Marks, 1990; Schaefer, 1990; Smith, 1985; Williams, 1997). Race and ethnic status can be linked to potentially stressful experiences. For example, recent immigrants may experience acculturative stress (Berry, 1998; Vega & Rumbaut, 1991) when forced to decide the rela-tive importance of their original cultural identity in juxtaposition to an Anglo identity (Gor-don, 1961), or may report learned helplessness (Fernando, 1984) or hypervigilance (Essed, 1991) as a result of systematic social exclusion from mainstream society on the basis of their race, ethnicity, or cultural distinctiveness. Furthermore, members of subordinate ra-cial or ethnic groups may internalize notions propagated in the general culture about their inherent inferiority (Akbar, 1991).

All people experience some amount of stress, attributable to multiple roles and sta-tuses (e.g., worker, woman, or immigrant), that directly influences mental health. In the stress and mental health literatures, however, researchers (Carter, 1993; Gary, 1991; Thoits, 1983; Vega & Rumbaut, 1991; Williams & Fenton, 1994) admit that sparse attention is devoted to the stress one experiences, or does not experience, because of race, ethnicity, or conflict in cultural influences. Even less attention is dedicated to understanding how defi-nitions of psychiatric disorder, psychological distress, and mental well-being, as well as norms dictating appropriate coping strategies, might vary across sociocultural groups. An individual's culture, for example, might influence their definition of illness, perceptions of symptoms, and health behaviors (Lawson, 1986; Williams & Fenton, 1994; Zheng et al., 1997).

There is a growing literature that suggests subjective reports of racial and ethnic dis-crimination are related to adverse mental health outcomes (Amaro & Johnson, 1987; Jack-son et al., 1996; Kuo, 1995; Salgado de Snyder, 1987; Smith, 1985). We believe that racial discrimination is inherently stressful, partly because of the immutability of phenotypic char-acteristics and the salience of the identities that are often the basis of exclusion and mal-treatment. Similarly, immigration is a process that is closely linked to ethnic status and can have mental health consequences (Vega & Rumbaut, 1991). Berry (1998) explores accul-turation at the group and individual levels. He suggests that psychological acculturation operates at the macrolevel (e.g., society of origin, type of acculturation, acculturation ide-ology) and microlevel (e.g., acculturative stress, social support, age, gender, personality). Furthermore, Berry notes that acculturation is complex because it affects all groups in-volved in the transformation, not just the acculturating groups. He cautiously concludes that we cannot be sure about "how" and "if" acculturation affects health without considering its multidimensionality.

Cultural beliefs about the causes and consequences of mental illness can also influence treatment outcomes and symptom expression (Lawson, 1986; Meketon, 1983). For instance, symptoms unique to a given culture (e.g., belief in spirit possession) may be unfamiliar to the clinician and can consequently result in misdiagnosis or misspecification of symptomatology (Levine & Caw, 1995; Narduzzi 1994; Rogler, 1993a,b; Zheng et al., 1997). Cultural conflict between researcher/clinician and respondent/client may occur, and this may be one factor leading to symptom misinterpretation. The often implicit assumption is that clinical disorder, psychological distress, subjective well-being, and experiences of social stress are universal. Research indicates, however, that there is considerable racial, ethnic, and cultural variation in the onset of a given disorder, nature of symptoms (Gallo et al., forthcoming; Lawson, 1986; Vega & Rumbaut, 1991), vulnerability to stress (Broman, 1989), willingness to discuss mental dysfunction, social support (Kuo & Tsai, 1986), hardiness (James, 1994; Neff, 1985; Sue et al., 1995), likelihood of seeking professional psychiatric care (Neighbors, Caldwell, Thompson, & Jackson, 1993), and a range of other factors.

Predictors of Mental Health

Race, ethnicity, and culture may influence important predictors of mental health status. These include some well researched predictors: age, appraisal of stress, choice of coping strategy, effectiveness of coping strategy, and personal and group identities. Race, ethnicity, and culture can shape how and whether stress is perceived and how particular racial and ethnic groups cope with it. For instance, Kuo (1995) examined the distribution of discrimination episodes and problem- versus emotion-focused coping in a sample of 499 Asian Americans (i.e., Koreans, Japanese, Filipinos and Chinese in Seattle, Washington). Respondents were asked whether (1) they experience discrimination when seeking housing, (2) they are treated badly or differently than whites at their job, and (3) they experience any other racial discrimination. Fifteen percent reported housing discrimination, 30% reported work-related incidents, and 39% reported some other kind of discriminatory episode (e.g., internment, trouble getting a license, and racial jokes and slurs). Kuo used nine items from a coping inventory that assessed the two types of coping styles. Statistically significant differences were found between ethnic groups in episodes of discrimination, coping styles, cultural values, and perceptions of minority status. Among other things, Filipino and Japanese respondents were more likely to report discrimination than Koreans in this sample. Kuo also found that Chinese respondents were less likely to use problem-focused coping, whereas Filipinos were more likely to use emotion-focused coping when compared to Koreans. Japanese and Chinese respondents used similar coping strategies. In another study of discrimination, mental health, and coping, Jackson, Williams, and Torres (under review) examined the impact of subjective reports of racial discrimination on the mental health of Whites. They found that the degree to which the consequences of such discrimination were adverse depended upon the ethnic status of their White respondents. For example, Italians and other White ethnic groups that historically have experienced discrimination were more adversely affected by discrimination than were other White ethnic groups. The results of these studies suggest that there may be ethnic differences in coping and coping strategies among members of the same racialized group.

Other predictors of mental health, such as racial identity and biological markers, can vary by race, ethnicity, and the array of cultural influences acting on an individual. For example, some researchers (Bowser, 1981; Broman, 1989; Kuo & Ysai, 1986; Jones, 1981; Neff, 1985) believe that the relatively low level of psychopathology among racial and ethnic groups, when compared to Whites, may be attributable to hardiness, group identification, and cultural embeddedness. Other researchers suggest that biology may interact with race, ethnicity, and culture to influence important predictors of psychiatric disorder. For example, Lawson (1986) suggests that there may be important racial and ethnic influences in terms of pharmacotherapy and the effectiveness of psychotropic drugs. He reports that in different racial groups, there are differences in cortisol suppression, enzyme release, and levels of particular hormones among individuals with a psychiatric disorder. Such biological markers have been linked to obsessive–compulsive disorder, schizophrenia, and dementia without depression. Lawson also discusses the empirical finding that Asians and blacks with psychiatric disorders often respond quickly to lower doses of certain psychotropic drugs than do Whites.

IMPLICATIONS OF RACE, ETHNICITY, AND CULTURE: A RESEARCH AGENDA

The quality of data on mental health status among non-White racial and ethnic groups is acceptable for some groups and unacceptable for others. Very few non-White groups in the United States are researched rigorously, and many groups receive little systematic research attention. We chose to illustrate this point using Blacks, Hispanics, Asians, and American Indians/Alaskan Natives. We briefly discuss what we know about racial and ethnic variation in mental health within a framework that acknowledges the influences of general and specific cultures. We believe there are many gaps in the literature, and we enthusiastically encourage researchers to carry out investigations to fill in these gaps.

In the following sections, we do not focus on collecting more complex or larger psychiatric inpatient samples, although such research could be informative. We also make an overarching declaration that the gathering of longitudinal data is important for all groups.

Black Mental Health Status

There is one major source of nationally representative information on a broad range of psychiatric disorders among Blacks—the NCS (Kessler et al., 1994). Blacks in the NCS were oversampled. Unfortunately, this oversampling methodology may systematically exclude important members of that population (Jackson, Tucker & Bowman, 1982). There are numerous other large- and small-scale, multisite and regional random samples that assess particular disorders, psychological distress, and subjective well-being among members of this population (see Vega & Rumbaut, 1991; Williams & Harris-Reid, 1997). There are also a fairly large number of smaller probability surveys that assess mental disorder, psychological distress, and subjective well-being in large metropolitan areas (e.g., the 1995 Detroit Area Study).

Overall, the data suggest that compared to Whites, Blacks report the same, if not lower, levels of current and lifetime psychiatric disorder, about equivalent psychological distress after introducing control variables, and lower levels of subjective well-being. The weakness in studies of Black mental health is that we know very little about interethnic group variation. Patterns in the distribution of mental disorder, distress, or well-being could vary among Southern African Americans, Caribbeans, Haitians, or other ethnic subgroups. Overall, multiple data sources can be used to infer a fairly comprehensive picture of Black mental health, but we need larger, more current samples that are truly representative of the sociocultural variation in this population.

Hispanic Mental Health Status

Hispanics are one of the fastest growing groups in the United States. There are a number of random, regional samples of specific ethnic groups, particularly Mexicans in the Southwest (e.g., Hispanic Health and Nutrition Survey [HHANES]) and Puerto Ricans in New York, that focus on mental health issues in this population (for review see Vega & Rumbaut, 1991). There are, however, few nationally representative samples of this racial group that contain numbers of respondents sufficient for complex statistical analysis of psychiatric disorder. In the NCS, Hispanics constituted 9.7% of the sample, and Kessler et al. (1994) reported that there were no psychiatric disorders for which either lifetime or current prevalence was significantly lower among Hispanics than among non-Hispanic Whites. It is not clear how this finding would change if data on ethnicity, culture, immigration status, and other factors were a taken into account in the NCS. The patterns for psychological distress and well-being are quite complex and depend upon factors such as level of acculturation, employment status, citizenship, and ethnicity.

Larger samples with more than one ethnic group and measures of multiple psychiatric disorders are needed for valid study of Hispanic mental health. We need to design a nationally representative sample of Hispanics, with at least three socially and historically distinct ethnic groups (e.g., Mexicans, Puerto Ricans, and Cubans). Immigration status is also a factor that may influence the mental health of members of this population. Prospective data would shed light on the acculturative process as well as other processes related to coping, psychological distress, and subjective well-being. Such a project must be sensitive to cultural influences on assessment, such as language, ethnic differences in social statuses, and ethnic differences in known correlates of mental health.

Asian Mental Health Status

There are relatively few sources of representative data on psychiatric disorder, psychological distress, or subjective well-being among Asians living in the United States. Supposedly, representative national studies such as the ECA and NCS do not include enough Asians to permit a thorough exploration of their mental health and the role of race, ethnicity, and cultural influences. Studies based upon probability samples of large numbers of Asians are themselves infrequent. The recent Chinese American Psychiatric Epidemiologic Study (CAPES) is a well-designed project that is beginning to shed light upon mental health issues within this population (Sue et al., 1995). This study obtained completed interviews from 1,700 Chinese Americans living in the Los Angeles area. A comparison of psychiatric disorder reported by White respondents in the ECA, NCS, and the Chinese respondents in CAPES suggests that overall levels of psychopathology may be significantly lower in the

CAPES. Compared to the NCS, respondents in the CAPES reported lower levels of manic–depression, major depression, dysthymia, general anxiety disorder, agoraphobia, simple phobia, social phobia, panic attack, and panic disorder. Compared to the ECA, CAPES respondents reported higher levels of major depression and dysthymia. Other studies, using much smaller, convenience community samples, show similar and dissimilar patterns to the general findings from the CAPES (Sue et al., 1995).

A large-scale study of multiple ethnic groups within the Asian population is necessary at this point to verify with any certainty patterns of disorder, distress, and well-being. A study that includes at least three socially and historically distinct ethnic groups (e.g., Japanese, Chinese, Vietnamese) from this population would be an excellent starting point. Three of the largest groups may be reasonable, considering that 50 distinct ethnic groups have been identified (Sue et al., 1995). A probability sample of Asians may be an expensive undertaking, but it would elucidate a number of mental health and stress-related issues in this diverse population. There are obvious cultural influences, such as language, nativity, acculturation, and generation, that must be taken into account in designing and implementing such a study. Interethnic comparability of mental health measures is essential yet potentially difficult to guarantee. However, the rich data generated from such a project would serve to inform the literature.

American Indian and Alaskan Native Mental Health Status

Norton and Manson (1996) report that there are over 250 federally recognized tribes, 209 Alaskan Native villages, and a number of tribes recognized at the state level. There are, however, no major and reliable sources of representative data detailing the distribution of psychiatric disorders, psychological distress, or well-being among American Indians (see Meketon, 1983). One reason that we have such poor data is that American Indians/Alaskan Natives have been systematically exploited and marginalized. Researchers must be sensitive to the cultural traditions of American Indians and Alaskan Natives. Planned research should be designed so that it directly benefits this community; including tribal leaders in the research process would be an important beginning (Norton & Manson, 1996; Wolf, 1989).

The single most researched topic among American Indians is that of alcohol abuse (Narduzzi, 1994; Wolf, 1989). Institutionalized patient studies find higher rates of alcohol abuse among American Indians. This alcohol abuse is often comorbid with other mental health problems, including suicide. Suicide rates for American Indians are significantly higher than among many other non-White groups as well as the White population (Narduzzi, 1994), and the elevation in rates is increasing. There are also important differences that need to be explored between American Indians and Alaskan Natives who live in traditional communities, and those who may be residentially assimilated into mainstream society. American Indians who leave the reservation are not allowed to use Indian Health Service programs, and few urban settings offer the type of support that compares to indigenous support systems (Narduzzi, 1994). In a small study using data from the National Indian Council on Aging, Narduzzi (1994) found significant differences between elderly American Indian men and women, as well as between reservation and urban American Indians. Using the Short Psychiatric Evaluation Schedule (SPES), he reported that coping is more important for women than for men, but that physical health is more important for men than women in predicting psychiatric disorders. Furthermore, reservation elders and urban elders revealed reversed patterns for coping and physical health. Narduzzi suggested that physical health is an essential mediator of poor mental health in urban settings, since the primary motive for migration is usually economic, and physical well-being is essential for earning a living.

Most of what we know about American Indians and Native Alaskans remains speculative (Meketon, 1983). Research is needed that focuses on the distribution of mental health and social stress, interethnic variation in mental health patterns, coping and risk factors, the influence of acculturative stress, and other neglected topics. Researchers have permitted American Indians and Alaskan Natives to remain in the "Other" category. The starting point for a research agenda focusing on mental health issues among this population would be to identify the location of individuals who self-identify as American Indian or Native Alaskan. We might begin with qualitative data that would serve as an impetus to create a culturally and ethnically sensitive probability sample of at least three ethnic groups and include some form of standardized indicators. Such a research agenda would offer a unique perspective on the historical experience of marginalization and the influence of culture in shaping patterns of mental disorders, psychological distress, and well-being.

SUMMARY: A NEW RESEARCH AGENDA
FOR A HETEROGENOUS NATION

The first step toward expanding our knowledge about race, ethnicity, culture, and mental health is to continue the task of determining whether the construct of mental health, broadly defined, should be conceptualized and operationalized in the same way across racial and ethnic groups. We must simultaneously account for the way that culture influences individuals' mental health. The next step would be to systematically draw large and national (if possible) probability samples from racial and ethnic groups of interest, as mandated by the National Institutes of Health (1994). With standardized and specific measures of mental health, social stress, coping strategies, and other correlates of mental health, sociologists studying mental health would be in a position to plot trends, address assumptions, and gain greater understanding of the meaning of race, ethnicity, and cultural influences.

Currently, Blacks, Hispanics, American Indians, and Asians comprise 18% of the U.S. population. Projections indicate that by the year 2050, these groups will comprise approximately 47% of the U.S. population. The increasing heterogeneity of the U.S. population presents challenges and opportunities for mental health research. Our first challenge is to better and more consistently to measure race, ethnicity, and cultural influences. We must develop assessment tools that are culturally sensitive and that account for important sociocultural nuances. We do a basic disservice to the social sciences, the mental health field, and future scholars if we continue to ignore the confluence of interracial, interethnic, and cultural influences in the sociology of mental health.

ACKNOWLEDGMENTS: The authors would like to thank Drs. David T. Takeuchi and David R, Williams for their comments, and Dale Jerome for assistance in preparing this chapter.

REFERENCES

Adebimpe, V. R. (1981). Overview: White norms and psychiatric diagnosis of black patients. *American Journal of Psychiatry, 138*(3), 279–285.
Adebimpe, V. R. (1994). Race, racism, and epidemiological surveys. *Hospital and Community Psychiatry, 45*(1), 27–31.

Akbar, N. (1991). Mental disorder among African Americans. In R. L. Jones (Ed.), *Black Psychology* (3rd ed., pp. 339–352). Berkeley, CA: Cobb & Henry.

Alarcon, R. D. (1995). Culture and psychiatric diagnosis: Impact on DSM-IV and ICD-10. *Cultural Psychiatry, 18*(3), 449–463.

Amaro, H., Russo, N. F., & Johnson, J. (1987). Family and work predictors of psychological well-being among Hispanic women professionals. *Psychology of Women Quarterly, 11,* 501–521.

Aneshensel, C. S. (1996). Consequences of psychosocial stress: The universe of stress outcomes. In H. Kaplan (Ed.), *Psychosocial stress: Perspectives on structure, theory, life-course, and methods* (pp. 111–136). New York: Academic Press.

Berreman, G. D. (1991). Race, caste, and other invidious distinctions in social stratification. In N. R. Yetman (Ed.), *Majority and minority: The dynamics of race and ethnicity in American life* (pp. 30–48). Boston: Allyn & Bacon.

Berry, J. W. (1998). Acculturation and health: Theory and research. In S. S. Kazarian & D. R. Evans (Eds.), *Cultural clincal psychology: Theory, research and practice.* New York: Oxford University Press.

Bowser, B. P. (1981). Racism and mental illness: An exploration of the racist's illness and the victim's health. In O. Barbarin, P. R. Good, O. M. Pharr, & J. A. Siskind (Eds.), *Institutional racism and community competence* (Chap. 11 DHHS Publ. No. [ADM] 81-907). Washington, DC: U.S. Government Printing Office.

Broman, C. L. (1989). Race and responsiveness to life stress. *National Journal of Sociology, 3*(1), 49–64.

Burke, A. W. (1984). Racism and psychological disturbance among West Indians in Britain. *International Journal of Social Psychiatry, 30,* 50–68.

Carter, J. H. (1993). Racism's impact on mental health. *Journal of the National Medical Association, 86,* 543–547.

Cooper, R. (1984, September). A note on the biologic concept of race and its application in epidemiologic research. *American Heart Journal, 00,* 715–723.

Essed, P. (1991). *Understanding everyday racism: An interdisciplinary theory.* Newbury Park, CA: Sage.

Fernando, S. (1984). Racism as a cause of depression. *The International Journal of Social Psychiatry, 30,* 41–49.

Gallo, J. J., Cooper-Patrick, L., & Hochman, S. (forthcoming). Ethnic differences in depressive symptoms: An item analysis of the diagnostic interview schedule. *Journal of Gerontology.*

Gary, L. E. (1991). The mental health of African Americans: Research trends and directions. In R. L. Jones (Ed.), *Black psychology* (3rd ed., pp. 727–745). Berkeley, CA: Cobb and Henry.

Geertz, C. (1973). *The interpretation of cultures.* New York: Basic Books.

Gordon, M. M. (1961). Assimilation in America: Theory and reality. *Daedalus, 90*(2), 263–285.

Hendricks, L. E. (1983). The NIMH Diagnostic Interview Schedule: A Test of its validity in a population of black adults. *Journal of the National Medical Association, 75*(7), 667–671.

James, S. (1994). John Henryism and the health of African-Americans. *Culture, Medicine and Psychiatry, 18,* 163–182.

Jackson, J. S., Tucker, B. M., & Bowman, P. J. (1982). Conceptual and methodological problems in survey research on black Americans. In W. T. Liu (Ed.), *Methodological problems in minority research* (pp. 11–39). Chicago: Pacific/Asian American Mental Health Research Center.

Jackson, J. S., Brown, T. N., Williams, D. R., Torres, M., Sellers, S., & Brown, K. (1996). Racism and the physical and mental health status of African Americans: A thirteen year National Panel Study. *Ethnicity and Disease, 6,* 132–147.

Jackson, J. S., Williams, D. R., & Torres, M. (under review). Perceptions of discrimination: The stress process and physical and psychological health. In A. Maney (Ed.), S*ocial stressors, personal and social resources, and their mental health consequences.*

Jones, F. (1981). White racism and Africanity in the development of Afro-American communities. In O. Barbarin, P. R. Good, O. M. Pharr, & J. A. Siskind (Eds.), *Institutional racism and community competence* (pp. 67–74) (Chapter 7, DHHS Publ. No. [ADM] 81-907). Washington, DC: U.S. Government Printing Office.

Kaplan, M. S., & Marks, G. (1990). Adverse effects of acculturation: Psychological distress among Mexican American young adults. *Social Science and Medicine, 31*(12), 1313–1319.

Kessler, R. C., McGonagle, K. A., Zhao, S., Nelson, C. B., Hughes, M., Eshleman, S., Wittchen, H. U., & Kendler, K. S. (1994). Lifetime and 12-month prevalence of DSM-III-R pscyhiatric disorders in the United States. *Archives of General Psychiatry, 51,* 8–19.

Kroeber, A. L., & Kluckhorn, D. (1952). *Culture: A critical review of concepts and definitions.* New York: Random House.

Kuo, W. H. (1995). Coping with racial discrimination: The case of Asian Americans. *Ethnic and Racial Studies, 18*(1), 109–127.

Kuo, W. H. (1984). Prevalence of depression among Asian Americans. *Journal of Nervous and Mental Disease, 172,* 449–457.

Kuo, W. H., & Tsai, Y. M. (1986). Social networks, hardiness, and immigrant's mental health. *Journal of Health and Social Behavior, 27,* 133–149.

Lawson, W. B. (1986). Racial and ethnic factors in psychiatric research. *Hospital and Community Psychiatry, 37*(1), 50–54.

Lawson, W., Hepler, N., Holladay, J., & Cuffel, B. (1994). Race as a factor in inpatient and outpatient admissions and diagnosis. *Hospital and Community Psychiatry, 45*(1), 72–74.

Levine, R. E., & Caw, A. C. (1995). Culture-bound syndromes. *Cultural Psychiatry, 18*(3), 523–536.

Loring, M., & Powell, B. (1988). Gender, race, and DSM-III: A study of objectivity of psychiatric diagnostic behavior. *Journal of Health and Social Behavior, 29,* 1–22.

Meketon, M. (1983). Indian mental health: An orientation. *American Journal of Orthopsychiatry, 53*(1), 110–115.

Narduzzi, J. (1994). *Mental health among elderly Native Americans.* New York: Garland.

National Institutes of Health. (1994). *NIH guidelines on the inclusion of women and minorities as subjects in clinical research* (59 FR 14508-14513). Washington, DC: U. S. Department of Health and Human Services.

Neff, J. A. (1985). Race and vulnerability: An examination of differential vulnerability. *Journal of Personality and Social Psychology, 49,* 481–491.

Neighbors W. H., Caldwell, C., Thompson, E., & Jackson, J. S. (1993). Physician contact for depressive symptoms among African Americans. In S. Friedman (Ed.), *Anxiety disorders in African Americans* (pp. 26–39). New York: Springer.

Neighbors, H. W., Jackson, J. S., Campbell, L. & Williams, D. (1989). The influence of racial factors on psychiatric diagnosis: A review and suggestions for research. *Community Mental Health Journal, 25*(4), 301–311.

Neighbors, H. W. (1997). The (mis)diagnosis of mental disorder in African Americans. In R. Taylor (Ed.), African American Research Perspectives (pp. 1–11). Ann Arbor, MI: Program for Research on Black Americans.

Norton, I. M., & Manson, S. M. (1996). Research in American Indian and Alaska Native communities: Navigating the cultural universe of values and process. *Journal of Consulting and Clinical Psychology, 64*(5), 856–860.

Raskin, A., Crook, T. H., & Herman, K. D. (1975). Psychiatric history and symptom differences in black and white depressed inpatients. *Journal of Consulting and Clinical Psychology, 43*(1), 73–80.

Robins, L. N., Helzer, J., Croughan, J., & Ratcliff, K. (1981). The National Institute of Mental Health Diagnostic Interview Schedule (DIS): Its history, characteristics and validity. *Archives of General Psychiatry, 38,* 381–389.

Robins, L. N., & Regier, D. A. (1991). *Psychiatric disorders in America: The epidemiologic catchment area study.* New York: Free Press.

Rogler, L. H. (1996a). Framing research on culture in psychiatric diagnosis: The case of the DSM-IV. *Psychiatry, 59,* 145–155.

Rogler, L. H. (1996b). Research on mental health services for Hispanics: Targets of convergence. *Cultural Diversity and Mental Health, 2*(3), 145–156.

Rogler, L. H. (1993a). Culturally sensitizing psychiatric diagnosis: A framework for research. *The Journal of Nervous and Mental Disease, 181,* 401–408.

Rogler, L. H. (1993b). Culture in psychiatric diagnosis: An issue of scientific accuracy. *Psychiatry, 56,* 324–327.

Salgado de Snyder, V. N. (1987). Factors associated with acculturative stress and depressive symptomatology among married Mexican immigrant women. *Psychology of Women Quarterly, 11,* 475–488.

Schaefer, R. T. (1990). *Racial and ethnic groups.* HarperCollins.

Smith, E. M. J. (1985). Ethnic minorities: Life stress, social support, and mental health issues. *Counseling Psychologist, 13*(4), 537–579.

Strakowski, S., Shelton, R., & Kolbrener, M. (1993). The effects of race and comorbidity on clinical diagnosis in patients with psychosis. *Journal of Clinical Psychiatry, 54*(3), 96–103.

Sue, S., Sue, D. W., Sue, L., & Takeuchi, D. (1995). Psychopathology among Asian Americans: A model minority. *Cultural Diversity and Mental Health, 1*(1), 39–51.

Swindler, A. (1986). Culture in action: Symbols and strategies. *American Sociological Review, 51,* 273–286.

Thoits, P. A. (1983). Dimensions of life events that influence psychological distress. In H. B. Kaplan (Ed.), *Psychological stress: Trends in theory and research* (pp. 33–103). New York: Academic Press.

Vega, W., & Rumbaut, R. (1991). Ethnic minorities and mental health. *Annual Review of Sociology, 17,* 351–383.

Wade, J. C. (1993). Institutional racism: An analysis of the mental health system. *American Journal of Orthopsychiatry, 63*(4), 563–544.

Williams, D. R. (1997). Race and health: Basic questions, emerging directions. *Annals of Epidemiology, 7*(5), 322–333.

Williams, D. R., & Fenton, B. (1994). The mental health of African Americans: Findings, questions and directions. In I. L. Livingston (Ed.), *Handbook of black American health: The mosaic of conditions, issues, policies, and prospects* (pp. 253–268). Westport, CT: Greenwood Press.

Williams, D. R., Lavisso-Mourey, R., & Warren, R. C. (1994). The concept of race and health status in America. *Public Health Reports, 109*(1), 26–41.

Williams, D. R., & Harris-Reid, M. (in press). Race and mental health: Emerging patterns and promising approaches. In A. Horwitz & T. Scheid (Eds), *The sociology of mental health and illness.* New York: Cambridge University Press.

Wilkinson, D., & King, G. (1987). Conceptual and methodological issues in the use of race as a variable: Policy implications. *The Milbank Memorial Fund Quarterly, 65,* 56–71.

Wolf, A. S. (1989). The Barrow studies: An Alaskan's perspective. *American Indian and Alaskan Native Mental Health Research, 2,* 35–40.

Zheng, Y.-P., Lin, K.-M., Takeuchi, D., Kurasaki, K. S., Wang, Y., & Cheung, F. (1997). An epidemiological study of neurasthenia in Chinese-Americans in Los Angeles. *Comprehensive Psychiatry, 38*(5), 249–259.

CHAPTER 10

Mental Disorder in Late Life

Exploring the Influence of Stress and Socioeconomic Status

Neal Krause

INTRODUCTION

The purpose of this chapter is to review data on the prevalence of selected mental health problems in late life and to develop a theoretical explanation for the patterns that are observed. Consistent with these goals, the discussion that follows is divided into two main sections. The prevalence and age of onset for mental health problems in late life are reviewed first. Following this review, a potentially useful conceptual framework is developed to explain these findings. This theoretical perspective relies on extensions of the stress process model and places a heavy emphasis on the pervasive influence of socioeconomic status (SES).

PREVALENCE OF MENTAL DISORDERS IN LATE LIFE

A necessary first step in devising a viable sociological explanation for mental disorder in late life is to describe the prevalence and age of onset for mental health problems. This point of departure is important because data on the age distributions of disorder and the age of onset provides hints about potential explanatory factors. If mental disorders emerge

NEAL KRAUSE • School of Public Health and Institute of Gerontology, University of Michigan, Ann Arbor, Michigan 48109.

Handbook of the Sociology of Mental Health, edited by Carol S. Aneshensel and Jo C. Phelan. Kluwer Academic/Plenum Publishers, New York, 1999.

early in life and tend to taper off as people grow older, then it makes sense to search for causal mechanisms in the earlier decades of life. However, if mental health problems increase substantially as people get older, then the focus should be shifted to factors that are encountered in late life.

Unfortunately, there is little consensus in the literature about the prevalence and onset of mental health problems among older adults. Instead, different views are provided by research aimed at assessing clinical psychiatric syndromes and studies that focus on symptoms of distress that may not constitute clinical cases of disorder. The findings from each body of research are reviewed below. In the process, age-related problems associated with assessing mental illness with each technique are discussed briefly.

Clinical Psychiatric Syndromes

Probably the most reliable data on psychiatric disorders among elderly people come from the Epidemiologic Catchment Area (ECA) surveys (Robins & Regier, 1981). This large-scale community survey was designed to evaluate mental disorder in adults of all ages by operationalizing the diagnostic criteria in the third edition of the *Diagnostic and Statistical Manual of Mental Disorders* (DSM-III; American Psychiatric Association, 1980). This survey is noteworthy because it attempted to assess the age of onset as well as the prevalence of a wide range of mental disorders. (Data from the more recent National Comorbidity Study, described in Chapter 7, are not relevant to aging because the sample is limited to persons 15–54 years of age.)

Viewed broadly, the findings from the ECA study revealed that rates of most mental disorders are lower among older than younger people (Robins, Locke, & Regier, 1991). For example, the lifetime prevalence rate of any DSM-III disorder was 37% for respondents under age 30, but only 21% for study participants 65 and older. Even though depressive and anxiety disorders are among the most common disorders in late life, prevalence estimates of these mental health problems are well below those of younger adults. More specifically, the lifetime prevalence of depressive episodes for people 30–44 years of age was 10%, but only 2% for individuals 65 and older (Weissman, Bruce, Leaf, Florio, & Holzer, 1991). Similarly, the lifetime prevalence of phobic disorder (a major type of anxiety) for women 65 and over (14%) was substantially lower than the corresponding rate for women in the 30 to 44 year-age range (23%). Comparable, but less dramatic, estimates were observed in men: 5% aged 65 and over had had a phobic disorder in their lifetime, whereas 6% in the 30–44 year-age range had suffered from this mental health problem (Eaton, Dryman, & Weissman, 1991).

There are, however, two important exceptions to these trend: The first has to do with organic mental disorders and the second concerns suicide. There is some evidence that the rates of organic mental disorders (e.g., the dementias) increase markedly in late life (George, Landerman, Blazer, & Anthony, 1991). However, the diagnosis of these disorders is virtually impossible in a community survey research setting. Consequently, the ECA investigators elected to assess cognitive impairment with the Mini-Mental State Examination (MMSE; Folstein, Anthony, Parhad, Duffy, & Gruenberg, 1985). As these investigators readily acknowledge, there may be significant slippage between MMSE scores and the clinical diagnoses of organic mental disorder. In particular, George and associates(1991) pointed out that persons with low levels of educational attainment may score highly on the MMSE, even though they do not suffer from any of the organic mental disorders. Keeping these limitations in mind, findings from the ECA study revealed that less than 5% of the population under age 55 suffered from mild cognitive impairment. However, by age 75, over 22% experienced mild cognitive impairment (George et al., 1991).

Like cognitive impairment, suicide does not constitute a specific diagnosis in the DSM series. Even so, it is discussed here because suicide is associated with a number of mental health problems, especially depression (Hendin, 1986). One of the most comprehensive studies of suicide was conducted by Manton, Blazer, and Woodbury (1987). Although the data from this study revealed complex race and gender variations in suicide rates, these investigators reported that persons 65 years of age and older commit suicide more often than individuals in any other age group. For example, the suicide rate for white males at age 80 was 4 per 1,000 individuals, while the corresponding estimate for 20-year-old white males was only about 1.5 per 1,000.

Although the young are more likely to suffer from clinical mental health problems, the ECA study further revealed that most syndromes emerge early in life as well. In particular, Robins and her associates reported that the median age of onset for any DSM disorder was age 16 (Robins et al., 1991). Moreover, these investigators stated that 90% of the sample with any disorder experienced first symptoms by age 38. This tendency is reflected in the age of onset for specific psychiatric syndromes. For example, the median age of onset for depressive episodes was 25, while phobia (age 10), and schizophrenia (age 19) first appeared at an even earlier point in the life course (see also Kessler & Zhao, Chapter 7, this volume).

Taken at face value, the data on clinical psychiatric syndromes suggest that mental health problems are more prevalent among younger people, and that psychiatric disorders tend to emerge relatively early in life. Nevertheless, as the discussion in the next section reveals, there are a number of methodological problems with this research.

Problems with the Psychiatric Perspective

There are at least six reasons why the prevalence rates and age of onset for mental disorders may be underestimated in elderly populations. First, measures may not capture the unique ways in which depression is expressed by older adults. In particular, some researchers maintain that somatic symptoms, as well as apathy, are not adequately represented in existing measures even though they represent significant features of depression in late life (e.g., Blazer, George, & Landerman, 1986; Krishnan, Hayes, Tupler, George, & Blazer, 1995). Second, prevalence rates based on surveys of community-dwelling elders overlook the fact that many older adults with mental disorders reside in nursing homes or congregate housing. For example, research by Parmalee and her colleagues suggested that the prevalence of major depression in their institutional sample was 12.4% (Parmalee, Katz, & Lawton, 1989). Third, some disorders, such as depression, are comorbid with either physical health problems or cognitive impairment, making accurate diagnosis difficult (Blazer, 1994; Ernst & Angst, 1995). Fourth, the utility of scales that assess the lifetime prevalence of disorder, as well as age of onset, rests on the assumption that respondents can accurately recall their psychiatric history. However, there is some concern that memory problems may be especially troublesome in studies of older adults. In fact, Blazer (1994, p. 195) concluded that memory problems "contribute to the differences in lifetime rates of depression by age, thus explaining a significant portion of the variance in lifetime rates of major depression among younger persons compared to older persons" (see also Knauper & Wittchen, 1994). Fifth, some investigators argue that rates of disorder are higher among the young because many with psychiatric disorders die prematurely. For example, Bruce and Leaf (1989) reported that the odds of dying during a 15-year follow-up are four times greater for those suffering from a mood disorder. Finally, a good deal of the data on psychiatric disorder is cross-sectional in nature, making it difficult to distinguish between age, period, and cohort effects (Palmore, 1978).

Although each of the problems identified here may explain some of the observed age differences in mental disorder, a more serious limitation may arise from the fact that these data are based solely on the psychiatric perspective, which is almost exclusively concerned with identifying cases of disorder, while often overlooking subclinical levels of symptomatology. This limitation is important because subclinical disorder may have a major impact on the quality of life in later years (Koenig & Blazer, 1996). As the discussion in the next section reveals, studies that focus on symptoms of distress provide a different picture of the mental health of our aging population.

Symptoms of Psychological Distress

In contrast to the psychiatric approach to assessing mental disorders, many sociologists take one of two broad approaches to measure symptoms of psychological distress. First, some investigators focus on global or undifferentiated symptoms of distress (e.g., Dohrenwend, Shrout, Egri, & Mendelsohn, 1980). In contrast, other researchers prefer to evaluate symptoms associated with particular types of mental health problems, especially depressive symptoms (e.g., Lewinsohn, Seeley, Roberts, & Allen, 1997). The literature reviewed below focuses solely on depressive symptomatology, because the wide majority of studies presenting data on age differences are restricted to this type of mental health problem.

Probably the most widely used measure of depressive symptoms is the Center for Epidemiogical Studies Depression Scale (CES-D; Radloff, 1977). Unfortunately, findings from a number of community surveys that use the CES-D Scale reveal an inconsistent pattern of results. Some reported no age differences in depressive symptoms (e.g., Sayetta & Johnson, 1980), while others suggested that levels of depressive symptomatology decline with advancing years (e.g., Eaton & Kessler, 1981). Inconsistencies also emerge when other depressive symptom scales are used (for a review of this research, see Newmann, 1989).

Although it is hard to reach a firm conclusion about the relationship between age and depressive symptoms, a small but intriguing cluster of studies provides a potentially important resolution. In particular, this research suggests that there may be a nonlinear relationship between age and depressive symptoms. This means that symptoms of depression initially decline from early life through midlife. However, there appears to be a fairly sharp upturn around age 60 that continues through the remaining decades of life (e.g., Kessler, Foster, Webster, & House, 1992; Lewinsohn, Rohde, Fischer, & Seeley, 1991; Newmann, 1989).

It is important to determine why some studies fail to find a nonlinear effect of age on depressive symptoms. At least two reasons are provided by Newmann (1989). Based on an extensive review of the literature, she argued that most investigators simply do not test for nonlinear effects, and those who do often failed to use appropriate data-analytic procedures. Second, many studies did not find a sharp upturn in depression among older adults because the samples did not contain enough respondents in the later decades of life.

Although discussing these methodological problems helps to resolve inconsistent empirical findings, it is important to determine if there is a plausible theoretical justification for the proposed nonlinear relationship between age and depressive symptoms. As the conceptual perspective developed later in this chapter reveals, thinking about the social factors that may be responsible for this relationship provides a unique opportunity to expand our understanding of the aging process. Before turning to these theoretical issues, however, it is important briefly to identify problems inherent in research on depressive symptoms in late life.

Limitations in Research on Depressive Symptoms

Two shortcomings are especially noteworthy in research on depressive symptoms among elderly people. First, investigators do not make an effort to determine the age of onset. Although it is very difficult to address this issue when studying symptoms of distress, failure to do so results in data that provide information on only recent mental health problems (typically, in the past week or so). As a result, the lack of data on the natural history of these mental health problems over the life course hinders the search for etiological factors. For example, we do not know whether current symptom patterns have emerged in late life for the first time, or if they merely represent a lifelong recurrence of bouts with depression that have been experienced for many years. The second problem with scales that assess depressive symptoms has to do with the fact that they typically contain items assessing psychophysiological symptoms of distress (i.e., somatic symptoms). For example, questions relating to appetite problems and difficulty sleeping are included in the CES-D Scale (Radloff, 1977). However, sleep disruption is a frequent concomitant of the aging process that often is unrelated to depression (Morgan, 1992). Moreover, appetite problems may be associated with medication use or a health problem that is entirely physiological in nature. Unless special probe questions are administered in conjunction with depressive symptom items to screen for these potential sources of contamination (see Wells & Strictland, 1982), rates of disorder among older adults are likely to be inflated. unfortunately, investigators who use depressive symptoms scales typically fail to incorporate these important probe questions in their interview schedules.

EXPLAINING PATTERNS OF MENTAL DISORDER IN LATE LIFE

It should be emphasized at the outset that it is not possible to develop a single conceptual framework that explains all of the variance in mental health problems among older adults. A bewildering array of factors are likely to play a role in the etiology of mental disorder, ranging from genetic influences (Reiss, Plomin, & Hetherington, 1991) to broad social status factors such as gender and race (Roberts, Kaplan, Shema, & Strawbridge, 1997). Consequently, three steps are taken to limit the discussion that follows and, therefore, the scope of the conceptual framework. First, an emphasis is placed on developing a life-course perspective. Second, within this context, the stress process model is used to integrate the seemingly disjointed findings on the etiology of mental health problems reviewed earlier. Third, the emerging perspective seeks to explain depressive disorders only. The rationale for making these decisions is presented briefly below.

An emphasis is placed on the life-course perspective because problems arise when investigators look for the genesis of mental health problems only in the recent past (see Chapter 27, this volume). For example, a number of researchers suspect that stress plays a causal role in the development of many mental disorders (Avison & Gotlib, 1994). Even so, the majority of investigators focus exclusively on the impact of stressors that have arisen either within the past year or the previous 6 months (e.g., Krause, 1986). This measurement strategy is problematic because it ignores the wider biographical context in which current life events emerge. In particular, it overlooks elders' prior history of stress exposure, as well as their previous experience using various resources to cope with these difficulties. As discussed later, this rich personal biography may substantially shape reactions to current stressors (Wheaton, 1994).

Research on the etiology of mental disorder may be crudely partitioned into two broad perspectives that locate the origins of mental health problems in social processes that appear at different points in the life course. The first assumes that the genesis of adult disorder lies in factors that emerge early in life. For example, some investigators argue that early parental loss creates the inability to form close relationships, which in turn leads to depression in adult life (Bowlby, 1980). In contrast, the second body of literature focuses exclusively on factors that are more likely to appear in late life, such as chronic illness (George, 1996) or ongoing financial problems faced by retired elders living on fixed incomes (Krause, 1995). A common conceptual framework is needed so that these seemingly opposing views can be merged into a coherent and compatible framework. The stress process model appears to be especially well suited for this task (Pearlin & Skaff, 1996). For example, many of the causal factors identified in both research orientations are in fact stressors (early parental loss and late-life economic difficulty) and the negative sequalae that follow (e.g., the inability to form close ties) may be conveniently recast in terms of diminished coping resources.

Rather than deal with all types of psychopathology, this chapter focuses on clinical depressive disorders as well as subclinical depressive symptomatology. There are two reasons for selecting depression. First, more studies have been devoted to assessing the impact of psychosocial factors on depression in later life than other types of mental disorder. Second, as discussed earlier, subclinical symptoms of depressive symptomatology are quite prevalent in late life.

The remainder of this chapter is divided into five main sections. The first deals with the life-course perspective. As Chapter 27 in this volume reveals, there are many elements in the life-course framework. Consequently, the first section is devoted to identifying the particular facets of the life-course perspective that are used to frame the subsequent discussion. Key elements in the stress process model are reviewed briefly in the second section. Following this, research on etiological factors that emerge early in life is presented in the third section. These studies provide a point of departure for developing a life-course view of depression, but they fall short because the principles identified in this work are rarely extended into later life. Next, the fourth section examines causal factors that typically arise in the later decades of life. Included here are age-related changes in the coping resources often used to deal with stressful events. An emphasis is placed throughout the third and fourth sections on the pervasive influence of SES. Finally, the goal of the fifth section is to suggest ways of integrating and merging the insights provided by early and late-life etiological factors.

Adapting Elements from the Life-Course Perspective

Two epidemiological findings from the literature on depressive symptoms provide a point of departure for infusing research on mental health problems among older adults with a life-course perspective. The first involves the inverse relationship between education and depressive symptoms. The second, which has already been discussed, deals with the sharp upturn in rates of depressive symptomatology after age 60 (Newmann, 1989).

Education is widely regarded as a key indicator of SES. Research consistently reveals that elders with fewer years of educational attainment experience considerably more depressive symptoms than older adults who have more years of formal schooling. For example, a study by Murrell, Himmelfarb, and Wright (1983) examined the prevalence of elders with CES-D scores of 20 or greater across select levels of educational attainment. Although this measurement strategy does not assess clinical cases of depression, these researchers maintain that a cutpoint score of 20 or greater identifies elderly people who are likely to need the help of a mental health professional. Murrell and associates (1983) reported that 24.5% of the men with four or fewer years of education had CES-D scores above this cutpoint, whereas only 5.7% of the men with 13 or more years of schooling had scores that high. Similar findings were observed in their subsample of older women as well.

Although the inverse relationship between SES and mental disorder is one of the most frequently observed findings in the epidemiological literature, considerable controversy exists over how to interpret these findings (Ortega & Corzine, 1990). Some investigators support what is called the social causation hypothesis. This perspective states that adversity and stress associated with low SES cause mental health problems to emerge. Others endorse the social selection hypothesis, which states that genetically predisposed individuals drift downward from higher to lower SES positions (Ortega & Corzine, 1990). Although empirical support has been found for both perspectives (see Ortega & Corzine, 1990), a compelling study by Dohrenwend and his associates revealed that it is important to take the type of mental health problem into consideration when attempting to resolve this issue (Dohrenwend et al., 1992). In particular, these investigators reported that the social selection hypothesis may be more useful for explaining the relationship between SES and schizophrenia, whereas the social causation hypothesis may be more helpful for understanding SES variations in depression. Since the theoretical framework developed here is designed to explain depression in late life, it is assumed throughout the remainder of this chapter that the social causation perspective provides the most valid explanation of the inverse relationship between SES and mental health problems in late life.

Education is a stable factor that is fixed for most individuals after young adulthood. If education causes mental health problems, it is unlikely that these effects only emerge in late life. In fact, there is ample evidence that this is not the case. Instead, a number of studies suggest that education is associated with mental health problems across the life course (e.g., Mirowsky & Ross, 1989). If this is true, then we cannot understand the relationship between education and mental disorders in late life without also considering the relationship between these constructs earlier in life. Put simply, the compelling findings on the relationship between education and mental health problems call for an explanatory framework that adopts a lifecourse perspective.

Expanding the scope of research on mental disorders in late life to encompass a life-course perspective presents a number of substantial challenges. One is of particular importance here. More specifically, this conceptual framework must somehow come to grips with research suggesting that there may be a sharp upturn in depressive symptoms among older adults (Newmann, 1989). Even so, if a way can be found to develop a life-course perspective that is capable of explaining this trend, then we will be in position to infuse the mental health literature with a unique gerontological focus. As the discussion provided below reveals, extending and elaborating recent work by Ross and Wu (1996) may provide a useful way of accomplishing this goal.

Ross and Wu (1996) identified and empirically evaluated a number of models that provide alternative ways of specifying the relationship between age, education, and physical health problems. Three of their models are depicted graphically in Figures 10.1 through 10.3. The first is a main effects model (Figure 10.1). This specification begins with the assumption that people with more education enjoy better physical health across the life course than those with lower levels of educational attainment. However, this model further specifies that physical health declines at a constant rate as people get older, and that the rate of decline is the same for all elderly people, regardless of educational attainment. The second view may be called the divergence model (Figure 10.2). Here, it is specified that the relationship between age and health is conditional on education. This means that age will exert a stronger impact on health for those with less education. However, it is important to note that the gap between people with different levels of education emerges relatively early in life and becomes wider at a constant rate. The third specification (the accelerating divergence model) is more complex (Figure 10.3). The rate of decline in health among people with different levels of educational attainment accelerates over the life course. This pattern means that instead of increasing at a constant rate, the gap between those with different levels of educational attainment increases in an exponential fashion. Based on data from two large community surveys, Ross and Wu found empirical support for the accelerating divergence model.

Ross and Wu (1996) extended the theory of cumulative advantage to explain the empirical findings that emerged from their data. In particular, they argued that highly educated individuals tend to accumulate more health-promoting resources over the life course than people with less schooling, and that this produces an ever-widening gap in health between them. The relationship between some of the resources identified by these investigators (e.g., income, a good diet, and regular exercise) and health is relatively straightforward. This is illustrated in the following sequence: (1) People who do not exercise are more likely to be overweight; (2) those who are overweight tend to develop joint and back problems; (3) these problems, in turn, further limit physical activity; and (4) because of this spiraling tendency toward inactivity, physical health deteriorates in an exponential fashion.

It is especially important for the purposes of this chapter to note that Ross and Wu (1996) also suggested that psychosocial resources figure into this process. Social support and feelings of personal control are mentioned explicitly in this context. This is significant

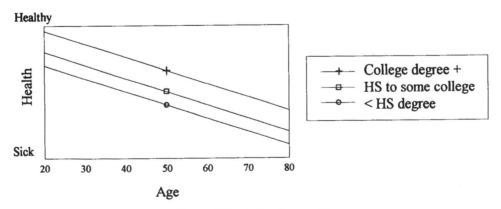

FIGURE 10.1. Main effects model.

Healthy

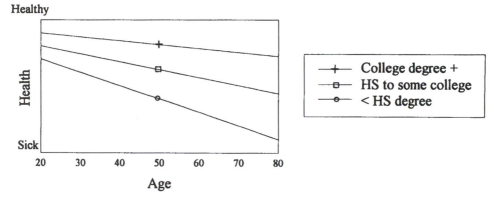

FIGURE 10.2.   Divergence model.

because, as discussed later, these are key elements in the stress process model. Unfortunately, the relationship between these resources and health is not developed fully, and it is not clear how they contribute to a widening gap in health with age.

A key issue is whether the theoretical framework developed by Ross and Wu (1996) may also be applied to the study of mental health problems. There do not appear to be any studies in the literature that empirically evaluate this issue. Although all three models discussed earlier may provide insight into mental disorders across the life course, a major premise in this chapter is that the accelerating divergence model may be especially useful. There are three reasons for making this assertion. First, as discussed, physical health problems are correlated highly with depressive symptoms in late life. For example, Roberts and associates (1997) reported that the relationship between age and depressive symptoms disappears once the effects of physical health status are controlled statistically. Although it is difficult to determine the direction of causality between physical and mental health problems (Cohen & Rodriguez, 1995), the work of Roberts and his colleagues suggests that age may influence depressive symptoms indirectly through physical health problems (Roberts et al., 1997). The second reason for preferring the accelerating divergence model may be found in the work of Newmann (1989). As noted earlier, her research indicated that depressive symptoms increase in an accelerating fashion with age. Unfortunately, Newmann did

Healthy

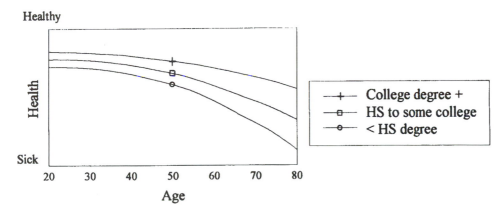

FIGURE 10.3.   Accelerating divergence model.

not explicitly test for SES variations in her study. Nevertheless, research reviewed earlier on the relationship between education and depressive symptoms suggests that it may be useful to do so, because it may reveal a pattern of accelerating decline similar to that observed with physical health status. Third, Ross and Wu (1996) suggested that feelings of personal control may contribute to the widening gap in health across the life course. As research reviewed later in this chapter reveals, personal control also plays a key role in shaping symptoms of depression (Krause, 1987). Perhaps more important, recent research by Mirowsky (1995) suggests that a sense of control may decline in an accelerating fashion with advancing age. This pattern is consistent with the accelerating divergence model, but variations by SES have not been explored in this work. A more fully developed theoretical rationale is needed at this point to bind the age-related trends in depression and control more tightly to the basic tenets of the theory of cumulative advantage. As the discussion in the next section reveals, insights from research on the stress process provide a useful point of departure for attaining this goal.

Key Elements in the Stress Process Model

An extensive body of research provides convincing evidence that exposure to stress increases the risk of mental health problems in younger as well as older adults (see Pearlin, Chapter 19, this volume; Krause, 1995). A good deal of this relationship may be explained by the interplay between three main components of the stress process model: stress, social support, and feelings of personal control.

As a number of researchers point out, the construct of control has been operationalized in many ways (Skinner, 1996; see Chapter 18). Among the variables subsumed under this broad rubric are mastery (Pearlin & Schooler, 1978), fatalism (Wheaton, 1983), and locus-of-control orientations (Rotter, 1966). Although there are differences in the way these constructs have been defined and measured, they nevertheless share a common conceptual core. Embedded within each concept is the notion that individuals with a strong sense of control believe that changes in their social environment are responsive to, and contingent upon, their own choices, efforts, and actions. In contrast, people with a weak sense of control believe that events in their lives are shaped by forces outside their influence and that they have little ability to affect what happens to them (Bandura, 1995).

Although many psychologists believe that the construct of control is a personality trait, sociologists are more inclined to argue that one's sense of control is shaped by forces in the wider social environment, including stress and social support. According to a number of studies, stress operates, at least in part, by eroding feelings of personal control (Pearlin, Menaghan, Lieberman, & Mullan, 1981). This appears to be true for older as well as younger adults (Krause, 1987). However, people frequently seek assistance from significant others in an effort to deal with the difficulties that confront them. This help in turn serves to replenish and bolster feelings of control that have been challenged by the stressful experience. Caplan's (1981) work provided one way to explain this relationship. He argued that social network members help to define the problem situation, develop a plan of action, assist in implementing the plan, and provide feedback and guidance as it is being executed. As a result, the stressed person is able to see that the problem situation can be overcome or controlled.

This brief overview of the stress process is cast largely in terms of a single stressful episode. What is missing is a sense of how this process fits into the broader context of events that precede and follow it. Stress is a ubiquitous part of life, and as people age, they learn from, and are shaped by, the stressors that confront them. As a result, the psychic residues left by these difficult experiences, and the strategies that have been devised over the years to deal with them, set the stage for how future events will be handled. Taking a life-course perspective is especially useful for understanding this process because it emphasizes the continuity of experience over time. A necessary first step in developing this orientation is to evaluate the interplay between events and resources early in life. Consistent with the basic tenets of the accelerating divergence model, education should play a role in shaping the relationships among these constructs. The purpose of the next section is to lay this basic groundwork. However, instead of merely taking education as a given, the intent is to show that the stress process may also be useful for explaining how social factors shape educational attainment.

Early Precursors of Adult Distress

There is a vast literature relating exposure to traumatic events in childhood with mental disorder in adult life. This work places a major emphasis on the pivotal role of early parental loss (Bowlby, 1980). At the risk of oversimplifying the complex issues involved in this research, this literature suggests that people who lost a parent early in life are more likely to experience mental health problems as adults (for a review of this research, see Patten, 1991). Evidence for this conclusion has emerged in studies of younger as well as older adults (Brown & Harris, 1978; Phifer & Murrell, 1986). Moreover, it appears that those who lost a parent early in life are especially likely to suffer from depression (Patten, 1991). Even so, it is less evident how the effects of early childhood trauma are transmitted across the life course. Four perspectives are examined here: The first suggests that childhood trauma creates early-onset disorders; the second holds that early trauma is causally linked to other types of stress that subsequently emerge over the life course; the third view states that early parental loss leads to the erosion of key coping resources; whereas the final perspective assumes a more social–structural orientation by linking early parental loss with educational disruption. In the process of reviewing these perspectives, an effort is made to show how each provides ways of adapting the accelerating divergence model to the study of mental health.

CHILDHOOD TRAUMA AND EARLY-ONSET DISORDER.   A recent study by Kessler and Magee (1994) indicated that traumatic events arising in early childhood (e.g., parental loss and family violence) promote early-onset depression. Once in place, early-onset depression causes stressors in adulthood, as well as subsequent relapses of major depression that are triggered by these stressors. The key point is that the effects of stress-induced, early-onset disorder reverberate across the life course and are the primary driving force behind the relationship between recent stressors and mental health problems in adulthood.

Viewed broadly, the work of Kessler and Magee (1994) is not inherently at odds with the basic tenets of the theory of cumulative advantage, because early-onset disorder is capable of starting a vicious cycle of events that culminate in mental health problems in adult life. It differs, however, from the theory of cumulative advantage in the emphasis placed on social structural factors: Whereas the process discussed by Ross and Wu (1996) identified education as the root cause of health problems in adult life, the work of Kessler and Magee (1994) instead suggested that early-onset disorder is the prime driving force in and of itself.

EARLY TRAUMA AND STRESS-PRONENESS. In a very insightful paper, Wheaton (1994) carefully delineated seven different ways to measure stress. More importantly, he also proposed a causal model that effectively relates these different stressors over the life course. This model means, for example, that early childhood trauma is thought to promote early adult-life events (in his study, events arising more than 2 years prior to the data-collection point), and that early adult-life events, in turn, create more recent chronic strains. Adult disorder, therefore, results from the cumulative effects of these stressors. It is important to point out that the causal relationships between stressors suggest a sort of stress proneness, because exposure to one type of problem (e.g., childhood trauma) increases the odds of encountering other types of difficulty (e.g., chronic strain) later on in life. What is missing is a detailed explanation for why these stressors are related causally, and what makes some people more likely to become entangled in this process than others. Although brief references are made to unsuccessful role performance, this rationale is not fully developed. As the views depicted in the remaining perspectives suggest, the relationships among education, social support, and personal control may provide some answers to these questions. Even so, Wheaton's work is especially useful because it suggested that stressors do not occur at random, and those who are exposed to noxious events early in life are more likely to encounter additional stressors as they grow older.

EARLY TRAUMA AND THE DEPLETION OF COPING RESOURCES. The third perspective suggests that early trauma causes mental disorder in adult life because it compromises a person's ability to develop and utilize effective coping resources. Consistent with the main theme in this chapter, social support and feelings of personal control figure prominently in this work.

Beginning at least with the work of Bowlby (1980), researchers have argued that early parental loss compromises a child's ability to develop and maintain meaningful social relationships in adult life. This view is perhaps best expressed in the work of Brown and his colleagues (Bifulco, Brown, & Harris, 1987). According to these investigators, women who lost their mothers before age 11 tended to make poor relational choices in the second and third decades of life. More specifically, Brown's work suggested that these women are more likely to get pregnant before marriage, and they tend to marry men who offer little emotional support (see also McLeod, 1991). Consequently, when stressors emerge in adult life, they are unable to obtain the benefits associated with a strong, supportive relationship. Instead of being a source of solace and resilience, these deficient relations exacerbate problems. In the process, they act more like a conduit that transmits and further infuses the deleterious effects of early parental loss.

The work of Brown and his colleagues (Bifulco et al., 1987) focused solely on the interplay between early loss, the quality of the marital relationship, stress, and depression. What is largely absent is a sense of whether early parental loss affects the quality of social support provided by someone other than a spouse. Although a number of studies examine the effects of parental loss on subsequent relationships in adult life (e.g., McLeod, 1991), the effects of stress are not typically viewed in conjunction with these interpersonal problems. As the work of Brown and his colleagues suggested, this may be a major oversight (Bifulco et al., 1987).

Brown and Harris (1978) also suggested a second mechanism for relating early parental loss and adult depression. These investigators maintain that up to age 11, the mother is the primary source for learning how to control or master the environment. As a result, loss of one's mother before this age may permanently lower a woman's sense of mastery, thereby eroding her ability to confront losses and other stressful experiences in adult life. When stressors are encountered in adult life, members of this vulnerable subgroup of women are especially likely to experience clinical depression. It should be emphasized that Brown and Harris (1978) found that lower class women are particularly vulnerable to this process. Viewed broadly, the driving force behind adult depression in this perspective is a permanently diminished sense of mastery operating in concert with recent stressors.

There are a number of intersections between the work of Brown and Harris (1978) and the theory of cumulative advantage. Both take a life-course view, both recognize the influence of socioeconomic factors, and both identify feelings of personal control and social support as key intervening constructs. However, they differ in one important respect. Whereas the theory of cumulative advantage posits an exponential rate of decay, the notion of an ever-widening mental health gap between the social classes is absent in the work of Brown and Harris. By taking this stance, the work of Brown and Harris subtly places a disproportionate emphasis on forces that emerge early in life. With the exception of recent life events, this conveys the impression that there is little that changes in adult life, an assumption that is at odds with the life-course perspective. Even so, the work of Brown and Harris provides a useful point of departure for extending the theory of cumulative advantage, because it conveys a clear sense of how social support and personal control are shaped by both early trauma and a person's SES.

EARLY PARENTAL LOSS AND EDUCATIONAL DISRUPTION.   A different approach to relating early parental loss with adult depression may be developed by extending the work of McLanahan (1985). She argued that economic hardships encountered in single-parent families encourage adolescents to prematurely assume adult roles. In particular, McLanahan maintained that, compared to children from intact families, children in single-parent homes are more likely to work full time and assume responsibility for the care of younger siblings. As a result, they are more inclined to drop out of school than children who are raised by both parents. This educational-deprivation perspective may be especially important for understanding the effects of early parental loss in the current cohort of older adults because the present generation of elders was raised at a time when there was no governmental social safety net (i.e., no social security system, welfare system, or alimony payments) to assist families confronted with the loss of a parent. The premature termination of the educational process is important because, as McLanahan pointed out, educational attainment exerts a lifelong influence on the subsequent income of persons after they reach maturity. Although not explicitly mentioned by McLanahan, the lifelong impact of education may extend far beyond this income effect. In particular, research indicates that people with lower levels of educational attainment experience more stress (Kessler, 1979), receive less social support (Turner & Marino, 1994), and feel less personal control (Gecas, 1989) than individuals who have received more schooling.

Kessler and his associates also examined factors that influence educational attainment, but they identified a different mechanism than the one discussed by McLanahan (1985). Instead of arising from the premature assumption of adult roles, Kessler argued that early-onset disorders cause many adolescents to drop out of school (Kessler, Foster, Saunders, & Stang, 1995). When coupled with his study that was discussed earlier (Kessler & Magee, 1994), a different causal sequence emerges: Early childhood trauma promotes early-onset disorder, and early-onset disorder, in turn, leads to diminished educational attainment.

There are at least two ways to reconcile the findings provided by Kessler and associates (1995) and the view derived from the work of McLanahan (1985). First, instead of contradicting the extension of McLanahan's work, Kessler's view may simply illustrate that the process is more complex than it appears initially, and that there may be more than one pathway from early childhood trauma to educational disruption. If this turns out to be the case, then the next step is to determine the relative contributions of each perspective, so that the relationship between early trauma and educational disruption may be more fully understood. Second, questions may be raised about the methodology used in the Kessler study. In particular, data on the onset of mental disorders are gathered through retrospective recall. However, as discussed earlier, memory problems encountered in late life may hamper the ability of older adults to recall this information accurately (Blazer, 1994; Bradburn, Rips, & Shevell, 1987; Knauper & Wittchen, 1994).

SUMMARY.   The literature reviewed in this section reveals that at least five mechanisms may link early childhood trauma with depression in adult life. In particular, adults may encounter episodes of depression because the trauma they experienced as children created early-onset disorder, stress-proneness, the inability to form meaningful social ties with others, diminished feelings of personal control, or educational disruption. Taken together, this array of potential causal factors may initially appear to be disjointed, and the processes they describe may seem to contradict each other. However, rather than being at odds, each may capture part of a larger causal process. What is needed at this juncture is a single conceptual model that weaves these different elements into a more coherent whole, thereby providing a forum for testing their relative impact. Consistent with the discussion provided here, this model may reveal, for example, that early trauma or loss lowers educational attainment, and that educational attainment in turn affects exposure to stress, as well as the key resources needed to cope effectively with stress (i.e., feelings of personal control and social support).

Although this conceptual scheme may provide a useful way for thinking about adult disorder in life-course terms, we need to know more about how these early processes are manifest in later life. The various perspectives reviewed here do not mention older adults explicitly. Moreover, they convey only a vague sense of how early life forces play out over the middle adult years and beyond. In reviewing this work, we are somehow left with the impression that early and middle adulthood may be characterized by sporadic periods of stress and subsequent bouts of disorder that are driven solely by early childhood experiences. Remarkably little effort has been made to look at developmental changes or general social processes in middle-adult life that might specify how these early life forces are transformed and reexpressed in the ensuing decades. We need to know if the stressors, resources, and disorders encountered by elderly people are nothing more than a straightforward extrapolation of the principles discussed here, or whether something unique happens that reshapes and redirects the course of these early life forces. More importantly, if the theory of cumulative advantage is valid (Ross & Wu, 1996), then we need to find out whether there are processes in later life that promote an ever-widening gap in mental health, and whether these effects are especially evident among older adults with different levels of educational attainment. Initial steps toward addressing these complex questions are taken in the following section.

Late-Life Influences on Depressive Disorders

A central premise in this section is that changes in key coping resources alter the processes described earlier in ways that are relatively unique to late life. Consistent with the basic tenets of the theory of cumulative advantage (Ross & Wu, 1996), an argument is developed that suggests these changes tend to promote an ever-widening mental health gap between elders in different SES positions. In the process of developing and extending this framework, a special emphasis is placed on the key role played by feelings of personal control and social support.

AGE-RELATED CHANGES IN CONTROL.   Feelings of personal control figure prominently in at least two critical points in the stress process. First, as noted earlier, stress operates in part by reducing a person's sense of control. However, in addition to being undesirable in its own right, this constitutes a second major setback, because feelings of control are an important resource for offsetting the noxious effects of life events. This process can be highlighted by briefly describing how a diminished sense of control impedes successful adaptation. Research indicates that people with a low sense of control avoid challenging tasks and give up quickly when confronted with difficulties. As a result, stressful situations that could have been rectified with concerted action instead fester and become worse. Consequently, individuals with a low sense of control are especially vulnerable to the effects of stress and are at an increased risk for developing depression (Bandura, 1995).

Unfortunately, a recent study by Mirowsky (1995) suggests that feelings of control may decline during later life. In particular, he reports that feelings of control remain fairly stable up to about age 50 but decline sharply in an accelerating fashion beyond this point. This trajectory is consistent with the basic tenets of the theory of cumulative advantage. Moreover, two additional findings from this work are especially noteworthy: Although part of this decline may be attributed to physical impairment, education emerges as the most important explanatory factor.

What is less evident from this pivotal study is why education has this effect on control. Mirowsky (1995) briefly mentioned research showing an inverse relationship between education and feelings of personal control. However, this discussion does not provide a clear sense of why the decline should begin at age 50 and proceed in an accelerating fashion. It seems likely that a conceptual model containing a number of interrelated factors will be needed to address fully this issue. In the meantime, reflecting carefully on the prevalence and correlates of cognitive dysfunctioning may provide a somewhat unusual way of beginning to think about these results.

Research reviewed earlier suggested that rates of cognitive disability increase markedly in late life (George et al., 1991). Two important findings emerge from this research. First, rates of cognitive disability appear to increase in an accelerating fashion. As noted earlier, only about 5% of the people between ages 35 and 54 suffered from mild cognitive impairment. However, this rate increased exponentially to just under 31% by age 85. The second major finding reported by George et al. has to do with education. The data suggest that only 2% of the people with more than a high school education experienced mild cognitive impairment, whereas 26% with less than 9 years of schooling were confronted by this limitation.

The data reviewed here suggest that both cognitive impairment and feelings of personal control have the same general trajectory in later life; that each begins to decline at roughly the same age; and that both are highly correlated with education. We need to know whether the accelerating decline in cognitive functioning produces a corresponding trajectory in feelings of personal control. A necessary first step in addressing this issue is to develop a theoretical rationale that explains why cognitive functioning and feelings of control may be related. As discussed below, recasting these relationships in a stress process model provides some useful insights.

Social and behavioral gerontologists have shown a great deal of interest in the specific coping responses initiated by older adults who are confronted by stressful experiences (Aldwin, 1994). Although elderly people rely on a range of coping strategies to deal with stressful events, a good deal of this literature has been concerned with problem-focused coping. Problem-focused coping involves taking deliberate to action either eradicate or alter the course of a stressful experience (Lazarus, 1966). Planful problem solving represents a specific type of problem-focused coping and is generally regarded as one of the more effective ways to deal with a wide range of stressors. The following item, which comes from the widely used Ways of Coping Scale, represents how planful problem solving is typically assessed: "I came up with a couple of different solutions to the problem" (Folkman & Lazarus, 1988). The successful implementation of this strategy obviously requires that individuals possess fairly sound cognitive and problem-solving skills, including the capacity for abstract reasoning.

Given the data provided by George and associates (1991), it seems that a significant number of older adults may not have the cognitive resources needed to successfully implement problem-focused coping strategies. If elders cannot devise and implement plans to eradicate the stressors that confront them, it follows that they may be especially likely to experience a decline in their sense of personal control.

In view of the potentially important role that cognitive ability may play in the coping process, it is surprising to find that it has been largely ignored in the stress literature. In fact, there appear to be only two studies that empirically examine this issue. The first is a recent study by Krause (1996). This work was designed to examine the relationship between stressful life events and the use of outpatient medical care. The theoretical rationale developed for this study specifies that at least some elders turn to their primary care providers for assistance when they are unable to resolve a stressful situation on their own. People who are impaired cognitively are thought to be among those who are especially likely to do so. The data indicate that when stressors arise, older men who are suffering from mild cognitive impairment are more likely to visit the doctor than elderly men who are cognitively intact. The second paper, by Krause and Thompson (1997), more directly tests the relationships between stress, cognitive functioning, and depressive symptoms. Two types of stress are examined in this study: financial strain and the death of a family member. It was hypothesized that elders with cognitive dysfunction are more vulnerable to the effects of stressors that can be ameliorated or altered (i.e., financial strain), because these stressors represent instances in which problem-focused coping may be effective. In contrast, it was further predicted that elders with cognitive disability are not more susceptible to the effects of stressors that are difficult, if not impossible, to change (i.e., the death of a family member). Data from a longitudinal nationwide survey tend to support both hypotheses. In particular, the findings suggested that the effects of financial strain on changes in depressive symptoms over time are exacerbated for elders with high levels of cognitive impairment. In contrast, the results further revealed that the deleterious effects of a death in the family on depression are not contingent on cognitive functioning in late life.

Although the findings reported by Krause are consistent with the notion that cognitive functioning is related to feelings of personal control, it should be emphasized that the interface between these constructs was not evaluated empirically in this research (Krause, 1986; Krause & Thompson, 1997). Doing so represents a top priority for future studies.

One caveat merits mention. Mirowsky (1997) recently reported findings from a study designed to probe further the accelerating decline in control during late life. This research focused on subjective life expectancy (i.e., the number of years people expect to live). His data suggest that once the effects of subjective life expectancy are entered into the equation, the nonlinear relationship between age and control is no longer statistically significant. This means that, compared to individuals who anticipate having a long life, people who do not expect to live long are more likely to experience diminished feelings of control. These results would appear to obviate the theoretical rationale presented in this chapter that focuses on cognitive functioning. This may not necessarily be the case. We know very little about the factors that influence how long people feel they will live. Some studies suggest that people who are physically ill do not anticipate having a long life (Hamermesh & Hamermesh, 1983). Even so, it is possible that cognitive disability influences these perceptions as well, and that people who experience cognitive deficits may also feel they will not live long. Support for this assertion is provided by Manton, who reported that cognitive impairment is associated with a shorter active life expectancy (i.e., people with cognitive dysfunctioning actually die at a relatively younger age) (Manton & Stallard, 1991). Perhaps cognitive dysfunctioning also lowers subjective life expectancy, which in turn diminishes feelings of personal control.

The discussion provided up to this point suggests that at least part of the reason for the accelerating decline in feelings of personal control in later life may be found by looking at the interface between late-life stressors and cognitive impairment. Although this may provide some useful insights, the implications for mental health have not been developed fully. Fortunately, Newmann's (1989) research on accelerating rates of depressive symptoms in late life provides an interesting possibility. As discussed earlier, depressive symptoms initially diminish with advancing age but then increase sharply around age 60. This trend is intriguing because it is very similar to the late-life trajectories of cognitive impairment and personal control. Moreover, the point at which depressive symptoms begin to escalate (age 60) is only 5 or 10 years after cognitive impairment begins to emerge and feelings of control start to decline. Perhaps the pattern observed by Newmann represents the end point in the process sketched out earlier. More specifically, the interplay between stress, cognitive impairment, and feelings of personal control may help explain the upturn in depressive symptomatology that begins around the sixth decade of life.

Social Support and Successful Aging.   The process described in the previous section paints a bleak picture of later life. Even so, the theory of cumulative advantage would lead us to believe that only some elders get caught in this downward spiral, while others are able to avoid these problems and even thrive as they grow older. Consequently, it is important to identify the resources that enable these more fortunate individuals to age successfully. In particular, we need to know how some older adults are able to offset, avoid, or compensate for the decline in control reported by Mirowsky (1995). A central premise of the discussion that follows is that social support plays a key role in this respect (Rowe & Kahn, 1997). However, social support is a complex, multidimensional phenomenon in its own right. This point was not dealt with adequately in the brief overview of social support that was provided earlier. The intent in this section is to redress this imbalance by delving more deeply into the complexity of the social support process. In order to accomplish this task, three issues are examined. Different ways of conceptualizing and measuring social support are identified first. Following this, research is reviewed that suggests one particular type of support (anticipated support) may be especially beneficial in late life. In the process, SES variations in the effectiveness of anticipated support are examined.

During the past several decades, researchers have identified a number of ways to define and measure social support. This vast literature is summarized succinctly in Barrera's

(1986) straightforward classification scheme. According to Barrera, there are three kinds of social support measures: measures of social embeddedness (e.g., the frequency of contact with others), received support (e.g., the amount of tangible help actually provided by others), and perceived support (subjective evaluations of supportive exchanges, such as satisfaction with support). As the literature continues to evolve, it is becoming increasingly clear that measures of perceived support exert more beneficial effects on mental health outcomes than scales that assess social embeddedness or received support (Eckenrode & Wethington, 1990). Recently, two papers by Krause suggested that this may be especially true with respect to one particular type of perceived support—anticipated support (Krause, 1997a; Krause, Liang, & Gu, 1997). Anticipated support is defined as the belief that significant others are willing to provide assistance in the future should the need arise (Wethington & Kessler, 1986). Two findings from these studies are especially relevant for this chapter. First, this work suggested that anticipated support offsets the noxious effects of economic stress on depressive symptoms. The emphasis on financial difficulties is noteworthy because it is an important concomitant of SES. Second, this research revealed that, in contrast to anticipated support, received support exacerbates the noxious effects of economic difficulty on depressive symptomatology.

In order to see why received support may exacerbate the impact of financial stress, it is helpful to first consider what individuals may do when they encounter a stressor. Although the selection of a particular coping response is undoubtedly influenced by many factors (Aldwin, 1994), research reviewed by Eckenrode and Wethington (1990) suggested that instead of immediately turning to others for help, some people may initially try to resolve their difficulties on their own. After this step, they may ask for assistance, but only if their own personal resources prove to be ineffective (Gore, 1979; Wethington & Kessler, 1986). Viewed from this vantage point, some researchers argued that received support actually serves as a marker of failed or ineffective individual coping efforts (Wethington & Kessler, 1986). If older adults are unable to resolve economic problems on their own, it may initially appear that obtaining assistance from others would be especially helpful. Unfortunately, elders who face economic problems may find that their social network members are not in position to help out. As Coyne and his associates argued, stressors frequently affect not only individuals but also entire social networks (Coyne, Wortman, & Lehman, 1988). This phenomenon may be especially true with respect to financial problems. Social networks are comprised largely of individuals with the same SES (Lin, 1982). Consequently, when older adults encounter economic problems and turn to significant others for help, the very individuals they rely on may be experiencing financial difficulties of their own (Belle, 1982). This correspondence may, in turn, create interpersonal conflict that may ultimately erode the quality of assistance provided by lower SES social network members.

If support received in response to economic difficulty proves to be ineffective, then it is not clear how some elders are able to cope adequately, while others subsequently experience psychological distress. Perhaps part of the answer may be found by turning to anticipated support. Although Krause (1997a) provided several reasons why anticipated support may prove to be effective in dealing with stress, one is especially relevant for the purposes of this chapter. As Wethington and Kessler (1986) argued, the realization that others stand ready to help constitutes a social safety net that promotes risk taking and encourages individuals to resolve problems on their own (see also Pierce, Sarason, & Sarason, 1996). The experience of successfully confronting a stressor without the direct intervention of others may be an especially effective way to promote feelings of personal control (Rodin, 1990).

Usually, the promotion of self-sufficiency is a desirable goal because, as noted earlier, this may increase feelings of control in late life. However, individuals must possess adequate personal resources in order to ensure that individually initiated actions are possible and ultimately successful. Unfortunately, lower SES elders may be at a disadvantage in this respect. An emphasis has been placed throughout this chapter on the importance of education for successful aging. In addition to being a key measures of SES, education is also an important coping resource in its own right. As noted earlier, elders must possess certain cognitive skills in order to develop and initiate plans for confronting and eradicating troublesome life events. Those with little schooling may be at a disadvantage in this respect because one of the primary goals of education is to develop the capacity for sound abstract reasoning and effective problem solving.

Taken as a whole, the theoretical rationale developed here suggests that anticipated support may influence feelings of personal control, but there may be important SES variations in the relationship between these constructs. Bolstered by the belief that others stand ready to help if needed, upper SES elders may be more likely to try to resolve their problems on their own. Since they possess adequate personal resources, these self-initiated efforts often meet with success. In contrast, lower SES elders may lack the personal resources needed to implement individually initiated coping efforts. Consequently, they may be more inclined to turn immediately to others for help. However, doing so does not foster the opportunity for personal growth and the enhancement of personal control.

Recently, Krause (1997b) took a preliminary step toward evaluating this perspective. In particular, he examined the statistical interaction between anticipated support and a global measure of stressful events on changes in received support over time. The intent was to see if those who anticipate getting help actually mobilize their social networks when life events are encountered. Consistent with the theoretical rationale developed earlier, important SES variations emerged from the analyses. In particular, the findings from this longitudinal nationwide survey revealed that lower SES elders mobilized anticipated support regardless of the amount of stress that is present. In contrast, upper SES elders were much more selective about mobilizing anticipated assistance from others and did so only when stress reached a relatively high level. Although this research provides an important point of departure for evaluating the theoretical perspective developed in this section, it is important to emphasize that the relationships among anticipated support, stress, and feelings of personal control were not evaluated empirically.

SUMMARY.   Viewed broadly, the research presented in this section provides a preliminary conceptual framework for explaining the sharp upturn in depressive symptoms that emerge at about age 60. Two factors are especially important in this view. First, it is argued that the increase in cognitive disability during late life may be at least partially responsible because it erodes the ability of older adults to cope effectively with the stressors that confront them. Since education is an important determinant of cognitive ability, lower SES elders may be especially vulnerable in this respect. The second factor has to do with social support. Although social support may play an important role in bolstering and replenishing feelings of personal control, research focusing on anticipated support suggests that these advantages are more likely to be enjoyed only by those in upper SES groups. Taken in tandem, the research on cognitive disability and anticipated support provides one way of explaining why there may be an ever-widening gap in personal control during late life. Even so, the discussion of these principles is not a fully articulated life course perspective because it is not clear how these dynamics are related to the research presented in the previous section on the early life precursors of adult mental health. The discussion provided in the next section begins to make these connections.

Merging Early- and Late-Life Perspectives on Disorder

The constructs of control, social support, and stress figure prominently in the discussions of early as well as late-life precursors of depression. If a true life-course perspective is to be developed, then it is important to explicitly demonstrate how these early- and late-life factors act in concert to increase the risk of mental disorder among older adults. Given the current knowledge base, it is not possible to accomplish a tight merger here. Consequently, three explicit linkages are discussed here to illustrate the kind of thinking that may be useful for accomplishing this task. Rather than being based on a firm empirical foundation, the examples provided may best be thought of as points of departure for stimulating further conceptual development.

Earlier, research by George and her colleagues (1991) was reviewed to show that education and cognitive impairment are highly negatively correlated. There is considerable debate over the meaning of this relationship. Some investigators believe that the high correlation between these constructs reflects little more than test bias (Kittner et al., 1986), whereas others maintain that education may be a legitimate risk factor in the etiology of cognitive impairment (Berkman, 1986; Rowe & Kahn, 1997). Actually, these scenarios are not mutually exclusive and both may be present at the same time. It is not possible to resolve this issue conclusively in the absence of a gold standard for measuring cognitive deficits. Even so, a recent study by Schmand and his associates (Schmand, Lindeboom, Hooijer, & Jonker, 1995), involving over 4,000 elders in Amsterdam, suggests that lack of education is a genuine risk factor for cognitive impairment. There are likely to be a number of explanations for this finding. For example, some investigators maintain that those with lower levels of educational attainment are more likely to take jobs that expose them to unsafe levels of toxic materials and solvents. Prolonged exposure to these toxins is thought to eventually promote cognitive impairment in later life (Dartigues et al., 1992). If this scenario is true, then this work may be coupled with the perspective developed from the work of McLanahan (1985) to show how forces set in motion during childhood (i.e., early parental loss and educational disruption) ultimately erode the cognitive resources needed in later life to deal effectively with the deleterious effects of stress.

A second example of how more tightly to merge early- and late-life factors may be found by extending Wheaton's (1994) stress-proneness perspective. As discussed earlier, he posits that the deleterious effects of stressors that emerge over the life course are cumulative. Although he presented compelling evidence to support this assertion, there may be more to it. In a thought-provoking paper, Turner and Avison (1992) argued that although stress may indeed have negative effects, life events may create the opportunity for personal growth as well. If an event is eventually resolved, an individual may ultimately emerge from the process with greater skill and a renewed sense of confidence, thereby increasing the odds that stressors encountered in the future will also be successfully confronted. Instead of being a relatively rare phenomenon, data provided by these investigators revealed that fully 40% of their study participants reported that all the events they encountered in the past year had been successfully resolved. When coupled with the work of Wheaton (1994), this finding suggests that life events may have two different trajectories over the life course: One leads to an escalating sequence of negative fallout, while the other consists of a cumulative series of growth experiences. It is important to point out that the escalating patterns portrayed by these trajectories are consistent with the theory of cumulative advantage (Ross & Wu, 1996).

Although this extension of Wheaton's (1994) work may be helpful, its relevance for the study of mental health problems in later life is not fully articulated. One way of showing the importance of cumulative growth in later life may be found by turning to Erikson's (1959) well-known theory of adult development. According to this conceptual scheme, advancement through each of eight developmental stages is contingent upon the successful resolution of a normative developmental crisis. The fruits of this lifelong process are realized in the final stage, when elders are faced with the prospect of either building a sense of integrity or slipping into despair. Although the notion of integrity is not defined clearly by Erikson, it is the product of deep introspection and reflection. During this final stage, individuals begin to accept the kind of person they have become over the years; it is a time for reconciling the real and ideal self by coming to grips with the gap between what they would like to have done, and what they have actually accomplished. It seems that the person who is best positioned to meet the developmental challenges of this final stage is the one who has experienced a trajectory of cumulative growth experiences, whereas the individual most likely to fall into a state of despair is the one whose life has consisted of a cumulative series of unsuccessfully resolved problems.

The final example of how to begin developing a life-course perspective has to do with anticipated support. Earlier, research by Krause was reviewed, suggesting that anticipated support may buffer the effects of economic stressors on depression, whereas received support may actually exacerbate the deleterious impact of financial problems (Krause, 1997a). The theoretical rationale for these findings suggests that anticipated support is an especially effective resource because it promotes independent problem solving, thereby bolstering feelings of personal control. Viewed more broadly, anticipated support may be considered a key factor in successful aging because it contributes to self-sufficiency in late life. If this is true, then we need to know a good deal more about how perceptions of anticipated support arise and evolve over the course of a person's life. Some psychologists argue that anticipated support is little more than a relatively fixed personality trait (Sarason, Sarason, & Pierce, 1994), but this orientation may overlook important changes in social support systems over the life course.

Antonucci's (1985) work on the support bank provides a useful way to show how changes in the nature of support systems over time may enhance anticipated support in late life. This view, which is derived from social exchange theory, is best described by focusing on the relationship between elderly people and their grown offspring. Early in life, parents make a substantial investment in their children without receiving compensation that is commensurate with their efforts. Even so, they are building up support credits (i.e., expectations for assistance in the future) that may be cashed in during late life. In particular, when parents reach old age, they are likely to feel assured that needed assistance will be forthcoming because they, as well as their children, understand that the children may be called upon to repay assistance that was provided decades earlier.

Although the support bank perspective is insightful, it is possible to develop this view more fully. Current discussions of the support bank create the impression that all parents are able to build up a sufficient store of social support credits because they have provided adequately for their children when young. This is not always the case. Instead, there may be significant variance in the store of support credits that parents are able to amass, and we must be able to explain it. Perhaps early parental loss may play a role in this respect. Do elders who lost a parent early in life experience relationship problems with their own off-spring, and do these interpersonal difficulties affect the amount of help that older adults expect their children to provide in the future? Unfortunately, there do not appear to be any studies in the literature that empirically evaluate these conceptual linkages. Even so, as illustrated throughout this section, the life course perspective provides a useful vantage point for formulating thought-provoking hypotheses about the problems older adults encounter and the resources they rely on to deal with these problems.

CONCLUSIONS

The purpose of this chapter was to review selected findings on the epidemiology of mental disorder in late life and to offer a theoretical explanation for these findings. There is little consensus on the prevalence of mental health problems among older adults. Research that focuses on clinical cases of psychiatric disorder suggests that mental health problems arise early in life and that the prevalence of most conditions gradually tapers off over the life course. However, organic mental health problems and suicide constitute two important exceptions to this trend. In contrast, studies concerned with subclinical levels of depressive symptoms provide a different view. Although this literature is not consistent, an intriguing cluster of studies suggests that levels of depressive symptomatology initially decline over adulthood and then increase sharply after age 60.

In view of the methodological problems associated with each of these research traditions, it is not possible at this time to reach a firm conclusion about the prevalence or age of onset of mental disorders among older people. Instead, deficiencies in the existing knowledge base underscore the need for additional research. In particular, we need to conduct a nationwide survey that is geared specifically to assessing the mental health of our aging population, and that does so using mental health scales that are designed specifically for older adults.

Although assessing rates of mental disorder in late life is an important goal, sociologists must also be able to devise conceptual frameworks that are capable of explaining the patterns that are observed. Most of the theoretical models used by social gerontologists focus largely on etiological factors that arise in late life. However, as the research reviewed in this chapter reveals, there is a vast literature suggesting that forces arising in the early decades of life may exert a profound influence on mental health in the adult years. Even so, this does not obviate the role of late-life etiological factors. Instead, a major premise in this chapter is that it is possible to merge both literatures, and that to assume a life course perspective is essential for doing so.

Using the theory of cumulative advantage as a point of departure, an effort was made to explain the upturn in depressive symptoms during the sixth decade of life. Research was reviewed suggesting that feelings of personal control, as well as levels of cognitive functioning, follow a nonlinear trajectory similar to that of depressive symptoms. Then, using the stress process model as a organizing framework, an attempt was made to show how these seemingly unrelated trends may be part of the same underlying process. In particular, it was argued that the onset of cognitive disability may compromise the ability of older adults to deal effectively with the stressors that confront them. This decline may in turn erode feelings of personal control, thereby contributing to the sharp rise in late life depressive symptomatology. It was further argued that social support helps some elders avoid this vicious downward spiral. A case was made for the important role played by anticipated support in this process. Consistent with the basic tenets of the theory of cumulative advantage, the pervasive influence of educational attainment was highlighted throughout this discussion.

Instead of locating the genesis of depression in factors that are encountered only in late life, the scope of inquiry was expanded by sketching out several ways in which factors arising early in life may influence the emerging theoretical process. For example, one line of thinking points to the following temporal sequence: (1) Early parental loss promotes educational disruption; (2) people with lower levels of educational attainment take jobs in which exposure to toxins are high; (3) during the ensuing decades, continued exposure to toxins contributes to cognitive impairment; and (4) people who are cognitively impaired have difficulty coping with late-life stressors. Other possibilities were explored by extending Wheaton's (1994) compelling work on stress proneness. In particular, he argued that while some individuals encounter cumulative exposure to noxious events over the life course, others may follow a different trajectory that consists of personal growth through the successful resolution of life events.

The theoretical framework developed in this chapter is far from complete. For example, the important influence of cohort effects is noticeably absent from the discussion provided here. It will take years of research and revision to bring this work to fruition, because the scope of inquiry is so vast. Although the conceptual and methodological challenges in pursuing this work are daunting, the vantage point it creates, the sweeping view of life it affords, and the sense of connectedness and continuity it provides are unattainable in any other discipline. When viewed in this way, the contribution of the theoretical perspective presented here may lie primarily in the possibilities that it illuminates.

ACKNOWLEDGMENT: This work was supported by a grant from the National Institute on Aging (RO1 AG09221).

REFERENCES

Aldwin, C. M. (1994). *Stress, coping, and development: An integrative perspective.* New York: Guilford.

American Psychiatric Association. (1980). *Diagnostic and statistical manual of mental disorders* (3rd ed.). Washington, DC: Author.

Antonucci, T. C. (1985). Personal characteristics, social support, and social behavior. In R. H. Binstock & E. Shanas (Eds.), *Handbook of aging and the social sciences* (pp. 94–128). New York: Van Nostrand Reinhold.

Avison, W. R., & Gotlib, I. H. (1994). *Stress and mental health: Contemporary issues and prospects for the future.* New York: Plenum Press.

Bandura, A. (1995). Exercise of personal and collective efficacy in changing societies. In A. Bandura (Ed.), *Self-efficacy in changing societies* (pp. 1–45). New York: Cambridge University Press.

Barrera, M. (1986). Distinctions between social support concepts, measures, and models. *American Journal of Community Psychology, 14,* 413–425.

Belle, D. (1982). The impact of poverty on social networks and supports. *Marriage and Family Review, 5,* 89–103.

Berkman, L. F. (1986). The association between educational attainment and mental status examinations: Of etiologic significance for senile dementia or not? *Journal of Chronic Disease, 39,* 171–174.

Bifulco, A. T., Brown, G. W., & Harris, T. O. (1987). Childhood loss of parent, lack of adequate parental care, and adult depression: A replication. *Journal of Affective Disorders, 12,* 115–128.

Blazer, D. G. (1994). Is depression more frequent in late life: An honest look at the evidence. *American Journal of Geriatric Psychiatry, 2,* 193–199.

Blazer, D. G., George, L., & Landerman, R. (1986). The phenomenology of late life depression. In P. E. Bebbington & R. Jacoby (Eds.), *Psychiatric disorders in the elderly* (pp. 141–150). London: Mental Health Foundation.

Bowlby, J. (1980). *Attachment and loss: Volume III. Loss, sadness, and depression.* New York: Basic Books.

Bradburn, N., Rips, L., & Shevell, S. (1987). Answering autobiographical questions: The impact of memory and inference in surveys. *Science, 236,* 157-161.

Brown, G. W., & Harris, T. O. (1978). *Social origins of depression.* New York: Free Press.

Bruce, M. L., & Leaf, P. J. (1989). Psychiatric disorders and 15-month mortality in a community sample of older adults. *American Journal of Public Health, 79,* 727–730.

Caplan, G. (1981). Mastery of stress: Psychosocial aspects. *American Journal of Psychiatry, 138,* 413–420.

Cohen, S., & Rodriguez, M. S. (1995). Pathways linking affective disturbances and physical disorders. *Health Psychology, 14,* 374–380.

Coyne, J. C., Wortman, C. B., & Lehman, D. R. (1988). The other side of support: Emotional overinvolvement and miscarried helping. In B. H. Gottlieb (Ed.), *Marshaling social support: Formats, processes, and effects* (pp. 305–330). Newbury Park, CA: Sage.

Dartigues, J.-F., Gagnon, M., Letenneur, L., Barberger-Gateau, P., Commenges, D., Evaldre, M., & Salamon, R. (1992). Principle lifetime occupation and cognitive impairment in a French elderly cohort (Paquid). *American Journal of Epidemiology, 135,* 981–988.

Dohrenwend, B. P., Levav, I., Shrout, P. E., Schwartz, S., Naveh, G., Link, B. G., Skodol, A. E., & Stueve, A. (1992). Socioeconomic status and psychiatric disorders: The causation–selection issue. *Science, 255,* 946–952.

Dohrenwend, B. P., Shrout, P. E., Egri, G., & Mendelsohn, F. S. (1980). Measures of nonspecific psychological distress and other dimensions of psychopathology in the general population. *Archives of General Psychiatry, 37,* 1229–1236.

Eaton, W. W., Dryman, A., & Weissman, M. M. (1991). Panic and phobia. In L. N. Robins & D. A. Regier (Eds.), *Psychiatric disorders in America: The Epidemiologic Catchment Area Study* (pp. 155–179). New York: Free Press.

Eaton, W. W., & Kessler, L.G . (1981). Rates of symptoms of depression in a national sample. *American Journal of Epidemiology, 114,* 528–538.

Eckenrode, J., & Wethington, E. (1990). The process and outcome of mobilizing social support. In S. Duck (Ed.), *Personal relationships and social support* (pp. 83–103). Newbury Park, CA: Sage.

Erikson, E. H. (1959). *Identity and the life cycle.* New York: International Universities Press.

Ernst, C., & Angst, J. (1995). Depression in old age: Is there a real decrease in prevalence? A review. *European Archives of Psychiatry and Clinical Neuroscience, 245,* 272–287.

Folkman, S., & Lazarus, R. S. (1988). The relationship between coping and emotion: Implications for theory and research. *Social Science and Medicine, 26,* 309–317.

Folstein, M., Anthony, J. C., Parhad, I., Duffy, B., & Gruenberg, E. M. (1985). The meaning of cognitive impairment in the elderly. *Journal of the American Geriatrics Society, 33,* 228–235.

Gecas, V. (1989). The social psychology of self-efficacy. In W. R. Scott & J. Blake (Eds.), *Annual review of sociology* (Vol. 15, pp. 291–316). Palo Alto, CA: Annual Reviews.

George, L. K. (1996). Social and economic factors related to psychiatric disorders in later life. In E. W. Busse & D. G. Blazer (Eds.), *Textbook of geriatric psychiatry* (pp. 129–153). Washington, DC: American Psychiatric Association Press.

George, L. K., Landerman, R., Blazer, D. G., & Anthony, J. C. (1991). Cognitive impairment. In L. N. Robins & D. A. Regier (Eds.), *Psychiatric disorders in America: The Epidemiologic Catchment Area Study* (pp. 291–327). New York: Free Press.

Gore, S. (1979). Does help-seeking increase psychological distress? *Journal of Health and Social Behavior, 20,* 201–202.

Hamermesh, D. S., & Hamermesh, F. W. (1983). Does perception of life expectancy reflect health knowledge? *American Journal of Public Health, 73,* 911–914.

Hendin, H. (1986). Suicide: A review of new directions in research. *Hospital and Community Psychiatry, 7,* 148–154.

Kessler, R. C. (1979). Stress, social status, and psychological distress. *Journal of Health and Social Behavior, 20,* 259–272.

Kessler, R. C., Foster, C. L., Saunders, W. B., & Stang, P. E. (1995). Social consequences of psychiatric disorders, I: Educational attainment. *American Journal of Psychiatry, 152,* 1026–1032.

Kessler, R. C., Foster, C. L., Webster, P. S., & House, J. S. (1992). The relationship between age and depressive symptoms in two national surveys. *Psychology and Aging, 7,* 119–126.

Kessler, R. C., & Magee, W. J. (1994). The disaggregation of vulnerability to depression as a function of the determinants of onset and occurrence. In W. R. Avison & I. H. Gotlib (Eds.), *Stress and mental health: Contemporary issues and prospects for the future* (pp. 239–258). New York: Plenum Press.

Kittner, S. J., White, L. R., Farmer, M. E., Wolz, M., Kaplan, E., Moes, E., Brody, J. A., & Feinleib, M. (1986). Methodological issues in screening for dementia: The problem of adjustment for education. *Journal of Chronic Disease, 39,* 163–170.

Knauper, B., & Wittchen, H.-U. (1994). Diagnosing major depression in the elderly: Evidence for response bias in standardized diagnostic interviews? *Journal of Psychiatric Research, 28,* 147–164.

Koenig, H. G., & Blazer, D. G. (1996). Minor depression in late life. *American Journal of Geriatric Psychiatry, 4,* S14–S21.

Krause, N. (1986). Social support, stress, and well-being among older adults. *Journal of Gerontology, 41,* 512–519.

Krause, N. (1987). Chronic strain, locus of control, and distress in older adults. *Psychology and Aging, 2,* 375–382.

Krause, N. (1995). Assessing stress-buffering effects: A cautionary note. *Psychology and Aging, 10,* 518–526.

Krause, N. (1996). Stress, gender, cognitive impairment, and outpatient physician use in later life. *Journal of Gerontology: Psychological Sciences, 51B,* P15–P23.

Krause, N. (1997a). Anticipated support, received support, and economic stress among older adults. *Journal of Gerontology: Psychological Sciences, 52B,* P15–P23.

Krause, N, (1997b). Received support, anticipated support, social class, and mortality. *Research on Aging, 19,* 387–422.

Krause, N., Liang, J., & Gu, S. (1997). Financial strain, received support, and anticipated support in the P.R.C. *Psychology and Aging, 13,* 58–68.

Krause, N., & Thompson, E. (1998). Cognitive functioning, stress, and psychological well-being in later life. *Journal of Mental Health and Aging, 4,* 277–292.

Krishan, K. R., Hayes, J. C., Tupler, L. A., George, L. K., & Blazer, D. G. (1995). Clinical and phenomenological comparisons of late-onset and early-onset depression. *American Journal of Psychiatry, 152,* 785–788.

Lazarus, R. S. (1966). *Psychological stress and the coping process.* New York: McGraw-Hill.

Lewinsohn, P. M., Rohde, P., Fischer, S. A., & Seeley, J. R. (1991). Age and depression: Unique and shared effects. *Psychology and Aging, 6,* 247–260.

Lewinsohn, P. M., Seeley, J. R., Roberts, R. E., & Allen, N. B. (1997). Center for Epidemiologic Studies Depression Scale (CES-D) as a screening instrument for depression among community-residing older adults. *Psychology and Aging, 12,* 277–287.

Lin, N. (1982). Social resources and instrumental action. In P. V. Marsden & N. Lin (Eds.), *Social structure and social network analysis* (pp. 131–145). Beverly Hills, CA: Sage.

Manton, K. G., Blazer, D. G., & Woodbury, M. A. (1987). Suicide in middle age and later life: Sex and race specific life table and cohort analyses. *Journal of Gerontology, 42,* 219–227.

Manton, K. G., & Stallard, E. (1991). Cross-sectional estimates of active life expectancy for the U.S. elderly and oldest-old populations. *Journal of Gerontology: Social Sciences, 46,* S170–S182.

McLanahan, S. (1985). Family structure and the reproduction of poverty. *American Journal of Sociology, 90,* 873–901.

McLeod, J. D. (1991). Childhood parental loss and adult depression. *Journal of Health and Social Behavior, 32,* 205–220.

Mirowsky, J. (1995). Age and the sense of control. *Social Psychology Quarterly, 58,* 31–43.

Mirowsky, J. (1997). Age, subjective life expectancy, and sense of control: The horizon hypothesis. *Journal of Gerontology: Social Sciences, 52B,* S125–S134.

Mirowsky, J., & Ross, C. E. (1989). *Social causes of psychological distress.* New York: Aldine De Gruyter.

Morgan, K. (1992). Sleep, insomnia, and mental health. *Review of Clinical Gerontology, 2,* 246–253.

Murrell, S. A., Himmelfarb, S., & Wright, K. (1983). Prevalence of depression and its correlates in older adults. *American Journal of Epidemiology, 117,* 173–185.

Newmann, J. P. (1989). Aging and depression. *Psychology and Aging, 4,* 150–165.

Ortega, S. T., & Corzine, J. (1990). Socioeconomic status and mental disorders. In J. R. Greenley (Ed.), *Research in community and mental health* (Vol. 6, pp. 149–182). Greenwich, CT: JAI Press.

Palmore, E. (1978). When can age, period, and cohort be separated? *Social Forces, 57,* 282–295.

Parmalee, P. A., Katz, I. R., & Lawton, M. P. (1989). Depression among institutionalized aging: Assessment and prevalence estimation. *Journal of Gerontology: Medical Sciences, 44,* M22–M29.

Patten, S. B. (1991). The loss of a parent during childhood as a risk factor for depression. *Canadian Journal of Psychiatry, 36,* 706–711.

Pearlin, L. I., Menaghan, E. G., Lieberman, M. A., & Mullan, J. (1981). The Stress Process. *Journal of Health and Social Behavior, 22,* 337–356.

Pearlin, L. I., & Schooler, C. (1978). The structure of coping. *Journal of Health and Social Behavior, 19,* 2–21.

Pearlin, L. I., & Skaff, M. M. (1996). Stress and the life course: A paradigmatic alliance. *Gerontologist, 36,* 239–247.

Phifer, J. F., & Murrell, S. A. (1986). Etiologic factors in the onset of depressive symptoms in older adults. *Journal of Abnormal Psychology, 95,* 282–291.

Pierce, G. R., Sarason, I. G., & Sarason, B. R. (1996). Coping and social support. In M. Zeidner & N. S. Endler (Eds.), *Handbook of coping: Theory, research, and applications* (pp. 434–451). New York: Wiley.

Radloff, L. (1977). The CES-D Scale: A self-report depression scale for research in the general population. *Applied Psychological Measurement, 1,* 385–401.

Reiss, D., Plomin, R., & Hetherington, E. M. (1991). Genetics and psychiatry: An unheralded window of opportunity. *American Journal of Psychiatry, 148,* 283–291.

Roberts, R. E., Kaplan, G. A., Shema, S. J., & Strawbridge, W. J. (1997). Prevalence and correlates of depression in an aging cohort: The Alameda County Study. *Journal of Gerontology: Social Sciences, 52B,* S252–S258.

Robins, L. N., Locke, B. Z., & Regier, D. A. (1991). An overview of psychiatric disorders in America. In L. N. Robins & D. A. Regier (Eds.), *Psychiatric disorders in America: The Epidemiologic Catchment Area Study* (pp. 328–366). New York: Free Press.

Robins, L. N., & Regier, D. A. (1991). *Psychiatric disorders in America: The Epidemiologic Catchment Area Study.* New York: Free Press.

Rodin, J. (1990). Control by any other name: Definitions, concepts, and processes. In J. Rodin, C. Schooler, & K. W. Schaie (Eds.), *Self-directedness: Cause and effects through the life course* (pp. 1–17). Hillsdale, NJ: Erlbaum.

Ross, C., & Wu, C.-L. (1996). Education, age, and the cumulative advantage in health. *Journal of Health and Social Behavior, 37,* 104–120.

Rotter, J. B. (1966). Generalized expectancies for internal versus external control of reinforcement. *Psychological Monographs, 80*(Whole No. 609).

Rowe, J. W., & Kahn, R. L. (1997). Successful aging. *Gerontologist, 37,* 433–440.

Sarason, I. G., Sarason, B. G., & Pierce, G. R. (1994). Relationship-specific social support: Toward a model for the analysis of supportive interactions. In B. R. Burleson, T. L. Albrecht, & I. G. Sarason (Eds.), *Communication of social support: Messages, interactions, relationships, and community* (pp. 91–112). Thousand Oaks, CA: Sage.

Sayetta, R. B., & Johnson, D. P. (1980). *Basic data on depressive symptomatology: United States, 1974–75.* (DHEW Publication No. PHS 80-1666). Washington, DC: U.S. Government Printing Office.

Schmand, B., Lindeboom, J., Hooijer, C., & Jonker, C. (1995). Relation between education and dementia: The role of test bias revisited. *Journal of Neurology, Neurosurgery, and Psychiatry, 59,* 170–174.

Skinner, E. A. (1996). A guide to constructs of control. *Journal of Personality and Social Psychology, 71,* 549–570.

Turner, R. J., & Avison, W. R. (1992). Innovations in the measurement of life stress: Crisis theory and the significance of event resolution. *Journal of Health and Social Behavior, 33,* 36–50.

Turner, R. J., & Marino, F. (1994). Social support and social support: A descriptive epidemiology. *Journal of Health and Social Behavior, 35,* 193–212.

Weissman, M. M., Bruce, M. L., Leaf, P. J., Florio, L. P., & Holzer, C. (1991). Affective disorders. In L. N. Robins & D. A. Regier (Eds.), *Psychiatric disorders in America: The Epidemiologic Catchment Area Study* (pp. 53–80). New York: Free Press.

Wells, J. A., & Strictland, D. E. (1982). Physiogenic bias as invalidity in psychiatric symptom scales. *Journal of Health and Social Behavior, 23,* 235-252.

Wethington, E., & Kessler, R. C. (1986). Perceived support, received support, and adjustment to stressful life events. *Journal of Health and Social Behavior, 27,* 78–89.

Wheaton, B. (1983). Stress, personal coping resources, and psychiatric symptoms: An investigation of interactive models. *Journal of Health and Social Behavior, 24,* 208–229.

Wheaton, B. (1994). Sampling the stress universe. In W. R. Avison & I. H. Gotlib (Eds.), *Stress and mental health: Contemporary issues and prospects for the future* (pp. 77–114). New York: Plenum Press.

CHAPTER 11

Splitting the Difference

Gender, the Self, and Mental Health

Sarah Rosenfield

In her book, *The Mismeasure of Woman,* Carol Tavris tells a story about how men and women express love:

> A friend of mine, who I will call Roberta, has been mildly unhappy for years about one flaw in her otherwise excellent husband, Henry. The flaw rises and falls in importance to her, depending on Roberta's state of mind and general stresses, but it has long been a chronic irritant. Henry's problem is that he doesn't like to "chitchat," as he puts it. This means, Roberta explains, that he doesn't like to gossip about friends and family, he doesn't like to analyze his marriage on a weekly or even a yearly basis, he doesn't like to analyze his feelings. . . . Once, pressed to reveal his passion, Henry said, "I vote with my feet. If I didn't love you, I wouldn't be here." Instead of killing Henry at that moment, which was her inclination, Roberta did what she usually does: She called a woman friend, and they met for lunch to discuss Henry. Several hours later, Roberta emerged refreshed, invigorated, and prepared to cope with Henry for another few months (Tavris, 1994, p. 246).

This story captures the gulf between men and women in their expression of affection. What we call the feminization of love is matched by the masculinization of silence (Tavris, 1994). More generally, Roberta and Henry's story illustrates the fundamental ways in which gender shapes experience. Whether we are male or female profoundly affects our social relationships, resources, and daily activities. As William James (1890/1958) stated a century ago, gender is a basic cultural dimension that is used to divide the universe, second

SARAH ROSENFIELD • Institute for Health, Health Care Policy, and Aging Research, Rutgers University, New Brunswick, New Jersey 08903.
Handbook of the Sociology of Mental Health, edited by Carol S. Aneshensel and Jo C. Phelan. Kluwer Academic/Plenum Publishers, New York, 1999.

only to the distinction made between what is the self and what is not. Recent studies show that gender is one of the first social distinctions children acquire. Surely, then, gender splits our experiences and understandings of the world and, in turn, the problems we suffer from and even the ways we suffer.

One of the most striking patterns in the epidemiology of mental illness is the difference between the sexes (see Chapter 7). Taking all psychological disorders together, there are no differences in males' and females' rates of psychopathology; however, they suffer from dramatically different types of disorders. Females suffer more than males from internalizing disorders, including depression and anxiety, which turn problematic feelings inward against themselves. Women more often struggle with a sense of loss, hopelessness, and feelings of helplessness to improve their conditions. They endure attributions of self-blame and self-reproach. More often than men, women live with fears in the forms of phobias, panic attacks, and free-floating anxiety states. In contrast, males predominate in externalizing disorders, expressing problematic feelings in outward behavior. They more often have enduring personality traits that are aggressive and antisocial in character, with related problems in forming close, enduring relationships. Males also exceed females in substance abuse. They are more often dependent on substances, suffer physical consequences, and experience problems with work and family because of drugs or alcohol use. Males and females diverge in these disorders in adolescence and continue to follow different patterns throughout their lives (American Psychiatric Association, 1994).

In this chapter, I seek to explain these differences. In doing so, I develop a framework that connects these differences in psychological problems to larger cultural and structural divisions associated with gender. I propose that sociocultural conceptions of masculinity and femininity—reflected in child socialization practices and adult social positions—differentially shape central dimensions of the self in males and females. These differences in dimensions of the self, in turn, predispose males and females to opposite extremes of internalizing and externalizing disorders (Aneshensel, 1992). In this way, social practices that are divided by gender produce both selves that are fragmented and mental health problems that are consistent with this fragmentation.

The first part of the chapter develops this framework. After briefly reviewing some of the relevant sources and characteristics of our conceptions of gender, I trace the implications of these conceptions for current social practices. I then draw out the consequences of these social practices for dimensions of the self. Finally, I show how these forces contribute to the psychological problems borne differentially by the sexes. The second part of the chapter examines evidence for these arguments.

THE ROOTS OF OUR GENDER CONCEPTIONS: DIVISIONS IN THE MODERN AGE

Our current distinctions between the genders are connected to larger social–economic and philosophical–conceptual divisions arising in the modern age, especially the last 200 years. As Jane Flax (1993) asserts, a basic agenda of the modern age has been the simultaneous generation and devaluation of difference. For example, urbanization, and especially industrialization, divided spheres of life that were public from those that were private. The home no longer unified productive and reproductive labor as had farms and even small craft production. Work for pay became centralized in factories or shops, taking laborers far from the home and domestic life. Furthermore, institutions in the public realm became increasingly independent and separate, with increasingly explicit and elaborated divisions of labor (Weber, 1946).

Worldviews shifted in the same period. With the rise of the middle class and its freedom from manual labor, rewards came to be seen as properly based on one's own activities and merit rather than on birth. The Protestant Reformation's emphasis on a direct relationship with a deity contributed to the notion of an autonomous self and individuality of expression (Connell, 1995; Seidler, 1989). The growth of cities and the possibilities for the accumulation of wealth reinforced the emphases on individualism and calculated rationality, which was captured in Weber's description of the Protestant ethic. As capitalism advanced, rationalization spread from business to other institutions, emphasizing technical reasoning and a focus on means rather than goals. Spawned by the Enlightenment, rationality became the pathway to truth, knowledge, and inevitable progress, representing the height of human potential (Flax, 1993). Reason and science—as rationality's highest form—were defined by their opposition to the natural world and emotion. These changes reflected a fundamental cultural assumption relatively new to modernity: the belief that the world was controllable and that forces determining individuals' lives rested within their own power.

Major conceptual distinctions were permeated with issues of control. Contrasts were drawn between things that were defined as more and less subject to rationality. Thus, reason and logic, as the basis of control, were split from emotion and desire, the hallmarks of irrationality. The mind, as the seat of reason, was split off from the body and its myriad mysteries. These distinctions fit within the public–private split. The workings of the mind and the application of reason governed activity in the public sphere of production. Bodies, emotions, and desires ruled the private sphere. Such dichotomies were infused with value and judgments. In each, the side associated with irrationality was devalued (Bordo, 1993).

Gender was linked to these splits between public and private, mind and body. Reason and emotion became closely associated with male and female, respectively. Before the eighteenth century, women were usually distinguished from men in being "less" than men— for example, less rational—but not as being men's opposite. A new ideology of separate capacities entailed a polarized conception of gender in which males and females had qualitatively different characters (Connell, 1995). Masculine character was attached to the power of reason, and its counterpart was the feminization of emotion. A cult of feminine domesticity validated the assignment of women to the private sphere. This originally middle-class ideology dictated that women were fragile and emotional beings, and that children required their mothers' (not fathers') special care for moral and psychic development (Douglas, 1986; Hays, 1996). Conceptions of femininity thus accentuated the association of women with the private sphere of domesticity and consumption, carrying primary responsibilities for caretaking and emotion work, and possessing related characteristics of nurturance, sensitivity, and emotional expressiveness. Ideals of masculinity came to associate males with the public sphere of production and with the consonant characteristics of assertiveness, competitiveness, and independence.

Thus, paralleling the public–private split, the connections of femininity with nature and emotion, and of masculinity with reason and the mind, were accentuated. As Bordo says, "All those bodily spontaneities—hunger, sexuality, the emotions—seen as needful of containment and control have been culturally constructed and coded as female, . . . [while] the capacity for self-management is decisively coded as male" (1993, pp. 205–206). Desire becomes a subject of conflict for women: To be good and to please the self are incompatible for females but are congruent for males. More specifically, Foucault (1978) points out that as new conjugal and parental duties emerged in the early modern period, bodies became the focus of new technologies of power which provided pervasive, internally focused forms of regulation. For example, as part of these new technologies, medical science eventually produced the image of the nervous woman, the woman afflicted with vapors, who, aided by psychoanalytic thinking, was thought of as hysterical and marked as pathological.

In summary, rationalization was a central theme in the cultural landscape of the modern age that permeated the construction of gender. Given the cultural premium placed on mind and on reason, that which is associated with males and masculinity has become by definition the norm—what Tavris (1994) calls the universal male. If the reference point is male, female is defined as "other." Since all categories of "other" are judged—and judge themselves—in relation to the cultural reference group, that which is female is cast in a devalued light (Goffman, 1966). These specific dichotomies and the standard of the universal male continue to color the interpretation of everything associated with maleness and femaleness, creating a fundamental opposition between males and females (Tavris, 1994).

These contrasts describe our dominant conceptions of gender, which in Connell's (1995) terms are the current forms that guarantee patriarchy. There are multiple masculinities and femininities that differ, for example, by race, social class, and sexual preference. I focus on the dominant forms: middle-class, white masculinity and femininity. Even though there are distinctions among these dominant images, for instance, a masculinity exemplified by professionals and based in technical expertise versus one illustrated by businessmen and based in dominance, I focus on elements that cut across these distinct forms. I trace the implications of dominant conceptions of masculinity and femininity for current social practices, for dimensions of the self, and for the mental disorders that distinguish the sexes.

CURRENT SOCIAL PRACTICES

Childhood Socialization

These dominant conceptions of gender are reflected in current social practices that polarize the life experiences of males and females. Beginning with childhood, parents treat sons and daughters differently. For example, sons are given more freedom and independence than daughters (Best & Williams, 1995). Some claim that mothers encourage separateness in sons but hold daughters back because of their overidentification with daughters (Chodorow, 1978). Others claim that parents treat sons and daughters differently to prepare them to fit into gendered roles in the adult world (Hagan, Gillis, & Simpson, 1985; Hagan, Simpson, & Gillis, 1987, 1988). Less control over sons encourages them to develop a risk-taking, entrepreneurial spirit that fits into the adult realm of production. Greater instrumental control or supervision over daughters' activities discourages risk taking and independence in preparation for a primary emphasis on domesticity. Meta-analyses of socialization research show that parents encourage sex stereotypes in play activities and household chores. As for emotions, parents show warmth and prohibit aggression more for girls (Lytton & Romney, 1991). These differences are greater in observational and experimental studies than in self-reports, which suggests that parents think they treat sons and daughters more similarly than they do in practice.

Teachers also socialize boys and girls differently. Research finds that males are treated as more important and more competent by teachers in nursery schools, elementary and high schools, and college classrooms (Geis, 1993). Teachers also respond more often to aggression in boys than in girls, which serves to maintain aggressive interchanges. In contrast, they typically ignore girls' aggression, which tends to terminate the interaction (Fagot & Hagen, 1985).

Differential socialization also occurs in play. Insofar as play is direct preparation for adulthood, sex-typed play is the antecedent for sex-typed social and achievement behaviors. Playing dolls calls for the practice and development of nurturing skills—as opposed to the demands of sports such as football or basketball, which call for quick reactions, coordination, endurance, and toughness. Adults differ strongly in what playthings they would offer to children depending on the child's gender: Dolls go to girls and footballs to boys (Tittle, 1986). Peer groups reflect the separation by gender that occurs in the family and the larger culture. In mixed-sex groups, boys dominate and girls are passive (Meyer, Murphy, Cascardi, & Birns, 1991). Insofar as girls are passive only in mixed-sex groups, we see the situational character of gender. Since conceptions of gender are largely relational, that is, the characteristics of females are defined in opposition to those of males, people enact or "do" these conceptions more strongly in the presence of the opposite sex.

Gendered socialization experiences intensify in adolescence as physical changes in girls and boys identify them to others as women and men (Chodorow, 1978; Gove & Herb, 1974). These changes invoke images of the perfect woman and man (Brown & Gilligan, 1992). Parents and others begin to apply more stereotyped ideas of womanhood and manhood to their daughters and sons (Nolen-Hoeksema, 1990). Adolescents evaluate themselves against these cultural ideals of masculinity and femininity. Thus, those who were given some leeway in childhood are pushed more in adolescence—for example, girls who were tomboys report increased pressure "to act like a lady, wear dresses, be nice" (Martin, 1996). In addition, one of the primary psychological goals in adolescence is to establish a separate identity, renewing the issues of individuation and autonomy that have not been so salient since the preoedipal period (Chodorow, 1978). From the earlier cognitive stage of concrete operational thought, adolescence ushers in a stage of facility with formal operations. Adolescents thus acquire a greater capacity for abstraction and generalization with which to better understand and adapt to the points of view and desires of others (Piaget, 1954; Brown & Gilligan, 1992). For these reasons, conceptions of gender seem to "kick in" or become personalized in adolescence; that is, in adolescence, we begin to apply to ourselves the general stereotypes that we internalized in childhood (Link, 1987). No experience could do more than "dating" to encourage people to think about how others see them. In this sense, the differentiation in socialization experiences appear to achieve its full expression in adolescence.

Social Practices in Adulthood

Similar practices endure throughout adulthood. Women retain primary responsibility for caretaking and emotional labor, and men, for the economic support of the family. Most women are employed currently, including those with small children. Still, women do the bulk—an average of 66%—of child care and housework, even if they work hours comparable to their husbands outside the home (Lennon & Rosenfield, 1994). As evidence, employed women sleep 30 minutes less per night than their husbands, and do an extra month of 24-hour days' work each year (Hochschild, 1989). In addition, women's predominantly service-sector jobs often require emotion-work, the labor force equivalent of the cult of domesticity (Hochschild,1983).

The persistent association of women with the private sphere has implications for inequality. Women more often have jobs that are part time, with low security and remuneration. These jobs also tend to involve less autonomy and less complexity than men's jobs. Although more women have entered managerial ranks, they are concentrated in the lower levels, primarily managing other women, and have little direct decision-making power (Reskin & Ross, 1992). In the labor force, women earn less than men, even in jobs requiring comparable training and experience (Kilbourne, England, Farkas, Brown, & Weir, 1994). Often, income is divided unequally within the family as well, with husbands receiving more than wives, and wives spending larger proportions of their share on their children (Becker, 1981). Thus, women's income is less than men's overall, whether we look at labor force earnings or at how money is distributed within the family to husbands versus wives and children.

Given these ties to the public and private spheres, respectively, men hold more institutional, generalizable forms of power than women. The skills from the public sphere are transferable, since the value of money remains the same across exchanges. In contrast, the skills of the private sphere, and thus the power, are less transferable because they are tailored to the particular characteristics of one's spouse and children (Mirowsky, 1985). Thus wives' investments are more specific to family members, while those of husbands produce more benefits outside of the marriage (England & Kilbourne, 1990; Lennon & Rosenfield, 1995).

Such disparities leave women with fewer options for economic survival other than marriage. The difference in options is reflected in husbands' generally greater decision-making power in the family. The difference is also reflected in wives' assessments that, even when the burdens of work outside the home are the same as their husbands', their unequal share of work in the home is fair (Lennon & Rosenfield, 1995). These inequalities shape social interactions in male–female relationships, such as the balance of providing and receiving support. Given lower institutional power—coupled with the responsibility for the care of others—the ratio of giving to receiving emotional support for women tilts more toward giving. The greater economic resources held by men, on the other hand, tilt the ratio more toward receiving emotional support. These disparities are revealed in the character of loss with divorce: Women's distress results more from the loss of economic security, whereas men suffer more from a deprivation of emotional sustenance (Gerstel, Riessman, & Rosenfield, 1985).

IMPLICATIONS FOR DIMENSIONS OF THE SELF

These social and cultural divisions must affect the self. By splitting the world into parts and dividing these parts by gender, we also polarize certain aspects of the self that have consequences for psychopathology. I conceptualize these aspects of the self as "basic operating assumptions" that individuals construct from past experience to make sense of their world. Because individuals have the ability to take themselves as well as the outside world as objects, they have the capacity to interpret and judge both as objects. Using this capacity, individuals create basic assumptions about the self, the world, and social relationships. For example, perceptions of self-esteem and mastery—described as fundamental aspects that protect and enhance the self (Pearlin et al., 1981)—constitute major assumptions about the self. Individuals' views of the extent to which forces affecting them are controllable—even if not by themselves—form a major assumption about the world. Other world assumptions focus more specifically on views about the social world, for example, the degree to which other people are seen as basically good versus bad, trustworthy versus worthy of suspicion, competent versus incompetent. The boundaries drawn between the self and others comprise a central assumption about social relationships. This relational assumption refers to the degree of individuation from, or connection to, other people (Chodorow, 1978). Finally, the importance individuals confer on others' versus their own needs, desires, and interests constitutes another basic assumption regarding relationships. This assumption varies from the extreme of self-salience on one end, in which the self is given complete primacy, to the extreme of other-salience, in which others are given total priority. A common element across these assumptions is their evaluative character, which infuses cognitive conceptions with a strong emotional valence.

I contend that individuals take an active part in constructing basic assumptions. Depending on the range and layers of experience, they join inferences about the world from multiple sources, juggle contradictory assumptions from different periods in their lifetime, and fill in the blanks when information is missing. Thus, basic assumptions are not completely automatic or unchangeable. However, we do not totally invent ourselves from one situation to another. Earlier messages, especially if repeated and received from significant others, have tremendous continuity. We carry these messages as working hypotheses into each situation to be altered or reinforced, but with a slant toward seeing new things as we have in the past. In spite of the complexities, we tend to have similar "gut reactions" to new experiences. Working like a filter in which all is seen in a certain light, basic assumptions operate as a kind of cognitive–emotional set point, which is altered only by significant experiences of considerable duration or intensity.

The same capacity to take themselves as objects allows individuals to construct these assumptions from social experiences. As symbolic interactionism describes, people can take others' perspectives toward themselves as well as toward the world by using shared meanings in symbols. In taking the role of others and identifying with their positions, individuals incorporate the outlooks of others. By this process, over time, they internalize the attitudes toward themselves and the world of larger and larger numbers of persons and groups, culminating in a generalized other within the self that represents perspectives in the larger culture (Mead, 1934). Even acknowledging a strong element of agency, this process of taking the role of the other tends to reproduce existing social structures (Thoits, 1996). Desiring positive responses, people tend to modify their thoughts, feelings, and behaviors to mirror their image of others' views and expectations (Cooley, 1902). In this way, our basic assumptions are shaped by the messages in social practices, which are internalized as part of taking the attitude of the other.

The divisions by gender in these practices generate divergent messages and thus split the core assumptions for males and females (Rosenfield, 1997). The greater power and value of activities associated with masculinity convey messages that males are of high personal worth, in control of their world, and need others less than others need them. The low power, high demands, and devaluation of activities associated with femininity carry messages that females have less worth and control over their world, depend on others for their survival, and are less important than others in social relations.

These messages are both direct and indirect, explicit and subtle. For example, parents may directly tell daughters more than sons that the world is a dangerous place. They also convey this information—as well as a message of girls' inability to fend for themselves—indirectly in their greater control over daughters' activities as compared to sons (e.g., earlier curfews) (Hagan, Gillis, & Simpson, 1981). Children get indirect messages from a range of experiences with parents: from observing parents' interactions, from listening to parents' spontaneous explanations about why things happen, and from hearing what parents say when they themselves fail or do something wrong (Seligman, 1990 ; Meyer et al., 1991). These messages also span different levels, including dominant cultural views and those particular to individuals' social characteristics. Given females' status as the "other" in relation to the universal male, they build their assumptions partly by comparing messages about themselves with messages about the cultural ideals. For example, as Becker (1997) suggests, assumptions of having little control over the world may stand out and be particularly damaging within a context that promotes control as a distinct possibility and a strong cultural ideal.

CONSEQUENCES FOR MENTAL HEALTH

These divisions have consequences for the psychopathologies that differentially plague the sexes. Basic assumptions arguably affect psychopathology by blocking some reactions and facilitating others. For example, the more individuals take on and attend to the feelings and desires of others, the less they can act in their own behalf. At the extreme, identifying strongly with others' interests precludes acting on one's own. The inability to act according to one's own interests also predisposes individuals to feelings of helplessness and hopelessness that characterize depressive reactions. Doubts about one's control and competence in the face of difficulties similarly create feelings of helplessness. Furthermore, a lack of individuation implies dependency and emotional reliance on others, which reflect and create uncertainty and anxiety about one's own abilities and self-worth (Turner, 1996).

At the other extreme, a strong sense of separateness from others and their interests and feelings allows one to act against them more easily. Coupled with a sense of entitlement and control, this distance enables individuals to blame others for difficulties. Such projective types of defenses characterize externalizing behavior. Problems in life exist because of other people and their personal failings. Others become an interference, something to get out of the way. In contrast, identifying with others' interests and feeling what others might feel, namely, empathy, impedes harming another person. An act against someone else is experienced as an act against oneself.

In summary, I have argued that, within a context of gender stratification, basic operating assumptions about the self, the world, and social relations are gendered. By taking the attitudes of others toward the self and the social world, individuals internalize gender inequalities as part of their core assumptions. These processes begin in childhood but achieve their full expression from adolescence through adulthood. The gender differences in basic assumptions, in turn, facilitate the differing forms of psychopathology in males and females. In this way, the divisions we construct by gender have implications for the sex differences found in externalizing and internalizing disorders.

What evidence do we have for this perspective? Splitting this question into three parts, I first review the general evidence bearing on links between gender, basic assumptions, and psychopathology. Second, I look at research specifically on children and adolescents. Finally, I examine work on adulthood.

EVIDENCE ON GENDER, BASIC OPERATING ASSUMPTIONS, AND PSYCHOLOGICAL PROBLEMS

Research on both children and adults indicates that there are gender differences in basic assumptions. Females experience lower levels of perceived control than males, whether it is conceptualized as locus of control, learned helplessness, fatalism, or mastery (Avison & McAlpine, 1992; Hughes & Demo, 1989; Kohn, 1972; Mirowsky & Ross, 1990; Pearlin et al., 1981; Radloff, 1977; Ross & Mirowsky, 1989; Rotter, 1966; Seligman, 1975; Umberson, 1993). A meta-analysis shows that males are higher in internal locus of control in both behavior and perception. In relation to self-esteem, females are lower in studies of both adolescents and adults (Barnett & Gotlib, 1988; Craighead & Green, 1989; Hirschfield, Klerman, Chodoff, Korchin, & Barrett, 1976; Hughes & Demo, 1989; Josephs, Markus, & Tafarodi, 1992; Nolen-Hoeksema, Girgus, & Seligman, 1991; Owens, 1994; Rosenberg, 1989).

Research on relational boundaries finds that females perceive themselves to be more dependent interpersonally and more emotionally reliant on others than males (Barnett & Gotlib, 1988; Craighead & Green, 1989; Hirschfield et al., 1976; Hughes & Demo, 1989; Josephs et al., 1992; Nolen-Hoeksema et al., 1991; Owens, 1994; Rosenberg, 1989; Turner, 1996). Compared to men, women are more likely to see the well-being of family members as important sources of concern and are more likely to perceive the stressful events that happen to others as distressing (Brody, 1981; Kessler & McLeod, 1984). Females generally report a stronger identification with the feelings of others (Rosenfield, 1995). Although there are no direct measures of self–other salience, we have some evidence for differences in that men have a better memory for information encoded with respect to the self, whereas women have a better memory for information encoded with reference to others (Joseph et al., 1992).

Evidence that these differences are based in social experiences comes from cross-cultural research. Boys and girls are more similar in aggression and in nurturance when both are assigned to care for younger siblings and when both perform housework (Edwards & Whiting, 1974; Whiting & Edwards, 1988, 1973; Whiting & Whiting, 1975). Both girls and boys exhibit more nurturing behavior when they care more for infants (Edwards & Whiting, 1980; Munroe, Shimmin, & Munroe, 1984). This reminds us that it is not the capacity for traits or behaviors that is at issue here, but the differences as they develop through social practices.

Other work links basic assumptions to psychopathology. Life events and circumstances that undermine perceptions of self-esteem and mastery are particularly damaging to mental health (Pearlin et al., 1981). Depression is linked to low perceived control across the life course (Mirowsky & Ross, 1990). Perceptions of low mastery and of helplessness in childhood are specifically related to later episodes of clinical depression (Harris, Brown, & Bifuco, 1990). In terms of externalizing behavior, a greater willingness to take risks—which is linked with high levels of independence—is associated with delinquency in acts against both people and property (Hagan et al., 1981). Past research also provides evidence that strong boundaries between the self and others—as indicated in low levels of empathy—are associated with high levels of aggressiveness (Miller & Eisenberg, 1988; Rosenfield, Vertefuille, and McAlpine, 1994).

In summary, previous research establishes some general links between gender and basic assumptions, and between basic assumptions and psychological problems. Most important to the current analysis, there is also evidence that gender differences in basic assumptions help to explain the differences between male and female psychiatric problems. Lower levels of mastery and self-esteem among females contribute to explaining their predominance in depressive symptoms in both adolescence and adulthood (Avison & McAlpine, 1992; Barnett & Gotlib, 1988; Craighead & Green, 1989; Hirschfield et al., 1976; Nolen-Hoeksema, 1990; Rosenberg, 1989; Rosenfield, 1989). The greater levels of emotional reliance and identification with others also helps explain women's higher incidence of depressive symptoms (Kessler & McLeod, 1984; Turner, 1996). In terms of externalizing problems, the differences in risk taking and risk aversion between males and females contributes to males' predominance in antisocial behavior (Hagan et al., 1981).

RESEARCH ON CHILDREN AND ADOLESCENTS

In research relating specifically to childhood and adolescence, Brown and Gilligan (1992) trace the development of assumptions about the self and social relations for girls over time. Their interviews of girls from first grade through tenth grade document dramatic changes. The youngest girls, 7- and 8-year-olds, are outspoken about how they think and feel: They face conflict with friends and family directly and negotiate differences of opinion with little hesitation in the face of clashes in feelings or ideas. At the same time that they know what they want, however, they are aware of what others want them to do and be. This awareness looms larger over time. By the time girls are 11 years old, they feel real fear about saying what they think. They are inhibited, in part, by the (white, middle-class) ideal of the perfect girl, who has no bad thoughts or feelings and who is liked by everybody. To be that perfect girl, they have to be nice all the time and not cause any trouble. At this point, girls have difficulty answering when the question, "Who am I?" is posed by interviewers. Having one's own thoughts and opinions risks conflict, and conflict risks losing relationships. To say what one thinks is to court being unloved and alone. Thus, girls eventually move from a stance of not speaking openly about their feelings to not knowing their thoughts and feelings. By adolescence, they depend on others to define their wishes and ideas. In a model of womanhood that assigns selflessness as the basis for being loved, girls put the interests and feelings of others before their own. As one girl says, "I think of more what to do to be nice than what I want to do." It becomes more important to preserve connections than to hold onto one's own feelings and beliefs.

Quantitative research indicates that the differences between girls and boys in basic assumptions underlie the emergence of the differences in mental health problems. A large study of adolescents examines identification with others' feelings, or empathy, as a dimension of relational boundaries (Rosenfield et al., 1994). High levels of emotional identification indicate a conception of self that is highly connected to other people. In general, individuals who identify strongly with the feelings of others are at greater risk of becoming depressed. Conversely, those who identify very little with others' feelings are more at risk for aggression and other antisocial behavior. The data show that girls are more often extremely high in emotional identification with others, whereas boys more often are extremely low. Furthermore, these differences in empathy help explain girls' higher levels of depressive symptomatology and, to a lesser extent, contribute to explaining boys higher levels of antisocial behavior.

A subsequent longitudinal study investigated these gender differences more extensively (Rosenfield, 1998). This research showed that, over the course of adolescence, boys and girls receive divergent messages about themselves and social relationships. For example, girls and boys perceive that adults expect similar levels of independence and self-confidence from them in early adolescence. These expectations change over time, however, increasing for boys and decreasing for girls. Shifts in basic assumptions correspond to these changes. Boys and girls start their teenage years with similar assumptions about self-worth, degree of autonomy in relationships, and self-salience. By mid- and late adolescence, boys have risen strongly in these assessments and girls have dramatically fallen. This divergence helps explain gender differences in psychopathology. Controlling for these different assumptions about the self and relationships reduces to nonsignificance the sex differences in depressive symptoms, delinquency, and aggressiveness.

RESEARCH ON ADULTS

A constellation of studies link certain adult social conditions to dimensions of the self. These studies focus on major institutions such as the workplace and the family, connecting social roles and conditions within these institutions primarily to self-esteem and perceptions of control. In doing so, this research suggests that activities of daily life continue to shape individuals' basic assumptions in adulthood.

Overall, employed individuals have a higher sense of personal control than those who are not in the labor force or are unemployed (Ross & Mirowsky, 1992). Across both public and private domains, however, work conditions characterized by autonomy, low routinization, and intrinsic and extrinsic rewards bring individuals a heightened sense of control and enhance self-esteem (Lennon, 1994; Pugliesi, 1995; Ross & Mirowsky, 1993). Those whose work provides few economic rewards and little autonomy—coupled with high demands—have a lower sense of self-worth and more fatalistic views about their lives (Karasek & Theorell, 1985; Kohn, 1972; Lennon, 1994; Link et al., 1989; Mirowsky & Ross, 1996). These findings are echoed in general research on socioeconomic status. Individuals with higher levels of education and income have higher self-esteem and perceive that they have greater control over the forces affecting them (Mirowsky & Ross, 1996). Higher earnings relative to one's spouse also brings greater perceptions of personal control (Rosenfield, 1989). Consistent with this pattern, greater gains in self-efficacy accrue when economic resources come from one's own earnings rather than those of one's spouse (Ross & Mirowsky, 1992).

Researchers have examined the impact of these work and family conditions on mental health primarily with respect to internalizing problems. Individuals with high levels of work–family demands have high levels of depressive symptoms. For example, employed women with children have higher depressive symptoms than those without children, and women or men who have more domestic responsibilities have higher symptom levels than those with fewer responsibilities (Kessler & McRae, 1982; Krause & Markides, 1985; Lennon and Rosenfield, 1994; Radloff, 1977; Rosenfield, 1989, 1992; Ross, Mirowsky, & Huber, 1983). Furthermore, people who have fewer economic resources in general, and fewer resources relative to their spouses, suffer greater depressive symptomatology (Rosenfield, 1989).

These general effects are reflected in research on gender (Karasek & Theorell, 1990; Kohn, 1972; Lennon, 1992; Phelan, 1992; Ross & Bird, 1990). Women's work in the labor force commands lower wages and provides less autonomy and complexity than that of men, resulting in a lower sense of control, lower self-esteem, and higher levels of depressive symptoms (Pugliesi, 1995). In contrast, as their relative contributions to the family income become more similar, husbands and wives approach each other in their perceptions of control and levels of depressive symptoms. Compared to paid work, domestic labor provides greater autonomy for women. However, the routine nature of housework and the absence of economic remuneration for homemakers also results in lower perceived control and higher symptoms relative to men (Lennon, 1992; Ross & Mirowsky, 1993). When women combine paid work and domestic work, their continued responsibility for the do-mestic sphere adds up to an extremely high level of demands, which also lowers control and raises symptoms of depression. As further evidence, when employed men and women share domestic labor, their perceptions of personal control become similar and their levels of depressive symptomatology equalize. In view of the negative effects of low power and high demands, I would emphasize that the major role alternatives currently held out to women, described earlier, are characterized by one or both of these conditions (Rosenfield, 1989; Ross & Mirowsky, 1992).

The impact of perceived control and self-esteem on internalizing symptoms suggests that the gender differences in these basic assumptions account in part for the gender differ-ences in rates of depression. Indeed, controlling for levels of self-efficacy reduces sex differences to nonsignificance, irrespective of whether women are homemakers or em-ployed. In this sense, assumptions about control and worth that are embodied in workplace and family experiences contribute to gender differences in internalizing problems (see chap-ters 2 , 13, and 18). The daily experiences of low power and high demands perpetuate the excess of depressive symptoms among women in adulthood. Thus, among adults, as among children, females have more depressive symptoms, partly because their social experiences give them messages of low control.

CONCLUSION

In summary, I have proposed a theoretical perspective connecting social divisions by gen-der, dimensions of the self, and internalizing and externalizing disorders. Social divisions into public versus private, reason versus emotion, and mind versus body have become associated with gender and pervade the social experiences of females and males from child-hood through adulthood. These experiences convey different messages that shape males' and females' basic assumptions about themselves, the world, and social relations. Given the power, responsibility in the public domain, receipt of support, and value placed on masculine pursuits, males generally tend toward high self-esteem, strong feelings of per-sonal control, a sense of self-containment and self-sufficiency, and a clear vision of the importance of the self in social relations. These basic operating assumptions in turn foster psychological disorders that turn against others and deter reactions that turn against the self. Given little power, work in the private sphere, stress on the provision of support, and the low cultural valuation of these activities, females feel relatively less of a sense of worth, less control over the world, stronger emotional attachments to others, and a priority of others' needs over the self in social relationships. These assumptions facilitate psychologi-cal problems that disadvantage the self and curtail those that damage others.

In reviewing the literature, there is evidence that boys and girls receive messages from the adult world that become increasingly divergent during adolescence. These messages correspond to splits in basic assumptions: Over time, conceptions about self-worth, control in the world, autonomy, and importance relative to others heighten for boys and decline for girls. This divergence contributes to explaining the emergence of sex differences in inter-nalizing and externalizing problems.

There is also some evidence that these relationships persist into the world of adult social institutions. Within both the workplace and the family, social positions characterized by low power and high demands compromise self-esteem and perceived control. Women, more often than men, inhabit such positions. Their lowered sense of control accounts in part for their higher depressive symptoms relative to men. When men are in positions of low power or high demands, they also rise in their levels of depressive symptomatology.

Information on these questions is limited. More work on childhood and adolescence is needed to firmly establish these relationships. Much more research is needed on adult institutions. Since the research on adulthood only covers assumptions about the self, further investigation about world and relational assumptions is necessary. More work needs to be done on externalizing as well as internalizing types of problems, especially studies that investigate both (Aneshensel, Rutter, & Lachenbruch, 1991). Another limitation is that past research has concentrated primarily on the disadvantages for women of the gendered division of spheres. There are some good reasons for this focus. Men are more privileged in these divisions and women's lower power has particularly damaging effects. For example, women suffer more than men from divorce even when both male-linked symptoms such as drinking and female-linked symptoms such as depression are considered (Horwitz, White, & Howell-White, 1996). In addition, while men are more often destructive to others as well as to the self, women's typical forms of suffering focus solely against the self. However, there are serious costs in gender divisions for men as well as women. The parity in overall rates of psychopathology suggests that the limitations inherent in dividing the world by gender damage both sexes. For a balanced account of the consequences of social experiences, therefore, both male-dominated and female-dominated disorders must be evaluated (Aneschensel et al., 1991).

Though I have split discussions of childhood and adolescence from adulthood, ultimately, these periods of the life course should be merged. In thinking about basic assumptions through the life course, I stress the tension between agency and determinacy. Taking one step back, our response to each new social experience is partly an interaction and struggle between the demands of the situation and the basic assumptions we carry from past experiences—and, I would add, our unrelenting attempts to feel the best we can. The outcome depends on the strength of each of these forces. Basic assumptions have the most influence when situations are relatively ambiguous. Extreme circumstances have more impact on reactions, as witnessed by the association of loss events with depression and threat events with anxiety (Brown & Harris, 1978). But I also suggest that in extreme situations, people tend to fall back on their earliest assumptions about the world and themselves, making it harder to use more recently acquired assumptions, for better or for worse. All these assertions, of course, require further investigation.

In concluding, some have argued that classification systems always embody hierarchy (Szasz, 1961). We cannot make a split between things without valuing one side and devaluing its opposite. However, Flax (1993) asserts that this is a historically specific tendency, rampant in the modern age. Clearly, we make distinctions that are more and less neutral, even in the modern age. Gender is one of the dichotomies that is far from neutral. One cost of making this value-infused distinction is the extremes of psychopathology endured differentially by males and females. Thus, the splits in gender result in a polarization of psychological suffering. The preceding research points to integrating the experiences and assumptions currently divided by gender as a means of overcoming tendencies toward both problematic extremes.

REFERENCES

American Psychiatric Association. (1994). *Diagnostic and statistical manual of mental disorders* (4th ed.). Washington, DC: Author.

Aneshensel, C. (1992). Social stress: Theory and research. *Annual Review of Sociology, 18,* 15–38.

Aneschensel, C., & Pearlin, L. (1987). Structural contexts of sex differences in stress. In R. C. Barnett, L. Biener, & G. Baruch. (Eds.), *Gender and stress*. New York: Free Press.

Aneshensel, C., Rutter, C. M., & Lachenbruch, P. A. (1991). Social structure, stress, and mental health: Competing conceptual and analytic models. *American Sociological Review, 56*, 166–178.

Avison, W. R., & McAlpine, D. D. (1992). Gender differences in symptoms and depression among adolescents. *Journal of Health and Social Behavior, 33*, 77–96.

Barnett, P., & Gotlib, I. (1988). Dysfunctional attitudes and social stress: The differential prediction of future psychological symptomatology. *Motivation and Emotion, 12*, 251–270.

Becker, A. (1997). *Body, self, and society: The view from Fiji*. Philadelphia: University of Pennsylvania Press.

Becker, G. (1981). *A treatise on the family*. Cambridge, MA: Harvard University Press.

Best, D., & Williams, J. (1995). A cross-cultural viewpoint. In A. Beale & R. Sternberg (Eds.), *The psychology of gender* (pp. 215–250). New York: Guilford.

Bordo, S. (1993). *Unbearable weight: Feminism, Western culture, and the body*. Berkeley, CA: University of California Press.

Brody, E. M. (1981). Women in the middle and family help to older people. *Gerontologist, 21*, 471–480.

Brown, G., & Harris, T. (1978). *Social origins of depression: A study of psychiatric disorder in women*. New York: Free Press.

Brown, G. W., Harris T. O., & Hepworth, C. (1995). Loss, humiliation and entrapment among women developing depression: A patient and non-patient comparison. *Psychological Medicine, 25*, 7–21.

Brown, L., & Gilligan, C. (1992). *Meeting at the crossroads*. Boston: Harvard University Press.

Chodorow, N. (1978). *The reproduction of mothering*. Berkeley: University of California Press.

Connell, R. W. (1995). *Masculinities*. Berkeley, CA: University of California Press.

Cooley, C. H. (1902). *Human nature and the social order*. New York: Charles Scribner's Sons.

Craighead, L., & Green, B. (1989). Relationships between depressed mood and sex-typed personality characteristics in adolescents. *Journal of Youth and Adolescence, 18*, 467–474.

Dohrenwend, B. P., & Dohrenwend, B. (1976). Sex differences in psychiatric disorders. *American Journal of Sociology, 81*, 1447–1454.

Douglas, A. (1986). *The feminization of American culture*. New York: Avon.

Edwards, C. P., & Whiting, B. B. (1974). Women and dependency. *Politics and Society, 4*, 343–355.

Edwards, C. P., & Whiting, B. B. (1980). Differential socialization of girls and boys in light of cross-cultural research. *New Directions for Child Development, 8*, 45–57.

Fagot, B. L., & Hagen, R. (1985). Aggression in toddlers: Responses to the aggressive acts of boys and girls. *Developmental Psychology, 22*, 440–443.

Flax, J. (1993). *Disputed subjects: Essays on psychoanalysis, politics, and philosophy*. New York: Routledge.

Foucault, M. (1978). *The history of sexuality*. New York: Vintage Books.

Geis, F. (1993). Self-fulfilling prophesies: A social psychological view of gender. In A. Beale & R. Sternberg (Eds.), *The psychology of gender* (pp. 9–54). New York: Guilford.

Geistel, N., Riessman, C., & Rosenfield, S. (1985). Explaining the symptomatology of separated and divorced men and women: The role of material conditions and social networks. *Social Forces, 64*, 84–101.

Goffman, (1966). *Stigma*. New York: Vintage.

Gove, W., & Herb, T. (1974). Stress and mental illness among the young: A comparison of the sexes. *Social Forces, 53*, 256–265.

Hagan, J., Gillis, A. R., & Simpson, J. (1985). The class structure of gender and delinquency: Toward a power-control theory of common delinquent behavior. *American Journal of Sociology, 90*, 1151–1178.

Hagan, J., Simpson, J., & Gillis, A. R. (1987). Class in the household: A power-control theory of gender and delinquency. *American Journal of Sociology, 92*, 788–816.

Hagan, J., & Simpson, J., & Gillis, A. R. (1988). Feminist scholarship, relational and instrumental control, and a power-control theory of gender and delinquency. *British Journal of Sociology, 39*, 301–336.

Harris, T., Brown, G., & Bifulco (1990). Depression and situational helplessness/mastery in a sample selected to study childhood parental loss. *Journal of Affective Disorders, 20*, 27–41.

Hays, S. (1996). *The cultural contradictions of motherhood*. New Haven, CT: Yale University Press.

Hirschfeld, R. M. A., Klerman, G. L., Chodoff, P., Korchin, S., & Barrett, J. (1976). Dependency-self-esteem-clinical depression. *Journal of the American Academy of Psychoanalysis, 4*, 373–388.

Horwitz, A., White, H. R., & Howell-White, S. (1996). The use of multiple outcomes in stress research: A case study of gender differences in responses to marital dissolution. *Journal of Health and Social Behavior, 37*, 278–291.

Hughes, M., & Demo, D. (1989). Self-perceptions of black Americans: Self-esteem and personal efficacy. *American Journal of Sociology, 95*, 132–159.

James, W. (1958). *Varieties of religious experience*. New York: New American Library. (Original published 1890)

Josephs, R. A., Markus, H. R., & Tafarodi, R. W. (1992). Gender and self-esteem. *Journal of Personality and Social Psychology, 63,* 391–402

Karasek, R., & Theorell, T. (1990). *Healthy work: Stress, productivity, and the reconstruction of working life.* New York: Basic Books.

Kessler, R. C., & McLeod, J. (1984). Sex differences in vulnerability to life events. *American Sociological Review, 49,* 620–631.

Kessler, R. C., & McRae, J. E. (1982). The effects of wives' employment on the mental health of married men and women. *American Sociological Review, 47,* 216–227.

Kilbourne, B., England, P., Farkas, G., Brown, K., & Weir, D. (1994) Returns to skill, compensating differentials, and gender bias: Effects of white women and men. *American Journal of Sociology, 100,* 689–719.

Kohn, M. (1972). Class, family, and schizophrenia. *Social Forces, 50,* 295–302.

Krause, N., & Markides, K. A. (1985). Employment and well-being in Mexican American women. *Journal of Health and Social Behavior, 26,* 15–26.

Lennon, M. C. (1994). Women, work, and well-being: The importance of work conditions. *Journal of Health and Social Behavior, 35,* 235–247.

Lennon, M. C., & Rosenfield, S. (1995). Relative fairness and the division of household work. *American Journal of Sociology, 100,* 506–531.

Lennon, M. C., & Rosenfield, S. (1992). Women and mental health: The interaction of work and family conditions. *Journal of Health and Social Behavior, 33,* 316–327.

Link, B. (1987). Understanding labeling effects in the area of mental disorders: An assessment of the effects of expectations of rejection. *American Sociological Review, 52,* 96–112.

Lytton, H., & Romney, D. M. (1991). Parents' differential socialization of boys and girls: A meta-analysis. *Psychological Bulletin, 109,* 267–296.

Martin, E. (1996). *Puberty, sexuality, and the self.* London: Routledge.

Mead, G. H. (1934). *Mind, self, and society.* Chicago: University of Chicago Press.

Meyer, S. L., Murphy, C. M., Cascardi, M., & Birns, B. (1991). Gender and relationships: Beyond the peer group. *American Psychologist, 46,* 537–549.

Miller, P., & Eisenberg, N. (1988). The relationship of empathy to aggressive and externalizing/antisocial behavior. *Psychological Bulletin, 103,* 324–344.

Mirowsky, J. (1985). Depression and marital power: An equity model. *American Journal of Sociology, 91,* 557–592.

Mirowsky, J., & Ross, C. (1990). Control of defense? Depression and the sense of control over good and bad outcomes. *Journal of Health and Social Behavior, 31,* 71–86.

Mirowsky, J., & Ross, C. (1996). Economic and interpersonal work rewards: Subjective utilities of men's and women's compensation. *Social Forces, 75,* 223–245.

Munroe, R., Shimmin, H., & Munroe, R. (1984). Gender understanding and sex role performance in four cultures. *Developmental Psychology, 20,* 673–682.

Nolen-Hoeksema, S. (1990). *Sex differences in depression.* Stanford, CA: Stanford University Press.

Nolen-Hoeksema, S., Girgus, J. S., & Seligman, M. E. P. (1991). Sex differences in depression and explanatory style in children. *Journal of Youth and Adolescence, 20,* 233–245.

Owens, T. J. (1994). Two dimensions of self-esteem: Reciprocal effects of positive self-worth and self-deprecation on adolescent problems. *American Sociological Review, 59,* 391–407.

Pearlin, L. I. (1989). The sociological study of stress. *Journal of Health and Social Behavior, 30,* 241–256.

Pearlin, L. I., Lieberman, M. A., Menaghan, E. G., & Mullan, J. T. (1981). The stress process. *Journal of Health and Social Behavior, 22,* 337–356.

Phelan, J. (1992). The paradox of the contented female worker: An assessment of alternative explanations. *Social Psychology Quarterly, 57,* 95–107.

Piaget, J. (1954). *The construction of reality in the child.* New York: Basic Books.

Pugliesi, K. (1995). Work and well-being: Gender differences in the psychological consequences of employment. *Journal of Health and Social Behavior, 36,* 57–71.

Radloff, L. S. (1977). Sex differences in depression: The effects of occupation and marital status. *Sex Roles, 1,* 243–265.

Reskin, B., & Ross, C. (1992). Jobs, authority, and earnings among managers: The continuing significance of sex. *Work and Occupations, 19,* 342–365.

Rosenberg, M. (1989). Self-concept research: A historical overview. *Social Forces, 68,* 34–44.

Rosenfield, S. (1989). The effects of women's employment: Personal control and sex differences in mental health. *Journal of Health and Social Behavior, 30,* 77–91.

Rosenfield, S. (1992). The costs of sharing: Wives' employment and husbands' mental health. *Journal of Health and Social Behavior, 33,* 213–225.

Rosenfield, S. (1997, February). *Gender and dimensions of the self: Implications for internalizing and externalizing behavior.* Paper presented at the American Psychopathological Association, New York City.

Rosenfield, S., Vertefuille, J., & McAlpine, D. (1994, August). *The emergence of sex differences in depression.* Paper presented at the Society for the Study of Social Problems, Los Angeles.

Ross, C. E., & Bird, C. (1994). Sex stratification and health lifestyle: Consequences for men's and women's perceived health. *Journal of Health and Social Behavior, 35,* 161–178.

Ross, C. E., & Mirowsky, J. (1989). Explaining the social patterns of depression: Control and problem-solving or support and talking? *Journal of Health and Social Behavior, 30,* 206–219.

Ross, C. E., & Mirowsky, J. (1992). Households, employment, and the sense of control. *Social Psychology Quarterly, 55,* 217–235.

Ross, C. E., & Mirowsky, J. (1995). Sex differences in distress: Real or artifact? *American Sociological Review, 60,* 449–468.

Ross, C. E., Mirowsky, J., & Huber, J. (1983). Dividing work, sharing work, and in-between: Marriage patterns and depression. *American Journal of Sociology, 48,* 809–820.

Rotter, J. B. (1966). Generalized expectancies for internal vs. external control of reinforcement. *Psychological Monographs, 80,* 1–28.

Seidler, V. J. (1989). *Rediscovering masculinity: Reason, language, and sexuality.* London: Routledge.

Seligman, M. E. P. (1975). *Helplessness.* San Francisco: Freeman.

Seligman, M. E. P. (1990). *Learned optimism.* New York: Knopf.

Szasz, T. (1961). *The myth of mental illness.* New York: Hoeber-Harper.

Thoits, P. A. (1996). Me's and we's: Forms and functions of social identities." In R. D, Ashmore & L. Jussim (Eds.), *Self and identity: Fundamental issues.* New York: Oxford University Press.

Tittle, C. K. (1986). Gender research and education. *American Psychologist, 41,* 1161–1168.

Turner, H. A. (1996, August). Emotional reliance as an explanation of gender differences in depression. Paper presented at the Society for the Study of Social Problems, New York City.

Umberson, D., Chen, M., House, J., & Hopkins, K. (1996). The effects of social relationships on psychological well-being: Are men and women really so different? *American Sociological Review, 61,* 837–857.

Whiting, B. B., & Edwards, C. P. (1973). A cross-cultural analysis of sex differences in the behavior of children aged three through eleven. *Journal of Social Psychology, 91,* 171–188.

Whiting, B. B., & Edwards, C. P. (1988). *Children of different worlds: The formation of social behavior.* Cambridge, MA: Harvard University Press.

Whiting, B. B., & Whiting, J. W. (1975). *Children of six cultures: A psychocultural analysis.* Cambridge, MA: Harvard University Press.

CHAPTER 12

Family Status and Mental Health

DEBRA UMBERSON
KRISTI WILLIAMS

Early epidemiological research on family status and mental health produced three "social facts":

1. Marriage is beneficial to mental health.
2. Marriage benefits the mental health of men more than women.
3. Parenthood causes psychological distress, especially for women.

Until very recently, the first "fact" went largely uncontested. Durkheim (1897/1951) came to a similar conclusion at the turn of the century when he found that suicide rates were higher among the unmarried than the married. Working from a variety of theoretical perspectives, sociologists throughout the twentieth century concluded that marriage has beneficial effects on the individual. The second "fact" generated much more controversy beginning in the 1970s. Jesse Bernard (1972) argued, in support of a gender difference in marital benefits, that men and women experienced "his and hers marriages" in which women sacrifice more of themselves than do men, particularly in providing services to their spouses. Furthermore, she argued that men receive more benefits from marriage than do women. Walter Gove (Gove & Tudor, 1973) similarly argued that women are more depressed than men and that this sex difference is largely due to women's more frustrating and less rewarding roles, especially their marital roles. Bruce Dohrenwend (Dohrenwend & Dohrenwend, 1976) contested Gove's conclusions because Gove presented evidence only for neurotic

DEBRA UMBERSON AND KRISTI WILLIAMS • Department of Sociology and Population Research Center, The University of Texas, Austin, Texas 78712.

Handbook of the Sociology of Mental Health, edited by Carol S. Aneshensel and Jo C. Phelan. Kluwer Academic/Plenum Publishers, New York, 1999.

disorders and functional psychoses—disorders for which women are overrepresented relative to men. He argued that Gove's definition of mental illness left out some of the most significant and serious disorders, particularly personality disorders, that happen to be more prevalent among men than women. Dohrenwend contended that the different types of disorders could be viewed as functional equivalents in the sense that men and women simply express psychological distress in different ways. In summary, women are generally not necessarily more distressed than men.

A review of subsequent research on sex, marital status, and mental health would lead the reader to believe that Gove won this debate—at least in the sense that the sociological research community chose to focus on depression as the basic expression of emotional disturbance. In so doing, researchers continued to emphasize that women demonstrate more emotional disturbance than do men. Therefore, researchers continued to seek explanations for women's greater distress, typically focusing on women's demanding family roles. Although research on family status and mental health continues to focus primarily on depression as the key measure of mental health, some researchers are renewing the emphasis on examining different expressions of emotional upset—expressions that may be more typical of one gender than the other. Essentially, these researchers are reasserting Dohrenwend's earlier concerns. This emphasis raises new questions about the validity of long-held assumptions about gender, family status, and mental health.

Most sociologists in the seventies, including Gove and Dohrenwend, worked from an epidemiological model. This model assumes that sex and marital status differences in official reports of emotional disturbance are real and strongly influenced by the social environment. However, the general consensus reached by the sociological community—that women exhibit more emotional disturbance than men—is a social construction. Had researchers focused on alcohol problems rather than depression, men would be labeled as more disturbed than women. Sociologists might have searched for elements of men's social roles that contribute to their greater distress. The bottom line is that our research conclusions are largely dependent on the questions we choose to ask, how we choose to measure family status and mental health, and how we choose to analyze our data (Hubbard, 1990).

Why did the socially constructed "fact" that women are more emotionally disturbed than men and that marriage is good for individuals but better for men than women come into being? The sociopolitical backdrop of the 1970s included the Women's Movement and questioning of traditional institutions such as marriage. In turn, a great deal of research attention was devoted to the study of family status and women's roles. The claim that women's roles are more stressful than men's roles, and that women's stressful roles are conducive to women's higher rates of emotional disturbance relative to men, fit perfectly with the sociohistorical moment. Jessie Bernard's (1972) claims could hardly have been made in a previous historical period:

> Despite all the jokes about marriage in which men indulge, all the complaints they lodge against it, it is one of the greatest boons of their sex. (p. 17)

> A generation ago, I propounded what I then called a shock theory of marriage. In simple form, it stated that marriage introduced such profound discontinuities into the lives of women as to constitute genuine emotional health hazards. (p. 37)

Much of the emotional health hazard of marriage for women was attributed to their wife/mother role. This orientation helped shape the third "social fact" regarding family status and mental health—that parenthood is detrimental to psychological well-being, especially for women.

A great deal of research on gender, family status, and psychological distress has accumulated over the past 30 years. The most recent research in this area leads us to qualify all three of the social facts about family status and mental health. In this chapter, we review the current state of epidemiological evidence on the linkages between gender, family status, and psychological distress to arrive at the contemporary answer to the question of whether and why such linkages exist. In light of the changing answers to these questions, we also consider the socially constructed nature of this work.

DEFINITIONS

The way we define family status and mental health greatly influences our research findings. In this section, we briefly describe how these constructs are typically conceptualized and measured in social science research and delineate some of the concerns that arise from these definitions.

Studies typically focus on either marital status or parental status in relation to mental health. Although some of the effects of marital status are due to parental roles and the effects of parental status greatly depend on marital status, the two variables are quite separable. In fact, in light of current demographic trends, marital and parental status are becoming increasingly distinct from one another. Approximately 61% of the U.S. population is married (U.S. Bureau of the Census, 1994). However, of those married persons who are parents, only 30% have young children living in the home (Sweet & Bumpass, 1987). The majority of parents have adult children living outside the home, and a substantial minority have young children living elsewhere (typically because of a prior marriage, so that children reside with the other parent) or adult children living at home. Furthermore, parental status is not contingent on marital status. Rates of births to unmarried mothers are at an all-time high: 30.2% of all births are now to unmarried mothers, and these rates vary substantially by race. Among whites, 22.6% of births are to single women; among African Americans and Hispanics, the rates are 68.1% and 39.1% respectively (U.S. Bureau of the Census, 1992a). Twenty-eight percent of households with minor children include only one parent (U.S. Bureau of the Census, 1992b). Approximately 19% of married couples are childless (U.S. Bureau of the Census, 1996). In summary, marital status and parental status increasingly represent separate dimensions of family status. However, the effects of marital and parental status on mental health are highly contingent on one another.

Marital Status

In a number of studies, the married are simply compared to the unmarried, with the unmarried group defined in various ways—sometimes combining the divorced/separated, widowed, and never-married, and sometimes including only some of these states. This approach produces indecipherable results because the effect of being married is highly contingent on which groups are compared. Typically, the married are compared to the divorced (who are sometimes combined with the separated), the widowed, and the never-married. An additional marital status that is often left out of these discussions is remarried. In the 1980s, 40% of all marriages were second or later marriages for at least one of the spouses (Wilson & Clarke, 1992). As we shall see in the following section, the mental health advantage of marriage may be great, negligible, or nonexistent, depending on the group (i.e., divorced, widowed, never-married, cohabiting, remarried) against which the married are compared.

Contemporary trends raise some questions about how marital status should be operationalized. The current definition focuses on legal marital status. However, Ross (1995) argues that the underlying construct that marital status taps into is better viewed as an attachment continuum. This continuum would take into account individuals who cohabit as well as individuals with significant (e.g., nonmarried, noncohabiting, and nonheterosexual) relationship commitments. This particular perspective works from the premise that the primary ingredient of marriage that is significant for mental health is a secure attachment to a supportive individual. Those working from a more Durkheimian tradition, however, would argue that the construct of marriage is much more than support and attachment. In fact, legal marriage involves obligations and constraints in addition to, and even in the absence of, socioemotional support and feelings of attachment. These various dimensions of social integration through marriage may have substantial mental health consequences—some positive and some negative. Attempts to define marriage in terms of its constituent parts may enable us to identify some of the specific components of marriage that affect mental health. On the other hand, breaking marriage down into a set of many variables may impair our ability to consider how marriage as a social institution affects individuals.

Parental Status

The daily and lifelong constraints, demands, and rewards of parenting differ very much depending on the age and living arrangements of children. In turn, it is these structural contingencies that shape the qualitative experience of parenting and affect the mental health of parents, at least in part. The most important distinction in predicting mental health appears to be that of having minor children as compared to adult children. Just as marital status becomes more difficult to measure in contemporary society, particularly when one takes remarriage into account, parental status also takes on greater complexity. Although there have always been stepchildren and adopted children in addition to biological children, the sheer numbers of the former groups call for greater research attention. Methodologically, it is very difficult to assess parental status if one wants to distinguish between step-, biological, and adopted children, age and number of children, and living arrangements of children. This assessment is made more difficult because an individual may have several children who differ on all of these characteristics. Generally, researchers do not attempt to make all of these distinctions. Most studies restrict their focus to one child in the family or to certain types of distinctions (e.g., stepchildren vs. biological children). As a result of such simplifications, research tends to remove elements of family status from the social context that actually shapes how those elements affect mental health.

Mental Health

Almost all of the empirical research on gender and marital status differences in mental health utilizes outcome measures of depression and psychological distress symptoms. In a sense, this is advantageous. Because so many researchers have examined a similar measure of mental health, we have substantial comparability across studies. However, this is also an important limitation that may lead to inaccurate conclusions about the effects of family status on the mental health of men and women.

It is well accepted that social groups differ in the types and degrees of social stress to which they are exposed. It is equally plausible that the different life experiences associated with social status would lead individuals in different social groups to express emotional upset in different ways. For example, empirical studies over the past 10 years provide evidence that men and women express emotional upset differently (e.g., Horwitz & White, 1991; Lennon, 1987). A central premise of these studies is that men tend to externalize distress, whereas women tend to internalize distress (Horwitz & Davies, 1994; Horwitz & White, 1991; Robbins, 1989). This difference in distress styles is attributed to gender-role socialization and gender norms:

> Because women are encouraged to develop feelings of attachment and obligations toward others, they should also channel distress into forms that harm only themselves while refraining from anti-social behaviors. . . . In contrast, men face fewer restraints against behaving in ways that are harmful to others so are more likely to externalize feelings of distress. (Horwitz & Davies, 1994, p. 610)

Most studies premised on this view examine the dependent variables of depression (presumably an internalizing style) and alcohol use/abuse (presumably an externalizing style). Several recent studies indicate that various types of stressors are more strongly associated with substance abuse for men and psychological distress for women, thus supporting the notion of gendered sytles of expressing distress (Aneshensel, Rutter, & Lachenbruch, 1991; Horwitz & Davies, 1994; Horwitz, White, & Howell-White, 1996a; Lennon, 1987). The emphasis on different styles of expressing emotional distress (styles that vary across social groups) represents an important direction in research on group differences in mental health and has the potential to provide new insights into the social processes that produce emotional distress (see Chapters 4 and 11).

The current focus on depression and alcohol use/abuse as internalizing and externalizing styles of expressing distress is an innovative but rudimentary beginning. Certainly, no style is entirely internalizing or externalizing. For example, depression may be expressed through crying, which might be viewed as externalizing; alcoholism may be an attempt to numb one's feelings, which might be viewed as internalizing. Mirowsky and Ross (1995) argue against the notion of functional equivalents, at least for explaining gender differences in distress. They contend that men should exhibit more anger than women, since anger is an externalizing style of distress. However, they find that women report more anger as well as depression. They further argue that alcohol and drugs do not protect men from distress, since substance abuse and distress covary. Additional qualitative and quantitative research is needed to explore possible group differences in expressions of distress. It may be more useful to view *feelings* of distress (e.g., anger, depression, sadness) as distinct from *behaviors* indicative of distress (e.g., violent behavior, substance abuse) when exploring these group differences.

Violent behavior may be one of the most important expressions of emotional upset to be explored in future research. A variety of different types of evidence suggest that violence, at least at times, is an expression of emotional upset that is particularly characteristic of some social groups (Umberson & Williams, 1993). Violent acts are more likely to be perpetrated by males, the young, and individuals of lower socioeconomic status (Stark & Flitcraft, 1991; Williams, 1992). Furthermore, domestic violence often seems to follow stressful life events (e.g., divorce, job loss) that may contribute to emotional distress (Public Health Service, 1989). Violence as an expression of distress is of particular theoretical and practical interest because it not only suggests emotional upset on the part of the perpetrator, but is also likely to contribute to emotional and physical disturbance in the human target of the violence.

THE EPIDEMIOLOGICAL MODEL

Social–structural theory provides the foundation for epidemiological research on family status and mental health. Structuralists contend that one's social environment has profound implications for one's life experiences. The social environment is largely shaped by one's position in the social structure as determined by elements of stratification such as sex, marital status, race, and socioeconomic status. Whether one is male or female, married or unmarried, African American or white, rich or poor, determines the types of structural opportunities, demands, and constraints that an individual faces on a day-to-day basis. In turn, structural positions associated with more demands and constraints and fewer opportunities lead to higher rates of mental illness. Sociological research on family typically adopts a social–structural approach to argue that marriage and family define one's social environment in key ways that affect mental health. For example, the married are less likely to be socially isolated and more likely to have a confidant and emotional support. In turn, these aspects of the social environment are conducive to mental health, partly explaining why the married exhibit better mental health than the unmarried. Gender differences in the effects of marital status on mental health are attributed to women's greater role obligations within marriage and family that undermine the value of the marital environment for their mental health.

Marital Status, Gender, and Mental Health: The Evidence

Generally, no one questions the assumption or the evidence indicating that the married exhibit lower rates of mental illness than the unmarried and that this advantage is greater for men than women. Ross, Mirowsky, and Goldsteen summarized the accumulated evidence in 1990:

> Compared to people who are divorced, separated, single, or widowed, the married have better overall well-being. This overall positive effect is strong and consistent. . . .The nonmarried have higher levels of depression, anxiety, and other forms of psychological distress. . . . They have more physical health problems. . . . The nonmarried have higher rates of mortality. (p. 1061)

Furthermore, they add that "although marriage generally protects and improves health, it protects men's well-being more than women's" (p. 1062).

The vast majority of studies on which these conclusions are based, and the majority of studies conducted since 1990, consider the effects of marriage on measures of depression or psychological distress. Typically, these measures tap into feelings of sadness, loneliness, lethargy, unhappiness, sleep problems, and somatic complaints. In fact, many studies use the same scale (i.e., the Center for Epidemiologic Studies Depression Scale) to measure depression.

More often than not, research since 1990 finds that the married do exhibit better mental health—in terms of depression—than the unmarried and that marriage benefits men more than women. However, this conclusion must be qualified. First, a few studies find no significant marital status differences in depression. Furthermore, it is likely that the research literature exaggerates the marital status difference in depression because the nature of scientific research renders the publication of nonsignificant group differences less likely than the publication of significant group differences—a factor shaping the social construction of research in this area (Hubbard, 1990). Second, even those studies that do detect marital status differences in depression often proceed to identify factors that explain away differences in depression; that is, they conclude that mental health differentials between the married and unmarried are due not to marital status per se but to other factors, such as socioeconomic status, that are correlated with marital status. We provide a review of these factors in the following section. Third, the measured mental health advantage of marriage, and gender differences in marital status effects, vary in degree depending on the group (e.g., divorced, widowed, remarried, cohabiting, never-married) against which the married are compared. For example, studies comparing the married to the never-married yield different conclusions about the advantages of marriage than do studies comparing the married to the divorced or widowed. Further confusing results, many studies simply combine the divorced, widowed, and never-married into one group of "unmarried" individuals. The mental health advantage or disadvantage associated with different marital statuses may also differ by race, class, and gender. Fourth, the effect of a particular marital status on mental health may vary according to the length of time in the marital status. For example, initial distress levels following marital dissolution may be quite high but attenuate over time.

DIVORCE AND WIDOWHOOD.   Table 12.1 provides a summary of recent studies on marital status and mental health. The evidence for a mental health advantage of marriage is greatest when the married are compared to the divorced or widowed (Williams, Takeuchi, & Adair, 1992). Across studies, the divorced and widowed exhibit significantly higher levels of depression and psychological distress than their married counterparts (Gove & Shin, 1989; Umberson, Wortman, & Kessler, 1992; Williams et al., 1992). Gender differences in the effects of divorce are inconsistent across studies. For example, two recent longitudinal studies yield different conclusions: Aseltine and Kessler (1993) report that women's mental health is more adversely affected than men's by divorce whereas Booth and Amato (1991) find no gender difference in the mental health effect of divorce. This discrepancy may occur, in part, because the samples differ in length of time divorced and in the choice of control variables for analyses. The adverse mental health consequences of widowhood are consistently stronger for men than for women across a range of studies (e.g., Stroebe & Stroebe, 1983; Umberson et al.,1992). Presumably, the divorced and widowed exhibit poorer mental health than the married because they have lost the valuable components of marriage (Gerstel, Reissman, & Rosenfield, 1985; Umberson et al., 1992). However, it may be the strains associated with marital dissolution that undermine mental health more than the resources of marriage benefiting mental health. In this sense, research on divorce and widowhood may reveal more about the effects of marital dissolution than the effects of marriage per se (see also Williams et al., 1992). Supporting this possibility, Booth and Amato (1991) find that divorce is associated with elevated distress for only 2 years. After this period of time, the divorced do not significantly differ from the married on psychological distress. These findings point to the possibility that marital status transitions are more conducive to distress than are certain marital statuses per se. Once an individual adjusts to the transition, distress levels may return to baseline levels. The amount of evidence on this point is too limited to draw clear conclusions at the present time.

NEVER-MARRIED.   Although the unmarried statuses of divorce and widowhood are clearly linked with psychological distress, the evidence is less consistent for a mental health advantage of marriage when the comparison group is the never-married (Williams et al., 1992), the cohabiting, or the remarried (Ross, 1995; Weingarten, 1980; for a review, see Coleman & Ganong, 1990). The never-married and remarried are sometimes simply excluded from analyses of marital status and mental health. Analyzing Epidemiologic Catchment Area (ECA) data and a range of indicators of mental health, Williams et al. (1992) conclude that,

TABLE 12.1. Summary of Studies Comparing Mental Health of Men and Women across Marital Status Categories

Reference	Sample	Mental health measure[1]	Marital status	Marital status effects	Sex X Marital status
A. Studies that test the effects of marital status on mental health in a combined sample of men and women						
(1) Aseltine & Kessler (1993)	$N = 1,455$ Community panel	Depression (SCL-90-R)	Separated + divorced[2b] Remarried	$>$[3a, e, g, m,o] n.s.	— —
(2) Booth & Amato (1991)	$N = 2,033$ married National panel	Psychological distress	Divorced 5–8 yrs.[2b] Divorced < 5 yrs. Divorced > 2 yrs.[2b] Divorced < 2 yrs.	n.s[3c,f,h] n.s. n.s.[3a] $>$[3a]	n.s. n.s. n.s. n.s.
(3) Gove & Shin (1989)	$N = 2,248$ National cross-sectional	Psychological distress	Never married[2a; 4b] Widowed Divorced	$>$[3b, c, d, e, f] $>$ $>$	— — —
(4) Horwitz et al. (1996a)	$N = 592$; age = 25–31 yrs. Community panel	Depression (SCL-90-R) Alcohol problems (RAPI)	Separated + divorced[2b] Separated + divorced	$>$[3a, b, c, e, k, g] $>$[3a, b, c, e, k, g]	> depression among women n.s.
(5) Horwitz et al. (1996b)	$N = 829$; age = 25–31 yrs. Community panel	Depression (SCL-90-R) Alcohol problems (RAPI)	Never married[2f] Never married	$>$[3a, b, c, e, g] $>$[3a, b, c, e, g]	— —
(6) Horwitz & White (1991)	$N = 396$; age = 24 yrs. Community panel	Depression (SCL-90-R) Alcohol problems (RAPI)	Never married[2a] Never married[2a]	n.s.[3a, e, f, i, j] $>$[3a, e, f, i, j]	— —
(7) Marks (1996)	$N = 6,877$; age = 53–54 yrs,) Community cross-sectional	Psychological distress (CES-D)	Divorced + separated[2] Widowed Never married	$>$[3c, f, j, k] $>$ $>$	n.s. n.s. > distress among men
(8) Ross (1995)	$N = 2,031$ National cross-sectional	Psychological distress (CES-D)	Cohabiting[2a] Separated + divorced Never married Widowed < 1 yr. Widowed 1–5 yrs. Widowed > 5 yrs.	n.s.[3b, c, d] $>$[3b, c, d; 5a, b, c] $>$[3b, c, d; 5b, c] $>$[3b, c, d, e, g, p] $>$[3b, c, d, e, g. p] $>$[3b, c, d; 5a, b, c]	n.s. n.s. n.s. n.s. n.s. n.s.
(9) Shapiro (1996)	$N = 2,081$ National cross-sectional	Depression (CES-D)	Remarried[2e] Married/never divorced	$<$[3b, c, d, f, k; 5f] $<$[3b, c, d, e, f, k]	> depression among women n.s.
(10) Umberson (1987)	$N = 2,246$ National cross-sectional	Problem drinking Substance abuse	Divorced[2a] Widowed Divorced Widowed	$>$[3b, c, d, e, f] n.s. $>$ n.s.	> drinking among men n.s. n.s. n.s.

Reference	Sample	Mental health measure[1]	Marital status	Marital status effects		Sex differences
				Men	Women	

B. Studies that test the effects of marital status on mental health separately for men and women

Reference	Sample	Mental health measure[1]	Marital status	Men	Women	Sex differences
(1) Aseltine & Kessler (1993)	$N = 1,455$ Community panel	Depression (SCL-90-R)	Separated + divorced + remarried[2b]	n.s.[3a, e, g, m, o]	>	> Depression for women but n.s.
(2) Gerstel et al. (1985)	$N = 757$ Community cross-sectional	Depression and anxiety symptoms	Separated + divorced[2a]	>[3e, k; 5l]	n.s.[3e, k]	—
(3) Gove et al. (1983)	$N = 2,268$ National cross-sectional	Affective well-being	Never married[2a; 4b] Widowed Divorced	<[3b, d, e, f, n] < <	< < <	n.s.[4b]
(4) Horwitz et al. (1996b)	$N = 829$; age = 25–31 yrs. Community panel	Depression (SCL-90-R) Alcohol problems (RAPI)	Never married[2f] Never married	>[3a, b, e, g] n.s.	n.s.[3a, b, e, g] >[3a, b, e, g]	— —
(5) Horwitz & White (1991)	$N = 396$; age = 24 yrs. Community panel	Depression (SCL-90-R) Alcohol problems (RAPI)	Never married[2a] Never married[2a]	n.s.[3a, e, f, i, j] n.s.[3a, e, f, i, j]	n.s.[3a, e, f, i, j] >[3a, e, f, i, j]	— —
(6) Marks (1996)	$N = 6,877$; age = 53–54 yrs.) Community cross-sectional	Psychological distress (CES-D)	Divorced + separated[2a] Widowed Never married	>[3e, f, g, j, k, l] >[3e, f, g, j, k, l] >[3e, j, k, l; 5b, d]	>[3e, f, g, j, k, l] >[3e, f, g, j, k, l] n.s.[3e, f, g, j, k, l]	— — —
(7) Umberson et al. (1992)	$N = 3,196$ National cross-sectional	Depression (CES-D)	Ever widowed[2d] Currently widowed	>[3b, d, f, k, q] >	n.s. >	n.s. > Depression among men[3b, d, f, k; 5m]
			Remarried after widowed		n.s.	n.s.

		Mental health measure	Marital status	Marital status effects (compared to married[2a])				Sex differences[4a]	
Reference	Sample			Black men	White men	Black women	White women	Black	White

(C) Test of the effect of marital status on mental health separately by sex and race

Reference	Sample	Mental health measure	Marital status	Black men	White men	Black women	White women	Black	White
(1) Williams et al. (1992)		Alcohol abuse	Widowed	>[3b, r, s]	>[3B, r, S]	n.s.[3b]	n.s.[3b]	> For women	> For men
	cross-sectional ECA data		Divorced + separated	>[3b, r, s]	>[3b, r, s]	>[3b, r, s]	>[3b, r, s]	>For men	> For men
			Never married	n.s.[3b]	n.s.[3b]	n.s.	>[3b, r, s]	> For men	> For women
		Drug abuse	Widowed	—	>[3b; 5k]	>[3b, r, s]	—	—	—
			divorced + separated	n.s.[3b]	>[3b, s; 5n]	>[3b, r, s]	>[3b, r, s]	> For women	> For women
			Never married	n.s.[3b]	n.s.[3b]	n.s.[3b]	>[3b, r, s]	> For women	> For women

Continued

Table 12.1. *Continued*

Reference	Sample	Mental health measure	Marital status	Marital status effects (compared to married[2a])				Sex differences[4a]	
				Black men	White men	Black women	White women	Black	White
		Anxiety disorders	Widowed	>[3b,r,s]	n.s.[3b]	>[3b,r,s]	>[3b;5k]	> For men	> For men
			Divorced + separated	n.s.[3b]	>[3b,r,s]	n.s.[3b]	>[3b;5k]	> For men	> For men
			Never married	>[3b,r,s]	n.s.[3b]	n.s.[3b]	<[3b,r,s]	> For men	> For men
		Major depression	Widowed	n.s.[3b]	>[3b,r,s]	>[3b,r,s]	n.s.[3b]	> For women	> For men
			Divorced + separated	n.s.[3b]	n.s.[3b]	n.s.[3b]	>[3b,r,s]	> For men	> For women
			Never married	n.s.[3b]	n.s.[3b]	n.s.[3b]	n.s.[3b]	> For men	> For men
		Schizophrenia	Widowed	n.s.[3b]	n.s.[3b]	>[3b,r,s]	n.s.[3b]	> For women	> For men
			Divorced + separated	n.s.[3b]	n.s.[3b]	n.s.[3b]	>[3b,r,s]	> For women	> For women
			Never married	n.s.[3b]	n.s.[3b,r,s]	n.s.[3b]	>[3b,s;5n]	> For men	> For women
		Any disorder	Widowed	>[3b,r,s]	>[3b,r,s]	>[3b,r,s]	>[3b;5k]	> For women	> For men
			Divorced + separated	>[3b,r,s]	>[3b,r,s]	>[3b,r,s]	>[3b,r,s]	> For men	> For men
			Never married	>[3b;5k]	>[3b;5k]	n.s.[3b]	n.s.[3b]	> For men	> For women

[1] Although some of these studies include other outcome measures, we summarize only those results involving standard measures of mental health.

[2] Compared to (a) currently married, (b) continuously married, (c) first married, (d) never widowed, (e) currently divorced, (f) married < 8 years

[3] Controlling for (a) Time/ mental health, (b) age, (c) sex, (d) race, (e) income, (f) education, (g) social support, (h) length of marriage, (i) social isolation, (j) employment status, (k) presence of /number of children, (l) personality traits, (m) marital quality, (n) childhood experiences, (o) role demands, (p) social attachments, (q) time widowed, (r) household size, (s) SES

[4] Significance tests: (a) not shown, (b) given only for overall effect of marital status, not for individual categories

[5] Relationship reduced to nonsignificance with controls for (a) economic support, (b) social support, (c) social attachments, (d) income, (e) number of children, (f) economic distress, (g) personality characteristics, (h) marital quality, (i) age, (j) education, (k) SES, (l) social network variables, (m) time widowed, (n) household size

"most striking is our finding that for both African-Americans and Whites, the married do not enjoy a mental health advantage over the never-married" (p. 153) (the sole exception to this pattern is for White women where the never-married have higher rates than the married for the substance abuse disorders but lower rates for the anxiety disorders). In a longitudinal study comparing the mental health of young, recently married and never-married adults (age ≤ 24), Horwitz and White (1991) find no mental health advantage of marriage. Others suggest that the mental health advantage of marriage may be diminishing over time, particularly as alternatives to marriage become more common and socially acceptable (Marks, 1996; Ross, 1995).

On the other hand, several studies find that the mental health of the never-married does not compare favorably with the mental health of the married. A recent follow-up study of the sample of young married and never-married individuals by Horwitz and associates shows that, over time, "young adults who get and stay married do have higher levels of well-being than those who remain single" (1996b, p. 895). The authors further reveal a gender difference that indicates women, but not men, who marry report fewer alcohol problems when compared to their never-married counterparts. However, men, but not women, who marry report less depression than their never-married counterparts. Marks examines a sample of middle-aged adults on several different measures of well-being and concludes that, "overall, singles (including the never-married as a separate group) at midlife in the early 1990s continue to fare more poorly on a wide array of measures of psychological well-being than marrieds" (1996, p. 930). However, Marks adds that "contrary to conventional wisdom, in many cases (i.e., for certain measures of psychological well-being) there are no differences in psychological well-being between marrieds and singles" (p. 930). Although some of the mental health difference between the married and never-married might be attributed to selection effects—that is, individuals with better mental health are more likely to marry—tests of this possibility suggest that something more than selectivity is operative (e.g., Marks, 1996). Most researchers find that, even with controls for possible selection effects (e.g., selection due to personality traits), being married continues to be associated with better mental and physical health (Hemstrom, 1996; Marks, 1996).

REMARRIAGE.   Most cross-sectional comparisons of the remarried and divorced show that the remarried have higher levels of psychological well-being than the currently divorced (Shapiro, 1996; Weingarten, 1985). Weingarten suggests that remarriage may facilitate recovery from the negative mental health effects of divorce. However, longitudinal tests of the effect of remarriage on well-being appear to contradict cross-sectional findings. Two longitudinal studies report that the well-being of men and women who remarry following divorce does not improve significantly more than the well-being of those who remain single. Rather, it appears that the divorced, regardless of whether they remarry, experience improvement in well-being between 2 and 4 years following divorce (Spanier & Furstenberg, 1982) and return to levels similar to those of the married within 2 years following divorce (Booth & Amato, 1991). Spanier and Furstenberg (1982) suggest that a greater length of time since divorce among the remarried may account for their apparent greater well-being in cross-sectional studies. Moreover, individuals with lower levels of psychological distress before and after divorce are more likely to remarry (Booth & Amato, 1991; Spanier & Furstenberg, 1982), suggesting a possible selection effect that may partly explain cross-sectional findings.

COHABITATION.   A few studies suggest that some of the contemporary alternatives to marriage, particularly cohabitation, provide mental health benefits that are very similar to those provided by marriage. Ross (1995) compares various unmarried statuses to the married on depression. She finds that although the never-married, separated/divorced, and widowed exhibit higher rates of depression than the married, cohabiting individuals exhibit rates that are very similar to those of the married. She concludes that it is attachment to a significant person rather than marriage per se that contributes to mental health. However, in a review of various quality of life outcomes, Waite argues that "cohabitation has some but not all of the characteristics of marriage, and so carries some but not all of the benefits" (1995, p. 498). For example, compared to the unmarried, married men and women report more emotional satisfaction with their sex lives and married men report more physical satisfaction with their sex lives (Waite, 1995). Waite contends that some of the benefits of marriage result from the greater commitment and emotional investment associated with legal marriage.

It is somewhat difficult to separate cohabiting status from marriage since three-fourths of cohabitors plan to eventually marry (Brown & Booth, 1996). Brown and Booth find that cohabitors who plan to marry do not differ from the married in the quality of their intimate relationships. In turn, many studies demonstrate the positive effect of marital quality on mental health (Glenn, 1990). Cohabitation warrants attention in studies of marital status and mental health based on the increasing number of individuals who occupy this status and the demographic evidence that individuals who cohabit are spending longer periods of time in this status (McLanahan & Casper, 1995; Waite, 1995). The National Survey of Families and Households (1992–1994 data) suggests that about 13% of individuals cohabit, with cohabitation rates much higher for younger individuals; 20–24% of adults aged 25–34 cohabit (Waite, 1995). Although older persons are less likely to cohabit, their numbers are increasing significantly. Although less than 1% of individuals aged 60 and older were cohabiting in 1960, 2.4% were cohabiting in 1990 (Chevan, 1996). Chevan points out that the reasons for cohabitation may differ for older and younger individuals and that we can only expect the proportion of cohabiting elderly to increase as cohorts more open to cohabitation continue to age.

THE MARRIED. Most of the research on marital status and mental health works from the premise that marriage confers unique benefits to individuals. And many studies suggest that, on average, the married are better off than some unmarried groups in terms of their mental health. But there is also substantial variability in mental health among the married. Several studies demonstrate that the quality of marriage is associated with mental health among the married (Aneshensel, 1986; Glenn, 1990; Gove, Hughes, & Style, 1983; Umberson, 1995). Gove and associates (1983) find that individuals in unhappy marriages exhibit poorer mental health than do unmarried individuals. Furthermore, they find that the quality of marriage is more important to the mental health of women, whereas simply being married is more important to the mental health of men. Aneshensel (1986) analyzes panel data and concludes that, although married women with low marital strain exhibit less depression than do unmarried women, women with high marital strain exhibit higher levels of depression than do unmarried women.

Numerous factors contribute to or detract from marital quality. Women's income is positively associated with marital instability (Booth, Johnson, White, & Edwards, 1984) and the probability of divorce (Spitze & South, 1985), perhaps because greater personal income enables women to leave unsatisfactory relationships, or because the higher income of women somehow contributes to gender and marital conflict. On the other hand, overall family income (largely determined by male income) seems to contribute to marital quality, perhaps because income serves as a resource that protects couples, and because higher male income is viewed as an important component of the married male role (Booth et al., 1984; Cutright, 1971; Wilcoxen & Hovestadt, 1983). The transition to parenthood and having minor children is often linked to reduced marital quality (e.g., Glenn & McLanahan, 1982; White, Booth, & Edwards, 1986); however, one longitudinal study suggests that couples who become parents and those who do not become parents experience a decline in marital quality over time (White & Booth, 1985). The presence of minor children may undermine marital quality because it tends to trigger a more traditional division of labor in the home, increase the amount of labor in the home, detract from marital and sexual intimacy, and increase financial strain (Hackel & Ruble, 1992; McLanahan & Adams, 1987).

In summary, the married exhibit better mental health than the unmarried, primarily when the unmarried groups are the divorced and widowed. And some scholars suggest that it is more appropriate to talk about the adverse mental health consequences of marital dissolution and marital status transition than it is to talk about the benefits of marriage per se. This viewpoint is buttressed by research showing that marriage per se is not necessarily conducive to mental health: The mental health of individuals in unhappy marriages fares more poorly than the mental health of unmarried individuals. The long-standing view that marriage benefits individuals has led to a great deal of research on the key mechanisms through which marriage confers mental health benefits. We now turn to a discussion of those possible mechanisms.

What Is It about Marriage That May Be Beneficial to Mental Health?

Certainly, many studies suggest that marriage confers mental health benefits to its participants. Much of the recent research on marital status and mental health focuses on identifying the psychosocial mechanisms through which marital status affects mental health. The most frequently identified explanations for the positive effects of marriage are that marriage provides its participants with (1) economic resources; (2) social integration, including socioemotional support and attachment; and (3) a sense of meaning and purpose. One alternative explanation for the apparent beneficial mechanisms linking marriage to mental health is that the stress of marital dissolution is the primary mechanism responsible for marital status differences in health. Another alternative is that selection effects are operative, so that the association of marital status and mental health is spurious.

ECONOMIC RESOURCES.   Economic resources are positively associated with mental health (Kessler, 1982; Ross & Huber, 1985) and the married have more economic resources than do the unmarried (see Ross et al., 1990; Zick & Smith, 1991). The economic benefits of marriage primarily derive from the dual-earning potential for the married, and these benefits exist for men as well as women (Ross et al., 1990). One of the major reasons that divorce and widowhood undermine mental health is that marital dissolution typically results in reduced economic resources, particularly for women (Shapiro, 1996; Zick & Smith, 1991). Mirowsky (1996) finds that financial strain explains 16% of the gender difference in depression (i.e., women's higher level of depression); furthermore, he argues that women's financial strain increases over the life course partly because of the lasting effect of divorce and widowhood on financial status. Several authors suggest that the relatively low rates of depression of the remarried and cohabitors compared to other unmarried persons may be due in part to the economic benefits of living with a partner (for a review, see Ross et al., 1990).

SOCIAL INTEGRATION AND SOCIAL SUPPORT.   Durkheim (1897/1951) argued that marriage confers some benefit to individuals because it provides them with a sense of social integration—a sense of social connectedness, belonging, and obligation. In recent empirical research, social integration typically refers to the presence or absence of certain key relationships. Marriage is typically viewed as the most significant of such relationships. The available evidence suggests that simply avoiding social isolation does not provide the unmarried with the mental health benefits offered by marriage: Two studies demonstrate that the mental health of unmarried persons who live alone does not significantly differ from that of unmarried persons who live with another person (Alwin, Converse, & Martin, 1985; Hughes & Gove, 1981). The aspects of social integration viewed as most significant by Durkheim— purpose, obligation, and belonging—have not received much research attention but may explain some of the impact of marital status on mental health. Several studies suggest that the sense of obligation and responsibility associated with marriage (and parenthood), may inhibit suicidal impulses and substance abuse. Suicidal impulses and substance abuse reflect mental health (e.g., Umberson, 1987).

The vast field of research on social support taps into Durkheim's idea of social connectedness as a dimension of social integration. Social support refers to "a flow of emotional concern, instrumental aid, information, and/or appraisal (information relevant to self-evaluation) between people" (House, 1981, p. 26). Married persons are more likely than unmarried persons to report that they have a relationship characterized by social support, and they are most likely to identify their spouse as their closest confidant (Umberson, Chen, House, Hopkins, & Slaten, 1996). Of course, unmarried individuals may also have an emotionally supportive relationship with another person. In fact, cohabitors are more likely than the divorced, widowed, and never-married to have an emotionally supportive relationship— partly explaining why their mental health is more similar to the married than the divorced, separated, and widowed (Ross, 1995). However, Ross and Mirowsky (1989) find that the nonmarried have higher levels of depression than the married even when emotional support is controlled, suggesting that social support alone cannot explain the mental health benefits of marriage. Rather, Ross (1995) shows that the benefits of marriage are best explained by both emotional support and social attachments—defined as "a sequence of increasing commitments in adult relationships" (Ross, 1995, p. 131). She finds that statistical controls for social attachment and social support reduce the mental health differences between the never-married and the married to nonsignificance (Ross, 1995).

PURPOSE AND MEANING.   Marriage may provide individuals with a sense of meaning and purpose in life. Building a life with another person often involves building a shared culture and value system, and planning for the future. These activities shape personal and social identity in ways that enhance an individual's sense of self (Marks, 1996). The social approval accorded to marriage may also enhance self-views (Marks, 1996). Purpose and meaning have received very little direct research attention; however, Marks reports that the separated/divorced and the never-married score significantly lower than the married on a Purpose-in-Life Scale.

Certainly, the symbolic meaning of marriage (or any other marital status) is not the same for all individuals. Several scholars argue that the social context of marriage—as well as other marital statuses—shapes the meaning of that marital status for the individual (Marks, 1996; Umberson et al., 1992; Wheaton, 1990; Williams et al., 1992). In turn, the meaning of the marital status shapes the mental health consequences of that marital status. For example, Wheaton (1990) reports that individuals who experience more marital strain prior to divorce or widowhood exhibit less psychological distress in response to marital dissolution than those whose marriages seemed nonproblematic. Marital dissolution may mean relief for those who had been in strained marriages, whereas it may mean substantial loss for those in relatively unstrained marriages.

The meaning of marital status may also differ across social groups. Gove and Shin (1989) report that divorce may be less detrimental to the mental health of African American women than white women, because divorce is less stigmatizing to African American women, and because African American women receive more family support than do white women. Umberson et al. (1992) report that widowhood is more detrimental to the mental health of men than women, in part because widowhood has a different meaning for women and men.

For example, widowhood may be more likely to symbolize loneliness and an inability to manage daily affairs for men, whereas women may be more likely to see widowhood as a period of newly discovered self-sufficiency (Umberson et al., 1992). Marital status, as well as the meaning attached to one's marital status, may also influence individuals' feelings of mastery or personal control. Marks (1996) finds that the married report significantly higher levels of mastery than do the never-married and the divorced/separated. In turn, numerous studies demonstrate a relationship between mastery and mental health (Mirowsky & Ross, 1989). Research on the meaning of marital status for individuals may help to explain variation in mental health within as well as across marital statuses.

THE STRESS OF MARITAL DISSOLUTION.   Williams et al. (1992) emphasize that marital status differences in mental health may derive more from the difficulties of marital dissolution than from the advantages of marriage. Numerous studies on divorce and widowhood work from the premise that marital dissolution—both the event and the process—are stressful for individuals. Booth and Amato (1991) distinguish between marital dissolution as a stressful life event from which individuals typically recover after a couple of years and marital dissolution as characterized by persistent life strains (e.g., economic hardship, single parenting, and social isolation) that lead to persistent psychological distress. Booth and Amato provide evidence for the first perspective following divorce. However, other studies provide support for the latter perspective (Mastekaasa, 1994; Menaghan & Lieberman, 1986; Pearlin & Johnson, 1977; see review by Kitson & Morgan, 1990), at least in certain populations (e.g., the socioeconomically disadvantaged). Furthermore, marital dissolution through widowhood and divorce entails very different processes. Researchers should consider stress models in addition to marital resource models in explaining marital status differences in mental health outcomes.

SELECTION.   Throughout the decades of research on marital status and mental health, sociologists have argued that the social environment varies across marital statuses and that various features of the social environment are responsible for shaping marital status differences in mental health. Sociologists also recognize that social selection processes may contribute to marital status differences in mental health. Selection may occur in that mentally and physically healthy individuals are more likely to get and stay married. Sociologists have sought to rule out selection effects in order to substantiate causal effects but such efforts are typically indirect (see review in Waite, 1995).

A few recent longitudinal studies devote more effort to direct empirical evaluation of selection effects. For example, Marks (1996) controls for mental ability and personality traits in predicting a wide range of mental health measures. She finds no evidence of selection effects for women. In fact, she finds that "single women are generally advantaged in mental ability and personality compared with married women" (Marks, p. 930). Marks finds some evidence for negative selection among unmarried men, but even there she concludes that controlling on mental ability and personality does not entirely eliminate the negative effects of being single for men.

Most sociological studies are careful to point out the possibility of selection effects; however, most conclude (with little empirical support) that the preponderance of evidence is for causal effects of marital status on mental health. Although most studies on marital status and mental health emphasize the importance of ruling out selection effects, it would be useful in future research to emphasize how selection effects operate in conjunction with causal effects of marital status. A number of scholars now emphasize the potential historic specificity of marital status effects on mental health (Marks, 1996). In the past, the vast majority of individuals married and U.S. societal values strongly emphasized the positive value and importance of marriage for individuals. As more individuals live in unmarried statuses, and as the sociocultural experience of living in various marital statuses changes, the balance of selection and causation effects may change. Furthermore, this balance may differ across gender lines as well as other sociodemographic characteristics.

Other Measures of Mental Health

Several authors make persuasive arguments for the inclusion of other measures of mental health in addition to depression (Aneshensel et al., 1991). The primary impetus for these arguments is the observation that social groups—particularly men and women—differ in their ways of expressing emotional or psychological upset in response to stress. Some studies consider marital status differences in alcohol or substance use/abuse; however, few consider a wider range of measures. One of the more significant studies of the past decade on marital status and mental health outcomes focuses on African American–White differences in psychiatric disorders and marital status (Williams, et al. 1992). Williams and his colleagues analyze the ECA data that use the Diagnostic Interview Schedule (DIS) to measure psychiatric disorder. The DIS includes information on alcohol and drug abuse as well as symptoms of depression, anxiety, and schizophrenia. This analysis shows the importance of considering different expressions of distress when studying social group differences in mental health. For example, the authors find that, compared to their married counterparts, separated/divorced African American males are about four times more likely to exhibit alcohol problems, yet the two groups do not differ in the incidence of the other assessed disorders. Compared to their married counterparts, separated/divorced White men are about three and one-half times more likely to exhibit alcohol problems, two times more likely to exhibit drug problems, three times more likely to have anxiety disorders, and about three times more likely to exhibit signs of schizophrenia. Compared to their married counterparts, separated/divorced African American women are more likely to exhibit alcohol and drug problems, whereas separated/divorced White women are more likely to exhibit all types of disorders except for anxiety disorders. Williams et al. (1992) suggest that "any disorder," defined as the presence or absence of any of the mental health problems delineated earlier, is best suited for comparing social groups. When mental health is defined in this way, compared to their female counterparts, *men exhibit more psychiatric disorder than women, across all marital statuses; the married do not differ from the never-married on overall disorder, and the divorced/separated and widowed exhibit significantly more disorder than do the married.* The Williams et al. results may differ from other studies in part because they use dichotomous measures of mental health (i.e., one is either depressed or not depressed rather than focusing on depression as a continuous variable.)

PHYSICAL HEALTH, HEALTH BEHAVIOR, AND MORTALITY.   A substantial body of work on marital status and physical health/mortality is highly relevant to research on marital status and mental health. Substantial comorbidity exists between mental health and physical health (Aneshensel, Frerichs, & Huba, 1984). For example, poor physical health status is conducive to poor mental health, and individuals with mental health impairment are more likely to engage in negative and self-destructive health behaviors and to fail to monitor adequately and respond to physical health problems. In this sense, physical health status, negative health behavior, and mortality reflect mental health status.

The married do report better overall physical health (Murphy, Glaser, & Grundy, 1997) and fewer negative health behaviors (Umberson, 1987) than the unmarried (also see Anson, 1989). Murphy et al. (1997) finds that up to age 70, long-term illness rates are lowest for the ever-married, followed by the remarried, the widowed and divorced. They also report that illness rates of cohabitors are very similar to those of the married.

Marital status differences in mortality provide some of the clearest evidence that we have for the salutory effect of marriage. The overall mortality rate is lower for the married than for any unmarried group, and this marital status difference is greater for men than women (Gove, 1973; Zick & Smith, 1991). Furthermore, the causes of death for which there are the greatest marital status differences involve a behavioral component that may reflect mental health status (i.e., suicide, homicide, accidents, cirrhosis of the liver) (Gove, 1973).

Explanations for the apparent salutory effect of marriage on physical health and mortality include (1) the positive role of spouses in influencing one another's health behaviors—research shows that a spouse is more likely than other persons to notice symptoms, encourage preventive health behavior, and discourage deleterious health behavior (Anson, 1989; Umberson, 1987, 1992a), (2) a sense of responsibility to stay healthy in order to care for family members (Umberson, 1992a), (3) greater access of the married to an emotionally supportive partner that may affect psychological and, ultimately, physical health (Wyke & Ford, 1992), (4) higher socioeconomic status of the married (Zick & Smith, 1991), and (5) the possible influence of the presence of a partner on immune functioning (House, Landis, & Umberson, 1988; Seeman, Berkman, Blazer, & Rowe, 1994).

Although many studies emphasize the advantages of marriage for health and mortality, other studies emphasize the deleterious effects of marital dissolution. For example, research suggests that health behavior is particularly problematic for the divorced (Umberson, 1987, 1992a). Stack and Wasserman (1993) find that divorce is associated with an increased probability of alcohol consumption and suicide. Hemstrom (1996) finds evidence for a long-term causal effect of widowhood and divorce on mortality. He also finds excess mortality for the remarried and for cohabiting individuals, particularly for women. Hemstrom reports that gender differences in mortality following marital dissolution are much smaller than those suggested in previous studies—with the exception of widowed men's elevated rates compared to widowed women's rates. This smaller gender difference may result because Hemstrom includes statistical controls for variables that explain gender differences. He identifies socioeconomic status, labor force participation, and number of children residing in the household as factors that diminish the effects of marital dissolution on mortality—factors that differ for men and women. Hemstrom (1996) concludes: "Because those who remarry had a higher mortality than those who remained [continuously] married, selection factors are interpreted as weaker than causal factors" (p. 375).

The problem of sorting out possible causal effects versus selection effects in the relationship between marital status and mortality is difficult to resolve: Marriage may confer some protective benefits; marital dissolution may have adverse stress effects on individuals; and healthy individuals may be more likely to get and stay married. Goldman (1993) emphasizes the importance of using longitudinal data to address this difficult research issue. Future research should include a comprehensive longitudinal assessment of marital status, mental and physical health, and mortality, and attempt to address the balance of selection and causation factors in affecting mortality. This work should also take into account variation by gender, race, age, and class.

Race, Age, and Socioeconomic Variation

Most studies on marital status and mental health include control variables for age, race, and socioeconomic status. However, very few studies consider how the relationship between marital status and mental health differs across sociodemographic groups. Certainly, the proportion of individuals in each marital status varies greatly by sociodemographic status (Waite, 1995), and marital status composition may influence overall mental health rates of different sociodemographic groups.

RACE. Compared to Whites, a significantly larger proportion of African Americans are unmarried (Waite, 1995). Furthermore, African Americans are more likely to never marry than are Whites, whereas Whites are more likely to divorce and to remarry (Waite, 1995). Not only do the proportions in each marital status differ by race, but also the social context and meaning of each marital status may differ by race (Gove & Shin, 1989). Williams and colleagues (1992) have conducted the most comprehensive study on race differences in marital status and mental health to date. Overall, they find that marital disruption—separation/ divorce and widowhood—is less predictive of psychiatric disturbance for African Americans than for Whites. More specifically, they conclude:

> All forms of marital dissolution are associated with an increased risk of psychiatric illness for Blacks of both sexes and White males, but the association is stronger for White men than for their Black peers. For White females, separation/divorce is the marital status category most strongly linked to an elevated risk of disorder and the odds ratios for Whites are consistently larger than Blacks. Adjustment for age, SES, and household size reduce but do not eliminate these relationships. The pattern of gender vulnerability to psychiatric illness also contains race differences. . . . Among the widowed, Black women are worse off than Black men, while an opposite pattern is evident for Whites. (p. 155)

AGE. The relationship between age and depression is U-shaped, with higher rates of depression for the youngest and oldest adults and lower rates of depression for those in their middle-adult years. Mirowsky and Ross (1992) find that controlling for marital status (and employment status) flattens the U-shaped relationship between age and depression to nonsignificance. Mirowsky (1996) argues that the gender gap in adult statuses (i.e., marital status, housework and childcare, unemployment, and financial status) creates much of the higher rate of depression among women relative to men. Furthermore, this gender gap increases as individuals age because adult statuses become more unequal and disproportionately stressful for women. With age, women are more likely to be widowed, to experience falling financial resources, and divorce is more likely to create lasting economic hardship for women. In summary, marital status, and the social context associated with different marital statuses, is largely responsible for the gender gap in depression.

Researchers also focus on the normative status of widowhood and divorce in predicting their effects on different age categories. Since divorce is more common among the young, its negative impact on mental health should be greater for older individuals. Conversely, since widowhood is more common and normative among older indivuals, its negative effect on mental health should be greater for the young. Generally, research confirms the latter hypothesis about widowhood (Gove & Shin, 1989); however, studies examining age differences in the mental health effects of divorce produce conflicting results. Analyzing national survey data, Gove and Shin find that younger divorced men and women report highelevels of psychological distress than their older counterparts. In contrast, Chiriboga's (1982) smaller community study showed that in the period immediately following divorce, younger adults report greater happiness, less social disruption, fewer psychological symptoms, and more control over their lives than respondents over the age of 50.

Several possible explanations may account for these discrepant findings. Given that rates of remarriage are higher for the young (Teachman & Heckert, 1985) and for those with lower levels of distress (Booth & Amato, 1991; Spanier & Furstenburg, 1982), Gove and Shin's findings may result from the remarriage (and exclusion from the sample) of younger individuals with the lowest levels of distress. Second, older individuals may experience higher initial levels of distress in response to divorce yet recover more quickly than younger individuals. Longitudinal research is needed to assess age differences in the effects of marital dissolution on psychological distress over time.

SOCIOECONOMIC STATUS.   Most studies that examine the effect of marital status on mental health control for income and education. Only a few studies directly test for possible socioeconomic differences in the effects of marital status or marital dissolution on mental health. Among those that focus on divorce, the results are somewhat surprising. Given that SES is positively related to mental health and income typically declines following marital dissolution, especially for women, the effect of divorce or widowhood on mental health should be greater among those in lower socioeconomic status (SES) groups. In a longitudinal study that followed divorced individuals up to 8 years after divorce, Booth and Amato (1991) find that, as expected, divorced men and women with higher levels of income and education report significantly fewer symptoms of psychological distress up to 2 years after divorce. However, they also find that 3 or more years after divorce, members of the more disadvantaged groups have lower levels of psychological distress than those of higher SES groups. The authors suggest that this may occur because of greater relief or a greater sense of accomplishment from overcoming the higher levels of divorce-related stress initially experienced by those in the lower SES group (Booth & Amato, 1991). Given the strength of the relationship between SES and psychological distress, and between marital status and SES, it is surprising that more research has not focused on describing and explaining the complex relationships among these variables.

Parental Status and Mental Health: The Evidence

Parenthood significantly affects psychological well-being. Studies on the general effects of parenthood on mental health are summarized in Table 12.2. Whether the effect of parenthood is positive or negative depends on many factors, one of the most important being minor versus adult status of the child. Studies consistently find that parents of minor children exhibit higher levels of psychological distress than do nonparents and parents of adult children (Umberson & Gove, 1989; see review by McLanahan & Adams, 1987). On the other hand, having adult children seems to be beneficial to psychological well-being—at least for the widowed. Parenthood is a strongly gendered experience with consequences for psychological well-being. Parenting of minor children seems to be more detrimental to the well-being of women than men (Umberson & Gove, 1989), however, mothers seem to experience greater psychological benefits from having adult children than do fathers (Umberson, 1992b).

MINOR CHILDREN.   Numerous longitudinal studies establish that the transition to parenthood is associated with a decline in marital quality and an increase in psychological dis-

TABLE 12.2. Studies Comparing the Mental Health of Men and Women across Parental Status Categories

Reference	Sample	Mental health measure[1]	Parental status	Parental status effects	Sex X Parental status
A. Studies that test the effects of parental status on mental health in a combined sample of men and women					
(1) Harkins (1978)	$N = 318$ married white women Community cross-sectional	Psychological well-being (affect balance scale)	Experienced empty nest in past 2 yrs.[2c]	$>$[3a, k]	—
(2) Ross & Van Willigen (1996)	$N = 2,031$ National cross-sectional	Anger	Parents with children in household	$>$	—
		Anger	Number of children in household	$(+)$[3a, b, c, d, e, f; 4a]	> Anger among women[3a, b, c, d, e, f; 4a]
(3) Umberson & Gove (1989)	$N = 2,246$ National cross-sectional	Depression (Bradburn, 1969)	Parents[2a]	n.s.[3a, b, c, d, g, h]	n.s.[3a, b, c, d, g, h]
			Children at home	n.s.	n.s.
			Adult children away	$<$	n.s.
			Minor children at home	n.s.	n.s.
			Adult children	n.s.	n.s.
		Positive affect	Parents[2a]	n.s.[3a, b, c, d, g, h]	n.s.[3a, b, c, d, g, h]
			Children at home	n.s.	> Positive affect for men
			Adult children away	$>$	> Positive affect for women
			Minor children at home	n.s.	n.s.
			Adult children	n.s.	n.s.
		Anxiety	Parents[2a]	n.s.[3a, b, c, d, g, h]	n.s.[3a, b, c, d, g, h]
			Children at home	$>$	> Anxiety among women
			Adult children away	$>$	n.s.
			Minor children at home	$>$	n.s.
			Adult children	n.s.	n.s.

Reference	Sample	Mental health measure[1]	Parental status	Parental status effects — Men	Parental status effects — Women	Sex differences
B. Studies that test the effects of parental status on mental health separately for men and women						
(1) Koropeckyj-Cox (forthcoming)	$N = 3,967$; age = 50–84 National cross-sectional	Depression (CES-D)	All parents[2a]	n.s.[3a, b, c, d, e, i, j]	n.s.[3a, b, c, d, e, i, j]	—
			Separated/divorced childless[2b]	n.s.[3b, c, d, e, j]	n.s.[3b, c, d, e, j]	—
			Widowed childless[2b]	n.s.[3b, c, d, e, j]	$>$[3b, c, d, e, j]	—
			Married childless[2b]	n.s.[3b, c, d, e, j]	n.s.[3b, c, d, e, j]	—
		Loneliness (NSFH item)	All parents[2a]	n.s.[3a, b, c, d, e, i, j]	n.s.[3a, b, c, d, e, i, j]	—
			Separated/divorced childless[2b]	n.s.[3b, c, d, e, j]	n.s.[3b, c, d, e, j]	—
			Widowed childless[2b]	$>$[3b, c, d, e, j]	$>$[3b, c, d, e, j]	—
			Married childless[2b]	n.s.[3b, c, d, e, j]	n.s.[3b, c, d, e, j]	—
(2) Ross & Huber (1985)	$N = 1,360$ (680 married couples) National cross-sectional	Depression (CES-D)	Parents[2a]	n.s.[3f]	$<$[3f]	—

[1] Although some of these studies include other outcome measures, we summarize only those results involving standard measures of mental health.

[2] Compared to (a) childless, (b) married parents, (c) preempty nest women + women experiencing empty nest > than 2 years ago

[3] Controlling for (a) age, (b) race, (c) education, (d) marital status, (e) employment status, (f) economic hardship, (g) income, (h) sex, (i) health, (j) living alone, (k) menopausal status

[4] Relationship reduced to nonsignificance after controls for (a) proportion of child care done and child care dificulties

tress (Cowan et al., 1985; Hackel & Ruble, 1992). These effects are generally found to be stronger for women than for men (e.g., Belsky, Lang, & Rovine, 1985), and this is usually attributed to women's greater involvement in rearing children. Women usually shoulder the bulk of child-care responsibilities, even if they also work outside the home (Nock & Kingston, 1988). Not surprisingly, women report more demands from minor children than do fathers (Umberson, 1989). Several studies document that employed mothers experience better mental health than do housewives (Gove & Geerken, 1977; Ross, Mirowsky, & Huber, 1983), presumably because employment provides women with relief from the social isolation and parenting strains associated with the homemaker status. A number of other factors are also associated with improved mental health status of mothers: access to reliable and high-quality child-care, financial resources, and having a supportive spouse and other supportive persons in their social networks. In fact, when all of these resources are available, mothers of minor children experience even better mental health than their married, nonparent counterparts (Ross & Huber, 1985). This finding suggests that it is not parenting per se that contributes to psychological distress, but the stressful conditions that are often associated with parenting of minor children.

The stress of parenting minor children is strongly influenced by the marital status of the parent. Most research focuses on divorced parents as compared to married parents. Divorced parents report poorer relationship quality with their minor children than do married parents, and relationship quality, in turn, contributes to psychological distress (Umberson, 1989). Umberson and Williams (1993) find that higher rates of psychological distress and alcohol consumption among divorced fathers compared to married fathers are explained in part by higher levels of parental role strain experienced by divorced fathers. Although divorced mothers and fathers may both experience parental role strain following divorce, the different nature of their experiences should not be underestimated. Mothers usually retain custody of children following divorce, while most fathers do not regularly visit with their children (Furstenberg & Nord, 1985). The strains of parenting for divorced women are often related to economic hardship and social isolation (Arendell, 1986), whereas the strains of parenting for men are more often related to difficulties with child support and visitation, interacting or avoiding interactions with the ex-wife, and personal and social identity concerns (Umberson & Williams, 1993). The bottom line is that resources are limited and divorced parents experience many strains. These conditions increase the stress of parenting.

Many of those who remarry following divorce experience the strains of stepparenting. The presence of stepchildren is associated with increased family strain (Furstenberg & Spanier, 1987), greater marital conflict (McDonald & DeMaris, 1995), lower marital quality (Clingempeel, 1981), and twice the likelihood of divorce as couples with biological children only (White & Booth, 1985). In turn, conflict, strain, and marital quality may undermine psychological well-being, although research on stepparenting does not typically focus on mental health outcomes of parents.

Although there are substantial numbers of adults in other "unmarried" statuses—that is, never-married, cohabiting, and gay/lesbian relationships—very little research exists on the effects of parenting across these groups.

ADULT CHILDREN. Overall, depression rates of parents with adult children and nonparents do not significantly differ (Koropeckyj-Cox, forthcoming; Umberson & Gove, 1989). Furthermore, the "empty nest" appears to be a social myth. A couple of cross-sectional studies suggest that the transition to the "empty nest" is associated with a psychological boost for parents, especially for mothers (Glenn, 1975; Harkins, 1978). The effects of having adult children depend on marital status, gender, and age of the parent. The effect of parenthood on married men and women is not significant (Koropeckyj-Cox, forthcoming; Umberson & Gove, 1989). However, among widowed women, mothers exhibit lower depression rates than nonmothers, and among divorced women, mothers exhibit higher depression rates than nonmothers (Koropeckyj-Cox, forthcoming). Koropeckyj-Cox finds that parental status does not differentiate the mental health of fathers from nonfathers in any marital status.

Among parents, the quality of relationship they have with children is important to psychological well-being. Supportive relationships with adult children contribute to parental well-being, whereas strained relationships with adult children contribute to parents' psychological distress (Umberson, 1992b). Gender differences persist across the life course in that mothers are more affected than fathers by the quality of relationships with adult children, although fathers are more affected by frequency of contact with adult children (Umberson, 1992b). Divorce of parents has lasting effects on relationships with children, undermining parent–child relationship quality, particularly in relationships with fathers (Cooney, 1994). The apparent adverse effects of parental divorce on parent–child relationships exist whether the divorce occurred when children were young or adults (Booth & Amato, 1994). It appears that adult children may be particularly helpful to the well-being of parents who experience widowhood and those who become mentally or physically impaired (Baum & Page, 1991). It is much more common, however, for adult children to rely on parents for support and services than it is for parents to rely on their adult children (Speare & Avery, 1993). Even when adult children and parents share a residence, it is typically out of the adult child's need rather than the parent's need (Speare & Avery, 1993). Sharing a residence, however, does not seem to contribute to parents' psychological distress (Aquilino & Supple, 1991).

PARENTHOOD AND OTHER MEASURES OF MENTAL HEALTH.   Most research on parenting and mental health uses measures of depression as the dependent variable. Ross and Van Willigen (1996) provide a recent exception, using anger as the dependent variable. They argue that women are exposed to greater parental strain than men and, therefore, women should experience greater feelings of anger. The results suggest that women are angrier than men. Furthermore, each additional child in the household increases feelings of anger, and children increase feelings of anger for women more than men. The association of children with feelings of anger is largely explained by economic and child-care strain, both of which are greater for women than men.

Although numerous studies indicate that parenting of minor children is associated with psychological distress, some studies suggest that other dimensions of individual well-being may actually benefit from parenthood. Compared to nonparents, parents, especially those with minor children, are less likely to take health risks and more likely to engage in preventive health behaviors (Umberson, 1987). Parents also have lower mortality rates than do nonparents (Kobrin & Hendershot, 1977) and report a greater sense of meaningfulness and purpose in life (Umberson & Gove, 1989).

CONCLUSION

Socially Constructed Facts

We began this chapter with three "social facts" about family status and mental health. Sociologists tend to accept these three facts without question, but are they true? Social constructionists tell us that truth does not exist, that our sociological facts result from so-cial processes reflecting the nature of the scientific enterprise and those who run it. In fact, a true constructionist would not be very interested in the empirical evidence mustered in support of those facts because the empirical evidence is simply a by-product of the scientific enterprise. We do not adopt this radical position, but we do see the constructionist perspective as having the potential to help us do better science.

In a general sense, the empirical evidence does support the three social facts presented at the beginning of this chapter. However, the empirical evidence also suggests that these three "facts" must be qualified under a number of different circumstances. Furthermore, almost all of our empirical evidence focuses on psychological distress or depression as the key indicator of mental health. When research focuses on multiple indicators of mental health, conclusions about gender and marital status differences are quite divergent from those presented in our three "social facts." For example, Williams et al.'s (1992) multiple outcomes study indicates that men actually exhibit greater psychological distress than do women and that the never-married do not differ from the married. Research methods also influence our conclusions. We see that the use of longitudinal samples versus cross-sectional samples leads to different research conclusions. For example, cross-sectional data suggest that divorce has detrimental effects on well-being and that remarriage benefits well-being, whereas longitudinal data suggest that the effects of divorce are ephemeral and that the remarried and divorced exhibit similar levels of well-being. As increasingly sophisticated multivariate methods have been applied to the study of family status and mental health, we have been able to identify specific "mechanisms" through which family status affects mental health. However, in explaining away the effects of various marital and parental statuses on mental health, we lose sight of the larger social institutions and their social and personal meanings that work together to affect the mental health of individuals.

In summary, our conclusions about family status and mental health are constantly being revised and are highly dependent on measurement and method. The revision of such "facts" may arise because the costs and benefits of families are actually changing, *or* because we modify the particular research questions we ask, as well as the way we measure and interpret them.

What Can We Conclude about Family Status and Mental Health?

We can conclude that marital status and parental status are associated with mental health. However, we must qualify any general conclusions about the degree and direction of those associations. Most importantly, the degree of benefit conferred by marriage is greatly dependent on the group (e.g., divorced, widowed, never-married, remarried) against which the married are compared. Many studies demonstrate that the married exhibit lower levels of depression and psychological distress than the unmarried; this difference is greatest when the married are compared with the divorced or widowed. Most past research emphasizes the advantageous state of marriage when explaining marital status differences in mental and physical well-being. More recent research questions whether the presumed benefits of marriage actually reflect salutory effects of marriage or whether it might be more appropriate to focus on the adverse consequences of marital dissolution. This is a very different construction in that the former approach emphasizes the value of marriage, whereas the latter emphasizes the stress of status change. Overall, the evidence suggests that it might be more appropriate to emphasize the disadvantageous state of divorce and widowhood or the stressful transitional period from married to unmarried status rather than the advantageous state of marriage. One could even view marriage as a major risk factor for depression in the sense that one must be married in order to experience marital dissolution. In fact, studies focusing on mental health among the married emphasize that it is not marriage per se that contributes to psychological well-being; rather, the quality of marriage is associated with psychological well-being. Individuals in marriages characterized by stress, conflict, and unhappiness exhibit poorer mental health than do their unmarried counterparts.

Remarried and cohabiting individuals are characterized by levels of distress that are similar to those of the married. Some researchers conclude that this confirms the mental health benefits of involvement in a close (marital) relationship. However, others argue that the remarried have simply been divorced long enough on average to recover from the adverse consequences of divorce and that the cohabitors have not had to experience the stress of divorce—supporting the stress model of marital dissolution more than the marital resource model.

Theoretical explanations for the apparent mental health benefits of marriage tend to focus on the higher levels of social integration and social support, the lower levels of financial strain, and the enhanced sense of meaning associated with marriage. Alternative explanations for the apparent benefits of marriage focus on the stress model of marital dissolution, processes of selectivity as opposed to causation, and methods of measurement and analysis used by researchers.

Less research focuses on the effects of parental status on mental health, but the findings are fairly consistent. Having minor children appears to be detrimental to mental health, and the adverse consequences are greater for unmarried than for married parents, and greater for women than for men. Having adult children is beneficial to the mental health of widowed parents but has little effect on married parents. Again, however, these general effects vary in degree and direction, depending on soicodemographic characteristics of individuals as well as social contextual factors (e.g., supportive ties, financial strain).

Where Do Researchers on Family and Mental Health Go from Here?

Increasingly, research breaks marriage, and other marital statuses, down into their component parts—for example, degree of financial strain and social support experienced by individuals (all factors that vary by marital status). Controlling on such variables may reduce or eliminate any apparent marital status differences. However, controlling for the key variables that distinguish various marital statuses may serve to mask any actual effects of that marital status on mental health (Lieberson, 1985). We must ask what it means to be married, divorced, or remarried. Each of these statuses is characterized by a different contellation of factors that uniquely distinguish the experience of being in that status. We may be able to control away the factors that explain why the divorced are more distressed than the married, but we cannot conclude that divorce does not affect mental health once financial status is taken into account, because financial strain is one of the factors that characterizes divorce. Empirical research must continue to identify the mechanisms through which each marital status contributes to mental health in order to understand group differences in distress. However, we must also remember that social institutions affect individuals in their entirety.

Group differences (e.g., by gender, race, age, or SES) in the effects of family status on mental health require that we include sociodemographic variables in analyses not merely as control variables but as variables that may potentially interact with family status in their impact on mental health. The importance of this line of research is suggested by the few existing studies suggesting group differences in the meaning and consequences of family status on mental health. In addition, we must consider possible group differences in the expression of distress. We cannot conclude that one social group is more reactive to family status than some other group, unless we assess the key ways in which both groups express distress. For example, if men are more likely to respond to stress with substance abuse, whereas women are more likely to respond with depression, both measures of distress should be assessed. To this end, researchers must first seek to identify the key expressions of distress in various social groups and develop measures of those expressions.

The issue of selection versus causation should receive greater research attention. It may be that certain types of individuals (i.e., those who are more or less mentally robust) are more likely than others to be selected into or out of marriage. Most researchers are very conscientious about noting the possibility of selection effects; however, very few researchers actually include direct empirical tests of selection processes. The few studies that do conduct direct analyses of potential selection effects yield conflicting results about the degree to which selection operates. Disentangling selection from causation processes, and analyzing how causal factors and selection factors may interact in affecting mental health, poses a theoretical and empirical challenge for future research on family status and mental health.

REFERENCES

Alwin, D. F., Converse, P. E., & Martin, S. S. (1985). Living arrangements and social integration. *Journal of Marriage and the Family, 47,* 319–334.

Aneshensel, C S. (1986). Marital and employment role-strain, social support, and depression among adult women. In S. E. Hobfoll (Ed.), *Stress, social support, and women* (pp. 99–114). New York: Hemisphere.

Aneshensel, C. S., Frerichs, R. R., & Huba, G. J. (1984). Depression and physical illness: A multiwave, nonrecursive causal model. *Journal of Health and Social Behavior, 25,* 350–371.

Aneshensel, C. S., Rutter, C. M., & Lachenbruch, P. A. (1991). Social structure, stress, and mental health: Competing conceptual and analytic models. *American Sociological Review, 56,* 166–178.

Anson, O. (1989). Marital status and women's health revisited: The importance of a proximate adult. *Journal of Marriage and the Family, 51,* 185–194.

Aquilino, W., & Supple, K. R. (1991). Parent-child relations and parent's satisfaction with living arrangements when adult children live at home. *Journal of Marriage and the Family, 53,* 13–27.

Arendell, T. (1986). *Mothers and divorce: Legal, economic, and social dilemmas.* Berkeley, CA: University of California Press.

Aseltine, R. H., Jr., & Kessler, R. C. (1993). Marital disruption and depression in a community sample. *Journal of Health and Social Behavior, 34,* 237–251.

Baum, M., & Page, M. (1991). Caregiving and multigenerational families. *The Gerontologist, 31,* 762–769.

Belsky, J., Lang, M. E., & Rovine, M. (1985). Stability and change in marriage across the transition to parenthood: A second study. *Journal of Marriage and the Family, 47,* 855–865.

Bernard, J. (1972). *The future of marriage.* New Haven, CT: Yale University Press.

Booth, A., & Amato, P. R. (1991). Divorce and psychological stress. *Journal of Health and Social Behavior, 32,* 396–407.

Booth, A., & Amato, P. R. (1994). Parental marital quality, parental divorce, and relations with parents. *Journal of Marriage and the Family, 56,* 21–34.

Booth, A., Johnson, D. R., White, L., & Edwards, J. N. (1984). Women, outside employment, and marital instability. *American Journal of Sociology, 90,* 567–578.

Brown, S. L., & Booth, A. (1996). Cohabitation versus marriage: A comparison of relationship quality. *Journal of Marriage and the Family, 58,* 667–678.

Chevan, A. (1996). As cheaply as one: Cohabitation in the older population. *Journal of Marriage and the Family, 58,* 656–667.

Chiriboga, D. A. (1982). Adaptation to marital separation in later and earlier life. *Journal of Gerentology, 37,* 109–114.

Clingempeel, W. G. (1981). Quasi-kin relationships and marital quality in stepfather families. *Journal of Personality and Social Psychology, 41,* 890–901.

Coleman, M., & Ganong, L. H. (1990). Remarriage and stepfamily research in the 1980s: Increased interest in an old family form. *Journal of Marriage and the Family, 52,* 925–940.

Cooney, T. M. (1994). Young adults' relations with parents: The influence of recent parental divorce. *Journal of Marriage and the Family, 56,* 45–56.

Cowan, C. P., Cowan, P. A., Heming, G., Garrett, E., Coysh, W. S., Curtis-Boles, H., & Boles, A. J., III. (1985). Transitions to parenthood: His, hers, and theirs. *Journal of Family Issues, 6,* 451–481.

Cutright, P. (1971). Income and family events: Marital stability. *Journal of Marriage and the Family, 33,* 291–306.

Dohrenwend, B., & Dohrenwend, B. S. (1976). Sex differences in psychiatric disorders. *American Journal of Sociology, 81,* 1447–1459.

Durkheim, E. (1951). *Suicide: A study in sociology* (J. A. Spaulding & G. Simpson, Trans.). New York: Free Press. (Original published 1897)

Furstenberg, F. F., Jr., & Nord, C. W. (1985). Parenting apart: Patterns of childrearing after marital disruption. *Journal of Marriage and the Family, 47,* 894–904.

Furstenberg, F. F., Jr., & Spanier, G. B. (1987). *Recycling the family: Remarriage after divorce.* Beverly Hills, CA: Sage.

Gerstel, N. R., Riessman C. K., & Rosenfield, S. (1985). Explaining the symptomology of separated and divorced women and men: The role of material conditions and social networks. *Social Forces, 64,* 84–101.

Glenn, N. D. (1975). Psychological well-being in the postparental stage: Some evidence from national surveys. *Journal of Marriage and the Family, 37,* 105–110.

Glenn, N. D. (1990). Quantitative research on marital quality in the 1980s: A critical review. *Journal of Marriage and the Family, 52,* 818–831.

Glenn, N. D., & McLanahan, S. (1982). Children and marital happiness: A further specification of the relationship. *Journal of Marriage and the Family, 44,* 63–72.

Goldman, N. (1993). Marriage selection and mortality patterns: Inferences and fallacies. *Demography, 30,* 189–208.

Gove, W. R. (1973). Sex, marital status, and mortality. *American Journal of Sociology, 79,* 45–67.

Gove, W. R., & Geerken, M. R. (1977). The effect of children and employment on the mental health of married men and women. *Social Forces, 55,* 66–76.

Gove, W. R., Hughes, M., & Style, C. B. (1983). Does marriage have positive effects on the psychological well-being of the individual? *Journal of Health and Social Behavior, 24,* 122–131.

Gove, W. R., & Tudor, J. F. (1973). Adult sex roles and mental illness. *American Journal of Sociology, 78,* 812–835.

Gove, W. R., & Shin, H.-C. (1989). The psychological well-being of divorced and widowed men and women. *Journal of Family Issues, 10,* 122–144.

Hackel, L. S., & Ruble, D. N. (1992). Changes in the marital relationship after the first baby is born: Predicting the impact of expectancy disconfirmation. *Journal of Personality and Social Psychology, 24,* 122–131.

Harkins, E. (1978). Effects of empty nest transition on self-report of psychological and physical well-being. *Journal of Marriage and the Family, 40,* 549–556.

Hemstrom, O. (1996). Is marriage dissolution linked to differences in mortality risks for men and women? *Journal of Marriage and the Family, 58,* 366–378.

Holden, K. C., & Smock, P. J. (1991). The economic costs of marital dissolution: Why do women bear a disproportionate cost? In W. R. Scott & J. Blake (Eds.), *Annual review of sociology* (Vol. 17, pp. 51–78). Palo Alto, CA: Annual Reviews.

Horwitz, A. V., & Davies, L. (1994). Are emotional distress and alcohol problems differential outcomes to stress? An exploratory test. *Social Science Quarterly, 75,* 607–621.

Horwitz, A. V., & White, H. R. (1991). Becoming married, depression, and alcohol problems among young adults. *Journal of Health and Social Behavior, 32,* 221–237.

Horwitz, A. V., White, H. R., & Howell-White, S. (1996a). The use of multiple outcomes in stress research: A case study of gender differences in responses to marital dissolution. *Journal of Health and Social Behavior, 37,* 278–291.

Horwitz, A. V., White, H. R., & Howell-White, S. (1996b). Becoming married and mental health. *Journal of Marriage and the Family, 58,* 895–907.

House, J. S. (1981). *Work, stress, and social support.* Reading, MA: Addison-Wesley.

House, J. S., Landis, K., & Umberson, D. (1988). Social relationships and health. *Science, 241,* 540–545.

Hubbard, R. (1990). *The politics of women's biology.* New Brunswick, NJ: Rutgers University Press.

Hughes, M., & Gove, W. R. (1981). Living alone, social integration, and mental health. *American Journal of Sociology, 87,* 48–74

Kessler, R. C. (1982). A disaggregation of the relationship between socioeconomic status and psychological distress. *American Sociological Review, 47,* 752–764.

Kitson, G. C., & Morgan, L. A. (1990). The multiple consequences of divorce: A decade review. *Journal of Marriage and the Family, 52,* 913–924.

Kobrin, F. E., & Hendershot, G. E. (1977). Do family ties reduce mortality? Evidence from the United States, 1966–1968. *Journal of Marriage and the Family, 39,* 737–745.

Koropeckyj-Cox, T. (Forthcoming). Loneliness and depression in middle and old age: Are the childless more vulnerable? *Journal of Gerontology: Social Sciences.*

Lennon, M. C. (1987). Sex differences in distress: The impact of gender and work roles. *Journal of Family Issues, 9,* 273–284.

Lieberson, S. (1985). *Making it count : The improvement of social research and theory.* Berkeley, CA: University of California Press.

Marks, N. F. (1996). Flying solo at midlife: Gender, marital status and psychological well-being. *Journal of Marriage and the Family, 58,* 17–933.

Mastekaasa, A. (1994). The subjective well-being of the previously married: The importance of unmarried cohabitation and time since widowhood or divorce. *Social Forces, 73,* 665–692.

McDonald, W. L., & DeMaris, A. (1995). Remarriage, stepchildren, and marital conflict: Challenges to the incomplete institutionalization hypothesis." *Journal of Marriage and the Family, 57,* 387–398.

McLanahan, S., & Adams, J. (1987). Parenthood and psychological well-being. In *Annual Review of Sociology* (Vol. 13, pp. 237–257). Palo Alto, CA: Annual Reviews.

McLanahan, S., & Casper, L. (1995). Growing diversity and inequality in the American family. In R. Farley (Ed.), *State of the union: America in the 1990s: Volume 2: Social trends* (pp. 1–45). New York: Russell Sage.

Menaghan, E. G., & Lieberman, M. A. (1986). Changes in depression following divorce: A panel study. *Journal of Marriage and the Family, 48,* 319–328.

Mirowsky, J. (1996). Age and the gender gap in depression. *Journal of Health and Social Behavior, 37,* 362–380.

Mirowsky, J., & Ross, C. E. (1989). *Social causes of psychological distress.* Hawthorne, NY: Aldine de Gruyter.

Mirowsky, J., & Ross, C. E. (1992). Age and depression. *Journal of Health and Social Behavior, 33,* 187–205.

Mirowsky, J., & Ross, C. E. (1995). Sex differences in distress: Real or artifact. *American Sociological Review, 60,* 449–468.

Murphy, M., Glaser, K., & Grundy, E. (1997). Marital status and long- term illness in Great Britain. *Journal of Marriage and the Family, 59,* 156–164.

Nock, S. L., & Kingston, P. W. (1988). Time with children: The impact of couples' work-time commitments. *Social Forces, 67,* 59–85.

Pearlin, L. I., & Johnson, J. S. (1977). Marital status, life strains, and depression. *American Sociological Review, 42,* 704–715.

Public Health Service. (1989). Injury prevention: Meeting the challenge. The National Committee for Injury Prevention and Control. New York: Oxford University Press. Supplement to *American Journal of Preventive Medicine, 5*(3).

Robbins, C. (1989). Sex differences in psychosocial consequences of alcohol and drug abuse. *Journal of Health and Social Behavior, 30,* 117–130.

Ross, C. E. (1995). Reconceptualizing marital status as a continuum of social attachment. *Journal of Marriage and the Family, 57,* 129–140.

Ross, C. E., & Huber, J. (1985). Hardship and depression. *Journal of Health and Social Behavior, 26,* 312–327.

Ross, C. E., & Mirowsky, J. (1989). Explaining the social patterns of depression: Control and problem solving—or support and talking. *Journal of Health and Social Behavior, 30,* 206–219.

Ross, C. E., Mirowsky, J., & Goldsteen, K. (1990). The impact of family on health: The decade in review. *Journal of Marriage and the Family, 52,* 1059–1078.

Ross, C. E., Mirowsky, J., & Huber, J. (1983). Dividing work, sharing work, and in-between: Marriage patterns and depression. *American Sociological Review, 48,* 809–823.

Ross, C. E., & Van Willigen, M. (1996). Gender, parenthood, and anger. *Journal of Marriage and the Family, 58,* 572–584.

Seeman, T. E., Berkman, L. F., Blazer, D., & Rowe, J. W. (1994). Social ties and support and neuroendocrine function: The MacArthur studies of successful aging. *Annals of Behavioral Medicine, 16,* 95–106.

Shapiro, A. (1996). Explaining psychological distress in a sample of remarried and divorced couples: The influence of economic distress. *Journal of Family Issues, 17,* 186–203.

Spanier, G. B., & Furstenberg, F. F., Jr. (1982). Remarriage after divorce: A longitudinal analysis of well-being. *Journal of Marriage and the Family, 44,* 709–720

Speare, A., Jr., & Avery, R. (1993). Who helps whom in older parent–child families. *Journal of Gerontology, 48,* S212–S222.

Spitze, G., & South, S. J. (1985). Women's employment, time expenditure, and divorce. *Journal of Family Issues, 6,* 307–329.

Stack, S., & Wasserman, I. (1993). Marital status, alcohol consumption, and suicide: An analysis of national data. *Journal of Marriage and the Family, 55,* 1018–1024.

Stark, E., & Flitcraft, A. H. (1991). Spouse abuse. In M. L. Rosenberg & M. A. Fenle (Eds.), *Violence in America: A public health approach* (pp. 123–125). New York: Oxford University Press.

Stroebe, M., & Stroebe, W. (1983). Who suffers more? Sex differences in the health risks of the widowed. *Psychological Bulletin, 93,* 279–301.

Sweet, J. A., & Bumpass, L. L. (1987). *American families and households.* New York: Russell Sage Foundation.

Teachman, J. D., & Heckert, A. (1985). The impact of age and children on remarriage. *Journal of Family Issues, 6,* 185–203.

Umberson, D. (1987). Family status and health behaviors: Social control as a dimension of social integration. *Journal of Health and Social Behavior, 28,* 306–319.

Umberson, D. (1989). Relationships with children: Explaining parents' psychological well-being. *Journal of Marriage and the Family, 51,* 999–1012.

Umberson, D. (1992a). Gender, marital status, and the social control of health behavior. *Social Science and Medicine, 34,* 907–917.

Umberson, D. (1992b). Relationships between adult children and their parents: Psychological consequences for both generations. *Journal of Marriage and the Family, 54,* 664–674.

Umberson, D. (1995). Marriage as support or strain? Marital quality following the death of a parent. *Journal of Marriage and the Family, 57,* 709–723.

Umberson, D., Chen, M. D., House, J. S., Hopkins, K. & Slaten, E. (1996). The effect of social relationships on psychological well-being: Are men and women really so different? *American Sociological Review, 61,* 837–857.

Umberson, D., & Gove, W. R. (1989). Parenthood and psychological well-being: Theory, measurement and stage in the family life course. *Journal of Family Issues, 10,* 440–462.

Umberson, D., & Williams, C. L. (1993). Divorced fathers: Parental role strain and psychological distress. *Journal of Family Issues, 14,* 378–400.

Umberson, D., Wortman, C. B., & Kessler, R. C. (1992). Widowhood and depression: Explaining long-term gender differences in vulnerability. *Journal of Health and Social Behavior, 33,* 10–24.

U.S. Bureau of the Census. (1992a). Marriage, divorce and remarriage in the 1990s: October 1992. *Current Population Reports,* Series P230, No. 180. Washington, DC: U.S. Government Printing Office.

U.S. Bureau of the Census. (1992b). *Vital Statistics of the United Sates, annual.* Washington, DC: U.S. Government Printing Office.

U.S. Bureau of the Census. (1994). Marital status and living arrangements: March 1994. *Current Population Reports,* Series P20, No. 484. Washington, DC: U.S. Government Printing Office.

U.S. Bureau of the Census. (1996). *Vital Statistics of the United States, annual.* Washington, DC: U.S. Government Printing Office.

Waite, L. J. (1995). Does marriage matter? *Demography, 32,* 483–507.

Weingarten, H. R. (1980). Remarriage and well-being: National survey evidence of social and psychological effects. *Journal of Family Issues, 1,* 533–559.

Weingarten, H. R. (1985). Marital status and well-being: A national study comparing first-married, currently divorced, and remarried adults. *Journal of Marriage and the Family, 47,* 653–662.

Wheaton, B. (1990). Life transitions, role histories, and mental health. *American Sociological Review, 55,* 209–223.

White, L. K., & Booth, A. (1985). The quality and stability of remarriages: The role of stepchildren. *American Sociological Review, 50,* 689–698.

White, L. K., Booth, A., & Edwards, J. N. (1986). Children and marital happiness: Why the negative correlation? *Journal of Family Issues, 7,* 131–147.

Wilcoxen, S. A., & Hovestadt, A. J. (1983). Perceived health and similarity of family of origin experiences as predictors of dyadic adjustment for married couples. *Journal of Marital and Family Therapy, 9,* 431–434.

Williams, D. R., Takeuchi, D. T., & Adair, R. K. (1992). Marital status and psychiatric disorders among blacks and whites. *Journal of Health and Social Behavior, 33,* 140–157.

Williams, K. R. (1992). Social sources of marital violence and deterrence: Testing an integrated theory of assaults between partners. *Journal of Marriage and the Family, 54,* 620–629.

Wilson, B. F., & Clarke, S. C. (1992). Remarriages: A demographic profile. *Journal of Family Issues, 13,* 123–141.

Wyke, S., & Ford, G. (1992). Competing explanations for associations between marital status and health. *Social Science and Medicine, 34,* 523–532.

Zick, C. D., & Smith, K. R. (1991). Marital transitions, poverty, and gender differences in mortality. *Journal of Marriage and the Family, 53,* 327–336.

CHAPTER 13

Work and Mental Health

Mark Tausig

Work[1] is a central activity and a principal source of identity for most adults. As such, the relationship between work and mental and emotional well-being is of substantial interest. The effects of work on well-being, however, cannot be effectively understood simply by examining individual experiences in particular work settings. Rather, work-related well-being is linked to macroeconomic and labor market structures that define opportunities for employment (and probabilities for unemployment), to characteristics of jobs, to workers' positions in other social stratification systems, and to the intersection of work roles and other major roles, especially marital and parental roles.

Four distinct research traditions address the ways in which work and psychological well-being are linked. First, labor market studies examine the effects of macroeconomic structures on mental health (Brenner, 1973; Catalano & Dooley, 1977). These studies generally assess the relationship between aggregate macroeconomic conditions, such as unemployment rates and aggregate rates of disorder, but occasionally link aggregate economic conditions to individual psychological outcomes (Dooley & Catalano, 1984b; Fenwick & Tausig, 1994). In addition, labor market-related studies also examine the psychological

---

[1] In this chapter, the notion of work is limited to "paid employment." Thus, housework and its relationship to mental health is not explored as a separate topic here. Such work is clearly of economic value and is related to broader economic, political, and social structures and processes but is beyond the scope of this chapter. Some research on the relationship between paid work, housework, and distress is discussed, however, in the section on work and family (see also Chapter 12).

MARK TAUSIG • Department of Sociology, University of Akron, Akron, Ohio 44325.

Handbook of the Sociology of Mental Health, edited by Carol S. Aneshensel and Jo C. Phelan. Kluwer Academic/Plenum Publishers, New York, 1999.

impact of unemployment and reemployment (Kessler, Turner, & House, 1989; Turner, 1995). Recent discussions of the psychological effects of the restructuring of the employment relationship (i.e., plant closings, downsizing, contingent work, deskilling) fall into this tradition, although such studies use macroeconomic changes largely as background for individual-based outcome studies.

There is a second research tradition that examines the relationship between well-being and the characteristics of jobs (Karasek, 1979; Kohn & Schooler, 1982). These studies examine how features of jobs—such as the level of job demand, decision latitude, autonomy, substantive complexity and co-worker support—affect psychological orientations and mental health status. These studies generally do not link characteristics of jobs to larger economic and social conditions, but treat job characteristics as constants and technological "givens" of the production process. Much of this research has been limited to the male labor force.

A third literature is reflected in studies that attempt to explain the relationship between positions in social structure (particularly, gender) and well-being. Since Gove and Tudor's (1973) early study of the importance of multiple roles for mental health, attempts to assess the mental health consequences of participation by women in the paid labor force have uncovered a variety of issues related to the consequences of social stratification. These include the occupational distribution of women, differences in the characteristics of "women's" and "men's" work, and gender-related differences in the relationship between aspects of job characteristics and psychological well-being. Similar research regarding the effects of social–structural positions described by socioeconomic status, social class, and race are also included here.

A fourth, and closely related area of research examines the intersection of paid work and other social roles, particularly family roles. This literature has developed in part because of increased female participation in the labor force and in part because of the more general recognition that the impact of roles and statuses cannot be properly understood without accounting for larger social contexts. This research has principally examined the experience of women who work but seldom deals with labor market factors that might affect the types of work available or their effect on mental health. Its focus is on the spillover or contamination of roles, principally between the family and work spheres.

In this review, I summarize what each of these four research areas tells us about the relationship between work and mental health. Each approach reflects subdisciplinary interests but collectively they present a broader sociological perspective. As a foundation for this approach, I briefly describe the contexts within which the individual experiences work and the ways in which these contexts are consequential to his or her mental health.

THE SOCIAL–STRUCTURAL CONTEXT OF WORK

The emerging portrait of the relationship between work and mental health that comes from juxtaposing these four research areas fits well with the view of psychological distress as a fundamental product of social–structural arrangements (Link & Phelan, 1995). In this instance, macroeconomic structures and changes, social status positions, and role sets provide a context for understanding how the immediate work environment affects psychological well-being. Figure 13.1 provides a working conceptual model.

This model allows us to link the aggregate level research on macroeconomic structure with research on the relationship among job characteristics, stress, and distress. These two

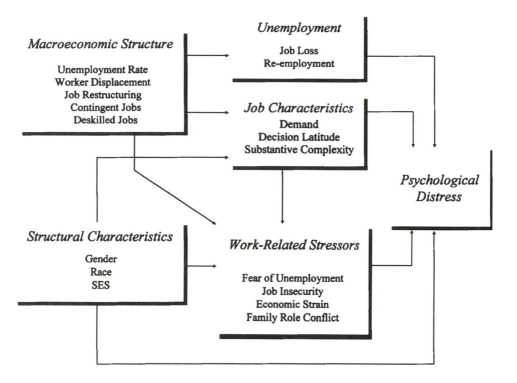

FIGURE 13.1. Structural contexts of work and mental health.

areas of research are linked by postulating a relationship between macroeconomic structure and specific job characteristics (Fenwick & Tausig, 1994). This connection indicates that the broader organization of labor, product, capital, and resource markets—which determine the number and types of jobs, human capital requirements, and wages—also provides a context for understanding why individual jobs affect well-being.

Macroeconomic structures also reflect social–structural conditions in at least two ways. First, labor markets are stratified by gender and race, and second, job characteristics are stratified by gender and race. For example, women and men work in markedly different types of occupations (Reskin, 1993) and are not equally placed in either internal or external labor markets. Studies of the relationship between gender, work, and well-being need to account for the contextual effects of macroeconomic structure that reflect gendered labor market conditions. Moreover, the specific job characteristics of men and women often differ precisely because "men's" jobs differ from "women's" jobs. A similar argument may be made about the importance of race. Consequently, it is necessary to take into consideration the status characteristics of individuals that affect their location within labor markets and their exposure to particular work characteristics.

Finally, role sets also provide a context for examining the relationship between work and well-being. In this instance, the impact of family life on well-being can be assessed as a separate set of role obligations that cause role conflict or role overload. However, role sets also affect labor market position and job characteristics by affecting the extent of participation in the labor force (i.e., full-time vs. part-time jobs).

In the remainder of this chapter, I summarize the existing research using Figure 13.1

as a means for building a general understanding of the relationship between work and mental health.

LABOR MARKET STRUCTURE AND DISTRESS

The plight of workers in the context of industrial economies has been of concern and interest at least since Engels analyzed the condition of the working class in England in 1844 (Engels, 1845/1958). Marxist studies of labor under capitalism show a relationship between this mode of economic production and both societal and individual alienation, and they suggest a direct link between economic organization and well-being (Marx, 1964; Mészáros, 1970).

More contemporary research by Brenner (1973, 1976, 1984, 1987), Marshall and Funch (1979), and especially Catalano, Dooley and their associates (Catalano & Dooley, 1977, 1979; Catalano, Dooley, & Jackson 1981; Catalano, Rook, & Dooley, 1986; Dooley & Catalano, 1984; Dooley, Catalano, & Rook, 1988) shows that a direct relationship does indeed exist between aggregate indicators of the state of the economy (generally, unemployment rates) and aggregate indicators of stress-related poor health (psychiatric hospital admissions, cardiovascular illness, mortality). Changes in unemployment rates (mainly, increases) increase risk of exposure to negative work and financial-related events, and reduce social tolerance for deviant behavior. Greater exposure to stressors and reduced tolerance in turn lead to higher aggregate rates of morbidity and mortality (Catalano 1989).

Studies conducted at an aggregate level run the risk of committing an "ecological fallacy" (Catalano & Dooley 1983), that is, erroneously concluding that persons experiencing greater morbidity are also those who were exposed to the economic stressor (e.g., unemployment or threat of unemployment). Catalano et al. (1986) have attempted to retain the ecological link to individual outcomes by suggesting that workers' perceptions of employment security are affected by unemployment rates and that perceived employment insecurity will be related to increased help seeking. They focus on the perceptions of workers (perceived employment security) and how these perceptions are affected by economic conditions (unemployment rates). Consistent with this explanation, Dooley et al. (1988) concluded that aggregate unemployment adversely affects all principal wage earners as a group, but that the effects of personal unemployment do not interact with aggregate unemployment effects. Brenner (1987) suggests that when macroeconomic conditions force a firm to reduce its labor force, remaining employees will experience fear of employment loss and destruction of careers, as well as increased work stress. Starrin, Lunberg, Angelow, and Wall (1989) suggest that fear of unemployment causes employed workers to work harder and that, at least in certain industries, as unemployment rates increase, owners of capital will find it efficient to extract more labor by requiring overtime work from a smaller number of workers instead of obtaining cheaper labor from the growing pool of the unemployed. As job demands and job insecurity are increased, these authors suggest, worker distress increases. Although these latter arguments make a case for the existence of direct effects of macroeconomic structure and change on well-being, the study of unemployment most clearly illustrates the direct effects of macroeconomy on well-being.

Unemployment and Reemployment

Unemployment is a stressor that clearly leads to greater physical and mental distress (Horwitz, 1984; Jahoda, 1988; Liem & Rayman, 1984; Pearlin & Schooler, 1978). Given that we often define ourselves by our job titles, the loss of a job can mean that our identity, based on our employment, is threatened. Unemployment, of course, also has significant financial effects. Most of the research on the effects of unemployment on workers' well-being focuses on these two matters: threats to identity and financial strain. The typical study of the health effects of unemployment shows that unemployment is related to increases in drinking, more physical illness, higher rates of depression, anxiety, "bad days," suicidal ideation, and the increased use of tranquilizers (Kessler, House, & Turner, 1987). This research also shows that becoming reemployed largely wipes out the effects of not being employed (Kessler et al., 1989).

Because the health effects of unemployment are unambiguous, the question turns to the causes of unemployment. It is here that we can see some of the ways in which social and economic structures affect worker well-being by affecting opportunities for work. The main reason for unemployment is "structural" and involuntary; that is, the economy goes through cycles of growth and decline, and during decline, jobs are lost simply because employers cannot afford the labor force costs they incurred when times were better, or because they close economically marginal plants or relocate production to lower wage areas. During recessions, numbers of unemployed persons swell and prospects of quick reemployment are poor. By definition, involuntary unemployment means that workers do not have control over the basic condition of their access to financial and identity security. There is also evidence that even among workers who do not lose their jobs during recessions, elevated levels of insecurity brought on by concern over the economy increase symptoms of depression and other forms of psychological distress (Heaney, Israel, & House, 1994; Kuhnert & Vance, 1992).

The actual extent to which personal unemployment affects well-being is subject to some debate because of the absence of well-designed longitudinal studies (Kessler et al., 1989; Liem & Liem, 1988; Ross & Mirowsky, 1995). Although a social-causation explanation argues that the event of job loss leads to increases in distress, a social-selection explanation suggests that emotionally fragile individuals are more likely to become unemployed. Evidence suggests that both explanations can be supported (Dooley & Catalano, 1984). A number of authors, however, have noted that personal reactions to unemployment may be affected by the aggregate economic context. Although Dooley, Catalano, and Rook (1988) did not find such a relationship, Perrucci, Perrucci, Targ, and Targ (1988) and Turner (1995) have shown that community-level reactions to plant closures and/or local unemployment rates do interact with personal unemployment experiences to affect psychological reactions. For example, Turner (1995) found that losing a job results in less physical and psychological distress when the chances for reemployment in the local community are good.

Studies of the consequences of reemployment generally show that it largely reverses the distress attributed to unemployment (Kessler, Turner, & House, 1988, 1989; Liem & Liem, 1988; Payne & Jones, 1987; Warr & Jackson, 1985; Turner, 1995). This effect can be attributed to personal job-seeking efforts and the consequent feelings of efficacy as well as improved finances. In some instances, reemployment may not improve well-being. Perrucci et al. (1988) report that the well-being of those reemployed following a plant closing was no better than that of those who remained unemployed, largely because those who became employed did so in jobs that offered substantially lower wages and less job security than their previous employment. In this instance, reemployment addressed neither financial nor identity issues. Both studies of the effects of unemployment and reemployment suggest the importance of accounting for the macroeconomic context in understanding effects of distress. This concern now leads us to examine some recent changes in the basic relationship between workers and employers, and the effects these changes may have on employee well-being.

The Changing Nature of Work

Work-related social structures in the United States and other postindustrial societies are currently changing in ways that probably decrease perceptions of employment security and increase anxiety related to the continuity of employment. I refer specifically to the rapid growth of contingent forms of employment, characterized by limited terms of employment. Such jobs, by their nature, may reduce perceptions of personal control because they are insecure, and because decision latitude within such jobs may be greatly limited.

Sizable numbers of those employed in the United States now work in jobs that are intentionally structured to last a limited period of time or to provide limited hours of work (i.e., part-time jobs). In 1995, the Bureau of Labor Statistics estimated that up to 14% of the current labor force was working in jobs that met various definitions of contingent employment (U.S. Department of Labor, 1995); adding those who are employed part time brings the total closer to one in three workers overall (Parker, 1993). For large numbers of workers, employment is not permanent, income is not predictable, and traditional employee benefits, such as retirement and health insurance, are highly uncertain. Moreover, the prospect of "downsizing" hangs over many permanently employed workers who no longer regard any job as permanent, even as their own employment continues. In short, many persons in the labor force are likely to feel insecure about their jobs, and many will feel that they have little control over the conditions of their employment. Because work is the major source of economic well-being and a principal source of identity, the potential uncertainty represented by contingent, insecure work constitutes a significant source of stress.

Contingent workers share a number of characteristics. Their wages are typically lower than permanent workers; they receive few, if any, fringe benefits; they have few opportunities for career advancement and no chance to exert control over the conditions of their work. Although contingent labor is increasing as a form of employment, not all contingent employment is identical in form or in implications for personal sense of control. For example, part-time work represents the largest category of contingent work, but much of it is voluntary on the part of workers. In 1989, 20 million nonagricultural workers were employed on a part-time basis (Tilly, 1991). Negrey (1993) concluded that voluntary, part-time employment may enhance sense of control by permitting scheduling and participation in other social activities. Tilly (1991) found, however, that most of the increase in part-time employment since 1970 is among "involuntary" part timers, workers who prefer full-time employment but cannot find it. He argued further that the inability to find full-time work is not a function of economic downturns but of the types of jobs employers are offering.

The growth of contingent labor is linked, ironically, to employers' interest in gaining greater control over the labor process. The "flexible" labor force is equated with a firm's ability to respond quickly to changes in demand and competition. Control over labor, to the extent of reducing or eliminating permanent employees, reduces fixed costs to organizations. Although part of the flexibility that firms seek is derived from the pressures of the competitive market, some is related to the de-skilling of jobs and presumed accompanying substitutability of employees that this permits (Braverman, 1974; Edwards, 1979). The standardization, mechanization, and fragmentation of jobs that de-skilling describes creates a condition that encourages the use of contingent employees by eliminating the advantage of retaining experienced workers (Parker, 1993). Employees become interchangeable and more insecure. Moreover, de-skilled work, by definition, lacks autonomy, opportunity for self-direction, and substantive complexity (Spenner, 1990). The existence and/or extent of de-skilling is a matter of considerable debate (Edwards, 1979; Form, 1980; Spenner,

1983,1 990). Consequently, it is not possible to make any generalizations at this time about the extent to which the average job has become de-skilled.

Contingent work, however, represents conditions of labor that clearly contain the possibility to threaten an employee's sense of control over his or her labor. Permanent employees may also worry about the stability of the firm, the restructuring of their work, or the loss of job benefits as a result of the changes they observe in the economy or elsewhere in the firm.

JOB CHARACTERISTICS AND DISTRESS

The previous discussion suggests that there is a direct relationship between changes in the economy and how people feel psychologically. This connection occurs principally through the effects of unemployment on distress and anxiety about the likelihood of unemployment, as well as the uncertainties associated with worker displacement, de-skilling, and employment instability . However, this relationship may not be as relevant to mental health as the impact of characteristics of specific jobs. What we actually do on our jobs and how we are able to do it have strong effects on well-being. The way work is organized represents structural rather than individual effects on mental health.

The bulk of research concerning the relationship between work and mental health is focused on specific work conditions rather than the general economy. In particular, the relationship between the demands of work and the freedom to meet those demands is of crucial importance (Karasek, 1979; Karasek & Theorell, 1990). It appears that the ability to control the balance between job demands and capacity to meet demands is also central to the development of identity, intellectual flexibility, and well-being (Kohn & Schooler, 1983).

One other argument that has been advanced to explain differences in worker reaction to their jobs is called the "person–environment fit" explanation (French, Caplan, & Van Harrison, 1982). This approach suggests that when individual biological and psychological characteristics do not match job requirements, workers will report more job dissatisfaction, alienation, and illness. Distress related to work, then, is a function of how well or poorly the individual has matched job and personal characteristics. Research, however, suggests that this explanation for work stress accounts for only some, not all, of the distress observed among workers (Baker, 1985).

Robert Karasek and his colleagues (Karasek, 1979; Karasek & Theorell, 1990) have outlined a "demand–control" model for explaining worker well-being that has received widespread empirical support. In this schema, the way that a worker can balance work demands with decision latitude (autonomy) in the way work is done is strongly related to worker mental health. The worker who experiences a high level of demands on the job but has little flexibility in the way he or she can meet these demands is at high risk of developing signs and symptoms of psychological distress. In this model, stress comes from the inability of the worker to manage high levels of demand. Note that some jobs have high levels of demand but do not produce distress because the job also permits the incumbent to control how the job will be done. People do not become distressed by the presence of challenge in their work, but by the inability to meet the challenge.

Job demands are usually indexed by survey items that ask workers if they must work very fast on their job, if they have too much work, or if they have enough time to get everything done. Job demands can also be used to indicate whether the work is paced by machine, and whether it is boring and repetitive. The effects of machine pacing have been of concern for some time. In the stereotypical image of assembly line manufacturing, a worker's rate of activity is determined by the speed of the assembly line, and the image of the worker falling behind the pace of the machine is a symbol of the stress of manufacturing jobs. Machine pacing has been associated with higher levels of boredom, anxiety, and depression (Caplan, Cobb, French, Van Harrison, & Pinneau, 1975; Hurrell, 1985). In addition, Link, Dohrenwend, and Skodol (1986) have shown that "noisome" physical occupational conditions can be linked to psychological disorder.

Decision latitude appears to be the most crucial variable related to work satisfaction and the onset of psychological distress. It is central to the notion of personal control and autonomy. Latitude is intended to reflect how the job, as defined by the employer, affects the employee. In its simplest version, decision latitude assesses whether the worker has the ability to complete assigned tasks in a way that permits individual preferences to be respected; that is, to what extent can an individual participate in the design of his or her work? Decision latitude is typically measured by questions about a worker's belief that he or she has the freedom to decide what to do on the job, has a lot of say about what happens on the job, feels that he or she has responsibility to decide how the job gets done, and that the job requires some creativity. Decision latitude also contains the notion of "closeness of supervision." Findings suggest that persons who are closely and constantly monitored by their supervisors, who perceive that they are unable to make decisions about their work on their own, and who have no opportunity to disagree with their supervisors, will display increased levels of anxiety, low self-confidence, and low job satisfaction (Kohn & Schooler, 1983).

Link, Lennon, and Dohrenwend (1993) have shown that the ability to control the work-related activities of others is important for well-being. This ability is a job characteristic defined by the *Dictionary of Occupational Titles* (DOT) as, "direction, control, and planning." The construct is clearly related to decision latitude but applies as a description of the job only insofar as the employee has control over other employees. The core of each construct is clearly personal control of one's actions related to work.

The "substantive complexity" of jobs is another feature of work that affects psychological well-being. Jobs that require more thinking to complete or that are more complicated to complete are associated with lower rates of anxiety, higher self-esteem, and higher life satisfaction (Caplan et al., 1975; Kohn & Schooler, 1983; Kornhauser, 1965; LaRocco, House, & French, 1980).

Work is also a social setting. Generally, we talk with our co-workers and our supervisors during the day. Often, people develop important friendships among co-workers that are carried on after working hours. The opportunity to interact with one's co-workers fills a general human need for socializing. As well, interactions with co-workers and supervisors offer the possibility of receiving support in times of strain or distress. Jobs that permit workers to interact and to form relationships (e.g., those in which one does not work alone, or where the surrounding noise is not too great) also permit workers to obtain support and advice regarding work-related (and maybe family-related) problems. Having someone who is trusted to consult about problems is essential to well-being. Thus, opportunities to make friends and to obtain social support from co-workers and supervisors on the job can have a positive effect on well-being (Billings & Moos, 1982; Etzion, 1984; Karasek, Triandas, & Chandry, 1982; LaRocco et al., 1980; Winhurst, Marcelissen, & Kleber, 1982).

Finally, jobs vary in the extent to which they offer a sense of security to their occupants. Job insecurity is defined as "perceived powerlessness to maintain desired continuity in a threatened job situation" (Greenhalgh & Rosenblatt, 1984, p. 438). Workers' beliefs that their jobs will still exist in a year and that they can expect to keep the job if they choose are important to a sense of well-being. Even when economic times are generally good, employees worry about the stability of their employment. When times are bad, fear of unemployment can have severe psychological effects on individuals (Joelson & Wahlquist, 1987; Heaney et al., 1994).

The Effects of Labor Market Changes on Job Characteristics

Studies of the relationship between macroeconomic conditions and well-being generally assume a direct effect between macroeconomic conditions and well-being. They rarely take into account the possible effects of macroeconomic structure on job characteristics. Few studies of the relationship between job structures and well-being use longitudinal data. For these reasons, changes in job characteristics that might be attributable to macroeconomic conditions and changes in the macroeconomy are rarely examined. The characteristics of jobs are generally assumed to be givens that are related to the specific technology of production, the characteristics of bureaucratic organization, and "industry standards."

A number of authors, however, argue that job characteristics are not constants. Rather, they change, in part because of the effects of labor and product market change (as well as technological change). During economic downturns, for example, the viability of economic organizations can be threatened by declining resource, capital, and product markets. In response to such decline, organizations often reduce the size of their labor force (Starrin et al., 1989) and/or push for improved efficiency among remaining workers (Brenner & Mooney, 1983). The results of this job restructuring may include work speedups, reduced margins for error in output, relaxation of rules governing safety, and increased supervision of work—all changes that increase the stressfulness of jobs.

In fact, firms may engage in both strategies, reducing the workforce and restructuring existing jobs (Hachen, 1992). One way to cope with reduced product demand is to reduce labor costs. This can be accomplished by laying off workers whose production is replaceable (i.e., those whose work requires fewer specialized skills and is less crucial to organizational survival, and those who are not protected by union contracts). The psychological effects of this replacement strategy on replaceable workers is principally felt through the effects of unemployment. The other strategy retains valued workers but restructures their jobs. The psychological effects of this type of change is largely felt through increases in job demands and decreases in decision latitude (Fenwick & Tausig, 1994; Tausig & Fenwick, 1993). Both strategies also are likely to increase perceptions of job insecurity among those who remain employed (Catalano et al., 1986; Fenwick & Tausig, 1994).

The increasing use of contingent forms of labor also affects job structures. By their nature, contingent jobs affect perceptions of job security. Contingent and part-time jobs, however, also generally require less skill, offer less responsibility, pay less, and exclude workers from internal labor markets (Tilly, 1996). To the extent that the shift to contingent labor is part of a systematic socioeconomic process, the distribution of jobs that contain stress-related characteristics may increase across the entire economy. Thus, the likelihood that an employee will encounter a job with stress-related characteristics may also increase over time.

In fact, exposure to stressful work characteristics is not uniform. Rather, women, persons with lower socioeconomic status, and minorities are more likely to work in jobs with stressful job characteristics. The next phase of this review examines the relationship between these social–structural positions, work characteristics, and distress. Because most of this research has examined the relationship, among gender, work, and well-being, it is also the focus of the discussion.

GENDER, SOCIOECONOMIC STATUS, AND RACE

Men and women who work often do so under very different structural conditions. Their labor is differentially distributed across economic sectors, organizations, occupations, and specific job characteristics. These differences have well-documented effects on job outcomes, ranging from differences in income (Blau & Beller, 1988) and authority (Wright, Baxter, with Birkelund, 1995) to distress (Barnett & Marshall, 1991).

Compared to men, women constitute one group of workers whose employment is typified by job characteristics that have been found to be stressful. Women's work is concentrated in low-paying occupations, smaller organizations, and peripheral, nonunionized industries (Beck, Horan, & Tolbert, 1978; England & McCreary, 1987). This occupational segregation is also related to characteristics of the jobs that women typically encounter. Women tend to predominate in occupations that are less flexible and that permit less autonomy than those occupied by men—precisely the characteristics related to high levels of job-related distress (Glass, 1990; Hachen, 1988; Rosenfield, 1989; Tomaskovic-Devey, 1993).

Gender differences in job stress have been observed for some time, and there are two predominant explanatory perspectives. The "jobs" model assumes that the same job characteristics account for job stress in both men and women, but that women are more likely to be in jobs with stressful characteristics (Haw, 1982). The "gender" model assumes that non-work-related variables affect women's (but not men's) reactions to job-related stressors, the most important being home and family demands and the conflicts domestic demands create with job demands. (I will examine evidence for the gender model in the section regarding work and family). There is evidence that the two models are not inherently contradictory (Barnett & Marshall, 1991; Haynes, 1991; Lennon & Rosenfield, 1992; Lowe & Northcott, 1988).

In general, the literature supports the jobs model explanation. Despite differences in samples and measures, most studies that compare the causes of job-related distress for men and women find that the balance between job demands and the structural capacity to meet demands (decision latitude) affect worker distress. Miller (1980) found that men and women are equally affected by time pressures to complete work. Adelmann (1987) found that occupational control leads to self-confidence in both men and women. Karasek, Gardell, and Lindell (1987) found that control over work, workload, support from co-workers and supervisors, and the absence of conflict between workers and supervisors predicted worker well-being for both men and women. Similarly, Lowe and Northcott (1988), Loscocco and Spitze (1990), Barnett and Marshall (1991), and Lennon and Rosenfield (1992) have found no differences by gender in the ways that job demands, autonomy, and/or substantive complexity affect well-being.

Some researchers have found that men and women react to features of jobs differently. For example, Miller (1980) and Lennon (1987) found that lower substantive complexity of work predicted distress for women but not for men. Miller also found that only men are affected by closeness of supervision and the absence of job protection. Adelmann (1987) and Lowe and Northcott (1988) found that income and autonomy predict well-being for men only. Lowe and Northcott also found that shift work affects men, but that work intensity and the absence of helpful co-workers affect only women. Roxburgh (1996) reported that men's and women's jobs do not differ in terms of the extent of job demands and routinization, but that women are more adversely affected by demands and routinization.

Men and women do, however, typically experience different work characteristics and have different structural capacities to react to the stressful aspects of these characteristics. The gender segregation of occupations means that the job characteristics, industries, and types of organizations in which women are employed expose them to different work conditions than men. Even when men and women work in the same occupations, it has been shown that women tend to occupy jobs with less power than men (Wolf & Fligstein, 1979).

Women are more likely to be employed in small organizations with no internal labor markets, in peripheral sectors of the economy, and in nonsupervisory positions (Beck et al., 1978). This pattern of employment reinforces the subordinate position of women in the external labor market (Wolf & Fligstein, 1979), and it may affect the way in which they react to changes in macroeconomic conditions such as increases in unemployment (Semyonov & Scott, 1983), or shifts in the sectoral composition of the labor force (Abrahamson & Sigelman, 1987). In short, the social and economic environments play a prominent role in structuring work opportunities and specific job characteristics that in turn affect individual well-being. Differences in these environments for men and women may explain differences in gendered reactions to changes in these environments.

The consequences of women's occupational segregation are not limited to restricted labor markets, mobility chances, and stress-causing job characteristic changes. Women may also perceive greater risk of job instability during economic downturns because, as employees of firms that are more likely to be threatened by economic crises (e.g., firms in peripheral sectors), their perceptions of personal threat may increase (Brenner, 1987; Lichter & Landry, 1991). Women's job mobility is often limited to lateral changes (Hachen, 1988), and even this mobility is limited by widespread unemployment (Rosen, 1987). Furthermore, it is possible that women's jobs will be sacrificed in order to create resources to retain other valued workers (males) during economic downturns (Hachen, 1992). The overrepresentation of women in economic sectors and industries that favor replacement rather than retention strategies (Schervish, 1983), coupled with personnel policies that seek to retain "valued" employees, increase women's perceptions that they are at greater risk of unemployment even if they manage to remain employed.

Women's job-related distress is therefore affected both by the macroeconomic and social conditions that channel women into specific occupations and industries, and to the specific job characteristics they encounter. Moreover, the differences in occupation and industry also lead to different consequences for men and women during periods of economic change (Tausig & Fenwick, 1992).

Socioeconomic Status

Socioeconomic status (SES) has separate effects on the well-being of workers. SES is defined, in part, by occupation. Therefore, the relationship between socioeconomic status and distress owes much to the relationship between occupational (job) characteristics and distress. Just as I suggested that the typical jobs that women hold have characteristics that make them more stressful, a similar argument can be made about the characteristics of jobs held by persons of lower SES (Karasek, 1991; Link et al., 1993). SES affects job-related distress by sorting workers into jobs with different levels of stressful characteristics. Kessler (1982), however, shows that only the occupational status component of SES indicators is related to job characteristics. Income and education have separate effects on distress that do not appear to operate entirely through work characteristics. Karasek (1991) also found that not all occupations that can be characterized as "blue-collar" or "white collar" contain the same basic job characteristics. However, jobs with high levels of demand and low levels of decision latitude are more prevalent in bluecollar occupational categories. Kohn, Naoi, Schoenbach, Schooler, and Slomczynski (1990) suggest that the traditional indicators of SES (education, income, and occupational prestige) are consistently related to distress only for manual workers. They found that manual workers differ from others largely because their jobs lack the dimension of control of one's own labor. Link et al. (1993) found that the crucial characteristic of work that connects SES to distress is the extent to which occupations permit workers to control the work of others. They showed that persons in occupations containing the characteristic of direction, control, and planning (DCP) are less likely to experience depression, and that these jobs are linked to higher SES.

SES is related to social class, but in a complicated fashion (Kohn et al., 1990). The concept of class distinguishes between those who own the means of production and those who work for owners. Research confirms a relationship (although not a linear relationship) between class-related positions, job characteristics, and distress (Kohn et al., 1990; Tausig & Fenwick, 1993). Tausig and Fenwick showed both that the characteristics of jobs in terms of demands and decision latitude differ by class and that the impact of macroeconomic change on workers is conditioned by class status. Those who work for others and do not supervise others (the proletariat) are more likely to work in jobs with high demands and low decision latitude. During economic downturns, their decision latitude decreases and their levels of anxiety and depression increase. Owners and supervisors, however, are not immune to the effects of macroeconomic change. The owners of smaller businesses in the peripheral sector of the economy experience increased anxiety following economic downturns, and they also report decreases in decision latitude that affect depression. Depression and anxiety levels for supervisors also increase during recessions because job demands increase and decision latitude decreases. Kohn et al. (1990) argued that position in the class structure determines the degree of control one has over the conditions of one's work, especially regarding occupational self-direction (decision latitude), which are related to psychological functioning.

SES is a multidimensional construct that also crosscuts gender and race. As such, it is extremely difficult to isolate the unique effects of SES. However, it is clear that SES reflects an assessment of human capital characteristics that affect occupational attainment and, therefore, job characteristics. Moreover, differences in occupational attainment by SES suggest that exposure and vulnerability to the effects of macroeconomic change will also vary by SES in ways that are similar to those observed between men and women based on gendered differences in occupational attainment.

Race

Finally, we need to consider the effects of race on the relationship between work characteristics and distress. Membership in nonwhite racial categories has substantial effects on the likelihood that an individual will be employed in a job with stressful characteristics.

Blacks earn less than whites on average and within identical occupations (Cain, 1984). Black men earn about 73% of the amounts earned by white men. Black women earn almost as much as white women, but earn substantially less than men. When alternate explanations for these income differentials are evaluated, the racial differences observed are mostly attributable to discrimination and occupational segregation. Studies show that blacks have less access to "good," well-paying jobs that are high in decision latitude and low in job demands (Tomaskovic-Devey, 1993). Tomaskovic-Devey found that black employees are more closely supervised, have less complex tasks, less managerial authority, and less supervisory responsibility than whites.

In fact, it is somewhat difficult to disentangle racial from SES effects on occupational attainment and income (Kessler & Neighbors, 1986). Race and SES appear to interact so that lower SES blacks are more vulnerable to the effects of undesirable life events than lower SES whites (Ulbrich, Warheit, & Zimmerman, 1989). These differences remain even when differences in training and skills are taken into account. With the long history of racial segregation, discrimination, and bias that characterizes the African American experience in the United States, part of the explanation for the relatively poor jobs that non-whites hold must be based on institutionalized racist policies that prevent people of color from acquiring a good education and/or job training. However, as indicated, even when training is held constant, African Americans are at a significant disadvantage in terms of occupying jobs with positive characteristics. Therefore, race affects both the likelihood of obtaining the prerequisites needed to acquire good jobs and the likelihood of acquiring these jobs themselves.

One work-related effect that certainly affects blacks and whites differently is the experience of unemployment. Unemployment rates for black Americans are routinely twice those for white Americans. Among black youth, rates may be four times as high (Poussaint, 1990). Whether this is the result of human capital differences or racist employment policies, the experience of unemployment contributes to observed rates of distress among black Americans. Blacks are also concentrated into several occupational categories—such as private household cleaners, postal clerks, nurse's aides, service jobs and clerical positions (Ruiz 1990)—that have stress-related job characteristics (Tomasevic-Devey1993) and that make blacks vulnerable to layoffs during economic downturns. Despite these general observations, however, there is little research on the relationships between race, macroeconomic conditions, job characteristics, and distress.

Gender, SES, and race clearly affect the exposure and vulnerability of workers to distress. Using a "jobs" model, these differences are explained as a function of job characteristics coupled with predictions about the ways in which labor market differences based on gender, SES, and/or race affect occupational distributions and vulnerability to economic change. The jobs model emphasizes common structural determinants of work-related distress. It provides a central theoretical core of explanation that allows comparisons across social–structural conditions. The jobs model, however, cannot account for the effects of gender or racial bias over and above structural effects. The model also fails to consider how commitments in other social roles such as spouse and parent are related to work experiences. So-called "gender" models, however, form a basis for considering the final research literature in this area.

WORK AND FAMILY

The gender model, as generally specified, assumes that non-work-related variables affect women's (but usually not men's) reactions to job-related stressors, the most important being home and family demands, and the conflicts these demands, create with work (Haw, 1982). This model has received some support (Barnett & Marshall, 1991; Lennon & Rosenfield, 1992; Rosenfield, 1980). The gender model also makes two other assumptions. First, it assumes that, for many women, work does not have the same psychological or social meaning it does for men (Rubin, 1994; Simon, 1995; Wiley, 1991). Thus, the impact of unemployment or stressful job structures would not be identical to that experienced by men. Second, it assumes that even if work has similar meanings for men and women, only women need to deal with substantial work *and* household and parental demands. Hence, men and women do not face common stressors within or across roles (Thoits, 1987).

Within the framework developed in this chapter, a gender model of work-related distress implicates family roles as they affect distress in three ways. First, the entry of women into the labor force represents a modification of traditional, societal-level definitions of normative adult female social-role combinations. Second, the joint demands of family and paid work affect labor market preferences and opportunities. Third, the specific structures of paid work and family work may cause distress that spills over or contaminates the level of psychological well-being associated with the other role.

Thoits (1986), Menaghan (1989), and Ross, Mirowsky, and Huber (1983) have all observed that distress levels (especially for women) are increased when women occupy nontraditional role combinations. Menaghan (1989) argues that nontraditional role combinations do not receive adequate social–institutional support, which makes continuation in these role combinations stressful. Women's contemporary entry into the paid labor force represents a historical and social alteration of traditional role combinations. Thus, one source of work-related distress occurs because participation in the labor force is itself not institutionally supported for women. Women's participation in the labor force has long been considered supplemental to the main earnings of husbands. This perspective suggests that the labor market for women is partly structured by expectations that women do not "need" to earn as much as men, nor are they as committed to labor market participation as men. Traditional and nontraditional notions of women's roles also clash at the level of spousal expectations. Ross et al. (1983) have shown that when husbands and/or wives endorse a traditional gender-role set and wives work, these wives have elevated levels of depression. Mirowsky and Ross (1989) have also shown that difficulty in obtaining child care is a strain on working mothers. This difficulty reflects in part a lack of general social–institutional support for female role combinations that contain a role in the paid labor force.

Human capital considerations and women's preferences about participation in the labor force also affect the labor market conditions that women encounter and, hence, the amount of distress related to working. This complicates the evaluation of the effects of employment status on women's well-being, because women's work characteristics are rarely accounted for in studies of the impact of family and work roles. Women are far more likely to be found in part-time positions than men (Parker, 1993). In part, this pattern represents employer preferences to reserve full-time positions for men. The overrepresentation of women in part-time jobs is also a primary rationalization for gendered occupational segregation. However, it also reflects the preferences of women who try to balance work and family obligations, even though some evidence suggests that female-dominated jobs are often not compatible with family demands (Glass & Camarigg, 1992; Pugliesi, 1995). From a human capital perspective, the preference for part-time work reduces the value of the employee because it slows tenure and undermines perceptions of career commitment. Women who "stop out" their jobs to raise families may do so at the cost of foregone promotions, as well as jobs with features that enhance well-being. Part-time jobs do not generally contain high levels of decision latitude, pay, or job security (Tilly, 1996). Thus, one consequence of attempts to balance work and family roles is exposure to labor market conditions that do not favor positive job conditions. "The very job characteristics that would reduce stress and job–family tension among employed mothers are difficult for them to obtain because these rewards are linked to an authority and reward structure that places women in marginalized 'women's jobs' " (Glass & Camarigg, 1992, p. 148).

Meeting expectations in both the paid labor force and in families requires the management of job and scheduling demands in both spheres of activity. For both paid labor and household labor, the balance of demands and decision latitude in each sphere can be used to estimate overall distress (Lennon & Rosenfield, 1992). Rosenfield (1989) showed that a woman's ability to control demands in the work sphere improves her ability to control demands in the domestic sphere. Hughes, Galinsky, and Morris (1992) reported that workers in jobs with high demands and low supervisor support have more frequent marital arguments, because high job demands increase the pressure also to complete family-related demands. Pleck and Staines (1985) reported that longer work hours for women lead to greater negative effects on family well-being, and Bolger, DeLongis, Kessler, and Wethington (1989) found that high levels of work hours, for either husbands or wives, lead to increased strain for both husbands and wives. Similarly, Sears and Galambos (1992) found that high job demands and low pay for women lead to increased work-related distress, which in turn affects marital adjustment. Piotrkowski (1979) and Kanter (1977) found that control over scheduling at work is most crucial for determining whether work hours conflict with family demands.

The gender model, as usually specified, focuses on the additional strain felt by working women from incurring a second shift of work demands, as I have just described. The extent to which the combined demands of employment and household duties elevate distress, however, is more complicated than suggested by a simple accounting of hours. Macrosocial changes in the normative definitions of gender roles and expectations, and dynamics of the gendered labor market also affect the degree to which work and family roles affect distress. The gender model, then, is not in opposition to the jobs model. Rather, it provides a context for accommodating the effects of non-work-related roles on work-related stress processes.

CONCLUSIONS AND PROSPECTS

This chapter has explored a structural explanation for the relationship between work and mental health. I have shown how macroeconomic, job, social, and role structures each contribute to the explanation of this relationship. The four research literatures I described here reflect different starting points, different units of analysis, and different objectives. They have in common an emphasis on how structures affect access to resources that contribute to feelings of well-being: The status of the economy affects the availability of jobs; the shape of jobs affects feelings of accomplishment; social status affects starting points for entry into jobs, and role structures affect opportunities for participation. Moreover, it is clear that these dimensions of structure are related to one another.

The articulation between these approaches is not seamless. However, it is also clear that researchers are increasingly aware of the need to account for these dimensions of structure as they develop a more complete understanding of how work affects mental health.

This enterprise is also consistent with the notion of a sociological stress process (Pearlin, 1989), with the notion of social structure as a fundamental cause of illness (Link & Phelan, 1995), and with the need for medical sociology to establish clear connections with the larger discipline of sociology (Pescosolido & Kronenfeld, 1995).

The emphasis on structural effects does not negate the importance of understanding the relationship between work and emotions. For example, Hochschild (1983) argues that one of the consequences of the macroeconomic shift to service-related jobs in postindustrial societies is the increasing frequency with which jobs require the transformation of human raw material (the customer) via a process of "emotional" labor. She argues further that "emotional labor" exacts a direct cost on the emotional well-being of the worker by estranging the worker from his or her own emotional identity. Precisely because jobs increasingly require "working with people," we need to incorporate an understanding of how people processing affects well-being.

Similarly, the current shift to contingent employment and flexible workforces represents a historical shift in the relationship between employer and employee. Job characteristics become a moving target, and the loss of control that generally is associated with conditional forms of employment may have serious effects on the well-being of workers and their families. This consequence is nowhere better illustrated than in the instance of middle-aged workers who lose their jobs because of the decline of certain industries or plant relocations. Many of these workers are attempting to "retrain" to qualify for existing jobs, but we know almost nothing about the psychological consequences of this increasingly prevalent situation (Geller & Stroh, 1995).

Relatively speaking, there is less research on the relationship between work and mental health than for many other aspects of mental health. Still, the outline of a reasonably complete sociological analysis of this relationship appears to be in place. There is still a need to improve the theoretical consolidation of the different research literatures that compose this analysis, a need to specify how the effects of aggregate characteristics on organizational and individual outcomes occur, and a need for empirical data that permit testing of such theory.

REFERENCES

Abrahamson, M., & Sigelman, L. (1987). Occupational sex segregation in metropolitan areas. *American Sociological Review, 52,* 588–597.

Adelmann, P. K. (1987). Occupational complexity, control, and personal income: Their relation to psychological well-being in men and women. *Journal of Applied Psychology, 72,* 529–537.

Baker, D. B. (1985). The study of stress at work. *Annual Review of Public Health, 6,* 367–381.

Barnett, R. C., & Marshall, N. (1991). The relationship between women's work and family roles and their subjective well-being and psychological stress. In M. Frankenhaeusen, U. Lundberg, & M. Chesney (Eds.), *Women, work and health: Stress and opportunities* (pp. 11–36). New York: Plenum Press.

Beck, E. M., Horan, P. M., & Tolbert, C., II. (1978). Stratification in a dual economy: A sectoral model of earnings determination. *American Sociological Review, 43,* 704–720.

Billings, A. G., & Moos, R. H. (1982). Work stress and the stress-buffering roles of work and family resources. *Journal of Occupational Behaviour, 3,* 215–232.

Blau, F., & Beller, A. H. (1988). Trends in earnings differentials by gender: 1971–1981. *Industrial and Labor Relations Review, 41,* 513–529.

Bolger, N., DeLongis, A., Kessler, R. C., & Wethington, E. (1989). The contagion of stress across multiple roles. *Journal of Marriage and the Family, 51,* 175–183.

Braverman, H. (1974). *Labor and monopoly capital.* New York: Monthly Review Press.

Brenner, H. M. (1973). *Mental illness and the economy.* Cambridge, MA: Harvard University Press.

Brenner, H. M. (1976). *Estimating the social costs of economic policy: Implications for mental and physical health, and criminal aggression*. Report to the Congressional Research Service of the Library of Congress Joint Economic Committee of Congress, Washington, DC.

Brenner, H. M. (1984). *Estimating the effect of economic change on national mental health and social well-being*. Prepared by the Subcommittee on Economic Goals and Intergovernmental Policy of the Joint Economic Committee, U.S. Congress, Washington, DC.

Brenner, H. M. (1987). Relation of economic change to Swedish health and social well-being, 1950–1980. *Social Science and Medicine, 25,* 183–195.

Brenner, H. M., & Mooney, A. (1983). Unemployment and health in the context of economic change. *Social Science and Medicine, 17,* 1125–1138.

Cain, G. G. (1984). The economics of discrimination: Part 1. *Focus, 7,* 1–11.

Caplan, R. D., Cobb, S., French, J. R. P., Van Harrison, R., & Pinneau, S. R. (1975). *Job demands and worker health*. Washington, DC.:U.S. Department of Health and Human Services.

Catalano, R. (1989). Ecological factors in illness and disease. In H.E. Freeman & S. Levine (Eds.), *Handbook of medical sociology* (4th ed., pp. 87–101). Englewood Cliffs, NJ: Prentice Hall.

Catalano, R., & Dooley, D. (1977). Economic predictors of depressed mood and stressful life events. *Journal of Health and Social Behavior, 18,* 292–307.

Catalano, R., & Dooley, D. (1979). The economy as stressor: A sectoral analysis. *Review of Social Economy, 37,* 175–187.

Catalano, R., & Dooley, D. (1983). Health effects of economic instability: A test of economic stress hypothesis. *Journal of Health and Social Behavior, 24,* 46–60.

Catalano, R., Rook, K., & Dooley, D. (1986). Labor markets and help seeking: A test of the employment security hypothesis. *Journal of Health and Social Behavior, 27,* 277–287.

Dooley, D., & Catalano, R. (1984). The epidemiology of economic stress. *American Journal of Community Psychology, 12,* 387–409.

Dooley, D., Catalano, R., & Rook, K.S. (1988). Personal and aggregate unemployment and psychological symptoms. *Journal of Social Issues, 44,* 107–123.

Edwards, R. (1979). *The contested terrain: The transformation of the workplace in the twentieth century*. New York: Basic Books.

Engels, F. (1958). *The condition of the working class in England*. W. O. Henderson & W. H. Chaloner (Trans. and Eds.). Stanford, CA: Stanford University Press. (Original published 1845)

England, P., & McCreary, L. (1987). Integrating sociology and economics to study gender and work. In A. H. Stromberg, L. Larwood, & B. A. Gutek (Eds.), *Women and work: An annual review* (Vol. 2, pp. 143–172). Newbury Park, CA: Sage.

Etzion, D. (1984). Moderating effect of social support on the stress-burnout relationship. *Journal of Applied Psychology, 69,* 615–622.

Fenwick, R., & Tausig, M. (1994). The macroeconomic context of job stress. *Journal of Health and Social Behavior, 35,* 266–287.

Form, W. H. (1980). Resolving ideological issues on the division of labor. In H. M. Blalock, Jr. (Ed.), *Sociological theory and research* (pp. 140–145). New York: Free Press.

French, J. R. P., Jr., Caplan, R. D., & Van Harrison, R. (1982). *The mechanisms of job stress and strain*. New York: Wiley.

Geller, M. M., & Stroh, L. K. (1995). Careers in midlife and beyond: A fallow field in need of sustenance. *Journal of Vocational Behavior, 47,* 232–247.

Glass, J. (1990). The impact of occupational segregation on working conditions. *Social Forces, 68,* 779–796.

Glass, J., & Camarigg, V. (1992). Gender, parenthood, and job–family compatibility. *American Journal of Sociology, 98,* 131–151.

Gove, W., & Tudor, J. F. (1973). Adult sex roles and mental illness. *American Journal of Sociology, 78,* 812–835.

Greenhalgh, L., & Rosenblatt, Z. (1984). Job insecurity: Toward conceptual clarity. *Academy of Management Review, 9,* 438–448.

Hachen, D. S., Jr. (1988). Gender differences in job mobility rates in the United States. *Social Science Research, 17,* 93–116.

Hachen, D. S., Jr. (1992). Industrial characteristics and job mobility rates. *American Sociological Review, 57,* 39–55.

Haw, M. A. (1982). Women, work and stress: A review and agenda for the future. *Journal of Health and Social Behavior, 23,* 132–144.

Haynes, S. G. (1991). The effects of job demands, job control, and new technologies on the health of employed women: A review. In M. Frankenhaeuser, U. Lundberg, & M. Chesney (Eds.), *Women, work, and health: Stress and opportunities* (pp 157–169). New York: Plenum Press.

Heaney, C. A., Israel, B. A., & House, J. S. (1994). Chronic job insecurity among automobile workers: Effects on job satisfaction and health. *Social Science and Medicine, 38*, 1431–1437.

Hochschild, A. R. (1983). *The managed heart: Commercialization of human feeling.* Berkeley: University of California Press.

Horwitz, A. (1984). The economy and social pathology. *Annual Review of Sociology, 10*, 95–119.

Hughes, D., Galinsky, E., & Morris, A. (1992). The effects of job characteristics on marital quality. *Journal of Marriage and the Family, 54*, 31–42.

Hurrell, J. J., Jr. (1985). Machine-paced work and the type-A behaviour pattern. *Journal of Occupational Psychology, 58*, 15–26.

Jahoda, M. (1988). Economic recession and mental health: Some conceptual issues. *Journal of Social Issues, 44*, 13–23.

Joelson, L., & Wahlquist, L. (1987). The psychological meaning of job insecurity and job loss: Results of a longitudinal study. *Social Science and Medicine, 25*, 179–182.

Jones, J. A., & Rosenfeld, R. A. (1989). Women's occupations and local labor markets: 1950 to 1980. *Social Forces, 67*, 666–692.

Kanter, R. M. (1977). *Work and family in the United States: A critical review and agenda for research and policy.* New York: Russell Sage Foundation.

Karasek, R. A. (1979). Job demands, job decision latitude, and mental strain: Implications for job redesign. *Administrative Science Quarterly, 24*, 285–306.

Karasek, R. A. (1991). The political implications of psychosocial work redesign: A model of the psychological class structure. In J. V. Johnson & G. Johansson (Eds.), *The psychosocial work environment: Work organization, democratization, and health* (pp. 163–190). Amityville, NY: Baywood.

Karasek, R. A., Gardell, B., & Lindell, J. (1987). Work and non-work correlates of illness and behavior in male and female Swedish white collar workers. *Journal of Occupational Behaviour, 8*, 187–207.

Karasek, R. A., & Theorell, T. (1990). *Healthy work: Stress, productivity, and the reconstruction of working life.* New York: Basic Books.

Karasek, R. A., Triandas, K. P., & Chandry, S. S. (1982). Co-worker and supervisor support as moderators of association between task characteristics and mental strain. *Journal of Occupational Behaviour, 3*, 181–200.

Kessler, R. C. (1982). A disaggregation of the relationship between socioeconomic status and psychological distress. *American Sociological Review, 47*, 752–764.

Kessler, R. C., House, J. S., & Turner, J. B. (1987). Unemployment and health in a community sample. *Journal of Health and Social Behavior, 28*, 51–59.

Kessler, R. C., & Neighbors, H. W. (1986). A new perspective on the relationships among race, social class and psychological distress. *Journal of Health and Social Behavior, 27*, 107–115.

Kessler, R. C., Turner, J. B., & House, J. S. (1988). Effects of unemployment on health in a community survey. *Journal of Social Issues, 44*, 69–85.

Kessler, R. C., Turner, J. B., & House, J. S. (1989). Unemployment, reemployment, and emotional functioning in a community sample. *American Sociological Review, 54*, 648–657.

Kohn, M., Naoi, A., Schoenbach, C., Schooler, C., & Slomczynski, K. M. (1990). Position in the class structure and psychological functioning in the United States, Japan, and Poland. *American Journal of Sociology, 95*, 964–1008.

Kohn, M., & Schooler, C. (1982). Job conditions and personality: A longitudinal assessment of their reciprocal effects. *American Journal of Sociology, 87*, 1257–1286.

Kohn, M., & Schooler, C. (1983). *Work and personality: An inquiry into the impact of social stratification.* Norwood, NJ: Ablex.

Kornhauser, A. W. (1965). *Mental health of the industrial worker: A Detroit study.* New York: Wiley.

Kuhnert, K. W., & Vance, R. J. (1992). Job insecurity and moderators of the relation between job insecurity and employee adjustment. In J. C. Quick, L. R. Murphy, & J. J. Hurrell, Jr. (Eds.), *Stress and well-being at work: Assessments and interventions for occupational mental health* (pp. 48–63). Washington, DC: American Psychological Association.

LaRocco, J. M., House, J. S., & French, J. R. P., Jr. (1980). Social support, occupational stress, and health. *Journal of Health and Social Behavior, 21*, 202–218.

Lennon, M. C. (1987) Sex differences in distress: The impact of gender and work roles. *Journal of Health and Social Behavior, 28*, 290–305.

Lennon, M. C., & Rosenfield, S. (1992). Women and mental health: The interaction of job and family conditions. *Journal of Health and Social Behavior, 33*, 316–327.

Lichter, D. T., & Landry, D. J. (1991). Labor force transitions and underemployment: The stratification of male and female workers. *Research in Social Stratification and Mobility, 10*, 63–87.

Liem, R., & Liem, J. H. (1988). Psychological effects of unemployment on workers and their families. *Journal of Social Issues, 44*, 87–103.

Liem, R., & Rayman, P. (1984). Perspectives on unemployment, mental health and social policy. *International Journal of Mental Health, 13*, 3–17.

Link, B., Lennon, M. C., & Dohrenwend, B. P. (1993). Socioeconomic status and depression: The role of occupations involving direction, control, and planning. *American Journal of Sociology, 98*, 1351–1387.

Link, B., & Phelan, J. (1995). Social conditions as fundamental causes of disease. *Journal of Health and Social Behavior* (Extra Issue), 80–94.

Loscocco, K. A., & Spitze, G. (1990). Working conditions, social support, and well-being of female and male factory workers. *Journal of Health and Social Behavior, 31*, 313–327.

Lowe, G. S., & Northcott, H. C. (1988). The impact of working conditions, social roles, and personal characteristics on gender differences in distress. *Work and Occupations, 15*, 55–77.

Marshall, J. R., & Funch, D. P. (1979). Mental illness and the economy: A critique and partial replication. *Journal of Health and Social Behavior, 20*, 259–272.

Marx, K. (1964). *Early writings,* T. B. Bottomore (Ed. & Trans.). New York: McGraw-Hill.

Menaghan, E. G. (1989). Role changes and psychological well-being: Variations in effects by gender and role repertoire. *Social Forces, 67*, 693–714.

Mészáros, I. (1970). *Marx's theory of alienation.* London: Merlin Press.

Miller, J. (1980). Individual and occupational determinants of job satisfaction: A focus on gender differences. *Sociology of Work and Occupations, 7*, 337–366.

Mirowsky, J., & Ross, C. E. (1989). *Social causes of psychological distress.* New York: Aldine.

Negrey, C. (1993). *Gender, time and reduced work.* Albany :SUNY Press.

Parker, R. E. (1993). The labor force in transition: The growth of the contingent work force in the United States. In B. Berberoglu (Ed.), *The labor process and control of labor: The changing nature of work relations in the late twentieth century* (pp. 116–136). Westport, CT: Praeger.

Payne, R. L., & Jones, J. G. (1987). Social class and re-employment: Changes in health and perceived financial circumstances. *Journal of Occupational Behaviour, 8*, 175–184.

Pearlin, L. I. (1989). The sociological study of stress. *Journal of Health and Social Behavior, 30*, 241–256.

Pearlin, L. I., & Schooler, C. (1978). The structure of coping. *Journal of Health and Social Behavior, 19*, 2–21.

Perrucci, C. C., Perrucci, R., Targ, D. B., & Targ, H. R. (1988). *Plant closings.* Hawthorne, NY: Aldine.

Pescosolido, B. A., & Kronenfeld, J. J. (1995). Health, illness, and healing in an uncertain era: Challenges from and for medical sociology. *Journal of Health and Social Behavior* (Extra Issue), 5–33.

Piotrkowski, C. (1979). *Work and the family system.* New York: Free Press.

Pleck, J., & Staines, G. (1985). Work schedules and family life in two-earner couples. *Journal of Family Issues, 6*, 61–82.

Poussaint, A. F. (1990). The mental health status of black Americans, 1983. In D. S. Ruiz (Ed.), *Handbook of mental health and mental disorder among black Americans* (pp. 17–52). New York: Greenwood Press.

Pugliesi, K. (1995). Work and well-being: Gender differences in the psychological consequences of employment. *Journal of Health and Social Behavior, 36*, 57–71.

Reskin, B. (1993). Sex segregation in the workplace. *Annual Review of Sociology, 19*, 241–270.

Rosen, E. I. (1987). *Bitter choices: Blue collar women in and out of work.* Chicago: University of Chicago Press.

Rosenfield, S. (1980). Sex differences in depression: Do women always have higher rates? *Journal of Health and Social Behavior, 21*, 33–42.

Rosenfield, S. (1989). The effects of women's employment: Personal control and sex differences in mental health. *Journal of Health and Social Behavior, 30*, 77–91.

Ross, C. A., & Mirowsky, J. (1995). Does employment affect health? *Journal of Health and Social Behavior, 36*, 230–243.

Ross, C. A., Mirowsky, J., & Huber, J. (1983). Dividing work, sharing work, and in-between: Marriage patterns and depression. *American Sociological Review, 48*, 809–823.

Roxburgh, S. (1996). Gender differences in work and well-being: Effects of exposure and vulnerability. *Journal of Health and Social Behavior, 37*, 265–277.

Rubin, L. B. (1994). *Families on the fault line.* New York: Harper-Collins.

Ruiz, D. S. (1990). Social and economic profile of black Americans, 1989. In D. S. Ruiz (Ed.), *Handbook of mental health and mental disorder among black Americans* (pp, 3–15). New York: Greenwood Press.

Schervish, P. G. (1983). *The structural determinants of unemployment: Vulnerability and power in market relations.* New York: Academic Press.

Sears, H., & Galambos, N. L. (1992). Women's work conditions and marital adjustment in two-earner couples: A structural model. *Journal of Marriage and the Family, 54*, 789–797.

Semyonov, M., & Scott, R. I. (1983). Industrial shifts, female employment and occupational differentiation: A dynamic model for American cities, 1960–1970. *Demography, 20*, 163–176.

Simon, R. W. (1995). Gender, multiple roles, role meaning, and mental health. *Journal of Health and Social Behavior, 36*, 182–194.

Spenner, K. I. (1983). Deciphering Prometheus: Temporal change in the skill level of work. *American Sociological Review, 48*, 824–837.

Spenner, K. I. (1990). Skill: meaning, methods, and measures. *Work and Occupations, 17*, 399–421.

Starrin, B., Lunberg, B., Angelow, B., & Wall, H. (1989). Unemployment, overtime work and work intensity. In B. Starrin, P.-G. Svensson, & H. Wintersberger (Eds.), *Unemployment, poverty and quality of working life: Some European experiences* (pp 261–275). Berlin: World Health Organization, European Regional Office and the European Center for Social Welfare Training and Research, Education Service.

Tausig, M., & Fenwick, R. (1992, June). *Gender differences in the causes of worker stress.* Paper presented at the International Conference on Social Stress, Venice, Italy.

Tausig, M., & Fenwick, R. (1993). Macroeconomic and social class influences on the relationship between work and stress. *Research in Social Stratification and Mobility, 12*, 361–389.

Thoits, P. A. (1986). Multiple identities: Examining gender and marital status differences in distress. *American Sociological Review, 51*, 259–272.

Thoits, P. A. (1987). Gender and marital status differences in control and distress: Common stress versus unique stress explanations. *Journal of Health and Social Behavior, 28*, 7–22.

Tilly, C. (1991). Continuing growth of part-time employment. *Monthly Labor Review, 114*, 10–18.

Tilly, C. (1996). *Half a job: Bad and good part-time jobs in a changing labor market.* Philadelphia: Temple University Press.

Tomaskovic-Devey, D. (1993). *Gender and racial inequality at work: The sources and consequences of job segregation.* Ithaca, NY: ILR Press.

Turner, J. B. (1995). Economic context and the health effects of unemployment. *Journal of Health and Social Behavior, 36*, 213–29.

Ulbrich, P. M., Warheit, G. J., & Zimmerman, R. S. (1989). Race, socioeconomic status, and psychological distress: An examination of differential vulnerability. *Journal of Health and Social Behavior, 30*, 131–146.

U.S. Department of Labor. (1995, August). Contingent and alternative employment arrangements. USDL, Bureau of Labor Statistics Report 90. Washington, DC.

Warr, P. B., & Jackson, P. R. (1985). Factors influencing the psychological impact of prolonged unemployment and of re-employment. *Psychological Medicine, 15*, 795–807.

Wiley, M. G. (1991). Gender, work, and stress: The potential impact of role-identity salience and commitment. *Sociological Quarterly, 32*, 495–510.

Winhurst, J. A., Marcelissen, F. H., & Kleber, R. J. (1982). Effects of social support in stress-strain relationship: A Dutch sample. *Social Science and Medicine, 16*, 475–482.

Wolf, W. C., & Fligstein, N. D. (1979). Sexual stratification: Differences in power in the work setting. *Social Forces, 58*, 94–107.

Wright, E. O., & Baxter, J., with Birkelund, G. E. (1995). The gender gap in workplace authority: A cross-national study. *American Sociological Review, 60*, 407–435.

PART IV

Social Antecedents
of Mental Illness

CHAPTER 14

Social Stress

BLAIR WHEATON

INTRODUCTION

Interest in stress continues unabated. Whether we take the publication of Holmes and Rahe's life event inventory (1967) or Selye's *The Stress of Life* (1956) as the point of demarcation, it is clear that a quarter- to half-century later, we are still fascinated by this elusive yet powerful concept. As a point of reference for this chapter, I searched Sociofile from 1990 through the early months of 1997 to detect any recent trends in publications on stress. There were 2,446 articles and books published on stress in this time period. This volume of work is clear evidence of the staying power and the continuing importance of stress as a concept. Furthermore, there is no evidence over these years of a trend one way or the other; in fact, the number of articles and books published per year varied from a low of 321 in 1990 to a high of 385 in 1996, with minor fluctuations in the interim.

A basic question one might ask is why stress continues to draw this much attention. A possible reason is the strict historical visibility of this concept as a mode of explanation in the late twentieth century. But it is more than that. A second, less apparent reason is that the process of elaboration of both the concept and measurement of stress over time has led to issues that are *both* more complex and, at the same time, more clearly articulated. Thus, compared to those points of origin for the modern study of stress some 30 or 40 years ago,

BLAIR WHEATON • Department of Sociology, University of Toronto, Toronto, Ontario, Canada M5T 1P9 98.

Handbook of the Sociology of Mental Health, edited by Carol S. Aneshensel and Jo C. Phelan. Kluwer Academic/Plenum Publishers, New York, 1999.

we now know much more clearly what we *need* to know, and, I believe, we have a clearer sense of the *route* to resolution of essential issues.

Beginning with Some Conclusions

The concept of stress has been the cornerstone of a larger model now called the stress process (Pearlin, Lieberman, Menaghan, & Mullan,1981). This process articulates the social origins, sequences, circumstances, contingencies, modification, and consequences of stress exposure. In this model, stress is a central connecting link in a web of concerns, with multiple sources leading into and defining important stressful experiences, as well as multiple processes intervening after stress occurs, defining an array of possible consequences.

The elaboration of this model over time has led us to the following almost certain conclusions. First, whereas we once considered the outcomes of stress one by one, following the standard medical illness model, we now see that stress is a generalized force in mental and physical health, demanding that we simultaneously consider multiple health outcomes if we are to understand the role of stress properly (Aneshensel, Rutter, and Lachenbruch, 1991). Second, whereas we once typically conceived of stress as a starting point in a devolving health process and asked what kinds of coping helped ameliorate this problem, we now see long-term life patterns, signifying that the experience of stress is defined by social status and social location rather than emerging as a random shock to lives that forces the attention to coping with misery rather than preventing it (Pearlin, 1989; Turner, Wheaton, & Lloyd, 1995). Third, whereas we typically have asked what forms of coping helped "buffer" the impacts of given stressors, we now are beginning to understand that such questions require first that we understand which occurrences of potential stressors can be contextually defined as stressful in the first place (Brown, 1974, 1981). Fourth, whereas we once assumed that stressful life events embodied all there is to study about stress, we now regularly expect that stress will come in multiple forms and ask how different sources of stress combine in their impacts (Pearlin et al., 1981; Wheaton, 1990, 1994). Fifth, whereas we once focused on recent and current stress only, with the understanding that its impacts were probably delimited over a few years, we now search for the lifelong impacts of childhood and adolescent "traumatic" stressors, including such specific concerns as parental divorce (Amato & Keith, 1991), parental deaths (Brown, Harris, & Bifulco, 1986; Saler, 1992), family violence (Gelles & Conte, 1990; Kessler & Magee, 1994), and sexual abuse (Browne & Finkelhor, 1986; Kendall-Tackett, Williams, & Finkelhor, 1993). Finally, whereas we once studied stressors in aggregates, looking at the total effects of events, or daily hassles, or work stress per se, we now more typically look at individual stressors in different life domains and investigate how the preexistence or co-occurrence of one type of stressor changes the meaning and consequences of others (Eckenrode & Gore, 1989).

Overview of Issues

In this chapter I consider both the history and the pathways that have led us to this juncture in research on social stress, with particular focus on what has been achieved and where the future will likely take us. I consider the following issues in turn. First, I discuss the definition of social stress, focusing on problems with the concept of a social *stressor* in particular. The problematics of this concept constitute a primary source of confusion and misunderstanding in the stress literature. Second, I review the variety of stress concepts now used in the literature, and their relation to each other. This overview is important to the study of both the combined effects of multiple sources of stress and sequences of stress accumulation. Third, I discuss the unfolding of stress research and the stress literature over the last 25 years, focusing on the reasons for the emergence of recent concerns in this literature. Fourth, I speculate about the directions stress research either will, or at least should, take in the near future, in order to address fundamental outstanding issues.

This chapter does not review in representative detail the recent substantive achievements of the stress literature. There have already been at least three overviews of research in this area in this decade (Aneshensel, 1992; Thoits, 1995; Wheaton, 1994), and, in particular, Thoits (1995) updates the recent work on stress so effectively that I will not repeat here everything I concur with in her article.

DEFINING STRESS

Given the number of uncertainties attending the specification of what is stressful, the "devil's advocate" question at this point is as follows: Why try to define stress at all? Recently, Kaplan (1996) questioned the utility of using the term *stress*, perhaps in view of the complexities and uncertainties in what this term exactly refers to, as well as it boundaries. Kaplan (p. 374) concludes: "In the last analysis, the term stress may be unnecessary to accomplish analyses that are executed under the rubric of stress research." Putting aside—for the moment—the issue of the wisdom of foregoing the term *stress* entirely, it would seem advisable to have a definition of stress, as well as stressors, if we are going to use the term anyway. And we will. According to Sociofile, there is no decline in actual references to *stress* in the abstracts and keyword descriptor fields over the 1990s.

Confusion about what is meant by the term *stress* starts with confusion about the relation among concepts in the overall stress process and is enhanced by the problem of having to decide which events or life circumstances qualify as potentially stressful in developing measures of stress for research purposes. Since we *must* preselect some things to measure as potentially stressful, it seems obvious to conclude that there is no benefit of avoiding clarification of the term *stress*. In effect, we need some guidance in choosing stressors.

Models of Stress

There are at least two models of stress one could look to for guidance: the well-known biological stress model (Selye, 1956), and the stress model of engineering (Smith, 1987). Selye's biological model has four components: (1) stressors, in Selye's approach, are a wide variety of events and conditions that represented threat or insult to the organism; (2) conditioning factors that alter the impact of the stressor on the organism, as in coping resources in the psychosocial model; (3) the general adaptation syndrome (GAS), an intervening state of stress in the organism (this is the place stress actually resides in the overall process); and (4) responses, adaptive or maladaptive.

For Selye (1956), the heart of the matter of stress was the GAS itself. This syndrome was conceived of as physiological indications of a three-stage response sequence to "noxious agents": the alarm reaction, the stage of resistance, and the stage of exhaustion. Thus, Selye's primary interest was in identifying and describing a biologically based and generalized response syndrome to threatening agents. To help with the metaphor, he added that stress could be defined as the "state of wear and tear of the body" (p. 55). If it were stress per se that we had to define, there would be little problem: we already have very good definitions of stress adapted to the psychosocial realm. For example, Aneshensel (1996) defines stress as "a state of arousal arising from socioenvironmental demands that tax the ordinary adaptive capacity of the individual, or from the absence of the means to attain sought-after ends" (p. 115).

In the biological model, a stressor is seen simply as "that which produces stress" (Selye, 1956, p. 64). At this point, the problem of defining environmental agents that produce stress is reduced and tied inexorably to a physiological response. But what if these environmental agents have consequences for mental health that bypass the "necessity" of intervening stress? Do we want to restrict the realm of stressors to things that produce a stress response? If we want to allow for all posssible links between the environment and maladaptive behavioral responses we call "poor" mental health, we simply cannot begin by assuming that all such links require intervening physiological states of stress. For example, long-term work stress may undermine cognitive understandings of the self that feed depression. In this long-term process, it would be very unclear whether physiological stress occurred or was important to the outcome.

The problem we face as social scientists, then, is not the definition of stress itself but the definition of stressors, and it is this concept that we have never been able to define adequately. The result of this ambiguity is fundamental, since there is little guidance as to what should be included as stressors in research. Furthermore, if we allow that stressors can affect mental health without necessarily resulting in physiological stress, then we must define stressors without reference to this form of stress as a criterion.

Although the biological model gives no guidance in defining stressors, the engineering model—where the concept of stress began—does provide some metaphorical guidance. In this model, the stressor is essentially an external force acting against a resisting body that may or may not operate within normative limits. Thus, one could say that the stressor becomes stressful when the level of force exceeds limits defining structural integrity. To be precise about how stress is defined in this model, it is the load exerted by a force divided by the capacity of the material to resist (Smith, 1987). This definition has the benefit of saying that stressors are forces applied to a material. But there is a problem with this definition in that it assumes stress results from dividing the force applied by stressors by the current "coping capacity" of the material. This may be entirely correct for metals and wrong for humans. To be safe, our approach keeps coping as a distinct issue in the model, possibly with its own main effects. Then, we can discover whether particular levels of stressors and coping resources combine to produce deterioration in mental health by estimating interactions between them—an operation that is very close to dividing the stressor's load by current capacity (Wheaton, 1996)—or whether their combined effect is simply additive and counteractive (which is not implied by the engineering model).

The engineering model includes the concept of "elastic limit" to distinguish situations in which a stressor occurs at nonthreatening levels of force from those in which the level of the stressor exceeds the material's usual capacity to adjust without changing shape. This elastic limit is literally the coping capacity of the individual in the human stress model. It is important to see that as long as we measure this coping capacity in conjunction with potential stressors, we do not need to decide a priori what level of the stressor stands for exceeding the elastic limit of individuals.

What Stressors Are—and Are Not

Taking the notion of an external force or pressure as a point of departure, we can define a stressor as a *condition of threat, demand, or structural constraint that, by its very occurrence or existence, calls into question the operating integrity of the organism.* This definition implies that stressors can occur in different ways, each still standing for a source of environmental force or pressure. *Threats* involve the possibility or expectation of potential harm. *Demands* involve the load component of stressors, also commonly referred to as "burden," or "overload." The sense of being "pushed" by current life circumstances reflects this component of stressors. Finally, *structural constraints* stand for reduced opportunities, choices, or alternatives resulting from severe or non-self-limiting social disadvantage. The structural constraints referred to here are features of social structure and thus are a function of social location. Classic concerns with insufficient means to attain goals, discrimination, underreward in social exchange (such as pay at work), or role captivity, are, by this definition, forms of social stress.

There are both theoretical and practical restrictions on what can be defined as stressors. First, some events or situations are typically incapable of providing sufficient challenge to most people to be considered potential stressors in the first place. It is important that we avoid a commonly stated misunderstanding about stress, namely, that "*Life* is stressful," implying that everything is a form of stress. Rather, a stressor must be an event or situation that *would* challenge the integrity of the organism *if applied at levels beyond the current elastic limit of the organism.* This statement implies further that stressors occur naturally as continuous variables (i.e., the force or pressure resulting from the occurrence of an event or the presence of a difficult situation). We sometimes mistakenly think that we should predesignate the threshold at which the force becomes stressful. All we must do is measure the level of *potential stressors,* and then, in conjunction with a full understanding of both contextual factors and coping resources, observe by their consequences whether an elastic limit has been exceeded.

This discussion implies that there are two forms of nonstressors: events or situations that are inherently weak forces in providing a challenge to the organism, and potential stressors that occur below a threshold of importance as a problem. The former include the vicissitudes of daily life, the small, self-limiting problems that arise and dissipate naturally and over a short time span. The latter include such things as job losses, when the job was disliked, or when followed immediately by a new job, small increases in the unemployment rate, the loss of an ambivalent relationship, the death of a relative that one barely knows, or occasional and resolvable marital conflicts.

Consider a concrete example of these distinctions. If a particular program on your personal computer (PC) does not run, or continually crashes, this could be considered a subthreshold problem. It *can* be resolved fairly straightforwardly: Either remove the program, or find another that works. If your PC crashes entirely, but you have a backup of all your work, we could call this a potential stressor with contextual information suggesting it is not an important stressor in this case. Finally, if your PC crashes and none of your work or data are backed up, this *could* be considered a stressor.

Second, if we want to measure stress as a generalized threat to health in a general population, there are practical limitations to the number of potential stressors we can consider. Implicitly, we try to consider stressors that fall above some threshold of total impact on the health of a population—some multiplicative function of the prevalence of the stressor and its average seriousness. This strategy allows for both extremely traumatic and serious stressors that may be quite rare and more moderate forms of stress that affect a broader segment of the population. What is excluded are idiosyncratic or highly specific stressors that are unique to individuals, and stressors that generally fall below the current elastic limit of most of the population.

The issue of violence provides a concrete example. Imagine three different versions of violence we may want to consider in a general assessment of stress exposure: having something thrown at you once or twice in your life, occasional hitting or slapping by a partner, and regular physical abuse as a child. These forms of victimization differ in prevalence. Assuming a hypothetical scenario, that we know that about 80% of the population reports something being thrown at them at least once in their life, we might conclude that the problem is so general and so "normative" that it is difficult to imagine that it could have a serious impact on mental health. Imagining further that the prevalence of occasional hitting is 20% in ongoing relationships, and regular childhood physical abuse occurs in less than 10% of the population, it is probably the case that we would want to consider both of these problems as potential stressors.

This definition treats stressors in generic form, but in fact, they come in a number of distinct forms. When we allow for distinctions in terms of types of stressors, there are a number of important implications in how we treat stress as an explanation of health differences. The three most important are that: (1) we thus allow for investigation of the effects of stress sequences over time and through lives, and accordingly, we expand our time focus from recent or current stress to the implications of stress in early stages of life; (2) attention is given to the nature and form of the combined effects of separate stressors; and (3) we allow for distinct phenomenologies for different stressors and thus can pose further questions about distinct forms of coping responses, consequences, and so on. In the next section, I differentiate stressors into distinct forms.

VARIETIES OF STRESS

When the word *stress* is used in research circles, the most common operational link that gives expression to this word is the life change event, a discrete, observable, and "objectively" reportable *event* that requires some social and/or psychological adjustment on the part of the individual—the operant word here being *event*. It is this type of event that is targeted by numerous, famous inventories intended to measure stress (e.g., Holmes & Rahe, 1967; Dohrenwend, Krasnoff, Askenasz, & Dohrenwend, 1978).

The association between the notion of a "life event" and the concept of stress is so strong that we sometimes deny that other forms of stress may be stress at all, or we strain to find events in stressors that in no way qualify as such. For example, Monroe and Roberts (1990) reflect the assumption that "events" are the sine qua non of stress in the following passage: "It may seem that life events are self-evident. Yet life is a continuous flow of experiences and transactions. Determining at what point ongoing experience becomes an event can be problematic" (p. 211). Although the correct problem is identified, the need to transform a continuous reality into a discrete event leads to the wrong conclusion. The assumption that stressors must occur as events at all is wholly questionable. Fundamentally, a stressor can exist as a "state," a continuous reality. It need not start as an event but may evolve slowly.

Both the biological and engineering stress models suggest the necessity of distinguishing types of stress based on the typical discrete versus continuous nature of their occurrence. The stressors in Selye's (1956) biological research included such things as toxic substances, noise, extreme heat or cold, injury, and weight. Although there are some agents here that qualify as "events," it is also clear that some qualify as conditions or continuous states. This distinction is generally reflected in biological research since that time (Hinkle, 1987). A fundamental point of the engineering model is that stress occurs in more than one form, sometimes as a catastrophic event, and sometimes as a continuous force. Futhermore, stress that occurs as a trauma to the material acts inherently differently than stress that acts as a continuous load on the material. A bridge may collapse because of high winds beyond designed tolerance or by long-term rusting that leads to a point of fundamental breakdown of structural integrity.

Events versus Chronic Stressors

As stressors, life events have the following characteristics: They are discrete, observable events standing for significant life changes, with a relatively clear onset and offset, and made up of, once in motion, a relatively well-defined set of subevents describing the "normal" progress of the event. The defining issue in a life event is its discreteness. Typically, life events do not slowly emerge as an issue; rather, they begin with the announcement of the unfortunate news that begins the life change. As stressors, they typically have a clear offset, a point at which the stressor ends, for example, the court settlement of the divorce, or the actual last day of work, or the actual death of the spouse. The fact that events take time to come to fruition has been well-documented by Avison and Turner (1988).

Taking events as a point of departure, then, we can define a very different class of stressors, referred to as *chronic stressors,* that (1) do not necessarily start as an event but develop slowly and insidiously as continuing and problematic conditions in our social environments or roles, and (2) typically have a longer time course than life events from onset to resolution.

The crux of the distinction between event stressors and chronic stressors is the time course of the stressor, but there are other aspects as well, including differences in the ways in which the stressor develops, exists, and ends. First, chronic stressors often develop insidiously, leaving the individual with the definite sense of a problem but little understanding of how it developed or when it started. Second, chronic stressors are continuous in an approximate sense, standing for problems and issues that so regularly occur in the enactment of daily roles and activities, or are defined by the nature of daily roles and activities, that they behave as if they are continuous for the individual. Finally, chronic stressors are also less self-limiting in nature than the typical life event. A life event, almost by definition, will end, whereas chronic stressors are typically open-ended, using up our resources in coping but not promising resolution. In Pearlin's words these are "the enduring problems, conflicts, and threats that many people face in their daily lives" (Pearlin, 1989, p. 245).

There is, of course, the inevitable fact that some life events will be more chronic than others, and some chronic stressors will act more like discrete problems. This overlap in phenomenology is not at issue. Some stressors may begin like an event, with sudden news, or a clear change, but then become open-ended and protracted. This situation describes what *could* be considered a borderline case, a hybrid. But in many cases in which this development of a stressor is the scenario, it is likely that two stressors, and not one, have occurred, and they have, in effect, been "spliced" together. For example, the distinction between event stressors and chronic stressors allows us to see that the *loss* of another and the *absence* of another are distinct stressors.

The Stress Continuum

Contrasting the idea of an event with the idea of a continuous force allows us to anchor two ends of a "stress continuum" (Wheaton, 1994), along which other commonly used stress concepts in the literature can be arrayed. This continuum, defined by a range from discrete to continuous, simply makes the point that stressors vary in their phenomenology, and thus, indirectly, that the assessment of the overall impact of stressors on health requires variability in the form in which stressors occur.

DAILY HASSLES.   A concept that is often mistaken for chronic stress is daily hassles (Kanner, Coyne, Schaefer, & Lazarus, 1981). The focus in this type of stress is on "the relatively minor stresses . . . that characterize everyday life" (p. 2). Daily hassles are defined as "the irritating, frustrating, distressing demands that to some degree characterize everyday transactions with the environment" (p. 3). An important phrase is the qualifying "to some degree." It is possible to argue that there is considerable variability in the degree to which the daily hassles used in measures are regular features of daily life.

The Daily Hassles Scale itself has been the subject of some controversy. Complaints that a significant number of items are really measures of other concepts in the stress process model, including outcomes such as distress, seem all too valid (Dohrenwend, Dohrenwend, Dodson, & Shrout, 1984). For example, items such as "thoughts about death," "use of alcohol," "being lonely," "not getting enough sleep," and "not enough personal energy" are clearly measures of distress or related concepts—many of these items existing in almost the same form on well-known distress scales. Other items sound very much like life events, for example, "laid off or out of work," or "problems with divorce or separation," while a large number indeed reflect standard chronic stress items but have little to do with the stated definition of daily hassles as minor for example, "difficulties getting pregnant," "overloaded with family responsibilities," and "prejudice and discrimination from others." The problem with this measure, then, is that it attempts to be too inclusive, although starting from a clear but more delimited conceptual mandate. There are indeed a number of items on the Daily Hassles Scale that operationalize this concept straightforwardly, for example, "troublesome neighbors," "misplacing or losing things," "care for a pet," "planning meals," "repairing things around the house," "having to wait," "too many interruptions," "filling out forms," "the weather," and "traffic problems."

The concerns expressed in these items nicely express the mundane realities of daily life that, when experienced cumulatively, could be quite stressful. But note that they do not consistently refer only to *regular* features of daily life. Some items clearly refer to the almost automatic or ritualized concerns of daily life and thus may be more chronic in their manifestations (e.g., troublesome neighbors, preparing meals, and grocery shopping). Such issues are defined as chronic by the unavoidability of their enactment. At the same time, a number of these items refer to more episodic, irregular, microevents that cannot be anticipated daily and only occur contingently (e.g., "misplacing or losing things," "having to wait," or "the weather"). In the case of each of these items, the usual scenario would be that the problem occurs at some times, and not others, and usually unpredictably.

Thus, daily hassles span a middle range of the stress continuum, from a border at the event end of recurrent microevents to a border at the chronic end, involving a set of scheduled and ritualized life concerns that still happen as a set of distinct occurrences.

NONEVENTS.   Gersten, Langner, Eisenferg, and Orzeck (1974) use arousal theory to point out that lack of change can be as stressful as change. They use this point, however, not to suggest the importance of chronic stressors, but a closely related kind of stressor that they term *nonevents* (p. 169). They define a nonevent as an "event that is desired or anticipated and does not occur. . . . Alternatively, a nonevent could be seen as something desirable which does not occur when its occurrence is normative for people of a certain group" (p. 169). Thus, an anticipated promotion that does not occur, or not being married by a certain age, can be considered nonevents. These examples raise the clear possibility that non-events are a form of chronic stressor. But nonevents have the additional ironic quality of seeming like events at the same time. For example, it takes the *possibility* of a change for a "nonevent" to occur. In a sense, the event is the passing of a point in time at which an expected event would happen. This quality is clearest in the case of nonevents that reflect the absence of expected events with a time limit, or events with normative and expected scheduling in the life course.

Nonevents that derive from nontransitions to desired roles that are *not* tied to normative timing, on the other hand, seem more clearly like classic chronic stressors. Even the absence of a promotion could be seen as role captivity, the inability to leave or alter a given role situation. In these situations, it is the unwanted waiting for an outcome or the very lack of change that becomes the problem. Seen from this perspective, they look very much like a type of chronic stressor.

Nonevents can be placed close to the chronic (i.e., continuous) end of the stress continuum. But because these stressors often involve regular or scheduled considerations of change, it is likely they are not as continuous in form as chronic stressors, where the problem is more intractable, open-ended, and difficult to escape.

TRAUMAS.   Some stressors are thought to be so serious, so overwhelming in their potential for impact, that they tend to be given separate status as stressors. The most applicable term for these stressors is *traumas*.

The third, revised edition of the *Diagnostic and Statistical Manual of Mental Disorders* (DSM-III-R) defines a traumatic event as one "that is outside the range of usual human experience and... would be markedly distressing to almost anyone" (American Psychiatric Association, 1987, p. 250). This definition emphasizes one of the essential characteristics distinguishing traumas from the kinds of events commonly seen in life event inventories: the magnitude of the stressor. Norris (1992) defines traumas in terms of a population of events marked by a sudden or extreme force and denoting "violent encounters with nature, technology, or humankind " (p. 409). Both this definition and the DSM-III-R definition point to important classes of traumas, but they are incomplete. First, not all traumas occur as events. For example, a single rape would be considered a traumatic event, but repeated, regular, and therefore expected sexual abuse is best thought of as a chronic traumatic *situation*. Including chronic situations allows us to broaden the definition to encompass Terr's (1991) consideration of both events and situations marked by "prolonged and sickening anticipation" (p. 11). Second, and obviously, not all traumas need be violent; some, like having a life-threatening illness, or a partner ending an important and valued romantic relationship, need not involve violence at all.

Thus, we can see a number of elements of traumas that are important: (1) They must be more severe in level of threat than other sources of stress; (2) they may occur either as isolated events or long-term, chronic problems; and (3) because of their severity, they are thought to have greater potential for long-term impacts than most other types of stressors.

Traumas include a potentially wide range of severe situations and events, such as war stress (Laufer, Gallops, & Frey-Wouters, 1984), natural disasters (Erickson, 1976), sexual abuse or assault during childhood or adulthood (Burnam et al., 1988; Kendall-Tackett et al., 1993), physical violence and abuse (Bryer, Nelson, Miller, & Krol, 1987; Gelles & Conte, 1990; Kessler & Magee, 1994), parental death (Brown et al., 1986; McLeod, 1991; Saler, 1992), and parental divorce (Glenn & Kramer, 1985; Amato & Keith, 1991).

The archetypal form of a trauma—characterized by a sudden, unanticipated, dramatic, and profoundly threatening experience—suggests that these stressors often occur as the most discrete form of stress on the stress continuum. Traumas of this sort include living through a natural disaster, a sexual assault, the unexpected and sudden death of a partner, victimization in a violent crime, and severe accidents. But it is also important to realize that some of the most important traumas in life may occur as a series of recurring and expected events that begin to be chronic in form, with the victim living with the belief and the fear that the next event could occur at any time. These kinds of traumatic situations act very much like chronic stress and could constitute the single most virulent form of stressful experience.

ECOLOGICAL STRESSORS.   I have previously used the term *macrostressors* or *system stressors* to refer generally to stressors occurring at units of analysis above the individual (Wheaton, 1994). The classic treatments of stressors of this type focus on macroeconomic problems, especially as embodied by changes in the unemployment rate (Brenner, 1974; Dooley & Catalano, 1984). Recent work points to the fact that there are many more levels of social organization to consider. Aneshensel and Sucoff (1996a) focus on the neighborhood as a source of *contextual* stressors. This is in fact an appropriate and general designation for this source of stress, but unfortunately the term *contextual* also is used to stand for current social circumstances at the individual level (Brown, 1981). Reynolds (1997) focuses on economic sectors as the contextual level, and there are many other possibilities—organizations, schools, voluntary groups, cities, social networks—all of which define social units with contextual relevance to individual behavior. Thus, one could refer to stressors that occur at any level of social unit above the individual as *ecological* stressors.

The recent discussion of combined models of ecological and individual level stressors by Aneshensel and Sucoff (1996b) suggests the importance of considering ecological stressors as integral to understanding the effects even of individual-level stressors. Just as we could claim that the influence of life events on mental health will be misspecified and misunderstood unless we take into account more chronic forms of stress, it is important to be clear that the same could be said if we exclude the influence of ecological stressors.

As a group, these stressors contain both acute and chronic concerns. Macrostressors clearly span a broad range of discrete occurrences (disasters) to chronic conditions (recessions, crime). For every macroevent stressor, there seems to be corresponding chronic version. A military coup is a macroevent, while a war is macrochronic stressor. In the economic sphere, a stock market crash is a macroevent, while a prolonged recession acts more like a chronic stressor.

A Two-Way Classification of Stressors

The concept of a stress continuum distinguishing the phenomenology of stressors has been introduced before (Wheaton, 1994; 1996). One can also array stressors by the level or unit of analysis at which they occur. Using the unit of analysis as the distinguishing feature of a second dimension crosscutting the stress continuum, one can imagine *layers* of stress extending from the individual level to the level of the social system, with variation at each level in the chronicity–discreteness of stressors to be considered.

Figure 14.1 gives a general scheme of how this two-way classification might look. On the horizontal dimension, we can distinguish stressors by their (typical) chronicity. Many stressors have a built-in, natural history, ritualized by a social process. Thus, at the extreme discrete end of the stress continuum at the micro, that is, individual level, we have one-time, sudden, unanticipated events, such as a sexual assault, or the death of a child in a car accident. Slightly less acute is a range of typical "life events," such as a job loss, or a divorce. These events often involve some anticipation, and some defined process that follows the event to fruition. Daily hassles represent a "borderline" form of stress, as discussed earlier, depending on their episodic versus regular and ritualized nature. At the more chronic end, we have demands in a long-term caretaking role, built-in noisome conditions at a job, or the cumulative work and parenting demands of a single mother. In each case, the problem posed by the stressor is structured as part of a social process, and thus is likely to operate as a chronic life condition.

Figure 14.1 shows an intermediate unit of analysis containing *meso*stressors, a term standing for sources of stress between the individual and the systemic level. Potentially, there are many mesolevels: Taking a child as the target issue, we can consider the school as an aggregate context, within a neighborhood or other geopolitical region, within a whole community or city, within a state, and so on. Although many ecological forms of stress may be chronic, because they depend on the form of social organization, there will also be ecological "events" that mark important sources of stress at the individual level—such as the shooting of elementary school students in a school yard. At the more chronic end, we have disorder in the classroom, visible minority status in a predominantly majority school, and forms of social disorder in neighborhoods (Aneshensel & Sucoff, 1996a). In organiza-

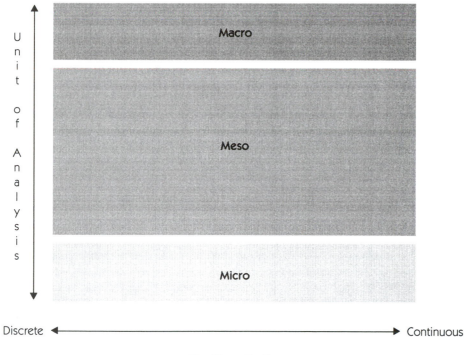

FIGURE 14.1. A two-way classification of stressors.

tions, an event stressor might involve the merger of one company with another; more chronic stressors involve issues such as the ratio of client demands to available staff. At the macrolevel in Figure 14.1, we have the classic concerns with the economy mentioned earlier, but we also can and should consider political, military, and social events and conditions that act as societal stressors. These include issues such as a governmental coup (event), a civil war (chronic stressor), widespread poverty (chronic stressor), loss of rights (event), secession of part of a country (event), the continual threat of secession (chronic stressor), and symbolic macroevents that indicate deep social differences (the O.J. Simpson trial).

By considering stress as a multilevel issue, we gain the possibility of investigating the effects of the conjunction of stressors across levels (Aneshensel & Sucoff, 1996b). This orientation may be extremely important if we discover that the meaning, and therefore effects, of individual stressors are inherently dependent on contextual stressors at higher levels of social organization.

PAST AND FUTURE

To understand the current state and prospects of stress research, it is necessary to consider how far we have come. Indeed, we rarely stop to consider the actual conceptual and empirical achievements already embodied by an existing literature. In this section, I consider the history of the social stress literature, with an admittedly personal perspective on the evolution of this literature. My intention is tell a story that will make clear both the current problems stress research faces and the likely directions it will take.

The Life Events Era

It is difficult to choose a starting point for such a complex literature, but it is at least convenient to restrict our attention to the latter half of the twentieth century. One can cite either Selye's publication of the *The Stress of Life* in 1956, or the 1949 Conference on Life Stress and Bodily Disease, following up on Cannon's (1929) earlier work on bodily reactions in stressful situations. Both approaches outline stress as a bodily response to a set of external agents.

Although the landmark publication of Holmes and Rahe's (1967) life events scale is often seen as the impetus behind the diffusion of research on social sources of stress, it is probably more relevant to remember the very important Midtown Manhattan study published in the late 1950s and early 1960s, especially Langner and Michael's (1963) *Life Stress and Mental Health*. In fact, if this book had had greater influence across disciplines, much of the later myopia of stress research could have been avoided. A basic reason for this assertion is that Langner and Michael use a broad set of stress indicators that, as a whole, reflect a prescience about the *eventual* treatment of stress as a multidimensional concept. The stressors considered include parental poor physical health, childhood economic deprivation, coming from a "broken" home, poor adult interpersonal relations, and current work worries. Two points can be observed: The stressors emphasize more chronic forms of stress, and they span the life course, rather than emphasizing only recent experience. The fact that some of these stressors are problematic because they refer to "worries"—possibly a symptom of anxiety or other outcomes—is less important than what is being worried *about*.

Obviously, the Holmes and Rahe (1967) life events inventory was one of the single most influential publications and measures in the history of stress research. This inventory had a number of advantages over other approaches: It referred, in simple item format, to objectively verifiable events (mostly), it could be administered in just a few minutes, it incorporated the possibility of the differential importance of events, it attempted to incorporate a list of what was thought to be the most important and prevalent stressful events occurring in a broad population, and it embodied the prevailing view developing at the time that the heart of stress was in the related notions of crisis and change. The reported effect of life crises on schizophrenia around the same time (Brown & Birley, 1968), and the ensuing large-scale research program of the Dohrenwends (Dohrenwend & Dohrenwend 1969, 1970, 1974; Dohrenwend et al., 1978) provided much of the impetus for research on life events.

Soon, it became commonplace to invoke some life events inventory as the operationalization of the concept of social stress. In fact, the use of life events as a measure of stress exposure overall became *so* automatic that, collectively, we forgot the distinction between the measure and the concept. Thus, when findings using life events were modest, if not disappointing, many reasons were suggested, but the fact that events may not capture everything that is stressful was rarely cited.

In fact, as we now know, the findings *were* surprisingly modest (Rabkin & Streuning, 1976; Thoits, 1983), and it was clear that the issue of properly specifying the effect of social stress was much more complex than even the most sophisticated early researchers had imagined. Although the hypothesis of differential weights for the events made intuitive sense, little research accumulated to suggest that such normative weighting made much of a difference. A basic question arose at this point in the history of stress research—a question that I believe was the fundamental impetus to much of the research on stress over the last two decades: How can stress, theoretically assumed to be of central if not definitive importance in the social explanation of mental health, be so modestly related to mental health outcomes in most research?

The fact of modest findings was in fact a fortuitous event for stress research. If anything, the research traditions that have followed from that question have collectively been more important than the original concern. The "problem" of modest correlations with health led to four central hypotheses in stress research. Three of these hypotheses posit that the observed modest correlations mask differential effects of stress of some sort, so that some people are subject to very large impacts, while others experience no effects at all. Obviously, for both theoretical and applied reasons, this explanation would offer an important alternative view to the modest findings as of 1980. The essential question then becomes: Why are some people immune to stressors, while others are very sensitive to them?

FOUR HYPOTHESES.   The four hypotheses can be stated in general terms as follows:

The Trait Hypothesis.   Thoits (1983) observed, following Dohrenwend and Dohrenwend (1974) and others, that different types of events have different characteristics as stressors. Obviously, they vary in undesirability as events but typically, they also vary in level of controllability, in how expected or scheduled, how serious and so on. If we could specify and find the subset of events that most embody what is stressful, by distinguishing events in terms of these "traits," we could discover both the full impact of stress and the most essential stressors. This hypothesis rests, to some degree, on the level of between-event variability, averaged across people, which may be smaller than between-person variability in the meaning of events. However, in fact, the full possibilities of this hypothesis, in conjunction with individual variability, have never been fully studied.

The Differential Vulnerability Hypothesis.   Kessler's (1979) introduction into the mental health literature of the decomposition of social class differences in distress into components due to stress exposure versus differential vulnerability to stress represented a general statement of a hypothesis with many variants, all sharing the idea that differences in resources—coping, constitutional, social, personal—left some people more vulnerable to the effects of stress than others. Of course, the popular term *stress buffering* had already been widely used to stand for the differential impact of stress based on coping resources or strategies. This hypothesis has drawn widespread attention throughout the last two decades of stress research, focusing especially on social support, as a social resource, and a sense of personal control over life outcomes as a personal resource. The general differential vulnerability approach also includes other possible resources that differentiate susceptibility, including biological factors.

The Context Hypothesis.   Another way of approaching the issue is to imagine that when stressors occur, they represent different levels of threat across individuals, depending on the context in which they occur. Thus, some occurrences of stressors may not be that stressful, given the right context, while other occurrences may be very virulent. George Brown's (1974, 1981) work in this area defined the agenda for understanding the differential meaning of stressors based on life circumstances and conditions leading up to and surrounding the event. This approach was originally concerned with "weeding out" trivial events, rather than looking at differential effects per se. However, it is possible to treat context as a separate set of variables in its own right, with separate main effects on health. Thus, the context hypothesis has grown in importance with time as it has become clear that there are many forms of context to consider, including *biographical context* (Wheaton, 1990), referring to how earlier life experience will in part define the meaning of current events, as well as *social context* (Aneshensel and Sucoff, 1996b), referring to the effects of social system conditions and events on responses to stressors at the individual level.

The Stress Domain Hypothesis.   Realizing that there are multiple forms of stress makes clear why findings using only life events may be considered partial. The explicit use of multiple stress concepts was incorporated into the original stress process model (Pearlin, Lieberman, Menaghan, & Mullan, 1981). Around the same time, other approaches distinguished more acute, or event, forms of stress, from ongoing or chronic forms (Brown & Harris, 1978; Wheaton, 1980, 1983). Research using multiple varieties of stress tends to suggest that they have independent effects, while being related in sequences of exposure as well (Wheaton, 1994). Since no one source of stress will capture the full impact of the stress domain, we can readily see why events alone may produce modest findings. Perhaps more importantly, the stress domain hypothesis suggests, together with the context hypothesis, that the effects of events may depend essentially on the history of other sources of similar or dissimilar stressors, including childhood traumas, current chronic stressors, and ecological stressors in the workplace or neighborhood.

Each of these four hypotheses was intended to suggest a more complete specification of "stressfulness." Each set in motion an agenda and a tradition of research, although the trait hypothesis was mainly a concern of the 1970s. It is now clear that the early 1980s was a pivotal period in stress research, since the increasing complexity of specifying stressfulness coincided with the introduction of a more general, overarching framework for stress research—the stress process model.

The Stress Process Era

In 1981, Pearlin and his colleagues published an integrative and multidimensional model of how stress works (Pearlin et al., 1981; see Chapter 19, this volume). The stress process model is a generalized view of the social processes leading to and flowing from the occurrence of stress, including social origins for stress, multiple roles for the intervention of coping resources, the differentiation of stressors into types that can be interrelated in sequences of exposure over time, and a range of interrelated outcomes, only one of which is mental health per se. It is a model describing both the *rooting* and the *routing* of stress.

A number of innovations accompanied the introduction of this model and its elaboration through the 1980s (Pearlin, 1989). First, the stress process model explicitly included multiple types of stress operating in a sequence of stress accumulation. Most notably, Pearlin and associates (1981) demonstrated the central role of chronic stressors in addition to the usual emphasis on life event stressors. Second, until then, few articles had simultaneously considered the roles of both social support and personal resources as buffers in the stress process. Third, Pearlin elaborated the notion of stress buffering, which had usually been applied to the reduction of impacts of stress on health outcomes per se, to include the possibility of the reduction of the impacts of earlier stressors on later stressors. Thus, stress buffering could occur at a number of points in a multistage process. Fourth, the stress process model emphasized that stressors are socially embedded: they arise from the conditions that accompany social position and social disadvantage. Fifth, the stress process model disaggregated stress and considered specific stressors rather than the more common practice of assessing total exposure across a number of stressors. Finally, as the model grew with time, increasing heterogeneity and generality of outcomes were considered as appropriate in stress research (Aneshensel, 1996; Aneshensel et al., 1991).

The 1980s was a decade of many coexisting traditions involving the intensive study of the stress-buffering role of both social and personal coping resources, the differentiation of stress concepts, and the study of various forms of context—social, situational, biographical—in determining the stress potential of putative stressors. Thus, the stress process was timely in part because it allowed a larger perspective, another power of the microscope, when much of the focus on research was on well-defined but delimited issues. At the same time, the message that the stress process was itself complex became clear as the decade progressed. For example, it became clear that many variants of personal or social resources may act in a stress-buffering role, but the relationship among these resources was (and still is) unclear. Furthermore, the causal ordering of resources and stressors clearly became an essential issue, since the role of coping in preventing stress consequences changes radically depending on the causal sequence (Barrera, 1981; Ensel & Lin, 1991; Wheaton, 1985). The issue of sequencing led to a large number of questions about stress that helped form the focus of research in the 1980s: The preexisting state of a resource could deter stress from occurring, the current state of a resource could buffer stress—in the sense of preventing the impact of stress when it occurred; the level of the resource could be affected by the stressor and thus either suppress or explain the effect of stress; and the resource could change after mental health had already been affected and thus act to counteract the stress only after it had had an effect.

Recent and Future Directions

Research in the 1990s includes a number of overlapping and interdependent themes. What is clear at this point in the history of stress research is that the benefits of questions raised in earlier decades are coming to fruition. Stress is now seen as a central node in a process with many starting points (Turner et al., 1995) and many consequences (Aneshensel, 1996).

As mentioned earlier, in attempting to gauge developing themes in stress research, I reviewed Sociofile for the years 1990–1997. Other than the fact that there has been a steady blizzard of articles on stress, indicating at least that academic interest in this subject is far from waning, I also reviewed changes over time in the content of stress articles. For example, for each year, I counted articles dealing with social support, coping in general, stress buffering per se, contextual issues, the life course, chronic stress, life events, and traumas. Interestingly, the emphasis over this period did not shift away from coping issues at all, nor did it shift toward contextual or life-course issues. The fact is, the relative frequency of these issues was stable throughout this period.

There is one major exception to this conclusion. The focus on traumas as a form of stress, and especially on childhood and adolescent traumas, was an explicit focus of only 14% of the articles covered in 1990, increasing to 40% by 1993, and reaching 60% or more by 1996 and 1997. This is remarkable growth in the explicit recognition of this source of stress as an issue. There are probably many reasons for this trend, but three should be mentioned. First, there was already a strong focus on this type of stress in the psychiatric literature in the 1980s. Second, as with the shift in framing of many issues, the fact that an early age of onset of many disorders was being established as a "known fact" in community epidemiological research (Kessler et al., 1994; Robins et al., 1984) suggested strongly a reorientation of concern about social origins to earlier stages of life. Third, the development and importance of the life-course perspective in sociology (Elder, George, & Shanahan, 1996) made possible a sociological orientation in explaining linked events in lives without reference necessarily to the psychodynamic and/or developmental approaches in psychology. In summary, the prevalent focus in stress research on *current and/or recent* stressors has proven to be both unnecessary and misleading, especially considering the fact that more remote traumatic stressors are likely to have indirect effects on mental health through the change in risk of more recent stressors (Kessler & Magee, 1994; Wheaton, 1994). In fact, the whole issue of the proliferation of stress—from the spread of primary stressors to the occurrence of secondary stressors—has been a continuing theme of the stress process model, and suggests the general importance of studying the indirect effects of stressors over time (Pearlin, Aneshensel, & LeBlanc, 1997). An important consequence of this approach is a concern with stress "starting points" in the long-term devolution of functioning.

The increased interest in traumatic stress may reflect a number of incipient and ongoing themes in stress research that, I believe, will form the primary agendas of stress research into the twenty-first century. Here, I focus on five areas: (1) contextual specification of the stressfulness of events and chronic conditions; (2) life-course approaches to the linkages, sequencing, and timing of stress and coping over lives; (3) disaggregation of stressors and the study of interdependence across stress domains; (4) study of the social origins of stress; and (5) concern with the proper specification of stress outcomes and full consideration of multiple outcomes. This list partially overlaps with the future directions noted by Thoits (1995), as it should. It should also be clear that these five issues are not independent of each other. For example, the interest in contextual specification is encouraged by the popularity of life-course perspectives since we can consider earlier life experience as a type of context for current problems.

How does a concern with traumas reflect these themes? Traumas form part of the life-history context of recent stressors, change the timing and likelihood of crucial life transitions, interact with other forms of stress concurrently and over time, draw attention to social origins through the concept of the "matrix of disadvantage," and have multiple outcomes and life-course pathways that each may increase or decrease the chances of optimal mental health in adulthood (Rutter, 1989). Thus, traumas, as an issue, are at the juncture of multiple concerns in the current stress literature.

FIVE THEMES.   I turn now to a brief consideration of the importance of these five themes in research on stress processes.

Multiple Outcomes. Aneshensel and colleagues (1991) have demonstrated the need for considering the multiple possible outcomes of stress. Fundamentally, the problem with the single outcome approach is that it could misrepresent and misspecify the actual impacts of stress across social groups. For example, if depression is studied on its own and women report more depression than men, it is likely that women will be seen as more vulnerable to stress than men. If we consider a range of mental health outcomes, including substance abuse, this may not be the case. Or the effect of getting married may appear to favor men if only one outcome is considered; this may be less apparent when multiple outcomes are considered (Horwitz, White, & Howell-White, 1996).

Recently, Aneshensel (1996) has expanded this theme to a consideration of the full universe of stress outcomes. Aneshensel properly notes that there is no need, nor is it wise, to consider only mental health or functioning outcomes of stress exposure. Stress may lead to behaviors that are considered perfectly healthy, such as enhancing achievement–striving, or at least socially acceptable, such as conspicuous consumption (Aneshensel, 1996). In general, stress exposure should be seen as an essential part of the model determining (coping) resource acquisition and maintenance. As pointed out earlier, stressors can also lead to the spread of stress in lives (Pearlin, Mullan, Semple, & Skaff, 1990), and this fact in and of itself reflects an important public health focus of stress research.

This type of work is signaling the development of a more comprehensive model of stress impacts. This model includes effects of stress on resources, on the spread of stressors, on others as stress contagion, and indirectly, on life outcomes via mental health changes. This last point deserves careful consideration in further research, since it reconceptualizes what is *usually* posited to be social selection. If the indirect effect starts with the emergence of a stressor, then biological interpretations of social selection findings would be inappropriate. Finally, we need to consider the possible effects of stress on life-course outcomes that *bypass* changes in mental health.

Social Origins. Pearlin (1989) argues for the importance of understanding the social embeddedness of stressors. Although some stressors occur randomly in the population, many of the most potent forms of stress are socially patterned (Aneshensel, 1992), a function of social position, or more generally, social location.

Recently, Turner and associates (1995) have mapped some of these social origins, focusing on the "classic" social group differences in mental health, including gender, social class, and marital status. Wheaton and Hall (1996) consider comprehensive differences in stress exposure and resource deficits as potential explanations of four sociodemographic differences—gender, age, income, and marital status—and find that stress exposure plays an equal role with resource deficits in explaining social group differences. In the case of gender, stress exposure differences are central to the explanation. Thus, research into social origins makes clear that stress is part of a larger social process that creates or maintains "emotional inequality" as a function of social inequality.

If we begin with stress as the problem to be addressed, the impression is that stress is endemic, ubiquitous, and beyond social or personal control. This is not the case. By focusing purely on the consequences of stress, we mistakenly believe that stress itself is the origin of the problem. Research on the social foundations of stress experience is therefore essential to the proper specification and interpretation of stress consequences, including the possibility that some of the effects of stress may be spurious in view of more fundamental causation.

In fact, research into the social origins of stress exposure reflects a fundamental cornerstone hypothesis of the whole research agenda on social stress. It may be helpful to recognize that the 1970s and the 1980s deflected attention temporarily to the issue of specification of the effect of stress itself.

Disaggregation and Interdependence.   Early applications of stress measures emphasized the concept of "total burden" by adding up exposure across items representing diverse stress experiences. The recent and growing tendency is to consider individual stressors. This approach is most clear in the numerous parallel literatures on different forms of traumatic stress, each focusing on the unique issues arising due to the content and context of that particular stressor. Thus, recent research tends to focus on sexual assault or parental death, or job loss, or divorce, or war stress, but not all at once.

There are strengths and shortcomings in each of these approaches, and ultimately they are not in competition. The total exposure approach is intended to measure total stress load *without* regard to content. In fact, the effects of content are likely to be canceled somewhat when different stressors are added up and considered in total. At the same time, there is a point to considering stressors individually, since only then do we learn whether, and which, stressors act as important starting points of stress proliferation or act as fundamental causes of mental health differences, or of life-course outcomes.

The primary problem with focusing on individual stressors is the tendency to see the stressor as presumptively unique and treat it as if it is operating in a social vacuum. The evidence of this tendency is the very large literatures on work stress on the one hand, focusing purely on workplace conditions, and family stress on the other, focusing on domestic operations. The fact is that the effects of stressors in each role depend crucially on the state of stressors in the other role, as has been made clear in a series of studies reported in Eckenrode and Gore (1989). The primary point of that volume is the interdependence of the impacts of stress in one role—work or family—on stress in the other, sometimes increasing impacts, sometimes decreasing impacts. If interdependence is the case, then two lessons are learned. First, within-role theories, emphasizing, for example, workplace conditions or the distribution of domestic labor, partially miss the point that the effects of these stressors will vary substantially depending on "outside" stressors. Second, perhaps the optimal approach is to focus on individual stressors, with the understanding that there is an array of other current and past stressors that simultaneously must be considered.

It is possible to have it both ways, to a degree. One can study individual stressors—for example, specific traumas in childhood, such as sexual abuse or parental divorce—and still consider the cumulative total of *other* (prior) stressors as part of the context determining the impact of those stressors. Wheaton, Roszell, and Hall (1997) report, for example, that prior stress histories often reduce the impact of specific traumas—a point suggesting that the overall main effect reported in many studies of traumas may be misleading.

Life Course Perspectives. Although life-course approaches grew into a full-fledged framework in the 1980s, the influence on stress research is still in process. It is this perspective that makes clear how stressors early in life can be linked through a number of maintenance processes to mental health in later life (Rutter, 1989). It is important to remember that early findings on stress suggested that only recent or current stressors are relevant in predicting current mental health. We now know this is not the case, and the life course perspective provided the rationale—and the courage—to investigate the remote effects of stress. The idea of stress proliferation, the contextual relevance of past stressors for current stress, and the long-term effects of childhood experiences are each made more plausible by the point made clearly in the life-course literature that long-term and indirect effects are not weak effects (Elder et al., 1996).

Elder's work in sociology (1985; Elder et al.,1996) has been pivotal in setting a broad agenda of investigations on the sequencing, timing, order, and structural and historical constraints and opportunities attending life course trajectories through lives. The potential stressfulness of events, or life conditions, therefore necessarily depends on the related issues of the normativeness of their timing in the life course, on the sequencing of life transitions, and on the life-history factors that determine the meaning of life changes and transitions. Wheaton (1990) argues that role histories in general will lead to contrasting implications of life changes and transitions, sometimes leading to negative downturns in mental health, because a beneficial role is lost, or to improvements in mental health, because of escape from a stressful situation. Thus, even issues such as "divorce" or "job loss" cannot be defined as stressful without reference to life-history factors that could either remove or enhance the threat accompanying these events.

The fact that life-course concerns have been and will continue to be a central issue in stress research is reflected in a series of volumes in the 1990s which have focused on life-course linkages between adversity in early life and the potential for change in life-course trajectories (Gotlib & Wheaton, 1997; Haggerty, Sherrod, Garmezy, & Rutter, 1993; Robins & Rutter, 1990; see also Chater 27, this volume). Interest in recent work has focused on stressors as major "turning points" in the life course, and whether and how resilience is actually borne of stress and adversity in early life. As Wertlieb (1997) notes, many turning points, even the divorce of one's parents, must be considered as "conditional" turning points. A stressor may or may not be a turning point in the life course, depending on the accumulation of prior stressors (Wheaton et al., 1997), its proximity to current stress, the age at which the stressor occurs, the matching of content of prior stressors to current stressors (Roszell, 1996), and the poststress "arrangements" that arise to deal with the stress.

Contextual Specification. The idea that contextual factors must be considered in specifying the actual stressfulness of events is clearly not a new idea (Brown, 1974). Brown's pioneering work on the importance of context in determining the threat of events has broadened over time to include multiple meanings of the term *context* and, thanks to the lengthening of time perspectives in studying stress, the extension of situational context to include the whole configuration of past life history. Thus, we can distinguish at least three uses of the term *context*, each of which may contribute to the potential for stressfulness: (1) *current life context*, described in terms of the conditions, demands, and attendant stressors in current social roles; (2) *biographical context*, referring to the effect of past experience, both in terms of timing and content, on the "meaning" of current stress; and (3) *social context*, referring to the influence of higher units of analysis—neighborhood, school, city, country—on the meaning of current stress. The importance of context is part of what Thoits (1995) refers to as "the search for meaning."

The recent discussion by Aneshensel and Sucoff (1996b) distinguishes a series of models for the effects of contextual stressors on individual outcomes. Using existing distinctions between direct and indirect effects, main and conditional effects, and primary and secondary stressors, their discussion gives specificity to a range of theoretical possibilities. The advantage of such conceptual discussions is that important distinctions are introduced that delineate very different mechanisms and conditions under which ecological stress affects individuals. For example, we want to know whether these effects fall under what Aneshensel and Sucoff call the "modal multilevel model," in which the effect of ecological stress is primarily expressed as a change in the probability of exposure to that stressor at the individual level, or through "the crossover effect," in which the ecological stressor directly affects individual functioning, regardless of the actual occurrence or nonoccurrence of that stressor at the individual level. This latter possibility would suggest a very important role for ecological stress, and it reflects the type of effect so often expected, but rarely demonstrated, in discussions of the importance of economic downturns, unpopular wars, and traumatic social system events.

As is the case with life-course approaches, where methods such as survival analysis and latent growth curve models allow us to address question in ways that we could not before (Willett & Singer, 1997), recent developments in the study of hierarchical linear models make possible assessment of theoretical issues pertaining to multilevel relationships that have existed throughout the twentieth century. The multilevel model (Byrk & Raudenbusch, 1992) is an approach that allows for estimation of cross-level effects. Thus, it may be a propitious historical moment given the recent theoretical input of Aneshensel and Sucoff (1996b), for the further development of research on contextual effects.

CONCLUSIONS

I return to the issue raised by Kaplan (1996): Do we need to retain the concept of stress at all, given it current complexity? In this chapter, I devoted a share of the discussion to the problem of defining stressors. I did so because I believe this issue is still widely misunderstood. I argued that even if we do not use the term *stress*, we will continue to be interested in things that are *stressful*. As such, we will want to preselect things to focus on as possible stressors. Guidance in this selection, and in a conceptual framework, surely help in avoiding confusion about the roles of variables in an overall model for mental health, as well as in providing rationales about what to include and exclude in our search for important risks to mental health. In a sense, this conclusion seems self-evident.

I argued as well that a fundamental mistake is made when we believe that we must predecide whether the stressor is actually stressful. We want to measure the context and coping capacities that are brought to bear on the event of interest, and thus *discover* whether it is stressful. I argued further that stress ideally should be measured as a continuous variable and that our dichotomous representations of stress should be seen as imposition of a coarse threshold to define "presence." It is helpful that this threshold is usually a minimal requirement for presence, since we want to be able to find a subset of such stressors that are in fact stressful. However, the idea that we should impose or predefine a threshold of stressfulness has led to problems and confusion in the stress literature. The important point is not to presume, but to find out. Thus, it is essential that we give more attention to the elements of context and coping that in summary define the current stress potential of an event or chronic situation.

I can suggest three other reasons why it might be advisable to retain the term *stress*. First, there are important advantages of working from a conceptual framework such as the stress process. One of the most important is that the potential roles of variables in an overall explanation are made clear by a conceptual framework. Furthermore, the aticulation of outstanding issues depends on these explicit conceptual roles. A conceptual framework makes possible the discovery of commonality or distinctiveness of processes leading to or following from different stressors. For example, we can only discover the overall role for stress exposure in explaining sociodemographic differences, and compare this role across different social risk factors, if we apply the same meaning for "stressors" to the analysis of different relationships. Second, the attempt to differentiate stress concepts while retaining the overarching notion of a stress domain allows us to investigate the interrelationships among stressors, in terms of stress proliferation, stress containment, or desensitization or sensitization processes describing the combination of effects of particular sequences of stressors. This task, it seems to me, is a central issue in future stress research, but it cannot proceed without understanding that what we are investigating is relationships *among* stressors. Third, I believe that avoidance of the term *stress* as a "place holder" for the various concepts used in this chapter will have the unintended consequence of delegitimizing the socioenvironmental explanation of mental health because issues that now can be clearly treated as representative of social causation become less clearly articulated as alternatives to biological or genetic causation. It is fortunate, for example, that some stressors are truly random, or cannot be possibly anticipated or predicted, because they provide an elegant argument for social causation that cannot be easily understood as the unfolding of biological or genetic givens. In other words, social stress remains one of the most important alternative hypotheses to biological models of mental disorder. As such, a full understanding of the variants of social stress in people's lives will only serve to make clear the potential power of stress as a force in mental health. Of course, the proper specification of social stress should be considered as potentially complex as the subtleties of genetic causation. Daunting life changes, chronic intractable problems, those irritating hassles tomorrow, the rezoning of the neighborhood, the drop in the worth of the dollar, and not getting that job are all *stressors*.

REFERENCES

Amato, P. R., & Keith, B. (1991). Parental divorce and the well-being of children: A meta-analysis. *Psychological Bulletin, 110,* 26–46.

American Psychiatric Association. (1987). *Diagnostic and statistical manual of mental disorders* (3rd ed., rev.). Washington, DC: Author.

Aneshensel, C. S., Rutter, C. M., & Lachenbruch, P. A. (1991). Social structure, stress, and mental health. *American Sociological Review, 56,* 166–179.

Aneshensel, Carol S. 1992. Social stress: Theory and research. *Annual Review of Sociology* 18: 15-38.

Aneshensel, C. S. (1996). The consequences of psychosocial stress: The universe of stress outcomes. In H. B. Kaplan (Ed.), *Psychosocial stress: Perspectives on structure, theory, life-course, and methods* (pp. 111–136). New York: Academic Press,

Aneshensel, C. S., & Sucoff, C. (1996a). The neighborhood context of adolescent mental health. *Journal of Health and Social Behavior, 37,* 293–310.

Aneshensel, C., & Sucoff, C. (1996b, August 16–20). *Macro and micro influences in the stress process.* Paper presented at the meeting of the American Sociological Association, New York, New York.

Avison, W. R., & Turner, R. J. (1988). Stressful life events and depressive symptoms: Disaggregating the effects of acute stressors and chronic strains. *Journal of Health and Social Behavior, 29,* 253–264.

Barrera, M. (1986). Distinctions between social support concepts, measures, and models. *American Journal of Community Psychology, 14,* 413–445.

Brenner, M. H. (1974). *Mental illness and the economy.* Cambridge, MA: Harvard University Press.

Brown, G. W. (1974). Meaning, measurement, and stress of life events. In B. S. Dohrenwend & B. P. Dohrenwend (Eds.), *Stressful life events: Their nature and effects* (pp. 217–245). New York: Wiley.

Brown, G. W. (1981). Contextual measures of life events. In B. S. Dohrenwend & B. P. Dohrenwend (Eds.), *Stressful life events and their contexts* (pp. 187–201). New Brunswick, NJ: Rutgers University Press.

Brown, G. W., & Birley, J. L. T. (1968). Crises and life changes and the onset of schizophrenia. *Journal of Health and Social Behavior, 9,* 203–214.

Brown, G. W., & Harris, T. (1978). *The social origins of depression: A study of psychiatric disorders in women.* New York: Free Press.

Brown, G. W., Harris, T., & Bifulco, A. (1986). Long-term effects of early loss of parent. In M. Rutter, G. E. Izard, & P. B. Read (Eds.), *Depression in young people* (pp. 251–296). New York: Guilford.

Browne, A., & Finkelhor, D. (1986). Impact of child sexual abuse: A review of the research. *Psychological Bulletin, 99,* 66–77.

Bryer, J. B., Nelson, B. A., Miller, J. B., & Krol, P. A. (1987). Childhood sexual and physical abuse as factors in adult psychiatric illness. *American Journal of Psychiatry, 144,* 1426–1430.

Burnam, M. A., Stein, J. A., Golding, J. M., Siegel, J. M., Sorenson, S. B., Forsythe, A. B., & Telles, C. A. (1988). Sexual assault and mental disorders in a community population. *Journal of Consulting and Clinical Psychology, 56,* 843–850.

Byrk, A. S., & Raudenbush, S. W. (1992). *Hierarchical linear models: Applications and data analysis methods.* Newbury Park, CA: Sage.

Cannon, W. B. (1929). *Bodily changes in pain, hunger, fear, and rage.* New York: D. Appleton and Company.

Dohrenwend, B. S., & Dohrenwend, B. P. (1970). Class and race as status-related sources of stress. In S. Levine & N. Scotch (Eds.), *Social stress* (pp. 111–140). Chicago: Aldine.

Dohrenwend, B. S., & Dohrenwend, B. P. (1974). Overview and prospects for research on stressful life events. In B. S. Dohrenwend & B. P. Dohrenwend (Eds.), *Stressful life events: Their nature and events* (pp. 313–331). New York: Wiley.

Dohrenwend, B. S., Dohrenwend, B. P., Dodson, M., & Shrout, P. E. (1984). Symptoms, hassles, social supports, and life events: Problem of confounding measures. *Journal of Abnormal Psychology, 93,* 222–230.

Dohrenwend, B. S., Krasnoff, L. Askenasy, A. R., & Dohrenwend, B. P. (1978). Exemplication of a method for scaling life events: The PERI Life Events Scale. *Journal of Health and Social Behavior, 19,* 205–229.

Dohrenwend, B. P., & Dohrenwend, B. S. (1969). *Social status and psychological disorder.* New York: Wiley.

Dooley, D., & Catalano, R.(1984). Why the economy predicts help-seeking: A test of competing explanations. *Journal of Health and Social Behavior, 25,* 160–175.

Eckenrode, J., & Gore, S. (Eds.). (1989). *The transmission of stress between work and family.* New York: Plenum Press.

Elder, G. H., Jr. (1985). Perspedtives on the life course. In G. H. Elder, Jr. (Ed.), *Life course dynamics: Trajectories and transitions, 1968–1980* (pp. 23–49). Ithaca, NY: Cornell University Press.

Elder, G. H., Jr., George, L. K., & Shanahan. M. J. (1996). Psychosocial stress over the life course. In H. B. Kaplan (Ed.), *Psychosocial stress: Perspectives on structure, theory, life-course, and methods* (pp. 247–292). New York: Academic Press,

Ensel, W. M.& Lin, N. (1991). The life stress paradigm and psychological distress. *Journal of Health and Social Behavior, 29,* 79–91.

Erikson, K. T. (1976). Loss of community at Buffalo Creek. *American Journal of Psychiatry, 133,* 302–305.

Gelles, R. J., & Conte, J. R. (1990). Domestic violence and sexual abuse of children: A review of research in the eighties. *Journal of Marriage and the Family, 52,* 1045–1058.

Gersten, J. C., Langner, T. S., Eisenberg, J. G., & Orzeck, L. (1974). Child behavior and life events: Undesirable change or change per se? In B. S. Dohrenwend & B. P. Dohrenwend (Eds.), *Stressful life events: Their nature and effects* (pp. 159–170). New York: Wiley.

Glenn, N., & Kramer, K. (1985). The psychological well-being of adult children of divorce. *Journal of Marriage and the Family, 47,* 905–911.

Gotlib, I. H., & Wheaton, B. (Eds.). (1997). *Stress and adversity over the life course: Trajectories and turning points.* New York: Cambridge University Press.

Haggerty, R. L., Sherrod, L. R., Garmezy, N., & Rutter, M. (Eds.). (1993). *Stress, risk, and resilience in children and adolescents: Process, mechanisms, and interventions.* New York: Cambridge University Press.

Hinkle, L. (1987). Stress and disease: The concept after 50 years. *Social Science and Medicine, 25,* 561–567.

Holmes, T. H., & Rahe, R. H. (1967). The social readjustment rating scale. *Journal of Psychosomatic Research, 11,* 213–218.

Horwitz, A. V., White, H. R., & Howell-White, S. (1996). Becoming married and mental health: A longitudinal study of a cohort of young adults. Institute for Health, Health Care Policy, and Aging Research, Rutgers University.

Kanner, A. D., Coyne, J. C., Schaefer, C., & Lazarus, R. S. (1981). Comparison of two modes of stress measurement: Daily hassles and uplifts versus major life events. *Journal of Behavioral Medicine, 4,* 1–39.

Kaplan, H. B. (1996). Themes, lacunae, and directions in research in psychosocial stress. In H. B. Kaplan (Ed.), *Psychosocial stress: Perspectives on structure, theory, life-course, and methods* (pp. 369–403). New York: Academic Press,

Kendall-Tackett, K. A., Williams, L. M., & Finkelhor, D. (1993). Impact of sexual abuse on children: A review and synthesis of recent and empirical studies. *Psychological Bulletin, 113,* 164–180.

Kessler, R. C. (1979). Stress, social status, and psychological distress. *Journal of Health and Social Behavior, 20,* 259–272.

Kessler, R. C., & Magee, W. (1994). Childhood family violence and adult recurrent depression. *Journal of Health and Social Behavior, 35,* 13–27.

Kessler, R. C., McGonagle, K. A., Zhao, S., Nelson, C. B., Hughes, M., Eshelman, S., Wittchen, H.-V., & Kendler, K. S. (1994). Lifetime and 12-month prevalence of DSM-III-R psychiatric disorders in the United States. *Archives of General Psychiatry, 51,* 8–19.

Langner, T. S., & Michael, S. T. (1963). *Life stress and mental health.* London: Free Press of Glencoe.

Laufer, R. S., Gallops, M. S., & Frey-Wouters, E. (1984). War stress and trauma: The Vietnam veteran experience. *Journal of Health and Social Behavior, 25,* 65–85.

Linsky, A. S., Colby, J. P., Jr., & Straus, M. A. (1987). Social stress, normative constraints, and alcohol problems in American states. *Social Science and Medicine, 24,* 875–883.

McLeod, J. D. (1991). Childhood parental loss and adult depression. *The Journal of Health and Social Behavior, 32,* 205–220

Monroe, S. M., & Roberts, J. E. (1990). Conceptualizing and measuring life stress: Problems, principles, procedures, and progress. *Stress Medicine, 6,* 209–216.

Norris, F. H. (1992). Epidemiology of trauma: Frequency and impact of different potentially traumatic evens on different demographic groups. *Journal of Consulting and Clinical Psychology, 60,* 409–418.

Pearlin, L. I. (1989). The sociological study of stress. *Journal of Health and Social Behavior, 30,* 241–256.

Pearlin, L. I., Aneshensel, C. S., & LeBlanc, A. J. (1997). The forms and mechanisms of stress proliferation: the case of AIDS caregivers. *Journal of Health and Social Behavior, 38,* 223–236.

Pearlin, L. I., Lieberman, M. A., Menaghan, E. G., & Mullan, J. T. (1981). The stress process. *Journal of Health and Social Behavior, 22,* 337–356.

Pearlin, L. I., Mullan, J. T., Semple, S. J., & Skaff, M. M. (1990). Caregiving and the stress process: An overview of concepts and their measures. *The Gerontologist, 30,* 583–594.

Rabkin, J. G., & Streuning, E. L. (1976). Life events, stress, and illness. *Science, 194,* 1013–1020.

Reynolds, J. R. (1997). The effects of industrial employment conditions on job-related disress. *Journal of Health and Social Behavior, 38,* 105–116.

Robins, L., & Rutter, M. (Eds.). (1990). *Straight and devious pathways from childhood to adulthood.* Cambridge, UK: Cambridge University Press.

Robins, L., Helzer, J. E., Weisman, M. M., Orvaschel, H., Gruenberg, E., Burke, J. D., & Regier, D. A. (1984). Lifetime prevalence of specific psychiatric disorders in three sites. *Archives of General Psychiatry, 41,* 949–958.

Roszell, P. (1996). *A life course perspective on the implications of stress exposure.* Ph.D. dissertation, University of Toronto, Toronto, Canada.

Rutter, M. (1989). Pathways from childhood to adult life. *Journal of Child Psychology and Psychiatry, 30*(1), 23–51.

Saler, L. (1992). Childhood parental death and depression in adulthood: roles of surviving parent and family environment. *American Journal of Orthopsychiatry, 62,* 504–516.

Selye, H. (1956). *The stress of life.* New York: McGraw-Hill.

Smith, W. K. (1987). The stress analogy. *Schizophrenia Bulletin, 13,* 215–220.

Terr, L. C. (1991). Childhood traumas: An outline and overview. *American Journal of Psychiatry, 148,* 10–20.

Thoits, P. (1983). Dimensions of life events that influence psychological distress. In H. B. Kaplan (Ed.), *Psychosocial stress: Trends in theory and research* (pp. 33–103). New York: Academic Press.

Thoits, P. (1995). Stress, coping, and social support processes: Where are we? What next?" *Journal of Health and Social Behavior*, extra issue, 53–79.

Turner, R. J., Wheaton, B., & Lloyd, D. (1995). The epidemiology of social stress. *American Sociological Review, 60,* 104–125.

Wertlieb, D. (1997). Children whose parents divorce: Life trajectories and turning points. In I. Gotlib & B. Wheaton (Eds.), *Stress and adversity over the life course: Trajectories and turning points* (pp. 179–196). New York: Cambridge University Press.

Wheaton, B. (1980). The sociogenesis of psychological disorder: an attributional theory. *Journal of Health and Social Behavior, 21*(2), 100–123.

Wheaton, B. (1983). Stress, personal coping resources, and psychiatric symptoms: An investigation of interactive models. *Journal of Health and Social Behavior, 24,* 208–229.

Wheaton, B. (1985). Models for the stress-buffering functions of coping resources. *Journal of Health and Social Behavior, 26,* 352–365.

Wheaton, B. (1990). Life transitions, role histories, and mental health. *American Sociological Review, 55,* 209–224.

Wheaton, B. (1994). Sampling the stress universe. In W. R. Avison & I. H. Gotlib, (Eds.), *Stress and mental health: Contemporary issues and prospects for the future* (pp. 77–114). New York: Plenum Press.

Wheaton, B. (1996). The domains and boundaries of stress concepts. In H. B. Kaplan (Ed.), *Psychosocial stress: Perspectives on structure, theory, life-course, and methods* (pp. 29–70). New York: Academic Press,

Wheaton, B., & Hall, K. (1996, August 16–21). The stress process as an explanation of sociodemographic differences in distress and depression: Preliminary results from the National Population Health Survey. Paper presented at the meeting of the American Sociological Association, New York, New York.

Wheaton, B., Roszell, P., & Hall, K. (1997). The impact of twenty childhood and adult traumatic stressors on the risk of psychiatric disorder. In I. Gotlib & B. Wheaton (Eds.), *Stress and adversity over the life course: Trajectories and turning points*. New York: Cambridge University Press.

Willett, J. B., & Singer, J. D. (1997). Using discrete-time survival analysis to study event occurrence across the life course. In I. Gotlib & B. Wheaton (Eds.), *Stress and adversity over the life course: Trajectories and turning points* (pp. 273–294). New York: Cambridge University Press.

CHAPTER 15

Social Integration and Support

R. Jay Turner

J. Blake Turner

The importance of social relationships in the lives of human beings is an idea as old as the written word. In Genesis (2:18), the Lord judges, "It is not good that [one] be alone," and philosophers from Aristotle to Martin Buber have emphasized that the essence of human existence is expressed in our relations with others. In sociology, patterns of human contact, processes of social interactions, and the subjective valences of personal relationships have been central foci of theory and research since the inception of the field. Over the last quarter century, a substantial portion of the variegated sociological literature in this area has focused on the role of the presence and quality of social relationships in health and illness. *Social support* has become the most widely used phrase to refer to the salutary content of these relationships.

Although sociologists can trace the ancestry of social support research back to Durkheim's (1951) treatise and empirical assessment of the role of social involvement in the prevention of suicide, the well-documented "boom" in social support research (House, Umberson, & Landis, 1988; Vaux, 1988; Veil & Baumann, 1992) probably owes more to the accumulation of evidence from other fields. For example, research in developmental psychology long ago demonstrated the dramatic significance of human associations for development. The profound negative consequences of maternal deprivation observed by Spitz (1946) among institutionalized infants, the implications of unresponsive mothering suggested by Harlow's (1959) research with baby monkeys, and Bowlby's (1969, 1973) dissertations on the indispensability of attachment for healthy human development are promi-

R. Jay Turner • Department of Sociology, University of Miami, Coral Gables, Florida 33146.   J. Blake Turner • Division of Sociomedical Sciences, School of Public Health, Columbia University, New York, New York 10032.

Handbook of the Sociology of Mental Health, edited by Carol S. Aneshensel and Jo C. Phelan. Kluwer Academic/Plenum Publishers, New York, 1999.

nent among the many examples that illustrate this point. As Pierce, Sarason, and Sarason (1996) have recently noted, developmentalists and family researchers have long viewed social support, particularly that provided by parents, as a crucial contributor to personality and social development (Rollins & Thomas, 1979; Symonds, 1939).

From evidence of the significance of social support as a developmental contingency, it was only a minor leap of faith to the now pervasive assumption that this important developmental factor must also be significant with respect to personal functioning and psychological well-being throughout the life course. Moreover, social epidemiologists had accumulated preliminary evidence for the role played by a lack of social relationships in the development of serious physical morbidity (Holmes, 1956), psychiatric disorders (Kohn & Clausen, 1955), and general mortality risk (Kitagawa & Hauser, 1973).

Although this view—that social bonds and supportive interactions are important for maintaining mental health—has a long history, accompanied by strands of supporting data, specific research evidence on this connection has largely accumulated over the past 20 years. The immense growth in research on, and evidence for, the significance of social support was importantly stimulated by the publication of seminal review articles by John Cassel (1976) and Sidney Cobb (1976). These papers introduced a hypothesis that a large portion of subsequent research has attempted to address—that the availability and quality of social relationships may act to moderate the impact of life stress.

CONCEPTS OF SOCIAL SUPPORT

The Oxford Dictionary defines support, in part, as to "keep from failing or giving way, give courage, confidence, or power of endurance to . . . supply with necessities . . . lend assistance or countenance to" (1975, p. 850). What distinguishes *social* support from the broader concept is that it always involves either the presence or the implications of stable human relationships. The domain of social support has been addressed under a variety of labels, including "social bonds" (Henderson, 1977, 1980), "social networks" (Wellman & Wortley, 1989), "meaningful social contact" (Cassel, 1976), "availability of confidants" (Brown, Bholchain, & Harris, 1975), and "human companionship" (Lynch, 1977), as well as social support. Although these concepts are not all identical, they are similar and share a focus on the relevance and significance of human relationships.

The diversity of opinion with respect to how social support should be conceptualized and measured has been widely commented on in the literature for more than a dozen years (e.g., Gottlieb, 1983; Turner, Frankel, & Levin, 1983), and this diversity remains apparent today. When the full range of offered definitions and potentially relevant elements are considered together, a kind of conceptual imperialism seems apparent; that is, social support has been used to refer to an ever-widening domain of content that seems almost coextensive with the structural and social aspects of all human relationships and interactions.

While seeking to delimit the meaning of social support, a number of researchers have concluded that social support is a multifactorial construct and described different types or categories of social support that should be considered and that may have differing consequences (e.g., Dean & Lin, 1977; Funch & Mettlin, 1982; Hirsch, 1980; House, 1981). Vaux (1988, p. 28) has argued that social support is best viewed as a metaconstruct "comprised of several legitimate and distinguishable theoretical constructs." Three such constructs are specified: support network resources, supportive behavior, and subjective appraisals of support. These dimensions, or constructs, correspond closely with Barrera's

(1986) distinction between social embeddedness (the connection individuals have to significant others or to their social environment), enacted support (actions that others perform in rendering assistance), and perceived social support.

Perhaps the best-known and most influential conceptualization of social support is that offered by Cobb (1976, p. 300). He viewed social support as "information belonging to one or more of the following three classes: (1) information leading the subject to believe that he[/she] is cared for and loved; (2) information leading the subject to believe that he[/she] is esteemed and valued; and (3) information leading the subject to believe that he[/she] belongs to a network of communication and mutual obligation." In other words, social support refers to the clarity or certainty with which the individual experiences being loved, valued, and able to count on others should the need arise.

Cobb (1979, p. 94) argued the importance of distinguishing social support from support that is instrumental (counseling, assisting), active (mothering), or material (providing goods and/or services). However, he did not suggest that these other forms of support are not important or that they lack relevance for health and well-being. His point was simply that it is worth distinguishing social support as self-relevant information from various support resources and support activities.

This perspective was prominent in focusing the interests of many researchers on social support as a social psychological variable—an interest consistent with W. I. Thomas's (Thomas & Thomas, 1928) familiar admonition that situations that are defined as real are real in their consequences. It is an axiom of social psychology that events or circumstances in the real world affect the individual only to the extent and in the form in which they are perceived. As Ausubel (1958, p. 277) has pointed out, "This does not imply that the perceived world is the real world but that perceptual reality is psychological reality and the actual (mediating) variable that influences behavior and development."

Accumulated evidence is highly consistent with this latter point. Indeed, long ago, House (1981) pointed out that the great bulk of evidence pointing to the significance of social support for health and well-being came from studies focused on "emotional support"—his term for perceived support. He further acknowledged that emotional support was the common element across most conceptualizations, that it was what most people meant when they spoke of being supportive, and that, indeed, it seemed to be the most important dimension. Since that time, studies have repeatedly demonstrated that the strongest correlations between measures that purport to assess social support and indices of psychological distress or well-being are found with measures of perceived social support. For example, Wethington and Kessler (1986, p. 85) have presented specific evidence for the primacy of perceived over received support. They documented "not only that perceptions of support availability are more important than actual support transactions but that the latter promotes psychological adjustment through the former, as much as by practical resolutions of situational demands." This finding further supports House's (1981, p. 27) suggestion that "social support is likely to be effective only to the extent perceived."

Notwithstanding the apparent mental health significance of perceived social support, the dominant view among sociologists and psychologists is that social support is best understood as a multidimensional construct. Although descriptions of relevant elements vary somewhat, most include, along with emotional or *perceived support*, the dimensions of *structural support* and *received support,* or supportive behaviors. Structural support refers to the organization of people's ties to one another, involving the frequency of contact with network members and the structural characteristics of social ties. Relevant structural characteristics include degree of reciprocity of exchanges between provider and receiver, the strength of the bonds involved, the degree of similarity among network members, and the density of relationships among network members (Wellman, 1981, 1992). As Thoits (1995) has noted, network measures often reflect the individual's level of social isolation or social embeddedness. Received support simply refers to the help that helpers extend in providing either instrumental or informational assistance.

There does seem ample basis for concluding that social support phenomena involve objective (relational connections and helping behaviors) as well as subjective elements. Indeed, as Pearlin (1989) has argued, an understanding of the significance of social institutions and contexts will ultimately require the consideration of social networks and resources along with perceived support. However, the grounds for according primary importance to perceived support seem equally clear. The twin facts that perceived social support is most persistently and powerfully associated with mental health and that other elements apparently exert their effects by influencing this perception, focuses attention on perceived social support as an outcome or dependent variable; that is, social support represents the most direct criterion for assessing the role and significance of network characteristics, of other social resources, and of potentially supportive actions generally. Perceived social support appears to provide a basis for identifying behaviors and circumstances that may constitute promising targets for intervention efforts to prevent or ameliorate mental health problems.

THE NATURE OF PERCEIVED SOCIAL SUPPORT

Two general views have been offered to explain the protective benefits of perceived social support—a situation-specific model in which perceived support performs as a coping resource in relation to particular stressful events or circumstances, and a developmental perspective that sees social support as a crucial factor in social and personality development (Cohen, 1992; Pierce, Sarason, Sarason, Solky, & Nagle, 1996). These views are not necessarily contradictory, reflecting instead the probability that social support has both short- and long-term consequences for psychological well-being (Pierce et al., 1996). Both of these perspectives view the social environment as the primary source of supportive experiences, and hence of the perception or belief that one is supported by others. However, the first perspective focuses largely on the contemporary social environment, whereas the second view, in contrast, emphasizes the effects of the social–environmental context on personality over time, attaching special significance to the developmental years.

That the tendency to believe or perceive others to be supportive may partially be a reflection of stable personality characteristics makes intuitive sense in the context of Cobb's (1976) conceptualization of social support described earlier. Recall that this definition describes social support as information that one is loved and wanted, valued and esteemed, and able to count on others should the need arise. Thus, reflected appraisal, which is a central component of self-esteem (Rosenberg, 1965, 1979, 1986), also represents an element of perceived social support, and experiences that foster or challenge one of these constructs must also be relevant to the other. Moreover, it is reasonable to assume a degree of reciprocal causation. Surely, the experience of being supported by others contributes toward more stable and positive self-esteem, whereas one's level of self-esteem must set at least broad limits on level of perceived social support. It is clear that individuals vary in their tendency or capacity to derive meaning and emotional sustenance from a given amount of evidence of positive regard and affection. Everyone has encountered individuals who cannot seem to incorporate messages of social and emotional support no matter how frequently or clearly these messages are delivered. Self-esteem presumably contributes to such differences in receptiveness because one's capacity to experience the esteem of others must require some minimal level of esteem of self.

Other grounds for assuming that personality factors are implicated in perceptions of support include evidence that such perceptions tend to be consistent over time, to be reasonably consistent across situations (Sarason, Pierce, & Sarason, 1990), and to be related to various personality characteristics such as social competence and personal control (Lakey & Cassaday, 1990). It has been hypothesized that appraisals of the supportiveness of the social environment reflect, at least in part, "support schemata"—referring to "knowledge structures whose content include information about the likelihood that others, in general, will be able or willing to meet one's needs for support. Support schemata encompass one's expectations about the forthcomingness of the social environment in providing aid should one need it" (Pierce et al., 1996, p. 5). The origins of such schemata are seen as substantially rooted in early experience with attachments, especially attachments to parents (Sarason, Pierce, & Sarason, 1990).

From this perspective, an important part of the linkage between perceived social support and the objective supportiveness of the environment derives from the tendency for those high in perceived support to be more effective at developing and maintaining supportive relationships on the one hand, and to interpret ambiguous actions and statements as supportive in nature on the other hand (Lakey & Dickinson, 1994). As Pierce and associates (1996, p. 6) have noted, those with the firm expectation that others will be supportive "create supportive relationships in new social settings, thereby further confirming their expectation that others are likely to be supportive." Indeed, it seems clear that early supportive behaviors—like those surrounding attachment-relevant experiences and those involving the experience by children of stability, sameness, and predictable daily rituals (Boyce, 1985)—are significant factors in the development of the personality factors at issue. Personal characteristics associated with a capacity to obtain and maintain supportive relationships and the tendency to experience one's environment as supportive appear, at least in some part, to be consequences of support experienced during and following infancy.

However, the evidence seems compelling that expectations, beliefs, or confidence about the availability of social support cannot be independent of one's recent history of real world experiences of the supportive actions and expressions of others (Cutrona, 1986; Sarason, Pierce, & Sarason, 1990; Vinokur, Schul, & Caplan, 1987). Thus, expressions of support and supportive actions may be seen as important in the short term for the coping assistance provided and, in the long term, for the contribution made to the receiver's expectation or confidence that such support will be available in the future. Although early attachment experiences may well influence the individual's tendency to foster and perceive environmental supportiveness, there seems good basis for concluding that such tendencies are profoundly shaped and modified by later experiences. The perception of being loved and wanted, valued and esteemed, and able to count on others must be a function of one's history of supportive and unsupportive experiences, with both early life and recent experiences representing significant influences.

SOCIAL SUPPORT AND MENTAL HEALTH

An ever-growing number of volumes and reviews document the apparent significance of perceived social support for emotional health and well-being (e.g., Cohen & Syme, 1985;

Cohen & Willis, 1985; Dean & Lin, 1977; Gottlieb, 1981; Kessler, Price, & Wortman, 1985; Sarason & Sarason, 1985; Sarason, Sarason, & Pierce, 1990; Turner 1983; Turner, Frankel, & Levin, 1983; Vaux 1988; Veil & Baumann, 1992). A large portion of this very substantial research effort has been focused on the hypothesis that low levels of social support increase risk for depressive symptomatology. Taking note of this, Henderson (1992) identified and evaluated 35 separate studies that have addressed the social support—depression relationship. These studies utilized measures of depression that varied from very brief self-report inventories to standardized interviews based on accepted diagnostic criteria. Similarly, procedures for indexing social support differed widely, varying from the use of a single item on the presence or absence of a confidant, to sophisticated multiitem measures. Despite such variable assessments of both social support and depression, Henderson observed remarkable consistency across studies. Virtually all studies reported a clear, inverse association between social support and depression, with studies employing more brief measures of one or both variables demonstrating equally strong relationships as studies employing more elaborate methods. The connection between perceived social support and mental health status generally, and depression in particular, appears to be highly robust. As other reviews of the social support literature make clear, similar conclusions generally are justified with respect to anxiety and psychological distress.

MAIN VERSUS BUFFERING EFFECTS

Much of the strong interest in social support effects on mental health has been associated with the hypothesis, strongly articulated in the influential papers by Cassel (1976) and Cobb (1976), that social support may act to buffer or moderate the effects of life stress. From this perspective, social support tends to be of mental health significance only within stressful circumstances. As Cobb (1976, p. 502) argued,

> Social support facilitates coping with crises and adaptation to change. Therefore, one should not expect dramatic main effects from social support. There are, of course, some main effects simply because life is full of changes and crises. The theory says that it is in moderating the effects of the major transitions in life and of the unexpected crises that the effects should be found.

In a highly influential study, Brown and his colleagues (Brown & Harris, 1978; Brown et al., 1975) considered factors that might influence vulnerability to depression in the face of adversity. Specifically, they examined the influence of a close, confiding relationship in reducing the risk of depression following a major life event or long-term difficulty. Among those women who lacked a confiding relationship with a husband or boyfriend, 38% developed depression following life stress or major difficulties, compared with only 4% of women with such a confiding relationship. Consistent with this result, Henderson's (1992) review of 35 social support–depression studies revealed only four that did not report such a buffering or protective effect.

However, it is also clear from Henderson's review, and from the wider literature, that a number of studies have found a low level of support to increase risk for depression, or for mental health problems generally, whether or not exposure to unusual stressors has also taken place. Whether these findings allow the conclusion that social support can be of importance in the absence of social stress cannot be easily answered. Antonovsky (1979, p. 77) has forcefully argued that "all of us . . . even in the most benign and sheltered environments, are fairly continuously exposed to what we define as stressors. . . . We are able to get low scores on stress experience [only] because we do not ask the right questions or do not ask patiently enough and not because there really are any low scorers." He insists that "even the most fortunate of people . . . know life as stressful to a considerable extent" (1979, p. 79). If this constancy-of-stress argument is accepted, both the main effects and interactive effects that have been observed would theoretically be interpretable in terms of the buffering hypothesis.

From this perspective, it might seem to follow that the buffering- versus main-effects debate is not worth worrying about. However, even if what look like main effects are really buffering effects, it would remain important to determine whether social support is largely or wholly of significance because it reduces the impact of extraordinary stress exposure. In other words, is social support of greater significance when stress is relatively high than when relatively low? Given the inevitability of limited resources, it would be very useful to be able to distinguish those who most need and who might most benefit from, a social support intervention. In other words, although all might benefit from enhanced social support, the issues of relative need and relative benefit with respect to psychological distress and disorder remain salient.

Evidence from a study of young mothers may shed some additional light on the inconsistency of findings relating to the buffering hypothesis (Turner, 1981; Turner & Noh, 1983). In initial analyses, social support was found to relate to psychological distress independent of stress level. The life stress by social support interaction term was not significant when the main effects of social support and stress were controlled, suggesting an absence of buffering. This finding was consistent with the hypothesis of "main" or direct social support effects and with the significant minority of other studies that have reported no evidence for a stress-buffering role.

Further analyses of these same data, however, indicated that the question of whether social support is of influence in its own right, or is important wholly, or largely, as a buffer against unusual stress, may not be so simply answered. With young mothers of lower socioeconomic status distinguished from middle-class study participants, Turner and Noh (1983) regressed psychological distress on perceived social support within each of three stress-level categories. Within the lower-class grouping, the significance of social support varied substantially by level of stress. No significant relationship was observed among the lower-class group in either the low- or medium-stress circumstance. However, perceived social support was of dramatic significance in the high-stress circumstance.

The results for the middle-class group contrasted sharply with these findings. Clear and quite consistent social support effects were observed regardless of stress level. Thus, the answer to the question of whether social support has main or buffering effects may be both conditional and complex. The significant associations observed among the middle-class at all three stress levels demonstrated a main effect. In sharp contrast, no main effects were observed among the lower class, as evidenced by small and nonsignificant associations observed within the low- and medium-stress conditions. Social support was found to matter, and matter importantly, only among those experiencing a high level of stress. This finding provides clear support for the buffering hypothesis. Thus, the significance of social support appears to vary with both social-class position and stress level.

At this point, available evidence suggests the appropriateness of three working hypotheses with respect to the main effects-buffering debate: (1) Social support tends to matter for psychological well-being in general, and depression in particular, independent of stressor level; (2) social support appears to matter more where level of stress exposure is relatively high; and (3) the extent to which (1) and (2) are true varies across subgroups of the population defined by class level and, perhaps, by other characteristics. For considerations of alternative mechanisms or pathways by which social support may exert a protective function, see Dohrenwend and Dohrenwend (1981), Wheaton (1985), and Ensel and Lin (1991).

SOCIAL STATUS AND SOCIAL SUPPORT

The starting points for a great deal of research on the sociology of mental health have been findings that connect certain social statuses with mental health problems. The most persistently observed and provocative of these linked low socioeconomic status (SES) (e.g., Gurin, Veroff, & Feld, 1960; Hollingshead & Redlich, 1958; Srole, Langer, Michael, Opler, & Rennie, 1961), being unmarried (e.g., Gurin et al., 1960), and being female (e.g., Al-Issa, 1982; Nolen-Hoeksema, 1987) with increased risk for psychological distress and depression.

This evidence has suggested that social stratification and other structural factors are consequential and has led researchers to turn their attention to the questions of how these factors come to influence individual health, and under what circumstances such effects are diminished or intensified (House & Mortimer, 1990). On the assumption that socially patterned differences in ongoing social experience and in social and developmental acquisitions are likely to be implicated, a number of hypotheses about the mental health significance of various psychosocial factors have been suggested (Aneshensel, 1992). The most prominent among these factors are those that define the "stress process" model (Pearlin, Lieberman, Menaghan, & Mullan, 1981), including social support.

As noted earlier, substantial evidence has accumulated indicating the relevance of social support for mental health. However, as Vaux (1988) has noted, relatively little is known about how social support varies across subgroups of the population. At about the same time, House and associates (1988, p. 310) concluded that "while there is a substantial theoretical base in sociology suggesting that macrosocial features influence social relationships, there is little empirical evidence to substantiate the nature of that influence." In their view, comparative research represents an important step in illuminating the impact of macrosocial structures on processes of social support.

In this connection, Pearlin (1989) has argued that there are grounds for assuming that variations in the availability and experience of social support arise substantially out of contemporary and developmental conditions of life. To the extent that important differences in such conditions are defined by one's gender and one's socioeconomic and marital status, the hypothesis follows that observed relationships between these statuses and mental health may arise, in part, from associated differences in social support, that is, to the extent that social support is linked to these social statuses and thus, presumably, to differences in social group experience, it may be directly relevant to understanding how the social conditions of life create variations in mental health. The potential practical significance of such information includes the likelihood that social resources that arise at least partially from patterned social experience are more likely to be socially or programmatically modifiable and thus represent promising targets for prevention and intervention efforts.

A number of studies have provided findings on the relationships between social support and the risk-relevant social statuses of gender, marital status, and SES. With few exceptions (e.g., Lin, Dean, & Ensel, 1986; Ross & Mirowsky, 1989), however, these findings have been incidental to the goals of the studies involved and have considered only one of these status dimensions at a time. For that reason, available information is considered separately with respect to each status dimension.

Gender

Although a substantial number of studies have provided social support data by sex, the question of sex differences in level of support experienced remains a matter of some debate. A decade ago, Vaux (1988, p. 169) accomplished a rather complete review of available evidence and concluded that "empirical findings regarding gender differences in social support are mixed and inconsistent." However, others have read essentially the same evidence as indicating a tendency for women to experience more supportive relationships than men (Flaherty & Richman, 1986; Leavy, 1983). Although a number of studies have reported little or no difference by gender in level of perceived social support (e.g., Fusilier, Ganster, & Mayes, 1986; Holahan & Moos, 1982; Turner & Noh, 1988), the weight of the evidence appears to suggest that women are advantaged with respect to social support, variously conceived and measured. In addition, more recent studies of representative community samples have tended to support this conclusion. For example Ross and Mirowsky (1989), and Turner and Marino (1994) found women to experience substantially higher levels of social support than men.

Since women appear to experience higher levels of social support, social support differences cannot, in any straightforward way, assist our understanding of the tendency for women to experience higher levels of psychological distress and depression. In this connection, it should be emphasized that evidence makes clear that among women, as among men, higher levels of social support are reliably associated with lower levels of distress and depression. It thus follows that, without the advantage of higher social support, distress and depression among women could be even more elevated relative to men.

Marital Status

As House (1981, p. 29) long ago noted, the "minimum condition for experiencing social support . . . is to have one or more stable relationships with others." Being married is generally thought to define the existence of one such relationship—one in which normative expectations involve the giving and receiving of social support. The assumption of marital status differences in social support that follows from these expectations has led some researchers to employ marital status as a complete or partial index of differences in social support (e.g. Berkman & Syme, 1979; Eaton, 1978; Gore, 1978; Lynch, 1977). However, evidence to justify this assumption has been slim in quantity and not entirely consistent. Findings of no marital status differences have emerged from studies of urban men (Stueve & Gerson, 1977) and of nurses (Norbeck, 1985). In contrast, Ensel (1986) and colleagues (Lin et al., 1986) reported the highest levels of support among both married men and married women. Similar findings were also reported by Gerstel, Riessman, and Rosenfield (1985). They found that both married men and married women reported more confidants and perceived their support resources as more adequate than their unmarried counterparts. More recently, both Ross and Mirowsky (1989), and Turner and Marino (1994) have reported higher levels of perceived support among married persons, other social statuses controlled. In the latter study, social support from one's spouse or romantic partner, from relatives, from friends, and from one's co-workers were separately measured. With the exception of support from relatives, higher levels of support were not observed among the married compared to the unmarried when each source of support was considered separately. However, when either total scores across sources or average scores across relevant sources were considered, a clear advantage was found among both married men and women. Moreover, Turner and Marino (1994) found that social support differences collectively accounted for approximately half of the depressive symptomatology advantage enjoyed by married persons, and more than 60% of their advantage with respect to major depressive disorder. These data support the conclusion that social support tends to vary by marital status and that such variation helps to explain observed marital status differences in depressive symptoms and disorder.

Socioeconomic Status

There seems little question that SES tends to be associated with differences in the average responsiveness of the social environment and in socially significant opportunities more generally. These patterns suggest that the structures and processes of relationships may also vary systematically across SES categories. Here, as with the other social statuses considered, evidence bearing on this possibility, particularly with respect to perceived support, is more sparse and less clear than one might wish. Some data have suggested that lower SES individuals tend to have social relationships of lesser quality than those of higher SES (Belle, 1982; Dohrenwend & Dohrenwend, 1970), but, based on a large community study, Ensel (1986) reports no class differences in the appraisal of close relationships. Ross and Mirowsky (1989) observed mixed evidence with respect to a social support–SES connection. Although education was found to be positively related to social support, family income was completely unrelated to support.

Available evidence on SES differences in support resources and social networks, as opposed to perceived social support, is also limited but more consistent. Fischer (1982) found higher income and education to be associated with more voluntary associations, larger networks, and more contact with network members. Other studies have reported similar findings (Dohrenwend & Dohrenwend, 1970; Eckenrode, 1983; Moody & Gray, 1972).

Turner and Marino (1994) elevated the SES–perceived support relationship, assessing social support in terms of four dimensions or sources (spouse/romantic partner, family, friends, and co-workers), each measured by reliable multi-item indices. SES was assessed in terms of occupational prestige level. None of these four dimensions of support were found to be individually correlated with occupational level. However, when these scores were summed into more global measures, a clear relationship was observed, irrespective of the number of support sources. Indeed, the distribution of social support scores was the precise mirror image of the observed distributions of depressive symptoms and disorder, with high locations in the social system being associated with high levels of perceived social support. These findings were seen as consistent with the hypothesis that SES differences in depression may partially arise from complementary differences in social support. Further analyses, however, indicated that social support differences explained only about 15% of SES differences in depressive symptoms and virtually none of the observed SES variations in depressive disorders.

The fact that level of perceived social support varies systematically by one's gender and by one's socioeconomic and marital status supports the argument that social support is importantly conditioned by differences in past social experience and/or contemporaneous life circumstances. These findings thus illuminate ways in which social structures impact social processes relevant to social support, suggesting two assumptions: (1) that variations in the availability of social support arise, as do differences in exposure to social stress, substantially out of developmental and contemporaneous conditions of life (Aneshensel 1992; Pearlin 1989); and (2) that one's gender and socioeconomic and marital status effectively define significant differences in such conditions of life. House et al. (1988) have suggested that these status differences are associated with variations in exposure to structural barriers and access to opportunities in society that tend to shape social relationship structures and processes and, hence, the availability of social support.

CAUSAL INTERPRETATION

A fundamental assumption among those who investigate the social correlates of psychological distress and depression is that there is an etiological message to be found within these well-demonstrated linkages. However, in the case of social support, as with other social variables, it has been difficult to reach clear conclusions about the nature of this message. Most of the studies reporting this relationship have been cross-sectional or epidemiological in character and, consequently, confront the classic dilemma of whether the finding should be interpreted from a social causation or social selection perspective. Does perceived support operate directly or indirectly to make psychological distress and depression less likely, or do high levels of distress or depression limit the likelihood that the individual will secure and maintain social relationships or experience the social support that is, in fact, available? The first of these possibilities represents a social causation hypothesis, whereas the latter points to social selection processes.

A second form of selection proposes that the observed social support–mental health connection may simply be an artifact derived from the personal inadequacies of persons who later become distressed or depressed—inadequacies that also limit one's ability to secure and maintain supportive relationships. One version of this latter social selection hypothesis proposes that dispositional characteristics, as opposed to the nature of the social environment, largely account for differences in perceived social support (e.g., Heller, 1979; Sarason, Sarason, & Shearin, 1986)—characteristics that may also be associated with increased risk for distress and depression.

As noted earlier, it is clear that supportive experiences in the family context represent crucial early developmental contingencies that importantly influence personality. Thus, social support is causally relevant to personality processes and, by extension, to psychological well-being. However, the question remains of whether social support represents a promising intervention target throughout the life course as distinct from only during early developmental phases. To answer this question in the affirmative requires that some part of the causal flow involved in the social support–mental health connection goes from social support to distress and depression, and that level of perceived support be at least partially a function of contemporary processes and circumstances.

At this point it seems clear that no single study provides persuasive evidence on these matters. However, more than 15 years ago, House (1981, p. 51) reached the conclusion that much of the causal flow is from social relationships to health, rather than vice versa. Although much of the evidence supporting this conclusion involved physical rather than mental health outcomes, its applicability to phenomena such as psychological distress and depression seems apparent. John Cassel's (1974, 1976) early argument on the health significance of social support derived substantially from evidence derived from animal studies on the effects of laboratory-induced stress. Examples include Liddell's (1950) finding suggesting that the presence of the mother protects young goats from experimental neurosis, the Conger, Sawrey, and Turrell (1958) observation of the relevance of isolation for the occurrence of ulceration in rats, and the Henry and Cassel (1969) report on the significance of littermate presence for the prevention of persisistent hypertension in mice. Other kinds of studies reviewed by House (1981, 1987) and others (e.g., Turner, 1983), including laboratory analogue studies with humans, intervention studies, and longitudinal and panel studies, strongly suggest that some important portion of the causation involved in the well-established link between perceived social support and mental health status goes from social support to mental health.

In considering the issue of causation, it is useful to acknowledge that neither human development nor functioning is likely to proceed in terms of linear or clear-cut causes and effects. Rather, most causes and effects in human affairs are likely to be reciprocal in nature. As Smith (1968:, p. 277) long ago argued, development is a matter of benign circles or vicious ones, and causation in personal and social development is "inherently circular or spiral, rather than linear, in terms of neatly isolable causes and effects." In the present case, evidence suggests that the perceived availability of social support has important consequences for distress and depression. At the same time, it is probable that one's mental health status and personality characteristics affect the availability of social support and the ability or tendency to experience the support that is available. Accumulated evidence from diverse sources appears to constitute a compelling case for the causal impact of social support. It thus also follows that social support represents a promising target for intervention efforts aimed at reducing rates of psychological distress and depression in high-risk populations or subgroups.

FURTHER CONSIDERATIONS

Supportive Interactions versus Perceived Social Support

Most of the research discussed in this chapter has employed operational definitions of social support based on personal perceptions of support availability. As we have noted, support for the dominance of perceived social support in the literature derives from its relative strength of empirical association with mental health outcomes. Although we believe that perceived support deserves a high level of research attention, caution should be observed in according it primary importance on the basis of strength of associations.

It has already been noted that dispositional tendencies to translate real world experiences into support perceptions may themselves be strongly associated with well-being, thereby inflating the perceived support–well-being linkage. In addition, the significance of supportive interactions (i.e., "received" or "enacted" social support) has probably been underestimated for two reasons. First, the cross-sectional nature of most analyses of supportive acts reflect the tendency for such acts to be increased in the face of a high level of experienced distress. This phenomenon tends to minimize, or even appear to reverse, the positive impact of supportive behaviors. Consequently, the mental health significance of enacted support can only be effectively estimated when studied over time.

The second reason that "received" social support tends to display comparatively modest associations with well-being may be that such support tends to be undermeasured in most studies. Undermeasurement can result from failure of the research instrument to consider all domains of supportive interactions or from limiting information to what can be provided by the individual in question. Survey methodology is very well suited to the measurement of perceived social support. Conscious lying aside, respondents' subjective assessments are by definition accurate and comprehensive measures of their perception. Nevertheless, support information is imparted by others with varying degrees of clarity, and the recipient takes in this information with greater or lesser effectiveness. Research examining the social circumstances and interpersonal actions influencing both these components of social support transfer remains a largely unfulfilled need.

Increased research attention in the area of actual support transactions is important for at least two reasons. The most obvious is that associations between support perceptions and mental health do not, by themselves, inform or facilitate effective intervention efforts. Much of the initial, as well as continuing, excitement associated with social support research relates to the possibility that it represents a significant and socially modifiable mental health contingency (Turner, 1981; Turner & Marino, 1994). In order for this promise to be realized, the social processes through which social support is conveyed will require dramatically more research attention than the field has so far garnered.

Second, there is evidence that the emotional benefits of supportive interactions are not entirely mediated by perceptions of being supported. Examining daily diary data from a sample of married couples, Bolger, Kessler, and Schilling (1991) found that supportive actions performed and reported by a respondent had a beneficial impact on the recipient spouse's mood the next day, if the recipient did *not* report having received the supportive assistance. When the recipient spouse did report the supportive behavior, the impact on mood the next day was actually negative. These investigators suggested that the social support benefits of a marriage accrue substantially through a kind of "dyadic coping" process in which each spouse is shielded from a certain amount of daily stress because of the contribution of his or her partner in responding to daily tasks and difficulties. Although the role that global perceptions of social support might play in the positive effects of this shared coping is unclear, this study suggests that some of the benefits of social relationships may bypass the cognitive recognition of having been supported. In this instance, the supportive behaviors that affected mood and, presumably, psychological well-being were the ones that could not have been reported by the recipient. It appears that measures of enacted support that are based solely on recipient reports may substantially underestimate the mental health significance of actual supportive behaviors. This bias suggests that some aspects of social relationships that are relevant for mental health may not be amenable to study using standard survey methods. That one of the mechanisms by which social support may exert influence is through reduction of stress exposure was long ago suggested by Wheaton (1985) in describing a "stress deterrence" model, and subsequently by Ensel and Lin (1991) in their specification of a "stress suppression" model. However, the idea and accompanying evidence that unrecognized supportive behaviors may deter or suppress social stress clearly deserves enriched consideration.

Social Integration versus Relationship Content

In a critical review of the social support literature published a decade ago, House et al. (1988) emphasized the importance of assessing social integration (the existence and structure of social relationships) independent of relationship content (quality and valence of the relationships, reliability of support, etc.) They advocated separate assessment in part because it facilitates an examination of the processes through which social relationships translate into the experience of social support, and the structural factors that influence these processes. This point has been reiterated subsequently in the context of explicating the epidemiology of psychological distress and psychiatric disorder (Turner & Marino, 1994) and in the context of considering the costs as well as the benefits of extensive social networks (Thoits, 1995). Nonetheless, the relationship between social integration on the one hand, and specific supportive relationships and global perceptions of social support on the other, remains largely unexamined.

House and colleagues (1988) also pointed out that investigators in the area have tended to assume that the health benefits of social relationships arise solely from their supportive quality. They object to this view, in which social integration is accorded value only as a structural precursor of social support. The reviewed evidence, they argue, supports the proposition that the presence of social relationships have important effects on health and well-being separately from, and irrespective of, the content of those relationships. They point out that the most compelling evidence for establishing a causal link from social relationships to health comes from experimental studies of animals and humans (for reviews, see Cassell, 1976, Lynch, 1979; Turner, 1983) and large prospective mortality studies (Berkman & Syme, 1979; House, Robbins, & Metzner, 1982; Kaplan, Johnson, & Baily, 1988), and that these studies have found important effects even though relationship content was unmeasured. In contrast, most investigations of the benefits of social support do not conduct (or at least do not report) analyses assessing well-being across varying levels of social integration.

If the mere presence of social relationships enhances health and emotional well-being, irrespective of the supportive content of the relationships, then mechanisms for such an effect need to be considered and examined—mechanisms that do not involve cognitive appraisal or behavioral coping. For physical health, Umberson (1987) has suggested that social networks act to facilitate health-promoting behaviors (diet, exercise, etc.) through the instrumental assistance they provide and restrict noxious behaviors (smoking, drinking, etc.). Antonovsky (1979) has suggested a more general mechanism in which social integration is an important contributor to an individual's "sense of coherence." Sense of coherence, in Antonovsky's view, diminishes reactivity to stress and is an important component of psychological well-being in its own right. Finally, the direct neuroendocrine sequelae of contact with other human beings, and the health consequences of these reactions, are an area in need of further investigation.

Interventions and Levels of Analysis

As noted previously, part of the attractiveness of social support to social researchers derives from the view that it is amenable to intervention. Indeed, the dominant research question of the social support field, buffering versus main effects, has been motivated partly by the goal of identifying appropriate intervention targets based on need. But is the idea of targeted intervention the most useful one? Earlier in the chapter, we noted the dubiousness of a "zero-stress" state (which we assume when we talk about uncovering social support main effects in regression analyses). It is equally dubious, however, to interpret a strong buffering effect as evidence that social support intervention is best directed at individuals under high level of stress. The types of severe stressors for which buffering effects of social support have been most consistently found tend to be rare. Thus, an intervention with a more general focus is likely to have a greater aggregate benefit than would an intervention targeting "stress buffering."

Our point is more than a caveat about "targeted" interventions. There are grounds, we believe, for questioning the benefits of individually focused interventions in general. Even if the preponderance of the individual-level influence of social support is due to stress buffering, the largest public mental health effects are likely to result from macrolevel changes addressed to the social integration of communities. By definition, macrolevel changes are, in Ryan's (1971) terminology, "universalistic" rather than "exceptionalistic," and "exceptionalistic" interventions can only benefit those who are specifically targeted. In contrast, the influence of macrolevel dimensions of social contact (social integration, community-level social cohesion, and connectedness) on health and well-being tends to be discernible largely or wholly at an aggregate level of analysis. For example, Lynch (1977), commenting on the substantial differences in coronary heart disease (CHD) mortality and morbidity rates between Framingham, Massachusetts, and Reno, Nevada, attributed the contrast to differences in social milieu. Reno was characterized as having a high concentration of individuals who had arrived relatively recently and had few ties to the community, whereas most of Framingham's population (during the time to which Lynch was referring) had long-term ties to the community. However, it does not necessarily follow, as Lynch argued, that geographically mobile, less socially connected individuals have a greater risk of CHD. It may instead be that lack of social cohesion and connectedness at the community level has noxious effects on the community as a whole, irrespective of individual social circumstances. Durkheim (1951) explained and understood his findings on the correlates of suicide risk at this level of analysis.

Recent cogent treatises (Lieberson, 1984; Schwartz, 1994) have made it clear that the causes of individual variation in a phenomenon are not always, or even usually, the same as the causes of changes in the frequency of the phenomenon, or of group differences in frequency. These distinctions are of considerable relevance in attempting to understand the social distribution of ill health, psychological or otherwise. Nonetheless, mental health research in sociology has generally ignored the ecological level, or has treated ecological analyses as a less rigorous precursor to individual-level studies. The study of the mental health implications of social relationships is one area that could benefit from the conceptual frame of social ecology.

CONCLUSIONS

Despite the huge volume of research and publications on social support, much remains to be learned about how and why social support matters for health and well-being, and about the circumstances and processes that promote and enhance its availability. As summarized in this chapter, however, several conclusions are warranted from available evidence.

1. The ever growing number of studies and reviews on the subject leave little doubt that social support is importantly associated with mental health status in general, and depression in particular.
2. Combined evidence from laboratory animal studies, experimental human studies, and longitudinal field studies provides clear support for the contention that an important portion of the causality involved in this persistently observed relationship flows from social support to mental health status.
3. Although social support phenomena clearly involve objective elements such as network size, structure and density, and actual events and activities, it is one's

perception or belief about the availability of support that appears most protective against distress and depression. This pattern means that the love or esteem of another, and/or the fact that emotional, material, or instrumental assistance is available if needed, if kept a secret, is likely to be of comparatively little protective utility. Nevertheless, it is important to acknowledge that researchers have probably undermeasured enacted support and, thereby, underestimated its mental health significance.

4. The fact that level of perceived social support varies reliably with location in the social system as defined by SES, marital status, and gender, in combination with an array of other evidence, makes clear that the experience of being supported by others arises substantially out of the ongoing social context within which the individual is located.

5. At the same time, the early experience of social support within the family context appears to be a crucial developmental contingency that facilitates the later capacity to develop and maintain supportive relationships, and to meaningfully experience the support provided by others.

6. Social support tends to matter for psychological distress and depression independent of stress level. However, it tends to matter more to both individuals and communities where stress exposure is relatively high.

REFERENCES

Al-Issa, I. (1982). Gender and adult psychopathology. In I. Al-Issa (Ed.), *Gender and psychopathology*, (pp. 83–110). New York: Academic Press.

Aneshensel, C. S. (1992). Social stress: Theory and research. *Annual Review of Sociology, 18,* 15–38.

Antonovsky, A. (1979). *Health, stress, and coping.* San Francisco: Jossey-Bass.

Ausubel, D. P. (1958). *Theory and problems in child development.* New York: Grune & Stratton.

Barrera, M., Jr. (1986). Distinctions between social support concepts, measures and models. *American Journal of Community Psychology, 14,* 413–446.

Belle, D. (1982). The stress of caring: Women as providers of social support. In L. Goldberger & S. Breznitz (Eds.), *Handbook of stress: Theoretical and clinical aspects,* (pp. 496–505). New York: Free Press.

Berkman, L., & Syme, S. L. (1979). Social networks, host resistance, and mortality: A nine-year follow-up study of Alameda County residents. *American Journal of Epidemiology, 109,* 186–204.

Bolger, N., Kessler, R. C., & Schilling, E. A. (1991). *Visible support, invisible support, and adjustment to daily stress.* Manuscript submitted for publication.

Bowlby, J. (1969). *Attachment and loss: Attachment, Volume 1.* London: Hogarth Press.

Bowlby, J. (1973). *Attachment and loss: Separation, anxiety and anger, Volume 2.* London: Hogarth Press.

Boyce, W. T. (1985). Social support family relations and children. In S. Cohen & S. L. Syme (Eds.), *Social support and health,* (pp. 151–173). Toronto: Academic Press.

Brown, G. W., Bholchain, M., & Harris, T. (1975). Social class and psychiatric disturbance in urban populations. *Sociology, 9,* 225–254.

Brown, G. W., & Harris, T. (1978). *Social origins of depression: A study of psychiatric disorder in women.* New York: Free Press.

Cassel, J. (1974). Psychological processes and "stress": Theoretical formulation. *International Journal of Health Services, 4,* 471.

Cassel, J. (1976). The contribution of the social environment to host resistance. *American Journal of Epidemiology, 104,* 107–123.

Cobb, S. (1976). Social support as a moderator of life stress. *Psychosomatic Medicine, 38,* 300–314.

Cobb, S. (1979). Social support and health through the life course. In M.W. Riley (Ed.), *In aging from birth to death* (pp. 93–106). Boulder, CO: Westview Press.

Cohen, S. (1992). Models of the support process. In H. O. F. Veiel & U. Baumann (Eds.), *The Meaning and measurement of social support,* (pp. 109–124). New York: Hemisphere.

Cohen, S., & Syme, S. L. (Eds.). (1985). *Social support and health*. New York: Academic Press.

Cohen, S., & Willis, T. A. (1985). Stress, social support, and the buffering hypothesis. *Psychological Bulletin, 98,* 310–357.

Conger, J. J., Sawrey, W., & Turrell, E. S. (1958). The role of social experience in the production of gastric ulcers in hooded rats placed in a conflict situation. *Journal of Abnormal Psychology, 57,* 214–220.

Cutrana, C. E. (1986). Objective determinants of perceived social support. *Journal of Personality and Social Psychology, 50,* 349–355.

Dean, A., & Lin, N. (1977). The stress buffering role of social support. *Journal of Nervous and Mental Disease, 165,* 403–417.

Dohrenwend, B. S., & Dohrenwend, B. P. (1981). Socioenvironmental factors, stress, and psychopathology. *American Journal of Community Psychology, 9*(2), 123–164.

Durkheim, E. (1951). *Suicide*. New York: Free Press.

Eaton, W. W. (1978). Life events, social supports, and psychiatric symptoms: A reanalysis of the New Haven data. *Journal of Health and Social Behavior, 19,* 230–234.

Eckenrode, J. (1983). The mobilization of social support: Some individual constraints. *American Journal of Community Psychology, 3,* 509–528.

Ensel, W. M. (1986). Social support and depressive symptomatology. In N. Lin, A. Dean, & W. Ensel (Eds.), *Social support, life events, and depression* (pp. 249–266). Orlando, FL: Academic Press.

Ensel, W. M., & Lin, N. (1991). The life stress paradigm and psychological distress. *Journal of Health and Social Behavior, 32,* 321–341.

Fischer, C. S. (1982). *To dwell among friends*. Chicago: University of Chicago Press.

Flaherty, J. A., & Richman, J. A. (1986). Effects of childhood relationships on the adult's capacity to form social supports. *American Journal of Psychiatry, 59,* 143–153.

Funch, D. P., & Mettlin, C. (1982). The role of support in relation to recovery from breast surgery. *Social Science and Medicine, 16,* 91–98.

Fusilier, M. R., Ganster, D. C., & Mayes, B. T. (1986). The social support and health relationship: Is there a gender difference? *Journal of Occupational Psychology, 59,* 143–153.

Gerstel, N., Riessman, C. K., & Rosenfield, S. (1985). Explaining the symptomatology of separated and divorced women and men: The role of marital conditions and social support. *Social Forces, 64,* 84–101.

Gore, S. (1978). The effects of social support in moderating the health consequences of unemployment. *Journal of Health and Social Behavior, 19,* 157–165.

Gottlieb, B. H. (1981). Social networks and social support in community mental health. In G. H. Gottlieb (Ed.), *Social networks and social support* (pp. 11–42). Beverly Hills, CA: Sage.

Gottlieb, B. H. (1983). *Social support strategies: Guidelines for mental health practice*. Beverly Hills, CA: Sage.

Gurin, G., Veroff, J., & Feld, S. (1960). *Americans view their mental health: A nationwide survey*. New York: Basic Books.

Hammer, M., Makiesky-Barrow, S., & Gutwirth, L. (1978). Social networks and schizophrenia. *Schizophrenia Bulletin, 4,* 522–545.

Harlow, H. E. (1959). Love in infant monkeys. *Scientific American, 200,* 68–74.

Heller, K. (1979). The effects of social support: Prevention and treatment implications. In A. P. Goldstein & F. H. Kanfer (Eds.), *Maximizing treatment gains: Transfer enhancement in psychotherapy* (pp. 353–382). New York: Academic Press.

Henderson, A. S. (1992). Social support and depression. In H. O. F. Veiel, & U. Baumann (Eds.), *The meaning and measurement of social support*, (pp. 85–92). New York: Hemisphere.

Henderson, S. (1977). The social network, support and neurosis: The functions of attachment adult life. *British Journal of Psychiatry, 131,* 185–191.

Henderson, S. (1980). A development in social psychiatry: The systematic study of social bonds. *Journal of Nervous and Mental Disease, 168,* 62–69.

Henry, J. P., & Cassel, J. C. (1969). Psychological factors in essential hypertension. *Journal of Epidemiology, 90,* 171–200.

Hirsch, B .J. (1980). Natural support systems and coping with major life changes. *American Journal of Community Psychology, 7,* 263–277.

Holahan, C. J., & Moos, R. H. (1982). Social support and adjustment: Predictive benefits of social climate indices. *American Journal of Community Psychology, 22,* 157–162.

Hollingshead, A. B., & Redlich, F. C. (1958). *Social class and mental illness: A community study*. New York: Wiley.

Holmes, T. H. (1956). Multidiscipline studies of tuberculosis. In P. J. Sparer (Ed.), *Personality, stress, and tuberculosis* (pp. 65–152). New York: International Universities Press.

House, J. S. (1981). *Work stress and social support*. Reading, MA: Addison-Wesley.

House, J. S. (1987). Social support and social structure. *Sociological Forum, 2,* 135–146.

House, J. S., & Mortimer, J. (1990). Social structure and the individual: Emerging themes and new directions. *Social Psychology Quarterly, 53,* 71–80.

House, J. S., Robbins, C., & Metzner H. L. (1982). The association of social relationships and activities with mortality: Prospective evidence from the Tecmser Community Health Study. *American Journal of Epidemiology, 116,* 123–140.

House, J. S., Umberson, D., & Landis, K. (1988). Structures and processes of social support. *Annual Review of Sociology, 14,* 293–318.

Kaplan, H. B., Johnson, R. J., & Baily, C. A. (1988). Explaining adolescent drug use: An elaboration strategy for structural equation modeling. *Psychiatry, 51,* 142–163.

Kessler, R. C., Price, R. H., & Wortman, C. B. (1985). Social factors in psychopathology: Stress, social support, and coping processes. *Annual Review of Psychology, 36,* 531–572.

Kitagawa, E. M., & Hauser, P. M. (1973). *Differential mortality in the United States.* Cambridge: Harvard University Press.

Kohn, M. L., & Claussen, J. A. (1955). Social isolation and schizophrenia. *American Sociological Review, 20,* 265–273.

Lakey, B., & Cassaday, P. B. (1990). Cognitive processes in perceived social support. *Journal of Personality and Social Psychology, 59,* 337–348.

Lakey, B., & Dickinson, L. G. (1994). Antecedents of perceived support: Is perceived family environment generalized to new social relationships? *Cognitive Therapy and Research, 18,* 39–53.

Leavy, R. L. (1983). Social support and psychological disorder: A review. *Journal of Consulting and Clinical Psychology, 54,* 438–446.

Liddell, H. S. (1950). Some specific factors that modify tolerance for environmental stress. In H. G. Wolff, S. Wolf, & C. Hare (Eds.), *Life stress and bodily disease* (pp. 155–171). Baltimore: William & Wilkins.

Lieberson, S. (1984). *Making it count: The improvement of social research and theory.* Berkeley: University of California Press.

Lin, N., Dean, A., & Ensel, W. (1986). *Social support, life events, and depression.* Orlando, FL: Academic Press.

Lynch, J. (1977). *The broken heart.* New York: Basic Books.

Moody, P. M., & Gray, R. M. (1972). Social class, social integration, and the use of preventive health services. In E. G. Jaco (Ed.), *Patients, physicians and illness* (pp. 250–261). New York: Free Press.

Nolem-Hoecksema, S. (1987). Sex differences in unipolar depression. *Psychological Bulletin, 101,* 259–282.

Norbeck, J. S. (1985). Types and sources of social support for managing job stress in critical care nursing. *Nursing Research, 34,* 225–230.

Pearlin, L. I. (1989). The sociological study of stress. *Journal of Health and Social Behavior, 30,* 241–256.

Pearlin, L., Lieberman, M. A., Menaghan, E., & Mullan, J. T. (1981). The stress process. *Journal of Health and Social Behavior, 22,* 337–356.

Pierce, G. R., Sarason, B. R., & Sarason, I. G. (Eds.). (YEAR). *Handbook of social support and the family.* New York: Plenum Press.

Pierce, G. R., Sarason, I. G., Sarason, B. R., Solky, J. A., & Nagle, L. C. (1996). Assessing the quality of personal relationships: The quality of relationships inventory. Submitted.

Rollins, B.C., & Thomas, D.L. (1979). Parental support, power, and control techniques in the socialization of children. In W. R. Burr, R. Hill, F. I. Nye, & I. L. Reiss (Eds.), *Contemporary theories about the family* (Vol. I, pp. 317–364). New York: Free Press.

Rosenberg, M. (1965). *Society and adolescent self-image.* Princeton, NJ: Princeton University Press.

Rosenberg, M. (1979). The self concept: Source, product and social force. In M. Rosenberg & R. H. Turner (Eds.), *Social psychology: Sociological perspectives* (pp. 000–000). New York: Basic Books.

Rosenberg, M. (1985). Self-concept and psychological well-being in adolescence. In R. L. Leahy (Ed.), *Development of the self* (pp. 205–456). Orlando, FL: Academic Press.

Rosenberg, M. (1986). *Conceiving the self.* Melbourne, FL: Krieger.

Ross, C. E., & Mirowsky, J. (1989). Explaining the social patterns of depression: Control and problem solving—or support and talking? *Journal of Health and Social Behavior, 30,* 206–219.

Ryan, W. (1971). *Blaming the victim.* New York: Pantheon Books.

Sarason, I. G., & Sarason, B. R. (Eds.). (1985). *Social support: Theory, research, and applications.* Boston: Martinus Nijhoff.

Sarason, B. R. Pierce, G. R., & Sarason, I. G. (1990). Social support: The sense of acceptance and the role of relationships. In B. R. Sarason, G. R. Pierce, & I. G. Sarason (Eds.), *Social support: An interactional view* (pp. 97–129). New York: Wiley.

Sarason, B. R., Sarason, I. G., & Pierce, G. R. (1990). Traditional views of social support and their impact on assessment. In B. R. Sarason, G. R. Pierce, & I. G. Sarason (Eds.), *Social support: An interactional view* (pp. 9–25). New York: Wiley.

Sarason, I. G., Sarason, B. R., & Shearin, E. N. (1986). Social support as an individual difference value: Its instability, origins, and relational aspects. *Journal of Personality and Social Psychology, 50,* 845–855.

Schwartz, S. (1994). The fallacy of the ecological fallacy: The potential misuse of a concept and the consequences. *American Journal of Public Health, 84*(5), 819–824.

Smith, B. (1968). Competence and socialization. In J. A. Clausen (Ed.), *Socialization and Society* (pp. 270–320). Boston: Little, Brown.

Spitz, R. A. (1946). Analytic depression: An inquiry into the genesis of psychiatric conditions in early childhood II. *Psychoanalytic Study of the Child, 2,* 313–342.

Srole, L., Langer, T. S., Michael, S. T., Opler, K., & Rennie, T. A. C. (1961). *Mental health in the metropolis* (Vol. 1). The Thomas A.C. Rennie series in social psychology. New York: McGraw-Hill.

Stueve, C. A., & Gerson, K. (1977). Personal relations across life the cycle. In C. S. Fischer, R. M. Jackson, C. A. Stueve, & L. M. Jones, with M. Baldassare (Eds.), *Networks and places* (pp. 79–98). New York: Free Press.

Symonds, P. (1939). *The psychology of parent–child relationships*. New York: Appleton–Century–Crofts.

Thoits, P. A. (1984). Coping, social support, and psychological outcomes: The central role of emotion. *Review of personality and social psychology, 5*: 219–238.

Thoits, P. A. (1995). Stress, coping, and social support processes: Where are we? What next? *Journal of Health and Social Behavior, 37*(extra issue), 53–79.

Thomas, W. I., & Thomas, D. S. (1928). *The child in America: Behavior problems and programs*. New York: Alfred A. Knopf.

Turner, R. J. (1981). Social support as a contingency in psychological well-being. *Journal of Health and Social Behavior, 22,* 357–367.

Turner, R. J. (1983). Direct, indirect and moderating effects of social support upon psychological distress and associated conditions. In H. B. Kaplan (Ed.), *Psychological stress: Trends in theory and research* (pp. 105–155). New York: Academic Press.

Turner, R. J, Frankel, B. G., & Levin, D. M. (1983). Social support: Conceptualization, measurement and implications for mental health. In J. R. Greeley (Ed.), *Research in community and mental health* (Vol. 3, pp. 67–112). Greenwich, CT: JAI Press.

Turner, R. J., & Marino, F. (1994). Social support and social structure: A descriptive epidemiology. *Journal of Health and Social Behavior, 35,* 193–212.

Turner, R. J., & Noh, S. (1983). Class and psychological vulnerability among women: Significance of social support and personal control. *Journal of Health and Social Behavior, 24,* 2–15.

Umberson, D. (1987). Family status and health behaviors: Social control as a dimension of social integration. *Journal of Health and Social Behavior, 28*(3), 306–319.

Vaux, A. (1988). *Social support: Theory, research, and intervention*. New York: Praeger.

Veil, H. O. F., & Baumann, U. (1992). The many meanings of social support. In H. O. F. Veil & U. Baumann (Eds.), *The meaning and measurement of social support* (pp. 1–7). New York: Hemisphere.

Vinokur, A., Schul, Y., & Caplan, R. D. (1987). Determinants of perceived social support: Interpersonal transactions, personal outlook, and transient affect states. *Journal of Personality and Social Psychiatry, 53,* 1137–1145.

Weiss, R. (1974). The provisions of social relationship. In Z. Rubin (Ed.), *Doing unto others*. Englewood Cliffs, NJ: Prentice-Hall.

Wellman, B. (1974). Applying network analysis to the study of support. In B. H. Gottlieb (Ed.), *Social networks and social support* (pp. 171–200). Beverly Hills, CA: Sage.

Wellman, B. (1981). Applying network analysis to the study of support. In B. H. Gottlieb (Ed.), *Social networks and social support* (pp. 171–200). Beverly Hills, CA: Sage.

Wellman, B. (1992). Which ties to what kind of support? *Advances in Group Processes, 9,* 207–235.

Wellman, B., & Wortley, S. (1989). Brothers' keepers: Situating kinship relations in broader networks. *Sociological Perspectives, 32,* 273–306.

Wethington, E., & Kessler, R. C. (1986). Perceived support, received support, and adjustment to stressful life events. *Journal of Health and Social Behavior, 27,* 78–90.

Wheaton, B. (1985). Personal resources and mental health: Can there be too much of a good thing? *Research in Community and Mental Health, 5,* 139–184.

CHAPTER 16

Social Stratification and Inequality

JANE D. MCLEOD

JAMES M. NONNEMAKER

Social stratification refers to differential access to resources, power, autonomy, and status across social groups. Social stratification implies social inequality; if some groups have access to more resources than others, the distribution of those resources is inherently unequal. Societies can be stratified on any number of dimensions. In the United States, the most widely recognized stratification systems are based on race, social class, and gender.

The challenge for those of us interested in understanding the implications of social stratification and social inequality for mental health is to trace the processes through which macrostructures of social stratification become manifest in the microconditions of individual lives. Those microconditions can be objective or subjective, and the effects of objective conditions often depend on how those conditions are subjectively perceived. Thus, the study of social stratification and mental health requires that we think at multiple levels of analysis and about the connections between objective and subjective experiences. Given renewed interest in macro–micro links among sociologists (e.g., Huber, 1990) and the centrality of subjective perceptions in social-psychological theory, the study of social stratification and mental health is a quintessentially sociological project.

In this chapter, we review the progress that has been made toward understanding the implications of social stratification and social inequality for mental health, and the work that remains to be done. Figure 16.1 presents the conceptual outline that guides our think-

JANE D. MCLEOD • Department of Sociology, Indiana University, Bloomington, Indiana 47405.   JAMES M. NONNEMAKER • Department of Sociology, University of Minnesota, Minneapolis, Minnesota 55455.
Handbook of the Sociology of Mental Health, edited by Carol S. Aneshensel and Jo C. Phelan. Kluwer Academic/Plenum Publishers, New York, 1999.

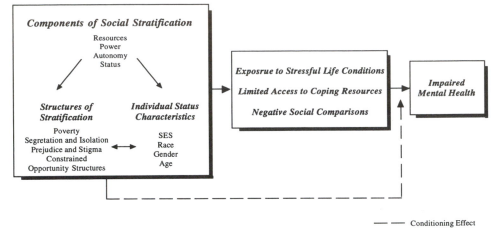

FIGURE 16.1. A conceptual model for the relationship of social stratification and inequality to mental health.

ing. We submit that social stratification and social inequality influence the concrete experiences of daily life through intermediary structures of stratification and individual status characteristics. These structures—poverty, segregation and isolation, prejudice and stigma, and constrained opportunity structures—determine how much access individuals have to resources, power, autonomy, and status. Because individual status characteristics are systematically linked to structures of stratification, those characteristics can also be seen as intermediate representations of stratification.[1] This volume includes separate chapters devoted to individual status characteristics, so we do not review research on those characteristics in detail.

Structures of stratification become relevant to mental health in two main ways. First, stratification structures represent broad classes of experience that are differentially distributed across groups, and that influence the types of stressors that individuals experience, their interpretations of those stressors, and the resources they have to cope with those stressors. Second, stratification structures influence the likelihood with which individuals confront negative social comparisons. Because these two broad processes underlie most of the research on social stratification and mental health, we begin with overviews of stress theory and social evaluation theory as they have been applied to understanding the mental health effects of social stratification.

SOCIAL STRATIFICATION AND STRESS

The definition of social stratification as systems of differential access to resources, autonomy, power, and status creates a natural link between theories of social stress and research on the mental health effects of stratification (Aneshensel, 1992). Theories of social

---

[1] Individual status characteristics are intermediate representations in the sense that they represent superficial causes of mental health [in Lieberson's (1985) terminology], the effects of which can be traced back to the existence of social stratification. Because the bases of social stratification vary from one society to the next, the relevant status characteristics vary as well. In other words, we use the word *intermediate* in the conceptual, rather than temporal, sense.

stress consider the ways in which socially structured experiences relate to the risk of stress and how that stress in turn diminishes mental health. Stress researchers have argued that social status differences in mental health can be explained by status differences in exposure to stressors and in the availability of resources (intrapsychic, interpersonal, and material) to cope with those stressors. According to this argument, members of lower status groups face more stressors than members of higher status groups but have relatively few coping resources. The mismatch between the environmental demands and adaptive capacity generates stress and psychological distress.

Group Differences in Exposure and Vulnerability to Stress

Whereas there is intuitive appeal in the notion that status differences across groups are mirrored in group differences in exposure and vulnerability to stress, evidence indicates that the relationships among status, stress, and mental health are complex. Research on major life events has evaluated group differences in the experience of stress using global or broadly disaggregated measures of life-events exposure. Typically, differences in exposure to life events do not account for status differences in mental health (e.g., Dohrenwend & Dohrenwend, 1969; Kessler, 1979; Kessler & McLeod, 1984; Langner & Michael, 1963; Thoits, 1987). Rather, occupants of lower status positions appear to be more vulnerable to the effects of life events, perhaps because they have less access to material and interpersonal resources that can be used to cope with events, or because the intrapsychic strategies they choose are less effective.

The greater relevance of differential vulnerability to events, rather than differential exposure to events, has been observed for all major status characteristics, including gender (Aneshensel, Rutter, & Lachenbruch, 1991; Conger, Lorenz, Elder, Simons, & Ge, 1993; Kessler & McLeod, 1984; Thoits, 1987), race (Ulbrich, Warheit, & Zimmerman, 1989, although see Neff, 1983), and social class (Dohrenwend & Dohrenwend, 1969; Kessler, 1979; McLeod & Kessler, 1990). However, group differences in exposure and vulnerability to life events have varied greatly across studies and seem to depend both on the type of event (Aneshensel et al., 1991; Golding, Potts, & Aneshensel, 1991; McLeod & Kessler, 1990; Thoits, 1987; Turner & Avison, 1989) and on the specific outcome under consideration (Aneshensel et al., 1991; Conger et al., 1993). These specifications call into question the usefulness of general claims about the contribution of life events to explaining status variations in mental health.

Conclusions about the relative importance of differential exposure and differential vulnerability are sensitive to which events are included in the measure of stress. On the one hand, the inclusion of random events (e.g., death of a parent) in measures of stress leads to underestimates of differential exposure because events whose mean exposures would be expected to vary across groups are combined with events whose means would not be expected to vary across groups. On the other hand, to the extent that certain kinds of events that *do* vary by status are systematically excluded from measures of stress, differences in exposure to stress are incorporated into estimates of differential vulnerability (Turner, Wheaton, and Lloyd, 1995). More generally, research on status variations in major life events has failed to offer a theoretically compelling account of which life events would be expected to vary by status and why. This failing has constrained our ability to make precise conclusions about how stratification manifests itself in the day-to-day lives of individuals. As a result, research on status variations in life events has not been able to move beyond the truism that persons who occupy lower status positions lead disproportionately stressful lives.

Research on chronic stressors has been more successful than research on major life events in offering theoretical predictions about the social origins of stress. Chronic stressors may arise from the demands and expectations accorded to social roles (Aneshensel & Pearlin, 1987), or they may reflect the long-term sequelae of life events or enduring disadvantageous life conditions (Avison & Turner, 1988; Eckenrode, 1984; Wheaton, 1983). Because roles, life events, and life conditions are distributed and experienced differentially by status (Aneshensel & Pearlin, 1987; Pearlin & Lieberman, 1979), members of different status groups are differentially exposed to various types of chronic stressors.

Pearlin and Lieberman (1979) found that many types of role strains are more commonly experienced by members of lower status groups. For example, women, persons of low socioeconomic status (SES), and nonwhites are more likely than others to experience various forms of job instability, lack of reciprocity in marriage, and difficulties with children. Furthermore, conflicts among various roles may be particularly common and problematic for members of lower status groups because they have fewer resources with which to resolve them, and because their accepted role repertoires are more constrained. For example, employed mothers report much more guilt, self-blame, and poor self-evaluations in describing their performances as wives and mothers than do employed fathers (Simon, 1995). The greater role conflict that women feel may arise in part from cultural expectations about the appropriate behaviors of men and women (Simon, 1995), but also from the greater responsibilities that women have for child care and housework in dual-earner families (Shelton & John, 1996) and from the diminished control employed women feel as compared to their husbands (Rosenfield, 1989).

Despite the general finding that chronic stressors are more common among lower status groups, it is important to emphasize that some role-related strains are more common among persons in higher status positions. For example, men are more likely than women to experience depersonalizing work relations and job pressure; education is positively associated with job pressures, and income is positively associated with self-reports of stressors involving children (Pearlin & Lieberman, 1979). The question remains, then, of which types of chronic stressors would be more commonly experienced among members of lower status groups and which are most useful for explaining status variations in mental health.

Group Differences in Coping Resources

As Aneshensel (1992) notes, status variations in material, interpersonal, and intrapsychic resources are often inferred from findings of differential vulnerability to life events rather than being evaluated directly. For example, income differences in the effects of life events on psychological distress are presumed to reflect differential access to financial resources (e.g., McLeod & Kessler, 1990). Direct comparisons of coping resources by status are rare.

To the extent that such comparisons have been made, they have focused predominantly on intrapsychic resources, with much less attention being given to material and interpersonal resources. Pearlin and Schooler (1978) present evidence to suggest that persons with low levels of income and education employ less effective coping strategies than persons with high levels of income and education. In contrast, based on a review of the extant literature on coping, Menaghan (1983) concludes that social status characteristics are more strongly related to broad coping resources—such as self-esteem, sense of control, and mastery—than to specific coping efforts. Given that the success of specific coping efforts varies depending on the type of problem that one encounters (e.g., Mattlin,

Wethington, & Kessler, 1990; Pearlin & Schooler, 1978), generalized explanations that link social status variations in mental health to differences in specific coping efforts may prove difficult to support.

The predominant focus on intrapsychic coping resources is problematic for another reason: It fails to acknowledge the social sources of those resources. Self-esteem and mastery are social products, linked to social status by social comparison processes (Rosenberg, 1981) and by the availability of opportunities for efficacious action (Gecas & Schwalbe, 1983; Mirowsky & Ross, 1986). Certain specific coping strategies, such as discussing problems with others or asking others for assistance, are also influenced by one's position in the status hierarchy. For example, lower status persons tend to be embedded in lower status networks (Massey, Condran, & Denton, 1987) that offer less social support (Turner & Marino, 1994). Direct evaluation of the social sources of coping resources would illuminate the connections between vulnerability to stress and status differences in life conditions.

We opened this section by noting that status differences in coping resources are usually inferred from status differences in vulnerability to life events. This inference may not be justified. Although status differences in vulnerability to life events may reflect status differences in coping resources, alternative explanations are plausible (Pearlin, 1991). The effects of life events on mental health may vary across groups because the objective circumstances surrounding the event are group-specific. The effects of life events may also vary across groups because of group differences in the subjective interpretations of those events. This possibility moves us toward the theme of the next section: the contribution of social evaluation processes and the self to status variations in mental health.

Despite shortcomings in the ways in which researchers have applied stress theory to the relationship between social stratification and mental health, we believe that stress theory has the potential to provide valuable insights into the process through which social stratification influences mental health. Those insights will depend on the ability of stress theory to connect the specific components of social stratification to specific experiences of stress, and to evaluate explicitly the origins of status differences in vulnerability to stress.

SOCIAL STRATIFICATION AND SOCIAL EVALUATION

The second theoretical tradition that has been applied in studies of social stratification and mental health emphasizes the role of social evaluation in creating psychological distress for members of lower status groups. Drawing on a variety of theories that share an interest in the bases for and outcomes of social evaluation (Pettigrew, 1967), theorists in this tradition argue that persons in lower status positions compare themselves unfavorably to relevant others. These unfavorable comparisons result in perceptions of inequity and/or negative self-evaluations, which in turn diminish mental health.

Rosenberg and Pearlin (1978) offer one of the more cogent statements of the relevance of social comparisons for mental health. They argue that social status becomes relevant for self-esteem to the extent that members of lower status groups internalize the negative appraisals of higher status groups (reflected appraisals), see themselves as having been less successful than those groups (social comparisons), and attribute their lack of success to their own actions (self-attribution) (see also Rosenberg, 1981). Each of these processes is conditioned by the extent to which the status in question is salient to the individual.

Consistent with the focus of Rosenberg and Pearlin's (1978) theory, most empirical studies of social evaluation and mental health have focused on self-esteem as the relevant outcome. In their own study, social class, as measured by occupational prestige, was unrelated to self-esteem for young children (ages 8–11), was only weakly related to self-esteem for older adolescents, and was strongly related to self-esteem for adults. The weak relationship between social class and self-esteem for children has been replicated more recently (Holland & Andre, 1994; Maly, 1992), attesting to its robustness across time. However, stronger relationships with self-esteem emerge when measures of income or welfare dependency are used in place of occupational prestige (Wiltfang & Scarbecz, 1990), implying that some negative, status-based, social evaluations may be relevant for children. Among adults, subsequent research has confirmed that occupational prestige predicts self-esteem, particularly for persons who report that work is central to their self-evaluations (Gecas & Seff, 1990).

Recent studies have broadened the focus to include considerations of justice and equity as they relate to other mental health outcomes. Although some studies suggest that judgments of equity in marital relations affect mental health (Mirowsky, 1985), broad evaluations of the world as a just place have not explained the effects of social stratification on mental health (Umberson, 1993). The general lack of attention to justice and inequity in the mental health literature, and the inconsistencies in the few reported studies, may derive from the highly contingent nature of the relationship between justice evaluations and mental health. Responses to injustice may depend on the perceived controllability of the circumstances that created the injustice and the perceived likelihood that one would be successful in changing those circumstances. As we discuss later, there is some evidence that, under certain conditions, feelings of injustice lead to anger rather than low self-esteem, and that negative social comparisons can lead to social action rather than self-deprecation (Singer, 1981).

Studies of social evaluation are motivated by concerns similar to those that motivate studies of social stress. Paralleling concerns with stress exposure, researchers interested in social evaluation attempt to document the conditions under which negative social comparisons are most likely to occur. Paralleling concerns with stress vulnerability, researchers ask under what conditions negative labels can be resisted. As a result of these parallel concerns, there is considerable overlap between the strategies and predictions that arise from the two theoretical traditions.

STRUCTURES OF STRATIFICATION

Much of the sociological literature on social stratification and mental health has focused on status characteristics as individual indicators of social stratification, and on stressors as the individual-level experiences that derive from the components of stratification—resources, power, autonomy, and status. However, satisfactory approaches to understanding the mental health effects of social stratification require not only that we identify the types of stressors common to occupants of lower status positions, but that we also describe the intermediary structures that link social stratification systems to the occurrence of those stressors. We focus on four such structures here: poverty; segregation and isolation; prejudice and stigma; and constrained opportunity structures. Although there is not a one-to-one correspondence between these structures and the components of stratification, the origins of each of the structures can be found in one or more of these components. We refer to these experiences as structures, rather than as stressors per se, because they represent broad processes that arise from the existence of social stratification and that have wide-ranging implications for the distributions of stressors and for the experience of negative social comparisons.

Poverty

Economic stratification holds a central position in attempts to elaborate the mechanisms that link stratification to individual well-being because it overlaps with other stratification systems in the United States. Women, members of minority groups, and the elderly have disproportionately high rates of poverty relative to their higher status counterparts (U.S. Bureau of the Census, 1990). The high rates of poverty among single parent families substantially explain the effects of single-parenthood on children's mental health and school performance (Blum, Boyle, & Offord, 1988). More generally, financial resources are related both to the risk of, and psychological responses to, life events (McLeod & Kessler, 1990).

The way in which poverty becomes relevant for mental health may differ for adults and children. For adults, poverty is an achieved status, whereas for children, it is ascribed. This implies that the subjective meaning of poverty varies for adults and children in ways that have relevance for understanding its relationship with mental health. Because the lives of adults and children are structured differently, the objective stressors of poverty also vary by age.

Studies of adults show that the stresses of poverty extend beyond financial problems to encompass a variety of negative life experiences. Poor persons are at greater risk of unstable employment, working in noxious environments, marital problems and divorce, problems with children, and ill health (McLeod & Kessler, 1990; Pearlin & Lieberman, 1979). Whereas some of these stressors arise directly from the financial pressures of living in poverty, others derive from links between occupational and economic stratification. Poor persons in the United States are also at greater risk of a variety of physical health problems, especially chronic conditions (Newacheck, Butler, Harper, Pronkowski, & Franks, 1980), and they are less likely to receive adequate medical care (Blendon, Aiken, Freeman, & Corey, 1989). A variety of explanations has been given for the generally poor health of lower socioeconomic groups, including greater exposure to physical health hazards (e.g., pollutants, hazardous waste, and toxic chemicals; Calnan & Johnson, 1985) and failure to follow healthy lifestyles (Williams, 1990), both of which may be rooted in the desperate conditions in which many poor persons live. Physical health problems in turn are related to levels of depression (Aneshensel, Frerichs, & Huba, 1984).

Research on children's poverty typically ties poor children's mental health to the mental health of their parents. In the most comprehensive presentation of the dominant theoretical model, McLoyd (1990) argues that poverty creates financial stress for parents, which leads parents to become psychologically distressed. Parental distress in turn is associated with harsh, unresponsive parenting that places children at risk of mental health problems. Evidence in favor of this specific model is mixed (McLeod & Nonnemaker, 1997; McLeod & Shanahan, 1993), but the more general proposition that parents' financial problems become relevant for children because of their implications for parenting practices has received substantial support (Conger et al., 1992; Elder, Van Nguyen, & Caspi, 1985; Lempers, Clark-Lempers, & Simons, 1989).

Studies that focus on family interactions as the key to understanding the effects of poverty on children's mental health present a very narrow conceptualization of children's lives. In the same way that poverty can affect adults' experiences at work, in marriages, and in their families, poverty affects all of the relevant contexts of children's lives: neighborhoods, schools, friendship groups, and families. Experiences in these contexts have been linked to delinquency and antisocial behavior (e.g., Giordano, Cernkovich, & Pugh, 1980; Hagan, 1991; Patterson, DeBaryshe, & Ramsey, 1989), outcomes that fall loosely under the category of mental health. The relevance of nonfamilial contexts to other outcomes is less well understood.

In our own work, we found that poor children's relative lack of access to culturally valued experiences—such as newspapers, magazines, and cultural outings—and poor physical health contribute to explaining the effects of poverty on children's mental health independent of neighborhood characteristics, mother's mental health, and the quality of mother–child interactions (McLeod & Nonnemaker, 1997). Neighborhood stressors are also important mediators of poverty's effects, particularly for children in urban areas.

The material deprivations of poverty may be particularly detrimental for children. Moffitt (1993) reviews evidence for the role that disruptions in fetal neural development play in subsequent antisocial behavior. Exposure to drugs, toxic agents, and poor prenatal nutrition place the fetus at risk of disrupted development and have been linked to later violence and antisocial behavior. Poor nutrition and a lack of stimulation in early life also disrupt neural development. All of these deprivations are much more common for poor children than for nonpoor children (for a review, see Pollitt, 1994). Furthermore, studies of educational achievement indicate that poor nutrition is a factor in poor school performance and disruptive school behavior (McGuire & Austin, 1987; Pollitt, 1987), both of which may initiate a cycle of self-perpetuating negative interactions with teachers and parents (Caspi & Elder, 1988), and both of which are related to mental health and behavior problems (Barone et al., 1995; Hinshaw, 1992).

The literatures on the mental health implications of adult and childhood poverty would benefit from synthesis and integration. The literature on adult mental health considers a variety of life experiences as they are shaped by poverty but provides little insight into the processes through which poverty has its effects. In contrast, the literature on children's mental health considers a narrow life domain—family interactions—in great detail.

Whereas the stress literature has focused primarily on contemporary life events and chronic stressors as mediators of the effect of poverty on mental health, the persistence, accumulation, and timing of stressors may be equally relevant. Liem and Liem (1978) argued that individuals who are poor are confronted with an unremitting succession of life events and chronic stressors, and find it more difficult to avoid the "contagion" of stress that negative events promote. Poor persons themselves attest to the unremitting character of the daily stressors they encounter and the psychological distress these stressors create (Olson & Banyard, 1993). As we noted earlier, physical deprivations early in life have potentially devastating, lifelong consequences, implying that when a deprivation occurs may be critical. Consistent with this emphasis on temporality, McLeod and Shanahan (1996) found that early experiences of poverty were related to higher levels of depression 5 years later, regardless of the intervening poverty history.

To this point, our discussion has focused on the ways in which poverty influences exposure to stress. Poverty also affects one's ability to manage stress. McLeod and Kessler (1990) observed income differences both in exposure to stress and in the effects of stress on mental health. Poverty itself defines the financial resources to which one has access, but other types of resources vary with poverty status as well. Because friendship networks and social interaction are constrained by social status (Blau, 1977; Moore, 1990), poor persons become members of poor collectivities, which exacerbate their personal stressors and diminish their access to resources (Massey et al., 1987). Boisjoly, Duncan, and Hofferth (1995) found no differences in reported access to time and money from family and friends based on income, but there may nevertheless be differences in access to other types of resources. For example, Belle (1982) argues that, for poor women, interpersonal relationships within informal support networks are also sources of stress. Access to resources also varies with income level because of the types of communities in which poor persons, especially poor blacks, are segregated.

Segregation and Isolation

Massey and his colleagues (1987) argue that stratification in the United States is ecologically based. Intergroup hostilities serve as both the cause and the consequence of segregation (Farley & Allen, 1987; Massey et al., 1987), and have implications for mental health that merit discussion in their own right. In this section, we focus on the role of residential segregation in creating different life conditions for members of different status groups.

The literature on residential segregation focuses on trends in racial segregation (e.g., Massey & Denton, 1987) and on the quality of life in economically deprived neighborhoods (e.g., Jarrett, 1995; Wilson, 1991). The two lines of research overlap. Because members of racial and ethnic minority groups are more likely than the white majority to be poor, they are also more likely to live in economically deprived neighborhoods and/or substandard housing.

Residential characteristics importantly affect the mental health of their residents. Early studies in the sociology of mental health found higher rates of psychiatric treatment in lower status areas of cities than in higher status areas of cities (e.g., Faris & Dunham, 1939; Schroeder, 1943). Although these studies can be criticized for inferring individual-level relationships from aggregate data (Robinson, 1950), the effect of residential characteristics on mental health has been replicated in individual-level studies of children and of adults. Children and adolescents who live in dangerous neighborhoods experience more mental health problems and have fewer satisfying interpersonal relationships than do children and adolescents living in less dangerous neighborhoods (Aneshensel & Sucoff, 1996; Homel & Burns, 1989). The social cohesion of the neighborhood also has modest effects on adolescent mental health (Aneshensel & Sucoff, 1996). Furstenberg (1992) argues that poor children fare better in socially cohesive neighborhoods because parents in those neighborhoods perceive their lives as less stressful, and their neighbors as more supportive, than do parents in less socially cohesive neighborhoods. For adults, perceived crime (White, Kasl, Zahner, & Will, 1987) and social cohesion (Furstenberg, 1992) in the neighborhood relate to mental health in predictable ways.

The mechanisms that account for these effects have not been adequately explored. Studies of adults have assumed, perhaps reasonably, that living in disorganized, unsafe, and isolated environments is inherently stressful. The constant vigilance that is required to negotiate such environments overwhelms adaptive capacities and may lead parents to focus on certain aspects of caregiving (e.g., physical protection) at the expense of others (e.g., tender interactions; Halpern, 1993). Residential characteristics may matter for mental health beyond their purely stressful implications, however. Mirowsky and Ross (1983) propose that victimization, exploitation, and the accompanying belief that events are outside of one's control, create feelings of mistrust that, in turn lead to psychological distress. They document the relationship between mistrust and distress in their study; although plausible, the empirical relationship between these patterns and the residential risk of victimization has not yet been established.

The feelings of mistrust that victimization instills also isolate individuals from the interpersonal networks on which they might draw for social support. Based on a review of urban ethnographies, Massey and Denton (1993) conclude that residents of ghetto neighborhoods develop a deep suspicion of others that leads them to depend exclusively on close kin for assistance. In a similar vein, Wilson (1991) argues that living in neighborhoods characterized by a high proportion of nonworking adults, isolated from jobs and mainstream culture, erodes personal and collective self-efficacy. The persistent unemployment common in such neighborhoods gives rise to self-doubts and futility, which are reinforced by the lower collective self-efficacy among neighborhood residents. With few or no "success stories" from which to draw hope, residents join a self-perpetuating cycle of despair. Consistent with these arguments, Caspi, Bolger, and Eckenrode (1987) found that the effects of stressful daily events on mood were heightened for women who lived in neighborhoods that they regarded as unsafe and in which residents did not engage in mutually supportive activities.

Prejudice and Stigma

Prejudice can be conceptualized in terms of institutionalized practices of discrimination, personal experiences of prejudice or general cultural bias, or ethnocentrism (Gougis, 1986). Institutionalized discriminatory practices constrain life opportunities for members of lower status groups—a topic to which we return in the section that follows. In this section, we focus on personal experiences of prejudice and ethnocentrism as predictors of mental health.

Personal experiences of prejudice can be conceptualized as stressors (Burke, 1984; Fernando, 1984; Moritsugu & Sue, 1983). They have been operationalized both as stressful life events (Thompson, 1996) and as chronic stressors (Landrine, Klonoff, Gibbs, Manning, & Lund, 1995) in prior research. Regardless of how they are measured, experiences of racism and sexism contribute directly to variations in mental health among members of lower status groups (e.g., Amaro, Russo, & Johnson, 1987; Mohutsica-Makhudu, 1989; Salgado de Snyder, 1987). In the most comprehensive evaluation of the effects of perceived discrimination on mental and physical health to date, Williams, Jackson, and Anderson (1997) found that everyday experiences of discrimination—such as being treated disrespectfully or being called names—significantly increased levels of psychological distress in a sample of adults from the Detroit metropolitan area, independent of measures of other stressors and of SES. Major acts of discrimination—such as being unfairly denied a promotion—were also related to decreased well-being in that study.

Prejudice may affect the course of mental illness, as well as onset, through its association with the likelihood of receiving appropriate treatment. Research on diagnostic practice indicates that, controlling for symptom presentation, diagnoses are assigned by race and by gender based on stereotypical expectations about appropriate behavior. Women are more likely to be diagnosed with depression, whereas men are more likely to be diagnosed with adjustment disorder (Loring & Powell, 1988). Blacks are overdiagnosed with schizophrenia and underdiagnosed with affective disorders relative to whites (for a review, see Neighbors, Jackson, Campbell, & Williams, 1989). In both cases, diagnoses correspond to stereotypical notions of expected behavior based on race and sex. Cultural barriers, reinforced by ethnocentrism, also contribute to lower rates of mental health care utilization by Hispanic Americans (for a review, see Woodward, Dwinnel, & Arons, 1992). To the extent that appropriate treatment aids recovery and forestalls relapse, inappropriate diagnoses may be related to the persistence of mental health problems.

Whereas the concepts of prejudice and discrimination are usually reserved for behaviors directed toward women and persons of color, stigma is invoked to understand the experiences of other groups that are viewed as having socially undesirable traits (see Chapter 23). For economically deprived persons, the stigma of welfare receipt is thought to have severe psychological implications (Belle, 1990). Women who receive Aid to Families with Dependent Children (AFDC) view receiving public assistance as unpleasant and embarrassing (Goodban, 1985). They report feeling ashamed and depressed by their interactions with social services organizations (Popkin, 1990). Furthermore, the longer that women receive AFDC, the more ashamed they feel and the less they believe in their abilities to move off AFDC. This suggests that AFDC receipt affects women's perceived self-efficacy to change their circumstances.

The mechanisms through which AFDC receipt affects psychological distress are not well understood. In a longitudinal study of AFDC recipients, Seff (1992) found that women on welfare who began paid employment reported greater improvements in self-efficacy over time than women on welfare who did not begin paid employment. However, although self-efficacy and psychological distress are logically connected conceptually, variations in self-efficacy based on AFDC receipt may not explain the effects of AFDC receipt on other indicators of psychological distress. Ensminger (1995) reports that "potency as a mother"—a measure of mothers' perceived self-efficacy in that role—did not explain the effects of welfare receipt on psychological distress in a sample of African American mothers. Ensminger's finding may reflect the generally low levels of self-efficacy reported by African Americans (Hughes & Demo, 1989), or it may indicate that the importance of self-efficacy as a mediator of AFDC effects varies depending on the specific type of self-efficacy that is measured. As an aside, AFDC receipt was not consistently related to women's self-esteem in either study (Ensminger, 1995; Seff, 1992), suggesting that the effects of welfare receipt on psychological well-being are not universal.

The effects of prejudice and stigma on mental health are conditioned by the ability of target persons to resist negative evaluations imposed by others. Rosenberg (1962, 1977) argued that children benefit from living in consonant social environments—environments in which children share important sociodemographic characteristics with the majority population. In such environments, children are insulated from prejudice and enjoy a familiar, comfortable environment within which to develop. The results of Rosenberg's (1962, 1977) empirical analyses were consistent with his argument. Youth who lived in dissonant environments (based on religion, social class, and race) had relatively low levels of self-esteem and relatively high levels of depression compared with youth who lived in consonant environments. McLeod and Edwards (1995) also found that poor Hispanic and American Indian children who lived in racially consonant areas had lower levels of internalizing and externalizing problems than comparable children who lived in racially dissonant areas.

Not all consonant environments are equally protective, however. Poor children living in poor areas had higher levels of internalizing and externalizing problems than poor children living in more affluent areas in the latter study (McLeod & Edwards, 1995), perhaps because the stressors inherent in economically deprived neighborhoods overwhelm any advantage those neighborhoods offer with respect to prejudice and stigma.

Similar arguments have been submitted to explain geographic variations in the relationship between sociodemographic characteristics and mental health among adults. Amato and Zuo (1992) found that the well-being of poor whites is lower in rural areas than in urban areas, but that the opposite holds for poor blacks. The authors attribute the race difference to differences in the proximal life conditions of poor blacks and whites in the two types of areas. For poor blacks, urban life is more stressful than rural life because poor, urban blacks are segregated in stress-ridden, urban ghettos. In contrast, poor, urban whites do not face the same residential disadvantages as poor urban blacks, but poor, rural whites encounter stigma and the accompanying negative social comparisons. More generally, the rate of mental illness in ethnic groups decreases as their proportionate size in the community increases (Mintz & Schwartz, 1964; Tweed et al., 1990). One plausible mechanism for such an effect is less exposure to prejudice and more support in the face of it.

Studies of consonant social environments challenge the traditional assumption that experiences of prejudice inevitably undermine the self-esteem of blacks. DuBois (1903) made this assumption explicit when he argued that blacks in the United States internalize the negative stereotypes promulgated by whites, and, as a result, see themselves as less worthy. As recently as 1987, Farley and Allen argued that the psychological consequences of segregation derive from the isolation of blacks by whites and the negative effects of the accompanying prejudice on black self-perceptions. As others have noted (McCarthy & Yancey, 1971; Rosenberg, 1981), however, the argument that prejudice would undermine self-esteem relies on two key assumptions: that members of upper status groups comprise a relevant reference group for members of lower status groups, and that members of lower status groups would accept the judgments of upper status groups as valid. Contradicting the first of these assumptions, studies of social comparison processes indicate that persons tend to compare themselves to similar others (where similarity is defined, in part, by shared ascriptive characteristics such as race) and to proximate others (such as peers and neighbors; Singer, 1981). By implication, one's racial peers constitute the most likely comparison group. Contradicting the second of these assumptions, Ogbu (1986) argues that, in the face of prejudice and discrimination, racial and ethnic minorities tend to blame the system rather than themselves.

Blaming the system, although protective for self-esteem, may increase the risk of other mental health outcomes. Mirowsky, Ross, and Van Willigen (1996) evaluated the relationship between two dimensions of instrumental beliefs and depression: personal instrumentalism (sense of control over one's own life) and American instrumentalism (the belief that most Americans control their own lives). Both a firm sense of personal control and, in the absence of such a sense, faith in American instrumentalism were related to lower levels of depression. In fact, Ogbu (1986) recognized the potentially negative effects of system-blame on psychological well-being. He argued that blacks who blame the system become disillusioned with schools and learn to distrust white society. These claims are consistent with studies that find a relationship between victimized or exploited statuses, mistrust, and paranoia (Mirowsky & Ross, 1983).

Self-esteem is not related to ascribed statuses, such as race, in the expected way. However, it is clearly related to social class. Rosenberg and Pearlin (1978) demonstrated convincingly that although social class has little relevance to self-esteem for children, it importantly predicts self-esteem for adults. In the United States, social class is an achieved status rather than an ascribed status. Given societal norms that emphasize individual achievement, and the potential for social mobility, occupants of the lower socioeconomic strata are devalued by others and interpret their own failures as an indication of their lack of ability. The relevant reference group for adults broadens beyond that for children because of contact in the workplace and through the media. Thus, through negative reflected appraisals, unfavorable social comparisons, and self-attributions of failure, occupants of the lower socioeconomic stratum come to see themselves as less worthy.

As noted at the outset of this section, prejudice can become manifest in institutionalized discriminatory practices, as well as in prejudiced actions and ethnocentrism. Discriminatory practices determine the extent to which one's avenues to success are open or constrained. Constrained opportunity structures, in turn, have been linked to mental health through their effects on objective life conditions and through their relationship with feelings of relative deprivation.

Constrained Opportunity Structures

Members of lower status groups are less likely to realize aspirations and goals than are members of upper status groups. The constrained opportunity structures that members of lower status groups face are a function in part of their lack of resources, power, and autonomy. They may also result from direct efforts by members of dominant groups to maintain their dominant position through discriminatory actions. Regardless of their source, constrained opportunity structures create challenges to mental health and, to the extent that they are successful in blocking goal achievement, diminish self-efficacy and mastery. Blocked opportunities have been implicated in racial and gender differences in mental health (Gibbs & Fuery, 1994; Willie, 1978). They are best understood empirically in studies of occupational segregation.

Research on occupational segregation and mental health has been particularly successful in delineating the job conditions that mediate the mental health effects of occupational segregation based on social class and gender (see Chapter 13). Kohn and Schooler (1983) argue that occupational conditions link broad patterns of occupational stratification to individual attitudes and well-being. Specifically, they argue that different occupations offer different opportunities for self-directed activities. In turn, the exercise of occupational self-direction directly diminishes distress and alienation. Notably, Kessler's (1982) disaggregation of the effects of income, education, and occupational status on depression and psychophysiological symptoms shows that job conditions do not substantially explain their effects, suggesting that the explanatory power of job conditions may vary depending on the specific operationalizations of social status and of mental health. Other studies confirm the importance of control, authority, and autonomy in promoting health, well-being, and self-esteem (Karasek & Theorell, 1990; Lennon & Rosenfield, 1992; Link, Lennon, & Dohrenwend, 1993; Schwalbe, 1985). Interestingly, intrinsic job features, such as self-direction, matter less to the mental health of teenagers than to the mental health of adults, perhaps because teenagers experience self-direction as stressful (Finch, Shanahan, Mortimer, & Ryu, 1991).

Comparable arguments could be advanced to explain gender differences in mental health. Occupational segregation differentiates the work experiences of women and men. Employed women are concentrated in fewer occupations than employed men, and they are particularly likely to hold clerical jobs and jobs in service industries (U.S. Bureau of the Census, 1985). As a result, working conditions differ for women and men, as do the quality of the physical and social work environments (Lennon, 1987). Women are more likely than men to report receiving inadequate rewards from work, including lack of job security, limitations for job advancement, and insufficient income (Pearlin & Lieberman, 1979). Women's jobs also offer less control and complexity than men's jobs on average (Pugliesi, 1995). Gender differences in ocupational conditions do not appear to account for gender differences in distress (Pugliesi, 1995; Roxburgh, 1996), but women are more vulnerable to the depressing effects of high job demands and routinization (Roxburgh, 1996).

Thus, constrained opportunity structures affect mental health in part through their effects on the objective life conditions of members of different status groups. Constrained opportunity structures also become relevant to mental health through their relationship with anomie, frustration, and feelings of relative deprivation. In a classic theoretical statement, Merton (1938) argued that societies, such as the United States, in which culturally prescribed aspirations and socially structured opportunities for realizing these aspirations are disassociated experience anomie. Specifically, when norms about desirable goals are more well-developed than norms about the means to achieve those goals, normlessness arises. Although there are several possible responses to that normlessness, according to Merton, deviance, especially, criminal behavior, is the most likely response for members of lower status groups (see also Cloward & Ohlin, 1960). More generally, anomie as an objective feature of group life is subjectively experienced by group members as mistrust, paranoia, anxiety, isolation, and purposelessness (MacIver, 1950; Mirowsky & Ross, 1983; Riesman, 1950), all of which constitute forms of psychological distress.

There are parallels to Merton's arguments in the psychological literature. Dollard, Doob, Miller, Mowrer, and Sears (1963) argued that any interference between an act designed to achieve a goal and actual goal attainment creates frustration, which leads to an aggressive response. The aggression can be directed outward in the form of violent actions against the persons or objects responsible for the interference, inward as in depression, self-blame, and suicide, or it may be displaced toward another person or object. The conditions that determine the specific target of the aggression have not been clearly identified. In a modified version of Seligman's (1975) learned helplessness theory, Abramson, Seligman, and Teasdale (1978) argued that depression is particularly likely to arise in response to negative, uncontrollable events that one attributes to personal failure. Whereas one might reasonably speculate that persons in lower status groups would be more likely to encounter uncontrollable events, learned helplessness theory does not specify how one's position in the social stratification system would be related to the likelihood of invoking personal attributions for failure. (For a more general critique of the lack of attention to social structure in attribution theories, see Howard, 1995.)

Williams (1975) offers relevant predictions in his discussion of relative deprivation and injustice. He defines relative deprivation as the outcome of having less than one wants or needs, and injustice as the outcome of receiving less than one is due based on the acknowledged rules for achievement and advancement. A sense of injustice is particularly likely when deprivation is conceived in collective terms and is most likely to result in a collective response, such as riots or other forms of protest, rather than psychological distress. Collective responses are fostered within close-knit, homogeneous social strata that are systematically blocked from advancement. In contrast, individual feelings of deprivation are most likely when there occurs relatively rapid change in the social status of individuals between and among loose-knit and heterogeneous groups. In the latter situation, negative social comparisons may occur, although such comparisons are contingent on a series of other conditions, including the proximity, visibility, and perceived similarity of others. Williams's arguments make clear that individual responses to constrained opportunity structures are highly contingent.

Empirical research has not yet evaluated the link between various social statuses and the likelihood of individual versus collective responses to blocked opportunity structures. Nor has it considered the psychological ramifications of those responses directly. However, William's theory receives some support from research on collective mobilization. For example, Portes and Rumbaut (1990) observed heightened ethnic solidarity among minority immigrant groups that had been somewhat economically successful, but whose additional efforts to advance were blocked. Porter and Washington (1979) reviewed evidence to support their argument that collective deprivation among blacks leads to dissatisfaction, racial militancy, and high racial self-esteem. In an experimental study, Grant and Brown (1995) found that collective relative deprivation increased expressed support for collective action because it promoted judgments of injustice. Furthermore, although they were not able to test this hypothesis, they proposed that collective relative deprivation would be most likely to lead to collective action when the deprived group perceives a threat to its identity from the nondeprived group. Together, these arguments and evidence suggest that constrained opportunity structures may produce feelings of anomie and alienation, but that they may also promote assertiveness and collective action.

The relationship between relative deprivation and psychological and behavioral outcomes appears to vary depending on the specific outcome under consideration. Most of the evidence relating measures of relative deprivation to social pathology derives from studies that predict aggregate rates of delinquent and criminal behavior from income inequality, across either time or aggregates. For example, Eberts and Schwirian (1968) conclude that U.S. crime rates are highest within communities characterized by higher levels of economic inequality, even after controlling for basic structural variables. Their findings are echoed in a time-series analysis by Danziger and Wheeler (1975) and appear to hold true with respect to international comparisons of income inequality and homicide rates (Horwitz, 1984). However, recent studies suggest that homicide rates may be tied more closely to economic discrimination than to income inequality per se (Messner, 1989).

Direct evaluations of the role of income inequality in mental health are less common. Easterlin (1974) examined data from 19 countries, both developed and less developed, comparing national economic growth with levels of happiness. He found that, within countries, income was positively associated with happiness. However, average happiness levels were not higher in wealthier countries as compared to poorer countries, and they did not increase within countries during periods of economic growth. He argued that this discrepancy can be explained by positing that the level of satisfaction individuals derive from their material wealth depends on relative status considerations rather than on absolute material well-being. Seidman and Rapkin (1983) arrive at the same conclusion based on their review of empirical research on the relationship between SES and psychological dysfunction. According to their review, SES is most strongly related to rates of suicide, major functional disorders, and demoralization in communities that are heterogeneous with respect to status. One explanation for this finding is that persons of low status feel more deprived when they live in the company of higher status others (an explanation that is consistent with several decades of research on reference groups, and with Rosenberg's idea that consonant social environments offer protection from negative social comparisons). Notably, neither Easterlin's study nor the studies reviewed by Seidman and Rapkin measured income inequality or relative deprivation explicitly. As a result, their findings are amenable to other interpretations.

STATUS INCONSISTENCY

To this point, our discussion has considered broad sets of experiences that differentiate status groups and that are related to stress and social evaluation processes. The existence of multiple systems of stratification implies that individuals may be subject to conflicting expectations within those different systems, which themselves may become manifest as stressors or in negative social comparisons. This leads us to the final topic of the chapter: status inconsistency. Status inconsistency is defined as occupancy of inconsistent hierarchical positions in different stratification systems. Parks (1928) theorized that persons who hold inconsistent statuses, for example, economically successful African Americans, live in multiple worlds in all of which they are strangers. The moral and spiritual confusion that result generate restlessness, malaise, and intensified self-consciousness. Hughes (1944), Lenski (1954), and Jackson (1962) locate this "moral and spiritual confusion" in the conflicting expectations that inhere in status inconsistency (a stress argument), whereas House and Harkins (1975) argue that status inconsistency results in feelings of injustice that breed frustration (a social evaluation argument).

Although early empirical studies found significant effects of status inconsistency on mental health, the effects were neither as pervasive nor as straightforward as these theories would suggest. For example, in one study, older men were more distressed by status inconsistencies than younger men (House & Harkins, 1975). Receiving a higher income than one would expect based on one's occupational status was related to lower occupational stress for blue-collar workers but to higher occupational stress for white-collar workers (Hornung, 1977). Methodological critiques of status-inconsistency research (focused on using appropriate controls for status characteristics and the operationalization of status inconsistency) fueled several studies that did not find any effects of status inconsistency on mental health (Horan & Gray, 1974; Jackson & Curtis, 1972).

In all of these studies, status inconsistency was operationalized based on objective status characteristics, most commonly, as the discrepancy between educational attainment and occupational status. This operationalization of status inconsistency is limited in several ways. It neglects inconsistencies across other stratification systems, such as race and gender, as they relate to SES. It fails to consider whether or not individuals perceived the constellation of statuses they hold as inconsistent. Finally, it does not incorporate other human capital inputs that might alter the expected relationship between educational and occupational statuses. One might reasonably conclude, therefore, that the effects of status inconsistency on mental health have received only a very weak test.

The benefit of moving beyond simple objective measures of status inconsistency can be seen in Dressler's (1988) work. He found that "goal-striving"—an incongruity between objective status and lifestyle—was related to depression in a southern black community, but that objective status inconsistencies were not. Dressler speculates that goal-striving diminishes mental health because it leads to negative social comparisons and self-doubt, and because it creates uncertainty and stress in social interactions where status claims are important. His results imply that objective status inconsistency may be much less important for mental health than incongruity between one's actual status and status aspirations.

SUMMING UP

At the outset, we identified two main traditions of thought that underlie contemporary research on social stratification and mental health. The first, based on stress theory, emphasizes differences in objective life conditions as they explain why members of lower status groups experience more mental health problems than members of higher status groups. The differences in resources, power, and autonomy that inhere in social stratification systems imply that members of lower status groups will experience more undesirable life events, such as job loss and divorce, and more regular and persistent chronic stressors, such as difficulty paying bills and verbal assaults. Members of lower status groups also have fewer resources to mobilize when coping with stress and may interpret certain stressors as more threatening. Status differences in stressors and coping resources are rooted in intermediary structures of stratification, such as poverty, segregation, discrimination, and constrained opportunity structures. The stressors arising from these structures are varied, and their effects on mental health are attributed to diverse processes, including their potential to overwhelm adaptive capacities and their effects on perceived self-efficacy.

The second tradition, based on social evaluation theories, emphasizes subjective perceptions as mediators of the effects of stratification on mental health. What matters for mental health is not how many stressors one encounters or how well-developed one's coping resources are, but rather where one stands in the social hierarchy relative to others. One's relative position in the social hierarchy becomes important for mental health through one's own and others' interpretations of the meaning of that standing—a meaning that is shaped by the choice of reference group, exposure to prejudice and stigma, and the extent to which similar others collectively resist negative evaluations.

The joint contributions of stress and social evaluation processes to mental health are rarely discussed or evaluated in the sociological literature on stratification and mental health. For the most part, research within the two traditions remains distinct. Yet the two approaches overlap in important ways. For example, discrimination and constrained opportunity structures create stress, but they also rely on and reinforce comparative social evaluations. Furthermore, social comparison processes depend on one's exposure to negative social evaluations and the availability of supportive others to counteract those evaluations.

Stress research and social evaluation theories find common ground in issues of self, identity, and meaning (Thoits, 1991; Chapter 17, this volume). Burke (1991) argues that stress results from the disruption of identity processes. Specifically, individuals constantly monitor the level of incongruity between their identities and their self-perceptions as derived, in part, from the behavior and appraisals of others. When efforts to resolve the incongruity are unsuccessful, stress results. Although Burke does not link his theory to social stratification, one might reasonably argue that persons in lower status positions would be less able than others to exert their identities in the face of challenges. One specific example is evident in the literature on race and ethnicity. In the United States, ethnic whites have more latitude in selecting ethnic self-identifications than do members of other racial groups (Waters, 1990). Attempts by persons of mixed racial heritage to claim a white ethnic identity are actively resisted. The discrepancy between self-identities and socially defined identities can create stress and self-doubt (Dressler, 1988).

Stress and social comparison processes also converge in subjective perceptions of objective experiences. Even the most objectively defined stressors take on meaning only as they are interpreted within a stream of other life transitions and persistent problems that frame their implications for the self (Wheaton, 1990). Those implications may become apparent through processes of social comparison, but also through the comparison of one's current life circumstances with past realities and future possibilities. Given that past, present, and future are shaped by one's position within overlapping systems of stratification, structure and meaning are naturally linked in studies of mental health (Pearlin, 1992).

Studies of social stratification and mental health would be better positioned to exploit the convergence of stress and social comparison processes if they paid closer attention to the relationship between structure and meaning, particularly as the relationship is shaped by the accumulation of stress over the life course and by stress trajectories. For example, Aneshensel and Pearlin (1987) found that women not only experienced different job conditions than men, but that they were more likely to experience unstable employment histories. The objective gender difference implied by their finding suggests that subjective perceptions of employment and employment-related stressors may also vary by gender. Operationalizations of stress that rely on current stressors fail to capture fully the history of life experiences that shape interpretations of life events (for a related argument, see Turner et al., 1995).

Research on social stratification and mental health would also benefit from more concentrated attention to the historical and social context. Stressors, coping resources, and social comparisons are not universally linked to social stratification. For example, self-efficacy plays an important role in linking individual experiences of status to mental health in the contemporary United States. However, self-efficacy is likely to be much less important for understanding mental health in cultures where independence and self-reliance are less valued. Many non-Western cultures emphasize an interdependent and relational self (Markus & Kitayama, 1991); in such cultures, one's ability to engage in cooperative social behavior, to take the perspective of others, and to adjust oneself to existing realities may be more relevant to mental health (Ryff, 1987). Whether or not those abilities vary by position in the stratification system is not known. Cultures also vary in their assumptions about the permeability of class boundaries. In caste-like systems, or cultures in which class boundaries are assumed to be relatively rigid, constrained opportunity structures are much less likely to breed frustration and distress (Rushing, 1971).

More generally, research on social stratification and mental health has been more successful at identifying the day-to-day implications of social status than at tying individual experiences of status to the macrostructures from which they derive, or at elaborating the psychological mechanisms that account for status effects on mental health. Perhaps the most notable exceptions to this claim are macrolevel studies of the economy and mental health. These studies trace the linkages between macroeconomic change, individual job and financial events, and mental health (e.g., Dooley & Catalano, 1979; for a review, see Cahill, 1983). Fenwick and Tausig (1994) took this work one step further by showing how macroeconomic structures affect individual well-being through their effects on proximal job conditions. Specifically, they found that as unemployment increases, employers demand more from their workers and allow less decision latitude. Even this work, however, shares a problem common with much research on job conditions and mental health: The reasons why those job conditions matter, and the psychological mechanisms responsible for their relationships with mental health, are only vaguely specified (for a more elaborate critique, see Spenner, 1988).

Our summary comments make our own biases clear: There is no easy answer to the question of why social stratification and inequality matter for mental health. Rather, there are multiple answers that are contingent on the outcome, the component of stratification, and the time and place in which we are interested. Exploring these contingencies may be more important to theory development than broad studies of the mental health effects of stratification.

ACKNOWLEDGEMENTS: Work on this chapter was supported by the Life Course Center at the University of Minnesota (Jeylan Mortimer, Director) and by NIMH Training Grant No. T32 MH19893. We wish to express our sincere appreciation to the editors, Carol Aneshensel and Jo Phelan, whose insightful comments and gentle prodding helped bring this chapter to completion, and to Mary Drew who typed the figure.

REFERENCES

Abramson, L. Y., Seligman, M. E. P., & Teasdale, J. (1978). Learned helplessness in humans: Critique and reformulation. *Journal of Abnormal Psychology, 87,* 49–74.

Amaro, H., Russo, N. F., & Johnson, J. (1987). Family and work predictors of psychological well-being among Hispanic women professionals. *Psychology of Women Quarterly, 11,* 505–521.

Amato, P. R., & Zuo, J. (1992). Rural poverty, urban poverty, and psychological well-being. *Sociological Quarterly, 33,* 229–240.

Aneshensel, C. S. (1992). Social stress: Theory and research. *Annual Review of Sociology, 18,* 15–38.

Aneshensel, C. S., Frerichs, R. R., & Huba, G. J. (1984). Depression and physical illness: A multiwave, nonrecursive causal model. *Journal of Health and Social Behavior, 25,* 350–371.

Aneshensel, C. S., & Pearlin, L. I. (1987). Structural contexts of sex differences in stress. In R. C. Barnett, L. Biener, & G. K. Baruch (Eds.), *Gender and stress* (pp. 75–95). New York: Free Press.

Aneshensel, C. S., Rutter, C. M., & Lachenbruch, P. A. (1991). Social structure, stress, and mental health: Competing conceptual and analytic models. *American Sociological Review, 56,* 166–178.

Aneshensel, C. S., & Sucoff, C. A. (1996). The neighborhood context of adolescent mental health. *Journal of Health and Social Behavior, 37,* 293–310.

Avison, W. R., & Turner, R. J. (1988). Stressful life events and depressive symptoms: Disaggregating the effects of acute stressors and chronic strains. *Journal of Health and Social Behavior, 29,* 253–264.

Barone, C., Weissberg, R. P., Kasprow, W. J., Voyce, C. K., Arthur, M. W., & Shriver, T. P. (1995). Involvement in multiple problem behaviors of young urban adolescents. *Journal of Primary Prevention, 15,* 261–283.

Belle, D. (1982). The stress of caring: Women as providers of social support. In L. Goldberger & S. Breznitz (Eds.), *Handbook of stress: Theoretical and clinical aspects* (pp. 496–505). New York: Free Press.

Belle, D. (1990). Poverty and women's mental health. *American Psychologist, 45,* 385–389.

Blau, P. M. (1977). *Inequality and heterogeneity: A primitive theory of social structure.* New York: Free Press.

Blendon, R., Aiken, L., Freeman, H., & Corey, C. (1989). Access to medical care for black and white Americans. *Journal of the American Medical Association, 261,* 278–281.

Blum, H. M., Boyle, M. H., & Offord, D. R. (1988). Single-parent families: Child psychiatric disorder and school performance. *Journal of the American Academy of Child and Adolescent Psychiatry, 27,* 214–219.

Boisjoly, J., Duncan, G.J., & Hofferth, S. (1995). Access to social capital. *Journal of Family Issues, 16,* 609-631.

Burke, A. W. (1984). Racism and psychological disturbance among West Indians in Britain. *International Journal of Social Psychiatry, 30,* 50–68.

Burke, P. J. (1991). Identity processes and social stress. *American Sociological Review, 56,* 836–849.

Cahill, J. (1983). Structural characteristics of the macroeconomy and mental health: Implications for primary prevention research. *American Journal of Community Psychology, 11,* 553–571.

Calnan, M., & Johnson, B. (1985). Health, health risks and inequalities. *Sociology of Health and Illness, 7,* 55–75.

Caspi, A., Bolger, N., & Eckenrode, J. (1987). Linking person and context in the daily stress process. *Journal of Personality and Social Psychology, 52,* 184–195.

Caspi, A., & Elder, G. H., Jr. (1988). Emergent family patterns: The intergenerational construction of problem behaviour and relationships. In R. A. Hinde & J.Stevenson-Hinde (Eds.), *Relationships within families: Mutual influences* (pp. 218–240). Oxford: Clarendon Press.

Cloward, R. A., & Ohlin, L. E. (1960). *Delinquency and opportunity: A theory of delinquent games.* New York: Free Press.

Conger, R. D., Conger, K. J., Elder, G. H., Jr., Lorenz, F. O., Simons, R. L., & Whitbeck, L. B. (1992). A family process model of economic hardship and adjustment of early adolescent boys. *Child Development, 63,* 526–541.

Conger, R. D., Lorenz, F. O., Elder, G. H., Jr., Simons, R. L., & Ge, X. (1993). Husband and wife differences in response to undesirable life events. *Journal of Health and Social Behavior, 34,* 71–88.

Danziger, S., & Wheeler, D. (1975). The economics of crime: Punishment or income redistribution. *Review of Social Economy, 33,* 113–131.

Dohrenwend, B. P., & Dohrenwend, B. S. (1969). *Social status and psychological disorder: A causal inquiry.* New York: Wiley Interscience.

Dollard, J., Doob, L. W., Miller, N. E., Mowrer, O. H., & Sears, R. R. (1939). *Frustration and aggression.* New Haven, CT: Yale University Press.

Dooley, D., & Catalano, R. (1979). Economic, life, and disorder changes: Time-series analyses. *American Journal of Community Psychology, 7,* 381–396.

Dressler, W. W. (1988). Social consistency and psychological distress. *Journal of Health and Social Behavior, 29,* 79–91.

Du Bois, W. E. B. (1903). *The souls of black folk: Essays and sketches.* Chicago: McClurg.

Easterlin, R. A. (1974). Does economic growth improve the human lot? Some empirical evidence. In P. A. David & M. W. Reder (Eds.), *Nations and households in economic growth: Essays in honor of Moses Abramovitz* (pp. 89–125). New York: Academic Press.

Eberts, P., & Schwirian, K. P. (1968). Metropolitan crime rates and relative deprivation. *Criminologica, 5,* 43–57.

Eckenrode, J. (1984). Impact of chronic and acute stressors on daily reports of mood. *Journal of Personality and Social Psychology, 46,* 907–918.

Elder, G. H., Jr.,Van Nguyen, T., & Caspi, A. (1985). Linking family hardship to children's lives. *Child Development, 56,* 361–375.

Ensminger, M. E. (1995). Welfare and psychological distress: A longitudinal study of African-American urban mothers. *Journal of Health and Social Behavior, 36,* 346–359.

Faris, R., & Dunham, H. W. (1939). *Mental disorders in urban areas: An ecological study of schizophrenia and other psychoses.* Chicago: University of Chicago Press.

Farley, R., & Allen, W. R. (1987). *The color line and the quality of life in America.* New York: Russell Sage Foundation.

Fenwick, R., & Tausig, M. (1994). The macroeconomic context of job stress. *Journal of Health and Social Behavior, 35,* 266–282.

Fernando, S. (1984). Racism as a cause of depression. *International Journal of Social Psychiatry, 30,* 41–49.

Finch, M. D., Shanahan, M. J., Mortimer, J. T., & Ryu, S. (1991). Work experience and control orientation in adolescence. *American Sociological Review, 56,* 597–611.

Furstenberg, F. F., Jr. (1992). How families manage risk and opportunity in dangerous neighborhoods. In W. R. Heinz (Ed.), *Institutions and gatekeeping in the life course* (pp. 121–149). Weinheim: Deutscher Studien Verlag.

Gecas, V., & Schwalbe, M. L. (1983). Beyond the looking-glass self: Social structure and efficacy-based self-esteem. *Social Psychology Quarterly, 46,* 77–88.

Gecas, V., & Seff, M. A. (1990). Social class and self-esteem: Psychological centrality, compensation, and the relative effects of work and home. *Social Psychological Quarterly, 53,* 165–173.

Gibbs, J. T., & Fuery, D. (1994). Mental health and well-being of black women: Toward strategies of empowerment. *American Journal of Community Psychology, 22,* 559–582.

Giordano, P. C., Cernkovich, S. A., & Pugh, M. D. (1986). Friendships and delinquency. *American Journal of Sociology, 91,* 1170–1202.

Golding, J. J., Potts. M. K., & Aneshensel, C. S. (1991). Stress exposure among Mexican Americans and non-Hispanic whites. *Journal of Community Psychology, 19,* 37–59.

Goodban, N. (1985, September). The psychological impact of being on welfare. *Social Service Review,* 403–422.

Gougis, R. A. (1986).The effects of prejudice and stress on the academic performance of black Americans. In Ulric Neisser (Ed.), *The school achievement of minority children: New perspectives* (pp. 145–158). Hillsdale, NJ: Erlbaum.

Grant, P. R., & Brown, R. (1995). From ethnocentrism to collective protest: Responses to relative deprivation and threats to social identity. *Social Psychology Quarterly, 58,* 195–211.

Hagan, J. (1991). Destiny and drift: Subcultural preferences, status attainments, and the risks and rewards of youth. *American Sociological Review, 56,* 567-582.

Halpern, R. (1993). Poverty and infant development. In C. H. Zeanah, Jr. (Ed.), *Handbook of infant mental health* (pp. 73–86). New York: Guilford.

Hinshaw, S. P. (1992). Externalizing behavior problems and academic underachievement in childhood and adolescence: Causal relationships and underlying mechanisms. *Psychological Bulletin, 111,* 127–155.

Holland, A., & Andre, T. (1994). The relationship of self-esteem to selected personal and environmental resources of adolescents. *Adolescence, 29,* 345–360.

Homel, R., & Burns, A. (1989). Environmental quality and the well-being of children. *Social Indicators Research, 21,* 133–158.

Horan, P. M., & Gray, B. (1974). Status inconsistency, mobility, and coronary heart disease. *Journal of Health and Social Behavior, 15,* 300-310.

Hornung, C. A. (1977). Social status, status inconsistency and psychological stress. *American Sociological Review, 42,* 623–638.

Horwitz, A. V. (1984). The economy and social pathology. *Annual Review of Sociology, 10,* 95–119.

House, J. S., & Harkins, E. B. (1975). Why and when is status inconsistency stressful? *American Journal of Sociology, 81,* 395–412.

Howard, J. A. (1995). Social cognition. In K. S. Cook, G. A. Fine, & J. S. House (Eds.), *Sociological perspectives on social psychology* (pp. 90–117). Boston: Allyn & Bacon.

Huber, J. (1990). Macro-micro links in gender stratification. *American Sociological Review, 55,* 1–10.

Hughes, E. C. (1944). Dilemmas and contradictions of status. *American Journal of Sociology, 50,* 353–359.

Hughes, M., & Demo, D. H. (1989). Self-perceptions of black Americans: Self-esteem and personal efficacy. *American Journal of Sociology, 95,* 139–159.

Jackson, E. F. (1962). Status consistency and symptoms of stress. *American Sociological Review, 27,* 469–480.

Jackson, E. F., & Curtis, R. F. (1972). Effects of vertical mobility and status inconsistency: A body of negative evidence. *American Sociological Review, 37,* 701–713.

Jarrett, R. L. (1995). Growing up poor: The family experiences of socially mobile youth in low income African-American neighborhoods. *Journal of Adolescent Research, 10,* 111–135.

Karasek, R., & Theorell, T. (1990). *Healthy work: Stress, productivity, and the reconstruction of working life.* New York: Basic Books.

Kessler, R. C. (1979). Stress, social status, and psychological distress. *Journal of Health and Social Behavior, 20,* 259–272.

Kessler, R. C. (1982). A disaggregation of the relationship between socioeconomic status and psychological distress. *American Sociological Review, 47,* 752–764.

Kessler, R. C., & McLeod, J. D. (1984). Sex differences in vulnerability to undesirable life events. *American Sociological Review, 49,* 620–631.

Kohn, M. L., & Schooler, C. (1983). *Work and personality: An inquiry into the impact of social stratification.* Norwood, NJ: Ablex.

Landrine, H., Klonoff, E. A., Gibbs, J., Manning, V., & Lund, M. (1995). Physical and psychiatric correlates of gender discrimination. *Psychology of Women Quarterly, 19,* 473–492.

Langner, T. S., & Michael, S. T. (1963). *Life stress and mental health.* New York: Free Press.

Lempers, J. D., Clark-Lempers, D., & Simons, R. L. (1989). Economic hardship, parenting, and distress in adolescence. *Child Development, 60,* 25–39.

Lennon, M. C. (1987). Sex differences in distress: The impact of gender and work roles. *Journal of Health and Social Behavior, 28,* 290–305.

Lennon, M. C., & Rosenfield, S. (1992). Women and mental health: The interaction of job and family conditions. *Journal of Health and Social Behavior, 33,* 316–327.

Lenski, G. E. (1954). Status crystallization: A non-vertical dimension of social status. *American Sociological Review, 19,* 405–413.

Lieberson, S. (1985). *Making it count: The improvement of social research and theory.* Berkeley: University of California Press.

Liem, R., & Liem, J. (1978). Social class and mental illness reconsidered: The role of economic stress and social support. *Journal of Health and Social Behavior, 19,* 139–156.

Link, B. G., Lennon, M. C., & Dohrenwend, B. P. (1993). Socioeconomic status and depression: The role of occupations involving direction, control, and planning. *American Journal of Sociology, 98,* 1351–1387.

Loring, M., & Powell, B. (1988). Gender, race, and DSM-III: A study of the objectivity of psychiatric diagnostic behavior. *Journal of Health and Social Behavior, 29,* 1–22.

MacIver, R. M. (1950). *The ramparts we guard.* New York: Macmillan.

Maly, M. T. (1992). Socioeconomic status and early adolescent self-esteem. *Sociological Inquiry, 62,* 375–382.

Markus, H. R., & Kitayama, S. (1991). Culture and the self: Implications for cognition, emotion, and motivation. *Psychological Review, 98,* 224–253.

Massey, D. S., Condran, G. A., & Denton, N. A. (1987). The effect of residential segregation on black social and economic well-being. *Social Forces, 66,* 29–56.

Massey, D. S., & Denton, N. A. (1987). Trends in the residential segregation of Blacks, Hispanics, and Asians: 1970–1980. *American Sociological Review, 52,* 802–825.

Massey, D. S., & Denton, N. A. (1993). *American apartheid: Segregation and the making of the underclass.* Cambridge, MA: Harvard University Press.

Mattlin, J. A., Wethington, E., & Kessler, R. C. (1990). Situational determinants of coping and coping effectiveness. *Journal of Health and Social Behavior, 31,* 103–122.

McCarthy, J. D., & Yancey, W. L. (1971). Uncle Tom and Mr. Charlie: Metaphysical pathos in the study of racism and personal disorganization. *American Journal of Sociology, 76,* 648–672.

McGuire, J. S., & Austin, J. F. (1987). Beyond survival: Children's growth for national development. *Assignment Children, 2,* 1–51.

McLeod, J. D., & Edwards, K. (1995). Contextual determinants of children's responses to poverty. *Social Forces, 73,* 1487–1516.

McLeod, J. D., & Kessler, R. C. (1990). Socioeconomic status differences in vulnerability to undesirable life events. *Journal of Health and Social Behavior, 31,* 162–172.

McLeod, J. D., & Nonnemaker, J. M. (1997, August). *Explaining children's responses to poverty.* Paper presented at the annual meeting of the American Sociological Association, Toronto.

McLeod, J. D., & Shanahan, M. J. (1993). Poverty, parenting, and children's mental health. *American Sociological Review, 58,* 351–366.

McLeod, J. D., & Shanahan, M. J. (1996). Trajectories of poverty and children's mental health. *Journal of Health and Social Behavior, 37,* 207–220.

McLoyd, V. C. (1990). The impact of economic hardship on black families and children: Psychological distress, parenting, and socioemotional development. *Child Development, 61,* 311–346.

Menaghan, E. G. (1983). Individual coping efforts: Moderators of the relationship between life stress and mental health outcomes. In H. B. Kaplan (Ed.), *Psychosocial stress: Trends in theory and research* (pp. 157–191). Orlando, FL: Academic Press.

Merton, R. K. (1938). Social structure and anomie. *American Sociological Review, 3,* 672–682.

Messner, S. F. (1989). Economic discrimination and societal homicide rates: Further evidence on the cost of inequality. *American Sociological Review, 54,* 597–611.

Mintz, N. L., & Schwartz, D. T. (1964). Urban ecology and psychosis: Community factors in the incidence of schizophrenia and manic depression among Italians in Greater Boston. *International Journal of Social Psychiatry, 10,* 101–118.

Mirowsky, J. (1985). Depression and marital power. *American Journal of Sociology, 91,* 557–592.

Mirowsky, J., & Ross, C. E. (1983). Paranoia and the structure of powerlessness. *American Sociological Review, 48,* 228–239.

Mirowsky, J., & Ross, C. E. (1986). Social patterns of distress. *Annual Review of Sociology, 12,* 23–45.

Mirowsky, J., Ross, C. E., & Van Willigen, M. (1996). Instrumentalism in the land of opportunity: Socioeconomic causes and emotional consequences. *Social Psychology Quarterly, 59,* 322–337.

Moffitt, T. E. (1993). Adolescence-limited and life-course-persistent antisocial behavior: A developmental taxonomy. *Psychological Review, 100,* 674–701.

Mohutsica-Makhudu, Y. N. K. (1989). The psychological effects of apartheid on the mental health of black South African women domestics. *Journal of Multicultural Counseling and Development, 17,* 134–142.

Moore, G. (1990). Structural determinants of men's and women's personal networks. *American Sociological Review, 55,* 726–735.

Moritsugu, J., & Sue, S. (1983). Minority status as a stressor. In R. Felner, L. Jason, J. Moritsugu, & S. Faber (Eds.), *Preventive psychology: Theory, research, and practice* (pp. 162–174). Elmsford, NY: Pergamon Press.

Neff, J. A. (1983). Urbanicity and depression reconsidered: The evidence regarding depressive symptomatology. *Journal of Nervous and Mental Disease, 171,* 546–552.

Neighbors, H. W., Jackson, J. S., Campbell, L., & Williams, D. (1989). The influence of racial factors on psychiatric diagnosis: A review and suggestions for research. *Community Mental Health Journal, 25,* 301–311.

Newacheck, P. W., Butler, L. H., Harper, A. K., Prontkowski, D. L., & Franks, P. E. (1980). Income and illness. *Medical Care, 18,* 1165–1176.

Ogbu, J. U. (1986). The consequences of the American caste system. In Ulric Neisser (Ed.), *The school achievement of minority children: New perspectives* (pp. 19–56). Hillsdale, NJ: Erlbaum.

Olson, S. L., & Banyard, V. (1993). Stop the world so I can get off for a while. *Family Relations, 42,* 50–56.

Parks, R. E. (1928). Human migration and the marginal man. *American Journal of Sociology, 33,* 881–893.

Patterson, G. R., DeBaryshe, B. D., & Ramsey, E. (1989). Developmental perspective on antisocial behavior. *American Psychologist, 44,* 329–335.

Pearlin, L. I. (1991). The study of coping: An overview of problems and directions. In J. Eckenrode (Ed.), *The social context of coping* (pp. 261–276). New York: Plenum Press.

Pearlin, L. I. (1992). Structure and meaning in medical sociology. *Journal of Health and Social Behavior, 33,* 1–9.

Pearlin, L. I., & Lieberman, M. A. (1979). Social sources of emotional distress. *Research in Community and Mental Health, 1,* 217–248.

Pearlin, L. I., & Schooler, C. (1978). The stress of coping. *Journal of Health and Social Behavior, 19,* 2–21.

Pettigrew, T. F. (1967). Social evaluation theory: Convergences and applications. In D. Levine (Ed.), *Nebraska Symposium on Motivation* (pp. 241–311). Lincoln: University of Nebraska Press.

Pollitt, E. (1987). Effects of iron deficiency in mental development: Methodological considerations and substantive findings. In F. Johnson (Ed.) *Nutritional anthropology* (pp. 225–254). New York: Alan R. Liss.

Pollitt, E. (1994). Poverty and child development: Relevance of research in developing countries to the United States. *Child Development, 65,* 283–295.

Popkin, S. J. (1990). Welfare: Views from the bottom. *Social Problems, 37,* 64–79.

Porter, J. R., & Washington, R. E. (1979). Black identity and self-esteem: A review of studies of black self-concept: 1968–1978. *Annual Review of Sociology, 5,* 53–74.

Portes, A., & Rumbaut, R. (1990). *Immigrant America: A portrait.* Berkeley: University of California Press.

Pugliesi, K. (1995). Work and well-being: Gender differences in the psychological consequences of employment. *Journal of Health and Social Behavior, 36,* 57–71.

Riesman, D. (1950). *The lonely crowd.* New Haven, CT: Yale University Press.

Robinson, W. S. (1950). Ecological correlations and the behavior of individuals. *American Sociological Review, 15,* 351–357.

Rosenberg, M. (1962). The dissonant religious context and emotional disturbance. *American Journal of Sociology, 68,* 1–10.

Rosenberg, M. (1977). Contextual dissonance effects: Nature and causes. *Psychiatry, 40,* 205–217.

Rosenberg, M. (1981). The self-concept: Social product and social force. In M. Rosenberg, & R. H. Turner (Eds.), *Social psychology: Sociological perspectives* (pp. 593–624). New York: Basic Books.

Rosenberg, M., & Pearlin, L. I. (1978). Social class and self-esteem among children and adults. *American Journal of Sociology, 84,* 53–77.

Rosenfield, S. (1989). The effects of women's employment: Personal control and sex differences in mental health. *Journal of Health and Social Behavior, 30,* 77–91.

Roxburgh, S. (1996). Gender differences in work and well-being: Effects of exposure and vulnerability. *Journal of Health and Social Behavior, 37,* 265–277.

Rushing, W. A. (1971). Class, culture, and "social structure and anomie". *American Journal of Sociology, 76,* 857–872.

Ryff, C. D. (1987). The place of personality and social structure research in social psychology. *Journal of Personality and Social Psychology, 53,* 1192–1202.

Salgado de Snyder, V. N. (1987). Factors associated with acculturative stress and depressive symptomatology among married Mexican immigrant women. *Psychology of Women Quarterly, 11,* 475–488.

Schroeder, C. W. (1943). Mental disorders in cities. *American Journal of Sociology, 48,* 40–47.

Schwalbe, M. L. (1985). Autonomy in work and self-esteem. *Sociological Quarterly, 26,* 519–535.

Seff, M. (1992, August). *Welfare, work status, and women's self evaluations.* Paper presented at the annual meeting of the American Sociological Association, Pittsburgh.

Seidman, E., & Rapkin, B. (1983). Economics and psychosocial dysfunction: Toward a conceptual framework and prevention strategies. In R. Felner, L. Jason, J. Moritsugu, & S. Farber (Eds.), *Preventive psychology: Theory, research and practice* (pp. 175–198). Elmsford, NY: Pergamon Press.

Seligman, M. E. P. (1975). *Helplessness: On depression, development and death.* San Francisco: W. H. Freeman.

Shelton, B. A., & John, D. (1996). The division of household labor. *Annual Review of Sociology, 22,* 299–322.

Simon, R. W. (1995). Gender, multiple roles, role meaning, and mental health. *Journal of Health and Social Behavior, 36,* 182–194.

Singer, E. (1981). Reference groups and social evaluations. In M. Rosenberg & R. H. Turner (Eds.), *Social psychology: Sociological perspectives* (pp. 66–93). New York: Basic Books.

Spenner, K. I. (1988). Social stratification, work, and personality. *Annual Review of Sociology, 14,* 69–97.

Thoits, P. A. (1987). Gender and marital status differences in control and distress: Common stress versus unique stress explanations. *Journal of Health and Social Behavior, 28,* 7–22.

Thoits, P. A. (1991). On merging identity theory and stress research. *Social Psychology Quarterly, 54,* 101–112.

Thompson, V. L. S. (1996). Perceived experiences of racism as stressful life events. *Community Mental Health Journal, 32,* 223–233.

Turner, R. J., & Avison, W. R. (1989). Gender and depression: Assessing exposure and vulnerability to life events in a chronically strained population. *Journal of Nervous and Mental Disease, 177,* 443–455.

Turner, R. J., & Marino, F. (1994). Social support and social structure: A descriptive epidemiology. *Journal of Health and Social Behavior, 35,* 193–212.

Turner, R. J., Wheaton, B., & Lloyd, D. A. (1995). The epidemiology of social stress. *American Sociological Review, 60,* 104–125.

Tweed, D. L., Goldsmith, H. F., Jackson, D. J., Stiles, D., Rae, D. S., & Kramer, M. (1990). Racial congruity as a contextual correlate of mental disorder. *American Journal of Orthopsychiatry, 60,* 392–403.

Ulbrich, P. M., Warheit, G. J., & Zimmerman, R. S. (1989). Race, socioeconomic status, and psychological distress: An examination of differential vulnerability. *Journal of Health and Social Behavior, 30,* 131–146.

Umberson, D. (1993). Sociodemographic position, world views, and psychological distress. *Social Science Quarterly, 74,* 575–589.

U.S. Bureau of the Census. (1985). *Statistical abstract of the United States 1986* (106th Ed.). Washington, DC: U.S. Government Printing Office.

U.S. Bureau of the Census. (1990). *Money income and poverty status of families and persons in the U.S.: 1989* (Current Population Reports, Series P-60). Washington, DC: U.S. Government Printing Office.

Waters, M.C. (1990). *Ethnic options: Choosing identities in America.* Berkeley: University of California Press.

Wheaton, B. (1983). Stress, personal coping resources, and psychiatric symptoms: An investigation of interactive models. *Journal of Health and Social Behavior, 24,* 208–229.

Wheaton, B. (1990). Life transitions, role histories, and mental health. *American Sociological Review, 55,* 209–223.

White, M., Kasl, S. V., Zahner, G. E. P., & Will, J. C. (1987). Perceived crime in the neighborhood and mental health of women and children. *Environment and Behavior, 19,* 588–613.

Williams, D. R. (1990). Socioeconomic differentials in health: A review and redirection. *Social Psychology Quarterly, 53,* 81–99.

Williams, D. R., Yu, Y., Jackson, J. S., & Anderson, N. B. (1997). Racial differences in physical and mental health: Socioeconomic status, stress and discrimination. *Journal of Health Psychology, 2,* 335–351.

Williams, R. M., Jr. (1975). Relative deprivation. In L. A. Coser (Ed.), *The idea of social structure: Papers in honor of Robert K. Merton* (pp. 355–378). New York: Harcourt, Brace, Jovanovich.

Willie, C. V. (1978). The president's commission on mental health: A minority report on minorities. *New England Sociologist, 1,* 13–22.

Wilson, W. J. (1991). Studying inner-city social dislocations: The challenge of public agenda research. *American Sociological Review, 56,* 1–14.

Wiltfang, G. L., & Scarbecz, M. (1990). Social class and adolescents' self-esteem: Another look. *Social Psychology Quarterly, 53,* 174–183.

Woodward, A. M., Dwinnel, A. D., & Arons, B. S. (1992). Barriers to mental health care for Hispanic Americans: A literature review and discussion. *Journal of Mental Health Administration, 19,* 224–236.

CHAPTER 17

Self, Identity, Stress, and Mental Health

Peggy A. Thoits

THE RELEVANCE OF SELF AND IDENTITY ISSUES TO STRESS AND MENTAL HEALTH

It is virtually impossible to develop a theory of the etiology of mental illness without thinking about self and identity issues. Almost all approaches in psychiatry and clinical psychology (with the exception of behaviorism) view individuals' mental health as at least partly influenced by positive self-conceptions, high self-esteem, and/or the possession of valued social identities. Conversely, psychological disorder has been attributed to unconscious conflicts within the ego (Freud, 1933), arrested or inadequate identity development (e.g., Erikson, 1963; Freud, 1933), threats to self-conception or self-esteem (e.g., Abramson, Metalsky, & Alloy, 1989), and identity loss (Breakwell, 1986; Brown & Harris, 1978; Thoits, 1986), among many related processes. Indeed, some theorists and researchers see injuries to identity or self-worth not only as precursors but as key *markers* of mental disorder (e.g., Beck, 1967; Abramson et al., 1989).[1] This can be seen in the criteria for various mental disorders in the fourth edition of the *Diagnostic and Statistical Manual of Mental Disorders* (DSM-IV; American Psychiatric Association, 1994). For example, "low self-esteem," "feelings of worthlessness," and/or "unstable self-image" are key criteria in the identification of major depression, bipolar disorder, dysthymia (chronic depressed mood), and borderline and avoidant personality disorders.[2]

---

[1] Of course, this view confounds causes with consequences, making etiological theories difficult to disprove.

[2] Manic and hypomanic episodes, and narcissistic personality disorder, on the other hand, include states of inflated self-esteem or grandiosity.

PEGGY A. THOITS • Department of Sociology, Vanderbilt University, Nashville, Tennessee 37235.

Handbook of the Sociology of Mental Health, edited by Carol S. Aneshensel and Jo C. Phelan. Kluwer Academic/Plenum Publishers, New York, 1999.

Despite considerable theoretical emphasis placed on self and identity factors in psychiatry and clinical psychology, sociology's currently dominant etiological approach to mental disorder, stress theory, only relatively recently has begun to attend explicitly to these constructs. In its simplest form, stress theory traces mental disorder to environmental demands (i.e., to challenges and threats originating outside the person). Numerous challenges and threats are thought to overwhelm the person's coping resources or coping abilities, producing symptoms of psychological distress or more serious forms of mental disorder (see Chapter 14). Despite the theory's focus on external or environmental causes, researchers in the past decade have been finding it necessary to incorporate self and identity concepts in order to explain stressors' psychological impacts.

Why have stress theorists had to think about self and identity? There are at least two reasons. First, about 25 years of research has shown that major life events and chronic strains in people's lives generally have *nonspecific* impacts; that is, stressors can negatively affect physical health *or* mental health (or both simultaneously). Events and strains are significantly and causally associated with the occurrence of numerous conditions, including colds, flu, asthma attacks, tuberculosis, angina, heart attacks, high blood pressure, occupational injuries, complications of pregnancy, episodes of multiple sclerosis, anxiety, depression, schizophrenia, alcohol and drug use, early death, and so on almost endlessly (see reviews in Cohen & Williamson, 1991; Coyne & Downey, 1991; Creed, 1985; Thoits, 1983a). Given this wide array of potential negative consequences, the stress theorist who wants to predict outcomes more precisely needs to find factors that narrow this range of possibilities. One crude (but useful) refinement is the ability to determine whether *physical* health or *mental* health problems are likely to result from stress exposure (Brown & Harris, 1989; Folkman, Lazarus, Gruen, & DeLongis, 1986; Lin & Ensel, 1989). Since people's self-conceptions are closely linked to their psychological states, stressors that damage or threaten self-concepts are likely to predict emotional problems, whereas stressors that place wear and tear on the body (because they require effortful readjustments in behavior) may better forecast physical disease or injury. Of course, many stressors threaten self-conceptions and require effortful behavioral changes, and in those cases, one would expect both emotional and physical sequelae. Since emotional problems and physical health problems are only moderately correlated, however (Hays, Marshall, Yu, & Sherbourne, 1994; Manning & Wells, 1992), identifying variables that lead to these differing broad outcomes still helps to refine our explanatory models.

A second reason why it has become necessary to incorporate self/identity issues into stress research concerns the conditions under which stressors have psychological impacts. Not all persons who experience multiple negative events or chronic strains react with emotional disturbance. Research shows that flexible and situationally appropriate coping strategies (Folkman, 1984; Mattlin, Wethington, & Kessler, 1990) and coping resources (such as high self-esteem, a sense of mastery or control, and social support) can buffer or reduce the negative psychological impacts of stressors (for details, see Chapters 15 and 18). Upon closer inspection, each of these stress-buffering factors has important self aspects. Coping strategies can shore up threatened perceptions of self. High self-esteem can give individuals the confidence necessary to attempt problem solving or to persist in their efforts. And the perception that social support is available helps to sustain a person's self-worth and sense of "mattering" to others (Rosenberg & McCullough, 1981), again encouraging coping efforts.

In summary, it often seems necessary to include self or identity factors when trying to distinguish stressors' physical effects from their psychological ones, and when trying to explain why some people are emotionally disturbed by stress experiences, whereas other people are not. This chapter scrutinizes newly developing theoretical ideas, empirical findings, and still-unanswered questions about the influences of self and identity factors in the stress process.

Definitions of Self and Identity

Up to this point, I have used the terms *self* and *identity* loosely, without definition. It is important to clarify the meaning of these terms before turning to their roles in stress theory. (How these notions are measured is described below where appropriate.)

Three major features of self can be distinguished: "the self," "selves/identities," and "self-esteem." "The self" is that aspect of the person that has experiences, reflects on experiences, and acts upon self-understandings derived from experiences (Gecas & Burke, 1995; McCall & Simmons, 1978; Weigert, Teitge, & Teitge, 1986). The self is generally perceived as unified, singular, and whole. However, the self is also aware of and can behave in terms of its "social selves," also called "identities," "self-concepts," or "self- conceptions." These are more specific understandings of oneself and one's experiences in the world, for example, as a Californian and a woman. These selves or identities are essentially parts of the self as a whole. In general, selves, identities, or self-concepts (terms I use interchangeably) are understandings of ourselves as *specific objects* that can be named or classified (e.g., Frank, an atheist, a flower gardener). In contrast, "self-esteem" (also termed "self-regard," "self-worth," "self-evaluation," and so on) is an understanding of one's *quality* as an object—that is, how good or bad, valuable or worthless, positive or negative, or superior or inferior one is. Self-esteem may be global ("I am a good person") or domain-specific ("I am pretty good at teaching").

Sociologists are particularly interested in those self-conceptions and self-evaluations that are socially derived and socially sustained. Symbolic interactionist theory (Blumer, 1969; Cooley, 1902; McCall & Simmons, 1978; Mead, 1934; Stryker, 1980) outlines the social origins of the self and its development (as well as the development of more specific selves/identities). Since most sociological stress researchers draw from this theory, a quick synopsis of this approach is in order.[3]

Symbolic Interactionist Approaches to the Self

Very generally speaking, symbolic interactionism sees both society and the self as created, maintained, and changed through the process of communication (i.e., symbolic interaction). Because communication depends upon shared symbols, and because shared symbols have the same general meanings to those who use them, people are able to "take the role of the other" when they interact (Mead, 1934). Putting it another way, because we know that others attach roughly the same meaning to our words and gestures as we do ourselves, we can imaginatively anticipate their responses to our communications; we can shift perspectives from our own to theirs and then back again. Thus, language not only gives us the ability to classify, think about, and act toward meaningful objects in the world,

---

[3] Readers interested a detailed history of self/identity terms, variations in their meanings, and their roles in theory will find Weigert et al. (1986) a valuable source.

but also enables us to reflect on the *self* as an object from the perspective of other people (i.e., role taking). Quite literally, through shared language, societies (i.e., other people) give us our knowledge that we exist and have meaning.

We personally experience and act on our lives in the natural world. But we also reflect on ourselves from the perspective of other people and/or the generalized community. For this reason, Mead (1934) found it useful to distinguish between the "I" and the "me" aspects of self. The "I" is the active, creative agent doing the experiencing, thinking, and acting—"the self" as described earlier. The "me" is the perspective on oneself that one assumes when taking the role of specific others or of the general community (Mead 1934). Because there are multiple "others" from whose eyes we see, we usually have multiple "me's." Or in William James's famous explanation (1890/1950, p. 294, emphases in the original), *"a man has as many social selves as there are individuals who recognize him and carry an image of him in their mind. . . .* But as the individuals who carry the images fall naturally into classes, we may practically say that he has as many different social selves as there are distinct *groups* of persons about whose opinion he cares." Mead's "me's" are our more specific social "selves" or "identities."

Selves/identities, then, are social categories that individuals learn in social interaction and accept as self-descriptive and self-defining. In essence, selves or identities are answers to the question "Who am I?" Answers typically refer to (1) sociodemographic characteristics that we hold (e.g., middle-aged, African American), (2) groups or organizations to which we belong (member of Little League, Episcopalian), (3) social roles that we possess (stepmother, physician), (4) social types of person that we are (intellectual, leader), and (5) personality or character traits that we display (optimist, responsible) (Thoits & Virshup, 1998). We learn these categories from our society through shared language, and we learn to apply them to ourselves by taking the role of the other and by having our selves/identities validated by other people in social interaction (McCall & Simmons, 1978). These notions of self/identity play an important role in stress theory, as is seen below.

Some theorists (e.g., Gecas & Burke, 1995; McCall & Simmons, 1978; Weigert et al., 1986), prefer to distinguish selves from identities. For these theorists, selves refer to private self-definitions, whereas identities refer to who or what one is in the eyes of others—to public definitions. In this chapter, I generally treat the terms *selves* and *identities* as equivalent because people typically invest themselves in their identities, so that private selves and public identities become two halves of the same coin. Nevertheless, the distinction is especially useful when private and public definitions of self do not correspond, for example, when one has been mistakenly labeled as a certain kind of person by others, when others emphasize the importance of a characteristic that one does not see as relevant (e.g., "Hispanic teacher" as opposed to "teacher"), or when one has imaginatively taken on a self-conception of which other people are unaware. In these cases, the term *identity* is used to refer to the definitions that others apply to the person.

Like selves/identities, self-esteem is also acquired and sustained in social interaction with specific and "generalized" others (Blumer, 1969; Cooley, 1902; Mead, 1934). We not only see who and what we are as we imaginatively share the reactions of others, but we see how good or bad we are from their reactions as well. Cooley (1902) described the result of this role-taking process as "the looking-glass self"—we see ourselves mirrored or reflected in the eyes of other people. Self-esteem that is derived from others' reactions (or, more accurately, from our somewhat biased *perceptions* of others' reactions), is termed "reflected" or "reflexive" self-esteem, since we tend to accept and share the opinions of our worth that others communicate either verbally or nonverbally.[4] Symbolic interactionism assumes that other people's positive regard for us or for our role performances is rewarding. In sharing others' opinions of us, we feel pleasantly good about ourselves. Positive reflected self-esteem, in turn, motivates us to keep trying to meet people's behavioral expectations (which we continue to anticipate through role taking).[5] In summary, our sense of self, our identities, and our self-esteem are derived, at least in part, from social relationships and are grounded in social interaction. Not surprisingly, then, stressors that disrupt or damage relationships with other people may have negative consequences for the self, a topic to which I will return.

Cognitive Approaches to the Self

Although symbolic interactionist understandings of self and identity predominate in the sociological stress literature, psychological stress theorists draw from a different (but compatible) approach to the self, cognitive theory.

Much stress research that attends to the self in psychology relies implicitly or explicitly on ideas elaborated by Markus (1977).[6] Markus uses the term *self-schemas* to refer to self-concepts. Self-schemas are a major subset of all schemas or concepts, defined as cognitive generalizations that we draw from our personal experiences. *Self*-schemas are cognitive generalizations about the self derived from past experiences (Markus, 1977, p. 63). Schemas serve to organize and guide the processing of information; they are important because, without concepts to streamline incoming data, individuals could be immobilized by information overload. Markus argues that individuals develop self-schemas for various domains of recurring important experiences (e.g., "I am independent," "I am nurturing"); these self-concepts in turn direct future information processing about the self. In her view, a person's overall self-concept consists of a set of self-schemas (Markus, Crane, Bernstein, & Siladi, 1982), just as one's set of social selves or identities constitutes the self in symbolic interactionist approaches.

According to Markus, self-schemas facilitate recognizing, interpreting, and rapid responding to situational stimuli. For example, if a man has a self-schema as "masculine," he will notice and more rapidly process information that relates to that self-concept, and he will try to behave in ways that are consistent with his masculine acts in the past. Although schemas guide and speed up information processing, they also introduce biases or misperceptions, because situational cues that are irrelevant or inconsistent with one's schematic representations of the self tend to be missed, ignored, or discounted.

Markus and her colleagues have tended to focus on self-schemas that are personality

[4] Self-esteem is only moderately correlated with others' evaluations (e.g., May, 1991) for two reasons. First, we tend to perceive others' opinions of us through rose-colored glasses (e.g., O'Connor & Dyce, 1993), which weakens the association between our own self-regard and others' actual evaluations. Second, we are able to assess our abilities or worth independently through social comparison processes (e.g., Gecas & Schwalbe, 1983; Suls & Will, 1991); others' evaluative feedback may not match our own assessments of our relative ability or worth.

[5] Hence, our socially based selves/identities and our reflected self-esteem motivate conformity, sustaining and perpetuating the social order. However, the potential for unpredictability, creativity, and deviance is always present in the "I" aspect of the self (Blumer, 1969). Although symbolic interactionist theory emphasizes the potential for social change, social forces tend to make behavioral conformity more common than deviance (Stryker & Stratham, 1985).

[6] I am grateful to Lauren Virshup for discussion of Markus's approach and for her assistance in summarizing the main thrust of the theory.

traits such as "independent," "nurturing," "introverted," "masculine," "feminine," and "androgynous" (e.g., Markus et al., 1982; Markus, Smith, & Moreland, 1985). However, self-schema theory does not preclude self-schemas based on sociodemographic characteristics, social roles, and group memberships. Each of these attributes is associated with recurrent experiences from which persons are likely to abstract generalizations about themselves (e.g., "I am young," "I am poor," "I am a student"). And social identities are thought to shape people's perceptions, interpretations, and behaviors in ways that are consistent with Markus's theoretical arguments about self-schemas (see McCall & Simmons, 1978; Stryker, 1980). In short, there are considerable similarities between the notion of self-schema and symbolic interactionist conceptions of self. Moreover, each theory suggests useful solutions to problems in the other theory.

For example, Markus does not explain how self-schemas are generated or where they are acquired. She implies that schemas emerge from a private process of self-observation and self-discovery (Markus, 1977). However, as Mead (1934) and others have observed, generalizations about the self are available in the socially shared categories provided in language. Furthermore, other people label and treat an individual as if he/she were a son/daughter, a child, or Asian-American, and also make personality attributions about him/her. These social sources of ready information about the self likely expedite cognitive organization and self-schema formation. Finally, because social structure is a key determinant of the types of recurrent experiences each individual will have (Stryker & Statham, 1985), people's locations in the social structure (e.g., their gender, race, age, social class) should influence their schema formation. In these ways, symbolic interactionist theory helps elaborate the origins of self-schemas.

Similarly, the cognitive properties of schemas may help to account for phenomena that are poorly explained in symbolic interactionist theory. Symbolic interactionists generally assume that people are motivated to conform to others' expectations by a desire for social approval (McCall & Simmons, 1978; Stryker & Serpe, 1982). However, people often continue to enact and seek validation for identities that are low in status or stigmatized and, thus, likely to garner disapproval. As Markus has argued and shown, schemas (or selves) have information-biasing consequences. The more developed the self-schema, the more accessible and influential it is in information processing and the more resistant the individual is to counterschematic information (Gurin & Markus, 1989; Markus, 1977; Markus et al., 1985). These information-processing biases predispose individuals to act in ways that reconfirm or verify their existing self-conceptions, initiating, in essence, self-fulfilling prophecies. Indeed, studies show that people deliberately seek out interactions that support their self-schemas (Markus et al., 1985; Swann, Wenzlaff, Krull, & Pelham, 1992a; Swann, Wenzlaff, & Tafarodi, 1992) even when those self-schemas are negative. Thus, biased information processing helps stabilize identities, regardless of social approval. One implication for stress theory, then, is that receiving schema-inconsistent information about the self will be more threatening than receiving schema-consistent feedback, even when the inconsistent information is positive or approving (Swann & Brown, 1990; Swann, Wenzloff, & Tafarodi, 1992). This is an implication to which I will return.

To this point, I have described symbolic interactionist theory and cognitive schema theory in broad strokes. More specific versions of these two approaches to self have been applied to problems in stress theory. I turn now to an examination of those more specific applications.

THE ROLES OF SELF/IDENTITY FACTORS
IN THE STRESS PROCESS

Ideas about self have been introduced at several points in the stress process. Self and identity factors are thought to play a part in stress appraisal, stress mediation, stress moderation, and processes of coping and giving support. Each point is examined in turn, with special attention to empirical findings and as-yet-unanswered questions.

Stress Appraisal

Observed relationships between stress exposure and psychological symptoms have not been strong (Avison & Turner, 1988; Thoits, 1983a; Turner, Wheaton, & Lloyd, 1995), and people's emotional reactions to what appear to be the same objective events have been strikingly variable (e.g., Reissman, 1990; Umberson, Wortman, & Kessler, 1992; Wortman & Silver, 1987). These findings have lead researchers in recent years to assert that the psychological impacts of stressors must depend on their *meanings* to the individual. (Brown & Harris [1978, 1989] had this insight long ago and developed elaborate strategies to assess stressors' meanings.) Attention has increasingly turned to the problem of defining and measuring meaning (see Simon, 1997).

Sociologists have tended to focus on the social contexts that give stressors their meaning (Brown & Harris, 1978, 1989; Dohrenwend, Raphael, Schwartz, Stueve, & Skodol, 1993; Wheaton, 1990a, 1990b), or how people's belief or value systems influence the meaning of events (Pearlin, 1989; Reissman, 1990; Simon, 1995). Psychologists, in contrast, have generally followed the lead of Lazarus and Folkman (1984) and examined people's subjective appraisals of stressors.[7] Lazarus and Folkman suggest that the impact of a situational demand depends upon how it is perceived (as a harm/loss, a threat, or a challenge) and whether it is viewed as controllable or uncontrollable (Folkman, 1984).

A closer reading of Lazarus and Folkman's widely accepted definition of stress indicates that they view stress as an appraisal of harm/loss, threat, or challenge *to the self*. Stressors are perceptions that one has personally been physically or psychologically damaged (harms/losses), that one is personally in imminent danger of physical or psychological damage (threats), or that one faces minor but still potentially hazardous demands that must be met (challenges). Individuals react with tension, anxiety, despair, and/or upset to the *self-implications* of unmet demands, not just to the sheer volume or magnitude of those demands (as suggested in earlier conceptions of stress effects—e.g., Holmes & Rahe, 1967).

In essence, stressors might be seen as signals to the self about the adequacy of one's "person–environment fit" (French, Rodgers, & Cobb, 1974). Recently, Burke (1991) has taken this idea one step further, suggesting that all social stressors should be reconceptualized as "identity-interruptions." He argues that any feedback from the social environment that is inconsistent with an individual's self meanings or identity standards will provoke anxiety or tension. However, it is probably sensible to retain the notion of stress as a

---

[7] One must be careful with this strategy because a person's current psychological state can influence his subjective reports about the events and difficulties in his life; his appraisals may be confounded with the very outcome (his psychological state) that the research is attempting to explain.

distinct concept and view identity interruptions or threats to the self-concept as a key *sub-set* of life's major events, ongoing difficulties, and minor hassles. As suggested earlier, many stressors require extensive behavioral readjustments but do not necessarily involve threats to the self. A cumulation of events that compel behavioral changes may have physical health consequences, whereas stressors that implicate the self may primarily impact the psyche.

A number of mental health researchers have picked up this lead from Lazarus and Folkman's conception of stress and asked, what is it about the self that the individual believes has been harmed, lost, threatened, or challenged? Researchers from the two differing self traditions have suggested highly similar answers: *an important or valued* self-conception. Stressors that harm or threaten individuals' most cherished self-conceptions should be more predictive of psychological distress or disorder than those affecting less cherished aspects of the self (Brown, Bifulco, & Harris, 1987; Hammen, Marks, Mayol, & deMayo, 1985a; Hammer, Marks, deMayo, & Mayol, 1985b; Oatley & Bolton, 1985; Thoits, 1992, 1995).

This idea has been central in my own work. Drawing from symbolic interactionism, I have argued that individuals obtain important psychological benefits from their social identities, especially from those based in social roles (for related arguments, see Oatley & Bolton, 1985; Sieber, 1974). Roles are positions in the social structure to which are attached sets of normative behavioral expectations, or "scripts" for carrying them out. When individuals invest themselves in their roles, they not only gain a sense of who they are as meaningful social objects but of what they should do and how they should behave in given situations as well. From other people's legitimation (or disapproval) of their role-identity enactments, people also obtain feedback on how well they are performing. In turn, existential meaning, behavioral guidance, and social approval should prevent anxiety, despair, and disorganized conduct, and should maintain or raise self-esteem. In short, having and enacting role identities should be beneficial to mental health—and in fact, considerable research suggests that they are (Baruch & Barnett, 1986; Jackson, 1997; Miller, Moen, & Dempster-McClain, 1991; Moen, Dempster-McClain, & Williams, 1992; Pietromonaco, Manis, & Frohardt-Lane, 1986; Repetti & Crosby, 1984; Spreitzer, Snyder, & Larson, 1979; Thoits, 1983b, 1986, 1992).

Not all role identities should provide the same amount of benefit, however: Some social selves are more important than others. McCall and Simmons (1978) have suggested that people organize their role identities in a "prominence" hierarchy. The prominence of any one identity depends on how rewarding it is, which is a complex weighted sum of the degree to which others positively support the identity, the degree to which one is personally committed to and invested in the identity, and the intrinsic and extrinsic gratifications gained through competent role performance, among other benefits. Similarly, I have argued that people order their identities in terms of their salience, or subjective importance, where salience depends on each identity's prestige or reward value (Thoits, 1992; see also Rosenberg, 1979, on "psychological centrality"). Stryker (1980; Stryker & Serpe, 1982) suggests that identities are arranged by degree of commitment. In general, the higher an identity in a person's prominence, salience, or commitment hierarchy, the more he or she will want to enact that identity, and the more psychological benefits he/she should obtain from competent role-identity performance (Thoits, 1992).

It follows from these considerations that losses of, damages to, and/or threats to highly valued identities should be more psychologically harmful than equivalent assaults on less valued identities. Stated more generally, the more an individual identifies with, is committed to, or has highly developed self- schemas in a particular life domain, the greater will be the emotional impact of stressors that occur in that domain.

Variations of this "identity-relevant stress hypothesis" have been proposed by a number of researchers. For example, Brown and Harris (1978, pp. 236–237) speculated that when life events and ongoing difficulties deprive a person of an essential identity, feelings of hopelessness and, thus, depression will result. Drawing explicitly from symbolic interactionism, Oatley and Bolton (1985, p. 372) more formally tied the etiology of depression to disruption in a role that "had been primary in providing the basis for a person's sense of self," especially when there were few alternatives for maintaining that sense of self. Working from a cognitive framework, Hammen and her colleagues (1985a, 1985b) proposed that negative events that threaten individuals' dominant self-schemas will produce depression.[8] Similarly, J. D. Brown and McGill (1989) reasoned that the accumulation of "identity-disruptions" (defined as life events that are inconsistent with individuals' self-concepts) will be threatening and thus illness-provoking. Note that sociological stress theorists view *losses of or threats to* valued social self-concepts as the key to disturbance, while psychologists see *disconfirming information* about a firmly established self-concept as threatening and disturbing.

Tests of these various versions of the identity-relevant stress hypothesis have produced mixed findings. In my longitudinal community studies, I assessed identity salience by asking adults to identify up to three social roles that they viewed as "most important to me," up to three as "second most important to me," and up to three as "third most important to me."[9] When I interacted these identity-salience rankings with respondents' reports of strains in each role domain, I found little support for the identity-relevant stress hypothesis (Thoits, 1992). For example, chronic marital problems increased a person's psychological symptoms significantly, regardless of whether she viewed her "wife" identity as important or unimportant. In a second study, I categorized respondents' negative life events by whether they occurred in high-salience, moderate-salience, or low-salience identity domains and examined the effects of these events on respondents' subsequent psychological distress and alcohol and drug use (Thoits, 1995). Again, I found no support for the hypothesis. The effects of life events did not depend on the salience of the identity domain in which they occurred. Further detailed qualitative analyses suggested that only major strain-producing life events in salient-identity domains might be distressing and that, frequently, people's reports of identity salience also changed in response to major stressors (Thoits, 1995). These were potential reasons why I failed to confirm the identity-relevant stress hypothesis.

On the other hand, several other studies have offered support for the hypothesis. For example, Brown and his colleagues (1987) explored what they called "commitment-matching events." They assessed the degree to which women in their community sample were committed to several life domains, specifically, to children, marriage, housework, employment, activities outside the home, and close friends. A woman was rated as committed if, during structured, in-depth interviews, she expressed marked enthusiasm for and dedication to "the idea of that area as worthwhile in general" (1987, p. 33). A life event was classified as "commitment-related" if "it was reasonable to assume that the event would

---

[8] Beck (Beck, Epstein, & Harrison, 1983) initially developed the hypothesis that depressive symptoms result when a negative life event matches an individual's personal "vulnerability" characteristic; Beck suggested sociotropy (a focus on interpersonal relationships) and autonomous achievement as key characteristics.

[9] Respondents had already indicated that they thought of themselves in terms of those roles (e.g., "I think of myself as a father"), so respondents were in fact ranking their role *identities* in terms of salience.

threaten any sense of worth, security or sense of hope the woman derived from the commitment or activity associated with it" (p. 37). Note that these are assessments of commitments to social-role domains—parent, spouse, homemaker, worker, friend, and, perhaps, group member. Brown and his colleagues found that severe events occurring in role domains to which women initially were highly committed were stronger predictors of depression onset than other types of severe events (although a more useful comparison might have been to events in low-commitment role domains).

Simon (1992) also examined the effects of identity commitment, in this case assessing respondents' subjective commitment to the role of parent with semantic differential scales. She found that fathers who were highly committed to the parent role were significantly more distressed in response to their children's chronic health and behavior problems than fathers who were less committed to the parental role. Mothers, on the other hand, were highly distressed by these problems, regardless of their reported level of commitment. In contrast to my studies of identity salience, these two studies suggest that investment in, or dedication to, a role influences emotional reactivity to stressors in that role-identity domain (for related findings, see also Krause, 1995).

With parallel logic, Hammen and her colleagues have studied the effects of negative life events that they classified as "schema-congruent" (e.g., Hammen & Goodman-Brown, 1990; Hammen et al., 1985a, 1985b). Specifically, people's salient personality traits were the focus. These researchers identified subsets of subjects (in some studies, college students; in others, depressed or formerly depressed patients) whose dominant self-schemas were "sociotropic" (emphasizing interpersonal relations) or "autonomous" (emphasizing independent achievement). They reasoned that negative events in domains of central relevance to a person's sense of self-worth would be depressing, whereas undesirable events in irrelevant domains would not. With prospective data, Hammen and her colleagues showed that subjects with interpersonally dependent self-schemas became depressed in response to negative interpersonal events, whereas those holding self-schemas based on independent achievement became depressed in response to failure events. (Achievement failures did not depress people who were interpersonally dependent, and interpersonal problems did not affect those who were schematic for autonomous achievement.) A number of studies have confirmed the impacts of "schema-congruent" events, although the most reliable finding has involved a self-schema for interpersonal dependence combined with negative interpersonal events (Coyne & Whiffen, 1995; Robins, 1990; Robins & Block, 1988; Robins & Luten, 1991; Segal, 1988; Segal, Shaw, & Vella, 1989). This line of research suggests that events that threaten dominant self-conceptions are indeed more emotionally damaging than events in other, less personally meaningful domains.[10] Corroboratively, prospective studies by J. D. Brown (Brown & McGill, 1989; Swann & Brown, 1990) indicated that positive life events increased physical ill health and health center visits (which are usually correlated with psychological distress) only among subjects with low self-esteem—in this case, positive events were inconsistent with and presumably threatened these subjects' negative self-conceptions.

Studies of women's "burdens of caring" also offer some evidence for the

---

[10] However, one must be cautious when interpreting this line of research because many researchers in the "schema-congruent events" tradition have shifted their focus to the depressing effects of life events that match individuals' personality weaknesses, such as an overdependence on other people, an overemphasis on the importance of achievement, and dysfunctional attitudes (see review in Robins, 1995). In these studies, a positive self-conception is not threatened by a negative life event; instead, a negative self-conception is confirmed by it. Theoretically, these are distinctly different dynamics.

identity-relevant stress hypothesis, although at present, the evidence is mixed and indirect. Kessler and McLeod (1984) drew from the gender-role literature (e.g., Belle, 1982; Gove, 1984) to argue that women's interpersonal orientations and their socialization into nurturing roles should make them emotionally more reactive to "network events" (i.e., stressful events that happen to family members and friends about whom they care). Using data from five large community surveys, Kessler and McLeod (1984) demonstrated that women's higher psychological distress and emotional vulnerability to negative life events relative to men could be attributed in large part to women's higher exposure to network events. Some studies have replicated this finding (e.g., Turner & Avison, 1989), whereas others have not (e.g., Thoits, 1987). The central defect of these studies is that they *presume* that nurturing is important to women rather than taking into consideration the degree to which women actually view themselves as nurturant or as caregivers/supporters. If the identity-relevant stress hypothesis is correct, only women whose salient self-conceptions include caring for others should be more psychologically vulnerable to network events than men. Furthermore, men whose salient self-conceptions include caring for others should be more psychologically vulnerable to network events than other men. Men who value their nurturing aspects might even be more vulnerable to network events than women for whom nurturance is not especially salient. These more specific hypotheses await further testing. One recent study offers encouraging findings: Gore, Aseltine, and Colten (1993) found that to the degree that adolescent girls were oriented toward interpersonal caring and becoming involved in the problems of significant others, they were at increased risk of depression, especially when they were also experiencing family stress.

In general, studies of the effects of "identity-relevant" and "schema-congruent" stressors have produced mixed findings. Some studies fail to confirm expectations, some studies are clearly confirmatory, and others (e.g., Simon, 1992) find support only for subgroups of the population. There are several possible explanations for these variations in findings. First, the effects of identity-relevant or schema-congruent stressors may be specific to depression, so that studies focusing on other mental health outcomes such as generalized distress or substance use (e.g., Thoits, 1992, 1995) may be less likely to obtain expected results (Robins, 1990). Second, it may be necessary to assess the meaning of life events and chronic strains very carefully to specify more precisely those that are likely to damage or threaten important self-concepts (Brown, 1989). For example, for someone whose "father" identity is highly salient, a son's leaving home to start college differs drastically in its identity implications from a son's leaving home as a runaway. Studies often fail to make such detailed distinctions among stressors. Finally, people's self-concepts may change as a result of their stressful experiences, making the effects of identities or self-schemas elusive to detect. I return to this important issue under the topic of coping.

Stress Mediation

Although the impacts of stressors on psychological well-being may depend on their appraised meaning to the self, stressors can also have direct harmful effects on people's self-conceptions. Damaged self-conceptions in turn can affect one's psychological state. This is the process of stress *mediation*: Changes in self-conception are the conduits or mechanisms through which stressors can result in symptoms. In general, self-esteem and self-efficacy (or perceived control over life) are the two self factors that have most frequently been studied as variables intervening between stressors and mental health outcomes.

Changes in identities or self-schemas are less commonly examined as intervening variables perhaps because identity change is itself classifiable as a stressor and because weakened allegiance to an identity or schema can be understood as a coping strategy (Breakwell, 1986). I briefly review investigations of self-esteem as a stress-mediator here (see Chapter 18 for influences of self-efficacy/perceived control).

Large community studies investigating the role of self-esteem in the stress process are relatively rare, compared to studies of other coping resources. Perhaps researchers take it for granted that stressful experiences have negative impacts on self-esteem and that low self-esteem in turn increases symptoms of psychological disorder. Existing evidence does generally indicate that stressors decrease feelings of self-worth (DuBois, Felner, Sherman, & Bull, 1994; Krause, 1991; Pearlin, Lieberman, Menaghan, & Mullan, 1981; Skaff & Pearlin, 1992) and that low self-esteem is associated with a wide range of psychopathologies, including delinquency and conduct problems (DuBois et al., 1994; Kaplan, Robbins, & Martin, 1983a, 1983b; Kaplan, Johnson, & Bailey, 1986; Krause, 1991; Rosenberg, Schooler, & Schoenbach, 1989; Rosenberg, Schooler, Schoenback, & Rosenberg, 1995; Skaff & Pearlin, 1992; Turner & Roszell, 1994). There are, however, interesting exceptions and variations around these general findings.

For example, stressors do not always have strong or even significant effects on a person's global sense of self-worth (e.g., Shamir, 1986), as measured by instruments such as Rosenberg's (1979) Self-Esteem Scale (containing items such as "I take a positive attitude toward myself"—"strongly agree" to "strongly disagree"). Instead, researchers find that *domain-specific* stressors have more consistent negative effects on *domain-specific* self-esteem (e.g., Harter, 1986; Rosenberg et al., 1995). Academic failure negatively impacts a person's sense of academic self-worth or competence, interpersonal problems negatively affect a person's estimate of his/her interpersonal acceptance, and so on. Domain-specific self-esteem appears to be related to overall self-esteem only if the person perceives the sphere in which he/she has been having troubles (or success) as important or valuable (Harter, 1987; Rosenberg et al., 1995). For example, one can do badly (or well) at sports and be relatively unaffected psychologically if one does not view sports as important. Note that these findings are consistent with the identity-relevant stress hypothesis: Failures or poor performances have effects on an aspect of psychological well-being (global self-esteem) only when they occur in a personally salient domain.

Further variations on this theme are suggested by learned helplessness theory. This theory suggests that failures should affect self-esteem only if one attributes them to one's own global, enduring inadequacies (Abramson et al., 1989; Brewin, 1985). Not surprisingly, self-blame for mistakes or failures tends to be rather rare (Peterson & Seligman, 1984; Tillman & Carver, 1980). Instead, people attribute lapses in their performances to uncontrollable circumstances ("I had three tests that day"), to temporary personal factors ("I was sick that day"), or to highly specific personal inadequacies ("I don't do well on multiple-choice questions"). In these ways, people protect their global self-esteem from the threatening implications of failure.

Along the same lines, self-affirmation theory (Steele, 1988; Steele, Spencer, & Lynch, 1993) proposes that individuals are motivated to maintain their global self-images and that this motivation is primed when information threatens their self-images as good or competent persons.[11] Importantly, Steele argues that individuals do not have to counter directly

---

[11] Self-verification theory would predict such motivation whether the threatened self-view is either positive *or* negative.

every self-threat that they receive; instead, the self-system is flexible, so that affirming an alternative, unrelated positive aspect of the self will restore the person's overall sense of adequacy. Thus, doing poorly on an exam can be neutralized if one walks 5 miles for a cancer fund or donates blood to the local Red Cross. By implication, threats to the self will be psychologically disturbing only if other, positive self-conceptions are unavailable or if one is prevented from affirming one or more of these selves.

Finally, self-verification theory (Swann, Wenzlaff, Krull, et al., 1992) suggests that stressors will have negative impacts on the self or the psyche only if those stressors fail to verify one's sense of self-worth. Thus, negative events will be upsetting to people with high self-esteem but much less so to people with low self- esteem. Positive events will benefit those with high self-esteem but have no impact on or even upset those with low self-esteem (Brown & McGill, 1989; Cohen & Hoberman, 1983; Swann & Brown, 1990).

In short, the relationship between stressors and self-worth is far more complicated than many sociological stress researchers have assumed; thus, stressors' effects on mental health *through* self-esteem can be weakened if these complexities are not taken into account. Of particular importance is the tension between self-enhancement and self-verification motives. Symbolic interactionist investigators almost always presume the dominance of self-enhancement motives; that is, they presume that people prefer positive feedback over feedback that is consistent with their existing self-images.[12] Cognitive theorists propose that a need for consistency in one's cognitions about the self can be just as motivating. In most cases, these two motives go hand in hand. When people have high self-esteem, their successful pursuit of social approval sustains a consistent, positive self-view. But when individuals initially have a low sense of self-worth and self-verification motives predominate, negative events can produce unexpected effects, or even an absence of impacts, on psychological well-being.

In general, then, from the social-psychological self literature, it appears that self-esteem may mediate the relationship between stressors and mental health only when certain conditions are met. Many of these conditions have been identified in laboratory studies (e.g., learned helplessness, self-affirmation research). In future work, conditions pinpointed in the laboratory as important should be explicitly incorporated into large-scale community studies of stress effects and evaluated for their more general explanatory utility.

Stress Moderation

As mentioned earlier, decades of research have made it clear that even traumatic or cumulative stress experiences do not necessarily result in psychological distress or disorder. This result is in part because individuals possess "coping resources" with which to handle stressors. Coping resources are social and personal characteristics that enable effective and appropriate action in the face of adversity (Pearlin & Schooler, 1978). Social support is one such major resource (see Chapter 15). Personality resources that have been extensively studied include personal control or mastery (see Chapter 18) and self-esteem.[13] I focus on self-esteem here.

---

[12] Indeed, labeling theory suggests that the mentally ill are forced by the stereotyped expectations of others and by structural constraints to accept the identity of mental patient and to continue enacting that role (Scheff, 1984). Self-verification theory suggests that mental patients might do so willingly, if their self-perceptions were negative at the outset.

[13] Psychologists also examine hardiness, a sense of coherence, and Type A characteristics such as impatience and hostility (for reviews, see Cohen & Edwards, 1989; Rodin & Salovey, 1989).

Not surprisingly, because self-esteem and perceived control over one's life are strongly correlated (Pearlin et al., 1981; Turner & Roszell, 1994), these two resources are found to behave very similarly as stress moderators. Like personal control, self-esteem buffers or significantly reduces the harmful effects of stressors on people's psyches; that is, individuals who have numerous stressors and high self-esteem exhibit fewer symptoms of psychological distress and are less likely to develop a mental disorder than people with similar exposure but low self-esteem (Brown, Craig, & Harris, 1985; Brown & Harris, 1978; Cohen & Edwards, 1989; Kessler & Essex, 1982; Kessler, Turner, & House, 1988; Kaplan et al., 1983a; Pearlin et al., 1981; Shamir, 1986; Turner & Roszell, 1994). Although this stress-moderating effect is fairly well established in the literature, investigators have not yet determined how or why self-esteem works in this way.

Most researchers assume that self-esteem must influence the choice and effectiveness of the coping strategies that people use in response to stressors (e.g., Folkman, 1984). Presumably, individuals with high self-regard have greater confidence or motivation to initiate problem-solving efforts. Alternatively, they may be more likely than others to appraise a demanding situation as controllable and challenging and, therefore, to choose problem-focused coping strategies; those low in self-worth may more commonly perceive demands as uncontrollable and threatening and, thus, resort to emotion-focused coping strategies (Folkman, 1984). Although several studies show that individuals high in self-esteem are more likely to use problem-focused coping techniques or to have an active coping style (Aspinwall & Taylor, 1992; Menaghan, 1982, 1983; Menaghan & Merves, 1984; Pearlin & Schooler, 1978; Pearlin et al., 1981; Ross & Mirowsky, 1989), many studies also indicate that problem- focused efforts have minimal effects on, or sometimes exacerbate, people's psychological symptoms (see summary in Menaghan, 1983, p. 191). Thus, one may not be able to explain the stress- buffering influences of self-esteem through its supposed promotion of effective coping. Far more work is necessary to clarify the relationships among self-esteem, perceptions of stressors, choice of coping strategies, and mental health outcomes. To date, we have not developed adequate or detailed theoretical explanations (much less empirical tests) of how or why self-esteem actually helps buffer the negative consequences of exposure to stress.

Also unaddressed is the reverse question: What are the consequences of people's coping efforts for their self-esteem (Cohen & Edwards, 1989; Thoits, 1995; Turner & Roszell, 1994)? Social psychologists typically assume that personality characteristics are both learned from and later modified by life experiences. Self-esteem might not only influence stress perceptions and choice of coping methods, but also the success or failure of one's coping efforts in turn might enhance or undermine one's self-esteem, respectively. Personality characteristics have rarely been treated as dependent variables in the stress and coping process (cf. Thoits, 1994). Doing so might help further illuminate the dynamics of the relationships among self-esteem, coping-strategy choice, and mental health outcomes.

Cognitive theorists offer a different twist on stress- buffering processes. For example, Linville (1985, 1987) has suggested that the organization of self-schemas, or "self-aspects," can render an individual vulnerable or invulnerable to the effects of negative life events. She introduced the concept of "self-complexity," which she defined as having many self-aspects and making greater distinctions among self-aspects, so that they are relatively compartmentalized or unrelated. ("Self-aspects" include roles, relationships, activities, goals, and personality traits, so it is a more inclusive term than self-schema per se.) A complex organization of the self occurs when many self-aspects are kept relatively distinct; a simple organization occurs when relatively few self-aspects are closely associated with one another. To assess self-complexity, Linville had subjects sort a set of trait words (one word per card) into categories or groups that represented important aspects of themselves. Subjects could create as many (or as few) groups as they wished with the cards, and they could place the same words into different groups. The more groups a subject created and the fewer times he/she used the same words in multiple groups, the greater the complexity of the subject's self-structure.

Linville argued that when negative events happen, they activate thoughts and feelings about the relevant self-aspect. For example, if a person thinks of himself as artistic, having his paintings rejected for a show causes him to think about the artistic aspect of himself. When several self-aspects are closely related to one another (i.e., not complex), an event that damages or threatens one self-aspect will spread to affect others that are associated with it. This spread, or spillover effect, magnifies the psychological damage caused by the event. Conversely, when the self-structure is complex, negative thoughts and feelings in one self-domain are isolated from other domains, thus containing the damage and dampening the effects of the negative event. Linville showed that people with complex self-structures experience smaller swings in emotion, smaller decreases in self-esteem, fewer physical illnesses, and fewer depressive symptoms in response to undesirable life events compared to people with simple self-structures. Interestingly and unexpectedly, a high number of distinct self-aspects (high self-complexity) was associated with higher depression and illness in the absence of stress; that is, people with simpler selves were in better mental and physical health when stress was absent. Self-complexity may generate a low-grade chronic stress or create role overload or role conflict.

Linville turns our attention to a rarely investigated feature of the self, its structure or organization. Although sociologists have attended to the *dimensions* along which selves/identities might be organized (e.g., their prominence, importance, or commitment value), they have tended to presume only one possible organization, a rank-ordering, or hierarchy. Cognitive researchers who study the structure of self-representations, however, find a variety of structural forms (e.g., Deaux, 1993; Deaux, Reid, Mizrahi, & Ethier, 1995; Ogilvie, 1987; Rosenberg & Gara, 1985), such as trees and webs. How variations in structure are related to stress experiences and to psychological well-being are questions well worth pursuing, given Linville's tantalizing findings.

Social Support and Coping Processes

As mentioned earlier, stress experiences do not necessarily produce psychological disturbance, in part because individuals possess personality resources (such as self-esteem and personal control) that act as stress buffers. Stress effects are also moderated by access to social support and by flexible or effective use of coping strategies. Although self and identity influences in social support and coping processes have less often been discussed in the stress literature, they may be extremely important to elaborate and test. Mental health interventions frequently are aimed at people's social support networks or their coping techniques, and to be effective, interventions must target those aspects of supporting and/or coping that are largely responsible for preventing psychological harm. Changes in self/identity factors may be key.

A number of theorists have offered hypotheses about how social support works to reduce psychological disturbance in the face of stress (e.g., Belle, 1987; House, 1981; Pearlin, 1985; Thoits, 1985). One of the most common assertions is that supporters provide reassurance to the individual that he/she is esteemed and valued; this boost to self-esteem is believed to help the individual cope with or adjust to life's exigencies. Although some research shows that a sense of "mattering" to others does reduce psychological symptoms (Rosenberg & McCullough, 1981), very few studies actually test the hypothesis that changes in self-esteem intervene between perceptions of social support and psychological outcomes.[14] Cohen and Hoberman (1983) employed a social support scale that differentiated among different types of support. They found that the stress-buffering effects of social support among college students were primarily due to the self-esteem and appraisal aspects of perceived social support. Similarly, Krause (1987, 1994) found that supportive relationships had positive effects on well-being in the elderly, primarily through bolstering their self-esteem. Although these studies offer suggestive evidence that self-regard acts as an intervening mechanism between perceived or received support and psychological well-being, further tests seem crucial if we wish to understand and put to practical use our knowledge of how support works.

Turning to coping processes, we have already considered the often-presumed but incompletely investigated relationship between high self-esteem and the use of problem-focused coping strategies. There are other, more complex ways in which the self may be involved in coping. Often overlooked by stress researchers is the distinct possibility that people change their views of themselves as a way to cope with difficult life circumstances (Breakwell, 1986). For example, to reduce the perceived threat of chronic work strains or repeated failures on the job, individuals may self-protectively deemphasize the importance of work as an identity or as a source of self-evaluation. If the work identity is successfully made less central to the self, ongoing problems at work or even job loss should have less psychological impact (e.g., Bielby & Bielby, 1989; Pearlin & Schooler, 1978; Thoits, 1995; Wheaton, 1990a).

On the other hand, recent experimental research shows that people sometimes respond to adversity in a domain with increased, rather than decreased, commitment to the domain (Lydon & Zanna, 1990). The more individuals see an activity domain as relevant to their personal values prior to the onset of problems, the greater their commitment to that domain after encountering difficulties.[15] In short, people may cope with negative experiences in an important or valued realm of experience by becoming reactively less or reactively more invested in that identity.

These competing observations raise questions about the utility of people's self-reports of commitment or identity salience. We may need ways to detect temporary distortions in self-reports caused by efforts to cope with threatening events. These results also imply that it will be difficult to demonstrate that stressors' psychological impacts depend on their meaning for the self because the meaning of stressors may be constantly changing as individuals attempt to cope (Lazarus & Folkman, 1984). Appreciation of these dynamics impels the use of research strategies suited to the study of processes that unfold over time (e.g., daily diaries, participant observation, in-depth interviewing, narrative analysis). Furthermore, it becomes crucially important to specify the conditions under which people are likely to withdraw their allegiance from a stressful domain of experience or invest further in it. Only with some grasp of these conditions might we improve our understanding of

---

[14] Literally hundreds of studies, however, examine self-esteem and social support as factors that are independently associated with physical and mental health outcomes.

[15] Although increased commitment may enable individuals to persist in the face of adversity, investigators have not yet assessed the psychological consequences of greater commitment combined with thwarted efforts to overcome problems.

stressors' psychological impacts. And only with some understanding of when and why individuals become more committed under stress might we begin to develop interventions to encourage persistent coping efforts in the face of challenge or hardship.

AREAS FOR FUTURE RESEARCH
ON SELVES/IDENTITIES AND STRESS

Up to this point, we have examined the roles of self-conceptions and/or self-evaluations in stress appraisal, stress mediation, and stress moderation, explicating how social support and coping responses reduce psychological disturbance. However, there are other ways in which self and identity factors may enter the stress process. These avenues have less commonly been explored in the literature. The following commentary simply notes their appropriateness for inclusion in our future research agenda.

First, we have considered threats to or losses of salient identities as highly meaningful stressors that should have major impacts on people's psyches. There are other sources of identity that are generally considered to be stressful, in particular, identities imposed by other people that are not viewed by the individual as positive or self-descriptive. These can include identities based on gender, race, and ethnicity, as well as stigmatized sexual orientations, physical disabilities, chronic illnesses, and the like. The literature on these kinds of identities points to their role in frequent experiences of oppression, discrimination, devaluation, and other insults to the self (Jones et al., 1984; Link, 1987; Link, Cullen, Struening, & Shrout, 1989; Thompson, 1996; Vega & Rumbaut, 1991), all of which can be considered stressors. Interestingly, researchers have tended to assume that identity impositions by others and/or individuals' personal investments in socially devalued identities generate harm to self-esteem and mental health, often without empirical verification. When self-esteem outcomes have been examined directly, results have been more complex and context-dependent than anticipated (e.g., Rosenberg, 1981; Thompson, 1996). Symptoms of distress and onsets of disorder have even less frequently been the outcomes of interest; it is likely that when researchers turn their attention to these mental health outcomes, consequences will be just as complex and conditional as they have turned out to be with self-esteem as the dependent variable (Halpern, 1993). A crucial next step is investigating and completing the links from devalued social identities to negative experiences predicated upon those identities, to conditions specifying when those negative experiences will result in damage to psychological well-being.

A second, unexplored avenue concerns stress avoidance. Although personality resources such as high self-esteem and perceived control over life are most often treated as stress mediators and stress buffers, these resources likely enable people to avoid stressful situations at the outset. Assuming that people with high self-regard and a sense of control over life are more competent at social, intellectual, and/or physical task demands (an assumption deserving further empirical examination), these personality characteristics should help individuals to anticipate and select themselves into positive, desirable situations, and to foresee and prevent negative, undesirable ones (Cohen & Edwards, 1989; Turner & Roszell, 1994). Some evidence of such selection effects exists (Thoits, 1994). However, stress researchers have been eager to demonstrate that life events and chronic strains cause psychological problems rather than the reverse; in attempts to rule out reverse causality, researchers have carefully controlled for a variety of social selection factors. Consequently, the potential stress-avoidant effects of high self-esteem and self-efficacy have often been controlled statistically rather than analyzed directly as important in their own right. It seems entirely plausible that personality resources may facilitate stress avoidance and thereby help prevent distress or disorder. Consequently, these processes deserve further documentation and consideration because they may have implications for preventive interventions.

A third, generally unexplored question concerns identity change. A number of theorists have suggested that stress experiences may not only cause individuals to reevaluate the importance of certain self-conceptions but also may actually precipitate identity change (Charmaz, 1995; Ebaugh, 1988; Kiecolt, 1994; Thoits, 1994). According to symbolic interactionist theory, repeated experiences that disconfirm a valued identity or make it impossible to obtain support or validation for it may lead one to discard the identity (e.g., McCall & Simmons, 1978). Kiecolt (1994) has argued that stressors lead to identity change only when one or more conditions are met: One views the stressor as identity-relevant, one accepts self-blame for the stressor, one has access to structural and personal supports for self-change, one believes that self-change is possible, and/or one perceives that the benefits of self-change will outweigh the costs. Kiecolt's observations underscore the obstacles that often make extrication from an identity difficult and thus relatively rare (see also Ebaugh, 1988). Nevertheless, stress researchers have generally overlooked the possibility that stress experiences may cause individuals deliberately to drop an identity, as a coping response (Thoits, 1994). Some "negative" life events or identity losses (e.g., marital separation, quitting a job) may actually be ways of coping with stress rather than stressors in themselves.

Finally, and related to this last point, stress experiences might also lead to identity acquisition or identity reinvestment. Individuals can compensate for unsolved problems in one domain by deliberately increasing their involvement in other domains, or by acquiring additional roles (Gecas & Seff, 1990; Sieber, 1974). If a person remains in a difficult job situation, for example, he/she may devote more time and energy to family, church, or athletic activities, begin volunteering, or return to school part time. Purposefully engaging in rewarding activities in other role domains should help counterbalance the distressing impacts of unresolved situations. Future research might examine compensations as an additional way in which individuals act to alleviate psychological distress due to unsolved problems in their lives.

CONCLUSIONS

By this point, the reader may be wondering where stressors leave off and coping responses begin, where self-esteem is, or should be, located in the stress process, and at what points self and identity concepts are identical to or distinguishable from stress experiences. I have suggested that some stressors are direct threats to an identity, some are threats only if an identity is salient, and some changes in identity salience may be coping strategies. Identity losses may be stressors in themselves, may be caused by cumulative stress exposure, or may be ways of coping with unrelenting stress. Self-esteem may enable the avoidance of stress, may mediate stress effects, may modify the impacts of stress, or may itself be influenced negatively by stress experiences. Minimally, it should be clear that one is at risk of confounding one concept with another if one does not take great care in defining terms and specifying the particular links in the stress process being examined. Maximally, the degree to which self and identity factors pervade the stress process should be apparent, increasing appreciation of just how complex stress and coping dynamics really are and how important it can be to draw from theories of the self to explain these dynamics. I believe incorporating self and identity mechanisms into stress theory is crucial for developing it further, given the virtual impossibility of talking about stress, coping, and social support processes without some reference to these constructs. Their roles in the stress process have received less empirical attention than they deserve; it is likely that the next generation of stress studies will begin to elaborate and test a number of proposed theoretical mechanisms in detail. As we understand further how and when stress experiences result in psychological problems, we uncover points in the unfolding process at which increasingly specific, deliberate, and potent mental health interventions can be aimed.

REFERENCES

Abramson, L. Y., Metalsky, G. I., & Alloy, L. B. (1989). Hopelessness depression: A theory-based subtype of depression. *Psychological Review, 96,* 358–372.

American Psychiatric Association. (1994). *Diagnostic and statistical manual of mental disorders* (4th ed.). Washington, DC: Author.

Aspinwall, L. G., & Taylor, S. E. (1992). Modeling cognitive adaptation: A longitudinal investigation of the impact of individual differences and coping on college adjustment and performance. *Journal of Personality and Social Psychology, 63,* 989–1003.

Avison, W. R., & Turner, R. J. (1988). Stressful life events and depressive symptoms: Disaggregating the effects of acute stressors and chronic strains. *Journal of Health and Social Behavior, 29,* 253–264.

Baruch, G. K., & Barnett, R. (1986). Role quality, multiple role involvement, and psychological well-being in midlife women. *Journal of Personality and Social Psychology, 51,* 578–585.

Beck, A. T. (1967). Depression: Clinical, experimental, and theoretical aspects. New York: Harper & Row.

Beck, A. T., Epstein, N., & Harrison, R. (1983). Cognitions, attitudes and personality dimensions in depression. *British Journal of Cognitive Psychotherapy, 1,* 1–16.

Belle, D. (1982). The stress of caring: Women as providers of social support. In L. Goldberger & S. Breznitz (Eds.), *Handbook of stress: Theoretical and clinical aspects* (pp. 496–505). New York: Free Press.

Belle, D. (1987). Gender differences in the social moderators of stress. In R. C. Barnett, L. Biener, & G. K. Baruch (Eds.), *Gender and stress* (pp. 257–277). New York: Free Press.

Bielby, W. T., & Bielby, D. D. (1989). Family ties: Balancing commitments to work and family in dual earner households. *American Sociological Review, 54,* 776–789.

Blumer, H. (1969). *Symbolic interactionism: Perspective and method.* Englewood Cliffs, NJ: Prentice-Hall.

Breakwell, G. M. (1986). *Coping with threatened identities.* London: Methuen.

Brewin, C. R. (1985). Depression and causal attributions: What is their relation? *Psychological Bulletin, 98,* 297–309.

Brown, G. W. (1989). Life events and measurement. In G. W. Brown & T. O. Harris (Eds.), *Life events and illness* (pp. 3-45). New York: Guilford.

Brown, G. W., Bifulco, A., & Harris, T. O. (1987). Life events, vulnerability and onset of depression: Some refinements. *British Journal of Psychiatry, 150,* 30–42.

Brown, G. W., Craig, T. K., & Harris, T. O. (1985). Depression: Distress or disease: Some epidemiological considerations. *British Journal of Psychiatry, 147,* 612–622.

Brown, G. W., & Harris, T.O . (1978). *Social origins of depression: A study of psychiatric disorder in women.* New York: Free Press.

Brown, G. W., & Harris, T. O. (1989). *Life events and illness.* New York: Guilford.

Brown, J. D., & McGill, K. L. (1989). The cost of good fortune: When positive life events produce negative health consequences. *Journal of Personality and Social Psychology, 57,* 1103–1110.

Burke, P. J. (1991). Identity processes and social stress. *American Sociological Review, 56,* 836–849.

Charmaz, K. (1995). The body, identity, and self: Adapting to impairment. *Sociological Quarterly, 36,* 657–680.

Cohen, S., & Edwards, J. R. (1989). Personality characteristics as moderators of the relationship between stress and disorder. In R. W. J. Neufeld (Ed.), *Advances in the investigation of psychological stress* (pp. 235–283). New York: Wiley.

Cohen, S., & Hoberman, H. M. (1983). Positive events and social supports as buffers of life change stress. *Journal of Applied Social Psychology, 13,* 99–125.

Cohen, S., & Williamson, G. M. (1991). Stress and infectious disease in humans. *Psychological Bulletin, 109,* 5–24.

Cooley, C. H. (1902). *Human nature and the social order.* New York: Scribner's Sons.

Coyne, J. C., & Downey, G. (1991). Social factors and psychopathology: Stress, social support, and coping processes. *Annual Review of Psychology, 42,* 401–425.

Coyne, J. C., & Whiffen, V. E. (1995). Issues in personality as a diathesis for depression: The case of sociotropy–dependency and autonomy–self-criticism. *Psychological Bulletin, 118,* 358–378.

Creed, F. (1985). Life events and physical illness. *Journal of Psychosomatic Research, 29,* 113–123.

Deaux, K. (1993). Reconstructing social identity. *Personality and Social Psychology Bulletin, 19,* 4–12.

Deaux, K., Reid, A., Mizrahi, K., & Ethier, K. A. (1995). Parameters of social identity. *Journal of Personality and Social Psychology, 68,* 280–291.

Dohrenwend, B. P., Raphael, K. G., Schwartz, S., Stueve, A., & Skodol, A. (1993). The structured event probe and narrative rating method for measuring stressful life events. In L. Goldberger & S. Breznitz (Eds.), *Handbook of stress* (pp. 174–199). New York: Free Press.

DuBois, D. L., Felner, R. D., Sherman, M. D., & Bull, C. A. (1994). Socioenvironmental experiences, self-esteem, and emotional/behavioral problems in early adolescence. *American Journal of Community Psychology, 22,* 371–397.

Ebaugh, H. R. F. (1988). *Becoming an ex: The process of role exit.* Chicago: University of Chicago Press.

Erikson, E. H. (1963). *Childhood and society* (2nd ed.). New York: Norton.

Folkman, S. (1984). Personal control and stress and coping processes: A theoretical analysis. *Journal of Personality and Social Psychology, 46,* 839–852.

Folkman, S., Lazarus, R. S., Gruen, R. J., & DeLongis, A. (1986). Appraisal, coping, health status, and psychological symptoms. *Journal of Personality and Social Psychology, 50,* 571–579.

French, J. R. P., Rodgers, W., & Cobb, S. (1974). A model of person–environment fit. In G. V. Coelho, D. A. Hamburg, & J. E. Adams (Eds.), *Coping and adaptation* (pp. 316–333). New York: Basic Books.

Freud, S. (1933). *New introductory lectures on psycho-analysis.* New York: W. W. Norton.

Gecas, V., & Burke, P. J. (1995). Self and identity. In K. S. Cook, G. A. Fine, & J. S. House (Eds.), *Sociological perspectives on social psychology* (pp. 41–67). Boston: Allyn & Bacon.

Gecas, V., & Schwalbe, M. L. (1983). Beyond the looking-glass self: Social structure and efficacy-based self-esteem. *Social Psychology Quarterly, 46,* 77–88.

Gecas, V., & Seff, M. A. (1990). Social class and self-esteem: Psychological centrality, compensation, and the relative effects of work and home. *Social Psychology Quarterly, 53,* 165–173.

Gore, S., Aseltine, R. M., & Colten, M. E. (1993). Gender, social–relational involvement, and depression. *Journal of Research on Adolescence, 3,* 101–125.

Gove, W. R. (1984). Gender differences in mental and physical illness: The effects of fixed roles and nurturant roles. *Social Science and Medicine, 19,* 77–91.

Gurin, P., & Markus, H. (1989). Cognitive consequences of gender identity. In S. Skevington & D. Baker (Eds.), *The social identity of women* (pp. 152–172). London: Sage.

Halpern, D. (1993). Minorities and mental health. *Social Science and Medicine, 36,* 597–607.

Hammen, C., & Goodman-Brown, T. (1990). Self-schemas and vulnerability to specific life stress in children at risk for depression. *Cognitive Research and Therapy, 14,* 215–227.

Hammen, C., Marks, T., deMayo, R., & Mayol, A. (1985b). Self-schemas and risk for depression: A prospective study. *Journal of Personality and Social Psychology, 49,* 1147–1159.

Hammen, C., Marks, T., Mayol, A., & deMayo, R. (1985a). Depressive self-schemas, life stress, and vulnerability to depression. *Journal of Abnormal Psychology, 94,* 308–319.

Harter, S. (1986). Processes underlying the construction, maintenance, and enhancement of the self-concept in children. In J. Suls & A. Greenwald (Eds.), *Psychological perspectives on the self* (Vol. 3, pp. 136–181). Hillsdale, NJ: Erlbaum.

Harter, S. (1987). The determinants and mediational role of global self-worth in children. In N. Eisenberg (Ed.), *Contemporary topics in developmental psychology* (pp. 219–242). New York: Springer-Verlag.

Hays, R. D., Marshall, G. N., Yu, E. I., & Sherbourne, C. D. (1994). Four-year cross-lagged associations between physical and mental health in the medical outcomes study. Special section: Structural equation modeling in clinical research. *Journal of Consulting and Clinical Psychology, 62,* 441–449.

Holmes, T. H., & Rahe, R. H. (1967). The Social Readjustment Rating Scale. *Journal of Psychosomatic Research, 11,* 213–218.

House, J. S. (1981). *Work stress and social support.* Reading, MA: Addison-Wesley.

Jackson, P. B. (1997). Role occupancy and minority mental health. *Journal of Health and Social Behavior, 38,* 237–255.

James, W. (1950). *The principles of psychology* (Vol. 1). New York: Dover. (Original published 1890)

Jones, E. E., Farina, A., Hastorf, A. H., Markus, H., Miller, D. T., & Scott, R. A. (1984). *Social stigma: The psychology of marked relationships.* New York: W. H. Freeman.

Kaplan, H. B., Johnson, R. J., & Bailey, C .A. (1986). Self-rejection and the explanation of deviance: Refinement and elaboration of a latent structure. *Social Psychology Quarterly, 49,* 110–128.

Kaplan, H. B., Robbins, C., & Martin, S. S. (1983a). Antecedents of psychological distress in young adults: Self-rejection, deprivation of social support, and life events. *Journal of Health and Social Behavior, 24,* 230–244.

Kaplan, H. B., Robbins, C., & Martin, S. S. (1983b). Toward the testing of a general theory of deviant behavior in longitudinal perspective: Patterns of psychopathology. *Research in Community and Mental Health, 3,* 27–65.

Kessler, R. C., & Essex, M. (1982). Marital status and depression: The importance of coping resources. *Social Forces, 61,* 484–507.

Kessler, R. C., & McLeod, J. D. (1984). Sex differences in vulnerability to undesirable life events. *American Sociological Review, 49,* 620–631.

Kessler, R. C., Turner, J. B., & House, J. S. (1988). Effects of unemployment on health in a community survey: Main, modifying, and mediating effects. *Journal of Social Issues, 44,* 69–85.

Kiecolt, K. J. (1994). Stress and the decision to change oneself: A theoretical model. *Social Psychology Quarterly, 57,* 49–63.

Krause, N. (1987). Life stress, social support, and self-esteem in an elderly population. *Psychology and Aging, 2,* 349–356.

Krause, N. (1991). Financial strain and psychological well-being among the American and Japanese elderly. *Psychology and Aging, 6,* 170–181.

Krause, N. (1994). Clarifying the functions of social support in later life. *Research on Aging, 16,* 251–279.

Krause, N. (1995). Stress, alcohol use, and depressive symptoms in later life. *Gerontologist, 35,* 296–307.

Lazarus, R. S., & Folkman, S. (1984). *Stress, appraisal, and coping.* New York: Springer.

Lin, N., & Ensel, W. M. (1989). Life stress and health: Stressors and resources. *American Sociological Review, 54,* 382–399.

Link, B. (1987). Understanding labeling effects in the area of mental disorders: An assessment of the effects of expectations of rejection. *American Sociological Review, 52,* 96–112.

Link, B., Cullen, F. T., Struening, E. L., & Shrout, P. E. (1989). A modified labeling theory approach to mental disorders: An empirical assessment. *American Sociological Review, 54,* 400–423.

Linville, P. W. (1985). Self-complexity and affective extremity: Don't put all of your eggs in one cognitive basket [Special issue: Depression]. *Social Cognition, 3,* 91–120.

Linville, P. W. (1987). Self-complexity as a cognitive buffer against stress-related illness and depression. *Journal of Personality and Social Psychology, 52,* 663–676.

Lydon, J. E., & Zanna, M. P. (1990). Commitment in the face of adversity: A value-affirmation approach. *Journal of Personality and Social Psychology, 58,* 1040–1047.

Manning, W. G., & Wells, K. B. (1992). The effects of psychological distress and psychological well-being on use of medical services. *Medical Care, 30,* 541–553.

Markus, H. (1977). Self-schemata and processing information about the self. *Journal of Personality and Social Psychology, 35,* 63–78.

Markus, H., Crane, M., Bernstein, S., & Siladi, M. (1982). Self-schemas and gender. *Journal of Personality and Social Psychology, 42,* 38-50.

Markus, H., Smith, J., & Moreland, R. L. (1985). Role of the self-concept in the perception of others. *Journal of Personality and Social Psychology, 49,* 1494–1512.

Mattlin, J. A., Wethington, E., & Kessler, R. C. (1990). Situational determinants of coping and coping effectiveness. *Journal of Health and Social Behavior, 31,* 103–122.

May, B. A. (1991). The interaction between ratings of self, peer's perceptions, and reflexive self-ratings. *Journal of Social Psychology, 131,* 483–493.

McCall, G. J., & Simmons, J. L. (1978). *Identities and interactions.* New York: Free Press.

Mead, G. H. (1934). *Mind, self, and society.* Chicago: University of Chicago Press.

Menaghan, E. (1982). Measuring coping effectiveness: A panel analysis of marital problems and coping efforts. *Journal of Health and Social Behavior, 23,* 220–234.

Menaghan, E. (1983). Individual coping efforts: Moderators of the relationship between life stress and mental health outcomes. In H. B. Kaplan (Ed.), *Psychosocial stress: Trends in theory and research* (pp. 157–191). New York: Academic Press.

Menaghan, E. G., & Merves, E. S. (1984). Coping with occupational problems: The limits of individual efforts. *Journal of Health and Social Behavior, 25,* 406–423.

Miller, M. L., Moen, P., & Dempster-McClain, D. (1991). Motherhood, multiple roles, and maternal well-being: Women of the 1950's. *Gender and Society, 5,* 565–582.

Moen, P., Dempster-McClain, D., & Williams, R. M., Jr. (1992). Successful aging: A life course perspective on women's multiple roles and health. *American Journal of Sociology, 97,* 1612–1638.

Oatley, K., & Bolton, W. (1985). A social-cognitive theory of depression in reaction to life events. *Psychological Review, 92,* 372–388.

O'Connor, B. P., & Dyce, J. (1993). Appraisals of musical ability in bar bands: Identifying the weak link in the looking-glass self chain. *Basic and Applied Social Psychology, 14,* 69–86.

Ogilvie, D. M. (1987). Life satisfaction and identity structure in late middle-aged men and women. *Psychology and Aging, 2,* 217–224.

Pearlin, L. I. (1985). Social structure and processes of social support. In S. Cohen & S. L. Syme (Eds.), *Social support and health* (pp. 43–60). Orlando, FL: Academic Press.

Pearlin, L. I. (1989). The sociological study of stress. *Journal of Health and Social Behavior, 30,* 241–256.

Pearlin, L. I., Lieberman, M. A., Menaghan, E. G., & Mullan, J. T. (1981). The stress process. *Journal of Health and Social Behavior, 22,* 337–356.

Pearlin, L. I., & Schooler, C. (1978). The structure of coping. *Journal of Health and Social Behavior, 19,* 2–21.

Peterson, C., & Seligman, M. E. (1984). Causal explanations as a risk factor for depression: Theory and evidence. *Psychological Review, 91,* 347–374.

Pietromonaco, P. R., Manis, J., & Frohardt-Lane, K. (1986). Psychological consequences of multiple social roles. *Psychology of Women Quarterly, 10,* 373–381.

Reissman, C. K. (1990). *Divorce talk: Women and men make sense of personal relationships.* New Brunswick, NJ: Rutgers University Press.

Repetti, R. L., & Crosby, F. (1984). Gender and depression: Exploring the adult-role explanation. *Journal of Social and Clinical Psychology, 2,* 57–70.

Robins, C. J. (1990). Congruence of personality and life events in depression. *Journal of Abnormal Psychology, 99,* 393–397.

Robins, C. J. (1995). Personality–event interaction models of depression. *European Journal of Personality, 9,* 367–378.

Robins, C. J., & Block, P. (1988). Personal vulnerability, life events, and depressive symptoms: A test of a specific interactional model. *Journal of Personality and Social Psychology, 54,* 847–852.

Robins, C. J., & Luten, A. G. (1991). Sociotropy and autonomy: Differential patterns of clinical presentation in unipolar depression. *Journal of Abnormal Psychology, 100,* 74–77.

Rodin, J., & Salovey, P. (1989). Health psychology. *Annual Review of Psychology, 40,* 533–579.

Rosenberg, M. (1979). *Conceiving the self.* New York: Basic Books.

Rosenberg, M. (1981). The self-concept: Social product and social force. In M. Rosenberg & R. Turner (Eds.), *Social psychology: Sociological perspectives* (pp. 593–624). New York: Basic Books.

Rosenberg, M., & McCullough, B. C. (1981). Mattering: Inferred significance and mental health among adolescents. *Research in Community and Mental Health, 2,* 163–182.

Rosenberg, M., Schooler, C., & Schoenbach, C. (1989). Self-esteem and adolescent problems: Modeling reciprocal effects. *American Sociological Review, 54,* 1004–1018.

Rosenberg, M., Schooler, C., Schoenbach, C., & Rosenberg, F. (1995). Global self-esteem and specific self-esteem: Different concepts, different outcomes. *American Sociological Review, 60,* 141–156.

Rosenberg, S., & Gara, M. A. (1985). The multiplicity of personal identity. In P. Shaver (Ed.), *Self, situations, and social behavior: Review of personality and social psychology* (Vol. 6, pp. 87–113). Beverly Hills, CA: Sage.

Ross, C. E., & Mirowsky, J. (1989). Explaining the social patterns of depression: Control and problem solving—or support and talking? *Journal of Health and Social Behavior, 30,* 206–219.

Scheff, T. J. (1984). *Being mentally ill: A sociological theory* (2nd ed.). New York: Aldine.

Segal, Z. V. (1988). Appraisal of the self-schema construct in cognitive models of depression. *Psychological Bulletin, 103,* 147–162.

Segal, Z. V., Shaw, B. F., & Vella, D. D. (1989). Life stress and depression: A test of the congruency hypothesis for life event content and depressive subtype. *Canadian Journal of Behavioral Science, 21,* 389–400.

Shamir, B. (1986). Self-esteem and the psychological impact of unemployment. *Social Psychology Quarterly, 49,* 61–72.

Sieber, S. (1974). Toward a theory of role strain. *American Sociological Review, 39,* 567–578.

Simon, R. W. (1992). Parental role strains, salience of parental identity and gender differences in psychological distress. *Journal of Health and Social Behavior, 33,* 25–35.

Simon, R. W. (1995). Gender, multiple roles, role meaning, and mental health. *Journal of Health and Social Behavior, 36,* 182–194.

Simon, R. W. (1997). The meanings individuals attach to role-identities and their implications for mental health. *Journal of Health and Social Behavior, 38,* 256–274.

Skaff, M. M., & Pearlin, L. I. (1992). Caregiving: Role engulfment and the loss of self. *Gerontologist, 32,* 656-664.

Spreitzer, E., Snyder, E. E., & Larson, D. L. (1979). Multiple roles and psychological well-being. *Sociological Focus, 12,* 141–148.

Steele, C. M. (1988). The psychology of self-affirmation: Sustaining the integrity of the self. In L. Berkowitz (Ed.), *Advances in experimental social psychology* (Vol. 21, pp. 261–302). San Diego: Academic Press.

Seele, C. M., Spencer, S. J., & Lynch, M. (1993). Self-image resilience and dissonance: The role of affirmational resources. *Journal of Personality and Social Psychology, 64,* 885–896.

Stryker, S. (1980). *Symbolic interactionism: A social structural version.* Menlo Park, CA: Benjamin/Cummings.

Stryker, S., & Serpe, R. T. (1982). Commitment, identity salience, and role behavior: Theory and research example. In W. Ickes, & E. Knowles (Eds.), *Personality, roles, and social behavior* (pp. 199–218). New York: Springer-Verlag.

Stryker, S., & Statham, A. (1985). Symbolic interaction and role theory. In G. Lindzey & E. Aronson (Eds.), *Handbook of social psychology* (3rd ed., pp. 311–378). New York: Random House.

Suls, J., & Wills, T. A. (Eds.). (1991). Social comparison: Contemporary theory and research. Hillsdale, NJ: Erlbaum.

Swann, W. B., Jr., & Brown, J. D. (1990). From self to health: Self-verification and identity disruption. In B. R. Sarason, I. G. Sarason, & G. R. Pierce (Eds.), *Social support: An interactional view* (pp. 150–172). New York: Wiley.

Swann, W. B., Wenzlaff, R. M., Krull, D. S., & Pelham, B. W. (1992). Allure of negative feedback: Self-verification strivings among depressed persons. *Journal of Abnormal Psychology, 101,* 293–306.

Swann, W. B., Wenzlaff, R. M., & Tafarodi, R. W. (1992). Depression and the search for negative evaluations: More evidence of the role of self-verification strivings. *Journal of Abnormal Psychology, 101,* 314–317.

Thoits, P. A. (1983a). Dimensions of life events that influence psychological distress: An evaluation and synthesis of the literature. In H. Kaplan (Ed.), *Psychosocial stress: Trends in theory and research* (pp. 33–103). New York: Academic Press.

Thoits, P. A. (1983b). Multiple identities and psychological well-being: A reformulation and test of the social isolation hypothesis. *American Sociological Review, 48,* 174–187.

Thoits, P. A. (1985). Social support and psychological well-being: Theoretical possibilities. In I. G. Sarason & B. R. Sarason (Eds.), *Social support: Theory, research, and applications* (pp. 51–72). Dordrecht, The Netherlands: Martinus Nijhof.

Thoits, P. A. (1986). Multiple identities: Examining gender and marital status differences in distress. *American Sociological Review, 51,* 259–272.

Thoits, P. A. (1987). Gender and marital status differences in control and distress: Common stress versus unique stress explanations. *Journal of Health and Social Behavior, 28,* 7–22.

Thoits, P. A. (1992). Identity structures and psychological well-being: Gender and marital status comparisons. *Social Psychology Quarterly, 55,* 236–256.

Thoits, P. A. (1994). Stressors and problem-solving: The individual as psychological activist. *Journal of Health and Social Behavior, 35,* 143–159.

Thoits, P. A. (1995). Identity-relevant events and psychological symptoms: A cautionary tale. *Journal of Health and Social Behavior, 36,* 72–82.

Thoits, P. A., & Virshup, L. K. (1998). Me's and we's: Forms and functions of social identities. In R. D. Ashmore & L. Jussim (Eds.), *Self and identity: Fundamental issues* (Vol. 1, pp. 106–133). Oxford, UK: Oxford University Press.

Thompson, V. S. S. (1996). Perceived experiences of racism as stressful life events. *Community Mental Health Journal, 32,* 223-233.

Tillman, W. S., & Carver, C. S. (1980). Actors' and observers' attributions for success and failure: A comparative test of predictions from Kelley's cube, self-serving bias, and positivity bias formulations. *Journal of Experimental Social Psychology, 16,* 18–32.

Turner, R. J., & Avison, W. R. (1989). Gender and depression: Assessing exposure and vulnerability to life events in a chronically strained population. *Journal of Nervous and Mental Disease, 177,* 443–455.

Turner, R. J., & Roszell, P. (1994). Psychosocial resources and the stress process. In W. R. Avison & I. H. Gotlib (Eds.), *Stress and mental health: Contemporary issues and prospects for the future* (pp. 179–210). New York: Plenum Press.

Turner, R. J., Wheaton, B., & Lloyd, D. A. (1995). The epidemiology of social stress. *American Sociological Review, 60,* 104–125.

Umberson, D., Wortman, C. B., & Kessler, R. C. (1992). Widowhood and depression: Explaining long-term gender differences in vulnerability. *Journal of Health and Social Behavior, 33,* 10–24.

Vega, W. A., & Rumbaut, R. G. (1991). Ethnic minorities and mental health. *Annual Review of Sociology, 17,* 351–383.

Weigert, A. J., Teitge, J. S., & Teitge, D. W. (1986). *Society and identity.* Cambridge: Cambridge University Press.

Wheaton, B. (1990a). Life transitions, role histories, and mental health. *American Sociological Review, 55,* 209–223.

Wheaton, B. (1990b). Where work and family meet: Stress across social roles. In J. Eckenrode & S. Gore (Eds.), *Stress between work and family* (pp. 153–174). New York: Plenum Press.

Wortman, C. B., & Silver, R. C. (1987). Coping with irrevocable loss. In G. R. VandenBos & B. K. Bryant (Eds.), *Cataclysms, crises, and catastrophes: Psychology in action* (pp. 189–235). Washington, DC: American Psychological Association Press.

CHAPTER 18

The Sense of Personal Control

Social–Structural Causes and Emotional Consequences

Catherine E. Ross
Jaya Sastry

INTRODUCTION

Some people attribute the events and conditions of their lives to their own actions, whereas others believe their lives are shaped by forces external to themselves, such as luck, chance, fate, or powerful others. The sense of personal control is the belief that you can and do master, control, and shape your own life. Its opposite is the sense of personal powerlessness. Thus, perceived control and powerlessness represent two ends of a continuum, with the belief that one can effectively alter the environment on one end of the continuum, and the belief that one's actions cannot influence events and circumstances at the other.

The sense of personal control has social causes and emotional consequences (Mirowsky & Ross, 1989). Powerlessness, as a social-psychological variable, is distinct from the objective conditions that may produce it and the distress an individual may feel as a consequence of it. As noted by Seeman (1959) and elaborated by Mirowsky and Ross (1989),

CATHERINE E. ROSS • Department of Sociology, The Ohio State University, Columbus, Ohio 43210-1353.
JAYA SASTRY • Late of Duke University, died in February 1998, at the age of 26. He had recently joined the department at Duke as a Ph.D. candidate after receiving his master's degree from The Ohio State University in 1997. He was a promising, insightful young scholar. He had already contributed greatly to our lives and to research and scholarship in the area of ethnic, cultural, and national differences in physical and psychological well-being.

Handbook of the Sociology of Mental Health, edited by Carol S. Aneshensel and Jo C. Phelan. Kluwer Academic/Plenum Publishers, New York, 1999.

perceived control occupies the central position in a three-part model in which social conditions shape perceptions of control, which, in turn, affect emotional well-being. This model is illustrated in Figure 18.1.

Compared to the belief that outcomes are determined by forces external to oneself, belief in personal control is associated with low levels of psychological distress (Benassi, Sweeney, & Dufour, 1988; Kohn & Schooler, 1982; Mirowsky & Ross, 1983, 1984; Wheaton, 1980, 1983; Pearlin, Menaghan, Lieberman, & Mullan, 1981). In fact, of all the beliefs about self and society that might affect distress, belief in control over one's own life may be the most important (Mirowsky & Ross, 1986, 1989).

This chapter is organized according to three main issues relating to the sense of personal control: (1) concept and measurement, (2) social–structural causes, and (3) emotional consequences. In the first section, we discuss concepts and measures related to personal control, including locus of control, self-efficacy, helplessness, and subjective alienation; we examine heuristics in psychology and sociology; and we end with a discussion of defense and acquiescence in measures of perceived control. In the second section, we develop a theory of objective power and perceived control, and we examine several social–structural correlates of perceived control—socioeconomic status; gender, work and family;

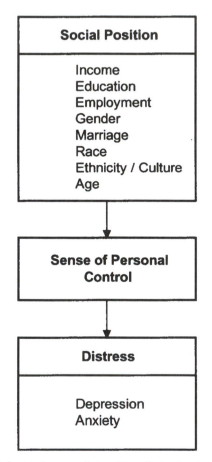

FIGURE 18.1. Personal control as a mediator of the effects of social position on distress.

age; and race, culture and ethnicity. In the third section, we describe the basic association between perceived control and psychological distress. Then, we address modifications of the basic pattern, including control over good and bad outcomes, various external attributions; diminishing returns, conditioning factors, mediating factors, social support and the sense of control, and effects of personal and universal control. We end the chapter with suggestions for future research.

THE CONCEPT AND MEASUREMENT OF PERCEIVED CONTROL

The importance of perceived control is recognized in a number of social and behavioral sciences, where it appears in several forms with various names. Seeman (1959) placed the sense of powerlessness and perceived lack of control at the top of his list of types of subjective alienation, defining it as "the expectancy or probability, held by the individual, that his own behavior cannot determine the occurrence of the outcomes, or reinforcements, he seeks" (p. 784). Perceived control is closely related to concepts of internal locus of control, self-efficacy, mastery, instrumentalism, self-directedness, and personal autonomy on one end of the continuum, and helplessness and fatalism on the other.

Locus of Control

In cognitive psychology, perceived control appears as locus of control (Rotter, 1966). Belief in an external locus of control is a *learned*, generalized expectation that outcomes of situations are determined by forces external to one's self, such as powerful others, luck, fate, or chance. The individual believes that he or she is powerless and at the mercy of the environment. Belief in an internal locus of control (the opposite) is a learned, generalized expectation that outcomes are contingent on one's own choices and actions. Compared to persons with an external locus of control, those with an internal locus of control attribute outcomes to themselves rather than to forces outside of themselves.

Personal Control

The sense of personal control corresponds to the personal control component of Rotter's locus of control scale, which includes questions such as "When I make plans, I can make them work" or "I have little influence over the things that happen to me." The concept of personal control refers to *oneself*, not others, and it is *general*, not realm-specific (Mirowsky & Ross, 1989). Thus, unlike Rotter's locus of control scale, it excludes beliefs about the control others have over their lives and realm-specific control, such as political control. For instance from the Rotter scale, we do not consider questions such as "The average citizen can have an influence in government decisions" or "There will always be wars" to be measures of the sense of personal control, since they do not refer to oneself, and they are realm-specific. Although political control may have implications for outcomes such as voter behavior (or academic control for scholastic performance), they are less directly related to mental health.

Perceptions about the amount of control *others* have over their lives might be related to mental health, but these beliefs are conceptually distinct from personal control. Belief about the amount of control that other people have has been termed *ideological control* (Gurin, Gurin, & Morrison, 1969), *universal control,* and *American instrumentalism* (Mirowsky, Ross, & Van Willigen, 1996), and should be distinguished from personal control or individual instrumentalism. Ideological, or universal, control refers to the degree one feels that others' successes or failures are their own doing; personal control refers to one's own life outcomes. Measures of personal and universal control are shown in Figure 18.2.

Self-Efficacy

The sense of personal control overlaps to a large extent with self-efficacy despite Bandura's (1986) claim that sense of control and self-efficacy are distinct (although related) concepts. Bandura collectively refers to concepts of locus of control, or sense of control, as outcome–expectancy theories. Self-efficacy, according to Bandura, focuses upon the individual's belief that he or she can (or cannot) effectively perform a specific action, whereas control focuses on the belief that certain actions will achieve ultimately desired goals. According to Bandura, self-efficacy is specific to particular contexts. To craft questions that would gauge people's feelings of efficacy in a sufficient number of situations and circumstances properly to fulfill the conceptual requirements of such a definition would demand far too much detail. The sense of control is a more parsimonious concept than self-efficacy, with more universal application. The degree to which people think they can or cannot achieve their goals, despite the specific nature of the actions required, has applicability to almost all circumstances. Hence, control is a more attractive measurable concept for most mental health research. More importantly, the sense of personal control may be the root of self-efficacy. Persons with a high sense of personal control will likely try other actions if their current repertoire of behaviors is not working. New behaviors may successfully obtain desired goals, which may in turn increase the perceived ability to shape other events and circumstances in life. Therefore, for all intents and purposes, the sense of control may be measuring the same underlying factor as self-efficacy. The conceptual distinction Bandura outlines may well be a purely academic one.

Helplessness

Another related concept appears in behavioral psychology as learned helplessness. The behavior of learned helplessness results from exposure to inescapable, uncontrollable negative stimuli and is characterized by a low rate of voluntary response and low ability to learn successful behaviors (Seligman, 1975). Although intended as an analog of human depression, it is important to remember that learned helplessness refers to the behavior, not to any cognitive attribution that reinforcements are outside one's control, and not to the imputed emotion of depression. In humans, however, there is a link between an external locus of control (a cognitive orientation) and learned helplessness (a conditioned response): the perception that reinforcement is not contingent on action. Hiroto (1974) found that, compared to subjects with an internal locus of control, those with an external locus of control were less likely to see a connection between behavior and reinforcement, and as a result, learned more slowly.

Personal Control

	Successes	Failures
Control	1) I can do anything I set my mind to. 2) I am responsible for my own successes.	1) My misfortunes are the result of mistakes I have made. 2) I am responsible for my failures.
Lack of Control	1) The really good things that happen to me are due to luck 2) If something good is going to happen to me, it will.	1) Most of my problems are due to bad breaks. 2) I have little control over bad things that happen to me.

Universal Control

	Successes	Failures
Control	1) In the U.S., most people can achieve anything they really set their minds to. 2) In the U.S. most people who have good things deserve them.	1) In the U.S. most people's problems result from their bad decisions and lack of effort.
Lack of Control	1) In the U.S., the good things that happen to people are mostly luck.	1) In the U.S. most people's problems are just bad luck. 2) In the U.S. most people's problems are caused by others who are selfish, greedy, or mean.

FIGURE 18.2. Indicators of personal and universal control. Personal control measure from Mirowsky and Ross (1991); universal control measure from Mirowsky, Ross, and Van Willigen (1996).

Subjective Alienation

In sociology, the concept of perceived powerlessness versus control can be traced to subjective alienation. Seeman (1959) defined alienation as any form of detachment or separation from oneself or from others. He further elaborated specific forms of alienation, defining powerlessness as the primary type of alienation (the others are self-estrangement, isolation, meaninglessness, and normlessness). Powerlessness is the separation from important outcomes in one's own life or an inability to achieve desired ends. Perceived powerlessness is the cognitive awareness of this reality. Both Rotter (1966) and Seeman (1959) recognized that perceived powerlessness—the major form of subjective alienation—and external locus of control were related concepts. In fact, Rotter (1966) derived the concept of locus of control from the sociological concept of alienation, stating that "the alienated individual feels unable to control his own destiny" (p. 263).

Other sociological concepts build on themes of perceived powerlessness versus control, and unlike some psychologists who focus on differences among related concepts, sociologists appear more likely to look for these common themes. As a result, many of the constructs used by sociologists overlap and often are conceptually indistinct. In sociology, concepts related to personal control appear under a number of different names in addition to powerlessness, notably, self-directedness (Kohn & Schooler, 1982), mastery (Pearlin et al., 1981), personal autonomy (Seeman, 1983), the sense of personal efficacy (Downey & Moen, 1987; Gecas, 1989) and instrumentalism (vs. fatalism) (Wheaton, 1980).

Heuristics in Psychology and Sociology

Ideally, social psychologists who study the links between social structural conditions, perceptions of control, and emotional outcomes will synthesize the strengths of psychology and sociology—as did Rotter and Seeman—while avoiding the pitfalls. Each discipline has a heuristic, or working assumption, which greatly simplifies reality to provide a base from which to proceed with research. In the extreme, psychology assumes that beliefs come out of people's heads without reference to social conditions, whereas sociology assumes that there is nothing *but* social structure. Sociologists too often discount the ways in which perceptions mediate the effects of social position on well-being; psychologists too often discount the influence of social structure on perceptions. Both links, shown in Figure 18.1, are crucial to understanding the processes by which social position affects psychological well-being.

Sociologists sometimes imply that social structure has consequences for individual behavior or well-being, without reference to individual beliefs or perceptions (Braverman, 1974). Erikson (1986) critiques sociologists who think that bringing in social-psychological mediating variables somehow makes theory less structural.

> There are those who argue that one ought to be able to determine when a person is alienated by taking a look at the objective conditions in which she works. The worker exposed to estranging conditions is alienated almost by definition, no matter what she says she thinks or even what she thinks she thinks. That view . . . has the effect of closing off sociological investigation rather than the effect of inviting it. Alienation, in order to make empirical sense, has to reside somewhere in or around the persons who are said to experience it. (p. 6)

The association between the objective condition and the subjective perception is an important empirical question; one that must be investigated, not assumed (Ross & Mirowsky, 1992; Seeman, 1983).

Some psychologists, on the other hand, discount the effects of social position, instead claiming that perceptions of control are as likely to be illusory as to be based on reality. Levenson (1973) says that a belief that one controls important outcomes in one's life is *unrelated* to the belief that others, chance, fate, or luck control those outcomes (see Lachman, 1986, for a review). Brewin and Shapiro (1984) contend that a perceived ability to achieve desirable outcomes is unrelated to a perceived ability to avoid undesirable ones. In both cases, people supposedly fail to see a connection, and the realities of life do not suggest one. Implicitly, these views deny the effects of social status on the sense of control. Levenson's view suggests that education, prestige, wealth, and power do not shift the locus of real control from others and chance to oneself. Brewin and Shapiro's view suggests that the real resources available for achieving success are useless for avoiding failure. These claims are based on small and often insignificant correlations between internal and external control, and control over good and bad outcomes. Next, we discuss the biases in their scales that are created by agreement tendencies and defensiveness.

Control, Defense, and Acquiescence

Responses to questions about personal control capture not only the concept of interest, but also two other crosscutting concepts—the tendency to agree and self-defense. Some people tend to agree with statements irrespective of content. Agreement tendency can make it appear as if internal and external control are uncorrelated (as in Levenson, 1973). Some people are more likely to believe that they control the good outcomes in their lives than the bad ones (self-defense); others take more responsibility for their failures than for their successes (self-blame, as in Brewin and Shapiro, 1984). Agreement tendencies and the tendency toward self-defense or self-blame crosscut the concept of interest and bias measures unless they balance agreement and defense. Thus, measures of personal control ideally should balance defensiveness and agreement tendencies to achieve unbiased measures. The Mirowsky–Ross measure of the sense of control (1991) is a two-by-two index that balances statements about control with those about lack of control, and statements about success (good outcomes) with those about failure (bad outcomes). It is illustrated in the top panel of Figure 18.2. Interestingly, Rotter's locus of control scale used a forced-choice format to solve the problem of acquiescence, but his logic apparently was lost when researchers switched to Likert scales. Likert scales are much more efficient in surveys and are more acceptable to respondents who dislike being forced to choose one of two extremes. Likert scales allow degrees of agreement with each statement, and the Mirowsky–Ross scale (1991) asks people whether they strongly agree, agree, disagree, or strongly disagree with each statement. However, Likert scales should balance control and lack of control over good and bad outcomes to ensure validity.

SOCIAL–STRUCTURAL CAUSES OF PERCEIVED CONTROL

In the United States, average levels of perceived control are high, and they vary systematically with positions of objective power. The large majority of Americans report that they control their own lives. Mirowsky et al. (1996) find that more than 90% of a representative national sample agree with the statements "I am responsible for my own successes" and "I can do just about anything I really set my mind to." A smaller percentage, but still more than two-thirds of the sample, agrees with statements claiming responsibility for personal misfortunes and failures. These levels of agreement are impressive, but as discussed earlier, they are inflated by the tendency of some respondents to agree with statements regardless of what they express (Mirowsky & Ross, 1991). That same tendency deflates the level of disagreement with fatalistic statements. Even so, disagreement with the fatalistic statements ranges from 54% to 79%. Averaging the percentage of instrumental responses across the eight personal control items shown in Figure 18.2 yields a mean of 77%. As a generalization, about three-fourths of Americans apparently feel that they are in control of their own lives and responsible for their own outcomes. Despite high mean levels of personal control in the United States, considerable variation exists.

Objective Power and Perceived Control

Belief in external control is the learned and generalized expectation that one has little control over meaningful events and circumstances in one's life. As such, it is the subjective awareness of a discrepancy between one's goals and the means to achieve them. Theoretically, social–structural positions indicative of objective powerlessness, including dependency, structural inconsistency, role stress, and alienated labor, increase the probability of this discrepancy and thus increase perceived powerlessness (Mirowsky & Ross, 1989; Rosenfield, 1989).

Beliefs about personal control are often realistic perceptions of objective conditions. An individual learns through social interaction and personal experience that his or her choices and efforts are usually likely or unlikely to affect the outcome of a situation (Rotter 1966; Seeman, 1983; Wheaton, 1980). Failure in the face of effort leads to a sense of powerlessness, fatalism, or belief in external control, beliefs that can increase passivity and result in giving up. Through continued experience with objective conditions of powerlessness and lack of control, individuals come to learn that their own actions cannot produce desired outcomes. In contrast, success leads to a sense of mastery, efficacy, or belief in internal control, characterized by an active, problem-solving approach to life (Wheaton, 1980, 1983; Mirowsky & Ross, 1983, 1984).

Sociological theory points to several conditions likely to produce a belief in external control. First and foremost is powerlessness. Defined as an objective condition rather than a belief, it is the inability to achieve one's ends or, alternatively, the inability to achieve one's ends when in opposition to others. The second condition is structural inconsistency, which is a situation in which society defines certain goals, purposes, and interests as legitimate and desirable and also defines the proper procedures for moving toward the objectives but does not provide adequate resources and opportunities for achieving the objectives through legitimate means. The third is alienated labor, a condition under which the worker does not decide what to produce, does not design or schedule the production process, and does not own the product. The fourth condition is dependency, a situation in which one partner in an exchange has fewer alternative sources of sustenance and gratification than the other. The fifth, role overload, is a situation in which expectations of others imply demands that overwhelm the resources and capabilities of the individual. Although these conditions are not exhaustive, they all point to the generative force of various forms of social power. In looking for the sources of perceived powerlessness, researchers have looked for variables associated with conditions of powerlessness, structural inconsistency, alienated labor, dependency, and role overload.

Among the major sociodemographic correlates of the sense of personal control are (1) socioeconomic status (SES), including general socioeconomic status, and a number of specific components such as education, income, occupation, and unemployment; (2) gender and gendered statuses in paid and unpaid work and in the family; (3) age; and (4) race, ethnicity, and culture.

Socioeconomic Status

Most research on the social–structural correlates of perceived control looks at SES—education, income, employment status, and occupation. General SES (as measured by an index of family income, occupational prestige of the respondent or breadwinner, and interviewer ratings of the social class of the neighborhood, home, and respondent) is negatively related to a sense of powerlessness and, thus, positively related to a sense of mastery and control

(Mirowsky & Ross, 1983). Looking at specific components of SES separately, family income, personal earnings, education, and job status each decrease the sense of powerlessness, adjusting for the other components (Downey & Moen 1987; Mirowsky & Ross, 1983; Ross & Mirowsky, 1989, 1992; Ross, Mirowsky, & Cockerham, 1983; Wheaton, 1980). Income is probably the most direct and obvious indicator of power—the ability to achieve one's ends—but education and work also have independent effects.

Education develops effective capacities on many levels. First, in formal education, one encounters and solves problems that are progressively more difficult, complex, and subtle. The process of learning builds confidence and self-assurance, even if the things learned have no practical value. Those things, however, often do have practical value. Education also instills the habit of meeting problems with attention, thought, action, and persistence. It develops the general habits and skills of communication and analysis, plus those that are tailored to an occupation. Education develops the ability to solve problems on all these levels, and the ability to solve problems increases control over events and outcomes in life. Finally, education serves as an avenue to good jobs and high income. Thus, it marks the social power that helps provide control over circumstances of life (Mirowsky, 1995; Ross & Wu, 1995).

Jobs are important for a number of reasons. Low-status jobs produce a sense of powerlessness because the job, and the opportunities and income it provides, are seen as barriers to the achievement of life goals (Wheaton, 1980). Jobs that are substantively complex (especially in work that involves primarily information and people rather than things) increase the sense of personal control and psychological self-directedness (Kohn, 1976; Kohn & Schooler, 1982). Jobs that provide autonomy—freedom from close supervision and participation in decision making—increase the sense of personal control (Bird & Ross, 1993; Kohn & Schooler, 1982; Ross & Mirowsky, 1992). Together, substantively complex, nonroutine, autonomous work signals control over one's own work, which Kohn and his colleagues call occupational self-direction. Among the employed, occupational self-direction—rather than ownership of the means of production or control over the labor of others—increases psychological self-direction, which is similar to the sense of personal control (Kohn, 1976; Kohn & Schooler, 1982; Kohn, Naoi, Schoenbach, Schooler, & Slomczynski, 1990). Job latitude, like occupational self-direction, includes autonomous decision making and nonroutine work, and it significantly increases perceived control (Seeman, Seeman, & Budros, 1988). Job disruptions such as being laid off, downgraded, fired, or leaving work because of illness, decrease the worker's sense of mastery, partly by lowering income and increasing difficulties in acquiring necessities such as food, clothing, housing, and medical care, or optional but useful items such as furniture, automobiles, and recreation (Pearlin et al., 1981).

In summary, theory strongly predicts a positive relationship between SES and the sense of control, and research strongly supports the prediction. Most aspects of SES, including high levels of education, household income, personal earnings, job status, occupational self-direction, and employment itself are significantly associated with high perceived control. Furthermore, some studies find that adjustment for the sense of control statistically explains the effects of education and household income on distress, meaning that perceived control mediates the effects of SES on distress (Mirowsky & Ross, 1989).

Gender, Work, and Family

Theory suggests that women have a lower sense of control over their lives than men as a result of economic dependency, restricted opportunities, role overload, and the routine nature of housework and women's jobs. Although past evidence indicates that women have a lower sense of control than men (Mirowsky & Ross, 1983, 1984; Thoits, 1987), the difference is often insignificant (Ross & Bird, 1994; Ross & Mirowsky, 1989). In this section, we review these theoretical expectations and examine the empirical evidence pertaining to them. Then, we return to the original question of whether women have a lower sense of control over their lives than do men, and the circumstances under which they do and do not.

PAID AND UNPAID WORK.   Women are more likely to do unpaid domestic work; men are more likely to work for pay. Compared to not working for pay, employment is associated with status, power, economic independence, and noneconomic rewards for both men and women (Bird & Ross, 1993; Gove & Tudor, 1973). For women who are exclusively housewives, domestic work is done without economic rewards, without the opportunity for advancement or promotion for work well done, and, because it is often invisible, devalued, and taken for granted, without psychological rewards (Bergmann, 1986; Gove & Tudor, 1973). Theory predicts that people employed for pay have a greater sense of control over their lives than do homemakers. Perceived control over one's life is the expectation that one's behavior affects outcomes, and working for pay likely produces a mental connection between efforts and outcomes. In contrast, work done without pay or other rewards produces a sense of disconnection between efforts and outcomes. Effort and skill at housework have few consequences; one does not receive a raise, and one's standard of living is determined by someone else, not by one's abilities at the job. Furthermore, homemakers are economically dependent, which may decrease their sense of control and increase the perception that powerful others shape their lives. Both economic dependency and the disconnection between work and rewards theoretically decrease perceived control among unpaid domestic workers compared to paid workers. Some empirical evidence indicates that employed persons have a higher sense of control than the nonemployed overall (Ross & Mirowsky, 1992), that the employed have a higher sense of control than homemakers specifically (Bird & Ross, 1993), and that the employed have a greater sense of self-determination than housewives (Ferree, 1976). For example, Elder and Liker (1982) found that elderly women who had taken jobs 40 years earlier, during the Great Depression, had a higher sense of self-efficacy and lower sense of helplessness than women who remained homemakers.

What explains the association between full-time homemaking and low personal control? Bird and Ross (1993) find that, compared to paid work, homemaking is more routine, provides less intrinsic gratification, fewer extrinsic symbolic rewards concerning the quality and value of the work, and it is unpaid. These differences account for houseworkers' lower sense of control over their lives. Bird and Ross also find that although homemakers are thanked for their work more often than male paid workers, being thanked for work does not significantly affect one's sense of control. However, housework offers one important advantage over the average paid job: higher levels of autonomy. Work autonomy significantly increases the sense of control. Were it not for their autonomy, homemakers would experience an even lower sense of control than is observed.

WORK AND FAMILY INTERACTIONS.   Overall, the employed have significantly higher average levels of perceived control than do homemakers. Not all jobs are alike, however; nor are all households contexts of employment. Critical combinations of low pay, nonautonomous working conditions, and heavy family demands (conditions faced disproportionately by women) may negate the positive influence of employment on control. Ross and Mirowsky (1992) find, first, that the difference in perceived control between employed and nonemployed depends on job conditions, including job autonomy and earnings (job authority, promotion opportunities, and job prestige are not significant). As job autonomy and earnings increase among the employed, their sense of control relative to that of the nonemployed increases. Second, household labor modifies the effect of employment on the sense of control. The higher one's responsibility for household work, the less the association between employment and control (Ross & Mirowsky, 1992). Responsibility for household work greatly decreases the sense of control associated with employment. (Household work does not decrease perceived control in itself; among people who are not employed, household work slightly increases the sense of control). Similarly, Rosenfield (1989) finds that the role overload of mothers who are employed at full-time jobs produces increases the sense of powerlessness and thus increases depression. Third, the greater the household income from sources other than one's own earnings, the less the association between employment and perceived control (Ross & Mirowsky, 1992). The lower the household income available from other sources, the greater the sense of control associated with having a job compared to not having one. Although other household income increases the sense of control, it decreases the positive effect of one's own employment on the sense of control.

Qualities of the job combine with household circumstances to give some employees a lower sense of control than found among those who are not employed. Figure 18.3 illustrates that, depending on circumstances, employment can be associated with either a lower or a higher sense of control. The gray bar represents the adjusted mean sense of control among persons who are not employed. The bar just below it represents the sense of control

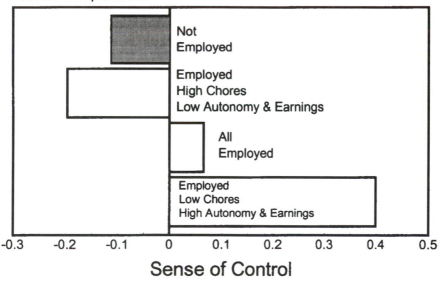

True-Score Standard Deviations
From the Sample Mean

Not Employed

Employed High Chores Low Autonomy & Earnings

All Employed

Employed Low Chores High Autonomy & Earnings

-0.3   -0.2   -0.1   0   0.1   0.2   0.3   0.4   0.5

Sense of Control

Figure 18.3. Conditions under which the employed have a higher or lower sense of control than the nonemployed. High refers to one standard deviation above the mean, and low refers to one standard deviation below the mean. Adapted from Ross and Mirowsky (1992).

predicted for the employed who have low earnings and autonomy (a standard deviation below average) and major responsibility for household chores (a standard deviation above average). Under these circumstances, employment is associated with a lower average sense of control than among people who are not employed. At the other extreme, the large bar on the bottom represents the sense of control predicted for the employed with high earnings and autonomy and low responsibility for household chores. Under those circumstances, employment is associated with a much higher sense of control.

Job autonomy, earnings, responsibility for household work, and other family income combine to make the association between employment and the sense of control greater for most men than for most women. Men have higher autonomy and earnings, less responsibility for household work, and lower amounts of other household income. Because of the differences in these factors, employment increases the expected sense of control most for married males, followed by nonmarried males, then nonmarried females, and finally married females. For married women, the typical combination of low pay, low autonomy, high responsibility for household chores, and high family income other than personal earnings nearly negates the positive association between employment and the sense of control.

Marriage and Children.   There is not much research on the ways that family affects women or men's sense of control over their lives. Ross (1991) finds that marriage has different effects on the sense of control for women than it does for men, and that among women, marriage increases the expected sense of control in some ways but decreases it in other ways. Adjusting for household income, nonmarried women have a significantly greater sense of control than both men and married women. Ordered from a low to a high sense of control are married females, nonmarried males, married males, and nonmarried females. Everything else being equal, marriage decreases perceived control among women, but not among men. However, everything else is not really equal. Married women have much higher household incomes than do nonmarried women ($33,680 compared to $20,380 in 1985, when the survey was taken). Thus, marriage represents a trade-off for women: It is associated with high household income, which increases perceived control, but it decreases personal control in other ways. The reverse, of course, is true for nonmarried women, who have low household incomes, but otherwise have something (perhaps independence or a lack of subordination) that increases their sense of control. "The economic well-being of married women carries a price, paid in personal control" (Ross, 1991, p. 837). The cost of marriage could be due to direct negative effects on women's autonomy, but some of the negative effect of marriage is due to the circumstances of married women's employment, which is usually combined with heavy responsibilities for household work, as described earlier.

Theory suggests that the presence of children in the household is associated with low levels of personal control among parents, especially mothers, because children limit freedom, impose constraints, and decrease the ability to maintain an ordered, predictable, and controlled world (Gove & Geerken, 1977). There is little evidence, however, for a detrimental effect of children on perceptions of control among women. Overall, the number of children in the household has no significant effect on women's sense of control in general (Ross, 1991), or among middle-age black mothers in particular (Coleman, Antonucci, Adelmann, & Crohan, 1987). Children born to mothers under the age of 19 decrease self-efficacy, but children born to women over the age of 19 do not (McLaughlin & Micklin, 1983).

SUMMARY.   Theory predicts that women have a lower sense of control than men. Adult statuses disadvantage women in terms of objective powerlessness, economic dependence, routine and unfulfilling work, and role overload. Women's positions at work, in households, and in the interactions between the two spheres provide empirical support for explanations of why women would have lower perceived control than men. Women are more likely to be homemakers; and if employed, women's jobs pay less, provide less autonomy, and are frequently combined with household responsibilities that produce role overload. These conditions are associated with low personal control. On the other hand, some research fails to find significant differences between men and women in their levels of personal control. These results mean that (1) something else, as yet unidentified, about women's lives offsets the negative conditions, and increases perceived control, and (2) under some as yet unidentified conditions, women have higher levels of control than do men. Identifying these conditions is a fruitful area for research. The fact that nonmarried women who have household incomes on par with married women (an unusual group) have high levels of personal control hints at a route for future research.

Age

Recent research using large representative samples of persons across the full range of adult ages, from 18 to 90, shows that older adults have a lower sense of control than do younger adults, and that perceived control decreases with age at an accelerating rate (Mirowsky, 1995). Prior studies had produced inconsistent and often contradictory results. In a review, Lachman (1986) concluded that about one-third of studies found low levels of control among the elderly, one-third found high levels, and one-third found no association between age and the sense of control. Rodin (1986) also concluded that there was little evidence that perceived control decreased with age. Inconsistencies in these studies may have resulted from the use of truncated, noncomparable, unrepresentative, and small samples. Many samples contained only elderly, so the comparative data showing higher levels of control among the young and middle-aged were unavailable; and even studies with comparison groups often used unrepresentative groups of young people (i.e., college students) or elderly (i.e., health plan members). Bias in the measures of perceived control may have also accounted for inconsistencies. For example, questions about planning, orderliness, perseverance, self-discipline, achievement, and the like were sometimes used to measure perceived control. Although perceived control may be correlated with these things, it is not the same, and many attributes such as planning, orderliness, and so on, increase with age and consequently confound associations with perceived control. Finally, indexes that do not account for agreement tendencies obscure the relationship between age and perceived control because older persons are much more likely to agree to statements regardless of content than are younger persons (Mirowsky, 1995; Mirowsky & Ross, 1996).

More research on representative samples that represent the full age range is needed, but if the accelerating negative association between age and perceived control is replicated, the question is what explains the association? Rodin (1986) suggests three possible explanations for a negative association between age and the sense of control: loss of meaningful relationships, a deterioration of health and physical functioning, and dependency created and enforced through contact with health professionals who prefer compliant patients. However, Wolinsky and Stump's (1996) test of these explanations finds little support for them. They conclude, as does Mirowsky (1995), that some of the apparent aging effect is really due to cohort differences. Older cohorts have lower levels of education, which explains some of the association between age and sense of control. However, Mirowsky (1995) also finds that some of the effect is due to aging's effect on physical impairment.

Race, Culture, and Ethnicity

RACE.   Racial discrimination and institutional barriers frustrate African American's aspirations and theoretically lead to a cognitive disconnection between their efforts and outcomes. Research finds that blacks have lower average levels of perceived control than whites. Explanations for this difference include discrimination encountered by blacks (a direct effect of race), along with the lower SES, especially education and income, held by black Americans (an indirect effect mediated by SES) (Gurin, Gurin, Lao, & Beattie, 1969; Hughes & Demo, 1989; Porter & Washington, 1979; Wade, Thompson, Tashakori, & Valente, 1989). The empirical evidence shows a direct effect of race, even adjusting for education and household income, indicating that blacks have a lower sense of control over their lives that is not just due to socioeconomic disadvantage (Ross & Mirowsky, 1989). Two unresolved issues stand out in this literature. First, what is the correspondence between blacks' perceptions of personal control and perceptions about the control other people have over their lives (universal control)? Second, what is the correspondence between blacks' perceptions of personal control and self-esteem?

Early research concluded that, compared to whites, African Americans had lower levels of personal control but similar levels of ideological, or universal, control (Gurin et al., 1969). White men had by far the highest levels of personal control, significantly higher than white women and black men and women, but black and white beliefs about the control others have over their lives did not differ (Gurin, Gurin, & Morrison, 1978). Gurin and his colleagues concluded that although blacks are likely to internalize general American attitudes about the relationship between effort and outcomes, they are more likely to believe that their own, personal efforts are not strongly related to positive outcomes. Wade et al. (1989) concluded that African Americans are more likely to attribute failures to personal effort, whereas whites are more likely to attribute successes to their own doing. In contrast, Mirowsky et al. (1996) found that African Americans have significantly lower levels of both personal and universal control (over both successes and failures) than whites. They found parallel race differences in people's beliefs about control over their own life and beliefs about the control most Americans have over their lives. Whites (along with the well educated and those with high household incomes) were significantly more likely than blacks to believe they are in control of their own lives *and* that other Americans are in control of their lives. Beliefs about Americans in general followed essentially the same race profile as beliefs about the self. However, even the large majority of blacks agreed that most people in the United States can achieve anything they set their minds to and that most people's problems result from bad decisions or lack of effort.

A second, related issue deals with the apparently contradictory relationship between self-esteem and sense of control among American blacks. Although much of the research literature indicates that blacks have comparatively low levels of control, they have levels of self-esteem on parity with or more positive than whites (Hulbary, 1975; Hunt & Hunt, 1977; Porter & Washington, 1979; Taylor & Walsh, 1979). These findings appear to be inconsistent, because self-esteem and sense of control are highly correlated. One interpretation argues that a high level of external control reflects the tendency of blacks to blame failures on a unfair system that discriminates against blacks and privileges whites (Porter & Washington, 1979). By attributing failures to a racist system rather than to themselves, blacks are able to maintain high levels of personal self-esteem. However, the sense of personal control is conceptually distinct factor from the degree of system-blame (Gurin et al., 1969; Ross et al., 1996), and blaming the system does *not* improve self-esteem (Hughes & Demo, 1989).

Another interpretation, proposed by Hughes and Demo (1989), is that interpersonal relationships predict self-esteem, whereas sense of control is determined more by socio-economic success. In their study of African Americans, Hughes and Demo find that variables predicting self-esteem are strongly related to the supportive quality of family, peer, and religious attachments. Their results support Rosenberg's (1979) theory that black self-esteem is related to reflected appraisals of the immediate community, such as teachers, parents, and friends (reflected appraisals of the dominant white culture, on the other hand, which tend to marginalize and devalue black culture, appear to be largely irrelevant for black self-esteem). Whereas perceptions of self-worth, or self-esteem, stem from social attachments to close friends and family that reflect positively on a person and provide interpersonal support (Schwalbe & Staples, 1991), perceived competence in the realm of SES (educational, occupational, and economic success) may be most important to beliefs about self-efficacy. Indicators of SES, such as education and income, more strongly predict perceived control than do social attachments. This supports the theory of personal control proposed earlier, stating that the experience of successful performance in a variety of tasks shapes a sense of personal efficacy. (Whether these factors explain race differences in personal control and self-esteem is still unanswered, however, since the study by Hughes and Demo did not include whites).

More research is needed to explain the processes by which race shapes the sense of personal control. One possible route suggests hypotheses derived from the theory of personal control. Any condition that severs the link between efforts and outcomes in theory reduces the sense of control. Discrimination is an act in which an individual is treated on the basis of race or another ascribed status (such as sex or age), rather than on the basis of their own individual achievements, effort, ability, skills, and other "meritocratic" or "performance-based" criteria. If people are treated on the basis of ascribed characteristics over which they have no control, rather than on the basis of achievements over which they do have control, the link between efforts and outcomes is severed. Whether this treatment is negative or positive does not matter, according to theory. Both negative and positive discrimination produce an uncoupling of what one does and the outcomes of these acts. If a person is hired or promoted on the basis of race, in theory, this will decrease the sense of control. Ironically, correcting past negative discrimination with current positive discrimination, rather than with meritocratic assessments of an individual's own ability to do the job regardless of race, may perpetuate low levels of personal control among African Americans. Only empirical investigation will tell whether this prediction implied by theory is supported.

ETHNICITY, CULTURE, AND CROSS-NATIONAL DIFFERENCES.   Differences in national and regional economic development levels, as well as cultural differences in values and normative expectations, may lead to differences in the sense of control. Economic development (and the change from agricultural to industrial society) has long been theorized to have an effect on individual psychology. In *Becoming Modern*, Inkeles and Smith (1974) hypothesized that the institutions of developed society would induce so-called modern values that would be held across all nations regardless of the nature of traditional cultural forms. Institutions within developed nations would socialize people in such a way that their value orientations would better mesh with the needs of advanced industrialized societies. Schools and the workplace would encourage critical thinking and proactivity, thereby eroding the influence of traditional value systems. Inkeles and Smith hypothesized that modern individuals would be characterized by a high degree of instrumentalism and have the conviction that they can take action to change their lives and the world around them. They would reject passivity, resignation, and fatalism. This orientation is substantively similar to the sense of personal control. Using a sample of six nations of varying degrees of national development (including Argentina, Bangladesh, Chile, India, Israel, and Nigeria), Inkeles and Smith found that the higher the level of economic development of the nation, the higher the sense of control of the respondent, even adjusting for the individual's own education and income. (Education had the largest effect on perceived control, however, and income was next). They conclude that those who live in developed societies have more contact with modern institutions and, as a result, develop higher levels of personal control, despite countervailing traditional cultural forces.

Despite the converging effects modern institutions have on individuals' beliefs about themselves and the world, others contend that traditional cultural values persist across different societies despite the effects of national development. A pervasive theme in comparative research is the contrast between familial and collectivist commitments on the one hand, and individual self-reliance and autonomy on the other. Mirowsky and Ross (1984) propose that, compared to Anglos, persons of Mexican ethnic identity in both Mexico and the United States have more of an orientation to family and pseudofamily, whereas Anglos place less emphasis on the mutual obligations of family and friends and more on the individual's personal responsibility for his or her own life. They find that Mexican heritage is associated with belief in external control, even after taking into account lower education, income, and status. On the other hand, they propose that Mexicans have higher levels of support, creating contradictory effects on distress: Lower levels of personal control among Mexicans increase depression levels, but proposed higher levels of supportive social networks decrease anxiety.

Hui and Triandis (1986) make a similar argument about Asian heritage. They argue that Asian countries emphasize collectivist values, whereas Western European nations emphasize individualistic values. Collectivist values commit individuals to social obligations to fulfill traditional, family-oriented role demands. The nature of the self is inherently familial. In contrast, Western cultures stress egocentric values and self-directed orientations. Al-Zahrani and Kaplowitz (1993) theorize (but find no empirical support for the idea) that people in individualistic nations are more likely to attribute favorable outcomes to personal achievements than those from collectivist cultures. Theoretically, people in individualistic cultures view themselves in terms of personal attributes, whereas those in collectivist cultures are more likely to view themselves in terms of personal relationships. The relational character of collectivist people may make them hesitant to take credit for personal achievement, whereas individualists, who define themselves by personal qualities, may be more likely to attribute outcomes to their own skills and effort.

Despite extensive theory on the ways in which cultural differences relating to collectivism versus individualism would affect the sense of personal control, there is almost no research on cross-national, cultural, or ethnic differences. Thus, we present results from our preliminary study of personal control among Asians in Asia and the United States

(Sastry & Ross, 1998). Using the 1990 World Values Survey, which includes samples from 42 different nations, we examined the effect of living in an Asian nation (Japan, South Korea, China, and India) on the sense of personal control, adjusting for national level of development (GDP) and for individual socioeconomic and household characteristics. Respondents who lived in an Asian nation were significantly less likely to agree that they had control over their own lives. Similarly, using a large representative national sample of the United States, we found that Asians scored significantly lower on the Mirowsky–Ross sense of control scale than did whites, again adjusting for socioeconomic status and household composition. Eastern culture, with its emphasis on familial commitment and subordination to the whole, may encourage individuals to attribute achievements to external causes. This is an important area for future research.

EMOTIONAL CONSEQUENCES OF PERCEIVED CONTROL

In the modern Western context, people with high levels of personal control have low levels of psychological distress (Aneshensel, 1992; Gecas, 1989; Mirowsky & Ross, 1986, 1989; Pearlin et al., 1981; Ross & Mirowsky, 1989; Wheaton, 1980, 1983). Distress tends to be elevated among people who believe they have little influence over the things that happen to them, that what is going to happen will happen, and they might as well decide what to do by flipping a coin, because success is mostly a matter of getting good breaks. In comparison, distress is low among those who believe that when they make plans, they can make them work, that misfortunes result from the mistakes they make because there is really no such thing as luck, and what happens to them is their own doing (Wheaton, 1980). Similarly, increases in the belief that "I have little control over the things that happen to me" increases distress over time, whereas increases in the belief that "I can do just about anything I really set my mind to," or that "What happens to me in the future mostly depends on me," decrease distress over time (Pearlin et al., 1981).

In addition to its direct, demoralizing impact, the sense of not being in control of the outcomes in one's life can diminish the will and motivation to actively solve problems. Wheaton (1983) argues that fatalism decreases coping effort. Belief in the efficacy of environmental rather than personal forces makes active attempts to solve problems seem pointless: "What's the use?" The result is less motivation and less persistence in coping and, thus, less success in solving problems and adapting. Taking Wheaton's arguments a step further, the fatalist has a reactive, passive orientation, whereas the instrumentalist has a proactive one. Instrumental persons are likely to search the environment for potentially distressing events and conditions, to take preventive steps, and to accumulate resources or develop skills and habits that will reduce the impact of unavoidable problems (for example, driving carefully, wearing a seatbelt, and carrying accident insurance). When undesired events and situations occur, the instrumental person is better prepared and less threatened. In contrast, the reactive, passive person ignores potential problems until they actually happen, making problems more likely to occur and leaving the person unprepared when they do. Furthermore, passive coping, such as trying to ignore the problem until it goes away, fails to limit the consequences of the problems. Thus, the instrumentalist is constantly getting ahead of problems, whereas the fatalist is inevitably falling behind. The theoretical result is a magnification of differences: Fatalists suffer more and more problems, reinforcing their perceived powerlessness and thus producing escalating passivity in the face of difficulties, and more and more distress.

By contrast, a self-directed orientation plays a central role in a three-way relationship with problem-solving flexibility and distress. Greater self-directedness increases problem-solving flexibility and decreases distress. In turn, the greater flexibility and lower distress boost self-directedness. The result is a self-amplifying feedback that magnifies the impact of occupational routinization, closeness of supervision, and substantive complexity on distress (Kohn & Schooler, 1982). (The impact of psychological self-direction on distress is much larger than the "rebound" effect of distress on self-direction, so the cross-sectional analyses that assume one-way causation are probably not seriously biased).

Evidence that belief in external, as opposed to internal, control is associated with increased distress is strong and consistent. In addition to the sociological studies cited earlier, Benassi et al. (1988), conducted a meta-analysis of 97 studies in the psychological literature on locus of control and depression, finding a mean correlation of .31 between external control and depression (or, equivalently, a mean correlation of internal control and depression of -.31). The effect was very consistent: Not one study found an effect in the opposite direction. Nonetheless, this relationship may not hold under all circumstances. Next, we ask a number of questions that address potential modifications of the basic association between perceived control and distress. Is the sense of control over both positive and negative outcomes associated with low distress? Are all types of external attribution equally distressing? Is there such a thing as too much perceived control? Does the sense of control reduce distress for all social groups? What mediates the sense of control on distress? What are the interrelationships among perceived control, social support, and distress? Do perceptions of personal control interact with beliefs about the amount of control others have in their effect on distress?

Control over Good and Bad Outcomes

It is not hard to believe that perceptions of control over good outcomes reduce distress, but does belief in responsibility for one's failures also reduce distress? The answer is "yes." Perceived control over both good and bad outcomes is associated with low levels of depression (Bulman & Wortman, 1977; Krause & Stryker, 1984; Mirowsky & Ross, 1990b). Increases in the belief that "I am responsible for my failures" and "My misfortunes result from the mistakes I have made" have as large and *negative* associations with depression as do the beliefs that "I am responsible for my own successes" and "I can do just about anything I set my mind to." Denying responsibility for failure does not protect well-being; it is associated with as much depression as denying responsibility for success. Claiming control of both success and failure is associated with low levels of depression (Mirowsky & Ross, 1990). In contrast there is no measurable benefit from claiming responsibility for success while denying responsibility for failure (self-defense). Furthermore, the perception that positive outcomes are due to chance is as distressing as the perception that negative outcomes are due to chance. The sense that good outcomes are unpredictable, random, and due simply to luck is distressing, probably because it implies that the individual cannot increase the likelihood of his or her own success.

Various External Attributions

There are various external attributions a person can make. People can attribute the outcomes in their lives to luck, chance, family background, other people, God, and so on. All these external attributions are logical opposites of internal control: Either I am in control of my life or not. If not, though, control could be in the hands of other people, or be due to luck, chance, or God. Only a few studies have looked at these separate external attributions. Both powerful others and chance attributions were associated with depression in psychiatric patients (Levenson, 1973), in alcoholics in treatment (Caster & Parsons, 1977), and in depressed and nondepressed subjects (Rosenbaum & Hadari, 1985). Overall, the attribution of outcomes to powerful others was slightly more distressing than the attribution to chance (overall mean correlation of .38 compared to .31) (Benassi et al., 1988). In a representative sample of Illinois residents, Ross (1990) compared attributions of success to one's own effort and ability with four types of external attributions—to luck, to God, to good connections, and to family background. Adjusting for sociodemographic characteristics, the willingness to express emotions, and the other attributions, personal control significantly reduced distress, attributions of success to luck and to good connections significantly increased distress, and attributions of success to God and family background were not related to distress.

In contrast to internal control, attributions of control to luck and to powerful others are distressing. There is nothing comforting about the attribution of outcomes to luck and chance. They imply that the world is unpredictable, uncertain, random, and uncontrollable; consequently, they are distressing. Anything, good or bad, could happen at any time is a perception that generates helplessness. The belief that good network connections determine success may be distressing because it implies that success is in the hands of other, more powerful people. Attributions of success to connections with other people may indicate dependency. On the other hand, belief that outcomes are in the hands of God may provide some comfort, hope, and meaning, which counteract the external attribution.

Diminishing Returns

Is there such a thing as too much perceived control? The idea of a threshold of dysfunction implies that there are diminishing subjective returns to an increasing sense of control, with a limit beyond which it increases distress (Wheaton, 1985). According to this view, the emotional benefits of a sense of control are largely the consequence of effective action. Effectiveness requires a combination of motivation and realistic appraisal. A greater sense of control implies greater motivation, but an excessive sense of control implies an unrealistic self-appraisal. Distress is minimized by a sense of control that balances motivation and realism. The threshold of dysfunction is the point at which the problems caused by illusory control exactly cancel the benefits from greater motivation (Mirowsky & Ross, 1990a, p. 1516). Wheaton (1985) found direct support for this idea in a parabolic model of perceived control (the linear term was *significant and negative,* and the quadratic term was *significant and positive*), with the least depression occurring when perceived control was at about the 80th percentile. Taking this idea a step further, Mirowsky and Ross (1990a) asked whether diminishing benefits to psychological well-being from high levels of control result from illusory rather than real control. Control perceptions predicted by status (income, education, age, and minority status) are considered realistic; perceptions not attributable to social status are considered illusory. They found that the diminishing returns to high perceived control apply only to the sense of control not attributable to status. There are no diminishing subjective returns to a greater sense of control due to greater status.

Conditioning Factors

Is perceived control associated with less distress for all social groups? Some theorists have argued that a belief in external control may help *reduce* distress among people with little real power and control, in part by protecting self-esteem. According to this argument, failures and inadequacies can be blamed on one's place in society rather than on oneself, and striving for success can be comfortably put aside (Gurin et al., 1969; Hyman, 1966). Given a social position of little real power, perceptions of control may increase distress. Mirowsky and Ross (1984) and Wheaton (1985), however, found no significant difference between Anglos, Mexicans living in the United States, or Mexican Americans in the effect of fatalism on depression and anxiety, despite much higher levels of fatalism among persons of Mexican ethnic heritage and identity. For both groups, belief in external control significantly increased depression. Turner and Noh (1983) found that, in a group of women who had recently given birth, those with a low sense of control suffered more distress from low status and undesirable events, not less. Mirowsky and Ross (1990a) found that low status persons (those with low levels of education, household income, older persons, and minority group members) are not consoled by a low sense of control. Fatalism and a sense of powerlessness are the recognition of a painful reality but do not soothe its discomfort.

Mediating Factors

What mediates the association between the sense of personal control and psychological distress? Few studies examine the processes by which perceived control affects psychological distress. However, Ross and Mirowsky (1989) found that problem solving explained about 17% of the effect of perceived control on distress. Depression was comparatively low among people who responded that they did not simply ignore problems and hope they would go away, but instead tried to figure out the cause of a problem and solve it; in turn problem solving was increased by perceptions of control. Thus, the basic precepts of personal control theory—that an attentive, active response to problems is increased by the sense of control and reduces depression—receive support but do not statistically explain the majority of the association between control and distress. More research is needed on the factors that mediate the association between perceived control and distress.

Social Support and Sense of Control

Perceived control and social support are two of the main links between social position and emotional well-being. What are the interrelationships among perceived control, support, and distress? Ross and Mirowsky (1989) describe three views of the relationship between control and support, and their impact on well-being: *displacement, facilitation,* and *functional substitution.* According to the first view, social support detracts from control and displaces active problem solving. Social support implies a network of reciprocity and mutual obligation that limits instrumental action while fostering dependence. People who solve their own problems have a greater sense of control and self-esteem, and are more effective in solving problems than those who turn to others (Brown, 1978). Pearlin and Schooler (1978) conceptualize turning to others as the opposite of self-reliance, and they find that those who rely on themselves to solve their own problems have lower levels of distress than those who turn to others. According to the second view, social support facilitates problem solving and instrumental action. The importance of support is not that one leans on others in times of trouble, but that perceptions of support give people the courage to act. This perspective would account for the finding that distress is reduced by the perception of available support if needed (perceived support), but not by the actual receipt of support (received support) (Wethington & Kessler, 1986). According to the third view, support and control can substitute for one another to reduce depression. They are alternative means of reducing perceived threat. Control provides confidence in one's ability; support provides confidence in one's worth. Each reduces distress, and each reduces the effect of otherwise stressful conditions (Turner & Noh, 1983). Thus, control is most beneficial—reduces distress the most—when support is low. Similarly, support is most beneficial when control is low. One resource fills the breach if the other is absent. In support of this view, Ross and Mirowsky (1989) find significant negative effects on depression of control and support and a significant positive interaction between control and support. This means that the effect of personal control on depression is not as great at high levels of support as at low levels; and the effect of support on depression is not as great at high levels of perceived control as at low levels. Thus, the functional substitution perspective receives the most empirical support.

Personal and Universal Control

Personal and universal control significantly interact in their effects on depression. Belief in universal control, that is, the belief that other Americans control their own lives, is related to a belief in the dominant American ideology of a meritocratic system in which there is ample opportunity for people to succeed if they work hard, on one end of the continuum, compared with a belief that the system is unfair and biased, on the other. Mirowsky et al. (1996) find that people with below-average personal control have lower depression, the more strongly they believe that most Americans control their own lives. In other words, people who feel unable to control their own lives are less depressed, not more depressed, if they think *most* Americans control their own lives. This interaction corroborates the view that control in principle is better than no control at all. It contradicts the view suggested by "revised learned helplessness" theory (Abramson, Seligman, & Teasdale, 1978; Peterson & Seligman, 1984) that people feel better about their own powerlessness if they regard it as systemic and universal, excusing themselves from responsibility for a helplessness shared by all. Belief that structural barriers and powerful others hinder achievement for other Americans does not mitigate the depressive effect of personal powerlessness. On the contrary, it exacerbates this effect: Americans who feel powerless find no comfort in the apparent powerlessness of others. Blaming fate or the system does not make people feel better, nor does blaming the successful. These results suggest that it is especially distressing to believe that most people's problems are caused by others who are selfish, greedy, or mean, and that the people who have good things do not deserve them.

FUTURE RESEARCH

Social Position and Personal Control: Contextual and Life-Course Perspectives

In the most general form, future research should (1) establish the associations between social conditions and personal control, (2) establish explanations for these associations, and (3) establish the conditions under which the associations occur. The second two objectives build on the first, so we start with a call for research that establishes associations between personal control and social conditions beyond individual SES and work. Research on family, marriage, and unpaid work (including volunteer work and community activism) is largely undeveloped. Furthermore, known social patterns of personal control refer to individual characteristics such as SES or gender. We call for research that examines the effects of the context in which a person lives on perceptions of control. Research on contextual determinants could include large geographic areas, such as countries, and smaller locales, such as cities and neighborhoods. Are there cross-national differences in perceived control, even adjusting for individual attributes, such as education and income? Are these effects due to economic development, culture, or both? Are there neighborhood effects? For instance, does neighborhood poverty, crime, or stability shape individual perceptions of control, even adjusting for the individual's own poverty, victimization, mobility, and so on? Answers to these questions require multilevel data.

Next, we call for research that establishes patterns of personal control across the life course. In order to establish these patterns, studies should include respondents over a large range of ages (ideally, from adolescence through old age). Although it is most ideal to follow people over time, a preference for panel data seems to have blinded researchers to the fact that establishment of the basic patterns first requires cross-sectional data on the whole age range (Baltes, 1987; Featherman, 1983). Without these data, we cannot know, for instance, whether teenage girls have a lower sense of control than young adult women, whether young women have a higher sense of control than elderly women, and so on. Failure to establish basic patterns means one cannot ask the next question: What explains the pattern?

Despite the potential of longitudinal data to help establish time order, cross-sectional data used in a thoughtful manner can further understanding of causal relationships. For instance, if part of the explanation for the negative association between age and perceived control is low educational attainment among older persons, we know this is a cohort, not an aging, effect. Age correlates negatively with education. Why? Educational attainment *cannot* decrease as a person ages; so it must be the case that older cohorts have lower average levels of education than do younger cohorts. Thus, if education explains some of the cross-sectional association between age and personal control, we know that part of the explanation must refer to cohort, not aging, differences. We do not need longitudinal data to know this; just logic and reference to known social facts outside the data.

Panel studies *are* useful for tracing the trajectories of the ways in which people arrived at their current status (Elder, 1994). Early work, school, or family experiences may shape the sense of control, which in turn affects future work or interpersonal resources to produce diverging trajectories with age. Theoretically, initial advantages in work that is nonroutine and autonomous increase perceived control, which increases subsequent effort, motivation, and success at work, leading to promotion to a job with even more objective control over one's own work, which boosts perceived control in a self-amplifying processes. Longitudinal research is potentially a powerful tool to show the processes by which advantage (or disadvantage) accumulate as people age to produce large differences in the sense of control among older people (Crystal & Shea, 1990; O'Rand, 1994).

Longitudinal studies are powerful tools for some purposes, but such data can also mask other relationships. Ascribed statuses, such as age, gender, and race, are fixed at birth. If we find a cross-sectional association between gender and sense of control, we know that perceptions cannot precede gender; thus, gender affects the sense of control.

Failure to recognize the fact that ascribed statuses (or other statuses fixed at young ages) precede all social psychological constructs ipso facto can lead to fallacious conclusions. For instance, let us say we find a cross-sectional association between gender and perceived control that shows women have significantly lower levels of control than men, but that in a longitudinal study, we find no association between gender and perceived control at Time 2, adjusting for perceived control at Time 1. This does not mean that the cross-sectional results were incorrect. It simply means that the gap between men and women did not increase over the follow-up period; as men and women aged (3 years, or 5 years, or whatever the follow-up was), women's sense of control did not decrease more than men's did. It does not mean that initially women did not have a lower level of personal control than men. If women's disadvantage compared to men is set in young adulthood and does not change much with age, there will be no association between gender and perceived control at Time 2, adjusting for perceived control at Time 1. Part of the reason researchers find significant longitudinal effects is because, in so many cases, social advantages and disadvantages do in fact cumulate with age, as, in reality, they probably do for men and women. A direct effect of gender on perceived control in an over-time study is the equivalent to an interaction between gender and age in a cross-sectional study (Ross & Wu, 1996).

Personal Control and Psychological Distress: Beyond Depression and Amplifying Effects

The negative association between personal control and depression is well established. Future research should examine the factors that mediate (or explain) and moderate (or condition) the association, extend the association beyond depression, and examine whether the relationship is reciprocal.

We call for research that examines types of psychological distress other than depression, problems such as anger, anxiety, alcohol problems, physiological malaise, and so on (Aneshensel, 1992; Aneshensel, Rutter, & Lachenbruch, 1991). Distress is an unpleasant subjective state, including, but not limited to, depression. Wheaton (1985) found that mastery decreases symptoms of depression, anxiety and schizophrenia. In contrast, some research indicates that belief in external control does not increase anxiety, except by way of anxiety's correlation with depression (Mirowsky & Ross, 1984). Few other studies examine the association between personal control and various types of distress.

There is good evidence that personal control decreases depression, but it is unclear whether there is feedback. Mirowsky and Ross (1990b) found that belief in responsibility for bad outcomes (or failures) correlates *negatively* with depression. Since people who are depressed often take responsibility for their failures (a *positive* correlation of depression with responsibility for failures) (Beck, 1972), it is hard to see how a reverse causal process could create the negative correlation between belief in personal control over bad outcomes and depression. Furthermore, follow-up studies show that one's initial sense of control and increases in one's sense of control are associated with decreased depression over time (Kohn & Schooler, 1982; Pearlin et al., 1981). Depression may somewhat reduce the sense of control, but the lag time required for the effect appears to be much longer, and the reciprocal effect only boosts the association between personal control and depression by a very small amount (Golin, Sweeney, & Schaeffer, 1981; Kohn & Schooler, 1982). Turner and Noh (1983) found a smaller but significant effect of earlier depression on change in personal control (beta = -.11) in addition to the larger effect of personal control on depression (beta = -.26). However, much more research is needed that systematically examines cross-lagged panel models of personal control and distress. Perceptions of control decrease distress, and low levels of distress may in turn may boost personal control in a self-amplifying process that creates larger and larger social inequalities in control and distress as people age.

REFERENCES

Abramson, L. Y., Seligman, M. E. P., & Teasdale, J. D. (1978). Learned helplessness in humans: Critique and reformulation. *Journal of Abnormal Psychology, 87,* 49–74

Al-Zahrani, S. S. A., & Kaplowitz, S. A. (1993). Attributional biases in individualistic and collectivistic cultures: A comparison of Americans with Saudis. *Social Psychology Quarterly, 56,* 223–233.

Aneshensel, C. S. (1992). Social stress: Theory and research. *Annual Review of Sociology, 18,* 15–38.

Aneshensel, C. S., Rutter, C. M., & Lachenbruch, P. A. (1991). Social structure, stress, and mental health: Competing conceptual and analytic models *American Sociological Review, 56,* 166–178.

Baltes, P. B. (1987). Theoretical propositions of life-span developmental psychology: On the dynamics between growth and decline. *Developmental Psychology, 23,* 611–626.

Bandura, A. (1986). *Social foundations of thought and action.* Englewood Cliffs, NJ: Prentice Hall.

Beck, A. T. (1972). *Depression: Causes and treatment.* Philadelphia: University of Pennsylvania Press.

Benassi, Victor A., Sweeney, P. D., & Dufour, C. L. (1988). Is there a relationship between locus of control orientation and depression? *Journal of Abnormal Psychology, 97,* 357–366.

Bergmann, B. (1986). *The economic emergence of women.* New York: Basic Books.

Bird, C. E., & Ross, C. E. (1993). Houseworkers and paid workers: Qualities of the work and effects on personal control. *Journal of Marriage and the Family, 55,* 913–925.

Braverman, H. (1974). *Labor and monopoly capital: The degradation of work in the twentieth century.* New York: Monthly Review Press.

Brewin, C. R., & Shapiro, D. A. (1984). Beyond locus of control: Attribution of responsibility for positive and negative outcomes. *British Journal of Psychology, 75,* 43–49.

Bulman, R. J., & Wortman, C. B. (1977). Attributions of blame and coping in the real world: Severe accident victims react to their lot. *Journal of Personality and Social Psychology, 35,* 351–363.

Brown, B. B. (1978). Social and psychological correlates of help-seeking behavior among urban adults. *Journal of Community Psychology, 6,* 425–439.

Caster, D. U., & Parsons, O. A. (1977). Locus of control in alcoholics and treatment outcome. *Journal of Studies on Alcohol, 38,* 2087–2095.

Coleman, L. M., Antonucci, T. C., Adelmann, P. K., & Crohan, S. E. (1987). Social roles in the lives of middle-aged and older black women. *Journal of Marriage and the Family, 49,* 761–771.

Crystal, S., & Shea, D. (1990). Cumulative advantage, cumulative disadvantage, and inequality among elderly people. *Gerontologist, 10,* 437–443.

Downey, G., & Moen, P. (1987). Personal efficacy, income and family transitions: A longitudinal study of women heading households. *Journal of Health and Social Behavior, 28,* 320–333.

Elder, G. H. (1994). Time, human agency, and social change: Perspectives on the life course. *Social Psychology Quarterly, 57,* 4-15.

Elder, G. H., & Liker, J. K. (1982). Hard times in women's lives: Historical influences Across forty years. *American Journal of Sociology, 88,* 241–266.

Erikson, K. (1986). On work and alienation. *American Sociological Review, 51,* 1–8.

Featherman, D. L. (1983). The life-span perspective in social science research. In P. B. Baltes & O.G. Brim, Jr. (Eds.), *Life-span development and behavior* (pp. 1–57). New York: Academic Press.

Ferree, M. M. (1976). Working class jobs: Housework and paid work as sources of satisfaction. *Social Problems, 23,* 431–441.

Gecas, V. (1989). The social psychology of self-efficacy. *Annual Review of Sociology, 15,* 291–316.

Golin, S., Sweeney, P. D., & Shaeffer, D. E. (1981). The causality of causal attributions in depression: A cross-lagged panel correlational analysis. *Journal of Abnormal Psychology, 90,* 14–22.

Gove, W. R., & Geerken, M. R. (1977). The effect of children and employment on the mental health of married men and women. *Social Forces, 56,* 66–76.

Gove, W. R., & Tudor, J. (1973). Adult sex roles and mental illness. *American Journal of Sociology, 78*, 812–835.

Gurin, P., Gurin, G., Lao, R. C., & Beattie, M. (1969). Internal–external control in the motivational dynamics of Negro youth. *Journal of Social Issues, 25*, 29–53.

Gurin, P., Gurin, G., & Morrison, B. M. (1978). Personal and ideological aspects of internal and external control. *Social Psychology, 41*, 275–296.

Hiroto, D. S. (1974). Locus of control and learned helplessness. *Journal of Experimental Psychology, 102*, 187-193.

Hughes, M., & Demo, D. H. (1989). Self-perceptions of black Americans: Self-esteem and personal efficacy. *American Journal of Sociology, 95*, 132–159.

Hui, H. C., & Triandis, H. C. (1986). Individualism–collectivism: A study of cross-cultural researchers. *Journal of Cross-Cultural Psychology, 17*, 225–248.

Hulbary, W. (1975). Race, deprivation, and adolescent self-image. *Social Science Quarterly, 56*, 105–114.

Hunt, J. G., & Hunt, L. L. (1977). Race inequality and self-image: Identity maintenance and identity diffusion. *Sociology and Social Research, 61*, 539–559.

Hyman, H. B. (1966). The value systems of different classes: A social psychological contribution to the analysis of stratification. In R. Bendix & S. M. Lipset (Eds.), *Class, status and power: Social stratification in comparative perspective* (2nd ed., pp. 488–499). New York: Free Press.

Inkeles, A., & Smith, D. (1974). *Becoming modern: Individual change in six developing countries.* Cambridge, MA: Harvard University Press.

Kohn, M. L. (1972). Class, family and schizophrenia. *Social Forces, 50*, 295–302.

Kohn, M. L. (1976). Occupational structure and alienation. *American Journal of Sociology, 82*, 111–130.

Kohn, M. L., Naoi, A., Schoenbach, C., Schooler, C., & Slomczynski, K. M. (1990). Position in the class structure and psychological functioning in the United States, Japan, and Poland. *American Journal of Sociology, 95,* 964–1008.

Kohn, M. L., & Schooler, C. (1982). Job conditions and personality: A longitudinal assessment of their reciprocal effects. *American Journal of Sociology, 87,* 1257–1286.

Krause, N., & Stryker, S. (1984). Stress and well-being: The buffering role of locus of control beliefs. *Social Science and Medicine, 18*, 783–790.

Lachman, M. E. (1986). Personal control in later life: Stability, change, and cognitive correlates. In M. M. Baltes & P. B. Baltes (Eds.), *The psychology of control and aging* (pp 207–236) . Hillsdale, NJ: Erlbaum.

Levenson, H. (1973). Multidimensional locus of control in psychiatric patients. *Journal of Consulting and Clinical Psychology, 41*, 397–404.

McLaughlin, S. D., & Micklin, M. (1983). The timing of the first birth and changes in personal efficacy. *Journal of Marriage and the Family, 45*, 47–55.

Mirowsky, J. (1995). Age and the sense of control. *Social Psychology Quarterly, 58*, 31–43.

Mirowsky, J., & Ross, C. E. (1983). Paranoia and the structure of powerlessness. *American Sociological Review, 48*, 228–239

Mirowsky, J., & Ross, C. E. (1984). Mexican culture and its emotional contradictions. *Journal of Health and Social Behavior, 25*, 2–13.

Mirowsky, J., & Ross, C. E. (1986). Social patterns of distress. *Annual Review of Sociology, 12*, 23–45.

Mirowsky, J., & Ross, C. E. (1989). *Social causes of psychological distress.* New York: Aldine de Gruyter.

Mirowsky, J., & Ross, C. E. (1990a). The consolation prize theory of alienation. *American Journal of Sociology, 95*, 1505–1535.

Mirowsky, J., & Ross, C. E. (1990b). Control or defense? Depression and the sense of control over good and bad outcomes. *Journal of Health and Social Behavior, 31*, 71–86.

Mirowsky, J., & Ross, C. E. (1991). Eliminating defense and agreement bias from measures of the sense of control: A 2 × 2 index. *Social Psychology Quarterly, 54*, 127–145.

Mirowsky, J., & Ross, C. E. (1996). Fundamental analysis in research on well-being: Distress and the sense of control. *Gerontologist, 36*, 584–594.

Mirowsky, J., Ross, C. E., & Van Willigen, M. (1996). Instrumentalism in the land of opportunity: Socioeconomic causes and emotional consequences. *Social Psychology Quarterly, 59,* 322–337.

O'Rand, A. M. (1994, August). *The precious and the precocious: Understanding cumulative dis/advantage over the life course.* Paper presented at the 89th American Sociological Association Annual Meeting, Los Angeles, CA.

Pearlin, L. I., Menaghan, E. G., Lieberman, M. A., & Mullan, J. T. (1981). The stress process. *Journal of Health and Social Behavior, 22*, 337–356.

Pearlin, L. I., & Schooler, C. (1978). The structure of coping. *Journal of Health and Social Behavior, 19*, 2–21.

Peterson, C., & Seligman, M. E. P. (1984). Causal explanations as a risk factor for depression: Theory and evidence. *Journal of Personality and Social Psychology, 91*, 347–374.

Porter, J. R., & Washington, R. E. (1979). Minority identity and self-esteem. *Annual Review of Sociology, 19*, 139–161.

Rodin, J. (1986). Health, control, and aging. In M. M. Baltes & P. B. Baltes (Eds.), *The psychology of control and aging* (pp. 139–165). Hillsdale, NJ: Erlbaum.

Rosenbaum, M., & Hadari, D. (1985). Personal efficacy, external locus of control, and perceived contingency of parental reinforcement among depressed, paranoid, and normal subjects. *Journal of Personality and Social Psychology, 49*, 539–547.

Rosenberg, M. (1979). *Conceiving the self.* New York: Basic Books.

Rosenfield, S. (1989). The effects of women's employment: Personal control and sex differences in mental health. *Journal of Health and Social Behavior, 30*, 77–91.

Ross, C. E. (1990). Emotional consequences of various attributions of success. *Sociological Focus, 23*, 101–113.

Ross, C. E. (1991). Marriage and the sense of control. *Journal of Marriage and the Family, 53*, 831–838.

Ross, C. E., & Bird, C. E. (1994). Sex stratification and health lifestyle: Consequences for men's and women's perceived health. *Journal of Health and Social Behavior, 35*, 161–178.

Ross, C. E., & Mirowsky, J. (1989). Explaining the social patterns of depression: Control and problem-solving—or support and talking. *Journal of Health and Social Behavior, 30*, 206–219.

Ross, C. E., & Mirowsky, J. (1992). Households, employment, and the sense of control. *Social Psychology Quarterly, 55*, 217–235.

Ross, C. E., Mirowsky, J., & Cockerham, W. C. (1983). Social class, Mexican culture, and fatalism: Their effects on psychological distress. *American Journal of Community Psychology, 11*, 383–399.

Ross, C. E., & Wu, C.-L. (1995). The links between education and health. *American Sociological Review, 60*, 719–745.

Ross, C. E., & Wu, C.-L. (1996). Education, age, and the cumulative advantage in health. *Journal of Health and Social Behavior, 37*, 104–120.

Rotter, J. B. (1966). Generalized expectancies for internal vs. external control of reinforcements. *Psychological Monographs, 80*, 1–28.

Sastry, J., & Ross, C. E. (1998). Asian ethnicity and the sense of personal control. *Social Psychology Quarterly, 61*, 101–120..

Schwalbe, M. L., & Staples, C. L. (1991). Gender differences in sources of self-esteem. *Social Psychology Quarterly, 54*, 158–168.

Seeman, M. (1959). On the meaning of alienation. *American Sociological Review, 24*, 783–791.

Seeman, M. (1983). Alienation motifs in contemporary theorizing: The hidden continuity of classic themes. *Social Psychology Quarterly, 46*, 171–184.

Seeman, M., Seeman, A. Z., & Budros, A. (1988). Powerlessness, work, and community: A longitudinal study of alienation and alcohol use. *Journal of Health and Social Behavior, 29*, 185–198.

Seligman, M. E. P. (1975). *Helplessness.* San Francisco: Freeman.

Taylor, M. C., & Walsh, E. J. (1979). Explanations of black self-esteem: Some empirical tests. *Social Psychology Quarterly, 42*, 242–253.

Thoits, P. A. (1987). Gender and martial status differences in control and distress. *Journal of Health and Social Behavior, 28*, 7–22.

Turner, R. J., & Noh, S. (1983). Class and psychological vulnerability among women: The significance of social support and personal control. *Journal of Health and Social Behavior, 24*, 2–15.

Wade, T. J., Thompson, V. D., Tashakori, A., & Valente, E. (1989). A longitudinal analysis of sex and race differences in predictors of adolescent self-esteem. *Personality and Individual Differences, 10*, 717–729.

Wethington, E., & Kessler, R. C. (1986). Perceived support, received support, and adjustment to stressful life events. *Journal of Health and Social Behavior, 27*, 78–89.

Wheaton, B. (1980). The sociogenesis of psychological disorder: An attributional theory. *Journal of Health and Social Behavior, 21*, 100–124.

Wheaton, B. (1983). Stress, personal coping resources, and psychiatric symptoms: An investigation of interactive models. *Journal of Health and Social Behavior, 24*, 208–229.

Wheaton, B. (1985). Personal resources and mental health: Can there be too much of a good thing? In J. R. Greenley (Ed.), *Research in community and mental health* (pp. 139–184). Greenwich, CT: JAI Press.

Wolinsky, F. D., & Stump, T. E. (1996). Age and the sense of control among older adults. *Journal of Gerontology: Social Sciences, 51B*, S217–S220.

CHAPTER 19

The Stress Process Revisited

Reflections on Concepts and Their Interrelationships

LEONARD I. PEARLIN

INTRODUCTION

Social research into stress and its consequences has burgeoned over the past 25 years or so. Indeed, the accumulated body of knowledge about social stress has contributed substantially to our understanding of the forces affecting the well-being of people. The expansion of knowledge has not occurred because sociologists are of one mind about stress and its consequences; far from it. Research into stress has moved in many directions, has examined multiple levels of social and personal life, and has focused on an array of issues. The notion of "the stress process," a label first used in 1981 (Pearlin, Lieberman, Menaghan, & Mullan, 1981), represents an attempt to give some conceptual organization to the diverse lines of research that were—and still are—underway. This is not a task that is easily or quickly brought to completion. Instead, it is a continuous challenge requiring an unending appraisal of what we know and of the future directions that merit attention. This chapter is part of that ongoing critical appraisal.

It should not be inferred from the term "*the* stress process" that stress invariably follows a single pathway. Quite the opposite is true. The circumstances that give rise to a particular set of stressors and the conditions that regulate the impact of the stressors on people's well-being are highly complex and variable. The stress process conceptual model,

LEONARD I. PEARLIN • Department of Sociology, University of Maryland at College Park, College Park, Maryland 20742.

Handbook of the Sociology of Mental Health, edited by Carol S. Aneshensel and Jo C. Phelan. Kluwer Academic/Plenum Publishers, New York, 1999.

therefore, is not a set of rules that can rigidly be followed by all inquiries into social stress. Instead, it should be regarded as a general orienting framework that can guide the thinking of researchers about potentially stressful circumstances, sensitize them to the kinds of data that are needed to study these circumstances, and suggest to them fruitful lines of analyses and interpretation of their effects. It is intended to be of special use to sociologists who seek to incorporate and emphasize features of social and economic life into accounts of the health and well-being of people.

Certain key assumptions underlie the notion of the stress process. One, discussed in greater detail below, is that the diverse factors that converge on people's well-being are interrelated. Among these converging factors are the social statuses of individuals, the contexts that envelope their daily lives, their exposure to stressors, the resources upon which they are able to call in responding to the stressors, and the way stress is manifested in their psychological and bodily functioning. An implication of the web of interconnections among these multiple factors is that a change in one can result in changes in the others, thus setting in motion chains of effect. The links comprising such chains are not necessarily simultaneously discernible. More typically, alterations in life circumstances that occur at one point in time may have effects that emerge at a later point in time. Both the interconnectedness among relevant factors and the chains of effect that surface lead us to refer to stress as entailing a *process*. Stress and its consequences are not merely discrete happenings involving a stimulus immediately followed by a response. Instead, they may entail the many factors that over time can connect the inner lives of individuals to the larger social systems of which they are a part.

A second pivotal assumption of stress process perspectives is that social stress is not about unusual people doing unusual things and having unusual experiences. On the contrary, the study of social stress falls within mainstream sociology because it typically concerns thoroughly socialized people engaged in the ordinary pursuits of life and driven by widely shared values and commitments. This is a critically important matter, for it establishes a strong intellectual tie between current research into social stress and classical social theory. Thus, Durkheim (1951) thought of suicide not as the rash act of deviants but as a consequence of people's attachments to others; and Merton (1968) envisioned anomie not as result of people being caught up in their own personally created unrealistic fantasies but from the disparities between their socialized aspirations and their access to opportunity structures. Although many people certainly come under stress as a result of rare and exotic circumstances, research into social stress is more characterized by its attention to difficult and threatening circumstances confronted by collectivities possessing similar social and economic attributes (Pearlin, 1989). This orientation departs sharply from that of psychiatry, which tends to view stress-induced psychopathology as an aberrant response to unusual circumstances. As Aneshensel (1992) notes, the view of mental disorder as abnormal invites the assumption that its causes are also abnormal. The sociological search for the roots of stress, on the other hand, turns its attention to normative features of social life.

A third and final prefatory observation concerns a hallmark of social research into stress that distinguishes it from that of other disciplines also engaged in stress research. There is, of course, considerable overlap between the interests and perspectives of sociologists and those representing other disciplines. Thus, sociologists as well as psychologists and psychiatrists are concerned with the adaptive resources of people under stress, and, as discussed in a later section, sociologists and psychiatrists often share an interest in the evaluation of mental health outcomes of stress. Currently, too, there are efforts to cross disciplinary boundaries in looking for the connections between social and behavioral conditions and what can be observed in bodily systems, such as the immune system (Kiecolt-Glazer & Glazer, 1994). These kinds of overlap and joint efforts notwithstanding, sociology stands alone in an important respect: It is the only discipline having a major interest in the naturalistic origins of stress. Others, by contrast, are markedly more occupied with what happens to individuals following the onset of stress—how well they deal with the stress or the impact of the stressor on mental and physical functioning. Indeed, the questions that drive the work of many researchers do not necessarily require human subjects; they are answered more directly and easily by subjecting laboratory animals to stressful conditions (e.g., Turkkan, Brady, & Harris, 1982). Clearly, the intellectual appetites of sociologists studying social stress are satisfied only by the real thing.

Of course, in searching for the origins of stress, researchers often have to settle for what is more proximal than distal. Suppose, for example, that one were studying job insecurity as a stressor. One might fruitfully look at recent downsizing and the closing of manufacturing plants as a source of insecurity, as some investigators have done (Hamilton, Broman, Hoffman, & Renner, 1990). However, such conditions are hardly at the root origins of job insecurity; it could reasonably be argued that such origins reside more in technological displacement, the development of global capitalism, and the pull of industries toward cheap labor. These kinds of temporally distal developments have greater claim as the primordial origins of job insecurity both because they represent fundamental changes in economic organization and because they have been underway for many decades, long prior to current conditions associated with job insecurity. Unfortunately, social stress researchers, like other researchers, have neither the prescience nor the resources to identify and track important social change to much later stress. When we speak of the origins of stress, therefore, we usually do not refer to historical circumstance, although retrospectively there might be clear paths leading from such circumstances to the stressors under present observation.

Let us turn now to a closer look at the stress process model, specifying the concepts that fall within it and their interrelationships. Many of the major features of the model will be familiar to stress researchers (Pearlin, 1989). However, there has been considerable progress in recent years, both in the understanding of the concepts that serve as the foundations of the model and of the complex connections between these concepts and their measures. Research progress, however, needs to be judged not only by the problems that have been solved but also by those that have been newly raised as advancement takes place. The following discussions are tilted more toward the identification of the problems that remain and their implications for future directions than toward the identification of recent achievements.

CONCEPTS AND THEIR INTERRELATIONSHIPS

Status and Inequality

Much of the remainder of this chapter is organized around the schematic portrayal of the stress process shown in Figure 19.1 below. As shown by the figure, the social and economic statuses of people are superimposed on the stress process. It is these characteristics that make the model and the orientation to stress research it embodies quintessentially sociological. These characteristics signal the linkages between the status placement of people in the larger systems of society and their health and well-being. Statuses, of course, are hierarchically organized and inherently entail inequalities in the possession of power, privi-

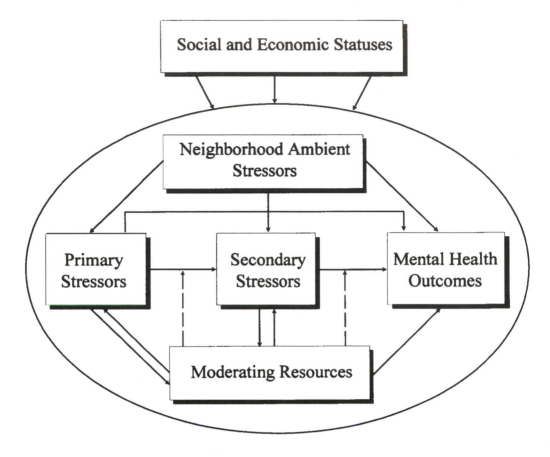

FIGURE 19.1. The stress process model.

lege, and prestige. People's standing in the stratified orders of social and economic class, gender, race, and ethnicity have the potential to pervade the structure of their daily existence and the experiences that flow from it. These systems of inequality are what Link and Phelan (1995) have described as the fundamental causes of inequalities in disease.

Because these systems of inequality are ubiquitous, one cannot easily escape their reach—as one might take a vacation from an onerous job. Of course, statuses may vary in their salience as people move from one situation to another. The gender of a person who is the sole male on his job may be more salient than with another whose work group has a different gender mix. But regardless of such situational variation, one does not stop being black or white, male or female, or, in all probability, rich or poor. To the contrary, these kinds of statuses become important elements of the persona and self-identification of individuals.

Understandably, then, the statuses of people are potentially connected to virtually every component of the stress process. Their preeminent place in the stress process is highlighted in Figure 19.1 by showing their encircling relationships to the other components. Before tracing out these relationships, it needs to be emphasized that the importance of people's statuses in systems of inequality cannot be fully appreciated by looking only at their influences on the other components. As will be described, these statuses have the potential to impact on well-being indirectly through their influence in shaping the contexts of people's lives, the stressors to which they are exposed, and the moderating resources they possess. Additionally, however, the social values attached to these statuses and the conditions surrounding them contribute *directly* to well-being and stressful outcomes.

Several examples of these direct effects can be offered. One concerns the social evaluations of people's worth implicitly built into their statuses. Briefly, to the extent that incumbency in lower status positions is socially devalued, there is the distinct possibility that the individuals who are incumbents of these statuses come to devalue themselves (Rosenberg & Pearlin, 1978). Another and obvious example involves those with limited or no financial resources, a condition that can condemn people to a grinding life of uncertainty and fear. Similarly, people of color may repeatedly experience subtle and not-so-subtle acts and gestures of discrimination (Jackson et al., 1996). The chances that such direct effects will surface in people's lives are enhanced by the "packaging" of statuses; that is, if a person occupies one low status, it is likely that other statuses will also be low. Being a member of an ethnic or racial minority, for example, is often associated with a low occupational status, having limited formal education, and possessing scarce economic resources. Indeed, a lack of association among these kinds of statuses, referred to as "status inconsistency," has itself been postulated as a problematic situation (e.g., Dressler, 1988). The sheer inconsistency represented by an extended education coupled with a low occupational status, for example, may be experienced with unrelenting pain and chagrin.

The Neighborhood Context

As emphasized earlier, the inequalities intrinsic to stratified status systems are not aspects of social organization that are encountered only occasionally. Instead, the consequences of these systems of inequality are likely to reach into every critical arena of people's daily existence. One reason why these systems are ubiquitous in their consequences is that they substantially shape the contexts of social action and experience. Outstanding among such contexts is the neighborhood of residence (Aneshensel & Sucoff, 1996). A major mechanism through which status systems bear on neighborhood contexts is the tendency toward status homology; that is, neighborhoods are typically composed of individuals whose key statuses are similar. Thus, the people in our neighborhoods, as well as those in our social networks, usually bear statuses more like ours than different. We can also speculate that neighborhoods tend to be experientially homologous: People who share similar statuses will also experience similar hardships and, furthermore, they will respond to these hardships in similar ways, with similar resources. Whether or not this kind of sharing intensifies or eases the stress process may be debatable. What is less debatable is that the neighborhood can stand as a context in which people come to witness stressful social disorganization as a normative reality of life.

The neighborhood, however, is more than a place where personal problems may be publicly shared; it is also a place that can give rise to its own distinctive stressors. Some of these can be described as ambient stressors (Aneshensel & Sucoff, 1996). They are ambient in the sense that, like social statuses, they surround the daily life and activities of people residing in the neighborhoods. A variety of ambient problems and threats encountered in everyday neighborhood life have been identified (Pearlin & Skaff, 1995). Uncertainty about personal security is one of them, and the physical state of the neighborhood surroundings is too often another, especially when people see themselves inescapably bound to a course of neighborhood deterioration. Where there is a high level of residential turnover, moreover, people can experience the breakup of established networks and come to see themselves as living uneasily among strangers.

Poor transportation, crowded and dilapidated housing, inadequate shopping facilities, lack of easy access to needed programs and services, and the absence of organized, safe entertainment and other leisure activities is also part of this picture. Some of these kinds of ambient problems have been labeled as "daily hassles" (Kanner, Coyne, Schaefer, & Lazarus, 1981), a term that does not succeed in conveying either the seriousness or persistence of a genre of stressors most often felt by those on the lower rungs of systems of inequality. We also know from our interviews that ambient problems centered in the neighborhood context are especially likely to beset elders, since they less frequently and regularly leave their neighborhoods (Pearlin & Skaff, 1995). For the same reason, it can be assumed that neighborhoods are important contexts for children.

Stressors

In addition to enfolding stressful conditions within themselves, the status characteristics and neighborhood contexts of people may also heighten the risk of exposure to other stressors. As portrayed in Figure 19.1, the risks of exposure to many stressors varies with the social and economic characteristics of people and the social contexts of their lives. To take a pair of simple examples, women more than men are likely to be the objects of sexual violence, and unskilled workers are more likely than the skilled to experience severe economic strains. Even where there are no clear connections between status placement and contextual factors and exposure to stressors, the ways in which people are able to deal with the stressors once they occur may be closely regulated by these background characteristics. Good examples of this can be found in natural disasters that are blind to the social and economic attributes of its victims. Yet, the ways in which the victims are able to manage their recovery may be highly sensitive to their social and economic characteristics and to features of their community context (see Quarantelli, 1978).

Stressors appear in two general forms: life events and the more chronic or repeated strains, the latter often associated with the enactment of social roles and the interpersonal relationships they entail. In a strict sense, an event is an event by virtue of having an identifiable point in time at which it occurred; this is in contrast to chronic stressors, which are likely to emerge more insidiously and be more persistent. The differences between events and strains need to be underscored, for there is some confusion surrounding the use of these constructs, most apparent in instances where events are viewed as coextensive with the entire universe of stressors. Moreover, many critical events are episodes that bubble up along the trajectory of chronic stressors, leaving us unsure as to whether it is the event or the continuing problems from which the event stemmed that accounts for the stressful impact. For example, losing a home through foreclosure, regarded as an event on the scale constructed by Holmes and Rahe (1967), is probably an episode that follows a lengthy period of financial strain. These are more than a definitional problem; this kind of slippage in the use of the concepts creates an ambiguity concerning the nature of stressors, their social origins, and the sorts of conditions that result in damage to mental health.

There are thoughtful critical reviews of the conceptual and methodological problems underlying much of the research into life events and their consequences (e.g., see McLean

& Link, 1994; Thoits, 1983). What is clear from these reviews, even after making allowances for the problems they identify, is that certain kinds of life events can exert a powerfully disruptive effect on people's lives and have deleterious effects on their well-being. Loss events, such as the loss of a loved one, are particularly onerous (Shrout et al., 1989). Such events take on greater force as stressors when, in addition to being unwanted, they are also unscheduled; that is, when their occurrence is not part of the immediately foreseeable life course (Pearlin, 1980). Thus, the death of an aged spouse may be difficult, but the death of a child is likely to be more so.

Traumatic events, some of which may involve loss, are distinguished from other events by their suddenness, the magnitude of their horribleness. Their harmful effects on mental health, moreover, tend to be persistent. Indeed, it was observed over 35 years ago (Langner & Michael, 1963) that the consequences of trauma that befall people in their childhood can often dog them through their adult life course. What makes the impact of trauma so long-lasting is not altogether clear. It might appear that by its very nature, trauma provokes reactions that become fixed traits of personality, capable of driving action, ideation, and emotion for the rest of one's life. A second explanation calls attention to conditions outside of personality that might sustain the effects of a traumatic experience. Concretely, people who are exposed to trauma, early or otherwise, may also be at greater risk of exposure to other stressors as they traverse the life course. Some evidence for this possibility is found in the work of Wheaton (1994), who reports strong correlations between exposure to traumatic events in childhood and to events and chronic stressors in adulthood. These findings suggest that the effects of earlier trauma may be carried forward in time by additional stressors that surface along the life course. Obviously, this is an area awaiting more systematic inquiry.

Some researchers have considered "nonevents," the things that do not happen, as stressors (Gersten, Langner, Eisenberg, & Orzek, 1974). Presumably, the stressfulness of a nonevent results from the failure of an expected or desired occurrence to materialize. However, as Wheaton (1994) points out, failures of this sort do not necessarily constitute nonevents. First, there are instances having the appearance of a nonevent that may as easily be construed as an event. For example, the bride-to-be left stranded at the alter may be more accurately described as having experienced an event—being jilted or rejected—than as the victim of a nonevent. Second, many nonevents can be conceived as continuously gnawing disparities between one's goals and hopes, and their achievement. This more richly describes the worker who did not get the promised pay raise, the son who did not get into an Ivy League school, and countless other instances of nonevents. Moreover, looked at this way, the sociological relevance of many "nonevents" becomes visible; that is, they can more easily be recognized as the products of structured disjunctures between socially valued goals and differential access to opportunities for their achievement.

Methodological and conceptual problems in the study of stressors are not confined to life events; there is an ample supply of such problems that can also be found in the study of chronic stressors (Link, Mesagno, Lubner, & Dohrenwend, 1990). One problem concerns the validity of their measurements, which are often based on reports of subjective states. The reliance on such reports raises the reasonable question as to whether the assessment of the stressors is too heavily dependent on the cognitive processes of individuals as they reflect upon their own lives. To the extent that this is true, it makes the interpretation of research findings difficult. For example, the presence of psychological depression might influence the appraisal of the chronic stressor rather than the stressor leading to depression. Is an individual depressed because of a reportedly difficult marriage, or does the individuals describe his or her marriage as difficult because the person is depressed?

Obviously, considerably more creative effort is needed to construct measures of chronic stressors that are as objective as we can make them. To a large extent, however, confidence in the validity of such measures must be grounded in the results of data analysis. Confidence is bolstered, by way of example, by observing that people reporting both a high level of marital strain and access to supportive social relationships are less depressed than those with the same level of reported strain but having limited social support. Confidence in the validity of the measures is also supported where the measures demonstrate some predictive utility, as when a high level of marital strain at one point in time is associated with later divorce. Data analyses, then, should test for theoretically expected variations that can stand as evidence that the self-reports of chronic stressors are not merely expressions of emotional distress.

Along with establishing their validity, it is typically difficult to ascertain how chronic a chronic stressor really is. Thus, for example, the onset of marital conflict typically eludes pinpointing, as do job problems or economic strains. Because such stressors often arise insidiously, people are simply unable to identify their onset with precision. A proxy for dating onset, one that is not entirely satisfactory, is to date the situation out of which the stressors grow. To illustrate, job overload would be considered to be a chronic stressor if the job itself is continuous. The treatment of job overload as a chronic stressor is thus tied to the assumption that because the situation in which the stressor is located is enduring, the stressor is also enduring. Longitudinal research, of course, can further enable us at least to bracket, if not pinpoint, the onset of chronic stressors within a time frame.

The search for chronic stressors usually takes the researcher into the institutional roles of people: marriage, parenthood, job, and finances. For several reasons, these are fertile grounds for such stressors: The roles and statuses are enduring; they often involve complex activities and relationships; and the roles are important both to the society at large and to their incumbents (Pearlin, 1983). Indeed, it is because of their importance that problems arising within them are not easily sloughed off or trivialized. Various types of role strains, as they are called, have been identified previously (Pearlin, 1983) and are not reviewed in detail here. It can simply be noted that they include being in a role whose demands exceed the capacities of its incumbents, being a captive of the role—an unwilling incumbent, being in conflict with those who comprise what Merton (1957) refers to as the role set, and being unable to reconcile the simultaneous demands of multiple roles. It needs to be underscored that the form and intensity of these kinds of chronic stressors undergo change as individuals traverse the life course. In fact, interpersonal conflict among members of a role set can emerge when there is resistance or uneven adaptation to life-course changes. Adult children whose parents continue to view them as minors in need of unsolicited guidance and advice can attest to such life-course conflicts.

Also among crucial life-course issues is the matter of unexpected or emergent roles. I refer specifically to caregiving roles. Although such roles are increasingly common as life is prolonged, we typically do not plan on being the incumbents of such roles, nor are we trained to meet their requirements. Often, caregiving roles become long-term commitments and deserve the label of "unexpected careers" (Pearlin & Aneshensel, 1994). Caregiving roles usually emerge during the midlife or late-life years, stages of the life course at which people are likely to have an array of established social roles. Emergent caregiving roles, therefore, surface within a context of preexisting multiple roles; the accommodation of the new role demands some restructuring of existing roles. Such restructuring may bring in its wake a constriction in the scope of social and leisure activities, conflicts with others, and the dilemmas of satisfying various demands, as between work and caregiving obligations

(Pearlin, Mullan, Semple, & Skaff, 1990). The activities directly associated with long-term caregiving can themselves become chronic stressors; in addition, they can lead to stressors in other domains of life. This is what we refer to as stress proliferation (Pearlin, Aneshensel, & LeBlanc, 1997), further discussed below.

The distinction between eventful and chronic stressors is important to researchers because it helps to trace the stressors back to their social origins. But it should be recognized that the distinction is a construct of the researchers and does not necessarily parallel the awareness people have of their hardships and problems. People do not ordinarily sort out the various stressors that impinge them, nor do they cognitively separate eventful stressors from enduring strains. For many, the boundaries between different types of stressors become blurred as they face a mix of these stressors in the flow of their daily activities. Indeed, these boundaries can also become blurred in the eyes of the stress researcher. This is because events frequently merge into chronic strains, and strains frequently heighten the risk of stressful events. It is this tendency of events and strains to merge and blend with each other that supports the construct of stress proliferation.

Stress Proliferation and the Creation of Secondary Stressors

Stress proliferation is a critically important but usually overlooked feature of the stress process. Cursory observation reveals that only rarely are people exposed to but one severe stressor. The loss of a loved one is an eventful blow, but it might also leave a painful social isolation in its wake (Pearlin & Lieberman, 1979); we know that involuntary job loss is a powerful stressor, but so are the economic strains that ensue if unemployment is prolonged (Pearlin et al., 1981); and, as a final example, divorce and separation can be highly stressful, but especially for those who are left as single parents caring for dependent-age children (Pearlin & Johnson, 1977). We refer to the initial set of stressors as primary and those that follow as secondary (Pearlin, 1989). These terms do not imply that one is more important than the other or more instrumental in creating harmful outcomes. They are intended to distinguish stressors according to the temporal order in which they can be observed. Behind the distinction of primary and secondary stressors, therefore, is the presumption that stressors do not arise simultaneously in people's lives but may appear sequentially as the stress process unfolds.

The classification of stressors as primary or secondary is essentially a heuristic device for turning attention to the multiple stressors to which people can come to be exposed. It underscores the dynamic character of the stress process, a process in which people may become enmeshed in a changing configuration of stressors. The threats and hardships people face often do not spring up together at one point in time; instead, stressors may surface and recede and, most important, come to stand in combination with other stressors. The identification of primary and secondary stressors is a step toward capturing this dynamic aspect of the stress process.

The distinction between primary and secondary stressors also helps to clarify the causal connections between exposure to difficult life problems and the deleterious outcomes of such exposure. It is common to find that people exposed to a similar stressor do not uniformly exhibit similar negative outcomes. For example, it has been observed that some people whose work combines high levels of job pressure tend to be depressed, especially when they are able to exercise little control over their labor (Karasek, 1979), but others exposed to the same job conditions somehow escape depression. We typically fall back upon people's moderating resources, such as coping, to explain such variation; that is, we assume that differences in depression reflect corresponding differences in the abilities of individuals to cope with the occupational hardship. In relying on such reasoning, however, a greater explanatory burden may be placed on coping and other resources than they are able to bear empirically. Even after making allowances for differences in moderating resources, at least some of the difference in outcomes among those exposed to similar stressors is likely to remain.

Attention to secondary stressors may help to take up some of the explanatory slack. Specifically, workers exposed to the same primary stressors, in this example, high demand and limited job control, may differ with regard to the presence of secondary stressors in their lives. Thus, the pressures some workers experience on the job may come to be associated with marital strife or conflict with their children, each of which then independently contributes to depression. If we fail to observe and assess these consequent stressors, we may also mistakenly assume that variations in the outcomes reflect differences in moderating resources or in vulnerability or resilience. Before interpreting such variation as a reflection of individual differences in adaptive capacities, we must first be sure that people are not embedded in very different configurations of primary and secondary stressors.

Still another utility of the distinction between primary and secondary stressors is that it provides a broader view of the junctures at which moderating resources may exercise their effects. The significance of this matter can be discerned in Figure 19.1 by following the arrows from the resources to the points at which they intersect with the stress process. These resources are referred to as moderating because of their ability to prevent or reduce the impact of stressors on the outcomes. Much of stress research judges the ability of the resources to moderate this impact by looking only at their *direct* influence on the outcome being observed. Moderating effects on outcomes, however, may also be exercised *indirectly* by governing the effects of conditions antecedent to the outcomes. Of particular interest here is the potential of the moderating resources to control the emergence of secondary stressors, thus blocking stress proliferation. These potentially indirect effects of resources on the stress process, therefore, come into clearer perspective with the inclusion of secondary stressors as part of the process. To overlook such indirect effects runs the risk of underestimating the moderating power of resources.

Why is it that serious stressors rarely stand alone? How do secondary stressors come to combine with those that are primary? The major mechanism giving rise to stress proliferation in the form of secondary stressors resides in a basic feature of social and economic life. Specifically, people are the incumbents of multiple roles located both within formal institutions, such as family and occupation, and informal domains, such as friendship groups and voluntary associations. With some exceptions, people's multiple roles are usually separated in time and space. This structural separation helps people shift ground more easily as they move between their multiple roles, each entailing interactions with different people and each having different expectations. To some extent, too, the separation might help to confine the effects of hardships to the domain in which they arise. The structural segregation of multiple roles notwithstanding, each of the several roles involves but a single actor and that person is usually unable to compartmentalize fully the hardships and stressors experienced in any one domain. For example, there is evidence that what goes on in the workplace influences what goes on in the family, and vice versa (Lennon & Rosenfield, 1992; Wheaton, 1990). It is not only a matter of a foul mood created in one place being carried over to another place, although the transfer of affect undoubtedly occurs. The crucial point is that the structure of experience in one domain comes to structure action in another domain. This kind of carryover across the boundaries of roles is illustrated by the research finding that workers who are subjected to close supervision on the job come to insist that their children be obedient (Kohn, 1969; Pearlin, 1971). The expectation of compliant obedience on the job, however problematic and stressful it might be to maintain, might help a worker avoid overt conflict with his supervisor. But the same expectations of obedience might lead to conflict when imposed on family relations; such conflict would then stand as a secondary stressor.

Secondary stressors may also arise out of circumstances in which key multiple roles are not fully integrated in a mutually accommodating way, as where the obligations of one role make the enactment of another role difficult. An example is observed among women in the workplace who find it difficult to satisfy the requirements of their jobs and the demands associated with the care of young children (Lennon & Rosenfield, 1992; Menaghan, 1991). In this instance, secondary stressors surface when the obligations of the parental role make the obligations of the occupational role difficult to meet. The same situation has been observed to be present in the case of caregiving roles, where one may find it difficult to satisfy the obligations of both the caregiving and the occupational roles (Aneshensel, Pearlin, Mullan, Zarit, & Whitlatch, 1995; Pearlin et al., 1997). The priority claims of one role, then, can render the enactment of another role problematic.

The foregoing discussion is intended to highlight the organization of experience around individuals' multiple roles as a major mechanism through which secondary stressors emerge from those that can be considered primary. However, the appearance and intensity of secondary stressors may also be influenced by one's standing in systems of inequality. Thus, the same fundamental conditions contributing to the creation or exacerbation of primary stressors may also contribute to the creation or exacerbation of secondary stressors. Continuing with the example used earlier, being in the economic underclass may be associated both with difficulties in finding or affording adequate child care arrangements and with being in a job that allows no flexibility for improvising such arrangements. In this illustration, an important status influences the chance of exposure to the primary stressor—problems in establishing appropriate child care—and to the consequent secondary stressors—problems on the job. Once established, these consequent problems become added independent, albeit related, stressors in the life of the worker. The general point to be drawn from this illustration is that the status characteristics that contribute to the rise of primary stressors may also contribute to the rise of secondary stressors.

Moderating Resources: Coping, Social Support, and Self-Concepts

As indicated earlier, moderating resources are conceived as having the capacity to hinder, prevent, or cushion the development of the stress process and its outcomes. Here, three such resources will be considered: coping, social support, and self-concept—specifically, mastery. Each of these merits its own extensive discussion, something that cannot be undertaken within this chapter.

A caveat needs to be introduced at the outset of this discussion. It is that there is nothing inherent about coping, social support, or mastery that destines them to be treated as moderating resources. Casting them as moderators is a conceptual strategy, not an empirical imperative. Indeed, the three resources could as plausibly be regarded as mediating conditions, where the effects of the other components of the stress process on outcomes are channeled through the resources. Their treatment as mediators assumes that resources are not immutable but can be diminished (or replenished) by the social and economic statuses surrounding the stress process and by the ensuing stressors. Thus, coping repertoires can be altered through trial and error as people contend with continuing threat; one's sources of social support may be lost as a consequence of exposure to a variety of stressors, such as the death of a close family member or friend; and mastery may be undermined by failure to control intractable exigencies. Each of these examples underscores that resources may be changed by the very conditions whose effects they may also moderate. To the extent that they are changed in these kinds of ways, they act as routes through which stressors impact on outcomes. These mediating functions are indicated in Figure 19.1 by the arrows tracing the pathways from the stressors to the resources and from resources to outcomes. Though the mediating features of resources are potentially important, the major concern of the following discussion centers around their moderating functions. This discussion begins with the examination of coping.

Coping refers to the behaviors that individuals employ in their own behalf in their efforts to prevent or avoid stress and its consequences (Pearlin, 1991; Pearlin & Aneshensel, 1986; Pearlin & Schooler, 1978). These behaviors may function to change the situations from which stressors spring, to shape the meaning of stressors in ways that reduce their threat, to hinder stress proliferation, or to reduce the intensity of distress that has been created by the stressors. The intellectual roots of coping are located in clinical psychiatry and psychology, and although there has been some sociological study of the construct, current research continues to mirror its early roots. Its history is clearly manifested in two ways. First, coping is largely treated as an individual disposition, thus ignoring how the behavior might be influenced by and learned from the experiences stemming from people's social statuses. Similarly, it is typically viewed as taking place in a contextual vacuum, in isolation from others with whom there are ongoing interactions. There may be certain stressors that do not substantially or directly involve one's social relationships; for example, one may be engaged in an internal and quiet effort to quell anxieties created long before one's present social relationships were formed. Exceptions notwithstanding, stressors usually arise within social domains, and the coping strategies of an individual will be constrained and guided by others sharing the domains. The choices and consequences of coping strategies adopted to deal with marital problems, to illustrate, cannot be understood fully without taking into account the marital relationship, the spouse's efforts to cope with problems in the relationship, and the spouse's responses to the partner's coping behaviors. Despite occasional attention to the interactional underpinnings of coping actions (e.g., Coyne & Fiske, 1992), research into coping falls far short of these ideals. Given these shortcomings, it is understandable that little is known of the influence of social and interpersonal contexts on individual coping behavior.

There is a second and related feature of research into coping that, from a sociological perspective, is limiting. It concerns the tendency of researchers either to ignore completely or to specify insufficiently the stressors with which people are coping. There is recognition by some leading researchers that coping is not a general disposition but, instead, is a specific set of responses tailored to specific exigencies (Lazarus & Folkman, 1984). Nevertheless, the same assessments of coping are used across very different situations, even by those who argue in behalf of the specificity of coping. The Ways of Coping (Folkman & Lazarus, 1980), probably the most widely employed measure, has been used to assess coping with a wide variety of exigencies without modification of the tool to fit the particular situation. If the differences and nuances of coping do, in fact, vary with the nuances and differences of specific stressors, it is doubtful that an all-purpose measure can be appropriate. The use of such a measure runs the risk of creating an understanding of coping as a general personality disposition rather than a specific strategy developed in response to specific life problems. The more general the uses to which measures are put, the more difficult it is to recognize variations in situation-specific coping strategies and their moderating functions.

Aside from the conceptual and measurement difficulties that can be found in the study of coping, the analytic techniques used to assess its efficacy are also limited. In this regard, the deficiencies identified in the study of coping are shared by the analyses of other moderating conditions. As noted earlier, and as indicated by Figure 19.1, each juncture of the stress process can be examined for potential moderating effects. Concretely, this means that coping and other resources might exercise multiple moderating functions: They may reduce or contain the intensity of a stressor, inhibit the emergence of secondary stressors, and cushion the effect of the stressors on outcomes. In contrast to this kind of detailed analysis, moderating effects are usually judged solely by their direct relationship to an outcome, ignoring their possible modification of primary and secondary stressors. Their direct effects on outcomes are important, but we run the risk of underestimating the totality of their effectiveness as moderators in ignoring other points of intervention.

There are other questions and problems attending the study of coping, some of which have been detailed elsewhere (Pearlin, 1991). By way of example, there is essentially no attempt made to distinguish the long- and short-term effects of coping, although it is easy to imagine that these are not always identical. Similarly, it is conceivable that a person's coping repertoires relieve that person of distress, while at the same time exacerbating the distress of others in his or her role set. However, as with other components of the stress process, the identification of these analytic problems should be interpreted only as an effort to target future efforts, not to abandon the construct. Indeed, despite current problems in our thinking about coping, our measurement of it, and the ways we analyze its effects, there are ample indications that it can be a significant naturalistic intervention at junctures of the stress process. Specifically, coping may be particularly efficacious in moderating the effects of stressors that arise in close interpersonal social relationships, such as those found in the family; but it may be less potent in moderating stressors involving relationships and activities that are mandated by formal organizations, such as found in bureaucratized work settings (Pearlin & Schooler, 1978).

Some of the limitations that can be identified in coping research are also present in studies of social support. (For a detailed discussion of social support, see Chapter 15 of this volume.) As first observed some years ago (Pearlin, 1985), research into social support is not as social as it should be, despite what might be expected given the label of the construct. What is strikingly absent in the prevailing research are the donors of support. Thus, the subjects of research into social support are typically its recipients, on whom we rely for information about the people who are supporting them (Sarason, Pierce, & Sarason, 1994). As a result, little is known as to the conditions that initiate or sustain support. Although it is usually assumed that stable support rests on equitable exchange, this assumption cannot apply to situations in which support is imbalanced or unidirectional, as in long-term caregiving to cognitively impaired people (Antonucci & Jackson, 1990; George, 1986; Pearlin et al.,1995). One explanation for the continuation of unreciprocated support resides in what has been called "mattering," the sense of being a person of importance to the well-being of a significant other (Rosenberg & McCullough, 1981). It is uncertain whether the desire to matter can be considered a universal motive, as self-esteem has been; we can be certain, however, that the disruption of mattering can be highly distressful. Evidence for this statement comes from an analysis of Alzheimer's caregivers, showing that where mattering is lost as a consequence of the death of the recipient of support, the former donor can experience an increase in depressive symptomatology (Pearlin & Le Blanc, 1999). What is to be emphasized here is that by looking solely at the recipients of support, we inescapably skirt one of its features that is quitessentially social, namely, that social support rests on the qualities of a relationship involving two or more people.

An exclusive focus on the recipient of support also deflects attention from something else about which little is known: what transpires in social support that makes it supportive—or that results in failed support. In interviews with husbands and wives, Pearlin and McCall (1990) identified some of the ingredients of exchange that can be present in emotional support. These include simply listening to the recipient's construction of his or her problem, gathering information about the circumstances surrounding problems through pertinent questioning, legitimating the concerns and distress of the individual, using gestures of affection and acceptance, distracting the person, giving advice, displaying humor, and expressing esteem and confidence. There are also discernible interactions that either undermine the effectiveness of support or turn what was intended to be supportive into conflict. It appears, for example, that the sequential order of supportive actions is itself a factor regulating its successfulness. For example, resentment can be created if advice is given before the recipient feels the donor understands the nature of the problem at hand. Similar reactions can be triggered in instances where the donor is seen by the recipient as feigning support to assert his or her own greater wisdom, power, or control.

To some extent, the failure to look more closely at supportive interactions stems from the misconception that it is only the perception of access to support by its recipient that is important in moderating the impact of stressors, not the actual support that is accorded. There is no doubt that such perceptions are important in bolstering well-being; this has been demonstrated in numerous studies (e.g., Antonucci & Israel, 1986; Sandler & Bererra, 1984). However, a more comprehensive picture emerges when the naturalistic interventions of social support are examined across the breadth of the stress process.

We were able to do this in our study of family members providing long-term care to relatives with Alzheimer's disease (Pearlin et al., 1995). Considerable information was gathered about a variety of formal and informal instrumental supports as well as perceived emotional support. The analysis revealed that different kinds of support are effective at different junctures of the stress process. Thus, *formally enacted instrumental support* given by trained workers is most efficacious in moderating certain kinds of primary stressors, particularly those involving the dependencies of the impaired relative for basic daily care. By contrast, *informal instrumental support* provided by friends and family was the only type of support that both moderated the impact of the behavioral problems of the relative and inhibited the emergence of secondary stressors, conflict between caregiving and job responsibilities in particular. Finally, *perceived emotional support* was the sole form of support that buffered the effects of the stressors on depression. The point to be underscored for purposes of the present discussion is that the efficacy of support depends on the ways its specialized source and form fit with the nature of the hardship that is involved and the juncture of the stress process at which the interventions of support are taking place. Looked at this way, all forms and sources of support—instrumental and expressive, perceived and enacted, formal and informal—may have a moderating role in the stress process. As in the case of coping, we run the risk of underestimating the influence of moderating resources when our conceptualization and analyses of them are restricted.

Mastery, the third and final moderator that is considered here, is different from coping and social support in that it represents a self-concept. (See Chapter 18 for a more detailed discussion of aspects of personal control in the stress process.) The construct of mastery refers to individuals' understanding of their ability to control the forces that affect their lives. Like coping, mastery is not a fixed element of personality but is a self-concept that can change as critical elements of individuals' lives change (Skaff, Pearlin, & Mullan, 1996). It has repeatedly been demonstrated as a powerful factor in moderating the stress process (e.g., Turner & Noh, 1988). Yet it is not altogether clear how it exercises its moderating functions. Why should one's sense of control help to govern the impact of stressors? There are two related provisional explanations of its power. One, simply, is that people who enjoy a high level of mastery see stressors as less threatening and ominous than do others whose sense of mastery is limited. Second, mastery may act as a self-fulfilling prophecy, where people who believe they can exercise control over the conditions of their lives act accordingly. They may cope more actively and with a richer repertoire than others, and they might also more effectively mobilize their social support and make better use of it. Although there is no doubt about the efficacy of mastery, explanations for its potency remain conjectural.

As in the case of coping, there is some beginning recognition that our general measures of mastery and kindred concepts do not capture possible variations in its levels from one situation to another (Krause, 1994; Seeman, Rodin, & Albert, 1993). Preliminary evidence indicates that mastery might be specific to the situations in which people are immersed. For example, the level of mastery we entertain as workers might be different from its levels as marital partners. Assuming that mastery is both global and role and situational specific, it is not yet known how the two may be related. Does the global sense of control influence the more specific or does the global represent some summation of the specific levels? My colleagues and I have further considered dimensions of mastery within a life-course context; we question, that is, whether people feel they have arrived at where they are as a result of capricious circumstances or as a result of circumstances they believe they have directed and managed. Exploratory interviews indicate that individuals are able to reflect back on their lives and estimate the extent to which they have been able to exercise control over their life-course trajectories. The same issues can be raised with regard to our futures; that is, as we contemplate the future, to what extent do we feel in control of the direction of our trajectories? These kinds of questions are worth addressing because of the consistent research findings that mastery is a powerful moderator of stress.

Although these moderators involve distinctly different resources, there is some evidence that there is an interrelationship among them (Ensel & Lin, 1991). We, too, find evidence of a relationship among them. Thus, it appears that if individuals are lacking in one of these resources, they are likely to be lacking in the others as well. Someone with a limited sense of mastery, for example, will probably also be deficient in coping skills and in access to effective support. These kinds of interrelationships have implications for the analytic strategies we usually employ in search for moderating effects. Specifically, they suggest that all three should be taken as a package to examine their combined effects, not one by one as is typically done.

Outcomes

The outcomes of the stress process represent the converging consequences of its other components. Sociological research has traditionally focused its attention on the mental health consequences of stress. Yet despite the rather lengthy history of this research, there is considerable confusion and uncertainty concerning the relevance of mental health and psychological disorder and their measures to the intellectual agendas of sociology. This discussion is an attempt to clarify how the study of stress and distress fits these agendas. To do this, I largely rely on the strategy of contrasting sociological orientations with those of psychiatry, ignoring the substantial heterogeneity existing within each of these fields. Although social and behavioral scientists have provided much of the know-how for developing standardized assessments of psychological disorders, they have largely done so under the aegis and for the purposes of clinical psychiatry and allied fields. Each is interested in disorders, and sometimes they collaborate in the pursuit of their interests, but their orientations to mental health and disorder are substantially at odds. In large measure, this reflects the differences in the purposes of psychiatry and sociology. Psychiatry, of course, is a specialized field of medicine that has the rather awesome responsibility of treating people suffering from mental illness. Like other medical specialties with responsibilities for treatment, psychiatry has limited tolerance for ambiguity and, therefore, seeks to minimize it. It needs to know, first, whether a person requires treatment; in other words, how to identify cases. Second, since the type of treatment depends on the type of the mental malady, a diagnosis of the specific type of disorder needs to be made—not an easy task where pathologies overlap and their differences are blurred. The need for diagnoses is currently reenforced by third-party payers who reimburse the clinician for treating specified disorders for prespecified lengths of time. Both its professional mission and the economic imperatives of the health care system in which it operates move psychiatry toward outcomes that are expressed in categorical terms: One either suffers from a cluster of symptoms signifying clinical placement in a diagnostic category or not. Research in behalf of clinical interests, then, is necessarily oriented toward locating people in the population who qualify for the treatment of specific diagnosed disorders.

Sociological orientations are fundamentally different from this medical orientation, though the differences are not always recognized. They are different, first of all, by virtue of the fact that observations of mental disorders are usually placed in the service of interests lying outside the disorders themselves; that is, information about mental disorders helps to direct attention to those features of social organization and social experience that are harmful to people; mental disorders serve as the litmus test by which we establish how social arrangements are functioning. This sounds more callous than it is in reality, for sociologists may also be driven to study disorders by profound humanitarian concerns. From a disciplinary perspective, nevertheless, sociological interest in mental health and disorder is rooted in its mission to identify elements of social life that have dysfunctional consequences. Among the multiple disciplines that study stress and its health consequences, sociology alone bears this mission.

Mental disorder, then, is employed as one of many possible indicators of the consequences of social and interpersonal arrangements. As Mirowsky and Ross (1990) have argued, for both theoretical and statistical reasons, the use of diagnostic categories is not well suited to this research mission. Suppose, for example, a study aims to compare the mental health consequences of two systems of occupational authority, one in which work is under strict supervisory control and the other in which workers have some decision-making control over their own labors. If this comparison were based only on the prevalence of diagnosed clinical depression, we would probably find little or no difference in the consequences of the two systems, for in neither setting would prevalence be sufficient to make a reliable comparison. A more sensitive indicator of such consequences would take the form of a symptom scale, perhaps of depression. Such a scale would permit the researcher to order individuals according to the number and intensity of the depressive symptoms they exhibit. Although symptom scales are of limited use in detecting clinical depression, they may be useful for identifying aspects of the organization of authority that have deleterious mental health consequences.

To some extent, the foregoing discussion paints an exaggerated picture of the preoccupation of psychiatry with treatment. Like social and behavioral scientists, they, too, are likely to be in search of the origins of disorders. But the two groups often look in very distinctive directions for these origins. Furthermore, disciplinary differences in where the origins are presumed to lie are strikingly more pronounced now than in earlier decades. Much of the effort of psychiatry to establish the causes of mental disorder currently takes place in the laboratory in the form of genetic and molecular research. Indeed, this effort has been sloganized by calling it the "decade of the brain." It is far beyond the expertise of this sociologist to evaluate the fruitfulness of this effort thus far, but it is not difficult to see that it is undergirded by perspectives in sharp contrast to those guiding sociological research. Briefly, mental illness is viewed as the outcome of biological failure, thus placing its causes squarely within the functioning of the individual organism. Sociological efforts to provide causal explanations, on the other hand, are more likely to be consistent with Mills's (1959) observation that the proper study of sociology is to show the influence of social problems on personal problems.

Few sociologists would dispute that biology is an important source of mental illness, especially the psychoses. It can be hoped, too, that some biological psychiatrists would acknowledge the causal role of social learning and experience. But whatever nods might be exchanged between the two, the difference in their causal paradigms remains: The one argues that the sources of one's distress lie within one's self, the other, that these sources lie in people's locations in social systems and the structuring of experience that often derives from these locations. These contrasting paradigms have equally contrasting implications for intervention, the one emphasizing pharmaceutical protocols that reduce the effects of individuals' biological malfunctioning, the other addressing the correction of problematic social conditions. It can be left to scholars of the sociology of knowledge to speculate on the ideological and economic climates that favor one or the other of these orientations.

Again, in pointing to differences between sociology and psychiatry, it is not meant to suggest that these are monolithic fields within which scholars march in a theoretical lockstep. These contrasts are intended only to highlight the general features of sociological inquiry. One of these features concerns differences in the explanation of outcomes; it pertains to the form in which questions of causation are raised. Specifically, there is a tendency for psychiatrists and psychiatric epidemiologists to focus on a single disorder, such as depression, and then attempt to work back to the multiple factors that might stand as risks for this single outcome. By contrast, the sociological investigator is more apt to examine a social condition or set of conditions and then trace forward to the multiple outcomes of these conditions. The first approach may help to broaden our understanding of the antecedents of the disorder and the second, ideally, to broaden our understanding of the array of outcomes produced by the circumstances of social life (e.g., Aneshensel, Rutter, & Lachenbruch, 1991). In accord with its disciplinary mission, the sociological orientation can lead to a keener appreciation of the wide scope of effects that social forces may exert on people's well-being. To observe the range and specificity of outcomes that the stress process might create, therefore, it is necessary that our studies be designed to gather information about multiple possible outcomes.

There is a related reason to examine multiple outcomes: It enables the investigator to detect possible differences in the ways in which social groups manifest stress-related disorder. Evidence is available indicating the utility of such a strategy. Thus, it has been observed that women are more likely than men to react to stressors through internalized states, such as depression, and men, more than women, through aggression and the excessive use of alcohol (Aneshensel et al.,1991; Horwitz, White, & Howell-White,1996). If depression alone were used to gauge the impact of stressors, one could erroneously conclude that women are more vulnerable to stressful circumstances than men. Clearly, it behooves the interests of sociological research to examine a reasonably full range of outcomes that may be generated by hardships that are rooted in social systems.

DISCUSSION

It might easily seem that this chapter leads to a conundrum: We presumably know the things we have to do to strengthen our research, but to do these things is beyond the reach of our capabilities. Thus, in addition to collecting extensive information about people's social and economic characteristics, and the contexts of their daily lives, research should ideally employ a host of measures appropriate to the particular issues and populations under investigation. This might entail the identification of multiple stressors, moderators, and outcomes, as well as the construction of their measures. Moreover, since change is inherently folded into the very notion of a stress process, a longitudinal design is demanded. Research that is driven by a conceptually rich framework needs data of corresponding richness. An analysis that seeks to thread its way through densely packed information in order to detect the effect paths that crisscross the interrelated elements of the stress process can be very daunting. As others have observed (McClean & Link, 1994; Somerfield, 1997), the comprehensive empirical testing of complex conceptual models is always difficult and sometimes out of reach. How, then, can the investigator test a stress process model of the complexity suggested in the foregoing discussions? The answer, of course, is that she or he cannot, at least within a single analysis; unfortunately, the technology is lacking that would enable the investigator to deliver in one package everything there is to be learned. One strategy, of course, would be to reduce the sheer volume of information one would ideally want in an inquiry. An alternative and, I believe, better strategy is one modeled after laboratory-based research that conducts one experiment after another to create a cumulative body of knowledge.

In a similar matter, research into the stress process can target its efforts toward incrementally building a knowledge base from the intensive analyses of delimited issues and interrelationships within the stress process. Particularly with large-scale surveys that gather comprehensive data touching on each component of the stress process, it is possible to plan multiple complementary analyses that together can reveal the interrelationships across the breadth of the stress process. In practice, this is one of the ways in which the field has been moving forward. What can be envisioned is many small narratives coming together in a way that creates a whole story.

A reminder is hardly necessary that the tasks of the chapter were undertaken with a specialized perspective in mind: the contributions and challenges of *sociological* research into the stress process. This disciplinary emphasis should not be interpreted as an expression of intellectual chauvinism, or as somehow advocating against multidisciplinary research. Multidisciplinary research is both exciting and promising, especially in an area such as stress and health, in which so many disciplines have equal claim to a stake. However, multidisciplinary research can only be as strong as its weakest component. In this regard, sociology has nothing to apologize for in what it is able to bring to the table. Although sociological research into stress and mental health may be less widely known than that of other research programs, it is neither less important nor less sophisticated than the others. By any estimate, the sociological study of stress and health has been vigorous, exciting, and productive.

Nevertheless, it behooves us to continue to push against the boundaries of our knowledge. It is my conviction that to push successfully, our theories and our methods must be kept under critical scrutiny. One measure of the progress being made by a field of inquiry, I submit, is its ability to recognize changes in the directions toward which it can bountifully move and the challenges it is likely to encounter along the way. This chapter has attempted both to chart the directions and to point to some of the obstacles that stand in its way. There is every reason to be optimistic about the future course of the field.

REFERENCES

Aneshensel, C. A. (1992). Social stress: Theory and research. *Annual Review of Sociology, 18,* 15–38.

Aneshensel, C. A., Pearlin, L. I., Mullan, J. T., Zarit, S. H., & Whitlatch, C. J. (1995). *Profiles in caregiving: The unexpected career.* San Diego: Academic Press.

Aneshensel, C. A., Rutter, C. M., & Lachenbruch, P. A. (1991). Social structure, stress and mental health: Competing conceptual and analytic models. *American Sociological Review, 56,* 166–178.

Aneshensel, C. A., & Sucoff, C. A. (1996). The neighborhood context of adolescent mental health. *Journal of Health and Social Behavior, 39,* 293–310.

Antonucci, T. C., & Israel, B. C. (1986). Veridicality of social support: A comparison of principal and network members' responses. *Journal of Consulting and Clinical Psychology, 54,* 432–437.

Antonucci, T. C., & Jackson, J. S. (1990). The role of reciprocity in social support. In B. R. Sarason, I. G. Sarason, & G. R. Pierce (Eds.), *Social support: An interactionist view* (pp. 173–198). New York: Wiley.

Coyne, J. C., & Fiske, V. (1992). Couples coping with chronic and catastrophic illness. In T. J. Akamatsu, M. A. P. Stephens, S. E. Hobfall, & J. H. Crawther (Eds.), *Family health psychology* (pp. 129–149). Washington, DC: Hemisphere.

Dressler, W. W. (1988). Social consistency and psychological distress. *Journal of Health and Social Behavior, 29,* 79–91.

Durkheim, E. (1951). *Suicide.* Glencoe, IL: Free Press.

Ensel, W. M., & Lin, N. (1991). The life stress paradigm and psychological distress. *Journal of Health and Social Behavior, 33,* 321–341.

Folkman, S., & Lazarus, R. S. (1980). An analysis of coping in a middle-aged community sample. *Journal of Health and Social Behavior, 21,* 219–239.

George, L. K. (1986). Caregiver burden: Conflict between norms of reciprocity and solidarity. In K. G. Pillermer & R. S. Wolf (Eds.), *Elder abuse: Conflict in the family* (pp. 67–92). Dover, MA: Auburn House.

Gersten, J. C., Langner, T. S., Eisenberg, J. G., & Orzek, L. (1974). Child behavior and life events: Undesirable change or change per se? In B. S. Dohrenwend & B. P. Dohrenwend (Eds.), *Stressful life events: Their nature and effects* (pp. 159–170. New York: Wiley.

Hamilton, V. L., Broman, C. L., Hoffman, W. S., & Renner, D. S. (1990). Hard times and vulnerable people: Initial effects of plant changes on autoworkers' mental health. *Journal of Health and Social Behavior, 31,* 123–140.

Holmes, T. H., & Rahe, R. H. (1967). The social readjustment rating scale. *Journal of Psychosomatic Research, 11,* 23–28.

Horwitz, S. V., White, H. R., & Howell-White, S. (1996). The use of multiple outcomes in stress research: A case study of gender differences in marital dissolution. *Journal of Health and Social Behavior, 37,* 278–291.

Jackson, J. S., Brown, T. B., Williams, D. R., Torres, M., Sellers, S. L., & Brown, K. (1996). Racism and the physical and mental health of African-Americans. *Ethnicity and Disease, 6,* 132–147.

Kanner, A. D., Coyne, J. C., Schaefer, C., & Lazarus, R. S. (1981). Comparison of two modes of stress measurement: Daily hassles and uplifts and major life events. *Journal of Behavioral Medicine, 4*, 1–39.

Karasek, R. A. (1979). Job demands, job decision latitude and mental strain: Implications for job redesign. *Administrative Science Quarterly, 24*, 285–308.

Kiecolt-Glazer, J. K., & Glazer, R. (1994). Caregivers, mental health, and immune function. In E. Light, G. Niederehe, & B. D. Lebowitz (Eds.), *Stress effects on family caregivers of Alzheimer's patients* (pp. 64–75). New York: Springer.

Kohn, M. L. (1969). *Class and conformity*. Homewood, IL: Dorsey Press.

Krause, N. (1994). Stressors in salient social roles and well-being in later life. *Journal of Gerontology: Psychological Services, 49*, 137–148.

Langner, T. S., & Michael, S. T. (1963). *Life stress and mental health*. London: Free Press.

Lazarus, R. S., & Folkman, S. (1984). *Stress, appraisal and coping*. New York: Springer.

Lennon, M. C., & Rosenfield, S. (1992). Gender and mental health: Interactions of job and family. *Journal of Health and Social Behavior, 33*, 316–327.

Link, B. G., Mesagno, F. P., Lubner, M., & Dohrenwend, B. P. (1990). Problems in measuring role strains and social functioning in relation to psychological symptoms. *Journal of Health and Social Behavior, 31*, 354–369.

Link, B. G., & Phelan, J. (1995). Social conditions as fundamental causes of disease. *Journal of Health and Social Behavior, Extra Issue*, 80–94.

McLean, D. E., & Link, B. G. (1994). Unraveling complexity: Strategies to refine concepts, measures, and research designs in the study of life events and mental health. In W. R. Avison & I. H. Gotlib (Eds.), *Stress and mental health* (pp. 15–42). New York: Plenum Press

Menaghan, E. G. (1991). Work experiences and family interaction processes: The long reach of the job? *Annual Review of Sociology, 17*, 419–444.

Merton, R. K. (1957). The role set: Problems in sociological theory. *British Journal of Sociology, 8*, 106–120.

Merton, R. K. (1968). Social structure and anomie. In R. K. Merton (Ed.), *Social theory and social structures* (3rd ed., pp. 85–124). New York: Free Press.

Mills, C. W. (1959). *The sociological imagination*. New York: Oxford University Press.

Mirowsky, J., & Ross, C. E. (1990). Psychiatric diagnosis as reified measurement. *Journal of Health and Social Behavior, 30*, 11–25.

Pearlin, L. I. (1971). *Class context and family relations: A cross-national study*. Boston: Little, Brown.

Pearlin, L. I. (1980). Life-strains and psychological distress among adults: A conceptual overview. In N. J. Smelser & E. H. Erikson (Eds.), *Themes of work and love in adulthood* (pp. 174–192). Cambridge, MA: Harvard University Press.

Pearlin, L. I. (1983). Role strains and personal stress. In H. B. Kaplan (Ed.), *Psychosocial stress: Trends in theory and research* (pp. 3–32). New York: Academic Press.

Pearlin, L. I. (1985). Social structure and processes of social support. In S. Cohen & L. Syme (Eds.), *Social support and health* (pp. 43–60). New York: Academic Press.

Pearlin, L. I. (1989). The sociological study of stress. *Journal of Health and Social Behavior, 30*, 241–256.

Pearlin, L. I. (1991). The study of coping: Problems and directions. In J. Eckenrode (Ed.), *The social context of coping* (pp. 261–276). New York: Plenum Press.

Pearlin, L. I., & Aneshensel, C. A. (1986). Coping and social supports: Their functions and applications. In L. H. Aiken & D. Mechanic (Eds.), *Social science, medicine, and policy* (pp. 417–439). New Brunswick, NJ: Rutgers University Press.

Pearlin, L. I., & Aneshensel, C. A. (1994). Caregiving: The unexpected career. *Social Justice Research, 7*, 373–390.

Pearlin, L. I., Aneshensel, C. A., & LeBlanc, A. J. (1997). The forms and mechanisms of stress proliferation: The case of AIDS caregivers. *Journal of Health and Social Behavior, 38*, 223–236.

Pearlin, L. I., Aneshensel, C. A., Mullan, J. T., & Whitlatch, C. J. (1995). Caregiving and its social support. In R. H. Binstock & L. K. George (Eds.), *Handbook of aging and the social sciences* (4th ed., pp. 283–302). Orlando, FL: Academic Press.

Pearlin, L. I., & Johnson, J. S. (1977). Marital status, life-strains, and depression. *American Sociological Review, 42*, 704–715.

Pearlin, L. I., & LeBlanc, A. J. (in press). Bereavement and the loss of mattering. In N. Goodman, T. J. Owens, & S. Stryker (Eds.), *Self-esteem and beyond: Festschrift for Morris Rosenberg*. Cambridge, UK: Oxford University.

Pearlin, L. I., & Lieberman, M. A. (1979). Social sources of emotional distress. In R. Simmons (Ed.), *Research in community and mental health* (pp. 217–248). Greenwich, CT: JAI Press.

Pearlin, L. I., Lieberman, M. A., Menaghan, E. G., & Mullan, J. T. (1981). The stress process. *Journal of Health and Social Behavior, 22,* 337–356.

Pearlin, L. I., & McCall, M. E. (1990). Occupational stress and marital support: A description of microprocesses. In J. Eckenrode & S. Gore (Eds.), *Stress between work and family* (pp. 39–60). New York: Plenum Press.

Pearlin, L. I., Mullan, J. T., Semple, S. J., & Skaff, M. M. (1990) Caregiving and the stress process: An overview of concepts and their measures. *Gerontologist, 30,* 583–594.

Pearlin, L. I., & Schooler, C. (1978). The structure of coping. *Journal of Health and Social Behavior, 19,* 2–21.

Pearlin, L. I., & Skaff, M. M. (1995) Stressors and adaptation in late life. In M. Gatz (Ed.), *Emerging issues in mental health and aging* (pp. 97–123). Washington DC: American Psychiatric Association Press.

Quarentelli, E. L. (Ed.). (1978). *Disasters: Theory and research.* Beverly Hills, CA: Sage.

Rosenberg, M., & McCullough, C. (1981). Mattering: Inferred significance and mental health among adolescents. In R. G. Simmons (Ed.), *Research in community and mental health* (pp. 163–180). Greenwich, CT: JAI Press.

Rosenberg, M., & Pearlin, L. I. (1978). Social class and self-esteem among children and adults. *American Journal of Sociology, 84,* 55–77.

Sandler, I. N., & Berrera, M. (1984). Toward a multimethod approach to assessing the effects of social support. *American Journal of Community Psychology, 12,* 37–52.

Sarason, I. G., Pierce, G. R., & Sarason, B. R. (1994). General and specific perceptions of social support. In W. R. Avison & I. H. Gotlib (Eds.), *Stress and mental health* (pp. 151–177). New York: Plenum Press.

Seeman, T. E., Rodin, J., & Albert, M. (1993). Self-effacing and cognitive performance in high-performing older individuals. *Journal of Aging and Health, 5,* 455–474.

Shrout, P., Link, B. G., Dohrenwend, B. P., Skodol, A., Stueve, A. & Mirotznik, J. (1989). Characterizing life events as risk factors for depression: The role of fateful loss events. *Journal of Abnormal Psychology, 98,* 460–467.

Skaff, M. M., Pearlin, L. I., & Mullan, J. T. (1996). Transitions in the caregiving career: Effects on sense of mastery. *Psychology and Aging, 11,* 247–257.

Somerfield, M. G. (1997). The utility of systems models of stress and coping for applied research. *Journal of Health Psychology, 2,* 133–151.

Thoits, P. A. (1983). Dimensions of life events that influence distress. In H. B. Kaplan (Ed.), *Psychosocial Stress* (pp. 33–104). New York: Academic Press.

Turkkhan, J. S., Brady, J. V., & Harris, A. H. (1982). Animal studies of stressful interactions: A behavioral-psychological overview. In L. Goldberg & S. Breznitz (Eds.), *Handbook of stress* (pp. 153–182). New York: Free Press.

Turner, R. J., & Noh, S. (1988). Physical disability and depression: A longitudinal analysis. *Journal of Health and Social Behavior, 29,* 23–37.

Wheaton, B. (1990). Where work and family meet: Stress across social roles. In J. Eckenrode & S. Gore (Eds.), *Stress between work and family* (pp. 153–174). New York: Plenum Press.

Wheaton, B. (1994). Sampling the stress universe. In W. R. Avison & I. H. Gotlib (Eds.), *Stress and mental health* (pp. 77–114). New York: Plenum Press.

CHAPTER 20

Social Transmission in Acute Somatoform Epidemics

WILLIAM W. EATON

INTRODUCTION

This chapter considers the social origins of *acute somatoform illnesses*, such as so-called hysterical epidemics and mass psychogenic illnesses. For the purposes of this chapter, somatoform illnesses are clusters of one or more *complaints* from individuals and typically accompany bodily, or somatic, illness—that is, in the disease model, *symptoms*—and one or more *behaviors* that typically accompany physical illness—that is, in the disease model, *signs.* There is evidence for social and psychological causes in these clusters (as is true in many, or even most, somatic illnesses), but they are distinct in combining the social and psychological causation with an absence of obvious physical cause.

The aim of this chapter is to describe the "epidemic" form of transmission of the somatoform illnesses, in which the agent of the transmission is human communication of some sort. Various terms and definitions have been put forward to describe this process. The term "hysterical contagion" has also been used in this context, as defined, for example, by Kerckhoff and Back (1968), wherein "a set of experiences or behaviors which are heavily laden with the emotion of fear of a mysterious force are disseminated through a collectivity. The type of behavior that forms the manifest content ... may vary widely... but all are indicative of fear, and all are inexplicable in terms of the usual standards of mechanical, chemical, or physiological causality." This term is not favored because the etymology of the word *hysteria* implies a physical structure in women, which is incorrect. Inevitable

WILLIAM W. EATON • Department of Mental Hygiene, School of Hygiene and Public Health, Johns Hopkins University, Baltimore, Maryland 21205.

Handbook of the Sociology of Mental Health, edited by Carol S. Aneshensel and Jo C. Phelan. Kluwer Academic/Plenum Publishers, New York, 1999.

linkage to the emotion of fear is also not appropriate, and the notion that the epidemic is "inexplicable" in mechanical, chemical, or physiological terms, is not quite on target either, as discussed below. Colligan and Murphy (1979) define "contagious psychogenic illness" as "the collective occurrence of a set of physical symptoms and related beliefs among two or more individuals in the absence of an identifiable pathogen." This definition suffers by requiring a cluster of more than one symptom, by not requiring actual transmission between persons, and by requiring the absence of an identifiable agent, which sometimes contributes to the epidemic process, even when not actually the agent of transmission. An early definition is *behavioral contagion*, defined by Grosser, Polansky, and Lippitt (1951) as "a social interaction in which a 'recipient's' behavior changes to become 'more like' that of another person, and where this change has occurred in a social interaction in which the 'initiator' (other person) has not communicated intent to influence the behavior of the recipient." This definition correctly requires social interaction to take place; puts to the side the study of persuasive influence, which is pertinent but not the central focus; and specifies the symmetrical quality of transmission, focusing on collective situations in which the transmitted behavior is similar or identical throughout the process. In this chapter, the concept of behavioral contagion is applied to somatoform illness. These complaints and behaviors are generally, but not always, socially disapproved, as was the situation in early studies of behavioral contagion (Wheeler, 1966), but social disapproval, with its consequent focus on lowering of restraints for enactment of proscribed behaviors, is not a required part of this otherwise useful definition.

Defining a few other terms makes future discussion more efficient. *Collective psychopathology* is the most general situation in which groups of individuals have high rates of disorder, for whatever reason. An *epidemic* is a more narrow form of collective psychopathology with a temporal and interpersonal element, in which a disorder spreads rapidly through a community. Collective psychopathology can exist for many reasons without having the epidemic form of transmission occur. Ill or disordered people can gather purposively in groups, for example, and groups of individuals can become ill or disordered because of risk factors that are common to them all. This distinction is sometimes referred to as the difference between "convergence" and "contagion." *Transmission* is the passage of a similar or identical complaint, behavior, sign, or symptom from one person to another. The *transmission completion rate* is the equivalent of the concept of the attack rate, used by infectious disease epidemiologists—that is, the proportion successfully reproducing the illness after transmission from another. The requirement that the sign or symptom be similar or identical in the transmitter and the receiver narrows the scope of the inquiry, eliminating many social situations that affect the occurrence of psychopathology, such as situations of stress produced in human interactions; situations of long-term developmental socialization, including that occurring in the context of the family; and certain unusual types of apparently florid and volatile mental disturbances such as latah and the startle reaction (Bartholomew, 1994). In all these situations, the actions of the individual producing the stress are not equivalent to the resultant reaction in the receiver.

In infectious disease epidemiology, a simple form of transmission is a *sole source epidemic*—that is, from a single source to many individuals. An example is the cholera epidemic studied by John Snow, in which the source was the pump at Broad Street, which carried water with cholera bacteria. This example is not perfect, since the cholera bacteria could also be transmitted from person to person after infection from the Broad Street pump water. A purer example might be an environmental catastrophe, such as the Bhopal Disaster, with a single source of exposure. A somewhat more complex form of transmission is the *person-to-person epidemic*, which involves transmission from person to person. Many contagious diseases take this form, such as tuberculosis and hepatitis, transmitted by bacteria; schistosomiasis transmitted by a parasite; and colds and HIV transmitted by viruses. The *social transmission of somatoform illness* is the experience or enactment in one or more individuals of an illness cluster that has been perceived in one or more other individuals during a group process. The transmission involves a symbol of some sort, making these epidemics uniquely human. All forms may legitimately be termed *psychogenic* since, as distinct from infectious and toxic disease epidemics, the individual's symbolic processing is a necessary agent for transmission.

Most psychogenic epidemics involve transmission where the presence of a group is necessary, or very important to, the transmission. In person-to-person epidemics, such as sexually transmitted diseases, the epidemic transmission can be limited to dyads. In socially transmitted somatoform illnesses, groups larger than two enhance, or are necessary for, transmission (as will be shown below). This is an example of the important distinction between the dyad and larger groups. A *group* is defined as two or more individuals who: (1) interact with one another more than would be expected by chance; *or* (2) think of themselves as possessing a common history or future. This definition of *group* allows a structural form (interaction) or a mental form (awareness). Where the group structure enhances, or is necessary for, transmission, the epidemic may be defined as *sociogenic* (as well as psychogenic). The term *sociogenic* has been proposed earlier (Stahl, 1982), but the distinction between the two forms (psychogenic and sociogenic) has not been made before. It turns out to be important in understanding the epidemics. The class of sociogenic epidemics are instances of the "social fact" (Durkheim, 1966). There is no analogue to the sociogenic epidemic in general epidemiology.

REVIEW OF RESEARCH ON SOMATOFORM EPIDEMICS

Overview

This section begins with an overview of studies of somatoform epidemics and then describes in detail several illustrative examples. Reviews of socially transmitted psychopathology trace back at least to Gruenberg (1957), who focused on severe psychopathology such as shared psychoses. Earlier work, such as that by MacKay (1852), or Hecker (1859), preceded the era in which the behaviors considered in this chapter were conceptualized in terms of psychopathology. A review by Markush (1973) presented a summary catalogue of brief descriptions of occurrences from medieval times to the present, but failed to specify the criteria for inclusion in the review, including anomalies such as smoking tobacco and driving while intoxicated. A brief sociological analysis by Gehlen (1977) focused on the distinction between panics and crazes. The psychologist's perspective on socially transmitted somatoform illnesses in occupational settings was laid out in Colligan and Murphy (1979; see also Boxer, 1985), and a multidisciplinary approach for the occupational setting was presented by Colligan, Pennebaker, and Murphy (1982). An analysis and review by Wessely (1987) described two subtypes of mass anxiety and mass motor epidemics.

Two comprehensive reviews of so-called "hysterical epidemics" have made it possible to examine the characteristics of this important type of socially transmitted psychopathology. Sirois (1974) summarized 70 accounts published from 1873 to 1973. Boss (1997) updated that work with a review of 70 further published accounts from 1973 to 1993. The epidemics included in these reviews cover the content area of delusions, emotions, and somatoform behaviors, all with short-term duration. Epidemics of suicidal behavior were not included. The somatoform behaviors in the epidemics reviewed included convulsions, fainting, coughing, numbness, headaches, nausea, vomiting, dizziness, paralysis, fatigue, and panic. The characteristics of the 140 epidemics are displayed in Table 20.1, which summarizes the two reviews.

The epidemics tend to occur in situations in which group communication is facilitated and well-defined groups already exist. In about half the epidemics described, fewer than 30 people fell ill. The number of persons ill is much smaller than the number of persons who are involved in, or who witness, the epidemic. The transmission completion rate is often about 5% or 10%, meaning that in most of the epidemics, many hundreds of people are involved as potential cases. Cases in these epidemics are often young women: In about half the epidemics the cases are exclusively women, and about half the cases consist only of persons under 20 years of age. About half the epidemics endure less than 2 weeks, and only one in five last more than a month.

The epidemics travel through social networks and not necessarily along lines through which physical contagion is most plausible. For example, in occupational settings where workers of different ethnic or cultural groups are in close physical proximity, typically only one ethnic group is affected, even though the setting is multiethnic (e.g., four out of six case

Table 20.1. Emotional, Delusional, or Somatoform Epidemics, 1872–1993

	Number of epidemics	Percent[a]
Location		
School	69	49
Town or village	24	17
Factory	28	20
Hospital or institution	10	7
Other	9	6
Number of persons ill		
Less than 10 persons	29	21
10–30 persons	38	27
More than 30 persons	63	45
Unknown	7	5
Gender of persons ill		
All female	68	48
Males and females	60	43
All males	4	3
Unknown	7	5
Age of persons ill		
All less than 20	65	46
20–40	17	12
All ages	28	20
Unknown	29	21
Duration		
Less than 3 days	30	21
3–14 days	45	32
15–30 days	16	11
More than 30 days	28	20
Unknown	21	15

[a] Percentages use 140 (the number of epidemics) as the denominator. Percentages do not always add to 100% due to rounding.
Sources: Adapted from Sirois (1973) and Boss (1997).

studies in Malaysia in Phoon, 1982, and the June Bug Epidemic described below, which affected only whites). Other studies show transmission through friends or social networks (as in the June Bug epidemic and 19 other separate case studies reviewed by Wessely in 1987). Social transmission is difficult to demonstrate after the epidemic is over, and it is likely that many of these case studies do not report it because the authors do not have sufficient documentation.

Many of the epidemics summarized in Table 20.1 have been reviewed by Wessely (1987). His definition excludes the strictly delusional epidemic, and he divides the remainder into two types: "mass anxiety hysteria," where the symptoms are forms of anxiety such as fear or panic, chest pain or palpitations, shortness of breath or hyperventilation, dizziness, nausea, and headaches; and "mass motor hysteria," where the symptoms involve dissociative or conversion behaviors such as convulsions, twitching, anesthesia, paralysis, and trances. The anxiety type spreads rapidly (often by line of sight), usually without a known index or primary case, and endures for only a few hours. It is more typical in children and adolescents. Preexisting stress is often absent. In contrast, the motor type spreads more slowly, lasts longer, occurs among adults as well as children, and preexisting stress is often present. Wessely contends, but does not show, that the group structure is necessary for the transmission of the anxiety type, whereas prior stress and the secondary gain obtained from sick role behavior are involved in the motor types. The conclusions Wessely makes about the two forms of the epidemics are intriguing, but it is difficult to make judgments about the relative absence of features, such as an index case or preexisting strain, when the review is based on published studies that may omit relevant information, and it is more difficult to gather evidence in the more volatile anxiety form of epidemics, than in the psychomotor form of epidemics.

The Seattle Windshield Pitting Epidemic

The focus of the chapter is on somatoform illnesses, but the transmission of a belief is so crucial to understanding the epidemics reviewed here that it is instructive to examine a "pure" epidemic in which transmission of delusional belief occurred with no associated signs or symptoms. An example is the episode of reports of windshield pitting that took place in Seattle (Medalia & Larsen, 1958). In March of 1954, newspapers in Seattle began carrying reports of damage about the size of a thumbnail to automobile windshields, first in cities to the north, and then gradually, by the middle of April, in Seattle itself. Newspaper coverage of the pitting peaked on April 15 (Figure 20.1), with more than 200 inches of newspaper columns on this topic in one day's edition of two newspapers. On April 14 and 15, there were 242 calls to the Police Department about pitting marks in windshields. Postulated causes for the pitting were diverse, including such possibilities as vandalism, ordinary road wear, industrial air pollution, hysterical beliefs, meteor dust, cosmic rays, sand fleas hatching in the windshield glass, and a recent atomic test conducted on a remote island in the Pacific Ocean. On April 15, the mayor of Seattle made an emergency appeal to the Governor and to President Eisenhower for help. In his appeal, the mayor referred to the atomic tests as a possible cause, and this eventually came to be accepted by more people as the cause than any other.

A telephone survey revealed that about one-fourth of the population of Seattle were skeptical that the pitting was anything other than ordinary road damage, and about one-fourth were undecided (Medalia & Larsen, 1958). Fifty percent believed that unusual damage was caused by a physical agent, and of these, one-third attributed the cause to the atomic test. Believers were distributed equally among males and females, but males were more likely to report actually having observed windshield pitting damage (8% of men vs. 3% of women). Believers were distributed equally across the range of adult ages.

The epidemic was over by April 19 (Figure 20.1), and a puzzle for the researchers was its relatively quick extinction. They discounted the possibility that the epidemic extinguished as a result of a developing counternorm, such as a belief that it was all due to hysterical delusions. They postulated that the dominant belief system—the atomic test—included the notion of transitory effect and actually resolved latent anxieties about the effects of the test, suggesting that its effects were consummated and exhausted by the windshield pitting. The survey showed that even though *interest* in the windshield pitting declined, the *belief* in it remained stable. One of Medalia and Larsen's conclusions is as follows: "Acute outbursts of mass delusion are not necessarily self-limiting. Interest and belief in a phenomenon for which no scientific basis can be found may well persist for periods of time even in a culture presumably committed to science as the ultimate test of reality" (p. 185). This conclusion sets the foundation for the importance of the transmission of a belief as the principal agent in the epidemics.

Anxiety in Harbor City Elementary School

An example of the anxiety epidemic is the occurrence at Harbor City Elementary School in California in 1993 (Small, Feinberg, Steinberg, & Collins, 1994). About 10 minutes after morning classes had begun, 10 of the 680 students in the school complained of nausea, thought to originate from odors (not too uncommon) associated with a nearby petroleum refinery. The school officials called the fire department, which arrived in a car and two fire

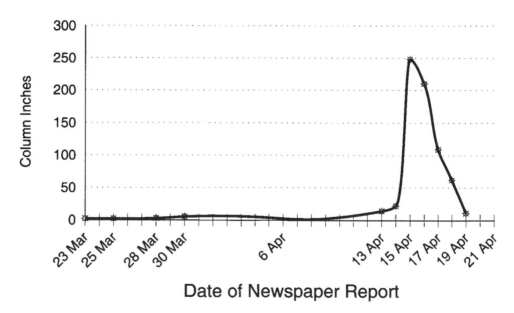

Figure 20.1. Seattle Windshield Pitting Epidemic newspaper coverage (Source: Adapted from Medalia and Larsen, 1958).

trucks, parking them in front of the school. A large yellow tarp was spread out to establish a makeshift treatment area. A few minutes later, the school was evacuated, by which time six to eight ambulances and emergency vehicles were in the parking lot, and the 10 students were being treated on the yellow tarp in front of the entire student body. School officials then approached each classroom and asked if anyone had experienced any symptoms, and children began walking over to the yellow tarp area. Sixty-six students and seven adults were ultimately taken to local hospitals, where laboratory blood tests revealed nothing abnormal. All the children and six of the seven adults were released that day, and school resumed the following day without incident. In a survey conducted shortly after the incident, 77% of the students reported one or more symptoms, including headache (57%), nausea (52%), dizziness (51%), abdominal pain (51%), and other symptoms (less than 30%).

The Harbor City occurrence is similar to many other epidemics of the anxiety form. These are often precipitated by odors (Alexander & Fedoruk, 1986; Araki & Honma, 1986; Bell & Jones, 1958; Boxer, Singal, & Hartle, 1984; Cole, Chorba, & Horan, 1990; Hall & Johnson, 1989; Modan et al., 1983; Selden, 1989). Skin or throat irritation often is reported along with the typical symptoms of anxiety such as fear, headache, nausea, and abdominal pain. The Harbor City example may be the largest epidemic in the literature, and the transmission completion rate of 77% is higher than in most other epidemics. In some of the epidemics, there is a detectable substance in the air at low levels, such as petroleum distillate or smog, and there are also some instances of strong and measurable, dangerous exposures, with predictable acute symptoms. But in some situations where an odor is reported, no physical source of the odor has been found despite prolonged environmental tests. In many of the epidemics, there are visual cues of emergency. In the Harbor City occurrence, the number of symptoms reported by students was greater for those falling ill after the arrival of the ambulances. A nearby school was also evacuated because of the fear that the odor might affect them, but no emergency vehicles were summoned, and no one required medical attention. In Harbor City, as in other epidemics, there are visual cues as to symptoms that might result.

The June Bug Epidemic

The classic study of somatoform epidemics is by Kerckhoff and Back (1968). In a textile and garment factory in the southern United States, 62 persons reported to the factory physician for fainting and nausea during an 11-day period in June 1962. Most people attributed the symptoms to the bite of an insect, possibly carried on new shipments of cotton that had arrived recently from abroad. The epidemic was widely reported in the press and attracted the attention of state and federal health officials. Local and national physicians, engineers, and epidemiologists tried to locate a possible cause for the symptoms in the air quality, in circulating toxins, and in infectious agents, but could come up with nothing, either through testing individuals or the factory environment. Most of the people affected were women, amounting to about 10% of the white female population of the first shift at the factory. The epidemic began mysteriously, spread quickly, and terminated in less than 2 weeks.

The work by Kerckhoff and Back (1968) shows three characteristics of these types of epidemics that were not known before: (1) the source of strain connected to the outbreak, (2) the social character of transmission, and (3) the distribution of belief about the cause. Comparison of persons reporting to the factory physician (cases) with a sample of those not reporting (controls) reveals several types of strain more prevalent in the affected group. First, cases were more likely to have been working overtime. Second, they were less likely than controls to approach their supervisor when they had a complaint about work. Third, they were more likely to notice variation in output among members of their section. Finally, there was evidence of family responsibilities that conflicted with, or added to, the pressure of work at the factory: Cases were more likely than controls to be the sole or major bread-winners in the home, and more likely to have a small child. The existence of prior stress or strain is not universal in the somatoform or anxiety epidemics but has been uncovered numerous times (7 of 28 case studies of anxiety epidemics, and 23 of 24 case studies of mass motor hysteria in Wessely's 1987 review).

Once it started, the June Bug Epidemic spread through sociometric networks. During the beginning of the epidemic, six women fell ill, of whom five were considered to be isolates from the results of a sociometric questionnaire (see Table 20.2: 83% of six cases in takeoff period). The first woman to be affected had fainted five times in the last few years. Another in this early group had been seeing a doctor for nervousness. Yet another in this group of six cases during the takeoff period felt her body "swelling like a balloon," and a fourth felt a "crawling sensation" on her thigh. Thus, in this takeoff phase, the individuals were marginal to any group structure, and the symptoms did not conform to any common type. When the epidemic began to spread more rapidly (Day 1 and Day 2 in Table 20.2), the spread was through individuals who knew one another. Affected persons were more likely to choose as friends, and to be chosen by, other affected persons. There were 83 individuals who chose cases as friends, but the tendency to choose Day 1 cases (61% of 41 choices of cases in Table 20.2) was stronger than the tendency to choose takeoff period cases (46% of 11 choices of cases in Table 20.2). The tendency for cases to choose other cases was stronger in Days 1 and 2 than during the takeoff or resolution periods (e.g., 61% of 41 choices made by Day 1 cases were of other cases, compared to 20% of 5 resolution period cases chosen by cases).

There was a good deal of heterogeneity of belief as to the cause of the June Bug epidemic. Those affected were more likely to believe the cause to be an insect (63% believed the cause was "definitely an insect"), even though some cases (37%) felt it was not an insect, and some controls (27%) believed that it was an insect. The degree of reaction and the group structure, are related independently to belief in the insect. For instance, the stronger the reaction, the more probable that the insect was blamed (76% of cases who reported to the medical clinic believed in the insect compared to 50% of cases who did not report). But even among controls, in groups where many were affected ("linked control"), workers were more likely to attribute the symptoms to the insect (44% of "linked controls" believed the cause was "definitely an insect" vs. 19% of the "not-linked controls").

RELEVANT THEORIES OF COLLECTIVE BEHAVIOR

Collective behavior in sociological terms is defined as *coordinated interaction that does not arise from preexisting norms or institutions* (Goode, 1992; Smelser, 1962; Turner & Killian, 1972). "Coordinated interaction" fits the definition of the group given earlier, so another definition of collective behavior might be *the formation of one or more new groups.* In sociology, it has typically included study of all types of new behaviors such as fads and fashions; crowd behaviors such as riots, panics, and lynchings; and social movements that

TABLE 20.2. June Bug Epidemic: Friendship Status by Time

Friendship status of cases	Period of occurrence for cases Percentages (n)			
	Takeoff period	Day 1	Day 2	Resolution period
Isolated (n = 56 cases)	83 (6)	21 (24)	23 (22)	25 (4)
Choosing cases (n = 83 choices)	46 (11)	61 (41)	54 (28)	33 (3)
Chosen by cases (n = 78 choices)	0 (2)	61 (41)	67 (30)	20 (5)

Sources: Adapted from Kerckhoff and Back (1968, p. 113). The *n*'s for the second and third rows are the total choices made by the entire sample (Row 2), and the choices by cases (Row 3).

aim to change the values or social structure of society. The area is thought to be crucial to sociology because it involves the basic processes of social change. Theories of collective behavior are relevant to explaining how mental disorders may be socially transmitted (Eaton, 1986).

Strain

Why does collective behavior occur? Explanations have focused on different levels of the social structure. At one level, there are *strain/stress* theories based on the placement of the individual in a macrosocial situation of structural strain or a microsocial situation of social stress. Strain produced at the level of society, such as economic fluctuations, can produce frustrations in individuals that contribute to formation of collective behavior. For example, Dollard, Doob, Miller, Mowrer, and Sears (1939) found a correlation between economic crises and lynchings of blacks in the South. Smelser (1962) defined *strain* as ambiguity as to the adequacy of means to a given goal, conflict over the allotment of rewards, or disagreement over norms and values. Social-psychological situations involving demands that the individual cannot meet, or life event stressors that overwhelm the individual's ability to cope, also may predispose that individual to engage in collective behavior.

The shape that the collective behavior takes is influenced by what Smelser called the *generalized belief*, that is, a myth or ideology that identifies the source of the strain and prescribes action to alleviate it. The generalized belief is not always accurate or realistic, and often it is semimagical in character, involving a very abstract line of reasoning or values, followed by a very concrete plan of action. The generalized belief arises in response to a situation of strain of some sort, and it "identifies the source of the strain, attributes certain characteristics to this source, and specifies certain responses to the strain as possible or appropriate" (Smelser, cited in Gehlen, 1977, p. 16). Five types of generalized belief were defined, each leading to a different type of social movement: (1) The hysterical belief involves anxiety and the resultant collective behavior is a panic or flight; (2) the wish-fulfillment type of generalized belief leads to a craze or fad; (3) the hostile belief produces scapegoating; (4) the norm-oriented belief generates normative social movement; and (5) the value-oriented belief leads to value-oriented social movement. The acute somatoform epidemics would appear to involve either the hysterical belief or the wish-fulfillment belief. But, as Gehlen notes, the epidemics of acute somatoform illnesses do not always involve simple approach (as in a craze or fad), or flight (as in a panic).

Structure

Another type of explanation for the occurrence of collective behavior is *transmission structure*: the communication networks available in the social system that enhance or impede transmission of information related to the collective behavior. Transmission structure includes the modality, such as person-to-person communication by written word, telephone, e-mail, or face to face; visibility of communication structure, such as in institutional settings where many individuals are in a large room together; and varieties of mass electronic communication such as newspaper, radio, television, and broadcast e-mail or chat room. Current developments in electronic networking have vastly enhanced the transmission structure of the entire world.

The strain/stress theories focus on the location of the individual in the group structure but do not require the existence of a group in producing the collective behavior. This perspective fits the broad definition of "collective" defined earlier, being an example of convergence. A sole source epidemic could be based on stress or strain but appears similar to a person-to-person epidemic, unless the analysis includes the temporal and interpersonal aspect. In contrast, the transmission structure is likely to be defined by the way individuals interact, and thus, by definition, characterizes a group quality.

Contagion

A third explanation for collective behaviors—*the contagion theory*—builds upon the mental characteristics of the group (i.e., group awareness as opposed to the interactive characteristics). This theory was popularized by the work of Gustave LeBon (1896/1960), who emphasized the irrational nature of crowds. There was considerable interest in hypnosis in his time, and he felt that individuals in crowds could be hypnotized and manipulated by the crowd leader. Individuals in the crowd acquired a sense of invincibility due to the masses of people with whom they identified. There was a sense of anonymity in the crowd situation, which lowered the feeling of individual responsibility for actions in which the crowd might engage. LeBon postulated that the crowd situation worked to release unconscious and irrational forces in the individual. In the contagion theory, the crowd is perceived to be homogeneous and emotional.

Emergent Norm

A fourth explanation for the occurrence of collective behavior is the *emergent norm theory* of Turner and Killian (1972). They observe that a crowd can appear to be homogeneous due to the collective actions of a minority, even when there is considerable heterogeneity. In a problematic situation where institutionalized norms do not prescribe accepted ways of acting, the perception of homogeneity by crowd members can contribute to development of unusual crowd behavior. A few members of the group may begin to respond to the problematic situation in such a way that the other members feel the response is accepted by the entire group. Each member evaluates his or her initial reactions in part by deciding whether the group approves. The inference of group approval—whether correct or not—contributes to the emergence of a normative response.

The emergent norm approach does not rely on any irrational or unconscious mechanisms in explaining collective behavior, even in its most extreme forms. It does not predict that the crowd will be homogeneous, as does contagion theory. Instead, it reflects the notion of anonymity in crowds, emphasizing that the individual assesses the likely approval or disapproval of others before acting. As with the contagion theory, however, and distinct from the concepts of strain or transmission structure, the emergent norm approach invokes the concept of group at the mental level; that is, individuals are understanding their current situation through their awareness of the group.

RELEVANT SOCIAL-PSYCHOLOGICAL PROCESSES

Emotional Contagion

Social psychology is the study of small groups. It is relevant to the genesis of collective behavior in general, and to somatoform epidemics in particular. One line of research has shown that humans have the instinctive ability to comprehend emotions in others. This facility extends backward in the mammalian order, as studied in the nineteenth century by Darwin, among others. In primates, the capacity or instinct for emotional and motor mimicry is expressed naturally throughout life. Primates instinctively understand the basic emotional content of facial expressions, for example (Brothers, 1989), and responses are so quick and automatic they must be measured through film in microseconds. Imitation of physical gestures is instinctive and is probably a primitive form of empathy (Bavelas, Black, Lemery, & Mullett, 1987). Emotional contagion presumably enhances survival by communicating danger linked to emotional reactions in others, and, in the infant, facilitating learning from others (Cappella, 1991; Hatfield, Cacioppo, & Rapson, 1994).

Hypnosis

A second line of research concerns the phenomenon of hypnosis. The modern study of hypnosis is about 200 years old, beginning with Mesmer's work in France (Ellenberger, 1970). Mesmer discovered that a certain situation could be created that often had bizarre effects on some people. First, a volunteer agreed to be placed under the hypnotist's influence (called the *hypnotic contract* by Hilgard, [1977]). Then the hypnotist would gradually shift the subject's attention away from normal roles and everyday matters to concentrate solely on the passive role of hypnotic subject (Hilgard's *relinquishment of initiative*). Finally, the hypnotist asks the subject to perform certain unusual behaviors (demonstrating that the *monitoring function is concealed* or reduced, in the language of Hilgard). These behaviors might be very bizarre, such as crowing like a rooster or barking like a dog, withstanding extreme pain, instantly falling asleep or waking up, and so forth.

In the nineteenth century the study of hypnosis was linked to epidemics of hysteria (Ellenberger, 1970). Hysteria is a name formerly applied to a disorder thought to originate in the uterus and common only in females. The symptoms of hysteria were divided into the dissociative type, such as trance and fugue states, amnesia, sleepwalking, and multiple personality; and the conversion type, with symptoms that are more physical in nature, such as uncontrollable fainting, vomiting, coughing, or headaches. In conversion hysteria, which is most similar to somatoform epidemics, Charcot demonstrated that the symptoms could be precipitated by hypnosis, and Bernheim demonstrated that hysteria could often be cured by hypnosis. As early as the late seventeenth century, the famous physician and epidemiologist Sydenham stated that hysteria could "mimic all known physical diseases" (reported in Sirois, 1982).

In the last half of this century, there have been dramatic advances in understanding hypnosis (Hilgard, 1977; Sarbin & Coe, 1972). A standardized method for inducing the hypnotic state has been developed, and it has excellent test–retest reliability. The trait of hypnotic susceptibility has stability (correlation of 0.60) over more than 10 years, as high as the most stable personality traits (Morgan, Johnson, & Hilgard, 1974), and there is evidence that it is moderately heritable (h^2 of about 0.64; Morgan, 1973). The distribution of hypnotic susceptibility is bimodal, with about 5% of the population being very hypnotizable, and about 1% being so extremely hypnotizable that they are termed *hypnotic virtuosos*, or somnambulists (Hilgard, 1977, pp. 156–158).

In hypnosis, the hypnotist appears to gain control over functions usually not considered under voluntary control. The hypnotized individual successfully follows instructions to become fatigued or sleepy, withstand extreme pain or create its experience, forget something or remember something that did not happen, feel nauseous or faint, exert him- or herself far beyond normal capacity, become deaf, and so forth. All the complaints, behaviors, signs, and symptoms discussed in this chapter have been shown in credible scientific studies to be either eliminated or strongly reduced by hypnosis, produced via hypnotic suggestion, or both. Many of the behaviors produced or influenced by hypnosis could be construed as being under voluntary control or, at least, affected by the threshold of reporting during measurement, which might be lowered due to the demand characteristics of the hypnotic situation. But there are also incontrovertible examples of blind studies concerning so-called "objective" signs, such as allergic skin reaction (Black, Humphrey, & Niven, 1963), hypersensitivity response (Smith & McDaniel, 1983), respiratory airway resistance (Kotses, Rawson, Wigal, & Creer, 1987) and warts (Spanos, Stenstrom, & Johnston, 1988; Spanos, Williams, & Gwynn, 1990).

Hypnosis appears to work through a combination of concentration of attention with two very strong human impulses: to imitate, and to plan. Imitation is a facility even very young infants possess, and the internal symbolic representation of another's gesture is enough to stimulate the imitative impulse. The classic, commonplace example of the imitative impulse at work is the after-dinner yawn. William James described a similar idea in his discussion of the ideomotor control of action: "Every representation of a movement awakens in some degree the actual movement which is its object; and awakens it in a maximum degree whenever it is not kept from so doing by an antagonistic representation present simultaneously to the mind" (cited in Hilgard, 1977). Imitation is not always conscious, as occurs in "body English" among those watching an athletic contest. Miller, Galanter, and Pribram (1960) felt that, in hypnosis, the planning function was taken over by the hypnotist. Planning takes place via the creation of a cognitive structure that involves a commitment to action in the future. There appears to be a reluctance to relinquish the plan once it has been created (Miller et al., 1960). An example of a cognitive structure for planning is a role (Sarbin & Allen, 1968).

The situation of imitation and rule following—or the more general concept of suggestion—is not limited to the original hypnotic state, with the hypnotist swinging a watch in front of a subject in a quiet room. It does not require the suggestion or experience of relaxation, for example (Hilgard, 1977, p. 165). It is in most ways indistinguishable from the role of experimental subject (Milgram, 1965; Orne, 1959; Sarbin, 1967). It has many similarities to various situations of persuasive influence, including the relative prestige of

the hypnotist and subject (Myers, 1993, pp. 265–282), and the gradual shaping of requirements from general and innocuous to specific and more difficult (Eaton, 1986, pp. 68–74).
Discussing extremely hypnotizable subjects, Hilgard noted that many

> are so talented in hypnotic performance that they gain what appears to be essentially hypnotic
> control through the exercise of imagination in circumstances of life in the real world where they
> are unconcerned about a definition of hypnosis: in riding a bicycle uphill, in distance swim-
> ming, in surgery without anesthetics. Have they then engaged in self-hypnosis? This is a ques-
> tion to be pondered and studied, not to be decided a priori. (Hilgard, 1977, p. 182)

Ruch (1975) conducted studies that led him to believe that the hypnotist is only an assistant
in the process—that, in effect, the individual hypnotizes himself.

Group Effects

Social-psychological research into the effects of groups is also relevant to the process of
social contagion. Sherif's (1937) studies of the autokinetic phenomenon showed that in the
presence of uncertainty, individuals will create and shape a belief structure through group
process, much in line with the emergent norm theory of collective behavior. Asch (1955)
showed the effects of *group conformity* on even such simple and straightforward perceptions as the length of a line. A large percentage of the subjects, answering at the end of the
sequence of reports by bogus confederates, reported comparisons that were distinctly against
their initial perceptions. Studies of the *audience effect* showed that performance of certain
tasks (such as bicycling or the tedious pursuit-rotor task) was facilitated by the audience.
Later results seemed to be contradictory at first, because performance of other types of
tasks involving learning was poorer in the presence of others. Gradually, researchers became aware that the results were not contradictory, because acquired responses were always facilitated by the audience and nonacquired responses (such as in a learning task)
were inhibited. Zajonc (1965) generalized the effect by noting that in the performance of
an acquired responses, the individuals's dominant tendency is the correct one, whereas, in
the performance of a learning task, the dominant tendency is usually *in*correct. Thus, he
concluded that the audience enhances the emission of dominant responses. The audience
effect is believed to be one of physiological arousal related to adrenocortical activity (Zajonc,
1965).

RESPONSIVE EMOTIONAL SCHEMATA IN CONVERGENCE, INITIATION, AND TRANSMISSION PHASES OF SOMATOFORM EPIDEMICS

What Is Transmitted: Responsive Emotional Schemata (RES)

In *The Selfish Gene*, Richard Dawkins (1976) claimed that the gene was definable as a unit
that replicates itself and is self-preservative. In discussing the difference between genetic
and cultural transmission, he included, almost as an aside, the notion that there might exist
ideas or cognitions that replicate themselves and are self-preservative—that is, the basic
units of cultural transmission, much as genes are the basic units of genetic transmission. He
called such ideas *memes* and stimulated an interest in what some have called the science of
memetics (Fog, 1996; Lynch, 1996). By what term should we name the unit of replication

in the transmission of somatoform behaviors, that is, the agent of transmission? It might seem at first that what is transferred is a *delusional belief*, but this idea would require the difficult proof that so-called nondelusional beliefs are different in quality. Most of our beliefs originate in social groups and are validated in a subjective, not on objective manner. For example, we easily conclude that the beliefs of the Heaven's Gate cult (e.g., transmission of the soul to a space ship after death) are delusional, even though many Hindus believe in the somewhat improbable idea of reincarnation, and Christians believe in the virgin birth and resurrection of Jesus. The point is, it is very difficult, *on the basis of the beliefs themselves*, to conclude that one thought is delusional and another is based in reality. The simple term *belief* might suffice except that it connotes a verbalizable and logical structure. Smelser (1962) used the term *generalized belief* in his study of collective behavior. The generalized belief is not necessarily logical, but it is verbalizable, as discussed earlier. Since what is transmitted cannot always be stated in words, belief is not the appropriate term.

The term *schema* is used in health psychology to denote "a hypothetical entity that readies the perceiver for perceptual experience by providing a structure for assimilating new information. . . . Illness schema will prompt the perceiver to selectively search his/her body for illness-relevant sensations" (Pennebaker, 1982, p. 142; Robbins and Kirmayer, 1991, also use this term). In the study of emotions, the term *schemata* has been used to denote memories or records of expressive/motor/emotional events (Leventhal & Mosbach, 1983). A schemata is a cluster of one or more beliefs, *and* expressive motor or emotional events that can be recorded in human memory and tend to be recalled as a unit. The term requires that there be at least some cognitive, ideational, abstract, or verbalizable element; at least some emotional element involving attraction to the memory pattern or repulsion from it; a physiological component; and (an addition to Leventhal's concept) some record of the social situation. An emotional schemata is a record in memory, but it also prepares the individual to receive information in a given form, as in a health schema.

Some or all of the elements of any given emotional schema may not be verbalizable. The notion that we can remember things that we cannot verbally express is a crucial aspect of the concept of schemata that distinguishes it from a belief. The nonverbalizable portion of memory would be called the *unconscious* in Freudian terms. Nonverbalizable memories arise in learning theory as *patterns of reinforced behavior*. The dissociation and conversion that occur in hypnosis are another example, and the fact that all of the symptoms and behaviors studied here can be brought about, or influenced by, hypnotic induction makes clear the relevance of this nonverbalizability. Experiments on the split brain show conclusively that individuals can react to complex stimuli, and create complex responses, without being able to state what they are doing in words (Gazzaniga, 1967).

In socially transmitted somatoform illness the emotional schemata in some manner or other address a puzzle or problem being experienced by one or more persons. This is the quality of the generalized belief that Smelser emphasized, saying that it "identifies the source of the strain, attributes certain characteristics to this source, and specifies certain responses to the strain as possible or appropriate" (1962). Smelser's analysis emphasizes the logical and verbalizable quality in the belief, which is too constraining in the present context. But his insight into the responsive quality of the generalized belief to a human problem was on the mark. Here we take advantage of his wisdom to add the modifier *responsive*, leading to focus on the notion of *responsive emotional schemata* (RES).

Characteristics that Facilitate Transmission

What are the characteristics of RES that make them highly transmissible, or "contagious" (Lynch, 1996)? Some characteristics have been studied in the field of communications theory under the rubric of *rumor transmission* (Rosnow, 1958). The basic two factors laid out in the 1940s that would promote the transmission of a rumor were the combination of importance of the topic and ambiguity of the current situation (Rosnow, 1958). Rosnow's experiments confirmed these notions and added the dimensions of personal anxiety and general uncertainty. That personal anxiety would promote the transmission of rumors is consistent with the notion that strain promotes collective behaviors (as discussed earlier). That general uncertainty promotes rumor transmission is consistent with the notion that epidemics begin with an unsolved problem or puzzle.

It seems clear that other dimensions are involved in promoting the transmission of a given RES. Human beings habituate quickly and pay attention to new stimuli: so, to attract attention, transmissible RESs should be new or have a new quality to them. All of the behaviors under study here have this quality of newness about them, but the newness is sometimes engendered by the precise context, or juxtaposition, and confluence of circumstances. For example, women had fainted in the weeks prior to the June Bug Epidemic, but not in the context of the possibility of insects in new shipments of cotton. To facilitate transmission, the RES should be uncomplicated. The symptoms and behaviors studied here all involve a relatively simple idea that can be explained in one sentence with a straightforward declarative structure—usually, an uncomplicated disease agent like an insect, virus, or toxin (e.g., "The bug made me faint" or "Nuclear fallout pitted my windshield"). To be reproducible, they should involve behaviors that do not have to be learned by the recipient. All of the physical symptoms of the acute somatoform epidemics are well known to the individual, in part because they are built into the human organism for various reasons related to survival. Obvious examples include the panic reaction, vomiting, nausea, and fatigue.

To be credible, the RES should link into a collection of ideas—a *paradigm*—already known to the recipient. It is also helpful to transmission if the paradigm is salient to the individual at the time that transmission is initiated. In the Seattle epidemic, the paradigm was relatively uncomplicated, in that most people understood that windshield glass could decay or be damaged in various ways. It is helpful to transmission if the paradigm has considerable power to affect outcomes in the material world. In many of these occurrences, the dominant paradigm involves health and the medical system. The simplicity of the germ theory of disease—sometimes called the "magic bullet"—is linked to its known power to affect outcomes in a wide variety of situations.

The RES will be more credible if it involves a *material substrate*, that is, a relatively unchanging aspect of the physical world that can serve as validation for the logic of belief involved in the RES. Material substrates are, in principle, visually perceptible. In the Seattle epidemic, there was a convenient, well-known place to look for the existence of the pitting (the windshield). In the somatoform epidemics, there is usually a search for a physical agent such as an insect, germ, or toxin. The RES can invoke a simple change in structure of threshold for identifying the material substrate, as occurred in the Seattle epidemic, in which attention directed to looking *at* the windshield, instead of *through* it, inevitably discovered evidence of pitting in some cars. In epidemics where a toxin is the purported cause, there are rapidly developing technologies that locate lower and lower doses of chemical agents in human beings. In principle, germs are also visible.

Three Phases of the Epidemic

It is helpful to divide acute epidemics into phases of *convergence, initiation*, and *transmission* (Figure 20.2). There appear to be group influences at work in all phases, but the nature of the group influences and the types of susceptible individuals change with each phase. In the *convergence* phase, a puzzle or problem is presented to some individuals with a group structure of some sort in a social context where certain model individuals are present. This convergence phase is probabilistic in that the convergence of model individuals in an existing group structure within a social context involving an unsolved problem requires the confluence of independently acting probabilistic processes. The prominent individuals who serve as *model*s are distinctive and can attract attention—sometimes these are popular individuals, but also at times they are social isolates (Murphy, as reported to Sirois, 1982). Wessely (1987) tabulates 34 separate studies in which an initial case was recorded, and it must be presumed that the case was missed in yet other studies due to weakness in data collection. Model individuals with disturbances or disorders in the convergence phase of the epidemic tend to be those who have engaged in the behavior many times earlier. For example, the individuals in the initiation phase might be "amplifiers" in Barsky's sense (1979), or somaticizers (Escobar & Camino, 1987; Smith, 1994). In epidemics of mass anxiety, the individuals in the convergence phase would score high on measures of trait anxiety or neuroticism. The enactments by models occur in the convergence phase, prior to the epidemic process, but they create the context for the outbreak. Figure 20.2 illustrates the responses of 15 individuals (five models, five early susceptibles, and five late susceptibles) during the three phases of the epidemic. The response structure of the models is represented by vertical bars for four potential responses—A, B, C, and D. Response B is the focus of the epidemic, that is, the response labeled as "falling ill," or the equivalent. The height of the bars shows the strength of the tendency to enact the response, and bars tipped by arrows designate the single chosen response that is enacted because it is strongest. The response structure of the five models does not change during the course of the epidemic, but the early susceptibles are more likely to fall ill during the initiation phase, and the late susceptibles are more likely to fall ill during the transmission phase.

The nature of the problem perceived by the group can be quite varied. For the June Bug epidemic, the puzzle might have been: "Why did Mrs. A and then Mrs. B faint?" Many or most individuals in the group seek a solution to the puzzle. If they locate a solution without difficulty, there are no further manifestations of group activity related to the initial problem, and it may never enter the group consciousness, being forgotten by the individuals exposed to the problem. For example, a solution in the June Bug epidemic might have been: "She faints all the time."

If individuals fail to solve the problem and the situation of uncertainty persists, they seek information of other persons in their environment, much as the individuals in Sherif's (1937) experiments on the autokinetic phenomenon and subjects in Asch's (1955) experiments on group conformity did. Other group members may be as puzzled as they are. The initial phase of the epidemic has features that suggest it is a *catastrophe* or *cusp*, that is, a stage of chaos where an eventual large outcome is delicately balanced on a few volatile variables (called the catastrophe aspect of *divergence*, or *the butterfly effect*; see Zeeman

[1976]). The group structure itself may contribute to a general arousal, as in the audience effect, and processes of emotional contagion may produce rapid and volatile developments where members of the group are visible to each other. The arousal engendered by the audience effect will push the group solution to include an emotional aspect, that is, a cognitive label and explanation for physiological arousal, as in the Schachter's theory of emotion (Reisenzein, 1983; Schachter & Singer, 1962). The volatile aspect is that there is no obvious dominant response, and the solution will arise from the rapid and unpredictable workings of the imagination of a limited number of individuals aiming to solve the puzzle. Eventually a cluster of activities, feelings, and cognitions is assembled—perhaps due to a single human performance in the public sphere, or a series of them, which is credible and transmissible—the RES. This stage may involve several experiments with solutions that are evaluated and rejected by the group, as occurred in the June Bug Epidemic.

In the *initiation* phase, many individuals will become aroused to the presence of a problem, and they will be attempting to estimate the group's approval of the models' behavior. The behavior enacted by the models is an existing and perhaps even dominant response tendency in many stress-reactive individuals, but it is inhibited by fear of disapproval, or lack of relevance to the current situation. The level of stress raises the need for an enactment of some sort, lowers inhibitions on performance, and raises the relevance of the given response to the current situation. The estimate that the response is appropriate, even if for any given individual it is *just barely* the dominant one among many alternatives, leads to enactment by a visible minority of the group. Enactment by a visible minority can occur even if the estimate of the group's approval of the models' behavior is made by only a fraction of those with this response tendency. Enactment of the dominant response under conditions of arousal is consistent with the social facilitation effect.

The percentage of the group that is susceptible to initial enactments will depend on the precise nature of the behaviors and the situation, but it may be as high as 25% of the general population. The susceptibles in this part of the population may be under identifiable stress from a variety of sources. When the social context and the availability of individual performances in the population in that social context match, the RES emerges briefly. It must be presumed that most nascent epidemics die out because no credible RES emerges or survives the group evaluation. For example, a credible and correctable cause of an odor or fume may come to be understood by the group before any deviant or bizarre behaviors are extended beyond one or two, or a small handful of individuals.

In the *transmission* phase, the group problem or puzzle persists, attracting focused attention, but now the RES is sufficiently credible that enacted behaviors are replicated in individuals to whom the behavior is new. There are temporarily strong pressures of conformity to the emerging RES, which is increasingly unconnected to an individual's own prior judgments of the situation, as in the Asch conformity experiments. At this point, the type of individuals who engage in the behavior changes from those predisposed toward the initial symptom production as highly (convergence phase) or barely (initiation phase) dominant response, to those predisposed to suggestibility, whose production of this particular type of symptom or response may be quite uncharacteristic and baffling to themselves and others, much as hypnotic performances are sometimes baffling to the hypnotized individual. In fact, the performance may be out of verbalizable awareness, as occurs in hypnosis. The resolution may, or may not be, logical, or verbalizable, as when participants, looking back, think "I don't know what came over me," "My mind went blank," and so forth. In many short-term small-group epidemics, the transition from initiation to transmission phase occurs apparently as soon as the third, fourth, or fifth performance of the same behavior. In this phase of the epidemic, any new information that resolves or explains the puzzle or problem may end the epidemic. In the situation of mass anxiety, the resolution occurs because the source of the fear is eliminated. In the Seattle Windshield epidemic, the dominant explanation for the delusion had the notion of impermanence built in: a cloud that passed with the weather pattern.

In the transmission phase, a situation similar to that of hypnotic induction is produced (Elkins, Camino, & Rynearson, 1988; Haberman, 1986). The situation includes the following: The individual has entered a social context voluntarily; attention is highly focused on one aspect of the social context; initially ambiguous demands have been gradually shaped into specific responses that the individual is capable of producing; and social constraints toward producing the responses have been lowered (Eaton, 1986). The effect is to change the individual's typical symptom attribution style (Robbins & Kirmayer, 1991), to change the threshold at which the material substrate is observed, or, to change the degree of attention that is focused on a particular aspect of the body. As much as 5% of the general population are highly suggestible, as shown by research into hypnotizability. The suggestible susceptible 5% are not necessarily highly overlapped with the approximately 25% stress-reactive susceptibles in the initiation phase. The designation "epidemic" may occur even with a very low transmission completion rate, that is, even when only a fraction of the proportion who are susceptible actually do respond with an enactment.

The proportion enacting the behavior or voicing the complaint grows from the convergence through the transmission phase. In a hypothetical population of 15 individuals in Figure 20.2, it grows from 4/15 to 6/15 to 9/15. But the three numerators are composed of different proportions of models, early (stress-reactive) susceptibles, and late (suggestible) susceptibles: 75% of the numerator are models in the convergence phase, versus 50% models and 50% stress reactive in the initiation phase, versus 33% models, 33% stress reactive, and 33% suggestibles in the transmission phase (Figure 20.2).

Medicine and Malingering

The medical system is implicated in the initiation and transmission phases of the epidemics. Medical diagnoses provide potent and salient RESs that benefit from powerful paradigms. They provide a readily available and inexhaustible material substrate that can be searched for agents. The efforts of the public health paradigm in the past have been to increase the structural conduciveness in the system, in order to prevent outbreaks. For example, laws require notification of partners in sexually transmitted diseases. But these efforts to communicate may not be helpful in the situation of somatoform epidemics, because they reinforce the RES and validate the emerging self of participants in the epidemic.

Malingering is the conscious imitation of symptoms of an illness, and *secondary gain* refers to the advantages that accrue to an ill individual because of the characteristics of the sick role. There are documented instances of malingering in some of these epidemics, such as the individual who, in a follow-up study years later, reported:

> I feel I must be honest. Though the illness apparently lasted for over three months in my case, I had actually recovered quickly but prolonged my stay in hospital by "cooking" a pyrexia [high fever] with cigarettes and hot water bottles. I can only explain it as a love of the attention I was receiving and a slight apprehension at going back into the outside world after such a long period of security. I have always been very sorry about doing this but have never told anyone before (McEvedy & Beard, 1973, p. 147).

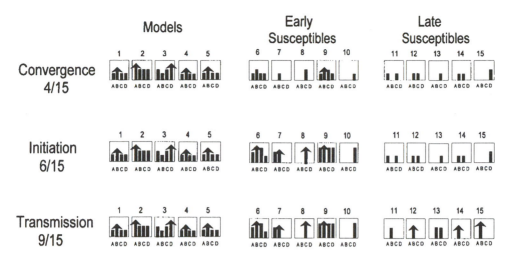

FIGURE 20.2. Social transmission in somatoform epidemics: strength of response alternatives for 15 individuals at three stages of the epidemic.

This is an isolated example, but it suggests that the epidemics sometimes include frank malingerers. However, the presence of malingering and secondary gain are characteristic of all diseases whose symptoms can be credibly imitated. The notions proposed earlier to describe and explain the epidemics do not use the notion of secondary gain, or malingering. In most individuals, and in most epidemics, the possibility of secondary gain certainly exists but is contradicted by the available evidence, which shows considerable loss in prestige, happiness, and social support in those who are ill.

CONCLUSION

There is considerable breadth to the symptomatic picture of epidemics reviewed here, but with many similarities in the underlying social processes. The symptomatology seems at first to be abnormal or bizarre, but the underlying social processes are quite general. What is distinctive is the unusual social context that occasionally comes into being through the convergence of diverse circumstances, including cultural and institutional histories, lifetime experiences of individuals, and the probabilistic formation of individuals into social gatherings, which then, rarely, acquires a history and importance belied by their almost accidental origins. The nature of the social process is more important than any other contributing cause to these phenomena. But it is also the most problematic to study, because the nature of the causal phenomena are temporary and evanescent, especially as compared to causal phenomena from other disciplines, which tend to have more permanence.

ACKNOWLEDGMENTS: This chapter was prepared while I was supported on sabbatical from the School of Hygiene and Public Health of the Johns Hopkins University. The environment provided by the Oregon Social Learning Center was a great help in its preparation. The chapter has benefited from the comments of Carol Aneshensel, Jo Phelan, and Simon Wessely.

REFERENCES

Alexander, R. W., & Fedoruk, M. J. (1986). Epidemic psychogenic illness in a telephone operators' building. *Journal of Occupational Medicine, 28*(1), 42–45.

Araki, S., & Honma, T. (1986). Mass psychogenic systemic illness in school children in relation to the Tokyo Photochemical Smog. *Archives of Environmental Medicine, 41*(3), 159–162.

Asch, S. E. (1955, November). Opinions and social pressure. *Scientific American, 20,* 31–35.

Bandura, A. (1977). *Social learning theory.* Englewood Cliffs, NJ: Prentice Hall.

Barsky, A. J. 1979. Patients who amplify bodily sensations. *Annals of Internal Medicine* 91: 63-70.

Bartholomew, R. E. (1994). Disease, disorder, or deception? Latah as habit in a Malay extended family. *Journal of Nervous and Mental Disease, 182,* 331–338.

Bavelas, J. B., Black, A., Lemery, C. R., & Mullett, J. (1987). Motor mimicry as primitive empathy. In N. Eisenberg, & J. Strayer (Eds.), *Empathy and its development* (pp. 317–338). New York: Cambridge University Press.

Bell, A., & Jones, A. T. (1958, August 23). Fumigation with dichlorethyl ether and chordane: Hysterical sequalae. *Medical Journal of Australia,* pp. 258–263.

Black, S., J., Humphrey, J. H., & Niven, J. S. F. (1963). Inhibition of Mantoux reaction by direct suggestion under hypnosis. *British Medical Journal, 6,* 1649–1652.

Boss, L. (1997). Epidemic hysteria: A review of the published literature. *Epidemiologic Reviews, 19,* 233–243.

Boxer, P. A. (1985). Occupational mass psychogenic illness: history, prevention, and management. *Journal of Occupational Medicine, 27*(12), 867–872.

Boxer, P. A., Singal, M., & Hartle, R. W. (1984). An epidemic of psychogenic illness in an electronics plant. *Journal of Occupational Medicine, 26*(5), 381–385.

Brothers, L. (1989). A biological perspective on empathy. *American Journal of Psychiatry, 146,* 10–19.

Cappella, J. N. (1991). The biological origins of automated patterns of human interaction. *Communication Theory, 1,* 4–35.

Cole, T. B., Chorba, T. L., & Horan, J. M. (1990). Patterns of transmission of epidemic hysteria in a school. *Epidemiology, 1*(3), 212–218.

Colligan, M. J., & Murphy, L. R. (1979). Mass psychogenic illness in organizations: An overview. *Journal of Occupational Psychology, 52,* 77–90.

Colligan, M. J., Pennebaker, J. W., & Murphy, L. R. (Eds.). (1982). Mass psychogenic illness: A social psychological analysis. Hillsdale, NJ: Erlbaum.

Dawkins, R. (1976). *The selfish gene.* Oxford, UK: Oxford University Press.

Dollard, J. L., Doob, N. E., Miller, N. E., Mowrer, O. H., & Sears, P. R. (1939). *Frustration and aggression.* New Haven, CT: Yale University Press.

Durkheim, E. (1966). *Suicide: A study in sociology.* New York: Free Press.

Eaton, W. W. (1986). *The sociology of mental disorders* (2nd ed.). New York: Praeger.

Elkins, G. R., Gamino, L. A., & Rynearson, R. R. (1988). Mass psychogenic illness, trance states, and suggestion. *American Journal of Clinical Hypnosis, 30*(4), 267–275.

Ellenberger, H. F. (1970). *The discovery of the unconscious.* New York: Basic Books.

Escobar, J. I., & Canino, G. (1989). Unexplained physical complaints: Psychopathology and epidemiological correlates. *British Journal of Psychiatry, 154,* 24–27.

Fog, A. (1996). *Cultural selection.* Copenhagen: Author.

Gazzaniga, M. S. (1967). The split brain in man. *Scientific American, 217,* 24–29.

Gehlen, F. L. (1977). Toward a revised theory of hysterical contagion. *Journal of Health and Social Behavior, 18,* 27–35.

Goode, E. (1992). *Collective behavior.* Fort Worth, TX: Harcourt Brace Jovanovich.

Grosser, D., Polansky, N., & Lippitt, R. A. (1951). A laboratory study of behavioral contagion. *Human Relations, 4,* 115–142.

Gruenberg, E. M. (1957). Socially shared psychopathology. In A. H. Leighton, J. A. Clausen, & R. A. Wilson (Eds.), *Explorations in social psychiatry.* New York: Basic Books.

Haberman, H. A. (1986). Spontaneous trance as a possible cause for persistent symptoms in the medically ill. *American Journal of Clinical Hypnosis, 29,* 171–176.

Hall, E. M., & Johnson, J. V. (1989). A case study of stress and mall psychogenic illness in industrial workers. *Journal of Occupational Medicine, 31*(3), 243–250.

Hatfield, E., Cacioppo, J. T., & Rapson, R. L. (1994). *Emotional contagion.* Cambridge, UK: Cambridge University Press.

Hecker, J. F. C. (1859). *The epidemics of the Middle Ages* (3rd ed.). London: Trubner.

Hilgard, E. R. (1977). *Divided consciousness: Multiple controls in human thought and action.* New York: Wiley.

Kerckhoff, A. C., & Back, K. W. (1968). *The June Bug: A study of hysterical contagion.* New York: Appleton–Century–Crofts.

Kotses, H., Rawson, J. C. Wigal, J. K., & Creer, T. L. (1987). Respiratory airway changes in response to suggestion in normal individuals. *Psychosomatic Medicine, 49,* 536–541.

LeBon, G. (1960). *The crowd: A study of the popular mind.* New York: Viking Press. (Original published 1896)

Leventhal, H., & Mosbach, P. A. (1983). The perceptual–motor theory of emotion. In J. T. Cacioppo & R. E. Petty (Eds.), *Social psychophysiology: A sourcebook* (pp. 353–388). New York: Guilford.

Lynch, A. (1996). *Thought contagion: How belief spreads through society, the new science of memes.* New York: Basic Books.

Mackay, C. (1852). *Extraordinary popular delusions.* Boston: Page.

Markush, R. E. (1973). Mental epidemics: A review of the old to prepare for the new. *Public Health Reviews, 2*(4), 353–442.

Milgram, S. (1965). Some conditions of obedience and disobedience to authority. *Human Relations, 18,* 57–76.

McEvedy, C. P, & Beard, A. W. (1973). A controlled follow-up of cases involved in an epidemic of benign myalgic encephalomyelitis. *British Journal of Psychiatry, 122,* 141–150.

Medalia, N. Z., & Larsen, O. N. (1958). Diffusion and belief in a collective delusion: The Seattle Windshield Pitting Epidemic. *American Sociological Review, 23,* 180–186.

Miller, G. A., Galanter, E., & Pribram, K. H. (1960). *Plans and the structure of behavior.* New York: Holt, Rinehart & Winston.

Modan, B., Tirosh, M., Weissenberg, E., Acker, C., Swartz, T. A., Costin, C., Donagi, A., Revach, M., & Vettorazzi, G. (1983, December). The Arjenyattah Epidemic: A mass phenomenon: Spread and triggering factors. *Lancet,* pp. 1472–1474.

Morgan, A. H. (1973). The heritability of hypnotic susceptibility in twins. *Journal of Abnormal Psychology, 82,* 55–61.

Morgan, A. H., Johnson, D. L., & Hilgard, E. R. (1974). The stability of hypnotic susceptibility: A longitudinal study. *International Journal of Clinical and Experimental Hypnosis, 22,* 249–257.

Myers, D. G. (1993). *Social psychology* (4th ed.). New York: McGraw-Hill.

Orne, M. T. (1959). The nature of hypnosis: Artifact and essence. *Journal of Abnormal and Social Psychology, 58,* 277–299.

Pennebaker, J. W. (1982). Social and perceptual factors affecting symptom reporting and mass psychogenic illness. In M. J. Colligan, J. W. Pennebaker, & L, R. Murphy (Eds.), *Mass psychogenic illness: A social psychological analysis* (pp. 139–154). Hillsdale, NJ: Erlbaum.

Phoon, W. H. (1982). Outbreaks of Mass Hysteria at Workplaces in Singapore: some patterns and modes of presentation. In M. J. Colligan, J. W. Pennebaker, & L, R. Murphy (Eds.), *Mass psychogenic illness: A social psychological analysis* (pp. 21–32). Hillsdale, NJ: Erlbaum.

Reisenzein, R. (1983). The Schachter theory of emotion: two decades later. *Psychological Bulletin, 94,* 239–264.

Robbins, J. M., & Kirmayer, L. J. (1991). Attributions of common somatic symptoms. *Psychological Medicine, 21,* 1029–1045.

Rosnow, R. L. (1958). Rumor as communication: a contextual approach. *Journal of Communication, 38,* 12–28.

Ruch, J. C. (1975). Self-hypnosis: the result of heterohypnosis or vice versa. *International Journal of Clinical and Experimental Hypnosis, 23,* 282–304.

Sarbin, T. R. (1967). Hypnosis as role enactment. In J. E. Gordon (Ed.), *Handbook of clinical and experimental hypnosis.* New York: MacMillan.

Sarbin, T. R., & Allen, V. L. (1968). Role theory. In G. Lindzey & E. Aronson (Eds.), *Handbook of social psychology* (2nd ed.). Reading, MA: Addison-Wesley.

Sarbin, T. R., & Coe, W. C. (1972). *Hypnosis: A social psychological analysis of influence communication.* New York: Holt, Rinehart & Winston.

Schachter, S., & Singer, J. E. (1962). Cognitive, social and physiological determinants of emotional state. *Psychological Review, 69,* 379–399.

Selden, B. S. (1989). Adolescent epidemic hysteria presenting as a mass casualty, toxic exposure incident. *Annals of Emergency Medicine, 18*(8), 892–895.

Sherif, M. (1937). An experimental approach to the study of attitudes. *Sociometry, 1,* 90–98.

Showalter, E. (1997). *Hystories: Hysterical epidemics and modern culture.* New York: Columbia University Press.

Sirois, F. (1974). Epidemic hysteria. *Acta Psychiatrica Scandinavica,* Supplementum 252.

Sirois, F. (1982). Perspectives on epidemic hysteria. In M. J. Colligan, J. W. Pennebaker, & L. R. Murphy (Eds.), *Mass Psychogenic Illness: A social psychological perspective* (pp. 217–236). Hillsdale, NJ: Erlbaum.

Small, G. W., Feinberg, D. T., Steinberg, D., & Collins, M. T. (1994). A sudden outbreak of illness suggestive of mass hysteria in schoolchildren. *Archives of Family Medicine, 3,* 711–716.

Small, G. W., Propper, M. W., Randolph, E. T., & Eth, S. (1991). Mass hysteria among student performers: Social relationship as a symptom predictor. *American Journal of Psychiatry, 148*(9), 1200–1205.

Smelser, N. J. (1962). *Theory of collective behavior.* New York: Free Press.

Smith, G. R., Jr., & McDaniel, S. (1983). Psychologically mediated effect on the delayed hypersensitivity response by direct suggestion under hypnosis. *Psychosomatic Medicine, 45,* 65–69.

Smith, G. R. (1994). The course of somatization and its effects on utilization of health care resources. *Psychosomatics, 35*(3), 263–267.

Spanos, N. P., Stenstrom, R. J., & Johnston, J. C. (1988). Hypnosis, placebo, and suggestion in the treatment of warts. *Psychosomatic Medicine, 50,* 245–260.

Spanos, N. P., Williams, V., & Gwynn, M. I. (1990). Effects of hypnotic, placebo, and salicylic acid treatments on wart regression. *Psychosomatic Medicine, 52,* 109–114.

Stahl, S. M. (1982). Illness as an emergent norm, or, doing what comes naturally. In M. J. Colligan, J. W. Pennebake, & L. R. Murphy (Eds.), *Mass psychogenic illness: A social psychological perspective* (pp. 183–198). Hillsdale, NJ: Erlbaum.

Turner, R. H., & Killian, L. (1972). *Collective behavior* (2nd ed.). Englewood Cliffs, NJ: Prentice Hall.

Wessely, S. (1987). Mass hysteria: Two syndromes? *Psychological Medicine, 17,* 109–120.

Wheeler, L. (1966). Toward a theory of behavioral contagion. *Psychological Review, 73,* 179–192.

Zajonc, R. B. (1965). Social facilitation. *Science, 149,* 269–274.

Zeeman, E. C. (1976). Catastrophe theory. *Scientific American, 234,* 65–83.

PART V

Social Consequences
of Mental Illness

CHAPTER 21

The Social Dynamics
of Responding
to Mental Health Problems

Past, Present, and Future Challenges
to Understanding Individuals' Use of Services

BERNICE A. PESCOSOLIDO

CAROL A. BOYER

KERI M. LUBELL

INTRODUCTION

Since social scientists first directed their attention to understanding how individuals recognize and respond to mental illness, they have struggled to capture both the underlying process or dynamic that drives the search for care and the social, cultural, medical, and organizational characteristics that shape the fate of persons dealing with mental health problems. At the present time, the dominant approaches to studying what many people call "help seeking" or "decision making," and others more generally call "illness behavior" or "service use" focus on well-developed but essentially correlation models of the factors

BERNICE A. PESCOSOLIDO AND KERI M. LUBELL • Department of Sociology, Indiana University, Bloomington, Indiana 47405.   CAROL A. BOYER • Institute for Health, Health Care Policy, and Aging Research, Rutgers University, New Brunswick, New Jersey 08903.

Handbook of the Sociology of Mental Health, edited by Carol S. Aneshensel and Jo C. Phelan. Kluwer Academic/Plenum Publishers, New York, 1999.

associated with use, compliance and outcomes. The Health Belief Model (Strecher, Champion, & Rosenstock, 1977), the Theory of Reasoned Action and its close counterpart, the Theory of Planned Behavior (Maddux & DuCharme, 1977), and the Behavioral Model of Health Service Utilization (Aday & Awe, 1997; Andersen, 1995) share an approach of outlining a comprehensive set of factors that shape the use of both preventive and curative services. Although these models do not ignore the underlying *process* of service use, key assumptions focus primarily on the factors that facilitate or discourage entry into formal treatment (for a review, see Gochman, 1997; Pescosolido, 1991; 1992; Pescosolido & Boyer, 1999). Rarely are the dynamics of coping with health problems a part of the empirical study of illness behavior. With the dynamics *assumed*, empirical studies in this tradition collect information on the extent and volume of use, and on a wide range of factors thought to influence the behavior of those entering care and treatment.

Our approach here is less traditional as we trace the theoretical and empirical work describing the process of coping with mental illness and the patterns of using different systems of care. As the health care system is fundamentally transformed, understanding how individuals respond to mental illness, what pathways they travel, and what factors shape their trajectories requires a step backward to reevaluate what is known about service use and where further research is needed. We begin by describing two classic studies that initially invoked an "illness career" approach and by highlighting their fundamental lessons. Later, we explore the recognition of mental illness, different modes of entry into the formal system of care, the availability and use of diverse systems of care, and the patterns and pathways to care. We conclude by focusing on the Network–Episode Model that combines the strengths of previous process and contingency models of utilization. New empirical findings are drawn from past studies as well as ongoing studies of persons with serious mental illness, from samples in the general population that report mental health problems, and from others who offer their opinions on the nature and cause of mental health problems.

THE PROCESS OF RESPONDING TO MENTAL HEALTH PROBLEMS

Parsons's Illness Career and Clausen and Yarrow's Pathways to the Mental Hospital

A concern with process was fundamental in early studies of how individuals coped with illness and their use of formal medical services. The emphasis was fairly implicit in these theories and was targeted mostly at a macrosociological level. The major transition from agrarian to modern societies set the conditions for individuals to turn to relatively new forms of scientific medical care and away from older forms of folk or indigenous treatments. Influenced by industrialization, higher standards of living, and increased education, urban residents were more likely to use modern medical services. Their rural counterparts, without the benefit of changing circumstances and access to newer treatments, were likely to respond in traditional ways to medical problems within their own families or local communities. Larger social forces changed how individuals responded to illness and the availability of medical services. Though not entirely rational, individuals who became ill were assumed to want to take advantage of the specialized knowledge and technological changes associated with the rise of modern medical practice (see Pescosolido, 1992; Pescosolido & Kronenfeld, 1995). The assumptions of this analysis of the transition to using modern medi-

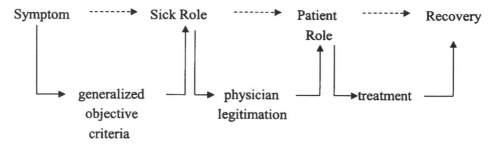

FIGURE 21.1. Diagrammatic representation of Parsons's (1951) illness career model.

cine were oversimplified, but the experience of illness and entering treatment was embedded in social life and framed as a causal, time-ordered process.

Talcott Parsons is credited with developing the first major social science schema for understanding people's behavior when they are ill. His concept of the "sick role," with accompanying rights (role release, nonresponsibility) and obligations (undesirability and help seeking), dominated social science approaches from the 1950s to the 1970s. What is less well understood about Parsons's (1951) work in *The Social System* is that embedded in it was an implicit model of an "illness career" that laid out stages and mechanisms for the transition between stages. Our visual understanding of this model is presented in Figure 21.1.

For Parsons, the illness career began with the onset of symptoms. In the first stage, which Suchman (1964) also called "the decision that something is wrong," the sick person evaluated "generalized objective criteria," weighing the severity of a problem, the prognosis, the frequency of its occurrence and normal "well-role" expectations. For Parsons, individuals would rationally and scientifically evaluate their circumstances, make a claim to those around them in the community, and proceed either to enter the sick role or return to normal roles. Upon entering the sick role, individuals would receive benefits and take on the obligations associated with the role. Because the obligation of seeking help from a competent professional (i.e., a physician) was an essential part of the sick role, individuals would proceed to make a claim to enter the patient role. At this stage, which Suchman called "the decision to seek professional advice," the "gatekeepers" are physicians who legitimate only "true" claims of illness, protecting society from "malingers" who might inappropriately seek the secondary gains of the patient role. Once in the patient role, the "decision to accept professional treatment," individuals with similar medical problems are treated equally. Once recovered, individuals reenter the world of the well, resume normal roles, and relinquish the rights and obligations of the roles associated with the illness career.

Across 20 years and hundreds of articles in the sociomedical sciences, researchers filled in the details of this model and showed where Parsons's theoretical, deductive, and logical scheme represented modern society's faith in the promise of modern medicine (e.g., see Segall, 1997; Siegler & Osmond, 1973). The sick role represented an "ideal type," not the social reality of sickness and the process of being treated. This voluminous research on the sick role yielded a large set of contingencies, or variables, for the now-dominant correlational models of health service use that shifted an emphasis from dynamic process to more static associations. Downplayed was Parsons's focus on the importance of the community as the adjudicator of the sick role. The patient role (being in treatment) was also

444 Bernice A. Pescosolido ET AL.

often confused in practice with the sick role (a shift in status granted in the lay community). Both Parsons's approach and the multidimensional contingency theories that developed from it shared a view of service use as essentially "help seeking" focused more on acute, physical illness rather than on chronic and long-term health and behavioral problems.

At about the same time, John Clausen and his colleagues at the Laboratory of Socio-Environmental Studies, within the research branch of the National Institute of Mental Health, used an inductive approach to study how people came to use formal services. Focusing on men who were hospitalized and diagnosed with psychotic disorders, they described a social process that looked substantially different from the Parsons model. In their own words, they aimed "to delineate the process whereby families adapt to mental illness and to distinguish variables in personality, culture, or in the social situations which significantly affect this process" (p. 4) (Clausen & Yarrow, 1955). Rather than a rational evaluation of psychiatric symptoms, Clausen and his colleagues described long scenarios of confusion, the use of coercion (from family and friends, as well as bosses and police), and accounts that varied from Parsons's ideal type. These researchers found that mental illness "seldom manifests itself in the guise of the popular stereotype of 'insanity' " (p. 4), and individuals struggled to understand and attach meaning to the unfolding of a serious mental illness.

Figure 21.2 depicts our understanding of Clausen and Yarrow's description of the process preceding a first hospitalization at St. Elizabeth's in Washington, D.C. The stories of the men in their study, who were white and 20–60 years old, were told by their wives. For these women, the onset of the illness was rarely clearly demarcated. After marrying, the wives noticed things that they attributed to a variety of factors unrelated to mental illness. About 6 months into their marriage, one wife noticed that her husband, a 35-year-old cab driver, had irregular work habits and complained of constant headaches. Although she occasionally thought this behavior "wasn't right," she adjusted her expectations and

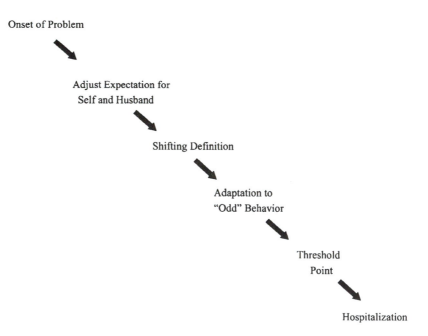

FIGURE 21.2. Diagrammatic representation of Clausen and Yarrow's (1955) process model of entry into formal care.

attributed his behavior to his personality ("a nervous person"), his past experiences ("Worrying about the war so much . . . has gotten the best of him"), and the subcultural norms of his occupation ("Most cab drivers loaf"). For the next 2 years, she shifted her definitions of their marriage, her husband's behavior, and their circumstances. She thought that he was lazy at one point and later, that he was seeing another woman. She developed strategies to deal with instances of odd behavior. When her husband spoke of existing plots of world domination, she learned that confronting him simply increased his agitation and escalated the situation, so she adapted by "chang[ing] the subject." Despite these accommodations, this "accumulation of deviant behavior" strained the wife's level of tolerance, which nevertheless remained below her "threshold" as long as she was able to bring some understanding to these incidents. With a "trigger" event, she reached a threshold where she was confronted with defining his behavior as an illness. At this point, her husband had stopped bathing and changing clothes; he chased her around the house and growled like a lion. She later learned that he went to a local church, made a scene, and was taken to the hospital by the police. Even though she had forced him earlier to go to a physician, she was not involved in the decision-making process for entry into formal psychiatric care. Only with his involuntary admission to a psychiatric hospital did she frame his problem as a psychiatric one. Describing this story as the "process of help seeking" for a mental health problem is problematic.

From this classic study, four important aspects of dealing with mental health problems (and perhaps most illnesses, especially chronic ones) are apparent. First, mental health problems are poorly understood by most people. Typical "symptoms" of schizophrenia and more so those associated with depression, are not easily or quickly recognized as illness. Families often normalize situations adapting to and accommodating behavior. Second, others beyond the family (e.g., police, bosses, teachers) are often the first to see the person's behavior as a mental health problem. Third, the image of entering treatment voluntarily is not entirely accurate. Fourth, the idea of an orderly progression through well-defined and logical stages is contradicted by the stories of people who faced, either for themselves or for their family members, mental health problems.

The following issues have been examined in research on illness behavior (Mechanic, 1968); the lay attribution of illness, the role of "others" in facing illness; the use of coercion in mental health treatment; and the refinement of stage models to reflect the complexity of the possible pathways to formal care. However, more studies have been conducted using correlation models than those focusing on process and on entering the formal medical care system in Western countries, not on community-based ethnographic, multimethod studies (Pescosolido & Kronenfeld, 1995). Nevertheless, anthropologists concerned with societies that had traditional, indigenous systems of treatment analyzed how different forms of care were used by individuals and dealt with by governments. Studies of illness behavior beyond the Western World and the sustained interest in understanding communities have also invigorated the continued focus on process and complexity.

ACKNOWLEDGING THE COMPLEXITIES: LEVELS OF ILLNESS BELIEFS

Several different literatures have evolved that attempt to understand the social "realities" faced by patients, families, and others who interact with the person with psychiatric symptoms or a diagnosed mental illness. Lay accounts of problem definition and the process of entering treatment are contained in a proliferating literature of first-person accounts, case studies, and surveys. The process by which a behavior, such as a delusion, is transformed and responded to as a symptom, the cognitive and emotional factors affecting its interpretation, and the process of referral and entry into treatment are of relevance to social scientists and clinicians alike. Ultimately, compliance could be enormously enhanced by learning more about how people make sense of psychiatric symptoms and their social selection into various pathways to prevention and treatment.

The recognition and definition of behavior as a symptom of mental illness is a complex, sometimes illogical, perplexing, and generally distressing and protracted process (Furnham, 1994; Horwitz, 1982). Only limited understanding or agreement exists about when behaviors are serious enough to require psychiatric treatment. Misconceptions about the illness and the person with a mental illness are common. One study of lay beliefs about persons with schizophrenia showed that they were regarded with apprehension, as potentially dangerous, amoral, egocentric and as "dropouts" or vagrants (Furnham & Rees, 1988). The recognition of mental illness by professionals is delayed because self- and other appraisals are not always consistent with the medical model or clinical interpretations.

Complicating the lay recognition of symptoms of mental illness is stigma. The negative cultural stereotypes associated with the label of a mental illness and the fear of discrimination and rejection prompt defenses against acknowledging symptoms and behaviors as mental illness. In their efforts to manage difficult behaviors, families and mentally ill persons themselves deny, withdraw, conceal, or normalize symptoms of psychiatric illness (Clausen & Yarrow, 1955; Link, Mirotznik, & Cullen, 1991). Within some communities and families, a high tolerance for disturbing behaviors can delay early recognition of mental illness. In other cases, symptoms and behaviors may not be seen as treatable or worthy of medical intervention (Freidson, 1970).

A direct pathway to specialty mental health care does not logically follow from the onset of symptoms or even with relapse when prior symptoms reappear. It is not unusual for two or more years to elapse between the onset of symptoms and hospitalization (Clausen & Yarrow, 1955; Horwitz, 1977a). Close relatives are more likely to deny the initial symptoms, whereas more distant relatives and friends are more willing to interpret symptoms and behavior within a psychiatric framework (Horwitz, 1982). Selection into care is also strongly influenced by gender. Women are more likely than men to recognize their problem as an emotional one and to be labeled with a psychiatric problem by family and friends (Horwitz, 1977b). This gender difference in recognition separates men from women in the process of decision making and entering care. Based on attributions about symptoms, people will also engage in self-medication and seek advice from friends and relatives long before entering medical or psychiatric treatment. Even with referrals from primary care to specialty mental health care, the process of selection is defined as much by social as clinical indicators (Morgan, 1989).

Research into the commonsense framework of recognizing and perceiving illness, as well as its cause, course, and treatment suggests that people may act on the basis of "schemas." One of the more studied schemas is the "self-regulation" model that shows how patients' representations of illness threats affect coping responses and intervention efforts (Leventhal, Leventhal, & Contrada, 1997). Limited work has been done on schemas for psychiatric disorders.

Recent public views of mental illness and the ability to recognize behaviors as mental health problems are available in the 1996 General Social Survey (GSS). A nationally representative sample of Americans was asked a series of questions about one of five vignettes written to conform to criteria in the fourth edition of the *Diagnostic and Statistical Manual of Mental Disorders* (DSM-IV) of the American Psychiatric Association (1994). The following two examples are vignettes for schizophrenia and major depression:

[Schizophrenia]

[Name] is a [Race/ethnicity] [Gender] with an [education level]. Up until a year ago, life was pretty O.K. for [Name]. But then things started to change. S/he thought that people around [him/her] were making disapproving comments and talking behind [his/her] back. [Name] was convinced that people were spying on [him/her] and that they could hear what s/he was thinking. [Name] lost [his/her] drive to participate in [his/her] usual work and family activities and retreated to [his/her] home, eventually spending most of [his/her] day in [his/her] room. [Name] began hearing voices even though no one else was around. These voices told [him/her] what to do and what to think. [S/he] has been living this way for six months.

[Major Depression]

[Name] is a [Race/ethnicity] [Gender] with an [education level]. For the past two weeks, [Name] has been feeling really down. [S/he] wakes up in the morning with a flat heavy feeling that sticks with [him/her] all day long. [S/he] isn't enjoying things the way [s/he] normally would. In fact, nothing gives [him/her] pleasure. Even when good things happen, they don't seem to make [name] happy. [S/he] pushes on through [his/her] day but it is really hard. The smallest tasks are difficult to accomplish. [S/he] finds it hard to concentrate on anything. [S/he] feels out of energy and out of steam. And even though [Name] feels pretty worthless, and very discouraged, [name's] family has noticed that [s/he] hasn't been [him/herself] for about the last month and that [s/he] has pulled away from them. [Name] just doesn't feel like talking.

Adapted from Link et al. (forthcoming), Table 21.1 reports on Americans' recognition of mental health problems for two of the five scenarios analyzed in the GSS. Although over two-thirds of respondents see the depression-based vignette as a mental illness, only 19.7% report that it is "very likely" one. In fact, they are more likely to see schizophrenia as a mental illness (85.7% in the "likely" categories), with over half of respondents seeing it as "very likely" (52.5%). Looking across the other categories, this sample is also likely to identify the schizophrenia-based vignette as a "nervous breakdown" (81.3% in the top two "likely" categories). Furthermore, a substantial percentage are likely to see this scenario as part of the normal ups and downs of life (39.5% in the "likely" categories) and as a physical illness (46.5%). However, when respondents were asked directly how likely it was that the

TABLE 21.1. Recognition of Mental Health Problems, 1996 General Social Survey

Vignette given to respondent	How likely is it that [Name] is experiencing . . .						
	Part of normal ups and downs of life %	A nervous breakdown %	A mental illness %	A physical illness %	Schizophrenia %	A major depression %	(N)[a]
Schizophrenia							
Very likely	13.3	36.1	52.5	13.4	43.8	—	(294)
Somewhat likely	26.2	45.2	33.2	33.1	29.9		
Not very likely	31.6	12.6	9.8	34.8	9.7		
Not likely at all	27.6	3.1	1.7	15.2	3.5		
Don't know	1.4	3.1	2.7	3.4	13.2		
Major Depression							
Very likely	36.9	22.6	19.7	14.6	—	58.9	(295)
Somewhat likely	41.0	44.6	45.4	50.2		33.3	
Not very likely	15.6	25.0	24.4	24.7		4.6	
Not likely at all	4.4	4.4	4.7	6.4		.7	
Don't know	2.0	3.4	5.8	4.1		2.5	

[a] N's are approximate, since the base changes slightly from question to question.

Source: Adapted from Link et al. (1997).

person was experiencing schizophrenia, 73.7% responded that this was likely the case. Although only a few respondents were unable to offer an opinion, the schizophrenia-based vignette is more likely than the depression-based vignette to elicit a "don't know" response (e.g., 13.2% of respondents said they did not know if it was schizophrenia and 2.5% said they did not know if it was depression).

Although respondents were likely to see the major depression–based vignette as a mental illness, over two-thirds of respondents said the person was either very or somewhat likely to be experiencing part of the normal ups and downs of life (77.9%), a nervous breakdown (67.2%), or a physical illness (64.8%). Asking respondents whether this person exhibited a major depression adds about another 39.2% to the percentage of respondents in the very likely category of depression. These responses suggest that Americans hold varying descriptions of the nature of illness (i.e., mental illness, physical illness, "ups and downs"). When the appropriate mental illness category is volunteered by an interviewer, however, high percentages of respondents agree with the actual diagnosis (see Link et al., forthcoming, for a detailed analysis).

Given the heterogeneity in recognition, it is not surprising that respondents attribute different causes to problems. Table 21.2 shows that a large percentage of respondents accept medical explanations for mental health problems. Over three-fourths agree that it is very or somewhat likely that the schizophrenia-based vignette targets a problem of chemical imbalance in the brain (77.8%); and almost that many (61.1%) agree that it might be a genetic or inherited problem. Psychosocial explanations are widely accepted also, with 86.4% of respondents seeing stress as a likely cause of the illness. The profile is fairly similar for depression, with slightly lower percentages of individuals reporting chemical imbalances (68.3%) or genetics (50.8%), and more identifying stress (92.6%) as a cause.

Although most Americans believe in biological or medical explanations of mental illness, the results show an unwillingness to forego other explanations of deviant behav-

TABLE 21.2. Attribution of the Cause of Mental Health Problems, 1996 General Social Survey

Vignette given to respondent	Bad character %	Chemical imbalance in the brain %	The way (he or she) was raised %	Stressful circumstance in his or her life %	A genetic or inherited problem %	God's will %
			How likely is it that [name]'s situation might be caused by . . .			
Schizophrenia						
Very likely	13.5	43.1	7.8	32.2	18.9	5.7
Somewhat likely	17.9	34.7	34.8	54.2	42.2	10.8
Not very likely	31.8	9.8	30.4	5.1	22.6	23.6
Not likely at all	32.4	4.4	21.3	3.7	7.4	54.7
Don't know	4.4	8.1	5.7	4.7	8.8	5.1
Major Depression						
Very likely	10.8	19.5	11.1	53.2	12.8	6.4
Somewhat likely	25.9	48.8	35.1	39.4	38.0	8.1
Not very likely	38.7	16.2	36.5	4.0	30.0	28.6
Not likely at all	20.5	9.4	14.5	1.0	15.2	50.8
Don't know	4.0	6.1	2.7	2.4	4.0	6.1

Source: Adapted from Link et al. (forthcoming).

iors. Almost one-third report that these problems are caused by bad character (31.4% for schizophrenia, 36.7% for depression), almost half cite child rearing (42.6% and 46.2%, respectively), and a small but still sizable group point to God's will (16.5% and 14.5%, respectively).

These profiles of responses to scenarios of mental illness suggest that there are several levels to beliefs about the behavior and its underlying causes. This result is no surprise given the prior work of many sociologists, psychologists, and anthropologists who have documented beliefs in supernatural or moral causes in "modern" societies while showing beliefs in scientific causes in "traditional" societies as well (Davis, 1963; Murdock, Wilson, & Frederick, 1978).

Illness attribution has been based in part on a number of unsubstantiated assumptions, especially an either–or approach that individuals can only replace one set of etiological beliefs with another, or that illness is seen as a punishment for wrongdoing only where the social order coincides with the moral order (Fosu, 1981; Lieban, 1977). As Pflanz and Keopp (1977) contend, there may be "layers" to individuals' understanding of illness. Hamnett and Connell (1981) found that both the severity of the illness and its "curability" influenced whether individuals resort to a moral explanation for illness. Given the nature of serious mental illness, the onset of behavioral problems is likely to evoke complex responses, tapping many layers of beliefs. Not surprisingly, with this diversity in attribution, individuals respond to and cope with mental illnesses by contacting many different kinds of "help" and using different pathways to care.

ACKNOWLEDGING THE COMPLEXITIES: DIFFERENT MODES OF ENTRY

Theories about how individuals use services are based primarily on an underlying assumption that a proactive choice is made, that they "seek" care. The case from Clausen and Yarrow's study suggests that "help seeking" and "decision making" do not accurately describe the social process of entering the medical or mental health system. As suggested by Pescosolido, Gardner, and Lubell (1998), taking a broader view of how individuals enter treatment, especially mental health care, reveals two distinct literatures on health service use. The main literature is referred to as "utilization," "help seeking" or "health care decision making," where the focus is on the individual and implicitly on "choices" even in the face of restricted access. The second research tradition comes from those more concerned with the interface between the legal and mental health systems. Often referred to as "law and mental health," this area focuses more on the power of legal systems to force individuals into treatment and on pressure, however well intended, from others in the community to receive care.

Data from a number of studies support "the two faces" of mental health service use. Researchers who focus on legal "holds" and court-ordered treatments report that many individuals with mental health problems are "pushed" into care by friends, relatives, and co-workers. They enter the treatment system not on their own volition but by the actions of police, other institutional agents (e.g., teachers), or through mechanisms of emergency detention and involuntary commitment (Bennett et al., 1993; Miller, 1988; Perelberg, 1983).

Researchers distinguish between legal coercion (i.e., formal measures such as involuntary hospitalization used to compel service use and compliance) and extralegal coercion (i.e., pressures from family, clinicians, and friends to get and stay in treatment). The official distinction between "voluntary" and "involuntary" commitment is problematic. According to Lidz and Hoge (1993), many individuals hospitalized for mental health problems are persuaded to "sign themselves in" to increase their freedom in leaving the hospital. Furthermore, the recent series of reports from the MacArthur Coercion Study show that almost 40% of those who were admitted voluntarily believed that they would have been involuntarily committed had they not "agreed" to admission (Dennis & Monahan, 1996). Of all the patients studied in two mental hospitals, 46% of individuals report no pressures to enter care, 38% report efforts to "persuade," and 10% report the use of "force" (Dennis & Monahan, 1996).

Such coercion is not limited to those who are perceived by others to require intensive, inpatient care. In our ongoing longitudinal study (the Indianapolis Network Mental Health Study) of how "community" influences early illness careers of individuals with mental health problems and their families, individuals were asked to tell the "story" of how they first came to be treated in a public or private hospital or a Community Mental Health Center (CMHC). Some of the individuals were later diagnosed with a major mental illness (e.g., schizophrenia, bipolar disorder), and others were diagnosed with "adjustment disorders." Similar to the MacArthur study, fewer than half of the stories (45.9%) match the notion of choice underlying dominant theories of health services use. Almost one-fourth of the respondents (22.9%) reported coercion. These stories were also examined for an additional kind of entry that has been called "muddling through." In about one-third (31.2%) of the cases, agency was virtually absent. Individuals neither resisted nor sought care and often struggled haphazardly to cope with a change in their mental health status, most likely perceived as resulting from a change in their social circumstances, such as divorce, job loss, or other life event. Often, it is unclear how they reached the mental health system at all.

Entry into care is shaped by both the type of mental health problems and the nature of the social contacts. For individuals with bipolar disorders, conflict with others is likely, and these individuals often describe a "supercharged" state. They are surprised and agitated when others around them want them to seek (and eventually pressure them into) medical care. The use of coercion appears also to be shaped by the availability of community ties. Larger social networks closely tied together have the social capacity to get individuals into the specialty sector even in the face of resistance (Pescosolido, Gardner, & Lubell, 1998).

Support for the use of legal coercion to get individuals with mental health problems into the formal system of care is substantial. According to results from the 1996 GSS, almost two-thirds of the public are willing to use legal means to force individuals with drug abuse problems to see a doctor, almost half report a willingness to do so with individuals described in the vignette as meeting criteria for schizophrenia, and over one-third agree for individuals with alcohol dependence. Interestingly, fewer individuals respond in a similar way to major depression, but still over one-fifth of Americans report a willingness to coerce those with major depression into medical treatment. A few (about 7%) were willing to use legal coercion for the person with "troubles" who did not meet criteria for any mental health problem (Pescosolido, Monahan, Link, Steuve and Kikuzawa, forthcoming).

ACKNOWLEDGING THE COMPLEXITIES: DIFFERENT SYSTEMS OF CARE

The differential response to mental health problems and to all illnesses is not a process that occurs in isolation. Many individuals with varying backgrounds and expertise can be involved in the process of identifying a mental health problem, providing advice or consultation, and taking part in the person's illness career. Kleinman (1980) has described three systems of care; the lay system, the folk system, and the formal medical care system. Table 21.3 offers a more detailed listing of the options, types of advisors, and examples of the different kinds of possibilities that exist in most, if not all, societies. The set of possibilities is the same whether the problem is physical or mental, in part because mental health problems are often first understood as physical problems. For others, the problem may be defined in terms of social relations, such as a problem with a significant other that may be handled with advice from a psychic rather than a psychiatrist. According to the stories in the Indianapolis Network Mental Health Study, few individuals saw the problem initially as a mental health problem. Rather, they attributed problems to a wide variety of stressors in their lives such as bad marriages, difficult bosses, troubled children, and conflicts with their parents.

Reforms in health care and in medical practice are directed to decreasing mental health treatment costs by training general practitioners to recognize, diagnose, and treat problems rather than refer patients to expensive specialists, such as psychologists or psychiatrists. These changes also underscore the movement toward community-level innovations to fill in the gaps left by a reformed medical care system (Peterson, 1997). As Table 21.3 also indicates, individuals may try to deal with illness on their own, engaging in a variety of coping practices to alleviate symptoms (Pearlin & Aneshensel, 1986). They may resort to vitamins, over-the-counter medications, home remedies, prayer, exercise, or folk practices.

In the study of Mental Health Care Utilization among Puerto Ricans (Alegría et al., 1991), a wide variety of practitioners and practices were used by poor individuals reporting an "episode" of a mental health problem. A fair amount of stability in the level of use

TABLE 21.3. The Range of Choices for Medical Care and Advice

Option	Advisor	Examples
Modern medical	M.D.'s, osteopaths (general practitioners, specialists), allied health professions	Physicians, psychiatrists, podiatrists, optometrists, nurses, midwives, opticians, psychologists, druggists, technicians, aides
Alternative medical practitioners	"Traditional" healers	Faith healers, spiritualists, shamans, curanderos, diviners, herbalists, acupuncturists, bone-setters, granny midwives
	"Modern" healers	Homeopaths, chiropractors, naturopaths, nutritional consultants, holistic practitioners
Nonmedical professionals	Social workers	
	Legal agents	Police, lawyers
	Clergymen	
	Supervisors	Bosses, teachers
Lay advisors	Family	Spouse, parents
	Neighbors	
	Friends	
	Co-workers, classmates	
Other	Self-care	Nonprescription medicines, self-examination procedures, folk remedies, health foods
None		

Source: Pescosolido (1992). Reprinted with permission.

existed across two waves of data collection in 1992–1993 and 1993–1994. Our more recent analysis indicates that a large percentage of respondents (40.1% in Wave 1 and 52.3%
in Wave 2) talked to a relative. Although this response is relatively common, it is by no
means what all individuals "decide" to do when they acknowledge that they have mental
health problems. Fewer individuals reported that they discussed their problem with friends
at each assessment (28.7 and 35.5%, respectively). The use of over-the-counter medications, religious practices, and exercise or meditation were reported by one-fifth to one-
fourth of respondents. These choices correspond closely to contacts with the formal treatment system. About one-fifth of respondents reported consulting a general practitioner or
mental health specialist. These findings suggest that individuals with mental health problems are likely to draw from a wide variety of sources of help and do not have exclusive,
common, or even regular contact with the specialized mental health treatment system (details on request).

ACKNOWLEDGING THE COMPLEXITIES:
THE RICH VARIETY OF PATHWAYS

As one of the first large-scale, population-based, representative sample surveys using a
dynamic, community-based perspective of health care use, the Puerto Rican Study also
provides new and important information not only on the nature and extent of the use of a
wide variety of advisors and practices, but also on the ordering of these contacts. A wide
variety of advisors was contacted initially. Almost two-thirds of those who talked to a
relative did so first (65.4% in Wave 1 and 64.2% in Wave 2), but over one-third also went
first to physicians (36.3% in Wave 1 and 39.1% in Wave 2). A similar percentage consulted
a mental health provider (e.g., psychiatrist, social worker, mental health clinician) for their
preliminary medical care contact (30.6% in Wave 1 and 35.3% in Wave 2). The only substantial difference between the two waves, was that 39% in Wave 1 and 26.7% in Wave 2
contacted a friend initially. Between one-fifth and one-fourth of those reporting mental
health problems went initially to the clergy (24.3% and 20%, respectively).

These findings reflect two different ideas not usually taken into account in discussions
of "help seeking." First, initial contact reflects the wide range of possible attributed causes
and descriptions of the nature of mental health problems. Second, because not all people
enter the treatment system voluntarily, the first person who "identifies" a mental health
problem (e.g., the police, a crisis clinician) starts the illness career rather than being a
logical end point in a "search" for care.

As Figure 21.3 shows, twenty years after the Parsons's scheme, models of the illness
career acknowledged different systems and multiple pathways to care (Twaddle & Hessler,
1977, p. 124). If help is needed, lay, religious, or medical advisors can be consulted and,
within the medical sector, psychiatrists, primary care physicians, nurses, social workers,
and auxiliary providers are available. The process circles back through a number of itera-
tions, including a reinterpretation of what it means to be "well" for a particular person.

In acknowledging multiple pathways, Romanucci-Ross (1977) suggested two distinct
"hierarchies of resort." For those she studied in Melanesia, an "acculturative" sequence
started with physicians or nurses. If no relief occurred, individuals moved to Western religious healers, practitioners, and advisors. Finally, if the search continued, native religious
practitioners and advisors were sought. In the "counteracculturative" sequence, individuals tried home remedies first, followed by visits to traditional, indigenous healers, finally

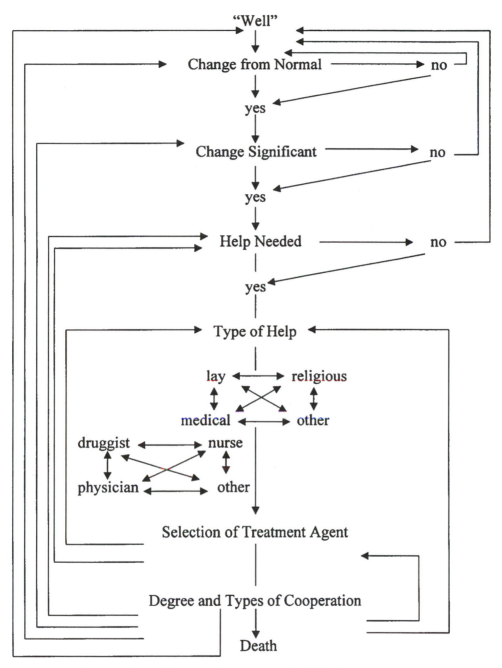

FIGURE 21.3. Twaddle and Hessler's illness career model (1972). Reprinted with permission.

going to a hospital if all else failed. Romanucci-Ross suggests that those acculturated to modern approaches to illness choose formal services first and will fall back on older cultural modes of responding when a "cure is not forthcoming" or "earlier choices are exhausted." Both Janzen's (1978) study of the "quest for therapy" in Zaire and Young's (1981) investigation of the "decision process" in a small Mexican village followed this tradition of describing and modeling the illness process. Young found four critical factors in structuring the process of dealing with an illness: (1) the seriousness of the illness; (2) knowledge about an appropriate home remedy; (3) faith in the effectiveness of folk treatment as opposed to medical treatment for that illness; and (4) the balance between the expense of alternatives and available resources.

Some mental health models (e.g., help-seeking decision-making model; Goldsmith, Jackson, & Hough, 1988) merge a concern with charting stages with the focus on correlates of use from models such as the Health Belief Model (Strecher et al., 1997) and the Sociobehavioral Model of Health Care (Andersen, 1995). Two problems still exist. First, although these models acknowledge that individuals might skip over stages or repeat them, a step-by-step ordering pervades the analyses of entering treatment and resembles Parsons's original scheme. The complexity of skipping stages is not modeled in the analytic design. Second, there is little guidance about how, when, and why different factors from the correlation models "kick in" to affect the process of coping with illness. Is social class more pronounced in interpreting the meaning of a "symptom" than in evaluating whether or not to seek formal care? In essence, attempts to blend dynamic and correlational models move in the right direction but are trapped in the theoretical "boxes" that faced Parsons and those who developed contingency models. These blended models still impose a single, logical order and decision-making framework on a process that is often disorderly and lacks rational stage-by-stage planning.

THE DYNAMIC, SOCIAL ORGANIZATION OF MENTAL HEALTH CONTACTS

This prior work suggests a need to study process without abandoning the search for how use is shaped by a variety of social, cultural, medical, and economic contingencies, and a need to consider multiple possibilities for the types of advisors and pathways to and from different systems of care. Prior quantitatively oriented attempts to incorporate process did not eliminate the "boxes" of contingencies that are so fundamental to these theories and to efforts to provide graphical displays of theories. In contrast, qualitatively oriented approaches failed to connect rich and textured descriptions of illness behavior to the larger, structural features that shape the process of responding to physical and mental health problems. Furthermore, theoretical, methodological, or statistical tools were also not available for venturing beyond descriptive, qualitative models or correlational, quantitative models.

The Network–Episode Model

The recently proposed Network–Episode Model (NEM) draws from the strengths of both dynamic and contingency models (Pescosolido, 1991; 1992; Pescosolido & Boyer, 1999; see Figure 21.4). The model moves away from "boxes" of contingencies and stages to "streams" of illness behavior incorporating changing community conditions and treatment system possibilities.

The NEM has three basic characteristics. First, rather than impose a rigid ordering of the process of coping with illness or the nature of the process, important research questions target understanding the illness career as patterns and pathways to and from the community and the treatment system; the degree to which individuals resort to different pathways; the

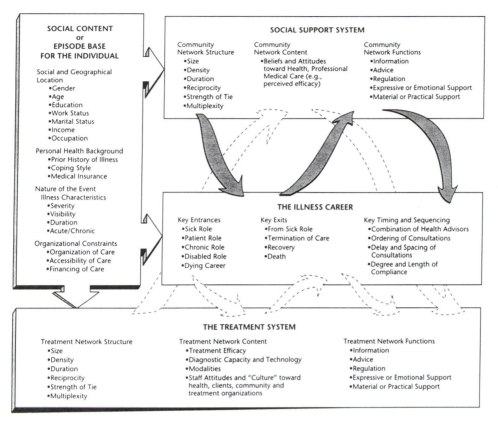

FIGURE 21.4. The revised Network–Episode Model (Pescosolido & Boyer, 1999).

continued use of services and outcomes; and when, how, and under what conditions individuals shift from invoking standard cultural routines and move into a rational choice-based calculus. Second, these patterns and pathways are not static, nor are they random. Both the social support system and the treatment system are ongoing streams that influence and are influenced by the illness career. Dealing with any health problem is a social process that is managed through contacts or social networks that individuals have in the community, the treatment system, and social service agencies, including self-help groups, churches, and jails. People face illness in the course of their day-to-day lives by interacting with other people who may recognize (or deny) a problem; send them to (or provide) treatment; and support, cajole or nag them about appointments, medications, or lifestyle. What this social support system looks like and what it offers is critical. The treatment sector represents the provision of clinical services that can be characterized as well by a set of networks of people who provide care, concern, pressure, and problems (Pescosolido, 1997). The NEM conceptualizes the medical system as a changing set of providers and organizations with which individuals may have contact when they are ill. Thinking about treatment in social network terms allows us to break down the treatment experience by charting the kinds (physicians, rehabilitation therapists, billing staff) and nature (supportive, antagonistic, cold or warm) of experiences that people have in treatment that affects whether they return, take their medications, or get better. Social networks in treatment create a climate of care that affects both patients and providers alike (Pescosolido, 1997). Third, the characteristics of the person and the illness (see the left-hand side of Figure 21.4) shape the illness career and its trajectory. All three streams are anchored in the social locations, histories, and problems of people and networks (for details, see Pescosolido 1991; 1992; Pescosolido & Boyer, 1999).

Pathways of Care: Some Preliminary Results

The mapping and exploring of the order in which pathways are activated do not fit usual statistical or econometric approaches. No multivariate technique deals with a long list of categories and thin cells in the many charted pathways to care that are reported by respondents. In the first wave (1992–1993) of the Puerto Rican study (described earlier), individuals ($n = 747$) reported the sequence of their sources of care. Four different types of providers were used (lay, folk, general medical practitioner, and mental health specialist) with one to four possible contacts. Individuals using no pathways were also identified.

The pathways into care and treatment can be collapsed in different ways to reflect the concerns of researchers, providers, or policymakers. From a clinical or health services research perspective, what matters about these pathways is whether individuals reach the specialized mental health system, and if so, whether they turn to other types of advisors later. Pathways here are collapsed into four types: "successes" show that individuals with mental health problems reach the specialty mental health sector and do not go elsewhere, except perhaps to notify friends and family; "failed pathways" use folk, lay, or general practitioners, but never reach the mental health sector; "successes with referral or rejection" show individuals traveling pathways that include mental health treatment but subsequent use of lay individuals or providers in the folk or general medical sector. This third type of pathway may represent a dissatisfying encounter, nonrecognition, reevaluation, or rejection of the person's mental health problem by the provider, resulting in referrals to general practitioners or others, or a rejection by the individual of the advice and treatment offered by mental health professionals. These pathways suggest either a failure of the system, or simultaneous use of different systems, possibly at the suggestion or even referral of a mental health provider. For individuals with both mental and physical health problems, pathways to the mental health system and into (either simultaneously or sequentially) the general medical care sector may indicate continuity of care (Hawley, 1997). The fourth alternative is using no pathway, where individuals indicate they did not contact any provider or source for help or treatment, even though they self-report a mental health problem.

Almost one-third (30.8%) of the pathways identified in this Puerto Rican study are simple, including only one advisor or practitioner (23.6% use lay advisors only; 5.8% contact mental health specialists only; 1.5% use folk practitioners only). Other pathways are much more complex, where respondents reported using three or more types of advisors or practitioners in various sequences (11.6%). Of the pathways, 17.5% were considered "successes" with treatment in the specialty mental health sector and no subsequent use of other advisors or practitioners; 40% were classified as "failed pathways," where mental health professionals were never used; an additional 5% were pathways showing "success with referral or rejection;" and finally, 37% reported doing nothing in response to a perceived mental health problem.

With these four types of pathways, a multinomial logit analysis provides an opportunity to examine the contingencies of the illness career. For illustrative purposes, we selected a set of variables from the NEM. A series of preliminary analyses were done and the models were pared down to eight variables, including sex, age, education, religious attendance, insurance, need, self-reliance, and social isolation as a measure of network availability that represented consistent correlates of health service use (Pescosolido & Boyer, 1999) and were important to the Puerto Rican context.

The new findings in Table 21.4 show the factors that shape the chosen pathways (see Pescosolido, 1992, for a detailed discussion of the use and interpretation of these procedures for services research; see Long, 1987, for detail on the statistical approach). The overall chi-square column indicates that sex, religious attendance, education, need, self-reliance, and social isolation are significantly associated with the kind of pathways traveled by individuals who report a mental health problem. As the coefficients in Table 21.4 indicate, individuals with definite mental health problems are significantly less likely to do nothing than to travel "successful" pathways to the mental health system. Though severity or need has generally been shown to be the best and most consistent predictor of service use, what is different, interesting, and important in this analysis of pathways that is not seen in the usual "use–no-use" framework is that individuals with definite mental health problems are also significantly more likely to travel failed pathways that never reach specialized psychiatric care or to enter the mental health system and proceed to the lay, folk, or general medical sector. In analyses not shown (available on request), individuals most in need of care come into the mental health sector, but they are also the most likely to reject

TABLE 21.4. Multinomial Logit Analysis of Pathways to Care, Mental Health Care Utilization among Puerto Ricans Study (N = 749)[a]

	Pathway comparisons			
Independent variable	Success vs. nothing	Failure vs. nothing	Success with referral or rejection vs. nothing	χ^2 for variable
Sex (Female = 1)	.99	1.79**	2.61*	13.55**
Age	1.00	.99	1.00	4.04
	(1.04)	(.85)	(1.05)	
Attendance at religious services or activities[b]	1.24**	1.23**	1.76**	27.64**
	(1.46)	(1.45)	(2.77)	
Education (in years)	1.04	1.02	1.16**	7.67*
	(1.15)	(1.11)	(1.85)	
Mental health problem[c]				
Probable	1.06	1.47	2.24	4.38
Definite	2.75**	2.55**	9.87**	36.61**
Respondent has private health insurance	1.18	1.10	1.68	1.96
Respondent is self-reliant	.40**	.90	.24**	28.08**
Social Isolation Index[d]	1.44**	.93	1.47	13.05**
Overall χ^2 = 153.47, 27 d.f., $p < .001$				

[a]Unstandardized factor changes reported; standardized factor changes reported where appropriate in parentheses. Factor change coefficients are the factor by which the odds change for a unit (unstandardized) or standard deviation (standardized) change in an independent variable.
[b]Responses ranged from 1 = never to 6 = more than once a week.
[c]Set of dummy variables; unlikely is omitted category.
[d]Sum of five ways in which respondent could be isolated: being a recent migrant, unmarried, unemployed, never attending church, and having no family or friends. *Note.* None of the respondents were isolated in all five areas.
*$p < .05$,   **$p < .01$

this treatment in favor of others. Although individuals with definite mental health problems are significantly less likely to do nothing, they are equally likely to be successful in entering psychiatric care, to fail to reach specialized mental health care, or to encounter referral or rejection after initial success.

Other findings show that women are significantly more likely to travel failed pathways or move beyond the mental health system than to do nothing or successfully reach and remain in specialized care. Attendance at religious services significantly decreases the probability of doing nothing. The more highly educated are more likely to enter psychiatric care but then leave this specialized sector for other referrals or assistance elsewhere. Individuals who are self-reliant are less likely to seek specialized care than to do nothing. Finally, individuals who are socially isolated are more likely to travel successful pathways than to do nothing. Fewer network ties in Puerto Rico increase the probability of entering the specialized mental health system.

Though this analysis reveals a difficult and complex task, we can begin to connect theories of the illness career to dominant contingency theories. The payoff for this effort is to show how structure connects to process and to challenge some of the well-accepted but poorly understood findings in health services research.

CHALLENGES TO THE SOCIOLOGICAL STUDY OF SERVICE USE: A MOVE TO UNDERSTANDING TREATMENT EFFECTIVENESS

Using the specialized mental health sector early and continuously until a problem is "solved" or "managed" should produce better outcomes for individuals and for the public health. To that end, models of service use that end at the door of the clinic do not tell us enough about what happens before individuals get there or what happens to them later. The chronicity of mental illness and of more and more physical problems requires a refocusing on illness careers that connect social interactions and communities that ultimately influence trajectories and outcomes. In this chapter, we have attempted to review the relevant literature, update some important findings, and present both new theories and results that provide direction for rethinking models of service use. As dramatic changes occur in the organization of the health care system, with new incentives and restricted choices, efforts to understand what happens to patients and their families in the process of entering treatment present a major challenge for mental health services research.

ACKNOWLEDGMENTS: We would like to thank the National Institute of Mental Health, Grant No. R24 MH 51669, Research Scientist Development Awards K01 MH 00849, K02 MH 01289 to the first author; Grants R01 MH 42655 (Margarita Alegría, P.I.) and to the second author P30 MH43450 (David Mechanic, PI) and the MacArthur Foundation for funding the Mental Health Module of the 1996 General Social Survey. We would like to thank Margarita Alegría, Norman Furniss, Bruce Link, Karen Lutfey, and Eric Wright for their comments on this chapter and on the various projects reported herein. Mary Hannah and Terry White provided important technical and clerical assistance.

REFERENCES

Aday, L. A., & Awe, W. C. (1997). Health service utilization models. In D. S. Gochman (Ed.), *Handbook of health behavior research: I. Personal and social determinants* (pp. 153–172). New York: Plenum Press.

Alegría, M., Robles, R., Freeman, D. H., Vera, M., Jimenez, A. L., Rios, C., & Rios, R. (1991). Patterns of mental health utilization among island Puerto Rican poor. *American Journal of Public Health, 81,* 875–879.

American Psychiatric Association. (1994). *Diagnostic and statistical manual of mental disorders* (4th ed.). Washington, DC: Author.

Andersen, R. (1995). Revisiting the behavioral model and access to care: Does it matter? *Journal of Health and Social Behavior, 36,* 1–10.

Bennett, N. S., Lidz, C. W., Monahan, J., Mulvey, E., Hoge, S. K., Roth, L. H., & Gardner, W. (1993). Inclusion, motivation and good faith: The morality of coercion in mental hospital admission. *Behavioral Science and the Law, 11,* 295–306.

Clausen, J., & Yarrow, M. (1955). Introduction: Mental Illness and the family. *Journal of Social Issues, 11,* 25–32.

Davis, F. (1963). *Passage through crisis: Polio victims and their families.* Indianapolis: Bobbs-Merrill.

Dennis, D. L., & Monahan, J. (1996). *Coercion and aggressive community treatment.* New York: Plenum Press.

Fosu, G. (1981). Disease classification in rural Ghana: Framework and implications for health behavior. *Social Science and Medicine, 15B,* 471–480.

Freidson, E. (1970). *Profession of medicine.* New York: Dodd Mead.

Furnham, A. (1994). Explaining health and illness: Lay perceptions on current and future health, the causes of illness and the nature of recovery. *Social Science and Medicine, 39,* 715–725.

Furnham, A., & Rees, J. (1988). Lay theories of schizophrenia. *International Journal of Social Psychiatry, 34,* 212–220.

Gardner, W., Hoge, S. K., Bennett, N., Roth, L. H., Lidz, C. W., Monahan, J., & Mulvery, E. P. (1993). Two scales for measuring patients' perceptions of coercion during mental hospital admission. *Behavioral Sciences and the Law, 11,* 307–322.

Gochman, D. S. (1997). Personal and social determinants of health behavior: An integration. In D. S. Gochman (Ed.), *Handbook of health behavior research: I. Personal and social determinants* (pp. 381–400). New York: Plenum Press.

Goldsmith, H. F., Jackson, D. J., & Hough, R.(1988). Process model of seeking mental health services: Proposed framework for organizing the literature on help-seeking. In H. F. Goldsmith, E. Lin, & R. A. Bell (Eds.), *Needs assessment: Its future* (pp. 49–64). DHHS Pub.No. (ADM) 88-1550. Washington, DC: U.S. Government Printing Office.

Hamnett, M., & Connell, J. (1981). Diagnosis and care: The resort to traditional and modern practitioners in the North Solomons, Papua, New Guinea. *Social Science and Medicine, 15B,* 489–498.

Hawley, T. (1997). Health behavior in persons with severe mental illness. In D. S. Gochman (Ed.), *Handbook of health behavior research: III. Demography, development and diversity* (pp. 247–265). New York: Plenum Press.

Hiday, V. (1992). Coercion in civil commitment: Process, preferences and outcome. *International Journal of Law and Psychiatry, 15,* 359–377.

Horwitz, A. V. (1977a). Social networks and pathways into psychiatric treatment. *Social Forces, 56,* 86–106.

Horwitz, A. V. (1977b). The pathways into psychiatric treatment: Some differences between men and women. *Journal of Health and Social Behavior, 18,* 169–178.

Horwitz, A. V. (1982). *The social control of mental illness.* New York: Academic Press.

Janzen, J. M. (1978). *The quest for therapy in Lower Zaire.* Berkeley: University of California Press.

Kleinman, A. (1980). *Patients and healers in the context of culture.* Berkeley: University of California Press.

Leventhal, H., Leventhal, E. A., & Contrada, R. J. (1998). Self-regulation, health, and behavior: A perceptual–cognitive approach. *Psychology and Health, 13,* 717–733.

Lidz, C. W., & Hoge, S. K. (1993). Introduction to coercion in mental health care. *Behavioral Sciences and the Law, 11,* 237–238.

Lieban, R. (1977). The field of medical anthropology. In D. Landy (Ed.), *Culture, disease and healing* (pp. 13–30). New York: Macmillan.

Link, B., Phelan, J., Bresnahan, M., Steuve, A., & Pescosolido, B. A. (forthcoming). Public conceptions of mental illness: Labels and causes. *American Journal of Public Health.*

Link, B. G., Mirotznik, J., & Cullen, F. T. (1991). The effectiveness of stigma coping orientations: Can negative consequences of mental illness labeling be avoided. *Journal of Health and Social Behavior, 32,* 302–320.

Long, J. S. (1987). A graphical method for the interpretation of multinomial logit analysis. *Sociological Methods and Research, 15,* 430–446.

Maddux, J. E., & DuCharme, K. A. (1997). Behavioral intentions in theories of health behavior. In D. S. Gochman (Ed.), *Handbook of health behavior research: I. Personal and social determinants* (pp. 133–152). New York: Plenum Press.

Mechanic, D. (1968). *Medical sociology.* New York: Free Press.

Miller, R. D. (1988). Outpatient civil commitment of the mentally ill: An overview and update. *Behavioral Science and the Law, 6,* 99–118.

Morgan, D. (1989). Psychiatric cases: An ethnography of the referral process. *Psychological Medicine, 19,* 743–753.

Murdock, G., Wilson, S., & Frederick, V. (1978). World distribution of theories of illness. *Ethnology,* 17, 449–470.

Parsons, T. (1951). *The social system.* Glencoe, IL: Free Press.

Pearlin, L. I., & Aneshensel, C. S. (1986). Coping and social supports: Their functions and applications. In D. Mechanic & L. H. Aiken (Eds.), *Applications of social science to clinical medicine and health policy* (pp. 417–437). New Brunswick, NJ: Rutgers University Press.

Perelberg, R. J. (1983). Mental illness, family and networks in a London borough. *Social Science and Medicine, 17,* 481–491.

Pescosolido, B. A. (1991). Illness careers and network ties: A conceptual model of utilization and compliance. In G. Albrecht & J. Levy (Eds.), *Advances in medical sociology* (Vol. 2, pp. 164–181). Greenwich, CT: JAI Press.

Pescosolido, B. A. (1992). Beyond rational choice: The social dynamics of how people seek help. *American Journal of Sociology, 97,* 1096–1138.

Pescosolido, B. A. (1997). *Bringing people back in: Why social networks matter for treatment effectiveness research.* Unpublished paper. Bloomington: Indiana University Press.

Pescosolido, B. A., & Boyer, C. A. (1999). How do people come to use mental health services? Current knowledge and changing perspectives. In A. V. Horwitz & T. Scheid (Eds.), *Sociology of mental illness.* Cambridge, UK: Cambridge University Press.

Pescosolido, B. A., Gardner, C. B., & Lubell, K. M. (1998). How people get into mental health services: Stories of choice, coercion and "muddling through" from "first timers". *Social Science and Medicine, 46*(2), 275–286.

Pescosolido, B. A., & Kronenfeld, J. J. (1995). Health, illness and healing in an uncertain era: Challenges from and for medical sociology. *Journal of Health and Social Behavior, 36*(Extra Issue), 5–33.

Pescosolido, B. A., Monahan, J., Link, B. G., Steuve, A., & Kikuzawa, S. (forthcoming). The public's view of individuals with mental health problems: Competence, dangerousness and the need for coercion in health care. *Amercian Journal of Public Health.*

Pescosolido, B. A., Wright, E. R., Alegría, M., & Vera, M. (1998). Social networks and patterns of use among the poor with mental health problems in Puerto Rico. *Medical Care, 36*(7), 1051–1072.

Peterson, M. A. (1997). Community: meaning and opportunity and learning for the future. *Journal of Health Politics, Policy and Law, 22,* 933–936.

Pflanz, M., & Keopp, H. (1977). A sociological perspective on concepts of disease. *International Social Science Journal, 29,* 388–396.

Romanucci-Ross, L. (1977). The hierarchy of resort in curative practices: The Admiralty Islands, Melanesia. In D. Landy (Ed.), *Culture, disease and healing* (pp. 481–486). New York: Macmillan.

Segall, A. (1997). Sick role concepts and health behavior. In D. S. Gochman (Ed.), *Handbook of Health behavior research: I. Personal and social determinants* (pp. 289–300). New York: Plenum Press.

Siegler, M., & Osmond, H. (1973). The 'sick role' revisited. *Hastings Center Report, 1,* 41–48.

Strecher, V. J., Champion, V. L., & Rosenstock, I. M. (1997). The health belief model and health behavior. In D. S. Gochman (Ed.), *Handbook of health behavior research: I. Personal and social determinants* (pp. 71–92). New York: Plenum Press.

Suchman, E. (1964). Sociomedical variations among ethnic groups. *American Journal of Sociology, 70,* 319–331.

Twaddle, A. C. & Hessler, R. M. (1977). *A sociology of health.* St. Louis, MO: Mosby.

Young, J. C. (1981). *Medical choices in a Mexican village.* New Brunswick, NJ: Rutgers University Press.

CHAPTER 22

Mental Health Services
and Systems

Michael F. Polgar
Joseph P. Morrissey

INTRODUCTION

In 1972, McKinlay wrote a literature review summarizing 20 years of sociological research on the use of health services. He found a number of competing research paradigms and concluded with recommendations for empirical work on utilization behavior. Specifically, McKinlay called for research gathering data on sociodemographic characteristics, the role of social networks, stages in health seeking behavior, and organizational impediments to utilization. In the ensuing 27 years, the literature on health services and systems has grown tremendously and has informed public policy. Mental health services and systems research have provided an abundance of indicators and information regarding the organization, distribution, and performance of mental health providers. Organizational and interorganizational data on mental health providers have supplemented individual-level data, enhancing sociological research and theory. Consumers, providers, and policy analysts benefit from this literature as new cycles of reform change the structure and performance of mental health care services.

Mental health services research has been defined broadly and as a complement to

MICHAEL F. POLGAR • Center for Mental Health Services Research, Washington University, St. Louis, Missouri 63105-4899.   JOSEPH P. MORRISSEY • Sheps Center for Health Services Research, 725 Airport Building, Suite, 210, Chapel Hill, North Carolina 27599-7590.
Handbook of the Sociology of Mental Health, edited by Carol S. Aneshensel and Jo C. Phelan. Kluwer Academic/Plenum Publishers, New York, 1999.

research involving particular forms and structures of treatment. Consider the following two definitions:

1. Mental Health Services Research examines the availability, quality, use, cost, structure and effectiveness of mental health and related services, programs, organizations, and systems (NIMH, 1991).
2. The domain of services research begins where that of treatment research ends. Such research is intended to permit the effective transposition of proven treatments into the larger service-delivery environment. . . . The design and institution of service systems needs to be carried out with the same care as that of treatment itself. Such systems need to be rationally based on knowledge gained from careful evaluation studies (NIMH, 1988).

Sociological studies of mental health include research traditions at three levels of analysis: individuals, organizations, and systems. Figure 22.1 illustrates that each level of analysis can be conceptualized in terms of the most common inputs (independent variables), the primary units of analysis (sampling units), and the most common outcome measures (dependent variables). Like sociological research on health care utilization more generally (Pescosolido & Kronenfeld, 1995), mental health care services may be considered at multiple levels of abstraction.

First, at a microsocial level, research examines individual risk factors and health behaviors (Andersen, 1995), such as stress and coping behaviors (Thoits, 1995), using individual-based or person-centered measurement (George, 1989). Both within health care settings and in community populations, individual-level research measures attributes of people and makes comparisons across health care settings, communities, or populations. Some research on individuals examines mental health or illness according to social categories (e.g., gender, race, age), and other research pays more attention to diagnosis, functional levels, or geographic variables. Outcomes measured at this level of abstraction include individual health status and quality of life, often analyzed by group, community, or population characteristics.

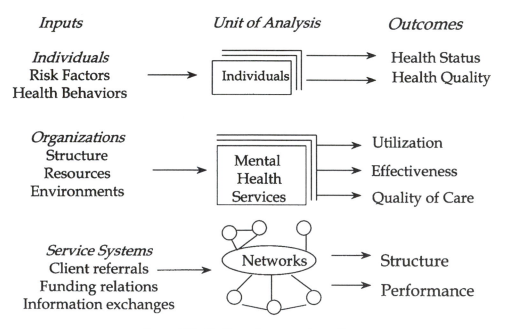

FIGURE 22.1. Health services research paradigms.

Second, research emphasizing provider-based measurement (George, 1989) uses broader, organizational perspectives to understand mental health services. Social research on health care utilization, organizational behavior, organizational development, and effectiveness examines broader questions about the structure, resources, and environments, of mental health service organizations. For example, studies of mental health utilization compare inpatient and outpatient care, primary and specialty care, as well as the effectiveness and quality of care in different arenas (Howard et al., 1996). Studies of specialty mental health services can make comparisons within and across facility type (Goldman & Skinner, 1989). At a multiorganizational level of analysis, research can also examine development of organizational forms, rates of organizational creation, organizational change, and organizational closures (Aldrich, 1979, 1987; Dowdall, 1996).

Third, at a macrosocial level of analysis, interorganizational research on systems of mental health care consider the effects of system-level interventions on the structure and performance of mental health provider organizations as social networks. Systems of care for persons with mental health problems are examined empirically based on surveys of groups of organizations or organizational sets (Evan, 1972). Interorganizational research examines the dynamic and complex structures of mental health service systems and the effects of system change on organizational performance (Morrissey, Calloway, Johnsen, & Ullman, 1997; Morrissey et al., 1994). The degree of communication and exchange among mental health provider organizations affects the system of care, which is modeled as a social network. The form and the performance of this system may be affected by changes in network variables such as density, centralization, and fragmentation, which vary across different service systems (Wasserman & Faust, 1994).

In the United States, four cycles of reform have developed and shifted responsibilities for administration of mental health services among governmental and private interests over the past 200 years (Morrissey, Goldman, & Klerman, 1985). These reforms focused on asylums in the early nineteenth century, mental hospitals in the early twentieth century, community mental health centers in the 1960s, and community support systems in the 1980s. A fifth cycle of reform, involving the growth and evolution of managed care, is currently generating important new questions about the organization and utilization of mental health service delivery (Mechanic, Schlesinger, & McAlpine, 1995; Morrissey, Johnsen, Starrett, Calloway, & Polgar, 1996). For sociologists, these questions include the effects of third-party management on the distribution, utilization, and organization of mental health care and cost-shifting between mental health, social welfare, and criminal justice systems.

This chapter reviews themes from recent research on mental health services and systems. We explore research on access and obstacles to care, systematic problems that may limit the distribution and use of mental health services. We then summarize national data on mental health service utilization according to the various types of organizations within and beyond the specialty mental health sector. Fourth, we explore emergent changes in services related to the growth of managed behavioral health care. Next, we consider some future directions for research in the sociology of mental health care services and systems.

ORGANIZATIONAL THEORY AND MENTAL HEALTH SERVICES

The early or "classical" period of social organizational studies of mental health services, from the late 1940s through the 1960s, relied on case studies and focused on the structure and functions of mental hospitals, the predominant institutions of that era (see Chapter 25). Stanton and Schwartz (1954), Belknap (1956), Caudill (1958), Strauss (1964), and Goffman (1961), among others, were the pioneers of this tradition. The contributions and limitations of this work have been extensively reviewed elsewhere (Perrow, 1965). Consequently, we concentrate on more recent research.

One of the hallmarks of recent scholarship in this era is the shift from "closed" to "open-system" perspectives on mental health institutions and the ways context or socioenvironmental influences shape their organization, financing, and effectiveness. The open-systems approach sees mental health care as taking place within an evolving web of professional and organizational relationships. Mental health service providers work in an increasingly diverse range of health and welfare organizations. Many of these organizations have a long and complex history in the United States (Grob, 1994; Morrissey, Goldman, Klerman, & Associates, 1980), tracing their roots back to British medicine (Scull, 1989). Recent growth and transformations among mental health and behavioral care organizations have intensified the process of organizational development and change, promising new levels of cost-effectiveness and leading to concerns about managed care and the public trust (Mechanic, 1996).

Organizational theory suggests that organizational survival, growth, and evolution require accessible, effective, and legitimate services (Aldrich, 1987; Scott, 1995). Organizational forms, such as hospitals and health management organizations (HMOs), adapt to dynamic environments, which are affected by health policy. Occupational groups such as psychiatrists, psychologists, social workers, and a wide variety of family and personal counselors, compete and coordinate their efforts under medical, administrative, and governmental authorities to provide treatments and insight-oriented services for diverse populations of children and adults in all states and for a variety of conditions. The importance of coordination, above and beyond competition, is greater when networks are larger (Alter & Hage, 1993).

Organizations may work together and develop interdependencies (Alter & Hage, 1993). Organizational dyads (Evan, 1972), triads (Calloway, Morrissey, & Johnsen, 1995), and larger organizational systems, including mental health providers (Morrissey et al., 1994, Provan & Milward, 1995), are formal representations of social structures among interdependent components. Organizational network theory emphasizes the presence and strength of network ties based on atomic and molecular metaphors first articulated by classical sociologists (Simmel, 1991).

Health service systems are modeled in terms of interorganizational relationships (IORs), and the structural forms of IORs may be measured using social network analysis (Van de Ven & Ferry, 1980; Wasserman & Faust, 1994). The identification and evaluation of organizational sets and systems are based on the study of the forms and changes in the social structure of IORs. The integration and coordination of complex networks is one goal of large-scale health and welfare demonstration projects (Morrissey et al., 1994).

Organizational theory takes many forms. Mental health services research has been inspired by institutional theory (Scott, 1995) and the population–ecology paradigm (Aldrich, 1979, Hannan & Freeman, 1984; Scott, 1995). Institutional theory examines the influence of the state and professions on the structure and function of organizational fields. Adaptation of organizations and organizational forms is the subject of the ecological perspective, which examines evolving populations of mental health services which are moving from a state-supported set of health authorities to a dynamic group of competing organizations.

Structural inertia and organizational change are two important but alternative outcomes of the relationship between organizations and their environment (Hannan & Freeman, 1984). In mental health systems, after over 150 years of predominantly institutionally based care, reforms over the last 40 years have generated increasingly dynamic systems of care, changing access, distribution, and organizational forms of care (Hasenfeld, 1983). Integrated services for adults and children are serving growing needs in more effective ways, promoting mental health care in the context of rapid social change (Breakey, 1996; Stroul & Friedman, 1996).

ACCESSIBILITY OF SERVICES AND OBSTACLES TO CARE

The structure of mental health systems and services has an impact on the course and consequences of mental illness which is independent of the efficacy of particular treatments. The burden of care for treatment of the mentally ill in the de facto system of care (Regier et al., 1993) is high, and the burden of care for untreated disorders is even higher. National data show that, during a 1-year period, 14.7% of the U.S. population uses mental health or addiction services, including 5.9% in the specialty mental health sector, 6.4% in the general medical sector, 3.0% in the human services sector, and 4.1% in voluntary support networks (Norquist & Regier, 1996). Nationally, it is estimated that more than 70% of persons with mental health disorders do not receive services, and only 12–13% of those with disorders receive services from a mental health specialist (Howard et al., 1996; Regier et al., 1993).

Health care organizations are designed to provide treatment and care to individuals, but in the case of mental illness, access to care is difficult for many people. Many children and adults in need of mental health services are unable or unwilling to receive care. Regardless of the complexities of diagnosis, children and youth with mental health problems are a central concern nationally (Stroul, 1993; Stroul & Friedman, 1996). Children with mental illnesses, particularly those with serious emotional disturbance (SED), need access to care without major obstacles. Children and youth are currently being treated by a de facto system in which schools provide or facilitate a majority of the care (Burns et al., 1995). Adults with mental illness, including the seriously mentally ill (SMI), use services both in the general medical sector and the specialty mental health sector (Norquist & Regier, 1996). As we will elaborate, these services are increasingly provided on an outpatient basis (Mandersheid & Sonnenchein, 1996).

The most visible problems associate with untreated mental health problems include school failures among youth and homelessness among adults. Programs to address unmet needs for mental health care, such as the ACCESS program for the homeless mentally ill, provide new models for mental health care service systems (Morrissey et al., 1997; Randolph, Blasinsky, Leginski, Parker, & Goldman, 1997). Still, there are differences in assessments of need, as well as gaps in mental health service coverage. The gaps can be narrowed by interventions such as ACCESS, particularly when the need is assessed and recognized by the homeless client (Rosenheck & Lam, 1997).

Obstacles to care include complex, including problems with the meaning of mental illness, the necessary course of treatment and care, consumer cooperation and satisfaction, and variations in the contexts of mental health care. Among the severely mentally ill, problems of housing and providing mental health service are most challenging (Randolph et al., 1997). These are a subset of the more general problems of displacement and homelessness.

Currently, access to community care and federal legislation to eliminate housing discrimination against people with mental disabilities is tempered by definitions of reasonable accommodation and established "dangerousness" to others (Petrilla & Ayers, 1994). Section 8 housing certificates provide extensive federal support for independent living among mentally ill people, against the rising problems of homelessness (Newman, Reschovsky, & Kaneda, 1994). In the current era of managed care, state and local supports for housing and health care are increasingly used to create community solutions to structural problems surrounding mental health care.

Access to care can be seriously limited by problems of poverty, stigma, misunderstanding, and racial inequality. Despite a tradition of epidemiological studies which suggest that mental health problems are as high or higher among poor people, those with higher incomes and insurance coverage are better represented among service users. People of color have higher rates of mental disorder than whites but use fewer services, in part due to their relatively low socioeconomic status (Norquist & Regier, 1996). However, even in "nonpoor", insured populations, there are ethnic and racial differences in mental health service use (Padgett, Patrick, Burns, & Schlesinger, 1994). The stigma surrounding mental illness, based on biased perceptions of its causes and manifestations, also impedes access to housing and care (Link, Cullen, Frank, & Wozniak, 1987; Link, Cullen, Struening, Shrout, & Dohrenwend, 1989). Reports on homeless people with severe mental illness suggest that the most frequent barrier to mental health service use was not knowing where to go for help, followed by not being able to afford services, hassle or confusion, and previously being denied services (Rosenheck & Lam, 1997).

Major obstacles to health services for people with mental health care needs include the following:

- Individual resources (cost, insurance, therapeutic relationship)
- Community resources (accessible providers, transportation, health education)
- Organization of services (choice of services, cost of care, insurance parity)
- Coordination of services (professional referral, integrated delivery systems)

Individual access problems, particularly cost and insurance, are most prohibitive among homeless people, those who are disabled, and those dually diagnosed with substance abuse and mental health problems (Dickey & Azeni, 1996). However, cost is not the only obstacle to care, nor is it even the most important barrier. Structural and organizational factors may impede older people from service, challenging the affordability–utilization assumption (Feinson & Popper, 1995). Available community resources, organization of services, and services coordination, improve systems of care. Community-based care, particularly for people with serious mental illness, can be both humane and cost-effective (Stein & Test, 1980).

There is also evidence for racial disparities in access and utilization (Padgett et al., 1994), although specific acts of discrimination on the basis of race, gender, or illness status are illegal under a number of statutes. Research and scholarship on mental health services find that ethnic minorities are not well served by the community mental health service system, and that culturally sensitive and responsive services are needed (Takeuchi & Uehara, 1996). Discrimination against mentally ill people is also a concern; the Federal Fair Housing Act has been successfully used in representative court cases where reasonable accommodation is not made to people with mental disabilities (Petrilla & Ayers, 1994).

Obstacles to effective mental health service delivery to children and their caretakers are found by researchers in both rural and urban regions. Poor utilization of long-term mental health services by urban children, particularly minorities in difficult economic conditions, has been conceptualized as both a lack of treatment compliance and insensitivity to complex problems among social service agencies and care providers (McKernan, McCadam, & Gonzales, 1996). Likewise, low rates of mental health service use by rural children may be related to problems in the distribution of providers, insurance coverage, and the disproportionate use of schools as a de facto system of care (Burns et al., 1997).

TYPES AND UTILIZATION
OF MENTAL HEALTH SERVICE ORGANIZATIONS

The mental health service system is composed of informal and formal providers working to supply institutional, outpatient, and home-based care. In the formal sector, there are two major distinctions that characterize mental health service research. First, institutional or inpatient care is distinguished from outpatient care. There has been a decrease over time in the use of institutional and inpatient care (Grob, 1991; Mandersheid & Sonnenchein, 1996). Second, specialty mental health services are distinguished from mental health services delivered by primary health care providers. Recently, there has been an increase in the use of primary providers for mental health care (Costello, Burns, & Costello, 1988; Mechanic, 1975). In addition, affect rates of utilization in all service sectors are diagnosis, severity of illness, and policy initiatives. Informal care—through nonmedical professions, self-help groups, families, and friends—is also a major resource for people with mental health and/ or substance abuse disorders.

Research on specialty mental health services is complex due to variations in definitions and methods of aggregation (George, 1989). Useful quantitative techniques include aggregation by unit of time, source of services, type of setting, service sector (as mentioned), provider profession, illness episode, service episode, and episode of care. Episodic aggregation may be most useful for longitudinal research at the interface of individual and organizational levels of analysis, while aggregation by setting, sector, and profession may be most useful to studies of the service system as a whole.

The specialty mental health system may be defined by aggregating organizations according to facility type, shown in Table 22.1. In 1992, organizational categories comprised nonfederal general hospitals containing separate psychiatric units and "other" facilities, which includes freestanding psychiatric *partial* care organizations and multiservice organizations (a new category including community mental health centers). Freestanding psychiatric clinics are the next largest organizational component but represent only half of the number of organizations as either of the two most common types. With regard to admissions, organizational representation differs by type of admission. Almost half of inpatient admissions are at nonfederal hospitals, whereas "other" organizatons predominate with regard to outpatient and partial forms of treatment. Public and private psychiatric hospitals serve fewer inpatient admissions than general hospitals. Veterans centers served almost 9% of inpatient admissions in 1992.

Although the number of organizations treating mental illness has doubled in the last 20 years, the number of treatment beds available has been halved. Although the proportion of psychiatric treatment beds in general and private psychiatric hospitals has increased, particularly in the 1980s (Mandersheid & Sonnenchein, 1996). Corresponding, patient care episodes took place increasingly in the context of outpatient care. In 1955, inpatient care comprised a strong majority of the 1.7 million care episodes. In 1992, outpatient care

TABLE 22.1. Specialty Mental Health System, 1992

Facility type	Organizations		Admissions		
	Number	Percentage	Inpatient	Outpatient	Partial
State or county mental hospital	273	5.0	275,382	45,527	5,380
Private psychiatric hospital	475	8.6	469,827	140,824	41,929
Nonfederal hospital with psychiatric unit	1,616	29.4	951,121	429,160	53,670
Veterans medical center	162	2.9	180,529	144,591	19,478
Freestanding psychiatric clinic	862	15.7	n.a.	464,449	n.a.
Residential treatment center (child)	497	9.0	36,388	112,667	13,395
Other[a]	1,613	29.3	178,815	1,544,776	159,646
Total	5,498	100	2,092,062	2,881,994	293,498
Total beds	270,867				
Total care episodes[b]	8,824,701		2,322,374	5,958,748	543,559

[a] Includes freestanding psychiatric partial care organizations and multiservice mental health organizations (previously classified at community mental health centers).
[b] Volume of care is measured as the number of persons receiving care at the start of the year plus the number of additional admissions into care during the year (patient care episodes). This is a duplicated count, since one person may have multiple care episodes in a year.
Source: Mandersheid and Sonnenschein (1996).

comprised 68% of the 8.8 million episodes, while the inpatient care share shrank to one-third of its share (Mandersheid & Sonnenchein, 1996, p. 96). Increases in staffing associated with this growth of outpatient care providers were associated with a growth in professional care staff, including psychologists, social workers, and registered nurses. Twenty-two-year trends in financing of mental health services also show that increased expenditures are almost entirely due to inflation (Mandersheid & Sonnenchein, 1996, p. 100).

National epidemiological surveys elaborate patterns of mental health utilization as shown in Table 22.2. An estimated 14.5% of the adult population used mental health or addiction services over the course of a year, primarily in the general medical and specialty mental health/substance abuse sectors). The estimated annual rates of mental or addictive disorder, based on a survey of the adult population in the United States is 28.1% or approximately 44.7 million people. This figure is based on the Epidemologic Catchment Area (ECA) study, a five-community study of mental health epidemiology and service use

TABLE 22.2. Annual Use of Mental Health or Addictive Disorder Services in U.S. Adult Population

Service sector	Utilization rate (%)		Number receiving treatment
	Inpatient	Outpatient	
Specialty mental health/substance abuse	0.9	5.6	9,381,000
General medical	0	6.4	10,043,000
Human services	na	3	4,754,000
Self-help groups	na	0.7	1,163,000
Family/friends	na	3.5	5,506,000
Voluntary support	na	4.1	6,535,000
Grand total	0.9	14.5	23,107,000

Source: Regier et al. (1993).

(Regier et al., 1993). These indicators fall to 22% (35.1 million) for mental disorders alone, exclusive of substance abuse disorders. In comparison, approximately 5.6% and 6.4% of the population made outpatient visits to the specialty mental health and general health sectors, respectively, and approximately 1% used inpatient hospital services.

Although occurrense of mental or substance abuse disorder does not imply or necessarily precede mental health service use, the ECA study determined that over a 1-year period, about 23 million adults used ambulatory mental health services for mental or addictive disorder treatment (Narrow, Regier, Rae, Manderscheid, & Locke, 1993). Mental health service users accounted for over 325 million visits, averaging over 14 visits per person per year, as shown in Tables 22.3 and 22.4. The average number of visits was lowest in the general medical sector, with visits to voluntary support networks substantially more frequent than visits to formal health system providers. This pattern is consistent across diagnostic area, as shown in Table 22.4. For people getting help for substance use disorders, the use of a voluntary support network is more frequent (Narrow et al., 1993).

When service delivery areas are reported in greater detail (Table 22.4), most ambulatory visits within specialty mental health services are made to providers in private practice mental health centers, alcohol/drug treatment centers, or specialist clinics. Roughly 11% of all visits are made to general medical care settings, with about 12% to professionals in other domains (clergy, teachers, etc.) (Narrow et al., 1993). A significant amount of care is done by self-help groups, family and friends, through less formal or informal systems of care. This pattern is particularly apparent for substance abuse visits, where recovery programs may be based on self-help principles.

Longitudinal studies help clarify patterns of mental health utilization, because they document trajectories that evolve over time. New users of the mental health system who require the support of Medicaid are an important group for public health and social policy trends. In a study conducted at the University of Pennsylvania, almost half of a cohort of Medicaid-supported new users did not receive any services again over a 4-year period, whereas long-term users were the most severely mentally ill and often shifted from inpatient to outpatient care. Fewer than one in five individuals were continuous service users over the 4-year study period (Rothbard, Schinar, & Adams, 1996).

Examining mental health service use in the aggregate shows the system of care in practice. Table 22.5 details the distribution of inpatient services received by diagnosis. These estimates are based on extrapolations from the ECA data and pertain to an estimated 1.4 million people identified. The majority of person-visits to inpatient services occur in general hospitals and regional mental hospitals. These two types of services provide the majority of services across diagnosis, but diagnosis shapes the distribution services. People

TABLE 22.3. Average Number of Visits per Treated Person per Year to Ambulatory Settings

		Disorder		
Ambulatory setting	All persons treated	Any disorder except substance abuse	Comorbid mental and substance	Any substance use
Specialty mental health	14.0	15.8	12.9	12.4
General medical[a]	3.6	4.1	3.9	3.2
Professionals	10.1	12.5	13.5	10.8
Voluntary support	19.8	18.9	21.2	20.6

[a]Includes general physician and emergency room.
Source: Narrow et al. (1993).

TABLE 22.4. Annual Visits to Ambulatory Settings, by Disorder

		Disorder		
	All persons treated	Any disorder except substance	Comorbid mental and substance	Any substance
Total number of visits	325,855,000	180,808,000	35,099,000	56,333,000
Psychiatric hospital outpatient clinics	1.3%	2.1%	0.3%	0.2%
Mental health center outpatient clinics	5.8	7.3	8.6	6.9
General hospital outpatient clinics	2	2.3	2.2	1.4
VA hospital outpatient clinics	1.1	1.2	2.6	2.3
Alcohol/drug outpatient clinics	4.3	4.2	1.6	5.4
Mental health specialist clinic	4.1	4.8	6.4	5.2
Mental health specialist private practice	18.9	19.8	13.9	12.1
Specialty mental health subtotal	37.5	41.8	35.8	33.6
General medical[a]	11.1	11.4	9.5	8.4
Health systems (subtotal)	48.6	53.2	45.3	42
Other professional	11.7	12.5	18.4	12.8
Professionals (total)	60.3	65.7	63.8	54.8
Self-help group	14.3	12.6	15.4	20.6
Family/friends	25.4	21.7	20.9	24.6
Voluntary support (total)	39.7	34.3	36.2	45.2

[a] Includes general physician and emergency room.
Source: Narrow et al. (1993).

with substance abuse disorders, for example, had relatively few stays at community mental health centers or nursing homes, and many stays at veterans hospitals or alcohol/drug units (Narrow et al., 1993).

Regional information from the Methods for the Epidemiology of Child and Adolescent Mental Disorders (MECA) Study shows that around 17% of youth use mental health-related services, primarily specialists or school counselors, in three study sites, Atlanta, New Haven, and New York. In Puerto Rico, the fourth site, the rates of service use among youth are much lower however, as shown in Table 22.6 (Leaf et al., 1996). Utilization, although broad-based, is not usually in the context of the mental health specialty sector. Schools and school-linked health services account for increasing mental health service use among children and adolescents in recent years (Burns et al., 1995).

TABLE 22.5. Distribution of Adults Seen in Inpatient Settings

	All persons treated (%)	Any DIS disorder except substance abuse (%)	Comorbid mental health and substance abuse (%)	Any substance use disorder (%)
General hospital	43.3	39.4	45.2	50.2
Regional mental hospital	35.2	38.9	25.1	21.4
Community mental health center	4.2	5.7	0.2	0.2
Private mental hospital	10.8	12.6	7.1	7.4
VA hospital (psychiatric unit)	7.1	6.7	15.2	15
Alcohol/drug unit	7.2	7.9	13.1	10.9
Nursing home	3.3	3.3	1.5	1.2
Total	1,400,000	1,033,000	354,000	437,000

Source: Narrow et al. (1993).

Table 22.6. Percentage of Youths Receiving Specific Mental-Health-Related Services in Past Year

	Total ($n = 1,285$)	Site			
		Atlanta ($n = 299$)	New Haven ($n = 314$)	New York ($n = 360$)	Puerto Rico ($n = 312$)
Any mental health service	14.9%	16.7%	17.2%	18.1%	7.4%
Mental health specialist	8.1	7.4	8.0	11.7	4.8
Medical	2.9	2.3	5.7	1.9	1.6
School	8.1	8.7	11.2	9.4	2.9
Clergy	1.2	1.0	2.6	0.3	1.0
Social service	1.6	1.3	1.6	2.2	1.0
Other	0.7	1.0	0.3	1.4	0.0

Source: Leaf et al. (1996).

Mental health outcomes and treatment quality are complex concepts which are measured in terms of both individual functional capacities and the health status of groups and populations (Ware & Sherbourne, 1992). Evaluation of outcomes and treatment quality is done sporadically, although the need for accountability under managed care has been a boon to outcomes research. Private hospitals do the best job of placing mentally ill patients, managing cases into community-based treatment, particularly if the patient has personal resources, is not severely ill, and if the hospital is an urban, nonfederally funded teaching hospital (Dorwart, 1995).

Research also shows that clinical characteristics of patients have more influence on the quality of care provided than do institutional constraints or social biases (Segal, Watson, & Akutsu, 1996). Public sector facilities care for the most disturbing patients and people without social or economic resources. Among those with severe and persistent mental illness (SPMI), outcomes are difficult to discern because the course of those disorders is usually chronic and recurrent under even the best of circumstances. Evidence from the Robert Wood Johnson Program on Chronic Mental Illness suggest that the establishment of integrated local mental health authorities are a necessary but not sufficient basis for improved outcomes for persons with SPMI (Lehman, Postrado, Roth, McNary, & Goldman, 1994).

Before closing this section, it is important to note that there are limits on measures of utilization and quality of mental health care. First, epidemiological data suffer from the difficulty of defining the population with active mental health problems and with operationalizing the variety of organizations providing mental health care services within formal and informal sectors. Second, it is difficult to separate treatment effects from ecological effects such as patient background. Third, the precise definition of mental health care or treatment depends upon a number of factors, generating estimates that can vary by as much as 700% (Olfson & Pincus, 1994).

GROWTH OF MANAGED BEHAVIORAL HEALTH CARE

The organization and structure of mental health care, historically a governmental responsibility, is increasingly the domain of private companies designing managed care systems (Mechanic et al., 1995). HMOs have been front-runners in demonstrating the benefits of managed care in the general health sector. Four types of HMOs include staff models, group models, networks, and independent practitioner associations (IPAs).

- Staff model HMOs employ physicians directly to serve members exclusively.
- Group model HMOs contract with a multispecialty medical group, which may provide services to the membership or to non-HMO patients.
- Network HMOs involve two or more group practices which contract for HMO enrollees.
- IPAs are loosely coupled, solo and small group practices organized to produce HMO efficiencies using capitation and prepayment.

In addition, there are foundations for medical care (FMCs), freestanding managed care organizations (MCOs), other specialty HMOs and preferred provider organizations (PPOs), and utilization review organizations (UROs). Freestanding MCOs are third-party administrators (e.g., U.S. Behavioral Health) providing support to self-insuring employers or insurance companies. Specialty HMOs and PPOs provide benefits in one limited medical specialty area. UROs employ external reviewers who assess the medical appropriateness of a treatment plan, generating a preadmission certification.

Increasingly, benefits for mental health and substance abuse (MH/SA) are managed separately, or "carved out," from general health care benefits. An independent managed behavioral care organization (MBCO) may contract with a mental health PPO, often in a capitated contract, making the MBCO essentially a mental health HMO and independent service agency (Wells & Astrachan, 1995, p. 59). Growth of the managed behavioral health care carve-out industry began in 1981 with the Metropolitan Clinic of Counseling (MCC, now CIGNA) in Minneapolis (Freeman & Trabin, 1994). Its roots spread back to the community mental health center (CMHC) movement, which began as a strategy to shift care from state hospitals to community alternatives under the Kennedy administration in 1963 (see Chapter 25). CMHC leaders have become executives of a number of private behavioral managed health care companies.

Employee assistance programs (EAPs) are another basis for MBCO organizations. EAPs began in the 1950s as occupational health services for substance abuse. They developed an informal provider network and a careful triage system, which have been incorporated into MBCO programs. Some EAPs are now expanding to become MBCO groups, while others bridge the human resources department with the "front end" of MBCO (Freeman & Trabin, 1994). A final historical precursor was utilization review for hospitalization of persons with psychiatric and substance abuse disorders. Seventeen utilization review companies were operating in 1979, making authorization a requirement for reimbursement. In the early 1980s, some of these groups developed specialized behavioral care services. In general, utilization review increased cost-savings by reducing inpatient utilization, although some costs were shifted to outpatient services. However, a lack of contractual relations between reviewers and treatment companies led to problems and eventually managed care carve-out companies (Freeman & Trabin, 1994).

In the early 1980s, private behavioral health benefits and private specialty clinics grew, and costs rose quickly. The need for more comprehensive care management in behavioral health care became clear. MBCOs were created from the need to assure cost-effectiveness through checks and balances, because cost-effectiveness was not being assured through the early utilization review industry. There was no price consciousness, since patients were not payers, nor was there concern with quality, since information on services was lacking.

The Tax Equity and Fiscal Responsibility Act (TEFRA) of 1982 led to the creation of diagnostic related groups (DRGs) to control health costs. These standards and the end of "cost-plus" reimbursement hurt hospital profits and investors. The MBCO industry was not strongly affected by DRGs however, since behavioral diagnoses were regarded as imprecise. Chains of specialty care hospitals began to proliferate, growing 40% between 1979 and 1986 (Bassuk & Holland, 1989).

During this time, indemnity plan benefits were inadequate and exploited. A narrow conception of psychiatric illness and skepticism over alternatives to inpatient treatment meant that inpatient utilization was excessive and that alternatives to hospitalization were unavailable in most communities. Aggressive marketing of inpatient programs with lengthy stays did little to expand services and less costly alternatives. Self-insured employers sought control over behavioral care costs.

Managed behavioral health care companies originated as clinics or informal local provider networks with a few business or insurance contracts. The development and institutionalization of MBCOs may be an example of what DiMaggio and Powell (1983) term *institutional isomorphism*, mimetic isomorphism in particular. Organizational characteristics became more similar as firms began to imitate one another under uncertain environmental conditions, such as the changing regulatory structure, the changing needs of employers, and the bewildering array of organizational arrangements and possible alternatives to inpatient hospital care. The fast growth of MBCOs in this period was visible first in the number of organizations and soon thereafter in their market share and the number of covered lives. As the market consolidated, the number of companies decreased and the industry become more clearly defined.

Gaining competitive advantage in this period meant aggressive sales and marketing, building an operational infrastructure (including expensive information systems), and a qualified staff, and credentialing within a network of providers. Quick development meant reliance on venture capital rather than marginal profits and shifted an informal culture into a more professional mode, with accompanying instability among staffs. MBCOs marketed their ability to reduce cost, assure quality, and improve access to major corporations which were in the midst of labor negotiations. Corporate buyers were influenced by benefit consultants, who promoted managed care and assisted in vendor selection. By the early 1990s, a more standard set of MBCOs began to tailor services to better-informed consumers (Freeman & Trabin, 1994).

In this period, economies of scale allowed tremendous consolidation, increasing coverage as the number of companies fell. MBCOs became responsive to conflicts between patient demands and payer-supported managed care policies. Whereas insurance companies are in the business of paying claims, MBCOs are involved in managing care, and their integration has not been easy. These two types of companies need each other for flexibility and strength (Freeman & Trabin, 1994).

Ethical questions remain for managed care, particularly regarding public trust (Mechanic, 1996). Managed care uses guidelines which limit patients' choices and doctors' decisions. MBCOs supplement the primary goal of health with managerial constraints, expanding organizational goals to explicitly include, if not prioritize, cost savings and efficiency (Pelligrino, 1994). Further, the costs of mental illness and substance abuse are spread across a number of agencies, and the "products" of mental health care are difficult to quantify, especially in the short run. Looking at the manner in which medical decisions affect quality of life years is an interesting advance in decision-making sciences, however, the applicability of such methods in mental health remains uncertain.

By the end of 1994, there were 625 HMO plans nationally, 1,107 PPOs, and 118 point of service (POS) plans (AMCRA Foundation, 1995). The growth in the cost of medical care, particularly behavioral care (i.e., mental health care and substance abuse services) has had a strong impact on state budgets. The federal government, under the authority of the Health Care Financing Administration (HCFA), has changed the development of health policy and mental health care organizations through waivers of certain federal program requirements (Dobson, Moran, & Young, 1992). Demonstration projects and programmatic waivers have allowed greater state involvement in the growth of MCOs and MBCOs through more flexible use of federal Medicaid funds to support public mental health and substance abuse services. Increasing numbers of waivers were allowed in the early and late 1980s, following election years, and programmatic waivers comprised an increasing proportion of waivers over time (Dobson et al., 1992).

A Social Security Act Section 1115 waiver from the HCFA allows states to fund demonstration projects which circumvent restrictions on the use of general Medicaid funds, including the use of MCOs. A section 1915 waiver is designed to allow greater choice (1915a) or mandatory managed participation (1915b). Evaluations of local health program demonstrations and state reforms are ongoing and important, particularly among health services which serve SMI populations who use public services, disproportionately, including emergency rooms and inpatient care, because of their high levels of need (Stroup & Dorwart, 1995). Exclusions in the use of 1115 funds for aged, blind, and disabled populations were part of the waivers in Hawaii and Rhode Island (Folcarelli, 1995).

How do 1115 waivers increase the power and legitimacy of managed care organizations? First, they lend both government support to state use of MCOs for Medicaid patients, enhancing cognitive and administrative legitimacy. Second, these waivers provide a model or demonstration that managed care systems can provide mental health care without compromising access or quality. It is important to note, however, that evaluation of state reform is still in its early stages (Wells & Astrachan, 1995; Wells & Hosek, 1992), particularly since the first state Medicaid managed care program for mental health only started in 1990, in Arizona, and most have started since 1993. Third, they increase the credibility of the private initiative by encouraging MCOs to serve the most challenging of clients, the severely mentally ill, rather than skimming the lower risk and higher-paying clients from private employers. In other words, if MCOs can act fairly and consistently in the public interest without compromising trust, their legitimacy and reputation will be secured, as well as their position in the market.

DIRECTIONS FOR FUTURE RESEARCH

One of the ironies of past reform cycles in mental health care is that new organizational forms and practices are embraced without a critical examination of their success claims, which ultimately prove to be exaggerated and are unable to resolve many of the fundamental problems of the older, discredited system of care. The more things change, the more they remain the same. Will this epitaph befall managed mental health care as well?

There are parallels with earlier reform efforts in the rush to adopt managed mental health care despite the lack of clear and convincing evidence to support claims that it will result in more efficient and effective care for mentally ill persons. The lack of evidence is especially disconcerting with regard to persons with SPMI, yet the states are rapidly adopting one or another form of managed care for their Medicaid and other public mental health responsibilities. Assessing the operation and performance of managed mental health care systems is a research and public policy agenda that must become a central concern for sociologists and other social scientists over the next several years.

Needed research relates to the three levels of analysis (see Figure 22.1) that have guided the sociology of mental health since its inception. At the microlevel, there is a need for studies of the outcomes of managed mental health care. To what extent do various types of managed care—carve-in versus carve-out, risk-sharing versus no-risk contracts, group model versus independent practice networks, and so on—actually lead to "managed care" versus "managed money"? Which types of managed care promote access to high-quality services, and which ones tend to discourage access and limit the intensity of services in order to turn a profit within a capitation or contractual payment system? What impact do these patterns of care have on mentally ill persons and their families, on other social safety net systems, and on the mix of public and personal contributions to the costs of care?

At the middle or organizational level, there is a need to understand the incentives associated with various forms of managed care and how these incentives shape provider behavior. In principle, managed care reverses the incentives associated with the traditional fee-for-service system; whereas seeing more patients or performing more procedures leads to more income in a fee-for-service payment system, it eats up potential profits in a capitated managed care system. But this formulation is deceptively simple given the myriad forms of managed care and the ways they are now combined into hybrid organizing and financing systems. Nonetheless, managed care systems can be expected to decrease the intensity of services by substituting less costly forms of care or no care at all. In mental health, the most intensive forms of care are inpatient hospitalization or other 24-hour care. Will patients be discharged "quicker and sicker" under managed care programs? Are some forms more likely to adopt this strategy than others?

In addition, the marketplace for mental health services is undergoing rapid changes in terms of ownership and control stimulated by developments in managed care and privatization. Buyouts and mergers are happening so quickly that it is difficult to keep up with who owns which managed behavioral health care firm. Traditional distinctions between the public and private sectors, and between specialty mental health and generic health care providers, are now all but useless as analytic categories. What are the implications of this agglomeration for the mental health system? Will the shift from locally or regionally owned and operated facilities to a few national chains lead to greater efficiencies and effectiveness? What kind of accountability systems are needed for these multistate networks? What will happen to consumer and family voice in these evolving systems of care? Will national corporations be more responsive to these interests than local hospitals and mental health centers have been? Will these agglomerated systems be receptive to care innovations that cost more money but lead to improved quality of life for persons involved?

At the macrolevel, the kinds of questions that need to be addressed by future research relate to the transformation of the mental health system and the redefinition of its boundaries with other community systems. What will be the impact of managed mental health care on community support systems for persons with the most serious and persistent mental illnesses? For the past 25 years, national policy has promoted linkages between mental health, social welfare, substance abuse, housing, health, criminal justice, and vocational systems to meet the needs of people with multiple needs that cannot be met by medical–psychiatric care alone. The emphasis in managed care on bottom-line costs and assuring that there is a payer for every service delivered may discourage the type of interagency pooling of resources and leveraging at the local level that has been encouraged by funding programs at the National Institute of Mental Health and the Center for Mental Health Services. In its place, managed care may well promote cost-shifting between service sectors as persons with multiple needs are "unbundled" and redefined as criminals, addicts, or whatever label will facilitate their transfer into another care or confinement system. "Dumping" people with multiple or expensive health problems into adjacent systems is an imperfect solution to difficult circumstances.

All of these research questions can be folded under the overriding concern about which face of managed care will endure: the benevolent face of comprehensive and continuous care to meet individual needs or the malevolent face of commodification and money making? This is a major and formidable research agenda, but it is one that holds the promise of making the sociology of mental health relevant to the next generation of policymakers, providers, and consumers.

ACKNOWLEDGMENTS: The work on this chapter was supported in part by a training grant (T32-MH19117) and a research center grant (P50-MH51410) from the National Institute of Mental Health. The statements contained in this chapter are solely those of the authors and do not necessarily reflect the views or policies of the NIMH.

REFERENCES

Aldrich, H. (1979). *Organizations and environments*. Englewood Cliffs, NJ: Prentice Hall.

Aldrich, H. (1987). New paradigmes for old: The population perspective's contribution to health services research. *Medical Care Review, 44*(2), 000–000.

Alter, C., & Hage, J. (1993). *Organizations working together* (Vol. 191). Newbury Park, CA: Sage.

Andersen, R. M. (1995, March). Revisiting the behavioral model and access to medical care: Does it matter? *Journal of Health and Social Behavior, 36*, 1–10.

AMCRA Foundation. (1995). *Managed health care overview 1994–1995*. Washington DC: Author.

Bassuk, E., & Holland, S. (1989). Accounting for high cost psychiatric care. *Business and Health, 52*(7), 38–41.

Belknap, I. (1956). *Human problems of a mental hospital*. New York: McGraw-Hill.

Breakey, W. R. (1996). *Integrated mental health services: Modern community psychiatry*. New York: Oxford University Press.

Burns, B., Costello, E. J., Angold, A., Tweed, D., Stangl, D., Farmer, E. M. Z., & Erkanli, A. (1995). Children's mental health service use across sectors. *Health Affairs, 14*(3), 147–159.

Burns, B., Costello, E. J., Erkanli, A., Tweed, D., Farmer, E. M. Z., & Angold, A. (1997). Insurance coverage and mental health service use by adolescents with serious emotional disturbance. *Journal of Child and Family Studies, 6*(1), 89–111.

Calloway, M., Morrissey, J., & Johnsen, M. (1995). *Using triads to assess structural change in networks of organization*. Paper presented at the International Social Network Conference, London.

Caudill, W. (1958). *The mental hospital as a small society*. Cambridge, MA: Harvard University Press.

Costello, E. J., Burns, B. J., & Costello, A. J. (1988). Service utilization and psychiatric diagnosis in pediatric primary care: The role of the gatekeeper. *Pediatrics, 82*, 435–441.

Dickey, B., & Azeni, H. (1996). Persons with dual diagnoses of substance abuse and major mental illness: Their excess costs of psychiatric care. *American Journal of Public Health, 87*(7), 973–977.

DiMaggio, P., & Powell, W. (1983, April). The iron cage revisited: Institutional isomorphism and collective rationality in organizational fields. *American Sociological Review, 48*, 147–160.

Dobson, A., Moran, D., & Young, G. (1992). The role of federal waivers in the health policy process. *Health Affairs, 11*(4), 72–94.

Dorwart, R. (1995, October). Managed mental health care: Myths and realities in the 1990s. *Hospital and Community Psychiatry, 41*, 1087–1091.

Dowdall, G. (1996). *The eclipse of the state mental hospital*. Albany: SUNY Press.

Evan, W. (1972). An organization-set model of interorganizational relations. In M. Tuite & R. K. Chisholm (Eds.), *Interorganizational decision making* (pp. 181–200). New York: Aldine–Atherton.

Feinson, M., & Popper, M. (1995). Does affordability affect mental health utilization? A United-States–Israel comparison of older adults. *Social Science and Medicine, 40*(5), 669–78.

Folcarelli, C. (1995). *Medicaid section 1115 waivers: Mental health and substance-abuse related provisions of five state demonstrations.* Paper presented at the Center for Mental Health Services (CMHS), Rockville, MD.

Freeman, M., & Trabin, T. (1994). *Managed behavioral healthcare: History, models, key issues, and future course.* Unpublished paper, prepared for the Center for Mental Health Services, Rockville, MD.

George, L. K. (1989). Definition, classification, and measurement of mental health services. In C. A. Taube, D. Mechanic, & A. A. Hohmann (Eds.), *The future of mental health services research* (Vol. 89, 289–301). Washington, DC: National Institutes of Mental Health.

Goffman, E. (1961). *Asylums.* Garden City, NY: Doubleday.

Goldman, H. H., & Skinner, E. A. (1989). Specialty mental health services: research on specialization and differentiation. In C. A. Taube, D. Mechanic, & A. A. Hohmann (Eds.), *The future of mental health services research,* (Vol. 89, 114–138). Washington, DC: National Institutes of Mental Health.

Grob, G. (1983). *Mental illness and American society, 1875–1940.* Princeton, NJ: Princeton University Press.

Grob, G. (1991). *From asylum to community.* Princeton, NJ: Princeton University Press.

Grob, G. (1994). *The mad among us: A history of the care of America's mentally ill.* New York: Free Press.

Hannan, M., & Freeman, J. (1984, April). Organizational inertia and structural change. *American Sociological Review, 49,* 149–164.

Hasenfeld, Y. (1983). *Human service organizations.* New York: Prentice Hall.

Howard, K. I., Cornille, T. A., Lyons, J. S., Vessey, J. T., Lueger, R. J., & Saunders, S. M. (1996). Patterns of mental health service utilization. *Archives of General Psychiatry, 53,* 696–703.

Leaf, P. J., Alegria, M., Cohen, P., Goodman, S., Horwitz, S. M., Hoven, C. W., Narrow, W. E., Vaden-Kiernan, M., & Regier, D. A. (1996). Mental health service use in the community and schools: Results from the four-community MECA study. *Journal of the American Academy of Child and Adolescent Psychiatry, 35*(7), 889–897.

Lehman, A., Postrado, L., Roth, D., McNary, S., & Goldman, H. (1994). An evaluation of continuity of care, case management, and client outcomes in the Robert Wood Johnson Program on chronic mental illness. *Milbank Quarterly, 72*(1), 105–122.

Link, B. G., Cullen, F. T., Frank, J., & Wozniak, J. F. (1987). The social rejection of former mental patients: Understanding why labels matter. *American Journal of Sociology, 92*(6), 1461–1500.

Link, B. G., Cullen, F. T., Struening, E., Shrout, P. E., & Dohrenwend, B. P. (1989). A modified labeling theory approach to mental disorders: An empirical assessment. *American Sociological Review, 54,* 400–423.

Mandersheid, R. W., & Sonnenchein, M. A. (1992). *Mental health, United States, 1992.* Washington, DC: Center for Mental Health Service.

Mandersheid, R. W., & Sonnenchein, M. A. (1996). *Mental health, United States, 1996.* Washington, D.C.: Center for Mental Health Service.

McKernan, M., McCadam, K., & Gonzales, J. (1996). Addressing the barriers to mental health services for inner city children and their caretakers. *Community Mental Health Journal, 32*(4), 353–361.

McKinlay, J. B. (1972). Some approaches and problems in the study of the use of serivces: An overview. *Journal of Health and Social Behavior, 13,* 115–152.

Mechanic, D. (1975). The organization of medical practice and practice organizations among physicians in prepaid and nonprepaid primary care settings. *Medical Care, 13*(3), 189–204.

Mechanic, D. (1996). Changing medical organization and the erosion of trust. *Milbank Quarterly, 72*(2), 171–189.

Mechanic, D., Schlesinger, M., & McAlpine, D. (1995). Management of mental health and substance abuse services: State of the art and early results. *Milbank Quarterly, 73*(1), 19–55.

Morrissey, J., Goldman, H., & Klerman, L. (1985). Cycles of reform in the care of the chronically mentally ill. *Hospital and Community Psychiatry, 36,* 70–98.

Morrissey, J., Goldman, H., Klerman, L., & Associates. (1980). *The enduring asylum: Cycles of institutional reform at Worcester State Hospital.* New York: Grune & Stratton.

Morrissey, J. P., Calloway, M., Bartko, W. T., Ridgley, S., Goldman, H., & Paulson, R. I. (1994). Local mental health authorities and service system change: Evidence from the Robert Wood Johnson Foundation Program on Chronic Mental Illness. *Milbank Quarterly, 72*(1), 49–80.

Morrissey, J. P., Calloway, M. O., Johnsen, M. C., & Ullman, M. D. (1997). Service system performance and integration: A baseline profile of the ACCESS demonstration sites. *Psychiatric Services, 48*(3), 374–380.

Morrissey, J. P., Johnsen, M. C., Starrett, B. E., Calloway, M. O., & Polgar, M. (1996). *A preliminary evauation of the impact of medicaid managed care on child mental health services.* Paper presented at the American Sociological Association Annual Meeting, New York.

National Institute of Mental Health. (1988). *A national plan for schizophrenia research: Panel recommendation* (ADM) 88-1570. Washington, DC: Department of Health and Human Services.

National Institute of Mental Health. (1991). *Caring for people with severe mental disorders: A national plan of research to improve services* (ADM) 91-1762. Washington, DC: Department of Health and Human Services.

Narrow, W. E., Regier, D. A., Rae, D. S., Manderscheid, R. W., & Locke, B. Z. (1993). Use of services by persons with mental and addictive disorders. *Archives of General Psychiatry, 50*, 95–107.

Newman, S., Reschovsky, J., & Kandea, K. (1994). The effectiveness of independent living on persons with chronic mental illnesses. *Milbank Quarterly, 72*(1), 171–98.

Norquist, G. S., & Regier, D. A. (1996). The epidemiology of psychiatric disorders and the de facto mental health care system. *Annual Review of Medicine, 47*, 473–479.

Olfson, M., & Pincus, H. A. (1994). Measuring outpatient mental health care in the United States. *Health Affairs, 13*(5), 172–180.

Padgett, D., Patrick, C., Burns, B., & Schlesinger, H. (1994). Ethnicity and the use of outpatient mental health services in a national insured population. *American Journal of Public Health, 84*(2), 222–226.

Pelligrino, E. (1994). Ethics. *Journal of the American Medical Association, 271*(21), 1668–1670.

Perrow, C. (1965). Hospitals: Technology, structure, and goals. In J. March (Ed.), *Handbook of organizations*, (pp. 910–971). Chicago: Rand McNally.

Pescosolido, B. A., & Kronenfeld, J. J. (1995). Health, illness and healing in an uncertain era: Challenges from and for medical sociology. *Journal of Health and Social Behavior*, 5–33, extra issue.

Petrilla, J., & Ayers, K. (1994). Enforcing the Fair Housing Amendments Act to benefit people with mental disability. *Hospital and Community Psychiatry, 45*(2), 156–160.

Provan, K. G., & Milward, H. B. (1995). A preliminary theory of interorganizational network effectiveness: A comparative study of four community mental health systems. *Administrative Science Quarterly, 40*, 1–33.

Randolph, F., Blasinsky, M., Leginski, W., Parker, L., & Goldman, H. (1997). Creating integrated service systems for homeless persons with mental illness: The ACCESS Program. *Psychiatric Services, 48*(3), 369–373.

Regier, D. A., Narrow, W. E., Rae, D. S., Manderscheid, R. W., Locke, B. Z., & Goodwin, F. K. (1993). The de facto U.S. mental and addictive disorders service system. *Archives of General Psychiatry, 50*, 85–94.

Rosenheck, R., & Lam, J. A. (1997). Client and site characteristics as barriers to service use by homeless persons with serious mental illness. *Psychiatric Services, 48*(3), 387–392.

Rothbard, A., Schinar, A., & Adams, K. (1996). Utilization of Medicaid mental health services. *Administration and Policy in Mental Health, 24*(2), 117–128.

Rothman, D. (1990). *The discovery of the asylum: Social order and disorder in the new republic* (2nd ed.). Toronto, Canada: Little, Brown.

Scott, W. R. (1995). *Institutions and organizations.* Thousand Oaks, CA: Sage.

Scull, A. (1989). *Social order/ mental disorder: Anglo-American psychiatry in historical perspective.* Berkeley: University of California Press.

Segal, S., Watson, M., & Akutsu, P. (1996). Quality of care and use of less restrictive alternatives in the psychiatric emergency service. *Psychiatric Services, 47*(6), 623–627.

Simmel, G. (1991). *On individuality and social forms.* Chicago: University of Chicago Press.

Stanton, A., & Schwartz, M. (1954). *The mental hospital.* New York: Basic Books.

Stein, L., & Test, M. (1980). *Alternatives to mental hospital treatment.* New York: Plenum Press.

Strauss, A. (1964). *Psychiatric ideologies and institutions.* Glencoe, IL: Free Press.

Stroul, B. A. (1993). *Systems of care for children and adolescents with severe emotional disturbances: What are the results?* Washington, DC: CASSP Technical Assistance Center, Georgetown University Child Development Center.

Stroul, B. A., & Friedman, R. M. (1996). The system of care concept and philosophy. In B. A. Stroul (Ed.), *Children's mental health: Creating systems of care in a changing society* (pp. 7–15). Baltimore: Paul H. Brookes.

Stroup, T. S., & Dorwart, R. A. (1995). Impact of a managed mental health program on Medicaid recipients with severe mental illness. *Psychiatric Services, 46*(9), 885–889.

Takeuchi, D., & Uehara, E. (1996). Ethnic minority mental health services. In B. Levin & J. Petrilla (Eds.), *Mental Health Services: A Public Health Perspective*, (pp. 63–80). New York: Oxford University Press.

Thoits, P. (1995). Stress, coping, and social support processes: Where are we? What next? *Journal of Health and Social Behavior, 36*(Extra Issue), 53–79.

Van de Ven, A., & Ferry, D. (1980). *Measuring and assessing organizations*. New York: Wiley.

Ware, J., & Sherbourne, C. (1992). The MOS 36-item short-form health status survey (SF-36): I. Conceptual framework and item selection. *Medical Care, 30*, MS253–MS265.

Wasserman, S., & Faust, K. (1994). *Social network analysis: Methods and applications*. New York: Cambridge University Press.

Wells, K., & Astrachan, B. (1995). Issues and approaches in evaluating managed mental health care. *Milbank Quarterly, 73*(1), 57–75.

Wells, K., & Hosek, S. (1992). The effects of PPOs in FFS plans on use of outpatient mental health serives by three employee groups. *Medical Care, 30*(5), 412–427.

CHAPTER 23

Labeling and Stigma

Bruce G. Link

Jo C. Phelan

"It is important to understand that we are faced with recovering not just from mental illness, but also from the effects of being labeled mentally ill" (Deegan, 1993, p.10). This quotation is from Patricia Deegan's personal account of her experience with mental illness. Deegan's statement indicates that some people who develop a mental illness also experience stigmatization, and when they do, the consequences can be as painful and debilitating as the illness itself. Why should this be? How do we understand the origins and consequences of stigma?

When we ask questions about the stigma of mental illness from a sociological vantage point, we turn attention to the social meanings associated with being labeled "mentally ill" and to the consequences of those social meanings for people who develop mental illnesses. To inform our consideration of these issues, we begin with some conceptual distinctions concerning the key ideas of labeling and stigma. We then review evidence concerning the existence of stigma and the severity of its consequences. Finally, we elaborate current theory concerning the mechanisms through which cultural conceptions of mental illness affect the lives of mentally ill people.

Bruce G. Link • Division of Epidemiology, School of Public Health, Columbia University, New York, New York 10032. Jo C. Phelan • Division of Sociomedical Sciences, School of Public Health, Columbia University, New York, New York 10032.

Handbook of the Sociology of Mental Health, edited by Carol S. Aneshensel and Jo C. Phelan. Kluwer Academic/Plenum Publishers, New York, 1999.

CONCEPTUAL DISTINCTIONS

A *label* is a definition. When applied to a person, it identifies or defines what type of a person he or she is. A label is "deviant" when it is used to designate the violation of a social norm, or "normal" when it makes a distinction that does not involve the violation of norms. Many of the signs and symptoms of mental illness result in the application of deviant labels because they violate taken-for-granted rules or normative standards. The breaking of taken-for-granted rules is most obvious when psychotic symptoms involving bizarre delusions are present and one believes, for example, that ideas are being planted in one's mind by external forces, or that one's thoughts are being broadcast on the radio. But this concept also applies to symptoms of anxiety and depression in that these symptoms violate taken-for-granted "feeling rules" dictating the kinds of emotions that are appropriate to given situations (Thoits, 1985). Although labels can be informal as well as official, our focus in this chapter is on official labels because they carry potent cultural meanings, can activate these meanings in diverse settings in a way that informal labels cannot, and are far more difficult to effectively dispute, ignore, or hide than informal labels.

The core concept for understanding the negative consequences of labeling is that of *stigma*. Jones and colleagues (1984) give a two-part definition of stigma as a "mark" (label) that (1) sets a person apart from others and (2) links the marked person to undesirable characteristics. When someone is linked to undesirable characteristics, a third aspect of stigma comes into play—people reject and avoid the labeled person. For example, stigma would exist if a person were hospitalized for mental illness (a mark or label) and then assumed to be so dangerous, incompetent, and untrustworthy that avoidance and social isolation ensue. Stigma is a matter of degree, because the mark or label can vary in the extent to which it sets a person apart, because the marked person can be strongly or weakly linked to a variety of undesirable characteristics, and because the rejecting response can be more or less strenuous.

The Role of Stigma in the Labeling Debate

Much of the theory and empirical research concerning the stigma of mental illness has been shaped by the debate surrounding the labeling theory of mental illness. This theory, first articulated by Scheff (1966), posits that the labeling of an individual as mentally ill is an important event with strong social antecedents and consequences. Scheff argues that many of the behaviors associated with mental illness—such as "inappropriate" affect or saying things that do not make sense to other people—are quite common and occur to many people for a variety of reasons, but usually are not considered noteworthy by others, do not become labeled as symptoms of mental illness, and, consequently, are only transitory. The circumstances that determine whether such behaviors become labeled as mental illness are social in nature, involving, for example, the race or social status of the person committing the norm-violating act (see Phelan & Link, in press, for a review). According to Scheff, once a person is labeled mentally ill, a set of social expectations and pressures are set in motion that eventually lead to a stable pattern of deviant behavior that conforms with cultural stereotypes of mental illness. A major factor determining this untoward outcome is the stigma of mental illness. In Scheff's framework, stigma is a form of punishment that people with mental illness experience when they attempt to break out of the mental patient role.

Critics of labeling theory contend that the consequences of labeling are positive, through exposure to beneficial treatments, not negative, as Scheff's formulation suggests. These critics not only attack the position that labeling is the prime determinant of stable mental illness (a criticism that may be valid; see Link & Phelan, in press), but also deny that labeling-induced stigma has detrimental effects on jobs, social networks, self-esteem, or the course of disorder. Gove (1970, 1975, 1980, 1982), for example, claims that there is little evidence that people with mental illness are rejected or devalued by others and that such reactions, when they do occur, are attributable to the disturbed behavior of people with mental illness, not to the mental illness label per se. According to Gove (1982, p. 280), for the "vast majority of mental patients stigma appears to be transitory and does not appear to pose a severe problem." Similarly, Crocetti, Spiro, and Siassi (1974, p. 88) claim that former psychiatric patients "enjoy nearly total acceptance in all but the most intimate relationships."

Thus, two dramatically opposing perspectives concerning mental illness labeling emerged in the context of this debate: labeling is a prime determinant of the experiences of people who are so identified versus labeling that is inconsequential except insofar as it ushers people into helpful treatment. These very different viewpoints have stimulated subsequent research that has sought to adjudicate these differing claims. We turn now to an evaluation of this evidence.

THE IMPORTANCE OF STIGMA IN MENTAL ILLNESS

Critics of Labeling

Three general types of evidence have been used to support the conclusion that stigma is unimportant in the lives of people with mental illnesses. First, when members of the public are asked so-called social-distance questions about whether they would, for example, be willing to work on the same job or fall in love with a former psychiatric patient, most say that they would be willing to do so. Such findings led Crocetti et al. (1974, p. 89) to conclude that "neither our study or other recent studies document the presence of clear prejudice toward those who have been mentally ill." Second, experimental studies that vary both labeling (e.g., "former mental patient" vs. no mention of mental illness) and behavior (normal behavior vs. behavior indicative of mental illness) have generally shown behavior to be a stronger determinant of rejection than labeling (for a review, see Link, Cullen, Frank, & Wozniak, 1987; for a recent example, see Aubry, Tefft, & Currie, 1995). Third, surveys of people with mental illness that were conducted in the 1970s and early 1980s reported few concrete and severe instances of rejection (Clausen, 1981; Gove & Fain, 1973). Moreover, studies indicated that many former patients viewed their hospitalization experience favorably (Pugh et al., 1994; Weinstein, 1979, 1983).

Based on this evidence, the dominant view during the late 1970s and early 1980s was that the stigma of mental illness was relatively inconsequential. For example, the term *stigma* was omitted from the title of the proceedings of a 1980 National Institute of Mental Health conference, even though the purpose of the meeting was to review evidence on that topic (Rabkin, 1984). Apparently, the argument that behaviors rather than labels are the prime determinants of rejection was so forcefully articulated that the editors of the proceedings decided that stigma was not an appropriate designation when "one is referring to negative attitudes induced by manifestations of psychiatric illness" (p. 327). And, although this view may no longer be dominant, it is still articulated. For example, Aubrey et al.

(1995) claim that people with mental illness are not burdened by stigma and can receive equitable treatment "if their presentation shows only minor deviations from the norm" (p. 48).

The Validity of the Claim That Stigma Is Inconsequential

Despite widespread acceptance at one time, the three sources of evidence mentioned earlier are too methodologically weak and too limited in scope to sustain the broad conclusion that labeling and stigma are unimportant. The first problem is that the social-distance questions used in these studies are completely undisguised as to their purpose. Consequently, these measures allow, indeed, almost invite, responses that are biased by social desirability. Three types of studies that circumvent social desirability bias challenge the assertion that people with mental illness are widely accepted. Link and Cullen (1983) experimentally manipulated the way in which social-distance questions about a hypothetical person with mental illness were asked. Respondents were asked either how an "ideal person" would respond, how they personally would respond, or how "most people" would respond. When the person was labeled with a reference to psychiatric hospitalization, the "ideal person" version of the questions produced the most accepting responses and the "most people" version produced the most rejecting responses. By contrast, when the hypothetical person was not labeled as a former patient, the "self" responses were the most rejecting. These findings suggest that people respond in a socially desirable way when reporting their own attitudes toward a group they have learned they should accept, such as mental patients. These findings challenge conclusions about the widespread acceptance of people with mental illness that were based on responses to undisguised social-distance items.

Second, studies that compare mental illness to other potentially stigmatizing conditions reveal a rather distinct hierarchy, with mental illness falling at or near the most-stigmatized end of a list of conditions including epilepsy, prostitution, alcoholism, drug addiction, and ex-convict status (Albrecht, Walker, & Levy, 1982; Brand & Claiborn, 1976; Drehmer and Bordieri, 1985; Hartlage and Roland, 1971; Lamy, 1966; Skinner, berry, Griffith, & Byers, 1995; Tringo, 1970). Although these studies asked questions in an undisguised way, they required that respondents compare conditions. Thus, we must conclude either that people accept everyone—including drug addicts, ex-convicts, and prostitutes—or that mental illness is indeed a stigmatized condition in our society. Because the latter view seems far more plausible, the comparative approach leads us toward the conclusion that public attitudes are not nearly as favorable as some have claimed.

Third, a few studies have investigated how people respond not to hypothetical scenarios, but in situations where they are personally involved—circumstances that are much less likely to induce socially desirable responses. For example, Page (1977) sampled advertisements for apartments to rent and randomly assigned landlords to different experimental conditions. In one condition, a caller working with the research team indicated that he was a patient in a mental hospital who would be released in a day or two, whereas no mention of mental hospitalization was made in the control condition. When the "mental patient" label was applied, landlords were much less likely to indicate that the apartment was available (27%) than in the control condition (83%). Similar effects of labeling have been found on willingness to hire a job applicant (Brand and Claiborn, 1976; Farina & Felner, 1973).

The claim that it is only the deviant behavior associated with mental illness that leads to rejection—not labeling per se—has been refuted by numerous experimental and nonexperimental studies. Social-psychological experiments have shown that labeling can affect responses, even when no deviant behavior is involved. These studies show a "self-fulfilling prophecy" effect: Labeling actually causes behavior that leads to rejection.

For example, Sibicky and Dovidio (1986) randomly assigned 68 male and 68 female introductory psychology students as mixed-sex pairs to one of two conditions. In one condition, a "perceiver" (random assignment) was led to believe that a "target" was recruited from the psychological therapy clinic at the college. In the other condition, the perceiver was led to believe that the individual was a fellow student in introductory psychology. In fact, the target was always recruited from the class. Both targets and perceivers were led to believe that the study was focusing on "the acquaintance process in social interaction." Each member of the pair completed a brief inventory of their courses, hobbies, and activities. The experimenter then exchanged the inventories and provided the perceiver with the labeling information (student or therapy client). Subsequently, the two engaged in a tape-recorded interaction that was later reliably evaluated by two raters, blind to the experimental conditions. Perceivers rated the therapy targets less favorably even before meeting them. Moreover, the judges' ratings revealed that in their interactions with therapy targets, perceivers were less open, secure, sensitive, and sincere. Finally, the behavior of the labeled targets was adversely affected as well, even though they had no knowledge of the experimental manipulation. Thus, expectations associated with psychological therapy color subsequent interactions, actually calling out behavior that leads to rejection.

Similar processes have been observed when targets believe they have been labeled but actually have not been labeled. Farina, Gliha, Boudreau, Allen, and Sherman (1971) had former psychiatric patients interact with a person they believed might be a prospective employer. In the experimental condition, former patients were led to believe that their interviewer knew of their hospitalization; in the control condition, no such information was conveyed. Subjects who believed they had been labeled behaved in less socially attractive ways and were judged less favorably by their interviewers than subjects who were not told they had been labeled. Thus, the behavioral sequences leading to self-fulfilling prophecies can be initiated either by the stigmatized or the nonstigmatized member of a dyad (see also Farina, Allen, & Saul, 1968; Harris, Millich, Johnston, & Hoover, 1990).

Link and associates (1987) extended this line of research by demonstrating the importance of taking into account what the label "former mental patient" means to people. They conducted a vignette experiment, similar to the experiments that had led previous researchers to conclude that behaviors and not labels are most important in determining societal reactions. However, they also incorporated a measure of the extent to which people believed that mental patients in general were "dangerous." When the vignette described a person without a mental illness label, beliefs about the dangerousness of people with mental illness played no part in determining social-distancing responses. When the vignette described a labeled person, however, these beliefs became a potent determinant of responses: Subjects who believed mental patients to be dangerous reacted negatively to the person described in the vignette as having experienced mental hospitalization. This pattern of results held regardless of the degree of deviant behavior. In fact, labeling-activated beliefs about dangerousness predicted social-distance responses just as strongly as did variations in the deviance of the behavior depicted in the vignette. Apparently, a mental illness label activates beliefs about dangerousness, with beliefs determining how much social distance is desired from a labeled person regardless of his or her behavior. It should be noted that, if Link and associates had not taken perceived dangerousness into account, they too would have found large effects of behavior and no effects of labeling.

Studies like those just described make it clear that labeling exerts an independent effect on the rejecting responses of the public. But research also suggests that the "labeling versus behavior" conceptualization is overly simplistic for two important reasons. First, labeling can produce behavior in the labeled person that then leads to rejection. Under such circumstances, it is shortsighted to attribute the subsequent rejection solely to behavior, since the behavior was induced by labeling. Second, labeling can provide an interpretive context that changes the meaning of "behaviors." In a pair of experiments, Riskind and Wahl (1992) demonstrated that labeling can change the interpretation of a behavior as seemingly objective as the amount of hand and leg movement a person exhibits. Both activity level (active vs. inactive) and labeling—patient on leave from a mental hospital vs. "clown" (Study 1) and "ordinary person" (Study 2)—were significantly related to perceived dangerousness. However, activity level increased perceived dangerousness more in the patient condition than in the other two conditions.

Given that labeling can both induce behaviors that lead to rejection and change the interpretive framework in which behaviors are evaluated, it seems overly simplistic to continue to cast the debate as an issue of "labeling" versus "behavior."

The Effects of Labeling and Treatment

We conclude, based on the foregoing evidence, that critics of labeling theory would be hard put to deny the untoward consequences of stigma in the lives of people with mental illness. At the same time, labeling theorists would be hard pressed to deny the benefits of treatment. Rigorous research evidence suggests that both psychotherapeutic and pharmacological treatments are effective at least in the short run (e.g., Robinson, Berman, & Neimeyer, 1990; Smith, Glass, & Miller, 1980). In recognition of this research, two recent studies have explicitly taken up the issue of the co-occurring and opposite effects of stigma and treatment.

In the first, Rosenfield (1997) examined the effects of both treatment services and stigma in the context of a model program for people with severe mental disorder. She shows that both the receipt of services (specific interventions that some people in the program receive and others do not) and stigma (perceived devaluation/discrimination) are related—in opposite directions—to multiple dimensions of quality of life. Services have positive effects on dimensions of quality of life such as living arrangements, family relations, financial situation, safety, and health, whereas stigma has equally strong negative effects on such dimensions.

In the second study, Link, Struening, Rahav, Phelan, and Nuttbrock (1997) conducted a longitudinal study of men who were dually diagnosed with mental disorder and substance abuse. The men were followed from entry into treatment, when they were highly symptomatic and addicted to substances, to a follow-up point 1 year later, at which time they were far less symptomatic and largely drug- and alcohol-free. Despite these dramatic treatment benefits, perceptions and reported experiences of stigma continued to affect the men's levels of depressive symptoms. The effects of stigma endured and were apparently unaffected by treatment benefits.

These two studies are important to the labeling debate in that they acknowledge both positive and negative consequences of labeling and thus achieve a partial accommodation of the so-called labeling and psychiatric perspectives (see also Herman & Miall, 1990; Link & Cullen, 1990). In particular, it is possible that the sharply opposed views that we mentioned earlier are both partly wrong and partly right.

HOW STIGMA AFFECTS PEOPLE WITH MENTAL ILLNESS

The foregoing review is cast in the historical shadow of the labeling debate and framed in terms of whether stigma has untoward effects. In light of our review, it no longer seems useful to ask whether stigma has important effects, but rather to ask how these effects occur. Thus, the new questions that need to be asked and answered should focus less on theory competition—labeling theory pitted against labeling theory's critics—and more on theory elaboration. To that end, we propose an evidence-based explanation of the ways in which stigma comes to affect people's lives. This explanation expands upon the approach provided by Link, Cullen, Struening, Shrout, and Dohrenwend (1989) by bringing new evidence to bear and by adding new concepts and emphases. The effort is distinctly socio-logical in that it focuses on the social and cultural processes that determine what it means to be mentally ill in our society—on the social construction of stigma and its consequences.

The starting point and core feature of our explanation are cultural conceptions of mental illness. These cultural conceptions form the context within which individual actions take place and thereby play a powerful role in influencing the trajectories of people's lives. We identify three processes through which this influence occurs: expectations of rejection, experiences of rejection, and the determination and sequencing of social and treatment experiences. In what follows, we begin by characterizing cultural conceptions and then turn to a consideration of each of these three processes.

Cultural Conceptions of Mental Illness

Cultural conceptions of mental illness include a disparate array of negative attributes, in-cluding dangerousness and unpredictability, weakness and incompetence, and a general-ized attribution of "badness." These conceptions are evidenced both in elements of mass culture, such as the media, and in public attitudes concerning mental illness. In one study of prime-time television dramas between 1969 and 1985, Signorelli (1989) found that 20.5% of episodes contained mental illness themes and that mentally ill characters were more likely than other characters to commit violence, to be victimized, to be unsuccessful, and to be characterized as "bad" rather than "good." For example, 72.1% of the mentally ill char-acters (compared to 45.1% of all characters) were portrayed as being violent, and 21.6% (compared to 8.7% of all characters) were portrayed as murderers. Similarly, Shain and Phillips (1991) found that 86% of a sample of 1983 United Press International stories making reference to former mental patients linked those individuals to violent crimes. In contrast, in his review of the empirical literature, Monahan (1992) concludes that violent or aggressive behavior occurs in, at most, 10% to 12% of people with mental illnesses. Surveys of public conceptions of mental illness indicate that these themes are also present in the minds of the public. Surveying a nationally representative sample of Americans, Star (1952, 1955) found that many people included themes of violence, unpredictability, and impulsiveness in their spontaneous descriptions of a person with mental illness. Moreover, only the severe type of psychotic disorder was identified by a majority of respondents as "mental illness." She concluded that "mental illness is a very threatening, fearful thing and not an idea to be entertained lightly about anyone (Star, 1955, p. 6). Similarly, Nunnally (1961), using a semantic-differential technique, found that people with mental illness "are regarded with fear, distrust, and dislike by the general public" (p. 46) and "are considered, unselectively, as being all things 'bad'" (p. 233). Specifically, concepts such as "mental

patient," "insane woman," or "neurotic man" were rated as more worthless, dirty, dangerous, cold, and unpredictable than concepts such as "average man" or "me."

Some researchers (e.g., Crocetti et al., 1974) have argued that public conceptions of
mental illness have become better informed and more positive over time. However, several
sources of data contradict this notion. Olmstead and Durham (1976), using Nunnally's
semantic-differential approach, found that college students' attitudes remained essentially
unchanged between 1962 and 1971. Signorelli (1989) found no trend toward more positive
portrayals of mentally ill characters on television dramas between 1969 and 1985. Most
recently, Phelan and associates (1996) found that perceptions of dangerousness, particularly regarding people with psychosis, have increased sharply between 1950 and 1996. As
further evidence of this cultural climate, Link and colleagues (1989) have found that people
with and without mental illness indicate awareness of this climate of rejection by endorsing
statements such as "Most people think less of a person who has been in a mental hospital"
(68%) and "Most young women would be reluctant to date a man who has been hospitalized for serious mental illness" (80%).

Expectations of Rejection

Link and colleagues have identified a mechanism through which patient attitudes about
stigma may strongly affect their life circumstances (Link, 1987; Link et al., 1989). This
modified labeling theory" posits that psychiatric patients experience culturally induced
expectations of rejection that lead to negative consequences (see below) for self-esteem,
job procurement, and the development of social networks. According to this view, people
form conceptions of what others think of mental patients long *before* they ever become
patients, and these conceptions are often quite negative. Such beliefs take on new relevance when a person becomes a psychiatric patient for the first time. What once seemed to
be an innocuous array of beliefs about people's attitudes toward mental patients is now
applicable personally and no longer innocuous. Being marked as a mental patient trans-
forms a person's beliefs about the devaluation of, and discrimination against, mental patients into a personal expectation of rejection. Once they expect rejection, the theory goes,
interactions with others may be strained, and strategies aimed at minimizing feared rejection—such as withdrawing from social contacts—may impair their ability to function. Strong
support for this aspect of the theory comes from the Farina et al. (1968; 1971) experimental
studies (discussed earlier) showing that stigma-related expectations negatively influence
performance. In this modified labeling approach, people can be harmed by labels even
when there are no direct negative reactions from others. The approach emphasizes that
people's internalization of negative stereotypes produces negative labeling effects.

To test this explanation, Link (1987) constructed a 12-item scale measuring the extent
to which a person believes that mental patients discriminated against and devalued. This
scale was administered both to mental patients and nonpatients in an epidemiological case-
control study of major depression and schizophrenia. Link showed that the degree to which
a person expects to be rejected is associated with demoralization, income loss, and unemployment in individuals labeled mentally ill, but not in unlabeled individuals, thereby supporting the notion that labeling activates beliefs that lead to negative consequences.

In a subsequent paper, Link and associates (1989) extend the foregoing reasoning in
two ways. First, they bring into the analysis empirical measures of coping strategies of
secrecy (concealing a history of treatment), withdrawal (avoiding potentially threatening

situations), and education (attempting to teach others to forestall the negative effects of stereotypes). Consistent with the notion that the stigma of mental illness activates expectations of rejection, patients tend to endorse these strategies as a means of protecting themselves. Second, the analysis is extended to a consideration of the effects of stigmatization on social-network ties. Patients who fear rejection most and who endorse the strategy of withdrawal have insular support networks consisting mainly of household members.

Thus, several studies support the idea that expectations of rejection have a substantial impact on multiple domains of people's lives. It seems reasonable to conclude, therefore, that at least some of the effects of stigma operate through the social-psychological mechanism of internalization. However, these observations do not necessarily mean that direct discrimination by others plays little or no role in producing negative outcomes. Instead, in addition to outright discrimination, cultural conceptions produce what we call "incidental rejection."

Cultural Conceptions and Rejection Experiences

As discussed in the previous section, Link and colleagues' (1987, 1989) early work emphasized the social-sychological mechanism of expectations of rejection rather than experiences of overt rejection by others. This emphasis followed from reports by Clausen (1981) and by Gove and Fain (1973) that experiences of discrimination in areas such as jobs and housing were quite uncommon. Because such rare experiences seemed unlikely sources of pervasive negative effects, researchers tended to focus their attention instead on the social-psychological mechanism of expectations of rejection. Here, however, we develop a conceptualization and present evidence concerning a type of rejection experience that appears to be much more common than the direct, overt experiences considered in earlier research and that, consequently, may have much more pervasive effects. We call these experiences incidental rejections.

As we have argued, a person who is tagged with a stigmatizing mark or label becomes subject to societal stereotypes about that mark or label. In considering the effect of expectations of rejection, we focused on the consequences of the stereotype for the stigmatized person, but people who have never been labeled are influenced by the stereotype as well. When unlabeled people make derogatory statements or behave in rejecting ways that are consistent with the stereotype, people with mental illness are likely to experience rejection. Thus, there exists a class of rejection experiences that occur simply because people articulate the stereotype in the presence of a person with mental illness. The rejection is therefore incidental in that it was not intended for the recipient. We begin our explication of the concept of incidental rejections with an example. It concerns a member of a clubhouse for people with mental illness. As one of his jobs at the clubhouse, he served as a bus driver. When paying the rent to his landlady, he was asked where he worked and what he did. He said that he drove a bus at the clubhouse, to which the landlady pointledly replied, "Oh! Do you really like driving those people?" The landlady's statement simultaneously conveyed that it might be quite undesirable to work with people with mental illness and that, of course, her tenant, because he was competent enough to drive a bus and pay the rent, could not also be a person with mental illness and a member of the club. It was a rejecting statement, and an *incidental* rejection because it was not targeted for the recipient; in fact, the landlady had no awareness that he belonged to the group of people whom she was rejecting. Unlike the more obvious and overt discrimination events that Clausen (1981) and

Gove and Fain (1973) examined, such incidental rejection experiences are probably very common (Link et al., 1997).

For people who do not share the mark, such occurrences might seem minor. But in the context of cultural stereotypes, these seemingly minor rejections can be quite hurtful and reinforce personal doubts in the stigmatized person about his or her competence, integrity, or self-worth. A comment about "crazy" people can remind the person that he or she is part of a group that is feared, discriminated against, and devalued. The power of day-to-day, taken-for-granted experiences in activating stereotypes has been demonstrated in the work of Steele and Aronson (1995) regarding stereotypes about the academic ability of African Americans. He finds that African American college students perform worse on SAT-like tests when they have been led to believe that the test measures their intellectual ability than when they are not led to have such a belief. The performance of white students, in contrast, is not significantly affected by statements about the meaning of the test. This "stereotype vulnerability," as Steele calls it—in which a seemingly minor event (the way a test is described) triggers a stereotype that produces very serious negative consequences--may also operate for people with mental illness. Powerful stereotypes can be activated by incidental rejections, and when they are, negative consequences are likely to follow.

Consistent with the idea that rejection experiences have been underplayed in research on the stigma of mental illness (Link, 1987; Link et al., 1989) are more recent findings concerning the impact of rejection experiences. In a longitudinal design Link and associates (1997) showed that rejection experiences strongly predicted depressive symptoms even when baseline depressive symptoms and expectations of rejection (devaluation/discrimination) were controlled. Although this work needs to be replicated and extended, it suggests that rejection experiences may have been given short shrift in previous studies of stigma.

Treatment and Social Control Initiatives

Cultural conceptions of the nature and causes of mental illness also play a powerful role in determining how people with mental disorders are treated or managed at a structural level. This connection is particularly evident when we examine how people with mental illness have been treated in different times and in different places. For example, Rothman (1971) explains how it came to be that nineteenth century Americans discovered the asylum as a means of managing or treating people with mental illnesses. Apparently, the impetus for the creation of the asylum came from an active group of social reformers who were, Rothman argues, concerned about the fabric of American society and the turmoil and stresses that resulted from large-scale immigration and urbanization. Given this conceptual framework, the causes of mental illness seemed apparent—too much stress and too little order. And so the asylums were created—highly structured communities set aside from the turmoil of urban life in bucolic settings, where moral treatment could be practiced, with its emphasis on order and the discipline of work. The point is that Rothman's analysis reveals how cultural conceptions shaped the experience of people with mental illness, determining where and how people were managed at the time.

In different settings and at different times, cultural conceptions have led to radically different approaches to the management of persons with mental illness. Thus, for example, in one epoch, people with mental illness might be sequestered in facilities that also charged admission to spectators who sat on the opposite side of a set of bars and apparently enjoyed watching and making fun of the people with mental illness. In another epoch, people with mental illness might be lumped together with criminals, or with the indigent, and managed as one large group of socially deviant persons. Today, for whatever combination of reasons, our society has come to tolerate the management (or mismanagement) of some mentally ill persons as homeless street people.

Examples taken from historical accounts such as Rothman's help us see how societal conceptions shape the experience of people with mental illnesses in terms of broad, period-to-period changes. Similar processes occurring in contemporary society are more difficult to identify, however, because theses processes are consistent with current beliefs and practices and are, therefore, taken for granted as the way things are or should be. A classic study by Rosenhan (1973) illustrates this point. Eight "normal" volunteers sought admission to state mental hospitals in California, feigning the single symptom of "hearing voices" upon initial interview. All were admitted and after admission no longer feigned any symptoms and behaved normally. The volunteers remained in the hospital for an average of 19 days, with one remaining a full 52 days before being discharged. More to the point, the experience of these "normal" volunteers was revealing with regard to the socially structured experiences of people with mental illness. When volunteers asked questions, they were routinely ignored and dismissed by physicians and nurses. Pseudopatients also observed the treatment of other patients and reported numerous instances of beatings and abuse. The fact that the psuedopatients did not suffer from serious mental illness made the poor treatment they received particularly obvious and particularly striking because, for these "normal" psuedopatients, such treatment was not taken for granted as "just the way things are" or "the way things should be." Thus, the study gave a us a different lens through which to observe the treatment routinely experienced by countless real patients.

When people ask and answer the questions, "What is mental illness?", "What are people with mental illnesses like?", and "What should be done about people with mental illnesses?", they create and shape social structures that become the realities of everyday experience for people with mental illness. People with mental illness are, for good or ill, linked to these conceptions and plugged into the societal structures that have been created for people who are thought of according to such conceptions.

CONCLUSION

At the outset of this chapter, we cited Deegan's statement that recovery included not only recovery from the illness but also from being labeled "mentally ill." This statement makes a strong claim about the effects of labeling and stigma—a claim that would be strongly disputed by critics of labeling theory who have discounted the importance of these factors. But the evidence we reviewed in this chapter indicates that stigma has strong and pervasive consequences. Although these consequences coexist with important positive benefits of labeling and treatment, as Rosenfield (1997) and Link et al. (1997) acknowledge, these adverse consequences are nevertheless present and debilitating. Moreover, although our research understanding of the way in which labeling and stigma affect people is far from complete, the evidence to date is consistent with the following formulation: When people develop the symptoms of a mental illness, they face decisions about treatment seeking and official labeling. If they choose or are coerced into psychiatric treatment, they are exposed to a kind of "package deal" of positive and negative effects. Although they can benefit from the positive effects of treatment, they are also exposed to the negative effects of stigma. In particular, as a consequence of being officially labeled, they are connected to societal stereotypes about what it means to be mentally ill, both in their own eyes and in the eyes of others. Depending on the nature of these societal conceptions at any given place or time, negative consequences may follow through expectations of rejection, experiences of rejection, and treatment and social control structures that strongly influence people's daily experience. When considered together, these powerful social factors may help us understand why a person with mental illness might feel as Deegan does about the label "mentally ill" and its consequences.

ACKNOWLEDGMENT: This research was supported in part by a grant from the National Alliance for Research on Schizophrenia and Affective Disorders (NARSAD) to Bruce Link.

REFERENCES

Albrecht, G., Walker, V., & Levy, J. (1982). Social distance from the stigmatized: A test of two theories. *Social Science and Medicine, 16,* 1319–1327.

Aubry, T., Tefft, B., & Currie, R. (1995). Public attitudes and intentions regarding tenants of community mental health residences who are neighbours. *Community Mental Health Journal, 31,* 39–52.

Brand, R. C. & Claiborn, W. L. (1976). Two studies of comparative stigma: Employer attitudes and practices toward rehabilitated convicts, mental and tuberculosis patients. *Community Mental Health Journal, 12,* 168–175.

Clausen, J. A. (1981). Stigma and mental disorder: Phenomena and terminology. *Psychiatry, 44,* 287–296.

Crocetti, G., Spiro, H., & Siassi, I., (1974). *Contemporary Attitudes Towards Mental Illness.* Pittsburgh, PA: University of Pittsburgh Press.

Deegan, P. (1993). Recovering our sense of value after being labeled mentally ill. *Journal of Psychosocial Nursing, 31,* 7–11.

Drehmer, D. E., & Bordieri, J. E. (1985). Hiring decisions for disabled workers: The hidden bias. *Rehabilitation Psychology, 30,* 157–164.

Farina, A., Allen, J., & Saul. B. (1968). The role of the stigmatized person in effecting social relationships. *Journal of Personality, 36,* 69–82.

Farina, A., & Felner, R. (1973). Employment interviewer reactions to former mental patients. *Journal of Abnormal Psychology, 82,* 268–272.

Farina, A., Gliha, D., Boudreau, L., Allen, J., & Sherman, M. (1971). Mental illness and the impact of believing others know about it. *Journal of Abnormal Psychology, 77,* 1–5.

Gove, W. (1970). Societal reaction as an explanation of mental illness: An evaluation. *American Sociological Review, 35,* 873–884.

Gove, W. (1975). *The labelling of deviance: Evaluating a perspective.* New York: Sage.

Gove, W. (1980). Labeling and mental illness: A critique. In W. R. Gove (Ed.), *Labeling Deviant Behavior* (pp. 53–109). Beverly Hills, CA: Sage.

Gove. W. R. (1982). The current status of the labeling theory of mental illness. In W. R. Gove (Ed.), *Deviance and Mental Illness.* Beverly Hills, CA: Sage.

Gove, W., & Fain, T. (1973). The stigma of mental hospitalization: An attempt to evaluate its consequences. *Archives of General Psychiatry, 29,* 494–500.

Harris, M. J., Millich, R., Johnston, E. M., & Hoover, D. W. (1990). Effects of expectancies on children's social interactions. *Journal of Experimental Social Psychology, 26,* 1–12.

Hartlage, L. C., & Roland, P. E. (1971). Attitudes of employers toward different types of handicapped workers. *Journal of Applied Rehabilitation Counseling, 2,* 115–120.

Herman, N., & Miall, C. (1990). The positive consequences of stigma: Two case studies in mental and physical disability. *Qualitative Sociology, 13,* 251–269.

Jones, E., Farina, A., Hastorf, A. H., Markus, H., Miller, D. T., & Scott, R. A. (1984). *Social stigma: The psychology of marked relationships.* New York: Freeman.

Lamy, R. E. (1966). Social consequences of mental illness. *Journal of Counseling and Clinical Psychology, 30,* 450–455.

Link, B. G. (1987). Understanding labeling effects in the area of mental disorders: An assessment of the effects of expectations of rejection. *American Sociological Review, 52*, 96–112.

Link, B. G., & Cullen, F. T. (1983). Reconsidering the social rejection of ex-mental patients: Levels of attitudinal response. *American Journal of Community Psychology, 11*, 261–273.

Link, B. G., & Cullen, F. T. (1990). The labeling theory of mental disorder: A review of the evidence. In J. Greenley (Ed.), *Mental Illness in Social Context* (pp. 75–105). Greenwich, CT: JAI Press.

Link, B. G., Cullen, F. T., Frank, J., & Wozniak, J. F.,(1987). The social rejection of former mental patients: Understanding why labels matter. *American Journal of Sociology, 92*, 1461–1500.

Link, B. G., Cullen, F. T., Struening, E., Shrout, P., & Dohrenwend, B. P. (1989). A modified labeling theory approach in the area of the mental disorders: An empirical assessment. *American Sociological Review, 54*, 400–423.

Link, B. G., & Phelan, J. C. (in press). The labeling theory of mental disorder (II): The consequences of labeling. In A. Horwitz & T. Scheid-Cook (Eds.), *The sociology of mental health and illness*. New York: Oxford University Press.

Link, B. G., Struening, E., Rahav, M., Phelan, J. C.,& Nuttbrock, L. (1997). On stigma and its consequences: Evidence from a longitudinal study of men with dual diagnoses of mental illness and substance abuse. *Journal of Health and Social Behavior, 38*, 117–190.

Monahan, J. (1992). Mental disorder and violent behavior: Attitudes and evidence. *American Psychologist, 47*, 511–521

Nunnally, J. C. (1961). *Popular conceptions of mental health*. New York: Holt, Rinehart & Winston.

Olmsted, D. W., & Durham, K. (1976). Stability of mental health attitudes: A semantic differential study. *Journal of Health and Social Behavior 17*, 35–44.

Page, S. (1977). Effects of the mental illness label in attempts to obtain accommodation. *Canadian Journal of Behavioral Science, 9*, 85–90.

Phelan, J. C., & Link, B. G. (in press). The labeling theory of mental disorder (I): The role of contingencies in the application of psychiatric labels. In A. Horowitz & T. Scheid-Cook (Eds.), *The sociology of mental health and illness*. New York: Cambridge University Press.

Phelan, J. C., Link, B. G., Stueve, A., & Pescosolido, B. (1996, November). *Have public conceptions of mental health changed over the past half century? Does it matter?* Paper presented at the annual meeting of the American Public Health Association, New York.

Pugh, R. L., Ackerman, B. J., McColgan, E. B., deMesquite,P. B., Worley, P. J., & Goodman, N. J. (1994). Attitudes of dolescents toward adolescent psychiatric treatment. *Journal of Child and Family Studies, 3*, 351–363.

Rabkin, J. (1984). Community attitudes and local psychiatric facilities. In J. Talbott (Ed.), *The chronic mental patient: Five years later* (pp. 325–335). New York: Grune & Stratton.

Riskind, J., & Wahl, O. (1992). Moving makes it worse: The role of rapid movement in fear of psychiatric patients. *Journal of Social and Clinical Psychology, 11*, 349–364.

Robinson, L., Berman, J., & Neimeyer, R. (1990). Psychotherapy for the treatment of depression: A comprehensive review of controlled outcome research. *Psychological Bulletin, 108*, 30–49.

Rothman, D. (1971). *The discovery of the asylum*. Boston: Little Brown.

Rosenfield, S. (1997). Labeling mental illness: The effects of services versus stigma. *American Sociological Review*.

Rosenhan, D. (1973). On being sane in insane places. *Science*, 250–258.

Scheff, T. (1966). *Being mentally ill: A sociological theory*. Chicago: Aldine.

Shain, R. E., & Phillips, J. (1991). The stigma of mental illness: Labeling and stereotyping in the news. In *Risky business: Communicating issues of science, risk and public Policy* (pp. 61–74). New York: Greenwood Press.

Sibicky, M., & Dovidio, J. F. (1986). Stigma of psychological therapy: Stereotypes, interpersonal reactions, and the self-fulfilling prophecy. *Journal of Consulting and Clinical Psychology, 33,*148–154.

Signorelli, N. (1989). The stigma of mental illness on television. *Journal of Broadcasting and Electronic Media, 33*, 325–331.

Skinner, L. J., Berry, K. K., Griffith, S. E., & Byers, B. (1995). Generalizability and specificity of the stigma associated with the mental illness label: A reconsideration twenty-five years later. *Journal of Community Psychology, 23*, 3–17.

Smith, M. L., Glass, G., & Miller, T. (1980). *The benefits of psychotherapy*. Baltimore: Johns Hopkins University Press.

Star, S. A. (1952). *What the public thinks about mental health and mental illness*. Paper presented at the annual meetings of the National Association for Mental Health (mimeograph).

Star, S. A. (1955). *The public's ideas about mental illness*. Paper presented at the annual meeting of the National Association for Mental Health (mimeograph).

Steele, C., & Aronson, J. (1995). Stereotype Threat and the intellectual test performance of African Americans. *Journal of Personality and Social Psychology, 69*, 797–811.

Thoits, P. (1985). Self-labeling processes in mental illness: The role of emotional deviance. *American Journal of Sociology, 91*, 221–249.

Tringo, J. (1970). The hierarchy of preference toward disability groups. *Journal of Special Education 4*, 295–306.

Weinstein, R. 1979. Patient attitudes toward mental hospitalization: A review of quantitative research. *Journal of Health and Social Behavior, 20*, 237–258.

Weinstein, R. (1983). Labeling theory and the attitudes of mental patients: A review. *Journal of Health and Social Behavior, 24*, 70–84.

CHAPTER 24

The Impact of Mental Illness
on the Family

WILLIAM R. AVISON

Research in the sociology of mental health is concerned primarily with understanding how individuals' social locations have consequences for their mental health. These investigations typically attempt to identify social and psychosocial processes that connect individuals' positions in the social structure with various measures of psychiatric disorder or psychological distress. However, as previous chapters in this handbook have demonstrated, mental illness also has important social consequences for individuals in terms of their experiences in help seeking, in accessing treatment, and in terms of the social stigma that they may experience. In this context, sociologists of mental health have made important contributions to our understanding of the social sequelae of mental illness.

It is also clear that individuals' mental health problems have consequences for others in their social networks, most notably, their family members. Indeed, social scientists have become increasingly interested in the ways in which the mental disorder of one family member has emotional and behavioral consequences for other family members. In recent years, substantial advances have been made in understanding these processes. To some considerable extent, these advances have been the result of conceptualizing the mental illness of a family member as a source of social stress and then tracing its consequences for others' psychological well-being. In thinking about mental illness as a stressor within the family, there are two separate bodies of literature that have traced the consequences of individuals' mental disorders for their families.

WILLIAM R. AVISON • Centre for Health and Well-Being, The University of Western Ontario, London, Ontario, Canada N6A 5C2.

Handbook of the Sociology of Mental Health, edited by Carol S. Aneshensel and Jo C. Phelan. Kluwer Academic/Plenum Publishers, New York, 1999.

The first concerns the intergenerational transmission of mental illness. There is ample evidence that documents the relationship between parental mental illness and children's emotional and behavioral problems. Nevertheless, there are many opportunities for the sociology of mental health to make additional contributions to this body of knowledge.

The second body of literature has a somewhat different focus. It examines the burden of stress experienced by family members who provide care to severely mentally ill individuals. These studies of caregiving and family burden provide interesting lessons for sociologists in understanding how the mental illness of a family member generates an array of chronic stressors that sometimes erodes the psychological well-being of parents, spouses, or adult children who provide care.

In this chapter, I briefly review the literature on each of these areas of research. In doing so, I identify those areas where the sociology of mental health has had a major impact, and where there appear to be important opportunities to develop a more distinctly sociological perspective. I conclude the chapter with an appraisal of the opportunities for sociologists of mental health to contribute to future theoretical developments in these areas.

MENTAL ILLNESS AS A STRESSOR

A central tenet of stress process formulations asserts that individuals' experiences of socially induced stressors manifest themselves in various forms of psychological distress. Indeed, the last two decades have witnessed an exponential growth in the number of studies that have investigated this basic process. A major issue in this field is a consideration of what constitutes a stressful experience. One of the most comprehensive treatments of this conceptual issue is Wheaton's (1994) examination of the "stress universe." He develops a stress continuum to array stressors from the most discrete to the most continuous in nature. Among other things, Wheaton demonstrates how this characteristic of stressors can be cross-classified by the stage of the life course when the stressor occurred. With this system of classification, one can distinguish between traumatic events experienced in childhood and those experienced in adulthood. One can also differentiate among relatively discrete life-change events that have occurred in childhood, in young adulthood, or in later life. Moreover, this classification system separates chronic stressors of childhood from more current, ongoing stressors of adulthood.

In the context of considering mental illness as a stressor in the family, this cross-classification is particularly useful. It seems clear that the presence of a family member with a mental health problem is more likely to constitute a chronic rather than a discrete stressor. After all, many psychiatric disorders are characterized by relatively insidious onsets rather than by some momentous behavioral or emotional break that occurs without warning. Moreover, the behaviors and emotions that are symptomatic of most disorders tend to persist over lengthy periods of time. In addition, many persons experience recurrent episodes of their mental illnesses. Accordingly, other family members are more likely to experience the difficulties of living with someone who has a mental disorder as a relatively continuous strain that may ebb and flow with the individual's symptomatology but remains an ever-present threat even when the individual is in remission.

However, the chronic stress associated with a family member's mental illness is not just a function of the duration of the disorder. It also seems apparent that living with a relative who suffers from a mental disorder creates a variety of role strains. Pearlin (1983) has presented a rich conceptual overview of this source of stress. For Pearlin, there are at least six types of stress that may arise from role occupancy: (1) excessive demands of certain roles; (2) inequities in rewards; (3) the failure of reciprocity in roles; (4) role conflict; (5) role captivity; and (6) role restructuring. These various types of stress are likely to become prominent in the lives of parents or spouses who must assume a variety of responsibilities for the care of an individual with a mental illness. The additional effort that is required to care for a mentally ill family member, and the absence of alternative sources of such care, frequently result in role overload, a sense of role captivity, and feelings that the resources and support provided to someone who fills the role of caregiver are not adequately reciprocated by the mentally ill family member.

Of course, as Pearlin (1989) and Wheaton (1994) remind us, not all chronic stress is role-related strain. Pearlin refers to ambient strains that are not attributable to a specific role but, rather, are diffuse in nature and have a variety of sources. These may be the kinds of strains that children of mentally ill parents experience. As we shall see in a subsequent section of this chapter, there is clear evidence that parents with schizophrenia, depression, or substance abuse disorders are often emotionally inaccessible or unavailable to their children. In addition, marriages in which one partner suffers from a mental disorder are frequently characterized by discord and conflict. Family environments in which there is an absence of strong parent-child attachments or the presence of ongoing conflict may constitute ambient strains for children.

In addition to these chronic stressors, the parents, children, or spouses of persons with mental disorders may also experience a number of discrete life events that may be a direct result of the illness itself. The hospitalization of mentally ill individuals, however infrequent this is today, and however short the admission to hospital, may be experienced by family members as a stressful event. This is perhaps even more likely to be the case for children who simultaneously experience the loss of a parent. Similarly, encounters that mentally ill individuals may have with the police also constitute stressful experiences for family members, as do instances of job loss. Thus, living with a mentally ill family member may expose individuals to more discrete stress in the form of life events as well as to more chronic stress in terms of role strain and ambient strain.

These considerations suggest ways in which the mental illness of a family member can be conceptualized as a stressor that influences the mental health of other family members, the perspective that is taken in this chapter. The remainder of this chapter is divided into three major segments. I first review the literature on the impact of parental mental illness on children's emotional and behavioral problems, and identify promising research opportunities for sociologists. Next, I summarize the research on caregiving to psychiatric patients and draw attention to some of the unique contributions that sociologists have made to this area. I conclude with a consideration of some theoretical issues that emerge when one considers mental illness in the family within the context of the stress process paradigm.

THE INTERGENERATIONAL TRANSMISSION OF MENTAL ILLNESS

There is substantial agreement among sociologists, psychologists, and psychiatrists that the family environment plays a critical role in the development of mental health problems among children. Indeed, almost every social science perspective on life-course development attributes considerable importance to the ways in which family contexts affect the lives of children. Moreover, a central theme of virtually all sociological and psychological theories of socialization asserts the prominence of family factors in influencing children's behavior. In this context, an important consideration is the intergenerational transmission of mental illness. Reviews of the literature on this topic clearly reveal that research on these issues has been dominated by clinical psychology and social psychiatry. The most extensive literatures are those assessing the effects of parental schizophrenia, depression, and alcoholism on the psychosocial functioning of children.

Children of Schizophrenic Parents

For some time, researchers have been aware of clear patterns of familial aggregation of schizophrenia. For example, although lifetime risk for schizophrenia is between 0.90% and 0.95% for the general population, this risk can rise to more than 10% for relatives of persons with schizophrenia (cf. Willerman & Cohen, 1990). Although it is widely accepted that genetic factors play a significant role in the transmission of schizophrenia, there has also been a consistent focus on the family environment of individuals with schizophrenia. These patterns of familial aggregation, coupled with an early focus on the family environment, led several investigators to follow over time young children with a schizophrenic parent to chart the emergence of any symptoms of schizophrenia. Among the most notable of these investigations are the Stony Brook High Risk Project (e.g., Emery, Weintraub, & Neale, 1982), the Massachusetts Mental Health Center Project (e.g., Cohler, Gallant, & Grunebaum, 1977), the Rochester Longitudinal Study (e.g., Sameroff, Seifer, & Zax, 1982), and the University of Rochester Child and Family Study (e.g., Fisher & Jones, 1980).

The results of these projects demonstrate that children of schizophrenic parents experience clear and consistent problems in their social functioning in terms of creating classroom disturbances and being defiant. As well, cognitive difficulties are apparent in terms of comprehension and performance on complicated tasks such as embedded figures tests. In addition, these results indicate that these children are at considerable risk for mental health problems, specifically oppositional and defiant behaviors, symptoms of attention deficits, and other indicators of maladjusted behavior at home and school. In many cases, however, the children of parents with schizophrenia were indistinguishable from those of depressed parents, although children in both these groups generally demonstrated high levels of psychopathology compared to children of parents who served as nonpsychiatric controls.

Children of Depressed Parents

The growing importance of this area of research is underscored by the number of reviews of studies of the emotional health of children of depressed parents (e.g., Cummings & Davies, 1993; Gelfand & Teti, 1990; Gotlib & Avison, 1993; Gotlib & Lee, 1990; Hammen, 1991). The conclusions of these reviews are remarkably consistent across a variety of research designs. In several early investigations, researchers interviewed depressed mothers about their children's mental health and found that depressed mothers reported more psychological problems with their children than did nondepressed women (e.g., Forehand, Wells, McMahon, Griest, & Rogers, 1982; Webster-Stratton & Hammond, 1988). Depressed mothers also reported more depressed and anxious mood in their children, greater suicidal ideation, and more difficulties in school (Billings & Moos, 1983; Weissman et al., 1987). Moreover, in a 1-year follow-up assessment, Billings and Moos (1986) compared the children of remitted and nonremitted depressed parents to controls with nondepressed parents. As expected, the nonremitted depressed group reported the highest incidence of dysfunction in their children; however, despite the abatement of their own depressive symptoms, parents in the remitted group continued to report more dysfunction in their children than did the control parents. It appears, then, that the effects of parental depression on children's well-being persist beyond remission.

Although the results of these studies indicate that children of depressed parents function more poorly than do children of nondepressed parents, these early findings were based on parental reports rather than on direct observations of the children. Because depressed parents' reports may be biased by a tendency to see both their parenting and their children's behavior in a negative light (cf. Rickard, Forehand, Wells, Griest, & McMahon, 1981; but see also Conrad & Hammen, 1989), a more rigorous research strategy requires direct assessment of the functioning of children. Observational investigations have incorporated these design considerations to provide information about the well-being of children of depressed parents and the quality of parent–child relationships. Whiffen and Gotlib (1989) conducted observational studies with infants of depressed and nondepressed mothers. They found that the infants of the depressed mothers were rated as less happy, more tense, and more easily fatigued during the interaction than were the infants of the nondepressed mothers. The infants of the depressed women also scored significantly lower on measures of infant development. These findings converge with those of other similar studies (Cutrona & Troutman, 1986; Field, Healy, Goldstein, & Guthertz, 1990; Whiffen, 1988).

Other investigations have examined the well-being of older children of depressed mothers. In general, the results of these investigations indicate that children of depressed parents demonstrate poorer social and psychological functioning than do children of nondepressed parents (Ghodsian, Zayicek, & Wolkind, 1984; Hirsch, Moos, & Reischl, 1985; Radke-Yarrow, Cummings, Kuczynski, & Chapman,1985). In a series of papers, Lee and Gotlib (1989a, 1989b, 1991a) report on a longitudinal examination of the psychological adjustment of four groups of school-age children: children of depressed psychiatric patient mothers, children of nondepressed psychiatric patient mothers; children of nondepressed medical patient mothers, and children of community mothers. Results reveal that the children of depressed mothers have more severe psychiatric symptoms and poorer overall adjustment than do the children of nondepressed mothers, and were also rated by their mothers as having a greater number of both internalizing and externalizing problems. Interestingly, the children of depressed mothers typically did not differ from the children of nondepressed psychiatric patient mothers, suggesting that the effects of psychiatric disorder on children's mental health may not be specific to depression.

Thus, there is little question that parental depression affects the functioning of children and significantly increases their risk of developing a psychiatric disorder or other emotional difficulties. This pattern of results has been found in assessments utilizing parental reports, child self-reports, and teacher, peer, and clinician ratings, attesting to its robustness. Furthermore, the nature and severity of problems found in children of depressed parents appear to be similar to those observed among offspring of schizophrenics. Indeed, some investigators have suggested that these difficulties in child functioning may not be due to depression or schizophrenia per se but, rather, to parental mental health problems in general.

Children of Alcoholic Parents

There is little doubt that children of alcoholic parents are at elevated risk for alcoholism in adulthood (cf. Sher, 1991). Although less is known about the impact of parental alcoholism on younger children, the incidence of psychiatric problems in this population has been a concern of clinicians for some time. West and Prinz (1987) have presented a comprehensive review of studies on the prevalence of psychopathology among the children of parents with alcoholism. They organized their review according to specific classifications of children's emotional and behavioral problems. In addition, they distinguished between those studies that sampled alcoholic and nonalcoholic parents and then assessed children's psychopathology, and those studies that assessed parental alcoholism among samples of children with and without indications of child psychopathology. For child hyperactivity and conduct disorder, West and Prinz concluded that these studies find only a weak association with parental alcoholism. There are, however, a number of interpretational problems associated with this conclusion. West and Prinz observe that the association may be stronger for boys than for girls; moreover, few studies distinguished between aggressive behavior and hyperactivity. Furthermore, these results may be confounded by prenatal exposure to alcohol because of maternal drinking and the possibility that attention deficit disorder and hyperactivity and alcoholism may be genetically linked. Accordingly, it is difficult to draw definite conclusions about the role of environmental factors associated with alcoholism in the family in causing this particular type of child psychopathology.

There is consistent evidence that parental problems with alcohol constitute a significant risk factor for young children's internalizing symptoms such as anxiety and depression. Moos and Billings (1982) reported higher levels of anxiety and depression among children of alcoholic than nonalcoholic parents. Children from alcoholic families have also been found to exhibit higher levels of internalizing problems and lower levels of self-esteem and sense of control (Chassin, Rogosch, & Barrera, 1991).

In summary, the studies reviewed examining the functioning of the offspring of parents with schizophrenia, depression, or alcoholism suggest that these children are at risk for developing a variety of emotional problems. Clearly, there is not a one-to-one correspondence between parental diagnosis and child functioning. Thus, for example, children of depressed parents not only exhibit higher rates of depression, but also higher levels of conduct disorder, global psychiatric symptoms, and multiple psychiatric diagnoses. Similarly, children of alcoholic parents are not only at elevated risk for alcohol and drug use, but also for diagnoses of major depression and anxiety. Finally, it is important to note that there are common problems exhibited by children in all three groups of parental disorders. These problems include difficulties at school, temper tantrums, headaches, problematic social functioning, and emotional disorder. The lack of diagnostic specificity in the impact of parental psychopathology on children's psychosocial adjustment, juxtaposed with the adverse effects of social disadvantage and problematic family structures reviewed earlier in this handbook, suggests there are common factors or processes that mediate the effects of these environmental variables on child functioning.

Common Mediating Processes

It seems clear, then, that children's exposure to parental mental illness in the form of schizophrenia, depression, and substance abuse increases the likelihood that the children themselves will exhibit symptoms of psychopathology. In the literature, two processes that are indicative generally of poor parenting repeatedly emerge as mediators of the impact of parental mental disorders on children's mental health: *marital or family discord* and the *emotional unavailability of parents.*

If marital or family discord is indeed a mediating process, there must be strong evidence that it is both a consequence of parental mental illness and an antecedent of children's emotional or behavioral problems. Several studies report a significant association between parental mental illness and marital or family discord (Biglan et al, 1985; Crowther, 1985; Gotlib & Whiffen, 1989; Ruscher & Gotlib, 1988). These investigations find that the interactions of depressed persons with their spouses are significantly more negative than those of nondepressed couples and that these marital stressors persist even after recovery. Although the literature examining the association of marital distress with alcoholism and schizophrenia is smaller than that focusing on depression, studies indicate that the marriages of individuals with these disorders are also characterized by tension and discord (Billings, Kessler, Gomberg, & Weiner, 1979; Hooley, Richters, Weintraub, & Neale, 1987; Jacob & Krahn, 1988; O'Farrell & Birchler, 1987).

The association between marital discord and children's mental health problems has also been widely documented. Grych and Fincham (1990) reviewed studies of marital conflict and children's adjustment, and concluded that 15 of 19 relevant studies support the existence of this association. Perhaps the most compelling support for the importance of family discord as a critical determinant of children's adjustment can be found in Amato and Keith's (1991) review of studies of emotional and behavioral problems among children of divorced families. They conclude that family discord is a stronger predictor of children's problem than either parental absence or economic disadvantage.

Other researchers have directly investigated the mediating role of marital discord. Indeed, West and Prinz (1987) suggest that marital conflict might be an important link between parental alcoholism and child dysfunction. Offord, Allen, and Abrams (1978) suggest that elevated rates of delinquency among children of alcoholics may be due to the high rates of marital conflict and divorce in these families. O'Brien, Margolin, and John (1995) also document a link between marital conflict and children's emotional and behavioral problems.

While these authors conclude that marital discord mediates the causal relationship between parental mental disorders and children's mental health, much of this research is based on correlational data. As Downey and Coyne (1990) note in their review of the literature on the children of depressed parents, there are other causal specifications that are tenable. Nevertheless, they conclude that there is empirical support for conceptualizations of marital conflict as a mechanism that links parental depression to children's psychopathology. Moreover, Loeber and Stouthamer-Loeber's (1986) meta-analysis suggests that marital conflict directly influences children's delinquency.

The second process that may mediate children's elevated risk for psychopathology involves the degree to which parents are emotionally available to respond to their children's needs. There is consistent evidence that the nature and quality of children's interactions with their parents affect their school performance, social competence, and interpersonal behaviors (Amato, 1989; Dornbusch, 1989). There is also a large body of literature indicating that the quality of parent–children interactions has a significant, direct effect on children's self-concept, sense of efficacy, and ego development (Avison & McAlpine, 1992). Analyses of interactions of parents and their adolescents, for example, indicate that families that are characterized by sensitivity and individuality promote the development of high self-esteem and a clear self-identity in adolescents (Walker & Greene, 1986).

The results of investigations examining more explicitly the effects of poor parent–child involvement and inadequate parental supervision reveal correlations between problems in parenting and children's mental health problems. In their review of over 30 studies, Loeber and Stouthamer-Loeber (1986) report strong support for the proposition that parental unavailability to, or insularity from, their children are significant predictors of children's misconduct and delinquency. Similarly, Patterson and Stouthamer-Loeber (1984) have presented striking evidence concerning the impact of coercive parent–child relationships on children's antisocial behaviors. Finally, several studies have documented the associations between family dysfunction and ineffective parenting on children's maladjustment, especially conduct problems and delinquency (Mann & MacKenzie, 1996; Patterson, Reid, & Dishion, 1992; Wooton, Frick, Shelton, & Silverthorn, 1997). In their earlier review of this issue, Loeber and Stouthamer-Loeber (1986) conclude that these dysfunctions are causally linked to children's conduct problems.

It is clear, then, that there is a significant association between problem parenting, typically characterized by emotional unavailability, and difficulties in children's mental health. In this context, it is important to note that a number of investigations suggest consistent links between parental mental disorders and parental emotional unavailability. The majority of investigations that have explicitly examined the parenting styles of individuals with mental health problems have focused on depression. These studies clearly indicate that depression interferes with the responsiveness of mothers toward their infants (Bettes, 1988; Field et al., Guthertz, 1990; Livingood, Daen, & Smith, 1983). Other investigators have replicated these findings with older children (Breznitz & Sherman, 1987; Goodman & Brumley, 1990).

A number of researchers have reported strikingly similar findings in examining the parenting styles of individuals exhibiting other mental illnesses. For example, Jacob, Ritchey, Cvitkovic, and Blane (1981) find that alcoholic fathers are less instrumental and directive than their nonalcoholic counterparts. Similar to the pattern for depressed parents, these findings suggest that alcoholism in fathers is related to lack of involvement with children. Corroborating these results, Steinglass (1981) and Moos and Billings (1982) report that members of families in which an alcoholic is currently drinking tend to function more independently of each other and to be less cohesive and responsive than are members of nonalcoholic families. These studies reveal a lack of family involvement and suggest that one mechanism by which parental alcoholism may be associated with child problems is through a tendency for the parent to be relatively unavailable or unresponsive to the child. As Lee and Gotlib (1991b) speculate, alcoholic parents may often be physically absent from the home because of the time spent drinking outside of the home, because of hospitalization for treatment of alcoholism or other illnesses, or because the nonalcoholic parent has requested that the spouse leave the home for a period of time. Alternatively, an alcoholic parent may be physically present in the home but uninvolved in parenting and caretaking responsibilities.

Finally, several investigators have examined the interactions of families in which a parent has been diagnosed with schizophrenia. Miklowitz and Stackman (1992) have reviewed the literature concerned with the construct of "communication deviance" in schizophrenia and note that parental communication deviance, which includes nonresponsivity, was the strongest individual predictor of the likelihood that the children developed a schizophrenic disorder at a 15-year follow-up. It appears, therefore, that parental emotional unavailability plays a critical role in children's problems in adjustment in the face of parental psychopathology and, in particular, in response to parental depression, alcoholism, and schizophrenia.

A Model of the Intergenerational Transmission of Disorder

One way to conceptualize these processes that link parental psychiatric disorders with their children's mental health problems is presented in Figure 24.1. In this model, the intergenerational transmission of mental disorder is influenced by a variety of factors. The effect of parental psychiatric disorder on children's mental health may be mediated by two broad categories of processes. First, parental disorder may result in emotional unavailability to one's children. Second, it may also generate parental discord and conflict. Both of these circumstances increase the likelihood of mental health problems among children. Of course, these processes are themselves influenced directly and indirectly by factors other than parental disorder, such as social status characteristics, exposure to stressors, and access to various psychosocial resources.

None of these considerations denies the possibility that genetic influences operate in this context. There is substantial evidence of genetic influences on a number of psychiatric disorders (Tsuang & Feroane, 1990), and many researchers have argued persuasively that future studies of developmental psychopathology need to consider genetic factors as important mediators of environmental influences (Plomin, 1989; Rutter & Pickles, 1991; Rutter, Silberg, & Simonoff, 1993). Rutter and colleagues (1993) have made a very compelling case for the need to design studies to measure both environmental and genetic factors that influence children's mental health:

> Genetic studies have indeed shown that some supposed environmental effects to an important extent reflect genetically mediated influences. Thus, how parents bring up their children is going to be affected by their own qualities as individuals, and those qualities are going to include a substantial genetic component (Plomin & Bergeman, 1991). However, this issue is not just one of determining whether supposedly environmental effects are truly environmental. Rather, the main interest and importance lies in the potential power of the genetic design for sorting out which aspects of a person's environment are having environmental influences on psychological development or psychopathology. (pp. 442–443)

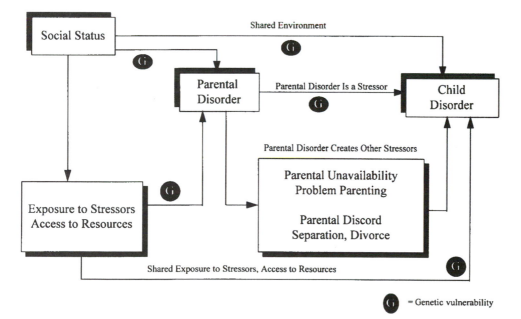

FIGURE 24.1. The intergenerational transmission of mental disorders.

Opportunities for the Sociology of Mental Health

It seems clear that the study of the intergenerational transmission of mental illness has been dominated largely by clinical psychology and, to a lesser extent, by social psychiatry. Does this imply that sociologists have no contribution to make in this important area of research? Quite the contrary, there are several important elaborations that sociologists of mental health can bring to this area of inquiry.

Perhaps the most important conceptual contribution that they can make is to elaborate the theoretical models that have dominated this area of research. Although it seems clear that parental mental illness is associated with children's emotional and behavioral problems, researchers in this area have generally failed to take into account the impact of social factors on this entire process. Indeed, a central theme of the sociology of mental health asserts that individuals' positions in the social structure have a vast array of mental health consequences (Aneshensel, Rutter, & Lachenbruch, 1991; Pearlin, 1989). Moreover, there is also strong evidence that social disadvantage has a profound effect on children's mental health (McLeod & Shanahan, 1993, 1996; Offord et al., 1987). Studies of the intergenerational transmission of mental illness that fail to take into account these social factors are likely to overestimate the direct effects of parental illness on children's mental health. A sociological approach would estimate the relative significance of social disadvantage and parental mental illness on children's well-being.

Studies of the impact of parental mental illness on children's mental health have also been relatively selective in considering other stressors to which these families may be exposed. One of the distinctive contributions of the sociology of mental health has been to recognize that individuals and families are exposed to a broad array of stressors (Turner, Wheaton, & Lloyd, 1995; Wheaton, 1994). These stressors may be both antecedents and consequences of episodes of psychiatric disorder. Thus, for example, chronic financial strains may account for both elevated rates of depression among mothers and emotional and behavioral problems among their children. Alternatively, episodes of depression, schizophrenia, or substance abuse among parents may increase the risk of job loss and subsequent socioeconomic disadvantage that in turn may have serious mental health consequences for their children. The potential mediators of the relationship between parental and child mental health problems need to be examined with the same kind of scrutiny that family conflict and emotional unavailability have enjoyed. Sociologists have developed the conceptual models and the empirical measures to do so.

The importance of delineating the stressors to which families are exposed is also crucial if scientists are to accurately estimate the relative impact of environmental and genetic influences on mental health. A particularly good illustration is Kendler, Kessler, Neale, Heath, and Eaves's (1993) twin study that examines the relative effects of genetic risk factors and environmental risks such as childhood parental loss, perceived parental warmth, and various dimensions of stressful experience on major depressive disorder. In descending order of impact, they find that recent stressful life events, genetic factors, a previous history of depression, and neuroticism all have direct effects on depressive disorder.

This example highlights the potential contribution to be made by sociological studies of the intergenerational transmission of mental health. Collaborations among sociologists and behavioral geneticists are likely to clarify the relative influences of social and genetic influences on this process. By carefully measuring environmental variables that include social status, social stressors, psychosocial resources, and family processes, sociologists and geneticists can play a central role in estimating the limits of genetic influences on the intergenerational transmission of mental illness.

There is a third substantive contribution that sociologists can bring to this area of research. As we have seen, the research on intergenerational transmission has focused mainly on diagnosed disorders among parents and their impact on children. For those who contend that indexes of psychological distress are more appropriate measures of mental health problems (cf. Mirowsky, 1994; Mirowsky & Ross, 1990), there is a pressing need for studies of the association between parental distress and children's outcomes. Such investigations broaden the scope of this area to include all families, not just those in which there is a diagnosable disorder.

This point raises an important methodological issue in which sociological expertise can be useful. Reviews of the literature on the intergenerational transmission of mental illness have noted that studies often fail to consider the impact of the severity of parental disorder on children's mental health. Many studies construct samples of families from caseloads of psychiatric practices or from other therapists' caseloads. The results of these studies are vulnerable to selection biases that result from sampling from clinical caseloads. A more appropriate method for sample acquisition would involve a population-based survey to identify families with at least one parent who has experienced a disorder. Such methodological approaches are typically part of the expertise of sociologists and epidemiologists, and can be expected to avoid commission of the "clinician's illusion," the error of generalizing from a sample with more severe and more chronic mental disorders to all families experiencing mental health problems (Cohen & Cohen, 1984).

THE IMPACT OF PSYCHIATRIC ILLNESS ON FAMILY CAREGIVERS

The sociology of mental health has a rich tradition of investigating the psychosocial consequences for individuals who provide care to family members who suffer from health problems. For example, there is a substantial body of literature that has examined the emotional impact on parents of caring for a child with a chronic illness or a life-threatening disease (Avison, Noh, & Speechley, 1991; Beresford, 1993; Breslau & Davis, 1986). More recently, increases in the number of individuals who suffer from Alzheimer's disease and other late-life dementias have stimulated several important investigations of caregiving for the elderly (Aneshensel, Pearlin, Mullan, Zarit, & Whitlach, 1995; Pearlin, Mullan, Semple, & Skaff, 1990; Zarit, Orr, & Zarit, 1985). As well, the AIDS epidemic has resulted in a significant increase in the number of family members who provide care to individuals with this illness (Moskowitz, Folkman, Collette, & Vittinghoff, 1996; Pearlin, Aneshensel, & LeBlanc, 1997; Pearlin, Mullan, Aneshensel, Wardlaw, & Harrington, 1994; Turner & Catania, 1997).

Perhaps the longest tradition of research on the emotional impact of family caregiving focuses on families of individuals with severe mental illness. For almost five decades, sociologists and social psychiatrists have documented the difficulties experienced by the close relatives of formerly hospitalized psychiatric patients. Early studies described the hardships experienced by the parents and spouses of these patients and provided some of the first evidence that these difficulties had distressful consequences for family members (Clausen & Yarrow, 1955; Clausen, Yarrow, Deasy, & Schwartz, 1955).

Family Burden

Subsequent research in this area focused on the concept of family burden: the emotional strains and socioeconomic difficulties borne by families of psychiatric patients. In their classic studies of schizophrenia, Brown, Bone, Dalison, and Wing (1966) documented a variety of difficulties experienced by family members and relatives, and Pasamanick, Scarpitti, and Dinitiz (1967) described how the presence, behavior, and dependency of the patient caused worries or difficulties in the family. Grad and Sainsbury (1968) further described the multidimensional nature of family burden and estimated that one-third of family members felt that the patient had adversely affected family life. As interest in family burden increased, Hoenig and Hamilton (1969) attempted to distinguish between objective and subjective burden. The former included the effects on the finances and routines of the family, whereas the latter was defined as family members' feelings that they were negatively affected by these objective burdens. Among those who reported the presence of objective burden, slightly less than 60% reported any subjective burden, and less than 20% reported severe subjective burden. This finding importantly suggests that factors beyond the objective burden itself influence subjective appraisals of the discharged psychiatric patient as a burden. Subsequently, a substantial body of research explored these possibilities (Freedman & Moran, 1984; Greenberg, Kim, & Greenley, 1997; Tessler & Gamache, 1994).

Research on the burden of living with former psychiatric patients has expanded substantially since these early studies. In a series of papers, Noh and his colleagues document how these two dimensions of family burden are associated but observe that only subjective burden is related to psychological distress among family members (Noh & Avison, 1988; Noh & Turner, 1987). Their examination of the differences in the factors that predict subjective burden among wives and husbands of former psychiatric patients places this work within the context of the stress process formulation.

This collaborative group has also articulated a more theoretical approach to the study of discharged psychiatric patients and their families. Avison and Speechley (1987) and Noh and Avison (1988) argue that the stress process paradigm is a useful theoretical context in which to examine the dynamics of psychiatric patients' family life. Central to their argument is the idea that the burdens of living with a discharged psychiatric patient can be conceptualized as stressors. Noh and Avison document that the burdens experienced by spouses of discharged psychiatric patients are determined in part by the patient's level of symptoms. In addition, they show that this relationship is exacerbated by the experience of other stressful life events. They also find evidence that the effects of life events on family burden are moderated by social support. These findings provide clear evidence of the theoretical relevance of the stress process paradigm for understanding the impact of psychiatric illness on family processes.

Family Caregiving

More recently, research in this area has extended the analysis of burden to focus explicitly on the experience of caregiving for family members with psychiatric illnesses. With the continued trends toward the deinstitutionalization of individuals with mental illness, an increasing number of discharged psychiatric patients return to live with their families. Consistent with earlier research, studies of these families reveal that the caregiving role is characterized by high levels of chronic strain (Cook & Pickett, 1987; Fisher, Tessler, & Benson, 1990).

This recent work has shown that the caregivers of individuals with mental illness are by no means a homogeneous group, a perspective missing from earlier work. For example, until relatively recently, there have been few studies of caregiving for the mentally ill that have systematically addressed gender differences. Noh and Avison (1988) find that husbands of psychiatric patients have higher levels of burden when their wives are more symptomatic and that their burden increases with the duration of time since their wives' discharge from the hospital. Increases in other stressful life events are also associated with husbands' reports of caregiving burden. Among the wives of patients, their age, the presence of children at home, and low levels of mastery correlate with caregiver burden. Thus, the factors associated with caregiving burden appear to be substantially different for men and women. To date, however, there have been few attempts to explore gender differences in the burden of caring for mentally ill people.

One of the more interesting examinations of gender in this context is Cook's (1988) investigation of who "mothers" the chronically mentally ill. She finds that this responsibility appears to fall mainly to the mothers of psychiatric patients, a pattern that has also been reported by Gamache, Tessler, and Nicholson (1995). Moreover, Gamache and associates also note that other female relatives appear to assume the caregiving role when mothers are unavailable.

Other investigators have explored the role that the gender of the mentally ill patient plays in influencing caregiving strain. For example, Pickett, Cook, and Solomon (1995) find that parents of mentally ill daughters appear to be more burdened than parents of mentally ill sons, even though sons are perceived to be more "off-time" in terms of their achievement of normative educational and occupational goals. The researchers speculate that this gender difference may emerge from parents' greater sense of responsibility for their daughters, whom they perceive to be more vulnerable to exploitation by others.

Researchers have also started to explore ethnic and racial differences in caregiving. In their study of families of discharged psychiatric patients, Horwitz and Reinhard (1995) report interesting differences in caregiving burden associated with race and kin relationship. White parents experience more subjective burden than do black parents, even though they have equivalent duties. Although black siblings report more caregiving responsibilities than white siblings, the former experience less burden. Horwitz and Reinhard interpret these findings in terms of the greater participation in and benefits from extended kin networks experienced by African Americans.

These differences in the caregiving experience appear to be consistent with the findings of Milstein, Guarnaccia, and Midlarsky (1995). Their interviews with European American, African American, and Hispanic American caregivers reveal substantial ethnic differences in family members' perceptions of the former patient's illness and their responses to it. Similar patterns have been reported by Pickett, Vraniak, Cook, and Cohler (1993). These studies clearly demonstrate the need for further research that examines racial, ethnic, and cultural variations in the caregiving role.

Several other new themes have emerged recently in the study of caring for former psychiatric patients. One is the possibility that the experience of providing care to a discharged psychiatric patient might have some beneficial aspects. For example, Greenberg, Greenley, and Benedict (1994) report that relatively high-functioning former patients often make important contributions to their families. A second theme concerns reciprocity. Horwitz (1994) reports that perceived reciprocity of support is an important predictor of sibling social support in the families of former psychiatric patients. Horwitz, Reinhard, and Howell-White (1996) document how former patients make expressions of support to their families, largely in terms of symbolic exchanges such as expressing affection and participating in family activities. The investigators conclude that the provision of social support by former patients alleviates feelings of burden among family caregivers.

The issue of reciprocity as a family dynamic directs attention to the nature of interactions between mentally ill patients and their family members. By far, the most frequently investigated relationship between family social networks and psychiatric disorder concerns the impact of expressed emotion (EE) on diagnosed disorder. EE refers to the quality of interaction or relationship between an individual with a disorder and his or her relative. Family members who display high EE tend to be very critical of the person with a mental illness and are often emotionally over involved in the life of the person with the disorder. Consequently, high EE families are likely to create highly stressful environments for people with mental illness.

Ever since the classic work of Brown (1985) and Vaughn and Leff (1976), research on EE has dominated the study of family networks and severe mental illness. Bebbington and Kuipers (1994a, 1994b) recently reviewed 25 papers on EE to evaluate the predictive and clinical utility of this construct in research on the course of schizophrenia. They argue that EE is a strong predictor of relapse across cultures and geographic locations, and across gender. From a clinical point of view, Bebbington and Kuipers conclude that there is clear evidence that extensive contact with relatives high in EE increases the likelihood of relapse, whereas contact with relatives low in EE may have protective influences.

There has been virtually no research, however, that investigates the impact of EE on family members themselves. Family members with high EE may be more likely to perceive caregiving as burdensome and to experience elevated levels of psychological distress. Alternatively, EE may magnify the impact of caregiving strain on psychological distress. This seems to be a promising area of research that has been largely ignored.

Opportunities for the Sociology of Mental Health

Sociologists have made major contributions to our understanding of the distressful effects of caring for a mentally ill relative. As I have suggested earlier, one of the more recent developments has been an exploration of ethnic, racial, and gender differences in caregiving experiences. In my view, sociologists are particularly well suited to undertake larger-scale studies of caregiving that will allow for more in-depth investigations of cultural variations of caregiver burden and distress. For several reasons, this is a challenging task. Cultures attach different meanings to the concept of mental illness and have very different notions of the appropriateness of various formal and informal treatment strategies. These differences are likely to have important consequences for caregiver burden across different cultures. As our societies become more ethnically and culturally diverse, these differences are likely to be increasingly important for understanding caregiver distress.

With some notable exceptions, studies of caring for mentally ill people have not developed a strong conceptual framework that considers the role of gender in the caregiving process. Although Cook and her colleagues have documented that women assume the major responsibilities and burdens of caregiving for mentally ill family members, we do not yet have a systematic exploration of the gendered nature of this role and its implications for women's mental health. This is an area where sociologists of mental health could make important theoretical and empirical contributions given the depth of sociological research on the impact of gender on mental health in general (see Chapter 11).

Independent lines of inquiry have investigated the reciprocity of support among family members with mental illness and their caregivers, expressed emotion, and caregiver burden; however, there have been few attempts to synthesize this work. Yet it appears that the dynamics of power and exchange are common to all three areas of research. Greenley (1986) has raised this possibility. He argues that behaviors characteristic of EE are often the family's attempt to control the patient's behavior. Moreover, EE is likely both to inhibit the reciprocity of support and to be associated with caregiver burden. Thus, there appears to be some potential for conceptual and empirical work that attempts to integrate these various findings concerning the caregiving experience.

There is another research opportunity for sociologists who are interested in studying the burden of caring for mentally ill individuals. Over the last decade, interest in caregiving has increased dramatically. There are now substantial bodies of literature concerning caregiving and a wide range of diseases and conditions, including AIDS, dementia, severe mental illness, Down's syndrome, and life-threatening or chronic pediatric illnesses. Given this wealth of research, it seems timely to take a comparative approach in the study of caregiving and mental health.

There are some examples of this comparative approach. For example, Avison, Turner, Noh, and Speechley (1992) have contrasted the experiences of the families of discharged psychiatric patients with those caring for children with cancer, families caring for children with Down's syndrome or autism, and single mothers caring for their normal children. This comparative approach identified specific aspects of the caregiving experience that were particularly important for the psychological distress of caregivers. Avison and colleagues find that the type of chronic strain associated with the caregiving role varies with the nature of the family member's illness. Thus, the context of caregiving is an important feature that could be explored fruitfully within a comparative research framework.

Several recent studies provide interesting examples of the value of this research strategy. For example, Greenberg, Seltzer, Krauss, and Kim (1997) and Seltzer, Greenberg, Krauss, Gordon, and Judge (1997) have compared the caregiving experiences of mothers of adults with mental illness with mothers of adults with mental retardation. They report that social support plays a more prominent role in influencing the burden and distress of caring for adult children with mental illness than mental retardation. In a companion article on the impact on siblings, Seltzer and associates find that siblings of adults with mental retardation report considerably closer relationships with their brother or sister than do siblings of a mentally ill patient. Contact with the brother or sister with mental retardation is positively associated with the sibling's psychological well-being. In contrast, the more pervasive the impact of a mentally ill brother or sister on the lives of siblings, the more distressed are the siblings.

These examples clearly demonstrate how contextual factors shape caregiving experiences and affect caregivers' levels of burden and distress. With the development of large-scale studies of caregiving that include standardized research measures, there are now several opportunities for more comparative work of this kind.

FUTURE THEORETICAL DEVELOPMENTS

Although there is a substantial body of research investigating the impact of mental illness in the family, there remain several areas in need of further development and exploration. One consideration that has been largely ignored in this body of research is any examination of life course processes (see Chapter 27). Studies of the intergenerational transmission of mental illness tend to focus on children in specific age groups—mainly infants or preschoolers and, occasionally, children of primary school age. Rarely do these studies follow children through their teens and into early adulthood. This omission is unfortunate because such long-term, prospective studies may provide a number of insights into how the children of mentally ill parents accommodate to the stresses and strains of family life over the early part of their life course.

This information may assist social scientists in understanding the roles played by other social institutions, such as schools, in protecting children from the ongoing stress of living with a mentally ill parent. In addition, long-term follow-up studies have much to tell us about how life in such families affects early role transitions such as leaving school and teen parenting. These are issues of central interest to sociologists who study life-course issues.

Issues concerning aging and the life course are also important to the study of caregiving for persons with mental illnesses. Although it is clear that parents (especially mothers) become the prime caregivers to chronically mentally ill individuals, surprisingly little attention has been directed toward the issue of aging in the caregiver role. Cook, Cohler, Pickett, and Beeler (1997) provide a particularly informative life-course analysis of this issue. They identify a number of important questions that need to be addressed: the possibility that the timing of various life transitions may be seriously disrupted by caring for a mentally ill adult child; difficulties associated with coresidence in older age; and changes in levels of expressed emotion. To these, we should add the lack of information about the conditions under which an extended career of caregiving leads to more or less burden and distress; that is, we have little information about the factors that lead to adjustment over the life course. Finally, it appears that little attention has been paid to the likelihood that caregiving responsibilities over the life course are more likely to fall to women because of the gender difference in mortality.

A second major theoretical issue that deserves consideration concerns the study of mental illness in the family from a multi-level approach. Very little research has considered the effects of macrolevel processes as moderators of the impact of mental illness on the family. Although there is a growing body of research that documents how characteristics of neighborhoods and schools exert important influences on children's mental health (Aneshensel & Sucoff, 1996; Brooks-Gunn, Duncan, & Aber, 1997), studies of the intergenerational transmission of mental health usually ignore the impact of these macrolevel factors. Children of mentally ill parents may be significantly more likely to experience mental health problems if they live in disadvantaged neighborhoods than if they grow up in more middle-class settings. Alternatively, social disadvantage may be such an important determinant of children's mental health that parental mental illness has little added effect. Sociologists have the expertise in multilevel investigations to explore these alternative hypotheses.

Similar issues need to be examined in studies of caregiving to individuals with mental illness. For example, it seems unlikely that the experiences of caregiving in disadvantaged neighborhoods will engender the same kinds of stressors and burdens as caregiving in a middle-class neighborhood. Moreover, the stigma associated with mental illness may vary substantially from community to community, affecting the caregivers' burden and distress.

Finally, all of these considerations suggest that sociologists need to devote additional effort to the development of a more comprehensive theoretical framework for the study of the impact of mental illness on the family. Despite some attempts to introduce the stress process paradigm and a life-course perspective to this area of research, there is a pressing need for the development of a more comprehensive framework. A theoretical paradigm that integrates concepts from life-course studies, the stress process model, theories about stigma, and considerations of power and exchange is likely to generate an abundance of interesting and important research questions.

The challenge for the sociology of mental health is to integrate research from various disciplines and to develop a new synthesis that demonstrates clearly how social structure and social processes play important roles in shaping the lives of families who experience mental illness. Sociologists have already made important strides toward achieving this goal; much more is still to be done.

REFERENCES

Amato, P. R. (1989). Family processes and the competence of adolescents and primary school children. *Journal of Youth and Adolescence, 18,* 39–53.

Amato, P. R., & Keith, B. (1991). Parental divorce and the well-being of children: A meta-analysis. *Psychological Bulletin, 110,* 26–46.

Aneshensel, C. S., Pearlin, L. I., Mullin, J. T., Zarit, S. H., & Whitlach, C. J. (1995). Profiles in caregiving: The unexpected career. San Diego: Academic Press.

Aneshensel, C. S., Rutter, C. M., & Lachenbruch, P. A. (1991). Social structure, stress, and mental health. *American Sociological Review, 56,* 166–178.

Aneshensel, C. S., & Sucoff, C. A. (1996). The neighborhood context of adolescent mental health. *Journal of Health and Social Behavior, 37,* 293–310.

Avison, W. R., & McAlpine, D. D. (1992). Gender differences in symptoms of depression among adolescents. *Journal of Health and Social Behavior, 33,* 77–96.

Avison, W. R., Noh, S., & Speechley, K. N. (1991). Parents as caregivers: Caring for children with health problems. In G. A. Albrecht & J. L. Levy (Eds.), *Advances in medical sociology* (vol. 2, pp. 65–94). Greenwich, CT: JAI Press.

Avison, W. R., & Speechley, K. N. (1987). The discharged psychiatric patient: A review of social, social psychological, and psychiatric correlates of outcome. *American Journal of Psychiatry, 144,* 10–18.

Avison, W. R., Turner, R. J., Noh, S., & Speechley, K. N. (1993). The impact of caregiving: Comparisons of different family contexts and experiences. In S. H. Zarit, L. I. Pearlin, & Schaie, K. W. (Eds.), *Caregiving systems: Formal and informal helpers* (pp. 75–105). Hillsdale, NJ: Erlbaum.

Bebbington, P., & Kuipers, L. (1994a). The clinical utility of expressed emotion in schizophrenia. *Acta Psychiatrica Scandinavia, 89,* 46–53.

Bebbington, P., & Kuipers, L. (1994b). The predictive utility of expressed emotion in schizophrenia: An aggregate analysis. *Psychological Medicine, 24,* 707–718.

Beresford, B. A. (1993). Resources and strategies: How parents cope with the care of a disabled child. *Journal of Child Psychology and Psychiatry, 35,* 171–209.

Bettes, B. A. (1988). Maternal depression and motherese: Temporal and intonational features. *Child Development, 59,* 1089–1096.

Biglan, A., Hops, H., Sherman, L., Friedman, L. S., Arthur, J., & Osteen, V. (1985). Problem-solving interactions of depressed women and their husbands. *Behavior Therapy, 16,* 431–451.

Billings, A. G., Kessler, M., Gomberg, C. A., & Weiner, S. (1979). Marital conflict resolution of alcoholic and nonalcoholic couples during drinking and nondrinking sessions. *Journal of Studies on Alcohol, 40,* 183–195.

Billings, A. G., & Moos, R. H. (1983). Children of parents with unipolar depression: A controlled one year follow-up. *Journal of Abnormal Child Psychology, 14,* 149–166.

Billings, A .G., & Moos, R. H. (1986). Comparisons of children of depressed and nondepressed parents: A socialenvironmental perspective. *Journal of Abnormal Child Psychology, 11,* 463–486.

Breslau, N., & Davis, G. C. (1986). Chronic stress and major depression. *Archives of General Psychiatry, 43,* 309–314.

Breznitz, Z., & Sherman, T. (1987). Speech patterning of natural discourse of well and depressed mothers and their young children. *Child Development, 58,* 395–400.

Brooks-Gunn, J., Duncan, G. J., & Aber, J. L. (Eds.). (1997). *Neighborhood poverty: Context and consequences for children.* New York: Russell Sage Foundation.

Brown, G. W. (1985). The discovery of EE: Induction or deduction? In J. Leff, & C. Vaughn, (Eds), *Expressed emotion in families* (pp. 7–25). New York: Guilford.

Brown, G. W., Bone, M., Dalison, B., & Wing, J. K. (1966). Schizophrenia and social care: A comparative follow-up study of 339 schizophrenic patients. (*Institute of Psychiatry Maudsley Monographs* No. 17). New York: Oxford University Press.

Chassin, L., Rogosch, F., & Barrera, M. (1991). Substance use and symptomatology among adolescent children of alcoholics. *Journal of Abnormal Psychology, 100,* 449–463.

Clausen, J., & Yarrow, M. (1955). Introduction: Mental illness and the family. *Journal of Social Issues, 11,* 3–5.

Clausen, J., Yarrow, M., Deasy, L., & Schwartz, C. (1955). The impact of mental illness: Research formulation. *Journal of Social Issues, 11,* 6–11.

Cohen, P., & Cohen, J. (1984). The clinician's illusion. *Archives of General Psychiatry, 41,* 1178–1182.

Cohler, B .J., Gallant, D. H., & Grunebaum, H. U. (1977). Disturbance of attention among schizophrenic, depressed and well mothers and their five-year-old children. *Journal of Child Psychology and Psychiatry, 18,* 115–136.

Conrad, M., & Hammen, C. (1989). Role of maternal depression in perceptions of child maladjustment. *Journal of Consulting and Clinical Psychology, 57,* 663–667.

Cook, J. A. (1988). Who "mothers" the chronically mentally ill? *Family Relations, 37,* 42–49.

Cook, J. A., Cohler, B. J., Pickett, S. A., & Beeler, J. A. (1997). Life-course and severe mental illness: Implications for caregiving within the family of later life. *Family Relations, 46,* 427–436.

Cook, J. A., & Pickett, S. A. (1987). Feelings of burden and criticalness among parents residing with chronically mentally ill offspring. *Journal of Applied Social Sciences, 12,* 79–107.

Crowther, J. H. (1985). The relationship between depression and marital maladjustment: A descriptive study. *Journal of Nervous and Mental Disease, 173,* 227–231.

Cummings, E. M., & Davies, P. T. (1993). Maternal depression and child development. *Journal of Child Psychology and Psychiatry, 35,* 73–112.

Cutrona, C. E., & Troutman, B.R. (1986). Social support, infant temperament, and parenting self-efficacy: A mediational model of postpartum depression. *Child Development, 57,* 1507–1518.

Dornbusch, S. M. (1989). The sociology of adolescence. In W. R. Scott & J. Blake (Eds.), *Annual review of sociology* (vol. 15, pp. 233–259). Palo Alto, CA: Annual Reviews.

Downey, G., & Coyne, J. C. (1990). Children of depressed parents: An integrative review. *Psychological Bulletin, 108,* 50–76.

Emery, R., Weintraub, S., & Neale, J. M. (1982). Effects of marital discord on the children of schizophrenic, affectively disordered, and normal parents. *Journal of Abnormal Child Psychology, 10,* 215–228.

Field, T., Healy, B., Goldstein, S., & Guthertz, M. (1990). Behavior-state matching and synchrony in mother-infant interactions of nondepressed versus depressed dyads. *Developmental Psychology, 26,* 7–14.

Fisher, G. A., Benson, P. R., & Tessler R. (1990). Family response to mental illness: Developments since deinstitutionalization. In J. R. Greenley (Ed.), *Research in community and mental health* (vol. 6, pp. 203–236). Greenwich, CT: JAI Press.

Fisher, L., & Jones, J. E. (1980). Child competence and psychiatric risk: II. Areas of relationship between child and family functioning. *Journal of Nervous and Mental Disease, 168,* 332–342.

Forehand, R., Wells, K., McMahon, R., Griest, D., & Rogers, T. (1982). Maternal perception of maladjustment in the clinic-referred children: An extension of earlier research. *Journal of Behavioral Assessment, 4,* 145–151.

Freedman, R. I., & Moran, A. (1984). Wanderers in a promised land: The chronically mentally ill and deinstitutionalization. *Medical Care, 22,* S1–S59.

Gamache, G., Tessler, R. C., & Nicholson, J. (1995). Child care as a neglected dimension of family burden. In J. R. Greenley (Ed.), *Research in community and mental health* (vol. 8, pp. 63–90). Greenwich, CT: JAI Press.

Gelfand, D. M., & Teti, D. M. (1990). The effects of maternal depression on children. *Clinical Psychology Review, 10,* 320–354.

Ghodsian, M., Zayicek, E., & Wolkind, S. (1984). A longitudinal study of maternal depression and child behavior problems. *Journal of Child Psychology and Psychiatry, 25,* 91–109.

Goodman, S. H., & Brumley, H. E. (1990). Schizophrenic and depressed mothers: Relational deficits in parenting. *Developmental Psychology, 26,* 31–39.

Gotlib, I. H., & Avison, W. R. (1993). Children at risk for psychopathology. In C. G. Costello (Ed.), *Basic issues in psychopathology* (pp. 271–319). New York: Guilford.

Gotlib, I. H., & Lee, C. M. (1990). Children of depressed mothers: A review and directions for future research. In C. D. McCann & N. S. Endler (Eds.), *Depression: New directions in theory, research, and practice* (pp. 187–208). Toronto: Wall & Thompson.

Gotlib, I. H., & Whiffen, V. E. (1989). Depression and marital functioning: An examination of specificity and gender differences. *Journal of Abnormal Psychology, 98,* 23–30.

Grad, J., & Sainsbury, P. (1968). The effects that patients have on their families in a community care and a control psychiatric service: A two year followup. *British Journal of Psychiatry, 114,* 265–278.

Greenberg, J. S., Greenley, J. R., & Benedict, P. (1994). The contributions of persons with serious mental illness to their families. *Hospital and Community Psychiatry, 45,* 475–480.

Greenberg, J. S., Kim, H. W., & Greenley, J. R. (1997). Factors associated with subjective burden in siblings of adults with severe mental illness. *American Journal of Orthopsychiatry, 67,* 231–241.

Greenberg, J. S., Seltzer, M. M., Krauss, M. W., & Kim, H. W. (1997). The differential effects of social support on the psychological well-being of aging mothers of adults with mental illness or mental retardation. *Family Relations, 46,* 383–394.

Greenley, J. R. (1986). Social control and expressed emotion. *Journal of Nervous and Mental Disease, 174,* 24–30.

Grych, J .H., & Fincham, F. D. (1990). Marital conflict and children's adjustment: A cognitive-contextual framework. *Psychological Bulletin, 108,* 267–290.

Hammen, C. (1991). *Depression runs in families: The social context of risk and resilience in children of depressed mothers.* New York: Springer-Verlag.

Hirsch, B. J., Moos, R. H., & Reischl, T. M. (1985). Psychosocial adjustment of adolescent children of a depressed, arthritic, or normal parent. *Journal of Abnormal Psychology, 94,* 154–164.

Hoenig, J., & Hamilton, M. W. (1969). *The desegregation of the mentally ill.* London: Routledge & Kegan Paul.

Hooley, J. M., Richters, J. E., Weintraub, S., & Neale, J. M. (1987). Psychopathology and marital distress: The positive side of positive symptoms. *Journal of Abnormal Psychology, 96,* 27–33.

Horwitz, A. V. (1994). Predictors of adult sibling social support for the seriously mentally ill. *Journal of Family Issues, 15,* 272–289.

Horwitz, A. V., & Reinhard, S. C. (1995). Ethnic differences in caregiving duties and burdens among parents and siblings of persons with severe mental illnesses. *Journal of Health and Social Behavior, 36,* 138–150.

Horwitz, A. V., Reinhard, S. C., & Howell-White, S. (1996). Caregiving as reciprocal exchange in families with seriously ill family members. *Journal of Health and Social Behavior, 37,* 149–162.

Jacob, T., & Krahn, G. L. (1988). Marital interactions of alcoholic couples: Comparison with depressed and nondistressed couples. *Journal of Consulting and Clinical Psychology, 56,* 73–79.

Jacob, T., Ritchey, D., Cvitkovic, J. F., & Blane, H. T. (1981). Communication styles of alcoholic and nonalcoholic families when drinking and not drinking. *Journal of Studies on Alcohol, 42,* 466–482.

Kendler, K. S., Kessler, R. C., Neale, M. C., Heath, A. C., & Eaves, L. J. (1993). The prediction of major depression in women: Toward an integrated etiologic model. *American Journal of Psychiatry, 150,* 1139–1148.

Lee, C. M., & Gotlib, I. H. (1989a). Clinical status and emotional adjustment of children of depressed mothers. *American Journal of Psychiatry, 146,* 478–483.

Lee, C. M., & Gotlib, I. H. (1989b). Maternal depression and child adjustment: A longitudinal analysis. *Journal of Abnormal Psychology, 98,* 78–85.

Lee, C. M., & Gotlib, I. H. (1991a). Adjustment of children of depressed mothers: A ten-month follow-up. *Journal of Abnormal Psychology, 100,* 473–477.

Lee, C. M., & Gotlib, I. H. (1991b). Family disruption, parental availability, and child adjustment: An integrative review. In R. J. Prinz (Ed.), *Advances in the behavioral assessment of children and families* (vol. 5, pp. 166–199). London: Jessica Kingsley .

Livingood, A. B., Daen, P., & Smith, B. D. (1983). The depressed mother as a source of stimulation for her infant. *Journal of Clinical Psychology, 39,* 369–375.

Loeber, R., & Stouthamer-Loeber, M. (1986). Family factors as correlates and predictors of delinquency. In M. Tonry & N. Morris (Eds.), *Crime and justice: An annual review of research* (vol. 7, 29–149). Chicago: University of Chicago Press.

Mann, B. J., & MacKenzie, E. P. (1996). Pathways among marital functioning, parental behaviors, and child behavior problems in school-age boys. *Journal of Clinical Child Psychology, 25,* 183–191.

McLeod, J. D., & Shanahan, M. J. (1993). Poverty, parenting, and children's mental health. *American Sociologial Review, 58,* 351–366.

McLeod, J. D., & Shanahan, M. J. (1996). Trajectories of poverty and children's mental health. *Journal of Health and Social Behavior, 37,* 207–220.

Miklowitz, D. J., & Stackman, D. (1992). Communication deviance in families of schizophrenic and other psychiatric patients: Current state of the construct. In E. F. Walker, B. A. Cornblatt, & R. H. Dworkin (Eds.), *Progress in experimental personality and psychopathology research* (vol. 1, pp. 1–46). New York: Springer.

Milstein, G., Guarnaccia, P., & Midlarsky, E. (1995). Ethnic differences in the interpretation of mental illness: Perspectives of caregivers. In J. R. Greenley (Ed.), *Research in community and mental health* (Vol. 8, pp. 155–178). Greenwich, CT: JAI Press.

Mirowsky, J. (1994). The advantages of indexes over diagnoses in scientific assessment. In W. R. Avison & I. H. Gotlib (Eds.), *Stress and mental health: Contemporary issues and prospects for the future* (pp. 261–290). New York: Plenum Press.

Mirowsky, J., & Ross, C. E. (1990). Psychiatric diagnosis as reified measurement. *Journal of Health and Social Behavior, 30,* 11–25.

Moos, R., & Billings, A. (1982). Children of alcoholics during the recovery process: Alcoholic and matched control families. *Addictive Behaviors, 7,* 155–163.

Moskowitz, J. T., Folkman, S., Collette, L., & Vittinghoff, E. (1996). Coping and mood during AIDS-related caregiving and bereavement. *Annals of Behavioral Medicine, 18,* 49–57.

Noh, S., & Avison, W. R. (1988). Spouses of discharged psychiatric patients: Factors associated with their experiences of burden. *Journal of Marriage and the Family, 50,* 377–389.

Noh, S., & Turner, R. J. (1987). Living with psychiatric patients: Implications for the mental health of family members. *Social Science and Medicine, 25,* 263–271.

O'Brien, M., Margolin, G., & John, R. S. (1995). Relation among marital onflict, child coping, and child adjustment. *Journal of Clinical Child Psychology, 24,* 346–361.

O'Farrell, T.J., & Birchler, G. R. (1987). Marital relationships of alcoholic, conflicted, and nonconflicted couples. *Journal of Marital and Family Therapy, 13,* 259–274.

Offord, D., Allen, N., & Abrams, N. (1978). Parental psychiatric illness, broken homes, and delinquency. *Journal of the American Academy of Child Psychiatry, 17,* 224–238.

Offord, D. R., Boyle, M. H., Szatmari, P., Rae-Grant, N. I., Links, P. S., Cadman, D. T., Byles, J. A., Crawford, J. W., Blum H. M., Byrne, C., Thomas, H., & Woodward, C. A. (1987). Ontario Child Health Study: II. Six-month prevalence of disorder and rates of service utilization. *Archives of General Psychiatry, 44,* 832–836.

Pasamanick, B., Scarpitti, F. R., & Dinitz, S. (1967). *Schizophrenics in the community.* New York: Appleton-Century-Crofts.

Patterson, G. R., Reid, J. G., & Dishion, T. J. (1992). *Antisocial boys.* Eugene, OR: Castalia.

Patterson, G. R., & Stouthamer-Loeber, M. (1984). The correlation of family management practices and delinquency. *Child Development, 55,* 1299–1307.

Pearlin, L. I. (1983). Role strains and personal stress. In H. B. Kaplan (Ed.), *Psychosocial stress: Trends in theory and research* (pp. 3–32). New York: Academic Press.

Pearlin, L. I. (1989). The sociological study of stress. *Journal of Health and Social Behavior, 30,* 241–256.

Pearlin, L. I., Aneshensel, C. S., LeBlanc, A. J. (1997). The forms and mechanisms of stress proliferation: The case of AIDS caregivers. *Journal of Health and Social Behavior, 38,* 223–236.

Pearlin, L. I., Mullan, J. T., Aneshensel, C. S., Wardlaw, L., & Harrington, C. (1994). The structure and functions of AIDS caregiving relationships. *Psychoscial Rehabilitation Journal, 17,* 51–67.

Pearlin, L. I., Mullan, J. T., Semple, S. J., & Skaff, M. M. (1990). Caregiving and the stress process: An overview of concepts and their measures. *Gerontologist, 30,* 583–591.

Pickett, S. A., Cook, J. A., & Solomon, M. L. (1995). Dealing with daughters' difficulties: Caregiving burden experienced by parents of female offspring with severe mental illness. In J. R. Greenley (Ed.), *Research in community and mental health* (vol. 8, pp. 125–154). Greenwich, CT: JAI Press.

Pickett, S. A., Vraniak, D. A., Cook, J. A., & Cohler, B. J. (1993). Strength in adversity: Blacks bear burden better than whites. *Professional Psychology: Research and Practice, 24,* 460–467.

Plomin, R. (1989). Environment and genes: Determinants of behavior. *American Psychologist, 44,* 105–111.

Plomin, R., & Bergeman, C. S. (1991). The nature of nurture: Genetic influence on "environmental" measures. *Behavioral and Brain Sciences, 10,* 1–15.

Radke-Yarrow, M., Cummings, M., Kuczynski, L., & Chapman, M. (1985). Patterns of attachment in two- and three-year olds in normal families and families with parental depression. *Child Development, 56,* 884–893.

Rickard, K. M., Forehand, R., Wells, K. C., Griest, D. L., & McMahon, R. J. (1981). Factors in the referral of children for behavioral treatment: A comparison of mothers of clinic-referred deviant, clinic-referred non-deviant, and non-clinic children. *Behavioral Research and Therapy, 19,* 201–205.

Ruscher, S. M., & Gotlib, I. H. (1988). Marital interaction patterns of couples with and without a depressed partner. *Behavior Therapy, 19,* 455–470.

Rutter, M., & Pickles, A. (1991). Person-environment interactions: Concepts, mechanisms and implications for data analysis. In T. Wachs & R. Plomin (Eds.), *Conceptualization and measurement of organism-environment interaction* (pp. 105–141). Washington, DC: American Psychological Association Press.

Rutter, M., Silberg, J., & Simonoff, E. (1993). Whither behavioral genetics?-A developmental psychopathological perspective. In R. Plomin & G. E. McClearn (Eds.), *Nature, nurture and psychology* (pp. 433–456). Washington, DC: American Psychological Association Press.

Sameroff, A. J., Seifer, R., & Zax, M. (1982). Early development of children at risk for emotional disorder. *Monographs of the Society for Research in Child Development, 47,* Whole No. 7.

Seltzer, M. M., Greenberg, J. S., Krauss, M. W., Gordon, R. M., & Judge, K. (1997). Siblings of adults with mental retardation or mental illness: Effects on lifestyle and psychological well-being. *Family Relations, 46,* 395–405.

Sher, K. J. (1991). *Children of alcoholics: A critical appraisal of theory and research.* Chicago: University of Chicago Press.

Steinglass, P. (1981). The alcoholic family at home: Patterns of interaction in dry, wet, and transitional stages of alcoholism. *Archives of General Psychiatry, 38,* 578–584.

Tessler, R. C., & Gamache, G. (1994). Continuity of care, residence, and family burden in Ohio. *Milbank Quarterly, 72,* 149–169.

Tsuang, M. T., & Feroane, S. V. (1990). *The genetics of mood disorders.* Baltimore: Johns Hopkins University Press.

Turner, H. A., & Catania, J. A., (1997). Informal caregiving to persons with AIDS in the United States: Caregiver burden among central cities residents eighteen to forty-nine years old. *American Journal of Community Psychology, 25,* 35–59.

Turner, R. J., Wheaton, B., & Lloyd, D. A. (1995). The epidemiology of social stress. *American Sociological Review, 60,* 104–125.

Vaughn, C., & Leff, J. (1976). The influence of family and social factors on the course of psychiatric illness: A comparison of schizophrenic and depressed neurotic patients. *British Journal of Psychiatry, 129,* 125–137.

Walker, L. S., & Greene, J. W. (1986). The social context of adolescent of self-esteem. *Journal of Youth and Adolescence, 15,* 315–322.

Webster-Stratton, C., & Hammond, M. (1988). Maternal depression and its relationship to life stress, perceptions of child behavior problems, parenting behaviors, and child conduct problems. *Journal of Abnormal Child Psychology, 16,* 299–315.

Weissman, M. M., Gammon, G. D., John, K., Merikangas, K. R., Warner, V., Prusoff, B. A., & Sholomskas, D. (1987). Children of depressed parents: Increased psychopathology and early onset of major depression. *Archives of General Psychology, 44,* 847–853.

West, O. M., & Prinz, R. J. (1987). Parental alcoholism and childhood psychopathology. *Psychological Bulletin, 102,* 204–218.

Wheaton, B. (1994). Sampling the stress universe. In W. R. Avison & I. H. Gotlib (Eds.), *Stress and mental health: Contemporary issues and prospects for the future* (pp. 77–114). New York: Plenum Press.

Whiffen, V. E. (1988). Vulnerability to postpartum depression: A prospective multivariate study. *Journal of Abnormal Psychology, 97,* 467–474.

Whiffen, V. E., & Gotlib, I. H. (1989). Infants of postpartum depressed mothers: Temperament and cognitive status. *Journal of Abnormal Psychology, 98,* 274–279.

Willerman, L., & Cohen, D. B. (1990). *Psychopathology.* New York: McGraw-Hill.

Wootton, J. M., Frick, P. J., Shelton, K. K., & Silverthorn, P. (1997). Ineffective parenting and childhood conduct problems: The moderating role of callous-unemotional traits. *Journal of Consulting and Clinical Psychology, 65,* 301–308.

Zarit, S. H., Orr, N. K., & Zarit, J. M. (1985). *The hidden victims of Alzheimer's disease: Families under stress.* New York: New York University Press.

PART VI

Institutional Contexts of Mental Illness

CHAPTER 25

Mental Hospitals and Deinsitutionalization

George W. Dowdall

INTRODUCTION

The mental hospital has been the pivot around which the care of the seriously mentally ill has revolved (Dowdall, 1996). Its study has been a central concern of the sociology of mental health. This chapter reviews selectively the work of sociologists and social historians on the mental hospital, particularly the state mental hospital, where most patients have been cared for, including its origins, the deinstitutionalization of its patients, and its present status. For more than a century, the state hospital was the primary institutional response to serious mental illness, and for the past several decades, it has been at the center of attempts to redirect public policy.

Although the state hospital remains at the center, it has become largely invisible. Thus, the editor (Gallagher, 1987) of the most important journal in medical sociology observed that one might think the mental hospital had simply disappeared from society, judging by how few papers about it were submitted for review, let alone published. The paucity of research may reflect the more general neglect of the seriously mentally ill by academic disciplines as well as the broader society (Cook & Wright, 1995). In the past half-century, deinstitutionalization has led to the eclipse of the state hospital and its present role is obscured by the diverse newer organizations, including other psychiatric hospitals, that also deal in some way with mentally ill persons. Nevertheless, the present mental health care

GEORGE W. DOWDALL • Department of Sociology, St. Joseph's University, Philadelphia, Pennsylvania 19131.

Handbook of the Sociology of Mental Health, edited by Carol S. Aneshensel and Jo C. Phelan. Kluwer Academic/Plenum Publishers, New York, 1999.

system (whether for good or ill) remains anchored to the state mental hospital and cannot be understood without appreciating its role, however changed or diminished.

Deinstitutionalization as a term has been used several ways (Bachrach 1976, 1978, 1992). It has usually been used to describe two different but related phenomena: the shift of patients out of state hospitals, and the closing of state hospitals. In addition, this chapter uses the term in a more sociological sense to describe the shift from the state hospital as the center to a more peripheral role in the specialty mental health system. Finally, deinstitutionalization also means the declining legitimacy of the state hospital as the taken-for-granted caregiver for the seriously mentally ill.

This chapter examines the social history of the state mental hospital, including its emergence and institutionalization in the nineteenth century; its critique by sociologists and other observers in the period just after World War II; and its deinstitutionalization in the past half-century. The chapter next discusses the consequences of deinstitutionalization—a decline in residents of state hospitals and the closings of state hospitals; the creation of new mental health organizations; and changes in the surviving state mental hospitals. Finally, several of the problems associated with deinstitutionalization are examined, including homelessness, problems in continuity of care, and transinstitutionalization.

THE SOCIAL HISTORY
OF THE STATE MENTAL HOSPITAL

The founding of institutions for the care of the mentally ill has been the subject of extensive research by historians and sociologists, and is reviewed in detail elsewhere (Dowdall, 1996; Dwyer, 1988; Golden & Schneider, 1982; Grob, 1973; Rothman, 1971; Scull, 1989). Some of the main themes in the voluminous literature, however, should be stated here.

Beginning with the two cells in the basement of America's first hospital, the Pennsylvania Hospital, a series of institutions were opened in the eighteenth century that provided shelter or confinement for "those deprived of their reason." With the opening of the Williamsburg, Virginia, institution in 1773, the organizational form that became known as the state mental hospital began to evolve. The mixture of public and private funds and control that marked early care for the mentally ill makes it difficult to separate sharply the evolution of public and private systems. Private institutions such as the Pennsylvania Hospital (Tomes, 1984) and public institutions such as the Worcester State Hospital (Grob, 1966; Morrissey, Goldman, & Klerman, 1980) shared similar treatment philosophies and roles before the Civil War, and their early successes contributed to a broad movement to found hospitals for the insane, most at public expense (Dowdall, 1996). No doubt, the motivations of their founders were complex, including humanitarian reform for the insane (Dwyer, 1987; Grob, 1973), the professionalization of medicine, class and civic interests (Dowdall, 1996), and capitalist concern for social order (Rothman, 1971; Scull, 1989; Staples, 1991). These motives contributed to the establishment of several hundred institutions by the period following the Civil War.

By the end of the nineteenth century, the institutional care of the seriously mentally ill was centered in state mental hospitals, and by the early twentieth century, their institutional biographies had very strong similarities (Dowdall, 1996). Founded to be small, curative institutions using moral treatment to care actively for the insane, they had evolved into large, in some cases, huge, institutions that provided long-term custodial care for their usually involuntarily admitted inmates (Bockoven, 1956). Waves of scandal and reform washed over these institutions without much effect. Psychiatry became largely an institutional or administrative specialty, with growing professional and lay skepticism about the curability of insanity as well as increased interest in biological and even racial theories of its origins.

Why did state hospitals grow so considerably between the Civil War and World War II? Some of the early growth came from the successful effort of reformers to shift the public institutional care of the insane from poorhouses and county facilities to state hospitals. Rather than examine putative changes in the numbers of "insane," Sutton (1991) examined characteristics of the American states that might be associated with the expansion of asylum populations from 1880 to 1920. These characteristics included the decline in the use of almshouses, the growth of state fiscal capacity, the amount of time since statehood, and competition for votes. Sutton's quantitative models quite firmly supported historical narratives, with both approaches viewing the expansion of the asylum as an alternative to the development of comprehensive national policies to deal with dependency. In contrast, Staples (1991) viewed the growth of state mental hospitals in large part as the reflection of the increasing ability and need of the developing state apparatus to control deviant and dependent populations.

The authors of a influential study of state hospitals after World War II (Council of State Governments, 1950, pp. 33–34) listed seven factors in the growth of hospital populations during the present century: (1)general population growth; (2) the aging of the general population; (3) the constant pressures of overcrowding and need exceeding capacity; (4) public and professional confidence in, and willingness to utilize, mental hospitals; (5) a broader conception of mental illness; (6) an increasingly long duration of stay; and (7) decreased tolerance for deviant behavior and perhaps higher rates of mental illness. Much more historical research must be done to assess how well these factors explain how state hospitals grew to house more than 500,000 Americans by the 1950s.

CRITICISMS OF STATE MENTAL HOSPITALS

World War II marks a watershed in the care of people with serious mental illnesses. Prior to the war, a few voices within psychiatry and medicine had begun to question whether state hospitals could be improved, and one of them even used the term *deinstitutionalization* to describe needed reform (Grimes, 1934). Conscientious objectors, assigned to state hospitals during the war, emerged with shocking stories of the poor quality of care (Wright, 1947). American psychiatrists returned from the war with new convictions. A continuum theory of mental illness gained favor, suggesting that earlier stages of the major mental diseases could be treated in community settings, thus avoiding lengthy hospitalization.

Postwar prosperity brought immense new federal resources into health care generally and specifically into the construction of community hospitals with Hill-Burton funds (Starr, 1982). State governments began to spend more on mental illness, trying to catch up after Depression and wartime cutbacks or stagnation. The establishment of the National Institute of Mental Health (see Chapter 26) provided a federal voice for efforts to place mental illness higher on the national agenda, provide training funds for a new generation of mental health professionals, and shift the locus of mental health care from asylum to community (Grob, 1991).

A remarkable generation of critics of the state hospital used print and other media to call public attention to its shortcomings. For example, Mary Jane Ward (1946) published her autobiographical novel *The Snake Pit* about her experience in the Rockland (New York) State Hospital. Condensed in *Reader's Digest* and then made into an Academy Award-nominated film starring Olivia DeHaviland, it reached millions with a shocking account of life in the huge institutions. The progressive journalist Albert Deutsch (1948) wrote a series of magazine articles later assembled into the sensational expose *The Shame of the States*; its graphic photographs showed American mental patients in scenes reminiscent of Nazi concentration camps.

Rising professional and popular discontent with care in state hospitals did little to slow their growth, however, and by the mid- 1950s, 500,000 Americans lived inside their walls. Reformers within the national psychiatric and governmental scenes began a sustained and ultimately successful campaign to replace state hospitals, or at least diminish their role. Formation of the Joint Commission on Mental Illness and Health led to the 1961 publication of *Action for Mental Health*, setting the stage for new federal policy about mentally ill people. The Kennedy family experience with the care of a mentally retarded relative joined presidential leadership to broader political and generational interest in change. President Kennedy signed the Community Mental Health Act into law in 1963.

Sociologists concerned with mental health provided much of the intellectual ammunition in the battle to replace the state hospital. Their work first focused on the contemporary state hospital of the 1940s and 1950s, and then gradually revisited the entire history of this organizational form. Belknap (1956) examined daily life at "Southern State Hospital," based on extensive fieldwork over a 3-year period. Belknap (1956, p. xi) argued "Nearly all these hospitals have become organized in such a way during their historical growth that they are probably themselves obstacles in the development of an effective program for treatment of the mentally ill." After a detailed analysis of the organizational problems of this state hospital, he concluded, "One fact seems to stand out: from the time of its foundation the hospital has been defined as an institution which must carry out two contradictory and essentially unrelated functions . . . treating the mentally ill . . . [and] serving as a more efficient poor farm, with more centralized organization." (p. 204).

Other social scientists (reviewed in Dowdall, 1996) sketched the culture of the state mental hospital and compared life within its walls to a specialized community experience, contrasting its custodial and therapeutic goals, or even examining its way of life as an isolated, separate society (Caudill, 1958). Rosenhan (1973) reported on how individuals posing as mentally disabled individuals received degrading treatment that did not end even when their "symptoms" ceased.

The most significant indictment of the state hospital was *Asylums*, among the most influential and important works of American social science. The sociologist Erving Goffman (1961) painted a vivid picture, in the most somber hues, of inmate life inside a state hospital. His participant observation inside St. Elizabeth's Hospital (a federal psychiatric facility that functioned very much like a large state mental hospital) was the basis for a series of searing images of the degradation of inmate life inside a huge federal hospital, differing only in minor details from life in the larger state hospitals of the late 1950s. Goffman argued that the state hospital was a "total institution," defined as a place "of residence and work where a large number of like-situated individuals, cut off from the wider society for an appreciable period of time, together lead an enclosed, formally adminstered round of life" (p. xiii). Implicit in his argument about "the total institution" is that state hospitals further undercut the mental stability of those unfortunate enough to be admitted (cf. Gronfein, 1992).

Many of Goffman's ideas remain central to the sociology of mental health, yet many remain untested (Goldstein, 1979). In an essay filled with intriguing suggestions for re-search, McEwen (1980) explicated the key concept of total institution. Though some work has explored these ideas (Gronfein, 1992), little empirical work has been done. Indeed, later critics (Scull, 1977) have noted how this most important of works has largely escaped scholarly scrutiny, and that, in fact, its enormous prestige was as much a product of its rhetorical strengths as any empirical analysis it provided. (Curiously, given his impact on thinking about mental hospitals, Goffman largely ignored the study of serious mental ill-ness in his later career.)

Other works about the mental hospital have also shaped the later debate about the care of people with serious mentally illnesses, and also have begun to revisit the history of their founding and development. Beyond the scope of the present essay is *Madness and Civili-zation* (Foucault, 1965), arguably one of the most important works of social criticism in the postwar world. Foucault maintained that beneath the humanitarian rhetoric of early institu-tional care for the mad was a profound and malevolent drive for social control.

Reviewing historical and sociological studies of social control, Scull (1988, p. 685) noted that it has "suddenly acquired a new cachet," in part showing the impact of the work of such scholars as Goffman and especially Foucault. This new work emphasized historical study of the apparatus of social control "fashioned through the visible hand of definable organizations, groups, and classes, rather than being 'naturally' produced by the invisible hand of society" (1988, p. 686).

Scull (1975, 1984, 1989) examined in detail the development of the profession of psychiatry in the United States and Britain, and the incarceration of the insane in asylums and mental hospitals, largely at state expense. He employed a historical analysis of the interaction of class interest, professional knowledge, state development, and social con-trol.

THE HISTORY OF DEINSTITUTIONALIZATION

The criticisms of the state mental hospital tarnished its image in both public and profes-sional eyes, and such later events as the Kesey novel and film *One Flew Over the Cuckoo's Nest* virtually blackened it. Fused with powerful political and economic forces, that de-graded image led to the state hospital's deinstitutionalization.

Though deinstitutionalization is arguably one of the most profound and wide-ranging reforms in American social history, it has yet to be explored fully by social historians. Grob (1991, 1994) has provided a detailed history of the reform at the national level, with par-ticularly strong portraits of how the profession of psychiatry tried to shape the process. Scull (1977, 1984) criticized the motivations of the state officials who implemented the reform, selectively summarizing unfavorable evidence about its impact on the mentally ill.

Deinstitutionalization has proved to be a revolution in the care of mentally ill people. Like other revolutions, its actual development was complex, messy, and perhaps as much unintended as planned, and many of those who brought it about now look back to its onset and wonder out loud whether its results were worth it after all. For example, Senator Daniel Patrick Moynihan, writing in *The New York Times* on May 22, 1989, recalled events a quarter-century earlier. Moynihan described his involvement in the 1955 decision by New York state officials, including himself, to introduce new tranquilizing drugs into the state hospitals, with almost immediate declines in population. This was followed by the forma-tion of the Joint Commission on Mental Illness and Health, the bill signed by President

Kennedy to build community mental health centers (CMHCs), and the consequent failure to build more than a quarter of the planned CMHCs. Moynihan wrote:

> It was explicitly understood that there would be 2,000 such centers by the year 1980. That would translate into some 2,400 today.
>
> But we have built only 768. In New York City, where the ratio would call for 73, we have only 14.
>
> What if, on the occasion of the bill signing in 1963, someone had said to President Kennedy, "Wait. Before you sign the bill you should know that we are not going to build anything like the number of community centers we need. One in five in New York City. The hospitals will empty out, but there will be no place for the patients to be cared for in their communities. A quarter-century hence the streets of New York will be filled with homeless, deranged people."?
>
> Would he not have put down his pen. Pens rather. He used half a dozen; one of which is on display in my New York City office. I look at it on occasion and wonder what ever became of our capacity to govern ourselves? (p.A16)

This letter takes up some of the most important themes in the literature on deinstitutionalization as public policy. Among the most crucial concerns are whether deinstitutionalization occurred primarily as a result of mental health events narrowly construed, such as the introduction of psychotropic drugs. These drugs allowed some numbers of patients to be released into community settings, led to improved behavior in state hospital wards, and resulted in an increased sense among clinicians that community care could be realized for many of the seriously mentally ill people. Other "mental health events" include the more vigorous state-level leadership exerted after the war; the increased spending by state governments on mental health care, and the great cultural change in psychiatry and other branches of medicine.

In contrast, deinstitutionalization has also been attributed to factors external to mental health care. Several researchers (Brown, 1985; Grob, 1991, 1994; Gronfein, 1985a, 1985b; Lerman, 1982; Torrey, 1988, 1997) agree that the introduction of federal health care policies (Medicare and Medicaid in the 1960s) and changes in the provision of public welfare (Supplemental Social Security in 1972, and later Supplemental Security Disability Insurance) probably played at least as large a role in deinstitutionalization as did any other, by providing financial incentives to shift patients from state hospitals to nursing homes and general hospitals, and by providing direct entitlements to mentally ill persons in community settings. Specifically, Gronfein (1985a) argues that the introduction of psychotropic drugs did not result in dramatic changes in deinstitutionalization, and, in a careful empirical assessment of the timing of deinstitutionalization across the states, demonstrates that the federal programs clearly played a more important role in initiating deinstitutionalization. His work is a particularly important example of careful empirical research on how mental health policy actually unfolds.

The Moynihan letter correctly identifies the leading role of state governments, especially New York and California, in initiating programs that shifted some state funding into community programs spending on CMHCs and continued spending on general hospital construction (some part of which fueled the expansion of psychiatric services). The national politics of mental health (briefly reviewed recently by Torrey, 1997) in part accounts for the failure to build CMHCs at anything like their planned level.

Another theme touched on by the Moynihan letter is the dramatic shift in how deinstitutionalization was, and is, perceived. Noting that deinstitutionalization began with the fervid enthusiasm of both professionals and the public, Mechanic and Rochefort (1990) state that reactions have become much more negative, and that "another ideological consensus may be emerging, one that identifies deinstitutionalization as one of the . . . most stunning public policy failures" (p. 302). A concluding section of this chapter will examine the consequences of deinstitutionalization.

Not mentioned in the Moynihan letter are a series of court victories that led to major changes within state hospitals. A very small number of lawyers and their clients successfully used the courts to create major changes in mental health care. The courts imposed standards for active care of patients, established the principle that care should be given in the least restrictive setting, prohibited hospitals from making use of unpaid patient labor, and restricted involuntary treatment of psychiatric patients. La Fond and Durham (1992) provide a comprehensive discussion of the impact of legal changes on care for people with serious mental illnesses. A central question in the operation of the state hospital system has been the legal status of involuntarily committed patients. But the crucial role of legal activists has largely been neglected by sociologists following a social control approach in this area. In contrast, more conservative critics of deinstitutionalization (Isaac and Armat, 1990; Torrey, 1988, 1997) place great stress on the role of legal activists in propelling deinstitutionalization.

In attempting to understand the changing role of the state mental hospital in the contemporary mental health care system, Dowdall (1996) adapted a central argument of the population ecology of organizations. The approach holds that powerful inertial forces usually preclude organizations from dramatic adaptational change. Diversity within organizational sectors tends to come instead from organizational births and deaths, both of the same species and competing species, and not from change of existing organizations. The American mental health care industry, particularly the part that deals with seriously mentally ill people, is an excellent example of this argument. State hospitals were (and to a surprising extent, are) the organizational form that deals with the seriously mentally ill people. Since coming into widespread existence in the past century, their survival, and very modest internal change, gave the mental health sector a stable backbone during the period from the mid-nineteenth century to the 1960s. This century of stability and organizational stagnation was ended by the process of deinstitutionalization, which has had profound consequences for the state hospital as well as the broader mental health care sector.

THE PROCESS OF DEINSTITUTIONALIZATION

When change came, it took four forms: a dramatic decline in the number of residents in state mental hospitals; the closing of several dozen hospitals; additions of hundreds of CMHCs and public outpatient facilities, as well as several new state psychiatric hospitals; and modest but significant changes in state hospitals themselves.

Decline in Residents

Figure 25.1 (based on unpublished data from the Center for Mental Health Services, 1997) shows the impact of all of these changes on the number of patients in state psychiatric hospitals. In just two decades, the average size of the state hospital fell from above 2,000 patients to under 500. But the number of state hospitals remained almost the same over that time. Data from the 1990s suggest that the dramatic decline has leveled off, but the result is still a stunning drop in population overall.

Morrissey (1989) has suggested that deinstitutionalization occurred in two broad phases:

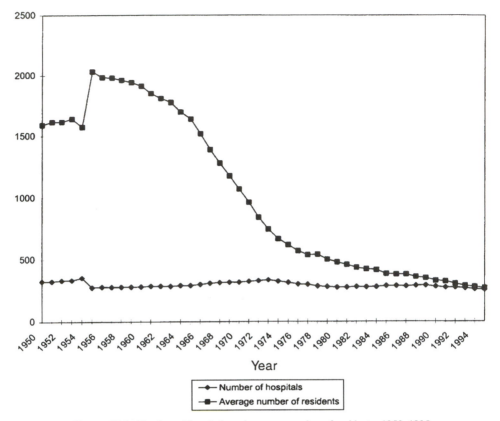

FIGURE 25.1. Number of hospitals and average number of residents, 1950–1995.

an early period of "opening the back door," when, for a variety of reasons, hospital patients were released more quickly than before, and both admissions and readmissions accelerated; and a later period of "closing the front door," when admission policies became more restrictive as alternative settings for treatment became more competitive. Mental health practices turned toward a combination of drug therapies and more active treatment using a variety of behavioral techniques, with increasing emphasis on avoiding prolonged hospitalization. Finally, the acute-care hospital became the most powerful organization in general health care and, increasingly, both the site and the model for psychiatric care, with profound and largely uncharted implications for the state mental hospital; a new generation of leaders tried to shape organizational change toward more active treatment of much smaller inpatient censuses. So as deinstitutionalization proceeded, mental hospitalization rates increased (Kiesler & Sibulkin, 1987), but with private psychiatric hospitals and general hospital psychiatric units significantly increasing their share of the inpatient population.

Figure 25.2 (based on unpublished data from the Center for Mental Health Services, 1997) presents a different perspective on deinstitutionalization. Over 500,000 persons were residents of state hospitals in 1955, but less than half that number were residents just 20 years later. While the census continues to fall in the 1980s and 1990s, the rate of change has become much more moderate. By contrast, admissions to state hospitals climbed dramatically after the onset of deinstitutionalization, but then began to fall after 1975. (Figure 25.2 presents data on residents in state mental hospitals over the entire time period. Two differ-

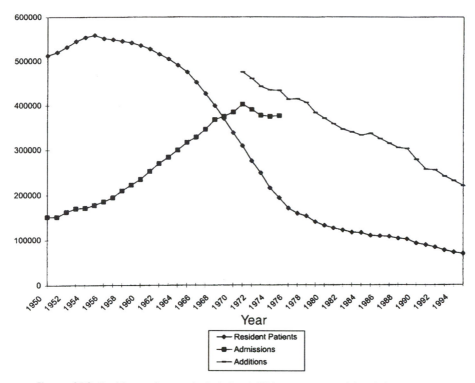

FIGURE 25.2. Resident patients and admissions/additions, state mental hospitals, 1950–1995.

ent series, an earlier one about admissions and readmissions until 1975, and a later one about "additions" that includes admissions, readmissions, and returns from leave, help explain the inflow into the state hospital but do not permit construction of a single comparable series over the same time period.)

Recent data on trends in the specialty mental health sector (Center for Mental Health Services, 1996) shed light on the availability, volume of services, staffing, and finances of mental health organizations, including state hospitals, in the period from 1970 to 1992.

During the period from 1970 to 1992, state hospitals were declining in number and in function, while the mental health sector grew in both. While the total number of specialty mental health organizations almost doubled, from 3,005 to 5,498, state mental hospitals decreased from 310 to 273. The number of organizations with inpatient services grew from 1,734 to 3,415, while the number of state hospitals with such services declined from 310 to 273. The number of organizations with outpatient services expanded from 2,156 to 3,390, while the number of state hospitals with outpatient services fell from 195 to 75. Organizations with partial care services rose from 778 to 2,548, while state hospitals with such services fell from 113 to 47.

Psychiatric beds per 100,000 fell during this period, but this decline was particularly steep for state and county mental hospitals. By contrast, the number of private psychiatric hospital beds was growing.

While state hospitals experienced "a steady and precipitous decline" (Center for Mental Health Services, 1996, p. 92) in the volume of services (measured by the number of inpatient additions), nonfederal general hospital and private psychiatric hospitals had "substantial increases." During this same period average daily inpatient census was declining across all organizational types. Outpatient additions expanded greatly from 1970 to 1980, grew moderately during the next decade, and slightly decreased from 1990 to 1992.

Patient care episodes provide a picture of the number of persons served during a year. There was a great increase in care given by specialty care organizations—from less than 2 million to almost 9 million episodes, from primarily inpatient to ambulatory (outpatient and partial care).

Empirical research has established the great variability across the states in the onset, timing, and depth of deinstitutionalization (Smith & Hanham, 1981). Observers pointed to the many perceived problems associated with deinstitutionalization (Bachrach, 1983; Bassuk & Gerson, 1978; Bachrach 1983; Mechanic & Rochefort, 1990), including the apparent lack of coordination with CMHCs; the erratic or nonexistent planning of aftercare for those discharged; and growth of psychiatric ghettoes near the rapidly emptying state hospitals.

Closings of State Mental Hospitals

Dowdall (1996) studied the entire population of state hospitals, estimated that approximately 40 state hospitals closed in the period between 1960 and 1990, and developed models that attempt to account for closings. Several states opened new state hospitals during the period, so the total number of state hospitals in the last year for which data were available (1990) was estimated to be 280. Many hospitals were renamed, perhaps reflecting the stigma associated with their old names. For example, Dowdall (1996) recounted the history of one institution. Opened in 1880 as the Buffalo State Asylum for the Insane, it was renamed the Buffalo State Hospital in 1890, but in 1974 was renamed yet again, this time as the Buffalo Psychiatric Center, its current name. But under whatever title, it is remarkable that given the great census decline and pressure to close state hospitals, almost as many exist at present as have ever existed in American history.

Openings of New Mental Health Organizations

Figure 25.3 presents data about the proportion of mental health organizations providing inpatient services. The bottom part of each bar presents the dramatic decline in the proportion of inpatient beds provided by state mental hospitals. In contrast the most dramatic growth occurs in nonfederal general hospitals with separate psychiatric settings and in private psychiatric hospitals. Kiesler and Sibulkin (1987) provided a detailed analysis of the increasing use of these types of inpatient settings in the care of seriously mentally ill persons.

Changes in State Hospitals

Dowdall (1996) presented a detailed case study of how one state mental hospital underwent deinstitutionalization. Almost all of the several hundred state hospitals underwent the same journey from relatively stable state hospital for much of the first half of the twentieth century to a somewhat more rapidly changing institution during deinstitutionalization. In the latter phase, the state hospital itself became stigmatized, increasingly seen as the place

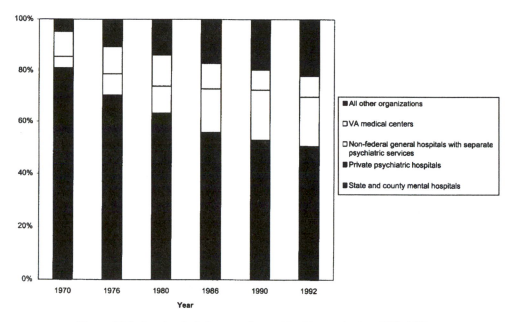

FIGURE 25.3. Inpatient beds by type of mental health organization, 1970–1992.

of last resort for seriously mentally ill people and the employer of last resort in public psychiatry. As its stigma increased, the state hospital was increasingly in eclipse, and the very real changes that took place in its daily life became largely invisible not only to the public but also to those concerned with mental health policy. Though largely hidden from public view and sociological scrutiny, state hospitals went through considerable turmoil and conflict during deinstitutionalization (Dowdall, 1996), playing a complex role in a changing mental health care sector (Goldman, Adams, & Taube, 1983).

Aside from size and market share, has the state mental hospital changed? At the beginning of the era of deinstitutionalization, the Joint Commission on Mental Illness and Health (1961) discussed the lag between support and interest for physical and mental health, saying it was "nowhere more evident" than in a comparison of state hospitals with community hospitals. The report went on to compare three indicators: daily patient costs, ratio of employees to patients, and accreditation.

One can roughly assess the amount of change by comparing these three indicators—costs, patient-staff ratios, and accreditation—over the recent past (for a detailed comparison, see Dowdall, 1996). One of the few researchers to examine the change empirically, Mechanic (1989) observed that the public mental hospital was transformed from custodial care to active treatment, in part because staff-patient ratios "improved enormously." Mechanic claimed "little resemblance" between state hospitals then and now (p. 479). Noting the great diversity across states, Mechanic (1987, p. 205) stated, "Between 1970 and 1982 the average number of patients per employee was reduced from 1.7 to .7 , and the average expenditure per patient increased from $4,359 to $31,000 ($12,500 after controlling for inflation)." On the question of accreditation, the Joint Commission reported that in 1960, 29% of state mental hospitals were accredited, whereas 67% of community hospitals were accredited. Hadley and McGurrin (1988) reported 1983 data on accreditation of 216 state psychiatric hospitals: 63.4% were accredited, more than double the rate of 30 years before.

Accreditation is only one measure of the quality of care in state hospitals, however. Dowdall (1996) reported on the visit of an accrediting agency, the Joint Commission on Accreditation of Hospitals, to a representative state hospital. The visit ended in glowing words about its "exceptionally high" quality and full accreditation. A short while later, an unannounced visit by an outside agency, the New York State Commission on the Quality of Care for the Mentally Disabled, yielded a dramatically different picture, comparing living standards in these state hospitals with those in prisons:

> While the Commission encountered islands of quality care for patients, other conditions witnessed by the Commission—including severe overcrowding; serious neglect of basic cleanliness; inadequate clothing; lack of privacy in sleeping, bathing, and toileting; absence of personal hygiene and grooming supplies; restricted access to drinking water and personal belongings; and the endless hours of boredom—would not meet standards which courts have mandated for state and federal prisons. In addition to not meeting court-mandated standards for incarcerated persons, these conditions fundamentally denied the human dignity of patients. (Quoted in Dowdall [1996], p. 173)

THE AFTERMATH OF DEINSTITUTIONALIZATION

The more complex ironies of deinstitutionalization begin to emerge when one tries to trace its consequences. Never a single national policy while it unfolded, it has been labeled as one and then blamed (or, less frequently, praised) for bringing about complex results that were perhaps only correlated with its onset. Perhaps it is not surprising to see comments about its almost mythic status (Goldman, Adams, & Taube, 1983; Goldman & Morrissey, 1985; Kiesler & Sibulkin, 1987).

The Rise of Community Mental Health

Since the onset of deinstitutionalization, institutional care for people with serious mental illnesses went from a largely monolithic dependency on huge state hospitals for most and small private psychiatric hospitals for some, to a far more diverse and variable mosaic of care. In the past decade, profound changes in the provision of mental health services have continued to transform the specialty mental health care sector, with the current trend toward managed care accelerating change (Center for Mental Health Services, 1996).

Professional reactions to the process varied considerably (e.g., see the essays for and against state hospitals in the July 1985 issue of *Hospital and Community Psychiatry*.) A more popular literature ties deinstitutionalization to a wide range of consequences for both mentally ill persons and social institutions, and reactions to deinstitutionalization range from supportive but critical (e.g., Johnson, 1990) to extremely negative (e.g., Isaac & Armat, 1990). Mechanic and Rochefort (1990) provided a particularly comprehensive assessment of deinstitutionalization as reform.

The most recent contribution to this large literature is representative of the largely critical reaction. Torrey (1997) cited the Carter administration Commission on Mental Health statement that the principle informing deinstitutionalization was "the objective of maintaining the greatest degree of freedom, self-determination, autonomy, dignity, and integrity of body, mind, and spirit for the individual while he or she participates in treatment or receives services" (pp. 10–11). This goal, Torrey claimed, has been realized in part for many, perhaps the majority, of those deinstitutionalized.

For a substantial minority, however, deinstitutionalization has been a psychiatric *Titanic*. Their lives are virtually devoid of "dignity" or "integrity of body, mind, and spirit." "Self-determination" often means merely that the person has a choice of soup kitchens. The "least restrictive setting" frequently turns out to be a cardboard box, a jail cell, or a terror-filled existence plagued by both real and imaginary enemies.

Torrey is the most recent critic to attempt a catalogue of the legacy of problems attached to deinstitutionalization and also cites some of the professional literature that will serve readers interested in further exploration. He argued that the large numbers of Americans with untreated serious mental illness represented a mental health crisis. He estimated that 150,000 were homeless and that another 159,000 were incarcerated in prisons or jails, often for crimes related to their untreated mental illness. Some became violent, others died prematurely—and all, in his opinion, unnecessarily (Torrey, 1997, pp. 1–3).

Deinstitutionalization appeared to have blurred the treatment and standing of mental illness on the national agenda, leading leaders of the constituencies, professions, and organizations that make up the ever-shifting "mental health or mental illness" arena into border skirmishes and calls for new agendas (Hilgartner & Bosk, 1988). One study of state budgeting found a correlation between state spending on mental hospitals and overall spending on mental illness (Hadley, Culhane, Snyder, & Lutterman, 1992; Schinaar, Rothbard, Yin, & Lutterman, 1992).

Deinstitutionalization was accompanied by several major therapeutic changes in the care of mentally ill persons. Among the most central was a vast increase in the number and types of drugs brought into use in the care of mentally ill people (Grob, 1994). Psychiatry was said to have "remedicalized," and interest shifted from community psychiatry and administrative psychiatry to biopsychiatry, culminating in the 1990s federal research effort termed "The Decade of the Brain." Progress in psychiatry came to be measured largely by advances in this part of the profession. But other treatment modalities developed as well, with new models such as aggressive community treatment (Dennis & Monahan, 1996; Estroff, 1981; Stein & Test, 1980) and psychiatric rehabilitation gaining support.

The boundaries between specialized psychiatric care and the broader medical care system remained unclear and perhaps became even more unclear as deinstitutionalization unfolded. Like other Americans, many seriously mentally ill persons use and abuse alcohol and drugs, and treatment for co-occurring mental disorder and substance abuse became particularly problematic in community care settings. As more seriously mentally ill people living in community rather than institutional settings, they experience the full range of daily problems of contemporary American communities, including housing, employment, and racism, but with the added burden of serious mental illness. The transformation of the general medical sector under managed care has had a profound effect on the provision of mental health care (Center for Mental Health Services, 1996).

Homelessness

Homelessness emerged as a major social issue in the United States during the 1980s. Since many of those wandering the streets of big cities exhibited many of the symptoms of serious mental illness at a time after deinstitutionalization commenced, it has been labeled by many as a cause and, in some cases, *the* cause of homelessness.

Bachrach (1992) provided a careful analytic review of the issues surrounding three key questions: "How much of the homeless population suffers from chronic mental illness?

Has deinstitutionalization precipitated an increase in homelessness among mentally ill persons? What kinds of programs—what specific services—should homeless mentally ill individuals be offered" (p. 453).

Before turning to the relationship between deinstitutionalization and homelessness, her responses to the first question help set a context within which to answer the question. Major conceptual and methodological issues make it virtually impossible to answer with certainty the question of how many of the homeless population are mentally ill—defining homelessness, assessing mental illness among homeless people, distinguishing between homeless mentally ill and other not easily distinguished populations, coping with the extreme diversity among the homeless mentally ill people, and dealing with the dramatic variations in time and space across this population. Taking into account the great obstacles in making these estimates, between 33% and 50% of people currently experiencing homelessness are estimated to be mentally ill, and between 22% to 57% of seriously mentally ill individuals are homeless.

Did deinstitutionalization result in these high rates? Some critics saw a direct causal link (Isaac & Armat, 1990; Torrey, 1988), whereas others saw a more complex pattern, with the way deinstitutionalization was implemented as the major factor (Goldman & Morrisey, 1985; Jencks, 1994; Lamb, 1984). Bachrach (1992) argued that major conceptual and methodological issues impede a simple answer. Conceptually, deinstitutionalization is at once a fact, a philosophy, and a process.

> When the definition of deinstitutionalization is broad enough to cover state hospital depopulation, diverted admissions, and unserved individuals, that policy may be viewed as having a pronounced, if not readily quantified, influence on homelessness among chronically mentally ill individuals. Many persons, disabled by their psychiatric illnesses and unable to gain access to suitable housing on their own, experience a unique form of eviction in being excluded from state mental hospitals that historically have performed many functions in their behalf, including that of providing a stable residential environment (Bachrach, 1992, p. 458).

Continuity of Care

Whatever its demerits, the huge state hospital of the 1950s and earlier provided a single, rigid framework within which long-term care for many seriously mentally ill people was provided. By contrast, the postdeinstitutionalization care of people with serious mental illnesses appears far less structured, and questions of continuity of care and the loss of community routinely arise (Cook, 1988). Sheehan (1982, 1995) presented a particularly vivid description of the journey of a mental patient through the system of services.

Deinstitutionalization was accompanied by a dramatic rise in for-profit psychiatric and nursing care, much of which sought to provide care to a population that in earlier decades might have been cared for at state expense in large hospitals. Anecdotes abound about skimming profitable patients; dumping unprofitable patients; "wallet biopsies" in which financial resources and insurance restrictions, and not psychiatric need determined care; and other difficulties in matching patient problems to adequate care. Privatization of psychiatric services remained a largely unexplored research area, with few adequate studies of its impact (Dorwart & Epstein, 1993), even while state governments increasingly followed a national model of "reinventing government" by moving from directly providing services to encouraging their privatization.

For some mentally ill persons, group care in the community almost certainly represented a major improvement over whatever life might be like in the state hospital (Estroff, 1981; Winerip, 1994). Some of the impetus for deinstitutionalization was provided by changes in the legal system. Involuntary psychiatric admission became particularly contested, with some observers noting a shift back toward its increasing use (La Fond & Durham, 1992) while others decried its virtual removal (Torrey, 1997). Aggressive community treatment models (Dennis & Monahan, 1996) appeared as a promising response to issues in community care.

Transinstitutionalization

The related problem of transinstitutionalization was noted by several researchers. Lerman (1982) studied deinstitutionalization as a broad process affecting several other institutions as well as mental health care, and provided a close examination of how changing patterns of welfare and health care programs at the federal level fueled much of deinstitutionalization. Brown (1985) conceptualized the process of deinstitutionalization as a series of transfers of care—from state to federal or local, from public to private authority, and from psychiatry to the welfare sector.

The expansion of the criminal justice and penal systems also played a major role. As the state hospital census declined during deinstitutionalization, state prisons and local jails were expanding dramatically, and many mentally ill individuals were incarcerated rather than hospitalized or treated in community settings (Scull, 1977, 1984; Steadman, McCarty, & Morrissey, 1989; Torrey, 1988, 1997; Torrey et al., 1992). A particularly urgent research question concerns the mental health status, treatment needs, and actual services provided to those incarcerated in jails and prisons.

Managed care, particularly involving the public sector, opens up a broad series of questions about the provision of mental health services to the seriously mentally ill people (Center for Mental Health Services, 1996). The rapidity of change in mental health care at present makes it difficult to assess what new roles mental hospitals, whether privately or publicly funded, will play, and what kinds of new organizational forms might take up some or all of the functions of traditional mental hospitals. Lamb (1997) reported on "institutes for mental disease" (IMDs), an example of what he terms "the new state mental hospitals in the community" (p. 1307). The IMD he studied was a 95-bed locked residential facility, one of 40 such facilities in California alone. Patients had many of the characteristics once found in those admitted to the more highly structured state hospitals, including psychotic symptoms, previous hospitalizations, violent behavior, and substance abuse. With lower costs per patient day, IMDs represent a cheaper alternative than mental hospitalization, but Lamb reported rising problems with patient behavior and provision of treatment and rehabilitation.

CONCLUSIONS

The state mental hospital is the pivot around which public policy about seriously mentally ill people has revolved (Dowdall, 1996). Its sociological study was a factor, perhaps a major factor, in the onset of deinstitutionalization, since it played a role in convincing a generation of clinicians, reformers, and activists that the state hospital had to be replaced.

This earlier sociological focus on the state hospital guaranteed sociological attention to the treatment of people with serious mental illnesses.

A more recent generation of sociologists has tended to ignore the state hospital, both its transformation during deinstitutionalization and its new role in the greatly expanded specialty mental health care system that emerged during the past 30 years. A few sociologists have worked as researchers or administrators in state hospitals (Dowdall & Pinchoff, 1994), but direct knowledge of how these institutions have changed appears rare in the field. Neglect of the state hospital may be part of a trend toward lessened sociological attention to serious mental illness. Assessment of the consequences of deinstitutionalization, as well as study of newer forms of inpatient and community care, remain urgent tasks for the sociology of mental health (Cook & Wright, 1995; Goldstein, 1979). This is all the more true as the advent of managed care has begun to transform mental health services (Center for Mental Health Services, 1996). Far from disappearing from the institutional scene, the state hospital is "down but not out," in Gronfein's (1989) terminology, becoming the place of last resort in an increasingly complex set of institutions providing care to the mentally ill people. Research about its persistence and change should illuminate how well or poorly the present mental health care system deals with serious mental illness. As such, the state hospital remains a central challenge for sociological research.

ACKNOWLEDGMENTS: Parts of this chapter are based on my book, *The Eclipse of the State Mental Hospital* and are used with permission of the publisher. I wish to thank Senator Daniel Patrick Moynihan for permission to reprint part of his letter to *The New York Times*. Michael Witkin of the Center for Mental Health Services provided unpublished CMHS data, and Gretchen Maenner prepared the final versions of the figures. I am grateful to the editors of the present volume and to Deborah L. Dennis for their many valuable suggestions, and the members of the Chester Avenue Seminar (with special thanks to Janet Golden, Randall Miller, and Eric Schneider) for reading an early draft of this chapter.

REFERENCES

Bachrach, L. L. (1976). *Deinstitutionalization: An analytical review and sociological perspective.* Washington, DC: National Institute of Mental Health.
Bachrach, L. L. (1978). A conceptual approach to deinstitutionalization. *Hospital and Community Psychiatry, 29*, 573–578.
Bachrach, L. L. (1992). What we know about homelessness among mentally ill persons: An analytical review and commentary. *Hospital and Community Psychiatry, 43*, 453–464.
Bassuk, E. L., & Gerson, S. (1978). Deinstitutionalization and mental health services. *Scientific American, 238*, 46-53.
Belknap, I. (1956). *Human problems of a state mental hospital.* New York: McGraw-Hill.
Bockoven, J. S. (1956). Moral treatment in American psychiatry. *Journal of Nervous and Mental Disease, 124*, 167–194, 292–321.
Brown, P. (1985). *The transfer of care.* Boston: Routledge & Kegan Paul.
Caudill, W. (1958). *The psychiatric hospital as a small society.* Cambridge, MA: Harvard University Press.
Center for Mental Health Services. (1996). *Mental health, United States, 1996.* R. W. Manderscheid & M. A. Sonnenschein (Eds.). DHHS Pub. No. (SMA) 96-3098. Washington, DC: U.S. Government Printing Office.
Cook, J. V. (1988). Goffman's legacy: The elimination of the chronic mental patient's community. *Research in the Sociology of Health Care, 7*, 249-281.
Cook, J. A., & Wright, E. R. (1995). Medical sociology and the study of severe mental illness. *Journal of Health and Social Behavior* (Extra Issue), 95–114.
Council of State Governments. (1950). *The mental health programs of the forty-eight states.* Chicago: Author.

Dennis, D. L., & Monahan, J. (Eds.). (1996). *Coercion and aggressive community treatment: A new frontier in mental health law*. New York: Plenum Press.

Deutsch, A. (1948). *The shame of the states*. New York: Harcourt, Brace.

Dorwart, R. A., & Epstein, S. S. (1993). *Privatization and mental health care: A fragile balance*. Westport, CT: Auburn House.

Dowdall, G. W. (1996). *The eclipse of the state mental hospital: Policy, stigma, and organization*. Albany: State University of New York Press.

Dowdall, G. W., Marshall, J. R., & Morra, W. A. (1990). Economic antecedents of mental hospitalization: A nineteenth-century time-series test. *Journal of Health and Social Behavior, 31*, 141–147.

Dowdall, G. W., & Pinchoff, D. (1994). Evaluation research and the psychiatric hospital: Blending management and inquiry in clinical sociology. *Clinical Sociology Review, 12*, 176–189.

Dwyer, E. (1987). *Homes for the mad: Life inside two nineteenth century asylums*. New Brunswick, NJ: Rutgers University Press.

Dwyer, E. (1988). The historiography of the asylum in Great Britain and the United States. In D. N. Weisstub (Ed.), *Law and mental health: International perspectives* (Vol. 4, pp. 110–160). New York: Pergamon Press.

Estroff, S. E. (1981). *Making it crazy*. Berkeley: University of California Press.

Federal Task Force on Homelessness and Severe Mental Illness. (1992). *Outcasts on main street*. Washington, DC: Interagency Council on the Homeless.

Foucault, M. (1965). *Madness and civilization: A history of insanity in the age of reason*. New York: Random House.

Gallagher, E. B. (1987). Editorial: Half-filled pages in mental health research. *Journal of Health and Social Behavior, 28*, vi–vii.

Goffman, E. (1961). *Asylums*. Garden City, NY: Anchor.

Golden, J., & Schneider, E. C.. (1982). Custody and control: The Rhode Island State Hospital for Mental Diseases, 1870–1970. *Rhode Island History, 41*, 113–125.

Goldman, H. H., Adams, N. H., & Taube, C. A. (1983). Deinstitutionalization: The data demythologized. *Hospital and Community Psychiatry, 34*, 129–134.

Goldman, H. H., & Morrissey, J. P. (1985). The alchemy of mental health policy: Homelessness and the fourth cycle of reform. *American Journal of Public Health, 75*, 727–731

Goldman, H. H., Taube, C. A., Regier, D. A., & Witkin, M. (1983). The multiple functions of the state mental hospital. *American Journal of Psychiatry, 140*, 296–300.

Goldstein, M. S. (1979). The sociology of mental health and illness. *Annual Review of Sociology, 5*, 381–409.

Grimes, J.M. (1934). *Institutional care of mental patients in the United States*. Chicago: Author.

Grob, G. N. (1966). *The state and the mentally ill: A history of the Worcester State Hospital in Massachusetts, 1830–1920*. Chapel Hill: University of North Carolina Press.

Grob, G. N. (1973). *Mental institutions in America: Social policy to 1875*. New York: Free Press.

Grob, G. N. (1983). *Mental illness and American society, 1875–1940*. Princeton, NJ: Princeton University Press.

Grob, G. N. (1991). *From asylum to community: Mental health policy in modern America*. Princeton, NJ: Princeton University Press.

Grob, G. N. (1994). *The mad among us*. Cambridge, MA: Harvard University Press.

Gronfein, W. (1985a). Psychotropic drugs and the origins of deinstitutionalization. *Social Problems, 32*, 437–454.

Gronfein, W. (1985b, September). Incentives and intentions in mental health policy: A comparison of the Medicaid and community mental health programs. *Journal of Health and Social Behavior, 26*, 192–206.

Gronfein, W. (1989, August). *Down but not out: State mental hospitals, deinstitutionalization, and social control*. Paper presented to the American Sociological Association, San Francisco, CA.

Gronfein, W. (1992). Goffman's *Asylums* and the social control of the mentally ill. *Perspectives on Social Problems, 4*, 129–153.

Hadley, T. R., Culhane, C. P., Snyder, F. J., & Lutterman, T. C. (1992). Expenditure and revenue patterns of state mental health agencies. *Administration and Policy in Mental Health, 19*, 213–233.

Hadley, T. R., & McGurrin, M. C. (1988). Accreditation, certification, and the quality of care in state hospitals. *Hospital and Community Psychiatry, 39*, 739–742.

Hilgartner, S., & Bosk, C. L. (1988). The rise and fall of social problems. *American Journal of Sociology, 94*, 53–78.

Isaac, R. J., & Armat, V. C. (1990). *Madness in the streets*. New York: Free Press.

Jencks, C. (1994). *The homeless*. Cambridge, MA: Harvard University Press.

Johnson, A. B. (1990). *Out of Bedlam: The truth about deinstitutionalization.* New York: Basic Books.

Joint Commission on Mental Illness and Health. (1961). *Action for mental health.* New York: Basic Books.

Kiesler, C. A., & Sibulkin, A. E. (1987). *Mental hospitalization: Myths and facts about a national crisis.* Newbury Park, CA: Sage.

La Fond, J. Q., & Durham, M. L. (1992). *Back to the asylum.* New York: Oxford University Press.

Lamb, H. R. (1984). Deinstitutionalization and the homeless mentally ill. *Hospital and Community Psychiatry, 35,* 899–907.

Lamb, H. R. (1997). The new state mental hospitals in the community. *Psychiatric Services, 48,* 1307–1310.

Lerman, P. (1982). *Deinstitutionalization and the welfare state.* New Brunswick, NJ: Rutgers University Press.

McEwen, C. A. (1980). Continuities in the study of total and nontotal institutions. *Annual Review of Sociology, 6,* 143–185.

Mechanic, D. (1980). *Mental health and social policy* (2nd ed.). Englewood Cliffs, NJ: Prentice Hall.

Mechanic, D., & Rochefort, D. A. (1990). Deinstitutionalization: An appraisal of reform. *Annual Review of Sociology, 16,* 301–327.

Morrissey, J. P. (1989). The changing role of the public mental hospital. In D. A. Rochefort (Ed.), *Handbook on mental health policy in the United States* (pp. 311–338). New York: Greenwood Press.

Morrissey, J. P., & Goldman, H. H.. (1984). Cycles of reform in the care of the chronically mentally ill. *Hospital and Community Psychiatry, 35,* 785–793.

Morrissey, J. P., Goldman, H. H., & Klerman, L. V. (1980). *The enduring asylum.* New York: Grune & Stratton.

Rochefort, D. (Ed.). (1989). *Handbook on mental health policy in the United States.* New York: Greenwood Press.

Rosenhan, D. L. (1973). On being sane in insane places. *Science, 179,* 250–258.

Rothman, D. J. (1971). *The discovery of the asylum: Social order and disorder in the New Republic.* Boston: Little, Brown.

Rothman, D. J. (1980). *Conscience and convenience: The asylum and its alternatives in progressive America.* Boston: Little, Brown.

Schinaar, A. P., Rothbard, A. B., Yin, D., & Lutterman, T. (1992). Public choice and organizational determinants of state mental health expenditure patterns. *Administration and Policy in Mental Health, 19,* 235–250.

Scull, A. T. (1977). *Decarceration: Community treatment and the deviant: A radical view.* Englewood Cliffs, NJ: Prentice Hall.

Scull, A. T. (1984). Afterword: 1983. In A. T. Scull (Ed.), *Decarceration* (2nd ed., pp. 161–189). New Brunswick, NJ: Rutgers University Press.

Scull, A. T. (1988). Deviance and social control. In N. J. Smelzer (Ed.), *Handbook of sociology.* Newbury Park, CA: Sage.

Scull, A. T. (1989). *Social order/mental disorder: Anglo-American psychiatry in historical perspective.* Berkeley & Los Angeles: University of California Press.

Sheehan, S. (1982). *Is there no place on earth for me?* Boston: Houghton Mifflin.

Sheehan, S. (1995, February, 20, 27). The last days of Sylvia Frumkin. *The New Yorker,* pp. 200–211.

Smith, C. J., & Hanham, R. (1981). Deinstitutionalization of the mentally ill: A time path analysis of the American states, 1955–1975. *Social Science and Medicine, 15D,* 361–378.

Staples, W. G. (1991). *Castles of our conscience.* New Brunswick, NJ: Rutgers University Press.

Starr, P. (1982). *The social transformation of American medicine.* New York: Basic Books.

Steadman, H. J., McCarty, D. W., & Morrissey, J. P. (1989). *The mentally ill in jail.* New York: Guilford.

Stein, L. I., & Test, M. A. (1980). Alternative to mental hospital treatment. *Archives of General Psychiatry, 37,* 392–397.

Sutton, J. R. (1991). The political economy of madness: The expansion of the asylum in Progressive America. *American Sociological Review, 56,* 665–678.

Taube, C.A., Mechanic, D., & Hohmann, A. A. (1989). *The future of mental health services research.* Rockville, MD: National Institute of Mental Health.

Tomes, N. (1984). *A generous confidence.* New York: Cambridge University Press.

Torrey, E. F. (1988). *Nowhere to go.* New York: Harper & Row.

Torrey, E. F. (1997). *Out of the shadows: Confronting America's mental illness crisis.* New York: Wiley.

Torrey, E. F., Wolfe, S. M., Erdman, K, & Flynn, L. M (1990). *Care of the seriously mentally ill: A rating of state programs* (3rd ed.). Washington, DC: Public Citizen Health Research Group and the National Alliance for the Mentally Ill.

Torrey, E. F., Wolfe, S. M., & Flynn, L. M. (1988). *Care of the seriously mentally ill: A rating of state pro-*

grams (2nd ed.). Washington, DC: Public Citizen Health Research Group and the National Alliance for the Mentally Ill.

Torrey, E. F., Stieber, J., Ezekiel, J., Wolfe, S. M., Sharfstein, J., Noble, J. H., & Flynn, L. M. (1992). *Criminalizing the seriously mentally ill: The abuse of jails as mental hospitals.* Washington, DC: Public Citizen's Health Research Group and the National Alliance for the Mentally Ill.

Ward, M. J. (1946). *The snake pit.* New York: Random House.

Winerip, M. (1994). *9 Highland Road: Sane living for the mentally ill.* New York: Pantheon.

Wright, F. L. (1947). *Out of sight, out of mind.* Philadelphia: National Mental Health Foundation.

CHAPTER 26

Instituting Madness

The Evolution of a Federal Agency

STUART A. KIRK

Erving Goffman's (1961) collection of essays, *Asylums: Essays on the Social Situation of Mental Patients and Other Inmates*, is one of sociology's classics. It has probably been read by more sociology students than any other single book in the field of mental health. Suffused with the author's eye for irony, amused skepticism, and gift with the language, the essays examine the nature of "total institutions" such as mental hospitals, the "moral careers" of patients, ways of "making out" in a mental hospital, and the "vicissitudes of the tinkering trades," as he referred to psychiatry and other mental health professions. Goffman's objective was "to try to learn about the social world of the hospital inmate, as this world is subjectively experienced by him" (p. ix).

He conducted his inquiries as a participant–observer for a year in the mid-1950s at St. Elizabeth's Hospital in Washington, D.C., a federal institution with over 7,000 inmates. His methodology consisted of passing the day with patients to learn about the "daily round of petty contingencies to which they were subject" (p. x). He acknowledged that this approach had its limits and admitted to intentionally adopting a partisan view, a view from the patients' standpoint, a partisanship he justifies to bring some balance to the professional literature, which was written almost entirely from the perspective of those in the tinkering trades.

Goffman was no clandestine operative at St. Elizabeth's. The hospital leadership was

STUART A. KIRK • Department of Social Welfare, School of Public Policy and Social Research, University of California, Los Angeles, Los Angeles, California 90095-1656.

Handbook of the Sociology of Mental Health, edited by Carol S. Aneshensel and Jo C. Phelan. Kluwer Academic/Plenum Publishers, New York, 1999.

not only aware of his efforts, but also supported them without censorship. Goffman's salary, secretarial help, and institutional sponsorship came from the Laboratory of Socio-Environmental Studies, where he served for 3 years as a visiting scholar. Later, he received an additional grant that provided the time to write his essays. The Laboratory's auspices and the source of this grant was the relatively new federal agency, the National Institute of Mental Health (NIMH). In his preface, Goffman acknowledges this support:

> The point I want to make is that this freedom and opportunity to engage in pure research was afforded me in regard to a government agency, through the financial support of another government agency, both of which were required to operate in the presumably delicate atmosphere of Washington, and this was done at a time when some universities in this country, the traditional bastions of free inquiry, would have put more restrictions on my efforts. For this I must thank the open- and fair-mindedness of psychiatrists and social scientists in government. (p. xi)

In this acknowledgment, Goffman reminds readers of the chilling Red scare at leading universities and contrasts it with the unexpected openness of government psychiatrists and social scientists at NIMH. This openness was particularly surprising since Goffman, at the time, was not well known and his studies were unconventional and intentionally critical, his research methods informal and unsystematic, and his conclusions appeared to be politically irreverent and institutionally subversive.

The Laboratory that sponsored his work was a very special entity within the new NIMH. Established in 1952, the Lab was headed by the sociologist John Clausen, who was given the autonomy and budget by the Institute to assemble an outstanding interdisciplinary group consisting of dozens of social scientists. Clausen, who invited Goffman to the Lab, recruited other young sociologists as well, among them Melvin Kohn, a young Ph.D. from Cornell, who would have a distinguished research career, later serving as chief of the Lab when Clausen departed, as President of the American Sociological Association, and as Chair of the Sociology Department at Johns Hopkins University; Leonard Pearlin, a Columbia University graduate, who became a well-known scholar of the social-structural determinants of social stress, and who later served on the faculty at the University of California, San Francisco and the University of Maryland; a former classmate of Pearlin's from Columbia, Morris Rosenberg, who, with Pearlin, pursued a line of inquiry into social factors and self-esteem, and who later taught at the University of Buffalo and the University of Maryland; a social anthropologist, William Caudill from Yale, who had written an influential book on the social organization of mental hospitals; and many others who had distinguished careers as scholars. Clausen himself joined the sociology faculty at the University of California at Berkeley in 1960, where Goffman also later taught, before going to the Univeristy of Pennsylvania. The Lab provided an intellectual think-tank atmosphere that was lively and active, where social scientists could work together on projects for sustained periods of time with substantial support. Yet the Lab was not an isolated enterprise. The scholars recruited by Clausen moved easily between the research laboratory in Washington and the halls of the finest universities, and their work was published by the mainstream sociology journals and book publishers.

Today, Goffman's work would be unlikely to receive any NIMH support, and the Laboratory for Socio-Environmental Studies, although still in existence, has a greatly diminished size and role. NIMH has changed dramatically.

Although NIMH has shaped mental health policy, training, service, and research for 50 years, very little has been written about it as an institution. In other chapters in this volume, the authors develop their topics by drawing on an established body of theoretical and empirical literature, often based on research funded by NIMH. For this chapter, however, there is no focused literature on the evolution of the NIMH. An adequate analysis of NIMH would require substantial attention to the evolution of the federal government and public policies, changing political leadership and philosophy at the federal level, and the transformations of American psychiatry. A thorough study of NIMH would be a case study in organizational adaptation to shifting political, economic, professional, technological, and cultural tides. This chapter is not an attempt to recount the full history of NIMH, its relationship with the federal government or professional community, or all its activities. Rather, I attempt to illustrate aspects of how NIMH has changed in its first 50 years by examining two major "signature" initiatives of NIMH, one early in its history and one very recent: the promotion of community mental health centers and the implementation of the Epidemiologic Catchment Area study. These two initiatives were selected because they each represent major, decade-long efforts by NIMH in which social scientists, particularly sociologists, played important roles. Both were highly public undertakings in which NIMH had a major political stake and each captures in different ways how NIMH established mental illness as a federal concern.[1]

CREATING AN INSTITUTE FOR MADNESS

Today, the NIMH, a component of the federal National Institutes of Health, has a staff of more than 850 scientists, administrators and support staff, and an annual budget of more than $600 million (NIMH, 1996a). Over the years, NIMH has described its mission in the same way: "improving the mental health of the American people; fostering better under-standing, diagnosis, treatment, and rehabilitation of mental and brain disorders; and pre-venting mental illness" (National Institute of Mental Health [NIMH] 1996b, p. 1). It car-ries out this mission by supporting research on mental disorders, neuroscience, and behavior; collecting, analyzing, and disseminating statistical information; training scientists; and com-municating information to scientists and the public (NIMH, 1996b).

Although there had been a Mental Hygiene Division within the Public Health Service since 1930, this agency was concerned chiefly with administering two hospitals devoted to narcotics addiction (NIMH, 1960). It was not until the World War II that the conditions were ripe for the establishment of a federal agency devoted to mental illness (Foley & Sharfstein, 1983). The military draft in World War II increased public awareness of mental illness. In mobilizing for the war, more men were rejected in the draft due to psychiatric disorders than the total number fighting at the peak of the war in the Pacific. The war itself also created a high incidence of psychiatric causalities. These battlefield causalities pro-moted on-the-spot crisis interventions that proved effective. The military's need for psy-chiatrists had stripped mental hospitals back home of staff and rendered care even less adequate than it had been. After the war, the many psychiatrists who were still in military uniforms could be called on to testify effectively at Congressional hearings about the men-tal health needs of the nation.

In striking contrast to current skepticism about the propriety or effectiveness of fed-eral intervention, the public's attitude in the 1940s was remarkably positive. There was

---

[1] The reader should be aware that many substantive topics about NIMH have been excluded in this chapter, including its role in developing and disseminating public information, its inhouse intramural research pro-grams, its shifting administrative attachments within the federal government, its relationship with important professional organization (e.g., American Psychiatric Association), its broad programs in support of mental health training and mental health research training, and so on.

enormous faith in the capacity of the federal government to get things done. A generation of adults had just lived through the Great Depression and World War II. The federal government had played an effective leadership role in resolving both national traumas, first by implementing FDR's New Deal, and then by mobilizing a nation for a military victory. On the tail of these enormous achievements, more effectively treating mental disorders and addressing other domestic social ills did not appear to be insurmountable tasks for the government.

Creating a new federal agency, however, required more than a receptive public and a booming postwar economy. It took advocates with an agenda to capitalize on and orchestrate the opportunities. Such advocates were found in the well-placed and highly respected psychiatrists Robert H. Felix, William Menninger, Francis Braceland, and Jack R. Ewalt, friends and colleagues in the nascent Group for the Advancement of Psychiatry (GAP), the progressive arm of the American Psychiatric Association (Foley & Sharfstein, 1998, p. 18). During the war, Felix was chief of the Mental Hygiene Division of the U.S. Public Health Service, Menninger was a general with the Office of the Surgeon General of the Army, and Braceland was a captain with the Office of the Surgeon General of the Navy. These were individuals who were viewed as leaders in the American Psychiatric Association as well (Barton, 1987, p. 171). Using ideas from Felix's earlier Master's of Public Health thesis, they developed a plan to establish a federal mental health institute. To accomplish this goal, they drafted the National Mental Health Act and built an impressive coalition of political supporters from both parties in the House and Senate. The bill was introduced to the Congress in the spring of 1946 and signed by President Truman that July. In its day, creating a new federal agency had taken less time than it would take today to pass some minor legislation.

Felix was appointed as the first director of NIMH and served in that capacity for over 15 years, through the presidencies of Truman, Eisenhower, and Kennedy. The other founders constituted a small psychiatric elite, who went on to hold many of the most important positions in American psychiatry and tied the Institute to the major professional organization, the American Psychiatric Association. For example, in 1955, Ewalt became chair of the very influential Joint Commission on Mental Health and Illness (more about this later). Braceland was the editor of the *American Journal of Psychiatry* from 1965 to 1978. Menninger became one of the most influential psychiatrists of the century. During the next decade or so, Felix, Braceland, and Ewalt would each serve as President of the American Psychiatric Association.

The 1946 Act establishing the NIMH authorized $7.5 million for research, training of personnel, and aiding states through grants and technical assistance in the treatment of mental illness. There were federal precedents for research (with the establishment of the National Cancer Institute) and for grants-in-aid to states (with public health programs to control venereal disease and tuberculosis), but funding training through stipends and fellowships to individuals was a new federal initiative. The law created a National Advisory Mental Health Council. All of these functions—providing grants to research institutions, stipends to individuals in training programs, financial aid to state mental health authorities, and using a professional-citizen Council—were used by Felix to build powerful, long-term national constituencies for the fledgling NIMH (Foley & Sharfstein, 1983).

But there were other important sources of immediate support for the new Institute. These consisted of "Washington's Noble Conspirators," as Elizabeth Drew (1967) described a broad coalition of advocates who wanted to expand the federal role in health and health research. The coalition included key legislators and committee chairmen, such as Senator

Lister Hill and Representative John F. Fogarty; wealthy philanthropists and lobbyists, such as Florence Mahoney and Mary Lasker; and journalists such as Mike Gorman, who became a skilled lobbyist as the executive director of the National Committee Against Mental Illness. The key persons developing mental health policy were relatively few in number, persons who worked in close collaboration and shared a common vision and agenda (Duhl & Leopold, 1968, p. 7). These were also people who had committed their entire careers to public service, tending to hold positions of public leadership for a decade or more. The fruits of the noble conspiracy were evident. From 1953 to 1960 the federal financing of medical research, including mental health, increased 700% (Foley & Sharfstein, 1983, p. 23; Felicetti, 1975).

Felix's agenda for NIMH was not simply to establish a federal bureau and have it thrive in order to improve services for the mentally ill. As he said in retrospect, "My hidden agenda was to break the back of the state mental hospital" (as quoted in Foley & Sharfstein, 1983, p. 23). This was no minor undertaking. At the time, state mental hospitals were *the primary* system of mental health care and had been so for a hundred years. State asylums were the institutional practice setting for many psychiatrists and other mental health professionals. They were also the major institutional home of the American Psychiatric Association, which originally began as the Association of Medical Superintendents of the American Institutions for the Insane. Many of the state hospitals were set in rural communities. Proponents of the philosophy of moral treatment had encouraged building hospitals in these serene environments (Rothman, 1971). Because these asylums grew to considerable size by the middle of the twentieth century, they had become major employers and economic mainstays in their communities. But of crucial significance, state mental hospitals were *state* institutions, regulated by *state* legislation and funded by *state* tax dollars. Thus, public mental health dollars were *state* dollars allocated to state asylums. Felix had no political authority or any obvious leverage over the system of mental health care in the United States. What strategy was he to use to dismantle the state hospital systems?

Americans had great faith in science and technical expertise. Science, including medicine and psychology, was power (Foley & Sharfstein, 1983, p. 24). NIMH was established to bring science and expertise to bear on the problem of mental illness and its treatment. By 1962, NIMH had funded nearly 3,000 research projects and had supported 1,500 training projects. During the fifties and sixties, the total number of mental health professionals increased 10 times faster than the number of all other health professionals (Foley & Sharfstein, 1983, p. 27). Nearly every graduate program in psychiatry, psychology, social work, and nursing enjoyed NIMH funding. Small grants-in-aid directly to the states' mental health authorities were made to assist them in developing mental health services in the community. None of these grants could be used directly to support state hospitals. In these ways, NIMH rapidly built mental health constituencies outside of Washington, D.C., and outside the state hospitals among the research, educational, and professional communities of every state.

In establishing NIMH, promises of success in preventing and treating mental illness had been made and, eventually, evidence of its achievement would be needed. Although European physicians were using new "tranquilizing" drugs to treat mental patients, Felix was skeptical of their early claims of success and, in fact, had been *decreasing* NIMH involvement in psychopharmacology projects (Foley & Sharfstein, 1983, p. 23–34). Despite Felix's reluctance, Congress earmarked $2 million in additional NIMH allocations in 1956 for drug treatment studies. Before long, he realized that the initial findings in clinical studies could provide the scientific support he needed for treating patients in the community. He was converted into a staunch supporter. By capitalizing on the enthusiasm and claims made by advocates of the new drugs, Felix and NIMH could begin to deliver on the promise of science and, at the same time, move directly in opposition to state hospitals by offering the possibility of alternative treatments. It was an early lesson in the political uses of weak and incomplete scientific data. "Promising more than could reasonably be delivered became a way of life for this (NIMH) leadership" (Foley & Sharfstein, 1983, p. 25).

Less than a decade after its establishment, NIMH, under Felix's leadership, was prepared to launch a national study of mental health. Capitalizing on its broad constituencies, in 1955, NIMH asked Congress to pass the Mental Health Study Act. Congress passed it without a single dissenting vote and President Eisenhower promptly signed the bill, requiring NIMH to appoint a commission to conduct a thorough evaluation of the nation's approach to mental illness. Felix, handed the opportunity that he had so masterfully sought, appointed his colleague, Jack Ewalt, to serve as Director of the 45-member commission. NIMH was now ready to remake the field of mental health.

CENTERING MENTAL HEALTH

Five years later, the Joint Commission on Mental Illness and Health issued its final report: *Action for Mental Health* (Joint Commission, 1961). The report, less a legislative blueprint for a specific set of initiatives than a clarion call to action, sought to mobilize attention, concern and funding for and expansion of mental health training, research and services (Ewalt, 1977). The "bold new approach" of creating Community Mental Health Centers that eventually emerged out of a marathon series of negotiations and compromises was not exactly what the Commission had in mind. Nevertheless, NIMH was instrumental in developing legislative proposals that eventually were authorized by the Public Law 88-164, the Mental Retardation Facilities and Community Mental Health Centers Construction Act of 1963, signed by President Kennedy less than a month before his assassination.[2] The legislative history of the CMHC Act and the supplementary ones that were to follow have been recounted elsewhere in detail (Connery, 1968; Felicetti, 1975; Foley & Sharfstein, 1983; Levine, 1981). Kennedy's death was hardly the end of an activist federal government. President Lyndon Johnson's Great Society and the commitment among the NIMH leadership kept the spirit of social reform alive. State hospitals, the decrepit and costly anchors of mental health care in the country, were to be supplanted by community mental health centers (CMHCs). Here, NIMH could capitalize on both the political arrangements and social theory that Felix had sponsored.

Political Strategies

With the CMHC legislation, the NIMH went from being a distant and powerless critic of state hospitals to being an activist agency with operatives in just about every community. Although the Institute offered small improvement grants directly to state hospitals (Windle, 1973), Federal funding for CMHCs bypassed the state hospital systems and went directly

---

[2] Felix soon retired, replaced as NIMH director by Stanley Yolles, who appointed Bertram Brown to be in charge of the CMHC program. In 1970, Brown himself would become NIMH director when Yolles resigned under fire from the Nixon administration.

to the new community centers, each in a local "catchment" area. Federal funds, with increasing state and local matching, provided new resources for building community facilities, hiring staff, and initiating programs. Although communities had considerable discretion in the administrative arrangements that they could cobble together to qualify as a CMHC, the federal requirements were designed to promote new systems of mental health services that would bear a striking and deliberate contrast to the existing state hospital systems.

Although CMHCs were diverse in structure, auspices, and success, there is no mistaking the fact that Felix's agenda was largely achieved. Due to a variety of developments, including the enactment of Medicaid and Medicare in 1965 and Supplemental Security Income (SSI) in 1972, the resident population in state hospitals dropped from 559,000 in 1955 to 125,000 in 1981 (Kiesler & Sibulkin, 1987, p. 46). Many patients were moved to other facilities, such as nursing homes, now that federal insurance coverage was expanded. Eighteen years after the CMHC enabling legislation, the NIMH had provided funding to over 700 CMHCs at a cost of nearly $3 billion. CMHCs had become one of the largest organized components of mental health services in the country (Bachrach, 1991, p. 549). In 1955, there were 379,000 episodes of outpatient care in the nation; by 1975 the count was up to 4.6 million, a twelvefold increase. The proportion of episodes of care dramatically reversed during these 20 years as well; inpatient episodes of care went from 77% of the total episodes of care to only 27% in 1975 (Kiesler & Sibulkin, 1987, p. 19).

But numbers only tell part of the story of the CMHC movement. Whereas state hospitals were located in rural communities some distance from the homes of their patients, CMHCs were located in their neighborhoods—their catchment areas. Whereas state hospitals reported to the directors of state bureaucracies, CMHCs reported to indigenous local boards. State hospitals involved largely self-contained services; CMHCs developed new networks of service providers. Hospitals provided little more than custodial care; CMHCs offered an array of new treatment modalities. State hospitals maintained little interest in the conditions of local communities; CMHCs promoted local political activity. State hospital-employed staff institutionalized themselves into the ways of custodial care; the CMHCs, with NIMH support, served as training sites for a new interdisciplinary cadre of community mental health professionals schooled in the new ideology of prevention and community care. State hospitals housed an aging group of chronic patients; the CMHCs catered to younger groups of less disordered clients. And where the state hospitals were content to rest on the remnants of the pessimistic science of phrenology and eugenics, the CMHCs championed a new, optimistic science derived from the social sciences. State hospitals were indeed supplanted within a generation, and NIMH's support and use of social science was one of the important tactics of reform.

The Uses of Social Theory

Breaking the backs of the mental hospitals required more than periodic exposés of their conditions in the press and in film. It required a scientific rationale for new models of care. NIMH found pieces of such support from diverse sources. From the social and behavioral sciences that NIMH had generously supported, different views of the nature of mental illness emerged that were politically useful to the promoters of CMHCs, although these views extended far beyond anything that the Joint Commission had in mind.

NIMH, in fact, had played an influential role in this effort to expand the scope of mental health concerns. By the late 1960s, the NIMH had become the largest financial supporter of behavioral science in the United States, next to the Department of Defense (Duhl & Leopold, 1968, p. 9). Although CMHCs were viewed as an expansion of traditional mental health services, the movement to develop them was vulnerable to capture by those who encouraged a much broader view of the role of mental health professionals in the community and the way problems of mental illness were understood. Examples of the broadening view can be found in the opening chapter of an influential book of the time, *Mental Health and Urban Social Policy* (Duhl & Leopold, 1968). The editors, both community psychiatrists on the cusp of the community mental health revolution, outlined the emerging new view of mental health practice, a practice that extended well beyond the hospital and clinic:

> Psychiatrists, psychologists, psychiatric social workers. . . , in attempting to cure the mentally ill, are concerned not merely with individuals, but with society as well. (p. 3)

> To operate in the larger system of mental health concerns one must deal with the total society rather than with the individual's emotional problem as the key to restoring mental health. For the individual's mental health is formed by the total society in which he exists. If you cure a mentally ill patient from a low-income background in a hospital, you must then return him to the poverty community. If he goes back to the poverty community, conditions in the community can undo everything that you have done. It is therefore the total society that needs a mental health treatment program and, almost more important than what you do in individual psychiatric treatment is how you treat the total environment. (p. 15)

> To operate in the broader system, then, the psychiatrist must return to the ecological model of man. He must become concerned with developmental processes rather than disease—with preventive mechanisms rather than symptom treatments. (p. 15)

> If you restrict yourself to psychiatric concepts, you look for the etiology of schizophrenia in an attempt to understand the disease. But, as the riots in the cities have begun to teach us, mental diseases, regardless of diagnostic label, are symptoms of a deeper disease. That disease lies in the social and economic system that puts so many stresses on these groups that disproportionately high percentages of them break down severely enough to require hospitalization. Such socioeconomic causal factors are not within the province of traditional psychiatry. But community mental health programs, if conceived as programs for prevention as well as treatment, must be prepared to engage with the social system in such a way as to modify these stresses and build into the community not only treatment but also social and political skills that will teach the dispossessed how to use the political process to ameliorate their own conditions. (pp. 16–17)

These striking views of the responsibilities of those staffing the new CMHCs became commonplace among the writings of the social scientists and mental health professionals who saw in the new national CMHC program an opportunity to promote general social reform. This thinking, which linked the causes and prevention of mental illness to broader social conditions and problems, provided more ideological ammunition than the leaders of NIMH needed to supplant the state hospitals. But this broad thinking was not foreign to NIMH. Indeed, NIMH had gone to considerable length during these early years to promote such behavioral science perspectives.

An example of this can be found in a small public information pamphlet from NIMH (1960) describing its activities and indicating its broadening agenda, all before the issuance of the Joint Commission report and prior to the CMHC legislation. Amid brief descriptions of its research and training efforts in neuropharmacology, neurophysiology, neurochemistry, cellular pharmacology, biophysics, and the neuroanatomical sciences are references to the Institute's interest in such disparate matters as emotional, biological, and cultural factors as they affect personality development, the transition of normal high school seniors to college, child development and mother–child relationships, the effects of aging, the nature of creativity, psychotherapeutic processes, and the annual gathering of statistics from state mental hospitals. There is mention of the Laboratory of Socio-Environmental Studies, as a plan that focuses on the role and social and cultural factors in the etiology, course, and consequences of mental disorders and does research on social class and behavior patterns, how different communities and populations define mental illness, and on the social structure and functioning of the mental hospital itself. Goffman's work and the work of others (e.g., Stanton & Schwartz, 1954) had found a comfortable home within this expanding domain of NIMH.

Under "Program Development" in the 1960 pamphlet, the Institute indicates that it is interested in areas that have cardinal mental health aspects and implications, and lists areas receiving considerations: rehabilitation of the mentally ill, drug addiction among youth, problems of aging, juvenile delinquency, alcoholism, child-rearing practices and beliefs, mental health in the school and college, mental health in industry, accident prevention, and "the impact of urban and suburban life on mental health" (p. 24).

The breadth of the Institute's concerns in 1960 was merely a glimpse of what was to come during the next two decades of expansion. The budget of NIMH expanded from $18 million in 1955 to over $300 million by 1966, as the Institute got involved in such activities as delinquency prevention, in the Mobilization for Youth program of the Ford Foundation, and in the President's Committee on Juvenile Delinquency (Duhl & Leopold, 1968, p. 9), activities that appeared to be responding, in part, to the demographic changes involved as the baby-boomers became teenagers.

One example of the expanding interests of NIMH is the research support given during this early period to behavior therapy, an approach based on learning principles that came from academic psychology (Stolz, 1973). This approach received approximately $3 million of research support in 1972. Among the diverse behavior therapy projects that NIMH supported during the 1960s and early 1970s were projects with autistic children, token economies, relaxation, desensitization and modeling, biofeedback therapy, training alcoholics to slow and moderate their drinking, contingency contracting with drug abusers, group therapy—all these in both traditional and community settings (Stolz, 1973).

Even the titles of some of the Institute's units reflect the broadened interests of the Institute by the early 1970s and its sensitivity to contemporary culture of the 1960s: the Center for Studies of Crime and Delinquency, the Center for Minority Group Mental Health Programs, and the Center for Studies of Metropolitan Problems. Problems of special interest to NIMH's Applied Research Branch, in the words of one NIMH official, included the changing role of the nuclear family; problems of the socially and economically deprived; the process of social change; alienation in contemporary society as related to phenomena such as efforts to change institution and social structure or those groups with different lifestyles who organize to bring about social change or greater social acceptance; problems of children and youth, with particular emphasis on the impact of social institutions, social conditions, family structure, and community resources that affect learning and coping capacities; and a variety of topics pertaining to early child care both in and out of the home (Stolz, 1973).

Concern about children garnered special attention during these years. In fact, children were made the number one priority by Bertram Brown when he assumed the Directorship of NIMH in 1970. In keeping with the broad mission of NIMH, this priority extended beyond research and into the services area. NIMH, in fact, funded six demonstration grants in child advocacy as a deliberate and focused attempt to involve community residents and staff in advocating at the local, state, and national level for better services for children (Dalmat, 1974).

NIMH was creating and operating in a mental health arena that was rapidly changing—ideologically, politically, and technologically. But it was also attempting to maintain strong ties with its older constituency, a constituency of white, male, psychoanalytically oriented psychotherapists. This group, once the locus of power in American psychiatry, was being rapidly left behind by NIMH initiatives, such as the rise of psychopharmacology, the progressive community mental health movement, and the new rigorous research protocols that called for outcome measures and control groups. NIMH tried to recognize the contributions of the traditional clinicians and to end the "warfare" between "those schools advocating psychotherapy and those espousing drug treatment" (Friedman, Gunderson, & Feinsilver, 1973, p. 674). One such NIMH project was the Psychotherapy of Schizophrenia project that involved discussion groups of a half dozen senior male psychoanalysts in five large cities, in which they were asked how they personally defined schizophrenia, their impressions of the characteristics of the patients that benefited from psychotherapy, and the essential characteristics of the therapists who worked well with schizophrenic patients. It was a project of respectful deference, an attempt to solicit the opinions of non-research-oriented senior practitioners, a group still powerful within the American Psychiatric Association, but one on the verge of being abandoned by NIMH.

The expansive agenda of NIMH can be seen in its award of research grants.[3] By 1960, the Institute was awarding approximately 1,100 research grants and the number was growing each year. By 1963, the number exceeded 1,750. The number remained at or above 1,500 grants per year until the presidency of Richard Nixon. Throughout the 1970s, grants numbered between 1,000 and 1,250 (NIMH, 1996c), but their current dollar value had grown steadily. By 1972, the Institute was awarding over $75 million per year (NIMH, 1996d).

The recipients of these grants were from diverse disciplines. Based on informal estimates from NIMH charts showing trend lines, in 1976, psychologists and other social sciences were receiving slightly over 50% of the total number of research grants made to academic institutions; the rest were distributed among psychiatrists (24%), biological scientists (10 percent) and other medical researchers (4 percent) (NIMH, 1996e). The research grants were similarly distributed when the tally was made by academic departments: Psychology (27%) and the social sciences (15%) accounted for nearly half; departments of psychiatry (32%) and other biomedical departments accounted for the rest (10% and 4%, respectively) (NIMH, 1996f). Similarly, in 1976, university schools of medicine and hospitals received 35% of the research funds awarded and other academic units received more (44%) (NIMH, 1996g). Although these indicators of the distribution of NIMH research funds in the mid-1970s, showing the greater proportion going to psychologists and other social scientists, can be partially accounted for by the relatively weak research training of most psychiatrists at the time, they also indicate the broad interests of NIMH in the perspectives of the social sciences and the Institute's desire to support new theory and research in the mental health field (see Table 26.1).

Articles published in the *Archives of General Psychiatry* and *American Journal of Psychiatry* reflected this steady increase in NIMH funding.[4] In 1955, NIMH was listed as the sponsor of the research in less than 5% of the articles, climbing to 11% in 1960, 24% by

---

[3] The follow data are taken from NIMH's site on the World Wide Web: www.nimh.nih.gov/.
[4] All regular articles published in the *Archives of General Psychiatry* and the *American Journal of Psychiatry* were reviewed every 5 years from 1955 to 1995. If any acknowledgment was given for funding of the study reported in the article, it was noted.

TABLE 26.1. Estimated Percent of Total Amount Awarded[a]

	1976	1995
Discipline		
Psychology	40	40
Psychiatry	24	27
Biological science	10	13
Social science	11	10
Other medical	4	6
Department		
Psychology	27	20
Psychiatry	32	45
Biological science	8	14
Social science	15	4
Other medical	2	7
Sponsoring institution		
University medical hospital	35	52
Other academic	44	31
Other hospital/clinic	10	10
Independent organization/state	1	1

[a] These figures are my estimates from trend lines provided by NIMH on the World Wide Web.

1970, 33% in 1985 and over 43% by 1995. By comparison, the percentage of articles resulting from NIMH's intramural research programs has remained small, varying from 2% to 8%.

Reckoning

After a quarter-century of research, the NIMH asked an 88-member task force to review its accomplishments in research and to make recommendations for the future (*Hospital and Community Psychiatry*, 1975). At the time, NIMH was struggling with President Nixon, who was cutting its research budget, and the report of the task force was an attempt to tout its research accomplishments. In the report, prominence was given to the promise of genetic research and the progress at "finding how psychoactive substances work on the central nervous system" (p. 714). On the one hand, the report expressed disappointment in the research on the mental health of children, finding serious flaws in the studies and lack of objective measures in classifying their problems. On the other hand, it applauded the research in behavior therapy that it had supported and encouraged more outcome research on psychosocial treatments.

Despite the great political investment that NIMH made in CMHCs, the report found little to praise. Although 8% of NIMH's research funds had been directed to research on and evaluation of mental health services, the results were hampered by lack of adequate methodology. Another "grave deficiency" according to the report "is the general lack of adequate information on the incidence and prevalence of mental disorders, a lack that hampers planning of services and analysis of their effects" (p. 715).

Indeed, NIMH's community mental health initiative, having succeeded in breaking the back of the state mental hospitals, was running into serious difficulties, and not merely in terms of research. There were no convincing data that CMHCs prevented mental illness or lowered the incidence or prevalence of mental disorder in the population, promises implicitly made by the exuberant rhetoric of the advocates of community psychiatry. But even the more modest objectives of CMHCs were not adequately achieved: It was not clear that releasing patients to the community saved money, sent them into a system of care that provided continuity of treatment, ensured that they fared better, or resulted in their reintegration into communities (e.g., Kirk & Therrien, 1975). "Deinstitutionalization," which had been a slogan of progressive reform promoted by NIMH, after 15 years, became a term of derision and a label exposing the failure of community mental health. Deinstitutionalization, once NIMH's solution, was now the name of a new problem, and it was an immensely public and visible one.

The emergence of homelessness in the 1980s, although caused by a confluence of reasons (Jencks, 1994)—which were not all mental-health-system related—was dropped at NIMH's doorstep. In response, NIMH began another community-based initiative, known as the Community Support Program. This initiative, designed to ameliorate the failures of the earlier CMHC initiative, offered contracts to state agencies to improve services to chronic patients (Turner & TenHoor, 1978). The Community Support Program constituted one of the last major efforts of NIMH to influence directly the delivery of mental health services in local communities. The Reagan revolution effectively ended NIMH's power to direct and shape mental health services by consolidating 10 federally funded alcohol, drug abuse, and mental health initiatives into a single block grant to each state. This was not the result of some specific failure on the part of NIMH; rather, it was the beginning of a much larger American political development in which leadership for an array of social programs was transferred from Washington D.C., to the states.

Even before the official demise of the federally directed CMHCs, some skeptics of the bold new approach observed that a day of reckoning would come.

> "We did not originally promise the community mental health center approach simply as a good common sense idea, a humane move, with the good sense of bringing the expert in closer proximity to the consumer and hopefully to a supporting community. . . . Somehow this sensible approach began to carry with it the promise that we can prevent mental disorders, not modify them.
>
> For a time it appears that we were aiming to rearrange the vast social service deficiencies of urban life under the rubric of mental health—and thereby prevent illness. That the entire Department of HEW is having problems with social welfare seemed to elude the MHC enthusiast who sought university centers for prestige and sanction, while undermining the discipline of tutored inquiry (which earned the prestige) as a luxury. (Daniel X. Freedman, quoted in Musto, 1977, pp. 9–10)

Reckoning day came and NIMH had to survive by emphasizing new tasks that would not entail the obvious political costs of trying to change mental health policy and services in the United States, new tasks that would not obviously conflict with Washington's new conservative politics.

The demise of the federal CMHC program should not blind us to the tremendous feat that was engineered by the leadership of NIMH during its first two decades. Mental disorders were hardly on the national scope of social problems in 1940, but within a year after the end of World War II, public health–minded, committed bureaucrats had fashioned and steered legislation through Congress establishing the NIMH with a broad agenda of research, training, and service. Capitalizing on a political context in which the federal government was viewed as able to solve national problems, a small band of progressive reformers built political constituencies of influential persons both inside and outside of government to build and expand rapidly a mental health institute. More significantly, they set out to change the shape of mental health institutions and practices in every state, to put mental health care on the agenda of every community. Using the structure of the CMHC legislation and the social reform ideology espoused by liberal social scientists, they found both a political strategy and an academic rationale for their work. In all these respects, they indeed succeeded. By the presidency of Richard Nixon, they had firmly established madness in the federal government.

By 1980, the bad press brought about by deinstitutionalization, in tandem with the public preferences for a non-activist federal government, put NIMH into retreat from any bold new services agenda. From the progressive and activist stance of the early reformers, the Institute, along with much of American psychiatry, turned full steam to the safer harbor of biomedicine. In this context, an initiative such as the "Decade of the Brain" was an understandable political move. Barred from any effective mechanism to manage or monitor mental health services around the country, NIMH turned to other projects that would be more likely to garner support from an increasingly conservative political establishment. The Institute turned increasingly from the community to the laboratory, from social reform to biological science, from concern with social structures to brain chemistry.

COUNTING THE MENTALLY ILL

In this new political era, NIMH had to develop projects that had little flavor of an activist federal government, that did not involve attempts to direct the activities of state mental health authorities, that could be justified on scientific grounds, and that would be likely to provide a basis for continuing Congressional support. Counting the mentally ill could potentially accomplish all of those objectives.

Since the nineteenth century, American psychiatrists have used statistical reports for purposes of policy advocacy. As superintendents of state asylums, they were avid collectors of data, which they used to demonstrate curability rates, establish the legitimacy of mental hospitals, and build broad support among state officials and the public (Grob, 1985, p. 229). Early epidemiological studies were guided not so much by the identification of disease processes and how they might be influenced by the environment (as was the epidemiology of infectious diseases) as by statistically minded social scientists concerned with problems of dependency and welfare (Grob, 1985, p. 235).

Scientifically, identifying in a population the characteristics and location of those who are ill is a way to detect patterns of disease in a population that might provide clues about etiology or lead to effective prevention. The first 100 years of psychiatric epidemiology were influenced more by the developing social sciences than by medicine and consisted primarily of noting the ailments and demographic characteristics of asylum patients in such states as Massachusetts and New York (Grob, 1985). The major impetus for counting the mentally ill came from the federal government's Census Bureau, but not all psychiatrists believed in the usefulness of these counts. Adolf Meyer, one of the more influential psychiatrists of the early twentieth century, expressed his concern in 1919: "Statistics will be most valuable if they do not attempt to solve all the problems of administration and psychiatry and sociology under one confused effort of a one-word diagnosis marking the individual" (cited in Grob, 1985, p. 233)

The early decades of psychiatric epidemiology were marred by many now well-recognized problems: using only hospitalized patients and the vagaries of state and local admission practices to establish community prevalence rates, depending on the unreliable diagnostic judgments of hospital personnel, and using various classification schemes of unknown or questionable diagnostic validity.

The Census Bureau, however, stopped counting the patients in mental hospitals in 1946, when the federal responsibility for such counts was transferred to the newly established NIMH, which continued the tradition for many decades by issuing a variety of annual standardized reports of data gathered from psychiatric facilities throughout the nation (see Leaf, 1986). By the 1950s, both NIMH and psychiatric epidemiology were moving into the community.

In what has been described as "an extraordinary intellectual leap" (Grob, 1985: 235) epidemiologists began to study the incidence or prevalence of mental illness among those hospitalized in relation to community and social factors. There were a series of such provocative leaps, including Faris and Dunham's 1939 Chicago study *Mental Disorders in Urban Areas*, the NIMH supported classic *Social Class and Mental Illness* (Hollingshead & Redlich, 1958) and its follow-up study (Myers & Bean, 1968) also supported by NIMH. It required an even greater methodological leap to study the prevalence of mental illness among community (not hospital) residents, as in the Manhattan study (Srole, Langer, Michael, Opler, & Rennie, 1962), *Mental Health in the Metropolis,* which was also partially funded by NIMH.

Despite the scientific advantages that can be gained in moving from the asylum to the community survey, there were very troublesome problems that emerged. There were, of course, the technical and practical complexities of obtaining representative samples of community residents so that the survey results were generalizable. But there was the more theoretically vexing problem of making an accurate diagnosis of mental illness.

Those who studied patients in mental asylums enjoyed the comfortable assumption that all those who were inmates were mentally ill, for why else would anyone be there? Studies of the psychiatric status of community residents confronted what appeared to be an intractable problem. Diagnosis, as practiced by clinicians, often required one or more lengthy clinical interviews, and even then, there was often disagreement among experts about the proper label. The presence of mental illness and its subtypes was not easily or quickly determined. There existed no simple-to-administer screening test, no blood pressure exam, no biological markers that could be obtained in a door-to-door survey. Moreover, there was no assurance that people could accurately identify themselves as mentally ill or be likely to make such an admission to a stranger in an interview.

Furthermore, the problems ran deeper than data-gathering techniques. The experts themselves did not agree on what mental illnesses were, how they should be defined, how they could be reliably identified, or what system of classification should be used to categorize them. Having valid categories of illness and reliable methods of placing individuals in them was a fundamental requirement of epidemiology. In mental health circles, that requirement had been largely neglected for a century. For example, the American Psychiatric Association's *Diagnostic and Statistical Manual of Mental Disorders*, in both the first (1952) and second (1968) editions, was silent on the definition of mental disorder, and the brief descriptions of disorders were decidedly vague. By 1970, numerous studies had suggested that even skilled clinicians could not make diagnoses reliably (Kirk & Kutchins, 1992, 1994). Even NIMH provided no official definition of the key term in its name.

Thus, in 1977, when Rosalyn Carter, the titular head of her husband's Commission on Mental Health, asked the seemingly simple question about how many people suffered from mental illnesses, neither NIMH nor the experts could offer more than an uncomfortable stammer. The problem was not merely a bureaucratic failure to inventory the nation's mentally ill; it was a conceptual and methodological problem that had bedeviled the psychiatric establishment.

NIMH felt compelled to move quickly to develop an answer to her question by launching the Epidemiologic Catchment Area study (ECA). The answer took a decade to produce and did not come until the presidency of George Bush—by which time President Reagan had completely gutted Carter's mental health initiatives. Nevertheless, the ECA represents the most significant recent social science–based initiative of NIMH. It is the "centerpiece" of NIMH's epidemiological efforts during the last 15 years (Regier, 1994). The ECA has been called "an agenda-setting" effort of "massive size and dramatic results" that helped to sensitize the general public as well as policymakers to the problems of the mentally ill in the United States (Kessler, 1994, p. 81). It also resulted in "an enormous increase in Federal funding for psychiatric epidemiologic research" and "greater prominence in academic psychiatry" (Kessler, 1994, p. 81). (The most recent large-scale installment in the research tradition initiated by the ECA is the National Comorbidity Study which is described in Chapter 7.)

Doing Big Science[5]

The ECA, which resulted in hundreds of publications, was highly praised. In the foreword to the book summarizing the major findings of the ECA, Daniel X. Freedman describes the book as "an unprecedented atlas," "a rich lode of new information on the natural history of psychiatric disorders," and "the soundest fundamental information about . . . psychiatric disorders ever assembled." He concludes: "In psychiatry, no single volume of the twentieth century has such importance and utility not only for the present but for the decades ahead" (Robins & Regier, 1991. pp.xxiii–xxiv). He is not the only psychiatric luminary praising the ECA. On the book jacket, Bruce Dohrenwend, John Wing, Gerald Klerman, Samuel Guze, and Norman Satorious—all mental health notables—refer to this report as an impressive achievement; a recognized hallmark; the largest and most sophisticated study undertaken in the United States, if not the world; an outstanding scientific and scholarly report; a storehouse of valuable data; and a major milestone in the development of psychiatry and medicine. This is the kind of praise that NIMH had not enjoyed for its efforts in many years.

The ECA was an enormous administrative and methodological undertaking, costing at least $20 million (Eaton, 1994). NIMH was not simply the conduit for grants to others. The ECA was the first effort in the Public Health Service to use a "cooperative agreement," permitting NIMH personnel to take a direct role as scientific collaborators in the collection and analysis of the data. The arrangement was not without difficulty, as a relatively young, inexperienced group at NIMH tried to manage five experienced university research teams of psychiatrists and sociologists in St. Louis, Durham, New Haven, Baltimore, and Los Angeles. Almost 20,000 randomly selected adults were interviewed by lay interviewers using a structured interview schedule. Using sophisticated sampling procedures that produced an overall 75% response rate, the researchers obtained samples consisting of both residents of households and institutionalized populations in such settings as prisons, mental hospitals, and nursing homes. The data were then weighted or adjusted by age, sex, and

---

[5] Part of this section were adapted from an essay by Kirk (1991).

racial distribution to match that of the United States as a whole. Great care went into both the development of instruments based on established diagnostic criteria and the selection of the samples so that prevalence estimates about disorders (i.e., what Rosalyn Carter had asked) in the entire national adult population could be made. Diagnoses of 10 selected disorders were made by computers, using diagnostic algorithms.

The result of this NIMH coordinated effort (Robins & Regier, 1991) was a blizzard of statistics. Some confirmed the obvious, such as that there is not much abuse of illicit drugs by residents of nursing homes or that cognitive impairment is more prevalent in the elderly than the young. But the major findings—the ones that served NIMH in defending its budget—were the ones that suggested that mental disorders were widespread in America. From the researchers and NIMH officials, the public began to hear authoritative reports from the ECA about mental illness (Robins & Regier, 1991): 32% of American adults have had one or more psychiatric disorder in their lives; 20% have a disorder at any given time; there are higher lifetime prevalence rates among men (36%) than women (20%), the young (37%) than the old (21%), African Americans (38%) than others (32%), those with less education (36%) than those with more (30%), those in institutions (65%) than those in households (32%), and those who were financially dependent (47%) than the wealthier (31%). NIMH could now tell Rosalyn Carter, for example, how many Hispanic women in the United States between the ages of 45 and 64 had ever had an antisocial personality (1.3%). The ability to provide an answer with this precision gave NIMH the kind of scientific authority that all federal health institutes were expected to have.

Given the magnitude of the ECA, its sponsorship by NIMH and the outstanding reputations of the researchers, the ECA data became the definitive word on psychiatric disorders in America. When government officials, advocacy organizations, or enterprising program developers wanted to document the prevalence of a particular disorder or the disproportionate suffering among some demographic subgroup, they could now turn to *Psychiatric Disorders in America*, scrounging through the tables to find the fact that supported their cause. With the ECA, NIMH claimed to have scientifically established the distribution of madness in the country.

It was essential for NIMH to be able to separate mental illness from other general problems of human suffering and distress, because, in the Reagan Era, concerns about general personal or community distress had less political cachet. In addition, NIMH wanted to establish a more defensible domain for mental health within the province of medical science. By documenting the fact that mental disorder was not only readily identifiable, but also widespread, outside the hospital and clinic, and often untreated, the Institute hoped to secure its own domain and relevance in the postasylum and post-CMHC era.

DIS'ing DSM

There are, however, curious findings in the masses of data generated by the ECA. For example, *Psychiatric Disorders in America* reports that 22% of those in psychiatric hospitals have *never* had a psychiatric disorder, and 27% have no evidence of having one during that last year. At the very least, such anomalies raise questions of definition and methodology. Questions of definition of disorder and methods of counting them were, of course, what NIMH had hoped to conquer with the ECA. To do so, NIMH capitalized on the fortuitous revolution within the American Psychiatric Association (APA) in which groups of research psychiatrists in the mid-1970s had captured the process of revising the psychiatric bible, the *Diagnostic and Statistical Manual of Mental Disorders* (DSM), and on the development of related instruments to detect mental disorder (Kirk & Kutchins, 1992a; Wilson, 1993). The ECA was a child of DSM, and, consequently, exhibited some of its limitations.

Until the 1980 edition, DSM-III (American Psychiatric Association, 1980), psychiatric diagnosis was in disrepair. Earlier editions had been little more than administrative codebooks. Not even the APA claimed that DSM was scientific. Researchers, in fact, found it nearly worthless as a guide to making valid or reliable diagnoses for research purposes, and clinicians used it when compelled to file official diagnoses in bureaucratic records, but rarely viewed it as a guide to practice. DSM-III, by contrast, created a revolution in diagnosis and quickly reshaped psychiatric research and training. DSM-III was transformed from a codebook to a textbook. It was designed by psychiatric researchers and grew out of their need to operationalize diagnostic categories by using behavioral criteria in order to make reliable diagnoses and to coordinate multisite research projects. For years prior to 1980, psychiatric researchers had worked to develop operational criteria for specific disorders and structured interview schedules to use in implementing the criteria. DSM-III had its origins in these research efforts.

DSM-III was developed in tandem with attempts to develop structured research instruments to detect mental disorders in patient and community samples. The Diagnostic Interview Schedule (known widely as the DIS) was one such highly structured instrument. The DIS told interviewers exactly what questions to ask, exactly what words to use in exactly what sequence, and how to code the responses they received from interviewees. Originally developed for narrow research interests, the DIS was tied to DSM's diagnostic criteria and was designed to be used by lay interviewers. This DIS capability was rapidly adapted to the needs of the ECA and the constantly changing DSM criteria (Robins & Helzer, 1994). Thus, by adopting the DIS, NIMH was able to quickly launch the largest psychiatric epidemiological study in the nation's history, by taking as its own both the APA's new diagnostic manual and the companion structured interview guides that had evolved for clinical research. It was an arranged marriage that had many advantages for NIMH.

For one, DSM provided a technical answer for the conceptually messy question of what constituted a mental disorder, a problem that NIMH had historically exhibited little interest in addressing. In the ECA, a mental disorder was any condition meeting the minimum diagnostic criteria for a DSM category. Furthermore, the DIS provided an already-developed and pretested method of implementing a survey of community residents in relation to these diagnostic criteria. NIMH was able quickly to join small teams of leading researchers to conduct a national survey, without entering into professional debates about the definition of mental disorder. In early epidemiological studies, mental illness had been defined simply as whatever maladies were suffered by residents in asylums, now it was defined as that which DSM and DIS identified. It appeared to be an administrative fix to an otherwise difficult conceptual and measurement problem.

The fix was flawed by the inherent limits of DSM's approach to diagnosis. The diagnostic criteria at the heart of both DSM and the DIS consist of many everyday behaviors, frequently exhibited by those who do not have mental disorders. The diagnostic criteria are themselves often insufficient in detecting mental disorder. Thus, using the diagnostic criteria in some checklist fashion among community samples runs the risk of producing "false positives" (e.g., Kutchins & Kirk, 1997; Wakefield, 1992; 1996). Furthermore, the primary purpose of the criteria—to greatly improve the reliability of diagnosis—was not achieved. This failure was due to many factors, including the fact that the criteria are often ambiguous and require substantial clinical inference to apply correctly, and that nonclinical factors often shape the uses of diagnosis in actual practice (Kirk & Kutchins, 1992, 1992b; Kutchins & Kirk, 1997). There are many problems in counting the mentally ill that NIMH inherited with the ECA.

For example, many operational definitions of specific disorders used in the ECA's major report, *Mental Disorder in America,* were obsolete 4 years *before* the book was published. No one could have predicted in 1978 that revising DSM would become a cottage industry, a process of revision that began anew almost before the ink was dry on the last edition. The DIS was explicitly and directly tied to definitions of disorder as given in drafts of DSM-III, finally published in 1980. By 1985, a draft of a DSM revision was circulated, then another, and then in 1987, a revised version of DSM was published (DSM-III-R) that altered the criteria for just about all the major disorders (American Psychiatric Association, 1987). Consequently, almost every chapter in *Psychiatric Disorders in America* begins by explaining how the DIS criteria are different than the ones in use in DSM-III-R. Furthermore, by 1994, DSM-IV appeared, making the original DIS criteria two generations out of date. Although some of these shifting criteria are minor and would not greatly alter gross prevalence rates, other diagnostic criteria changes can have a major impact.

In DSM-III, alcohol abuse and dependence were two independent disorders. In DSM-III-R, dependence was the central diagnosis and the criteria were altered. The ECA authors confess that it is difficult to judge from their data what the prevalence of alcoholism would be using the DSM-III-R criteria. Similarly, with obsessive–compulsive disorder, they report a lifetime prevalence rate (2.6%) using DSM-III criteria, a figure 50 times greater than earlier estimates. DSM-III-R provided greater specification of the disorder and the authors expected that the prevalence rate would be lower using those newer criteria. In chapter after chapter, the reader of the ECA is reminded that these rates are based on diagnostic criteria that are in varying stages of obsolescence and that by simply altering slightly the nature of the criteria, the duration of symptoms that must be experienced, or the number of criteria used, these seemingly solid and precise prevalence rates will rise and fall as erratically as the stock market.

But changing official diagnostic criteria is only one basis for the fragility of these numbers. Operational definitions of such seemingly simple but fundamentally crucial terms such as the age of onset, lifetime prevalence, and current presence of an active disorder undergird the ECA and the meaning of the statistics. A casual reader might assume, for example, that "age of onset" of a disorder is the person's age when he or she first had the "disorder" (i.e., simultaneously met *all* the criteria for the disorder as defined by DSM-III). This appears to be true for some disorders (e.g., affective disorder), but not for others. For schizophrenia, alcoholism, and anxiety disorders, the age of onset was operationalized as the age when the first "symptom" occurred among those who later met the other criteria for the disorder. For example, for a lifetime diagnosis of alcohol abuse there must be evidence of the occurrence of two symptoms, but they need not be present at the same time. One symptom could occur in a person's youth, the second 30 years later in adulthood. The person would be considered as having had an alcohol abuse disorder, despite the fact that there was no time period in which the two required criteria were met simultaneously. Not only does this raise serious conceptual questions about the operational definition of "disorder," but it also makes the meaning of "age at onset" troublesome. If, for example, the diagnosis of flu required that a person have a fever and an upset stomach, would a person who had a fever for a few days at age 19 and an upset stomach at age 35 be designated as someone who has had flu? And was the onset at age 19? Conceptual confusions such as these help to explain why so many men (24%) were determined to have lifetime diagnoses of alcohol abuse or dependence.

For drug abuse and dependence, a different meaning of "age of onset" was used—the age when illicit drug use began, not when the abuse or dependence began. The start of illicit drug *use* is a very different concept than the beginning of illicit drug *abuse*.

The way in which "active cases" (1-year prevalence rates) were determined is also deserving of scrutiny. Our intuitive sense of an "active case" is of a person who currently meets the minimum criteria for a specific disorder. This is generally *not* the operational meaning in the ECA. An active case is a person who met the minimum criteria sometime in his or her life and who currently has at least a single symptom. Again, as with age of onset, "active case" varies in its meaning. In the introductory chapter on methodology, "active illnesses" are defined as disorders in which the diagnostic criteria have been met "at some time in the person's life" and there has been "some sign of the disorder" within the year before the interview. The authors candidly suggest how this method of counting may be used: "A count of active disorders is useful information for purposes such as the development of annual budgets for the provision of mental health services" (Robins & Rogier, 1991, p. 13).

Two questions may be raised about this approach to establishing 1-year prevalence rates (i.e., active cases). First, as we have already seen, meeting criteria "at some time in the person's life" was operationalized differently for different disorders. Sometimes it means simultaneously meeting all the minimal criteria for the disorder and sometimes it means simply qualifying for enough criteria spread out over a lifetime. Second, having "some sign of the disorder," presumably meaning meeting at least one diagnostic criterion during the past year, is certainly different than having the disorder during the past year, particularly since, as the ECA book demonstrates, many single "symptoms" are experienced by a majority of the population. Consequently, using the presence of a single symptom to be the definition of "active case" is abandoning any defensible conceptual definition of mental disorder. Using the occurrence of one symptom may do wonders for budget justifications by inflating prevalence rates and allowing for claims that 20% of all American adults are currently active cases, but it does not necessarily represent good science.

Other chapters in this seminal volume from the ECA present numbers that raise other issues. Somatization disorder, for example, was difficult to find in the population. One-third of 37 DSM-III criteria must be met to make the diagnosis. Although this book aspired to present the major mental disorders, only a slim fraction of 1% qualified for this diagnosis. Since many of the physical symptoms that characterize this disorder are experienced by many people (e.g., back pain, nausea, painful menstruation), by lowering the threshold number of criteria to four for men and six for women, relabeling it "somatization syndrome" instead of disorder, the authors jump the lifetime prevalence rate to 11.6%, or 100 times the rate of somatization disorder. This redefinition yields enough "cases" to perform the routine statistical breakdowns with the demographic correlates. The effect of such liberties with diagnostic criteria illustrates the sensitivity that prevalence rates have to technical decisions about diagnostic criteria and to the ambiguities inherent in diagnostic systems with wavering concepts of disorder.

Finally, years after the barrage of ECA reports began appearing, a more troublesome problem was revealed. Part of the ECA involved reinterviews of all subjects 12 months later (i.e., Wave 2). One key statistic based on the data from Wave 1 was the "lifetime prevalence," that is, the percent of subjects who had ever had each disorder at any time in their life. A year later at Wave 2, the lifetime prevalence should reflect all those subjects who had been identified at Wave 1 as disordered, plus the addition of any new cases that developed during that year. If the DSM criteria are valid indicators of disorder and the DIS can reliably detect these indicators in community samples, *which is the fundamental assumptions underlying the entire ECA*, the Wave 2 data would be highly consistent with the Wave 1 data. There is evidence, however, that the data are *very inconsistent*. For example, in a study of obsessive–compulsive disorder that compared the ECA Wave 1 and Wave 2 data, there was dramatic unreliability (Nelson & Rice, 1997). At Wave 1, 291 subjects were diagnosed as meeting the criteria for obsessive–compulsive disorder (Nelson & Rice, 1997). A year later, only 56 of the 291 (19.2%) reported that they had *ever* had symptoms during their lifetime that met the criteria for obsessive–compulsive disorder. For the other 235 subjects, their earlier disorders that had been documented by the DIS at Wave 1 had disappeared from their clinical histories. Furthermore, at Wave 2, there were 118 "new-onset" cases, subjects diagnosed with obsessive–compulsive disorder who had not been so identified at Wave 1. Were these all new cases that developed in the intervening year? Generally, no. Over 74% of these "new" cases dated their onset to the period *before* Wave 1. These unsettling findings suggest that a majority of obsessive–compulsive disorders remarkably vanish after they have been identified by the DIS and that they also appear in people's past clinical histories after they had been declared nonexistent. This can only lead to one conclusion: that there is evidence to suggest that the validity problems of DSM and the reliability problems of DIS conspired in the ECA to produce rates of mental disorders of questionable accuracy.

Most readers of the ECA will not notice these technical problems, not remember for long the ECA authors' cautions about the limits of these data or be aware of the other methodological problems (e.g., Kessler, 1994). It is too easy to be seduced into the ECA's illusions of exactitude and fail to appreciate the conceptual and operational foibles on which some of the findings are based. Mrs. Carter could be told that 20% of adults currently have mental disorders, but she would not be told by NIMH that the figure is based on outdated diagnostic criteria, a diagnostic manual of untested reliability, a selective choice of disorders, wavering definitions of onset, an inflated concept of active cases, and measurement methods of questionable validity. Thus, what will be historically significant about the ECA will not be the exact count of the mentally ill in America but what it reveals about the state of American psychiatry and the NIMH in the 1980s.

Like CMHCs, the ECA was a creature of its time and served NIMH's contemporary purposes both within the government and with regard to the general public. As three decades of NIMH-inspired community mental health initiatives came to an end, NIMH embarked on a new program of activity that was equally attuned to opportunities and the shifting political winds. Relying on the best psychiatric researchers and the available research techniques developed for using DSM-III, NIMH accomplished its first national count of the mentally ill.

The ECA had strikingly different objectives than the community mental health initiative. Developing mental health services for the mentally ill was replaced with developing methods of counting them in the community. Federally directed policy interventions were replaced by federally directed interview schedules such as the DIS. Mobilizing participation of community residents in change efforts was replaced by locating samples of residents to serve as research subjects. Negotiating with key state mental health authorities to develop new systems of care was replaced with negotiating with teams of university-based researchers to use common research instruments. Analyzing patterns of political power in communities was replaced by analyzing mountains of data about behavioral symptoms. The objective of bolstering the capacity of communities to serve the mentally ill was replaced with bolstering the capacity of NIMH to answer narrowly focused scientific questions.

FULLY UNDERSTANDING OUR BRAINS

The NIMH is a different organization than it was in its early years, and for many reasons. In the early years, NIMH was led by "luminaries," as one NIMH official recalled in a personal communication, individuals who made lifetime commitments to public service and who deliberately planned a sustained effort to reform the way in which mental health services were organized in the nation. Under their leadership, the Institute grew rapidly and dramatically reshaped mental health services, funded the training of an entire new cadre of mental health professionals, and sponsored research programs across a broad array of disciplines, including the social sciences. They created an activist organization that was part of a vast array of social reform efforts initiated by the federal government in the 1960s. Mental health problems were viewed as embedded in a complex set of personal, family, and community dynamics that needed to be better understood and modified to promote mental health and prevent mental illness.

NIMH no longer plays a similar leadership role in mental health policy or service delivery (e.g., Kiesler, 1992). Prevented by legislation from intervening in state and local mental health service delivery, or even from monitoring state programs, the scope of the Institute's agenda has greatly narrowed. Services for the mentally ill are now governed much more by health policy developments outside of NIMH's domain. Medicare, Medicaid, Social Security Disability Insurance (SSDI), commercial insurance, and managed care affect the mentally ill much more immediately than any direct activities of NIMH. The Institute, by circumstance and choice, is now much more a biomedical research organization than the broad training and policy-initiating agency of the past. These dramatic differences are illustrated by its efforts in community mental health and the ECA study.

A flavor of the NIMH's current orientation is contained in a report to Congress advocating for more research funds for the "Decade of the Brain":

> As we approach the twenty-first century, we are on the brink of discovering the biological basis for many of the major mental illnesses and the impact of the environment on their course. We will be able to design better drugs for their treatment, and ultimately to prevent such devastating diseases as schizophrenia, depression, anxiety, and manic–depressive disorders. Through neuroscience research, we can realistically anticipate a time in the near future when we will fully understand our brains—how they function and dysfunction. However, we still have a long way to go, and the powerful new research approaches being developed are expensive." (National Advisory, 1988, p. iii of Executive summary)

NIMH has always advocated for more money from Congress for mental health, but better designed drugs and fully understanding our brains are recent emphases. The early directors of NIMH tended to serve in their roles for a decade, enough time to master Congressional and interest group politics and to set a long term agenda in motion. Since 1984, NIMH has not had a single director for more than 2 years. The new short-term directors also come from bench science backgrounds rather than from career posts as civil servants. The current NIMH Director (as of 1997), Steven Hyman, is an example. Appointed in spring of 1996, Hyman was serving as an Associate Professor of Psychiatry at Harvard

Medical School and director of the university's "Interfaculty Initiative in Mind/Brain/Behavior" (NIMH, 1996a). In announcing the appointment, the head of the National Institutes of Health praised Hyman's "research on the biological bases of mental disorders" that "puts him on a major frontier in biomedical science today" (p. 1). The announcement continued: "Exploration of the nervous system promises enormous advances in our understanding and treatment of some of the most devastating illnesses facing Americans, their families, and society."

Dr. Hyman seemed like the right choice to head NIMH, the congressionally designated lead agency in the "Decade of the Brain." He left little doubt about his agenda for NIMH in accepting the appointment:

> Unlocking the mysteries of the brain and mental illnesses stands as the supreme challenge of biomedical science today. The accelerating fields of neuroscience and molecular biology offer unprecedented opportunities for advancing our understanding of the complex interplay between biological phenomena and environmental influences that shape human behavior and give rise to mental illness. Thus this is an extraordinarily exciting time to assume leadership of the National Institute of Mental Health. (NIMH, 1996a)

To Dr. Hyman, it undoubtedly is an exciting time. But to Robert Felix, the Institute's founding director, the current Institute might not be as inspiring, nor would the political climate in which the federal government's role in providing policy leadership, that he so masterfully created, is being dismantled.

Erving Goffman, and many of the other early social scientists working at the Lab, might not find it as exciting either. His work was useful not only to NIMH as the Institute was seeking political leverage over an entrenched system of state mental hospitals, but it was also useful to the discipline of sociology in demonstrating how a critical perspective could shed penetrating light on mental health institutions, their caretakers, and their beliefs. Goffman's antiestablishment attitude, his critical eye and irreverent pen, charted a course for a generation of young sociologists interested in the field of mental health. At the time, NIMH found such work useful and generously supported it.

Goffman worked without a structured interview schedule, without a diagnostic system, without random samples, without control groups, without quantitative data, without a detailed methodological plan, and without faith in established authority. Today, for the reasons discussed, were he seeking NIMH research support, he would be without a wing or a prayer.

ACKNOWLEDGMENTS: The author wants to acknowledge the help offered, if not always taken, by the following readers of an earlier version of this chapter: Carol Aneshensel, Leona Bachrach, Tomi Gomory, Zeke Hasenfeld, Tally Moses, Leonard Pearlin, and Karen Staller.

REFERENCES

American Psychiatric Association. (1952). *Diagnostic and statistical manual of mental disorders*. Washington, DC: Author.

American Psychiatric Association. (1968). *Diagnostic and statistical manual of mental disorders* (2nd ed.). Washington, DC: Author.

American Psychiatric Association. (1980). *Diagnostic and statistical nanual of nental disorders* (3rd ed.). Washington, DC: Author.

American Psychiatric Association. (1987). *Diagnostic and statistical manual of mental disorders* (3rd ed., rev.). Washington, DC: Author.

American Psychiatric Association. (1994). *Diagnostic and statistical manual of mental disorders* (4th ed.). Washington, DC: Author.

Bachrach, L. L. (1991). Community mental health centers in the USA. In D. Bennett& H. L. Freeman (Eds.), *Community psychiatry: The principles* (pp. 543–569). Edinburgh: Churchill Livingstne.

Barton, W. E. (1987). *The history and influence of the American Psychiatric Association*. Washington, DC: American Psychiatric Association Press.

Connery, R. H. (Ed.). (1968). *The politics of mental health: Organizing community mental health in metropolitan areas*. New York: Columbia University Press.

Dalmat, E. (1974). Pioneering in child advocacy: Tri-agency collaboration of the Department of Health, Education and Welfare: BEH, NIMH, SRS. *Journal of Clinical Child Psychology, 3*(1), 10–12.

Drew, E. (1967, December). The health syndicate: Washington's noble conspirators. *The Atlantic Monthly*, pp. 75–82.

Duhl, L., & Leopold, R. (1968). *Mental health and urban social policy: A casebook of community action*. San Francisco: Jossey-Bass.

Eaton, W. (1994). The NIMH epidemiologic catchment area program: Implementation and major findings. *International Journal of Methods in Psychiatric Research, 4*, 103–112.

Ewalt, R. (1977). The birth of the community mental health movement. In W. Barton & C. Sanborn (Eds.), *An assessment of the community mental health movement* (pp. 13–20). Lexington, MA: Lexington Books.

Faris, R., & Dunham, H. (1965). *Mental disorders in urban areas: An ecological study of schizophrenia and other psychoses*. Chicago: University of Chicago Press. (Original published 1939)

Felicetti, D. (1975). *Mental health and retardation politics: The mind lobbies in Congress*. New York: Praeger.

Foley, H., & Sharfstein, S. (1983). *Madness and government: Who cares for the mentally ill?* Washington, DC: APA Press.

Friedman, R., Gunderson, J., & Feinsilver, D. (1973). The psychotherapy of schizophrenia: An NIMH program. *American Journal of Psychiatry, 130*, 674–677.

Goffman, E. (1961). *Asylums: Essays on the social situation of mental patients and other inmates*. Garden City, NY: Anchor Books.

Grob, G. (1985). The origins of American psychiatric epidemiology. *American Journal of Public Health, 75*(3), 229–236.

Hollingshead, A., & Redlich, F. (1958). *Social class and mental illness: A community study*. New York: Wiley.

Hospital and Community Psychiatry. (1975). A 25-year review of mental health research: Highlights of a report from NIMH. *Hospital and Community Psychiatry, 26*, 711–715.

Jencks, C. (1994). *The homeless*. Cambridge, MA: Harvard University Press.

Joint Commission on Mental Illness and Health. (1961). *Action for mental health*. New York: Wiley.

Kessler, R. (1994). Building on the ECA: The National Comorbidity Survey and the Children's ECA. *International Journal of Methods in Psychiatric Research, 4*, 81–94.

Kiesler, C. (1992). U.S. mental health policy: Doomed to fail. *American Psychologist, 47*, 1077–1082.

Kiesler, C., & Sibulkin, A. (1987). *Mental hospitalization: Myths and facts about a national crisis*. Newbury Park, CA: Sage.

Kirk, S. A. (1991). Essay review of *Psychiatric Disorders in America. Research in Social Work Practice, 1*, 434–439.

Kirk, S. A., & Kutchins, H. (1992a). *The selling of DSM: The rhetoric of science in psychiatry*. New York: Aldine de Gruyter.

Kirk, S. A., & Kutchins, H. (1992b). Diagnosis and uncertainty in mental health organizations. In Y. Hasenfeld (Ed.), *Human services as complex organizations* (pp. 163–183). Newbury Park, CA: Sage.

Kirk, S. A., & Kutchins, H. (1994). The myth of the reliability of DSM. *Journal of Mind and Behavior, 15*, 71–86.

Kirk, S. A., & Therrien, M. (1975). Community mental health myths and the fate of former hospitalized patients. *Psychiatry, 38*, 209–217.

Kutchins, H., & Kirk, S. A. (1997). *Making us crazy: DSM, the psychiatric bible, and the creation of mental disorders*. New York: Free Press.

Leaf, P. (1986). Mental health systems research: Adequacy of available organizational and systems data. In W. R. Scott & B. Black (Eds.), *The organization of mental health services* (pp. 97–129). Beverly Hills: Sage.

Levine, M. (1981). *The history and politics of community mental health*. New York: Oxford University Press.

Musto, D. (1977). The community mental health center movement in historical perspective. In E. Barton & C. Sanborn (Eds.), *An assessment of the community mental health movement* (pp. 1–11). Lexington, MA: Lexington Books.

Myers, J., & Bean, L. (1968). *A decade later: A follow-up of social class and mental illness.* New York: Wiley.

Nelson, E. N., & Rice, J. (1997). Stability of diagnosis of obsessive–compulsive disorder in the Epidemiologic Catchment Area Study. *American Journal of Psychiatry, 154,* 826–831.

National Institute of Mental Health. (1960). Public Health Service Publication No. 20.

National Institute of Mental Health. (1996a). New release 3-15-96. New NIMH Director Named. Rockville, MD: Author.

National Institute of Mental Health. (1996b). Facts about the National Institute of Mental Health. Rockville, MD: Author.

National Institute of Mental Health. (1996c). Total number of NIMH research grants, FY 1960–1995.

National Institute of Mental Health. (1996d). NIMH research grants, FY 1960–1995 in current and constant dollars.

National Institute of Mental Health. (1996e). NIMH research grants, FY 1976–1995 by discipline of principal investigator.

National Institute of Mental Health. (1996f). NIMH research grants to colleges and universities by academic department, FY 1976–1995.

National Institute of Mental Health. (1996g). NIMH research grants, FY 1976–1995 by type of sponsoring institution.

National Advisory Mental Health Council Report to Congress on the Decade of the Brain. (1988, January). *Approaching the 21st century: Opportunities for NIMH neuroscience research.* Washington, DC: U.S. Department of Health and Human Services.

Regier, D. (1994). ECA contributions to national policy and further research. *International Journal of Methods in Psychiatric Research, 4,* 73–80.

Robins, L., & Helzer, J. (1994). The half-life of a structured interview—The NIMH Diagnostic Interview Schedule (DIS). *International Journal of Methods in Psychiatric Research, 4,* 95–102.

Robins, L., & Regier, D. (1991). *Psychiatric disorders in America: The Epidemiologic Catchment Area Study.* New York: Free Press.

Rothman, D. (1971). *The discovery of the asylum: Social order and disorder in the new republic.* Boston: Little, Brown.

Srole, L., Langer, T., Michael, S., Opler, M., & Rennie, T. (1962*). Mental health in the metropolis: The Midtown Manhattan Study.* New York: McGraw-Hill.

Stanton, A., & Schwartz, M. (1954). *The mental hospital: A study of institutional participation in psychiatric illness and treatment.* New York: Basic Books.

Stolz, S. (1973). Overview of NIMH support of research in behavior therapy. *Journal of Applied Behavior Analysis, 6,* 509–515.

Turner, J., & TenHoor, W. (1978). The NIMH Community Support Program: Pilot approach to a needed social reform. *Schizophrenia Bulletin, 4,* 319–344.

Wakefield, J. C. (1992). Disorder as harmful dysfunction: A conceptual critique of DSM-III-R's definition of mental disorder. *Psychological Review, 99,* 232–247.

Wakefield, J. C. (1996). Are we making diagnostic progress? *Contemporary Psychology, 41,* 656–652.

Wilson, M. (1993). DSM-III and the transformation of American psychiatry: A history. *American Journal of Psychiatry, 150,* 399–410.

Windle, C. (1973). The impact of NIMH grants to improve state hospitals. *Health Services Reports, 88,* 559–561.

PART VII

Social Continuities

CHAPTER 27

Life-Course Perspectives on Mental Health

LINDA K. GEORGE

This chapter examines mental health and mental illness from a life-course perspective. Of necessity, discussion will focus more on the *potential* of life-course perspectives to inform us about the antecedents and consequences of mental health than about its demonstrated utility. Although the life-course paradigm has played a notable and increasing role in sociology for the past 25 years or so, it has had, as yet, limited impact on sociological studies of mental health. Thus, the major content of this chapter will consist of conceptual links between (1) the life-course and mental health and (2) the ways in which mental health research to date is compatible with life-course perspectives.

This chapter is divided into five sections of varying detail. It begins with a brief review of the major principles of life-course perspectives, followed by a discussion of critical methodologic issues and a brief note on the differences between life-course and epidemiological perspectives on mental health. The largest section addresses four major areas of convergence between mental health and the life-course: (1) periods of risk for mental illness, (2) the persisting effects of traumatic stress, (3) life-course consequences of mental illness, and (4) the linked lives of the mentally ill. The chapter concludes with recommendations for future research.

LINDA K. GEORGE • Department of Sociology and Center for the Study of Aging and Human Development, Duke University, Durham, North Carolina 27710.

Handbook of the Sociology of Mental Health, edited by Carol S. Aneshensel and Jo C. Phelan. Kluwer Academic/Plenum Publishers, New York, 1999.

LIFE-COURSE PERSPECTIVES:
MAJOR PRINCIPLES

There is no unified theory of the life-course; consequently, it is more appropriate to discuss *life-course perspectives.* Nonetheless, life-course perspectives also share important general principles. Three of these principles are key to understanding sociological views of the life-course and their implications for mental health.

First, life-course perspectives take a long view of individual biography, typically decades or longer. Two concepts have become integral to this long-range view: transitions and trajectories (e.g., Elder, 1985; George, 1993; Hagestad, 1990). Transitions refer to changes in status that are discrete and relatively bounded in duration, although their consequences may be observed over long periods of time. There is a natural link between transitions, as discussed by life-course scholars, and life events (Elder, George, & Shanahan, 1996; George, 1993). Trajectories refer to long-term patterns of stability and change, often including multiple transitions, that can be reliably differentiated from alternate patterns. For example, sequences of role entrances and exits are often used to delineate trajectories of work and family life. Characteristics of the trajectories include not only the ordering of role transitions, but also the duration of role occupancy. Transitions and trajectories are inherently interrelated. As Elder notes, "Transitions are always embedded in trajectories that give them distinctive form and meaning" (1985, p. 31). Note that trajectories are not synonymous with the concept of careers (see Chapter 28). Unlike careers, trajectories are not assumed to involve specific stages or steps toward a defined outcome. Also, the term *career* is typically applied to a single life domain, such as occupational careers. In contrast, trajectories often include the intersections of multiple life domains.

Second, life-course perspectives focus on the intersections of biography and history. Much life-course research has examined the ways that major historical events affect subsequent life-course trajectories (e.g., Elder, 1974; 1987; McAdam, 1989). This attention to history is a major way that life-course perspectives differ from more traditional studies of development and aging, which typically disregard the historical context in which development unfolds. Life-course perspectives also are more theoretically driven than traditional cohort studies. In the latter, the focus is on distinguishing between age-related change and cohort differences, some of which are the result of historical events. Life-course studies emphasize the mechanisms by which historical events alter personal biography in both the short and long term. Historical events are clearly implicated in mental health trajectories. As examples, there is a strong link between war-related combat and specific psychiatric disorders, and the deinstitutionalization of mental patients during the 1970s and 1980s had a strong impact on the trajectories of those patients.

A third principle of life-course studies is a focus on *linked lives* (e.g., Elder, 1987; Elder et al., 1996). Linked lives refers to the interdependence of individuals in various networks, including, but not limited to, family and work. Although social interdependence is an important component of much, if not most, sociological research, the focus in life-course studies is broader (because of the attention paid to multiple life domains) and more temporal (spanning longer periods of time). Social support and social networks have been central issues in the sociological study of mental health, indicating an important point of convergence with life-course research.

KEY METHODOLOGIC ISSUES

Definitions and Operationalizations

Mental health and mental illness have been conceptualized in multiple ways. For our purposes, key issues concern (1) whether mental illness is conceptualized as psychiatric disorder or as psychological distress; (2) whether mental health/illness is measured as a continuous or as a discrete, categorical variable; and (3) whether mental health is conceptually and operationally distinct from the absence of mental illness.

Mental illness can be conceptualized in diagnostic terms, which typically translate into measurement of discrete mental illnesses as defined in the psychiatric nomenclature. Alternatively, mental illness can be measured in terms of number or severity of symptoms; this approach results in continuous variables that are often labeled as measures of nonspecific psychological distress. Continuous measures of the number of symptoms that correspond to a specific form of illness/distress, such as depression, also are common. These two approaches have important implications for understanding the burden of mental illness in the population or in population subgroups and for the choice of analytic techniques and their attendant assumptions. Both approaches make important contributions to our understanding of mental illness. Studies of psychiatric diagnoses are ideal for studying transitions into and out of illness episodes and are viewed by clinicians as being more useful. Investigations of symptom counts better represent gradations in distress and dysfunction and the total burden of mental health problems in the population.

Following the lead of the World Health Organization (1946), many scholars *define* mental health as more than the absence of psychiatric illness or acute psychological distress—as incorporating positive states such as finding life pleasurable and feeling that one is a person of worth. Despite conceptual allegiance to a distinctive definition of mental health, little research has used this definition, and studies that purport to examine "mental health" in fact examine psychiatric disorder or psychological symptoms/distress. The closest that scholars come to studying mental health per se is those who study what is variously called life satisfaction, psychological well-being, and subjective well-being (see, e.g., the classic studies by Andrews & Withey, 1976; Campbell, Converse, & Rodgers, 1976). Such studies are beyond the scope of this chapter. Consequently, as in the mental health field more generally, the term *mental health* will refer to the absence of psychological symptoms.

The definition and operationalization of mental health/illness has important implications for life-course research. In general, life-course perspectives are applied best to measures of specific transitions and their properties, which are then patterned into long-term trajectories. Thus, it is easier to plot and analyze trajectories based on discrete measures of mental illness than changes in levels of symptoms. Sophisticated statistical techniques, such as hierarchical linear regression (e.g., Bryk & Roudenbush, 1987), are beginning to be used to delineate long-term "growth curves" for continuous variables, but applications are rare and pose problems for other temporal issues of concern to life-course scholars (e.g., change as a function of duration dependence). Thus, in practical terms, applying life-course perspectives to the study of mental illness will be more or less difficult depending on the operationalization of mental health/illness.

A final issue concerning the measurement of mental illness merits brief note. For the most part, measures of mental health (whether symptom levels or diagnostic categories) used with children are very different from those used with adults. One important element of this difference is that a number of key issues relevant to children's mental health (e.g., school performance, "antisocial" behaviors that are acceptable for adults) have no analog in adulthood. Indeed, most studies of mental health focus on either children or adults, but not both. The research reviewed here is restricted to studies of adults. Given the long-term perspective of life-course studies, however, the noncomparability of measures over time is problematic for the field.

Heterogeneity

Heterogeneity constitutes two major challenges to the application of life-course principles to mental health and mental illness. First, as demonstrated in multiple life-course studies, there is almost staggering heterogeneity in the numbers of trajectories observed among the population. A study by Rindfuss, Swicegood, and Rosenfeld (1987) illustrates this point. Using data from the National Longitudinal Survey of the High School Class of 1972, Rindfuss et al. coded participants' role sequences for 8 years following high school graduation, examining five roles: work, education, homemaking, military, and other. They report that 1,100 sequences were required to describe the experiences of the 6,700 men in the sample; 1,800 sequences were needed to capture the patterns of the 7,000 women. This level of heterogeneity challenges the assumption that transitions are patterned in predictable ways and complicates research on the consequences of transitions.

Illness and treatment trajectories are likely to exhibit even greater heterogeneity given the episodic nature of psychiatric disorders and the "revolving door" character of inpatient mental health care. Furthermore, because mental illness affects multiple life domains, such as work and family, these patterns necessarily encompass multiple trajectories. It is obviously impossible to study all the unique trajectories observed in many populations. The typical ways of handling this issue in life-course research to date are either to study only selected trajectories (usually those that are most common or those that provide a strategic site for testing specific hypotheses) or to aggregate trajectories into a smaller number of meaningful categories. Nonetheless, heterogeneity in sequences of transitions remains a challenge in life-course research, especially in its application to mental health.

A second source of heterogeneity relevant to studies applying life-course principles to the study of mental health is the vast heterogeneity in the dependent variable used in many studies. The most heterogeneous measures are continuous symptom counts. Distributions on those variables will typically take the form of a large group of participants with no symptoms, sizable groups of participants with one to five symptoms, and a very long "tail" in which small numbers of participants report very high levels of symptoms. When individual patterns are observed over time, there are large amounts of heterogeneity in amount and direction of change. It is somewhat easier to cope with heterogeneity when dichotomous measures of the presence or absence of mental illness are used. Even then, however, heterogeneity poses problems in areas such as heterogeneity of diagnoses, treatment (including no treatment), and chronicity.

Another largely ignored source of heterogeneity is variation in the *course* of mental illness. Research to date suggests that, among those who experience episodes of depression, for example, rates of recovery and relapse, as well as episode duration and length of time between episodes is highly variable (e.g., George, Blazer, Hughes, & Fowler, 1989;

Keller, Shapiro, & Lavori, 1982). Aneshensel (1985) provides important evidence that trajectories of depression are differentially related to loss events, role strains, and social support. Thus, an important contribution of life-course principles is the reminder that mental illness can be usefully viewed in terms of distinctive trajectories.

Limited Data and Statistical Methods

A final challenge in applying life-course principles to the study of mental health/illness is limitations in the availability of appropriate data and statistical methods for analyzing data. As noted previously, life-course research requires data that span very long periods of time, with decades of data needed to reap the full rewards of life-course analysis. Data sets covering large segments of the life-course are very rare. A few data sets are now available that focus on status attainment and family formation, and cover multiple decades. But it is unlikely that *any* extant data set focused on mental health or illness covers the period of time needed to perform meaningful life-course research. Progress also is being made in the ability to study life-course patterns with retrospective data. It now is possible to "reconstruct" life histories in ways that are adequately reliable and valid (e.g., Freedman, Thornton, Camburn, Alwin, & Young-DeMarco, 1988; Wheaton & Roszell, 1992).

A related issue concerns statistical techniques designed to rigorously test life course models. Identifying statistical techniques that are adequate to (1) mapping change over long periods of time, (2) discriminating among distinctive trajectories, (3) permitting appropriate attention to heterogeneity both over time and within the sample, and (4) identifying the factors associated with different patterns of change and stability over time remains a challenge. Typically, the statistical procedures used in life-course research fail to meet all four of these criteria. Indeed, one critically important part of life-course research is the development of new statistical techniques that can do justice to the complex questions and linkages posed by life-course theories. This methodologic challenge applies to life-course research on mental health, as it does to life-course research in general.

LIFE-COURSE RESEARCH IS DIFFERENT FROM EPIDEMIOLOGICAL RESEARCH

It should be obvious by now that life-course research is different from epidemiological research, presented earlier in this volume (see, in particular, Chapters 7 and 10). It is useful, however, to briefly note the areas in which these distinctive research fields converge and diverge. The major area of convergence between these approaches is an emphasis on age and cohort. Indeed, there are important epidemiological hypotheses about age and cohort differences in the prevalence and incidence of mental disorders. Life-course scholars also are interested in age and cohort differences in mental illness. But their main focus is trajectories of mental health. Prevalence and incidence data are needed to identify trajectories but are a means to that end rather than an end in itself.

Two other divergences are worth noting as well. First, epidemiologists are typically interested in *rates* of mental illness. As such, they virtually require population-based data that allow them to make precise and accurate aggregate estimates. Life-course scholars would also prefer population-based data to ensure that the entire range of trajectories in that population are observed. Their focus, however, is on intraindividual change—its parameters, patterns, and correlates or predictors. Indeed, one reason for the emergence of life-course perspectives was discontent with studies that described populations only in terms of aggregate rates and a single regression line that was assumed to capture the complexities of change and stability over time.

Second, the vast majority of epidemiological studies focus exclusively on identifying factors associated with the experience (prevalence studies) or onset (incidence studies) of mental illness. Life-course scholars also are interested in the conditions associated with the experience of illness, although they would prefer to observe those predictors over long periods of time in order to capture the *processes* that place individuals at differential risk of mental illness onset and generate differing trajectories of mental illness. In addition, life-course scholars are equally interested in the *consequences* of mental illness; that is, in mental illness as a life-course contingency that affects trajectories in other domains such as work, social relationships, and socioeconomic achievement (Aneshensel, 1996). This focus of life-course perspectives is quite distinct from epidemiological inquiry.

FOUR CONVERGENCES BETWEEN THE LIFE-COURSE AND MENTAL ILLNESS PERSPECTIVES

"Periods of Risk" in Life-Course Perspective

Two related issues frequently examined in epidemiological research on mental illness are age of onset and periods of risk. Age of onset is used both in the definition of certain psychiatric disorders (American Psychiatric Association, 1994) and to identify periods of risk (i.e., ages at which individuals are at greater risk for the onset of psychiatric disorder). In this section, I lay out how life-course scholars might think about these issues. Because there are no empirical studies of periods of risk from a life-course perspective, this discussion is necessarily conceptual. I hope, however, that it illustrates the ways in which life-course principles could contribute to our understanding of mental illness.

AGE AND MENTAL ILLNESS: ESTABLISHED PATTERNS. Epidemiological data describing rates and distributions of mental illness were covered in detail earlier in this volume (see Chapters 7 and 10). Thus, I only briefly summarize what is known about age differences in the distribution of mental health, as measured using both diagnostic criteria and measures of psychological distress.

Studies based on diagnostic measures of mental illness suggest that mental illness peaks, in both prevalence and incidence, during early adulthood (e.g., Kessler et al., 1994; Robins, Locke, & Regier, 1991), with 20–25% of persons age 18–39 experiencing active disorder. Rates of psychiatric disorder are approximately 30–40% lower among those age 40 and older, with no significant age differences among the middle-aged and elderly.

Recent epidemiological studies include attention to age of onset of psychiatric disorders. Because these measures of age of onset are based on retrospective self-report data, some researchers are highly skeptical of their validity. Nonetheless, retrospective studies provide the best estimates to date of age of onset of psychiatric disorders using population-based data. These data suggest that the onset of mental illness is concentrated in early adulthood. Indeed, the median age of onset of all major psychiatric disorders is in the decade of the twenties (Robins et al., 1991). Specific psychiatric disorders vary in age of onset. Depressive disorders exhibit the widest range, with relatively high levels of first incidence throughout adulthood. This is an important point because many sociological studies of mental illness focus on depressive symptoms.

Studies based on measures of psychiatric symptoms exhibit somewhat different patterns from those based on diagnostic measures. Most recent studies focus exclusively on depressive symptoms, although the measures are often labeled as nonspecific psychological distress (e.g., Mirowsky & Ross, 1992). Data based on depressive symptoms exhibit a curvilinear relationship between age and depression, with levels of symptoms lowest during middle age, highest during very old age (i.e., age 70 and older), and intermediate during both early adulthood and early old age (i.e., ages 60–69). Because scholars who use symptom measures do not conceptualize mental illness as discrete conditions, age of onset is not meaningful. Although one could ask respondents about the onset and duration of symptoms, I am not aware of any studies that have done so.

It is vital to note that the age distributions summarized here are based on cross-sectional data, resulting in two significant problems. First, age and cohort differences are confounded, although there are now sufficient cross-sectional studies spanning decades to suggest that age differences have been quite stable for the past 35 years or so (cf. Gurin, Veroff, & Feld, 1960; Robins et al., 1991; Veroff, Douvan, & Kulka, 1981). Second, and more important, are the effects of selective survival. Psychiatric disorder is a known risk factor for mortality, especially during early and middle adulthood (e.g., Bruce & Leaf, 1989; Somervell et al., 1989). Thus, in cross-sectional studies, selective survival produces age distributions in which older respondents are elite with regard to both physical and mental health. The problems generated by selective survival are widely acknowledged. Life-course scholars, however, view this as a fruitful area of inquiry rather than as a methodological problem; that is, an important research issue for life-course scholars is identifying the trajectories in which psychiatric illness results in mortality at young ages.

AGE AND MENTAL ILLNESS: A LIFE-COURSE INTERPRETATION. In general, life-course scholars would view periods of risk for psychiatric disorders as the intersection of socially structured conditions of the life-course with intraindividual pathways of vulnerability and resilience. Given clear age-related patterns in the distribution and onset of mental illness, it is likely that characteristics of the social structure play an important role in creating periods of risk. When it comes to the specific individuals who develop mental illness, however, life-course scholars would turn to life-course trajectories, distinguishing trajectories associated with vulnerability versus resilience in managing social-structural conditions.

Of course, recent and contemporaneous factors (e.g., recent stressors, current social resources) have sizeable impacts on vulnerability to mental illness. One can acknowledge the power of those factors, yet hypothesize that distal factors also affect vulnerability to mental illness. Moreover, proximate factors are also of interest to life-course scholars. Examining life-course trajectories is one way to identify the long-term processes associated with proximate risk factors for mental illness.

In addition to age, mental illness is robustly related to gender and race. Life-course principles have the potential to increase our understanding of the ways in which these statuses affect mental health. Men and women often exhibit distinctive health trajectories, as do racial/ethnic groups (Clark, Maddox, & Steinhauser, 1993; Ferraro, Farmer, & Wybraniec, 1977). Undoubtedly, there also are gender and racial/ethnic differences in trajectories of change and stability in the social factors that place individuals at increased risk of mental illness, as well as the social factors that help protect people against psychiatric problems.

To give this illustration more substance, life-course scholars might hypothesize that there are periods of the life-course during which levels of social integration—meaningful, yet manageable attachments to social structure—are likely to be problematic. Following the seminal work of Durkheim (1951), periods characterized by either too few or too many links to social structure might be expected to increase the risk of mental illness. As Durkheim and later scholars have argued, both adolescence/early adulthood and late life are periods when, on average, relatively high levels of anomie are likely to result from a deficit of attachments to the social order. To the extent that adults are likely to confront the conditions of too many links to social structure, the most likely time would be middle-age, when responsibilities peak. There is evidence supporting these propositions in both life-course research (e.g., Elder et al., 1996; Rossi & Rossi, 1990) and studies of stressful life events (e.g., Goldberg & Comstock, 1980; Hughes, Blazer, & George, 1988). Thus, life-course scholars would expect periods of risk to result from social structural conditions that undermine the capacities of persons to sustain mental health.

Life-course perspectives also remind us that risk is a phenomenon that can be observed at both the individual and aggregate levels. For periods of risk to be observed in *population* data, it is likely that the structured conditions would have to be widely experienced by age groups. In contrast, *personal* risk would be more closely related to specific trajectories that represent differential vulnerability to those structural conditions. For example, among young adults, trajectories characterized by increasing levels of stress and low or eroding social support should be more strongly related to the onset of mental illness than trajectories that exhibit low levels of stress and high levels of social support.

A final note on periods of risk: Life-course research suggests that specific historical periods might also be periods of risk for increased rates of mental illness. Massive social dislocations, such as those generated by the Great Depression or world wars, are associated with higher rates of mental illness (e.g., Dooley, Catalano, & Jackson, 1981; Elder, 1974; Fontana & Rosenheck, 1994). Again, however, *personal* life-course trajectories prior to the historical event would be expected to predict which individuals are most likely to experience mental health problems as a result of these social disociations. As this discussion illustrates, life-course research is an effective strategy for linking macrolevel social conditions with microlevel outcomes and antecedents.

The Persistant Effects of Traumatic Stress

To date, the best example of applying life-course principles to studies of mental health is research on the persistent effects of traumatic stress. Two general topics have been investigated. One focuses on the persistent effects of childhood traumas (e.g., abuse, loss of parents) on mental health in adulthood. The other examines the effects of combat experience during young adulthood on subsequent mental health. Among the latter, studies that span multiple decades of postmilitary life provide especially compelling evidence about the persistent effects of trauma on mental health.

The reemergence of attention to the persistent effects of early trauma is interesting from the perspective of the history of research on mental illness. In the late nineteenth and early twentieth centuries, following the lead of Freud, childhood was viewed as the time when personality is established in nearly final form. It was widely believed that, in the absence of major intervention, patterns established in childhood were fixed for life. During the last half-century, one of the major intellectual contributions of the social and behavioral sciences was documenting that change is both possible and prevalent throughout life. Current research interest on the persistent effects of childhood experiences on mental health is, in a sense, a return to an old issue. Current conceptualizations are quite different from the earlier views, however, emphasizing patterns of continuity and change across the life-course and heterogeneity across individuals.

LINKS BETWEEN EARLY TRAUMAS AND SUBSEQUENT MENTAL HEALTH. A variety of childhood experiences exhibit robust relationships with mental health during adulthood. The most frequently studied childhood trauma is loss of a parent at an early age (typically, but not uniformly, before age 11). There is strong evidence that parental divorce at an early age is associated with increased risk of psychological distress and depressive and anxiety disorders (Harris, Brown, & Bifulco, 1990; McLeod, 1991; Tennant, 1988; Tweed, Schoenbach, George, & Blazer, 1989). Evidence with regard to parental death is mixed; most studies report no significant relationship between parental death and mental illness, but others report significant associations (e.g., Hallstrom, 1987; Ragan & McGlashan, 1986).

Mental illness during adulthood also is significantly associated with both childhood abuse (Bryer, Nelson, Miller, & Krol, 1987; Kessler & Magee, 1993; 1994) and childhood sexual assault (Stein, Golding, Siegel, Burnam, & Sorenson, 1988; Winfield, George, Swartz, & Blazer, 1990; Yama, Tovey, & Fogas, 1993). Indeed, there is increasing evidence that family violence during childhood, whether or not one is the victim, increases the risk of mental illness during adulthood (Kessler & Magee, 1993, 1994).

Childhood poverty also has been examined in relation to adult mental illness (Elder, 1974; Hallstrom, 1987; Landerman, George, & Blazer, 1991). Evidence about the strength of childhood financial deprivation as a risk factor for adult mental illness is less consistent than for other childhood traumas, but most studies find significant associations.

Most of the cited studies utilize multivariate analysis in which other known social risk factors for mental illness are statistically controlled. Thus, the effects of childhood traumas are not "explained" by a broad range of more recent and contemporaneous factors.

The persistent effects of trauma have also been studied with regard to the stresses of war, especially combat experience. Combat experience is strongly related to subsequent mental illness, including mental health problems that emerge many years later (Clipp & Elder, 1996; Elder & Clipp, 1989, Elder, Shanahan, & Clipp, 1994; Fontana & Rosenheck, 1994; Goodwin, 1980; Kulka et al., 1990). Cumulatively, this research includes veterans of three major wars; thus, the persisting effects of combat stress appear to generalize across historical as well as biographical time.

PATHWAYS BETWEEN EARLY TRAUMA AND SUBSEQUENT MENTAL ILLNESS. For life-course scholars, establishing that conditions and events early in life are related to subsequent mental health is only the first step. The more important step is to identify the pathways that create those relationships—and that result in mental health problems for some, but not all, individuals who experience those traumas. Progress is being made in identifying the pathways and mechanisms by which early traumas exert long-term influences on health. For the purposes at hand, I discuss four issues that illustrate the ways pathways from early trauma to mental health at much later times can be identified.

The Immediate Aftermath of the Trauma. There is mounting evidence that the ways that early traumas are confronted and handled are related to whether or not the trauma generates a pathway of persisting vulnerability. For example, with regard to the persistent effects of parental divorce, both the quality of child care subsequent to the divorce (e.g., Bifulco, Brown, & Harris, 1987; Harris et al., 1990; Hess & Camara, 1979) and economic hardship resulting from the divorce (e.g., Landerman et al., 1991) have been shown to distinguish between persons who do and do not experience mental health problems during adulthood. Other investigators have identified a cognitive style that children frequently develop when they are abused or witness ongoing family violence. This style has been labeled as "rejection sensitivity" (Feldman & Downey, 1994) and "emotional reactivity" (Rutter & Rutter, 1993; Starr, MacLean, & Keating, 1991). Regardless of label, this style (which includes hypersensitivity to actual or implied criticism and a tendency to anger quickly) is associated with patterns of interpersonal stress that persist into adulthood and are associated with adult mental illness. Life-course studies of combat stress also provide evidence that immediate postmilitary service factors alter the probability of later mental illness. In particular, veterans who do not experience difficulty securing work, who obtain higher status jobs, and who experience little stress overall in the years immediately after combat exhibit better physical and mental health in middle and old age than their less advantaged peers (Elder & Clipp, 1989; Elder et al., 1994; Kulka et al., 1990).

Findings that link the ways that early traumas are handled with subsequent mental health are highly compatible with results from studies of social stress. Many of the factors associated with subsequent mental health are social resources that also have been shown consistently to mediate the effects of stress on mental health in the short term (e.g., Ensel & Lin, 1991; Pearlin, Menaghan, Lieberman, & Mullan, 1981). The importance of avoiding an onslaught of additional stressors, as shown in studies of combat veterans, is compatible with the concepts of stress proliferation and secondary stressors (e.g., Aneshensel, 1996).

Accumulation of Posttrauma Resources. There is substantial evidence that the acquisition and accumulation of social resources after early traumas can lessen the risk of mental illness. When victims of childhood traumas develop social resources during adulthood, persisting effects of the traumas can be ameliorated. Socioeconomic achievement (Elder, 1974; McLeod, 1991) and, especially, supportive interpersonal relationships (typically, a high-quality marriage) (Elder, 1974; McLeod, 1991; Parker & Hadzi-Pavlovic, 1984) are especially effective in ameliorating the effects of early trauma on subsequent mental health. Conversely, poor socioeconomic status and chronic interpersonal stress during adulthood exacerbate the effects of childhood traumas on adult mental health.

Life-course studies of combat stress also emphasize the importance of later socioeconomic achievements and supportive social ties in reducing the relationship between combat experience and later physical and mental health problems. Among veterans exposed to combat, stable careers, higher educational attainment (often completed after military service), and higher earnings dampen the effect of war stress on subsequent mental health (Elder & Clipp, 1989; Elder et al., 1994). Establishing supportive relationships after military service also decreases the risk of subsequent mental illness. For most veterans, the primary source of social support is marriage (Elder & Clipp, 1988; Kulka et al., 1990). Elder and Clipp (1988) also found that continued postmilitary contact with fellow soldiers decreases mental health problems. They describe the special nature of sustained contact with "comrades." Rather than keeping psychic wounds open and increasing emotional problems, such relationships provide a unique experience-based support that other relationships cannot provide.

Again, these findings are entirely compatible with traditional social stress theories that view socioeconomic achievement and supportive social ties as social resources that can mediate and/or moderate the effects of stress on mental health. The unique contribution of life-course research is the demonstration that these resources reduce the effects of traumatic stress experienced decades earlier on subsequent mental health.

Early Trauma as a More Subtle Harbinger of Mental Illness.   Thus far, discussion has focused on factors that mediate the relationships between early traumas and subsequent mental illness. There also is important evidence that the experience of early trauma moderates the effects of contemporaneous stress on mental health outcomes. The strongest evidence in this regard is that childhood traumas interact with subsequent life stressors to increase the risk of mental illness. This interaction was first reported by O'Neil, Lancee, and Freeman (1987), based on a sample of university students seeking help with depression. Landerman and colleagues (1991) demonstrated that this interaction was robust across multiple childhood traumas in a representative, community-based sample.

These results suggest that at least one of the pathways by which early trauma affects mental health many years later is by creating a generalized vulnerability to stress. Thus, life stressors that tend to put the population as a whole at increased risk of mental illness have even stronger effects on persons who experienced early traumas. This connection also provides a potential explanation for the long intervals often observed between early traumas and subsequent mental health problems. The vulnerability to stress generated by early trauma may remain dormant unless and until acute stressors are experienced. Although the necessary statistical modeling has not been done, this hypothesis is compatible with much of the research on the long-term consequences of combat experience: Frequently, it is not until late life—when physical illnesses, loss of significant others, and other stressors are more likely to occur—that veterans exposed to combat exhibit higher rates of mental illness than their peers (Elder & Clipp, 1989).

Pathways to Mental Illness—Or Selection Effects?   As noted earlier, issues that medical sociologists often view as problems generated by selection effects are likely to be viewed as evidence of the impact of pathways to mental illness by life-course scholars. Three issues examined in studies of the persisting impact of combat stress illustrate this point. The first issue concerns the impact of psychiatric history prior to combat exposure on subsequent mental health. Although the military typically will not accept men with obvious psychiatric disorders, there is evidence that *post*military mental health problems are more prevalent among veterans with a *pre*military history of psychological problems (Elder et al., 1994; Kulka et al., 1990). Note, however, that combat exposure is a significant predictor of subsequent mental health problems for all veterans—those without a history of psychological problems, as well as those with such a history. These findings suggest that one pathway to mental illness is the experience of traumatic stress *after* a history of psychological problems.

Second, other social factors appear to be related to combat experience. Compared to their more advantaged age peers, persons of low socioeconomic status (SES) during early adulthood are significantly more likely both to participate in the military and, once in the military, to be exposed to combat. The fact that premilitary SES affects the likelihood of combat exposure among military personnel is important. Even in wars with nearly universal participation by men of certain ages, such as World War II, SES is a strong determinant of exposure to combat stress. Available research suggests that, even in the absence of military experience, young men of lower socioeconomic backgrounds will be at greater risk of mental health problems than those with greater economic resources. This research suggests that low SES is associated with pathways or trajectories of greater exposure to specific stressors. Interestingly, although stress research has devoted substantial attention to differences in stress exposure, I am not aware of studies that take traumatic stress (such as combat experience and physical violence) into account.

A third line of research indicates that age of entry into the military also affects the pathways between early stress and subsequent mental illness (Clipp & Elder, 1996). In general, entering the military at a later age increases disruptions of life-course achievements, which in turn increase the risk of delayed symptoms. Specifically, in their sample of World War II veterans, older age at entry was associated with higher rates of postmilitary divorce and lower socioeconomic achievements, despite the fact that the older entrants had higher levels of education at induction and less combat exposure than younger entrants. This issue nicely illustrates the complexities of timing—in this case, the age at which a specific transition occurs. Temporality in general, and duration dependencies in particular, are topics highly relevant to understanding the social antecedents of mental illness, but they have been largely ignored to date.

Life-Course Consequences of Mental Illness

In addition to enhancing our understanding of the pathways that frequently culminate in mental illness, life-course perspectives also focus attention on the *consequences* of mental illness—on mental illness as a contingency that has the potential to alter the subsequent life-course. It is well established that mental illness is associated with a number of negative social consequences, especially in the areas of socioeconomic achievement and family formation and stability. A history of mental illness is associated with several components of socioeconomic achievement: lower educational attainment (Kessler, Foster, Saunders, & Stang, 1995; Turnbull, George, Landerman, Swartz, & Blazer, 1990), lower income (Clark, 1994; Harwood, Napolitano, Kristiansen, & Collins, 1984; Rice, Kelman, Miller, & Dunnmeyer, 1990; Turnbull et al., 1990), lower levels of occupational attainment, and less stable work histories (Clark, 1994; Turnbull et al., 1990).

With regard to family formation and stability, evidence about the relationships between mental illness and subsequent divorce is plentiful and consistent (Booth, Johnson, White, & Edwards, 1985; Gotlib & McCabe, 1990; Kulka et al., 1990; Mastekaasa, 1992; Turnbull et al., 1990). Evidence about the effects of mental illness on the probability of marriage is less clear. Mastekaasa (1992) and Turnbull et al. (1990) report that persons with a history of mental illness are less likely to marry than their peers. Forthofer, Kessler, Story, and Gotlib (1996), however, report that a history of psychiatric disorder is associated with *earlier* marriage. There is no inherent discrepancy in this pattern of findings: Forthofer et al. were estimating the *timing* of first marriage; the other studies predicted the probability of *ever marrying*. Nonetheless, the effects of mental illness on marriage merit further study.

With one exception, the only attention paid to temporality in these studies was to ascertain temporal order (i.e., to verify that mental illness preceded the outcome of interest). Life-course scholars would recommend broader, more long-term investigation. The study by Turnbull and associates (1990) makes an initial contribution. They examined the effects of psychiatric illness on several social outcomes: educational attainment, occupation and income, marriage, marital stability, and fertility. In addition to *current* psychiatric status, *age of onset* of the mental illness also was examined. Thus, some persons who suffered active or recent mental illness had long histories of chronic or episodic illness; others were in their first episodes. Another sizable group of respondents in this community-based sample did not have active or recent mental illness but had a *history* of mental illness earlier in life. All of the outcomes except fertility were related to mental illness, but age at first onset of mental illness was more strongly related to the outcomes than current psychiatric status. Patterns based on age of onset were dramatic: the later the age of onset, the less likely that the individual suffered subsequent socioeconomic deprivation, decreased likelihood of marrying, or marital dissolution. Indeed, unless the age of first episode of mental illness was before age 30, there were no differences between those who had a history of mental illness and those who did not. Early adulthood is a "critical period" for important social outcomes as well as for the onset of mental illness. If social achievements are made *before* the onset of mental illness, the long-term social consequences are minimal. Mental illness becomes a milestone in the life-course if it occurs at an early age: In addition to confronting a serious illness, the quality of one's life-course achievements is at risk.

The study by Turnbull and colleagues (1990) is an important initial foray into understanding the consequences of mental illness in life-course perspective. Richer, more detailed life-course data would yield even more information. Of particular importance would be *trajectories* incorporating mental illness, its antecedents, and its consequences. Trajectories could be used both to elucidate the specific pathways by which mental illness leads to lower achievements and to identify pathways by which persons with early histories of mental illness avoid subsequent social disadvantage. The trajectories also would be useful in better capturing heterogeneity more broadly. Very importantly, long-term trajectories would permit examination of selection effects of various kinds. Undoubtedly some of the factors that select persons into mental illness at an early age also increase the likelihood of low SES and marital instability or both. Thus, trajectories would help to distinguish between the effects of preillness factors and those of the illness itself on social outcomes. Multivariate techniques can be used to control particular variables in a given analysis (e.g., in the Turnbull et al. study, the effects of age of onset were examined controlling on numerous distal and proximal factors related to family and socioeconomic achievements). Nonetheless, trajectories permit a more complex view of the ways a variety of factors reinforce, exacerbate, or ameliorate each other. Given that mental illness is variously single episode, chronic, or episodic, trajectories also provide a method of taking illness course into account.

Linked Lives: Broader Effects of Mental Illness

One characteristic of life-course research is its breadth—its emphasis on interlocking trajectories across multiple domains and, ultimately, across individuals. Stress research has demonstrated that negative life events, experienced by one person, can affect his or her significant others as well (Kessler & McLeod, 1984). Similarly, a major transition or life-course milestone can affect the life-course of significant others. The effects of mental illness on family members is examined in detail in Chapter 24. Thus, this discussion focuses on the kinds of research questions about the relationships between mentally ill persons and their families that could be usefully pursued with in a life-course framework.

It is firmly established that mentally ill adults rely heavily upon their families for financial assistance, access to and compliance with treatment, general household and self-care assistance, and much of their social contact (cf. Anderson & Lynch, 1984; Clark, 1994; Gubman & Tessler, 1987). This pattern is especially true of people with chronic mental illnesses. Caregiver burden refers to the negative consequences that often result from taking care of a mentally ill relative. Previous research documents a range of negative outcomes associated with caring for mentally ill family members (cf. Biegel, Milligan, Putman, & Song, 1994; Gubman & Tessler, 1987), with emotional problems the most frequent outcome (cf. Biegel et al., 1994; Noh & Avison, 1988; Noh & Turner, 1987). Family members also play a significant role in what happens to mentally ill persons with regard to timely treatment and the likelihood of rehospitalization (e.g., Greenley, 1979; Horwitz, 1977). These studies, although based on longitudinal data, rest on short term observations. Thus, in the short-term, the lives of people with mental illnesses are clearly intertwined with those of their families.

We remain largely ignorant, however, about the ways the life-course trajectories of mentally ill persons intertwine with those of their family members over the long term. A number of important questions could be addressed. How long will family members provide care for a mentally ill relative—and what characteristics of both patients and caregivers explain variability in duration of caregiving? What are the life-course consequences of long-term caregiving to a mentally ill family member? There is substantial speculation that sustained caregiving will have negative consequences for caregiver employment and occupational achievements, accumulation of economic resources, and the ability to sustain meaningful social relationships outside of the family, but empirical evidence is lacking. How does the aging of caregivers of people with chronic mental illnesses affect the caregiving context? An important issue in this regard is establishing plans for mentally ill persons after caregivers die or are physically unable to continue caregiving. At least one study (Lefley, 1987) indicates that this is a major concern of aging parents of individuals with chronic mental illnesses.

I am aware of one study of caregiving in the life-course context, although it a study of women who take on caregiving responsibilities for their physically ill older parents rather than a study of caregivers providing assistance to mentally ill family members. Moen, Robison, and Fields (1994) examined the relationships between caregiving and employment. The sample consisted of 293 women who were interviewed twice, 30 years apart. Extensive life history data were collected about the timing and duration of major roles and commitments during the 30 years between interviews. Moen and her colleagues found no evidence that employment affected the acquisition or duration of the caregiver role. Half of the women who were ever employed reported a period in which they worked and had caregiving responsibilities for older parents. Very few women reported leaving work because of caregiving, and the few who did were mostly of retirement age or older. Indeed, the vast majority of women retained their jobs while caregiving and were more likely to exit the caregiving role than to stop working. These results were considerably different from what was expected on the basis of previous theory.

Obviously, caring for physically ill parents is different from caring for a mentally ill family member. There also may be important differences between acquiring the caregiving role in middle age and acquiring it earlier, as is typical for family members of the mentally ill. Obviously, Moen et al.'s results cannot be generalized beyond the parameters of their study. But that study illustrates the contributions that a life-course framework can make to understanding the impact of mental illness on the linked lives of family members.

IMPLICATIONS AND FUTURE DIRECTIONS

From its inception, the life-course framework has been a perspective that is best used in conjunction with the theories and research questions of other sociological paradigms (George, 1993; 1996). Such cross-fertilization has the potential to provide a broader understanding of many social phenomena, including mental illness. I hope that this chapter has pointed out the potential of cross-fertilization of life-course perspectives and the sociological study of mental illness, and the extent to which available research is compatible with a life-course view of mental illness.

To summarize, let us reexamine the major ways I have seen natural linkages between these two important areas of sociological specialization. First, life-course perspectives lead one to adopt a long-term view of individual biography, tracing distal as well as proximate antecedents of outcomes of interest and, where relevant, tracing long-term consequences as well. This first and most basic tenet of life-course theory seems well suited to what we know about mental illness. Patterns of exposure to risk factors, vulnerability to those risk factors, and resilience in the face of risk factors for mental illness develop over long periods of time—and sometimes change dramatically over time as well. Mental illness itself often has a long-term history; other times, because of the timing of mental illness in the life-course, even a single episode of illness can substantially alter occupational careers, socioeconomic achievements, and family and social ties. Already there is substantial research evidence supporting the importance of a long-term view. Despite this, we have barely revealed the tip of the iceberg—we know far less than we need to know.

Second, the focus on distinctive trajectories, which is a major conceptual allegiance of life-course research, provides a way of elucidating much of the heterogeneity that is ignored in most studies of social factors and mental illness. The overwhelming focus of research on the antecedents and consequences of mental illness to date has conceptualized mental illness as a single phenomenon (whether measured as a diagnosis or a symptom count), which can be statistically modeled as a single regression line. The limitations of this approach should be painfully obvious. Theories of social factors and mental illness often assume, explicitly or implicitly, that there are multiple pathways to any specific outcome. If there are multiple pathways, how can a single regression line adequately represent them? The emerging tradition in life-course research is to examine multiple pathways or trajectories. This approach is manageable because a discrete set of trajectories is examined (i.e., there is aggregation into subgroups), but it also permits a richer, more fine-grained examination of important sources of heterogeneity. Clearly, it will take much diligent work to conceptualize and measure trajectories in the most efficient and informative way, but I hope that the appeal of studying sets of distinctive trajectories is clear.

Third, because of its attention to history—both historical events and historical contexts—life-course theory provides an opportunity to incorporate macro- and microlevel factors into a single study. Rates of mental illness vary across historical time and structural location, which is strong prima facie evidence that macrolevel structures and processes affect the risk of mental illness. Nonetheless, microlevel processes seem to be the primary factors associated with the onset of mental illness at the individual level. Thus, even in historical periods that differ with regard to rates of mental illness, some individuals are at greater risk of mental illness than others. Extant research on historical events such as the Great Depression and World War II combat demonstrates that both macro- and microlevel factors can be linked to patterns of mental illness. Once again, however, the surface of this research opportunity has barely been scratched.

Finally, more than many other research paradigms used in the social sciences, life-course perspectives capture the "whole person," because the focus is on the whole life. Again, some level of aggregation is used in life-course studies, so there is never attention to personal biography at the individual level. Nonetheless, in more conventional studies, large proportions of study participants will look identical with regard to the risk factors of interest (e.g., highest educational degree). Attention to life-course patterns reminds us that people with the same level of educational attainment got there by many different routes, over varying lengths of time. Developing trajectories that discriminate among the major pathways to educational attainment will disaggregate a group that looks alike in terms of current status into a set of subgroups that reached their current status by different routes. Whether that disaggregation has explanatory power beyond that offered by current status is an empirical question. But life-course scholars argue that it is a question that should be asked and answered.

At the same time that life-course principles offer potentially important new conceptual and methodological tools to the study of mental illness, benefits accrue in the other direction as well. If life-course principles are to earn their place in the research armamentarium of social science, they must be demonstrated to add to our understanding of important social phenomena. Mental illness is one such phenomenon and, it seems to me, an especially promising one.

ACKNOWLEDGMENT: Preparation of this chapter was supported by a grant from the National Institute of Mental Health (MH 43756).

REFERENCES

American Psychiatric Association. (1994). *Diagnostic and statistical manual of mental disorders* (4th ed.). Washington, DC: American Psychiatric Association Press.

Anderson, C. A., & Lynch, M.M. (1984). A family impact analysis: The deinstitutionalization of the mentally ill. *Family Relations, 33*, 41–43.

Andrews, F. M., & Withey, S. B. (1976). *Social indicators of well–being.* New York: Plenum Press.

Aneshensel, C. S. (1985). The natural history of depressive symptoms: Implications for psychiatric epidemiology. *Research in Community and Mental Health, 5*, 45–75.

Aneshensel, C. S. (1996). Consequences of psychosocial stress: The universe of stress outcomes. In H. B. Kaplan (Ed.), *Psychosocial stress: Perspectives on structure, theory, life course, and methods* (pp. 111–136). San Diego: Academic Press.

Biegel, D. E., Milligan, S. E., Putman, P. L., & Song, I. (1994). Predictors of burden among lower socioeconomic status caregivers of persons with chronic mental illness. *Community Mental Health Journal, 30*, 473–494.

Bifulco, A. T., Brown, G. W., & Harris, T. O. (1987). Childhood loss of a parent, lack of adequate parental care, and adult depression: A replication. *Journal of Affective Disorders, 12*, 115–128.

Booth, A., Johnson, D. R., White, L. K., & Edwards, J. N. (1985). Predicting divorce and permanent separation. *Journal of Family Issues, 6*, 331–346.

Broadhead, W. E., Blazer, D. G., George, L. K., & Tse, C. K. (1990). Depression, disability days, and days lost from work in a prospective epidemiologic survey. *Journal of the American Medical Association, 264*, 2524–2528.

Bruce, M. L., & Leaf, P. K. (1989). Psychiatric disorders and 15-month mortality in a community sample of older adults. *American Journal of Public Health, 79*, 727–730.

Bryer, J. B., Nelson, B. A., Miller, J. B., & Krol, P. A. (1987). Childhood sexual and physical abuse as factors in adult psychiatric illness. *American Journal of Psychiatry, 144*, 1426–1430.

Bryk, A., & Roudenbush, S. (1987). Application of hierarchical linear models to assessing change. *Psychological Bulletin, 110*, 147–158.

Campbell, A., Converse, P. E., & Rodgers, W. L. (1976). *The quality of American life*. New York: Russell Sage Foundation.

Clark, D. O., Maddox, G. L., & Steinhauser, K. (1993). Race, aging, and functional health. *Journal of Aging and Health, 5*, 536–553.

Clark, R. E. (1994). Family costs associated with severe mental illness and substance abuse. *Hospital and Community Psychiatry, 45*, 808–813.

Clipp, E. C,. & Elder, G. H., Jr. (1996). The aging veteran of World War II: Psychiatric and life course insights. In P. E. Ruskin & J. A. Talbott (Eds.), *Aging and post–traumatic stress disorder*. Washington, DC: American Psychiatric Association Press.

Dooley, D., Catalano, R., & Jackson, R. (1981). Economic, life, and symptom changes in a nonmetropolitan community. *Journal of Health and Social Behavior, 22*, 144–154.

Durkheim, E. (1951). *Suicide*. Glencoe, IL: Free Press (Original published 1897).

Elder, G. H., Jr. (1974). *Children of the great depression*. Chicago: University of Chicago Press.

Elder, G. H., Jr. (1985). Perspectives on the life course. In G. H. Elder, Jr. (Ed.), *Life course dynamics: Trajectories and transitions, 1968–1980* (pp. 23–49). Ithaca, NY: Cornell University Press.

Elder, G. H., Jr. (1987). War mobilization and the life course: A cohort of Wold War II veterans. *Sociological Forum, 2*, 449–472.

Elder, G. H., Jr., & Clipp, E. C. (1988). Wartime losses and social bonding: Influence across 40 years in men's lives. *Psychiatry, 51*, 177–198.

Elder, G. H., Jr., & Clipp, E. C. (1989). Combat experience and emotional health: Impairment and resilience in later life. *Journal of Personality, 57*, 311–341.

Elder, G. H., Jr., George, L. K., & Shanahan, M. J. (1996). Psychosocial stress over the life course. In H. B. Kaplan (Ed.), *Psychosocial stress: Perspectives on structure, theory, life course, and methods* (pp. 247–292). San Diego: Academic Press.

Elder, G. H., Jr., Shanahan, M. J., & Clipp, E. C. (1994). When war comes to men's lives: Life course patterns in family, work, and health. *Psychology and Aging, 9*(Special Issue), 5–16.

Ensel, W. M., & Lin, N. (1991). The life-stress paradigm and psychological distress. *Journal of Health and Social Behavior, 32*, 321–341.

Feldman, S., & Downey, G. (1994). Rejection sensitivity as a mediator of the impact of childhood exposure to family violence on adult attachment behavior. *Development and Psychopathology, 6*, 231–247.

Ferraro, K. F., Farmer, M. M., & Wybraniec, J. A. (1997). Health trajectories: Long-term dynamics among black and white adults. *Journal of Health and Social Behavior, 38*, 38–54.

Fontana, A., & Rosenheck, R. (1994). Traumatic war stressors and psychiatric symptoms among World War II, Korean, and Vietnam war veterans. *Psychology and Aging, 9* (Special Issue), 27–33.

Forthofer, M. S., Kessler, R. C., Story, A. L., & Gotlib, I. H. (1996). The effects of psychiatric disorders on the probability and timing of first marriage. *Journal of Health and Social Behavior, 37*, 121–132.

Freedman, D., Thornton, A., Camburn, D., Alwin, D., & Young–DeMarco, L. (1988). The life history calendar: A technique for collecting retrospective data. *Sociological Methodology, 18*, 37–68.

George, L. K. (1993). Sociological perspectives on life transitions. *Annual Review of Sociology, 19*, 353–375.

George, L. K. (1996). Missing links: The case for a social psychology of the life course. *Gerontologist, 36*, 248–255.

George, L. K., Blazer, D. G., Hughes, D. C., & Fowler, N. (1989). Social support and the outcome of major depression. *British Journal of Psychiatry, 154*, 478–485.

Goldberg, E. G., & Comstock, G. W. (1980). Epidemiology of life events: Frequency in general populations. *American Journal of Epidemiology, 111*, 736–752.

Gotlib, I. H., & McCabe, S. B. (1990). Marriage and psychopathology. In F. Fincham & T. Bradbury (Eds.), *The psychology of marriage: Basic issues and applications* (pp. 226–255). New York: Guilford.

Greenley, J. R. (1979). Family symptom tolerance and rehospitalization experiences of psychiatric patients. In R. G. Simmons (Ed.), *Research in community and mental health* (Vol. 1, pp. 357–386). Greenwich, CT: JAI Press.

Gubman, G., & Tessler, R. (1987). The impact of mental illness on families. *Journal of Family Issues, 8*, 226–245.

Gurin, G., Veroff, J., & Feld, S. C. (1960). *Americans view their mental health*. New York: Basic Books.

Hagestad, G. O. (1990). Social perspectives on the life course. In R. H. Binstock & L. K. George (Eds.), *Handbook of aging and the social sciences* (3rd ed., pp. 151–168). San Diego: Academic Press.

Hallstrom, T. (1987). The relationship of childhood socioeconomic factors and early parental loss to major depression in adult life. *Acta Psychiatrica Scandinavia, 75*, 212–216.

Harris, T., Brown, G. W., & Bifulco, A. (1990). Loss of parent in childhood and adult psychiatric disorder: A tentative overall model. *Development and Psychopathology, 2,* 311–328.

Harwood, H. J., Napolitano, D. M., Kristiansen, P., & Collins, J. J. (1984). *Economic costs to society of alcohol and drug abuse and mental illness: 1980.* Research Triangle Park, NC: Research Triangle Institute.

Hess, R. D., & Camara, K. A. (1979). Post-divorce family relationships as mediating factors in the consequences of divorce for children. *Journal of Social Issues, 35,* 79–96.

Horwitz, A. (1977). Social networks and paths to psychiatric treatment. *Social Forces, 56,* 86–105.

Hughes, D. C., Blazer, D. G., & George, L. K. (1988). Age differences in life events: A multivariate controlled analysis. *International Journal of Aging and Human Development, 27,* 207–220.

Jacob, M., Frank, E., Kupfer, D. J., & Carpenter, L. L. (1987). Recurrent depression: An assessment of family burden and family attitudes. *Journal of Clinical Psychiatry, 48,* 395–400.

Keller, M. B., Shapiro, R. W., & Lavori, P. W. (1982). Recovery in major depressive disorder: Analysis with life table and regression models. *Archives of General Psychiatry, 39.* 905–910.

Kessler, R. C., Foster, C. L., Saunders, W. B., & Stang, P. E. (1995). The social consequences of psychiatric disorders: I. Educational attainment. *American Sociological Review, 152,* 1026–1032.

Kessler, R. C., & Magee, W. J. (1993). Childhood adversities and adult depression: Basic patterns of association in a U.S. national sample. *Psychological Medicine, 23,* 679–690.

Kessler, R. C., & Magee, W. J. (1994). Childhood family violence and adult recurrent depression. *Journal of Health and Social Behavior, 35,* 13–27.

Kessler, R. C., McGonagle, K. A., Zhao, S., Nelson, C. B., M. Hughes, Eshleman, S., Wittchen, H. U., & Kendler, K. S. (1994). Lifetime and active prevalence of DSM–III–R psychiatric disorders in the United States: Results from the National Comorbidity Survey. *Archives of General Psychiatry, 51,* 8–19.

Kessler, R. C., & McLeod, J. D. (1984). Sex differences in vulnerability to undesirable life events. *American Sociological Review, 49,* 620–631.

Kouzis, A. C., & Eaton, W. W. (1994). Emotional disability days: Prevalence and predictors. *American Journal of Public Health, 84,* 1304–1307.

Kulka, R. A., Schlenger, W. E., Fairbank, J. A., Hough, R. L., Jordan, B. K., Marmar, C. R., & Weiss, D. S. (1990). *Trauma and the Vietnam war generation: Report of findings from the national Vietnam veterans readjustment study.* New York: Brunner/Mazel.

Landerman, R., George, L. K., & Blazer, D. G. (1991). Adult vulnerability for psychiatric disorders: Interactive effects of negative childhood experiences and recent stress. *Journal of Nervous and Mental Disease, 179,* 656–663.

Lefley, H. (1987). Aging parents as caregivers of mentally ill adult children: An emerging social problem. *Hospital and Community Psychiatry, 38,* 1063–1070.

Mastekaasa, A. (1992). Marriage and psychological well-being: Some evidence on selection into marriage. *Journal of Marriage and the Family, 54,* 901–911.

McAdam, D. (1989). The biographical consequences of activism. *American Sociological Review, 54,* 744–760.

McLeod, J. D. (1991). Childhood parental loss and adult depression. *Journal of Health and Social Behavior, 32,* 205–220.

Mirowsky, J., & Ross, C. E. (1992). Age and depression. *Journal of Health and Social Behavior, 33,* 187–205.

Moen, P., Robison, J., & Fields, V. (1994). Women's work and caregiving roles: A life course approach. *Journal of Gerontology: Social Sciences, 49,* S176–S186.

Noh, S., & Avison, W. R. (1988). Spouses of discharged psychiatric patients: Factors associated with their experience of burden. *Journal of Marriage and the Family, 50,* 377–389.

Noh, S., & Turner, R. J. (1987). Living with psychiatric patients: Implications for the mental health of family members. *Social Science and Medicine, 25,* 263–271.

O'Neil, M. K., Lancee, W. J., & Freeman, S. J. (1987). Loss and depression: A controversial link. *Journal of Nervous and Mental Disease, 175,* 354–357.

Parker, G., & Hadzi–Pavlovic, D. (1984). Modification of levels of depression in mother–bereaved women by parental and marital relationships. *Psychological Medicine, 14,* 125–135.

Pearlin, L. I., Menaghan, E. G., Lieberman, M. A., & Mullan, J. T. (1981). The stress process. *Journal of Health and Social Behavior, 22,* 337–356.

Ragan, P. V., & McGlashan, T. H. (1986). Childhood parental death and adult psychopathology. *American Journal of Psychiatry, 143,* 153–157.

Rice, D. P., Kelman, S., Miller, L. S., & Dunnmeyer, S. (1990). *The economic costs of alcohol and drug abuse and mental illness, 1985.* Rockville, MD: Alcohol, Drug Abuse, and Mental Health Administration.

Rindfuss, R. R., Swicegood, G. G., & Rosenfeld, R.A . (1987). Disorder in the life course: How common and does it matter? *American Sociological Review, 52*, 785–801.

Robins, L. N., Locke, B. Z., & Regier, D. A. (1991). An overview of psychiatric disorders in America. In L. N. Robins & D. A. Regier (Eds.), *Psychiatric disorders in America* (pp. 328–385). New York: Free Press.

Rossi, A. S., & Rossi, P. H. (1990). *Of human bonding: Parent–child relations across the life course.* New York: Aldine.

Rutter, M., & Rutter, M. (1993). *Developing minds: Challenge and continuity across the life span.* New York: Basic Books.

Somervell, P. D., Kaplan, B. H., Heiss, G., Tyroler, H. A., Kleinbaum, D. G., & Oberist, P. A. (1989). Psychological distress as a predictor of mortality. *American Journal of Epidemiology, 130*, 1013–1023.

Starr, R. H., MacLean, D. J., & Keating, D. P. (1991). Life–span developmental outcomes of child maltreatment. In R. H. Starr & D. A. Wolfe (Eds.), *The effects of child abuse and neglect: Issues and research* (pp. 1–32). London: Guilford.

Stein, J. A., Golding, J. M., Siegel, J. M., Burnam, M. A., & Sorenson, S. B. (1988). Long–term psychological sequelae of child sexual abuse: The Los Angeles Epidemiologic Catchment Area Study. In G. E. Wyatt & G. J. Powell (Eds.), *Lasting effects of child sexual abuse* (pp. 135–154). Newbury Park, CA: Sage.

Tennant, C. (1988). Parental loss in childhood: Its effect in adult life. *Archives of General Psychiatry, 45*, 1045–1050.

Turnbull, J. E., George, L. K., Landerman, R., Swartz, M. S., & Blazer, D. G. (1990). Social outcomes related to age of onset among psychiatric disorders. *Journal of Consulting and Clinical Psychology, 58*, 832–839.

Tweed, J. L., Schoenbach, V. J., George, L. K., & Blazer, D. G. (1989). The effects of childhood parental death and divorce on six-month history of anxiety disorders. *British Journal of Psychiatry, 154*, 823–828.

Veroff, J., Douvan, E., & Kulka, R. A. (1981). *The Inner American.* New York: Basic Books.

Wheaton, B., & Roszell, P. (1992). *Lifetime models of stress exposure.* Paper presented at the annual meeting of the American Sociological Association, Pittsburgh, PA.

Winfield, I., George, L. K., Swartz, M. S., & Blazer, D. G. (1990). Sexual assault and psychiatric disorders among women in a community sample. *American Journal of Psychiatry, 147*, 335–341.

World Health Organization. (1946). *World Health Organization Charter.* Geneva: Author.

Yama, M. F., Tovey, S. L., & Fogas, B. S. (1993). Childhood family environment and sexual abuse as predictors of anxiety and depression in adult women. *American Journal of Orthopsychiatry, 63*, 136–141.

CHAPTER 28

Mental Illness as a Career

Sociological Perspectives

CAROL S. ANESHENSEL

INTRODUCTION

The topics encompassed within this handbook reveal the sociology of mental health to be multifaceted: juxtaposing etiological theories with those that contest the very existence of mental disorder, differentiating causal explanations of illness episodes with interpretations of societal reactions, and contrasting the objective criteria of diagnosis with the subjective experience of human misery—despair, confusion, compulsion, addiction, fear. The subjects of investigation are diverse as well: individuals beset by feelings, thoughts, or behaviors they cannot escape or control; social groups whose risk of impairment is unusually great; cross- and subcultural groups differing in the experience of distress, its manifestations, and the social reactions it evokes; institutions whose business is counting, classifying, treating, and paying for mental illness; and the historically specific and local understandings we as sociologists have of these phenomena.

In the previous chapter, Linda George employed the principles of life course to unify several of these diverse themes. In this chapter, I use a similar but distinct concept, that of *career*, to achieve the same end. Whereas the life-course perspective emphasizes connections among the diverse trajectories comprising a person's life, such as family and work, the career perspective extracts one of these trajectories and emphasizes its internal organization. In this instance, the trajectory of interest forms around the experience of unusual,

CAROL S. ANESHENSEL • Department of Community Health Sciences, School of Public Health, University of California, Los Angeles, Los Angeles, California 90095-1772.

Handbook of the Sociology of Mental Health, edited by Carol S. Aneshensel and Jo C. Phelan. Kluwer Academic/Plenum Publishers, New York, 1999.

unpleasant, or unwanted thoughts, feelings, and behaviors. I use the concept of career to fuse the social conditions that create such a state, mold the course it follows over time, shape its impact on the individual, and trigger consequences for those whose lives are interconnected. In many ways, this conceptual model reflects the organization of this handbook.

THE CONCEPT OF CAREER

Characteristics of Careers

The concept of career has a long history in sociology. Its dominant application, of course, is with regard to the occupational sphere, especially work performed within formal organizations over the course of one's entire work life. Career is more than work or job, however; it is a *series* of related positions typically arranged in a hierarchy of respect, responsibility, and reward (Wilensky, 1961). People move through these jobs in an ordered sequence, following a developmental trajectory of progressive accomplishment, expertise, control, complexity, and esteem.

In addition to this conventional usage, the concept of career has a rich history, dating from 1930s Chicago sociology (Barley, 1989), of application to occupations outside the institutional mainstream. For example, career was used to study marginal or unconventional jobs such as taxi-dancer (Cressey, 1932) and professional thief (Sutherland, 1937). More recent work in this vein has examined criminal occupations (Matsueda, Gartner, Piliavin, & Polakowski, 1992) and misconduct among lawyers (Arnold & Hagan, 1992).

The application of this concept to domains of life separate from work, however, forms the basis for our present interest in career. Classic studies in this tradition largely pertain to participation in deviant subcultures, such as marijuana users (Becker, 1953). The career motif also surfaces in studies examining the course of illness, most notably Goffman's (1961) description of the "moral career" of mental patients and Scheff's (1966) analysis of the deviant careers of the chronically mentally ill. Recent work has applied the concept of career to the management of chronic illness (Gerhardt, 1990), illness careers (Pescosolido, 1992; see Chapter 21), and to caregivers for the chronically ill (Aneshensel, Pearlin, Mullan, Zarit, & Whitlatch, 1995; Brody, 1985; Pearlin & Aneshensel, 1994).

Career, then, refers to any sphere of activity in which people move through a series of related and definable stages in a progressive fashion, moving in a definite direction or toward a recognizable end point or goal. This developmental quality is captured in the description of career as "the unfolding of a social role" (Arthur, Hall, & Lawrence, 1989). Careers are enacted within formal work organizations but also emerge in other settings as a series of informal social statuses.

The notion of an end point or goal gives career a directional or progressive quality. This feature distinguishes career from a series of states that just happen to be arrayed together over time. This goal-oriented quality is apparent in the occupational sphere, where dead-end jobs are avoided precisely because there is no rung leading to the top of the ladder. For illness, recovery, accompanied by the resumption of ordinary activities and responsibilities, seems like the obvious analog; indeed, it is an essential feature of Parsons's (1951) original formulation of the sick role. However, the chronic and recurrent course of many psychiatric disorders—such as depression, substance abuse, and schizophrenia—may make recovery, at least full and permanent recovery, an unattainable goal. As a result, other outcomes must be considered as career endpoints. For example, Rosenfield (1992) cites enhanced quality of life as a critical goal of treatment for persons with chronic mental illnesses for whom medicine's power to cure is limited. The identification of these alternative end points helps to define a circumscribed set of career paths with regard to mental health.

Mental Illness as a Career

Karp (1996) has recently provided a prototype for the application of the concept of career to mental health. He describes the subjective experience of the depressed person, emphasizing how people impose meanings onto their experience as it evolves over time: It is a long pilgrimage to figure out what is wrong, what to name it, what to do about it, and, ultimately, how to live with it. Karp describes this progression as a social process that entails an increasing commitment to a medical model of depression and the transformation of self to include the role of patient. He delineates a career path that starts with inchoate feelings of distress followed by the person's recognition that something is wrong; passes through the identification of this condition as a psychiatric illness that necessitates treatment, usually involving psychotherapy and medications; and ends with the person's accommodation to chronic disability. This scenario describes the experiences shared in common by many depressed persons.

However, a number of alternative career paths exist. Many people experience signs and symptoms of psychological disorder in some shape or form, but only some develop into psychiatric patients beset by recurrent episodes of impairment. The approach to career used in this chapter emphasizes the existence of alternative career paths, especially the determinants of transitions from one career stage to another: Why do some progress to chronic impairment, whereas others never come to see their distress as mental illness, or, if they do adopt this interpretation, do not seek treatment? This orientation is isomorphic to the life-course concern with transitions and trajectories described earlier by George (see Chapter 27).

The concept of career, then, does not mean that a single set of experiences characterizes the course of disorder; quite the opposite. At each career juncture, a person may continue in the same direction or turn onto an alternative pathway. Delineating the boundaries of these alternatives demonstrates that there is more than one way to be "mentally ill." The experience of mental illness, however, is not entirely individualistic, despite being perceived as excruciatingly private. Persons with the same "illness" share at least some experiences in common with one another. These shared experiences constitute a social patterning analogous to career paths, a specific way of acting within career stages, and a particular way of getting from one stage to another (Shafritz, 1980). Or, to put it differently, those who follow a given career path share similar experiences that differ in some essential feature from the collective experiences of those following alternative career paths. As sociologists, our work frequently concerns how these pathways are shaped by the structure and functioning of society, by people's locations within systems of stratification, and by the institutions, organizations, and professions that deal with mental illness.

A CONCEPTUAL MODEL OF CAREER

The career transitions and stages that link the experience of ambiguous feelings of distress to its consequences over time are illustrated in Figure 28.1. This conceptual framework

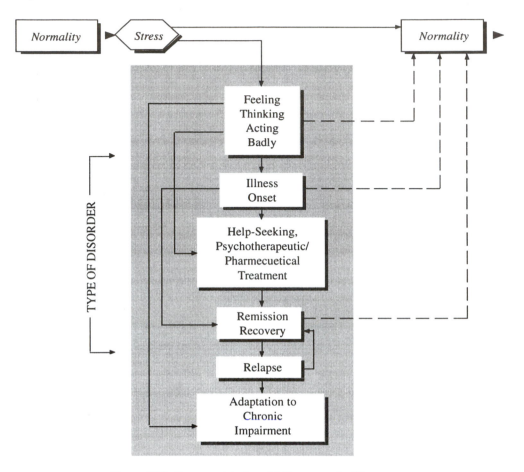

FIGURE 28.1. Career model of mental illness over the life course.

calls attention to certain facets of experience in a selective fashion. It is not fully comprehensive. In particular, it does not address in a systematic way the impact of type of disorder.
Yet the typical course of a mental illness tends to be disorder specific. Major depression,
for example, differs from schizophrenia. Consequently, this model fits some types of disorder better than others. In addition, not all alternative career paths are indicated for clarity of
presentation. Instead, Figure 28.1 emphasizes those elements with the strongest connections to the types of sociological theory and research presented in this volume.

   This figure shows a career that begins with normality and turns onto a path of acute
psychic distress that entails progressive movement into chronic disorder (the shaded area
of the figure). Following Karp (1996), this career path starts with inchoate feelings that
something is wrong that eventually become identified as mental illness requiring medical
treatment, which sometimes results in an abatement of symptoms, if not a complete cure.
However, this improvement often is temporary and the illness resurfaces at some later time.
This path is described as a mental illness career, using the language of psychiatry, because
its sequencing reflects the individual's increasing commitment to a medical explanation of
what is wrong and the development of self-consciousness as a mentally ill person (Karp
1996).

The uppermost line of Figure 28.1 represents one major alternative to this career—continuing normality over time, even in the face of exposure to difficult life circumstances. This career path is followed by most people most of the time. True, persons traveling this route on occasion feel sad, angry, or anxious; have confused, or intrusive thoughts; or act in a bizarre or socially proscribed manner. In other words, they experience signs and symptoms of mental illness. Although these states may be experienced as unpleasant or unwanted, they are mild, fleeting, or inconsequential. As a result, these states are better considered problems in living than indicators of mental illness.

Among those persons who develop signs and symptoms of mental illness, or more precisely, what psychiatry identifies as signs and symptoms of mental illness, some progress to become chronic psychiatric patients, whereas others discontinue and return to a state of normality. The dashed lines in Figure 28.1 represent some of these alternatives: distress that resolves itself without being identified or labeled as mental illness, symptoms that abate without treatment, and the isolated episode of treated disorder that does not portend recurrent disorder.

This model of career emphasizes that there are alternative career paths at each transitional point. The career described by Karp (1996), in contrast, is singular, seemingly inevitably leading to adaptation to chronic depression. This description fits the experience of the subjects in his study, all of whom progressed in this manner. This correspondence means that virtually everyone who arrives at chronic impairment goes through these stages in one fashion or another. Indeed, George (see Chapter 27) differentiates the concept of life course from career on this very dimension, that is, life course considers multiple routes, whereas career implies a single route. Although research into career can be read in this manner, the concept of alternative career paths is often at least implicit in this orientation. One particular pathway can be mistaken as the sole pathway simply because it is given more emphasis than its alternatives.

However, not everyone who encounters problems in living is beset by symptoms or continues on the path to chronic impairment. Most do not identify their problem as mental illness, receive treatment for it, or experience its recurrence (Aneshensel, 1985; Yokopenic, Clark, & Aneshensel, 1983). These alternatives are shown Figure 28.1 as initial movement along the mental illness career that ceases with a return to normality (the dashed lines). The model of career used in this chapter emphasizes the presence of alternative routes at each major juncture and brings into high relief questions concerning the direction of movement.

The junctures that define these alternative career paths are themselves the subject of sociological investigation. Under what circumstanced do individuals come to identify feelings of dis-*ease* as mental health problems? What characteristics motivate distressed people to seek help versus continuing to suffer in silence? Among those seeking help, who is most likely to receive it and in what form? Among those receiving treatment, who benefits and who is damaged? How do individual characteristics, especially those indicative of location in society, influence how long an illness episode lasts, whether it will persist indefinitely, or reoccur? An important agenda for future sociological research, I submit, concerns identification of the social characteristics and processes that push some persons on the track to chronic impairment and pull others onto more favorable paths.

To be sure, some of the answers to these questions are contingent upon the nature of the problem, for example, whether a person experiences crippling anxiety at the thought of leaving the house or dreads objects that are only rarely encountered, such as creepy, crawly things. Thus, we can expect the course of agoraphobia, for example, to differ from that of simple phobia. Other answers lie in the ascribed characteristics of the disturbed person. For example, the same clinical profile is more likely to be assigned a diagnosis of depression if the individual is identified as female rather than as male. Still other answers are found in the contingencies that shape social reactions to mental illness. For example, Scheff (1966) attributes the stabilization of symptoms of psychiatric disorder to the nature of the societal reaction. The intent of this chapter is to identify areas in which social factors, as distinct from disease factors, contribute to the course of mental illness and its consequences.

CAREER TRANSITIONS

Feeling, Thinking, and Acting Badly

The first transition, the beginning of this career, is from some existing state of normality to a new state of distress. As several earlier chapters make clear, normality usually means deviations from societal standards, however culturally idiosyncratic. This meaning is paramount in the "social response model" (see Chapter 4) and the labeling perspective (see Chapter 23), for example. A second meaning, one more apparent in the medical model and the psychiatric approach (see Chapter 3), is deviation from what is usual for the individual. This meaning is centered within the person, not anchored to societal points of reference. The deviation is from what is characteristic of the person (with the notable exception of personality disorders, for which it is the stable trait itself that is problematic). The person is not feeling, thinking, or acting like him- or herself. In this context, then, normality means consistent with one's usual demeanor, sentiments, and actions.

Normality is manifest as large individual differences in daily mood, customary ways of thinking, and characteristic forms of behavior. The relativity and subjectivity of normality has been addressed throughout this volume and constitutes one of the primary focuses of sociological research in mental health.

Attaching the adverb *badly* to signs and symptoms of disorder is meant to convey both the disagreeable quality of these experiences and their unfavorable social evaluation. These states are often, albeit not always, experienced as distressing. For some disorders, particularly internalizing disorders such as depression and anxiety, the state itself is unpleasant, upsetting, frightening, painful—qualities captured in earlier chapters as references to "suffering." The behavior associated with other disorders also generates distress, but less so for the individual than for those who populate his or her social world. For example, the hostile and irresponsible acts that accompany personality disorder are problematic because they evoke adverse reactions in others, including attempts to sanction, control, and restrict one's behavior, although, even in this instance, there often are complaints of distress, including tension, boredom, and depression (American Psychiatric Association, 1994, p. 343). Still other disorders create distress for both oneself and others. The cravings and stupor of the alcoholic, for example, often evoke hopelessness and helplessness among spouses and children.

At this initial stage, feelings of distress are not identified as signs and symptoms of psychiatric disorder. Instead, these states are usually experienced as amorphous and pervasive discomfort for which the individual lacks a vocabulary. According to Karp (1996), this ambiguous state is likely to persist for some period of time because distress typically is kept private: The individual searches for meaning on his or her own. Karp cites several factors as interfering with the communication of distress to other people. First, distressed people often lack the language to adequately describe their condition. Second, they often believe that others cannot comprehend the depth of their misery: There is no reason to express oneself because no one will understand. Finally, the fear of stigma keeps many silent. Distressed people conceal their discomfort because they does not want to be placed in the socially devalued category of mentally ill and because they are cognizant of the negative consequences of being so labeled (see Chapter 23).

A large part of this book has been concerned with the transition from normality, especially the chapters concerned with the mental health impact of exposure to stressors and access to resources. In Figure 28.1, stress is shown as the juncture between normality and distress. Stress is given a central role in this model of career not because it is the sole antecedent of distress; it definitely is not. Rather, stress is emphasized because it has dominated our thinking about and research into the social origins of mental illness. The defining attribute of this transition, the shift from normality to distress, is that of change. Hence the continuing interest in life event stressors, occurrences requiring some major readjustment of one's life. The chronic stressor model works on a different principle, that of erosion: One's capacity to bear ongoing difficulties is gradually worn away, until it is too thin to sustain the load.

A distinctively sociological contribution to this type of etiological research concerns the structural sources of exposure to stressors (Aneshensel, 1992; Pearlin, 1989; Turner, Wheaton, & Lloyd, 1995). Although past research has tended to emphasize quantity, the chapters in this volume demonstrate unequivocally that social groups differ importantly in the essence of the problems they are likely to encounter. These qualitative differences flow from the relative positioning of these groups vis-à-vis one another that constitutes social structure. For example, Rosenfield (see Chapter 11) calls attention to the ways in which gender stratification not only produces internalizing disorders in women, but also generates externalizing disorders in men.

A second, distinctively sociological contribution concerns structural variation in resources that mitigate the otherwise deleterious mental health effect of exposure to stressors (Aneshensel, 1992; Pearlin, 1989). One key question has guided research in this area: Why do some people become distressed, whereas others seem to be unscathed? In Figure 28.1, this issue is shown as the alternative to distress, the career path of continuing normality, shown at the very top of the figure. Several disciplines have contributed to our understanding of coping resources such as social support and mastery, resources that mediate and moderate the impact of exposure to stressors. Examining the connections between social placement and access to these resources, however, is typically a sociological enterprise (Aneshensel, 1992; Pearlin, 1989; Turner & Marino, 1994).

Two connections are especially important: the extent to which there are differences among social groups in *access* to resources or in their *efficacy*. Most existing research has addressed questions of access. For example, Ross and Sastry (see Chapter 18) show that gender differences in distress are essentially eliminated by statistically adjusting for gender differences in the distribution of personal control. Some research has reported between-group variation in the mental health impact of stress, which has been interpreted as evidence of group differences in the efficacy of coping resources, but there has not yet been a direct empirical test of the validity of this interpretation (Aneshensel, 1992).

In summary, the first career transition is from normality to distress, a transition often precipitated by exposure to stressors, especially when this exposure occurs in the absence of resources. Although some people who are exposed to stressors become distressed, most do not, remaining, for all intents and purposes, asymptomatic or normal. Accounting for this fork in the road has been the dominant focus of sociological research with an etiological bent.

Illness Onset

Medical sociologists draw a distinction between disease, a pathological condition, and illness, the subjective awareness of being unwell. These concepts are connected, of course, insofar as the underlying pathology gives rise to its signs and symptoms, that is, to the experience of being sick. However, some pathological conditions do not have perceptible manifestations, such as hypertension, and not all physical symptoms can be accounted for by a detectable organic pathology. Szasz (1970) draws an important contrast between physical and mental illness in that most people diagnosed as physically ill feel sick and consider themselves sick, whereas most people diagnosed as mentally ill do not feel sick and do not consider themselves sick.

The second career transition concerns this connection, the developing awareness that something is wrong and the identification of this state as a form of mental illness. Brown (1995) refers to this process as the social discovery of the condition, which is essentially a matter of diagnosis—the ways in which people, organizations, and institutions determine that there is a disease or a condition. In Figure 28.1, this transition is labeled *illness onset* to emphasize the subjective awareness that emerges at this time. The person is thinking, feeling, or acting badly for some time, usually a rather long time, but only now are these states recognized as signs and symptoms of mental illness. The individual may awaken to this realization on his or her own, often after some type of crisis, during which it becomes evident that something is terribly wrong (Karp, 1996; Thoits, 1985). It is not uncommon, however, for others—family, physicians, police—first to identify a person as being mentally disturbed. In this scenario, the individual may eventually acquiesce to this interpretation or vehemently resist it (Clausen & Yarrow, 1955). Involuntary commitment illustrates the latter scenario: The illness onset stage is bypassed, as shown to the left in Figure 28.1, insofar as the person does not feel unwell but is so labeled by others. This pathway, which entails the public and official labeling processes described by Scheff (1966) as leading to chronic mental illness, is set to the side for the moment and taken up again at the end of this section.

For the moment, however, let us concentrate on the person who experiences perceptible distress and comes to view this state as abnormal. Karp (1996) describes this transition as an "identity threshold," the development of a self-consciousness as a "troubled person." According to Karp, individuals construct an "illness identity" to make sense of their psychic discomfort. This illness identity evolves over time, reflecting patterned changes in consciousness and perception. Thus, identity is not static, emerging at this career stage and remaining fixed thereafter. Instead, additional sequenced identity transformations constitute the core of Karp's description of the depression career, involving the person's increasing commitment to a medical understanding of the problem.

In Figure 28.1, the first stage—feeling, thinking, acting badly—is separated from the second stage—illness onset—because the person initially lacks the self-perception that something is wrong with him- or herself. I make this distinction to emphasize that only some "symptomatic" persons go on to recognize this condition as an illness (Yokopenic et al., 1983). Others persist in a nebulous state until their "symptoms" abate or they make some adaptation that enables them to live with their discomfort. The attribution of illness to states of dis-*ease* is not intrinsic to the psychophysiological experiences, then; instead, this understanding of what is wrong is open to interpretation precisely because the meaning of these states is uncertain. Balint describes the initial stage as the "unorganized" phase of illness—an agglomeration of unclear, unconnected, and sometimes mysterious complaints and symptoms—that "settles down" into an "organized" illness (cited in Brown, 1995; Scheff, 1966). Scheff (1966) emphasizes that the stabilization of symptoms into an organized illness is not inevitable, that other outcomes are possible at this juncture: The individual may succeed in defining the condition or situation in terms other than illness—as eccentricity, for example.

In summary, there are three main career paths at this point. One leads to increasing involvement with the institutions concerned with mental illness and corresponding transformations of self. This path is signified by downward movement in the shaded area of Figure 28.1. The second path leads to ambiguous discomfort that exists largely outside of these institutions. In many instances, this distress resolves itself after some passage of time, which is indicated in the figure as the dashed line leading back to normality. In other instances, nebulous discomfort persists, becoming a chronic source of impairment, shown as the solid line to the far left in Figure 28.1.

For Karp (1996), the critical aspect of this juncture entails the attributions the individual makes concerning the causes of his or her discomfort. During the inchoate feeling stage, most people attribute their distress to external or situational conditions: a friend moves away; mother's health seems to be failing; a hoped for promotion fails to materialize. The decisive moment in the development of an illness identity occurs when the circumstances individuals perceive as troubling them change, but the distress continues. According to Karp (1996), the persistence of distress in the absence of its supposed cause necessitates a redefinition of what is wrong. This redefinition typically locates the source of the problem as somewhere within the person, within his or her mind and body, in the sense that "something is really wrong *with me*." In his sample of chronically depressed persons, most people came to favor a biochemically deterministic explanation for the cause of their distress. For these individuals, the failure of external explanations and the conversion to an internal explanation is a critical identity juncture in the depression career.

The persistence of distress over time is also a key feature of Thoits's (1985) account of self-labeling as being mentally ill, but she emphasizes the mismatch between affect and situation (as distinct from change in the situation) as the precipitating element. Her perspective is predicated on the idea that emotional behavior, like other behavior, is governed by social expectations, specifically, that emotional norms stipulate the range, intensity, and duration of feelings that are appropriate to given situations (see Hochschild, 1979, 1983). In this context, Thoits (1985) defines "norm–state discrepancy" as the individual's awareness of a noticeable discrepancy between his or her private experience of emotions and the states prescribed by emotional norms; the persistence and recurrence of discrepant feelings constitute emotional deviance. According to Thoits, the violation of emotional norms may elicit mental illness attributions by others, and, most importantly, by the self. Significantly, Thoits emphasizes that self-labeling processes are relevant *only* when the individual is aware of these discrepancies; otherwise, processes of labeling by others should apply (see below).

This perspective assumes that individuals are aware of both their feelings and emotional norms, and are motivated by social inducements to bring discrepant emotional states into conformity with societal expectations. This resolution may be accomplished by aligning situational features with existing emotional states, or, more often, by bringing emotions into conformity, that is, by "feeling work" or emotion-focused coping (Thoits, 1985). The failure of these efforts forces individuals to confront the meanings of their unconventional feelings and conclude that they are "inadequate, distressed, disturbed, having nervous breakdowns, unable to cope, going crazy" (Thoits, 1985, p. 242). Such self-attributions motivate people to voluntarily seek contact with mental health professionals, which, in turn, helps people to feel better, that is, to feel normatively, or so the theory goes.

The critical juncture at this stage of the career, then, may be whether distress continues over time. From Karp's (1996) perspective, it is the continuation of distress in the absence of its putative cause that leads one to think of oneself as being troubled. From Thoits's (1985) perspective, in contrast, attributions are more likely to be prompted by repeated exposure to discrepancy-producing situations, such as chronic role strain; the resultant negative emotional state is in and of itself a violation of emotional norms that proscribe long-term negativity. It is one's repeated failure to live up to emotional norms that leads to self-labeling. These two perspectives identify very different mechanisms but are not incompatible, inasmuch as one deals with changing situational contexts whereas the other deals with persisting or recurring situational contexts. Indeed, Thoits emphasizes that isolated instances of norm-violating emotions are not likely to produce self-attributions of being mentally ill.

The issue here is one of attributions. The "cause" in question is not some objective, scientifically, or medically established "cause," but the person's subjective explanation of his or her distress. The attributional theories described earlier help to explain why people in general come to see themselves as being troubled but are less helpful with regard to social variations in these processes. Why do similar situations lead some to see themselves as impaired, but others to fault their environment? And, relatedly, how do these tendencies vary according to one's social characteristics, statuses, and roles? According to Mechanic (1972), external influences on definitions of internal emotional states are especially important when the person lacks an appropriate explanation of what is being experienced. Social networks appear to be important in this regard. Having even vicarious experience with the formal mental health system—whether the person knows someone else who has had treatment—influences whether a personal problem is identified as a mental health problem (Yokopenic et al., 1983). Thus, the circumstances that lead one to adopt an illness identity are not inherent to the state of distress, even though some states may lend themselves more readily than others to this interpretation. The social determinants of this progression (vs. its alternatives) require more systematic investigation than they have received in the past.

Explanations for distress—internal versus external attributions—are limited, by and large, to the scope of the individual's own personal life. What is wrong is located within one's self or within the particulars of one's daily life. Rarely are these explanations placed within larger social contexts and processes. For example, a wife may feel her husband fails to understand her, or that she has failed as a wife, but she is unlikely to attribute her distress to the gender stratification of social roles discussed earlier by Rosenfield (see Chapter 11). The distressed person's consciousness rarely connects his or her psychological well-being to the ways in which society is organized as a whole, to broad cultural transformations, or macrolevel economic forces (Karp, 1996). Thus, the ways in which we as sociologists think about these processes, especially the social-structural sources of disorder, are not the ways in which the typical person understands what is the matter. The lay understanding of disorder emphasizes first the problematic aspects of the individual's life, and when these explanations fail, turns to problematic aspects of the self.

The concept of illness onset presupposes a self-awareness of distress, recognition that something is "seriously wrong with me," a self-attribution that, according to both Karp (1996) and Thoits (1985), leads distressed persons to seek help, specifically, to enter psychotherapy. The majority of distressed persons, however, never obtain treatment. Moreover, some of those receiving treatment did not seek it, and furthermore, do not see themselves as needing treatment or, indeed, as being disordered. These persons arrive at treatment through involuntary commitment. This group, of course, contains a disproportionate number of those with severe and persistent mental illnesses, especially persons with schizophrenia or other psychoses.

In such instances, illness onset pertains to the recognition by others that one's behavior, thoughts, or feelings deviate from normality, are inappropriate to the situation. Movement along the career pathway is governed not by one's own interpretation of the situation, but by the interpretations imposed by others (Thoits, 1985). This career path is defined by social processes of labeling and by the contribution of involuntary treatment to the development of chronic mental illness. Scheff's (1966) formulation of labeling theory attributes the stabilization of unorganized psychiatric symptoms into the social role of mentally ill to societal reactions to "residual rule-breaking" behavior, by which he means the violation of norms so basic and understood as to be unspoken, such as basic interpersonal and linguistic norms, and those used in the social construction of reality. He contends that residual rule breaking is extremely pervasive in society but generally ignored or rationalized away. When this is not the case, a pattern of symptomatic behavior develops that is in conformity with the stereotyped expectations of others, that is, with social stereotypes of the mentally ill. The person with symptoms of psychiatric disorder may adopt the view of others, incorporating the label of deviant into his or her self-conception. However, Scheff asserts that most instances of residual rule breaking do not proceed in this manner but are resolved by a return to normality, or by a redefinition of the problematic state in terms other than mental illness. That the label "mentally ill" is applied so infrequently leads Scheff to conclude that the most critical determinants of movement toward chronic mental illness are the social contingencies that influence the direction and intensity of societal reactions.

This orientation directs attention to the social attributes of the person who is identified as being mentally ill and the attributes of the persons who apply this label. Scheff's (1966) model does not require the individual's self-awareness that something is wrong. Movement along a career as a mentally ill person is driven by the public and official application of the label "mentally ill." The person need not, and, indeed, in many instances, does not concur with the judgment of others. This distinction is shown in Figure 28.1 as the pathway to the left that bypasses illness onset. When individuals do accept the label, they progress through the illness onset stage. This movement, however, is driven by external forces, specifically, by the social labeling process. It does not originate within the individual, but is imposed from outside: The person reacts to the label as distinct from generating it for himself or herself. Scheff argues that the individual may be especially suggestible when being labeled by others and may accept the proffered role of insane as the only alternative. For example, involuntary commitment to a mental hospital may make it difficult for the individual to resist adopting the social role of mental patient. An additional possibility is that individuals arrive at the determination that something is the matter with them at the same time that others arrive at the same determination, but that these are relatively separate judgments. Thus, there is more than one way to broach the transition between the stage of thinking, feeling, or acting badly and subsequent stages of a career as a mentally ill person.

Help Seeking and Treatment

Help seeking is by its very nature a social process, whether the person turns to informal social networks or to mental health professionals. In this approach, the distressed person actively seeks help or treatment after coming to the realization that he or she is sufficiently troubled to do something about it, to seek a remedy. According to Karp (1996) this remedy entails entry into the institutions concerned with mental illness: mental health experts, hospitals, medications. He describes this socialization process as transforming people into patients.

Although the transition to treatment may be self-initiated, it often is imposed by family or professionals and may be strenuously resisted (Clausen & Yarrow, 1955; Mechanic, Angel, & Davies, 1991). Moreover, these processes are shaped by social attributes and statuses. For example, Takeuchi, Bui, and Kim (1993) find that African American adolescents are overrepresented in community mental health clinics because of coercive referrals by social and legal agencies, which rely more often on the mental health system than on families or schools. Clausen and Yarrow (1955) described the pathways to psychiatric hospitalization as haphazard and discontinuous, often leading to "dead ends" before chance occurrences lead to hospitalization, a description at sharp odds with the more rational and purposeful descriptions cited earlier.

It should be noted, however, that this remedy is but one of many remedies tried by people who are distressed. Indeed, Karp (1996) emphasizes that this remedy is usually sought only after numerous other remedies have been tried and have failed. Nevertheless, not everyone who is distressed makes this transition. Others continue to suffer without naming their problem as an illness and without seeking help, especially without seeking professional help. Moreover, the path followed at this career juncture is influenced not only by the severity and persistence of the disorder, but also by the individual's social status. For example, among those with high levels of depressive symptomatology, education facilitates the recognition of personal problems, the identification of these problems as depression, and both lay and professional consultation (Yokopenic et al., 1983). Finally, not everyone who is in treatment has sought help; some have had it imposed by others, typically by family or by agents of social control. Patients who have been involuntarily committed as a result of the actions of others follow distinctly different career paths than those who voluntarily seek help with a problem they themselves have identified as psychological.

Informal social networks are instrumental at this transition. Pescosolido (1992, see Chapter 21) describes a dynamic social process of coping triggered by illness, physical or mental, in which networks not only help to define the situation, but also influence decisions regarding whether something is wrong, what, if anything, should be done about it, and how to evaluate results. For example, seeking professional help for emotional problems is promoted by having friends or family suggest it, and by knowing someone who has used a mental health service (Yokopenic et al., 1983). Moveover, networks shape the development of a strategy for managing the illness over time (Pescosolido, 1992).

According to Karp (1996), the progression to treatment also entails an "identity turning point," an increasing commitment to the idea that whatever is wrong is biological or biochemical. Perhaps the pivotal event in this sequence is receiving an official diagnosis. Karp describes a diagnosis as a relief on the one hand, because having a label to attach to one's condition brings the possibility of treatment and the absolution of responsibility, and as problematic on the other hand, because it places one in the devalued category of being mentally ill and erodes self-efficacy. He describes this interpretive dilemma as one that resurfaces repeatedly as the person moves toward an increasing medicalization of his or her condition. This dilemma is consistent with recent studies suggesting that the therapeutic benefits of treatment may be offset by the adverse consequences of being identified as mentally ill (Link, Struening, Rahav, Phelan, & Nuttbrock, 1997; Rosenfield, 1997).

Similar socialization and identity processes operate with regard to medication regimens. Karp (1996) identifies the start of medications as a decisive juncture in one's self-redefinition as an emotionally ill person (rather than merely a troubled person). He describes several typical stages: resistance, trial commitment, converted, and disenchanted. What begins as reluctance becomes a routine way of life with a new identity, that of a person who suffers from a biochemically based emotional illness. Disenchantment follows from the failure of drugs to provide a cure, in particular, to prevent the recurrence of distress. Again, this perspective fits the model of voluntary help-seeking behavior better than the case of involuntary commitment, where medications may be unwanted and resisted from the outset.

The literature on the course of mental illness over time does not indicate that psychiatric treatment necessarily leads to a more favorable course than the course followed by untreated disorder. One of the difficulties in interpreting this literature is the problem of social selection. Persons who receive treatment are systematically different from those who do not. One of the dimensions that differentiates these two groups is the severity and duration of impairment. The more severe and long-lasting the impairment, the greater the likelihood of treatment. Thus, those who are in treatment are, on average, more persistently distressed to begin with than those who remain untreated. This selection factor makes it difficult to accurately gauge the efficacy of treatment.

In addition, some disorders appear to run their course over time irrespective of whether treatment is obtained. The curative effects of the passage of time occur for both those in treatment and those who remain outside the institutions of mental illness. This process tends to attenuate observed differences in impairment and functioning between the treated and untreated.

Furthermore, the efficacy of treatment is context dependent. For example, Frank (1973) and Karp (1996) contend that patients' likely responses to different modes of treatment are shaped by the same culturally prescribed meanings that shape the understanding of the problem as an illness. In particular, they link the efficacy of medical treatments to a culturally induced readiness to view emotional pain as a disease requiring medical intervention. Although this perspective is widely shared in modern Western societies, as discussed in previous chapters, there is considerable variation within these societies in dispositions toward this interpretation of distress. For example, several chapters have discussed the greater tendency for women than men to turn to an illness explanation and to seek help in the form of medical treatment. In addition, Rosenfield (1997) shows that both treatment and stigma are related to quality of life, but in opposite directions, so that the beneficial effects of treatment are evident only to the extent that these effects are not offset by the detrimental effects of stigma. Rosenfield (1992) also shows that treatment services for the chronic mentally ill are most effective in enhancing life satisfaction when the program increases individuals' actual power, economic resources or status, self perceptions of mastery, and empowerment.

Finally, treatment is not necessarily beneficial (e.g., Broman, Hoffman, & Hamilton, 1994; Frank, 1973). For example, although many depressed persons respond to antidepressant medications, many do not experience relief, or instead experience adverse side effects. The antipsychiatry critique discussed earlier in this volume (see Chapters 1 and 3), provides sound basis for questioning the putative benefits of psychotherapy and medications, at least when these treatments are involuntary. In addition, feminist critiques have called attention to the adverse effects of psychotherapeutic and pharmaceutical treatment on women as individuals and for women as a social group (Chessler, 1972; Russell, 1995). For example, the self-help therapeutic movement has recently been criticized for encouraging women to understand that the solution to their unhappiness is to change themselves rather than to change the social conditions that lead to unhappiness (Rapping, 1996). Finally, Szasz (1970) asserts that individuals confined in mental hospitals are taught to act crazy and may become crazy as a result.

Karp (1996) describes a process of disenchantment with treatment for the chronically depressed persons in his study. He attributes this disillusionment, which he calls inevitable, to the immense gap in expectations that patients bring to treatment and what their doctors can actually deliver. Patients seek a cure, whereas psychiatry frequently only provides ephemeral relief from symptoms. Each time depression returns, it diminishes belief in a medical remedy.

Remission, Recovery, and Relapse

In comparison to etiological research, there is relatively little information about the course of various disorders over time and still less information about the social factors that differentiate an isolated acute episode from chronic impairment. This omission is serious because the course of many disorders is clearly chronic. This chronicity is shown in Figure 28.1 as the progression from remission/recovery to relapse, and as the feedback loop from relapse to remission/recovery.

Most of what we know about chronicity concerns relapse among treated patient populations. Research into relapse among persons with schizophrenia, for example, clearly implicates social processes, especially family functioning. The concept of "expressed emotion" is relevant here, referring to styles of family interaction—especially hostile criticism and emotional overinvolvement—that are likely to cause a florid relapse of symptoms. Greenley (1986) reconceptualized expressed emotion as a form of high-intensity interpersonal social control. He contended that families turn to these forms of social control when they are anxious and fearful as a result of the bizarre behavior of the patient. According to Greenley, these attempts at social control are experienced as uniquely stressful by persons with schizophrenia, who then become likely to relapse. Furthermore, the associations among these constructs differ according to whether the family views the person as being mentally ill and, therefore, not in voluntary control of his or her behavior. As we have seen throughout this volume, such understandings are shaped by social and cultural attributes.

Studies of relapse, however, are of limited generalizability because they pertain only to treated patients and do not describe the natural history of untreated disorder. This limitation is critical because, as noted numerous times in this volume, most disorder is untreated.

The natural history of depressive symptoms (as distinct from diagnosed depression) within the general population reveals that emotional distress is ephemeral for some persons but recurrent, persistent, and chronic for others (Aneshensel, 1985; Hornstra & Klassen, 1977; Lin & Ensel, 1984). The isolated episode of disorder represents a clear departure from the individual's more typical state of normal functioning and is followed by apparently complete and lasting recovery (Aneshensel, 1985). The less common pattern is a recurrent–chronic profile: Impairment occurs on a regular basis, with brief interludes between episodes, so that disorder is fairly continual, or with episodes that are more widely spaced in time but nevertheless recurrent (Aneshensel, 1985). In this instance, episodes are not self-limiting departures from normal mood, but rather the typical state of the individual includes some impairment. In the extreme, relief from persistent, pervasive symptoms is temporary, with periods of normal mood being infrequent and of short duration (Aneshensel, 1985).

This differentiation is important because the factors that account for the occurrence of disorder at one point in time are not necessarily the same factors that account for the persistence of disorder or its recurrence (Aneshensel, 1985; Lin & Ensel, 1984). For example, an acute life event tends to evoke only an isolated episode of distress, whereas frequent repetition of events over time seems necessary to produce chronic distress (Aneshensel, 1985; Lin & Ensel, 1984). Likewise, strains associated with major social roles—occupation, family, and finances—are etiologically important to long-term impairment to the extent that these strains persist or reoccur over time (Aneshensel, 1985). Similarly, it is the persistent absence of social support that matters to chronic distress (Aneshensel, 1985; Lin & Ensel, 1984). Thus, the sources of chronic impairment are likely to be found in the ongoing trajectories of the individual's life course.

Labeling theory is especially relevant to the course of chronic impairment. Indeed, Scheff (1966) maintains that his model is not meant to explain the initial occurrence of rule-breaking behavior, but rather is intended to account for its continuation or repetition. He contends that labeling is the single most important cause of a career as a chronically mentally ill person. From this perspective, labeling systematically blocks reentry into nondeviant roles: The mental patient is rewarded for continued deviation and punished for attempts to conform. The key issue, then, is identifying the conditions under which some instances of residual deviance are labeled as mental illness, whereas others are ignored or understood as something other than mental illness, for example, as eccentricity. Critics maintain, however, that labeling is of minor importance to the course of mental illness, that psychiatric treatment often is restitutive, and that many patients believe they have been helped by psychotherapy, hospitalization, or psychopharmaceutical treatments (Gove, 1982). At the present time, research is this area focuses on the extent to which any beneficial psychotherapeutic effects are offset or nullified by the application of a diagnostic label (Link et al., 1997; Rosenfield, 1997).

Karp (1996) has described chronic depression as a career stage of coping and adaptation to a condition that ebbs and flows over time but never completely vanishes from one's life. This adaptation occurs when the person has tried a variety of remedies, all of which have failed to eliminate the pain of depression. He contends that the recognition of depression's chronicity prompts a redefinition of its meaning, a reordering of its place in one's life, a shift from a medical understanding to a spiritual language of transformation. This search for meaning is a characteristically human endeavor that is now applied to an ongoing problem in living, the presence of enduring distress [see also Frank (1973)]. According to Karp (1996), this new understanding enables individuals to see meaning in their suffering. For example, some feel that it has been a critical learning experience, or that it has enhanced their capacity for empathy. This transcendental solution, however, is not universal. Some continue to seek treatment for what they consider an illness; others suffer in silence from an unnamed misery.

CONCLUSIONS

The concept of career encapsulates a set of characteristics, making it a convenient device for describing the course of mental illness. Most importantly, it emphasizes the ways in which cumulative experience merges into a holistic entity. In the occupational sphere, career refers not to a single job but to the constellation of jobs held over one's working life; each particular job is based on previous jobs and sets the foundation for future ones. This panoramic perspective emphasizes the entire sequence of events leading up to the present time; it also highlights the present state's consequences for the future. Similarly, mental health is best understood as a series of stages and transitions arrayed in its entirety across the life span. The meaning and impact of one's current state are shaped by what has happened in the past and by what is anticipated for the future.

Several lines of research demonstrate the necessity of looking at the individual's current mental health in its biographical context. For example, Wheaton (1990) shows that the mental health impact of various life-course transitions, such as divorce, depends upon the event's meaning in the context of previous experience, such as the earlier quality of the marital relationship. Similarly, one's psychiatric history is a good forecaster of one's chances of having disorder in the future (Aneshensel, 1985; see Chapter 7). This perspective is also evident in recent interest in the impact of early trauma of adult functioning (Kessler & MaGee, 1994; McLeod, 1991; Turner & Lloyd, 1995). It addresses not only the interdependence of events over time but also their cumulative impact. This orientation is similar to the life-course emphasis on the long-range view of individual biography (see Chapter 27). Although our work usually falls short of capturing the dynamic quality of experience over time, this goal should nevertheless be more vigorously pursued.

Although characteristics of the "disease" direct its natural history, the course of psychiatric impairment over time is shaped by social processes that transcend the condition itself. As we have seen, persons experiencing similar states often follow widely divergent paths in response to these states. Here, the issue is not social etiology but rather what transpires in the wake of symptom onset.

Of the determinants of these reactions, perhaps none is more important than whether the response is instigated by the individual or by others. On the one hand, progression is driven by the individual's developing self-awareness: the onset of dis-*ease* that disrupts one's sense of well-being and the realization that something is wrong; the recognition of this distress as an indicator of psychiatric disorder; decisions about seeking help and obtaining treatment; and, reactions to psychotherapeutic and pharmaceutical treatment, including remission, recovery, and relapse. On the other hand, the intrusive interventions of others mark entry into the role of psychiatric patient—an unwanted role characterized by the imposition of treatments, medications, and confinement—with exits from the role similarly controlled by the actions of others.

In general, the role of the individual tends to be emphasized in attributional orientations, which also tend to deal with affective disorders, whereas the role of the other tends to be more apparent in labeling perspectives, which also tend to deal with serious and persistent mental illnesses. This bifurcation means that we know less about the consequences of self- versus other-initiated processes than we might if disorders were not studied one by one, as is usually the case. In addition, the intersection of self and other remains an unrealized agenda for sociologists: How do the reactions of others shape self awareness, and, conversely, how does the individual's understanding of what is the matter affect the reactions of others?

The experience of mental illness is profoundly personal, because one's very being is threatened, but this experience is also profoundly social. The idiosyncratic features that make each individual's experience of mental illness unique coexist with common treads that link the biographies of individuals. Some of these commonalities pertain to general tendencies, for example, how do people typically respond to unpleasant, intrusive, and upsetting emotions? Other commonalities differentiate subgroups of the population, for example, why are some persons more likely than others to attribute problems to personal failings?

As sociologists, we deal in these commonalities. How is the experience of mental illness shaped by the organization of society, its systems of stratification and inequality? How does the occupancy of various social statuses and roles influence not only the likelihood of experiencing psychological problems but also how these problems are resolved? How does the occupancy of the role of psychiatric patient, or former psychiatric patient, become a permanent part of one's social identity? The unique aspects of each person's experience should not obscure the commonality in experience that arises because people encounter similar social systems, institutions, and processes, or because they occupy the same social role, that of psychiatric patient. Thus, the sociological study of mental health deals as much with society as it does the psyche.

ACKNOWLEDGMENTS: I wish to thank Leonard I. Pearlin and Jo C. Phelan for their constructive critique of an early version of this chapter. Preparation of this chapter was supported in part by a grant from the National Institute of Mental Health (2 RO1 MH40831).

REFERENCES

American Psychiatric Association. (1994). *Diagnostic and statistical manual of mental disorders* (3rd ed., rev.). Washington, DC: Author.

Aneshensel, C. S. (1985). The natural history of depressive symptoms: Implications for psychiatric epidemiology. In J. R. Greenley, (Ed.), *Research in community and mental health* (Vol. 5, pp. 45–75). Greenwich, CT: JAI Press.

Aneshensel, C. S. (1992). Social stress: Theory and research. In J. Blake (Ed.), *Annual review of sociology* (Vol. 18, pp. 18–38), Palo Alto, CA: Annual Reviews.

Aneshensel, C. S., Pearlin, L. I., Mullan, J. T., Zarit, S. H., & Whitlatch, C. J. (1995). *Profiles in caregiving: The unexpected career,* San Diego: Academic Press.

Arnold, B. L., & Hagan, J. (1992). Careers of misconduct: The structure of prosecuted professional deviance among lawyers. *American Sociological Review, 57,* 771–780.

Arthur, M. B., Hall, D. T., & Lawrence, B. S. (1989). Generating new directions in career theory: The case for a transdisciplinary approach. In M. B. Arthur, D. T. Hall, & B. S. Lawrence (Eds.). *Handbook of career theory* (pp. 41–65). Cambridge, UK: Cambridge University Press.

Barley, S. R. (1989). Careers, identities, and institutions: The legacy of the Chicago school of sociology. In. M. B. Arthur, D. T. Hall, & B. S. Lawrence (Eds.), *Handbook of career theory* (pp. 41–65). Cambridge, UK: Cambridge University Press.

Becker, H. S. (1953). Becoming a marihuana user. *American Journal of Sociology, 59,* 235–242.

Brody, E. M. (1985). Parent care as a normative family stress. *Gerontologist, 25,* 19–29.

Broman, C. L., Hoffman, W. S., & Hamilton, V. L. (1994). Impact of mental health services use on subsequent mental health of autoworkers. *Journal of Health and Social Behavior, 35,* 80–94.

Brown, P. (1995). Naming and framing: The social construction of diagnosis and illness. *Journal of Health and Social Behavior,* Extra Issue, 34-52.

Chessler, P. (1972). *Women and madness.* Garden City, NY: Doubleday and Co., Inc.

Clausen, J. A., & Yarrow, M. R. (1955). Paths to the mental hospital. *Journal of Social Issues, 11,* 25–32.

Cressey, P. G. (1932). *The taxi-dance hall: A sociological study in commercialized recreation and city life.* Chicago: University of Chicago Press.

Frank, J. D. (1973). *Persuasion and healing: A comparative study of psychotherapy* (rev. ed.). Baltimore, MD: Johns Hopkins University Press.

Gerhardt, U. (1990). Patient careers in end-stage renal failure. *Social Science and Medicine, 30,* 1211–1224.

Goffman, E. (1961). *Asylums.* New York: Anchor.

Gove, W. R. (1982). The current status of the labelling theory of mental illness. In W. R. Gove (Ed.) *Deviance and mental illness* (pp. 273–300). Beverly Hills, CA: Sage.

Greenley, J. R. (1986). Social control and expressed emotion. *Journal of Nervous and Mental Disease, 174,* 24–30.

Hochschild, A. R. (1979). Emotion work, feeling rules, and social structure. *American Journal of Sociology, 85,* 551–575.

Hochschild, A. R. (1983). *The managed heart: The commercialization of human feeling.* Berkeley: University of California Press.

Hornstra, R. K., & Klassen, D. (1977). The course of depression. *Comprehensive Psychiatry, 18,* 119–125.

Karp, D. A. (1996). *Speaking of sadness: Depression, disconnection, and the meanings of illness.* Oxford, UK: Oxford University Press.

Kessler, R. C., & MaGee, W. J. (1994). Childhood family violence and adult recurrent depression. *Journal of Health and Social Behavior, 35,* 13–27.

Lin, N., & Ensel, W. M. (1984). Depression–mobility and its social etiology: The role of life events and social support. *Journal of Health and Social Behavior, 25,* 176–188.

Link, B. G., Struening, E., Rahav, M., Phelan, J. C., & Nuttbrock, L. (1997). On stigma and its consequences: Evidence from a longitudinal study of men with dual diagnoses of mental illness and substance abuse. *Journal of Health and Social Behavior, 38,* 177–190.

Matsueda, R. L., Gartner, R. Piliavin, I., & Polakowski, M. (1992). The prestige of criminal and conventional occupations: A subcultural model of criminal activity. *American Sociological Review, 57,* 752–770.

McLeod, J. D. (1991). Childhood parental loss and adult depression. *Journal of Health and Social Behavior, 32,* 205–220.

Mechanic, D. (1972). Social psychologic factors affecting the presentation of bodily complaints. *New England Journal of Medicine, 286,* 1132–1139.

Mechanic, D., Angel, R., & Davies, L. (1991). Risk and selection processes between the general and specialty mental health sectors. *Journal of Health and Social Behavior, 32,* 49–64.

Parsons, T. (1951). *The social system.* New York: Free Press.

Pearlin, L. I. (1989). The sociological study of stress. *Journal of Health and Social Behavior, 30,* 241–256.

Pearlin, L. I., & Aneshensel, C. S. (1994). Caregiving: The unexpected career. *Social Justice Research, 7,* 373–390.

Pescosolido, B. A. (1992). Beyond rational choice: The social dynamics of how people seek help. *American Journal of Sociology, 97,* 1096–1138.

Rapping, E. (1996). *The culture of recovery: Making sense of the self-help movement in women's lives.* Boston: Beacon Press.

Rosenfield, S. (1992). Factors contributing to the subjective quality of life of the chronic mentally ill. *Journal of Health and Social Behavior, 33,* 299–315.

Rosenfield, S. (1997). Labeling mental illness: The effects of received services and perceived stigma on life satisfaction. *American Sociological Review, 62,* 660–672.

Russell, D. (1995). *Women, madness, and medicine.* Cambridge, UK: Polity Press.

Scheff, T. J. (1966). *Being mentally ill: A sociological theory.* Chicago: Aldine.

Shafritz, J. M. (1980). *Dictionary of personnel management and labor relations.* Oak Park, IL: Moore.

Sutherland, E. H. (1937). *The professional thief: By a professional thief.* Chicago: University of Chicago Press.

Szasz, T. S. (1970). *The manufacture of madness: A comparative study of the inquisition and the mental health movement.* New York: Dell.

Takeuchi, D. T., Bui, K. T., & Kim, L. (1993). The referral of minority adolescents to community mental health centers. *Journal of Health and Social Behavior, 34,* 153–164.

Thoits, P. (1985). Self-labeling processes in mental illness: The role of emotional deviance. *American Journal of Sociology, 91,* 221–249.

Turner, R. J., & Lloyd, D. A. (1995). Lifetime traumas and mental health: The significance of cumulative adversity. *Journal of Health and Social Behavior, 36,* 360–376.

Turner, R. J., & Marino, F. (1994). Social support and social structure: A descriptive epidemiology. *Journal of Health and Social Behavior, 35,* 193–212.

Turner, R. J. Wheaton, B., & Lloyd, D. A. (1995). The epidemiology of social stress. *American Sociological Review, 60,* 104–125.

Wheaton, B. (1990). Life transitions, role histories, and mental health. *American Sociological Review, 55,* 209–223.

Wilensky, H. L. (1961). Orderly careers and social participation: The impact of work history on social integration in the middle mass. *American Sociological Review, 26,* 521–539.

Yokopenic, P. A., Clark, V. A., & Aneshensel, C. S. (1983). Depression, problem recognition, and professional consultation. *Journal of Nervous and Mental Disease, 171,* 15–23.

Index

ISBN 0-306-46069-6